NOTHING RANDOM

NOTHING RANDOM

BENNETT CERF

and the Publishing House He Built

Gayle Feldman

RANDOM HOUSE • NEW YORK

Random House
An imprint and division of
Penguin Random House LLC
1745 Broadway, New York, NY 10019
randomhousebooks.com
penguinrandomhouse.com

Hardcover ISBN 978-1-4000-6027-6
Ebook ISBN 978-0-593-97837-5

Printed in Canada

3 5 7 9 8 6 4 2

Book Team: production editor: *Mark Birkey* • managing editor: *Rebecca Berlant* • production manager: *Richard Elman* • copy editors: *Lawrence Krauser, Martin Schneider* • proofreaders: *Melissa Churchill, Pam Rehm, Judy Kiviat*

Book design by Barbara M. Bachman

The authorized representative in the EU for product safety and compliance is Penguin Random House Ireland, Morrison Chambers, 32 Nassau Street, Dublin D02 YH68, Ireland. https://eu-contact.penguin.ie

In memory of Joseph Feldman,
father and dreamer 1915–2000

and

Rebecca Bigelman Feldman,
immigrant and pillar 1887–1956

Myer "Mike" Feldman, artist and patriot 1914–1945

Anna Bigelman Cohen, godmother to
a family 1917–2016

and always,

Bernice Borkofsky Feldman, mother
1920–1967

Life on earth passes;
It is not long;
Being remembered is the only success.

—*The Teaching for King Merikare,*
Egypt, around 1800 B.C.

And identity is funny being yourself is funny as you are never yourself to yourself except as you remember yourself and then of course you do not believe yourself. . . . You are of course never yourself.

—Gertrude Stein, *Everybody's Autobiography,* 1937

There are so many realities that in trying to render all of them visible, one ends up in the dark. That is why, when one paints a portrait there comes a moment when one ought to stop, having attained a sort of caricature. Otherwise, at the end, there would be nothing at all.

—Pablo Picasso to Daniel-Henry Kahnweiler, 1957

Contents

PART THREE

1941–1951

Try and Stop Me

PART FOUR

1952–1959

"And the Mystery Guest Is . . ."

PART FIVE

1960–1971

Real Business

To the Reader

IN 1962, A YOUNG UNKNOWN NAMED CORMAC MCCARTHY, WITH NO publishing connections at all, sent the precious manuscript of his first novel to Random House, "because [out] of everybody, they published . . . the good authors," he'd recall forty-six years later to an interviewer (me). "They were the foremost literary house in America," he added, almost as though it had been ordained.

The next year, 1963, Random took a chance on him, and gave McCarthy a contract. That same summer, *Esquire,* then the nation's hippest magazine, serendipitously echoed his words in an issue devoted to contemporary American writing. By that point, it proclaimed, "Bennett Cerf [had] secured Random's position as the most important literary publisher" in the country.

Many people today may be familiar with the name Random House, but Bennett *who*? Most would have no idea. They'd be clueless that in the mid-1920s, Cerf had co-founded, and until the mid-1960s was first among equals in running, what has now become the world's largest English-language publisher. They wouldn't know that from a young age he'd been a tremendous reader, with keen instincts for books and people; that he'd made the Modern Library into a cultural touchstone; that he'd succeeded in connecting books to Broadway, Hollywood, and TV, and in so many ways saw the publishing future long before most others in the business did.

However, in that midcentury moment when McCarthy and *Esquire* had come to the same conclusion, I was a kid growing up in Philadelphia and, like tens of millions of Americans at that time, *was* familiar with Bennett Cerf. He was the funny, middle-aged, horn-rimmed panelist I watched on *What's My Line?,* a television game show broadcast live from

New York City every Sunday night. I didn't know about Cerf and books; that would come much later.

After college in Philadelphia, I studied at Cambridge University, then worked for several London book publishers. Once back in America, I had trouble finding a New York job. When I was given a chance to write a few articles for *Publishers Weekly,* no one was more surprised than I when it spawned a career, one that enabled me to meander through publishing present and past.

Cerf's name would crop up from time to time, but it wasn't until I stumbled upon his personal archive at Columbia University, as well as the vast collection of Random House papers preserved there, that I began to grasp the immense surface of his life: the endless chain of writers, composers, producers, directors, actors, politicos, journalists, and publishers he'd known, as well as the multiplicity of the contribution to American letters that he'd made. I came to appreciate his uncanny ability to grasp what authors as disparate as Truman Capote, Gertrude Stein, and Dr. Seuss each sought through his or her work—be it connection, fame, money, attention, love, to change the world, to exorcise demons—and how he helped each achieve it.

I also began to understand the paradox that had largely denied him lasting recognition: what had made him well known and beloved in his day, and had helped put Random House on the map, had also worked against him. That became all too clear in another *Esquire* article that ran only eight months after the first. This second piece, a five-page profile of Cerf from 1964, characterized him not as that serious, driven publisher who had "secured" Random's paramount position in the publishing pecking order, but as a lightweight fixated on "fun." Most egregious was the TV fun of being on a game show, but there were other kinds, too: the lucrative fun of the pun-filled newspaper and magazine columns and joke books Cerf churned out under his own byline, and the fun derived from sunny speeches he'd deliver on (paid) lecture tours traversing the country. A "TV personality," he was a celebrity before celebrity culture seeped so indelibly into America. In intellectual circles, then, it made him highly suspect.

How could that man be the same one who'd fought the court case that allowed James Joyce's previously banned *Ulysses* to be legally available in the America of 1934? How could he have published Ralph Ellison's *Invisible Man* in the America of 1952? Or Philip Roth's *Portnoy's*

Complaint in 1969? How could that grinning guy on millions of screens be the publisher of William Faulkner, Ayn Rand, or Eugene O'Neill? Did he actually read the books he published? (He did, a large number of them.) To many in his day, that simply did not compute.

And yet, it's precisely because Cerf was open to so many worlds, high and low, mass and class; and to so many people—he loved being a New York switchboard to the famous, but also took pleasure in chatting with all the regular Joes and Janes—that he accomplished so much. He had warmth, charm, a fine brain, and handsome looks when young; humor bubbling up; and an eagerness and optimism that seemed to ensure life would sail along on a fair wind. His ego was far from small, but when he focused his attention, it felt like you and he were the only ones in the room. "Stepping into sunlight" was how actress Mia Farrow once described being with him. Influencing and reflecting the direction American culture would take from the 1920s through the 1960s, he intuited the role celebrity would play, and the business consolidation that would take place, but could not foresee how the changes he helped set in motion might affect *him*.

Underpinning all he did were two qualities of a rare magnitude. Extraordinary energy was the first. In the 1950s, a *New York Times* critic characterized Cerf's energy as akin to the greatness-defining quality of men like Hamilton and Washington. The second attribute of this man who made life look easy was a determination that was anything but. He never wasted time; competed fiercely to win; always wanted more; was never satisfied with himself. "Was I okay?" That question hounded him, haunted him. For a man who seemed to embody self-confidence, insecurity lay just beneath.

He was twenty-five when he began in publishing in 1923, working for a man named Horace Liveright. Two years later he started on his own, persuading his best friend to join him as business partner in buying Liveright's crown jewel, the Modern Library reprint series. Two more years, and the young partners announced that in addition to expanding the series, they would publish a few fine-press books on the side, "at random," to get in on the profitable market for beautifully made collectibles that was a Roaring Twenties craze. His decision to name the new company "Random House" signified to others that distinctive insouciance, as though what came of it would be nothing too serious, a mere "play toy" for two well-heeled young men.

And yet it was at the very start, a few weeks after he'd begun his apprenticeship with Liveright, that Cerf had vowed to his college friend Richard Simon (who was about to go into business with Max Schuster) that "within ten years" he hoped to become "one of the greatest publishers of the country." Ten years into his career, the ostensible "play toy" Random House fought and won the *Ulysses* case, going a long way to fulfilling that vow. There was nothing random at all about the ambition and scope of what he envisaged for himself and his company.

Cerf loved reading all kinds of stories, and loved telling them, too. His almost shameless need for attention, approval, and affection gave rise to a self-acknowledged habit of exaggerating and mythologizing—if nothing was ever enough, why not inflate things, make them funnier, edit out the painful parts, shape the story to gain the greatest effect? The stories created problems for him that outwardly, at least, he shrugged off with that grin.

They also created problems for me. Many of his stories were fashioned into *At Random,* a memoir published posthumously in 1977 and read as gospel. Some of the years I devoted to this book were taken up trying to untangle fact from fiction. In the early sections (and later, if a major discrepancy is involved), I point out the disparities; others are unpicked in the endnotes. When there is no paper trail to determine veracity, I indicate that the tale is likely apocryphal.

Bennett Cerf binds this book together, but his is not the only story between these covers. How Random House—now joined with Penguin, as Cerf himself had envisaged in the 1950s—became the preeminent English-language trade book publisher is one strand; how Random and the other New York houses established by Jews in the early decades of the twentieth century—particularly Liveright, Knopf, and Simon & Schuster—transformed American book culture is another. The publishing stories of authors both canonical and less well known (but ripe for rediscovery) thread through these pages. New York City history; Jewish American history; and Hollywood, Broadway, and TV history have strong supporting roles.

The contract for this book was signed in the autumn of 2002; years of research and interviews went into it, and countless drafts. I was fortunate so many who knew Cerf gave generously of their time to help, and am saddened some didn't live to see it in print. Whether from the daughter of a go-between in the *Ulysses* case; the children of Faulkner's longest-serving editor; friends like Kitty Carlisle Hart; acquaintances such as Henry Kissinger and Barbara Walters; authors like Toni Morrison, Ira Levin, and William Styron; or what the paper trail turned up, there is new information in these pages, as well as an evocation of a vanished world. Some attitudes, customs, language, and actions common to that world may no longer be acceptable in ours. This book is a portrait embedded in an era, not a judgment on that era or our own.

The act of biography is reclamation, a choice to recall one person and the world he or she inhabited to public memory. Why should any individual be worthy of the slog, sweat, and occasional hard-won moments of inspiration that go into the years it takes to birth a biography?

Walk into the tower at 1745 Broadway in New York City that is Penguin Random House's global headquarters. The massive lobby is lined with illuminated glass shelves. On them sit hundreds and hundreds of books. Some—titles like *In Cold Blood, The Cat in the Hat, Absalom, Absalom!, Atlas Shrugged, The Iceman Cometh, What Makes Sammy Run?, Act One, Rosemary's Baby, A Raisin in the Sun*—were books that Cerf first published.

From a very young age, I found books to be, as they are for so many of us, a window onto the world, a refuge, a promise, and a ticket to a life beyond the confines of my childhood. As an editor, journalist, and writer, they gave me a career. Although at times he frustrated, maddened, and perplexed me, tracking down Bennett Cerf also taught me so much. He amused, amazed, moved, and never bored me. It is humbling to peek inside and try to understand and portray another's life. Whether I have succeeded is for readers to decide. But that I should have made the attempt to recall this particular man back to life, I have no doubt.

NEW YORK CITY, DECEMBER 5, 2024

Key to Major Characters

BAC is Bennett Cerf
DSK is Donald S. Klopfer
RH is Random House
ML is Modern Library

CERF AND EXTENDED FAMILY

Glen Boles, 1913–2009, actor, later psychoanalyst, partner of Herbert A. Wise.

Bennett Cerf (born "Benoît," aka Beans, Bennett Alfred Cerf, Cerfie, Jesus Jr., Sonny), 1898–1971; Columbia Phi Beta Kappa; began in publishing at Liveright; reimagined ML; co-founded RH; TV panelist, *What's My Line?;* author, columnist, lecturer, bon vivant; husband of Sylvia Sidney and later Phyllis Fraser; father of Christopher and Jonathan Cerf; visionary publisher straddling books, TV, Broadway, Hollywood.

Christopher "Chris" Bennett Cerf, born 1941, first son of BAC and Phyllis Fraser Cerf; former RH editor; author/composer/lyricist; associated with children's TV, e.g., *Sesame Street*. Deputy editor of *Harvard Lampoon*. Girlfriend and first wife, Genevieve Charbin.

Fredericka "Frieda" Wise Cerf, 1873–1914, New York City–born mother of BAC; wife of Gustave Cerf; daughter of Nathan Wise; sister of Herbert Wise.

Gustave Cerf (aka Augustin, Gus, Pop), c. 1868–1941, Brooklyn-born father of BAC; husband of Fredericka Wise; lithographer; later, RH general factotum; close to BAC.

Jonathan Fraser Cerf, born 1946, second son of BAC and Phyllis Fraser Cerf; married Rosanne Novick in 1970; former editor, *Harvard Lampoon;* worked briefly in publishing, later in computing.

Phyllis Cerf (aka Helen Brown, Helen Nichols, Phyllis Fraser, "Thrup," "The General," Phyllis Cerf Wagner), 1916–2006; wife of BAC 1940–71; mother of Christopher and Jonathan; first cousin of Ginger Rogers; co-founder of Beginner Books; RH editor; columnist; Hollywood starlet; wife of former New York mayor Robert F. Wagner Jr.

Ginger Rogers (see under *Show Business*)

Lela Rogers (see under *Show Business*)

Herbert A. Wise (aka Uncle Herbert), 1892–1961, youngest son of Nathan Wise; brother of Fredericka Wise Cerf; uncle of BAC but only five and a half years older; exerted great influence on BAC; partner of Glen Boles.

Nathan Wise, born Germany c. 1842, immigrated to New York c. 1863, died 1908; BAC maternal grandfather; father to Fredericka and Herbert Wise; made a fortune in tobacco and land speculation; BAC's inherited share financed his publishing start.

RH AUTHORS

W. H. (Wystan Hugh) Auden, 1907–73, born U.K., naturalized U.S.; major twentieth-century poet; circle included Christopher Isherwood, Stephen Spender, C. Day Lewis. Threatened to leave RH when BAC tried to exclude poems by Ezra Pound from an RH anthology.

Truman Capote (aka Truman Streckfus Persons), 1924–84; published first novel with RH in 1948, and all later books, including *Breakfast at Tiffany's* and "nonfiction novel" *In Cold Blood*. Favored author close to both Cerfs. Childhood friend of Nelle Harper Lee.

Ralph Ellison, 1913–94; in 1953 the first African American to win the National Book Award for Fiction for his debut novel, *Invisible Man,* overcoming competition from Steinbeck and Hemingway. Championed by editors Frank Taylor and Albert Erskine.

William "Bill" Faulkner, 1897–1962; wife Estelle; daughter Jill. Nobel Prize–winning modernist steeped in the South and fictional Mississippi Yoknapatawpha County, he was published by Liveright, later Smith & Haas; came to RH 1936, with S&H–RH merger.

Theodor "Ted" Seuss Geisel (aka Dr. Seuss), 1904–91, first wife Helen Palmer Geisel; second, Audrey Stone Dimond Geisel. He transformed children's literature from *The Cat in the Hat* on, while becoming (and remaining) a financial bulwark of RH; regarded by

BAC as "genius" and friend. Partnered with Phyllis Cerf to start Beginner Books.

Moss Hart (see under *Show Business*)

James Joyce, 1882–1941, wife Nora, son Giorgio, daughter-in-law Helen Kastor Fleischman Joyce. Irish Modernist master, self-exiled to continental Europe 1904 on; RH mounted a landmark court case that allowed Joyce's *Ulysses* to be legal in the United States.

Sinclair "Red" Lewis, 1885–1951, Nobel Prize–winning novelist who anatomized Middle America. Came to RH late in career, diminished by alcoholism, for final five books, of which *Kingsblood Royal* remains noteworthy.

James A. "Jim" Michener, 1907–97, authored highly researched, bestselling fiction of epic sweep, often introducing Americans to foreign locales and their history. An early "brand name" author, his prolific success was crucial to RH bottom line and cash flow.

Nancy Mitford, 1904–73, Jessica Mitford's older sister, author of novels and biographies. RH published the first U.S. editions of her two most famous novels, *The Pursuit of Love* and *Love in a Cold Climate,* with DSK her primary contact. The most important British novelist on the RH list in the 1940s.

John O'Hara, 1905–70, second wife Belle; third, Katherine "Sister" Barnes Bryan. Set early template for *New Yorker* stories; published novels of unusual frankness about sex and class. Many, from 1949 to the 1960s, became RH bestsellers. Combative but close to BAC.

Eugene "Gene" O'Neill, 1888–1953, third wife Carlotta Monterey O'Neill, daughter Oona, sons Eugene Jr., Shane; America's first world-class dramatist, winner of the Nobel Prize, his plays remain staples of the repertoire. First great living author BAC signed; remained singularly important to him. Brought editor Saxe Commins to RH.

Ayn Rand (born Alisa Rosenbaum), 1905–82, Russian-born, naturalized U.S.; conceived "objectivism" philosophy, promulgating ethical egoism and unmitigated capitalism, and used novels to amplify beliefs and win adherents. BAC published her most famous work, *Atlas Shrugged,* despite its philosophy running counter to his beliefs.

Philip Roth, 1933–2018, Newark-born novelist focusing on Jewish American experience; after winning National Book Award for first book,

Goodbye Columbus, published by Houghton Mifflin in 1959, recruited by RH for next four, including *Portnoy's Complaint.*

William Saroyan, 1908–81, Armenian American writer. RH published his first two books. His debut story collection, *The Daring Young Man on the Flying Trapeze* (1934), was important for both Saroyan and RH.

Budd Schulberg (aka Seymour Wilson Schulberg), 1914–2009, early Hollywood princeling whose father, B. P. Schulberg, was discoverer and lover of Sylvia Sidney; writing career encouraged by BAC; five books with RH; "friendly" HUAC witness.

Gertrude Stein, 1874–1946, partner Alice B. Toklas; U.S.-born modernist who settled in Paris; famed art collector and convener of avant-garde salon; many of her books republished or published by RH in the 1930s and '40s; BAC helped organize her American tour 1934–35; close to BAC.

William "Bill" Styron, 1925–2006, wife Rose, daughter Susanna; Southern-born/raised; after first novel in 1951 with Bobbs-Merrill, went to RH and remained. Pulitzer for *The Confessions of Nat Turner;* best known for *Sophie's Choice;* close to BAC.

Robert "Red" Penn Warren, 1905–89, wife Eleanor Clark, daughter Rosanna; Southern Agrarian who recanted pro-segregationist stance in favor of integration; only writer to have won both fiction and poetry Pulitzer; prior to RH, published most famous book, *All the King's Men,* in 1946 with Harcourt; came to RH with friend, editor Albert Erskine.

Jerome "Jerry" Weidman, 1913–98, wife Peggy, son John; prolific novelist/playwright focused mainly on underside of first- and second-generation Jewish NYC experience.

INSIDE RH

Elmer "Pa" Adler, 1884–1962, founder of the Pynson Printers; he was one of three partners, along with BAC and DSK, who founded Random House in 1927, and active until 1932.

Robert L. "Bob" Bernstein, 1923–2019, wife Helen. After working at S&S in sales, recruited by BAC as RH sales manager in 1957 and chosen by BAC to succeed him as president and CEO of RH in 1966, after the firm was sold to RCA. Bernstein greatly expanded RH. Was fired by later owner Samuel Irving "Si" Newhouse Jr. in 1989. From 1970s on, pioneering human rights advocate and force behind Human Rights Watch.

Louise Bonino, 1904–84. Longtime head of juvenile books at RH, she had been an editor at Smith & Haas and came to RH when S&H and RH merged in 1936.

Saxe Commins, 1892–1958, wife Dorothy Berliner, aunt Emma Goldman; practiced as a dentist before becoming an editor, brought in to RH by his close friend, playwright Eugene O'Neill. A pillar of RH from 1933 on, he edited the ML and many authors, including O'Neill, William Faulkner, Edgar Snow, and Budd Schulberg. Close to BAC.

Jean Ennis, 1916–70, came to do publicity at RH in 1950, promoted to VP publicity and PR shortly before she died, one of the first women to be made a VP in publishing.

Jason Epstein, 1928–2022, wife Barbara. Recruited by BAC as an editor in 1958, he'd already distinguished himself by creating Doubleday's Anchor Books, the first modern U.S. trade paperback line. Involved in running the ML, later RH, a visionary, but very much a maverick. Instrumental in founding *The New York Review of Books*.

Albert Erskine, 1911–93, wife Marisa Bisi, daughter Silvia. Raised in Tennessee, joined RH with friend and fellow editor Frank Taylor in 1947. After Commins's death, BAC's favorite editor. Worked with Ralph Ellison, James Michener, William Faulkner, Cormac McCarthy, and Robert Penn Warren. Managed some of Michener's RH earnings.

Joseph Fox, 1926–95, hired by BAC as an editor in 1960, blue-blood Fox helped Truman Capote through *In Cold Blood,* Philip Roth through his first three RH novels. Renowned for devotion to his work, Fox died in his RH office.

Michael Frith, born 1941, Bermuda; best friend of Christopher Cerf in high school, college, and "adopted" member of Cerf household. Worked as editor under Phyllis Cerf at Beginner Books, later as RH New York editor for Ted Geisel, and editor of early *Sesame Street* books. Later, creative director of the Jim Henson Company.

Robert K. Haas, 1890–1964, wife Merle, son Bob Jr., daughters Betty, Priscilla "Pat" (aka "the Brat"); owned Little Leather Library, later co-founded Book-of-the-Month Club; in 1932 co-founded, with Harrison Smith, publisher Smith & Haas; from 1936, when S&H merged into RH, until retirement in 1956, RH partner. Brought

Faulkner, Isak Dinesen, et al. to RH; wife Merle translated *Babar* books for S&H, RH.

Emanuel "Manny" Harper, 1908–2002, bookkeeper at Boni & Liveright. BAC recruited him in 1925 as ML's first employee; longtime RH company treasurer, retired in 1970.

Hiram "Hi" Haydn, 1907–73, recruited by BAC in 1955 to be RH chief editor; stayed till 1959, when he co-founded Atheneum. Editor of Ayn Rand. Brought Styron to RH.

Richard "Dick" Kislik, 1927–2010, hired by BAC in 1961 as administrator akin to CFO. Lost out to Robert L. Bernstein in rivalry to succeed BAC as RH CEO; left RH in 1968.

Donald Simon Klopfer, 1902–86, mother Stella Danziger Klopfer Jacobson, daughter Lois Klopfer Levy; BAC acknowledged DSK as best friend and indispensable partner. They bought the ML in 1925, co-founded RH with Elmer Adler in 1927, and stayed together at RH, apart from DSK's military service during WWII, until BAC's death.

Florence "Pat" Selwyn Klopfer, 1906–79, second wife of DSK, mother of Charles A. "Tony" Wimpfheimer, DSK's stepson; Tony later became a company officer at RH.

Marian Ansbacher Klopfer (aka Hart, aka Gruber), 1903–93, first love of Bennett Cerf, first wife of DSK, mother of Lois Klopfer Levy.

Bertha "Bert" Krantz, 1911–2003, doyen of RH copy editors; indispensable to Michener, Rand, and many others, from Robert Penn Warren to Cormac McCarthy.

Pauline "Jezebel" Kreiswirth, 1907–54, husband RH controller Abe Friedman. Essential, beloved secretary to BAC and his partner DSK from 1927 until her death.

Robert "Bob" N. Linscott, 1886?–1964. After forty years at Houghton Mifflin, recruited in 1944 by BAC; senior editor until 1957. Edited Truman Capote's first books.

Robert "Bob" D. Loomis, 1926–2020, recruited by Hiram Haydn, editor 1957–2011. Edited William Styron, Shelby Foote, John Toland, Neil Sheehan, Maya Angelou, et al.

Lewis "Lew" Miller (n.d.), bringing fifteen years' experience in publishing, joined RH as sales manager in 1936, retired 1967. During the intervening years was one of four—BAC, DSK, and Robert K. Haas the others—running RH. Offered a partnership but declined.

Toni Morrison (aka Chloe Anthony Wofford), 1931–2019, a textbook editor at L. W. Singer in Syracuse, then moved to RH in New York in 1967. She became a trailblazing RH trade editor of books about the African American experience, and later a world-renowned Nobel Prize winner for her own fiction steeped in the subject. Close to DSK.

James "Jim" Silberman, 1927–2020. Recruited by BAC in 1963, he became chief editor of RH and publisher of adult trade until 1975, working with Hunter S. Thompson, Alvin Toffler, E. L. Doctorow, David Halberstam, Muhammad Ali, et al. Highly valued.

Frances Singer, 1900–(n.d.), head of L. W. Singer, Syracuse-based textbook firm. She sold it to RH in 1960, continuing to run it for some years. In 1964, she hired Toni Morrison as an editor.

Nan Ahearn Talese, born 1933, husband Gay. Joining RH as a copy editor aged twenty-five in 1959, she was the first female RH employee to become a "homegrown" literary editor, working with A. E. Hotchner, Rod McKuen, et al. Leaving RH in 1973, she retired from publishing in 2020, one of the most distinguished editors of her era.

Charles A. "Tony" Wimpfheimer, 1928–2020, son of Florence "Pat" Selwyn Klopfer, stepson of DSK; worked at RH from 1952 until his retirement, first in production, later becoming a shareholder, VP, and company officer.

PUBLISHING AND JOURNALISM OUTSIDE RH

Ian Ballantine, 1916–95, wife Betty, nephew of RH editor Saxe Commins. He founded a U.S. office for Penguin Books in 1939, and in 1945 was the key editorial figure recruited to start Bantam Books, of which RH was part-owner. In 1952, he and his wife founded Ballantine Books. He was a true pioneer of paperbacks.

Cass Canfield Sr., 1897–1986. At Harper, later Harper & Row, more than forty years, many as president or chairman, lastly as senior editor. As the latter, published some of BAC's books.

Norman Cousins, 1915–90, editor of *Saturday Review* (aka *The Saturday Review of Literature*) and BAC's column there.

Robert A. "Bob" Gottlieb, 1931–2023, editor, publisher, journalist, and author. He was the wunderkind chief editor of S&S before Robert L. Bernstein and Bennett Cerf recruited him, along with his colleagues Nina Bourne and Anthony M. "Tony" Schulte, to run Knopf in 1968.

Harold K. Guinzburg, 1899–1961, wife Alice, son Tom. Early scout for S&S; co-founded the Viking Press in 1925; co-founded the Literary Guild in 1927; chief of the Office of War Information domestic publications division, and subsequently chief of its London publications division during WWII. Son Tom later ran Viking, then sold it to Penguin.

Geoffrey T. Hellman, 1907–77, journalist who profiled BAC for *The New Yorker*.

Benjamin W. "Ben" Huebsch, 1876–1964, the first prominent Jewish person in American publishing, establishing his eponymous firm in 1900. The first American to publish James Joyce. Merged into Viking in 1925.

Alfred Abraham Knopf (aka AAK), 1892–1984. ***Blanche Wolf Knopf*** (aka BWK), 1894–1966. Alfred and Blanche co-founded eponymous firm in 1915, aided by Alfred's father, Sam (aka S.K.). Noted for fine design and production; history books; novelists in translation, e.g., Albert Camus, Thomas Mann; American novelists included Willa Cather, Raymond Chandler. Longtime friends of BAC, sold Knopf to RH in 1960. The combination made RH paramount U.S. publisher.

Alfred Abraham Knopf Jr. (aka Pat), 1918–2009, only child of AAK and BWK; heroic WWII pilot; worked in family firm under challenging circumstances; founded Vintage Books at Knopf. Left to co-found Atheneum Publishers in 1959. Close to BAC and DSK.

Allen Lane, 1902–70, U.K. publisher, in 1935 founded Penguin Books with brothers.

Irving Paul "Swifty" Lazar, 1907–93, lawyer and powerful talent/literary agent, represented Moss Hart, Irwin Shaw, et al. Admired BAC's ability to sell to Hollywood.

Horace Brisbin Liveright, 1884–1933, co-founded the ML and Boni and Liveright (B&L) with Albert Boni, but soon split with Boni to publish the imprints on his own. Built a stellar, adventurous list, including first books of Faulkner, Hemingway, O'Neill. Broadway producer of *Dracula* starring Bela Lugosi, as well as other plays. Gave first job in publishing to BAC, Richard L. Simon, Donald Friede, others. Model for BAC.

Leonard Lyons, 1906–76, Broadway columnist bylining The Lyons Den six days a week in the *New York Post* for forty years. He and BAC began as friends, but after Lyons accused BAC of stealing jokes from his columns, they became implacable enemies.

Horace Manges, 1898–1984, wife Natalie; founding partner of Weil, Gotshal and Manges, BAC and RH's lawyer; Columbia classmate, longtime friend.

Francis Meynell, 1891–1975, second wife Vera Mendel. English book designer, founded Nonesuch Press. Collaborated with BAC, DSK, Elmer Adler on early RH books.

Jessica Mitford, 1917–96, one of six daughters of British aristocrats, she became an American citizen, a Knopf author, and a muckraking journalist. Late in BAC's life, she investigated his connection to the Famous Writers School.

Harold Ross, 1892–1951, co-founder and founding editor of *The New Yorker;* member of the Algonquin Round Table; frequented many of the same circles as BAC; early poker companion of BAC; introduced him to Phyllis Fraser; ultimately disenchanted with BAC.

Barney Rosset, 1922–2012, Grove Press, *Evergreen Review* founder; avant-garde publisher of Beat poets, Samuel Beckett, unexpurgated *Lady Chatterley's Lover*.

Max Lincoln Schuster, 1897–1970, co-founded Simon & Schuster with Richard L. Simon in 1924; with Simon and Leon Shimkin backed Robert de Graff in founding Pocket Books in 1939. Talented copywriter; editorially focused; obsessive. Overlapped a year with BAC at Columbia Journalism School.

Leon Shimkin (aka "the Silent S," the "Little Bookkeeper"), 1907–88, began as bookkeeper at S&S, ended as sole owner of both S&S and Pocket Books. Number-savvy, focused on dollars and cents. Later, antagonist of Richard Simon.

Richard "Dick" Leo Simon, 1899–1960, wife Andrea, musical daughters Carly, Lucy, Joanna. Co-founded Simon & Schuster with Max Schuster in 1924; with Schuster and Shimkin backed Robert de Graff in founding Pocket Books. Piano prodigy; started at Liveright; pioneered crossword books, affordable illustrated books, known for taking risks. Graduated from Columbia with BAC; rivalry and friendship throughout.

Walter Winchell, 1897–1972, New York–born, was for most of his work life the most powerful newspaper gossip columnist as well as a radio commentator.

SHOW BUSINESS

John Daly (aka John Charles Daly), 1914–91, South African–born American journalist and broadcaster. Daly was moderator of *What's My Line?* on CBS TV. After the death of panelist Fred Allen in 1956, Daly was introduced by BAC each week; the two engaged in pun-filled repartee. Served concurrently as VP in charge of ABC News and anchor.

Arlene Francis (née Kazanjian), 1907–2001, husband actor Martin Gabel (blacklisted during the McCarthy era), son Peter Gabel (best friend of Jonathan Cerf). Brilliant, ambitious Jewish Armenian American actress, pioneering female radio host, and fellow panelist of BAC on *What's My Line?;* close Mt. Kisco neighbor and friend.

Mark Goodson (1915–92) and ***Bill Todman*** (1916–79), principals of the eponymous production company responsible for midcentury TV game shows such as *What's My Line?* and *To Tell the Truth.*

Kitty Carlisle Hart (née Catherine Conn), 1910–2007; husband Moss Hart, 1946 until his death in 1961. A singer and actress, famously the female lead in the Marx Brothers' *A Night at the Opera;* longtime panelist on the Goodson–Todman game show *To Tell the Truth;* later in life, chairwoman of the New York State Council on the Arts; Carlisle and Hart were among the closest friends of BAC and Phyllis Cerf.

Moss Hart, 1904–61, wife Kitty Carlisle. New York–born playwright (often co-wrote with George S. Kaufman, including *You Can't Take It with You*); screenwriter (e.g., for *A Star Is Born* with Judy Garland); theater director (including original Broadway production *My Fair Lady*); memoirist (*Act One,* an RH bestseller). BAC greatly admired Hart, one of two male non-relatives—DSK the other—whom he most loved.

Miriam Hopkins, 1902–72; an intellectual, Southern-born stage and screen actress, she became one of Paramount's top female stars. Although an early love interest of BAC, relationship quickly developed into friendship.

Leonora Hornblow (aka Leonora Salmon; Schinasi; Morris; also "Bubbles," "Bubs"), 1920–2005. BAC's confidante. Briefly married actor Wayne Morris, son Michael; second husband, movie producer Arthur Hornblow Jr. New York–born; tobacco heiress; published novels, an anthology, children's books with RH; extremely close to Cerfs.

George S. Kaufman, 1889–1961, prolific American comedic playwright, director, producer. Collaborated often, with Moss Hart, Edna Ferber, the Gershwins, the Marx Brothers. Member of Algonquin Round Table. First wife Beatrice. Friends to BAC.

Dorothy Kilgallen, 1913–65, Hearst Corporation daily columnist bylining The Voice of Broadway in the *New York Journal-American;* radio personality; longtime panelist on *What's My Line?* Under contract to RH for *Murder One* book, published posthumously.

Eugene O'Neill (see under *RH Authors*)

Richard "Dick" Rodgers, 1902–79, wife Dorothy (aka "La Perfecta"), friends of BAC. New York–born composer whose songs, with lyrics by Lorenz "Larry" Hart, form an integral part of the Great American Songbook, and whose partnership with lyricist Oscar Hammerstein II in shows such as *Carousel* and *South Pacific* brought a new level of drama, social awareness, and tragedy to American musical theater.

Ginger Rogers (aka Virginia Katherine McMath, "Cousin Ginger"), 1911–95, first cousin and surrogate sister of Phyllis Cerf; daughter of Lela Rogers; Hollywood star.

Lela Rogers (aka Aunt Lela, Lelee), 1891–1977, mother of Ginger Rogers; maternal aunt of Phyllis Cerf; early Marine; Hollywood talent school operator and producer; friend of FBI director J. Edgar Hoover; friendly witness at HUAC hearings.

Madeline Hurlock Sherwood (aka "the Dowdy Duchess"), 1897–1989, silent movie star known for her beauty in many Mack Sennett films. Robert Sherwood was her third husband, from 1935 until his death in 1955. A friend of the Cerfs, close to their sons.

Robert Sherwood, 1896–1955, stood six foot seven and was a prolific American playwright (*Abe Lincoln in Illinois*); screenwriter (*The Best Years of Our Lives*); and biographer (*Roosevelt and Hopkins: An Intimate History*). Greatly admired friend of BAC.

Sylvia Sidney (born Sophia Kosow), 1910–99, a New Yorker who began to act at the age of fifteen. Discovered on Broadway by Paramount head of production, B. P. Schulberg, and his agent wife, Adeline, she became a leading Paramount actress during the 1930s (also Schulberg's mistress). In October 1935 she married BAC, who was wildly in love with her. They divorced six months later. He never forgot her.

Frank Sinatra (born Francis Albert Sinatra), 1915–98, one of the greatest American entertainers of the twentieth century and likely a musical genius. He and BAC were close friends during the last half dozen years of BAC's life. Actress Mia Farrow was Sinatra's girlfriend and later wife during part of that period.

OTHER MAJOR CHARACTERS

J. Edgar Hoover, 1895–1972, director of the Bureau of Investigation (1924–35) and later the FBI (1935–72). Longtime friend of Ginger Rogers's mother, Lela. Cooperated with RH on *The FBI,* a 1954 Landmark series children's book by Quentin Reynolds, and *The FBI Story: A Report to the People,* by Don Whitehead, a 1956 book for adults.

David Sarnoff, 1891–71, son Robert ("Bobby"). "General" Sarnoff was longtime head of the Radio Corporation of America (RCA), and bought RH in 1966.

Prologue

August 31, 1971
"They Can't Take That Away from Me"

IT WAS A FUN FUNERAL. PEOPLE-WATCHING. REMINISCENCES. SHOW TUNES. Ask anyone who was there that day, and that's the first thing you'll be told. The second is that Bennett Cerf would have loved it—had it not, unfortunately, been his own. William Styron, Eudora Welty, John Hersey, and James Michener provided much of the script; *Sesame Street*'s young music director, Joe Raposo, played the tunes; Broadway's Tony Award winner Phyllis Newman sang a song, as a full house of more than six hundred mourners from near and far gathered in New York City to send Cerf off with a last good time.

Throughout most of his seventy-three years, this twentieth-century original had pursued happiness with all the restless energy an American could muster. Not for nothing did "Make Someone Happy" echo off the ivory keys. First and last a book publisher, one of the greatest, he also became, along the way, a radio and TV personality, newspaper and magazine columnist, anthologist, lecturer, and bon vivant. Some acquaintances, like *Cosmopolitan* editor Helen Gurley Brown, regarded him as "the friendliest, smilingest, pleasantest, encouragingest man," whether to nobodies or somebodies. Others found him buffoonish, a faucet leaking a steady stream of puns and jokes. No one, though, disputed the place he occupied in his world and time; he was a cultural force beloved by many.

Cerf enjoyed one of Manhattan's truly fabulous bird's-eye views, and from the mid-1940s through the late 1960s, his perch was literal as well as figurative: a third-floor office in the northern wing of a beautiful Italianate brownstone palace on the corner of Fifty-First Street and Madison Avenue. Everyone knew it as Random House, the publishing company he'd co-founded in the 1920s. It was a grand way to see the world, looking out on the lady chapel of St. Patrick's Cathedral, the soaring towers of Rockefeller Center in the distance, and his fellow New Yorkers hurrying about their business on the bustling avenue below. It was equally important to him that he be seen, and when he descended to the street—tall, well built, beautifully tailored, brown eyes bespectacled with bottle-thick lenses—he was very much part of that fine view.

They know me, he'd often say, explaining a daily phenomenon: he'd walk down the street—any street—and up they'd come.

"Hey, aren't you Bennett Cerf?" some would ask.

"I'd know you anywhere," others gushed.

His face and voice were familiar to just about every American. At 10:30 P.M. each Sunday night for sixteen years, millions of them welcomed him into their homes, sleek and smiling, a mainstay of a game show called *What's My Line?* The weekly half hour at weekend's close was part of the nation's routine, New York sophistication dressed up in tuxedos and gowns. He loved being "known," the recognition a necessary nourishment that seemed to give him a high-wattage glow. Bennett Cerf was almost always "on," the only U.S. publisher ever to be a truly public man. But as much as he loved being known, he loved his life in books. In 1925, when he was twenty-seven, he bought the Modern Library from its co-founder Horace Liveright; two years later, he started Random House. By the 1960s, it was the preeminent American book publisher.

Word had gone out on TV, radio, and the front pages of the Sunday papers: five minutes into Saturday, August 28, 1971, Bennett—he'd always insisted on being called that—had died in his bed at "The Columns," his weekend home in Mt. Kisco, an hour north of the city. Although that Friday afternoon he'd been released from a Manhattan hospital looking pale and drawn, no one had thought he was going to die. The news had come as a shock. Nobody knew what his health was; he hardly ever consulted a physician or complained. He always chose to look on the bright side. However, late in the fall of the previous year, a doctor had said he needed surgery on his gut; after that, he was never quite the same.

Bennett scrupulously kept a diary for most of his life. The pages are busy with *doing,* but rarely plumb any depths. Although his handwriting was tiny (chicken-scratch to the unfamiliar eye), anything major he noted in block capitals the way a precocious child might, expressing excitement, triumph, anger, or amazement such things were happening in his life. During the eight months between the first operation and his death, the diary veered up and down. Tuesday, May 25, a good day: "Poor old Cerf is 73!" That evening, Styron, Richard Rodgers, Frank Sinatra, Truman Capote, Rosalind Russell, and the New York mayor's wife, Mary Lindsay, gathered for birthday commiserations, partying until the wee hours. But by August 2: "Trouble, trouble!" Something was wrong with his right leg. He'd developed phlebitis, a vein inflammation that can deposit clots in the legs. And on August 15: "Damn leg no better." It was the last entry he would record.

Bennett didn't believe in organized religion; rather, he said, he believed in being good. Many didn't realize he was Jewish. His wife, Phyllis, raised Catholic, later adopted some habits of Christian Science. To make matters even more ecumenically confusing, they'd raised their two sons Presbyterian. A traditional religious ceremony wouldn't do. Phyllis traced her husband's horror of funerals to the minister never seeming to know the person he was burying, so when Random House's co-founder—Bennett's elegant business partner and long-avowed best friend, Donald Klopfer—drove over that Saturday morning from his country house in Greenwich, Connecticut, she asked him to preside.

"I can't, I just cannot do it," came the unexpected, blunt reply. Donald had never liked the limelight, to be sure, but much had also come between these two, who'd once been so inseparable. When the phone rang and John Daly, the former host of *What's My Line?,* wondered if there were any way he could help, Phyllis asked if *he* would do the honors, and Daly agreed. But Random House, not TV, had always been the center and heart of Bennett's life, and his first son, thirty-year-old Christopher, who'd worked there until joining the fledgling *Sesame Street* a year earlier, made sure Random was integral to the rites, soliciting from several authors brief remembrances for Daly to read aloud.

Richard Rodgers, who'd met Bennett when they were boys growing up in Jewish Harlem, helped the family choose the music. The songs would be by Rodgers, the Gershwins, and other friends of the American songbook that Bennett had loved. They would linger in the mourners' minds; even in the heyday of the Stones and the Dead, Broadway's ballads could speak across every generation and class.

Bennett's younger son, the shy, handsome Jonathan, and his wife,

Rosanne—they'd married just the previous year—asked that the funeral not occur on their wedding anniversary, Wednesday, September 1. The family agreed that it would take place on the Tuesday instead. Phyllis, whom Bennett had nicknamed "the General" for her ability to take charge of any situation, took charge now, and chose to hold the service at Frank E. Campbell's on Madison Avenue, the non-denominational way-stage to eternity for New York's famous and rich. Robert L. Bernstein, however, who'd succeeded Bennett as president of Random House in 1966, realized that a man who'd been supremely talented at collecting people would require much more space for his final goodbye.

"Is she out of her mind?" he asked Christopher. "Campbell's can't possibly hold enough people." Like any well-connected New Yorker, Bernstein picked up the phone. Fred Friendly, a pal, had spent years running CBS News and was now a professor at the Columbia Journalism School, Cerf's alma mater. After several more calls, it was agreed: the rites would take place at St. Paul's, the university chapel, at 11 A.M. on Tuesday.

Phyllis plunged into arrangements for the post-funeral feeding and watering of friends. Condolences poured in to the Cerf home and to Random House. As soon as the death was announced, Mayor John V. Lindsay had issued a statement calling it "a tragic loss," and proclaiming Bennett "one of the great men of the literary world, who made New York City the leader in books, art and communications." William Faulkner's widow and daughter wired from Mississippi. Robert Penn Warren, crediting his publisher as having the "very great gift" of making others feel good, wrote from France. Broadcaster Alistair Cooke, that quintessential British transplant, declared: "I can't possibly imagine New York without him."

But New York, without him, had managed to arrive at the last day of August in the troubled year of 1971. The city was going down a precipitous road that would stop just short of bankruptcy. Battles over desegregation and integration were being fought in North and South. Richard Nixon was invoking executive privilege to hide his military plans from Congress. People were worried, because for the fourth month in a row, the nation was buying more than it was selling abroad, the very first time such a prolonged trade imbalance had been recorded. American soldiers were dying, every day, in Vietnam.

That Tuesday morning, the overcooked air that habitually wraps itself around late-summer Manhattan lifted, and the sky above St. Paul's—a compact, new-world version of Italian Renaissance grandeur—was blue and clear. A hubbub surrounded the redbrick chapel, as cameramen and reporters milled about its white-columned portico while mourners streamed inside. The first two rows at the front on the left were reserved for Phyllis; Chris and his girlfriend, Genevieve; Jonathan and Rosanne; and the most elect and intimate of friends. A grand piano stood a few feet away. Several shallow steps led to two banks of choir stalls facing each other, perpendicular to the main body of the church.

At 10:45 A.M., the corps of ushers assembled. They were Random House men, along with Jon and Chris's best friends and Bennett's Hollywood pals Freddie Brisson (Rosalind Russell's husband) and the producer/director/screenwriter Joseph Mankiewicz. Their job was to identify the RH staff and funnel them to the choir stalls, and also to seat the first few rows of the main body of the church.

The honorary pallbearers were to be in front at the right, across the aisle from the family. First among them was Donald Klopfer, who had played the wise father in contrast to Bennett's role as the shining star in their long partnership. Others in the cadre included old Alfred Knopf, who'd sold his firm to Bennett in 1960; Sinatra, who'd showed his buddy "the Bookie" lots of good times during the past half dozen years; and *What's My Line?* producer Mark Goodson, the game show king. Bennett's old fraternity brother Horace Manges, now RH's attorney and the co-founder of a powerful New York firm, and Albert Erskine, his favorite editor, also did the honors. Truman Capote, seated in the chapel, had chosen not to be a pallbearer. He'd sent white roses and a note. As it happened, white roses covered the foot of the coffin that day.

Daly stood at the pulpit, glancing at his introduction and the authors' eulogies, waiting for the overflow crowd to settle and the music to stop. Then he spoke, declaring his friend "a glorious amalgam of pragmatist and leprechaun." Understanding that his main role was to share what others had written, he moved on. William Styron, sitting tall and somber beside his wife, Rose, and teenage daughter, Susanna, listened as his hastily composed words began to resonate in Daly's precise baritone.

Bennett might have appreciated that a few years earlier, Styron and Philip Roth were walking along a beach, "loftily pigeon-holing people into three categories—the well-poisoners, the lawn-mowers [most people], and the life-enhancers." Bennett, of course, belonged to that "rare and precious species," the life-enhancers, his vital force "so powerful, so seemingly indomitable, that he appeared virtually deathless." Styron recalled a night flight with his publisher "through a dark, lovely, star-crowded sky over Pennsylvania. The clear light of the cities below seemed to merge with the glittering stars, creating a wonderful radiant effect that touched us both deeply." Suddenly Bennett said something that from another man might seem odd, but expressed his essence. "Ah, Bill," he exclaimed, "I love being alive so much!"

Looking across the pews, it was also clear how Bennett had loved company. Eudora Welty, a Southerner like Styron, had taken up that theme in her reminiscence: Bennett's "keenness of mind," Daly read, "had so much gentleness of heart to go with it. I wonder," Welty had asked, "if anyone else of such manifold achievements in the publishing world could ever have had so many friends?"

Certainly, the world of books was there in force. Styron and Capote were joined by Ted Geisel, better known as Dr. Seuss; Rod McKuen, whose pop poetry had gained a huge following; Edgar Doctorow, just starting on the Random list; Ira Levin, progenitor of *Rosemary's Baby;* and Philip Roth, chronicler of *Portnoy's Complaint*. Distinguished publishers and editors had come from virtually every major house in the city, and some from further afield. Harper & Row's aged former president, Cass Canfield Sr., represented them all, the only other speaker besides Daly.

"I loved this man," he began in a quavering voice. "Bennett was gay, generous and charming. . . . He had the courage to defend our freedom to publish without government censorship. . . . He was a man with a quality of greatness."

Phyllis wept silently between her sons, who looked stunned and terribly young.

It was easy to recognize movie and television faces in the crowd. Bennett's fellow *What's My Line?* panelist Arlene Francis and her actor husband, Martin Gabel; *Love Story*'s Ali MacGraw; musical comedy star Danny Kaye, whose cheeks glistened with tears. Bennett had adored the theater—Eugene O'Neill was the first major author he'd signed—and Broadway sent playwrights, producers, composers, lyricists, and their partners to his last goodbye, among them Dick and Dorothy Rodgers and Kitty Carlisle. *Act One,* the memoir by Kitty's late husband, playwright/director Moss Hart, had been a number-one bestseller for Random. Bennett had loved Moss more than just about anyone.

The rare ability to unite different worlds and the disparate factions within them was one of Bennett's gifts. From politics came a Republican New York senator, Jacob Javits, and the city's Republican–turned–Liberal Party mayor, John Lindsay (who that year became a Democrat). Henry Kissinger, but also Hubert Humphrey; J. Edgar Hoover, but also George McGovern, sent condolences. Lady Bird Johnson's press secretary, Liz Carpenter, declared herself to have been, like many, "a little bit in love" with Bennett. Arthur Ochs Sulzberger, owner of *The New York Times,* and Dorothy Schiff, owner of the (then liberal) *New York Post,* were among the mourners, as was café society chronicler Suzy Knickerbocker, noting the presence of Gloria Vanderbilt and Walter Cronkite.

Novelist James Michener noted in his eulogy that Bennett could be counted on for some "outrageous pun," for "the involved yarn, narrated impeccably," or for "the classy one-liner." His jokes "were never vicious, nor at the expense of another man or another group"; rather, "they seemed to bubble up from the wellspring of humor itself," as if he were "attuned to some cosmic sense of the ridiculous, unknown to the rest of us."

John Hersey, best known for *Hiroshima,* recognized the "restless multiplicity" of Bennett's yearnings, and the "incongruity" defining his life. He took "great pride" in the *Ulysses* censorship fight, but also "in posing for an after-shave" ad; in "yachting with Frankie and owning Alfred"; in confiding what the mayor had told him the previous night, and in entering a friend's kitchen "to talk with the help" about *What's My Line?* The incongruities were "a unity" and the yearnings part of "the one great life-feeding desire: to be loved. . . . His entire life . . . was one long, zestful, ravenous boyhood."

Bennett *had* craved love, and wanted more of everything—attention, friendship, fun—not always wisely, but in whatever he did. Many responded to that need, and to the tremendous energy, warmth, boyish charm, and joyful enthusiasm that made him the world's best fan. That day, Random editor Nan Talese glanced around and marveled at such an outpouring of love. Then she looked over at Alfred Knopf, whom Bennett had considered the greatest publisher. "You will never have this outpouring," she predicted.

The fame and insatiable appetite for life, however, didn't endear Cerf to everyone. It was a different era, in which the power of celebrity hadn't yet overwhelmed so much of American life. In rushing to embrace the role of "TV personality," he'd anticipated the direction the culture would take, and helped make Random House and its books known in a way no other publisher could. But by going on TV—to play a game show, at that—and grinding out popular columns and joke books, he'd forfeited the right to be taken seriously by high-church worshippers at the literary altar.

Bill Styron and others close to Bennett recognized his duality and accepted it, knowing the "strange dichotomy" was something uncomfortable their publisher had had to deal with; but some intellectuals saw him as having "sold out." They thought he should have "been more dignified and given literature a better name." That paradox—of being both the famous, fun-loving, ultimately fleeting TV personality *and* the driven, dead-serious publisher-for-the-ages—defined him. Decades later, it would render him largely invisible and forgotten, which is the nature of modern celebrity itself. Yet it's in the power of funerals to try to reconcile all things, and for a brief time that August day, all were.

Thirty minutes after the funeral had begun, Bennett's friend Phyllis Newman got up to say goodbye. She took the microphone and sang:

"The way you wear your hat . . ."

"As I listened to the jokes," James Michener had written in his eulogy, "I never forgot that this unusual man had put together one of the strongest and most adventurous publishing houses in American literary history. He assembled a group of distinguished editors and notable writers who made Nobel and Pulitzer Prizes the habit. When the echo of the laughter is forgotten, that excellent row of books will be remembered."

Philip Roth agreed. Bennett had "fathered the Modern Library and ran a first-rate publishing house. That's all that mattered," he would later say.

"No, no, they can't take that away from me."

PART ONE

1898–1919

A Rather Unusual Specimen

What's amazing is that . . .
he did everything he did with so little a kick in the pants from fate.

—*Kitty Carlisle Hart*

Chapter 1

Inheritance

Go downtown, toward New York's early days, and head east along Rivington Street from the Bowery. Five-story walk-ups with dangling fire escapes—utterly gentrified now, boasting hip cafés and expensive boutiques—give way to a phalanx of towers erected during the 1960s, in the name of urban renewal. In buildings that once stood here, numbered 170 and 258, the two sides of Bennett's family lived after they arrived, three decades apart, in the nineteenth century. Serendipity, yes, but not so surprising: during most of its existence, Rivington was a street for starting over, a cramped, narrow foothold on the ladder of immigrant dreams. Some of the American dreams these ancestors harbored there came true—and helped make Bennett Cerf's possible.

When he was sixty-nine, his alma mater asked Bennett to record his New York story for posterity in a series of interviews, and he agreed. "I'm rather an unusual specimen," he began. Not only he and his parents, he proudly explained, but also his four grandparents, had been born on the island of Manhattan. To an establishment figure of his time, in a country deeply ambivalent about its immigrant roots, a three-generation born-in-America pedigree brought advantages and silenced prejudices. Still, he cautioned, his background was "shrouded in some mystery," and he'd never bothered poking into the history of his forebears. He did know that his father's father, Marcel Cerf, was a jeweler, and his mother's father was in the tobacco business.

New York, a city adept at covering over its past, hosts many citizens adept at covering over theirs, and Bennett's background wasn't such a mystery to him after all. In 1941, he was a man of forty-three when he had to give the City of New York vital family details after his father, Gustave, died. The death certificate specified that Gustave's mother was born in Germany, not America. A few days after losing his dad, Bennett was inspired to jot down a brief "Cerf Family" tree, where he noted that his father's father was born in a village in upstate New York in 1834. However, the grandfather wasn't called Marcel, the name Bennett had cited in his oral history; he was Benoît. The likely explanation is that Bennett was putting distance between himself and the embarrassing foreign name on his own birth certificate. In the Jewish tradition, a child is named after a deceased relative, and when Gustave's son was born on May 25, 1898, the man Americans would know as Bennett Cerf was officially "Benoît." His grandfather had died three years earlier.

In the mid-nineteenth century, many denizens of growing Gotham found each other through annual directories brought out by enterprising printer/publishers. In 1843–44, out of a total population of 371,000 persons, Doggett's *New-York City Directory* listed 55,000 of their names, one being Lazarus Cerf, Bennett's great-grandfather, a peddler at 258 Rivington. A year later, Caroline, his newly widowed wife, is listed at that address.

Lazarus and Caroline had come to America from France, probably Alsace; at times, Bennett joked that his ancestors had been Strasbourg horse thieves. Their surname, derived from Hebrew, literally means "deer" or "stag," and was not unusual for French Jews. (On the German-speaking side of the border, the name would have been "Hirsch" or "Hart," carrying the same meaning.) Lazarus had probably made clocks and watches in the old country: certainly, in 1850, his sixteen-year-old son, Benoît, was listed as a clockmaker living with his mother, and a year later—along with a brother—had become a watchmaker. Once the Civil War broke out, Benoît served in the New York State Militia. After he returned home, the brothers expanded into jewelry. By 1870, he'd married Bavarian-born Mathilda Newwitter and fathered four children. Two-year-old Augustin was later known as Gustave. Benoît had amassed real estate worth $3,500, a fair sum; within a decade, he'd moved home and business across the river to Brooklyn.

Bennett's mother, Fredericka Wise Cerf, was the fifth of nine children of Nathan and Delphine Wise. Grandmother Delphine was born in Luxembourg or Germany—boundaries were fluid, depending on the latest war—but definitely not in New York. She died in January 1893, twenty-nine days after giving birth to her last child, Herbert, so Bennett never knew her, but he did know her husband. Until he was ten, Bennett had to spend every Sunday at his grandfather's home. Nathan Wise

Fredericka Wise Cerf

sported a beard "like the Smith brothers," Bennett recalled—that iconic WASP pair whose image adorned boxes of cough drops sold all over twentieth-century America. But Nathan was no WASP: he was a stern Jewish immigrant who'd arrived from Bremen while the Civil War raged. His passport application said he was big-nosed, long-faced, bearded, and his first known address was 170 Rivington. Therefore, despite Bennett's boast, only *one* grandparent had been born in America (and not in Manhattan). An unusual specimen indeed.

"Cerf was a great exaggerator," the former *New York Times* managing editor Arthur Gelb once said. He knew how to play to an audience of thousands, or to a tape recorder and audience of one. Like every successful salesman, he was above all selling himself, and as both public man and publisher, Bennett's blurring of the line between fact and myth would be a defining characteristic—and prove immeasurably useful.

Christopher and Jonathan Cerf don't recall their father, the great storyteller, telling them anything about the maternal side of his family. Nonetheless, Nathan Wise, forgotten though he may be, isn't so easily lost. Between his arrival in the United States in 1863 and his death in 1908, Wise made a small fortune. His shadow not only loomed over Bennett's childhood, but extended across his life, and the legacy he left was what enabled his grandson to buy into the book business. To some extent, Bennett's self-imposed forgetting was a reinvention typical of Jews of his era, when antisemitism was rife. Instead of digging up roots to examine, easier to bury them under ancestral amnesia and Americanized names. But it's likely more came into play in this case.

Nathan Wise started in the tobacco trade. During the nineteenth century, the cigar was most men's smoke of choice, and New York became the country's manufacturing center. Virtually every immigrant nationality was involved, but Germans predominated, Jews among them. Once the cigarette began its ascent in the 1860s, Jews were heavily involved in that, too. In an 1874 city directory, "Nathan Wise, tobacco" is listed at 170 Rivington Street, but by 1880 he'd helped form a trade group, the Wholesale Tobacco Association in the City of New York, and had joined another German Jew, Adolph M. Bendheim, to deal in tobacco at 254 Canal Street.

Soon, however, there was a new tobacco player in town. James Buchanan Duke arrived from North Carolina in 1884 with huge ambition, and within a few months the tough young man had established a factory to mass-produce cigarettes. Five years later, Duke made and sold almost half the country's cigarettes, and had pressured four competitors to join him in starting the American Tobacco Company. He conspired to take over the cigar business, too, using independent competitors who cooperated to crush the rest. In 1899, both *The New York Times* and *The Wall Street Journal* announced the arrival of a "big new" firm, Metropolitan Tobacco. Its eleven directors included three Bendheims, a Bendheim spouse, and Nathan Wise. However, the *Brooklyn Eagle,* on its front page, rebuked Metropolitan for what it was: a smokescreen for a robber baron, the trust that Duke used to control tobacco distribution in the entire New York area.

Bennett glancingly referred to this in his oral history, saying that a young man had offered Nathan a partnership that his "conservative" grandfather didn't think good. "The man's name was Duke. . . . My grandfather thought [him] a wild young fellow, which indeed he was. But at that, my grandfather when he died had amassed a million dollars."

The description of the proposed partnership is oddly equivocal. Initially, it sounds as though Nathan rebuffed Duke, yet the phrase "but at that" *does* imply Nathan made his money through Duke—and of course, Duke amassed a great fortune. It's also odd that Bennett, an inveterate name-dropper, was so ambiguous, given that RH had published a Duke biography that mentioned Metropolitan. He'd even written a brief article about the book, and Duke's "hydra-headed trust." But though he undeniably enjoyed being linked to the famous, Bennett always said he believed in "being good." The ruthlessness most likely inherent in the business between Wise and Duke was something else entirely.

Tobacco made Nathan rich, but he parlayed that money into land deals that made him richer still. The late nineteenth century was a special moment in New York history, when the separate city of Brooklyn, the Bronx, parts of Westchester County, and the villages and farms of Queens and Staten Island were, by a series of annexations, brought into the metropolis; on January 1, 1898—five months before Bennett's birth—New York City was incorporated within its current boundaries. The scramble was on for the choicest real estate parcels to exploit, particularly in upper Manhattan and the Bronx. As immigrants poured in, huge projects—railways, bridges, subways—were undertaken to bind together the vastly expanded city. Nathan and his partners were in the thick of it, and it was in Washington Heights, the Bronx, and bordering areas of Westchester that he was most active—both individually and as part of a syndicate with Bendheim et al.—trading in dimensions, locations, and the future. He was also a pioneer of building loans.

Just as Nathan and his partners were willing to become Duke's men to flourish in the cutthroat tobacco trade, so, too, they weren't averse to greasing political wheels to deal in land. When Bennett's parents married, the announcement identified the bride as "daughter of Mr. Nathan Wise, Commissioner of the Street Opening Department in the annexed district," i.e., the Bronx. He lobbied for future subway stations to be near his properties, at times succeeding; but his most spectacular coup, early in 1902, involved New York's proposed Pennsylvania Station. Nathan's syndicate had ferreted out advance information and bought a dozen crucial parcels of the hundred on which the great rail terminal was to be built, in effect holding the Pennsylvania Railroad to ransom, in the end selling for "a consideration of $140,000 over mortgages aggregating $239,900."

Bennett never forgot those Sundays at the townhouse where his grandfather resided with his second wife, Bettie. They owned the first car he ever saw, and everyone "kow-towed" to the Wise family patriarch. Children, however, can't always be on best behavior, and at dinner,

Nathan would reach across and wallop some offending child over the knuckles "with a marvelous backhand that moved so fast, you didn't see it coming." Never-quiet Bennett tried to sit as far away from "Grandpa" as possible.

Nathan expected deference and obedience; despite this—or, perhaps, because of it—his daughter Fredericka left home at twenty-three to elope with twenty-eight-year-old Gustave Cerf, her elocution tutor. Gustave's family "was loaded with charm but not much money," Bennett recalled. Nathan was "outraged" by the match. Gustave would never develop a head for business and was bad at hanging on to what money he made. Financially and socially, Fredericka had come down in the world through her marriage.

Gustave Cerf

Gustave had hoped to be a professional baseball player and had gotten a tryout with the Brooklyn Dodgers, but hadn't made it. Baseball nevertheless remained an obsession: when Bennett was growing up, his father managed to see nearly every game played at the Polo Grounds. He only "just about made a living" as a lithographer; later, he'd be employed by his son at Random House packing books, writing letters, and generally keeping busy. Bennett "absolutely adored him."

This upbringing under the influence of two such very different men helps to explain Bennett's extraordinary drive—a quality that Kitty Carlisle, a close observer of the cultural scene, found hard to figure out, given her good friend's family resources. From the 1920s to the 1960s in America, she pointed out, "the creative body of work was done to a large extent by Jews, [who] gravitated towards each other. Bennett, like the rest of us, wanted to get up in the world. Most of us had to struggle; what's amazing is that [his] family had money, and yet he did everything he did with so little a kick in the pants from fate. To be born with money is a handicap, from the point of view of extraordinary accomplishment in the intellectual and creative fields."

And yet, with a grandfather like Nathan and a father like Gustave, Bennett's conflicting needs—to do big things, make money, be universally known, while at the same time to be jokey, fun, widely beloved—are not so inexplicable. What he set out to accomplish is rooted in the interplay of trajectories and tensions of two very different New York immigrant families, and the prisms through which they defined success.

...

FOR A HUNDRED AND fifty years, an area straddling the border between Brooklyn and Queens has been a land of the dead, where cemetery abuts cemetery as far as the eye can see. The lanes within these tracts have the same air of age—and agelessness—as the streets of Pompeii. In one, Mt. Neboh, Nathan was laid to rest, the bronze doors and Greek columns of his mausoleum near the very front of the cemetery. Nathan's heirs transacted one more deal on his behalf in October 1908, when they paid $1,500 for the plot. He'd come a long way from Rivington Street. The doors open to dampness, yet light filters in through a stained-glass window revealing burial chambers on either side. Nathan is kept company by a son lost in childhood; his first wife, Delphine; his second wife, Bettie; Bennett's mother, Fredericka; and her sister. On the ground sit two square bronze urns, holding the ashes of Bennett's father, Gustave, and his uncle Herbert Wise.

After Bennett's own death, Phyllis and his son Jonathan stood beneath his favorite tree, a copper beech at the foot of the lawn below the house in Westchester, and scattered his ashes into the Kisco River, which runs through the property—a gesture Nathan might have found incomprehensible, on a parcel of land he surely would have appreciated.

As for Bennett's legacy, when taping his oral history, he'd tried to sum up his philosophy, coming as close to the topic of mortality as he ever would: "If you can leave people a little bit happier after they leave you than . . . when they met you, you are my idea of a valuable citizen." When roaming the halls of Random House, the question he asked wasn't "How are you?" but "Are you happy?" He, in turn, always had to be "happy." However, as one acquaintance pointed out, "Nobody can be that happy all of the time."

Chapter 2

A Pretty Smart Kid

IN THE LAST DECADES OF THE NINETEENTH CENTURY AND FIRST DECADE of the twentieth, many upwardly mobile German Jewish families migrated to live middle-class lives in Harlem, in an area bordered on the south by Central Park and on the north by 125th Street. Houses and apartments were new or nearly so, synagogues sprouted up, and horse-drawn carriages echoed through the tree-lined streets. Fredericka "Frieda" Wise and Gustave Cerf moved to 68 West 118th Street after marrying on November 11, 1896, in a ceremony presided over by the rabbi of Harlem's richest reform congregation. At twenty-three, Frieda was a bit older than the average bride, and in a few photos one eye turns slightly. Maybe it hadn't been so easy to find a husband; in any event, Nathan Wise sufficiently tamped down his "outrage" at her choice to be present at (and presumably pay for) the wedding.

Eighteen months later, Bennett was born at home. He once let slip that his mother nearly died giving him life. His father made a living designing advertising layouts and labels for ketchup, cigarettes, and the like. The Cerfs lived with a nineteen-year-old Hungarian servant, as well as Frieda's bookkeeper brother, George, and his German bride; seven other families populated the rest of the building. Life got better in 1910, when Gustave, Frieda, and Bennett decamped to a brand-new, six-story apartment building at 201 West 121st Street, with neighbors including a doctor and a lawyer.

The "very handsome, charming, wonderful" Gustave (as his son described him), with proud handlebar mustache, light brown hair, twinkling eyes, and open face, delighted in fun and games. "Papa" (later "Pop") would call Bennett "Sonny" for the rest of his life. Frieda was different. In one early picture of mother and son, little Bennett is "Mama's" carefully cosseted boy in white knickerbockers and mariner's jer-

Mother and son, about age four

sey, pouty under bowl-cut bangs, his big dark eyes and dark hair hers, but Frieda doesn't smile in this or other photos. Bennett insisted he was born into "a very happy family" with parents who were "gloriously in love and wondrously happy for their entire lives," but he went on to depict his mother as "the most sensitive woman in the world—very easily hurt," always with "some fancied slight" to complain about. He and Gustave had to reassure Frieda that others weren't trying to "insult" her. And so, rather than happiness, her grave face and perception of "insults" seem to convey melancholy, insecurity, or both, surely connected to being Nathan's daughter and Gustave's wife.

While Bennett had inherited his father's love of fun, he admitted that he, like his mother, could be "terribly easily hurt." Yet although "terribly sensitive," he did enjoy teasing others. Often kidding his father, the would-be pro, about "not being able to hit Big League"—Gustave always took the bait and resented it—Bennett seemed unaware of the hurt such teasing might cause his dad (or, later, his own sons).

The childhood he liked to recall was classic New York. Not Lower East Side, up-from-poverty, but recognizable. How much had actually happened, and how much was embroidery, added to please an audience, is impossible to know. Bennett told the tape recorder that Frieda made the mistake of dressing him in a fancy Buster Brown collar on the first day of school, but the bloody nose he got taught him to be one of the boys. He and his friends played stickball and hitched onto ice wagons, roller-skating through town; on hot days, they stole treats of ice. On the edge of a "tough" neighborhood, "we were tough little kids," he bragged. After all, wasn't that how New York boys were supposed to be?

At P.S. 10—an impressive, recently built elementary school with stepped Dutch roofs—his "real life began." Bennett made new friends, some of whom would later become famous. He wanted to be one of the crowd, and described his parents and their politics as "absolutely middle class . . . in conformity with the day." However, he also wanted to set himself apart, even if it involved questionable behavior and a sort of shamelessness. Cocky about always causing "commotion," he recalled being one among other "nasty little boys" who enjoyed peeing into flasks kept by a hated science teacher in his supply closet. On the other hand, he was also "a pretty smart kid. I didn't have to work too hard. I never have," he boasted. He developed an ability to read fast, and as an adult would almost photographically imprint pages onto his brain, absorbing perhaps eight hundred words a minute: an invaluable gift for a publisher.

Other than the neighborhood, there was nothing very Jewish about his childhood. He maintained that he didn't see the inside of a synagogue until he was thirteen, when, noticing that boys were given a bicycle for their bar mitzvah, he decided to do whatever it took to get one. Having cajoled his amazed parents to agree, he learned the transliterated Hebrew texts and went through the ceremony, but was terribly disappointed in the end, when his mother declared bike-riding too dangerous for her one-and-only. The experience "soured" him permanently on religion, Bennett claimed in the oral history.

He insisted that in spite of his grandfather's wealth, his parents managed on what Gustave made: his pop wouldn't let Frieda ask her father for help, and Nathan saw his son-in-law as "the soft touch of the world." But when Bennett was eight, Nathan did let Gustave in on the real estate game, through a string of small land transfers. It didn't last; nor did work as a hosiery salesman for Frieda's brothers. His pop was a great salesman, Bennett recalled—until the ballgame started, and he'd disappear to the Polo Grounds.

Frieda always liked to read, and she introduced her son to books like *Black Beauty* and *Rebecca of Sunnybrook Farm*. Soon he was smitten with sports and adventure magazines and became a fan of the prolific Ralph Henry Barbour, whose novels he devoured at a library two blocks from home. He was devoted to the *St. Nicholas* magazine, a widely read children's monthly. Its "St. Nicholas League" sponsored contests for children to submit their own work, and many would-be writers and artists—William Faulkner, F. Scott Fitzgerald, Edna St. Vincent Millay, and Bennett himself—participated. He also put together a small newspaper with friends.

Cerf family, "absolutely middle class"

On July 20, 1908, two months after Bennett turned ten, something important happened: his grandfather died in Marienbad, a Bohemian spa town where the wealthy went to take a cure. Only a month earlier, Nathan Wise had signed a will in New York listing seven equal beneficiaries: his second wife and six surviving children. The widow and two older sons received inheritances outright; trusts were put in place for each daughter, and for Herbert, the youngest son. The will specified that should Frieda die, her funds would flow through the trust to her offspring. Nathan had ensured that Gustave could not touch the money. "The estimated value of the real property . . . is upward of ten thousand dollars" (about $341,000 today), court papers declared. In those days, $10,000 was common shorthand to maintain privacy while indicating a very large sum. Personal property was also valued at "upward of ten thousand." Bennett, so given to exaggeration, said his grandfather was a millionaire; this time, there is very good reason to believe him.

. . .

AS SUBWAY CONSTRUCTION PROCEEDED north, developers transformed wooded land into a forest of "high-class" apartment blocks, and Washington Heights was prime territory. Four months after Nathan died, his former partners bought Audubon Park, between Broadway and Riverside Drive, from 155th to 158th Streets. Two of Nathan's partners developed the "Riviera" apartments. Extending from 156th to 157th Street, facing the Drive, the Hudson, and New Jersey's Palisades, the building was advertised as "the largest and most up-to-date" on Riverside when it opened in 1911. A month later, when Bennett turned thirteen, the Cerfs moved there, to a spacious apartment on the twelfth floor. Along with airy views, it came with upper-middle-class comforts like polished wood floors and bathrooms with showers. Much was made of its being fireproof, the Triangle Shirtwaist fire having blazed downtown that same year.

The move brought outdoor space, where Bennett and his buddies played ball. It also brought him close to the river. He'd watch from his high window as night boats steamed up to Albany, their searchlights playing from one side of the Hudson to the other. "Wonderful," is how he described it. During several summers, Bennett would board one of those boats, thrilled to be on it, then take a train to reach camp in the Adirondacks with P.S. 10 schoolmates Mortimer "Morty" Rodgers; Morty's kid brother, "Dick"; and Richard Rodgers's future Broadway musical collaborator, Lorenz "Larry" Hart.

Nevertheless, Bennett was a city boy through and through, and at fifteen, after several tries, won a silver badge from the St. Nicholas League for an essay on the theme "After Vacation," turning it into a paean to his hometown. "Back into the bustle of the large city, the clanging of bells and the tooting of horns, Broadway, with its millions of tiny, yet brilliant, electric lights—we are at home!" he wrote. "Our hearts throb . . . after all, there was something missing in the country, an indefinable something that seemed somewhat to spoil our pleasure. Perhaps it was the air of loneliness and quiet; we were born in the city and brought up in the city—brought up to be one of a great multitude . . . to rush and hustle . . . and we *can't do without it*!"

It was at the Riviera—as much as P.S. 10—that his "real life" began. The family of Howard Dietz, who'd go on to write songbook standards and run publicity at MGM, moved into the building. Other pals were Merryle Rukeyser, who grew up to become financial editor at two city papers, as well as a financial columnist for Hearst; and Elliott Sanger, who would start New York radio station WQXR. Across the street lived

DeWitt Wallace, eventual co-founder of *Reader's Digest*. Such connections would later prove invaluable. But during these Riviera years, Bennett would also awaken more fully to books and the worlds they opened.

That autumn of 1911, he entered Townsend Harris Hall, the academically elite, all-male public high school attached to the City College of New York. Twenty blocks south of the Riviera, it was the city's sole college-preparatory public school, with entrance determined by competitive exam. Once enrolled, students accustomed to acing tests suddenly found them more difficult. "The dropouts were fantastic," was how Bennett recalled his first year. But if a boy got in and stayed the three-year course (four years' work was squeezed into three), a place was guaranteed at City College, and as a magnet for smart sons of immigrant New York, the fiercely competitive school had no equal.

Bennett studied French, English, math, history, and drawing his first year, earning grades in the 70s and 80s. He added German in his second. His grades improved, the man who liked to brag he never had to work hard doing just that. But he didn't return to be a senior in September 1913, and only a full year later, in the fall of 1914, did he study again, not at Townsend Harris, but at the Packard Commercial School, a private trade school, to learn penmanship, double-entry bookkeeping, and other practical skills. He also got a part-time job with an accountant, visiting clients to check their books after class each day.

Decades later, he justified abandoning high school because he'd determined he "was going to make money," but neither the rationale nor the timing makes sense. College graduates generally make *more* money, and Jewish families traditionally value higher education, not least to help their children do just that. Then as now, when a bright student gives up, it's almost always linked to illness or family circumstance. Frieda Cerf came under a physician's care in September 1913; on May 24, 1914, she died. Her son's dropping out, the empty year, and the decision to go to Packard are all tied up in her illness and death.

Bennett recalled in his oral history that Frieda had been "desperately anxious" to have another child. He was five when she'd given birth to a baby who died soon after. A series of miscarriages followed, until Frieda was told she "wasn't strong enough" to sustain another pregnancy. She tried again, and the baby girl lived but a few weeks. The ordeal "weakened my mother to the point that less than a year later, she died," Bennett explained. "It was the day before I [turned] sixteen. . . . Well, that was a blow."

However, Frieda's death certificate specified a very different cause: peritonitis stemming from advanced cancer of the colon and bones. She was only forty. In those days, cancer was for the most part a death sentence and taboo, a word not spoken. The patient sometimes wasn't told the nature of her illness; her husband might not have been informed at first. Perhaps Bennett hadn't known exactly what was going on.

Was Frieda desperate to keep him close, rather than in school that final year? Could Gustave not manage without him at home? Impossible to know. But how alarming and perplexing for a teen, in close quarters with his "terribly sensitive" mother, during months of increasing pain, awful decline, and fear. Bennett's opting for the fast track to work and adulthood was a not-unreasonable response. His later avoidance of discussing or dealing with anything touching on illness or death becomes more understandable.

In January 1915, eight months after Frieda died, Bennett began keeping a diary, but he didn't record any feelings about her death until 1918, following a different "blow." "Barring May 24, 1914—the day on which Mama died—today was the bitterest one in my life," he wrote. Father and son would visit the cemetery to mark the anniversary of her death, customary even for secular Jews. Frieda's brother Herbert, just five years older than Bennett, moved into the Riviera apartment to keep them company. Just as Bennett adored his father, his father adored his one precious child. "The important thing," Bennett once said, was that he and Gustave were together until his father's death decades later, an exceptional closeness noticed by many.

A year and a day after Frieda's death, Bennett turned seventeen and graduated from Packard. His after-class bookkeeping had taken him all over the city, mostly within the garment trade. Evenings and weekends had been a social whirl—a steady, rich diet of lunches, dinners, Wises and Cerfs. Restaurants, movies, vaudeville, theater, tennis, and skating filled hours and blotted out memories. He also learned about vacations. After graduating, Bennett took off most of the summer, first at the Jersey shore, then in New Hampshire, where relatives awaited. He didn't return until September.

Lanky, clean-cut, wanting to please, he had a ready smile and chatted winningly. He'd been hired as salesman by a bookkeeping client, National Petticoat Manufacturing, and started when he got back. That fall, he also attended a night class in salesmanship at Columbia. Days were busy, yet it wasn't enough—and Herbert had been working on him. On December 16, 1915, in red ink and capitals, Bennett told his diary: "DECIDED TO QUIT WORK, & PREPARE FOR COLLEGE." Saying goodbye to salesman's samples, he declared: "SETTLING DOWN TO A LONG, HARD, STEADY GRIND. . . ."

Chapter 3

Columbia

IN THOSE DAYS, IT WAS POSSIBLE TO BE ADMITTED TO COLUMBIA without a high school diploma, by attending extension courses and passing entrance exams. Dark and serious, Herbert had persuaded his nephew to work toward that goal, and had offered himself as a tutor. His influence would be enormous. Bennett thought him brilliant, an intellectual and arts lover who "knew everything." In 1910, Herbert himself had enrolled at the university and done well, captaining the chess team, but midway through his junior year he vanished from the rolls. Perhaps it was illness: Bennett would later note Herbert's bouts with tuberculosis, which had made him slightly hunchbacked.

The months they worked together weren't all slog. Interspersed with the coaching sessions were tennis matches, relief from cramming for a boy who couldn't sit still. Bennett fiercely wanted to win, and recorded in his diary what was won (and, far less often, lost) in his endeavors. Whether at a ball game, tracking stocks, pursuing a book deal, or in a match against the uncle he saw as "never terribly strong," he always kept score. Herbert hardly ever won a game, let alone a match, and yet he triumphed in the most crucial way: in July 1916, Bennett was notified that he'd made the grade to enter college that autumn, and would grasp the ticket to greater things after all.

Founded in 1754, Columbia had moved from tight midtown quarters up to a Morningside Heights campus less than twenty years before, led by then-president Seth Low. With an idealistic vision of a college-metropolis alliance, Low changed the name from Columbia University to "Columbia University in the City of New York," and searched for patrons who could do for it what Leland Stanford did in Palo Alto, and John D. Rockefeller in Chicago. *New York World* publisher Joseph Pulitzer obliged, funding an endowment for a school of journalism and stipulating that "suitable candidates" lacking certain credentials required by Columbia College could be admitted. Bennett, without Latin or Greek, was thus able to enter, one of 176 male and 47 female freshmen in the Journalism School's fifth class.

During Bennett's college years, Low's successor, Nicholas Murray Butler, was president. An "imperious chief executive," Butler saw the school as "a training ground for America's elite." "Hebrews" now comprised just under half of those graduating from New York public high schools, but antisemitic prejudice was quasi-institutionalized at most major American universities, and quotas were enforced. Still, 10 to 15 percent of those matriculating at Columbia were Jews, and many, like Bennett, lived at home. After America entered World War I in April 1917, there were students who left for military service, including some Jewish students, but the overall effect was the proportion of Jews rising to as much as 25 percent. Despite the discriminatory policies, the perception on the street became: "All Columbia students are Jews."

On September 21, 1916, Bennett Alfred Cerf—it's a mystery how he'd acquired a middle name that does not appear on his birth certificate—traveled three express stops downtown from the Riviera and arrived at the 116th Street campus entrance raring to go. He was six feet tall, 136 pounds thin, dark-haired, dark-eyed, handsome (and, whenever a photo was in the offing, whipped off the glasses that his nearsightedness required). He came by his college nickname, "Beans," thanks to the amazing energy that fueled him. Even before being admitted to the university, he'd been accepted into a fraternity: Morty Rodgers had introduced him to Pi Lambda Phi while he was still taking extension classes. The president of the fraternity was Oscar Hammerstein II. Another brother was Horace Manges, who would become Bennett's (and Random House's) attorney.

The Journalism School seemed a natural choice for the *St. Nicholas* silver medalist and boy who'd compiled a small newspaper. "You're born wanting to do things like that," he later said, emphasizing: "A good editor, like a good author, has to be born with some of the necessary talents." Before classes started, he'd approached the college paper, the *Spectator,* to introduce himself. Soon he was doing brief stories, and quickly landed bigger ones. By Christmas, he'd been elected to the paper's associate board.

His time at college coincided with rapid change in New York—now a city of 4.8 million—and the world. The Great War was inflicting dreadful casualties. Leon Trotsky left his temporary home in Manhattan to spearhead the Bolshevik Revolution. Agitation was growing for women's suffrage. Being on the paper expanded Bennett's life. When they gave talks, he encountered writers like Heywood Broun and Alexander Woollcott, as well as Herbert Swope, editor of the *New York World*. Two months into his freshman year, he was elected to the Class of 1920 organizing committee, and busily collected friends in Harlem and the Upper West Side, almost all with German Jewish surnames.

The new world of Columbia was juggled with the old one shared with Herbert and Pop. Home was felicitous: father and uncle joined him and his friends late at night for cozy games of miniature bowling and parlor golf in the apartment, and launched speculative discussions of great import, around such topics as "What we'd do if we had to get married tomorrow to win $12,000,000." Gustave was in his hosiery-selling phase, and Herbert described himself as a "writer." He'd become a friend and supporter of poets like Hart Crane, all the while devoting much energy to looking after his stocks, buying and selling through a good friend who was a broker. He was gifted at it. By the time Bennett graduated, Herbert had become a valued customer of the brokerage and made a lot of money. One other relative inspired great affection in Bennett: his first cousin Delphine, whose family had moved to Portland, Oregon, but returned for visits. In those days, attachments between first cousins were not infrequent. However, Bennett also saw other girls, and in August 1917, sixteen-year-old redhead Marie Mayer entered his diary, and would remain his girlfriend through the rest of college.

At Columbia, his journalistic career blossomed. Early in his second semester, he started a sports column in the *Spectator,* thrilled to "tag" his initials to it. Soon he contributed imaginary "interviews" to Stroller, a thrice-weekly column, and then was tasked with running it. He figured out how to fill column inches by asking everyone—even Herbert—to contribute, "because I'm blankety blanked if I do it alone!" He also wrote for the school humor magazine, the *Jester,* and in January 1918 became editor-in-chief.

The Beans were jumping, despite some youthful misjudgments. Thanks to Marie, he got a ticket to Barnard College's Greek games, where young women tried to re-create the athletic competitions of the ancients. When he covered them "like a burlesque show," the dean was

Surrounded by Columbia classmates

outraged. Another time, it was President Butler himself who hauled him in. He'd printed a friend's cartoon of a couple dancing the shimmy, with an English lord commenting—in Bennett's immortal aristocratic-Cockney caption—"All I can say is, I 'opes he marries the girl." Any more vulgarity, Butler threatened, and Bennett and his cartoonist friend would be expelled. For the most part, though, his progress seemed charmed. "I want to congratulate you upon the copy of the *Jester* which just came to my desk," the acting dean of the Journalism School wrote in March 1918.

A pattern was set. Many of his columns were sunny fluff, not unlike the magazine anecdotes he'd churn out decades later. That deep love for his hometown—so evident in the *St. Nicholas* story—also infused his college work. Bennett began one piece that still carries a certain resonance by wondering how many students new to the city worried that the average New Yorker was a "cold . . . unapproachable maverick." But as "a New Yorker first, last and all the time," he knew "no better-intentioned creature than the average person you will rub shoulders with. Maybe Stroller can help show . . . the more human side of New York. . . . Smile—that's what we want to make you do!"

Making people smile wasn't always easy. A police inspector at a meeting he reported on warned that the city's aqueduct system had to be guarded from anarchists, "for one stick of dynamite" might cut off the water supply. Shortages came with war: lacking enough coal during the 1918 winter, Columbia on some days had to cancel classes. Bennett's liberal inclinations came into focus, and he learned that a sports story—or almost any story—could convey social or political commentary. On the other hand, sometimes he seemed determined *not* to see things: there's no diary mention or clipping on the influenza pandemic that claimed about thirty thousand city lives.

After the United States entered the war on April 6, 1917, Bennett signed up for naval patrol with the Student Army Training Corps. Instruction began that October. In June 1918, he left for Connecticut and intensive training at "Camp Columbia," where he stood out for not-strictly-military activities: composing the camp marching song, producing the draft of the musical comedy revue, and getting himself appointed editor-in-chief of the magazine. Judged "good [officer] material," he hoped to ship out to Europe, but an eye test showed him to be so nearsighted that, even with the new draft law, he feared he'd be shunted into limited service and, along with "the riff-raff," miss out. A month later, it was worse: the medical board decided there was something wrong with his heart. In the end, a specialist reversed the heart decision, and by "judicious manipulation" in another eye test, he was deemed correctable to normal with glasses. On October 1, he was inducted into the artillery school of Columbia SATC, and two weeks later Bennett headed to infantry officer training at Camp Lee, Virginia. His military career proved short-lived, however: the armistice was signed on November 11, and three weeks later, Private Cerf received an honorable discharge.

Even so, his college progress was helped, rather than hindered, by the war. At the start of the semester, he'd been working as night editor on the *Spectator* when he came across news that was not yet public: students who went away to military service would get credit for classes in which they were already enrolled. At once Bennett signed up for several difficult courses—physics was one—that he hardly attended. As promised, he got the credit, and, after adding more by going to summer school, had satisfied the academic requirements of both the Journalism School and Columbia College for a joint degree. Although he'd officially graduate with his class the following spring, he was done with college by September 1919, and rather successfully: he was elected to Phi Beta Kappa.

So many pieces informing the man fell neatly into place at college: grasping how to write amusingly and fast for publication; honing his innate ability to schmooze, charm, and make the right connections; learning, as he put it, "not to clutter" his mind with useless information, but instead where to find it when necessary, and "just how to go about getting [it]." Not least consequential for his future career was his immersion in texts. His diaries are full of books, the excitement of a mind opening to the possibilities and worlds in them, and of quick, instinctive reactions that would serve him well later on.

His first year already had shown signs of what would come: "Spent the day at home reading [H. G. Wells's] *Mr. Britling Sees It Through.* Wish I could spend more Saturday evenings thus." The second year, his education picked up mass and speed: "Read first two books of *Don Quizote* [*sic*] and laughed myself sick. And yet the slapstick barely covers the rich vein of pathos. . . . Great stuff!" No disquisitions, just gut reactions. If needed, help was close: "Herbert went over a little of Keats' poetry with me." But it was two professors, Harrison Steeves and Raymond Weaver (only ten years older than Bennett), whom he credited with changing his life. Through Steeves, he learned about contemporary (mainly British) authors: Wells, Kipling, Arnold Bennett. Weaver's comparative literature class introduced Cervantes, Voltaire, and other classics. Later, Bennett said this exposure was one of the happiest things ever to happen in his life.

Weaver, especially, stood out. He'd publish a biography of Herman Melville a few years later, almost single-handedly resurrecting the by-now-forgotten author of *Moby-Dick,* and went on to influence another publisher, Robert Giroux, and writers as diverse as Joseph Campbell, Allen Ginsberg, and Jack Kerouac. Weaver had a mellifluous voice; Bennett thought him "a spellbinder" who could have been an actor, as well as a wonderfully nice man. Stories he wrote about the professor for the *Spectator* seemed to make Weaver mad, but Bennett reckoned that his mentor was secretly not displeased.

Weaver was the one teacher he kept up with, who for some years "became a very close friend." As a publisher, Bennett sought his advice, and persuaded him to write the occasional introduction to a book, like the Modern Library edition of Stendhal's *The Red and the Black.* Weaver was in a relationship with another professor, John Angus Burrell, whom Bennett would later also tap for help, but he recalled being so unsophisticated that he didn't realize the two men led, in the parlance of the day, an "irregular life."

"Today those things are taken . . . for granted," Bennett asserted, "the way it should be," but it was "shocking" back then. Certainly, one night just after he'd finished up at Columbia, he found himself shocked by his uncle. While walking along Broadway, Bennett listened as Herbert seemed to fixate on the topic of homosexuality. "Did it ever occur to you there must be some of this in you . . . ?" Bennett recalled asking.

"Well, you goddamned fool, I've been trying to tell you for five years, and you wouldn't listen," he remembered Herbert exploding.

Bennett was floored. "How could I have been such a fool not to have caught on? The fact he was a homosexual didn't mean anything to me at all; it was only rage at my own stupidity," he later insisted. They talked all night, Herbert citing occasions when he'd tried to tell him; but back then, Bennett admitted, he "unconsciously didn't want to hear." Herbert had also agonized about telling his best friend, and now sought Bennett's advice; his nephew assured him that the friend would react similarly. "I was absolutely correct," Bennett maintained. "This made my uncle so confident."

Uncle Herbert Wise and "Pop" Cerf

Throughout life, Bennett had the useful ability to avoid seeing what he didn't want to see, or hearing what he didn't want to hear. He also insisted on storybook endings. His admission that "unconsciously" he hadn't wanted to learn of Herbert's homosexuality is telling, set against his having just said "it didn't mean anything to me at all." It was a shock, and meant something, factoring into his avoidance of emotional turmoil in general, and raising questions about his insecurity and, more particularly, his own sexuality. Also, the reality of Herbert's situation was not quite so rosy. He struggled with his sexuality to such a degree that he lived in Germany for a while in the early 1930s, to be analyzed by a student of Freud's. At the same time, it's likely Bennett did accept his uncle for who he was. Herbert's longtime partner later said, "Bennett was somebody who felt it was okay to be homosexual," an uncommon attitude in that era.

Just as Bennett's mentors recognized his promise, he identified other up-and-comers among his peers, and learned to ally himself with them—men who'd be part of his future. Through Weaver he met Richard Simon, a student in one of the professor's other classes. Simon, who had the talent to pursue a career as a concert artist, would sit at their teacher's piano and play, to the delight of all. Max Schuster was a few years ahead of Bennett at the Journalism School, and he saw Horace Manges and Oscar Hammerstein often, but one friend—Donald Klopfer—would take precedence over them all.

During the spring semester of 1919, Bennett took a music appreciation course. The occasional reward was a concert ticket, the most prized being to the Philadelphia Orchestra, led by star conductor Leopold Stokowski. Students chose numbers from a hat; one day, Bennett drew a winner. Another went to a freshman he'd barely noticed. At home that evening, he jotted in his diary that he'd gone to Carnegie Hall "with Eddie Klopfer." The misnaming would soon be righted: despite a four-year age gap, they clicked. The exuberant boy who "never was quiet" would quickly find in thoughtful Donald the perfect ear and ideal complement—not to mention a business partner for life. He had no idea how much of a winner he'd drawn that day.

Seventeen years earlier, on January 23, 1902, Stella (née Danziger) and Simon Klopfer, both born in America of German Jewish stock, had welcomed their second child, Donald, to life at 116 West 119th Street, a few blocks from the Cerfs' first home. The Klopfers had moved from Syracuse with their seven-year-old daughter, Elma, into this street of row houses, distinctive with their Juliet balconies and wrought-iron trim.

In 1912, when Donald was ten, Simon died. He'd been in the shirtwaist business, and was "very unsuccessful." When the boy was two or three, the family had had to leave the pleasant street, and at Simon's death were "really hard up." Stella took in a boarder, common for a widow with kids, but this wasn't just any lodger; he was an old flame, and Stella married him. Manny Jacobson was in the wholesale diamond trade, and a certain affluence entered the family's life. They moved to 300 West End Avenue, heart of the haut bourgeois Upper West Side. A self-described "omnivorous reader," Donald fed his habit at the library and at DeWitt Clinton High School, ten blocks away.

Donald S. Klopfer

At fifteen, he graduated from Clinton, and his life became less local: in September 1917, he enrolled at Phillips Academy in Andover, Massachusetts, for a year. Perhaps he was too young for college. Maybe Stella wanted him to be academically stretched and socially finished at an exclusive Calvinist boarding school. But there may have been another reason. As Donald was entering his teens, his sister, Elma, was graduating from Barnard. Like her brother, she was very bright, and as a girl—Jewish, to boot—very unusual, to have made it to college in the young days of the twentieth century. Then Elma was "taken sick," experiencing a breakdown—probably schizophrenic. First, Donald had endured a failing, dead father; now his sister had gone mad. Her illness would cast a shadow over his life, but at fifteen may have offered a good reason to send him away.

It wasn't easy for a Jew to pass through quotas at places like Andover. Perhaps, even as a teenager, something about Donald made him stand out and yet be accepted: he was one of "nature's gentlemen," as others always described him. If photos are to be believed, along with the glow of youth, he had a seductive hint of melancholy, of life lessons learned, that made him an attentive, attractive listener. The Andover yearbook has him accepted for matriculation at Yale, but September found him at home in New York, enrolled at Columbia. The following spring, he pulled a number from a hat and met Bennett. However, in the fall of 1919, Donald transferred to Williams College in Massachusetts, only to quit and go to work for the family business a year later. Whether it was a fit of adolescent pique in a dispute with his stepfather over his future, or for some other reason, after a year at Columbia and one at Williams, his college days were over.

The same spring semester that Bennett met Donald, he reached another milestone: May 25, 1919, was his twenty-first birthday. With his father, step-grandmother, and trustee uncles Arthur and George Wise, he visited the family lawyers to take control of his $125,000 inheritance (more than $2.3 million today). In some respects he would always be the playful boy-for-life, but in others he'd reached a turning point.

In his oral history, Bennett claimed that from the day his mother died, he was "already stronger" than Gustave, and became financial head of the family. That may have been a bit of a stretch, but certainly, now he was in charge. "It all worked out," he added, for he was "pretty good with money." The "necessary talents" for the future were in place, along with the wealth to ease his way in exploiting them. Manhood beckoned.

PART TWO

1920–1940

From Playboy of the Western World to Man of Property

The transition from the playboy of the western world to the man of property has not been accomplished without a great deal of sturm *and* drang . . . if you could have seen the antics I have gone through, you would have howled with laughter.

—Bennett Cerf to Gertrude Stein, 1941

Chapter 4

Love Wrong

"ALL WALL STREET SHINES WITH A NEW RADIANCE, WHEN BENNETT A. Cerf resumes the role of wage earner," he joked to his diary in September 1919. Although he'd have to wait till spring to graduate, Bennett was set on starting a career. Rather than begin at the bottom as a journalist, he took a job at Sartorius & Einstein, the family brokerage firm of Irving Sartorius, Herbert's friend, and was surprised to learn his uncle was its biggest client.

The position was very much an apprenticeship. His salary, twenty dollars a week, was a bit less than what the average New York City worker earned in the period just after the Great War, and far from the $2,500 per year a family required for "decent living." Monday through Saturday, Bennett rode the subway downtown. It was a good moment to arrive on the Street: although 1919 saw a predictable postwar recession, the dip was short-lived, and as the new decade roared, the market climbed. He soon grew familiar with both Dickensian ledger books and modern ticker tape. Herbert and a slew of friends met him for lunches that "lit up" the whole day, while theater and moving pictures, restaurants and gaming—poker, bridge, and that new rage, mah-jongg—filled his nights.

He'd always loved the theater. At age ten, he went with friends to nickelodeons and picture-and-vaudeville palaces like Harlem's Alhambra, and during high school he saw shows most Saturdays, often with Howard Dietz. At Columbia, Bennett started the *Jester* drama column to obtain free tickets. He respected anybody connected with the theater, be it "the fellow opening the door to the dressing rooms or the chorus girl," and that moment after the house lights dimmed and before the curtain rose "electrified" him. One-sentence critiques—"Empire to see that pre-eminent actress Ethel Barrymore, she of the divine voice"—filled his diaries. In 1922, he took in no fewer than forty-four plays.

While working at Sartorius, he befriended another would-be broker, Charles Allen, who'd grown up poor and started on the Street at fifteen. Both young mavericks were irresistibly drawn to the wider world; they'd slip out of work and sneak down to the Battery together to watch boats glide in and out, or explore the wharves on South Street. The metropolis in which Bennett and Charlie played hooky was an exceedingly crowded place. Manhattan reached its demographic apogee around 1910, when home to more than 2.3 million people. The island's population then decreased a bit, but the density remained extraordinary, in part due to the influx of Russian and Eastern European Jews. Well-established German Jews, while often providing for poor co-religionists, felt ambivalent about their shared ethnicity, and distanced themselves from the masses. Some, boasting the right looks, manners, and education, decided to "pass." "It wasn't all that easy to be Jewish," recalled actress Kitty Carlisle (née Conn), who "for a long time" had passed. Others converted to Christianity. Still others were driven to reject their own kind.

When young, Bennett's relationship with his roots was patently uneasy; a Jewish society had refused to support him when he ran for the student board in his final term at Columbia because, he confided to his diary, they thought him "the biggest anti-Semite" on campus. (He squeaked in anyway.) He recalled that "to the German Jew years ago, the Russian Jew was an affront," and echoed the denial common in his community that "the influx of Russian Jews . . . really caused the prejudice in this country." The end of his second week at Sartorius coincided with Rosh Hashanah, the Jewish New Year. "The Hebrew hypocrites stay away from work," he complained to his diary, noting the next day: "The wandering Jews come back." On Yom Kippur, the holiest day of the Jewish calendar, he wrote: "Yum! Yum! Yom Kippur! chirp the Hebes of 20 Broad Street, and the office looks as lively this morning as Greenwood Cemetery at full blast. Despite which the faithful few performed the work satisfactorily."

"Bennett would have preferred not to be a Jew," Kitty Carlisle, later one of his inner circle, concluded. If speaking about his first few decades, she probably was right.

With his inheritance, he bought an interest in Sartorius on June 1, 1921, and seemed poised for a Wall Street life, yet the need to see his name in print was like an itch. His byline appeared in a few long-forgotten journals; despite the ambivalence about his origins, some—a garment trade paper, a benevolent society magazine—had Jewish ties. He yearned to be associated with a major outlet. In March 1922, his Riviera and Columbia friend Merryle Rukeyser, now assistant financial editor on the *New-York Tribune,* offered him that: a job on the side. While still at Sartorius, he'd give stock tips in a question-and-answer format several times a week. Readers sent queries; he was instructed to advise them generally to "Buy Liberty Bonds," the safe government securities. But how could a young man eager for attention refrain from some swagger? And so, he told an old lady who'd asked about a certain company that it was bankrupt; she'd be crazy to buy the stock.

The next day, the financial editor was "grimly waiting" for him. The firm wasn't *yet* bankrupt; it might hold on a week, and was about to sue the paper. Bennett's services were no longer required. His last *Tribune* piece ran just over a month after his first. He'd never forget "bravely" making his way to the men's room, and bursting into tears.

Bennett would become renowned, in the words of Barbara Walters, as "an inveterate flirt," and began early. In grade school, there was a girl whose books he carried, and if he "wormed" an extra quarter from his mother, he took the girl to the Alhambra. In high school, the interest wasn't so chaste; he said that he and Dietz once paid the brother of a girl in their building a dime to watch her bathe. "That's the first time we understood a girl's anatomy. . . . She was giving us a strip tease. . . . She flipped water on us, but we remained happily until the performance ended."

After his crush on cousin Del, Marie Mayer had entered his life, and just after Valentine's Day, 1919, Bennett—three months shy of twenty-one—scribbled: "Marie is a peach, I love her lots, and I don't think I've ever been so reckless in this diary!" Though her Barnard ring was soon attached to his watch chain, a rival lurked in the wings—his good friend and fraternity brother Horace Manges. Yet after a few weeks, the competition was resolved: "Interesting developments in our own little triangle play," he told his diary. "Horace withdraws . . . leaving the piece a duet. I can evince no sorrow. . . ." Declaring it "reckless" to admit he loves her, and describing the triangle—in self-conscious prose—as a play, with himself both actor and observer, conveys a push-pull between a desire for intimacy and a need for distance. While the romance with Marie would evolve into a long friendship, his next triangular relationship would be more complex—and consequential.

At a July Fourth dance at the Woodmere Country Club on Long Island the following year, Bennett took to the floor with an "absolutely beautiful young girl" named Marian Ansbacher, and persuaded her to let him see her home. When he tried to kiss her, she protested: it "wouldn't be right" since she was in love with someone else, a counselor at an upstate camp. As she began to describe the boy, Bennett burst out: "I bet I know him!" Sure enough, it was Donald Klopfer. Something about her "imperious" manner reminded him of how Don had spoken of a girl he was dating. But just as Bennett was about to go, Marian stopped him: "If I wasn't in love with Donald, this is the way I would kiss you." Soon blossoming Marian, with her bright dark eyes and bobbed hair, would be well known to Mr. Cerf, along with her very wealthy, country-clubbing father and amateur golf champion mother. Five servants kept their Fifth Avenue apartment humming.

When Donald came home from camp and discovered that Marian had been Bennett's girl while he was away, he was furious. They were all so very young—Marian, seventeen; Donald, eighteen; and Bennett, the older man of twenty-two. Bennett had thought he was "amusing" himself with a kid, and would forget her the moment summer ended. She'd thought she could have fun, and "hoodwink" Don. But Bennett had "really fallen in love," and that fall of 1920, Marian set off for Vassar with two beaux in pursuit.

Donald had had his go at Columbia and Williams, and now started a job at United Diamond Works in Newark, where his stepfather was part-owner. (For the next four years, he crossed the Hudson to start work at 8 A.M.) He and Bennett refused to see each other for months, but when Marian came home at Thanksgiving, she persuaded them to accompany her and a Vassar friend for a day in the city. "Although Donald and I had started out glaring," Bennett recalled, by day's end they found that they "still liked each other very much." After the double date, the men planned a Philadelphia Orchestra outing, as they had so fortuitously done once before. When they left Carnegie Hall after the concert, they decided to take a stroll. Talking all the while, they circumnavigated Central Park, a promenade that lasted hours. "When we finished that [walk], we were best friends for life," Bennett later said, delving no further. "Our interests were identical. The girl was one," was how Donald explained it, also shutting the door on further explanation, as though their friendship was inevitable.

How did two ambitious young men of such different temperaments—one shining, the other soulful—and in love with the same young woman, keep pursuing her, and at the same time decide that each would be the other's best friend? How important was the attraction each felt for Marian, how strong the bond each felt for the other? Both had known family tragedy and survived; both had quit studies and gone on; both felt they had to prove something: all that, surely, was a glue. Whatever transpired during that walk—the whys, words, and feelings—formed the keystone and conundrum on which Random House would be built. Much can be read into a relationship a long time after the fact. The truth woven into any heart is so complicated, it's impossible to separate all the secret strands. Bennett Cerf, as his confidante Leonora Hornblow later said, "always wanted more." One thing is certain: he wanted as much as he could get of both Donald and Marian.

She introduced them to a new world where country clubs were taken

Marian Ansbacher and her two beaux

for granted and girls had coming-out parties at the Ritz. In the 1910s and '20s, the havens where the richest New York Jewish families escaped the city were towns like Purchase and Scarsdale in Westchester County; a few communities on Long Island; and splendid seaside locales in Monmouth County, New Jersey, like Elberon and Deal. The New York–Long Branch railway made it easy for Bennett and Don to visit the weekend "cottage" of the Ansbachers and mingle with their Elberon crowd. They swam in the sea, danced at the roadhouse, and went boating on nearby Deal Lake. During these summers, Marian indulged another passion: books. With two other girls she formed "The Bookleggers," who'd circulate, for a fee, the latest novels a beachgoing pleasure-seeker might want. Books bound the triangle together, along with the more usual attractions.

Get accustomed to this kind of life, Bennett did. Before decade's end, helped by Marian's father, Louis, he'd hold club memberships on Long Island, in Scarsdale, and at the Harmonie in the city, all elite German Jewish bastions—with more to come. During the workweek, he and Donald would have dinner, play bridge, go to concerts together, at times with a tight social group—Herbert, Horace Manges and his new wife, Natalie—but often just the pair. After the downturn of 1921, when work at the Newark factory ceased for eight months, Bennett got Don a temporary job at Sartorius. Marian wrote long letters to both—ones they'd sometimes share. "Everybody was hilarious about our ridiculous threesome but us," Bennett said a half century later. The triangle—pleasurable, painful, absurd—set the pattern for his life throughout 1921 and 1922. Don would go to Vassar one weekend, Bennett the next, and together they'd see Marian in New York or Elberon.

How much had he fallen in love with her? How much with a way of life? For a man whose competitive instinct was so keen, how much of a spur was the presence of a rival (one whom he also loved)? Although the men's friendship didn't break, their romances were turbulent. Marian would "choose" Bennett. Then she'd favor Donald. Each had periods when he felt deceived: behind their backs, she was still seeing both. Having such power suited Miss Ansbacher: one day, she commandeered Bennett's diary—the first of only two times in five decades of diary-writing such a thing occurred. "Bennett gave in to me today," reads the entry. Her father tried to intervene, insisting one or the other do right by her, but the French farce continued—until it didn't, quite.

Nineteen twenty-three began with rare moments of reflection from Bennett: "I have not kept this diary [regularly] since November, 1919," he wrote on January 2, "and I regret the lapse . . . highlights . . . were my securing an interest in . . . Sartorius . . . and a love affair with Marian Ansbacher, with glorious highlights to balance much unhappiness." Three days later, he added: "Marian and I get along so much better now that we are no longer in love with each other that it has made me suspect gravely that as a Romeo, I succeed only, like Merton, in having 'a low-comedy face!'" *Merton of the Movies* was one of the first popular novels about Hollywood; Merton, a bumpkin, came to L.A. wanting to be a star, landed a part, and mistakenly thought he was playing a serious role.

Yet less than a month after trying to reconcile himself to being no great Romeo, Bennett met Marian at Grand Central. Feeling "something electric," he decided they were "doomed" to sporadic revivals until one of them got married. In March, "the mere" being with her convinced him how much he still cared, "but heigh-ho, she'll probably marry Donald," he concluded. Why did Bennett keep diaries? One reason was to be able to relive his experience later on. Another was his habit of meticulously organizing everything: bookshelves, desk, even shirts in drawers. The need to be intimate with himself, and possibly to leave a trail for posterity, may also factor in, but one thing he didn't do was use diaries to read deeply into his own heart. "Heigh-ho" was a wall between his heart and what was cause for pain. The "low-comedy face" was a way to deal with hurt—or better yet, ward it off.

Four days after sighing "Heigh-ho," Bennett met Helen, a beautiful girl he rather liked. Another week, and "Helen came down for lunch. . . . Stopped in to see Marian on the way home . . . , then in the evening, to make the day complete, had a date with Marie."

It took two more years for Marian to settle down, but on September 14, 1925, she finally got married—a true flapper in a short, sleeveless dress aglow with meteors of tiny, luminous pearls. She and her parents were joined by 250 guests at a magnificent outdoor wedding amid the manicured arbors of the Norwood Golf Club in Elberon; there was even a momentary movie made of the affair—an indulgence of her very relieved daddy.

The groom's name was Donald Simon Klopfer. Bennett Cerf was the best man.

Chapter 5

Liveright

A PHONE CALL FROM DICK SIMON SET THE COURSE FOR BENNETT'S future life. Indeed, he never ceased to be amazed (and a tiny bit annoyed) that his Columbia classmate Dick, whose head was perpetually lost in music, should have had the temerity not just to precede him into the book trade, but also to be responsible for bringing *him* into the business!

A year or so after graduating, at the urging of fellow alum Max Schuster, Simon had left a job selling pianos and gone to work for the publisher Boni & Liveright (*Bone-eye and Live-right*). Schuster, owl-eyed behind round spectacles, was an editor at a motor trade magazine. Unusually tall, Simon made an impression, and focused enough charm on bookstore owners to become known as a crackerjack salesman. In the summer of 1923, Max and Dick decided to go into business together. After Dick broke the news, his boss, Horace Liveright, asked if he could suggest a replacement. Dick rang Bennett. After his *Tribune* fiasco a year earlier, he was restless, ready to try something new.

A lunch was arranged at the Algonquin Hotel on West Forty-Fourth Street, a few blocks from the B&L offices, for the next day, September 28, 1923. When Bennett arrived to meet Simon and Liveright, he was awed by his proximity to the Round Table, the already-famous literary coterie—Dorothy Parker, George S. Kaufman, Robert Sherwood, et al.—who lunched there daily. More important, he was awed by the powerful, theatrical charisma of the man he'd come to meet. Horace Brisbin Liveright habitually cloaked his tall, scarecrow-thin frame in an elegant suit, with a crisp boutonniere that never seemed to wilt. A ten-inch cigarette holder jutted from between narrow lips, and a silver-tipped Malacca walking stick and pearl-gray fedora accompanied him wherever he went. Given to posing in dramatic profile, glossy jet hair streaked with silver, the thirty-eight-year-old was handsome and fancied he resembled matinee idol John

Barrymore. But far from being the Round Table regular Bennett had supposed, Liveright was often eviscerated by the sharp tongues of the "Vicious Circle" (as it was also called), even those of members he published. Everyone, one way or another, felt strongly about Liveright.

"We're a very individual firm," he declared to Bennett in an actor's diction. "I have my own ideas of publishing. You can go up very quickly . . . if you've got the stuff." Liveright looked him over with piercingly dark eyes that appealed and unsettled. "I hear you've got some money. . . . If you'd like to come in with style, if you put a little . . . into the business, I'll make you a vice-president." The "little" was $25,000 ($453,000 today). For a gamble on the future—even in an era crazy for gambles—$25,000 was a huge sum.

Liveright left the tantalizing offer hanging in the air, explaining that he had to hurry back to the office to look after his star author Theodore Dreiser. The prickly novelist wanted to go to a baseball game, and he'd have to go along too, even though the sport bored him. Suddenly a possible escape arose: Would Bennett like to accompany Dreiser instead? The outing would give him a small taste of what it was to be a publisher. Bennett obliged. He was baseball-crazy Gustave's son, and had never met a famous author up close. Although after the fact he judged Dreiser "a dour and sulky bastard," that didn't put him off: on the contrary, Bennett couldn't get Horace Liveright off his mind.

BONI AND LIVERIGHT
61 WEST 48TH STREET, NEW YORK CITY
TAKE PLEASURE IN ANNOUNCING THAT
BENNETT A. CERF
HAS ON NOVEMBER FIRST, 1923, BECOME ASSOCIATED WITH THEM AND HAS BEEN ELECTED A VICE-PRESIDENT AND DIRECTOR OF THE COMPANY.

"You can go up very quickly . . . if you've got the stuff."

More meetings took place before a contract was drawn up; on October 17, Bennett signed it. He'd start at a salary of $75 per week, "understood to be minimum only." He'd lend the company $25,000 at 10 percent interest for five months, and had the right to buy, for another $25,000, preferred B&L shares—which he soon did. At the same time, the incoming VP understood that it was "OK for Mr. Liveright to receive a salary of $300 per week," a princely sum. Uncle Herbert was consulted before Bennett signed on the dotted line, and with proper filial devotion, he talked it over with his pop.

The first time Bennett crossed the threshold into the five-story B&L brownstone at 61 West Forty-Eighth Street, with its book-lined ground-floor windows confidently presenting its wares to all who passed, he had no well-defined notion of what would greet him on the other side. Nothing in the smart city boy's middle-class life could have prepared him for what a fellow staffer called the "Jazz Age in microcosm," with its extremes "of hysteria and of cynicism, of Carpe Diem, of decadent thriftlessness, and of creative vitality."

"I walked in and met Horace Liveright and saw this publishing office," Bennett recalled. "Baby had gotten where he wanted to be."

. . .

"A MAN CAN STAND almost anything except a succession of ordinary days. . . . In publishing, there are no ordinary days," said Ben Huebsch, the first Jew to achieve prominence in twentieth-century trade books, who entered the business a decade before Liveright. For Bennett, what more persuasive argument could there be? And in U.S. publishing history, no days would be more extraordinary than those at B&L. Horace Liveright's singularly potent, reckless genius for a brief moment flared, and outshone all his contemporaries.

Before the United States entered World War I, workdays inside publishing houses were decidedly more quotidian. Most were WASP family firms with names like Harper, Scribner, and Dutton, careful to observe the decorum of the status quo. Publishing, Bennett once said, "was mostly in the hands of old stuffed shirts . . . conservative souls with gold watch chains across their fat bellies, [who] . . . would sit in their offices . . . and wouldn't dream of going out for a book. The author came crawling to them."

Several intersecting trends changed that picture. Waves of immigration had swelled the nation's population and made it increasingly urban. Cities were far more heterogeneous in ethnicity and class, more open to social movements and ideas. They were incubators of women's struggle for suffrage, the union movement, and radical politics; stages where immigrants, adventurous individuals from the heartland, and—despite greater obstacles placed before them—Black Americans might reinvent themselves: centers, then, where a mass market for books could be created and then spread. In New York especially, ambitious young Jewish men, many of whose fathers or grandfathers had earned enough in commerce or manufacturing to send them to college, could enter the book trade, but not as defined by the generally antisemitic old houses Bennett described. Instead, Liveright and his fellow Jews had to start companies themselves.

Born in a Pennsylvania mining town on December 10, 1884, Liveright later grew up in Philadelphia. Precocious and impatient to make his mark, he quit Central High School, went to work for a brokerage, and in 1902 came to Manhattan to sell bonds. A good talker, he was good at the job. He was also, like Bennett, besotted by show business. While still a teen, he'd co-written a comic opera that was to be professionally staged in New York. The backer was unreliable, the show never produced, but theater magic intoxicated, and would intoxicate absolutely in due course. Liveright was also a gambler, perhaps compulsive. At twenty-three, he made $40,000 in the market, but lost it the next year. Two years later, his stock account had soared to $160,000—but soon plummeted again.

In 1911, the arc of his life rose when he married Lucile Elsas, whose father had made a fortune in paper products and agreed to bankroll him in several start-ups. Nothing worked. By 1916, he was past thirty, a father of two, and Mr. Elsas was anxious. That fall, temporarily perched behind a desk at his cousin's advertising agency, Liveright chanced upon a twenty-four-year-old Harvard dropout and fellow Jew, Albert Boni, also at loose ends. Boni was a bookselling veteran. With his younger brother, Charles, he had used family money intended for law school to open the Washington Square Book Shop on MacDougal Street in Greenwich Village. Artists, writers, and radicals made the store a popular hangout. The Bonis had also dabbled in publishing.

It was common for cigarette and candy manufacturers to place a "premium"—a small prize—in products to entice customers. In 1915, the brothers came across a tiny book of scenes from Shakespeare inserted in tobacco packs, and Albert saw possibilities. With the help of his brother and two copywriter friends, Maxwell Sackheim and Harry Scherman, he produced a sample miniature *Romeo and Juliet* in a leatherette binding, which they pitched to Whitman's Chocolate, a major Philadelphia candymaker. Whitman ordered 15,000 Shakespeare books. Soon Woolworth's stores began ordering what was now called the "Little Leather Library," thirty titles selling as a set for the bargain price of $2.98. More than a million copies were distributed via Whitman, Woolworth's, and mail order. Despite that encouraging start, the Bonis sold out to their partners and left the store behind, too—which is how Albert found himself sitting across from Liveright, contemplating the long horizon of the future. But he had an idea, and Liveright grasped its potential. What about publishing a pocket-sized leatherette reprint series of classics? Liveright borrowed cash from his father-in-law for one last start-up, and the brothers Boni chipped in, too.

The idea owed a debt to Everyman's Library, J. M. Dent's British hardback reprint series, distributed in the United States by Dutton and consisting of well-crafted books meant to be canonical. Dutton/Dent fed their Everyman a distinguished albeit "safe" title diet, but what "classic" meant for Boni and Liveright was different: the greatest titles from the past, but also "advanced" literature dear to Greenwich Village habitués, contemporary books that could become classics. Befitting a diverse young nation awakening to its new place in the world, the list wouldn't be limited to Anglo-American authors, but instead encompass all that was needed to be educated and au courant in the new century: "The Modern Library of the World's Best Books."

Bennett was a Columbia student in April and May 1917, when Boni & Liveright issued the first dozen Modern Library (ML) titles at sixty cents each. These included Oscar Wilde's *The Picture of Dorian Gray;* August Strindberg's *Married;* Henrik Ibsen's *A Doll's House, An Enemy of the People,* and *Ghosts;* and books by Kipling, Stevenson, Wells, Dostoyevsky, Maupassant, Nietzsche, and Schopenhauer—nary an American in sight. Most of the original editions couldn't be easily or inexpensively found. The response from the reading public was so positive that six more titles were added almost immediately. Also added, in July, as literary adviser and vice president, was the Bonis' uncle Thomas Seltzer, an avowed leftist—and, more usefully, an experienced editor. A critic at the *New York Evening Mail* soon urged readers to "gallop to the nearest store and inspect the volumes." By the end of 1917, the ML would have thirty-five titles in print. Young people "hungry for what was sophisticated, subversive, avant-garde," sought it out. Authors wanted to be part of it. The idea was Albert's, but Liveright proved to be the inspired entrepreneur. And yet for him, a groundbreaking line of reprints wasn't enough.

That fall, B&L said it would bring out seven original hardcover titles—not series reprints—to stand on their own literary recognizance. Partly self-educated, Liveright had a romantic reverence for learning and books, and sought out what was fresh, vital, and worthy of being published—rather than simply what would sell. He felt passionate about a free press and fighting for the underdog, and saw the usefulness of a controversy in the hard job of securing attention. The book that held pride of place among those first seven titles wasn't, in fact, absolutely new, but wasn't exactly a reprint, either. A reissue of a novel that had been quickly buried, it trailed a difficult, but readily exploitable, past.

When Doubleday published the novel in 1900—it chronicled the decline of a rich, respectable man and parallel rise of a "fallen woman"—critics hated this story that went counter to established morality. Like publishers of every era who feel they've made a mistake, Doubleday did nothing for the book. However, by 1917, forward-thinking critics like H. L. Mencken saw the work in a different light. Its author was utterly antisemitic and boorish, but Liveright believed he was bringing to the public the most important living novelist in America. The book was *Sister Carrie,* its author Theodore Dreiser, and Horace Liveright's instinct would prove in this, as in so many cases, absolutely correct.

He also saw a chance to capitalize on the revolution being waged in Russia. In Thomas Seltzer's personal library was a pamphlet by Leon Trotsky. They could pad it a bit, publish, sell syndication rights: the story was unfolding on front pages daily. Boni was dispatched to see Herbert Swope, editor of the *New York World,* and ask for $7,000. Swope offered $5,000; Liveright told Boni to hold tight. Swope soon relented, providing a huge windfall. Yet Liveright and Boni found it increasingly hard to work together. With the toss of a coin, Liveright bought Boni out in July 1918. Seltzer soon left, too, to start his own firm. Needing capital, Liveright sold a vice presidency to Julian Messner, the firm's sales manager, and another to Leon Fleischman, who became secretary and treasurer. Once Fleischman departed in 1920, Liveright's father-in-law, concerned about his impetuous, spendthrift ways, made him hire Arthur Pell, a bookkeeper from Elsas's company, to try to curb Liveright's recklessness. Pell soon began to buy shares in B&L.

Outsiders assumed Liveright based acquisition decisions on whether he liked or was impressed by an author, and on synopses done by others. But despite his very active social life, he read manuscripts in the evening, and correspondence shows he read enough to make many decisions himself. He bet mainly, but not exclusively, on homegrown writers. Over the course of just thirteen years, he'd publish Dreiser, Nathanael West, Hart Crane, Djuna Barnes, Dorothy Parker, and S. J. Perelman; bring out John Reed's I-was-there story of the Bolshevik Revolution, *Ten Days That Shook the World;* and publish e. e. cummings's Great War memoir, *The Enormous Room.* Late in the day, the word "shit" had to be inked out from cummings's books by hand to avoid prosecution for obscenity.

Liveright had heart. Sherwood Anderson—whose masterpiece, *Winesburg, Ohio,* was published by Huebsch in 1919 and later reprinted in the Modern Library—began to fear he was washed-up. Liveright wouldn't let him sink, paying him a hundred dollars a week for five years against future royalties, no questions asked, for a book a year. "At least this man is not going to tell me how to write my book," Anderson realized, adding that he had a way of "trusting his authors." When Anderson brought young William Faulkner and Ernest Hemingway to Liveright's notice, he took Anderson's word for their talent and signed them. Famously generous, Liveright was always giving handouts. An epicene young Brit turned up with a sheaf of papers. "I don't think he's got any money," the boss told Bennett. "Treat him to lunch." The Englishman was Noël Coward, and B&L published his *Personal Portraits* (one was of Liveright). Another time, he got a letter from Faulkner, who'd drawn a draft on him against his next advance, to pay off two hundred dollars in gambling losses. Liveright made good on Faulkner's debt.

The B&L staff were colorful. T. R. "Tommy" Smith, a fine, middle-aged editor and equally fine connoisseur of drink and erotica, replaced Seltzer as editor-in-chief. In tandem with his rare nose for writers, Liveright engaged a whole corps of bright young people, men—and women—with vivid personalities and keen minds. He had "no truck with nonentities." Among this unusual cadre were Dick Simon, Bennett, and a handful of future publishers; playwright-to-be Lillian Hellman; Edward Weeks, who'd edit *The Atlantic;* critic Louis Kronenberger; Edward Bernays, father of modern PR; and literary salon-keeper Beatrice Kaufman. Would-be novelist Manuel Komroff ran production.

Amid such a group, gossip was endemic. When office girl Hellman insisted on returning to work after an illegal abortion (the abortionist having been suggested by someone at B&L), everyone knew about it. Toasted with breakfast champagne by Liveright, she spent the day resting on Smith's couch; she couldn't go home to her parents. Hellman later recalled that everybody gravitated to Horace because he gave them a chance: "Even the stenographers and shipping clerks often wandered about reading manuscripts, offering opinions about how to advertise or sell a book."

Liveright could publish to brilliant, bestselling effect. In Hendrik Willem Van Loon's *The Story of Mankind,* he produced a long-running hit and the winner of the first Newbery Medal for children's literature. Seventeen others had turned it down. In 1920, he issued *A General Introduction to Psychoanalysis,* the first time Sigmund Freud's writings were available to a lay readership in America. Edward Bernays—Freud's nephew and Leon Fleischman's brother-in-law—had brought Liveright the project, sure that he'd push the book vigorously, "more than most publishers did then."

What really made the relationship, though, was Liveright's decision to offer Bernays himself a contract to undertake an experiment. Bernays wanted to apply his uncle's insights from the consulting room to the rough-and-tumble of the book business. If you understood what made people tick, he reasoned, you could learn how to persuade them to buy something. Until then, the norm had been to mail basic information to literary editors at magazines and newspapers, distribute catalogues to booksellers, and hope for the best. Bernays—in concert with Liveright—did something new: made the connection between what was going on in a book and what was going on in people's lives, and injected a touch of panache. He mailed weekly newsletters to three hundred leading bookstores and offered newsworthy articles on B&L books free to newspapers. He created demand, as well as a recognizable brand. Together, the two men originated modern book publicity, a template that would be adopted in other fields.

Liveright also invented the book party, understood the potential of American celebrity-worship when he asked his famous pals to blurb humble authors' works, and, along with Alfred Knopf, transformed book advertising. But while Knopf, who'd started his business a year earlier, "invoked the American weakness for snob value," Liveright was unapologetically flamboyant—and much more democratic. The B&L ads were visually bold and contained snippets of trade gossip and witty repartee. They addressed readers directly, making them feel like insiders in the "exciting" world of books. Bennett, who would always be the ultimate arbiter of publicity, advertising, and promotion at Random House, followed in Liveright's footsteps in this, and many other ways.

Although Boston was famously a censorship hot spot—"Banned in Boston" often ensured brisk sales elsewhere—New York, that bastion of freedom, modernity, and iniquity, was the site of many First Amendment battles. John S. Sumner, of the New York Society for the Suppression of Vice, led the assault. Thanks to him, Alexandre Dumas's *Three Musketeers* and Horace's *Odes* were among many titles only sold expurgated.

In 1923, Sumner, with the backing of many church groups, was lobbying for a "Clean Books Bill" in the New York state legislature. Liveright decided to confront all that Sumner stood for, and placed an article, "The Absurdity of Censorship," in *The Independent,* a venerable magazine famous for supporting abolition and women's suffrage. The National Association of Book Publishers had refused to fight the bill; gossip among book salesmen was that the old-line houses saw it as a way of retaliating against "those cheap little publishers who have sprung up from nowhere that cause all the trouble . . . all goddamn Jews!" As the boldest and showiest of the lot, Liveright was an obvious target. Once, when too much alcohol gave voice to the toll such prejudice took, he lamented how unfortunate it was to be a Jew.

Time was running out that spring when, alone among publishers, he went to the state capital to make the case in person, seeking and receiving help from his friend James J. "Jimmy" Walker, minority leader of the state senate, who'd later be famous (and infamous) as mayor of speakeasy New York. Liveright's stand against the bill generated publicity; other book, magazine, and newspaper publishers, as well as printers, began to admit its dangers and offer support. In a stunning reversal, the measure was defeated: as Walker famously put it, "No woman was ever ruined by a book."

Bennett arrived at B&L that autumn. The stories he heard about the boss's censorship fights he never forgot, and the precedents Liveright helped forge would enable Bennett—and Donald—to do some First Amendment battling of their own.

. . .

THERE'S NO BETTER INITIATION into the mysteries of the book business than a sales trip. When Bennett took the job at B&L, Dick Simon agreed to accompany him on his first visits to stores in New England. As they drove north, Dick schooled him in shipping schedules and discounts; these lessons were punctuated by Bennett's jokes and joint a cappella renderings of Gershwin and Gilbert & Sullivan. It was a wonderful trip, despite the fact that Liveright had followed up Van Loon's *The Story of Mankind* with *The Story of the Bible,* a flop. Bennett's education thus also involved learning about failure.

B&L's catalogues bore the slogan "Good Books" writ large on their covers, and there were a variety to sell in 1923. The novelist Gertrude Atherton had written *Black Oxen,* a saga of sexual rejuvenation (via monkey gland transplants, all the rage), a big bestseller. More enduringly, B&L proudly published Eugene O'Neill, who'd won the Pulitzer Prize in both 1921 and 1922, "the one playwright," Liveright proclaimed, whose work merited a large audience. Books by Somerset Maugham, Ben Hecht, and Dorothy L. Sayers also came out that year; so did Jean Toomer's *Cane,* a harbinger of the Harlem Renaissance, "a book by a negro about negroes." Ezra Pound, a known antisemite, nonetheless respected Horace Liveright, who paid him to do French translations. On Liveright's visit to Paris in January 1922, Pound had taken him to see his friends T. S. Eliot and James Joyce. B&L's American edition of *The Waste Land* was the result, published that December, even before Virginia and Leonard Woolf's Hogarth Press issued it in England in 1923. In addition to all these Good Books—and financially underpinning them—was the Modern Library, now numbering about 112 titles.

New York in the 1920s was, as English novelist Ford Madox Ford put it, "the city of the Good Time—and the Good Time is there so sacred . . . you may be excused anything you do in searching for it." Visiting the B&L brownstone, a journalist doing a story on those making books in America saw that Good Time come to life: "Mr. Liveright is a hedonist in business—a dynamic hedonist—who holds that since a man must spend at least a third of his life at work, he ought to make it as pleasant as possible."

A visitor would climb to the first-floor landing in the house on Forty-Eighth Street, exchange the time of day with the pretty switchboard

"We're a very individual firm": Horace Liveright, inspired impresario

"girl," and then proceed to the second floor, where the boss's suite overlooked the street. Liveright sat at an Italian table that he used as a desk, diagonal to the window, the better for a guest to appreciate the Barrymore profile. There was nothing office-like about the room, with its grand piano and giant Chinese ginger jar doubling as wastebasket (the chinoiserie craze was at its peak). The elongated black telephone set was the table's most prominent object; Liveright constantly made use of it. Photos of his son and daughter hung over the fireplace, while those of favored authors floated on the wall beside him. Most striking was his scarlet-walled, black-ceilinged bathroom with zinc-lined shower. Once, defending a book from the censors, he declared his belief in utter frankness was so strong that he showered in front of his children. A columnist cheekily suggested that he take showers in Central Park. Instead, he positioned painted floral panels in front of the shower, bringing the "park" to him.

Publishing plays wasn't enough: he wanted to produce them. In the fall of 1924, around the time Bennett marked his first anniversary at B&L, Liveright and two others produced a smash hit, *The Firebrand,* based on the life of Renaissance goldsmith Benvenuto Cellini. The following year, he brought *Hamlet in Modern Dress* to the stage. But his most famous producing legacy was Bela Lugosi's turn as *Dracula* in 1927. It was all very exciting—and expensive. He took over the adjoining brownstone as his theatrical HQ, and cut a hidden door to connect the buildings. Doubling as a bookcase, its shelves bore esoterica such as *With Gun and Tackle Through the Ovarian Canal*.

Most every evening in fall and winter, cocktail parties convened around the reception room fireplace down the hall from Liveright's office. In spring and summer, gatherings moved outside, to a terrace extension decorated in rattan and smart-set upholstery in coral, jade, and mauve. Midtown was still a decade from being completely built-up, and surrounding trees made the terrace even more pleasant. Sometimes the mood would be enlivened by a three-piece jazz band from Harlem. Authors, editors, reviewers, lowly manuscript readers, theater people, celebrities, journalists, all would be there—often with Mayor Walker in tie and tails. Everyone would dance and, in Liveright's parlance, get "a glow" on, courtesy of his ever-flowing Prohibition booze.

Variety was welcome not just in drinks and decor, but in people. Liveright was one of the very few in New York willing to publish Black authors, like Jean Toomer and Eric Walrond. In his theater ventures, he gambled on Paul Robeson, and Robeson attended the parties. So did stunning Anna May Wong, who was viewed as lending "exoticism" to Hollywood movies. Women—young, beautiful, short-skirted, bobbed, permed, and wanting a part in a play—showed up, alongside more literary ladies. It was hard to conjure another publishing house where they were so much or so many in evidence.

Many of Liveright's parties were "respectable, high-class chatty" affairs. Bennett never forgot that amusing "great day" when Ford Madox Ford sat on one of the rattan couches and, being decidedly stout, "went right through with a terrible crash." Other gatherings were something else entirely. The mood would turn sexual, eased along by the lethally strong stingers that Smith, the editor-in-chief, liked to mix. Guests progressed from "high" to "tight" to "drunk," as Liveright described it. Girls in their thin flapper dresses would alight on men's laps and be casually fondled. Pairs would go off into dimly lit corners. Once, when Bennett brought a girl into Liveright's darkened office to do "a little necking," he came across the boss *in flagrante*.

"What must you think of me?" Liveright said the next day, "explaining" that the girl was a good writer. The only way he could lure her to the list was "a little affair." In truth, Liveright was becoming infamous for affairs, and, as the decade advanced, would grow more and more in thrall to alcohol, despite having little capacity for it. A fantastic figure, he was also a melancholy one, always driven, never satisfied, presiding over the most glamorous, but "never entirely 'respectable,'" house. His gambles on Broadway put him, in the eyes of most publishers, "beneath contempt." It stung, but he carried on.

There was something callow and naive about the new vice president. Others began calling him "Jesus Junior," and it stuck. "I was the wide-eyed kid," Bennett admitted, who thought all that Horace did was glamorous and exciting. Liveright liked him; as Bennett later realized, it's easy to like enthusiastic kids "who respond with worship."

Many of Liveright's staff shared his German Jewish roots, but Bennett had more in common with the boss than most. Both "adored" their fathers. Neither father was good with money. Liveright's had been an unsuccessful mine owner and coal dealer who went broke. Like Gustave, he'd married a woman whose family was better off than his. While Frieda Cerf had been overly "sensitive," Liveright's mother was "very rigid and stern." In different ways, both had been troublesome for their sons. Each man had dropped out of school, and each gone to Wall Street at a young age. They lived off a wellspring of nervous energy, charm, outsize ambition—and could never satisfy themselves. Liveright was conflicted about being a Jew, as was Bennett. Each liked to surround himself with women—many women. Both needed to turn a workplace into a home.

Liveright had affairs, but also a family in the wealthy enclave of New Rochelle, to whom he'd (eventually) return most evenings. On Sundays, he and his wife hosted large dinners, and Bennett would sometimes be a guest. Before or after the meal, he'd perch on a stool at Lucile Liveright's feet, joking and chatting in the slightly peculiar, effeminate voice that didn't quite mesh with the handsome face and height. He seemed unseasoned, a nice twenty-five-year-old boy trying to endear himself to a sympathetic older woman. Liveright's daughter wondered if he was looking for a mother.

The habitués of B&L liked him. He managed to be friendly with everyone, his colleague Manuel Komroff attested, from editors at the top of the house to the boys in the basement shipping room. Pleasant and bubbly, he didn't flaunt his wealth. Edward Weeks, who had the desk beside his in the sales department on the third floor, recalled Bennett as "sleek and dark," with very bright eyes and a ready laugh, addicted to punning. Jokes streamed from him, as he retold every anecdote he heard, and yet that "did not disguise how much he was learning about books." Besides selling, the two young men were tasked with reading galleys—the first set of printed proofs. One time, Bennett was assigned a novel "so cheap and pornographic" that he complained to Liveright. Later, when page proofs—the second set—arrived, he looked at Weeks, "held his fingers to his nose," and dropped them into the wastebasket. He was a shrewder judge than Dick Simon, Weeks thought. However, only in manuscript reports and opinions voiced at meetings did others notice the "keen quality" of Bennett's mind.

One task that fell to him was writing copy. Flair, wit, and a healthy dose of exaggeration went into almost every page of a B&L catalogue. Bennett's first blurbs (proudly pasted into one of the many scrapbooks he'd amass during his lifetime) tended toward the purple and puerile, but he improved quickly. The fall 1924 catalogue was more sophisticated. He commissioned a cover with caricatures—Freud, O'Neill, Dreiser, and others—executed by Ralph Barton, who would become one of *The New Yorker*'s most famous cartoonists. Liveright had to bawl Bennett out for

The "knockout" cover

paying the extravagant sum of three hundred dollars, but he'd begun to make his mark: the cover is a knockout. Young Bennett had a feel for the business, and Liveright gave him the freedom and trust to indulge it.

With authors, if the spark was there, Liveright was willing to stay with a young writer through several books, allowing for awkward experiments, negative reviews, disappointing sales. He knew that "attention, undivided attention" was the most valuable currency a publisher could offer in building and keeping a relationship. Horace taught him, Bennett acknowledged, that "if an editor felt strongly enough about a book, [he] let him sign it up. . . . He'd say, 'Well, if you're that crazy about it . . . go ahead.' " The author-publisher relationship was complex and many-layered, Bennett was discovering. Surprises popped up all the time. He watched Liveright and paid attention.

In 1925, the title parade included *Roan Stallion, Tamar and Other Poems* by Robinson Jeffers, a major poet of the day; *An American Tragedy,* Dreiser's masterpiece; and Hemingway's story collection *In Our Time.* There was also a lighthearted romp by Anita Loos (with charming illustrations by Ralph Barton) that chronicled the adventures of a call girl named Lorelei Lee. Long before it became a vehicle for Marilyn Monroe, *Gentlemen Prefer Blondes* was an emblem of the 1920s. Initially, there was concern within B&L about how it would fare; Bennett, alone among the staff, felt it had the potential to be big. It was—selling more than 150,000 copies. But to boost sales, the book was priced attractively low—too low—ignoring production costs. The firm lost out on each copy. When the price was finally raised, the market was already satiated.

An auditor's account revealed that despite the stellar list and revenues of just under $1 million, B&L's net profit for 1925 would amount to only $8,609. Bennett, with so much invested in the firm, was alert to all things financial, and concerned. He was learning *not* to follow in Liveright's fiscal footsteps. On plays he produced, stocks he bought, books he published, girls he pursued, Liveright spent heedlessly. By 1925, he found himself pressed on both Broadway and Wall Street. The Elsas family was well known; so were Horace's infidelities. His situation was becoming untenable.

. . .

ACCOUNTS OF THE MODERN LIBRARY sale vary, but Bennett collapsed the story into one memorable day in May 1925. Having decided to take a vacation and make his first trip to Europe, he'd booked passage on the *Aquitania,* sailing at ten that night. Liveright invited Bennett to a bon voyage lunch at a popular speakeasy called Jack and Charlie's.

"Horace obviously had had one or two drinks before we went out, and this was unusual—he was not a drunk; a few drinks would stimulate him . . . [but] he didn't hold his liquor too well," Bennett had observed. Yet, once seated, Liveright ordered another.

"My father-in-law is driving me crazy," he explained. "He . . . wants me to account for where all the money is. . . . Oh, how I'd like to pay him off."

Bennett recalled "blandly" responding: "One very easy way . . . is to sell me the Modern Library." He'd made that suggestion multiple times, and multiple times been rebuffed: as Bennett was well aware, Liveright "knew at heart" the ML was his "greatest asset." This time, however, he feverishly asked, "What will you give me for it?"

"The door had been opened," he realized. They began to bargain, and came to a price: $200,000. He recalled Liveright wanting to rush back and call his lawyer to draw up papers. There was no need for Bennett to postpone his trip, Liveright said. When he returned, they'd sign: $200,000 for the Modern Library, along with inventory on hand.

Back at the office, Liveright's lawyer, Arthur Garfield Hays, and Julian Messner, his closest friend at the firm, were appalled. They tried to persuade him to favor other options. He'd toyed with the idea of raising money by offering B&L stock on the open market, and had even put together a memo-prospectus: "Why the Modern Library Is Worth $250,000." But a deal with Bennett would be faster and easier.

"This will get me out of the hole I'm in," Liveright insisted. Macmillan was about to start a competing series, he added. "I'm selling at the top. Bennett knows this . . . I've warned him about it. Anyway, I've given Bennett my word. I don't break my word."

Fate took a hand: a furious literary agent with a revolver in his pocket turned up at B&L demanding to see the boss, who'd been romancing his wife. Messner was dispatched to try to calm him, leaving only Hays to argue their case, and the presence of the agent in the waiting room just seemed to spur Liveright to ink the deal.

Two things jar in Bennett's account. First, everyone knew about Liveright's drinking, yet Bennett made it seem atypical. He placed responsibility for the decision as much on the "unusual" effects of the alcohol as on pressure from the father-in-law, deflecting any sense of his having driven the sale himself. Second, he recalled having "blandly" suggested that Liveright sell. "Blandly" said is not at all bland: it conveys intent. Fifty years later, Manuel Komroff, who was friendly with both Bennett and Liveright, wrote to their former colleague Edward Weeks after Bennett died, summoning up "the wild day" when the ML was sold. "Bennett wanted to get out," Komroff stated.

Now fully aware of Liveright's volatility and financial weakness, Bennett knew he had to move on. Buying the ML was the safest way to ensure that the money he'd already put into B&L didn't disappear into the maw of Liveright's Broadway and Wall Street appetites. Donald Klopfer recalled Bennett telling him he "was going to try to get [the deal], and succeeded in getting Horace's handshake, which was just as good as a written document." Bennett then called him and said, "Hey, I haven't got enough money . . . how about going into business together?" It was the first time they'd really talked about such a move, but Bennett was going off to Europe and needed an answer.

"All right, I'd like to do it, if I can," Don agreed. He'd have to sell his interest in his family's business, and promised an answer for Bennett by the time he returned.

The only signatures on the sale document drafted May 19, 1925, belong to Liveright, Bennett, and Arthur Pell—the bookkeeper–turned–company treasurer whom the father-in-law had installed. The closing would take place late in June, after Bennett got back from his trip. The truth is that a clear-eyed young man saw that the Modern Library was a rare gem and coolly went after it. It gave him a career, a life, and provided the basis for him to establish with his best friend what would grow into the largest trade publisher in the world. Nothing else—certainly not the stories about an angry father-in-law or a cuckolded husband—counts for nearly as much, in the greater scheme of things.

Chapter 6

The Book Boys

Ford Madox Ford, the roly-poly British author who'd been happy to enjoy Liveright's hospitality, wasn't so keen on his ethnicity. "I don't like Jews," he declared in a nonfiction book about New York, published by (Jewish) Albert and Charles Boni, after Albert had left Liveright. He went on to admit, however, that "the arts flourish in New York largely because of its Jewish population. . . . The only people I have found [there]—and I have not found them anywhere else . . . who really loved books . . . were Jews—and the only people who subsidized young writers during their early non-lucrative years."

In buying the Modern Library, Bennett and Donald were joining an unofficial New York club, the Jewish "book boys" (and one girl, Blanche Knopf). They would remain excluded (with very few exceptions) from membership in institutions like the Century Association and other social bastions. As a cohort, however, they would be as influential culturally as the Jewish bankers' "Our Crowd" was economically. Even to antisemites like Dreiser and Ford, they proved unusually devoted publishers.

By the end of the 1920s, the book boys included Huebsch, Liveright, the Knopfs, the Bonis, Simon and Schuster, as well as Pascal Covici and Donald Friede; Harold Guinzburg, co-founder of the Literary Guild and Viking Press; Harry Scherman and Robert Haas, who established the Book-of-the-Month Club (BOMC); and the Wolffs and Shriftes, connected families whose printing-binding-warehousing facilities serviced them all. To be sure, they didn't consciously think of themselves as a club, and weren't always friendly: Knopf loathed Liveright, who wanted to best Knopf. But for decades, Bennett's and Donald's lives and fortunes would be closely intertwined with this group. The prejudice they encountered was a given, running the gamut from insidious to ugly to shocking and worse. Yet although many wanted to fit in, they also wanted to be noticed.

Alfred A. Knopf

With his typical sartorial splendor—green tie, salmon shirt, orange handkerchief, dark suit—as well as his fierce mustache, Alfred Abraham Knopf created a persona that stood out more than most. He'd graduated from Columbia in February 1912; his father gave him a trip to Europe. In London, he haunted bookshops around Charing Cross Road, and, meeting writers like John Galsworthy (with whom he'd precociously corresponded), he "determined to be a publisher." Back in America, every trade house he approached turned him down. Knopf's father, Samuel, was in advertising, and used his network to help Alfred get a job at Doubleday, which is how he became the first Jew to be employed at any major non-Jewish publisher. He began in accounting and moved to production.

As it happened, Joseph Conrad, one of Knopf's two favorite writers (Galsworthy being the other), was a Doubleday author, but Knopf felt that the firm neglected the great "Polish Englishman." Using subterfuge to remedy the situation, on stationery engraved with his home address, he wrote to a dozen famous American writers, telling of Conrad's financial situation and asking for a blurb, assuring them that Conrad's publisher would use it. With the "extremely generous" response, Knopf compiled and printed a booklet on the author. Conrad found it quite exciting to be "rediscovered" by his own publisher. "An investment must be attended to, it must be nursed if one believes in it," he declared, adding that the initial gamble "is not the connection." Authors of every era would agree.

Knopf realized there was nowhere within Doubleday for a Jew to rise. Already an admirer of finely wrought books, he took a job at Mitchell Kennerley, where he learned about stylish production. In June 1915, he and his fiancée, Blanche Wolf, with $3,000 and probably a contribution from his father, founded their own business in part of his father's office, and within a year, the young couple married. They began by publishing established foreign authors whom American houses had ignored, persuading the originating U.K. publishers to print extra sheets, which the Knopfs bought on credit, shipped, and bound in the United States in colors not dissimilar to Alfred's shirts and ties. It wasn't until the third year that they published their first American novel; and that same year Knopf's father, Sam, known as "S.K.," joined as treasurer. (He wouldn't be generous with author advances or staff pay.)

By most accounts a shy man, Alfred hid behind a blustery facade, but

Blanche Wolf Knopf

early photographs show a darkly handsome youth, once compared to a Persian prince. Young Blanche was lovely. Soon they moved into part of a Manhattan townhouse, convening "fortnightly Friday soirees" with sandwiches and punch, but as the 1920s progressed, Blanche ruined her digestion with a dieting regime intended to make her flapper-thin.

The flip side of Alfred's arrogant personality was his passion for fine bookmaking and his daring in promotion. Just as Liveright reissued *Sister Carrie,* Knopf—only two years in business—reissued W. H. Hudson's novel *Green Mansions,* which had failed to sell for Putnam a decade earlier. Under Knopf, it not only sold, but was judged a modern classic. He took to heart his father's advertising lesson: persuade the consumer to buy a line of "products" by establishing brand recognition with each one. In clothing his books as he clothed himself, he ensured they'd attract attention. A joke circulated among the publishing crowd: If a man wanted a new suit, he could buy ten Knopf books and take their cloth bindings to his tailor; standards were *that* high. In 1926, he began noting in each book he published the typeface and kind of paper used, and number of copies printed. Until then, such details had been the preserve of limited-edition collectibles. Other publishers imitated Knopf's practice.

In cultivating an aura, there was also the firm's colophon, the Borzoi. A Russian wolfhound that Blanche came to dislike in its living, barking incarnation, once it leapt onto the page, enjoyed an endlessly decorative afterlife. The mystique was propagated by wildly British-inflected ads: "Mr. Alfred A. Knopf has the honor to announce the following new Borzoi books," they'd begin, their snob appeal aimed at the upwardly mobile middle class. Blanche, too, was essential in image creation. "Young, exotic, and charming, it is she who takes care of the authors," *The New Yorker* wrote.

The Knopfs set about assembling a fine list: by the late 1920s, they'd published E. M. Forster, H. L. Mencken, D. H. Lawrence (expurgated to satisfy censors), Thomas Mann, and four other Nobel Prize winners. In 1920, Willa Cather literally appeared at their doorstep. She'd had a long relationship with Houghton Mifflin, but having seen how Knopf produced and advertised books, asked him to be her publisher. Cather never wanted an advance, and became the favorite among his authors. Popular fare was dressed up in finer cloth. Kahlil Gibran's *The Prophet,* published in 1923, was the fourth Gibran work Knopf had taken. The first three failed, but *The Prophet* became the biggest-selling book the Knopfs ever published, bringing in sales of at least 150,000 copies, year in, year out. Few books attain such a record. They also began publishing for children, helping to establish quality juvenile books as a field. Yet barriers remained. The Publishers' Lunch Club wouldn't make Knopf a member: he wasn't a "gentleman publisher" (code for his being a Jew). In reply, he started a rival organization, the "Book Table," in 1927. The august members of the Lunch Club would realize that they needed him more than he needed them.

. . .

ON JANUARY 19, 1924, *Publishers Weekly*—often abbreviated to *PW*—announced the formation of Simon & Schuster, which would similarly be shortened to "S&S." Max Schuster, born Jewish in 1897 in Austria, grew up, like Bennett, in Harlem, his family deeply religious in "the Spinoza sense . . . Reformed." His earliest recollections of his mother included seeing her read *Anna Karenina*. His father, a labor activist, later ran a Harlem stationery and cigar store. Before enrolling at Columbia, Max had worked as a copy boy on the *New York World* and idolized its owner, Pulitzer, and its editor, Swope. Dick Simon, two years younger, grew up in a house on fashionable West Eighty-Seventh Street, son of a German Jewish garment district entrepreneur who embraced assimilation. Dick showed rare early talent on the piano, but his father, so the story goes, wouldn't support a concert career. Others thought he decided against it himself, being a man, a colleague attested, "who knew if he couldn't be in the very first rank, he wouldn't do it."

Simon and Schuster began with lofty ideas about "democratizing" the publishing business. Max compiled a manifesto stating they'd publish "only good books" that they'd read and were enthusiastic about; use book publishing as the nucleus for other literary and journalistic endeavors; expand markets via better books, lower prices, and better merchandising, advertising, publicity, and "exploitation tie-ups"; offer reprint series at twenty-five or fifty cents per copy; and publish the best reprint titles. They'd also consider publishing "at different prices for paperback reprints and cloth books." Pegging their own salaries at twenty dollars per week, they paid their secretary twenty-six (being more generous than the Knopfs), and were prepared to contribute $3,000 each to the enterprise, plus more from Dick's family if needed. Harold Guinzburg, a schoolmate of Dick's, had graduated from Harvard, and he also invested, holding the third-largest stake. (Guinzburg's grandfather manufactured "unmentionable" but undeniably profitable ladies' undergarments.)

On their first day in a two-room office on West Fifty-Seventh Street, Morrie Ryskind, a Columbia friend to Bennett, Max, and Dick, dropped by and saw a sign painter affixing SIMON & SCHUSTER, PUBLISHERS to the door. Publishers of what, exactly? Ryskind asked. "We had no answer," Schuster recalled. But serendipity presented itself when Dick's aunt told him she wanted a birthday present for a niece who was a fan of the "Crossword Puzzle" feature in the Sunday *World*. Might he obtain a suitable book for her? The partners could find no collected puzzles. They ventured down to Schuster's old stomping ground, the *World* offices, and the Sunday editor introduced them to the trio responsible for the puzzles. Simon offered each an advance of twenty-five dollars to create enough for a book.

Max Lincoln Schuster (left) and Richard Leo Simon

Stores ordered only 800 copies. Another 1,000 would be taken on consignment by the American News Company, supplier to newsstands and station kiosks. "Practically every bookseller was skeptical," Simon later wrote. A novelty element was added to lure buyers: each book came with a small pencil. The mother of all crossword books was published on April 10, 1924, at a price of $1.35 per copy, and Simon had learned enough from Liveright to take a one-inch ad on the *World* puzzle page. Curiously, the book didn't bear the name Simon & Schuster. Max had grown afraid that *The Cross Word Puzzle Book* would be "a little unliterary and undignified," so the partners adopted a beard, the "Plaza Publishing Company." They needn't have worried. Twenty-odd clerks had to be hired to handle an avalanche of orders. Within six months, they'd published *four* bestsellers. Like mah-jongg and bobbed hair, crosswords became a craze.

When the firm announced its first "real" books for fall 1924, these included a biography of Schuster's hero, Pulitzer; a couple of novels; and several titles in a self-help series. However, their second year wasn't as spectacular. Others had pumped out crosswords and glutted the market; also, the fear that had prompted the corporate beard proved prescient: many in the book world looked on S&S as a mere novelty house. They were forced to fire the clerks, save for a very useful one named Leon Shimkin.

Brooklyn-born Shimkin had been recommended by Arthur Pell, after working a summer job at B&L. Shimkin knew bookkeeping, shorthand, how to run a switchboard. All of seventeen, he'd just finished his first year at NYU. When Dick and Max offered him a clerk's job, Shimkin switched to night school. Soon invaluable, he eventually became the third partner, known to outsiders as "the silent S." But insiders, including Dick and Max, would refer to him, less than affectionately, as "the little bookkeeper."

While Shimkin turned into a permanent fixture, Harold Guinzburg—who visited publishers in Europe on S&S's behalf—came back to New York and moved his money into a publishing house of his own. In 1925, Guinzburg and George Oppenheimer (who'd worked in advertising at Knopf) founded the Viking Press. Less than six months later, they persuaded financially strapped Ben Huebsch to merge, conferring his literary patina upon the new house. S&S, however, continued to be viewed as solely "commercial" despite efforts at diversifying its list; not by chance was it also regarded as the most "Jewish" of the new firms. That these "vulgarians" had succeeded "enraged" established publishers; in 1934, tongue only half in cheek, *PW* would refer to them as "the bad boys" of the trade.

Max was a collector, amassing thousands of color-coded notes so as never to let a maxim or idea escape unrecorded. "He had his own brilliance, in a limited way, and got publishing mileage out of being obsessive," an S&S old-timer observed, but as he and Dick got to know each other better, "they became less friendly." One thing he collected was Little Blue Books, a series of small paperbacks founded by E. Haldeman-Julius, a self-educated Jew who, like Liveright, grew up in Philadelphia. Also like Liveright, Haldeman-Julius combined the sales instincts of a P. T. Barnum with left-wing ideals. He ended up in Kansas, wanting to change the world; certainly, he influenced the book boys.

The Little Blue Books encompassed every kind of subject, from Shakespeare in installments to titles on sex. Selling by mail at five cents apiece, Haldeman-Julius aimed for "the democracy of books"—a precursor to Schuster's own manifesto. He'd sell 300 million books by mid-century. Dick and Max got the idea for their self-help line from his, and further inspiration came from eleven Little Blue Books on philosophers by Will Durant, who would become a mainstay of the S&S list through the 1960s.

Dick and Max weren't beyond gambling on books that were a bit chancy. Viking turned down an as-told-to memoir by an old ivory trader named Aloysius Horn (real name Smith). S&S published *Trader Horn*—essentially tall tales—in 1927, and sold 170,000 copies. Two years later, another "true-life" adventure, *Cradle of the Deep,* by Joan Lowell, would be exposed as a hoax—Dick and Max had been hoodwinked, too. When they moved the book from nonfiction to fiction, S&S became a laughingstock. Dick had a breakdown, but the firm rebounded, always looking for the next bestseller.

While Liveright's ads had been revolutionary, and Knopf's had inserted snob appeal, S&S would create from their imaginations (and the space between their offices) a make-believe world called the "Inner Sanctum" to charm the trade and the public. Under that rubric, weekly boxed ads written with wit and intimacy, each a kind of letter from the publisher, would begin appearing in 1927, including opinions about books and their makers; gossip; and asides on all the arts. After S&S used it to name a new mystery book series, and then licensed it to a mystery radio program, "inner sanctum" entered the American vernacular. While Schuster imagined the "Sanctum," Simon coined "Give the Reader a Break." Adept at dreaming up books inspired by personal passions like music and art, he insisted that they be very affordable. People found him attractive but "very mysterious," his fingers often drumming at an invisible keyboard.

When everybody was young and publishing was there to be remade, Dick decided to put some well-earned crossword money to good use. He'd travel to Europe himself, rather than rely on someone else to scout out the territory for him. His friend Bennett Cerf would provide the companionship.

Chapter 7

Embarkations

AT 2:40 A.M. ON MAY 20, 1925, ON THE FIRST NIGHT OF HIS TRANS-atlantic crossing aboard the *Aquitania,* Bennett began his travel journal: "Dick Simon and I sat up on the top deck for over an hour hoping to see the boat swing into midstream, but have given it up. . . . And so I'm off for bed after the most eventful day of my life. I bought the Modern Library from Boni & Liveright after a whirlwind conference—a step that will alter my entire career."

His immediate plans were for a grand tour: the fold-out passport had visas for Austria, Germany, France, as well as Britain. The next morning, after breakfast and a "bawth" drawn by his steward, he and Dick "repaired" to the boat deck; subsequently, they judged the English jazz band "really too fearful" for delicate American ears. His chameleon effort at adopting a British tone showed Bennett for the novice he was, half joking, half serious, and very much wanting to belong. Happily, Anita Loos was on board with her husband John Emerson, the president of Actors Equity, and had lent Bennett amusing reading matter: the final manuscript of *Gentlemen Prefer Blondes*.

There was something both exhilarating and calming about being in the middle of the sea: four days into the weeklong crossing, Bennett couldn't help but write: "I am very happy tonight." From time to time, he and Dick chatted amiably about Liveright and the Modern Library. Admitting only that in the "remote future" he intended to try to buy the series, he kept the momentous event that had just transpired to himself.

On May 26, the day after Bennett enjoyed a jolly twenty-seventh birthday on board, the ship docked in Southampton, and he proceeded to share a boat-train compartment with Dick and the Emersons. Everything on the journey made an impression: "the odd seating arrangement, the tea served on the way, the thatched roof cottages in orderly rows." He was nonplussed that rather than gazing out, Dick gazed down at a newspaper. Bennett had somehow neglected to book a room, but Emerson secured a few nights in a two-bedroom suite at the Savoy, London's first modern luxury hotel, and he and Loos invited him to join them. Dick had reserved at the Waldorf. "Dizzy" with excitement as his taxi crossed the Thames, Bennett could see Parliament from the bridge. He felt he was in a movie, or "some great spectacle at [Coney Island's] Luna Park," but the imperial city he'd conjured from books was real—and calling to him.

Exhausted after so many exciting hours, at the hotel he fell into a heavy sleep. But at 1:30 A.M., an intoxicated, "high-hatted" lord and an equally inebriated "very blonde" young lady loomed above, trying to rouse him to join their revels next door. Emerson rushed in to retrieve the friendly intruders, and Bennett returned to his dreams. But the next morning, amazed to learn the girl had been Tallulah Bankhead, a House Speaker's daughter and rising star, he "regretted" not having taken advantage of the situation. That evening, he made a beeline to see the play she was currently appearing in, even venturing backstage to demand an "apology."

After a few days, he and the Emersons moved to the Cavendish Hotel, whose proprietor, Rosa Lewis, had been mistress to King Edward VII. As it happened, Lewis was suing B&L: they'd contracted her memoirs but were refusing to delete chapters she now disavowed. Every day, it seemed, he felt Liveright's presence. One of Bennett's first outings was to Jermyn Street, to purchase a walking stick, gloves, and lounging robe worthy of the boss who held sway over his imagination. And after enjoying a play at the Strand Theatre, he asked about the availability of American rights, "with Horace in mind."

He met Dick for some meals, but each mostly went his own way. Bennett visited the National Gallery to see paintings he knew he didn't really appreciate, and Trafalgar Square and Westminster Abbey, which he did. One of Donald's diamond-dealer relatives introduced him to West End favorite Beatrice Lillie; he couldn't get enough of the ladies with names in marquee lights. More purposefully, he darted in and out of the wonderfully idiosyncratic Charing Cross Road bookstores picking up first editions, and called on agents and publishers, "men who may help me later." For the bank holiday weekend, along with the Emersons and Dick, he motored to Oxford and Stratford in a Rolls-Royce. Rubbing shoulders with the crowds, Bennett's greenness was again all too apparent. Adopting the local snobbery as though trying on a Savile Row suit, he dismissed these "lower class" Brits as an "ill-favored, dirty . . . lot."

He'd only been in England a week when a cable brought "disgusting" news: Pell, the B&L treasurer who made sure Horace never knew how much money the firm had, for fear he'd withdraw it all—and who managed the loans keeping B&L afloat (some, reportedly, from Pell himself at exorbitant interest)—demanded immediate payment of $75,000 of the ML purchase price, although it wasn't due until September. Herbert, Don, and lawyer Edwin Falk urged Bennett to return at once. He cabled back that he could sail on the *Berengaria* Saturday, but preferred the *Mauretania* a week later, to salvage a trip to Paris.

Bennett reckoned that his wanting to stay would set Herbert "gnashing his teeth" over a lack of dependability and acumen. More cables followed; Gustave warned he was "antagonizing" his friends. However, they didn't know he'd promised Liveright that $75,000 would be available early if needed, and Horace had cabled back that they could wait to discuss it when Bennett returned. Setting it all down in his diary, so that if anything went wrong he'd have nobody but himself to blame, he wrote: "I would curse myself for every kind of an idiot for not following my *own* judgment. . . . I *know* it's going to turn out *right*." While the others had branded Liveright "an awful crook," he "violently disagreed," and how he approached this first crisis hinted at how he'd handle the future: with confidence in his instincts about books and people. Bennett was willing to bet all that Liveright would "play fair," as he had these past two years.

On June 6, he stuffed cotton into his ears and sat beside Dick on an Imperial Airways seven-seater, his first experience of an "aeroplane" in the days when only the moneyed few could fly. After landing at Le Bourget, they traveled to Paris, where, seeing the grand boulevards, "even Dick" was awed. London's luxury gave way to the rather more bohemian Hotel Istria on the Left Bank, a *pension* known to Marcel Duchamp, Man Ray, and other artists and writers. B&L's Manuel Komroff was already staying there.

After a few wide-eyed days making the rounds of cafés and clubs full of expatriate Americans, Bennett met up with Gustave's brother Leo, who happened to be in Paris and insisted on taking his nephew for a night on the town with a guide and another American. Bennett was game, curious to experience an "out and out dive," and soon found himself in the Etoile de Vénus, where twenty naked girls burst into the room and did a "lewd" dance. Picking out four, they were taken up to a Louis XV bedroom, where the girls "staged what is known as a circus." His unsentimental education continued at an "even worse joint," where patrons were obliged to choose a naked lady as a drinking companion; his "girlfriend's" advances distressed Bennett "beyond measure." Rather than continue on with the others, he rushed back to the Istria to try to purge himself of "overpowering disgust," and dismissed his uncle as "a jackass and a lout." Several days later, as the *Mauretania* steamed toward New York, he had put the unpleasant episode behind him. Exciting times lay ahead at home.

. . .

THE MODERN LIBRARY (ML) was incorporated in New York by Bennett and Donald on July 15, 1925, with Gustave Cerf as company secretary. They rented space in a commercial loft at 71 West Forty-Fifth Street, across the street from *PW*'s offices. The two partners always said that each had contributed half the purchase price, and that working capital—the crucial funds required to run the firm—came from a $50,000 bank loan secured on five hundred shares of Norfolk and Western stock lent by Uncle Herbert. In his oral history, Bennett emphasized that between him and Don, "everything was to be fifty-fifty, absolutely. It would have killed either of us if there had been any difference."

But from the start he was president, his salary higher, and so the situation stayed—however, it wasn't just his large personality, gambler's instinct, energy, vision, and ego making him first among equals. There was also the matter of invested cash. Two sheets of figures written in Bennett's hand in 1925—using his, Don's, Gustave's, and Herbert's initials—tell the story. These papers were in Donald's files until he died, and almost certainly reflect a closer approximation of what the opening figures were.

ESTIMATED JUNE 25, 1925	AUGUST 1, 1925
BAC $125,000	*BAC* $125,000
DSK $50,000	*DSK* $62,500
GC $25,000	*GC* $25,000
HAW $75,000	*HAW* $62,500 loan

The papers suggest that Bennett's investment was significantly greater than Donald's. Nevertheless, both men knew that neither could have operated nearly so well—if at all—alone; and that recognition, combined with deep affection and mutual respect, made "fifty-fifty" the only possible face to show the world.

They were determined to get everything right—title selection, design, and business operation—and to establish themselves positively in the eyes of the book trade and reading public. Their first ad ran in *PW* at the beginning of August: "News! The Modern Library has changed hands!" The series would be the new owners' sole focus, the ad proclaimed, so booksellers could rely on receiving their full attention. A small article ran as well: it would now be "impossible" for a title to be out of print, and a new selection would be added on the twenty-fifth day of each month, like clockwork.

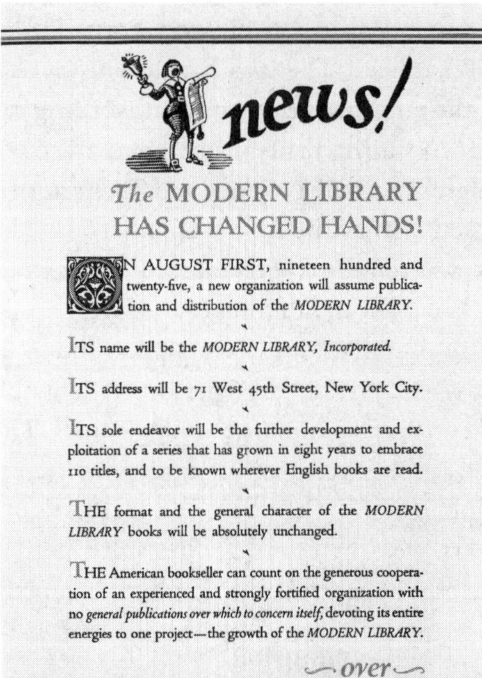

"Our first ad"—as Bennett's scrapbook noted

Albert Boni had envisioned a series mainly dedicated to foreign writers and translations; after he left B&L, more U.S. writing had appeared. By 1925, about fifty titles were by Europeans; thirty-odd by British or Irish authors; and thirty by Americans. By the time Bennett and Donald bought it, the ML had become much less of a dead authors' society; more than half the books were by writers very much alive and producing. Many of its titles were now featured on college lists for supplementary reading, and being purchased by the American Library Association for government schools.

Five new reprints were due to be published that fall, including *The Philosophy of William James* and Emily Brontë's *Wuthering Heights,* with an introduction by Rose Macaulay. Six more were previewed for early 1926, including James Joyce's *Dubliners*. Meeting publication dates that first year brought challenges and lessons: introductions arrived late, copyrights took longer to negotiate, and printers experienced delays. The Joyce wasn't out for the announced date, but did appear in 1926, and the substituted title, Herman Melville's *Moby-Dick,* was a worthy replacement.

Bennett managed to take people, as well as a publishing education, from B&L. Emanuel "Manny" Harper, a wire-rimmed, bow-tied young bookkeeper who looked older than his years, moved from Liveright's brownstone to the loft on Forty-Fifth Street, and spent the rest of his career with Bennett and Don, much of it as company treasurer. Helen Berlin, the wife of Liveright's advertising manager, came over as gal Friday for two years, followed by another young woman, Pauline Kreiswirth. Two young shipping clerks also migrated; one, Abe Friedman, would move up and stay for decades.

Working in the loft at 71 West Forty-Fifth Street

The office was partitioned down the middle. The partners shared one side, their desks facing each other, as they would for years; everyone else was on the other side. Stacked in piles all around was the inventory they'd inherited from B&L—only half what had been expected: while Bennett was abroad, contrary to his deal with Liveright, Pell had discounted copies, and sold off many for cash. Bennett fumed, but perhaps it was for the best. In high summer, in the days before air-conditioning, no one could escape the stench coming from the books. Castor oil used to "cure" the covers—the fake leather bindings had been a selling point—went rancid in humid heat. Donald summed it up: "They stank to high heaven." The binding would be cloth from then on.

As Liveright's attention had increasingly focused on new books and Broadway, the ML had been taken for granted. The series filled such a need that it had simply been a matter of collecting orders when making the rounds. Now Bennett and Don set out to maximize sales. Established "book travelers," working on commission, were engaged to sell the ML to distributors and stores in the Midwest and on the West Coast, but the partners kept the all-important East Coast territory for themselves. They hit the road and *sold,* one heading north, the other south; the following season, they'd swap directions. In January 1926, Bennett spent a typical week covering Philadelphia, Baltimore, and Atlantic City; February saw visits to Hartford, Springfield, and Boston in a blizzard. Both men got to know owners and buyers, building trust; retailers liked these two personable young fellows whose commercial instincts were married to a genuine love of books. When they weren't on the road, Bennett liked to say that he was the one who dealt with editorial matters, but both did their part in that regard, constantly consulting each other. Don, who *hated* "showing off," was the inside man, running production and the general office; Bennett, the born extrovert, took charge of PR, publicity, and ads.

The change in management and focus would quickly show results. In 1925, the ML sold 285,000 copies, an 8.5 percent increase over 1924; for 1927, sales would comprise nearly a half million copies. Bennett always said that they recouped their initial investment in two years. Marking the ML's first dozen years in February 1929, *PW* declared it "an institution," and the title count reached 175 by 1931. The partners played fair by retailers. In January 1927, they discontinued five titles, having promised "absolutely no deadwood," by which they meant any title selling less than 1,000 copies per year, their benchmark to stay in print. They told booksellers that they'd accept returns of those five, and replace them with new or other ML titles. This was unusual. Normally, an order was a "final sale": if nobody bought the book, the store was stuck with it. With this and other policies, they established a lasting reputation for decency.

They continued Liveright's policy of advertising in intellectual periodicals like *The Nation,* while also placing ads for a wider audience on the book pages of the *Herald Tribune* and *The New York Times*. In *The New Yorker,* a just-launched magazine aimed at the smart set, they captured attention with an ad headlined, "The Worst Sellers in the Modern Library: Four books that are designed to sell at 95¢ a copy but don't." The publishers worried it was "their fault" that books by the Belgian Maurice Maeterlinck, Hungarian Andreas Latzko, and two others weren't selling, because they had "definite merits and were added only after mature deliberation by a competent editorial board. . . . Make some honest bookseller believe in Santa Claus again by asking for these books!" the ad urged.

In contrast to the four "overlooked" titles, the ad listed ML bestsellers by the likes of Walt Whitman and Theodore Dreiser. Playful and direct, it already showed Bennett's style. The reference to an editorial board was meant to assure the public that the ML was a dependable cultural gatekeeper, the same kind of appeal used by the Book-of-the-Month Club. However, where BOMC employed an actual panel of journalists, writers, and experts to make selections, the "competent editorial board" that Bennett mentioned consisted, more or less, of Herbert, Don, and himself. They did, however, consult friends at B&L and Columbia about title selection and prefaces—friends like his favorite professor, Raymond Weaver, who provided the introduction to *Moby-Dick*.

By the early 1930s, the reprint field had become crowded, spawning the Blue Ribbon, Sun Dial, and Star Dollar series, besides the ML and Everyman. Along with choosing the right titles, the ML was commissioning introductions, sometimes from the writers themselves—Faulkner, Fitzgerald, and Bertrand Russell supplied prefaces to their own works—which made its books stand out. Bennett and Don understood that a series must feed readers new titles on a regular basis, otherwise interest flags; they scrutinized American and British catalogues for suitable books whose rights they might buy, and for works already out of copyright and in the public domain that would cost nothing in royalties.

Many publishers had been loath to grant B&L reprint rights, fearing that Liveright would lure away their authors with generous offers for their new projects once their older works were in the ML. To these firms Bennett and Don emphasized there was nothing to fear: they didn't publish new books and had no plans to do so. They were just the Modern Library boys. Nevertheless, some remained wary. Bennett had campaigned to win over Alfred Knopf and thought he'd succeeded, but soon received an icy, complaining letter. Knopf had read with "amazement" an ad that included *Green Mansions*—the novel he'd reissued in 1916—as an ML title. However, the misapprehension was in fact Knopf's.

According to U.S. copyright law, *Green Mansions* was in the public domain. It was *already* an ML bestseller when Bennett joined B&L. Yet Knopf now insisted he'd do no business with the partners. Deciding to be strategic, they paid a royalty to melt the ice. Charm, persistence, and serious intent did the rest. By 1931, Knopf's letters were signed, "Yours always, Alfred." A few years later, a jokey telegram was sent by "Lodovici Klopfer and Magillovitch Cerf" to "Alfred Staniscowitz Knopf," spoofing the names of Alfred's European authors. No one but Bennett could have gotten away with it.

. . .

IN MAY 1926, BENNETT crossed the Atlantic again to spend two full months abroad, making up for the truncated trip a year earlier; Don would have to manage on his own. Once again, he found shipboard life perfect for indulging his passion for celebrities, with Feodor Chaliapin, the first Russian to achieve international renown as an opera singer, the "prize package." He also took note of an alluring (married) actress, Elise Bartlett, but although appreciating her charms, fast retreated, recognizing her as a "hard-boiled gold-digger." (In a few years, he'd have cause to learn his instinct was all too accurate.)

In Paris he met up with Herbert, already in Europe, and Manuel Komroff, who was back among the Surrealists and bohemians at the Hotel Istria, having left Liveright's employ—but retaining the connection: his first book, *The Travels of Marco Polo,* had just been published by B&L. Knowing that Komroff's experience could be useful, Bennett appointed him the ML's European scout. The three set out to drum up business by calling on Parisian booksellers stocking English-language titles. Most famous among them was Sylvia Beach, American proprietor of Shakespeare & Co., whose profound faith in James Joyce's controversial novel *Ulysses* was equaled by her gumption: four years earlier, she'd turned herself into a publisher specifically to produce and disseminate that single title. Beach's edition—between demure blue covers—was often hidden in the steamer trunks of returning Americans, a trophy of mad, bad, sophisticated Paris. On May 17, in Beach's shop, Komroff, Herbert, and Bennett happened upon Joyce, "less robust, and more diffident, even, than I had been led to expect," as Bennett told his diary.

He couldn't know the future significance of that encounter, being too focused on Chaliapin's daughter Stella, and their "Paris-in-the-spring" romantic interlude. Having judged himself "reckless" after confessing similar feelings for college sweetheart Marie a decade earlier, he again felt uneasy: "Mental Reservation: I wonder if, when I am . . . home the foregoing will . . . strike me as a lot of sentimental slop?" Intimacy with women didn't sit easily with Bennett anywhere. But after the Orient Express deposited him and Herbert in Venice, he pined for female companionship, while his uncle went in search of romance with men.

In Vienna, they called on Arthur Schnitzler to try to sign him, then journeyed on to Salzburg and Munich, where—reunited with Komroff—they met Thomas Mann. Knopf had published *Buddenbrooks* and *Death in Venice* in 1924 and 1925, the only translations of his work available in America. Bennett hadn't read them, but knew that "one of the great living figures in German literature" belonged in the ML. Mann spoke practically no English; the smattering of German Bennett had heard in his grandfather's house had been supplemented by just one year of high school study; but they "spluttered along." It was good enough: *Buddenbrooks* and *Death in Venice* would join the ML.

More publishing visits followed in Leipzig and Berlin. However, after alighting from a train in a central German town called Eisenach, the trip took a different turn. When Nathan Wise had quit his homeland for America, he'd left something behind: his family. Uncle Herbert had brought his nephew back to meet them. For the next few days, in and around Stadtlengsfeld, a tiny village "famed in song and story" as ancestral seat of the Wise "*mishpocha,*" Bennett mingled with a buzzing horde of unknowns who shared his blood. "Christ, I never kissed so many strangers in my life!" he vented to his diary. He tried to be lighthearted, but the crush of faces, bodies, and voices claiming him grew tedious. When he and his uncle finally made it back to Eisenach, they had a close call: one of the relatives caught sight of Herbert's letter of credit, revealing how much money they could access on their travels. Heaven help them if the Germans started asking for handouts! With that fate "narrowly averted," Bennett, "*aus-gekissed*" and "*aus-gefressed,*" thanked God he and Herbert were leaving, and that his grandfather had emigrated.

A week later, all thoughts of the Wise *mishpocha* were shaken off like roadside dust, as he did the publishing rounds of London, but it was on the day before he headed home that he made his luckiest connection. Despite having assured everyone that his and Don's "sole endeavor" would be the ML, Bennett had harbored bigger ambitions from the outset. While Dick and Max had made a mass-market killing with crosswords, he and Don had their eyes on the other end of the spectrum—the craze among the well-off for fine letter-press art books that could be bought, sold, and bought again at a pretty profit.

Nonesuch Press books were among the most beautiful and coveted on both sides of the Atlantic. The limited number that made their way to the United States were subscribed by dilettantes and collectors alike, including Bennett and Don. A gentleman named Francis Meynell was Nonesuch's founder and presiding genius, and on that penultimate day, Bennett called on this man whose books he'd "dearly love to" distribute. Son of a poet and printer, and with a grandfather who'd been a close friend of Dickens, Meynell was a literary blueblood, but he also wanted to cater to a growing interest in fine books from middle-class enthusiasts who couldn't pay the "fine prices" of established presses. His philosophy shared something of the democratizing impulse that had animated the ML.

Other would-be American distributors had courted him, but to no avail. Suddenly this "brisk young man swinging a silver-headed cane" (one that Meynell rather envied) arrived at his Bloomsbury townhouse, and "with a mixture of humour and assertiveness" announced that henceforth he and his partner would be Nonesuch's "sole selling agency" in the U.S. Bennett wasn't really sure how much he'd managed to convince Meynell, but somehow knew they "*did* part mighty good friends." As he sailed home, his thoughts kept returning to their chat: he had an inkling it might lead to "something important."

Chapter 8

"The Random House"

By the time Bennett had embarked on his second trip to Europe, the initial challenges of the Modern Library were sorted and tackled, and he and Don had fallen into a routine. From their ninth-floor loft within earshot of the rumbling Sixth Avenue El, the day stretched to include long lunches and postprandial backgammon or bridge; card-tossing competitions at the (literal) drop of a hat; and entertaining favored authors while avoiding problematic ones, like the anthologist who hadn't bathed in five years. They even tried a wine-making machine—it was Prohibition, after all.

But writing to Komroff in August 1926, Bennett felt "so discontentedly in the old grooves" that he and Don had resolved Labor Day would end "all shilly-shallying and kibbitzing . . . the sparks will fly!" He liked good times, but the dynamo driving a desire to make his mark couldn't slacken for long without his feeling uneasy. Determined that the vogue for art-press books would be their entrée into original publishing, he and Don wanted to start a new enterprise parallel to the ML. But although both were keen collectors, he knew they couldn't do it alone. They needed relationships with designers and creators—sights were trained on Nonesuch—but also expertise closer to home.

Enter Elmer Adler, proprietor of the Pynson Printers, who already designed the ML's catalogues, leaflets, and title pages. An odd match for the "boys," forty-two-year-old Adler was known as "Pa," since he neither smoked nor drank, and affected a "country-squirish" demeanor. But he was also a cultivated printer-aesthete, respected in the art-printing and book-collecting world. Born in Rochester to a well-off Jewish family, he'd been thrown out of four schools, but already collected beautiful books as a teen. After managing ads for his family's suit-making factory, Adler arrived in Gotham in 1922 and founded Pynson with three fellow

Elmer Adler,
the third founder

"typophiles." Within six months, his partners had gone—*PW* called Adler "exacting," "unbending"—but he was soon doing work for the equally unbending Knopf. Adler introduced Alfred to W. A. Dwiggins, the typographer associated with the "Knopf look," just as he was respon-

Lucian Bernhard's design (above); Rockwell Kent's revision (opposite page); both replaced earlier ML colophons used by B&L

February 9, 1929  657

Re-drawing of the Modern Library Trademark recently made by Rockwell Kent

The Modern Library

A Popular Series of Reprints Appears in a New Flexible Cloth Binding

THE *Modern Library* is sending out its January editions to the trade in a new flexible binding of balloon cloth. For a long time the *Modern Library* has been attempting to secure a suitable cloth binding to replace the imitation leather one that has been for a decade a familiar sight on booksellers' shelves. A long series of experiments, they believe, is now ended with the introduction of the handsome binding which these popular books now possess. The announcement of the new style of binding comes to mark a sort of birthday, or anniversary, for it was just ten years ago that the *Modern Library* published Oscar Wilde's "Dorian Gray," as the first title in a book series that would retail for 95 cents a copy. Since that time 150 titles have been added to the list, many changes in organization have taken place, typographic and other book making improvements have been made, and the price has remained the same.

For the past three years the business has been owned and run by Bennett Cerf and Donald Klopfer, and now occupies a floor of extremely modern offices at 20 East 57th Street, New York.

The *Modern Library* is no longer an experiment; it has become an institution in the book world. And it is interesting to know some of the facts concerning these ubiquitous books, which at one time or another have penetrated into nearly every American home and into the libraries of many readers in other countries.

In the first place, to keep its popularity, the *Modern Library* has had to live up to its title of "Modern," and the editors, in their use of the word "Modern" have not necessarily meant "contemporary." Voltaire is certainly a modern of moderns, and so are Samuel Butler, François Villon, Rabelais and Dostoyevsky. There have been published 167 titles in all—17 of these have been dropped. It is the constant problem of the editors to keep this list up-to-date. A new title is added to the *Modern Library* every month, and sometimes two new titles are added at once. Between now and August, 1929, there will be nine new titles added—bringing the list up to 159.

The titles chosen for publication in the *Modern Library* are by no means limited to the literature of one or two countries. A glimpse at the following table will show the wide scope of nationalities represented.

English	53	Russian	10
American	35	Italian	4
French	29	Scandinavian	3
German and		Misc.	2
Austrian	13	Latin	1

Does the *Modern Library* owe its success to short stories, novels, biographies, philosophy or poetry? The following list will give an idea of the range of books included in the series.

Plays	11	Biographies	4
Novels	62	Poetry	12
Art	3	Miscellaneous	
Philosophy	13	(Essays, Science,	
Short Stories	22	etc.)	13

A novel, Hudson's "Green Mansions," was for a number of years the *Modern Library's* best seller. Although its popularity still continues, another book which appeared on the list last year has super-

sible for Bennett and Don meeting Lucian Bernhard, the Berlin transplant who designed what Bennett called the ML's "flying girl" torchbearer colophon, replacing ones used by B&L.

As an outsider, Pynson was uniquely privileged to occupy the eighth floor of the *New York Times* printing annex on West Forty-Third Street, where Pa maintained an elegant library, offices, and the most "uncommercial" printing plant imaginable. Each winter Thursday he invited artists, writers, publishers, and fellow printers to take tea in a bibliophile's paradise of floor-to-ceiling glass cases lined with rare books. It was therefore entirely understandable that when the new company Bennett and Donald envisaged for fine editions was incorporated in the State of New York on December 31, 1926, it had *three* partners: Cerf, Klopfer, and Adler, each essential—in the beginning.

Pa's interests colored the scope of the enterprise the incorporation papers described: a business of "editors, publishers, printers, bookbinders, stationers" that would encompass not just books, but magazines and newspapers, too. Bennett's press release declared a devotion to "books of typographical excellence," mentioning Pa's having made many such. The "sparks" he'd promised had indeed been flying, as he and Don worked on a plan to distribute Nonesuch books in the United States. But since every publisher in the fine-press game coveted that role, it required more than Bennett's charm and energy to convince Meynell. Luckily, a partner at the Sartorius brokerage was an old family friend of Meynell's wife, and vouched for Bennett's trustworthiness. News of Adler's involvement satisfied Meynell's other crucial criteria: quality and prestige.

On December 10, 1926—three weeks before formally joining with Pa—Bennett dispatched a letter and contract via the *Majestic,* assuring Meynell that he and Don were honoring his request to retain individual liability, even though the agreement was in the name of the new corporation. They'd insisted on doing so over the objection of their lawyer, who'd argued that the company would be liable in the eyes of the law, so they needn't put themselves at personal financial risk. They were doing so to guarantee Nonesuch that "there will be no breach," and deposited $20,000 in Liberty Bonds as further evidence of good faith. "We will certainly have our own reputation at stake," Bennett added, but knew that Pa's artistic bona fides and reputation argued even more persuasively.

Over the years, Bennett loved telling a story about how the company he formed with Don and Pa got its unconventional name. During the waning months of 1926, Rockwell Kent—intrepid traveler, Soviet sympathizer, and artist much in vogue—dropped by the office. When Bennett and Don had needed a designer to create new endpapers for the Modern Library, Pa had suggested Kent. Now they told Kent of their plan to expand beyond the ML and publish "a few books on the side," but what the start-up was to be called they hadn't decided. Bennett had to pop out briefly; when he returned, he suddenly announced, "I've got the name: Random House." Donald liked it, as did Kent, and then and there Kent sketched the image that has, in one variation or another, been on every RH book ever since. It's one of Bennett's stories that has attained mythic status, but his eureka moment may not be all that went into the decision.

Traditionally, publishers often began as printer-booksellers; those calling themselves "presses" reflect that origin. Many used personal surnames as identifiers, while others preferred symbols. Alfred Knopf put his difficult-sounding name on the spine of his books; so did Boni &

Liveright, and old-line WASP houses like Harper and Houghton. Why didn't Bennett, Don, and Pa? One likely reason: "Cerf, Klopfer, & Adler" is a mouthful. Another is that while "Cerf" is indeterminate, "Klopfer" and "Adler" are obviously Jewish: maybe *too* Jewish for Bennett's liking. Guinzburg and Oppenheimer—also clearly Jewish—called themselves "Viking." On the other hand, with Max describing his family as "deeply religious," it's no surprise that Simon & Schuster used their surnames, and that S&S was comfortable being seen as the most "Jewish" of the new firms.

"Random House" has a vaguely English cachet, and Bennett's admiration for Nonesuch may have played a part in the choice. Meynell's colophon depicts Nonesuch Palace, one of Henry VIII's long-gone abodes; Kent's conjures an eccentric old house that could easily be English. "Nonesuch Press" and "Random House" have the same pattern of syllables, stresses, beats. A century later, *Random House,* a brand, glides off the tongue. We hardly consider the literal meaning, or what an odd—inspired—pairing the words are.

The alliance with Meynell, also inspired, got off to an excellent start. The first Nonesuch book RH distributed was Herman Melville's *Benito Cereno*. Jazzy hand-colored drawings by well-known graphic artist E. McKnight Kauffer embellished the handsome text. Nine hundred copies were reserved for England and 750 for RH, at a list price of $7.50 (about $133 today), a run that immediately sold out. Other early titles included Blake's *Pencil Drawings* and Dante's *Divine Comedy,* the latter in English and Italian with illustrations after Botticelli, priced at $46.00 (quickly reselling for far more). Books were sold to shops at a 30 percent discount, and direct to readers at full price.

Bennett's hope for greater financial rewards lay in Meynell's *unlimited* editions: handsome trade books of more general interest. One of the first was *The Week-end Book,* compiled by Meynell and his wife, Vera. A magpie anthology of whimsical yet practical ideas for how to make the most of a country weekend, it topped the British bestseller list when published in 1924. Dial Press had brought out a U.S. edition, but in 1929 RH took over distribution. Promotional copy, with Bennett's signature double-entendres, promised that "the inveterate reader-out-loud can be kept busy during the wettest (climatically speaking) weekend," and declared: "If cocktails fail to cure his apathy, [the book] prescribes an elixir that will enable him . . . to rise to the occasion." The *Herald Tribune* said, more primly: "No self-respecting home should be without" it.

Meynell was an inveterate punster and, like naughty schoolboys, he and Bennett peppered their letters with wordplay, some blush-worthy. For the erstwhile kid from Harlem and the Heights, the relationship with this wonderfully approachable English gentleman was terrifically gratifying. Don, a far more devoted, knowledgeable collector than Bennett, corresponded with Meynell with equal pleasure. Nonesuch now enjoyed a continuity of support it hadn't had before; a distinct distribution advantage via the ML's popularity and marketing clout; and a source of capital for new projects. In return, Meynell agreed to give RH "first crack" at future unlimited editions. During a London visit in May 1927, Donald began a complex negotiation for what would be their most ambitious project: a twenty-six-volume Nonesuch Shakespeare. Bennett could be dilatory, "bored" by contract details; luckily, Don took on such matters. Yet it was Bennett who insisted that they get better terms, and that the Shakespeare be a "joint venture with us as co-publishers." His boldness moved them forward, taking risks.

Some of his notions were harebrained. Don would chew the end of his reading glasses, stare at Bennett across the desk, and let him expound to his heart's content, then reply: "That's the most goddamned foolish idea I ever heard!" Given time, Bennett usually came to his senses. Of course, Don's biggest gamble had been hitching his future to Bennett's in the first place. But this particular suggestion, like many, was a good one: Meynell agreed to the Shakespeare joint imprint. "Here indeed we pledge our past to your future," he declared. He saw their joining in "the greatest" of undertakings as "a marriage and the consummation of a marriage."

With their new plans afoot and the ML proceeding nicely, Bennett and Donald knew it was time to move. They did so on July 1, 1927, signing a ten-year lease at 20 East Fifty-Seventh Street, fifteen minutes by

Reception room view in remade world, 20 East 57th Street

foot and a world away from their old neighborhood. There would be no noisy El, the building was new, and they turned to Pa's designer friend Lucian Bernhard to build out the fifth floor into a paragon of Deco modernity. "You step off the elevator into an ante-room of sand-color walls, and brick-red ceiling with gold borders," a *PW* reporter noted. Beyond was a reception room with sea-green ceiling illuminated by concealed lighting, the latest architectural style. Bennett commissioned a large print from Kent to decorate one wall, and other Kent pieces hung in the yellow-and-blue office he shared with Don. A gaily-striped divan sat below the library's built-in bookshelves: perfect for settling in to a long read. A "distinct spirit of youth" pervaded the place, *PW* concluded: writers and booksellers were "guests . . . invited to see beautiful books and a beautiful setting." Another columnist declared it "a modern work of art." They were creating the publishing world anew in more ways than one.

. . .

IN SPRING 1928, RH introduced the first fine-press book it had commissioned on its own: Voltaire's *Candide,* the timeless novel that Bennett had studied with Raymond Weaver. Komroff had suggested it; the title was already an ML bestseller, and its long-dead author wouldn't require a royalty. Fierce social, sexual, and religious satire, the fable was a hallmark of the French Enlightenment, taking on one of the great questions: How could evil coexist with God? The naive, eponymous protagonist had to learn that "cultivating his own garden" was the only path to happiness in a life that, contrary to what he'd been taught, wasn't lived "in the best of all possible worlds." For illustrator, Bennett made the felicitous choice of Rockwell Kent. Bernhard would design it, and Pa print it.

Thousands of prospectuses were sent out in fall 1927; 1,370 signed and numbered copies were subscribed, along with 95 hand-colored ones. In fact, the book was oversubscribed. Kent illustrated each page, balancing eroticism with childlike whimsy, paragraphs separated by small silhouettes of naked humans rather than line breaks. Bernhard's type was metal-cast in Germany; Pa's men would hand-set and print on handmade French paper. But Kent was slow in making the illustrations, so publication had to be delayed until May.

The book was priced at twenty dollars, but a year later copies were selling at auction for four times that amount. And yet Pa's reputation for perfectionism had a downside: his final bills often bore little relation to estimates. *Candide* cost one-third more than he'd reckoned, but the book *was* beautiful, hailed by a foremost fine-press expert as "the greatest contribution to the illustrated book yet made in America." Random House had entered the world as Nonesuch's distributor; thanks to *Candide,* it arrived as an original publisher.

A year later, *Candide* was reset in a different type (to prevent confusion with the expensive original), and reprinted on cheaper paper in a "popular" five-dollar version. The first run sold out in two days. After the Collector of the Port of Boston banned it—confirming Voltaire's undying ability to provoke—RH's press release noted that they'd been "deluged" with orders. Bennett went further, offering book club rights to Robert Haas of the Book-of-the-Month Club (BOMC) and to Haas's competitor Harold Guinzburg in his Literary Guild guise. Guinzburg ordered 60,000. Although a "controversial" choice, club members liked it, returning fewer copies of *Candide* than almost any other selection.

Bennett rewarded Pa with a bonus. "Dear Beans, this is . . . pretty hard . . . to write," the usually crusty Adler confessed. Only one other time had he received a complimentary check. "Pynson . . . is very happy . . . working with you," he concluded. That happiness proved evanescent. It was Bennett and Don's money—initially $5,000 from each—that underwrote the business. Pa's stake was his investment of expertise and services, not cash, and he'd been promised that RH would

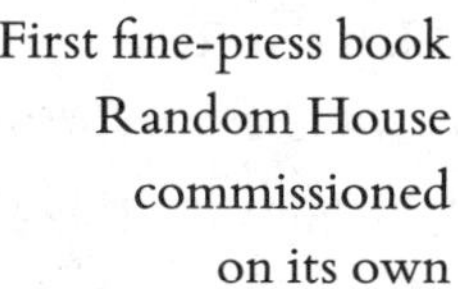

First fine-press book Random House commissioned on its own

bring Pynson work. Soon, though, he was grousing about not getting his due. When they'd started, Pa recalled, Bennett had said that "the Random House" was merely "a play toy" alongside the ML, so Pa—who claimed "very little of the spirit of the merchant"—hadn't been troubled by an unequal ownership split. It had become much more than a toy; meanwhile, the book trade assumed Pa was "an equal" member. Arguing that he should own a full third, he'd compromise by accepting 30 percent, but soon threatened to "withdraw entirely."

His protestations of business innocence were infuriating, but the boys needed him; Bennett came up with a plan that involved further compromises and fancy accounting. Weekly salaries were pegged at a fixed ratio of 40%, 35%, and 25%, for Bennett, Don, and Pa, respectively. Pa was expected to contribute his $5,000, but only $3,000 in cash. The remainder was to be credited from salary—he wasn't to receive any until after his $2,000 had accrued into the firm's account. The partnership survived; soon Bennett invested in Pynson, buying preferred stock—another effort to assuage disgruntled Pa.

RH's birth gave rise to an unexpected development: in nine carefully typed, number-crunched pages, Dick Simon and Max Schuster offered to take over the Modern Library for a handsome payout. "Messrs. Cerf and Klopfer will be relieved from the effort and responsibilities involved in the operation of the company and . . . have greater freedom for a) vacations and trips abroad; b) development of the Random House," the letter urged.

Dick and Max had coveted the ML even longer than Bennett had. After Bennett got Liveright's handshake and left for Europe with Dick, he'd kept the news to himself; but as cables flew back and forth and Bennett cut short his trip, Dick's suspicions had been aroused. He'd written Max, suggesting it would be fair to wait until "Beans" was home before entering the fray. However, they'd been outmaneuvered. Now three years had passed, and they proposed to allow Bennett and Don to retain a stake, offering them $100,000 outright; $300,000 in cumulative preferred stock; and dividends stretching over ten years: a total of almost $627,000 (about $11,117,000 today), arguing that only S&S's superior merchandising skills would keep momentum going. They also dangled the idea of a joint venture, such as retail chain stores. Bennett studied the numbers, but wasn't about to repeat Horace's mistake. The ML was the bedrock of all that he and Don did.

Back in 1923, after only three weeks at B&L, Bennett had been clear about his goal: "Within ten years I hope I may become one of the greatest publishers of the country," he'd vowed to Dick. The seeds of rivalry were planted between them, and less than a year after buying the ML, Bennett was on his way, mentioned in the press as one of the "more prominent" young men in publishing. He and Don were doing nicely, plowing most profits back into the firm. Their combined salaries and bonuses in 1928 would be about $40,000, plus $4,000 extra for travel abroad. They held real estate jointly, and each had stocks and bonds; Bennett even oversaw investments for a few friends—all this at a time when 40 percent of Americans lived on less than $1,500 per year.

Early in 1928, Bennett had moved to apartment 13A in the just-finished Navarro, a twenty-five-story Deco apartment-hotel at 112 West Fifty-Ninth Street, more often known as Central Park South. Whether in New York, London, or Shanghai, it was fashionable to reside in such establishments: all the privacy of one's own place, plus the services of a hotel. He was soon paying $5,600 per year in rent for a four-room flat (at first, Pop lived with him; later, he settled his father in a small place upstairs). His new home was modern, masculine, uncluttered. Bennett had commissioned custom paneling, and the living room boasted a fireplace and the latest phonograph-and-radio set, perfect for parties. From his cushioned window seat he could see the great park's tapestry of treetops, the roofline of the Metropolitan Museum, and residential towers rising on Central Park West. To go with the apartment was a 1929 Cadillac, garaged nearby.

Luckily, the place could look after itself, since that first year Bennett was gone a great deal, visiting printers, bookshops, and buyers for the large book sections in the best department stores. After Washington, Baltimore, and Philadelphia in January, he boarded the Clevelander at Grand Central in mid-February, and didn't return until the Crescent pulled in from the South six weeks later. The rhythm of the trains suited him: time to think and plan, observe and talk with all kinds of Americans, who responded to his eager smile and encyclopedic recall of jokes. Covering far more territory than the usual rep—Detroit to Denver, San Francisco to Dallas, New Orleans to Richmond—he visited seventy-one booksellers in fourteen cities. Midway through, he was based in L.A. for two weeks, at "Castle Wise": Herbert had taken a place in Altadena to improve his health.

In San Francisco, he called on printer Edwin Grabhorn, his brother Robert, and Robert's wife, Jane, and watched as their resident artist illuminated page after page of a text based on a fourteenth-century travel memoir. Mesmerized, Bennett marveled that the artist, Valenti Angelo, used techniques a medieval monk might have employed. He bought the entire edition of 150 copies for RH. In the spring of 1929, he'd commission the Grabhorns to produce arguably the most famous—and most expensive—volume RH published during its fine-press era. Walt Whitman's *Leaves of Grass,* with woodcuts by Angelo in a 400-copy edition, would retail at a hundred dollars and be "a knockout."

Bennett worked hard but also played hooky, seeing sights or going out on the town. Setting up one visit to Philadelphia, he wrote to Harold Mason, co-proprietor of the elegant Centaur Book Shop, and instructed him to purchase five tickets for a show, "with the most distinct understanding" that the party would be on Bennett. "Don't forget our family motto," he added: "A Cerf never sits back of the fourth row." He'd learned that the Centaur was a personal store, a meeting place for the city's intellectuals, reflecting the sophistication of its owner, who stocked "all the newest things." It was Mason who told him of a new novel by a fellow who the bookseller thought was "going to be one of the great authors." He took the book home, and saw what Mason meant: the author had "something tremendous." It was Bennett's first acquaintance with William Faulkner.

A month after the cross-country trip, he embarked on his third jaunt abroad, paying special attention to the Meynells, for the Nonesuch connection was both advertisement and guarantee. Suddenly the European fine-press trade was aware of RH, and Bennett resolved to cultivate as clients only those with first-rate books. "Let's keep at the top," he enthused to Don. England's Shakespeare Head and Golden Cockerel, France's Black Manikin, Germany's Cranach, and others became clients. He reached Italy, and on May 25, was forced to mark a milestone: "Naples on a melancholy day—my 30th birthday."

After sightseeing in Rome and Tuscany, it was on to Florence. Norman Douglas, the author of *South Wind,* a Modern Library top-ten seller, lived there. Over an exciting dinner, Douglas introduced Bennett to Giuseppe Orioli, the Florentine bookseller who'd just published D. H. Lawrence's new novel, *Lady Chatterley's Lover,* in a private, limited edition, with permission from Lawrence. French pirates were already scrambling to print bootleg copies of a book that was instantly infamous for its sex scenes and treatment of class. Lawrence's *Sons and Lovers* was an ML top-twenty title, and Bennett had made a date for the next day to see Lawrence, who lived in the countryside nearby.

"What do you want to waste your time with [him] for?" he recalled Douglas demanding, an interjection that seems to make little sense given that Lawrence was a writer and Bennett a publisher. But Bennett was a storyteller, and the story of this visit he'd dine out on and later publish under his own byline. How much embroidery he added is hard to untangle. For sure, less than two years later, Lawrence would be dead of tuberculosis, and twenty years after that, the story would not amuse Frieda, his soon-to-be widow: she would read and deem it "despicable."

As Bennett told the tale, Douglas and Lawrence—old friends—had had a terrible fight. Yet when Bennett and Douglas met again at their appointed lunch on Bennett's second day in Florence, and Bennett asked him to instruct the Italian driver Bennett had hired on how to navigate the winding hill-roads to Lawrence's villa, in the end Douglas said it would be easier if he accompanied them himself. And so they set off, Douglas spicing up the journey with tales of his former friend's wife and her lovers. However, as soon as they arrived, he rushed out to embrace the couple he'd just disparaged, and they embraced him back. Douglas proceeded to take Frieda for a walk so Bennett could talk with her husband, but then it was Lawrence's turn to be mad: How had Bennett dared bring Douglas? After that, they got down to business, in what Bennett described as "a pigpen" of a house that was no fit living place for a man with TB. The upshot was *My Skirmish with Jolly Roger*—a limited-edition pamphlet of six hundred copies that Random would publish in 1929, in which Lawrence defended *Chatterley* and attacked the pirates who paid no royalties.

The Lawrence episode marked the end of Bennett's sojourn. Three days later, his train pulled into a London station at 11 P.M., and he was met by a lovely young woman: Marian Klopfer. After more publishing visits in England, it was back to Paris with Marian to rendezvous with Herbert. On June 21, Don arrived to reclaim his wife, and Bennett started for home.

The partners consolidated transatlantic connections through letters and wires, but Bennett also deputized his uncle as emissary: when in Europe, Herbert called on Meynell and others, and Bennett continued to seek his literary advice. In the office, Pop was a gentle fixture. Marian flitted in and out, charming publishers. Bennett liked to tell the world that Random House was "a family." In the early years, that statement was literal.

Francis Meynell braved an icy Atlantic crossing in January 1929, thrilled to make his first sighting of Manhattan's modern marvels as a guest of Bennett, Don, and Pa. To cement the relationship, they'd not only issued him short-term loans for the Shakespeare project, but paid his passage and rented a handsome apartment for his stay. Pa had compiled a list of printing cronies and book collectors to visit, but Bennett wanted Meynell to enjoy as much of the city's wonderful nonsense as could be crammed into a New York fortnight, promising "a roaring good time." The first night, he organized a party of eight, including Dick Rodgers. After dinner, theater, and a nightclub, they ended up at Rodgers's apartment, where Dick sat down at the piano and played numbers from his new show.

"What a . . . lucky . . . fellow you have for an uncle. . . . *He knows Dick Rodgers,*" a dazzled Meynell wrote to his niece. This was the kind of magic Bennett loved, and loved to conjure for friends; that it helped smooth business—well, that *was* a bit of luck.

He and Don also introduced Francis to another New York custom: "the gamble of the stock market." On their way to lunch one day, they made a quick detour to a broker on the floor below. Guaranteeing him against loss, they had Meynell buy two hundred shares. Returning well fed and well lubricated, he sold at a profit of $2,000. "Can one do this during the lunch hour every day?" Meynell inquired. He left New York pleased and grateful, writing from the ship: "My dear friends: I thank you for making me a happy guest . . . even more, for allowing me to become most truly your friend."

Francis Meynell

Chapter 9

They Float

THE $2,000 THAT FRANCIS MEYNELL HAD MADE WITH BENNETT AND Donald in January 1929 on a lunch-hour stock trade was an astonishment, but not an anomaly. Since 1922, the Dow Jones industrial average had risen 400 percent in an unprecedented expansion, and in many cases people were investing only 10 or 20 percent of the cost of each share from their own money, borrowing the rest from a broker or bank. But come September, worries started circulating: How long could such speculation last? As October waned, traders' confidence began to crack, and on "Black Thursday," October 24, a record-breaking thirteen million shares were sold in the rising panic. The next Monday and "Black" Tuesday, October 28 and 29, a quarter of the value of the entire exchange was wiped out.

Bennett wrote Meynell that although he and Don were relatively unscathed, the past two years' paper profits had vanished: "Suffice it to say that everybody we know, with not a single exception, has taken a terrible trimming." By early November, $15 billion in market value had evaporated; the Great Crash would soon usher in the Great Depression. "Happy Days Are Here Again," a song both defiantly hopeful and painfully ironic, became a huge hit. Horace Liveright's friend, New York's charming, corrupt mayor Jimmy Walker, asked theater managers to show only cheerful movies. Women began using nail polish, just invented in Paris, looking for a little color and courage.

Wall Streeters glanced in the mirror and wondered if they'd be next to go under. When Sartorius—the brokerage firm where Bennett and Don had worked, and Herbert was the biggest customer—found itself needing cash in January 1930, rescue came from a surprising source: a $50,000 "call loan" from the Modern Library Inc. It was repaid by the end of April, but how extraordinary that when many were losing everything, Bennett and Don were in the rare position of being able to *lend* a very great sum.

They were comfortable enough for Donald to send Meynell exciting personal news: he now had a grand country house to complement his rented apartment on Park Avenue, as well as a new baby. Marian had given birth to a daughter, Lois, the previous summer; rebounding after a difficult delivery, she'd spent the winter redecorating. On Meynell's next visit, Don promised, "we'll be able to show you a real Random House," for the country place did resemble Kent's lucky colophon.

With the economic crisis, the partners became more stringent about the Modern Library: to stay in print, a title now would have to sell at least 2,000 copies annually, doubling the previous benchmark. At the same time, they continued to urge booksellers to substitute a different series title for a retired one with no cost to the store, a policy that had proved popular. Having estimated the ML would sell 750,000 books in 1930, they sold a million: the first time so many were bought in a single year.

Unfortunately, the cost of the culling to an author was a different matter. Several years later, Scott Fitzgerald was delighted when Bennett took a chance and put a rather underappreciated novel of his into the ML, even paying him to write what turned out to be a wonderful introduction. This was a precious sign that the book would continue to live and had a chance at entering the canon. Five years passed, but although Fitzgerald had his heart set on rewriting the introduction for a new edition, sales were so anemic that, following the usual guidelines, the book was discontinued—to Bennett and Don's regret, and Fitzgerald's real distress. It was *The Great Gatsby*.

Ironically, the economic crisis had made it easier for them to keep the line fresh by adding titles whose rights they'd been unable to buy previously: publishers, needing cash, were suddenly willing to negotiate reprint deals. Bennett and Don also decided to eliminate some competition. In April 1930, the ML—then comprising 175 volumes—bought Doubleday's 52-title Sun Dial Library. They remaindered undesirable titles, sold down existing stock, and folded the better Sun Dials into the ML. Nonetheless, with readers perceiving "dollar books" as good value—entertainment and education at a time when money was tight—they still worried about keeping preeminence over other lines.

When Bennett returned from a European business trip late that spring, it was to a changing cityscape. Walking home from the office, a glance two dozen blocks south revealed the towering miracle of the new Empire State Building—but many windows remained dark, untenanted. Lines formed outside soup kitchens, and in the fall, pyramids of apples, a nickel each, appeared all over the city, carefully arranged on street-corner crates as though whole families depended on them—which they did. The International Apple Shippers Association had offloaded the 1930 surplus, selling fruit on credit to the jobless, the only type of credit most of the six thousand who hawked them could get.

Whatever he thought of the faceless windows, ubiquitous lines, apple sellers, or the "Hooverville" shantytown the unemployed erected in the park during the winter of 1931, Bennett was well aware that *he* was paying top dollar for rent on Central Park South at a time when prices were plummeting. He wrote to the Navarro's owner that it was "absolutely imperative" he be granted a reduction. The owner was unpersuaded. Eight months later, with foreclosures sweeping the city, he wrote again: "I have been staying awake nights . . . trying to balance my expenses." Back and forth the letters flew, Bennett withholding some rent, but remaining at the Navarro and paying more than he wanted to. The owner could see that despite protestations of "seriously reduced" means, the jaunty young man-about-town in his custom-made suits was doing just fine.

A consequence of having resources was to be besieged by others without enough. In the summer of 1930, Meynell requested a £2,000 loan. The partners politely said no; a further market collapse had cost them plenty. But the next summer they agreed to pay Bert Wolff, who printed and bound the ML, for 20,000 copies of *War and Peace* before books were delivered, to tide him over. Wolff and even the Knopfs turned proud faces to the world amid financial woes. Others, like Edwin Grabhorn, displayed their pain.

In October 1929, just before the crash, when Grabhorn was embarking on their *Leaves of Grass* project, Bennett had asked: "Need any money?" After Black Tuesday, indeed he did, and Bennett sent an additional $3,000 on account to help Grabhorn pay off a bank loan. As his finances grew more parlous, the printer upped his price another 10 percent. But work was completed, and *Leaves of Grass* proved the stunner that Bennett had predicted. Despite many canceled orders, RH managed to sell every copy: the book was prized. Grabhorn, however, had to part with his precious first editions to survive. They continued to work together, Bennett answering pleas for cash by letting Grabhorn's suppliers bill RH directly; this helped Grabhorn while ensuring that books got finished for RH. By July 1932, having to pay off $5,000 in pre-Depression debts, Grabhorn despaired. Money owed him was "practically uncollectible," and his wife was soon to have a baby. "I'm still living," he concluded, "thanks to not having an insurance policy."

If only he could bring around "a jug of gin [to] drown our sorrows," Bennett sympathized. "If [we] can only hang on . . . things will work out. . . . I hope it will cheer you . . . that my high regard for you cannot be shaken." It was an attempt at comfort, but Bennett couldn't put himself in the printer's shoes. He'd never wanted for money, and as Grabhorn pointed out, "I guess you thank God for the Modern Library."

At a time when shops were dreaming up promotions to lure frugal customers, Macy's flagship in Manhattan's Herald Square—home to one of the biggest book departments in the nation—decided in the fall of 1930 to use the ML as a loss leader to entice foot traffic. Large newspaper ads proclaimed that Macy's would sell any customer a single Modern Library book for nine cents, and additional books for fifty cents each; everyone knew ninety-five cents was the regular price. Gimbels, hearing of the ploy, retaliated by offering unlimited copies of any ML book at a dime apiece. The war for hearts, minds, and wallets was on. Instead of queuing for an autographed copy of a new title by a famous author, lines of would-be purchasers snaked through and beyond each store's book section for ML reprints. "Merchants Gone Mad," *PW* said. Bennett and Don weren't complaining.

Between 1929 and 1932–33—the Depression's nadir—America's income went from $81 to $41 billion, with many, like Grabhorn, in economic freefall. In 1931, not counting government employees and farmworkers, 22 percent of the workforce was unemployed. "Happy Days Are Here Again" gave way to "Brother, Can You Spare a Dime?" Broadway and Hollywood put a sunny gloss on comedies and musicals, and so did Bennett on books. Attendees of the American Booksellers Association convention in Philadelphia in May 1931 were given a copy of the *New York Herald Tribune* with a special sixteen-page insert, *The Publishers' Weakly: The Heart & Liver of the Book Trade,* "compliments of a friend." The antic "friend" was instantly identifiable. In one (fictive) ad puncturing Alfred Knopf's pomposity and predilection for European authors, "Knopf" had

THE Publishers' Weakly

The Heart & Liver of the BOOK TRADE

★★★★ CONVENTION SPECIAL ★★★★★

VOL. A.B.A. PHILADELPHIA, MAY 18, 1931 No. OO

COMPLIMENTS OF A FRIEND

Conjuring merriment amid the Great Depression

"the honor to announce the death of Birvadj Oglinck (Estonia's greatest living author). . . . Other outstanding deaths: Stanislaw Cohen (Nobel prize winner, 1916); Stanislaw Kelly (Nobel prize winner, 1916)"; etc., etc. Merrily on, the *Weakly* went.

A year later, readers of (the real) *PW* were treated to a cartoon ad depicting a young blonde, pert and permed, enjoying a soak in a steaming tub, a hint of bosom teasing below the surface. Five well-chosen books by male authors bobbed around her: Balzac's *Droll Stories;* Mann's *The Magic Mountain;* Faulkner's *Sanctuary;* Maugham's *Of Human Bondage;* and Proust's *Swann's Way*. "They float!" proclaimed the caption, taking in breasts and books, parodying the ubiquitous Ivory Soap ads featuring a floating white bar, "99 and 44/100% pure." The ad was fresh—in both senses of the word. Bennett, the compulsive flirt, had confidence in his common touch. In an era long before most women dared object to being objectified, the naughty-boy humor charmed many. These books indeed "floated," while other products were going under.

The partners experimented with expanding the market for the ML in all sorts of ways. They started a mail-order "Book a Month Plan," and tried a "Multiple-Commission Plan," a misguided scheme promising

The ad was fresh . . .

consumers a commission if they got friends to buy books. It didn't last. More significant was the decision to expand the scope editorially. Certain classics had been too long to put into the ML, since production and paper would have cost too much to clear a profit at the usual run and price. Now, with printers eager for jobs, if the run were large enough to reduce cost-per-copy, longer books could sell profitably at only five cents more. In 1931 these ML "Giants" were born, retailing for a dollar apiece.

To be a Giant, a book had to be a major classic, at least a thousand pages long, never before published in an edition priced under three dollars, and out of copyright, so no author royalty would be due. The potential pool of readers also had to be large enough to risk a 20,000-copy printing. The first Giants included Tolstoy's *War and Peace,* Hugo's *Les Misérables,* and Boswell's *Life of Johnson*. Publishers and booksellers declared the editors of the Modern Library "had lost their heads," the firm's ads noted. "Subsequent developments have proven Messrs. Cerf and Klopfer . . . knew . . . what they were up to."

They also knew what they were doing when they hired Sarah "Sally" Ball, the ML's "most creative and energetic sales agent." Ball was one of many women working in the book business in the 1920s and '30s. Now mainly forgotten, they were essential. Ball's particular talent lay in finding and servicing unusual locations where the series could be sold. Driving a panel-sided van or a car with a trailer, she called on hotels, inns, and tearooms all over New England, persuading owners to let her stock and replenish racks of top sellers for guests to purchase. In the winter she'd do the same in Florida. A true pioneer, she also devised a plan for private schools, whereby students acted as "librarians" maintaining ML "stations." Bennett and Don were devoted to her.

. . .

THE ECONOMIC CRISIS DID nothing to alter the very adult merry-go-round where work blended almost seamlessly into play. Bennett, supremely social but bureaucracy-averse, was happy to let Don be the one to organize Twelve Against the Gods of Publishing, a monthly club for leaders of the newer firms, Jewish and Gentile alike. Begun, like Alfred Knopf's Book Table, as an alternative to the Publishers' Lunch Club and the Century Association, it was a way to discuss deals and trends over speakeasy lunches. The Saturday poker games at the Algonquin that Bennett and Viking's Harold Guinzburg sometimes attended, held by the "Thanatopsis Literary and Inside Straight Club" for serious money, were another matter: they could be marathons lasting all night. As well as Round Table and *New Yorker* regulars, visiting notables—from Harpo Marx to Paul Robeson—kept things interesting.

If anything, while much of the world was living through hell, Bennett partied harder. Everything about a Friday night fete that he, Don, Marian, and Pa organized at the office in January 1930—"a so-called tea or inspirational orgy for the spiritual benefit of Rockwell Kent"—was designed to be memorable. The invitations themselves were keepsakes, depicting a naked beauty floating among stars, long hair modestly draped, legs spread, chastely revealing all. A delighted (clothed) fellow reclined below, enjoying a shower of stars from the lady's overturned goblet. The stars were like those decorating Kent's *Candide,* for the honoree, at that time the youngest living artist to have work shown at the Metropolitan Museum, doubled as the invitation's illustrator. Book-loving recipients "got" the joke on each card: "Privately printed and limited to 99 copies," each claiming to be copy number one. After the fact, Kent pronounced the evening "beautiful."

The "orgy," unique in the eyes of its guest of honor, was both a throwback to Bennett's Liveright days and an indication of how he intended to carry on, in parties held either at the office or at home. Guest lists were increasingly notable, as flocks of invitation telegrams ("day-letters") were dispatched like carrier pigeons. One list later that year included George and Ira Gershwin, Ginger Rogers (a newly minted Broadway star, courtesy of the Gershwins' smash hit *Girl Crazy*), Maurice Chevalier, restaurateur Vincent Sardi, and executives from the Empire, Playhouse, and Music Box theaters, as well as journalists from *The New Yorker,* the *Sun,* the *American,* the *World,* and the *Herald Tribune*.

Gossip columns began to feature the soirées, generating ink on Bennett, the firm, and its books. Parties were also good for pursuing another favorite pastime: females. Jesus Junior loved having a pretty woman on his arm, in his lap, or twinned with his name in print. A frequent companion was Miriam Hopkins, a Broadway actress who'd just signed with Paramount. Bennett had met blonde, brainy Miriam at a Liveright party, and after he left B&L, her name began dotting his diary. By 1930, he told Meynell she was "a very, very special member of the Bennett A. Cerf Foundation for Beautiful Females." Pop Cerf declared the Savannah-born charmer "something from heaven."

In his oral history, Bennett later admitted, "I fell—oh, did I fall—for Miriam." At the time, he kept the letters and wires light: "Desolate at not getting goodbye kiss. After . . . Clark Gable my technique would be refreshing." Yet however keen he was, Bennett also had other romantic interests, and so did she. In 1932, he went on a number of dates with Anna May Wong, the magnificent daughter of an L.A. laundryman who had had to overcome tremendous prejudice to forge an acting career: Wong wasn't even allowed to kiss white love interests on screen. Mixing was easier in New York creative circles, and Bennett continued to see her occasionally through the 1930s.

He was more taken with another actress, Rosamond Pinchot, whom he met in the spring of 1933. Classically beautiful and the niece of Pennsylvania's governor, she was a veteran of a clutch of Broadway plays as well as a socialite who, like Bennett, projected a frivolous, carefree image—despite being a divorced mother of two. They saw each other nearly every week, and the relationship was serious enough for Rosamond to invite him to meet her father, politically active lawyer Amos Pinchot, at Grey Towers, the baronial family seat in the Pocono Mountains. Though it was very rare for a Jew to be invited there, Bennett was able to navigate with intelligence and humor. He handled himself well on the tennis court and brought an offering that pleased Amos: a selection of recent ML titles. Disposed not to like him, Rosamond's father was charmed by her beau.

"For my dear Lamb-boy, for all his dates may they be very pleasant," she wrote in his 1934 diary, confiding to her own that he seemed to think they'd marry. But she fell for a Broadway producer, and by the end of April, dates with "Lamb-boy" were done.

There were also women he knew through work, but their badinage was anything but businesslike. With Carol Quimby, who worked in radio advertising in Philadelphia, he engaged in an especially flirtatious correspondence. One letter expressed interest in her news of having lost six pounds, but "distress" at how it might alter her anatomy. Describing "our minimum requirements for fannys in this office," he concluded: "If you . . . can answer . . . these qualifications, we are . . . eager to discuss a little tail with you."

Handsome, funny, boyish, Bennett was "fresh" but got away with a lot: many women liked him. He could modulate the flirtation, but the compulsion to play the game was so strong, he rarely abandoned it, even with a woman like Blanche Knopf. He and "La Knopf"—as he called the slightly older Blanche—had grown close, often dining and reading manuscripts together in her city apartment, while Alfred went home to Purchase. "She disliked the country in winter as much as I did," Bennett explained. Everyone knew about the Knopfs' unhappy marriage; chic Blanche, whose scouting trips abroad were frequent, was often the subject of gossip. Meynell wrote Don about a fellow at Chatto & Windus who called on her at the Savoy, only to be met by "an exquisite figure in perfumed pajamas" who clearly expected a different gentleman.

In February 1933, Bennett and Blanche boarded a train together heading south to escape the winter, on a trip that combined pleasure with business. For a week they made a half dozen stops, from Richmond to Miami. Blanche then returned to New York, while Bennett met other friends in Nassau for almost a month. After he got back, their regular reading evenings resumed, and just before Thanksgiving, an unusual letter arrived for her at the Knopf offices: "Our private detective . . . first cousin of Mr. Dashiell Hammett," it began, had discovered that a "Mr. A. Olaf Bennett" had been with her at the Fort Sumter Hotel in February. If made public, it "would place you in a most embarrassing position," the letter suggested, concluding: "We are willing to entertain propositions from you."

Hammett, progenitor of gumshoe Sam Spade, was Blanche's author: Bennett was indulging in epistolary fun with a woman capable of same. Soon a reply came on behalf of client Blanche from "J. Florence Rubin," an (imaginary) partner in the (imaginary) law firm of Heinemann, Goldfarb, Feinberg, Carmichael, Spritzwasser, Rubin and O'Shaughnessy, denying knowledge of A. Olaf. The exchanges continued for several rounds, one letter from Random House including photographic "proof." The last letter from Blanche's alter-ego J. Florence to "Mr. Dashiell Cerf" noted that Blanche had been at the Fort Sumter with a different man, and had his affidavit to prove it. "The name of this man is Tom Jones," it concluded (Henry Fielding's bawdy classic was in the ML). Thirty years later, when Bennett was dictating his oral history, the interviewer opined that Blanche had been a cold woman. "Not as cold as you might imagine," came the reply.

The trip with Blanche was part of a routine initiated three years earlier, when Bennett had embarked on the first of what would become annual winter pilgrimages with friends to someplace warm. In 1930, he'd set sail on a Caribbean cruise, staying almost a fortnight in Havana; the next year he spent a month in Florida. But the vacation in February 1932, the pit of the Depression, was really extraordinary: one companion aboard the SS *Van Dam* was George Gershwin. George and Bennett were Brooklyn and Harlem boys made good, born a few months apart, but Bennett was in awe of his friend. In 1928, he'd tried to cajole him to publish a special edition of the score of *An American in Paris,* and before their holiday had at last got his nod for a signed edition of sixteen works. One was a song from the new musical *Of Thee I Sing*—the first comedy to win a Pulitzer.

Bennett's tales of the trip were full of musical moments with a signature dash of slapstick, but whether embellished, invented, or recounted as happened, the effect of his stories was often the same: to make the famous—even a genius like Gershwin—relatable, and to portray a world of human foibles and happy endings. And so, according to Bennett, between sunbathing, boozing, backgammon, and schmoozing, Gershwin "banged out" *Rhapsody in Blue* at 7 A.M. in Nassau's Colonial Hotel to impress a girl he'd met, and became "indignant" when the manager asked him to stop. In Havana, George was delighted when a rhumba band

George Gershwin (far left), Bennett (far right),
and pals vacationing in Cuba

played outside his room at 4 A.M., even though his (sleepy) neighbors were not. Yet everyone could rejoice in the upshot: a little rhumba he'd promised the band, folded into a work that premiered six months later as the *Cuban Overture*.

After the holiday, Bennett saw more of George at the "wondrous" Sunday deli-catered dinners Gershwin organized at his place. Talk ceased and guests surrounded the piano while he performed. Dick Rodgers could conjure a similar enchantment, but Gershwin was Gershwin. The joy of those evenings with George, Bennett never forgot.

. . .

A FEW YEARS EARLIER, home movies showed a happy young man and woman, Donald and Marian, sprawled on a sunny summer lawn, gazing raptly at baby Lois. Beneath the smiles, however, marital conflict was stirring. Donald was still tethered to his mother, whom he had to call on every day. There were the regular visits to his poor sister. And Marian, as he and Bennett knew all too well, was more than a bit demanding. Now he'd added fatherhood. Writing to Meynell in August 1929, shortly after Lois's birth, Don confessed to being "irritated" that Bennett could go to London while he had to tend to family. He also joked: "Marian is once more casting her eagle eye about for some handsome unattached male (for herself, I mean, not for her daughter)." It wasn't entirely funny. She often flirted outrageously, and as photographs show, with good reason. A description once sent to Don spoke of her as "the most beautiful woman . . . glorious . . . glamorous . . . but very cold." Everything was true, Donald replied, except "she wasn't in the least bit cold."

Marian reveled in the world; sitting home with a baby grew tiresome. Indulged since childhood, she "had to have everything her way," Lois Klopfer recalled. Still, any breakup involves two. Don, the kind listener at the office, could be short-tempered at home: "Oh, for Christ's sake, Marian," was a frequent refrain. His interfering mother didn't help. But as she parted from Don, Marian was beguiling Bennett once again.

Telegrams tell part of how the story played out. On March 7, 1933, two cables were sent to Bennett in Miami by the soon-to-be ex–Mrs. Klopfer. One asks, "Didn't you get my letter about meeting?" The second says, "Phone between six-thirty and eight-thirty." On March 10, another wire came, but from Don: "Too late to save Union Pacific." Four days later, back in New York, Bennett spent the evening with Marian, who soon embarked on a cruise. On March 24, he sent a telegram to Port-au-Prince: "Missing you, Darling." On April 3, he sent another: "Can't wait." The ship docked in New York, but then Marian was off to Reno, mecca for the mismatched. Another cable from him awaited her: "Welcome to the land of the about-to-be-free . . . thinking of you."

There was a residency requirement even for the quick divorces in which Reno specialized. Marian sat tight. Back East, Bennett bought a puppy named Skippy and took him to the little girl who'd been left with a nanny at the country house in Deal: Lois was four, and adored her father, but didn't dislike Bennett. She recalled his being there that summer. On July 17, Bennett went to Chicago for the "Century of Progress" Fair. Marian arrived from Reno at 2:30 A.M. They spent the next day together, then flew home.

An early love can flicker back into flame but die down again just as easily. Bennett and Marian knew too much about each other for good sense not to prevail. Still, they'd never be entirely out of each other's life. "I think [Bennett] always carried a bit of a torch for her," Lois reckoned. What her father felt about it, she did not say.

Business relationships were also changing. With Nonesuch and *Candide,* RH had built an admirable reputation, and Bennett no longer needed Pa to make connections, teach him what to do, or confer prestige. An unlikely couple from the start, they visibly chafed. As other presses were hired to print RH books, Pa complained that he and Pynson received neither the respect nor the amount of work they deserved: he thought he should have ultimate control over all print bearing RH's name. Irritated, Bennett made clear neither he nor Don had the slightest intention of giving all printing to Pynson.

On May 24, 1932, Pa agreed to a divorce. In June, a discreet note in *PW* said that the company had been "reorganized." The Modern Library took over Random House, which became an imprint, and RH ceased to exist as a corporate entity. The official name of the business now became the Modern Library Inc. The public "knows nothing," Bennett confided to Meynell, with RH unchanged in its eyes. The contract stipulated that Adler's RH shares be returned, and that Bennett relinquish his in Pynson. To Rockwell Kent, Pa complained that the boys had schemed to cut him out, wanting to combine RH and the ML, and "compelled" him to settle for "one-third the book value." Half the inventory of RH books printed by Pynson, and $6,000 cash ($126,000 today), went to Pa.

In the summer of 1933, a different crisis emerged that imperiled RH's relationship with Nonesuch. Meynell wrote that he and his partners had "heavily overspent," and owed the bank a lot. The Shakespeare had kept them "alive," but with the last volume in sight, they needed capital for new books: without it, they might go under. He'd received a merger offer from a British publisher, but would prefer that RH buy a half interest for £9,000. Bennett, who'd refused him once before, cabled that his and Don's surplus money was tied up in their own expansion, and though sympathetic, they couldn't help.

Two years later, Meynell sold the company, bleeding red ink, to George Macy, a classmate of Bennett's who'd started the Limited Editions Club. Macy granted Meynell shares, and employed him; Nonesuch became a subscription-based, direct-sales business. "Judged from any angle," Bennett wrote Meynell, working with Nonesuch had been "the pleasantest business deal" that he and Don had had, and the advantages the connection had conferred "cannot possibly be overestimated." He was speaking truth, but what was also true: the Nonesuch moment had passed. They'd grown beyond it.

. . .

THE "EXPANSION" BENNETT HAD mentioned in his denial of Francis's loan request had partly to do, once again, with his former employer. Things had not been going well for Horace Liveright. Four years earlier, on the day before Black Thursday, Liveright had admitted to Manuel Komroff that he was engaged in "much mental castigation of myself." He'd been in a downward spiral even before the crash—flopping plays, bad investments, a failed marriage, with no Modern Library to bring in cash—and the onset of the Depression added a terrible velocity. The bookkeeper Pell had procured loans at usurious rates, and little by little, shares of Liveright's company (now Horace Liveright Inc.) passed into other hands. By the fall of 1930, he'd been squeezed out, no longer a part of the house that bore his name.

He went to Hollywood to scout novels and plays for Paramount, but success eluded him, and Liveright returned to New York. There, in December 1931, he married Elise Bartlett, that alluring actress whom Bennett had sensibly rejected on a transatlantic voyage five years earlier. It proved a sordid affair, and within months they were in divorce court. With no money to publish or produce, Horace took to calling on friends. Pell had moved the firm to a nondescript building, but not all had changed: some staff remained. One day, Liveright was chatting with old pals there when Pell walked in.

"Horace, I don't think you'd better come in anymore; it doesn't look well for business," the bookkeeper announced.

Liveright had taken to applying ink to his threadbare clothes in a futile effort to hide their shabbiness, and lived in a cheap apartment-hotel on West Fifty-First Street that he could hardly afford. An infernal tumult accosted him there: the area was being remade into Rockefeller Center. Old houses—including his former offices—were coming down in clouds of memory and dust, to make way for shimmering towers and others' dreams. "I always feared," he once told his author Eugene O'Neill, "that someday I would be destitute. When fear takes hold of you, it shakes you like a terrier shakes a rat."

Dick Simon had been contacted by Komroff, who'd asked him to visit their old boss—Horace had talked about wanting to publish his memoirs. Dick hadn't seen Liveright for years, and the transformation shocked him. He wished him to be his old self, vain and full of life, instead of this poor broken ghost who made Dick so uncomfortable. Though the likelihood of a finished book was iffy, Dick did what Horace asked: gave him a contract and $2,000 as an advance to pay off his debts, providing money and purpose and a shred of self-respect. There was no way he could have done otherwise. Dutifully, Liveright began dictating the story that he called *The Turbulent Years,* but, emaciated and alcoholic, soon collapsed: he'd contracted pneumonia. On Sunday, September 24, 1933, the turbulence ended. He was forty-eight years old.

Bennett attended the funeral and arranged to write about it and his old mentor for *PW*. Very proud of the piece, he later recalled the "great pains" he took in composing it. They were a debt he owed Liveright, and yet the effort wasn't entirely altruistic: he knew it was also an opportunity. The vivid account was widely read, touching the minds and hearts of readers as disparate as Alfred Harcourt and Theodore Dreiser. People in the book trade discovered that Bennett Cerf could write. However, the "pains" didn't extend to facts, but rather to storytelling for dramatic effect: he got Liveright's age wrong and claimed that only a "straggling handful" had attended the funeral, when both *The New York Times* and Liveright's daughter attested to many former theatrical and literary associates being there. Eulogist and author Upton Sinclair, Bennett wrote, was "fearfully embarrassed," mumbling "inadequate nothings," while others whom Horace had helped, and friends he'd neglected his business for, hadn't shown up, "a dismal last curtain to a spectacular career—and to a publisher whose like will never be seen again."

Still, he also noted Liveright's "amazing faculty for winning the unquestioning loyalty of a great number of fine men and women [who] . . . love him still." Underneath the "sham and pretense, they saw a rather helpless person, craving affection and admiration, with a rare love of life and a reckless generosity."

Six months earlier, Bennett had heard that Liveright Inc. was in a precarious state, and the switchboard in his business brain lit up. He tried to persuade a bookbinder who held many Liveright plates, sheets, and copies to make a deal: the binder would sue to put the firm into bankruptcy; the ML would buy the assets at a discounted rate; the binder would then recoup some of what he was owed. He also tried a different tack: he'd join with a remainder dealer and another publisher to buy the assets. Neither plan worked. Others had been watching, and a petition was filed the first week in May, forcing a bankruptcy. By June, it was clear: the firm owed $100,000 to a large group of creditors.

Pell, using a dummy company, bought the assets for $18,500—a real bargain. However, the most valuable properties of a publisher aren't sheets, books, or plates, but authors. When the *Times* announced the bankruptcy, it noted that one of the firm's best-known recent books was a play: Eugene O'Neill's *Mourning Becomes Electra*. It had enjoyed one of the largest sales of any modern drama, with a first printing of 20,000 copies. It was obvious to Bennett that there was going to be a raid on the few major authors left. O'Neill was at the top; whatever it took, he was going to have him.

Chapter 10

Dentist, Patient—and Publisher

CIRCLING THE COLLAPSING HOUSE OF LIVERIGHT THAT SPRING OF 1933, publishers kept their sights trained on the dramatist who combined prestige, a large readership, and the likelihood of steady productivity. Even Eugene O'Neill's failures on stage turned a profit between covers. Several tried enticing him, but he could be as choosy as he liked. "Situation too confused yet . . . to negotiate," he'd told Harrison Smith of the recently formed Smith & Haas; yet he invited Tom Coward, of Coward-McCann, to meet at his Sea Island, Georgia, home.

On May 23, Bennett lunched with Richard Madden, O'Neill's agent, having spent the morning with Saxe Commins, the dark-haired, slight, friendly man who'd become the playwright's editor at Liveright. Bennett soon wired O'Neill that Madden's terms seemed satisfactory, and that the agent had suggested he, too, fly down to discuss them. He'd hoped to bring Saxe, but was told to come alone. The prospect was both thrilling and daunting: *he* was competing to bring to Random a great living author writing *now.* All Bennett had done so far—the ML, Nonesuch, *Candide*—paled in comparison.

Anyone who's seen *Long Day's Journey into Night,* O'Neill's autobiographical masterwork, knows of his early life. His dashing Irish immigrant father, James, could have been a great actor; instead he settled for money and years spent crisscrossing the country playing the Count of Monte Cristo in a potboiler based on Alexandre Dumas's novel. James's American wife, Ella—younger, convent-bred—brought romantic dreams, but no preparation for being the wife of a hard-drinking actor-manager. Eugene, third of their three sons, was born in a New York hotel room on October 16, 1888. The middle son, Edmund, had died from measles as a toddler, before "Gene" was born; Ella, on the road with her husband when it happened, never forgave herself. Also plagued by guilt was her firstborn, Jamie, who'd unwittingly passed the virus on to his brother; he sought forgetfulness in alcohol when very young. The legacy of Gene's birth was a different torment: given morphine after delivering her eleven-pound baby, soon Ella couldn't live without it. Her quarter century of addiction would be the family's secret shame.

During his freshman year at Princeton, Gene often played hooky, drinking himself into oblivion in New York. The university asked him not to return. In 1909, just before he turned twenty-one, he secretly married Kathleen Jenkins—wrong for him, as he already knew. After fathering a child, Eugene Jr., he fled, shipping out to Honduras and Buenos Aires, adventure and dissipation. Early in 1912, divorced and in New York, he made a creditable attempt to kill himself; friends saved his life. Later that year, having been diagnosed with tuberculosis, he felt "reborn" after six months in a sanitarium. He heard the call of the stage, but refused to reprise his father's role, wanting to create the dramas himself. At a Harvard playwriting course in 1914, he vowed to be "an artist or nothing."

In New York, he'd frequented the Boni brothers' MacDougal Street bookstore, an avant-garde mecca, and in the summer of 1916 went to Provincetown, the bohemians' warm-weather home. *Bound East for Cardiff,* conceived as first in a quartet of one-act plays, was his debut drama, staged in a ramshackle playhouse. Back in the city that fall, calling themselves the Provincetown Players, the group turned a MacDougal Street house into a performance space. Moody good looks made O'Neill attractive to women. He took up with Agnes Boulton, a magazine writer, and they married in 1918. The next year, she gave birth to Shane, his second son. In 1920, his earliest full-length work, *Beyond the Horizon,* was staged in New York and won the Pulitzer Prize—the first ever given to a play. All traces of his father's sentimental fare had been scraped clean; O'Neill brought ambition and seriousness to the nation's drama, baring the souls of losers and dreamers in common speech. He turned to the Greeks, Chekhov, and Ibsen for inspiration, but made the borrowings his own: an American was creating plays worthy of the world stage at last.

Years later, Bennett described O'Neill as "the handsomest, most arresting" man he'd ever seen, "beautiful . . . to look at him was soul-satisfying. He looked just the way a great playwright ought to but practically never does—brooding, piercing eyes, a wonderful smile and a superb figure." Yet in the early days of success, his parted lips revealed, as

O'Neill himself admitted, "frightfully dilapidated teeth"—a legacy of his dissolute youth. With his star rising, it was time to do something about them. Enter the dentist.

Dr. Saxe Commins was born in 1892 in Rochester, New York, into a family originally named Cominsky. Shy and intellectual, he set out to fulfill every immigrant Jewish mother's dream and become a doctor, but when his brother contracted TB, money grew tight. It took less time to train as a dentist, so a dentist is what he became. His older sister Stella married E. J. "Teddy" Ballantine, an artist/actor in the Greenwich Village crowd, but it was their mother's half sister who was a household name. Aunt Emma Goldman had arrived from Lithuania as a teen, and, as an anarchist and pioneering feminist, she was alternately idolized, vilified, and feared all over America.

Dr. Saxe Commins

In 1901, after another anarchist assassinated President William McKinley, Goldman was arrested, starting a two-decade cycle of arrests, imprisonments, and releases. (Thanks to a young official named J. Edgar Hoover, in December 1918 she'd be deported.) Emma was fond of Stella and Saxe. Though finding him wanting in the "coarser equipment" for life, she marveled at his "boundless capacity for love." She also noticed that too often he seemed "sad"; Saxe's wife would later describe him as "tense." There was reason for it: police often searched his home, looking for Emma. But, however anxious, he was loyal, greatly admired her, and, as a student, helped on her anarchist magazine.

At heart, Saxe didn't want to be a tooth-puller; he wanted to write. That summer of 1916, when *Bound East for Cardiff* was performed, he and Emma had visited Stella and Teddy in Provincetown. Saxe was working on a play to be staged that winter by the Provincetown Players; naturally, he met O'Neill. With drink in him, Gene could be a wild man; but when sober, he was shy. The two shy men discussed literature and philosophy; Saxe, a good listener, already admired Gene's work. They became close.

Five years passed, as plays poured out of O'Neill. It was March 1921 when he came to Rochester, having told Saxe to "polish up all your racks and thumbscrews." He stayed with the Commins family while Saxe wielded his drill. A friendship that endured two weeks of fillings, extractions, and bridgework could endure just about anything. Habits of empathy and dependence were established. Dentist and patient became "the closest of friends," and O'Neill came to trust Saxe Commins as no other.

In May 1919, Liveright had published O'Neill's first book, *The Moon of the Caribbees and Six Other Plays of the Sea,* and the next year *Beyond the Horizon*. Control over publication mattered greatly to O'Neill, artistically and financially. By 1931, the firm had his oeuvre, so new and different, in myriad forms: single plays, collections, and in limited and trade editions. As his corpus and reputation grew—he'd win a second Pulitzer, for *Anna Christie,* in 1922—bonds with Saxe went even deeper. In April 1926, Saxe visited the O'Neills in Bermuda, just before their daughter, Oona, was born. Gene toiled on *Strange Interlude* in the mornings, but spent much of the day with his friend.

Saxe's life was enlarging: he'd fallen in love with Dorothy Berliner, a pianist, and they married at the end of 1927. He'd also decided to give up dentistry and devote himself to books. Having become interested in Freud, he'd co-authored *Psychology: A Simplification,* published earlier that year by B&L. The couple would take their savings to Paris the next summer to live a dream: Saxe writing, Dorothy studying piano. O'Neill's life was about to change, too. Six months earlier, he and his family had gone to Maine to escape the Bermudan heat. There he encountered an actress whom he'd first met when she performed in his play *The Hairy Ape* five years earlier. Hazel Nielsen Tharsing, magnetic with a dark chignon and luminous face, was Danish American but had reinvented herself as the much more interesting "Carlotta Monterey." Feelings were ignited between the thrice-divorced actress and the playwright that neither could ignore.

In late January 1928, newly married, Saxe got a telegram from Gene beckoning him from Rochester to New York, where *Strange Interlude* was to be staged by the Theater Guild. Always jittery on opening nights, he wanted Saxe's reassurance, but his anxiety seemed unusually high. After the performance, Gene took Saxe aside: he and Carlotta were eloping to Europe. Five months later, as he'd planned, Saxe closed his practice and sailed for Paris, knowing he'd see Eugene O'Neill across the Atlantic.

The runaways had settled temporarily near Biarritz, and asked Saxe to visit. They discussed the draft of a new play, *Dynamo*. Returning to Paris, Saxe put aside his own writing, rented an English typewriter, and took the role of editor. From Gene's tiny longhand, he typed the text of *Dynamo,* and commented on the draft of another play, *Mourning Becomes Electra*. There was never any question of payment. In July 1929, after finally obtaining a divorce from Agnes, O'Neill wed Carlotta in Paris, but the Comminses had already returned to the United States, to make New York City their home.

Gene had entrusted Saxe with a laundry list of missions, including delivering a letter to their mutual publisher: he urged Liveright to give his friend a job. *Strange Interlude* was a phenomenon, on its way to selling 120,000 copies. That, O'Neill reckoned, might be persuasion enough, but when Saxe called on Liveright, he found that Horace's fortunes had dimmed. Pell held the purse strings; there was no job. He found work with Liveright's former vice president, Donald Friede, at Covici-Friede, but when Manuel Komroff left Liveright in 1931, Saxe replaced him, jumping at the chance to work with Sherwood Anderson, poet Robinson Jeffers, and above all, Gene. That fall, *Mourning Becomes Electra* was produced on Broadway and published by Liveright.

Pell pressed Saxe to buy stock in the company, and though dubious, he did, with $600 borrowed from Gene. Staff salaries had been cut, and he now had a little girl to support and a baby on the way (he'd be named Eugene). Uneasy, Saxe shared his worries with Gene, and in March 1932, O'Neill forced Pell to agree: if the firm were to fail, rights to his plays would revert to the playwright's control. Yet that gave only partial protection. O'Neill was owed substantial royalties, and in the ever-likelier case of insolvency, he'd be paid, at best, a few cents on the dollar. Loyalty to Gene made Saxe bold. He called a meeting of principal shareholders and demanded that a certified check for Gene's royalties be drawn within twenty-four hours, or he'd announce on the book page of the *Times* that O'Neill would transfer his plays to another house. This would cause panicked creditors to put the firm into bankruptcy at once, as Pell knew. He handed the check to Saxe that afternoon; with bankruptcy looming, control of the plays soon followed. Enter Bennett.

. . .

At Sea Island with Eugene O'Neill

ON MAY 29, HE boarded a plane in New York mid-morning and didn't set foot on Sea Island until 6:30 P.M., arriving at "Casa Genotta" on a humid Georgia evening. In name and very existence, the house was meant to symbolize undying union between playwright and actress. They welcomed him to the secluded, white-walled, Mediterranean-style villa, where the beach lay just beyond the palm-fringed garden. O'Neill was now a wealthy, dignified gentleman; with Carlotta at his side, what a handsome couple they made.

"Cerf just arrived." Carlotta had slipped away to wire Saxe almost at once. On the Q.T., she and Gene would keep him informed about nearly everything. Bennett had brought his usual gift—good books—and made a point of revealing that Robinson Jeffers, the well-regarded Liveright poet, had just agreed to come to RH.

O'Neill loved the sea, and was fit enough to swim "miles at a stretch." Bennett, a good swimmer, also loved bronzing on a beach. The next day, the two swam and talked, with Carlotta sometimes joining the conversation. In one prized photo memorializing the visit in his scrapbook, well-built Bennett in a two-piece bathing suit stands improbably next to his host, who's in white shirt, crisp trousers, and tie. Just turned thirty-five, Bennett looks younger than his years; Gene, his senior by a decade, looks older than he should. Both are smiling, Bennett more seriously than given to do later in life.

He'd come prepared to unveil a comprehensive plan for new works, reprints, limited and collected editions, book club rights, and more, and the setting proved congenial. O'Neill spoke slowly, hesitantly, in long sentences; Bennett, opinionated and impatient, was used to interrupting companions, but not now. O'Neill fascinated him completely: he was "the only man I ever knew," Bennett later said, "who without trying could shut me up." He may have abandoned two wives and neglected three children, but O'Neill embodied the theater. Bennett had found a "great man" and "hero" for life.

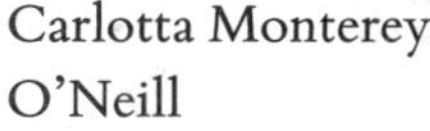

Carlotta Monterey O'Neill

Carlotta sent a progress note to Saxe: "Cerf is a *very clever business man*. And can get away with a lot on account of . . . boyish enthusiasm & a care free manner." She "*much*" preferred Tom Coward, as a man—"he is a gentleman"—but Cerf "knows more tricks of the trade and would always come out ahead. . . . Don't think I don't like Cerf . . . but he is a bit like all those N.Y. friends of his . . . & his humour runs a little to the vulgar . . . we are only interested in him as far as *publishing* goes." Meant for Saxe, another Jew, the coded words were insensitive and telling. O'Neill wrote his friend, the critic George Jean Nathan, that he liked that Random was a smaller place where his plays would get attention, and he'd be proud to be published alongside Jeffers. The ML track record was reassuring, and Bennett had offered terms he wanted "and then some." But he'd made an unusual stipulation: whoever he went with would have to give Saxe a job.

A few days after Bennett returned to New York, O'Neill wrote to Saxe that although he liked Coward "immensely," he was simply a trade publisher. Cerf brought "drive and enthusiasm, coupled with keen shrewdness" and more: "a love of beautiful books, an appreciation for good literature, an ambition to keep his firm above the level of the others, to expand only along lines of distinction." The answer, he concluded, "seems 'Cerf.'" Bennett soon sent O'Neill a proposed three-year contract for Saxe, insisting that the time frame was for the record only, since he and Saxe had talked, and regarded it as permanent. O'Neill had also asked the Guaranty Trust Company to report on the financial status of every publisher making an offer, and saw RH was "in an exceptionally sound position" compared to others. He had indeed found his publishing "answer."

What O'Neill brought to RH was clear; Commins, less so. But he'd become editorial anchor of the firm. A secular Jew, Saxe took the credo of his life's work from Saint John's Gospel: "In the beginning was the Word, and the Word was with God, and the Word was God." Bennett would later judge him "almost more important to us than O'Neill." Don didn't hesitate: Saxe was "our prize acquisition of the two." What Saxe saw in Bennett was "the potential of an imaginative, resourceful, adventurous and most trustworthy publisher," and in Donald, "quiet competence . . . reliability . . . good sense." Later, Saxe would recognize another of Don's qualities: "complete selflessness."

Polite wrangling over O'Neill's contract continued. He had a reputation for dictating terms to theater producers; he'd do the same to this publisher. At once, he objected that the draft had the advance "all wrong," since they'd "never cleared it up" at Casa Genotta. Bennett had stipulated $10,000 on signing: $5,000 applied to Liveright titles RH would republish, and $5,000 as an advance on three new titles. O'Neill held that $5,000 for three books was less than he'd have gotten under his old contract; he expected $5,000 on his *next* play, and $5,000 *per play* thereafter—much more in total than he'd have had from Liveright. He also complained that the boilerplate charging the author for corrections once the text had been set into galleys was unfair to a playwright, since script changes inevitably arise during rehearsals. It was necessary for him to have a "free hand" for such changes without being penalized; Liveright had allowed that privilege.

Bennett not only consented to the advances, but looked to the long term and accepted the stipulation on corrections. He also agreed to O'Neill having an extremely high 20 percent royalty—well beyond the usual 15 percent ceiling—and other favorable terms. He trusted that once the contracts were signed, both sides could "tuck them away" until it was time to talk about renewals, for trust *was* being forged. He saw proof in Carlotta's wiring him that "Mr. O'Neill" was allowing RH to announce their connection even before signed contracts were exchanged. He sent news of his coup to the press at once.

That trust, however, didn't extend to familiarity. Carlotta wrote Saxe that Gene (and certainly, *she*) expected him to handle the day-to-day, for "Cerf is inclined . . . to use every one's Christian name & invite them to parties & invite himself. . . . All this in good heartedness . . . but it must be nipped in the bud." Bennett persisted in his campaign to win her over. Liveright had hung portraits of favored authors near his desk; now his former vice president asked Carlotta for a signed picture of "Mr. O'Neill" for the wall, and another for publicity. He thought the old one was "getting a little tired," and would "very much value" her opinion. He and Don also worked to strengthen their identity as O'Neill's exclusive publisher by signing an academic study of his plays. All this didn't come cheap, as Bennett lamented to Francis Meynell. A $10,000 advance to O'Neill, $2,500 to Jeffers, and almost $7,000 for plates and rights to their earlier books had "put rather severe strain on our resources."

The first two plays covered by O'Neill's contract couldn't have been more different. *Days Without End* was second in a trilogy, *Myths for the*

God-Forsaken, begun with *Dynamo.* At its heart lay the dilemma of man in a world where God is dead. Most critics see it as true to its subtitle, a "modern miracle play" about a man's struggle to return to his faith: O'Neill was a lapsed Catholic. The protagonist, a man divided literally (masks are used) and metaphorically into two people, the sensualist "Loving" and the seeker "John," regains his faith—but half of him has to die. O'Neill had struggled through seven drafts, but in an unprecedented response to that torture, awoke one morning with the plot for the other play, his only comedy, fully formed. *Ah, Wilderness!* took just a month to create. The question was: Which to stage/publish first?

O'Neill told Bennett that if it were *Days Without End,* critics would compare it with his last, the tragedy *Mourning Becomes Electra.* He wanted the new one judged on its own, so *Ah, Wilderness!* had better be first. "A gamble, of course," he added, "but then dear old show business always is. I'd much rather play roulette but I can't afford it." And so, plans for *Ah, Wilderness!* proceeded. The story's family seems very different from the hard-drinking, drug-addicted O'Neills, yet in many ways the play is an idealized vision of what might have been, a first step toward the autobiographical. O'Neill insisted it be described as a "folk play" rather than a comedy, fearing an audience "sitting on their frosty mitts saying through grinding teeth 'now let's see him make me laugh!' "

Intent on pleasing the O'Neills, Bennett and Don paid extra attention to design. The binding was "sapphire"—a color Carlotta fancied—and the front stamped with O'Neill's signature in gold. When the couple checked in to the Hotel Madison for the premiere, Bennett rushed over a finished book, and a few titles Carlotta might enjoy.

"Mr. Stay-at-home,—you mustn't go about buying me books—I feel as if I were [a] gay young blonde starting off on board a liner!" she teased, then turned serious. "May I congratulate you and Mr. Klopfer again on your beautiful special [edition]." By month's end *Ah, Wilderness!* was on most bestseller lists; in O'Neill's lifetime, it was second only to *Strange Interlude* in theatrical success. Each side got what it wanted.

Two weeks later, though, it was a different story, when Bennett suggested that for *Days Without End,* a play about a return to faith, they solicit blurbs from figures in the Church. "No, I *certainly cannot consent,*" O'Neill thundered. "Lay off the Catholic stuff!" He was trying to convey "the life-preserving depths" in Catholic mysticism, yes, but the psychological truth would be the same whatever the faith. Bennett swallowed his pride, and replied that he didn't mind being told he was wrong, as long as he could offer opinions. But he still believed Catholics would see the play as a "soul-stirring triumph" for the Church, and welcome it more since O'Neill had earlier been on their "blacklist."

As it turned out, he was right. When the play opened in January 1934, Catholic reviewers loved it, but other Broadway critics panned it, and *Days Without End* eked out just fifty-seven performances. Yet that new year, relations between publisher and author were looking up. On January 17, publication day, they lunched together, and Bennett later dictated a note detailing plans for a seven-volume definitive edition of O'Neill's works. He ended with a question, confessing that during lunch he'd wanted to ask if Gene was still as pleased at signing with Don and him as he'd been the day it was decided, but "didn't have the nerve." The answer came inside a copy of *Days Without End* that stayed on one of Bennett's bookshelves for the rest of his life: "And replying to yours," O'Neill wrote, "will say I sure am as pleased with my publisher as on the day the banns were signed—even a damned sight pleaseder! So now, complain!"

By the end of February, *Ah, Wilderness!* had sold almost 12,000 copies, and *Days Without End* 9,000. Bennett assured his author that RH would do all it could to keep them active, including ads in the Sunday papers, posters, and an ad on *Days Without End* for Catholic publications. No longer above capitalizing on that connection, O'Neill conceded that the play needed whatever help Bennett could give. RH was "up against one of those rare occasions" where the production was "a debit." Still, 9,000 "for a complete theatre flop" at a time of economic hardship seemed "a bit of a modern miracle."

In August 1934, Mr. Cerf and Mr. Klopfer took luncheon with Mr. and Mrs. O'Neill. Carlotta received new reading matter—Robert Graves's *I, Claudius* and James Hilton's *Lost Horizon*. Having once determined to "nip" Bennett's "familiarity" in the bud, she now gushed, "With you, one forgets the business end and enjoys the friendship. You are charming people!" A pattern had taken shape: cordial relations, but squalls when a blunder—perceived or real—was even suspected.

At the beginning of 1935, O'Neill began work on his most ambitious project, an eleven-play series, "the Cycle," that he formally called "A Tale of Possessor Self-Dispossessed." The plan was to focus on two families, one immigrant Irish, the other aristocratic New Englander, and for the plays to span the course of a century, ending in the early 1930s. At a press conference, he explained his theory that the United States, instead of being the most successful country in the world, was "the greatest failure . . . the clearest example of 'For what shall it profit a man if he gain the whole world and lose his own soul?' " As for his own material profits, they were extraordinary. In America, his plays had sold almost a half million copies, "which, for plays, is sure going some, eh?" he wrote Bennett that April. Eighteen months later, however, feeling ill, he feared that TB had returned. Believing that the steamy climate was affecting his health, he and Carlotta decided to leave Georgia and resettle in Seattle, where on November 12, 1936, O'Neill learned he'd won the Nobel Prize for Literature. RH telegraphed congratulations straightaway.

It was wonderful news, but the intense attention, added to uncertain health and mental stress, began to overwhelm O'Neill. Within a month, he was furious with his publisher, demanding that Bennett wire to let him know "if you are doing anything at all" to take advantage of the award. He'd seen no ads, and booksellers had no books, nor could they get any for the new demand. "I can't believe you are so disgracefully lax . . . or so disloyal."

Bennett wired at once: not only had they run big ads in the *Times* and *Tribune,* RH had published a new edition of *Nine Plays* and used the award as rationale to raise the price a full 20 percent, to five dollars. The book was "a beauty," and copies were on their way. But this time he chose not to absorb the criticism, admitting to being "hurt" by O'Neill's tone, having hoped he had more confidence in "our friendship and our business judgment."

Another blast descended from Seattle. O'Neill insisted he'd seen almost every daily *Times* and all Sunday papers and found no ads. He'd received plans from his European publishers, but nothing from RH until this latest wire. Seattle stores still had no books, and friends said Portland and San Francisco had none either, despite it being the Christmas season and "months" (actually, four weeks) since the award announcement. Once again Bennett had to kowtow, and dispatched a peace missive. The day before, he'd sent O'Neill copies of the ad and the new edition. If stores said they couldn't get the *individual* plays, they were "lying." RH had ample stock of each in print.

What *had* been temporarily unavailable was *Nine Plays,* the omnibus edition that of course everyone now wanted. However, he reminded O'Neill that RH had deliberately allowed its stock of the omnibus to run down until they could discuss with him whether to keep it in print. The previous month, when Gene had visited New York, he'd agreed on a new edition and suggested a price increase. They'd had 300 copies on hand at the time: under normal circumstances, that would have carried them through until the new printing. But then the news hit, and a rush of East Coast orders cleared out copies in a day. However, within an hour of the announcement, RH was already discussing a Nobel edition with the printer, and it was "in the works" within two days. An ad listing all of O'Neill's available plays was rushed through the composing room for the next day's *Tribune* and *Times*. Bennett asked for the name of any store that claimed it hadn't been able to get copies of the *other* titles, and hoped to hear that all was right between them again. "For both sentimental and business reasons," he concluded, "you mean more to me" on the RH list than "everybody else on it rolled into one. Donald and Saxe feel the same way." O'Neill would hardly be the first enraged author to deem his publisher wanting. *No books in stores, no communication, no ads, no support at a critical time;* so runs the litany of the aggrieved writer, then and now. But Bennett was learning what he had to do—and did it.

Chapter 11

One-Book Odyssey

IN THE FALL OF 1931, EIGHTEEN MONTHS BEFORE SIGNING O'NEILL, Bennett and Donald had made a daring gamble that would play out over several years and profoundly influence their future: they decided to try to publish James Joyce's *Ulysses*. Banned in the English-speaking world and a cause célèbre, the book was for some "the thing to read" (and, too often, an unreadable cultural trophy); for others an object of utter indecency; still others judged it the emblematic novel of the age. Its publishing history had already taken many twists and turns. If *Ulysses* did reach safe harbor with this pair of young publishers and their two lawyer-champions, the journey would be tortuous, but winning the fight to publish it legally would turn Random House into a cultural force.

Censorship plagued Joyce almost from the start. A volume of verse saw print in 1907 when he was twenty-five, but a short story collection, *Dubliners,* suffered nine years of setbacks before it was published in London in 1914. Having eked out a living as a teacher on the Continent—the difficulty of finding a publisher factored into the Irishman's self-imposed exile—he came to depend on others' kindness. British feminist-philanthropist Harriet Shaw Weaver, introduced to his work by a literary adviser, American expatriate Ezra Pound, became Joyce's patron and during 1914–15 published his third book, *A Portrait of the Artist as a Young Man,* in installments in her magazine *The Egoist*. Ben Huebsch, under his eponymous imprint, brought out *Portrait* in 1916, having already introduced Joyce to the United States with *Dubliners*. But as the cognoscenti's admiration grew, Joyce's use of swear words and sexual references drew more attention from censors. When Weaver wanted to publish *Portrait* as a book, twelve printers refused, fearing prosecution; she had to import sheets from Huebsch. Yet such skirmishes over words like "bloody" were mere preludes.

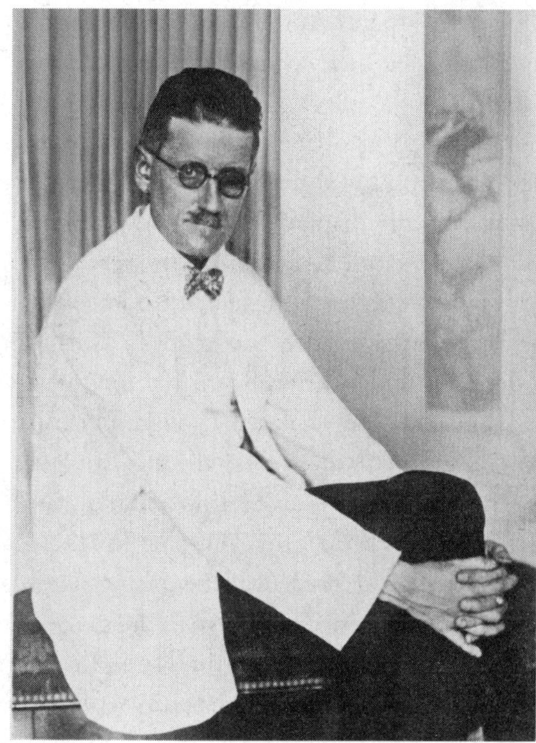

James Joyce in 1930

Ulysses adopted Homer's *Odyssey* as paradigm for a modern pilgrimage through the heart and mind. Experimenting with stream-of-consciousness techniques and insights from Freud, Joyce's epic aims to reveal the intricate workings of one day—June 16, 1904—in the life of a certain Leopold Bloom. Intelligent and sensitive, he is at the same time ordinary, a strange amalgam of Hungarian Irish Jew and lower-middle-class Dublin husband, father, and advertising salesman: Ulysses-Odysseus and Everyman. Threading through Bloom's adventures are those of his unfaithful wife, Molly, and of Stephen Dedalus, Joyce's semi-autobiographical stand-in from *Portrait*. By the Greek scheme, Molly is Penelope and Stephen his long-lost son, Telemachus. The eighteen parts limn encounters with the latter-day likes of Calypso and Nausicaa, until the last brings Ulysses home, with an extraordinary soliloquy by Molly. During "Bloomsday," all manner of bodily functions are poetically, tragically, or humorously related in prose making unabashed use of Anglo-Saxon four-letter words. "Bloody" seems anodyne.

Bennett was a Columbia undergraduate in 1918 when the first attempt to put the novel into print occurred not in London, but in Greenwich

Village, where Margaret Anderson and Jane Heap, lovers of the arts and each other, published the avant-garde *Little Review*. When Ezra Pound became their foreign editor, the idea of serializing *Ulysses* came up. Despite having already had one issue banned for an "obscene" story—the Comstock Act prohibited sending such material through the mail—the *Review*'s cover boldly displayed the credo "Making no compromise with the public taste": Anderson and Heap were game. Serialization began that March with a copyright notice in Anderson's name; for the first four parts, she officially registered copyright in Washington, D.C.

Episodes continued until the January 1919 issue was banned. The Post Office declared May "unmailable," and January 1920—"Cyclops"—they burned. The gutsy ladies carried on. But in "Nausicaa"—episode thirteen—Bloom observes a young woman on the beach, and, aware he's watching, she "leans back," revealing her knickers, and he ejaculates into his pants. That issue arrived at a lawyer's home—part of a *Review* effort to sign new subscribers. The lawyer's daughter passed it to her father, who apprised the district attorney, and soon Liveright's old nemesis, John Sumner—who'd succeeded Comstock as secretary of the New York Society for the Suppression of Vice—was told. Anderson and Heap were arrested on October 4, 1920, for obscenity that would corrupt a girl.

At their trial, fearing to argue a redefinition of obscenity based on literary transcendence or truth to life, the magazine's lawyer, John Quinn—who also advised Joyce—insisted that the "strong hard filth" would deter rather than promote lewdness. The strategy backfired, and the women were fined. Quinn looked for a New York book publisher to do a limited edition, sold by subscription, to try to skirt the censors. He approached Huebsch, who now had four Joyce works on his list. Huebsch wanted *Ulysses,* but in Quinn's words, "slightly draped"—with changes to ensure he wouldn't go to jail. Joyce refused. Liveright had also met Joyce; nobody liked a free speech fight more than Horace. In April 1921, he made an offer, but on that day Quinn received the "Circe" episode, set in a brothel. He told Liveright that prosecution and conviction for it was almost certain.

Needing money as always, Joyce—who'd moved to Paris in 1920—poured his woes into another sympathetic female ear. American Sylvia Beach, thirty-four-year-old proprietor of the Left Bank bookshop Shakespeare & Co., had never published anything, but she believed in him. Encouraged by her French lover Adrienne Monnier, she took up the challenge to print the manuscript using French compositors who wouldn't understand the text, and planned to sell by subscription to individuals willing to pay in advance.

Joyce revised much of the text as it had appeared in the *Review,* and more changes took place in proofs; his spiderweb of corrections would have caused consternation at a British or American printer, let alone a French one. Yet Beach proved efficient, and on February 2, 1922, *Ulysses* emerged as a book. One thousand numbered copies of a 732-page tome had come off the presses in Dijon. Significantly, while Anderson had registered copyright in her own name, Beach registered it to Joyce. By October, a second printing of 2,000 had gone through the French presses, this time with Harriet Shaw Weaver's *Egoist* colophon. Trouble followed, with 500 of her copies shipped to America burned by the New York Post Office, and a new printing seized in England. Yet Beach continued to reprint, and *Ulysses*'s reputation—famous and infamous—grew as copies circulated in Europe, and were smuggled by Americans returning from abroad, enjoying a frisson of intrigue. (One found its way into Don's library.)

Sylvia Beach and James Joyce in Paris

In 1926, the book sailed into choppier waters. Samuel Roth, a New Yorker known for publishing erotica, altered some text and pirated fourteen episodes in his magazine, *Two Worlds Monthly*. Joyce couldn't sue, given the muddied legal status: the early episodes had been copyrighted in Anderson's name, and the Beach book was already circulating in the

United States, making it impossible under American law for him to register his own copyright. Instead, he sought an injunction in New York to prevent the pirate from using his name "for advertising . . . or purposes of trade," and persuaded friends to organize a petition protesting Roth's action. E. M. Forster, André Gide, Virginia Woolf, and Albert Einstein were among 167 luminaries who obliged. But despite Joyce's obtaining the injunction, Roth issued *Ulysses* as a book, passing it off as the ninth printing of the Paris edition.

By 1931, Bennett was in the book business and well aware of Joyce, whom he'd met five years earlier, and whose relationship with the pragmatic Miss Beach had begun to fray. Though the "real" *Ulysses* had gone through eleven printings totaling 28,000 copies, and she'd devoted much time, money, and energy to supporting him and his family, he'd come to resent his long dependence on such women. What Beach couldn't do was publish the book openly in the United States or U.K., and Joyce desperately wanted that legitimacy. Hemorrhaging money on lawyers to stop Roth, he was losing much more in aggregate through every pirated book sold, and feared that the market for royalty-paying editions was drying up. And so, in December 1930, he made an odd request of Beach. When she'd agreed to publish *Ulysses,* he'd dismissed her suggestion that they draw up a proper contract. Suddenly he wanted to formalize their arrangement in writing, giving her the exclusive world right to print and sell *Ulysses,* and himself a 25 percent royalty on the published price of copies sold. But only in the last clause were his true designs discernible. Beach—the "Publisher"—was to agree to "abandon" her rights if thought advisable "by the Author and the Publisher in the interests of the Author." In that case, the right to publish *Ulysses* was to be "purchased from the Publisher at the price set by herself," to be paid by an acquiring publisher. Joyce was setting in motion the means to *separate* from her and seek U.S. or U.K. publication with someone else.

His timing made sense. In the United States, judicial attitudes toward censorship had been changing, and publishers' interest in *Ulysses* reawakening. Huebsch decided to risk another offer, and sent it to Beach and Joyce in May 1931. He'd pay legal fees and a royalty; in return, he wanted Joyce to write a preface, to provide a stamp of legitimacy. Huebsch, after all, had introduced him to America, and agreed to publish the book he'd been working on since finishing *Ulysses*—what we now know as *Finnegans Wake*. Less expected was a bid from Claude Kendall, whose eponymous house specialized in sensational thrillers. Kendall offered a $1,000 advance; $500 more if Joyce signed a hundred limited-edition copies; and he wanted a preface as well.

Beach thought both offers too small, and insisted any deal had to include $25,000 for her: a U.S. edition would likely end sales of her version. As a party to Joyce's contract, she decided it was best to organize her own American inquiry. In August, her sister, Mrs. Holly Beach Dennis, visited Alexander Lindey, an attorney in the New York law firm of Greenbaum, Wolff & Ernst. Budapest-born Lindey worked with Morris Ernst, a founding partner fast building a reputation as a brilliant censorship litigator. A "rough-around-the-edges" immigrant's son, Ernst had worked his way through law school and become associated with the American Civil Liberties Union soon after its start. He'd won a string of obscenity cases—one of them freeing Radclyffe Hall's novel of lesbian love, *The Well of Loneliness*—and co-authored a book on censorship, *To the Pure,* published by Harold Guinzburg's Viking Press. Lindey told him of Beach's interest in legalizing *Ulysses* and wish to cooperate with a responsible publisher. "This would be the grandest obscenity case" in history, Lindey proclaimed, and was willing to do anything to start it.

Ernst was hooked. Given Huebsch's history with Joyce, he seemed the obvious one to approach, but there was a complication: he'd merged his imprint into Viking, and Ernst had taken issue with his erstwhile publisher over his censorship book. However, Huebsch and Ernst still met. When Bennett heard that Huebsch would again try to publish *Ulysses,* he wondered if he and Don ought to pursue it themselves: it could make RH's name. However, in the end he proposed that should Huebsch succeed, he and Don would license reprint rights for the ML, and Huebsch was encouraging.

Quinn had died, and Joyce was being advised by two agents, the Pinker brothers, Ralph in the U.K. and Eric in New York. They thought he and Beach should accept Huebsch's offer. However, Viking pushed Huebsch to propose that instead of the $25,000 Beach wanted, she might agree "to take a portion" of Joyce's royalty. No way would Joyce cede that money; talks with Huebsch ended. Kendall had already dropped out. And so, on December 17, 1931, Huebsch wrote Bennett: he'd heard from the agents it was "hopeless to try to wrench *Ulysses*" from Beach. RH had "graciously stood aside," so Huebsch now passed the torch, but Beach's demand worried Bennett. When he and Ernst communicated,

Ernst quipped, "The only thing to do is for you and I to hop a boat and spend a weekend with Miss Beach in Paris." Bennett didn't join in the joke, not knowing "what we can do if Sylvia Beach maintains her preposterous stand."

Joyce himself was becoming increasingly frustrated. He steered clear of Beach's store, but his friend Padraic Colum haunted the place, delivering the message: "You are standing in Joyce's way!" Again *Ulysses* was at a crossroads, and this time what propelled it forward was an unexpected force: Joyce's extended family.

. . .

JAMES JOYCE AND NORA BARNACLE, the model for Molly Bloom, eloped to the Continent in 1904—the year *Ulysses* is set—and had their first child, Giorgio, in 1905. A daughter, Lucia, was born in 1907. The couple didn't legalize their union until 1931, the same year that Ernst and Bennett took an interest in legalizing *Ulysses*. By then, their illegitimate offspring were adults: Giorgio had married in 1930, and the estate issues his marriage crystallized had pushed Joyce to marry Nora. Giorgio's bride, Helen Kastor Fleischman, was a wealthy New York Jewish divorcée whose first husband had been Liveright's Paris agent. Known for her fine apartment, fancy friends, and "open" marriage, chic Helen was fascinated by Joyce. When she took up with his son, it was a *liaison scandaleuse:* at thirty-six, the bride was eleven years older than her groom, and a dozen years younger than her father-in-law. Her mother's mental illness had required stays in an asylum; her father's money had educated two sophisticated daughters and sent two sons to Harvard.

Joyce found Helen useful as a "volunteer" assistant. He'd also admitted her friend Paul Léon, a Russian Jewish émigré, to his inner circle as secretary. Well aware of Joyce's publishing problem, she mulled it over with her brother Robert, a Manhattan businessman who visited from time to time; they decided he could serve as a transatlantic go-between. But of all publishers to approach, why did Robert Kastor think of Bennett and Don, only six years in business and untested in handling new trade books? Perhaps he heard about them from Huebsch; another answer is the Modern Library. *Dubliners* and *Portrait* were in it, so they, like Huebsch, had experience selling Joyce. They'd also met the author, albeit briefly, in Paris; corresponded with Beach, using her to convey ML business to him; and the series attested to their sales and marketing prowess.

However, an even stronger reason propelled Kastor: he *already* had a connection with Bennett, namely the Sartorius brokerage firm. Robert had joined as a partner in 1929.

With time and the unreliability of memory—as well as his need to amuse and be center stage—Bennett spun a highly embellished version of the *Ulysses* tale in his oral history. But that same need had inspired him to publish an elaborate yarn about Kastor and *Ulysses* in a magazine article soon after the events occurred. "High up in one of lower Broadway's mightiest sky-scrapers there is hidden a brokerage office . . . presided over by two . . . remarkable figures," he began. One was Irving Sartorius, the other Robert Kastor, "who, tho he is so shy that few outsiders have heard his name, and tho he speaks in such a low, gentle voice that companions must strain . . . to hear . . . is said to possess one of the great fortunes. . . ." He was summoned in December 1931 by Mr. Kastor, who'd watched RH's progress, and was soon leaving for Europe. "Would we like him to tell Mr. Joyce that [RH] was ready to take up the battle? Would we!" Bennett exclaimed.

In truth, Kastor's family, though "comfortable," didn't boast a fortune. Far from shy and gentle-voiced, he was "gregarious," "stentorian," and remarkable only for it being well known that he had a mistress. The brokerage had indeed watched RH's progress, but curiously—for those not in on the joke—Bennett left out the most relevant fact of all: his long relationship with the Sartorius firm. (Kastor's lawyer, conveniently, was a partner of Ernst.) Kastor's discussions about Joyce may have occurred even before Huebsch exited the scene, and by year's end, the field was wide open: Harcourt, Vanguard, and Morrow were interested. Bennett had to make his move.

And so, discussions with Kastor and Ernst culminated in a letter he drafted to Joyce, detailing the challenges involved in fighting the case, as well as RH's offer. "No copyright can possibly be obtained on the text," he declared at the outset. A pirated version was presently being hawked in the city; no doubt if *Ulysses* were legalized, there'd be another soon after. Then there was the cost. The fee in each court would be at least $1,000; if the case went as far as the Supreme Court, that would be four battles, and more than $4,000 spent. Add the 15 percent royalty the firm would give Joyce with a $2,500 advance, payable on publication day. In return, Bennett expected him to write a ten-to-fifteen-page introduction on the "trials and tribulations" the book had suffered: crucially, the intro *could be* copyrighted, to show that Random's was the only authorized edition.

As for Beach, a big payment was "utterly" impossible, but she should "ardently desire a decent publisher" to make the fight, Bennett argued. "We are willing . . . but . . . [can't] have the cards stacked too heavily against us." In other words, if RH won, she'd have to be content with her European sales. It's fair to say he was vying for advantage at the start of a negotiation, as any businessman would. Yet Bennett knew the rules of engagement with a foreign publisher: without the Meynell deals, RH would hardly have existed. Huebsch had at least asked Joyce to give Beach part of his royalty. Bennett's view as to what she should "ardently desire" ignored her great accomplishment and the contract initiated by Joyce, and seems like something he'd never have countenanced had she been a man. His intentions, though, aligned with Joyce's. After Joyce's friend Colum had upbraided her for standing in Joyce's way, a deeply hurt, defiantly proud Beach told her author that she'd relinquish her rights. He made no move to persuade her otherwise.

Kastor assured Bennett his letter was just right, and announced that Helen was pregnant. She already exercised "considerable influence on Papa Joyce," and his sister would "swing the deal" if she gave birth to a boy: Joyce desperately wanted a grandson. On February 15, 1932, after a perilous pregnancy mainly confined to bed, Helen delivered that much-desired grandson, Stephen James Joyce. Less than a week later, on February 21, her brother hand-delivered Bennett's letter to Paris.

Unfortunately, the Pinker agency countered with a rival proposal: a \$2,000 publication day advance from Morrow if there were no ban, plus \$500 a month later if no new pirated edition had popped up. Morrow also wanted to do a more expensive signed edition of 1,000 copies. Soon the agents heard about Bennett's offer; in response, Morrow agreed to pay \$250 on signing. But since there seemed "great urgency," the agents told Léon they'd draft and send two contracts: one for RH, one for Morrow. The "urgency" had been fomented by Kastor, whose Paris visit was about to end, and on March 8 he cabled Bennett: "Have received full authority from Joyce" to negotiate. After returning to New York, Kastor cabled Giorgio on March 17: "Pinker Colum both favor Morrow. . . . Offers equal and satisfactory. I favor Cerf." The magic prospect of a \$1,000 signing advance then entered the picture. A cable from Joyce to Kastor asked if Cerf or Morrow would agree to such a sum: all else being equal, that would clinch the deal. Pressure on Joyce had also increased via Ernst, who'd written that if a *Ulysses* fight were to be mounted, it had to be now, before more pirated editions appeared. Joyce cabled Kastor again, having taken Ernst's warning to heart.

On March 21, Kastor made a final push to Giorgio: RH had agreed to the $1,000 signing advance, and would pay extra for a limited edition. But, "unable" to contact Morrow, he reckoned the Pinkers favored them for their own advantage. From a "totally disinterested angle," Kastor insisted, he was "more than ever convinced" Joyce's "best interest" lay with Cerf. The next day, Bennett, Don, Ernst, and Lindey lunched in New York. That afternoon, Bennett met with Kastor and Eric Pinker, and signed the memorandum of agreement drawn up by Pinker. Kastor later told Giorgio that Morrow's offer on the signing advance had stalled at $250; Bennett had promised four times that, yet without doubt, the Sartorius relationship had provided the crucial hinge.

The memorandum was amended by Paul Léon in Paris and in two letters written in New York. Joyce would keep the $1,000 signing advance even if RH failed to have *Ulysses* legalized, and would be paid on the date a signed contract and a letter from him of "not less than three hundred words" authorizing publication were received by RH. The length was far shorter than Bennett had sought, but Joyce balked at writing anything, and Bennett knew he had to have something to copyright so he could justify the edition. The $1,500 balance of the advance would be paid on publication, and Joyce would get an extra $500 for signing 250 limited-edition copies. Another clause permitted a foreword by a different author, but Kastor, foreseeing that this might upset Joyce, explained that the author in question would be Ernst, who'd reassure purchasers that it was legitimate to publish, sell, and read *Ulysses*. The most important proviso for the future concerned the Modern Library. Bennett specified there'd be no ML edition until two years after trade publication, but if a lower-priced pirated edition appeared, he and Don could bring out the ML reprint "immediately." They knew the real money would be made there. "My final word is this," Kastor urged Helen and Giorgio. Further delay would "jeopardize once and for all" Joyce's rights in connection with U.S. publication. "Go to it and get his signature." Helped along by the persuasive presence of a newborn grandchild, they did.

Ernst foresaw "a very bitter fight," and wanted a fee plus a profit share if they won; he'd had a similar deal with Covici-Friede when he'd taken on *The Well of Loneliness*. Bennett realized there was no way Joyce would pay a lawyer's fee jointly with any publisher: RH would have to swallow the entire cost of litigation. They'd provide a $500 retainer, and should there be a jury trial, the lawyers would also receive $50 per diem. If they won, RH additionally agreed to pay Ernst a 5 percent royalty on each trade copy sold, and 2 percent on reprint copies. That way, if they lost, RH wouldn't be too much out of pocket: without that royalty, Ernst would have demanded more up front.

Bennett and Don's willingness to grant a royalty that could be in effect for the rest of Ernst's life raises two questions: How confident were they that they'd win, and how much faith did they put in the novel's ability to last? To a bookseller, Bennett quoted Ernst saying that "the chances are 3 to 1 in our favor." Wanting to impress a reporter, he gave odds as "10 to 1." A more circumspect Don estimated "a 50-50 chance." It's likely they weren't as sanguine—whether about winning or longevity—as Bennett made it appear, since the royalties could eventually amount to several hundred thousand dollars. Ernst would later say that if Bennett had had more faith in *Ulysses,* he would simply have paid the legal bills and not made a deal to pay a percentage. Yet Bennett *did* agree to pay not only a retainer and per diem expenses (though arguing the rate), but also Joyce's $1,000 non-returnable advance—more than Viking and Morrow were willing to do. Faith enough.

. . .

ON A MID-APRIL EVENING in 1932, a month after sending the contract to Paris, Bennett sat in his living room facing Central Park, reading *Ulysses*. As happens more often than those outside the business might imagine, he'd signed the contract without having read most of the book. He brought passion to the enterprise, but not the devotion that Heap, Anderson, and Beach felt for the novel, and found it challenging. "There are several dull stretches that can be skipped over very quickly," he confided to an acquaintance. Yet for Ernst and Lindey, "skipping" wasn't an option: they needed to know every line.

The first step in Ernst's strategy was simple and brilliant: rather than put RH to the potentially crippling cost of setting, printing, and attempting to distribute the book in the United States, he would base his case on defending the importation of a single copy of Beach's *Ulysses* from Paris, which would be seized on arrival by customs as per Section 305 of the Tariff Act. But who should be the addressee? If an unimpeachable man of national repute were willing, that would help. Bennett asked retired Supreme Court Justice Oliver Wendell Holmes; when he demurred, he asked Columbia president Nicholas Murray Butler, who also declined. In the end, he told Léon to send it to RH.

Since it was uncertain what evidence the court would admit, as much as possible had to be planted on the book: Léon was instructed to paste in articles and reviews. Bennett said to write on the package the name of the boat it would come on, so there could be no mistake by the postal service. Once Léon provided the name, RH would notify customs; the package "surely" couldn't slip through "without being noticed."

While Léon prepared the special copy in Paris, Bennett fed Ernst a comprehensive list of articles and books about Joyce and *Ulysses,* and focused on rallying support that could prove critical in a court of law as well as in the court of public opinion. RH would send a questionnaire and statement that Lindey had drafted to librarians nationwide, to see if the novel was already in their collections, gauge demand, and seek opinions on its literary significance. A different letter would circulate to editors, critics, authors, social workers, lawyers, clergymen, psychiatrists, and teachers detailing RH's plans and asking for "frank opinions" of *Ulysses* as a "social document." Ernst had asked for a hundred librarian letters; Bennett sent out eight times as many, and also mailed a questionnaire to booksellers. Letters began arriving, one from Theodore Dreiser. Usually so prickly, he knew what it was to be censored, and was unusually gracious in reply: "To read [*Ulysses*] . . . is to spend a day inside a seeking and profoundly observant human mind. . . . Some things enter into it which are not generally recorded. But, and for precisely that reason, these things add to its value as an amazing, if not unique, social and literary document."

Joyce had given Bennett and Don the authorization letter they needed, pleasantly surprising them with nearly eight hundred words, rather than the contractual minimum of three hundred, and Paul Léon dispatched the special copy by registered mail. Into the precious book he'd attached an article from a Swiss literary review; circulars about French and German translations; extracts from press notices—favorable and unfavorable, but always weighty—from the likes of Arnold Bennett and critic Gilbert Seldes, whose 1922 review in *The Nation* had been very strong; also material on the international protest as well as the Roth injunction. On May 2, Lindey phoned and wrote the Collector of Customs in New York, alerting him to the parcel's impending arrival on the *Bremen,* and asserting for the record that they didn't want the book to slip through without "official scrutiny." That single copy is one of the most famous objects in literary history, and Bennett's account of its seizure has been referenced many times. Don also recorded his memories, as did Ernst, but the three do not entirely cohere.

Bennett recalled the book having an escort. He and Ernst were at the dock on "one of the hottest days" in the city's history. "The customs people wanted only . . . to get returning passengers off . . . and get the hell out. . . . Our man came out with his suitcase," and the inspector began to stamp it, unopened. "Frantic," they demanded he search the bag.

"It's too hot," the inspector declared.

"We think there's something in there that's contraband," they again asserted.

The hot-and-bothered inspector grudgingly opened the case to an "Aha!" from Bennett and Ernst, pointing to *Ulysses*. "Oh, for God's sake, everybody brings in that," he replied. But the two men refused to budge. The chief inspector was summoned, who in turn wasn't inclined to act. In the end, "we *made* them seize this book," Bennett insisted.

Don recalled having a copy mailed to RH that came through "unscathed," then asking a friend to bring in a second, meeting him at the dock, and going through the rigmarole Bennett described. Ernst also recalled the test volume coming through unseized, but added: "I had to redeliver the copy to the . . . official in charge." Marian Klopfer told her daughter that *she* had carried the book into New York. Kastor family lore has it that *he* did. Each wanted the glory, but Ernst added a useful caveat: "Memory plays tricks." Indeed. It is a matter of record that Lindey sent a query to customs about the status of a book that had been on board the *Bremen,* and Assistant Collector of Customs H. C. Stewart replied on May 13: "The book in question is detained as in violation of Section 305 of the Tariff Act as obscene." Eleven days later, Stewart told him it had been transferred to the U.S. attorney for the Southern District of New York to start forfeiture, confiscation, and destruction proceedings.

In June, Lindey telephoned Samuel C. Coleman, chief assistant U.S. attorney, for a status report. Already familiar with Ernst, Coleman seemed unusually "cordial and cooperative." He was plowing through the book, having with some difficulty read almost half, yet was unable to say when he'd render his decision. At the end of July, they spoke again. He'd finished, judging the book a "masterpiece," but he also found it "obscene" as defined by federal law. Conflicted and uneasy, Coleman turned the case over to his boss, U.S. Attorney George Z. Medalie, who might now read *Ulysses;* a few weeks later, Medalie told Ernst he feared he'd have to prosecute, but saw this was no ordinary book.

As autumn neared, Bennett grew uncomfortably aware of time's passage. The letters and questionnaires that he'd seeded in the spring had reaped a bumper crop of replies from librarians and intellectuals. As he told Kastor, hundreds of librarians had expressed a willingness to stock the book, and almost two hundred authors, lawyers, and critics viewed its banning as "a vicious and unpardonable affair." They all clamored to know when *Ulysses* would be available, and as both Bennett and Kastor had emphasized to Joyce during negotiations, if publication were delayed too long, interest would wane or a new pirate rise. Nevertheless, Ernst hadn't wanted to push for a quick decision, afraid the U.S. attorney would insist on reading the whole book aloud before a jury. Such a trial would be excruciating—the novel was long and convoluted even for private reading, let alone for a public performance by a single lawyer—and a positive outcome would be in doubt. All those sexual and scatological words would be known by every juror, while so much else remain beyond the ken of most. The odds would be better if, instead of a jury trial, the case were decided by an open-minded judge who appreciated literature.

The gears of the law creaked along. Nineteen thirty-three dawned: Franklin Roosevelt moved into the White House, and Hitler marched into the Reichstag. Hoping to provoke action, the attorneys requested another copy be sent from Europe, to Lindey rather than RH. It was *this* copy—the *second*—that slipped through customs, as Donald and Ernst's muddled memories recalled. Lindey again wrote Customs Collector Stewart, offering to surrender the second book to the government, but he would contest the seizure on the grounds that the Tariff Act let the Treasury Secretary "in his discretion" permit importation of "so-called classics, or works of recognized scientific or literary merit." On May 13, 1933, a year after the first copy's arrival, a messenger brought *Ulysses* to Stewart—accounting for Ernst's memory of "redelivering" a copy.

One month later—on Bloomsday, June 16, as it happened—the first breakthrough occurred. The acting commissioner of customs in Washington wrote to New York: *Ulysses* was "of sufficient literary merit" for Lindey's copy to be released to him under the Secretary's discretionary authority: *he could keep it legally*. A headline in *The New York Times* proclaimed, "Ban Upon *Ulysses* to Be Fought Again; Publisher Seeking to Bring Out Joyce 'Classic' Here Gets One Copy Admitted." The argument that the book was a classic had succeeded: for a moment, it looked as though the government might even drop the case. It didn't, Bennett heard, because of all the "dirty words" in the last part. In any event, just after Lindey had sent his copy to Washington for adjudication, the government finally agreed to decide the fate of the *first* copy by motion of a single judge—what Ernst and Lindey had hoped for—rather than by jury trial.

It was crucial the case come before the right judge, and almost from the start Ernst had fixed on John Munro Woolsey, a maritime law expert who'd handled several First Amendment cases, as the ideal arbiter. At fifty-six, he was a rounded, cultivated fellow, "fond of old furniture and old books," particularly the work of Samuel Johnson. The lawyers knew they'd have to jockey for the case to go to him, so when the motion came up and they considered the judge then sitting ill-disposed, they played for time: Chief Assistant U.S. Attorney Coleman's appreciation of the book proved essential. After three trial postponements, on August 29 *United States v. One Book Called "Ulysses"* was at last submitted to Woolsey. About to go on vacation, he could read it while away.

Bennett and his staff had prepared a list of articles and reviews, plus photostats of testimonials and an index of those providing them; librarians' comments and a map showing locations of libraries wanting *Ulysses;* details on foreign editions; and a select list of RH books. The firm's lawyers sent Woolsey a preliminary memo describing it all. Prosecutors and defendants would exchange briefs on September 25, and file them with the court on October 2.

. . .

THE PROOF OF THE brief that Lindey prepared and Ernst polished was sent to Bennett for approval. Its five parts—"Nature of the Case," "The Author," "The Book," "The Claimant," "Recent Cases"—were followed by a reiteration of the relevant section of the Tariff Act and a six-point argument. Bennett's publisher's eye was amused to catch many typographical errors—corrected soon enough—but overall, he judged the brief "swell." Ernst began by establishing the book as "unique." He gave Joyce's bona fides, declaring him to be the "most important" figure in contemporary literature: not since Shakespeare had English "reached such heights." Rather than ask the judge to take his word, he quoted Edmund Wilson, Rebecca West, and others, placing *Ulysses* beside Dante's *Divine Comedy* and Balzac's *Human Comedy*. In describing Random as claimant, he extolled the typographical distinction of its books, noting that the *Times* had anointed the Kent *Candide* the "most beautiful" fine-press book made in America. He also mentioned the hundred-dollar *Leaves of Grass;* limited-edition titles by Hawthorne, Blake, and others; and bourgeois favorite W. S. Gilbert. (But not O'Neill: far too controversial.)

The legal interpretation of obscenity in books was based on a nineteenth-century English ruling, the "Hicklin" test, which said something was obscene if it had a tendency to "deprave and corrupt" those whose minds were vulnerable to "immoral influences"—young girls, for instance. A London publisher who'd brought out Emile Zola's *Nana* had been convicted under the doctrine in 1888, and Ernst had to overcome the precedent in order to succeed. The brief cited forty-two legal battles: some that Ernst had waged and won, and some fought by Liveright and others. The test of obscenity "is a living standard," Ernst asserted, so *Ulysses* had to be judged by current customs. Then there was the second copy, which the government had acknowledged "a classic." A classic, Ernst insisted, cannot be obscene. *Ulysses* didn't behave like a dirty book: there were no pornographic pictures, and Joyce never hid his authorship. Length—those 732 "closely printed" pages—also argued against obscenity: the first sex passage didn't occur for some time. Most important was a "Gargantuan complexity" that limited readers by natural selection. The book was already in the Library of Congress. Having been accepted by many leading figures, to call it obscene would brand "eminent persons . . . champions of obscenity." Last, Ernst confronted the problem that had plagued *The Little Review:* the book could only be judged *as a whole*.

So much for the brief. Not until November 25 did the novel have its second day in court, thirteen years after Anderson and Heap's prosecution, and almost two since Bennett and Ernst had spoken of taking it on.

Going to court was, in Don's words, "very thrilling," but the court they went to wasn't in the bustling Lower Manhattan judicial hub. Instead, Judge Woolsey presided in the elegant Byrne Room, on the sixth floor of a midtown building adjoining the City Bar Association at 42 West Forty-Fourth Street.

Ernst, Lindey, Coleman, and Coleman's fellow assistant U.S. attorney Nicholas Atlas sat before a bench of justice said to be one of the most beautifully designed pieces of furniture in the United States. Behind them, on a row of "the finest colonial chairs in New York," were reporters and interested parties, among them Bennett, Don, Saxe, and Whit Burnett, co-editor of *Story,* a magazine known for publishing the best young writers. (Together with BOMC founder Harry Scherman, Bennett and Don had recently bought *Story* from Burnett and his wife.) The fight had begun to raise both RH's and Bennett's profiles. Many in the room knew who he was, but on this occasion he ceded the spotlight to bow-tied, fast-talking, gravelly-voiced Ernst, a showman who loved it as much as Bennett did.

Just before the hearing began, in the time-honored manner of respectful rivals, Coleman and Ernst chatted privately about one of the most reliable tests used to determine obscenity: producing "shame" in listeners by reading aloud four-letter words. Coleman told Ernst that he couldn't do it: he just could not say such things in public.

"Why?" Ernst asked.

"Because there is a lady in the courtroom."

Ernst stared at Coleman through his glasses and protested: the lady was Ernst's wife. Yet the U.S. attorney couldn't bring himself to utter such "horrid, torrid" words.

Onlookers crowded the courtroom—Sumner, of the Suppression of Vice Society, among them. The judge's round, bald head was unremarkable but for sharp, heavy-lidded eyes peering from behind spectacles. "This isn't an easy case to decide," he mused aloud, setting an approachable tone as he lit a cigarette jutting from a long ivory holder.

Coleman began by pleading for the court not to think him "a puritanical censor," since no one would "dare" attack the book's "literary value," but it contained obscenity. Ernst countered that libraries and people all over the United States had accepted it as a classic through bootleg copies; the court should follow the people's will. Woolsey agreed that things generally "ought to take their chances in the market place":

suppression invited bootleggers. But wouldn't a girl of eighteen be corrupted by Molly's speech? Ernst replied that the law didn't require adult literature to "be reduced to mush for infants."

For the government, Coleman had marked up the book, bracketing suspect sections like the following with a marginal "X": "Ocularly woman's bivalve case is worse. Always open sesame. The cloven sex." "That old servant Ines told me that one drop even if It got into you at all after I tried with the Banana but I was afraid it might break and get lost up in me somewhere yes because they once took something down."

The last came from Molly's soliloquy, literally "X"-rated for pages at a time.

Ernst did not share Coleman's qualms about four-letter words. He, too, had gone through his special vocabulary beforehand, studying each word's etymology with his wife, Maggie, a "newspaper gal" turned schoolteacher. He plunged in, parsing a sailor's vocabulary with a professor's skill, arguing that a possible derivation of *fuck* was "to plant," an Anglo-Saxon agricultural usage. "The farmer used to fuck the seed into the soil," he explained. "In fact, it's got more honesty than phrases that modern authors use to connote the same experience."

Woolsey wanted an example.

"Oh—'they slept together.' It means the same thing."

The judge smiled. "That isn't even usually the truth."

At that moment, Ernst felt that the case was "half won."

Woolsey elicited laughs after admitting to his "shocking surprise" that he'd "perfectly understood" passages described as obscene. Parts of the book were "rough"; others were "of moving literary beauty," leaving him "bothered, stirred and troubled." Ernst, pleased that the judge hadn't said "revolted," agreed. That was the book's "peculiar" power: it was "a weird epitome of what is going on in a human mind."

As the definition of obscenity continued to be debated, Woolsey kept asking Ernst if he'd "really read" the entire novel, unsettling him: it was easier for a judge to ban a book if he thought few would actually read it. Ernst decided to change tack, admitting that he'd tried to "get through" *Ulysses* a decade earlier and failed, but of course had had no choice but to read it in full now. And while reading it, he added, he was invited to speak at the Unitarian Church in Nantucket on the New Banking Act.

"What's that got to do with my question?" Woolsey interjected.

Speaking to that Nantucket audience, Ernst recalled, he'd been intently focused on banking, but had also been thinking "about the long ceiling-high windows . . . the clock and eagle in the rear . . . the baby in the sixth row. . . . Judge, that's *Ulysses*." He returned to his reading with a new regard for Joyce's "stream of consciousness put into words."

Woolsey smiled. The last part of the novel had worried him, but he understood it all much better now: although he'd listened closely to Ernst, he'd also been thinking about the Hepplewhite chair behind him. "That's the book," Ernst repeated. Woolsey's fondness for fine furniture had produced its own epiphany.

Now Bennett's efforts to find allies and persuade the public to support *Ulysses* came to the fore. On the back page of the 1932–33 catalogue, he'd put a large boxed ad:

> Random House has signed a contract with James Joyce [for] publication . . . of a complete and unabridged edition of his monumental novel. . . . Mr. Morris Ernst has been retained . . . to remove a legal ban. . . . The success of the attempt will depend . . . upon the extent to which intelligent and qualified public opinion can be rallied.

That ad, the publicity Bennett had drummed up, all those letters he'd sent, and a word-of-mouth campaign had done their work. Woolsey remarked on the "unbelievable" amount of mail he'd received when it became known that he had taken the case. Still, the verdict didn't come immediately. The judge took his time, wanting more documents. On Thanksgiving morning, alone in the bathroom of his country home, he looked "straight in the mirror" while shaving. He could see it was fine outdoors, and it came to him how he was going to decide, and what he was going to say. Immediately, he went to his desk. The following Wednesday, December 6, 1933, his decision was announced.

The judge's opinion was a model of elegance, clarity, concision, and common sense. He established that he'd read the entire novel once, and the suspect passages several times. He didn't detect "the leer of the sensualist" or hold it to be pornographic. With "astonishing success" Joyce showed, embedded in "the screen of consciousness with its ever-shifting" impressions, not only the actual things one focused on, but also a "penumbral zone" of past impressions, "not unlike the result of . . . a multiple exposure on a cinema film." The "dirty" words were known to almost

Judge John Munro Woolsey

all men and, he ventured, many women, and would be "habitually used" by the types Joyce sought to portray. As for "recurrent emergence of the theme of sex . . . his locale was Celtic and his season Spring."

Woolsey pronounced *Ulysses* "sincere and honest . . . brilliant and dull, intelligible and obscure by turns," even sometimes "disgusting," but hadn't found "dirt for dirt's sake." Noting that the legal definition of *obscene* was "to stir the sex impulses or to lead to sexually impure and lustful thoughts," he emphasized that a book had to be tested "on a person with average sex instincts—what the French would call *l'homme moyen sensuel*"—rather than on a girl. After he'd come to his own decision, he checked with two friends answering the French description, and they agreed with him. Summing up, he was "quite aware" *Ulysses* was "a rather strong draught" for some to take. But "whilst in many places the effect . . . on the reader undoubtedly is somewhat emetic, nowhere does it tend to be an aphrodisiac. *Ulysses* may, therefore, be admitted into the United States."

Woolsey had freed *Ulysses* at last.

. . .

WHEN THE DECISION CAME through, Bennett cabled Joyce, who congratulated and thanked publishers and lawyers alike. Exultant letters arrived from writers, critics, librarians, and fellow publishers, many of whose testimonials had been used in the case. "My admiration for you is only exceeded by my admiration for . . . Woolsey," Alfred Knopf wrote, but much of Bennett and Don's work lay ahead. The case was fought over one copy; now they had to make the book and get people to buy thousands. Bennett rushed releases to New York papers and wire services, and RH could finally link Joyce's name to its other star, O'Neill, whose *Days Without End* would be published in a month. The newspapers responded. The *Herald Tribune* headlined it "epochal." Stories noted that liberation of another sort had taken place the day before: on December 5, Prohibition was repealed. That same week, President Roosevelt publicly protested lynching. Columnist Harry Hansen called it "a week of wonders."

Once word was out, books had to follow fast, or momentum would be lost and pirates rush in. Months earlier, Donald had made plans with H. Wolff, the printer he depended on for the Modern Library, and the firm most dependent on him. It was Don who'd give production instructions and approvals. He'd ordered ten tons of paper for the 10,000-copy first run of a fat 768-page book that would sell for $3.50. Everything had to be coordinated for seamless flow: typesetting; galleys; first corrections; printing, reading, and correcting page proofs; manufacture of plates; then printing, binding, distribution. On December 7, 1933, at 10:15 A.M., he called the printer and gave the order: "Go ahead." Work was scheduled in relays: while the last part was being set, preceding chapters were made into pages; the middle of the book "plated" in metal; and the beginning put on the presses. The job had to be done in five weeks—incredibly tight—to meet the already-announced publication date of January 25, 1934.

The inclusion of Joyce's letter, Ernst's foreword—"The New Deal in the law of letters is here," Ernst memorably began—and Woolsey's decision lent an air of copyright legitimacy, although the issue was essentially fudged. "Copyright 1918, 1918, 1920, by Margaret Caroline Anderson. Copyright 1934, by the Modern Library, Inc.," the copyright notice read, not delving into what was—and wasn't—protected.

Ernst Reichl, a relatively new employee at H. Wolff, was responsible for designing *Ulysses* to make it RH's rather than Sylvia Beach's. Born in Leipzig, he'd studied at the Bauhaus before arriving in New York. His concept was modern, bold, and would remain, in Reichl's words, "the best-known" design he ever made. The title page extends across a spread, the left side anchored in an enormous "U." Needing neither numbers nor titles, chapters stream on. The only division is into three sections, each begun with another full-page capital—doubly unusual, falling on left-hand pages. The jacket is cream-colored. "James Joyce," although small, "pops"—a line of creamy letters stenciled on a long scarlet box tucked between the final "E" and "S" of the title. "ULYSSES," in hugely elongated, thin black verticals, jumps in an urgent staccato, taking up the rest of the jacket's height and width. Is it jazz notation? Bauhaus Germany? Skyscraper New York? Most important was that a previously banned book would now be worthy of display, catching eyes without inducing shame. Bennett happily told an anecdote about one particular storefront. *The Little Review* had serialized episodes of the novel from a location at the back of the Washington Square Bookshop. When "vice-hounds" descended in 1920 in search of Anderson and Heap, the shop's owner, Josephine Bell Horton, was "hauled into court." Now she filled her entire window with *Ulysses*.

Distribution was the next major hurdle. Prior to *Ulysses,* the firm's large sales had come from the ML and a very few trade reprints, like the Kent *Moby-Dick*. Now Bennett went to call on the American News Company, whose branches mostly distributed magazines, but also placed likely bestsellers in book and stationery stores. He thought its buyer, Harold Williams, "very tough, very efficient"; they hadn't done much business together, but now Bennett told Williams that they had "a big book" for him.

"I suppose it's that dirty book *Ulysses*. I don't think it's for us," Williams replied.

"What do you mean, dirty?" Bennett protested. "It's . . . been cleared by the court."

"Well, it's not really our kind of thing," Williams repeated. "But you're nice fellows, we'll help you a little." He took 250 copies. The door had been opened, and haggling began. It wasn't easy, but Williams finally agreed to take 5,000—half the first printing.

"At last, you've given me the right order," Bennett sighed, congratulating himself.

Williams pulled a sheet from a drawer and handed it to him. "I thought I'd make you work for it," he explained. It was an order, already written, for 5,000 copies.

On January 17, 1934, the first books landed at RH's offices, and Bennett at once dispatched six, as contractually bound, to Paris. Joyce had asked that they arrive by February 2, so he could savor the sweetness and vindication on his fifty-second birthday, twelve years to the day since Beach had put *Ulysses* into print. In the letter to Léon accompanying

Joyce's books, Bennett made a request: he and Don would be extremely grateful if two copies could be inscribed by Joyce for them. They would, of course, send replacements. "Naturally we would like to treasure these volumes in our private libraries," he explained. The fan and ultimate autograph hound once again, he was also the careful businessman: despite the announced publication date, most of the run wouldn't be ready until February. Bennett knew he needed early copies for publicity and to solicit orders, as well as to meet demand, since orders were starting to come in. A press release early in February claimed an advance sale of 13,000 copies: very healthy for a "difficult" book that had already sold many thousands in Beach's and pirate editions.

Three cardinal rules of bestseller promotion advised: an ounce of imagination pre-publication is worth a pound of advertising after a book is out; advertising sells a book that's already selling; a bestseller is helped by strokes of luck—the publisher's job is to know when and how to exploit them. In the case of *Ulysses,* some of that luck and imaginative thinking involved capitalizing on the letter-writing campaign that Ernst and Bennett had orchestrated. They had primed librarians, academics, and others to want a "legitimate" copy, even if they already owned a Beach. That accounted for many orders. Also crucial to promoting the novel was the passage of time. When Heap and Anderson were prosecuted, the *Times* had editorialized against *Ulysses,* but attitudes had evolved. Roth's piracy and the petition protesting it had created sympathy for Joyce. The publicity windfall from the court fight made him familiar to more readers. When his face appeared on the cover of *Time* magazine on January 29, with the headline "*Ulysses* Lands" and a three-page article, many felt they "knew" him.

Beach had focused on snob appeal, selling to the avant-garde and wealthy, for whom a copy of *Ulysses* implied a stay in Paris. That elite patina, combined with the legitimacy bestowed by Woolsey, allowed RH to aim for educated, middle-class Americans who bought serious books: a much larger readership. Luck helped, for book sales in general would improve a bit in 1934. Bennett contributed ideas and gave approvals, but asked Aaron Sussman, of the Spier & Sussman agency, to choreograph the ad campaign. He, too, had served his apprenticeship with Liveright, and would handle RH advertising for decades. Both men understood that sex sells, and it certainly helped sell *Ulysses*. The ad shouting it loudest was small, hawking "the novel America was forbidden to read! . . . suppressed for 20 years." But Sussman and Bennett also knew the difference between garnering publicity and inviting notoriety, and that the main challenge was to convince the public that *Ulysses* would be worth their time: accessible, enjoyable, and appropriate.

Leaflet to help bookstores sell *Ulysses*

A two-page spread in *The Saturday Review* was so effective that it brought 25,000 orders in three weeks. "How to enjoy James Joyce's great novel *Ulysses,*" its headline proclaimed. Varied fonts and illustrations, as well as plenty of white space, kept the large chunks of text from intimidating potential readers. The ad told a puzzle-and-epic-loving nation that Joyce's book was its own kind of puzzle and adventure. It reassured: *Ulysses* wasn't harder to "understand" than any classic and would reward readers in "wisdom and pleasure." Those familiar with Homer, Dante, and Shakespeare would find a book with the "symbolic narrative" of the *Odyssey,* the "spiritual planes" of the *Divine Comedy,* and the "psychological problem" of *Hamlet*. A list of dramatis personae placed Bloom, Molly, Stephen, and others beside their Homeric and real-life counterparts, and a summary was provided for each part. A photo of dandified, dignified, eye-patched Joyce in three-quarter profile was arresting and appealing. A Dublin map with references, photos, and explanations emphasized accessibility.

The ad also provided a partial answer to an intractable problem: Bennett had hoped to reproduce in the book a scholar's chart to help readers navigate the novel. Joyce, insisting his work speak for itself, had refused. "If you . . . have so little faith in our judgment, it is hard to explain why you ever signed a contract," Bennett snapped in frustration. But peace was soon restored, and happily the ad succeeded as substitute for the chart so well, stores asked for reprints.

The book's legal saga, however, wasn't quite over. On March 17—the last day he was empowered to do so—Martin Conboy, a pious Catholic who'd succeeded George Medalie as U.S. attorney, announced that he'd appeal Woolsey's decision. Bennett and Sussman realized the new crisis was also an opportunity to whip up publicity to counter the threat. "James Joyce's *Ulysses* remains on sale!" a big ad insisted, quoting the *Herald Tribune* and *World-Telegram* to mark Conboy as a biased "snoop." With 35,000 copies in print, the book was a bestseller "in every part of the country."

On Saturday, April 14, Bennett sailed for Europe on a long-planned journey with Viking Press's Harold Guinzburg, leaving Donald, Ernst, and Lindey to handle *Ulysses*. A week later he was allaying any fears Joyce might have about Conboy over lunch in Paris.

Ernst filed a brief before the court of appeals on May 2, using earlier arguments and one more: Woolsey's decision had met with "overwhelming public approval." If it was acceptable for theaters to show Mae West's *She Done Him Wrong,* and Macy's book department to advertise "Forbidden Classics" like Flaubert's *Madame Bovary,* the ruling should stand. Two weeks later, before a three-judge appellate panel, Conboy—"blushing, stammering, rocking nervously"—read aloud twenty-five passages. Among the spectators were a couple of women, or as the *Daily News* wrote: "Two little girlies / Went to court for fun / The lawyers read *Ulysses* / Then there was one." (The other had fled.) Not until August 7 did judges Augustus and Learned Hand and Martin T. Manton return their verdict. The cousins Hand sided with Ernst and Woolsey, Augustus noting: "Art certainly cannot advance under compulsion to the traditional forms, and nothing in such a field is more stifling to progress than limitation of the right to experiment. . . . *Ulysses* is a book of originality and sincerity." The majority ruled.

Ulysses has been invoked in obscenity cases ever since: to defend the novels of D. H. Lawrence and Henry Miller, but also the performances of Lenny Bruce. Decades later, it set the standard for European art films to enter the United States. Audiences were able to grow beyond Hollywood and, like Odysseus, venture to unknown shores. Donald would come to judge the novel's vindication "the finest hour" in his and Bennett's publishing career, and the signal achievement that catapulted them and their infant upstart, Random House, onto the map of America and the world.

. . .

THREE BRIEF CODAS REMAIN. The first concerns the fates of Joyce and several intimates.

Finnegans Wake was published by Viking in 1939, but Bennett harbored hopes that Joyce might return to RH. In February 1940, ever so deferentially, he proposed that, after the "imposing" *Finnegan,* a new book "in a more popular vein"—in the nature of *Dubliners* or *Portrait*—would "appeal to a very wide audience." But Bennett had got it wrong: Joyce wouldn't tailor his art to a publisher's suggestion. In any event, war had broken out in Europe, and the question of another book was moot.

The rest of their correspondence centered on a not-unfamiliar topic: money. With the war, Joyce was having "the greatest difficulty" getting funds from London, where his lawyer was and royalties went, so he asked Bennett to send payments directly to Paris. But after the city fell to the Germans in June 1940, he fled to the Auvergne and, even more desperate, wanted money sent care of the U.S. embassy in Vichy. Bennett applied for a license to cable funds, and in October wrote Joyce he was "very happy" when the bank said the money went through. Still, he asked for confirmation. It's unlikely he got it: on January 13, 1941, Joyce died in Zürich from peritonitis brought on by an ulcer.

The times were also desperate for Helen Joyce. Her marriage ended stunningly badly: Giorgio left and took their son; she broke down and was institutionalized as her mother had been; and as a Jew in a Europe being overrun by Hitler, only through her brother Robert's efforts did she escape from Paris in 1940. Paul Léon, another Jew, fled when the Nazis marched in, but returned for family reasons. He saved Joyce's papers before the Nazis found them, but unfortunately they found him.

The second coda takes up a textual saga. In the hectic weeks between Woolsey's decision and the announced publication date, there was no reason for anyone to think the sheets coming off the presses at H. Wolff had not been set from one of Beach's copies. They weren't. A Roth pirated version, looking just like Beach's but pockmarked with errors, had inadvertently been used. It wasn't until 1940 that a concerted effort at correction was made, when RH consulted the Odyssey Press version in preparation for the ML reprint, but that wasn't enough. More corrections came with later reprints, but this was still inadequate. In 1961, RH based its reprint on one made by The Bodley Head, publishers of the British edition. Some experts estimated that thousands of misprints remained. Another attempt at getting the book right occurred in the mid-1980s, using a computer to sieve through variations. It, too, became mired in controversy, and we've still not heard the end of it.

The final coda concerns the fate of the famous trial copy, the marked-up beneficiary of Sam Coleman's "X's" and John Woolsey's wisdom. After the ruling, the book, like its protagonist, wandered: berthing at the U.S. Attorney's Office; then at Internal Revenue; sailing next to the collector of customs before Lindey intervened and made sure it landed at RH on November 1, 1934. Already the *Herald Tribune* had run an article: "Columbia Gets *Ulysses* Copy Freed by Trial." The newspaper was a tad premature: Columbia's library didn't receive it until the following May, when proud alumnus Bennett presented it at the annual Writers' Club dinner.

Another copy came to Columbia on Bennett's death, bearing the RH colophon and notice "First American Edition." One of the six he'd sent to Joyce, it's inscribed: "To Bennet Cerf/Congratulating him on his courage and enterprise/Paris 25 January 1934."

The dropping of a "t" in Bennett's name—he was very particular about its spelling—rather undermines those inflated claims he'd made over the years that he was "a very favored friend" to Joyce, as he truly would be to many others he published. He did meet with the Joyces on a few social occasions in Paris, and liked to recount stories about them. One had him witnessing a tug-of-war over a piano bench between a very "potted" James and a slightly less inebriated Nora, and hearing her say: "Someday I'm going to write a book for you, Bennett, and I'm going to call it 'My Twenty Years with a Genius-So-Called.'" It was an amusing story, though as Ernst said, memory does play tricks. But no matter Bennett's inflated claims, often apocryphal stories—or his author's misspelling. In other respects, Joyce got the inscription right.

Chapter 12

Daring Young Men

WHEN SPRING ARRIVED IN 1934, AFTER *ULYSSES* HAD TRIUMPHED in Woolsey's courtroom, Bennett and Harold Guinzburg went on a *very* grand tour. They'd make stops in Europe, but also, more thrillingly, in Egypt, Palestine, and the Soviet Union. Viking and Random would have to do without their self-styled "young prima donna" presidents for three full months. The idea of four weeks in the USSR most excited Bennett. As the Depression persisted, many liberal Americans had grown intrigued by the Soviet experiment. True believers paid no heed to reports of food shortages and forced labor, convinced that Communism—or at least socialism—was the future. Bennett's breed of New Deal Democrat was curious, but cautious; yet once FDR opened diplomatic relations with the USSR in November 1933, travel got easier, and a trip to Red Russia became the thing to do.

The week leading to his departure was awhirl with activity. On Tuesday, April 10, sixty friends squeezed into his apartment to say bon voyage. On Thursday, after his final private Russian lesson, Bennett stopped at Dashiell Hammett's for drinks, managed two more cocktail parties, then at 10 P.M. met up with Harold and Alice Guinzburg at George and Beatrice Kaufman's townhouse, where the celebrating kicked into high gear. RH had published George's play *The Dark Tower,* written with Alexander Woollcott, in January. *Merrily We Roll Along,* a comedy coauthored with his brilliant young writing partner Moss Hart, would debut in the fall, and RH would publish that, too. Signing them and other dramatists during the next five years—Clifford Odets, Sidney Kingsley, Liveright alum Lillian Hellman among them—cemented RH's reputation as a publisher of plays, at a time when trade houses rarely entered the field. No surprise the biggest markets were New York and L.A., and that printings were small, but RH didn't skimp: the dramas came between well-designed covers, often with production photos inside. Some thought him crazy, but Bennett published plays for the same reason Liveright had: to indulge his not-so-secret "secret love," to feel he had "one foot in the back door of the theater."

That evening, the Kaufmans assembled a perfect cast on a perfect stage. Harpo Marx spoke! Walter Winchell gossiped! George and Ira Gershwin and novelist DuBose Heyward, poised to collaborate on *Porgy and Bess,* mingled! At backgammon, Bennett lost $146, but Harold won $485 off *New Yorker* editor Harold Ross—"that biggest pigeon who ever lived"—a useful contribution toward travel expenses. Leaving the party very late, Bennett stopped "chez Mademoiselle Lois Moran," an actress he'd been dating, before falling into his own bed at dawn. Bennett's remarkable stamina didn't fail him: up at eight-thirty on Friday, he was soon talking BOMC business with Harry Scherman over breakfast.

The *Ile de France* sailed the next day. A week later he was in Paris at the house of Gallimard to discuss plans for a new edition of C. K. Scott Moncrieff's celebrated seven-book translation of Marcel Proust's *Remembrance of Things Past,* the great novel that Gallimard had brought out in the original French. The Modern Library had profitably reprinted the first volume, *Swann's Way*. Bennett and Don now controlled exclusive rights to all U.S. editions, and he told Gallimard that RH would publish a new four-volume set that fall, with fancy Deco bindings and slipcase. They'd relaunch with fanfare—having learned lessons from *Ulysses*—and felt sure they could attract a wider audience, including many who'd bought Joyce. His instinct proved right: Proust's novel paid off in edition after edition for RH and American readers, and Bennett would come to consider it "one of the most successful projects" of his first fifteen years in business.

After finishing at Gallimard, he and Harold headed to a celebratory luncheon with the Joyces at Helen and Giorgio's flat, where secretary Paul Léon and two friends were also present. Joyce showed "rare good humor," pleased not least by Bennett's promise to pay $7,500 in royalties two months early. It was "most delightful," yet a nice irony winked back at the two publishers: RH had jumped when Viking demurred, gaining *Ulysses* glory; but Viking held the rights to Joyce's so-called "Work in Progress" *Finnegans Wake,* and there was nothing RH could do about it.

That night, Bennett and Harold met at the Gare de Lyon. Trains carried them through France and Italy to Brindisi on the heel of the boot,

When reprinted in *PW* courtesy of Donald on May 26, 1934, the caption spoke of "Mr. Cerf with his arm around his long-lost son, Bennett Cerf Jr. . . ."

where they boarded a "flying boat" to cross the Mediterranean. They marked their sojourn in Egypt by arranging for several desert photographs worthy of silent movie sheikhs. Sunburnt and seated in an elaborate tent, their leather wing tips poked only slightly incongruously from beneath Bedouin robes. Soon it was on to Palestine, where they settled into the three-year-old, already-famous King David Hotel. Their guide was an old friend of Harold's mother, Mrs. Judah Magnes, whose husband, an American rabbi, was chancellor of the Hebrew University. Palestine had a quarter million Jews under British Mandate; four hundred currently studied at the university her husband had helped found. Many spent their mornings helping to construct it, and took classes during the hot afternoons.

As he strolled the campus listening to Mrs. Magnes and observing what fellow Jews were creating, Bennett felt a strange sensation: such pride welled up in him that he was "thoroughly amazed." Another such moment occurred at the King David when he went down for a haircut. There was only one barber, who had a German in his chair; he spoke fluent German. After that client left, a Frenchman arrived; the barber spoke French. Bennett was next, and the man spoke "perfect English." Asked his nationality, the barber replied: "I am a Jew." Bennett never forgot his joy "at this man saying [it] so proudly."

Traveling to Tel Aviv, he and Harold saw that what had been desert twenty-five years earlier was now a modern city of 70,000. Everywhere, he met "alert, confident young Jews, their inferiority complex completely gone." After an "enlightening and thrilling ten days," he promised himself that he'd return. The young man who'd expressed contempt for the "Yum! Yum! chirp[ing] Hebes" (not to mention the Hebe in himself), had awakened to another kind of Jewish identity. "Sholom, Eretz Israel!" was the transliterated Hebrew farewell he wrote in his diary. He wouldn't shake off ambivalence entirely, and yet the difference was soon apparent.

In April 1936, co-publishing with the Time-Fortune magazine operation, RH rushed into print *Jews in America,* a slim book based on a recent *Fortune* survey. Delving into the history and prevalence of antisemitism and "common" prejudice, it took on the frequent remark "Oh, the Jews run everything" by analyzing what they *did* run—the majority of U.S. movie productions—and *didn't:* international banking and the legal and medical professions. In a publicity letter, Bennett declared: "Effective distribution" of the title could "squelch . . . a lot of the loose talk about 'the Jewish problem.'" Antisemitism was too entrenched in the United States to be "squelched" so easily, but the Palestine epiphany had made its way into his heart—and his publishing.

. . .

THE TRAVELERS MOTORED TO Tyre, Sidon, Beirut, and finally Damascus, where on their way to the station they saw two Arabs playing backgammon by the road. The hasty purchase of their "grubby" set made the next forty-seven hot, enervating train hours to Istanbul tolerable. After exploring the city's famous sites, they boarded a massive Soviet steamer to cross the Black Sea. Thirty-six hours later, the handsome limestone buildings of Odessa, long a cosmopolitan melting pot, emerged on the horizon, their first stop on Soviet soil. Minna Vinner, a pretty Intourist guide, met them at the dock and took them to a luxurious hotel where Bennett's room had a balcony, bath, and sea-front view.

"If Klopfer could only see me now!" he exulted to his diary. After being cooped up on the less-than-salubrious ship, a walk felt wonderful. On the broad boulevards, everyone looked decently dressed and fed, but the locals stared at him and Harold—so visibly foreign. There'd been talk about a terrible famine during the previous two years, but many had chosen not to believe it. That night, "very happy," Bennett could hardly wait for morning. A friend had provided an introduction to a Jewish bureaucrat, who early the next day led them on a dizzying round of visits to vocational schools and factories. All were Jewish, he explained in "good, old-fashioned Yiddish," adding that more than a third of Odessa citizens were Jews. These institutions taught former capitalist merchants a craft so they could take a "regular" job in a state industry. "There is no more 'Jewish question' in Russia: everyone is on precisely the same footing," went the litany.

The former Mr. Jesus Junior found it surprisingly easy to swallow, but then, Comrade Minna sweetened the propaganda as interpreter, factotum, and, almost immediately, his "girl." By the time Bennett and Harold left Odessa that night, it had been arranged for her to go with them, sailing to Sebastopol and motoring on to Georgia. On May 25, he rented a rowboat and in a secluded spot along the Black Sea coast, stripped to his birthday suit, and dived in, slim and strong. He turned thirty-six that day. In June, the travelers reached Moscow, where a telegram greeted Bennett: CERFURA SUNOVABICH ALWELLSKY HERE DONALD. Alice Guinzburg joined her husband and quickly sized up the situation between Bennett and Comrade Minna.

Publishing business intervened to distract him. Received by the head of Russia's book-importing trust, Bennett and Harold "swooned" at figures quoted that were so much larger than back home: 17,000 bookstores; a 2.5 million print run for Stalin's speeches. He squirreled away statistics for a piece he'd agreed to write for *PW:* doing two things at once had become a habit. "This is a chapter from a book to be called 'The Last Cerf in Russia,'" he'd joke, adding that after two and a half days collecting information, he'd become "a unique authority." But despite the tongue-in-cheek admission of limited knowledge, Bennett *was* treated as an expert on his return, courtesy of the article.

Strange but true, Harpo Marx had put him in touch with foreign minister Litvinov, whose English wife invited them to the family dacha, and O'Neill connected them to Alexander Tairov, founder/director of Moscow's famed experimental Kamerny Theater: the troupe had performed four of Gene's plays. Although Tairov was away, his male secretary tended to Bennett, who was growing more and more convinced that "the Soviet is on the way to tremendous things." But he also saw the cost: that its people were "making a religion" of martyrdom. "I'm damned if I am unselfish enough to sacrifice my whole life for poops of the future," he admitted. After a heart-to-heart with Alice, he knew that he wasn't prepared to sacrifice too much for Miss Minna, either. They'd had fun, but it was time to part. He bought her a new wardrobe, promised to write, and sent her on a "tearful" return to Odessa. (He did write for a time.) Her official report on this important foreigner (whom her boss may well have encouraged her to "befriend") could hardly have specified every single thing that they'd done together.

Leningrad—formerly St. Petersburg—was the last stop. Tairov and his troupe were there, performing *All God's Chillun Got Wings*. O'Neill's play portrayed the evils of capitalist America's racism, and was therefore guaranteed a good turnout in the Palace of Culture (it helped that most in the audience were workers, who'd received free tickets). That it was in Russian didn't matter to Bennett: the performance still worked magic. But dining afterward in Leningrad's fanciest hotel, he had to work hard to keep up with Tairov and the other actors until 3 A.M. almost entirely in his high school French.

He'd told his diary how "torn" he felt: full of admiration for the regime's plans and achievements and the amazing people he met, but then "rubbing shoulders with the dear old proletariat" and "recoiling in disgust." That night, the scent wafting through the theater had been sweat. Alone, he walked off the meal and the linguistic acrobatics while passing palaces eerie in the light of a Leningrad "White Night." Sleep eluded him, so he finished Aldous Huxley's *Brave New World*—an interesting choice in the circumstances.

On June 13, his last day, he got mail from New York. Donald gleefully wrote that he'd forwarded the Egyptian desert photo Bennett had sent him to *PW,* where it had already appeared. He'd have to suffer the kidding back home. Unfortunately, Harold had contracted chicken pox, so Bennett flew alone to Helsinki. The several hours that he had to kill before continuing to Stockholm were "among the happiest I have ever had," he realized, being back "where men wore collars and ties . . . shops had real goods in their windows," and a "mysterious weight was lifted." Three and a half weeks of "incessant propaganda" would affect just about anyone's thinking, he told himself, having reached two conclusions: first, many features of the Russian experiment were so clearly right, he was all for incorporating them into the U.S. system. Yet the basic concept—a "horrible leveling" of people into "one undistinguished . . . systematized mass"—was not for him. In Helsinki, "filthy capitalist Cerf" felt very relieved to be back in "a filthy capitalist world."

Pop had insisted on meeting "Sonny" in Stockholm. They galloped through Denmark, Holland, Belgium, and crossed to Britain, where Bennett made the publishing rounds. On July 13, when the *Aquitania* sighted Miss Liberty with one committed capitalist publisher on board, he was happy, after three months away, to be back home.

. . .

DESPITE THE HIATUS FROM RH, he easily slipped back in charge. He and Don were forging relationships with the better agents, trawling magazines for fresh voices, and leveraging ever-widening connections seeking talent. Saxe Commins had grown indispensable, and they depended on a cadre of readers to sift through submissions. As at Liveright, a reader could be a staffer whose designated job was different: Belle Becker, for example, had arrived in 1930 as receptionist, but between greeting guests and answering the phone, she started helping Saxe read proofs. Soon she shared his office, reading manuscripts and writing reports. Belle eventually became an editor, but never a senior one, being a woman in a man's club. Other readers—some authors in their own right—worked freelance. One manuscript might merit reports from two or three, but another would be judged on a report from only one. In the end, however, the partners knew their own minds.

Any list is a blend of taste, judgment, and luck. In April 1935, stories arrived from a twenty-two-year-old unknown. One reader saw promise but was concerned they might not "string together," and felt the author was "very young" to be so disillusioned. Stories were more difficult to sell than first novels, and no one knew if the writer would produce a novel with some financial success. The decision was that John Cheever posed too big a risk. (Two months later, he'd publish his first story in *The New Yorker*.) Before decade's end, RH's rejection file also included Elizabeth Bishop, Bertolt Brecht, Karel Čapek, Martha Gellhorn, Anaïs Nin, Flann O'Brien, and Jean Rhys.

A few years after commenting on Cheever, the same reader reported on a British author's "profoundly pessimistic" tales of life in Germany. RH had rejected his previous book, before it was brought out by a rival at a loss. The reader predicted another financial flop, yet thought the

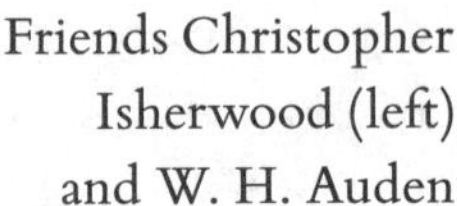
Friends Christopher Isherwood (left) and W. H. Auden

author showed "more talent . . . than any contemporary" he'd recently read. Belle Becker advocated for publication and a third reader agreed, provided the print run was small. Thus, Christopher Isherwood's *Goodbye to Berlin* was published (decades later, it would inspire the musical *Cabaret*). Bennett and Don had already introduced Isherwood's poet friends and compatriots W. H. Auden and Stephen Spender to the United States; collections by two more, Louis MacNeice and Cecil Day Lewis, followed.

Bennett's liberal sympathies had led him to court another Brit, John Strachey, an old Etonian former Labour MP who'd broken with his class to become the U.K.'s most influential Marxist writer: *The Coming Struggle for Power* and *The Menace of Fascism* were essential reading. Hoping to persuade Strachey to reprint in the ML and publish new titles with RH, Bennett promised a $1,000 advance on a multi-book contract. "We could do more for you than any other publisher in America," he urged. Strachey signed on.

Story, the magazine that Bennett, Don, and BOMC's Harry Scherman had bought from Whit Burnett and his wife, Martha Foley, was also expected to generate talent for RH. In February 1934, it published "The Daring Young Man on the Flying Trapeze," a short work by William Saroyan, a twenty-five-year-old Armenian American, that turned out to be a spectacular debut. Borrowing Joyce's stream-of-consciousness style, he used his immigrant-rich, Depression-spare American voice to take his protagonist—a jobless, unnamed San Francisco writer, literally starving to death—through the motions of his final day. The character's mind teemed with *Huckleberry Finn, Hamlet,* and other library treasures, even as coffee and cigarettes could no longer stave off the pain of a body about to collapse. Death came, yet the story affirmed the power of life and literature.

Bennett immediately wrote to see if Saroyan was working on a novel; he was, and congratulated RH for producing *Ulysses* and *Story* so beautifully. Though Knopf, Covici-Friede, and Harrison Smith were also vying to sign him, Saroyan said that because Random was backing *Story,* he'd rather have Bennett as his publisher than anyone else. Set on his first book being a story collection—he'd written plenty—he didn't want an advance. All he needed was "a good page, a good print, and a good binding," and in a five-page torrent of type, he laid out a plan for RH to publish all his work, forever and ever, amen. The confidence, cockiness, and cascade of verbiage were an indication of what lay ahead.

William Saroyan

That hectic April day before leaving on his grand tour, Bennett had rushed a contract to the young writer, insisting he at least receive a hundred-dollar advance, and specifying an option on his next three books. He'd already said that the proposed title, *27 Stories,* was "no good at all." Though not given to taking advice, Saroyan listened: it would be called *The Daring Young Man on the Flying Trapeze and Other Stories,* to reference his attention-getting debut. Devising titles would be one of Bennett's special strengths.

The RH team soon discovered how demanding and impulsive Saroyan was. He kept wanting to add new stories and rewrite others in proofs. Fully a third of the book was expensively reset. He also had definite ideas about good and bad design. Don had to educate him on financial realities, and on the author's primary responsibility: to submit the best possible manuscript in the first place. Nevertheless, Saroyan was a rare catch, and once back in New York, Bennett was delighted to tell him that T. S. Eliot and Frank Morley, who jointly ran Faber & Faber, would publish the collection in Britain. The sale into important New York stores Bennett would handle personally, as well as orchestrate advertising and publicity. He'd promised to make a beautiful book and it was, the jacket cleverly evoking a circus poster. Two weeks after mid-October publication, it was on the bestseller list in New York, with 4,000 copies in print.

"What a publisher: what a pal," Saroyan raved. He knew Bennett was giving his book every possible break.

Even if they didn't sell another copy, this was one of the happiest publishing experiences he'd had, Bennett assured Saroyan. His letters kept pace with his voluble author's, and just before Thanksgiving, Bennett proudly wrote that he'd signed the plays of the late J. M. Synge, including *The Playboy of the Western World,* "one of the greatest" ever written. That it had caused riots at its Dublin premiere might appeal to Saroyan, Bennett thought; and by saying that Synge added "one more important name to our list," he underscored his young author's own significance. Such epistolary conversation knitted relationships with the faith and attention writers need to thrive, but Bennett also craved *their* approbation. Securing the next book was always on his mind, but he also desperately wanted to be liked in the here and now.

A man capable of dictating sixty-five letters in a day, he kept fleet-fingered Pauline Kreiswirth—the secretary he shared with Don—busy. Having lured the "darling little rosy-cheeked kid" from B&L, he'd come to depend on her absolutely; her husband, Abe Friedman, had graduated from shipping clerk to accounts. Bennett also kept Pauline laughing: they were co-conspirators. One day he jokingly addressed her as "Jezebel," after the spoiled Southern belle played by his friend Miriam Hopkins on Broadway, and it stuck: "Jezebel" she became, but no one else was allowed to call her that to her face.

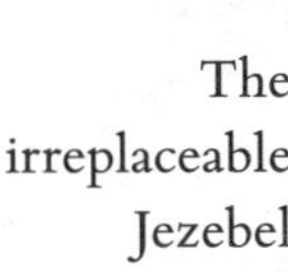

The irreplaceable Jezebel

By the end of December, 6,700 copies of *Daring Young Man* had been sold, a terrific showing. In true Liveright fashion, Bennett had invested heavily to launch a new writer. He'd sent out 600-plus review copies—a rare number—and advertised generously. Years later, he also remembered working to seed columns with anecdotes spun liberally from his own imagination. Saroyan boasted about "getting by with murder on what is carelessly known as my personality," and Bennett capitalized on it. One tale had his author taking his copies onto the Oakland–to–San Francisco ferry, buttonholing strangers about the book, and selling them all. (People accept this sort of fabrication about themselves if it shows them "in an amusing or friendly light," Bennett explained.)

Buying *Story* had brought the luck of landing Saroyan, but by the summer of 1935, Bennett, Don, and Harry Scherman decided to sell the magazine. Under them, circulation had increased, but they weren't able to grow the all-important advertising base. Losses spoke louder than prestige and a happy hunting ground for new talent; besides, they'd made their find. When the handsome wunderkind had visited New York in 1934, Bennett thought him "amazing," full of antic energy—but also a large ego. "I am a great writer," Saroyan had boasted. Bennett was taken with this "wild" man who'd told readers to be "wholly alive," because "You will be dead soon enough," a bit of his own philosophy. After meeting again in 1935, Bennett wrote: "To hell with this author-publisher relationship. I have the feeling [we] are real friends now. Or am I crazy?"

But antic could become manic and overpowering, like too-strong wine. Saroyan pushed RH to do a new collection too quickly, and with a much larger advance; it didn't sell like the first, or recoup its advance. When he pressed for a third, Bennett advised patience, but his own began to wear thin. Anger replaced jokes after Alfred Knopf and Dick Simon told him Saroyan had approached each of them with the book RH had declined. Bennett reminded him RH had an option on the next work; in the summer of 1936, Saroyan submitted a "new" collection. Some of its stories had already been rejected.

Bennett had had enough. "When I think of what you could do . . . I could scream with rage," he wrote in September, telling Saroyan that the option had been satisfied and he'd have to find a new publisher. The relationship between the "real friends" would never recover, and although Saroyan would win a Pulitzer for his play *The Time of Your Life* in 1940, and his novel *The Human Comedy* would garner great reviews in 1943 (one was from Bennett), critical consensus holds that his promise was never entirely fulfilled.

. . .

ANOTHER YOUNG BAY AREA writer had also piqued Bennett's interest, but while Saroyan may have thought too much of himself, twenty-two-year-old Tillie Lerner thought too little. In July 1934, just after his grand tour, Bennett sent Lerner a query letter about a novel extract he'd read in the *Partisan Review*. Impressed by it, he asked to see the rest of the manuscript. He'd also written to Saroyan, requesting a favor: Could he possibly contact Lerner, and check her out? She was a committed Communist, and, his head still echoing with Soviet propaganda, Bennett was sympathetic to her ideals. He also very much wanted to introduce a young woman writer onto the list. Saroyan did meet her. It turned out Lerner had written three-quarters of the novel at nineteen, but then struggled with menial jobs, bad health, and a baby. She liked Bennett's letter, what Saroyan said about him, and especially appreciated his role in the ML, "the main book factor" in her education, having dropped out of high school after one year to go to work.

Other publishers had also expressed interest, but a Macmillan salesman—a friend of a friend of Lerner's husband—got there first. Lerner had contracted pneumonia and was desperate for cash; when the salesman visited her sickbed with a $250 check and promised another if she published with his company, she took the check and signed an acknowledgment of its receipt as "an advance on a contract."

Refusing to think of himself as poaching, Bennett insisted that such a document, signed when she had a 103-degree fever, wasn't valid, and set about proving that a bastion of "conservatism" like Macmillan—"the colossus of American publishing"—wouldn't suit her. A publisher had to go after a book "hammer and tongs and believe in it fervently," he argued, promising he'd do a lot more than Macmillan. After coaching her on how to extricate herself without going to court—telling her to inform Macmillan's president that her novel was "unashamedly Communistic"—she ended up with RH.

Bennett matched the Macmillan money, but then she needed more, and he sent an additional five hundred dollars. By late May 1935, she couldn't pay her rent, and he agreed to another two hundred: ten dollars a week for twenty weeks. Chapters soon stopped coming. Bennett met Lerner in California that fall and understood her misgivings about the manuscript, but also that she'd been devoting too much time to political organizing. The odd letter was exchanged over the next few years, but she divorced, remarried, bore more children, and was busy with daily life. Thinking that the novel was "too lousy," she declined to proceed, even though Bennett pleaded for her to send the remainder and let RH decide. It wasn't until 1961 that Lippincott published a book of linked stories, *Tell Me a Riddle,* under her married name, Tillie Olsen, and she became a heroine to many in the burgeoning feminist movement for portraying working-class women's lives as they were. In 1974, Delacorte brought out the novel that Bennett had contracted, even though it remained unfinished.

Not every bet pays off. Two of Saroyan's three best books were not published by Random House, and the firm had to write off its advance to Lerner. Yet in both cases, Bennett's instincts had been right.

Chapter 13

Glamour Girls

La Grande Gertrude Stein

IN MAY 1933, WHEN THE *ATLANTIC MONTHLY,* ONE OF THE OLDEST literary magazines in America, began serializing sections of a book by Gertrude Stein that Harcourt would publish four months later, O'Neill hadn't yet signed with RH, and the fate of *Ulysses* remained undecided. Stein's writing had confounded readers even more than Joyce's novel had, yet she and Bennett would soon forge an unusual publishing partnership.

Thirty years earlier Stein had settled in Paris, where she and her brother Leo became patrons of Matisse, Picasso, and other avant-garde artists. Long before many did, the siblings recognized genius in the work that soon filled their home, and Gertrude set out to fashion an equivalent modern art in poetry and prose. Most was printed through vanity presses, and sales were sickly. Her social life, however, was wonderfully robust. The apartment and studio she soon shared with Alice B. Toklas—the life partner who displaced Leo—had become a salon, fizzing with the energy of artists and writers (the young Ernest Hemingway was a protégé), and propelling her to celebrity for *being* Gertrude Stein, the best-known American expatriate in Paris.

Still, she hungered for literary immortality, to be lauded for her writing as well as her person, and that eluded her. A case in point: for fourteen years, she'd repeatedly failed to place work in *The Atlantic.* Sorely needing money, she'd tried again during the winter of 1932–33, this time with a full-length manuscript created in six weeks and unlike anything she'd sent before. Surprised by the material, the editors agreed to publish more than half of it in installments, and as soon as the first part reached readers, mystification gave way to pleasure. *The Autobiography of Alice B. Toklas*—all about Stein, but written in the guise of her companion—was in prose they could understand, with only the thinnest veneer of her usual impenetrable style. Gossipy and sly, it was as though she'd opened the gates to her private world, mingling amusing tidbits about now-famous friends with deliciously disloyal, cutting comments settling old scores. (Reactions of Matisse, Hemingway, and Leo ranged from shock to fury.) Self-serving, not exactly "true"—what autobiography is?—it was brilliant storytelling and caused a sensation.

Bennett noticed, encouraged by his friend Carl Van Vechten, a novelist and longtime Stein familiar. Van Vechten was a man-about-town and a switchboard; as a frequenter of Harlem and a married bisexual, he helped link gay and straight, Black and white New York. His focus had recently turned to photography, and Don and Bennett had posed for him. Two chiaroscuro portraits stand out, unlike any taken of Bennett by anyone else. His face, half hidden, is unreadable, as though Van Vechten can't figure out who this man really is—or, perhaps, is trying to capture a defining duality.

He urged the partners to reprint Stein's previous works, and they soon signed a trio of early stories, *Three Lives,* for the ML. Bennett cautioned her agent, William Bradley, that "Miss Stein is still caviar for the masses," so not to expect a big sale, but they had a plan. Saving money by reusing the old plates, they freshened the package with an introduc-

A defining duality

tion by Van Vechten and a bold blue "cubist" cover by *Ulysses* designer Ernst Reichl. Bennett's promotional copy didn't deny her reputation for obscurity, but connected the stories to the accessible author of the *Autobiography*. In the end, it all worked to make the launch a "tremendous success," he wrote her in October 1933, adding that the book was arousing more comment than any new ML title of the past two years. Within weeks of publication, Macy's had bought an "astonishing" 1,200 copies.

Bennett next floated the idea of reissuing Stein's most substantial (and cryptic) novel, *The Making of Americans,* but Harcourt had already agreed to do an abridged edition. Instead, she suggested collecting older pieces into another ML volume, or publishing the libretto she'd written five years earlier for *Four Saints in Three Acts,* an opera composed by Virgil Thomson. Though Bennett thought it too soon for a second collection, there was growing excitement about *Four Saints*. Van Vechten had toured Thomson around Harlem nightspots, inspiring the radical decision to secure an all-Black cast. It would have its U.S. premiere in February in Hartford, to coincide with a major Picasso exhibit there. Bennett agreed to publish *Four Saints* as a Random House book—"the imprint just used" for *Ulysses,* he told Stein. Once the opera left Hartford for New York, her profile shone brighter still: her name was in Broadway lights, where it would remain for the two months of the opera's run. "Gertrude Stein's strange and baffling prose cadences provide a challenge to reader and publisher alike. Random House accepts the challenge," Bennett's blurb said on the dust jacket. His author was delighted.

Early in his travels with Harold, a desire to meet this legend in Paris had to be satisfied. After his lunch with the Joyces, he went around the corner to take tea with Miss Toklas and Miss Stein at 27 rue de Fleurus. He found himself in another world, encircled by countless modern masterpieces. Stein, "very pleasant and very voluble," reminded him of another formidable female whom he'd succeeded in charming, novelist and playwright Edna Ferber. "Gerty," as he called her in his diary and in letters to others (but would never dare do to her face), had her own agenda: to sell him four or five hundred remaining copies of works she'd self-published under the imprint Plain Edition. While "Miss Toklas' imposing mustachio quivered with emotion," he promised to think on it.

By now, it was clear that Americans were terribly curious about "the Mama of Dada," as the press called her (she preferred to view herself as the first genuine twentieth-century writer). People knew of the closeness with Hemingway and the paintings; they knew "a rose is a rose is a rose" and the reputation for inscrutability, and how she artfully exploded it in the *Autobiography*. They wanted to see this phenomenon in (her rather substantial) person, but Stein hadn't set foot in her homeland for thirty years. Her agent had realized that lectures could be highly remunerative and began to plan a U.S. tour, but she resisted, and soon dropped him. Yet money *was* a lure, and in Paris an intimate, Bernard Faÿ, who'd translated the *Autobiography* into French, argued that lecturing would truly enable her to disseminate her ideas. In the end, Faÿ and a Connecticut newspaperman, W. G. Rogers—whom Stein befriended when he was fighting in the Great War—managed to cajole her. That summer, she began preparing talks on "What Is English Literature," "Pictures," "Plays," and three other topics. Orchestrating publicity was Bennett's purview, and he invoked the same kind of relationship he'd described to O'Neill and would routinely promise others: "How happy we would be to become the American publisher of all of your books." Though "all" likely didn't include her *most* obscure works, he was eager to bring out a book of her lectures to coincide with the tour.

The production schedule was tight. Bennett tried his persuasive best to make her work quickly, even agreeing to relieve her of her Plain Edition problem. Not wanting to tarnish her reputation by disposing of those books with remainder brokers, he'd use the tour to inspire demand among the likeliest stores, with all revenues going to Stein, taking care of it "as a friend," knowing that friends usually reciprocate. It soon became clear, however, that *Lectures in America* wouldn't be delivered to RH in time. Instead, she would submit a quick collection of word portraits of Picasso, Van Vechten, and others, that could appear at the tour's start. It was absolutely imperative, Bennett told her, for Don to go to press on September 25. He vowed to make *Portraits and Prayers,* as the volume would be called, handsome, and promised a window display in every New York bookstore.

"I know I can trust to you to have it all carefully supervised," Stein replied. "I know you will make a pretty book . . . and that too pleases me." The last day of September, her trip only weeks away, she wrote again: "I am full of anticipation and a little frightened but that is inevitable but full of anticipation."

. . .

ON A FINE, CLEAR, late-October morning, the SS *Champlain* reached New York Harbor and headed for a berth on the Hudson at Fifteenth Street. Standing on the dock, Bennett and Van Vechten watched for the ship to glide into view. Earlier, a posse of reporters Bennett had corralled had packed into a government cutter and boarded the *Champlain* while the liner was still in the bay, come to interview Miss Stein. They sat in chairs and on tabletops or squatted on the floor in a lounge, pencils ready. Were they bent on making fun of her? Surely some were. Square and steady in brown tweed suit, close-fitting "Robin Hood" cap, and sensible shoes, she had the chiseled face and cropped hair of a Roman senator. Toklas, a thin gray mouse in a fur-trimmed cloak, gazed "raptly" at her side. Some reporters had done homework, and intoned examples of Stein's more perplexing sentences. In reply, she explained that she'd returned "to tell very plainly and simply and directly, as is my fashion, what literature is." The atmosphere shifted. She was "normal and intelligent . . . born legitimate of two respectable parents," she assured them.

"Why don't you write the way you talk?" one inquired.

"Oh, but I do," she responded. "After all it's all learning how to read it."

Her sixty years and massive bulk didn't diminish the power, as Hemingway once said, of her "beautiful eyes" and "mobile face." Nor did the "constant chuckle in her throat" or keen intelligence fail to impress. "You see and you hear and you have got to know the difference," she said in a voice imbued with the resonance and diction of a great stage actress. "It's very difficult to know how much you hear when you see and see when you hear. The business of writing is to find the balance in your own inside." She avoided talk of politics—some of her views about Hitler's accomplishments in Germany had already caused a stir. She also deftly handled the presence of Toklas, describing her as her "secretary," who "makes life comfortable."

The artist's business "is to be exciting," Stein had told Rogers, and she was. After an hour of "parry and riposte," she left the lounge and proceeded to the deck with Alice, to pose for pictures. As her dark eyes took in the Statue of Liberty, she felt greatly moved to be reentering her native land. The liner eased into the dock, and the two women descended the gangplank. Bennett and Van Vechten, now joined by a Stein cousin from Baltimore, were waiting. The next morning, *The New York Times* would proclaim: "Gertrude Stein Arrives and Baffles Reporters by Making Herself Clear."

The greeters and their guests drove to the Algonquin Hotel, where Stein and Toklas had a three-room suite. A gaggle of noisy reporters tagged along. During lunch, Bennett found himself slipping under her spell, "literally [falling] in love . . . [with] one of the most wonderful women I ever met." The Buddha-like lesbian of the inscrutably modern text and the playboy publisher of the incessantly proffered pun may have seemed an unlikely pair, yet they shared certain traits: an American talent for self-reinvention, a hunger for adulation, and loads of charm. About the same age Bennett's mother would have been, Stein was in many ways her opposite. Frieda Cerf had been sickly and insecure; Gertrude—as he now addressed her—was energetic and larger-than-life. To the precious, indulged only son, strong, accomplished women who could take him in hand and not take him too seriously—Bea Kaufman, Ferber, Stein—were appealing. And he wasn't alone. A *New Republic* profile judged Stein to be as "striking as Stonehenge," and as "hypnotic as a Yogi," with a charisma that caught both men and women off guard.

In her suite, they reviewed arrangements. The first talk, sponsored by the Museum of Modern Art, would occur in just over a week, followed by three at Columbia and a Manhattan merry-go-round of lunches, dinners, interviews, and parties, before the real work of crossing the country began. That evening, thanks to Bennett, Pathé would film the pair for newsreels that preceded the feature at theaters nationwide. After he and Carl left, the women took a walk, and many recognized them. In Times Square, Toklas saw the electric ribbon running along the Times Building. "Gertrude Stein has arrived in New York, Gertrude Stein has arrived in New York," it proclaimed. "As if we did not know it," she thought, finding herself in this *other* city of light, so different from the one she'd left, a crowded bustling place that scared her but also drew her in. As for Stein, she was delighted, a great need fulfilled. "They all know me and I know all of them, that is so comfortable and so comforting," she wrote in a piece for *Cosmopolitan*—a lucrative $1,700 commission arranged by Bennett. She'd give him the manuscript, and write: "For Bennett, who is so nicely spoiled and so nicely spoils."

They knew her, but the next day it turned out not quite everyone *recognized* her. When Stein and Toklas arrived for their appointment with Bennett at 20 East Fifty-Seventh Street, the elevator man—seeing two women in late middle age wearing heavy foreign clothes, one with closely cropped hair, the other sprouting it all-too-visibly above her lip, didn't bother to ask their destination: he took them straight to the Swedish Maids Employment Bureau. Bennett soon was worried: They were late. Were they lost? When the duo finally made their way to RH's reception desk, Gertrude, seemingly unfazed by the mix-up, was roaring with laughter. Bennett made sure the newspapers heard about it.

Everyone wanted to meet "the Sybil of Montparnasse." Bennett introduced her to his blonde, brilliant old flame Miriam Hopkins, riding high at Paramount. Hopkins thought her wonderful, and Stein was soon amused to have a movie star running her errands: she ordered *everybody* around. She also disarmed them. Bennett never saw a woman enjoy life more, or be a better sport. Years later, when he mimicked a rival's *PW* ad depicting a sexy bestselling author, he knew she'd enjoy the joke. "Shucks, we've got glamour girls too!" proclaimed the copy on his next Stein ad, featuring a photo of Gertrude and Alice.

When the critic Alexander Woollcott insisted on a private meeting with the illustrious visitor, Bennett obliged with a lunch in his apartment. Woollcott began perorating, as was his fashion, but Stein announced, "Mr. Woollcott, I am talking." He shut up, and conversation resumed. Stein disagreed with him several times.

"People don't dispute Woollcott," Woollcott informed her.

Glamour indeed

"I'm not people," came the reply. "I'm Gertrude Stein."

Woollcott dissolved in laughter; two days later, he touted her on his radio show.

On Armistice Day, Bennett invited Herbert, his Columbia mentor Raymond Weaver and his partner John Burrell, and Miriam to dine with Gertrude, Alice, Don, and himself: a happy camaraderie mixing different worlds. Another day, after a Ritz Towers luncheon in their honor, he drove the women around Manhattan, showing off his ultra-modern "Wonder City" from the Holland Tunnel to the George Washington Bridge. But Stein hadn't returned to sightsee. There to lecture and make money, she was such a hot ticket that even before her first talk almost every New York event had sold out. She'd insisted each lecture have a maximum audience of five hundred, but *Herald Tribune* reporter Joseph W. Alsop Jr. thought fully a thousand had packed the Colony Club. It was curious, he noted, that even though many had come to stare, there was a quality of affection: "They liked Miss Stein at first sight, whether they liked what she said or no." The New York *Sun* was more succinct: "Miss Stein [was] a Wow."

A week after the Colony lecture, *Portraits and Prayers* was published. That afternoon, escorted by Toklas and Van Vechten, Stein was exhilarated to take her very first flight, destination Chicago, to hear *Four Saints* conducted by Thomson at a benefit. Back in New York five days later, she was interviewed on the NBC Radio Network. Bennett had set it up and did the on-air introduction. Years later, in his oral history, he evoked the Radio City studio scene: "Gertrude Stein, here you are on a coast-to-coast hook-up," he began. This was her chance to explain her writings. As he'd told her, he was very proud to be her publisher, but confessed: "I don't understand very much what you're saying."

"Well, I've always told you, Bennett, you're a very nice boy but . . . rather stupid."

Stein had indeed said something like it—"dumb" instead of "stupid"—but he'd transposed the memory: she'd done so, hand on his shoulder and voice "rather pitying," in the privacy of her suite, as he reminded her in a letter the next year. He'd been caught off guard and stung, was unsure what to think, but decades later, had turned it into a public joke—on himself.

Traveling to thirty universities during the next half year, Stein was feted all over. She took tea with Eleanor Roosevelt at the White House; called on F. Scott Fitzgerald in Baltimore; had lunch with Sherwood Anderson in New Orleans; partied with Charlie Chaplin in Beverly Hills; was interviewed for the University of Texas paper by a student named Walter Cronkite. Periodically, she'd circle back to check in with Bennett over a meal. She also sent letters, writing from Indianapolis to the "nicest of editors." In that letter, Toklas's postscript included fond thoughts for both partners, but asked Bennett to keep mum about "a beautiful and messed up Vassar girl" (by strange serendipity, they'd met the ex–Mrs. Klopfer). "I hope you are remembering that the only male that you are allowed to kiss in this country is myself. To hell with the rest," Bennett delighted in replying to Stein.

. . .

THE LAST DAY OF 1934, after dinner and theater with Dick Simon, Bennett wound up at a New Year's Eve party in the townhouse of Nell Farnol and her husband, Lynn, who headed publicity for movie mogul Sam Goldwyn. He hadn't meant to attend, having agreed to squire a lady friend elsewhere, but another invitee, Richard Halliday, an acquaintance in Paramount's story department, phoned to say he'd regret it if he didn't stop in. Halliday offered a curious inducement: his own date, a Paramount actress. He knew Bennett had followed her progress for four years, since seeing her in a play titled *Bad Girl*. Its plot involved premarital sex and pregnancy, and caused such a scandal that the police were summoned and the show "cleaned up." The moment she walked on stage in a yellow raincoat, Bennett felt stunned: she was the most beautiful girl he'd ever seen, and he vowed to meet her. And so, that New Year's Eve, he and his lady friend dropped by. The "bad girl" shimmered like a mirage across the crowded room, her black evening dress alight with small silver stars. Halliday guided him toward her, so small-boned and slim.

"Mr. Cerf, this is Mrs. Cerf," Halliday said with a flourish, right out of a script.

Overcome, all Bennett managed was "Glad to meet you" before rushing away. The next hour, careful not to stray into her path, he was equally careful to orbit around her. The time came to reclaim his date and head for another party. It was a last chance: at least he could say goodbye. "It's been a great pleasure meeting you," he declared.

"You're the strangest young man I ever met in my life," she replied. For the past couple of years, she'd heard about this publisher who longed to meet her. Now they'd done so, and "you never say one word."

"Well . . . I've just been so dazzled. . . . But if you'd like me to tell you every move you have made . . . I can because I've never taken my eyes off you."

"Don't you think I know that?"

They walked out together, leaving their respective dates to look after themselves.

He arrived home at 5:30 A.M., noting in his diary, "Finis to a fine & exciting year." As for the Farnols' party, it was "chiefly distinguished by the fact that, just as 1935 rang in, I finally met Sylvia Sidney."

. . .

FIVE FEMALE STARS REIGNED in the Paramount firmament: Claudette Colbert, Marlene Dietrich, Miriam Hopkins, Carole Lombard, and Sylvia Sidney. Below a sleek head of dark bobbed hair, Sidney wasn't conventionally pretty, but a canvas of contrasts: heart-shaped face with large forehead, wide cheekbones, small tilted nose, full lips, huge gray-green eyes—one marred by a dark fleck, in which she took pride. Contradictions defined her: her voice could be tremulous or tough; she could play sophisticated or pure. Though seemingly waif-like, she had a lovely figure, and in makeup radiated a timeless glamour. The only major female star who was Jewish, she also looked a bit like Marian.

The "dazzling" Sylvia Sidney

At twenty-four a dozen years younger than Bennett, she was born Sophia Kosow to Russian Romanian immigrants in the Bronx. Her parents divorced when she was nine, and her mother "married up" to a dentist surnamed Sidney. The girl dreamed of acting and left school to study at the Theater Guild. Making her debut in 1926, she was cast in play after play. In 1927 she appeared briefly on film, and signed with Fox for its third "talkie," *Thru Different Eyes,* but she didn't like Hollywood and returned to New York.

Bennett wasn't alone in being drawn to her. Adeline Schulberg and her powerful husband, Ben "B.P." Schulberg, Paramount's production chief, also saw *Bad Girl*. "Ad," later a prominent agent, urged B.P. to give Sidney a contract, and he did. In 1931, when "It Girl" Clara Bow pulled out of *City Streets,* Sidney replaced her, opposite Gary Cooper—whose career Schulberg had also guided—and became a star. She appeared in four more films that year. In one, Josef von Sternberg's take on *An American Tragedy,* she played the pregnant factory girl. Theodore Dreiser hated this movie of his novel, but approved of her performance. However, another thing factored into Sidney's rise. Schulberg was thirty-nine, a father of three, not averse to straying, and a gambler who could drop $50,000 a night. He gambled madly on her: soon everyone knew of the affair.

The Schulbergs were among the first to build in Malibu, a mile-long slice of beachfront carved between cliffs and ocean west of Los Angeles, now become a retreat for Hollywood's elect. By summer 1931, Sidney had a house there, too; her mother played chaperone. Budd Schulberg—at seventeen, the eldest of B.P.'s children—had overheard fights about the "little Kike hoor," and was outraged by his father's behavior. One day, driving on the coast road near Sidney's cottage, he pulled over, stopped the car, rushed up the path, and burst in. B.P., scotch highball in hand, stared in disbelief. Sidney and her mother froze. With the furious conviction of youth, Budd forced his father home to his mother. "Goddammit, you two stay together," he shouted. B.P. and Ad tried, but failed.

The films kept coming, giving Bennett dreamy communion with the fantasy girl on the picture palace screens. Everyone knew her haunting, vulnerable look that spoke to the nation's Depression woes. Sidney's role was mainly to suffer; Dietrich, Colbert, and Lombard got most of the romance and laughs. But as she enhanced her critical reputation, she was also marked as a temperamental prima donna. In the late summer of 1933, she walked off a set and headed for New York. "No, I am not going to marry B. P. Schulberg. I don't care if he is supposed to have been divorced," she told the papers. He *had* divorced, and together they sailed to Europe, but the next year, he was forced out of Paramount. The relationship with Sidney didn't survive: on October 15, 1934, B.P. informed the press that it was over. Signing with Walter Wanger, an independent producer, she hoped to trade sob sisters for literary roles; besides being talented, tough, and temperamental, she was a reader, with hundreds and hundreds of books at home.

That world of books was Bennett's. He'd parted from her before dawn on New Year's Day, but thirty hours later escorted Sylvia to lunch at the Stork. The next day, he commissioned a leading designer to revamp his bedroom. That Sunday, she was at his apartment, among intimates Raymond Weaver, Bea Kaufman, the Guinzburgs, and Herbert, lunching with Stein and Toklas. Utterly intoxicated with Sylvia, on Friday he put her on a train back to L.A., but was determined that they would see each other soon.

Fortuitously, he'd forged a Schulberg connection of his own. On a business trip to New England a few months earlier, Bennett had chanced upon a copy of the Dartmouth College paper and was impressed by a student's lead story about a strike in Vermont. It was bylined "Budd Schulberg," and he soon invited young Budd to lunch in New York. For January 28, the day they met, Bennett's diary contains a one-word question: "Incest?"

Years later, Budd couldn't remember if Sylvia came up. What he did recollect was feeling terribly self-conscious and shy, stuttering as usual, but gradually relaxing into his host's energetic friendliness. With his Hollywood background, friendly wasn't how he'd imagined a powerful publisher would be. Bennett asked what other material he had; it turned out he'd written stories. If he ever had a novel, Bennett told him he'd like to see it.

A week after lunching with Budd, Bennett journeyed to Paradise Beach in Nassau to meet Sylvia. For him, the tropical idyll would forever be linked to Proust. He'd read the first part of *Remembrance of Things Past* in Europe. Now, each night after she fell asleep, he read late, lost in the great writer's reflections on time, art, memory—and the follies of love. The romance ripened quickly. By mid-March she was back in L.A., and for a few months they spoke by phone, often in the small hours after midnight, intimacy heightened by distance, the time, and the power of separation. He also sent a stream of wires west. But however preoccupied, he managed to concentrate on business: reading Faulkner's new novel, *Pylon,* about a ménage à trois, just published by Smith & Haas (might he buy it for the ML?); visiting Gene and Carlotta O'Neill on Sea Island to discuss *A Touch of the Poet;* negotiating the ML contract for Thomas Mann's *Buddenbrooks*.

Finally, on May 25, a Saturday, Sylvia returned, the thirty-seventh birthday gift he'd longed for. Bennett met her plane that morning at Newark, and they drove for hours—north to lunch amid Storm King's beautiful highlands, down to West Point, and south again, to pretty country around Briarcliff. Bennett had redone his bedroom, but they didn't stay in his apartment on Central Park South; Sylvia opted for a suite at the Essex House down the block. Sunday afternoon, they crossed the street to stroll under the trees among the hoi polloi. Stares and smiles trailed her wherever they went. The next Thursday was Memorial Day, and on Wednesday night they drove east, heading for an inn at Montauk, on the end of Long Island. Thick fog closed around them and persisted the next morning, making a walk along the beach chill and strange. When it finally lifted, they went to the old lighthouse at the island's tip, where waves crashed into the rocky promontory. Whatever else they did that weekend went unrecorded.

During the next two months, he campaigned to win approval for this woman he was wild about, on a whirlwind of visits to friends. But on July 24, discord pierced the happy tune; scribbling angry symbols next to her name in his diary, Bennett complained of having to go "ALONE" to a dinner party at Don's, and the next day he admitted to being in a blue funk. In Deal with Don and Horace Manges for the weekend, he vainly tried to cure what ailed him with hours of "violent" exercise. Back at work, he took Clifford Odets to lunch to discuss his play *Paradise Lost*. That night, paradise was regained: Sylvia returned. It was good that they'd gotten over their squabble, since she had to go back to Hollywood on August 4. Two days later, they spoke, and afterward Bennett's diary exploded in capitals: "WE DECIDED THAT WE ARE ENGAGED!!!"

Writing to Gertrude a week later, he noted that he'd be flying to California the next month. Whether he'd return single was "very moot"; he sought her "wisdom" about it. In early September he and Sylvia finally agreed to tell the world. By then, Bennett craved its approbation, since he wasn't getting much from Pop, who found his fiancée careful, polite, driven—so different from adorable Miriam. When word got out, an avalanche of wires and calls provided reassurance. Sylvia had to finish a picture, *Mary Burns, Fugitive,* in L.A., and though both she and Bennett had roots in New York, eloping had come into vogue, and they decided to marry in Phoenix on October 1. He planned a leisurely honeymoon motoring up the Pacific coast to San Francisco. From there, they'd cruise to New York via the Panama Canal. He joked to Gertrude he'd be gone so long, the book business would face an absolute crisis. After convening a stag dinner at home on the Wednesday before the wedding, he took delivery of a Cartier diamond bracelet Friday, and drove to his uncle's Connecticut farm, spending his penultimate bachelor nights with three gay men—Herbert, Raymond Weaver, and John Burrell. He couldn't help scrawling in his diary: "GROWING EXCITEMENT."

Don dropped Bennett and Pop at the airport in Newark on Monday, where they met Sylvia's mother for a journey that turned out to be complicated by many stops: the trio didn't arrive in Phoenix until early the next morning. Sylvia fared worse: her plane from L.A. had to make a forced landing en route, and she got to Phoenix three hours late and jittery. Still, at the appointed hour, 11 A.M. on October 1, Judge Marlin T.

Phelps pronounced them man and wife at the Westward Ho Hotel. Yet Sylvia seemed rattled; she didn't *feel* married, and looking to Judge Phelps, asked: "Was that the whole ceremony?" He assured her it was, and told Bennett to kiss the bride. Trouble reared again when bad weather forced the chartered plane back to L.A. Totally spent by the time a car got them to her house in Beverly Hills, Bennett scribbled in his diary, "Sylvia is Mrs. Cerf!!!!!"—making it real—before collapsing into bed.

After one perfect day alone together, Hollywood intruded. Soon they were lunching with her new producer, Walter Wanger; touring Paramount; and posing for the press. They'd agreed that they'd live on two coasts: she'd act on Broadway as well as in front of cameras, while he had authors, booksellers, printers, and studios to cultivate in California. With so many writers coming to work on films, Bennett told reporters that a smart New York publisher would have to alternate trips between London and L.A. But not all was going as planned. Although Sylvia had worked like the pro she was to finish *Mary Burns* on time, Wanger took Bennett aside at the premiere to talk of a new project.

The Trail of the Lonesome Pine was a 1908 bestseller about the Hatfields and McCoys that had been made into a movie three times. Now the story would be adapted again, for the first film to be shot outdoors in Technicolor, a new technology. Tests had already been done at Big Bear in the San Bernardino mountains; how could Bennett ask her to forgo such an important picture for a honeymoon cruise? Basking in the reflected glow of her fame, he'd tried to laugh off its less pleasing aspects, but being Mr. Sylvia Sidney was forcing him to reckon with a very altered reality. She'd do the picture, he knew; but however hurt, to the world he would smile, and seek consolation in work.

He visited bookstores with his West Coast salesman; had drinks with Nathanael West (RH would publish *The Day of the Locust* in 1939); met with Saroyan and the Grabhorns; and especially enjoyed a day with poet Robinson Jeffers and his wife, Una, in Carmel. He also made rare visits to some of Nathan Wise's children and grandchildren who'd settled out West. The period that should have been his honeymoon passed, and on October 25 there were very few others on board the Santa Fe Chief when Bennett left for New York. As the train rumbled east collecting passengers, he played hearts, read, and felt hollowed out inside, during what truly was one of the loneliest times of his life.

A thousand clippings waited at RH: his was "one of the three most-talked-about" Hollywood nuptials of 1935. He phoned Sylvia at Big Bear that evening, then it was back to days and nights without her—but with just about everyone else, including Marian, who'd acquired a new husband. Despite an initial reluctance to go near a horse, Bennett began taking riding lessons to please Sylvia, and one weekend had a "swell" ride with Don and actress Mary Astor, former paramour of his friend George Kaufman. On Armistice Day, he wrote Mama Gertrude: "Having shaken the contaminating dust of Hollywood from my shoes [I] am very eager to get back into my stride," and hoped to send a long letter when affairs cleared up. Two weeks later, he flew west; it was Thanksgiving, and Sylvia had the weekend off. In Griffith Park they saddled up, and Bennett was pleased to be able to hold his own on a horse. He stayed six days.

Married life had been hectic with lots of ups and downs, he wrote Gertrude just before Christmas. There was too much to tell, but when he saw her in the spring, he'd recount an amusing tale of what it's like to be married to a famous moving picture star. "At any rate, I have been very happy and life has certainly been full," he added, donning his smiling face. Sylvia came east for Christmas, to a Savoy Plaza suite. Classical music was not his usual fare now, but Bennett accompanied her with Don and his date to Carnegie Hall and to the Metropolitan Opera, where Flagstad and Melchior sang of passionate love in *Tristan und Isolde*. The diary entry for New Year's Eve—anniversary of their electric meeting a year earlier—recorded no particular activity. He slept late as 1936 dawned, "with Sylvia Sidney (STILL!) Cerf." Ten days later, she left for L.A., and the diary announced: "GOODBYE, SYLVIA CERF!" The girl whom critics thought so gifted at capturing a "fragile happiness" on screen had found it too fragile to sustain with Bennett. She'd gone for good: the marriage was a mistake, and it was over.

Gertrude was alarmed: Bennett hadn't answered several letters. Fearing that she'd been slighted when her name wasn't on a list of authors RH advertised it was proud to publish, she also sensed that something was wrong in his personal life, and worried it was matrimony. She wrote again: "It will be nice if you are equal to everything and we do want you to be," she declared, "because Bennett you are made to be happy and if anybody is made to be happy there is no way to reconcile anyone to them not being so."

The day before Sylvia left, he finally dictated his reply in a confessional rush:

> You must be possessed of some psychic power. . . . This marriage, for which I had hoped so much, came to grief almost immediately . . . the sickening realization came that I had fallen in love with an illusion. . . . Sylvia is . . . a moving picture actress first, last and all the time . . . and I was to be a very minor part indeed of her life.
>
> We tried . . . to reconstruct something from the wreckage, but it seems . . . we can only make each other miserable now, so . . . are going to break the whole thing up. . . . It has all hurt a great deal and the publicity has been humiliating and cheap.
>
> . . . By the time I see you in France . . . I will be able to regard it . . . as a very interesting adventure that should have stayed an affair. . . . There! . . . this is the first—the very first time I have put . . . these thoughts . . . on paper.

Bennett publicly denied the split until the *L.A. Times* front page confirmed it on January 22. "There is no other man, no other woman," Sylvia had told the paper. He stayed silent, desperately trying to save face. As the AP reported, the jaunty young publisher had been the wonder of the hour on Broadway. With the breakup, hounded by gossips, he was even more so. "Dapper and unperturbed," he played the part well. Later, Sylvia opened up to columnist Sheilah Graham. They hadn't known enough about each other when they married to realize that their temperaments "hadn't a chance to click." Her living in Hollywood had nothing to do with it, nor her being an actress and Bennett a publisher. Indeed, that should have been ideal. Even when the romance had seemed in full flower, she'd pointedly told an interviewer: "I like going to bed early five nights a week, and my literary leanings aren't [toward] joke magazines." When "crabby," she didn't want to hide "behind a fixed grin." It's hard not to see each point as a rebuke, but Bennett, so much in love, couldn't or wouldn't do so. The highly social publisher and the star who hated parties and chitchat were impossibly matched.

On March 26, 1936, Sylvia Cerf filed for divorce, uncontested, alleging standard grounds: her husband had treated her in a cruel and inhuman manner, causing mental anguish and humiliation. He'd said they were "incompatible" and quarreled about her career. An interlocutory judgment of divorce was granted; she could resume using her maiden name. In late May, she wrote to B. P. Schulberg from London, where Alfred Hitchcock was directing her in *Sabotage*. Her letter, like so much that went before, reads like a movie script: "A wish and hope for a kind of beauty in living . . . we've been cheated of . . . except for a few glorious years . . . I know now . . . how desperately I loved you . . . we had a kind of grandeur." She'd marry and divorce twice more, and never stop acting.

Years later, Bennett confessed to Budd that Sylvia had told him of her feelings for B.P., "a tie that nobody could really break into." He'd also admit to the pain of being brought up short by reminders. The "bad part" was entering Times Square and seeing a flag three stories high, SYLVIA SIDNEY, or opening the paper to a ravishing photo. In time, when people asked about the marriage, his answer was a smile and a quip: "One should never legalize a hot romance." But for the rest of his life, when visitors came to the office, he'd occasionally open a desk drawer and remove something special to show them. It was a picture of Sylvia Sidney. The drawer was full of them.

. . .

WHILE BENNETT'S LOVE STORY with Sylvia was blazing into life, Donald had embarked on a romance of his own. One February afternoon in 1935, a stylish honey blonde with luminous blue eyes breezed into the office. Martha Dodd, twenty-six, confident, and flirtatious, fancied herself a writer. Fascinated by the great Russian authors, she was also, like many young people, attracted to socialism. After college, she'd joined the *Chicago Tribune* as an assistant literary editor, but her tenure was cut short when her father, William, a history professor at the University of Chicago with a Ph.D. from Leipzig, became U.S. ambassador to Germany: the family moved to Berlin. Now on a home visit, she was in New York to meet publishers, wanting a writing career.

Martha would later admit that when she first arrived in Berlin, she carried the ugly, "slightly anti-Semitic" baggage common to many Americans, believing that "Jews were not as attractive physically as Gentiles . . . and less socially presentable." Both Don and Bennett, however, seemed to make favorable impressions, and Martha had rather an impact on them: not quite beautiful, she was sexually magnetic. With Bennett about to rendezvous with Sylvia, Donald took Martha dancing to Eddie

Duchin's music at the Central Park Casino. She soon invited him to the family farm in Virginia, where passion was kindled in front of an accommodating fire. Too soon, she had to return to Europe.

Martha Dodd

That spring, it was Don's turn to go abroad while Bennett minded the firm. Now he wanted to see Russia for himself—after visiting Martha in Germany. Don cabled the office from Ukraine to say he was having a wonderful time. Bennett couldn't resist telling Francis Meynell that he'd been "particularly enthusiastic" about adventures in Berlin. At thirty-three, Don had fallen hard for the ambassador's daughter. He repeatedly wrote and cabled her, asking Martha to join his travels, or at least see him again in Berlin. He heard nothing. On June 10 in Istanbul, he tried one last time: "Darling . . . I fly to Athens . . . and sail for home . . . stopping at . . . Naples. . . . I'm just going to have to be the best damned publisher . . . and be content with that—womanless. You seem to have given me the air in a big way. I still love you, you little fool."

When he reached the Naples hotel, hope and persistence were rewarded by a letter and telegram from Martha. He'd had a lovely trip, he replied, at one point sailing past the volcanic island Stromboli, "red flames licking the top of the crater, and a full moon shining over the quietest sea you've ever imagined." If only she'd been there! "What made you not write? Where was your heart?" he asked, vowing to return to Berlin if he could arrange it. He loved her "deeply and honestly," and wanted her "unbelievably!" He couldn't change his booking, but Martha Dodd was a woman not easily forgotten.

One year later, it was just-divorced Bennett who sailed for Europe in the spring, combining business with the pleasure of pursuing a new love interest. In the strange way such things happened between them, he now carried the torch lit by Don and was intent on courting Martha. After the Marian triangle collapsed, both men had fancied Rosamond Pinchot. Now, as Donald's heartbreak was being assuaged by Pat Selwyn, a stylish divorcée whose family wealth came from owning Broadway theaters, Bennett felt free to go after Martha. They'd meet in Germany after he saw to business in London.

First came tea with George Bernard Shaw to convince "the old boy" to allow *Saint Joan* to be included in *The Theatre Guild Anthology* (he agreed, at a price). Stephen Spender would do a new book of verse. RH would have an option on Wystan Auden's next three prose works in addition to his poetry. Don, who loved poetry in a way Bennett did not, was "tremendously" pleased at Random securing Auden's future. He was far less sanguine, however, about Bennett's visit to Allen Lane—nephew of Bodley Head owner John Lane—who'd just started a separate firm to publish cheap paperbound reprints that he'd christened "Penguins." The partners had earlier sold the Lanes rights to some ML Giants and other titles, and been kept waiting and worrying for their money. Don neither liked nor trusted Allen Lane, joking that he should change the name of his series to "Ostriches" and predicting it would fail. Bennett viewed Lane's initiative far more positively; he, too, had wondered about publishing a really inexpensive line.

Though impatient for Martha, Bennett's English stay passed pleasantly, with weekends at Miriam Hopkins's recently acquired country house (adorned with a Picasso and a Derain she'd bought from Gertrude) and, rather oddly, a string of encounters with the ex–Mrs. Cerf. When not being directed by Hitchcock, Sylvia was often at his side in the Savoy Grill or Claridge's. "No bloodshed . . . and no thrills!" he insisted to RH cronies. More intent than ever to be in the here and now, he went forward by cauterizing the past.

On May 25, his thirty-eighth birthday, Martha phoned. Two weeks later, he dispatched a last London letter to New York, concluding with a joke of sorts: "My next . . . will come from Berlin and I hope it won't be from a concentration camp." The Nuremberg citizenship laws had been enacted in 1935, depriving Jews of civil rights and outlawing marriage or sex between them and Aryans. They'd been banned from colleges and professions, found it almost impossible to write for newspapers or publish books, and couldn't work in theaters. Communists, socialists, "undesirables"—both Jews and those who weren't—had begun to be shipped to Dachau outside Munich, and Sachsenhausen would soon open north of Berlin. Bennett had written his "joke" in the bravado of fear.

"Mr. Klopfer's little Martha"—as he'd called her in that letter—met his plane at Tempelhof, the airport massively rebuilt by Hitler. In less than two months, Berlin would host the Olympics, and the new buildings, statues, banners, and uniforms that they passed coalesced in a message of Nazi triumphalism. Martha took him to the U.S. embassy compound to dine that night—not alone, but with her mother.

For ten days Bennett alternated publisher visits with romantic pursuit. He escorted Martha to events, and she arranged an evening with Russian friends, her interest in socialism having blossomed. They also went boating on the lakes separating Berlin from Potsdam. Describing the outing in his oral history, he recalled that when the wind blew on deck, a Nazi flag brushed his face, making him shudder. Martha thought it "hilariously" funny: alluring she was, but could be very cruel. In letters, she'd taunted him about Sylvia.

Whatever else happened in Berlin, it wasn't what happened with Donald. Bennett and Martha did not have sex. "You are a strange and a very interesting person," she wrote the next year. "It would be nice to meet . . . when neither of us was full of the past, and both free to have something together, with love and passion and recklessness." Another letter remarked how odd it was that "we . . . who enjoy it so much with other[s] . . . have always postponed the evil or the holy day of pure enjoyment between ourselves." She dangled the prospect of a rendezvous—but not in Germany, given the circumstances.

If Martha could stop "trying to be mother and sweetheart to the whole blasted Communist Party," Bennett replied, he'd love to see her in New York. Then he turned serious. She was aware of his overwhelming ambition for RH, despite all his "silly talk." They were making a real contribution to the cause, he assured her, "though I refuse to spell it with a capital 'c.'" Several months later he passed along news: Donald had married Pat Selwyn, the divorcée who had set her heart on having him.

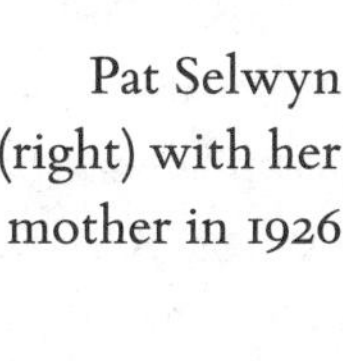

Pat Selwyn (right) with her mother in 1926

Bennett and Don may have known about Martha's belief in the "Cause," but they hardly knew the whole story. A year before visiting RH, she'd fallen in love with Soviet embassy press attaché Boris Vinogradov—a Jew like them—who'd been ordered to recruit her as a spy. She'd signed on, but had no idea that Vinogradov had a wife and family in Moscow. When he was recalled there, her orders came from another handler.

Martha became a valuable conduit for the Soviets, passing on information, trying to influence her father, and all the while making useful conquests, including the chief technical officer of the Luftwaffe. She was instructed to appeal to her wide network of friends to help fund the Cause—Bennett among them. "What in the world are you hoarding your money for?" one letter asked. Progressive movements couldn't "live by bread alone." Yet despite her loyalty, she feared the purges sweeping through Stalin's Russia, and petitioned the Soviets to allow her to marry Vinogradov. Permission didn't come. Instead, she returned to America when her father was replaced as ambassador at the end of 1937. Vinogradov, meanwhile, had been secretly purged and killed.

In January 1938, Walter Winchell would broadcast that Martha and Bennett had married—except, of course, the gossip wasn't true. But when he again reported the "seriousness" of the liaison between the "book peddler" and "ex-ambassador's daughter" several months later, if frequency were the measure, Winchell was now right. From February through early May, Martha's name peppered Bennett's diary. Then it disappeared. Unexpectedly her mother died, and in June, Martha married an American Jew whose name was neither Cerf nor Klopfer. Alfred Stern was a millionaire who not only provided security but proved a willing recruit, starting a music publishing company in New York that served as a front for Soviet spies.

Still, Bennett kept a sheaf of taunting, tantalizing letters from Martha for the rest of his life. There'd be no contact between Don and the former Miss Dodd for decades, but as it turned out, "Mr. Klopfer's little Martha" hadn't quite finished with Don yet.

Chapter 14

Ready for the Big Things

By 1936, ELEVEN YEARS HAD PASSED SINCE BENNETT AND DON HAD started in business together. They could congratulate themselves: the Modern Library was flourishing; they'd signed O'Neill, Stein, and others; and *Ulysses* had won Random House a place in literary history. Not bad for "boy publishers." But that wasn't all. In 1933, the ML published *Great German Short Stories and Novels,* edited by none other than Bennett Cerf (with a little help from Uncle Herbert). More recently, Bennett had coaxed Raymond Weaver's partner, John Burrell, to be his co-editor on the *Bedside Book of Famous American Stories*. A columnist wondered why it hadn't been done before, since there was such an obvious need "for just this book." More edited anthologies bearing Bennett's byline would follow.

Continually pushing for more from himself but also for the firm—more authors, scope, scale—early in 1936, before leaving for the Caribbean, Bennett wrote Gertrude that he'd be "ready for the Big Things" on his return. Under the insouciance, he was more than usually serious, about to take what he saw as a great step forward. The Depression had battered many publishers; some went under, and even Knopf had had to survive on bank loans. Though RH had seen a big fall-off, and ML numbers declined after 1932, the company not only survived, but in 1935 was doing better than many, thanks to Joyce and an upturn in ML sales. Yet the partners realized that the quickest way to grow and become more significant was to combine with another firm, and Bennett and Don began to look around. Already, in 1934, they'd joined with Knopf and Viking to open "K.M.V.," a shared shipping and warehousing facility in Chelsea that not only effected savings for all three through economies of scale, but also added revenue by distributing for other firms. Now Bennett and Donald began merger talks with Pat Covici, whose partnership with Donald Friede was ending. A talented editor, Covici had published promising writers like John Steinbeck and Nathanael West, and the ML had already done deals with him for John Strachey and Clifford Odets. However, when Bennett scrutinized the accounts, he found the company to be entangled in debt. Smith & Haas might be a better bet.

Robert Haas had had stints in banking and advertising before buying a stake in the Little Leather Library and then, in 1926, co-founding the Book-of-the-Month Club with Harry Scherman and Maxwell Sackheim. The idea was Scherman's, but Haas contributed the most cash. He was named president, and proved an excellent manager, doing "the real dirty work" of setting up relations with publishers and printers. However, six years later, Haas wanted a change, and started a publishing firm with Harrison Smith, a former Harcourt editor who had briefly run a New York branch for London's Jonathan Cape.

Together, Smith & Haas published Englishman Robert Graves's *I, Claudius; Seven Gothic Tales* by Karen Blixen, the Dane who wrote under the pen name "Isak Dinesen"; Frenchman André Malraux's *Man's Fate,* an important novel about the Communist uprising in Shanghai; and signed the young American journalist Edgar Snow, who would introduce the English-speaking world to Mao Zedong in *Red Star Over China*. Another French author, Jean de Brunhoff, whose Babar stories were translated by Haas's wife, Merle, had given them a toehold in the children's market. They had also taken on William Faulkner, with whom Bennett and Don enjoyed cordial relations, thanks to the ML reprint of *Sanctuary*. All were authors they'd be proud to publish.

The best friends wouldn't go into a new marriage lightly: just four years had passed since the incompatible Elmer's exit. "Hal" Smith, handsome and debonair, could be rather "absent-minded," but had value as a champion of young writers like Faulkner. Haas was the bigger draw. Quiet, angular, impeccably tailored, Bob was eight years Bennett's senior, and with his gray crew cut, looked older still. His German Jewish immigrant father had made a fortune in groceries, and sent him to private schools and Yale, one of the few Jews there. Merle Haas had also come from money; her uncle had been a U.S. senator. But even more important, with Bob they had history. In 1930, when RH had gambled on doing a one-volume trade edition of Rockwell Kent's three-volume art press *Moby-Dick,* BOMC had offered it to members, a big boost for a young firm. Soon after, BOMC began to pay higher rates and, thinking it only fair, sent RH an extra check. For Bennett and Don, a deal made

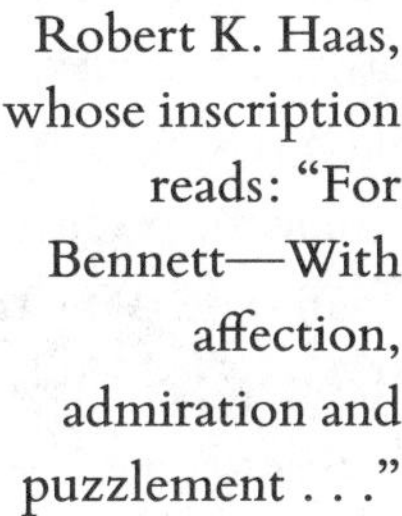

Robert K. Haas, whose inscription reads: "For Bennett—With affection, admiration and puzzlement . . ."

was a deal done: they sent it back. Bob and Harry didn't feel right. Over lunch, they agreed to split the difference. "Everybody was being decent, and when people are decent, things work out for everybody," Bennett explained.

Now, five years later, Bob understood what his own fledgling house needed: a way to generate predictable income, mitigating the risk of originating new trade titles. The ML could provide that cash flow. What Bennett and Don saw was that S&H's authors could grow RH's list, and some of Bob's wealth, invested judiciously, could grow the firm. A merger was agreed to, desirable to all, effective April 1, 1936. Although the ML was, and would remain, the bedrock on which all else stood, the center of gravity was shifting. Bennett and Don had operated as proprietors of the Modern Library Inc., but the merged company would be known as Random House Inc., with new, original trade books rather than reprints as its focus. Bennett would be president, Bob vice president, Don treasurer, each with an equal number of shares. Bob's initial contribution would be $175,000 to Bennett and Don, nominally for shares in the ML. Hal, with no money to invest, would be company secretary, and receive a bonus. He'd have a four-year option to buy up to half Bob's shares. Pop Cerf would also be a director, bolstering Bennett's position as first among equals.

Gertrude Stein was adamant on that point: news of the merger propelled her to seek reassurance that Bennett would not let anyone else do the "real deciding." Despite sometimes chiding him, she thought him unbelievably smart as a publisher. He put things "in the right way . . . the important way." Later she would insist: "Always and always you are the only publisher I will ever love."

The new corporation would begin, he promised, by cutting deadwood from the combined lists, just as it did from the ML, to shape a catalogue "we can feel proud of." Saxe and Belle would be joined by three S&H editors, including Louise Bonino, who worked on adult as well as Babar books, and would be tasked with developing a juvenile list. Bennett would continue to oversee advertising and publicity, Don run production and sales, Hal edit, and Bob manage the office. All four would make editorial decisions.

What neither firm had had before was enough volume to afford a sales manager to oversee the commission representatives—"book travelers"—shared with other houses who sold to stores, each covering a defined territory. Now they did, and recruited Lewis Miller, who'd spent fifteen years at Harper and Doubleday. With stylish clothes, an adopted "British" accent, and an encyclopedic knowledge of New York's best places, he seemed to have stepped out of a glossy magazine, but was disciplined and tough under the charm. Others came to judge Lew the best book salesman *ever,* someone who broadened the department's role, in order to do a better job of publishing. His first innovation was a merchandising unit to package ML titles into sets, like a $3.98 ten-volume "Library of the World's Great Novels," under a new imprint, "Carlton House." A rare value, distribution was exclusively limited to one major store per city; Macy's in New York and Wanamaker's in Philadelphia had signed on. Though RH's West Coast rep worried that their reputation for dignified selling would be muddied by "bargains," Bennett backed Lew: his energy, ideas, and ability to exploit assets to the full.

Bob Haas quickly showed himself a marvelous addition, capable and, as Don said, "of the greatest integrity." He'd won a Distinguished Service Cross during the Great War for saving a man. Bob was just as enthusiastic about Bennett and Donald: "I like my new partners so well that I'm really having fun," he wrote to his boarding-school son. The office hijinks did loosen him up. One day, Bennett told Bob about a press agent's efforts to help a company offload thousands of cans of white salmon. Having partaken of pink and red, Bob had never eaten any white, and challenged Bennett: the fish didn't exist. A bet was made, and a letter sent to the head of the city aquarium, an old Columbia classmate, who soon replied to "Beans" that the rare white salmon was indeed real. Bob paid up; more letters from the "aquarium head" followed. After the third, however, he smelled something fishy: Bennett, of course, had set it all up, and Bob loved it.

Hal Smith, however, soon proved problematic; Bob had already taken issue with him at S&H. Now friction grew between Hal and Bennett, who'd later judge him one of the most "amusing but irritating" men he ever knew. "Absent-minded," in Bennett's eyes, became "utterly undependable." Nine months after merging, Bennett, Don, and Bob called an "exceedingly" painful meeting, seeking—and getting—Hal's resignation. Landing first at Doubleday, Hal then found his way to the presidency of *The Saturday Review of Literature:* they would have to deal with each other for decades to come.

...

IN THE SUMMER OF 1936, after Bennett had said goodbye to Berlin and Martha, he headed to Paris and Gertrude. A sculptor friend of Stein's met his train. Recognizable by the bushy brows and beard that made this son of the Lower East Side look like a Hebrew patriarch, Jo Davidson—anointed by the press as "the plastic historian"—had captured in clay, bronze, and anything moldable anyone who counted, from FDR and Helen Keller to Joyce and Stein. Posing for him seemed to confer its own immortality. During the weekend they'd spend at Gertrude's French country home near the Swiss border, Bennett hoped to cajole Jo into doing a book. A plane deposited them at the Geneva airfield, where their hostesses and "Basket," a magnificent white standard poodle, welcomed them into an old Ford. Off they lurched, on what Bennett, like Mr. Toad in the children's classic *The Wind in the Willows,* memorialized as a "fantastic" wild ride. Their talk, so "rich" and distracting, led Gertrude astray four times, but they finally arrived, and Bennett proved the charming guest, bad plumbing and all.

Saturday, Jo made a watercolor of him reading on a garden chaise near Basket. It would hang in Bennett's study until he died, unusually precious to a man who preferred to fill his walls with books. After Gertrude's chihuahua, Pepe, tried to bite him, the tiny dog would suffer the indignity of becoming a running epistolary joke. But the story he'd dine out on involved "none other than Picasso," turning up with a sheaf of his own verse, seeking Gertrude's considered opinion. She read the poems, Bennett observed, leaned over, put her hands on the artist's shoulders, then decreed: "Go home and paint."

The very competitive Stein claimed literature as her preserve, and was known for dismissing Picasso's writing as "not poetry." Nevertheless, Bennett's tale, repeated in interviews he gave as late as the 1960s, while utterly true to himself, was most likely apocryphal. To omit a catch as celebrated as Picasso from his diary would have been unthinkable, but Picasso is not there; nor does he factor into Davidson's account of their visit in the sculptor's own memoir. Moreover, to the story about Picasso, Bennett's tale transposed almost word for word his description of Gertrude's gestures when she'd called *him* "dumb." In their tête-à-têtes, he'd probably *heard* Stein belittle the poems, but Picasso is one celebrity whom he almost certainly never met. Landing a successful story was what counted, and portraying a genius as having his own "dumb" moment with Stein made the sting of her words about him less sharp.

After returning from Europe, such storytelling took a new turn: Bennett began to be paid for it. *The Saturday Review of Literature,* occupying a middle ground between the high-toned *Atlantic* and popular *Saturday Evening Post,* ran Trade Winds, a column on book publishing. Novelist Christopher Morley wrote it, but asked Bennett to be vacation substitute for an August issue. Titling it "Mr. Bump Goes to Europe," Bennett related the transatlantic adventures of one of the "most articulate" of all publishers—"Tony Bump." Readers liked the self-satirizing piece, and further Bump chronicles began to appear, as Bennett's persona ventured beyond the walls of Random House.

He'd begged Gertrude to paint his portrait in words, and when she complied, he was elated about that, too—but nervous. *The Geographical History of America or the Relation of Human Nature to the Human Mind* was published that October. When he sent her advance copies, he pointed to the unconventional way he'd publicize the book. On the front flap was a note from him to the reader. "I do not know what Miss Stein is talking about. . . . That, Miss Stein tells me, is because I am dumb. [My partner and I] are characters. [We wish] we knew what she was saying about us. [We hope] her faithful followers will make more of this book than we [can]!" Attention-grabbing, it also took chutzpah.

The book's best-known Steinism declares, "I am I because my little dog knows me," but what mattered to Bennett were the lines she'd written about him and his uncle. Although they were difficult to decipher, it was clear she'd characterized Herbert as much more sophisticated, a man who "listened" to "the human mind," whereas Bennett, a creature of "human nature," did not. Instead, as her letter about Sylvia had said, he was "made to be happy." Not many in her orbit were: to be so was to have a certain simplicity. She'd formed that impression, and experience had proved it: when he'd rushed the publication of *Portraits and Prayers* to have it on sale for her tour, he'd understood her thirst for success, but failed to appreciate her aesthetics. His editors had made punctuation and spacing "corrections" that were anything but, neglecting to check with Stein, given the deadline.

Still, she overcame her pique and, in 1937, in *Everybody's Autobiography,* again mentioned him as a character, but this portrayal was different. "Before we went on the *Champlain* I asked Bennett . . . about my writing," began one passage. "I always want what I have written to be printed and it has not always happened no not mostly happened . . . he said it is very simple whatever you decide each year you want printed you tell me and I will publish that. . . ." What "hadn't mostly happened," he'd finally made happen.

The manuscript also had passages about others. Donald was "tall and pleasant and a little not very happy but every one was happy enough." The contrast between the man "made to be happy" and his "a little not very happy" partner was acute. Even briefer was her characterization of Gustave: "Bennett Cerf had a father but he was not much of a father." She'd perceived the son's dominance, but the description was cruel, and Bennett—unlike others who'd felt her barb—could do something: change the text. Published, the book would read: "Bennett Cerf has a father but he is more than a father and Bennett himself is more a brother and a nephew or a great nephew than a father, that is the reason we like him and like him as a publisher." Stein saw the proofs, cabled that her text had been altered, and insisted the original be restored. Copy editor Belle Becker, confused by its idiosyncrasies, had made many changes (yet again). Bennett promised: all restorations would be made, save for Gustave's description; Gertrude's original allowed for "misinterpretation," and he wouldn't have his father "hurt for the world."

This second autobiography was no *Autobiography of Alice B. Toklas* in sales; reviewers found it too like its predecessor. Still, he swore to Stein that he was proud of it, and it was wonderful, and if more people didn't want to buy it, "to hell with them."

. . .

EARLY IN 1937, HORACE MANGES brought Bennett together with an old friend, New York State Supreme Court Justice Samuel I. Rosenman, a long-standing counselor to President Franklin Delano Roosevelt. Rosenman had drafted many of FDR's speeches, coining the term "New Deal" in one. Recently, he'd assumed another role: compiling and editing the president's papers, from state addresses to fireside chats, dating from his New York governorship through his first term in the White House, material that would fill five volumes. FDR was seeking a publisher for books he wanted elegantly designed and bound. The patrician president who was helping the nation find its way again was a hero to Bennett. He and Don asked Joseph Blumenthal, a contact from their fine-press days, to prepare specimen pages at his Spiral Press. FDR liked both the samples and Bennett's enthusiasm, his "profound" belief that RH could sell 15,000 sets the first year. Similar papers, published after presidents left office, had never approached such a number.

In late May, Roosevelt chose RH as his publisher. In the contract, the royalty was split equally between the president and Rosenman. Bennett could hardly contain himself as he motored with the judge on July 4 to meet FDR at his Hyde Park home. Each of the five volumes would retail for three dollars, and the set cost a pricey fifteen in Depression greenbacks ($328 today); RH would give every store a free copy to stimulate sales. There would be revelations—the text of press conferences was to be printed with off-the-record remarks for the first time—and four more books were planned for FDR's second term.

Don accompanied Bennett on a second visit in December, this time to the White House; Bob's turn would come in the new year. *The Public Papers and Addresses of Franklin Delano Roosevelt* was RH's most important project, Bennett crowed to Gertrude, and early signs looked promising. Introductions and notes were to be written by FDR, and in February, Eleanor Roosevelt's literary agent negotiated two pre-publication deals: the introductions would be excerpted in *Liberty* magazine, and United Features was to syndicate selected notes in newspapers. Each would pay $30,000 for the privilege, with the agent and RH receiving a small cut.

However, a problem soon arose. Each book had been budgeted to run

400 pages—2,000 across five volumes—but the manuscript came in, and would make 3,600-plus. That meant more paper, press time, and money. Other costs were also involved: sample copies, promotional brochures, a major ad campaign. To recoup basic expenses, they'd have to sell many books, but though Bennett had forecast sales of 15,000 sets within a year, the initial run was a more cautious 7,500, and less than half would be bound. Special paper and leather would be used on another 500 limited-edition fifty-dollar set.

Bennett's enthusiasm hadn't allowed for another factor: in the spring of 1938, not everyone viewed FDR as a hero. The wealthy, who could easily afford a fifteen- or even a fifty-dollar set, generally loathed programs like Social Security and the financial controls he'd put into place. Libraries and colleges where their donations exercised influence might not acquire the books, whereas many FDR supporters couldn't afford them. And he'd become *less* popular since the project began, with a tranche of former admirers disenchanted by his (unsuccessful) attempt to pack the Supreme Court with extra justices sympathetic to his initiatives, as well as the effects of the "Roosevelt Recession": worried about deficits, the president had cut funding from the very programs he'd championed, stalling the recovery and allowing unemployment to surge again.

Even the syndication and magazine deals had soured. Newspaper articles and editorials questioned whether FDR had chosen to publish the papers now for private gain—contravening the Constitution—rather than after he left office. Forced to respond, his press secretary declared that the president would devote all net profits "to a useful public purpose under government direction," none going to him or the judge personally.

In late March, Rosenman wrote FDR about a talk he'd had with Bennett. "They are feeling very low," he reported, RH having been slammed by production costs of about $52,000—an enormous sum—more than double the estimate. In April, just before publication, Bennett sounded even worse: "Barring some miracle," he told the judge, RH faced one of the most spectacular publishing debacles of their time. His miscalculation staggered him. Most major accounts—bookstores and other vendors—had refused to mail out brochures. Philadelphia's best department store wouldn't stock even one set. Another, deluged with complaints, removed a sample copy after one day. Patrons of New York's Doubleday, Doran shop threatened a boycott if a poster for the books wasn't taken down. RH received profane letters, but few orders. Feelings ran so high, Lew Miller made the reps sign a pledge specifying there'd be no cause for criticism that they misrepresented anything in selling the sets.

Proposing to extricate them from the debacle without completely losing face, Bennett made a desperate suggestion to Rosenman: that they do the books on a "non-profit" basis, putting all monies received into a common kitty—royalties as well as RH's revenues—and charge all expenses to that fund. Underwriting the publication would become the "public purpose" to which the author's and editor's earnings would go. The firm would spend more on publicity and ads, and pledge never to remainder copies. In the end, was it fair to hand $50,000-plus to charity, while RH suffered a huge loss?

He failed to persuade Rosenman or convince the president to exert influence to find government money to buy sets for libraries at cost. Not that the books were wanting: FDR was thoroughly pleased with them. Nevertheless, by the end of July, RH faced a $25,000 loss. Lunching with Bob Haas, Rosenman said FDR felt the firm could have done more promotion and ads (the usual lament) and also raised the subject of the *next* four books, wanting to start work. Bob was blunt: RH might not publish them.

Bennett exploded when he heard of the president's complaints, and wrote the judge. "Not a single word" publicizing the books had come from the White House, while RH had even hired door-to-door salesmen and paid a mail-order house to send thousands of circulars. He didn't seem to understand that FDR couldn't use taxpayer money or government functionaries to move books, and that publishing the papers as a commercial proposition—and while FDR was in office—was misguided from the start.

Having allowed his optimistic heart to guide his head, Bennett faced another problem a year later: pallets of unbound sheets and unsold sets stored in the warehouse and with the printer and binder, clogging space needed for new titles. He offered to sell most remaining sets and sheets to Rosenman and FDR, with RH relinquishing legal rights and the original plates for $10,000, but nothing came of it. There was no recourse but to dispose of them with a remainder broker—though a broker selling them at a bargain-basement price would embarrass RH and the president. In the end, Bennett offloaded most to the Outlet Book Company, and pulped the rest. The president was very offended.

FDR won his next two elections, and his later papers were published in eight additional volumes, first by Macmillan, and then by Harper. After his death in April 1945, RH searched to see if any unbound sheets still existed, stored with the printer or binder. About five hundred sets turned up, and the firm ordered them to be bound.

The market for FDR's papers had suddenly revived.

...

JUST AS THE FIRM was publishing the president in 1938, a Texas congressman, Martin Dies, was making political hay by convening the newly formed House Special Committee on Un-American Activities to investigate Communist infiltration in the country. Already, Dies had grabbed headlines by accusing the Federal Theatre Project of being infested with Reds. In September, concerned that the congressman would target publishing next, Bennett proactively defended the industry in the pages of the (then) left-leaning *New York Post*. A month later, the trouble that a Communist connection could stir for the book business became very real, when RH author John Strachey, about to enter New York for a lecture tour, was taken off the SS *Normandie,* remanded to Ellis Island as an "excluded alien," and landed on the front page of the *Times*.

On a previous visit, the former MP and leading British interpreter of Communist philosophy had narrowly escaped deportation. But this time, the ACLU-affiliated lawyer who'd helped on the earlier visit couldn't arrange bail. Bennett was in Europe, so Don crossed to and from Ellis Island to keep Strachey company. Though denying he was a party member, he was marooned for a fortnight before bail was granted, and several months elapsed before the U.S. Court of Appeals ruled that the revocation of Strachey's visa was illegal. By that time, Don and his author were friends for life.

However, it wasn't the domestic front that was most worrying. In March, Germany had annexed Austria, and clearly coveted territory on its eastern border. The North African expansionist dreams of Italy's fascist leader, Benito Mussolini, had also become obvious; and on the other side of the world, the Japanese had established a puppet regime in China's far north, and were now fighting to control the rest of the country.

Then there was Spain. The civil war between the legitimate elected government of the republican Loyalists and the fascist Nationalists under Francisco Franco had raged since the summer of 1936. The Loyalists included many Communists, and for want of others willing to supply them, they were forced to buy equipment from the Soviets, while Germany supplied Franco with the latest materiel, and also men. The elite German "Condor" squad had perfected a previously unimaginable horror: aerial bombardment, planes raining destruction on civilians in cities and towns. Rushing to aid the Loyalists were the U.S. "Lincoln Brigade" and the "International Brigade" of European volunteers.

Bennett had written Gertrude in March that he'd probably come abroad, though front-page news was terrifying and depressing in the extreme. Their friendship survived by skirting politics. The "woman of authority" was a Franco supporter, while Bennett had just helped organize a luncheon that raised $10,000 for the Loyalist cause. In May he wrote again, again facing, as he had ten years earlier, one of the "most melancholy" birthdays of his life. About to turn forty, he'd still been thinking of himself as "the boy publisher," but now the philosophy he'd flippantly espoused to her nine months earlier—have as much fun as you can, and "the hell with tomorrow and the generations to come—known technically as no social conscience"—no longer felt so funny.

The previous year, RH had published Elliot Paul's *The Life and Death of a Spanish Town,* about the Spain Paul loved and the war that was destroying it. A critical success and bestseller, it won more American friends for the Loyalists. Two other RH authors were even more involved in the republican cause. The Englishman Ralph Bates had lived in Spain for fifteen years, and been sent to the United States as a propagandist for the Loyalist government. RH would publish his collection, *Sirocco and Other Stories,* the next year. Bob's brilliant author André Malraux was the other; thirty-two when he won the Prix Goncourt, France's top literary prize, for *Man's Fate,* he chased a life of heroic grandeur, and despite a penchant for self-mythology, lived it. Malraux had obtained precious French planes and pilots for the Loyalist air force, and led a squadron into air battle. RH would publish *Man's Hope,* his sprawling portrait of the struggle—as much cri de coeur and reportage as fiction—in November. Malraux was frantically directing a film based on the novel, hoping to win hearts and minds, and to reverse the course of a war looking bleak for his side.

Bennett would indeed return to Europe that fall, and Spain was on his itinerary. He was probably crazy, he admitted to a friend, but had to see what was happening: he felt the Loyalists were fighting *his* battle for him. Yet it wasn't his politics, or wanting to be at the center of the action, or what he'd learned from authors that had decided him: it was how he wanted to appear in the eyes of a woman. Bennett had fallen in love again.

Miss Helen Thompson

For a long time now, the women he'd pursued had had names that lit up the gossip columns, enhancing the glow of his own. This one was different. The Depression had given new impetus to the labor movement, and an effort was underway to unionize the book business. Though Bennett and Don felt that they already took care of their "RH family," after the Book and Magazine Guild kept pushing for a meeting, he agreed. He'd heard they were sending their best organizer, but in July when he sat down with the committee, he was taken aback: Miss Helen Thompson was young, fair-haired, most definitely well-bred, and a natural beauty. Though the niece of Kathleen Norris—a known isolationist and one of the most popular female novelists of recent decades—Helen was an internationalist, deeply committed to republican Spain. Her brother David was a member of the Lincoln Brigade; her father, Fred, scion of a San Francisco banking family, had helped establish the Emergency Committee for the American Wounded. Within weeks of the meeting, RH had a union affiliate, Helen had become Bennett's frequent companion, and he'd developed an urgent interest in Spain. Having survived his fortieth birthday, he found himself mad about this "swell girl" a decade younger, who "quivered with emotion." Just as with Sylvia, he launched Helen into his social whirl, seeking universal approval. His friends found the contrast astonishing. Helen's father, treasurer of the Emergency Committee, was now based in Paris. When Fred Thompson announced plans to visit his son, Bennett decided to accompany him to Barcelona.

Travel to Spain was highly restricted, and the U.S. government had to issue a special permit to go. He wrote to the passport office in D.C. early in September, explaining it was "practically impossible" to deal with authors like Malraux by mail; he had to conduct such business in person, and dropped FDR's name as an RH author, sure it would help. The application was respectfully denied. Quickly changing tack, Bennett phoned FDR's secretary, Missy LeHand, who agreed to forward a letter from Bennett to the State Department; three days later, a passport was granted.

On September 13, Hitler issued an ultimatum to Czechoslovakia, Germany's neighbor, to give up the Sudetenland, its German-speaking territory, and carried out military forays into the area, posing a grave threat. Bennett sailed for England the next day. He made the London rounds, and found Viking's Ben Huebsch there, too. They hatched plans to travel back together should Europe explode, but on September 30, Prime Minister Neville Chamberlain and his French and Italian counterparts agreed in Munich to give Hitler what he wanted (and bring the rest of Czechoslovakia and Poland within his sights), in exchange for a promise that supposedly brought "peace in our time." As Bennett wrote to RH, all England felt "rage, disgust, despair" at such appeasement. He'd never thought to hear Strachey and Noël Coward agree politically. They did now.

In Paris, he and Fred Thompson dined with Jo Davidson, who would travel down with them. Jo had already been to wartime Barcelona on a wangled press pass. Luckily for Bennett, Ralph Bates had written to Don Fernando de los Rios, Spain's ambassador to the United States, describing his publisher as a "sound anti-Fascist" and man of influence. The Loyalist government, anxious that such a person form a "correct estimate" of their effort, invited Bennett to visit as their guest. The three bought food, soap, cigarettes, whiskey, and other goods to give to those in need, but also to barter or bribe when necessary. With the heavy baggage, they boarded a train heading for Perpignan, the last major French city before the border, traveling south in a haze of smoke, talk, sleep, and wakefulness.

A car sent by the government met them twelve hours later, and they crossed into Spain early in the afternoon on Friday, October 14, destination Barcelona. Another passenger rode along, a handsome woman a bit older than Bennett. Dressed entirely in black, hair pulled into a soft, low bun, eyes unusually bright and dark, her face seemed as changeable as Pyrenees weather, going from serene to defiant to tragic in a moment. Now he understood how Dolores Ibárruri, founding firebrand of the Spanish Communist Party, had come to be "La Pasionaria," a living legend. On the radio at the outbreak of war, she'd declared: "It is better to die on your feet than to live on your knees!" and added, "*No pasarán!*" (They shall not pass!), giving the Loyalists their rallying cry. Her presence signified that they truly were viewed as important emissaries—and, equally, how desperate the government was to influence any outsider who might help. A deeper sense of what Bennett had gotten himself into took hold when they reached Figueres, the largest town close to the border. It had been bombed hours earlier, and acrid smoke hung about ruined houses as soldiers searched the wreckage. ESTA ES LA OBRA DEL FASCISMO, had been written on a sign. Townspeople seemed furious, not frightened.

They went on, and at last the car stopped outside Barcelona's Hotel Majestic, home to many foreign correspondents. Climbing to the sixth floor—periodic power failures meant no working elevator—Bennett discovered no functioning electric lights, either. He tried to make a chambermaid understand his need for a bathroom with enough natural light to at least wash and shave before the sun disappeared entirely. Failing miserably, he tramped back down six flights and set off in search of a tourist dictionary.

The bookstore he was directed to was on the point of closing. However, the manager changed his mind as soon as he heard the latecomer speak: an ecstatic "New York!" was all the welcome Bennett needed. It turned out Señor Manzanes had once worked at Brentano's on Fifth Avenue, and Bennett peppered him with questions about how books and stores were faring in Spain. Playing the journalist he'd once trained to be, he would write it all up for *PW,* just as he'd written about the Soviet Union. When he asked if the state had taken over private industry, Manzanes grew indignant: such talk was Fascist propaganda, their "usual tactics" to brand anyone not with them as Reds. "My business here stays my own," he insisted. On close inspection, Bennett saw that most new titles were propagandistic nonfiction: so many writers were caught up in the struggle.

He'd returned to the hotel and was listening to a desk clerk describe the worst of the bombing, when a fearsome sound he'd never heard before knocked the breath out of him: an air-raid siren. Another wailed at dinner, accompanied by booming anti-aircraft guns and the clang of an ambulance down the avenue. He tried to take his cue from the reporters feigning indifference, grumbling in the dark as they pulled out flashlights to continue eating the poor food that passed for a meal. He was still downstairs when a third air raid sounded at midnight. Everyone rose, thin flashlight beams guiding them up till they emerged on the roof and beheld a metropolis of two and a half million, hushed and utterly dark. Soon, from hills circling the city, a dozen searchlights played across the sky, one catching a bomber in its white arc. Two Loyalist planes swooped in pursuit, as the watchers gave what sounded like a million-throated roar, thrilling and terrifying. All three planes then vanished into the night, the show ending as abruptly as it had begun.

Two winters before, Bennett had already witnessed how fast life could be lost: he and an agent friend, William Morris Jr., holidaying in the Adirondacks, had come upon a pair of struggling skaters who'd fallen through a jagged hole in the lake ice. They acted fast enough to save one boy, but the other perished, and Bennett was haunted enough to keep a piece of the pole they'd used to save the one as a good-luck charm for the rest of his life. Now, climbing down to his room in pitch darkness, he realized how scared he'd been on the roof: he'd wet himself. He threw off his clothes, and slept.

In the morning, a government guide walked him through thronged streets in strong sunlight, and he took in what the blackout had hidden: buildings blasted in half, skeletal staircases, doorways leading nowhere. The countryside had emptied a harvest of refugees into the city, gaunt men in rubble, staring at the well-fed foreigner. Appointments had been made for him to meet the aristocratic Communist press chief Constancia de la Mora, as well as a general and the minister of police. That night, he dined with reporters, among them the *Times'*

Herb Matthews, whose bony face he'd known as a fellow teen at the Riviera apartments. Returning to his room, flashlight trained on the latest book he'd found about the conflict, Bennett read into the night to prepare for more meetings.

Days tumbled one into another on little sleep, but the next morning, he knew it was Sunday because the propaganda ministry's Miss Ruiz collected him, Fred, and Herb to go to mass. Later they toured through what remained of the harbor district. Bennett finally caught up with another Majestic guest that night: hyperkinetic, chain-smoking Malraux. Thanks to serendipity or Sunday prayers, there'd been no air raids all day.

De la Mora, who plied him with statistics as well as charm, began the week, and foreign minister Julio Álvarez del Vayo gave a half hour of his time. Between meetings, de la Mora's office screened propaganda films, whose scenes were the closest he'd get to the front, for Bennett's adventure would go only so far: not to the Ebro, where the big battles were fought. On his fifth and final day, he said goodbye to Herb and de la Mora as war planes circled above. He flew to Toulouse, and that night a dinner of white beans and pork felt like gorging on steak. In Paris, as a bearer of fresh news, he was interviewed by United Press, debriefed by Elliot Paul, and welcomed by the Joyces. He wrote Gertrude, in Bilignin, that Spain had rattled him: the sketch she'd done needed "radical alteration." Those unwilling to join in the fight at such a time "deserve everything they will get!"

Seven weeks after he'd left New York, he sailed back into the harbor on November 2 and was met at the dock by Pop, Don, Bob—and Helen. They went home, and the two stayed up until 5 A.M. At the office later that morning, the switchboard buzzed with callers who asked, "How was Spain?" and "Are you engaged?" The gossip columns had been busy while he was gone. Bennett couldn't help but notice that though lovely, Helen wasn't bothered by what she wore to meet him—or the world, for that matter. Always so keen to put his best face forward, that troubled him. Subject to a kind of color-blindness, he'd learned early to make sure his tie, shirt, suit, and handkerchief matched; he wasn't used to a girl on his arm being less than supremely stylish. Still, she *was* wonderful.

They holed up at Herbert's in Larchmont his second weekend back, where he immersed himself in *Man's Hope,* which was selling even faster than they'd dreamed. Alarming radio reports spoke of extreme antisemitic violence on German soil, with Jews beaten, their shop windows shattered. "Nazi bastards," Bennett told his diary, about what would come to be called *Kristallnacht,* the night of broken glass.

Shrewd and credulous by turns, four years earlier he'd temporarily swallowed Soviet propaganda, but the anti-fascist education he'd received in Barcelona really stuck. After telling his hosts that he'd do all he could to spread the Loyalist creed, Bennett tried to make good on the promise, speaking at the next scheduled New York benefit for Spain; footing the printing bill for a catalogue of Jo Davidson's Spanish busts being exhibited to raise money for the cause; and most important, writing "They Are Still Selling Books in Spain," his feature for *PW*. Conjuring a Barcelona bookstore as well as aerial bombardment (and repeating a little too impulsively the optimistic words of foreign minister del Vayo), he urged America to lift its embargo and send desperately needed supplies, for if Spain fell, the repercussions would be "incalculable." The writers he'd met were "in absolute agreement": Hemingway, Malraux, and others wondered if Americans, British, and French would watch while "the gentlemen who sold out Czechoslovakia" agreed to sell out Spain. This time, though, they had to reckon with a people who were determined "to die on their feet rather than live on their knees!" He knew La Pasionaria wouldn't mind his borrowing her words.

Spain's Loyalists weren't alone in seeking U.S. help: so did Europe's Jews. Bennett had never fancied himself a "joiner," but his Jerusalem epiphany had had its effect. In 1937, he felt connected enough to his roots to become fundraising chair for the New York book publishing branch of the Joint Distribution Committee, the main U.S. charity assisting Jews to flee Europe. His chairing the committee also helped burnish RH's reputation among houses owned by the Jewish book boys. Writing to Huebsch, Knopf, Guinzburg, and a dozen others, he said he realized that they'd all heard tales of persecution, but it was only after meeting a few Jews who'd escaped that the truth had really been brought home. They, the lucky ones, must give what help they could.

The situation had only worsened a year later, when he received a letter from Dick Walsh, founder of the John Day Company, who was writing at the behest of his wife (and Pulitzer Prize–winning author) Pearl S. Buck. With missionaries for parents, activism ran in Buck's blood. She had sponsored Jewish refugees, but couldn't assist every person who appealed to her, so Walsh was canvassing contacts to find help for one of

Buck's German translators, Annie Polzer, who wanted to leave Vienna with her doctor husband. Now barred from work, they lived in fear of what would come next.

Bennett stepped up. The State Department wouldn't admit anyone who might be a charge on the public purse, so a sponsor had to show he or she was able to take care of the foreigner. In due course the American consulate in Vienna received documents proving that the average yearly earnings and personal property in excess of $100,000 of Bennett A. Cerf were sufficient to meet the obligation. "Owing to your generosity and affidavit we have, a few days ago, got the American Visa. . . . It is really a sort of fairy tale," Annie wrote him on October 12. When the Polzers arrived in Hoboken on October 30, the fairy tale came true. Bennett also agreed to sponsor two other couples, but whether they made it is unclear—too often, they didn't. And then there was the letter written on the last day of 1938, bearing the old-fashioned signature of one Siegfried Cerf, postmarked Vienna. Herr Cerf hoped that their rare name meant they were related, and begged for help. This time, Bennett replied that he dare not offer another affidavit. If Herr Cerf did reach America, he'd help if he possibly could.

But what of grandfather Nathan Wise's relations, whom he'd met in Germany a dozen years earlier? A brief statement in one of his affidavits declares: "The only immigrants sponsored by me who are now in this country are members of my own family. They are three in number and all of them are being adequately cared for." Affidavits were sometimes "massaged": he'd helped the Polzers, who *weren't* family. No documents in his files show him sponsoring Wise relatives. He may have, but it's hard to know. Bennett never spoke to his sons about the German branch of the family, and barely spoke about the American uncles, aunts, and cousins who'd populated his youth. He was quite capable of forgetting people. Old photos would spill from an envelope that arrived at the office one day with a letter from his uncle Max, who was comfortably spending his old age "in pleasant memories." As a kid, Bennett had told him he was his favorite uncle, but Max, though admiring his nephew's success, couldn't understand his absolute silence for twenty-five years, and plaintively asked, why?

The long-lost nephew was "deeply touched," and confirmed he'd adored Max; that they weren't in contact for so long only showed how lives tend to "drift apart." He lived at a furious pace in the here and now, with an eye turned to the future. In such a life, consciously or otherwise, Bennett was selective about the past, often leaving it behind.

Helen was at his side through the holidays, and they saw 1939 in together. At the end of January they mourned Barcelona's fall to the Fascists, and on Lincoln's birthday she kept him company as he lazed about, reading a new memoir by a certain Miss Dodd. (Thankfully, no mention of RH partners.) However, the relationship was growing volatile. The playboy publisher liked his good times and preferred his girls polished and painted. Sometimes talk grew *too* political, but he couldn't crack a joke to cut it off: she was being pushed further left by true-believing pals. At times short-tempered, he was also afraid. A U.S. government–sponsored exhibition of American books in Madrid had infuriated Bennett: he saw it as legitimizing Franco and refused to take part, but when the Communist press wrote too devotedly about his stand, he blamed her friends for the ink. Yes, he backed the Loyalists, but wanted the world to know he was no Communist.

Outside Saks on a frigid February Saturday, they began to argue. Anger propelled them ten blocks north to a bench at the edge of Central Park, and words spilled out. When they rose and went to his apartment, it was to face a cold reality: they were too different, and compromise would demand too much. "We should stop seeing each other," Helen ventured. Bennett agreed. They made their farewells and she walked out, but he couldn't remain alone. Quickly, he packed a bag and drove to his uncle's place in Larchmont. Herbert had acquired a lover, a blond, handsome, intelligent young actor, Glen Boles. The weekend passed talking books, playing ping-pong—and worrying about Helen.

The next week he kept busy, signing Christopher Isherwood for a novel, and meeting Ted Geisel, an advertising man and cartoonist whose brilliant ads for Flit insecticide were known to every American. In 1937, as both writer and illustrator, Geisel had published with Vanguard Press an unusual children's book, *And to Think That I Saw It on Mulberry Street,* under the pen name "Dr. Seuss." A year later, Vanguard issued *The 500 Hats of Bartholomew Cubbins*. Reviews were mixed, but the books sold, the talent and originality unmistakable, and Bennett had noticed. For his part, Geisel was impressed by RH's playful advertising, quality lists, and the energy and humor of its president. A contract for an adult picture book he wanted to do—*The Seven Lady Godivas,* in which the naked lady of legend multiplied into seven naked sisters cavorting with seven brothers—was the result. It failed to sell, but Bennett campaigned to take everything he wrote, for adults *or* kids; soon he'd sign the next juveniles, and they got on so well that a year later, Geisel would celebrate him in a comic ode—*Pentellic Bilge for Bennett Cerf's Thirty-ninth Birthday*—before a roomful of booksellers. That Bennett was halfway through his forty-second year wouldn't matter a jot.

March blew in, and he exchanged what had become an annual contract with *The New Yorker* for a cartoon album, then left for Nassau. Under the hot sun of Paradise Beach, Helen's memory could begin to burn away, but he'd not forget the hurt of what she'd said: he had the makings of a good person, but had let soft living get in the way.

One Saturday in July, he picked up a poker companion, *New Yorker* editor Harold Ross, at his summer home in Stamford, and drove to a picnic for Mrs. Roosevelt. Afterward, they returned to Ross's place for the rest of the weekend. Harold was crazy—who wasn't—about Ginger Rogers, so crazy he'd invited the star's mother, Lela, who ran RKO Pictures' young talent incubator, to join them. Lela was bringing her niece, Phyllis Fraser, who'd known some hard times in her young life, and didn't object to a little "soft living." In just over a year, she would become Bennett's second wife.

Chapter 15

For Love or Money

Phyllis Fraser

When Bennett got back to Stamford after the picnic, he knew Harold expected him to entertain Ginger Rogers's "god damned kid cousin" for the rest of the weekend. What he didn't suspect was just what a surprise Ross had in store. In her red-and-white gingham playsuit with matching heels in smaller checks, showing off shapely legs and dainty size-3 feet, the girl he met with her Aunt Lela looked all of eighteen (in fact, she was twenty-three). After relocating from Los Angeles, Phyllis Fraser was working in New York on scripts for radio commercials and soap operas. She'd seen Bennett's picture in the papers a few years before, and had felt sorry for the nice-looking man Sylvia Sidney was using "to bring B.P. Schulberg to his knees." Paradoxically, neither she nor Bennett realized that Sylvia had inspired this encounter: Harold, convinced the young woman resembled Bennett's ex-wife, had set out to put a joke over on his gag-loving friend.

When introductions were made, what Ross saw was this: Bennett leaned down and kissed her. Phyllis slapped him. Aunt Lela was watching it all.

"I was a fresh guy," Bennett explained in his oral history.

"I was a virgin," Phyllis insisted more than six decades later, though allowing that a twice-divorced older man and a married producer had shown her around the city. Ross got the rise he'd wanted; it was all fun and games after that. Bennett was forty-one and Phyllis almost eighteen years younger, but he was interested: her name was jotted down in block capitals in his diary. Dates quickly ensued, but in early August she was laid off, and went back to L.A. for a small role in a picture. Bennett, burned by Marian and Sylvia and frustrated by Helen, saw Phyllis as youth and fun. They'd resume when she returned.

Phyllis Fraser, Ginger Rogers—by design in one case and serendipity in the second, they had literally named each other. First cousins, they were more like sisters. Phyllis entered the world as Helen Maurine Brown on April 13, 1916, in Kansas City, Missouri. Her cousin—born Virginia Katherine McMath—had arrived five years earlier. Their mothers were sisters, respectively Virginia and Lela, second oldest and oldest of four girls. Blonde Lela had named her redheaded daughter after her sister.

When Helen was eleven months old, her father died in a gas explosion. She, her two-years-older sister Emogen, known as Gene, and their mother went to stay with her mother's parents, surnamed Owens. Their cousin was already there, after her own parents' notorious breakup: her father had twice "kidnapped" the girl, but Virginia Katherine's steely mother had gotten her back, divorced, left her daughter with her folks, and headed west alone, to work as a screenwriter in the days before movies talked. Virginia Katherine came to treat baby Helen as a "walking, living doll," but Virginia was too much of a mouthful for the toddler. Helen called her cousin "Jinja," and the name stuck.

In L.A., Lela worked on scripts at Fox, then headed to New York to do the same. En route, she stopped in Kansas City to pick up Ginger. In 1918, with the United States at war, she saw an opportunity. Confident and opinionated, Lela became one of the first ten "Marinettes"—women who enlisted for clerical duty in the Marines—the "darnedest drumbeater you ever met," Phyllis later said. She was seconded to the Liberty

Bonds office in Manhattan, and Ginger shuttled between school and a locked hotel room while her mother wrote publicity for the Corps. When Lela was posted to the unit in Washington, D.C., Ginger returned to her grandparents, but after Lela married John Rogers, a Texas insurance salesman, her daughter was repossessed and got a new surname.

Lela's sister's ambitions were different. "In those days you didn't have affairs, you got married," Phyllis recalled. "My mother married five times." (Like Bennett, she wasn't the most reliable narrator, but there's evidence of four marriages, at least.) For husband number two, Mr. Williams, Virginia and her girls moved to Wichita. When that marriage ended, she moved to Oklahoma City, working in—maybe starting—a beauty shop, but young children underfoot wouldn't do. Granny Owens had died, so Virginia boarded out the girls. Helen only saw her mother on Sundays. The night before, she was treated to a bath in a kitchen tub; plumbing was a privy. Creature comforts would be so important later on.

The girls had to please their inconstant mother, as well as others drifting in and out. Phyllis claimed her sister's brain had been affected by the explosion that killed their father, and no love was lost between them. After Virginia married husband number three, Mr. Nichols, the girls lived with their mother and him. A Black domestic came into their lives, who "became my mother, really," Phyllis stated in her oral history.

In Fort Worth, Lela became society and theater editor for the local paper. Often, she'd take freckle-faced Ginger with her to the Majestic, where the girl sat transfixed by the vaudevillians. She'd tiptoe backstage; sometimes they taught her a routine. Seeing a way to get ahead, Lela began entering thirteen-year-old Ginger in Charleston contests; within a few years, she was Texas state champion, and soon mother and daughter joined the vaudeville circuit themselves. There was a brief untethering when Ginger, aged seventeen, eloped with a handsome hoofer (Lela parted from Mr. Rogers around the same time), but soon Ginger returned to the defining relationship of her life: her bond with Mama. Lela, like a wife, did all "the little things," Phyllis once said, and she wanted to be like her aunt.

On Christmas Day of 1929, Ginger made her Broadway debut, and soon the Gershwins' *Girl Crazy* got her noticed. Paramount in New York offered a contract, and she bleached her hair to please the camera. In 1930, Ginger left for L.A. and a contract with Pathé. When that wasn't renewed, she freelanced. On an Oklahoma City visit during the summer of 1932, she and Lela picked up some extra baggage: sixteen-year-old Helen. They judged her pretty and lively enough to be in pictures. But "Helen Nichols" wouldn't do: to get a contract, she needed a better name. On the train to L.A., they decided: Why not "Fraser," after a Christian Science practitioner Ginger had known, and "Phyllis" for alliteration?

Years later, Phyllis said home life with her sister had become "a disaster"; maybe that's why she was "taken away," or perhaps it was because she was "so adorable." Lela always told her, "You were so smart . . . I had to take you." Children are adaptable, the ultimate survivors, but her choice of words, "taken away," is telling. She was rescued, but also rejected: sent off by her mother, and not for the first time. Her surname changed again, but her first name was found wanting, too, erased by her aunt and cousin. Pretty, lively, smart she may have been, but rescue hinged on becoming someone else.

The Garden of Allah was a long way from Oklahoma. The two dozen palm-fringed stucco-and-tile casitas, hotel, and pool on Sunset Boulevard had a movie-land guest list and reputation for partying *and* privacy. When Lela and the girls arrived, it was home to the Marx Brothers and Lillian Hellman, who pushed Phyllis to learn to swim. She had much to learn while Lela tried to write scripts and Ginger ground out pictures. But the next summer, Phyllis was sent back to Oklahoma, and became

From left: Cousin Ginger Rogers, sixteen-year-old Phyllis, and Aunt Lela in Hollywood

Helen Nichols again. However, life changed fast in L.A. Ginger had landed parts in *42nd Street* and *Gold Diggers of 1933,* two hits, resulting in a contract with RKO. Her next picture premiered December 29, 1933: fourth-billed, she was paired with a fifth-billed player named Astaire. At twenty-two, *Flying Down to Rio* was already her twentieth picture, and they made magic together. A dozen years later, she'd be the highest-paid star in L.A. But long before then—in 1934—she and her mother invited her cousin back to Hollywood.

Phyllis was slight, with a low-pitched voice. Thick auburn hair framed fine blue-gray eyes, a button nose, and a heart-shaped, deeply dimpled face, whose wide forehead and cheekbones tapered suddenly into a pointed chin. Side by side, she and Ginger were clearly family, but at some angles her face's geometry came up a bit short. Still, studios signed young people at little cost, and Ginger opened the door: Phyllis was given a screen test by George Cukor. Though she didn't get the part, she got a contract—a salary for forty weeks, and by law, RKO had to hire a tutor and send her to the studio school. The test made an impression, not just because of the contract. As Cukor—one of Hollywood's great directors of women, and a gay man—showed how to read the lines, she laughed: he sounded like a girl. When she saw his face, she realized it wasn't funny. Life was much more complicated than she'd imagined.

Soon the starlet's name and image appeared in *New Movie* and *Photoplay,* and in bit parts in B pictures—a girl in a drugstore, a bridesmaid. Her best chance came in 1936, when cast as John Wayne's love interest in *Winds of the Wasteland.* The role called for Phyllis to start cool, even haughty, which she did well enough, but by picture's end it was obvious she should look for a new career. She began to write for fan magazines, and secured a monthly gossip column, Hollywood Youngstars, in *Hollywood Magazine.* Then Lela—who'd become assistant to RKO's production head—got a special friend, and decided it was time for Phyllis to move out. The aunt who'd taken her away cut her loose, just as her mother had. Anne Shirley, a former child star who was her closest friend, took her in, but then Anne got married. With money from Ginger and a lead from Lela, Phyllis headed to New York to start over, on her own. Soon she found a place, got a job, and began to get used to the city. The man would come next.

. . .

BENNETT SPENT PART OF Labor Day weekend at the Haas family's Vermont home, Red Mountain Barn. The high hills made radio reception in the house terrible, and Bennett couldn't stand being out of the loop. That Friday, September 1, 1939, with Bob, Merle, and their teenage daughter Pat in tow, he drove to the middle of a meadow and turned on the Cadillac's radio. A crackly bulletin declared that Hitler had invaded Poland. They huddled in the car, Pat remembered, afraid and trying to take it in. Everywhere, Americans felt that same fear: war was waiting for them, too. Yet ordinary life, having skipped a beat, went on. RH had recently hired Harry Maule, who'd been let go in his fifties as a senior fiction editor at Doubleday. Bennett, Bob, and Don had sensed that value remained in old-fashioned Harry's relationships with western and mystery authors, and with his one marquee writer, Sinclair Lewis. That Saturday, Bennett drove ninety miles to court Lewis over lunch at his farm in South Pomfret.

His amazing string of novels satirizing middle-class American provincialism, complacency, and self-delusion—*Main Street, Babbitt, Arrowsmith, Dodsworth, Elmer Gantry*—had enjoyed huge sales, and in 1930 Lewis became the first U.S. writer to win the Nobel Prize. Nothing since—except *It Can't Happen Here,* where a fascist is elected president—matched the earlier work. He'd become alcoholic and difficult, yet Bennett admired his work, and bet Lewis still had good, profitable books in him. His new novel would be published by Doubleday in 1940; Lewis listened to Bennett and was tempted, but not ready to jump. Given time, he would. Back home Sunday night, Bennett turned on the radio, and heard FDR announce Britain and France were at war with Germany.

The following Friday, he dictated a letter to Gertrude. He'd been thinking about her and Alice, hoping with all his heart that they'd come through what lay ahead "with colors flying." If he could help, he begged them to let him know. Phyllis Fraser had returned, and was working on scripts for the McCann-Erickson ad agency. She joined him that night at Lindy's, and on Monday he took her to a place he'd come to love, the World's Fair in Flushing, Queens. Bennett adored the razzle-dazzle, fantasyland, and wonders of tomorrow that had sprung up in April on what had been the municipal ash-heap. Yet sometimes when he was with her, he felt sheepish: Phyllis looked so young. His slicked-back hair was dark, but his temples were striped with gray, and he didn't want to be mistaken for anybody's daddy. Still, she was "small and quiet and darling" and deferred to him, and he liked that. When they landed as an item in Ed Sullivan's column, it did not displease him.

In December he trod the red carpet at Grand Central onto the 20th Century Limited, and in Chicago caught the Super Chief for L.A. First up was an important contract with Walt Disney, whose second full-length animated feature, *Pinocchio,* was scheduled for 1940 release. Rather than the usual cheap tie-in, RH would publish a deluxe limited edition as well as a trade hardcover. Bennett made sure to call on Phyllis's cousin Ginger before heading north to spend a few days with Gene and Carlotta O'Neill at Tao House, their hilltop home not far from San Francisco. Talking with Gene that first night until 2 A.M., Bennett again felt spellbound. The next day, as he and the O'Neills walked through acres and acres of garden and fields, they discussed a reprint that would become *Nine Plays,* and he heard about *The Iceman Cometh,* Gene's most complex tragedy to date, harking back to the bars of his youth. By February, Saxe would possess a copy of the script, and Bennett be "deeply thrilled" to read it, but O'Neill feared how an audience might react. Another six years would elapse before *Iceman* would be published and have its Broadway premiere, in 1946.

Back home on Christmas Eve, Bennett had a date with Phyllis, who introduced him to a visitor: her mother. It was obvious how seriously she took their relationship, and Pop, who'd met her, liked Sonny's new girl. Yet he remained skittish, making a point of not meeting again for ten days, and seeing the new year in with someone else. At the office, the decision to hire Harry Maule had paid off: the popular mystery novelist Mignon Eberhart followed Harry to RH, and Vincent Sheean, another well-known writer, had signed on. Bennett also sensed "something there" in *The Ox-Bow Incident,* a first novel from a new western writer, Walter van Tilburg Clark, in which a posse who seem bent on righteous justice descend into a lynch mob. His hunch proved correct: the book garnered good reviews, and would be the basis for a movie starring Henry Fonda.

Wary of Phyllis cornering his calendar, Bennett was surprised by how much time she did take up. During evenings devoted to reading, he liked her quiet company reading beside him at home, and she loved cards and backgammon, being as fiercely competitive as he was. The last weekend in February, they visited Harold Ross for an enchanting day of gaming, and buoyed by a winning streak against his favorite pigeon, Bennett asked her a question mid-play. He was heading to Nassau the following week, and if his luck held, would she like to come along? When he won $346 off Ross, the offer was on.

Together in Nassau: What better place to fall in love?

Phyllis's boss thought a young girl accompanying a man like Bennett a terrible idea, but she countered that they wouldn't be entirely alone. Bob and Merle Haas would be there for the first part of the stay, and Herbert and his young partner, Glen—whom she'd met during his acting days in Hollywood—for the rest. Other friends would also turn up. She decided to go. Night brought beach picnics, bonfires, ghost stories; days were filled with long swims and even longer bike rides. Bennett took to calling her "Thruppence"—"Thrup" for short—the tiniest coin on this British colonial outpost a suitable nickname for one so endearingly small. In photos they lean in, the well-built older man tanned and grinning like a boy, and the young woman shyly smiling, yet clearly knowing something of the world. There were memories of his time there with Sylvia of course, but what better place to fall in love again than a Caribbean island?

That spring of 1940, news from Europe grew more alarming each week: Norway and Denmark had been overrun by the Nazis. Bennett agreed to put together and print a program for the "Allied Ball," a big May 10 fundraiser to help the Brits and French. Germany attacked Belgium, Holland, and Luxembourg that day; Neville Chamberlain was finally ousted and replaced by Winston Churchill. The Dutch surrendered four days later, then Brussels fell, and the Nazis were crashing through French lines. Bennett and Thrup drove for the weekend to Blackberry Hill, the New Jersey farm he'd bought with Don and then ceded when his best friend married Pat. Late Saturday afternoon, the four took themselves to Princeton for tea with Mr. and Mrs. Thomas Mann, who'd fled Germany the year before. But although the world seemed to be "going to hell in a hack," and he and Don began the week in a funk, it was one of Bennett's defining strengths that his spirit couldn't stay down. He'd always driven Cadillacs, but Thrup had lobbied for a Buick convertible. He bought one, telling himself, "Might as well have fun while I can."

Of course, the bad news continued, with Bennett compelled to record its *rat-a-tat* in his diary. Belgium surrendered on May 27; on June 10, Mussolini declared war on Britain and France. RH's sales conference, in light of everything else, seemed "futile." On June 14, as he picked at lunch with Ben Huebsch, the situation was more futile still: the Germans had marched into Paris. Several days later, he went to Rockefeller Center to inspect the sleek new offices Dick Simon and Max Schuster had just inaugurated there. At least he wasn't alone in trying to carry on "normally." France surrendered that day.

McCann-Erickson had sent Phyllis to work on a few scripts in L.A., and he found himself sorely missing "unique, invaluable, irreplaceable, little Thrup." The night after she left, he wrote the first in a stream of letters, admitting the room felt "haunted!!!" The man who'd told his younger self he was better at playing the joker than the lover now played joker-as-lover. When Phyllis wrote that Fox would pay her $150 to act in a picture, ex–Mr. Sidney replied: "Overwhelmed by Fox offer. Always yearned to know a film star. Fully expect you to support me in my old age. Incidentally, I love you." Another letter revealed more: "Never knew I could miss anybody so much! Always seemed to get along fine with anybody who happened to be around. So this is love, hey? What you have done to me!" Almost daily, Phyllis replied. She found him "cute," missed saying goodnight, now depended on him for all her fun. Always "cagey" before, she now admitted to herself (and him): "I'm in love."

Determined as ever, at the end of June, Bennett wrote to her: "YOU AND I will have some happiness, come what may." After Phyllis returned from California, they did spend many happy hours with Don and

Pat, Herbert and Glen, Pop, Harold Ross, the Manges. Everyone seemed to like her. For him, having ignored their cautions about Sylvia, approvals were even more necessary now. Wearing her Hollywood makeup, Phyllis could radiate the public glamour at '21' that Helen Thompson had disdained, but they could also enjoy a simple meal at Hamburger Heaven and create a serene day. On a mid-July Saturday, they put the new convertible through its paces, driving to Beatrice and George Kaufman's Bucks County farmhouse. They'd lunch with George's young writing partner Moss Hart—his weekend place was nearby—for Moss was someone Bennett had grown to admire and wanted in his inner circle. Yet the whole drive down he was tense. George, the driest of wits, always slightly intimidated him, and brilliant Beatrice had known him since Liveright days. Would they think him foolish? To forestall sarcastic cracks, he'd already resorted to jokes about his "daughter," and his own anxiety made him repeatedly warn Phyllis not to be too afraid. The great George was waiting on the portico when they arrived. "So, this is Phyllis," he said, holding out his arms. In ten minutes, she was less scared of George, Bennett saw, than he'd been since first meeting Kaufman.

On Tuesday, when she came to his apartment, he found himself discussing the future. London was being blitzed and an invasion seemed imminent: Surely the United States would enter the war, so how could anyone plan? Yet that weekend had tipped the balance. Lovely she was. Intelligent. She admired him. And no question he'd be in charge. What did he have to lose? A few days later, he took her to Herbert and Glen's, where Weaver and Burrell were visiting. The young woman who'd tittered at George Cukor knew better now. He was pleased: she could hold her own with these cultivated men. Phyllis was "very much in love," Glen saw, but also knew that something troubled her: Bennett was a Jew. Of like age and background, they talked it through.

A weekend at Harold Ross's followed, returning them to the scene where they'd met cute. Bennett had been tiptoeing around the topic of matrimony, but hadn't proposed. When the men were alone, Harold groused: "Why the hell don't you get married?"

"We are going to," Bennett replied. But it was Harold who informed Phyllis.

On the drive back that Sunday, Bennett reprised his fears about the difference in age, but she would have none of it. He told the office Monday morning, and soon apprised the papers. In their items, both the *Times* and the *Herald Tribune* mentioned the essential connection: Cousin Ginger. A week later, Carl Van Vechten photographed the betrothed, and Phyllis began moving her things into the Navarro. A wedding eve party for their hundred closest friends (almost entirely Bennett's) was organized by an old pal.

On Tuesday, September 17, a small group assembled on the edge of the World's Fair grounds at an old clubhouse—a kind of "summer city hall." The previous Christmas, Phyllis had wanted Bennett to meet her mother, but today Virginia was absent, and Phyllis's aunt represented her family. Lela, who'd taken up residence in the Ritz Towers, had persuaded Mayor Fiorello La Guardia—son of a Jewish mother and Catholic father—to officiate, a clever solution to the problem of Bennett's Jewishness and Phyllis's Christianity. Pop, Lela, Phyllis's best friend Anne Shirley, and Harold Ross acted as witnesses. A year and nine days after they first visited "The World of Tomorrow" together, Bennett and Phyllis embarked on their own tomorrow close by.

. . .

WILLIAM FAULKNER HEARD BENNETT'S news from Bob Haas. "Even if he told me why, I still wouldn't believe it," Faulkner declared. "To have escaped once, and then daring fate again. If [he] don't watch out, the gods are going to look around and see him some day." As RH's partners knew, he was talking as much about his own marriage to Estelle Oldham Franklin Faulkner as he was about marriage generally and Bennett's particularly. Bob said that all was well, Bennett blooming on "porterhouse steak and domesticity," but while the gods seemed to smile on the newlyweds, lately they'd been capricious about RH and Faulkner. What it came down to—as with so many authors—was money.

In April RH had published, to fine reviews, *The Hamlet,* first in a trilogy about the Snopes family of Yoknapatawpha County—based on Lafayette County, where Faulkner lived—a setting he populated through many books and stories. He wove together tales from his family, community, and history, grappling with questions of good and evil, time and truth, life and death, race and sex, in lyrical prose having the hallucinogenic power of Mississippi heat. He was the only American to stand beside the European modernists.

A few days after *The Hamlet* was published, Bennett wrote Faulkner that *Information, Please,* one of the country's most popular radio shows,

William Faulkner in Saxe Commins's office

had invited him on. It was an opportunity for nationwide publicity, and he assumed Bill would "get a great kick out of it," since *he* certainly would if invited. But in truth, it was highly unlikely that slow-to-speak Faulkner would, and besides, when he replied, it was clearly out of the question: not only did Faulkner lack the train fare, but the government had summoned him to New Orleans, demanding an extra $450 in back income tax. As usual, he was strapped for cash. There was Estelle, who'd jilted him for a wealthy match when they were young, only to divorce and marry Bill in 1929; she liked nice things. They had three children: two from her first marriage, and Jill, now seven, the daughter they'd had together. He supported relatives and retainers; had debts inherited from his father; and Rowan Oak, their once grand house in Oxford, the county seat, always needed repairs.

He'd made sporadic visits to Hollywood to earn money crafting screenplays, but no work was available. He'd written a handful of magazine stories, but his current agent, Harold Ober—a neighbor of Bob Haas's—had sold only one. The remaining option was RH. Faulkner didn't want to ask for a new advance; instead, he asked for an assignment of $1,000 on royalties due in November, to be used as collateral for a bank loan. Bob agreed. But a few days later, a new letter revealed his affairs were worse. He'd been mortgaging mules one at a time to buy essentials, and had just about run out of animals. He needed that $1,000, and more: $400 a month for two years. Begging even $300, he said: "If not, can I have your blessing to try somewhere else" for a similar deal?

Bob responded straightaway: he expected them to publish together for the rest of their lives, and understood Bill needed "a pretty substantial endowment." The partners accepted that, and wanted to go "just as far as we can . . . even a bit further." The reality, though, was that RH had only shipped about 7,000 copies of *The Hamlet* to stores. On each of Faulkner's last four books—*Absalom, Absalom!; The Unvanquished; The Wild Palms;* and this latest—he'd earned, on average, just under $3,400. Bob knew that Bill couldn't expect much more per title for the foreseeable future, so proposed a different plan: three books for the next three years (Faulkner had spoken of stories, a mystery, and the next Snopes), with a $1,000 advance now; $2,000 as needed this year; and $250 per month in 1941 and '42. It was what he'd wanted, but stretched over three years, not two.

Dammed-up frustrations overran Faulkner's reply: being sole support of all these draining dependents, his time was wasted fretting over money, causing a fine artist like him, who should be free of such burdens and "any moral compass whatever," to "seethe and rage." He might have agreed to Bob's plan, but then the tax bill ballooned to $1,300 and the back-and-forth became even more strained. Bob offered another $1,000 advance.

Not unmindful that the partners had been "good friends for a long time," he didn't want to be a "goddamn nuisance," but now had to have $5,000 for the next year, or $9,000 for two. He had one novel, five stories, and two others mapped out. Four more in his head were "first class," and with a quieter mind bought by $4,000 *in the next six months* would come more: in other words, he wanted the money even sooner. Over time, Bob had given much more than financial support to a brilliant writer but needy man; now he felt it necessary to be firm, and returned to Bill's idea about trying elsewhere.

"You know how deeply I hope that our publishing association will continue," he wrote, but prudence dictated limits. Books weren't selling, and who knew when they would. If Faulkner's finances required his offering the stories to another house, Bob could see no legitimate grounds for stopping him, but hoped no other books would be involved. Should such a possibility arise, he wanted Bill to alert him before making a move. What Bob didn't say was that RH had its own woes. The partners had taken a hit with the FDR books; signed too many costly advances; didn't cull enough deadwood; and overprinted. This time, *they'd* had to go on their knees to the bank to tide them over, and also transfused personal funds. They could only extend themselves for an author so far.

Bill replied that he'd decided to try another firm and upped the ante: since he must have $4,000 in the next six months, he felt sure the other house would want more than one book, and likely it would be the unnamed novel he'd contracted with RH. On June 18, he confirmed in a telegram the alternative offer for the stories and novel, with the understanding that henceforth he'd be published elsewhere. He'd wait until noon the next day to receive RH's acknowledgment before closing the deal. The rival turned out to be Viking. Bob was away when the news arrived: he'd been anxious to help prepare America for conflict, and got permission from the War Department to organize training camps for former officers like himself, to constitute a potential "home guard." Now Bennett had to respond, and did so in characteristic fashion, wiring Bill, promising an air-mail special-delivery letter to follow. "Please do nothing further until you get [it]," he pleaded. He knew Faulkner's real value lay not in current sales, but in prestige, the likelihood it would increase, and that larger sales might ensue. RH needed this author.

Without overtly casting blame on Bob, he told Bill that the training camps had preoccupied his partner. They were heartsick at the idea of Faulkner's leaving, and Bennett was racking his brain to find a way to tide him over. RH owed him $1,000 on the new novel, and Bennett now proposed a $3,000 advance on the story book in monthly installments. Added to the $1,000 they'd already paid, the total would be $5,000 for a novel and book of stories. If Faulkner completed only one book by year's end and needed more cash, they could advance it against his general royalty account. After months of RH being reactive, Bennett now showed that they could take the initiative: he'd been in touch with Harold Guinzburg. The two agreed that if Viking could offer more, Random would bow out as "a token of friendship" to Bill, but if RH's offer was just as good, the fair thing would be for Viking to stand aside. Finally, Bennett asked Bill to recall that RH already had a considerable investment in thousands of copies of his books stored in their inventory; that would present an additional problem if he moved to another house.

Faulkner replied that he must have $10,000, half now, half in monthly payments; he'd asked RH, and they'd declined; another publisher had accepted. He couldn't play "fast and loose" with Guinzburg. He would come to New York the following week, and was sending a copy of this letter to Viking. The intent was clear.

He understood Faulkner's position, Bennett replied, and wanted to be sure "you likewise understand ours." By now, he was embarrassed, angry, and worse—hurt. He wasn't going to retire without a fight. The "additional problem" of those copies of *The Hamlet* sitting in the warehouse came to the fore, and he turned the pain of—as he saw it—his author's disloyalty back on Bill. He'd expect Viking to buy the plates and existing stock at the manufacturing prices. RH had printed more than usual, assuming they'd publish the trilogy; the picture had "radically changed." That evening, he went to see O'Neill's *Ah, Wilderness!* and met Sinclair Lewis for drinks. Yet Bennett also told his diary: "Faulkner probably lost to us," a very rare descending note and sign of defeat. Thinking back to how their association had developed, and considering all RH had done for this proud, gifted, complex man, it was hard to believe it had come to this.

. . .

FAULKNER'S PUBLISHING HISTORY HAD, like Joyce's, twisted and turned. Horace Liveright brought out his first two novels, but when Liveright rejected *Flags in the Dust* as too long, Faulkner's then-agent, Ben Wasson, reworked and cut it, and in 1929 Hal Smith published it at Harcourt as *Sartoris*. Though Liveright had given him his start, the thirty-one-year-old author wrote his aunt: "Well, I'm going to be published by white folks now," adding "much, much nicer there." A Jew, clearly, was not "white" enough. Harcourt, however, rejected the next novel, *The Sound and the Fury*.

When Hal joined with Jonathan Cape, he was able to publish it, and *As I Lay Dying* followed in 1930. That year, Estelle Faulkner became pregnant, and they needed money. Faulkner wrote *Sanctuary,* a novel that Malraux viewed as marking "the intrusion of Greek tragedy into the detective story." It was this shocking tale—how a young woman from a "good" Southern family is corrupted—that a Philadelphia bookseller had urged Bennett to read, and in April 1931, he'd written Faulkner praising it, and offering to put one of his works into the Modern Library.

He'd also promised to send Faulkner any titles he fancied, a proposal of considerable interest to a book-hungry man with too few coins jingling in his pockets. Joyce and Dostoyevsky were requested.

Faulkner came north that November and they met a half dozen times, Bennett finding him a "queer fish" and hard to decipher, but he was solicitous and introduced him to influential friends. After the dissolution of Hal Smith's partnership with Cape, everyone wooed the author of *Sanctuary*. Although Faulkner had suggested *The Sound and the Fury,* Bennett held out for *Sanctuary* for the ML, betting it would outsell any other series title "five to one." But Wasson also had an agenda: he wanted RH to bring out a limited edition of *Idyll in the Desert,* a story that had been sitting around. Prospects for fine-press sales during the terrible year of 1931 had dried up, but for the very productive author of *Sanctuary,* Bennett gambled. He'd rush four hundred signed copies of *Idyll* for Christmas; Faulkner would earn a dollar a book. *Sanctuary* would go into the ML on the usual terms, and he'd pay an extra hundred dollars for an author's preface. In it, Faulkner courted controversy again, saying he'd written the novel solely for money.

In New York, he was having a heady time, but also working on a novel, *Light in August;* a short story; and a dramatization of *Sanctuary,* as well as meeting with Paramount, who wanted a screenplay for Tallulah Bankhead. He wrote Estelle about being in such demand, but she sensed he was too frenetic. Both were in thrall to alcohol, and she grew anxious.

Bill liked bourbon and used it to relax, to cope with shyness, and when he was sick—he didn't trust doctors. At times he miscalculated his capacity, and ill effects lasted a day or two. Then there were the binges. He didn't write when drunk. However, when he finished a book, sometimes the reaction to being drained into page after page was to drink—for several days, a week, or more than a month. He'd plan the binges as a necessary—but to any outsider, ghastly—relief. Other times, when too many demands built up and he couldn't face them down, or when set upon by the panic that seeps through any man from time to time, he'd feel, as he put it, that all his nerve endings were exposed, and, like the young O'Neill, escape into the oblivion of drink. The price might be collapse, but his strong constitution was such that after a few days of drying out, he'd usually rebound.

This trip, full of meetings, translated into pressure, and already there'd been very public drunkenness. One day Bennett, Bill, and Dashiell Hammett—Faulkner loved mysteries and admired the author of *The Maltese Falcon*—were deep into a lubricated lunch at '21.' Bennett had to return to work, but was going to a black-tie party afterward at Blanche Knopf's, and Hammett, a Knopf author, invited himself and Bill along. Early that evening, Bennett met them again at '21' and steered them to Blanche's. The writers sat down, politely accepted glasses from a butler, and drank until Hammett slid to the floor, out cold. Bill rose, said he was going, collapsed, and had to be helped out the door.

A few days later, Bennett hosted Faulkner at home. Alfred Knopf arrived, bearing first editions for Bill to inscribe. Faulkner refused, saying that signing his books was a way to make money on limited editions; otherwise, he only did so for friends. Bennett rushed over, interjecting how distinguished and what an admirer of his work Alfred was, trying to help Knopf save face. Faulkner's reply was, as usual, measured (excruciatingly so): "Mrs. Knopf has been very nice . . . and so I will sign one of those books for you."

Gossip about his condition at parties got around, yet so long as he worked in his room and spent evenings with friends, worry was kept at bay. Then a few days passed with no sightings, his phone unanswered. Hal Smith went with a colleague to his hotel: no Bill. They made the rounds and found him at the Algonquin—and not in good shape. They talked to his agent, who wired Estelle, which is how Bennett came to meet the dark-haired, slender, vivid woman who was Faulkner's wife. A crisis was averted, work continued, and publication of *Idyll* was set. The night before the couple's return to Mississippi, Bennett hosted a small dinner in his apartment. At one point, Estelle grew bored and wandered from the room. Bennett understood. He put a record on the phonograph, then asked if she'd care to dance; he charmed her as they danced a good while.

The next day, the agent thanked him for the "courtesies" he'd shown. Bill and Estelle were grateful, and decided that this publisher was all right. By the end of the year, after finished copies of *Idyll* arrived, they also liked the books he made. Nevertheless, during Smith & Haas's brief life, Faulkner had remained loyal to Hal and Bob, publishing four books with them. Then came the merger, and it was Random House that brought out *Absalom, Absalom!* in 1936, which many critics and scholars regard as Faulkner's finest novel. *The Unvanquished* came two years later, and *The Wild Palms* in 1939.

The quality and frequency of his output was astounding, even more so given how he shuttled between book-writing in Mississippi and screenplays in Hollywood. With books, he didn't look kindly on editorial interference with his text, and on proofs would respond to a query with a laconic "Why in hell not?" or "No, damn it!!!" He did, however, suffer the same kinds of "corrections" that Stein had complained about over her own work, as was evident in *Absalom, Absalom!* (later editions would restore some material that had been altered). When the original title of this latest book—*If I Forget Thee, Jerusalem*—was dropped in favor of *The Wild Palms,* the title of its first story, Bill was angry, but Bob insisted that the book needed more of a "selling" title. It did well at first, but then, as Don wrote to a vacationing Bennett, "died pretty completely." In fact, business was "lousy" all around, for newspapers covering world events in 1939 were "more interesting than any book." Nevertheless, *The Hamlet* would appear next year.

Faulkner once told a friend that he saw Bennett as "a con man," "the greatest salesman," who probably didn't read manuscripts. Bennett would never be the partner he'd turn to for advice. After Hal was pushed out, Bob and Saxe maintained primary responsibility for the day-to-day, and Faulkner's relationship with them deepened. In long, at times anguished epistolary dialogues, he chewed over money matters—buying land, negotiating loans, taking Hollywood jobs—as though Bob were akin to a father figure. All three partners were aware of his complex personal life: the female companionship he sought outside marriage, and the friction between him and Estelle. The crises with alcohol were another matter. Bennett had seen him drunk during that New York trip in 1931, but his full introduction had come in October 1937, after Bill arrived for several weeks at the Algonquin. Meta Carpenter, his Hollywood lover, had married, and she and her husband were passing through New York. He desperately wanted to see her. For ten days, there'd been the regular to-and-fro with Random, but the last week in October, he'd stopped answering letters or calls, and missed meetings. Neither Estelle nor his agent could reach him. Feeling "anxious" on a Friday, Bennett had written again, asking Bill to ring him at home Saturday morning.

That same Friday, a drinking pal, Eric Devine, went to the hotel and got access to his room. Naked but for his undershorts, Faulkner had fallen against a bathroom steam pipe in his stupor and lay unconscious, a burn the size of a man's palm near the small of his back. A doctor was summoned at once, who dressed the burn and administered paraldehyde to help him get through withdrawal. RH was soon informed.

"Bill Faulkner in a coma. Got him a male nurse," Bennett scribbled in his diary, the nurse being Devine. For fourteen hours he slept a drugged sleep (what Bennett had called a coma). As days passed, he got through the delirium, dehydration, shakes, and malnourishment of alcoholic poisoning, but the back wouldn't heal. Infections, skin grafts, and pain would plague Faulkner for years. A week or so after the "accident," RH arranged for him to return to Mississippi accompanied by Devine, who was given $350 of *The Wild Palms* advance as pay. The partners had asked him to report on Bill's condition, and the "domestic situation," when he got back. Years later, Bennett recalled going to say goodbye before the two men's long train ride south. He didn't like emotional messiness; others were better when patience and deep empathy were called for.

"Bill, aren't you ashamed of yourself?" he blurted, still baffled by what his author had brought upon himself.

"Bennett, it was *my* vacation," Faulkner responded, quietly.

It was hardly the last "vacation" they'd have to rescue him from.

Now it was 1940, almost three years later, and Random's gentlemen faced an almost certain likelihood they'd lose him to Viking. Faulkner came to New York to see Harold Guinzburg on June 25 and seal his deal, but Harold told him that, given Bennett's new condition about compensating RH for Faulkner inventory, he couldn't finalize any contract until he and Bennett met. Unfortunately, Harold had to leave town and wouldn't be available for a week. Faulkner went home not knowing who his publisher would be.

On July 3, Harold sent his answer. Bennett had insisted that Viking pay $1,500 for the stock and plates of the first Snopes book if Bill jumped houses for the other two. It was more than Harold could justify, and he had to bow out. Five days later, Bennett wrote from a position of strength, hoping Bill would be at Random "for all time" and able to work through money woes on what the firm offered. They wanted to make things as easy for him as they could, but also to protect RH at a time when their business was "beset with unusual problems and hazards." A postscript tried to restore the old footing, with jokes about Bob's KP duty, but jokes weren't what Faulkner wanted.

He replied, not addressing what had occurred, nor accepting that he'd have to stay, but instead offering comments on *The Ox-Bow Incident.*

Bennett had sent a copy, seeking his opinion; contrary to others, Bill judged the novel "dull." The subtext of grievance and disappointment was clear: "What has happened to writing, anyway?" Bill asked. Saying he knew of no young writers "worth a damn," he asked Bennett to explain that.

Bennett tried again, seeking definite assurance that he'd acceded to RH's terms. A few days later, Faulkner replied: "I have not approached any other publisher, and at present I do not intend to." It was the closest he could put acquiescence into words.

RH would do everything to make things as easy as they could, Bennett repeated. Faulkner and O'Neill were "keystone" authors and the firm could not lose them. There was something—or rather, someone—else he knew well: Harold. They'd gambled and traveled together. It was shrewd calculation on his part that had made Bill too high a risk for Viking. Bennett—not Bob or Don—had figured out the way to keep him.

. . .

THE ROMANTIC CRUISE THAT Bennett had planned and Sylvia Sidney had nixed for his first marriage wasn't the honeymoon he had with Phyllis the second time around. After the wedding luncheon, they dusted rice from the car and set out for the nation's capital. He'd mapped out a motor tour, taking in sites like Monticello and Gettysburg, suiting himself. However, even the most pragmatic twenty-four-year-old has her dreams, and this wasn't what Phyllis expected. Years later, about their 11 P.M. arrival at the Shoreham Hotel, she was tart: "So a seven-hour drive. Happy honeymoon."

Lela Rogers's old friend J. Edgar Hoover (they'd met when she was a Marinette) provided a car and chauffeur to take them around. Bennett was thrilled to meet the top cop and be given a private tour of his fiefdom. He and Phyllis even fired tommy-guns at targets in the bureau's basement shooting gallery. But walking past rows of cabinets, did it occur to him that some housed dossiers on "suspects" who'd done no more than he had—visiting Spain and Russia, supporting anti-fascist causes, dating a girl like Helen? (Phyllis presented no such problem: her conservative politics were like her aunt's.)

As they traveled on, she felt the hotels he'd chosen were suited to a salesman rather than a bride; nor did she share her husband's appetite for guided history and sightseeing. Six days into the marriage, when they reached the Luray Caverns in Virginia, she balked at entering. Bennett insisted: it would be fun, and besides, Herbert had suggested the outing. "I don't want to go on a honeymoon with Uncle Herbert," she retorted. They arrived at Williamsburg late that afternoon and had a swim. But when Bennett—whose energy was only now wholly revealing itself—decided there was time to tour the town, she begged off. He set out, returning full of what he'd show her the next day. Frustration had kindled a slow burn; anger was a familiar feeling. Phyllis sulked, but Bennett seemed oblivious—or chose to ignore the signs. The burn flared: she'd make herself clear by not going to dinner. Unfazed, he went alone. Stuck in the room, she felt "staggered," never treated like this by a man; worse, he was the one she'd married.

Six days later, when they boarded a ship in Norfolk to return to New York, she saw her future more clearly. She wasn't Ginger, who could flit from husband to husband (eventually, five). Bennett would become father, mother, mentor, furnishing a shelter such as she'd never had, and under which she could bloom—at a price. He had a temper that could rage suddenly. If she got angry, sulking wouldn't work (she'd discover that tears sometimes did). She'd have to choose fights carefully, and shout him down. But he would always be the center, and she would accommodate herself to his career, habits, likes, dislikes, and keep up with his inexhaustible (and exhausting) energy. To get what she wanted, she'd have to work through Bennett—or find a way around him.

"She made him a marvelous wife," Don said later, then added: "It wasn't easy."

When they returned at the end of September, Pop came down from his small apartment upstairs to greet them, but not alone: his longtime lady friend, Eva, was with him. She lived in a place he'd secured nearby, where he spent half the week. Pop had never spoken of her to Bennett: she was "secret." But with this marriage—a real one, Pop figured—it was time for the man he'd called Sonny for forty-two years to grow up. They embraced and cried.

Bennett had always eaten out or summoned room service, and his parties were catered by Reuben's. Now, using a hot plate and sink in the butler's pantry, Phyllis made scrambled eggs for breakfast, and made Bennett happy. On a visit to friends in Westchester that weekend, they took a detour to inspect an "intriguing" house for sale in Mt. Kisco. In the end they gave it a pass, but rather liked the area.

When Ted Geisel came to Random House a few days later, Bennett was delighted that Ted and Phyllis already had a connection. Much of his lucrative advertising work was for McCann-Erickson, and he kept some things in a desk drawer in their Manhattan offices for occasional visits—a desk now usually occupied by Phyllis. She'd also been the person who'd forwarded letters to him in California.

Anne Shirley (left) and Leonora
"Bubbles" Schinasi, Phyllis's best friends

In November, the Cerfs held their first "at home" with four guests: beloved professor Raymond Weaver and partner John Burrell from Bennett's world, and Leonora Schinasi and mother Ruby from Thrup's. While Weaver had played a formative role in Bennett's intellectual development, Leonora would come to understand him better than anyone. With a mischievous wit and ravenous appetite for books, she made a charming foil for the academics. "Bubbles" (as she was called) had, like Ginger, been battled over by divorcing parents. Her mother remarried, and she grew up a lonely little rich girl in a Riverside Drive mansion. With jet-black hair and a wide-eyed allure (in photos she, too, could look like Sylvia), Bubbles eloped with a young actor, Wayne Morris, and became close to Phyllis in L.A. When the marriage failed, she went back East with a baby.

That December, Phyllis gave Bennett and Pop their first home Christmas, and the two secular Jews loved it. Bubbles and year-old Michael were often there, and Pop, so happy to have a baby around, placed a small cradle under the tree, hinting at what he'd like from Phyllis. He needn't have worried: as the test she took a few days later confirmed, she was already pregnant. She'd seen too many broken marriages up close; perhaps this baby would ensure a future. Whether the news, when Bennett heard it, brought back disturbing memories of his mother's miscarriages is impossible to say. What's certain is that having lived a well-ordered life for so long, he didn't want any disruption. On the last day of the year, he visited his childhood friend Morty Rodgers—Dick Rodgers's brother was now an obstetrician/gynecologist. All Bennett told his diary was: "Reached BIG DECISION." The pregnancy continued. However, in early February he couldn't help noting "disquieting thoughts" about the creature inside Phyllis he referred to as "Pulsifer," and she herself sensed he was frightened of fatherhood.

For sure, they couldn't remain long in the Navarro. Phyllis was still working—Bennett didn't want a wife who had nothing to talk about—but she also began to look for a new home. With Bennett accustomed to his view of the park, he hoped to go one better—a penthouse—so she made the rounds with agents to see places on Fifth and Park Avenues atop all the "nicest" buildings. But when she became really interested, too often the agent didn't follow up. A comment might slip out about her husband's unusual surname. Questions might be posed, or hints dropped. Finally, someone explained that New York City's best buildings often had "restrictions." Phyllis had not appreciated that marrying a Jew would provide her with a humiliating education in antisemitism.

Bennett's old Sands Point pal, commercial artist Neysa McMein—an independent woman who'd created the image of the ultimate housewife, Betty Crocker—knew how artists grappled with problems over studio space. "Why don't you look at houses?" Neysa suggested. The second one Phyllis saw was 132 East Sixty-Second Street, a five-story brownstone with a small back garden between Park and Lexington Avenues, an easy walk to the office on Fifty-Seventh Street. They bought it for $20,000 cash. Robert Heller, who'd redone Bennett's Navarro bedroom in Deco Modern, was tapped to do the same for the house.

In mid-October 1941, a little more than a year after their wedding day, the Cerfs moved into East Sixty-Second Street: a new start tinged with more joy and sorrow than Bennett had ever anticipated. Two weeks earlier, Pop had died, aged seventy-three. He'd had a stroke, and at Lenox Hill Hospital Bennett spent "an anguished hour" with his father but could take no more than that. After a general collapse in the night, Gustave Cerf never regained consciousness. Don was the one to speak a few words at the crematorium.

132 East 62nd Street (middle house)

But then, there had been that *other* event that Pop had lived long enough to see. On August 19, Christopher Bennett Cerf was born, Dr. Morty Rodgers delivering him by caesarean section. Eight days later, sitting at midnight in the familiar apartment in a world upended by unfamiliar emotions, Bennett jotted a note on Modern Library paper to his twenty-five-year-old wife, still recovering at Lenox Hill. In an unusually deliberate hand, he wrote: "Darling, I just thought I'd tell you how much I love you and how proud I am of you—Goodnight," and popped it in the corner box for the first collection.

Earlier that year, RH had published another "impenetrable" brainchild from Gertrude, entitled *Ida,* giving Bennett the pleasure of corresponding with a favorite author. In September, he wrote her about wife, baby, house: "The transition from *The Playboy of the Western World* to *The Man of Property* has not been accomplished without a great deal of *sturm* and *drang*. . . . [Had you] seen the antics I have gone through you would have howled with laughter." Sonny truly was a grown-up now.

PART THREE

1941–1951

Try and Stop Me

Our business is now greater than that of Knopf and Viking put together. When you consider the fact . . . that we are still only boy publishers, just think where we'll get when and if you ever reach puberty. That's a pretty dazzling thought. Take it slowly.

—Bennett A. Cerf to Major Donald S. Klopfer

No one underrates his ability to make the twelve Herculean labors seem like light housework. When we say no one, we include Mr. Cerf.

—*"Note About the Author" in* TRY AND STOP ME

Chapter 16

Patriotism and Profit

CURLY-HAIRED, CLEVER, STUTTERING, SHY HOLLYWOOD PRINCELING Budd Schulberg never forgot the seed of encouragement that Bennett had planted, after seeking him out to praise his college newspaper writing. After Dartmouth, Budd returned to Los Angeles, became a junior scriptwriter for David Selznick, and began to publish stories on the side. Into one, "What Makes Sammy Run?," he distilled all he'd seen of the ruthless ambition coursing beneath Hollywood's sheen. More Sammy stories followed, and in 1939, seeing they might become a novel, he went to New York to show Bennett the seed was taking root. Budd considered the RH contract Bennett offered, despite only a $250 advance, a real turning point. Saxe gave the editorial guidance the insecure young man needed; Bennett read closely, making suggestions. Budd felt he was "being brought into a family."

B. P. Schulberg, however, tried to dissuade his son from publishing the novel, fearing that exposing Hollywood's underbelly—and the prevalence of Jews in the system—might unleash antisemitic attacks and exile Budd from the business. Having endured Hollywood's uglier side in the Sylvia debacle, Bennett recognized that studio moguls might cause trouble, but believed in the book and was determined to proceed. He could reassure Budd (and himself) when the reps placed 7,000 copies of *What Makes Sammy Run?* into stores before publication in April 1941—really impressive for a first novel—and was buoyed by reactions to advance copies. Dorothy Parker raved, and Scott Fitzgerald, who'd briefly worked with Budd on a screenplay for *Winter Carnival,* wrote the kind of blurb a publisher dreams of: the book was "utterly fearless," written with both beauty and satire, conveying "the feeling of Hollywood with extraordinary vividness."

Budd was in L.A. when the book came out, finishing a script for Sam

Budd Schulberg

Goldwyn, and about to leave work one evening when the supremo summoned him. Instead of discussing the screenplay, Goldwyn screamed, purple-faced: "That horrible book—you're a traitor to this industry and the Hollywood community!" and fired him. But Budd and RH had the last word: *What Makes Sammy Run?* became a critical success, bestseller, and groundbreaking classic about Hollywood, marking the start of an important career. It also brought Budd and the Cerfs closer; he was one of a select few whom Phyllis permitted to call her "Thrup." Still, he learned there were certain places this friendship could not go. As his marriage began to unravel, he saw Bennett protect himself with jokes whenever Budd tried to pour out the turmoil in his heart. That kind of listening was Saxe's role. Budd would save only the happy things for Bennett.

. . .

WHEN 1941 BEGAN, RH, still in debt to the bank from the FDR misadventure and other difficulties, could only publish about thirty new trade titles a year. Most were novels, but the demand for nonfiction was growing in response to the upheavals in Europe and Asia. The firm brought out Edgar Snow's eyewitness account of the situation in Hong Kong and the Philippines, *The Battle for Asia;* John Strachey's *A Faith to Fight For,* "championing . . . democracy against the imminent catastrophe of a Nazi victory"; and Quentin Reynolds's reportage of the Blitz, *London Diary*. Bennett was especially drawn to Reynolds, star war reporter for

Collier's, a big, all-around good guy, as Bennett saw him: when "Quent" started waving the flag, it felt like you were "standing on a summit . . . with a ten-thousand-voice chorus of *The Star-Spangled Banner.*" He'd broadcast human-interest stories from England, and narrated *London Can Take It,* a British propaganda short released to fifteen thousand theaters. When he and wife Ginny were in town, Bennett loved partying with them.

In June 1941, after publishing *London Diary,* Random signed Elliot Paul for a nonfiction book about Paris to follow *Life and Death of a Spanish Town.* Paul had spent most of the interwar years there, and Bennett envisaged a "heartwarming" portrait of the street where he'd lived, representing a "lost" city that millions of Americans had loved pre-war. They'd borrow a title from a Kern/Hammerstein tune and call it *The Last Time I Saw Paris.* But Paul wanted to do more than send a love letter to the city and sell books: he'd show, through the street's people, that anywhere could be fertile ground for fascism, lacing the story with asides on collaboration, refugees, and the U.S. role in the world. "There is so darn much appeasement," he wrote Saxe. Refusing to be a party to it in order to gain sales, he knew that "Bennett will feel the same way about the situation if he understands it."

Saxe certainly did: his wife had family in Paris, and no idea of their fate. While he moved and trimmed passages from the too-long manuscript, careful to keep the novelistic portrait that Bennett favored, he also ensured that Paul's views came through strong and clear. "I should name you as co-author," Paul told him; instead, Bennett gave Saxe a $500 bonus. He also sold the book to MGM—the seventh movie deal he'd made in quick succession. *The Last Time I Saw Paris* would become a number-one bestseller, and readers would love the book—apart from those at Boston's Watch and Ward Society, who banned it for being injurious to public morals—but then, it *was* about Paris.

On the first Sunday afternoon in December, the Cerfs were engaged in a favored activity—bridge—at their friends Harry and Bernardine Scherman's country home in New Jersey. The radio hummed as the couples sat, squabbling over points. There were no cries from infants: in the very adult world in which Bennett thrived, four-month-old Christopher had been left with the nurse. Suddenly a radio bulletin demanded attention: the Japanese had attacked Pearl Harbor naval base in Hawaii. They all felt foolish, having argued over a game. Bennett couldn't keep still: he plunged outside for a stiff walk in the cold, before he and Phyllis got in the car to return to the city.

Donald, as it happened, was also in New Jersey when he heard. He, Pat, and Pat's teenage son, Tony, had spent the weekend at their farm, and were driving back when the car radio crackled with the startling news. Two years earlier, after Spain had fallen to Franco with Germany's help, Don had said to Bennett: "I can't get it out of my head that Hitler will never be stopped until someone is really willing to fight." America, then, wasn't willing to be that someone. Now Pearl Harbor brought a national epiphany and collective shock: eighteen ships sunk or incapacitated; many men lost. Nine hours later, Japan destroyed the U.S. bomber command in the Philippines. The country was at war.

Back in the office that week, Bennett paced back and forth, puffing on his pipe while reeling off rapid-fire dictation to Pauline. He mused in a letter to Gene and Carlotta that it felt "kind of funny" living in a lovely new home with a new baby while the country faced war. Glancing out at Fifty-Seventh Street, he saw people with Christmas packages rushing in all directions, seemingly unaware that there'd been two air-raid alarms in the past two hours. The whole thing was "so fantastic, it [was] almost unbelievable."

Later that week, the Japanese sunk the British battleship *Prince of Wales* and cruiser *Repulse* off Malaya. While the gears of the country began to shift in ways nobody could yet grasp, Bennett went on with his usual life like the busy people he'd watched through the window, but he also saw clearly that there would be an array of opportunities brought by war. Cecil Brown, one of Edward R. Murrow's CBS News boys, had been on the *Repulse* en route to a Singapore posting when the ship went down, but he survived. Friends told Bennett how good Brown's night-owl radio dispatches were, and he tracked him down on the other side of the world. Twelve days after he'd nearly died, Brown had an agreement with RH; his wife, Martha, hammered out details with Bennett in New York.

By the time Brown made it home in April, Singapore had fallen, Java was lost, and Rangoon almost gone. Three months later, he delivered five-hundred-plus pages that blamed the British for what had happened. Books were slower, but had wider latitude than newspapers to call out mistakes in the conduct of the war, especially if publishers were willing to face off against censors. Still, Bennett realized he'd have to be nimbler, competing with the papers and radio. He vowed to publish Brown's *Suez to Singapore* in three months—three times faster than usual—even though the book required a lot of paper, not easy to come by, and RH would have to mount an expensive advertising blitz.

On publication day in October 1942, the Cerfs took the Browns to celebrate at the Stork, and the evening felt to Bennett like the opening of a play. They drank, smoked, ate, and talked, but it was all an effort at waiting, the way a playwright does, for the morning papers to hit the streets with the first reviews. It was late when they set out in search of a twenty-four-hour newsstand with an early delivery. From Fifty-Second and Fifth they walked until Fifty-Ninth and Third, where bundles of fresh newsprint beckoned. They bought a paper and bent under a streetlight reading, then the two couples in evening dress paired off and began dancing up the street. The rave review was the first of many; *Suez to Singapore,* like *The Last Time I Saw Paris,* would be an immediate bestseller.

While the war brought opportunities, it also brought problems, not least in terms of personnel: men were leaving to fight, creating hard-to-fill holes. Selective Service legislation had been passed by Congress in 1940, and after war was declared, all males eighteen to sixty-five had to register for the draft. Bennett received his classification: 3A, deferred because of dependents and age. Bob Haas, already over fifty, was promoted to lieutenant colonel in the New York National Guard, dividing his time between the office and home-front duty. Don turned forty soon after the United States declared war. With dependents—Pat, Tony, and Lois, too, since Marian's husband wasn't much of a provider—he didn't have to fight, but couldn't stand aside. He talked to Pat. At thirty-six, she wanted to give him a baby, but had miscarried several times; if he enlisted, there might not be a chance for a child. Still, she couldn't get in his way. He talked to Marian, who said she'd go to work to support Lois. Last, he talked to Bennett, formally asking his partner's permission to leave RH for as long as the country needed him. Both knew he had to go.

Don went down to D.C. to lobby for a commission in the Army Air Forces, and on Bennett's birthday, the last Monday in May, a wire from Uncle Sam arrived appointing Donald Simon Klopfer a captain, and ordering him to leave for California on Saturday. "STUNNED," Bennett wrote in his diary, but after he saw Captain Klopfer for the first time in

Captain Donald S. Klopfer

uniform, added: "LOOKS GREAT." The office staged a tearful farewell on Friday, and in between the goodbyes, Bennett kept very, very busy. Midafternoon Saturday, he drove his best friend to the plane. By 4:30 P.M., Donald was gone.

On a small slip of letterhead paper Bennett noted in a very clear hand, "BAC bet Donald that Klopfer is back at Random House Jan. 1, 1945. $25 even," the kind of cocky wartime wager used to keep hope close and fear at bay. The two would refer to that bet many times as a kind of talisman: Donald must return—one of them had to pay up! But back at work Monday, the office felt lonely. The chair across the desk loomed empty, while the smell of Don's tobacco hovered faintly. At RH's summer party at Bob Haas's Scarsdale home, the tennis was tempered by Don and Pop not being there.

Captain Klopfer, on the other hand, wrote "the Gang" as soon as he arrived in California about how tremendously thrilling it was to know how much friends cared, an emotional kick that comes "too seldom." He described his routine: up at 6:15, working all day at drill and in lectures. By dinner, he was "usually dead." It was harder for him than for the single men, because together with Pat and Tony, he had to live off-base.

"We all envy you," Bennett assured him, "particularly sad" at not having to rise at six. Turning serious, he was most anxious that Don send reports for the gang to devour.

Don, too, was hungry for what he no longer had. He wanted "Cerfie" to keep him abreast of everything, being lonesome for the life he'd led, the language he'd spoken, the dear friends. He aimed for an intelligence job or to be a squadron commander. Don liked the cadets, and might enjoy "wet-nursing" them through training. Right now, though, he'd been put in charge of training aids, specifically a 600-page aviation manual that needed editing and printing. He urged the Cerfs to take advantage of the farm on weekends. It was in wonderful condition, Bennett wrote at the end of August, yet being there left him with a strange empty feeling. They wouldn't return anytime soon.

With Don gone, Bennett shouldered more work, but his extracurricular activities also proliferated. He was churning out anthologies, which by 1942 included two *Bedside Books; Three Famous Murder Novels;* and *Sixteen Famous American Plays*. Since his 1936 debut in *The Saturday Review of Literature,* alter ego "Tony Bump" had grown popular through occasional pieces, and recently, when Christopher Morley decided to step down from chronicling the literary scene in his Trade Winds column, the *SRL*'s twenty-seven-year-old editor, Norman Cousins, asked Bennett to step up. They agreed on twenty-five dollars a column, but though money definitely mattered, the influence he'd gain was the bigger lure. Bennett's playful debut in February had contrasted with Morley's more serious tone, and aimed to forestall potential problems. He'd asked for indulgence for future gaffes, and promised to be "pretty careful" not to favor his own house. He'd "roam" the literary world, but also take in theater and Hollywood news, paying more attention to connections between books, Broadway, and movies than most publishers did.

Toggling between publications and personalities in that first column, he'd noted that Viking was bringing out Steinbeck's story of Norwegian resistance, *The Moon Is Down,* while its president, Harold Guinzburg, was away creating government war propaganda, having put Ben Huebsch in charge for the duration. Leaping from Hollywood "dope" on Hitchcock's *Suspicion,* he landed on the latest book club picks (*The Last Time I Saw Paris* just happened to be the Literary Guild choice). And inevitably, that first Trade Winds ended with a joke. As the column developed, he showed a knack for bringing readers along, whether it was describing Scribner's Fifth Avenue bookstore, where the window display of war titles, railroad posters, and tank models was "stopping passers-by in their tracks," or taking them to Washington to meet Major Trautman, who was in charge of buying books for the army. The fact that military post

MIND-READING ACTS have always struck me as a lot of apple-sauce, and nothing that I observed while officiating as a guest judge on Dunninger's radio program has led me to change my mind. Dunninger has climbed to the top of his profession, which is quite understandable. He is a smooth and experienced showman, quick as a flash, a marvelously dexterous prestidigitator, and his line of patter is often very amusing. His weekly radio program is popular all over the country. His new book, "What's On Your Mind," sold 100,000 copies in less than a month. But as to that "master mentalist" and "thought reading" stuff, you certainly can't prove it by me.

Many of my friends heatedly maintain that they have participated in actual cases of mind reading, although some of them call it by fancier names, like E.S.P. and mental telepathy. It's never happened to me. The other three judges and I concentrated for an hour on trying to make Dunninger read one single thought in any of our minds but when the program ended he was still telling people in the audience the numbers on their automobile licenses and the addresses of their cousins. In the last few minutes my thoughts reached a point where I half expected the great man to come over and poke me in the jaw. He's big enough to do it. But everything ended on a tranquil note, and I wandered off knowing—and believing—as little about mind reading as I did before I came.

I have never understood why an honest-to-goodness mind reader didn't go down to Wall Street, put the bee on a couple of tycoons and professional market riggers, and make enough in a month to retire for life. I can't believe they bang around the country going through all their elaborate hokus-pokus because they like it. . . .

DUNNINGER, who can do just about anything with a pack of cards but make them read the *Congressional Record*, told us about one happy encounter he had with a couple of notorious swindlers on a Fall River night-boat. The boys took him for an easy mark, and lured him and a New Bedford merchant into a little game of poker. Dunninger ended up with a profit of over eight hundred dollars. A hundred and thirty of it came from the innocent victim. "I really didn't mind losing to such interesting gentlemen," said the latter the next morning. "Interesting is the word," said the "Master Mentalist." "You were playing with two of the biggest crooks in the East—and *my* name is Dunninger." The man got back his stake plus ten percent of the winnings, and probably is still telling the story in New Bedford. . . .

IT WAS JUST a stone's throw from Dunninger at Radio City to the Harvest Moon Ball at Madison Square Garden, and the completion of a typical evening of research work for a conscientious publisher. The Harvest Moon Ball is one of the most fantastically successful newspaper promotions in the history of journalism. Every summer the *Daily News* stages a series of elimination contests to determine the best amateur dancers of the fox-trot, waltz, rhumba, and jitterbug in the various sections of metropolitan New York. The finalists then dance it off at the Garden, while twenty-two thousand rabidly partisan fans pack the arena, and additional thousands mill around the streets trying to squeeze in. Ed Sullivan, the Broadway columnist, M.C.s the show, introduces guest acts and celebrities, and hustles the prize winners off to a week's engagement at Loew's State Theatre, where everybody cashes in handsomely.

Last year the big winner turned out to be AWOL from the Navy, and a few hours after his picture appeared on the front page he was meditating on the caprices of fame in a nearby brig. This year's show produced nothing as dramatic as that, but the crowd roared with delight when the blossoming Shirley Temple did an old dance routine with her erstwhile mentor, Bill "Bojangles" Robinson. It roared even louder when that wonderful little man, Irving Berlin, climbed onto the platform and warbled the song he had composed in Italy, "There Are No Wings on a Foxhole."

If you heard Berlin sing his "How I Hate to Get Up in the Morning" either in "Yip Yip Yaphank," or twenty-five years later in "This Is the Army," you know that he's not exactly a Sinatra or "der Bingle." Just after he had rendered the song for the film version of "This Is the Army," he overheard an electrician exclaim, "If the guy who wrote that song hoid this boid singing it, I bet he toined over in his grave." . . .

FOR WEEKS the entire literary world has been aflame with rumors that Marshall Field is planning to enter the book-publishing business in a very substantial way. The announcement that Freeman Lewis has resigned from Doubleday to become Field's consultant lends substance to these rumors. Lewis is one of the ablest and most dynamic figures in the expanding reprint market. No contract has been signed as yet but an announcement is expected any day. . . .

THE FIRST DRAMATIC HIT of the new theatrical season is "Anna Lucasta," by Philip Yordan, who has quite a reputation as a writer in Hollywood. The play is laid in Harlem and is acted by an all-Negro cast. When it first went the rounds of managers' offices, however, it concerned a Polish-American family, which explains the title. Rose Franken, author of "Claudia," made a similar drastic switch when her first play, "Another Language," failed to impress as a Bronx dialect comedy in the Kober vein. The accents were eliminated, the locale switched, and the play turned into a solid success. . . . Every other week, the Book-of-the-Month Club has been sponsoring dances and entertainments for service men, with employees of the Club acting as hostesses. The parties are directed by the Defense Recreation Committee of New York, and have been a huge success from the start. Suddenly the chairman noticed that the man who supervised the food and drinks, representing the hotel where the parties are held, was zealously suggesting means of cutting down expenses. "This is nice of you, I'm sure," he was told, "but why this sudden interest in the size of the check?" "I just joined the Book-of-the-Month Club," the man explained candidly, "and I figure that the less it spends, the better those dividend books will be." . . .

MGM has completed the film version of Sally Benson's "Meet Me in Saint Louis." I asked a studio executive if it was a faithful adaptation. "Faithful?" he echoed. "Wait till you hear Judy Garland sing 'Clang, Clang,

20 *The Saturday Review*

"Columning" opens new doors

exchanges (PXs) would likely start selling them to soldiers—providing a new business stream—was truly welcome news to every publisher.

Bennett was such a hit that by fall, the *SRL* doubled his space and agreed to double his pay, and very quickly *Reader's Digest* began to excerpt material for its millions of monthly subscribers. Eventually the column's success would open a door for Phyllis, too. She and a friend, Edith Young, whose husband was an RH printer, enjoyed doing *Herald Tribune* cryptograms, and proposed to create puzzles on vaguely bookish themes for the *SRL*. The first "Literary Crypt" by the pseudonymous "Fraser Young" would appear in June 1943. Trade Winds would give the "intriguing new" feature a boost, but its columnist kept mum about his connection to its compilers.

. . .

IN 1941, THE TEN-MILLIONTH copy of a Modern Library book had been printed, a milestone celebrated with as much ballyhoo as Bennett could muster: a five-month PR campaign inspired by movie promotions, done almost entirely outside normal book channels. Across the country, papers carried photos of a Phi Beta Kappa beauty relaxing amid ML volumes. Sarong-clad star Dorothy Lamour posed tongue-in-cheek with *The Complete Novels of Jane Austen*. For features hailing "the Henry Fords of literature" who'd "cashed in on the classics" by making them available and affordable, Bennett fed reporters tales of the "exciting" publishing game—yet still had cause for worry.

A few years earlier, Depression economics had convinced Robert de Graff, a hardcover reprint publisher, that the titles in his "Blue Ribbon" series cost too much. He found in Dick Simon and S&S's "little bookkeeper" Leon Shimkin men who understood the time was ripe for something new. In 1939, he joined with all three S&S partners to found a company—de Graff controlled 51 percent—that would open a new world in American publishing. They named it Pocket Books, and its paperback products would retail for only twenty-five cents each. It was Dick, whose credo about giving the reader a break came to the fore, who'd insisted on that revolutionary price. Leon's contribution was about distribution: the books would be sold through drugstores, news agents, even Sears.

Bennett had downplayed the threat, insisting that if they succeeded, he'd adapt the ML into paper, and Pocket would "fold in three months." The bravado, as usual, masked fear: after all, in 1936, the year after Penguins were born, he'd written Don from London to say that they ought to consider a twenty-five-cent line themselves. But if done in parallel to the ML, a paperback line would have entailed serious investment; alternatively, if they'd dispensed with hardcovers and reengineered the ML as paperbacks, each book would bring far less money, a gamble they couldn't take. Yet Pocket was such a hit—23 million copies sold by 1942—he had to keep the upstart very closely in his sights. For two decades, his relationship with Dick and Max had involved friendship, rivalry, and symbiosis. That last, surprisingly, had come into play again when, knowing Bennett was exactly the right man for the job, they'd asked him to edit a *Pocket Book of American Plays*. He obliged.

When in July 1942 de Graff invited him to take on a second anthology, this one devoted to military humor, Bennett again found the idea irresistible and soon wrote Don, begging for any and all war-related anecdotes he could send. With possible army and Red Cross bulk purchases, the paperback could sell half a million copies! To do it all—run the company; compile Trade Winds; pitch pieces to others (he added monthly columns in *Esquire* and another magazine, *Omnibook*); edit anthologies; keep up his social life—Bennett worked well into every night. Having taken on the humor book, his "present obsession," he'd just have to juggle faster. Some weekends, the man on the best-dressed list wouldn't get out of his pajamas at all, working through, apart from meals and an hour or so Sunday mornings, the slot officially given over to playing with Chris. It was only with a houseguest like Cousin Ginger—she'd made a rare ten-day visit mid-February, when they were "up to their asses in glamour"—that he couldn't be quite so "lazy." He did, however, enjoy the perks of her reflected glory: wanting ten orchestra seats for *Citizen Kane*'s opening night the previous year, he'd told the RKO liaison that "for purposes of identification, Mrs. Cerf is Miss Ginger Rogers' cousin." He added that tag habitually, as though Phyllis was complete only with the magic connection.

But Phyllis, sans Ginger, was useful in other ways. Bennett had bought her a typewriter, enlisting her aid in his outside work. Soon she'd start learning shorthand, "just in case." Help came as well from his and Don's secretary, Pauline, who'd return with him to Sixty-Second Street for Friday dinner, type anecdotes to his dictation until the small hours, and then be driven home to the Bronx by her boss. The contract with de Graff was officially between RH and Pocket, but an addendum specified that he'd receive 60 percent, Phyllis 30 percent, and Pauline 10 percent of the royalty: the only way to get the book done. In Bennett's job, life, and public person, nothing was random now.

Buying Phyllis her typewriter had been prescient. The government announced in March 1942 that no new typewriters would be sold to civilians. Americans already knew there'd be no new cars. Since gasoline was also limited, for the first time since his Columbia days, Bennett regularly boarded buses, and on weekends, "hot and crowded" trains. Men were required to forgo cuffs on new trousers to save cloth, while women, flocking to the workplace, suddenly found it acceptable to wear slacks. Booze and cosmetics became scarcer, and by the fall coffee was gone, "just like that." In a Trade Winds column in August, he focused on what was happening in Britain—far fewer staff and far less paper—to preview how the war would likely affect U.S. publishers. Granted, printers here weren't being bombed by Germans, but already paper was scant.

Donald wrote in September, worrying about the workload, wondering if Saxe was killing himself, and begging Bennett to watch out for him. Bennett himself had been "slaving" night after night on the war humor book. He'd feverishly solicited anecdotes from soldiers, columnists, booksellers; had put a plea into Trade Winds; even asked his maid. "There can't be too many parades, and bands, and rousing marching songs—and, yes, good belly laughs—to make the load a little lighter," his introduction would declare. For those not in the know, he provided a lesson in army slang: "pineapple"—grenade; "snore sack"—sleeping bag; and "on the carpet," "grease monkey," and many more.

Along with the "damn book," volunteer activities crowded his diary. He'd become chair of the book division of New York's Red Cross War Fund, and also represented publishers in the Navy Relief drive for sailors' families. He chaired a small Treasury Department committee tasked with persuading publishers to put patriotic messages on book jackets, and asking authors to urge readers to buy war bonds. Although Random ranked only fifteenth in size among publishers, its profile rose alongside its president's. In his *PW* article "War and the Book Business," Bennett forecast how firms would have to juggle: while books wouldn't be a priority for paper, citizens would nonetheless want to read more, "given less other entertainment." He also cautioned that portraying the USSR as an enemy was a mistake; it was now "a friend," and U.S. Communists a small group who could be dealt with later. The split between those who agreed and those who didn't would haunt the industry for years.

He'd also helped coordinate the "Victory Book Campaign," a national effort to collect donated books for soldiers. But despite publishers' good intentions and citizens' efforts, the number of donated books fell far short of the campaign's ten-million-copy goal. Soon a small working group of publishers convened in New York to create a better way. The Council on Books in Wartime (CBW) would be an umbrella organization charged with overseeing industry efforts and, crucially, finding ways to fund them. At that point, Don hadn't yet gone off to the army, and he, *PW* editor Fred Melcher, and Warder Norton, founder of W. W. Norton, were among those early participants. Norton suggested a slogan—"Books Are Weapons in the War of Ideas"—a natural, and quickly adopted by FDR himself. The council would establish a board—Norton was elected chair—and work with the New York–based Writers' War Board and the Office of War Information, the federal government's central propaganda and censorship bureau in Washington. Booksellers', librarians', and other organizations joined the effort.

Bennett chaired the CBW's early endeavor, *They Burned the Books,* a radio play by Stephen Vincent Benét that aired in May 1942 to remind the public about the huge Nazi book-burning nine years earlier. The response to that and other programs helped persuade seventy publishers to underwrite council expenses for the war's duration. As FDR himself later declared: "Through books, we have appraised our enemies and discovered our allies. We have learned something of American valor in battle. We have, above all, come to understand better the kind of war we must fight and the kind of peace we must establish." Town halls, newsreels, book fairs and luncheons, print: all would be enlisted to get the message across. Radio had already proved its effectiveness, and so, come autumn, the council asked Bennett to try out as emcee for a new program, *Books Are Bullets,* to be broadcast in New York. On a Wednesday afternoon the first week in October, he strolled purposefully into the Empire State Building and up to the studios of WQXR, the station owned by his P.S. 10 chum Elliott Sanger. With so many men in the service, women had taken over myriad jobs, and Nan Taylor, an experienced producer who'd been recruited as the council's radio director, was on hand to guide him.

Though a "try-out," it would be live, Bennett interviewing the two authors of *Sabotage,* which warned Americans to beware of Axis fifth columnists. Nan said to stress ideas rather than personalities, and to follow her script. Bennett's voice was lively and distinctive, if less than beautiful: where some detected a lisp, others only heard the vowels and consonants of old-fashioned, vernacular New York. But that afternoon, it wouldn't cooperate, creeping higher like a nervous teen's. Still, he made it through the interview and the council kept him on. Each week, he'd prepare introductory remarks and Nan the rest, but after several months she noticed that he didn't hesitate "to ad lib *at liberty,*" and had developed a comfortable radio personality. He talked freely, having established "some sort of precedent" in saying that of course everyone knew "Mussolini had syphilis." Fellow publisher John Farrar told him to have "all confidence" in his abilities, and was delighted that the book trade had someone so effective. By war's end, Bennett would host almost 120 guests, from Treasury Secretary Henry Morgenthau Jr., to Gypsy Rose Lee, and not a few RH authors. Still, he longed for regular exposure on a national network (occasionally he did appear on CBS or NBC),

In the studio for *Books Are Bullets*

but *Books Are Bullets* remained stubbornly local. New Yorkers, though, got to know him.

Five days after his radio debut, the man who hated meetings was co-opted onto the CBW's board and executive committee to direct its publicity effort. Bennett was flattered, but confided to Don that he'd stipulated he would not be "pestered" by any committee. He'd find time, yet it wouldn't be easy. That same week, de Graff collected the war humor manuscript. Pocket would publish in less than three months, and Bennett agreed to do a cartoon companion, under a contract with him personally, rather than RH.

The council decided that from time to time, they'd recommend a war-related title that the whole country should read, and at a meeting a week into his new role, Bennett came up with a perfect name for them: "Imperatives." Hearing it, the executive secretary of the board responded that "new life [was] being breathed into us." But given the shortages they all worked under, asking each publisher to set aside a chunk of their own advertising space and money to promote a rival's title was a hard sell. Important though they were, only six Imperatives would be chosen during the course of the war.

. . .

PAT KLOPFER HAD BEEN forced to return to New York a few times for treatment. February 1943 would see another visit, one that, in Bennett's words, would "end her trouble . . . for good." After six miscarriages, it was time for a hysterectomy: no children for Don and Pat. However, the first year of the war for Phyllis had involved new motherhood and being Mrs. Bennett Cerf. She ran the household, hosted his parties, helped with looking after his authors and projects, and read for him (increasingly, he sought her opinion), while the nanny tended to Chris. She knew Bennett wouldn't let her lead the life of ladies whose days were organized around lunch, shopping, and cards, but he also had no desire for her to do work that inconvenienced him. Each month, he gave her a $500 household allowance, but it mattered that she also earned her own income from compiling the *Saturday Review* cryptograms, working on his books, and other projects.

With her good friend Leonora—who wanted to be a novelist—she collaborated on a short story, "Honeymoon Inc.," about a young couple who save to go on a romantic wedding trip, only to die when their ship is sunk in Hawaii on December 7, 1941. Under the pseudonym "Phyllis Morris," they sold it to *Liberty* magazine for Valentine's Day 1942. A year later, *Liberty* published "One Man's Honeymoon" by "Fraser Wilson"—this in collaboration with Budd Wilson Schulberg. Here, too, was an O. Henry twist: a young woman's egotistical fiancé plans every detail of a honeymoon trip. She follows it, but without him—after a blow-up pushes her to marry a rival. Certain that he'll win her back, the ex-fiancé wires the last hotel on "his" itinerary, but she never sees the wire: her husband had changed the final booking, and by then she knows she loves the man she married. A psychologist might have a field day with the plots, but Bennett merely pasted the clippings into his scrapbook, and noted Phyllis was paid a hundred dollars for the second story.

Like many well-off matrons, she volunteered for the city's Defense Recreation Committee on Park Avenue, soliciting free restaurant dinners, tickets to shows, and organizing dances for servicemen with a few precious days on the town before shipping out. She was good at it, and the society women she worked alongside—Minnie Cushing Astor, Brooke Marshall (the next Mrs. Astor), and Madeline Sherwood, ex-chorus-girl wife of Pulitzer winner and FDR speechwriter Robert Sherwood—noticed. She felt she was *really* getting to meet New York, and women who would be important to her later.

During the summers of 1943 and '44, the Cerfs would spend several pampered weeks on Long Island at the magnificent Sands Point mansion of another friend, Alicia Patterson, and her ultra-wealthy third husband, Harry Guggenheim. Alicia's father, born into the *Chicago Tribune* family, had founded the New York *Daily News;* in 1940, Harry bankrolled his wife to start her own New York paper, *Newsday*. Bennett was happy to contribute guest editorials when Alicia needed them. Meanwhile, Phyllis joined with Uncle Herbert on a project for the family firm: a thousand-page anthology of ghost stories, *Great Tales of Terror and the Supernatural.* Published in May 1944 to good reviews, its cover depicted an anthropomorphic haunted house inspired by the RH colophon (Bennett would encourage similar "themed" logo transformations for other favored books). Within a week of publication, *Great Tales of Terror* would sell out a first printing of 13,000, and two months later reach 20,000 copies in print. Bennett thought he could sell 100,000 by Christmas—but alas, couldn't scare up enough paper.

The colophon, transformed—and not for the last time

. . .

WITH FEWER ENTERTAINMENT OPTIONS, people *were* reading more books, and the firm's profits amazed Bennett. At last they were able to pay off the bank loan, and new opportunities continually arose. Ward Greene, head of the powerful Hearst-owned King Features newspaper syndicate, had called him and eight other publishers in November 1942—multiple submission was highly unusual—on behalf of Richard Tregaskis, a Hearst reporter, offering the chance to bid on a time-sensitive manuscript. Tregaskis, a young Harvard graduate, was one of two journalists to land with the Marines on an obscure atoll, Guadalcanal, site of the first major Allied offensive in the Pacific war. He'd been in the lead boat, kept a diary, and turned it into a book. Bennett stayed up until 3 A.M. reading the manuscript, recognizing the urgency of the opportunity. He phoned King Features at 9 A.M.—well before others—preemptively offered a $2,500 advance, promised to publish in eight weeks, and got the deal. Then he sent telegrams to New York papers, saying that RH had signed Tregaskis for "*Guadalcanal Diary,* first eyewitness story of fighting there . . . one of the most exciting stories I have ever read."

Four days later, he wired Don, bursting with news that BOMC had taken the Tregaskis as a main selection. Luckily, Hearst had already submitted it to naval censors in Honolulu, and each page carried the requisite red stamp. Fox soon bought movie rights and would make the picture in record time. *Guadalcanal Diary* was published on January 18, 1943, to sensational coverage. Greene had suggested, and Bennett exploited, a novel publicity plan: stories were fed to papers all over the country about local Marines in the book. By the end of February, BOMC had 334,000 copies in print, and that month, Saxe's nephew Ian Ballantine, who'd started a small U.S. outpost for Penguin Books, bought the right to rush a twenty-five-cent paperback exclusively for military posts. The full-priced book would clock 100,000-plus copies by June, the first time an RH title had reached six figures without including book club copies. Penguin began selling its edition to the general public in the fall, and Doubleday published a one-dollar hardcover reprint.

Bennett had even higher hopes for *Thirty Seconds over Tokyo* by Captain Ted Lawson, who'd told his story to another Hearst journalist, Bob Considine. Ward Greene had sent the Lawson-Considine manuscript in December, a month after the Tregaskis, and Bennett tore through it that day—a Friday—and asked Herbert, Glen, and Thrup to do a quick read. They shared his enthusiasm. On Sunday, he managed to reach Lawson, who'd lost a leg and was recovering at Walter Reed Hospital in Washington; Monday, he met with Considine. Missing Don, Bennett wrote him straightaway, swearing that he'd read *the* "most exciting" manuscript he'd ever seen, the story of the first Tokyo bombing raid, a book "done with complete simplicity and dignity." The complication was getting the censor's stamp, since the mission, the U.S. answer to Pearl Harbor, had been secret.

He was right. The government wanted it quiet that the B-25s had taken off not from land, but from an aircraft carrier seven hundred miles off the Japanese coast. The plan had been for planes to set out from four hundred miles away, but after the carrier encountered a Japanese patrol boat, the operation had to be executed sooner. Almost doubling the distance meant that planes needed more fuel to reach the target; Lawson's had run out before he could return to a safe airstrip inside Nationalist China. Crash-landing into the sea off Japanese-occupied territory, it was a miracle he was alive.

Lawson's story was intensely personal: he bombed, crashed, then was rescued by the Chinese underground, who carried him inland through mountainous terrain by stretcher and truck to the wartime capital, Chongqing, his gangrenous leg amputated on the way. In February, he and his wife became Phyllis and Bennett's houseguests, and were shown around the city as Gertrude and Alice had once been. MGM and Warner were in a bidding war for the film rights (MGM won), but the government still wanted to suppress some of the story.

Bennett couldn't keep silent. In Trade Winds on March 23 he took a chance, noting that RH's safe held a manuscript marked "mustn't touch," the most "breathtaking" war story so far, not yet cleared for publication, a "subtle torture" until Washington gave the green light. A month later they did, and he ordered a 100,000-copy printing, another first for RH. The advance sale into stores was huge, but Bennett couldn't suppress a niggling fear about all those copies, confessing to Don in July that he felt in "suspended animation," very much missing his friend's counsel and approval. That same letter also wondered why Don hadn't commented on a Gershwin profile Bennett had done for *The Saturday Review.* George had died six summers earlier of a brain tumor, and Bennett had put his heart and soul into memorializing him. Dick Simon thought it the best thing he'd ever written, and predicted that one day Bennett would publish some fully original writing; if the lucky publisher wasn't RH, Dick wanted to put in a bid for S&S.

All wrapped up in his own hectic world, at times Bennett didn't quite appreciate the strictures on Don's. He'd been moving from base to base, until reaching the 445th Bombardment Group in Sioux City that month.

Assigned to intelligence, he *had* managed to pilot a bomber for part of a flight from Mississippi to Idaho, and prayed that his ultimate destination wouldn't be England, since intel officers with the Eighth Air Force there weren't allowed to fly. Used to military life now, to being the empathetic officer whom the kids called "Pop," he could admit to his best friend that he was often plagued by "restlessness and futility." He did, however, know how to comfort Bennett. He'd liked the Gershwin piece, and saw no reason to worry over the Lawson book. "Don't let the business get you down," he added: "It's so much pleasanter than any other [including] the AAF!" But though *Thirty Seconds over Tokyo* did make the bestseller list, it wasn't the spectacular success Bennett had wanted: the censorship delay had stymied sales.

However, news had come at the beginning of June that had briefly pushed everything else aside for all three Random House partners. Bob Haas's son, who'd dropped out of Yale to join the Navy Air Corps, was in a plane being catapulted from a small aircraft carrier off the coast of Africa when the mechanism failed. Robert K. Haas Jr., twenty-three years old, would never return home to join his father at RH and help determine its future, as Bob Jr. had dearly dreamed. Bennett wired Don.

The next day he went to an office plunged in gloom, while Don, away and alone, had no other recourse but to write to Bob and Merle. "I was as proud of him as you were. I boasted of him all around the Air Force as my nephew because that's the way I felt . . . a part of my family. He died in a cause that we know is more important than any of us. . . . I'm . . . wishing I were with you and loving you very very much." Bob kept that letter for the rest of his life. He returned to the office, but the navy required silence about how young Bob had died: equipment malfunctions were all too common, and there was the matter of morale to maintain. "Bob has been wonderful," Bennett informed Don, but the toll on the whole family was terrible.

Bob kept another letter alongside Don's. "Bob, dear boy," William Faulkner had begun, his handwriting far clearer than usual. He said that his eighteen-year-old nephew was about to be posted to carrier training, and most probably, "He will get it too. Then who knows? The blood of your fathers and . . . mine side by side at the same long table in Valhalla . . . draining the cup and banging the empty pewter on the long board to fill again, holding two places for us maybe, not because we were heroes or not heroes, but because we loved them." "Blood" commingling was a long way from the days when Faulkner had found it "much nicer" to be published by the "white folks" of Harcourt than by that Jew, Horace Liveright. He and Bob had traveled far together.

. . .

WITH WOMEN DOING MEN'S jobs, Carlotta O'Neill complained repeatedly about her struggle to hire help for isolated Tao House. It was especially burdensome since Gene's health was deteriorating, with a Parkinson-like tremor threatening his ability to hold a pencil and write. Bennett replied each time with the same plea, that they close up the house and come east, where people who really cared could help them.

O'Neill's nerves were challenged in other ways, too. The previous year, during his long recuperation from a blood infection, Carlotta had done everything—including open his mail. That May, she'd replied to Bennett about a letter and Trade Winds clipping that he'd sent. In the magazine piece, he'd wanted to remind readers that O'Neill remained the country's greatest playwright, mentioning that because he couldn't leave California, his "crowning work," *The Iceman Cometh,* and other new plays languished in RH's safe. But he'd begun the column on a different note, reporting that sixteen-year-old Oona O'Neill had just been chosen the Stork Club "Debutante Number One" of the season.

Carlotta's response came on two handwritten postcards to "Bennett dear." Gene was embarrassed by the glamour girl gossip, and unlike most friends, Bennett didn't seem to know "the inner" O'Neill very well, or understand how he loathed cheap publicity, she chided. She hadn't given Gene the clipping, holding it back until he was well. "You do understand this, don't you? . . . Our love always, bless you."

She'd shamed him. It would be wonderful if she'd cut off the first paragraph and give the rest to Gene, Bennett replied; the Oona business was "a tempest in a teapot" and would be "soon forgotten." But the tempest shattered the teapot. Oona, who'd wanted to be an actress, soon met Charlie Chaplin, much-married and thirty-six years older. Chaplin proposed; so young that she needed permission from her father to marry, she asked and he refused. When she turned eighteen, she married without O'Neill's consent.

Wanting to show that he'd learned his lesson, Bennett wrote Carlotta to sympathize about the "nauseating" publicity, adding that as he watched his small son pursue his "carefree path," he wondered what

Chris might one day do to break *his* heart. But as Carlotta had sensed, Bennett hadn't gauged O'Neill's dark depths well. He didn't understand how he felt about his birth family; how he'd neglected his children; or the fury his daughter's marriage unleashed. O'Neill disowned Oona and never saw her again.

. . .

First humor book bearing Bennett's byline

WITHIN TWO MONTHS OF publication in January 1943, Bennett's *The Pocket Book of War Humor* had sold 400,000 copies. In September, *The Pocket Book of Cartoons* would debut; by November, it would have 700,000 copies in print. The two books turned out to be the fourth- and fifth-biggest bestsellers on Pocket's list.

Bennett could claim authoritatively to an interviewer that the war's effect on all low-priced books had been "phenomenal." Thanks to demand from servicemen, the ML had sold almost twice as many copies in 1942 as in any previous year, and for the financial year ending June 30, 1943, RH would realize a formidable net profit. By the end of that calendar year, they'd taken two more floors of the Fifty-Seventh Street building, and the company had grown to sixty-one employees. In addition, he'd won a $300,000 order from Woolworth's to produce a half million cheap children's books, to be "packaged" by Georges Duplaix at the Artists and Writers Guild, part of Western Printing Corporation. Bennett saw Duplaix as key to RH's juvenile future.

However, in August, Duplaix suddenly announced he'd changed his mind, and was coordinating with another client—S&S—to originate a line that they'd call "Little Golden Books." It would transform children's reading by making books cheaper and easily available beyond the bookstore, or as Bennett put it to Don: "Those bastards are going to crack the chain store market within the next two years." (As always, the rivalry was complicated: under her maiden name, Phyllis would author two of those Little Golden Books.) RH would have to play catch-up to take advantage of this new retail opportunity, and, before war's end, would hatch plans for a rival series, Wonder Books.

Another conduit for expansion was the ML. A BOMC executive, Harry Abrams, pitched the idea for an Illustrated Modern Library gift line. Sitting in swimming trunks in Bennett's small garden on a scorching day and hosing themselves down when the heat got too much, Abrams, Bennett, RH sales chief Lew Miller, and production head Ray Freiman agreed that Harry would oversee the series on a freelance basis for a royalty, and they'd launch for Christmas. Artists would be of the caliber of a Thomas Hart Benton or a George Grosz, and the first batch include Dickens's *Pickwick Papers* and the Bible.

"Now all we need is a dictionary and our dream of having Shakespeare, the Bible and the dictionary in the Modern Library will have come true," Bennett wrote Don. In return, Donald floated a dream of his own, one that he'd often advocated: What about entering the college text business? It seemed a pretty sure bet that after the war, returned servicemen would flood colleges and universities.

Even Bennett couldn't juggle everything. By August 1943, he'd missed too many Council on Books in Wartime meetings, so was asked to step down as publicity director, but would stay on the board and continue his radio gig. It would have made him very unhappy indeed to give up *Books Are Bullets;* besides, he was good at it. Earlier that year, the council had made what would prove to be its most consequential decision: since donations of books had lagged, it contracted with the government to take responsibility itself for such books. It would select titles, create, and publish what came to be called "Armed Services Editions" (ASEs), small-format paperback reprints distributed free to soldiers overseas (but not on the home front). They'd marry the quick, cheap, large-scale publishing that Pocket had pioneered, with Uncle Sam's ability to provide raw materials and a distribution network. Ray Trautman—the officer Bennett had interviewed for Trade Winds—together with Isabel DuBois, librarian of the U.S. Navy, would make the title selections from lists compiled by a council committee. The books would be lightweight, stapled along the short edge to be horizontal and slip neatly into a pocket, and have two columns of easy-to-read type on each page. Covers, when possible, were to be bright yellow, to lure tired soldiers in.

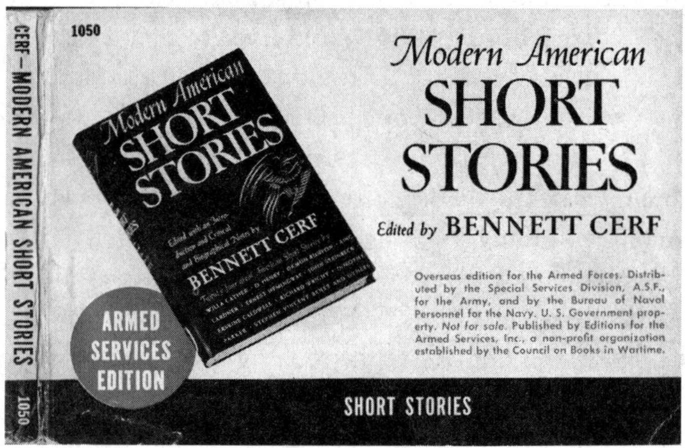

One of three ASEs edited by Bennett

The council would commission publishers to originate some books for specific needs, which is how Bennett was asked that first year to compile a collection of recent plays, as he was the man who published more good ones than anybody. Into *Four Modern American Plays* went Lillian Hellman's suspenseful *Watch on the Rhine,* to keep a soldier reading; James Thurber and Elliott Nugent's *The Male Animal,* to keep him laughing; Sidney Kingsley's *The Patriots,* to rally him to his cause; and Jerome Chodorov and Joseph Fields's *Junior Miss,* to remind him of the best things at home. ASEs began to roll off the presses in September 1943, and at its peak, the operation printed 155,000-plus copies of each of forty different titles per month. Along with a pack of cigarettes and letters or photos from home, these little books were as precious as anything a soldier carried. War correspondents wrote about them, and so did the men who read them, in letters to folks back home. An army officer at a hospital in England saw "boys reading as they have never read before. Some toughies . . . admitted without shame that they were reading their first book since they were in grammar school." The GIs had adopted ASEs as their own, and among more than a thousand titles, three were personally edited or compiled by Bennett. Far more than the efforts of Penguin and Pocket, it would be ASEs that hooked Americans on paperbacks, priming them for a publishing revolution.

. . .

HAVING RECEIVED NOTICE THAT he was going overseas, Don was granted home leave just before shipping out. He and Pat needed a favor from Bennett and Phyllis: the use of their home as a gathering spot to say goodbye. "It would be the most ghastly party," he wrote, "but my good Jewish conscience says that I should at least have a drink" with them all.

He turned up at RH on September 8, 1943, a Wednesday, rendering the whole office, as Bennett put it, "agog," but two days later the old friends managed to escape for lunch together. The following Monday, the farewell party took place. The facade of the Cerfs' nineteenth-century brownstone house had been remade into a streamlined gray-and-white Deco exterior, and guests flowed upstairs to the second floor, where a large modern bar area with wall-to-wall bookshelves occupied its center. Bennett regularly tended his literary garden there, arranging, rearranging, and imposing order. Anyone opening a volume might see a grateful, witty inscription from Gertrude or Gene, Quent or George Kaufman. In some he tucked whole letters. The space was perfect for mixing cocktails *and* people, as guests got a drink and spilled into the equally book-lined living room fronting Sixty-Second Street or the large library on the other side of the bar that looked down onto the garden. The Cerfs had filled the parlor floor with well-stuffed sofas as well as a phonograph and piano, where Broadway friends often played their latest tunes.

In almost all respects, the party went better than anticipated, yet there'd been a slight unpleasantness. Something didn't sit easily between Pat and Bennett and Phyllis. Little bickering exchanges flared that Bennett alluded to with sarcasm in letters. Pat wasn't charmed by the jokes, exuberance, and ego that took over a room and left her husband in the shadows, irritating her the more because Don didn't seem to mind. And of course, Bennett and Phyllis had had a baby, while the Klopfers couldn't. In his thank-you letter, Don acknowledged the tension: "Don't ever worry about anything coming between us. . . . Nothing can and nothing will and that goes for wives, children, or mistresses!"

Unexpectedly, he managed one more visit to New York. Senior enough not to embark with junior officers and thousands of troops squeezing aboard the old *Queen Mary,* he flew to Britain instead by way of Dakar and Marrakesh. The intelligence posting to the Eighth Army's 445th Bomber Group was exactly what he *hadn't* wanted: he wouldn't pilot planes. But he'd do his all "over there" to make the best of it. "You win the war and let us take care of Random House . . . !" was Bennett's adieu.

Tibenham lay toward the top of East Anglia, the hump jutting out from the trunk of England to the north and east of London. Thirteen miles southwest of Norwich—a small city that had suffered bomb damage the previous year—tiny Tibenham was well and truly in the sticks. A scent of coal fire and chill wet earth permeated everything, so unlike the crisp, step-lively New York air. The locals' language had to be untangled, thick with undecipherable overtones of place and class. To American eyes, East Anglia was a patchwork of fields and hedges, medieval church towers, pastel cottages, and farming rhythms that, like everything else, seemed not to have changed for hundreds of years. But of course, with war, change would come, as it had twenty-five years before, when so many who'd left to fight "the war to end all wars" never returned, leaving young widows and soon-to-be old maids.

Don had to learn to ride a bicycle to get around the base, leased from the Royal Air Force. "I almost froze my well-known balls off last night," he informed Bennett in one letter, "but today, since I was ordered to go to church with 4 other officers to represent the AAF on Armistice Day—I was warmed by the hot air of a High Episcopalian minister." He soon grew resigned to the chill.

His assignment was to lead a team processing intelligence from the RAF, then brief American boys on that day's mission. His group was responsible for directing them to and from targets and schooling them in evasion and escape tactics. One of his young officers, fellow New Yorker Fritz Jacobi, was entrusted to sneak in photos of naked ladies to keep crews awake during early-morning aircraft recognition sessions about "curves" and "angles." Don had a wonderful sense of humor, Jacobi learned, inspiring respect while being demanding "in the most constructive way." The four squadrons he oversaw flew heavy B-24s from the field's three runways, with cities like Münster and Kiel as targets. Sometimes they'd drop propaganda leaflets over France. In the afternoon—if they returned—he'd debrief them: what they'd hit, mistakes made, and planes and comrades left behind. He was burdened with knowing that the attrition rate was awful, and, "from the vast loneliness of the outskirts of Merrie Englande," confided to Bennett that writing was "like thinking of another world. . . . You lose your sense of proportion."

Bennett, for his part, told Don that he envied him and others overseas so much, it was "eating out my insides." He feared the "piddling" things he worried about must seem an incredible waste of time, and found it intolerable to be away from the center of the action and, that worst possible thing, irrelevant. Frustration mixed with shame and a jolt to his confidence: all those looks able-bodied men got at home. Perhaps he was asking Don to say those piddling things weren't so small after all, and that he counted on Bennett. "Think of us once in a while," he begged, but recovered: "Business couldn't be better."

Part of the solution to his juggling problem had been to add a senior editor capable of assuming some of his entertaining-and-coddling-authors burden, Bennett told Don in another letter. Fortunately, both had known just the fellow. On their trips to Boston, they'd long cultivated Robert Linscott, a bear of a man who'd been at Houghton Mifflin forever—or at any rate since 1904, when he'd started as an office boy. They'd sometimes sought Linscott's advice and enjoyed his company, and he in turn had found it convenient to stay at the Cerfs' when in New York. Gradually, it became clear that he was no longer happy at Houghton, and so in 1943, he came over to RH. In addition to his salary, Bennett agreed to pay a small percentage—to be determined later—on profits of certain books for which Linscott was directly responsible. Further, he'd decided it was time to set up a small stock plan for all key people. "Nothing, of course, will be done until you get back," he told Don, but they ought to think about such matters now.

He also detailed other developments: he'd registered a subsidiary, "Random House of Canada," and persuaded Saxe and Linscott that the firm ought to publish a Modern Library *Concise American Dictionary*. Soon, though, it became clear they couldn't oversee such an effort themselves, and contracted well-known lexicographer Clarence Barnhart to supervise the project. A new philosophy series, the Lifetime Library, was in the works, with volumes on Aquinas, Plato, and St. Augustine. He'd dearly have liked Don there to cope with the paper problem, for the quota was cut again: in 1944, they'd receive only 75 percent of the 1942 allocation. Yet invoices for the ML were amazing. The navy had just bought 60,000 books, and store orders were streaming in.

In January 1944, the captain became Major Klopfer, and Bennett's telegram told him: "sales conference halted to cheer the promotion." The major, however, thought the sales and profit figures Bennett quoted were "too good to be true," and felt unnerved that the business was growing so quickly without him. When weather got bad enough to ground all missions, he moped around like an old, lost dog with nothing to do, and hated that most of all. At such moments, despite the steady stream of letters from Bennett and others, melancholy took hold and he feared he'd gotten stale. "Jesus, I'll have to learn the whole list over again, when, as, and if I get back," he wrote, and besides, Don knew his partner. With so much excitement, was Bennett neglecting other priorities they'd promised to get to when the cash came in—like resetting ML volumes that were still reprinted using old, mistake-ridden plates? This was the moment to do it, just as now was the time to get into college texts, but Bennett kept ignoring his suggestions.

"I've got to have something to come back to, Cerfie," Don finally wrote. "I expect to be flat broke." He was going to have to sell what stocks he had to pay income tax, which he'd owe "for '42, '43, '44, '45, and I won't have the dough."

Occasionally, Don was able to travel to London for a few days, visit a sympathetic publisher or author, "and see if there's any civilization left." A few times, Bennett and Bob asked him to carry out missions on the firm's behalf. Too often, though, he was so taxed with work that he hardly slept, being briefed at 4:30 A.M. and, like his fellow officers, also functioning as an assistant chaplain to crews, absorbing their stress as well as his own. Sometimes, it spilled into letters. He'd heard that New York was "gay and mad," people spending like it was "1929 all over again." He found that depressing. Americans were, despite rationing, spending more than before the war.

"Don't be a God damned fool, Cerfie," he erupted in another letter, "to want to change places with me . . . in this God-forsaken part of England! . . . [It's] nothing but hard work—a degraded type of excitement and tragedy every damned time the boys take to the air. . . . As we lose some, another batch of expendables comes. . . . It isn't pretty and you're lucky not to have anything to do with it. I still think I'm doing exactly what I should be doing but no one can ever make me say I like it."

Reading about so many initiatives from three thousand miles and an entirely different life away, Don was confounded and concerned. "That's quite an organization you and RKH are building up," he wrote in early March. "I wonder about two things: (1) will there be any reason for me in it at the end of all this horrible mess and will I be any asset to the business; (2) will Random House be any fun at all as a 'big business' instead of our very personal venture?" A week later, he repeated those fears, reckoning he'd always been a "small-time operator."

With overseas mail so unpredictable, both letters arrived in New York on the same day, and Bennett, terribly anxious to reassure Don quickly, told Jezebel to make three carbons of his reply to send at two-day intervals. At least one would reach Britain. First, he reminded Don that the military had introduced the ML to millions of new readers, multiplying its potential market five times over pre-war, and promised that he wasn't dreaming. He *was* doing what Don had always wanted: making new plates for ML warhorses, replacing bad translations with good. Prospects for the Illustrated Modern Library, Lifetime Library, and juveniles were good, and he had every confidence Linscott would bring in fine new authors. Further, new distribution channels that had profited from cheap books would probably be willing to carry slightly more expensive ones, providing RH with a whole new market. The beautiful thing, Bennett assured Don, was that they could remain simple, with "no possibility" of ever developing into "an unmanageable menagerie" like Doubleday. He shared that abhorrence for "impersonal 'big business,'" and didn't think RH would ever take that form. "You are part of [its] . . . very fibre and bloodstream, you blithering idiot," he practically shouted. Even without a nickel outside the firm, Don would be "sitting pretty," he promised.

The original and carbons arrived on the same day, a joy to their recipient, but knowing the ambition that fueled Bennett, Don replied with continued concern. "Please don't let the damned thing get so big that we can't run it ourselves and get some fun out of it and still think we're contributing a little something to the future of America," he reiterated. "Sounds mighty pompous, but I like to kid myself that we can contribute something if we're intelligent about it." And yet, when fall 1944 arrived, an opportunity arose, so fantastic that Bennett could hardly believe it possible. Don's cautions were cast aside as the same instinct that inspired him to buy the ML led to a second great coup.

It all began with Marshall Field, scion of the Chicago department store family, who also owned the *Chicago Sun,* radio stations, a reference book company, and the left-leaning New York newspaper *PM.* About to catch a train at Grand Central, Field bought a few Pocket Books; by the time he arrived in Chicago, he'd decided to buy the firm. He phoned Pocket president Bob de Graff, whose great-uncle had been Field's grandfather's business partner. When de Graff told him the company wasn't for sale, Field offered to buy a share of the business, and then recruited a key Doubleday executive, Freeman "Doc" Lewis, to join Field Enterprises as his publishing right-hand man. As soon as Lewis informed his new boss that de Graff's other partners in Pocket were Simon, Schuster, and Shimkin, Field offered to buy S&S; they were willing to talk, not sell. Field was soon told of another interesting possibility: Grosset & Dunlap. A leading publisher of hardcover reprints, G&D *was* for sale.

The inexpensive reprint business, hardcover and paperbound, was dominated by four companies: Doubleday, G&D, Pocket, and World. If Pocket combined with G&D, it would rival Doubleday for supremacy and make Field one of two or three men who could determine the future of the entire trade book industry, dictating terms that others would have to accept. Bennett heard about Field's plan. He and his partners didn't have enough money to mount a rival bid, but maybe they could join with others to buy G&D. It had been a cash cow but needed new pastures on which to feed, and energy and ideas from men who understood the potential of new markets and how to reach them. G&D hadn't gone after bestselling authors as Doubleday and World had, nor had it sold titles into the chain and drugstores that Bennett knew were the future for cheap books.

Teaming up with BOMC's Harry Scherman and his second-in-command, the RH partners invited G&D owner Donald Grosset to meet over several days in late September. That weekend, Bennett conferred with Lew Miller at home. On Monday, Grosset agreed to a purchase price of $49 per share of G&D stock, or about $4.25 million. With so much capital involved, RH and BOMC extended an invitation to Harper to join them. It was old-line, but its head, Cass Canfield, was savvy and a man they trusted, who recognized the rare opportunity being offered. Soon enough, they invited Little, Brown and Scribner as well, making it much harder for any other group to mount a challenge.

The news rocked the publishing world. The wonderful part was, Bennett wrote Don, that they'd snatched G&D from Marshall Field and the "smarty pantses" at S&S at the very last minute. Don would have been happier with a smaller group, but expressed "utmost confidence" in what Bennett and Bob were doing. He was "so damned interested" but frustrated: there wasn't anybody on base who could really appreciate the publishing part of his life and what this meant. Not many days passed before a B-24 made an emergency landing at Tibenham. Being the intelligence officer on duty, he cycled out to interview the pilot. As the flyboy exited the cockpit, Don was amazed to recognize Alfred and Blanche's son, Pat, who was equally taken aback when the bicyclist turned out to be Donald. Alfred A. Knopf Jr. had known Don since he was a kid.

As they walked the bicycle back to HQ, Don suddenly grew excited. "Guess what we did yesterday?" he asked, and Pat worried what he would hear.

"We bought Grosset!" he whooped, at last able to share the big news.

G&D's new owners would be an unusual mix: three old-money firms, a pair of entrepreneurial Jewish firms, and Don Grosset and his original shareholders, who'd retain 10 percent of stock. BOMC would hold 30 percent, with the four publishers controlling 15 percent each. RH would provide $350,000 in capital, and be paid to manage the company. Bennett badly wanted Don home to help, but until then proposed that RH's managerial fee be structured so that he and Bob got $12,000 each per year, with another $12,000 divided among eight RH staffers. Once Don returned, he, Bob, and Don would receive $10,000 each. Yet they still required a general manager for the day-to-day. Ironically, John O'Connor, the VP in charge of Marshall Field's reference book company, took the job, and in less than a year, Saxe's nephew Ian Ballantine left Penguin to join O'Connor in starting a Grosset subsidiary to compete toe-to-toe with Pocket. They named it Bantam Books.

Simon, Schuster, and Shimkin continued to talk with Marshall Field. Early in November, Field bought an interest in S&S and Pocket, enough to bring them into Field Enterprises, though he promised not to interfere editorially or replace management. In a *New York Post* article, Bennett noted this development, and saw book publishing edging into the realm of "real 'Big Business.'" He predicted golden days but drew a line in the sand: "Original publishing of new, good books will not become involved in any of this frenzied finance. Big business and literature definitely do not mix," since the relations between creative writers and publishers were far too personal. To Don, he wondered why Dick and Max wanted to sell part of their business, concluding that they were "drunk with dreams of empire and . . . led blindly by Shimkin."

However, at the same time, he had reason to feel grateful toward S&S—very grateful. Sitting on top of the world in the swanky Rainbow Room, perched high up in Rockefeller Center's RCA building, he'd been one of four Pocket authors feted at an October luncheon, the first members of an exclusive club—the "Silver Gertrudes"—whose books had sold at least a million copies ("Gertrude" being Pocket's kangaroo colophon).

The previous December, Bennett had begun collecting stories for a third compendium, this one of anecdotes, and fancied publishing the new book himself, as an RH hardcover. There was a problem, however: the firm didn't have enough paper in its wartime quota. A $1,000 advance and 15 percent royalty had made it easy to agree over lunch with Dick and Max back in June that S&S would do the original, and Pocket reprint in paper. Between mouthfuls, Bennett as usual reeled off jokes, pausing only to say: "Stop me if you've heard this one." Whereupon Dick, knowing well how hard it was to interrupt Bennett in full flow, suggested that *Try and Stop Me* would be a perfect title, and that Jack Goodman work with him on the project.

The work went well, and after delivering the final draft to Goodman in July, Bennett immediately began gathering material for a second anecdote book as well as an American short story collection, the latter for Tower Books. He'd also begun working with Van Cartmell, an editor at a Doubleday subsidiary, to co-edit a huge anthology of the most successful plays in American theater, this time for Random.

In November, a month after welcoming him into the Silver Gertrude club, S&S launched Bennett's *Try and Stop Me,* with a full-page ad full of clever cartoons in *The New York Times Book Review* and even cleverer copy by Jack Goodman. "This is NOT an advertisement for a picture book," it began.

> These pictures appear . . . because it goes against our grain to quote one word of Bennett Cerf's prose. He's the President of Random House. . . .
>
> We're Simon and Schuster. . . . We're publishing this book because Mr. Cerf, a modest man, doesn't feel he can rightly give his own book the sort of tremendous promotion he feels it deserves. Like this. . . .
>
> It's the sort of book that grabs you by the shoulder, pushes you into a chair, and keeps you in a condition of helpless merriment for hours. Even if its author *is* president of Random House.

Nothing like a little "helpless merriment" to cheer a weary nation at war. Bennett had decanted the best stories he knew into sections on Hollywood, Broadway, the literary life, etc., mixing tales from the lives of friends and authors like the Marx Brothers, Gertrude, even Saxe and Don, with borrowings from RH books and newspaper columns. S&S salesmen had placed more than 40,000 copies of *TASM*—as Bennett referred to it—in stores. By the end of the first month, it had sold 60,000 copies. The second week in February, it was number one on the *Tribune* bestseller list and number two in the *Times*. From shy high school boys needing icebreakers to ease into social situations, to Judge Woolsey, liberator of *Ulysses,* the book found an extraordinarily wide range of fans. "I . . . must tell you," Woolsey wrote Bennett, "how much it delights me. I have been ill lately, and it has been a great source of pleasure." By the end of July, *TASM* had also been turned into a yellow-covered ASE, and BOMC had nearly 400,000 of its version in print. In November 1945, on the first anniversary of publication, S&S could boast 321,000 copies of its edition; the book remained on the *Times* list; and an inexpensive hardcover reprint was forthcoming from Doubleday.

Magazines were dangling paychecks for Bennett's byline, and forums paid him to speak. But he also spoke unpaid on War Bond Drives, sharing a podium with famous novelists, and addressed wounded soldiers recovering in the hospital. Once, his audience was a thousand military "mental cases." Early in 1945, King Features had phoned to ask him to write a daily column for syndication. The arrangement began with eighteen papers, but the number grew and grew. Naturally, it ran under the rubric Try and Stop Me.

Bennett had become the subject of profiles and features, pieces like "Cerface Facts," from *The Philadelphia Record;* "The Thief of Badgags," in the *Chicago Sun;* and "Try and Stop Bennett Cerf," a huge profile in Marshall Field's *PM,* all dutifully pasted into his scrapbook. In December, *Life* devoted five pages to "Bennett Cerf: Publisher of Classics and Best Sellers, He Is Now the Nation's No. 1 Peddler of Jokes."

. . .

THE WAR ENDED IN August 1945, with two bombs and a personal bombshell. Just after devastation was visited upon hundreds of thousands of lives in Hiroshima and Nagasaki, Phyllis, who'd been fearful about a second pregnancy after the difficult caesarean of her first, announced that she was carrying a new baby, due in April. Bennett pointedly referred to this second as "Finale." Their first, now a precocious blond, blue-eyed four-year-old, was looked after by Margaret Brennan, a no-nonsense Irish nanny who loved him. She lived on the top floor of the house along with Ivar and Vera, the Cerfs' married servants, and would remain the center of Chris's world throughout childhood. Bennett found his very chatty boy rather amusing now, worth showing off. Occasionally, Chris would walk with him from Sixty-Second Street to Fifty-Seventh Street and delight the office; less frequently, Bennett and Phyllis would allow "the Brat" to accompany them on a weekend jaunt. Still, Phyllis baited Bennett that he was a "neglectful" parent, and Lew Miller pleaded that both parents ignore the advice of the child psychologists and "display some outward marks of affection for the boy."

Donald had returned to America in June and to Random later in the summer, one of four officers in his division—and the only intelligence officer—to have been awarded a Croix de Guerre. He'd also merited a Bronze Star, a ribbon with four battle stars, and a distinguished unit citation. A year earlier, Bennett had said that the first day Don was back at his desk would be "the happiest of my entire life." Donald had told him in turn: "You know full well how much you mean to me. I haven't many *close* friends!" Yet Don, along with many who'd worn the nation's uniform so well, came home to a changed world where, despite Bennett's assurances, he was uncertain of his place, and where heart-rending experiences he'd had would have to be stowed away. His friend had been one of those responsible for changing that world: same old Bennett, but not the same. He'd moved to a different plane of fame, money, and influence, and had established a rhythm with a wife who had her own ideas about the future. Bennett had experienced nothing of the soldier's life, but the final piece in *Try and Stop Me* alluded to that life nonetheless:

> An officer, home from . . . overseas, was assigned to a desk job in the Pentagon. . . . Each day . . . he shifted the location of his desk—next to the window, away from the window, into a corridor, and finally into the men's wash room. "He must be shell-shocked," the authorities figured, but the officer . . . [explained] grimly: "It's the only place around here . . . where people seem to know what they're doing."

At war's close, Bennett Cerf stood triumphant. He thought he knew *exactly* what he was doing. Everything was in place: wife, child, another on the way, house, social life, business, columns, books, lectures, broadcasting career, a horizon of unlimited prospects. He'd lost his bet with Donald, but Don was home, and in place, too. There was also the matter of money. In *Try and Stop Me,* he'd included a story about Duke the tobacco magnate, borrowed from the biography RH had published during the war. Now the grandfather who'd made his fortune as one of Duke's men had nothing on his grandson. The boy whose fun-loving father had been so hopeless with money and unworthy in Nathan Wise's hard eyes, had proved at least as clever as his grandfather. He'd earned well over $100,000 from the S&S edition of *Try and Stop Me* alone.

There would be no stopping him now.

Chapter 17

Mr. Chirp in the Lyons Den

COME TO OUR NEW YEARS EVE PICNIC AT 8:30 PM
AT THE CERF'S PICNIC GROUNDS, 132 EAST 62nd.
INSTEAD OF DRESSING UP WE ARE DRESSING DOWN. . . .
GENERAL SHENANIGANS WILL USHER IN
THE ATOMIC AGE.

Moss Hart and Phyllis and Bennett Cerf

THE WIRES WERE SENT IN THE LAST WEEK OF DECEMBER 1945, SUMMONING a houseful of the three hosts' closest pals. Bennett's self-professed credo had always been to grab as much fun as possible. Now all New York grabbed it with him. Restrictions had been lifted; nightspots hummed. The city's stepped skyline seemed more wonderful than ever as big ships, horns booming, brought soldiers home from the war along with a new cargo: refugees. Their gaze was not so different, willed on the future, averted from the memory of horrors they'd seen. Streets were crowded with servicemen clutching their GI Bill of dreams and ripe young women expectant with the first postwar babies. New York, intact and alone, towered over the broken old world, the undisputed new center of the action.

Bennett, Phyllis, and Chris had sat for the famous society photographer Philippe Halsman in July, just around the time that Phyllis discovered she was pregnant again. The images show a confident young woman who'd never be lovelier and a middle-aged man in his prime. The Cerfs were even more "outrageously happy" than in 1940, when Bennett had penned that line into his new clipping book. Yet delightful though it was to be famous, celebrity changed how people looked at a man, not always to his benefit: a platform might unexpectedly turn into a pillory. Authors could be more than a little troublesome, as could fellow publishers and literary critics. Most vexing, though, to the newly crowned king of joke books, was that the joke could be on him—and not very funny.

Leonard Lyons made sure of that. Like Bennett, he was a fixture on the New York social scene. Six nights a week, from dusk to dawn, he haunted restaurants, clubs, parties, Broadway, so that devoted readers of the *New York Post* could venture into his "Lyons Den" six days out of seven. There they expected to read the latest about the rich and famous, beautiful and talented. Lyons was no Walter Winchell—who wielded the most powerful byline in the country—but his column was carried by over a hundred papers.

Cerf and Lyons grazed on the same gossipy turf for fodder, but "columning," as Bennett had called it since Columbia days, was a part-time gig for the master of Random House, while being the full-time job that earned Lyons a living. The differences didn't end there. Leonard, eight years younger than Bennett, had been born to poor immigrants on the Lower East Side. After escaping to City College and law school, a love of Broadway propelled him into a column at the *Jewish Daily Forward* (unlike Bennett, no mistaking Leonard's ethnicity). When he got the *Post* job, he gave up lawyering for good.

For some years, the two had been useful to each other. In the afternoons, before pounding the city by foot, Lyons would consult a roster of big talkers by phone, seeking fresh material. Bennett was one. If he passed along an item about an RH author, it would be good for Lyons and good for the firm. Bennett was also happy to serve as a guest columnist when Leonard needed a substitute. It was a given that their personal lives would intersect, since the boundary between personal and professional was so fluid for both. Back in 1943, Bennett told Don with relief that a party at Leonard and his wife Sylvia's home had been "an oasis" after a very long social desert. Of course he and Phyllis reciprocated, and Lyons was among the multitudes Bennett considered a "good personal friend." But then *Try and Stop Me* brought Leonard up short. The question of who could lay claim to a joke or funny story, who actually owned it—or whether anyone could—turned out to be a matter of strong disagreement.

In a foreword to *TASM,* Bennett acknowledged many sources for stories. He didn't reveal that Phyllis, using her maiden name, had sent away for obscure Midwest joke magazines and combed through them for reusable material, but did explicitly recognize Leonard as a source, and allowed that "column conductors" were "highly competitive," and their anxiety to establish originality "thoroughly understandable." Still, no one could trace every joke to its creator, and it struck him as ridiculous for columnists to cry " 'Thief! Thief!' at rivals" who had possibly overheard the disputed gem at the same table.

In retelling stories, he loved to pin them on his nearest and dearest—Don, Herbert, Saxe—or, even better, a famous chum. Columnists had long realized, Bennett explained, that people responded better when a line is delivered by someone whose humor is well known. He'd learn his lesson for later books, and would often clear the use of a "name" in advance, but for *Try and Stop Me* neither Bennett nor S&S had sought permission from—let alone given compensation or credit for individual stories to—Lyons. His reaction was swift and very public. Less than three weeks after the book appeared, Lyons wrote in the *Post* that Bennett had dropped sixty-two of his anecdotes without credit into *TASM,* the first accusation of many. Six months later, he referenced Bennett admitting to "poring over these columns" to supplement his memory, and dividing the royalties thus: "one third to his wife, one third to his secretary, and one third to himself. In short, one third for clipping, one third for pasting and one third for sheer gall."

He'd gotten his facts wrong for the royalty cuts, but it didn't make the attack any less insulting. Sure, Bennett clipped the paragraph and pasted it into his album—he saved anything with his name on it. And sure, he scribbled underneath, "Good old Lennie, greenest . . . with envy, celebrates sixth printing of *TASM* with characteristic charm and inaccuracy." Yet he couldn't brush it off, and to the lawyer Morris Ernst admitted, "I have been bitter about the things he has been saying." He tried to convince his *Ulysses* comrade that he, not Lyons, was the aggrieved party: from the moment Lyons had heard about the book, he was the sole gossip-monger to fail to mention it in his column.

But Bennett *had,* Ernst reminded him, been sufficiently cognizant of a potential problem to have indicated in the "long distant past" that he wanted the lawyer's opinion on columnists' property rights. And he *did* know Lyons had been planning a collection himself—indeed, for years had claimed to have a contract. Ernst, whose big ego jousted with Bennett's over the glory each was due for freeing *Ulysses,* admitted that while he hadn't been retained, he'd been consulted by Lyons "informally" and saw Bennett's position as untenable. What he'd said about Lyons publicly had been "less than wise." With his impetuousness, loose tongue, oversensitivity—compounded by obliviousness that led him to tread on others' sensitivity—he'd got himself into real trouble.

Bennett assured Ernst that he wanted nothing more than to sit down with him and Lyons over lunch and hash out the whole thing. Ernst made encouraging noises and spoke vaguely of "some kind of [financial] adjustment." Yet no such meeting or adjustment occurred. Instead, acrimony intensified. At one party, Sylvia Lyons, in view of others, told Phyllis that her husband was "taking bread from her children's mouths."

More horrible still, Walter Winchell, whom Bennett "put in a class by [himself]" among columnists for the international issues he'd highlighted, turned against him once the scale of the book's success was evident, and began sniping. In a pleading letter in July 1945, Bennett not only argued that Lyons's "yapping" proved him "strictly small-time," but also made Winchell a blanket offer to publish any book he could concoct, and pay any advance and royalty within reason. Columning was "strictly play" for him, Bennett declared, "a book publisher first, last, and all the time." Winchell didn't relent.

Serendipitously or otherwise, on April Fool's Day the feud landed in *Time* magazine. *Time* took a few jabs but also Bennett's side, opining that no one had the right to copyright "barroom babble," and that his failure to give Winchell and Lyons credit was "an old failing of their own." Others entered the fray. A *Detroit Free Press* piece, "Stealing Jokes," supported Bennett: his accusers were acting like kids on the seashore quarreling about "who owns the ocean." A columnist for the *Dallas Times Herald* defended Bennett's habit of pinning stories to friends or well-known pals: in overhearing "intimate incidents of the ephemeral great," perhaps readers had the "delicious" feeling that they knew those people. Bennett's instinct for attribution was integral to his "extraordinary sense of how to tell a story."

Yet the needling from Lyons didn't let up, and when an anonymous assault ran in November 1946, Bennett boiled over and Ted Thackrey, the *Post* editor, heard about it. An apology from Thackrey soon arrived: by not making an issue of the attacks, he'd hoped Lyons would stop, but now realized he'd been wrong, especially since "the poison barb" had been aimed at a man whose integrity and ethics he'd never had occasion to question. Thackrey offered to print an apology—but warned it might not help.

Bennett agreed such a statement would only draw more attention to a "disgusting" affair. In place of the vitriol, the *Post* printed a plug: "Read Bennett Cerf's amusing column, 'Trade Winds,' in *Saturday Review of Literature* every week." Lyons was put on notice never to mention Bennett in his column again. The feud settled into intractable enmity. "I have very few enemies," Bennett said in his oral history, but there was one he "cherished" very, very deeply. Lyons had managed to inflict real pain. Whether or not Bennett recognized he should have been careful to assign credit and stroke others from the outset, one thing was certain: for each, the "cherishing" ended only when he died.

By now, many citizens knew Bennett the bestselling jokester and columnist, but had practically no notion of Bennett the book publisher. With this transformation came signs of more lasting fires that the jokebook controversy and fame appeared to kindle or bring to light. Increasingly, he seemed defiantly, almost perversely, to fan the flames. In April 1945, a double-page portrait of one of the "dashingest" men in New York literary circles had appeared in *PM*. Headlined "Try and Stop Bennett Cerf," a box in the middle of the piece listed all his activities, hour by hour, during a "typical" working day. It included breakfast at home with Dick Tregaskis, proofreading Trade Winds at the office, a sighting of Sinclair Lewis, an ad meeting with Aaron Sussman, lunch at the Plaza, an appointment at King Features, a meeting at Grosset, a *Books Are Bullets* interview, an RH cocktail party, dinner at Bob Haas's, writing an *Omnibook* column, and staying up until 4:10 A.M. to read a manuscript. The amazing thing is, it *was* typical.

Mary Morris, the profile's author, inevitably asked about the "little storm" over the joke business. "Sheer nonsense," Bennett insisted—then a memorable exchange took place. He mentioned that he'd also edited anthologies of plays and stories, an occupation he considered laudable, but one that his *New Yorker* friend Harold Ross dismissed as "picking other people's brains," and therefore "second rate."

"Well," Bennett said, "guess I agree—that's kinda true. But so is columning a second-rate occupation—I'm a columnist too." He paused, then airily declared: "Just a superficial fellow with catholic tastes—I write and I talk about a whole lot of subjects but I'm never more than two inches below the surface."

Morris, startled, looked up from note-taking to find him facing her, sitting on top of her desk, "his long mouth turned up like a happy Hallowe'en pumpkin." Surely if the wattage behind the big boyish grin were high enough, all sorts of shortcomings and mischief would be forgiven, it seemed to imply.

The *Life* profile in December was far more biting, accusing Bennett of coveting the accolades of his authors: "Today Cerf is a literary lion, too, but it has remained for a glorified jokebook to fulfill his passion for public attention." His name, it continued, "is now a byword with thousands of Americans and an epithet with others." After more digs, it presented an "unsettling" possibility. Many of the most famous works of the ancients have failed to come down to us. Now there was the chance that Bennett, through sheer ubiquity, would be known to future historians as "the wittiest man of our time."

When he got hold of an advance copy of the magazine, Bennett tried to make the best of it, deeming it "not too bad!" Yet although the magazine's "close-ups" were known for sharp angles, some judged the portrait too sharp by half. A *San Francisco Chronicle* columnist, Joe Jackson, was one who chose to defend him against *Life:* "I've sat in Saxe Commins' office, next to Bennett's, and overheard him in conferences. . . . I know that he gets more done through his fanatically loyal staff than many another stodgier exec."

Phyllis, too, had had to thicken her skin against slights descending like sudden social frosts. At one party, Frances Goldwyn, wife of Hollywood mogul Sam, had refused to shake hands with Bennett "because of the things he said about her fine husband in *Try and Stop Me,*" Phyllis confided to Leonora. "Goldwyn cornered BAC & explained he didn't care for himself, but he thought it was bad for the Jews."

Around that time Elmer Adler, the long-departed third founder, wrote to complain about having been airbrushed out of Random House history. Bennett countered that much RH publicity was now written without his knowledge, but "Pa" wasn't persuaded. In a string of letters from January 1944 through June 1945, his venting became ever shriller as Bennett's success grew more pronounced. Mr. Cerf was beginning to discover that, much though he craved it, fame really could be a little tedious at times.

. . .

IT'S BOTH SURPRISING AND predictable that a man who squeezed so many disparate activities into a day would have such strongly imprinted habits and preferences, and demand that they be satisfied. Bennett wanted what he wanted when he wanted it—and was determined not to overpay. He regularly talked down prices, whether buying a painting for the office or paying a decorator, and, when filing his taxes, argued for substantial deductions (including for the maintenance of his home library). His official income for 1944—which his accountant presented to gain as much tax advantage as possible—was $58,000 (more than $1,020,000 today). He'd written for ten different magazines.

With the success of *Try and Stop Me* and visibility from columns, lectures he was being paid to give, and broadcasting, companies began to solicit his help: Why not endorse products? In some instances, the only payoff was flattering publicity; other companies paid in kind. In response to blandishments from the Benton & Bowles advertising agency, he became a member of the "Inner Circle of Coffee Lovers" for Yuban coffee. Superior java for home consumption was very much a premium commodity. For lending his name, the Madison Avenue men forwarded a case of Yuban "in the grind we understand you prefer."

Good coffee was just one of many comestibles that, even a year after war's end, were still scarce. The Hershey Chocolate Corporation, whose products had played a well-known role helping American GIs win hearts and minds in war-ravaged Europe, was manufacturing at only 60 percent of pre-war production because of a sugar shortage. There just weren't enough Hershey bars to go around. Bennett had a sweet tooth. He loved to reach for candy in his desk and share it. He didn't know whether Hershey's president would recognize his name, he wrote in October 1946, but hoped the president wouldn't think him "presumptuous" for doing so. When Bennett couldn't buy chocolate almond bars during the war, he'd assumed they were going to the troops "and said nothing." Now, however, he couldn't understand what was going on, and it bothered him very much.

He wanted to place a standing order for a box to arrive every fortnight. Several letters and a courtesy visit from a Hershey manager followed, but two months later, there were still no shipments—even though, Bennett complained (this time to the manager), his cook had seen the chocolate on sale in the Bronx, some subway kiosks were supplied, and he'd spotted the bars being sold from a pushcart. "I don't like to be a nuisance, but there is a stubborn streak in my character and once I start a thing like this, I want to see it through." This kind of letter peppered his correspondence with some regularity.

During the war, the availability of good fruit, like good chocolate and coffee, was also interrupted. He'd tried to satisfy his needs by subscribing to the "Fruit of the Month Club," a mail-order scheme offered by a company in Oregon. One author, the humorist S. J. Perelman, was aware of this: it provided the basis for Perelman's own sketch of Bennett in *The New Yorker* three weeks after the *Life* profile, for if *TASM* and the other joke books had affected how columnists, corporations, and the public responded to him, the anthologies also colored relations with his writers.

Perelman had published his first book unhappily with Liveright, but in 1937 moved to RH for his humor collection *Strictly from Hunger*. He decided he liked Bennett's humor and way of doing business, but by his third collection, *Crazy Like a Fox,* in 1944, the relationship had soured. Like many authors then and now, whoever the publisher, Perelman felt his wasn't promoting or advertising enough. *Crazy Like a Fox* was a bestseller, but he wanted more. He was far from an easy man (relationships with publishers would be rocky the rest of his life), but other factors also influenced his view. His brother-in-law Nathanael West had switched to RH after having had three books brought out by three different houses. At first West was happy, but by 1939, when RH published his Hollywood novel *The Day of the Locust,* he despised his publisher.

Even before publication, at the same time that Bennett was encouraging Budd Schulberg to write *What Makes Sammy Run?,* he was warning West that Hollywood novels didn't sell. Certainly, *The Day of the Locust* was a far darker story even than *Sammy,* and West a trickier personality. When *Locust* debuted, Bennett's fears were borne out. The book, misunderstood by many critics, sold just 1,464 copies. More than $200 of West's $500 advance was unearned, and the firm lost an additional $600. West, who made a good living as a screenwriter, was furious and blamed RH. But he needed a publisher, and early in 1940 summoned the nerve to ask for a $1,000 advance for a new book, infuriating Bennett. He countered by offering $250, icily informing West he was extremely lucky to get any offer. Later that year, a car crash killed West and his wife, and Perelman claimed that Bennett asked for the advance to be returned shortly thereafter.

Perelman's *New Yorker* piece was titled "No Dearth of Mirth—Fill

Out the Coupon." The narrator described a visit to "Barnaby Chirp," a brilliant young publisher, reviewer, anthologist, columnist, and flaneur who had "fathered" many a compendium, his latest titled "Laughing Gasp." Now the narrator had a great idea: a "Jape-of-the-Month Club" modeled after the fruit operation, and he pronounced "Chirp"—giggling, miserly, joke-stealing, with a "dazzling" smile—the man to carry it out. *New Yorker* readers needed less than a second to identify the model for Perelman's grinning booby.

Bennett appeared to take it as a joke, even signing "Barnaby Chirp" in a Christmas telegram to his author, whose new collection, *Keep It Fresh,* would soon be published by RH. Still, that spring of 1946 Perelman wrote to James Thurber, his *New Yorker* colleague, acidly calling Bennett "America's Sweetheart" and suggesting, "What say we sneak over to Random House and clap a commode snugly down over his ears?"

Perelman had talked to Don about his next project, a travel book, but neglected to mention that he'd taken it to S&S. When Donald found out, he felt betrayed—so betrayed that he spent several years not speaking to his erstwhile author. Such behavior, Perelman felt, was highly uncharacteristic of the man whom everyone considered a consummate gentleman.

Bennett's espousal of publishing as a bastion of creative endeavor—free expression guaranteed by the Constitution—was all very well, but for some his image as the punning bon vivant, always available for a comment with a joke on top, belied the seriousness with which he took his work. Others didn't like his insistence that it was also a business that had to add up, if it were to continue to bring out more books. During the courtship, he may have promised that he wanted to publish a writer for life and meant it, but poor sales could and did get in the way, as they had with West. Even with authors he adored, like Gertrude, he'd refuse to take a book that he felt sure would make a loss.

"Undoubtedly, you will find another publisher who will tell you the honeyed lies that you seem to want to hear," he once exploded to a writer who, after learning that Bennett culled ML titles that didn't meet a sales benchmark, chose not to come to RH. Even authors whom he went out of his way to help might loathe him in private, and the very public image that he projected seemed to goad them on. In 1939, with war on the horizon, Christopher Isherwood, having said goodbye to Berlin, wanted to stay in the United States rather than return to his native England. Bennett undertook to act as financial guarantor so he could become a permanent resident. Yet behind his back Isherwood spoke of him as "a twister" whose grand gestures were coupled with paltry advances. By 1947, still with RH, Isherwood described his publisher as "that incomparable ass."

In the immediate postwar years, the joke books, columns, and endorsements made Bennett a book publisher like no other before or since: a nationally known celebrity with the money, power, and influence that this conveyed. For fifteen years, Americans had had to sacrifice. Now many wanted to play hard and forget; they wanted optimism, escapism, jokes, which he gave them. But to a segment of the literary community, he'd be forever stained, a lightweight at best. The "superficial fellow . . . never more than two inches below the surface" played along, but also recognized the danger of this duality.

In October 1946, Bantam published *Anything for a Laugh,* by "the nation's Number One collector, refurbisher, and inventor of jokes," as the back cover announced. Yet in Bennett's preface he took a more serious turn, having discovered that this status as an authority on old jokes made him uneasy: he was "a book publisher by choice," who'd rather be remembered as the publisher of O'Neill, Lewis, Faulkner, and Joyce's *Ulysses* than as "a facile raconteur or anthologist of other people's bons mots." *Anything for a Laugh* and an already-contracted *Try and Stop Me* sequel would be the last of this sort to bear his name for a long time to come, he assured readers. After addressing Lyons's and Winchell's accusations, he reiterated, with a signature pun, that he was "a prattle-scarred veteran who is about ready to try and stop himself." But how could he give it up?

. . .

JOKE BOOKS WEREN'T THE only cause for controversy. The Modern Library had tapped Conrad Aiken and William Rose Benét, both Pulitzer Prize–winning poets, to assemble a new compendium to appeal to contemporary tastes. *An Anthology of Famous English and American Poetry* was almost a thousand pages, with work by more than a hundred poets, and advertised as the most comprehensive poetry collection in the series. It was the kind of book that would likely sell for years to students and families, libraries and institutions. When the manuscript arrived, however, Bennett wrote that he "objected to printing a single line of Ezra Pound in the year 1946 in any new volume that bore [our] imprint."

Pound, of course, was the expatriate American poet who'd championed Joyce, Eliot, and other modernists, and whose advocacy had been useful to *Ulysses*. Yet he'd spent part of the war in Italy as an apologist for Mussolini, broadcasting Fascist propaganda and defeatist messages to GIs. Don had fought in that war; Bob Jr. died in it. Pound had been flown to America, judged "insane," and put in a mental hospital, but to Bennett he was a traitor, period. What he didn't spell out was that Pound was a fervent antisemite.

Having appointed Aiken section editor for the American poems, Bennett felt morally bound to rely on his judgment; yet as publisher he retained the right to question Aiken's selections. After much wrangling, he offered him a choice: agree to delete the twelve Pound poems (the sop being the insertion of a note with the titles and the reason for their omission), or resign, in which case he'd still receive full pay. Aiken chose to remain, with a statement in print that his wishes had been overruled by the publishers, "who flatly refused at this time to include one word by Ezra Pound." The note appeared with a line that was pure Bennett: "This is a statement that the publishers are not only willing but delighted to print." He was dumbfounded when Lewis Gannett, a critic whom he respected, took issue in the *Herald Tribune,* going so far as to evoke Nazi book-burning.

"No one would demand that a publisher of Mr. Cerf's proved democratic passion publish books by authors whose politics or personalities he detests," Gannett conceded. "But a publisher's list is not an anthology: it does not pretend to represent the whole field." To let political concerns—however well-intentioned—shape a collection presented as comprehensive is "ill-thought hysteria, a blot on American publishing and a disservice to American democracy . . . the sheerest cultural barbarism" that others might be influenced to adopt.

Bennett couldn't change Gannett's mind, but was allowed to publish a reply in the paper. Maintaining that he spoke for Don and Bob as well, he argued: "Damn it, Lewis, this war is not over." The ideology that caused it—that Pound preached—was all too prevalent. To publish him was to enhance his reputation, and Bennett "gagged" at the idea of paying Pound for permission to print his lines. How could he help being emotional about "the most important struggle in the world today?"

Again, he was unprepared for what came next. Four men whom he held in high esteem—editor Bob Linscott; RH authors W. H. Auden and distinguished historian Henry Steele Commager; and liberal journalist Max Lerner—sided with Gannett. Auden did respect the fact that Bennett hadn't claimed the poems themselves were fascist—"a claim which, however unjust, would be almost impossible to refute in public because of the space . . . [it] would require." However, he urged his publisher to recognize the issue was far more serious than at first it seemed. Accept "that one thing to which a man stands related shares in his guilt," and you will extend that guilt to others; begin by banning his poems "not because you object to them but because you object to him, and you will end, as the Nazis did, by slaughtering his wife and children." The late senator Huey Long's "cynical observation" that if fascism came to America, it would be called "Anti-fascism," had more truth than one would like to believe, Auden warned. Bennett's abhorrence of Pound's conduct had led him "to take the first step." If not stopped, other steps would follow that would "horrify" him. "Very reluctantly," therefore, Auden said he'd have to sever his connection with RH, who'd shown him "unfailing courtesy and kindness."

Terribly shaken, Bennett tried to persuade Auden to stay, but still refused to agree that politics and art were quite so divorced. Taking a different tack, in Trade Winds he asked his readers to weigh in. "The stake we are fighting for is nothing less than the future of America," he wrote. It was all very well for some to argue "that we dare not employ any of the tactics of the enemy," but against such an implacable foe, he asked, "how often can we *afford* to . . . trust that abstract right and justice will triumph?" In the end, 289 letters were received: 142 opposed the poems' exclusion; 140 felt Bennett was right; seven were on the fence. Some threatened to pull their subscriptions to the *Review* and never buy another ML or Random House book. Bennett capitulated.

It was "damn unpleasant" to admit a mistake publicly, his column confessed, but he saw no way out, now "thoroughly convinced" that omitting the poems was an error. Future editions would have them and a note that he previewed to readers: "Pound the poet is deemed worthy of representation in this volume by the editor, Conrad Aiken. Here he is. Pound the man we consider a contemptible betrayer of his country." Bennett was offended when a reader argued that the commercial imperative had inspired his stance.

The final language, worked out with Pound's representative, was considerably more politic: "After the publishers . . . omitted the poems of Ezra Pound from the first edition of this volume, a veritable avalanche of praise and blame, equally divided, descended. . . . Nothing could have been farther from [their] intention . . . than to exercise arbitrary rights of censorship. We now have decided to include these poems . . . to remove any possible hint of suppression, and because we concede that it may be wrong to confuse Pound the poet with Pound the man."

It stuck in his gorge that RH had to pay three hundred dollars to reprint the poems, and the episode remained a sore point. What's more, he'd let slip to Auden that, contrary to what he'd said in the *Herald Tribune,* there had been no "unanimity of opinion" at RH. In his own oral history, Donald deemed Bennett's action to have been "very stupid." Auden was kinder, writing: "Decisions are hard enough to make; to change them is even harder." He would stay with Random, and less than a year later send Saxe the manuscript of his next book, a long poem in six parts that would win the Pulitzer Prize. Called *The Age of Anxiety,* it has spoken urgently to Americans ever since.

The Pound affair was full of mixed messages about Bennett. However, another author's wartime politics—Gertrude's—would also give him pause. But while he loathed Pound, he loved Stein, and the mixed messages *there* tell a different story. After France was liberated, he and she had been in fairly frequent communication, and he even hoped that Gertrude might make a trip to America. There was also a backlog of books to be published, and she was determined to get her share—as always, she needed money as well as glory. And yet, how had a pair of lesbian expatriate Jews (however lapsed) survived in Vichy France? In the spring of 1940, just before France fell, Bennett had written, sending "deep love" to Gertrude and Alice, hoping they would "come through the holocaust completely unscathed." Of course it's hindsight that makes that word so horribly freighted. By war's end, the Holocaust—as we use the term now—would have consumed six million Jews, including ninety thousand residing in France, more than one in four. But even without knowing about the "final solution," wartime dangers were omnipresent.

In part, the women came through thanks to the villagers of Bilignin and, later, Culoz, whom Gertrude's charisma had charmed. But more than anything, they owed their survival and the survival of their Paris art collection to their dear friend Bernard Faÿ, Stein's French translator. Faÿ, who'd been so useful in pushing Gertrude to go to America, became the Vichy administrator of the French National Library. A dedicated antisemite and

Nazi collaborator who hated both Masons and Jews (apart from a few exceptions), he was responsible for the deaths of both. Truth be told, Gertrude's own politics were hardly liberal: she admired Vichy president Philippe Pétain; had sided with Franco; and in 1937 had dismissed Hitler as "the German Romanticist" who'd "never really go to war."

For most Americans, though, she was a literary celebrity, not a political figure. Her U.S. tour had made her so famous, she was almost as much a French landmark as the Eiffel Tower. Which is how it happened that, in the summer of 1944, five American journalists set out to "liberate" Stein and Toklas, and make good copy while at it. The leader of the group, Eric Sevareid, had had the bright idea to cable CBS in New York, asking them to get Stein's whereabouts from Random House—how else would anyone know how to locate her? The journalists tracked her down in Culoz and found her personal magic still intact. They liked her and she liked them. Pieces duly appeared in *Life,* the Baltimore *Sun,* and the Washington *Evening Star;* and Sevareid's article for the *New York Herald Tribune* was picked up by *The New York Times* and other papers.

Bennett hadn't heard directly from Gertrude for two years, when on September 2 he read the headline in the *Herald Tribune:* "Gertrude Stein Safe in France with New Book." He dashed off a wire saying how "terribly happy" he was, and eager about the book—but such was Europe's chaos, it didn't make it through. Stein's manuscript arrived amazingly swiftly, though, through the good offices of Frank Gervasi, a reporter for *Collier's* and one of Sevareid's pals, who brought it home. In mid-October, Bennett spent a Saturday perusing what his cover copy would describe as Gertrude's "first-hand report of four years of Nazi rule in France and the joy of liberation." Within weeks, he'd sold an excerpt to *Collier's* for $2,000. By the time it was published in 1945, the book was titled *Wars I Have Seen*. Bennett's flap copy was again epistolary, to draw in fans of the charismatic lecture star rather than the cryptic modernist: Gertrude's friends, "aware of her indomitable courage and resourcefulness, were not at all surprised when she emerged unscathed . . . with even her Picasso collection absolutely intact, and her poodle Basket wagging his tail," he began. But having experienced her share of troubles and excitement, she had described them in this "most graphic and revealing of all her books."

The Autobiography of Alice B. Toklas had shown that, when so inclined, she could write "straightforward" English, and *Wars I Have Seen* was another such book, he told readers. The first half, conveying the impression that Stein was more concerned with foraging food for her dogs than with the fate of democracy, struck Bennett as "all too comprehensible." However, before long, her sense of "Olympian" detachment vanished in the excitement of the battle for liberation, and the Americans' arrival gave her "the thrill and supreme delight" of her whole life. The letter was genuinely felt—Bennett was no doubt carried away with affection and relief at her fate—but not everyone at RH saw Stein as "indomitable," "courageous," and "resourceful." Saxe had read the manuscript and made his feelings known in three highly emotional single-spaced typed pages. Of course, he'd known the "drop-by-drop" agony of trying to process her copy.

"No doubt" RH would publish the book, he began; "no doubt" it would get much "amusing and irrelevant" publicity; "no doubt" it would sell to those expecting another *Autobiography of Alice B. Toklas;* and "no doubt whatever" that few who bought it would "read it through." But in the substance of what she said about the occupation, war, and wars in general, he continued, not once was there outrage, never a hint of the political, social, or economic forces responsible. She was "incredibly tolerant" of collaborationists, and the advice she claimed to have offered Frenchmen about to be deported to Germany for slave labor—"Try to study them and learn their language and . . . literature. Think of yourself as a tourist and not as a prisoner"—was preposterously, offensively jejune. Few will trouble to seek the thoughts buried in the "rubbish heap" of incomprehensible words, Saxe concluded, but there was plenty of evidence she'd completely missed the meaning and tragedy of "the greatest cataclysm of history. . . . It's time a little moral indignation, instead of sycophancy, was aimed at Gertrude Stein." Emma Goldman's nephew had plenty of reasons to find Stein morally repugnant: his wife's French relatives had doubly risked their lives, since they were Jews who'd worked in the underground, and whose fate remained unknown until well after the war ended.

Perhaps more surprising is a note—never seen by Gertrude—written in Bennett's hand and appended to four typed manuscript pages filed away in the RH archive. The pages are Stein's introduction to a proposed collection of speeches by Marshal Pétain that she was translating and editing. A hero of the First World War, the Vichy head of state would be condemned for treason after the Second. It was his regime that had put into place the antisemitic policies that might have killed her. The project had been proposed to Stein early in the war by Faÿ—but whether it was an intellectual challenge she embraced or some sort of complex insurance policy, is impossible to know. In either case, the result would have been hard to swallow. Extraordinarily, in her introduction, she compared Pétain to George Washington, each having given his countrymen "courage in their darkest moment," "told them the truth," and made them realize that "the truth would set them free." She included herself in those who came to have faith in Pétain, "and in the fact that France will live."

Presumably, she'd written Bennett to see if the firm might want to publish it; the reaction of his handwritten note seems unequivocal: "For the records. This disgusting piece was mailed from Belley on Jan. 19, 1942—BAC." But it appears her proposal didn't arrive at RH until long *after* the fact, for in a March 1946 letter, he said that they'd all got a great laugh out of her cable and letter telling them the Pétain suggestion had been made in 1941. "Some German gauleiter was probably sleeping with it under his pillow for the last three or four years; come to think of it, there was about it the faint aroma of frankfurters and sauerkraut." He may have wanted to be perfectly clear about his own sympathies for posterity, but his disgust seems to have been easily transformed into humor for the consumption of his author. In all probability, he condemned her Pétain apologia "for the records" at the same time that he sent "the faint aroma of frankfurters and sauerkraut" wafting back in friendly fashion to France. When arrayed against his affection and his business interests, Bennett's moral outrage was quickly diverted.

Wars I Have Seen was published in February 1945, and by V-E Day on May 8, RH had sold 14,000 copies—"pretty darn good," Bennett congratulated himself and his author. His instincts had not failed him. It was Stein's most popular work since *The Autobiography of Alice B. Toklas*. He even managed to get a good joke out of it—one that spread quickly, taking on the quality of legend. When Gertrude received her author's copies, she cabled back, "Book received lovely page lovely book lovely Bennett love to Random House." Replying in kind, he sent a check made out for "Two thousand thousand dollars dollars." Promptly RH got another cable: "Cut out this nonsense and make my check out properly." He could only obey.

Chapter 18

Golden Era for a Brownstone Palace

THE NOTICE ARRIVED THE DAY AFTER CHRISTMAS 1945. AFTER YEARS of going about their business surrounded by Rockwell Kent's torch-bearer and other tutelary spirits, the partners had to abandon their cozy Deco lair. The International Business Machines Corporation had bought the building and, as Bennett put it, "asked in a friendly way for us to get the hell out." The order to vacate specified June, so the hunt was on for a new home. Unfortunately, good office space was scarce in midtown: except for Rockefeller Center, there hadn't been much new building in that part of town since the crash of 1929.

As luck would have it, Bennett was also sourcing paper for a saint. Thomas Aquinas, he'd been persuaded, was a sufficiently big deal in Roman Catholicism to merit a two-volume selected edition of his work. (The only Aquinas then available was in two *dozen* volumes put out by a religious publisher.) Still, even boiled down, the saint's wisdom extended to about 1,200 pages per book. Bennett calculated that if RH printed 10,000 sets, they'd satisfy demand for five years and recoup the investment. After that, it would be clear profit, because the Church wasn't expected to tire of Aquinas anytime soon. What he hadn't realized was that every Jesuit school in the country was waiting for an edited version of the saint's words. Within three weeks, all 10,000 sets were sold.

RH didn't have any more paper to put through a reprint—a less-than-desirable situation in the eyes of the Church, which had looked favorably on the firm for publishing Aquinas in the first place. When a monsignor from Saint Patrick's offered to sell enough of the Church's own paper to make another 5,000 sets, a grateful Bennett got chatting, and mentioned his other little problem. "How about the big building across from the Cathedral? The palazzo, the brownstone building," the priest suggested. That's how Bennett came to hear of the availability of

457 Madison Avenue—the north wing of what is known as the "Villard Houses" or "Villard Mansion"—extending from Fiftieth to Fifty-First Street, and architecturally unique the length and breadth of Manhattan. Unlike the city's characteristic brownstones—terraced sandstone-faced row houses like the one Bennett lived in (although his was painted gray)—the Villard residences coalesce into one glorious U-shaped whole, six houses (originally four, with two more added at the back) around a central courtyard overlooking Madison Avenue. They were built between 1882 and 1886 for Henry Villard, a remarkable German immigrant who'd decided to live with neighbors he selected himself.

Né Heinrich Hilgard, he'd arrived in America wanting to be a writer. Working as a journalist, he got involved in the anti-slavery movement; married the daughter of famed abolitionist William Lloyd Garrison; reported on the Civil War; but also allied himself with a group of successful German investors. Eventually he became president of the Northern Pacific Railway, and owned the *New York Evening Post* and *The Nation*. Villard took the unusual step of appointing a fledgling architectural firm, McKim, Mead & White, to design the houses (there was a family connection), and with this project they announced a strikingly different aesthetic for the city, turning away from fussy Victoriana to refined neoclassicism, taking as model the Palazzo della Cancelleria in Rome.

Alas, Villard lived only briefly in the property on the Fiftieth Street side of the complex—he went bankrupt and fled the city—but there was something about the place that attracted publishing types. Villard's residence was bought by Whitelaw Reid, editor and publisher of the *New-York Tribune,* who with seventeen servants maintained it as "the richest and handsomest set of rooms for entertainment" in New York. The house that Bennett toured was at the other end of the complex, bordering Fifty-First Street, and had been owned by a banker, Harris Fahnestock, who'd also bought the adjacent property on the side street. His son later broke through the walls and hired another architect, Charles Platt, to open up the grand house, making it lighter, airier, more footloose and fancy-free, in the "flapper" high style of the early 1920s. The stairwell and halls were painted in a then-revolutionary new color, beige, and Platt added a classic black-and-white checkered stone floor, with delicate wrought-iron railings that ran the length of the cream-colored marble stairs. Descending that curved staircase was like doing a star turn in an especially glamorous movie. But times changed, and the complex became increasingly hard to staff and maintain. The families who'd lived there didn't so much move out as die out.

During the war, Villard's house became the Women's Military Services Club—more than 250,000 uniformed women had stayed there, for fifty cents a night—while Fahnestock's home headquartered American Relief for France. By 1946, the real estate speculator and ex-ambassador Joseph P. Kennedy owned the whole complex. When Bennett protested to the monsignor that he couldn't possibly afford anything as grand as the Fahnestock house, the priest told him to stop quibbling. "We'll make [Kennedy] give it to you for what he paid for it," and got Kennedy on the line in Palm Beach. The deal was done, just like that—or so Bennett spun the story. It was in fact a bit more complicated. In late January, when he first inspected the place, he saw it was the best the realtors had shown him, but was offered as a rental. On February 1, RH signed a three-year lease. He deadpanned to *PW:* the house had "wonderful rooms, a wonderful staircase, in fact, it is wonderful for anything but an office." It transpired, however, that Kennedy decided he wanted to sell, and Bennett, all fired up, wanted to buy. Bob Haas overcame his natural caution: the building was too marvelously elegant to resist. The sale would include a one-third interest in the private driveway that led from Madison Avenue into the center of the courtyard. But Don, still uncertain about his finances and footing, balked, not thinking the three "had any business being in the real estate business." In the end, Bennett and Bob outvoted him. They agreed to stretch to Kennedy's price: $420,000. After all, it was what it had cost him, Bennett was led to believe. (Twenty years later, discovering Kennedy had paid $200,000, Bennett complained; Kennedy's broker drily offered to take the house back for $420,000. By then, the building was worth millions.)

Choosing the mansion was "very imaginative and un-publisher-like," recalled Robert Giroux, an editor who'd lend his name to another great house, Farrar, Straus & Giroux. Part Hollywood, part Madison Avenue, Bennett had an uncanny instinct and a talent for presenting his firm and his authors to the world, and had trusted himself in the Villard purchase. For almost a quarter century, in the eyes of passersby, let alone all who entered there, the six-story building took on one overarching identity: literally and figuratively, Random House. Saint Thomas Aquinas, Bennett joked, was RH's patron saint.

That autumn, in a special lecture Bennett gave to some five hundred students at the Barbizon Plaza to open the New York University publishing course, he declared that, in spite of the difficulties that lay ahead, "we truly are entering the Golden Era of American publishing." So it would be—in the memories of author after author, editor after editor, visitor after visitor, and for the master of the house—an impossibly golden era in an impossibly beautiful brownstone palace. "It was an old-fashioned elegance that you cannot duplicate . . . being published out of that mansion gave you a wonderful sense . . . to feel that you were a writer," William Styron recalled. It would not last forever, but while it did, there was nowhere like it.

North wing of the Villard Houses, 1947

Once the deal was announced in the papers, Bennett, like the proudest kid with the latest toy, delighted in taking cronies to gaze boggle-eyed at the building. On these tours, he kept chuckling at the very idea of "rattling around" in it, the *New York World-Telegram* reported. There were libraries, boudoirs, a ballroom, vast rooms, decorated with fine wood paneling and marble mantels. The kitchen would make a good stockroom, Bennett observed, and the butler's pantry a lunchroom for RH ladies. Yet he drew the line: the bidet would have to go. (Such "loot" was divided among the partners.)

Bob Haas supervised the transformation into a workable publishing house. The most complex tasks involved cutting through six-foot walls in the building's center to add an additional staircase from the second floor to the sixth, and installing a modern "air-cooling" system (except for the attic). Each partner would have his own room on the third floor—no longer would Bennett and Don laugh at each other across desks. Moving day was set for May 13, and before leaving for a Florida vacation May 2, Bennett bet Bob that the firm would still be on Fifty-Seventh Street when he got back. "I knew," he chortled to *PW,* "that he'd move the stuff personally if he had to, to win that bet."

On Sunday, May 19, back from the trip, he went down to the new Random House, Phyllis and Chris in tow. They walked under the wrought-iron gateway bisecting the piazza, turned left, crossed the courtyard, and skipped up four broad stone steps. The big double doors of 457 Madison Avenue stood mysteriously at attention, awaiting orders.

When they broke the enchantment and burst inside, all thoughts of mystery were left behind: the entrance hall's light walls, checkerboard floor, peppermint-striped chairs, and cheery red sofa welcomed them with a gay, bright air. The receptionist's desk and a handsome wood-and-glass display case for books—it had been built with a cornice to resemble a house—completed the scene. Later, Bennett would return to inspect Manny Harper's room and the accounting office Manny would oversee, next to the entrance hall. This level was in fact the second floor, although anyone coming into the building would have judged it to be the first. The layout was complicated due to the joining of the two houses. The actual first floor had its main entrance on Fifty-First Street and accommodated the "back end" operations: orders and billing, mailroom, stockroom. The only parts of this floor that showed faces to the world were street-level vitrines along Madison Avenue, perfect for passersby to admire the latest RH and ML books. The fourth and fifth floors housed manufacturing, sales, juveniles, copy editors, secretaries, and publicity.

The Cerfs proceeded up the marble staircase to the rooms on the third floor: the heart and soul of the old house. In addition to the partners, the three acquiring editors had offices there, along with Bennett and Don's Jezebel and Margaret the switchboard operator. Each partner's room had been decorated to reflect the distinctive character of the man. Pat Klopfer, who'd dabbled in interior design before marrying Donald, planned his office. Against dark-green painted walls she placed draperies and upholstered furniture with big botanical prints, a green leather chair, and a fine yellow carpet, to go with the old-fashioned sconces and exquisite mantel. The room, smaller and more intimate than Bob's and Bennett's, became an approximation of a classic English gentleman's study. It was centrally located near the top of the stairs, providing easy access to the partner most frequently sought by staff needing advice. When Don himself required a moment's refuge, he could gaze down at the courtyard, now embellished with plantings of rhododendron and pachysandra laid out by avid gardener Harry Maule.

An Upper East Side decorator was hired for the other offices. The enormous former sitting room of the master bedroom suite, facing onto Madison Avenue as well as the courtyard, was intended for Bennett, but he decided that dark oak paneling carved with garlands was more suited to Francophile Bob. This room also had a fine fireplace, as well as a thick beige broadloom, rose-and-green chintz curtains and upholstery, and a "Charles of London" red leather chair, all of which combined to speak of refined civility.

Bennett chose an entirely different look. In the corner opposite to Bob, facing Madison and Fifty-First Street, everything had to be "very modern, very convenient, and very cheerful." Bennett's walls were painted blue-gray. Floor-to-ceiling bookshelves and glass-and-Formica-topped cabinets were painted to match, while a long leather sofa and easy chairs welcomed visitors. A pattern of black, brown, and gray horses pranced gaily between very bright red and blue ribbons, up and down the length of the drapes. He would sit (contrary to reports, he *was* capable of sitting still), pipe jutting from the left side of his mouth, with his back to the windows along the avenue. Surveying his kingdom, he saw across the room a surprisingly plain fireplace and two large, paneled doors. Behind the left one was his own private bathroom (as good as anything Liveright had enjoyed) with a telephone and bookshelves that featured two adjacent copies of Charles Lindbergh's *We*—a pun Bennett couldn't resist—and other similarly tongue-in-cheek bathroom-themed titles, along with a shower for his personal convenience. "Every God damned [book] buyer in the United States comes . . . to look over the joint and Lew . . . shlepps [*sic*] them in" to the bathroom first, Bennett chuckled. "I must admit . . . [it's] a sight to see."

Pictures, photos, mementos, and gadgets personalized the office but didn't clutter it. There was a lot of space to pace about, as well as enough to accommodate impromptu parties. The room could only be of that particular postwar 1940s New York modern moment: fresh, uncomplicated bright colors, straightforward masculine lines, and splashy prints—a center of power and work, to be sure, yet informal and easy.

"DELIGHTED WITH MY OFFICE," Bennett enthused to his diary. He'd stayed "five happy hours" arranging the books on the room's many shelves. Monday, his first workday in the place, was "MOST EXCITING!"—and not just for Mr. Cerf.

(From left) Linscott, Maule, Commins with the boss in his new office

. . .

THAT YEAR, SO MANY exciting things were happening. Having demonstrated his radio moxie, Bennett was invited to make guest appearances on that fresh new medium, television, and starting on Valentine's Day 1946, he'd emcee a Thursday night program of his own, a weekly CBS "tele-quiz," *See What You Know*. Presiding over a panel that included Sid Perelman (business was business, whatever Perelman thought of him); Gypsy Rose Lee; and talk show pioneer Tex McCrary, he welcomed guests ranging from songsmith Johnny Mercer to Bess Myerson, the reigning Miss America, from 8:10 to 8:40 P.M. In March he delivered his latest cornucopia of corn, *Anything for a Laugh,* to Grosset and Bantam, and that month Allan Ullman, who'd headed book advertising at the *Times,* joined RH in the new role of promotion manager, freeing more of Bennett's time.

On the author front, Bennett saw an obvious winner in Sinclair Lewis's new manuscript, *Kingsblood Royal,* and was also enthusiastic about *The Pursuit of Love,* a novel by Nancy Mitford that Don had bought from Hamish "Jamie" Hamilton, a favorite British publisher. Bennett went so far as to write personal letters to give it a push. Then there was *The Snake Pit,* that rare miracle that comes in over the transom and succeeds beyond anyone's imagining. The novel, a thinly veiled memoir by one Mary Jane Ward—aka Mrs. Edward Quayle, of Evanston, Illinois—had traveled from the Chicago suburbs to Random House on the wings of friendship. Another woman had submitted a novel on the very tricky subject of incest. Linscott rejected it but was impressed enough to send five pages of advice. The author, grateful for so thoughtful a rejection, wrote again, mentioning that a friend had written an absolutely riveting work. The friend—Mary Jane—had published two books with Dutton, yet her new one had been rejected in the most devastating way: her agent refused to send it out. Linscott agreed to read it. "So in came *The Snake Pit,*" Bennett recalled, and when RH brought out the novel that spring of 1946, he didn't think even ten changes had been made in the manuscript—"it was so perfect."

"Do you hear voices?" the story begins. "Virginia Cunningham" is thirty-five, married, from a comfortable background, and experiences a severe breakdown. Institutionalized, at first she doesn't understand what's happened or where she is. The novel, written from within the illness and inside the asylum, portrays through shattered shards of her mind the fellow patients, doctors, and therapies she undergoes, including shock treatments. Ward had spent nine long months in such a place, at a time when mental illness was a deeply taboo topic, and conditions in institutions were often appalling. She felt compelled to purge herself through writing. Linscott agreed to use one of the titles she suggested—*The Snake Pit*—though Bennett had worried it would put women off. To clarify the meaning, a note opposite the title page explained: "Long ago they lowered insane persons into snake pits; they thought that an experience that might drive a sane person out of his wits might send an insane person back into sanity."

Omens were good: in January 1946, BOMC selected it; Bennett sold movie rights to his producer pal Anatole "Tola" Litvak; and *Reader's Digest* took an option to abridge the novel. At the end of that month, Ward and her husband came to stay at Sixty-Second Street and learn about success. She'd found it "exciting" simply to have received a letter from the famous Mr. Cerf, but now she was wined and dined by Cerfs, Haases, Linscott, and Frances Merriam, the new publicity director whom Bennett had lured from Macy's book department. What mattered most was that the whole RH family came across as "just people" who put an "ordinary" person like her at ease. Bennett was especially concerned that she undertake only as much publicity as she felt able to.

Later, when she and her husband traveled to Hollywood for the making of the movie, Bennett's instinct was to protect her from the kind of poison he'd known a dozen years earlier. "It is a bewildering place and certainly fascinating for short stretches," he cautioned. "Don't let it get you. It's no place for a wonderful girl like you—and I mean that as one of the most sincere compliments I ever paid." He also tried to reassure her about changes the book might undergo on the screen: "Put your faith in God and Tola . . . top men in their respective professions."

Published in April, *The Snake Pit* had sold more than 100,000 copies in the RH edition by the end of August. "I don't know when I have been made happier by a book's success," Linscott wrote to Ward. Foreign rights were sold in sixteen languages. When she made a second trip to New York that fall, Bennett pulled out all the stops: Eleanor Roosevelt came to the party at Sixty-Second Street. Ward felt under a spell the whole time, her host and hostess being "real artists in hospitality." Years later, Bennett would describe *The Snake Pit* as an example of "why the publishing business is so damned exciting." The "real fun is discovering somebody brand new and bringing the book out and publicizing it properly . . . watching overnight some unknown become a big star." Having published two novels, Ward wasn't exactly "brand new," but she was far from "known." It had taken instinct, guts, enthusiasm, and know-how to bring off such a triumph.

As soon as the extent of that success became clear, Ward asked that the money earned be held for her and doled out over several years; such requests would become more common, to avoid an author having to make high income-tax payments under the current law. These arrangements, negotiated to help the author, were extremely beneficial to RH as well. By law, the interest accrued couldn't go to the author; instead, it went to the firm. She'd asked for $25,000 to be released in each of the next few years, and also sought advice: Did Bennett think she could afford to buy a farm for $48,000? "Proceed with our blessings and please take my personal order now for four pounds of butter a week," came the reply. Moviegoers judged the film, released in 1948, shocking and unprecedented. It was nominated for six Oscars, including best picture, and Olivia de Havilland won the New York Film Critics' best actress award. In Britain, despite being released in a censored version, it broke twenty years of attendance records at London's most famous cinema.

RH had contracted Ward's next novel, *The Professor's Umbrella*. She'd turned for inspiration to her student days at Northwestern, devising a plot about a trumped-up charge of sexual misconduct against a professor who not coincidentally was Jewish. The manuscript arrived in spring 1947, just when Bennett's poker-playing, Jewish pal Laura Z. Hobson, with that "most Jewish" publisher S&S, blew the topic of antisemitism wide open with *Gentleman's Agreement,* exposing how many "nice" Americans treated Jews.

Like any author after a huge success, Ward felt tremendous pressure to repeat it; and, as is often the case, the new novel was found wanting by Linscott, Saxe, and others. But this was a special case: there was the scary sense—conveyed by both Ward and her husband, and pinning RH into a corner—that if the book didn't succeed, she might suffer another breakdown. Yet the manuscript's problem was serious: her treatment of Jews wasn't authentic in the eyes of those in a position to know. Fritz Jacobi, the young lieutenant who'd served under Don and been taken on as an editorial reader, diagnosed characters who "apologize for their Jewishness, try to minimize it. . . . She's playing right into the hands of the antisemites." Ward tweaked the text, but couldn't make the major changes it needed. RH stood by her, and it was a relief when the book had a decent sale on the coattails of *The Snake Pit*. She published two more novels with RH in 1951 and 1952, and a couple more with others years later. None came close to matching her great success.

When dictating his oral history, Bennett recalled *The Snake Pit,* though he evidently forgot the firm had published two books after *The Professor's Umbrella* and rejected another. He'd "lost track of" Ward. What matters more is the chance RH took in signing *The Snake Pit* in the first place, and, most of all, what the novel accomplished. It drew attention to a problem and a population that society didn't want to see, inspiring editorials and institutional reforms. For years, the phrase "snake pit" would pop up in any general discussion of mental institutions. And the book's reach extended further: Ward got letters from junior high and high school students, who felt the novel spoke to them.

Bennett saw it as the kind of book that makes the publishing business exciting. It was also the kind that makes a difference in people's lives.

. . .

THE CERFS' SECOND CHILD had been due in April 1946, and obstetrician Morty Rodgers told Phyllis the baby might come on the thirteenth, her birthday. Like Christopher, this one would be delivered by caesarean section, and she'd seen no reason to share her birthday, given a choice: it would have to arrive sooner. And so, on April 2, the day after the first reviews of *The Snake Pit,* Bennett took Thrup to the hospital. That night, four-and-a-half-year-old Chris—who hadn't been told the cause of his mother's increasing girth but figured it out, as children do—slept in her bed in the room she shared with his dad. He'd seemed to cry each time she left the house. A few months earlier, Bennett had written to Gertrude: "If it's a girl, what will you give us to name it Gertrude Stein Cerf? The bidding is now up to two Picassos." Later he added: "For a guy whose motto . . . was possession without responsibility I certainly have gotten myself into the god-damnedest set of complications!"

On April 3, Jonathan Fraser Cerf was born, eyes tightly shut for two full days before being ready to look out on the world. His father, much more comfortable than he'd been the first time, admitted to Saxe it was "highly presumptuous and impertinent" of nature to give him a son, when he'd wanted a daughter. More seriously, he told his diary that Thrup had been "wonderful throughout. I love her so!" And his wife, as well as giving birth a second time, soon reached another milestone, turning a grown-up thirty.

The baby remained in the hospital until April 16, and that night, Bennett was able to record: "home with Thrup and my two sons!" The next day, he celebrated at Yankee Stadium, where in the RH box he watched the season opener with Bob Haas and Gene O'Neill. There was, though, a shadow that kept breaking through the sunny surface. While Thrup was in the hospital, he'd written to Edgar Snow, then in Tokyo, cautioning that back home, people were "in a mood of bitter disillusionment," patronizing black markets because there wasn't enough of anything to go

With Thrup and his two sons

around, and wringing their hands that the last war "accomplished nothing" and a new one loomed, "more and more unavoidable." He caught himself, telling Snow to discount some of that uncharacteristic gloom: "I guess I'm just tired." He'd been going at quite a pace, and had had no winter break because of Phyllis's pregnancy. He hoped the post-partum depression *he* was feeling would burn off under Florida's sun during his holiday with Thrup just before RH's move. Chris and the baby would stay in New York. The vacation helped, as did the marvelous new offices and an unexpected and quite touching fillip provided by Bob Haas. On April 1, he'd penned a valentine rather than a joke to his partner, to mark the tenth anniversary of their merger:

> These have been years with as congenial partners as a man ever had, years that have given me more real happiness than I would have thought possible. . . . The best . . . I could hope for . . . is that we three may have many more. . . . Associations . . . [like] ours are so rare as to be almost unique, and you may be certain I'm duly appreciative of such a gift . . . for which you were and are so largely responsible.

It was, as Bennett noted in his scrapbook, "a letter to treasure."

His business dealings with Gertrude had had ups and downs since war's end. She and Alice had needed cash to rebuild their Paris life; although their paintings had stayed safe thanks to Faÿ, other items had

Congenial partners, rare association

been looted, and in June 1945, Bennett granted a royalty revision she'd asked for that would help. Her next book would be *Brewsie and Willie,* whose starting-off point was her conversations with GIs in France (two of their nicknames furnished the title). But while RH awaited arrival of the manuscript, a man Bennett didn't know claimed to be offering rights to another book by Stein. He wrote her again: she had to understand it was "impossible" for RH to call itself her publisher when others kept popping up claiming rights to her books. To discourage wanderlust, Bennett made an enticing proposal. If she delayed plans with anyone else until 1947, RH would publish a pricey, one-volume "selected writings" and later reprint it as an ML Giant. For most people and purposes, those eight hundred pages would be the definitive Stein, and keep her most important writings "permanently" in print. If her reaction wasn't "wildly favorable," he joked, "you'll be hearing from me again, young lady." A deal was struck.

Alas, she didn't live long enough to see his promise fulfilled. Cancer, far gone, had been discovered. After an operation on July 26, she didn't regain consciousness and died, age seventy-two, the next day. All kinds of people whose lives she'd improbably touched through her writing, her charisma, or her very existence mourned her passing. Mary Jane

Ward wrote to Bennett as soon as she read the news—her feeling of loss was so strong, she felt compelled to communicate with someone who'd known Gertrude.

It is part of Stein lore that she died holding a copy of *Brewsie and Willie* in each hand—precious talismans guiding the way to her afterlife, the literary equivalent of the tomb figurines favored by the ancients. No doubt Alice had taken care of that. Surely, Gertrude would have approved when death did not interfere with her publishing afterlife. In their windows, Fifth Avenue bookstores featured memorial displays of *Brewsie and Willie*. More important, the selected writings, edited by Carl Van Vechten, was rushed for publication in the fall. As Bennett had promised, the book remains in print to this day.

One of the last pieces of Stein's work didn't appear in that volume. Bennett may have cheekily started 1946 with a celebration to usher in the atomic age, but Gertrude's life went out with a "Reflection on the Atomic Bomb." "They asked me what I thought of the atomic bomb. . . . I had not been able to take any interest in it," she began. "What is the use, if they are really as destructive as all that . . . really nobody else can do anything about it so you have to just live along like always." Both Gertrude and Bennett put much effort, during wartime and all times, into conducting their lives to "just live along like always." Neither lost sight of what they wanted from life, and each saw that in the other.

Bennett was in Vermont with the Haas family when she died, so Don sent the wire with condolences. Nevertheless, Alice directed her reply to Bennett: "I only wanted to say that she was very fond of you and never forgot what you had done for her." But it was in an introduction to the *Selected Writings* that Bennett had cajoled from her six weeks before her death that Gertrude provided her own envoi to her publisher:

> . . . [He] said he would print and he would publish even if he did not understand and if he did not make money, it sounds like a fairy tale but it is true, Bennett said I will print a book of yours a year . . . and he has, and often I have worried but he always said there was nothing to worry about and there wasn't. And now I am pleased here are the selected writings and naturally I wanted more, but I do and can say . . . all . . . here are those that I wanted the most, thanks and thanks again.

Chapter 19

A New Voice, Another Home

Truman Capote

NOT EVERY AUTHOR ELICITED THE KIND OF AFFECTION FROM BENNETT that Gertrude had. Yet in the autumns of 1945 and 1946, two rare birds who had that potential came to roost at Random House—one of tender exotic plumage, the other a tough old fighting cock.

"Big Daddy" is how Truman Capote would come to refer to his publisher. The nickname was affectionate yet barbed: if there was one thing Bennett didn't want to be reminded of, it was his age. "For Pete's sake, cut that out!" he'd snap—but quickly rebound. The relationship with the Cerfs would sustain Capote at Random House, and they, in turn, would grow very fond of him. John O'Hara, on the other hand, was at forty-one an established pro at short-form fiction, who'd published nine books. Still, he suffered with the knowledge that *Appointment in Samarra,* the first, was universally judged his best. With a permanent chip on his shoulder and showing warning signs of middle-aged drunken burnout, he was looking for a new publisher. Both writers would require special care and handling, and call forth from Bennett a level of devotion akin to that he'd shown Gertrude. Each would return the favor—in his fashion.

On June 2, 1947, *Life* ran a long feature headlined "Young U.S. Writers—A Refreshing Group of Newcomers on the Literary Scene Is Ready to Tackle Almost Anything." War was over; who would take up the mantle of Hemingway, Fitzgerald, and go one better? *Life* piqued readers' curiosity with photos of those it was betting on. The vote for "most brilliant" of the new fictionists went to two: Jean Stafford—who'd already been compared to Proust and was Mrs. Robert Lowell—and Thomas Heggen, whose critical and bestselling success *Mister Roberts* would later be adapted for stage and screen. Names like Norman Mailer, J. D. Salinger, and Saul Bellow were not yet lighting up the horizon, although Bellow had published his first novel during the war. Instead, the magazine pointed to Calder Willingham, Elizabeth Fenwick, Peggy Goodin, Ann Chidester, Peggy Bennett, Gore Vidal, and husband-and-wife Nancy and Benedict Freedman—who, with the exception of Vidal, have faded into obscurity.

One photo stood out, occupying most of the article's first page. In jacket, tie, waistcoat, gray flannels, and shiny dark shoes, the writer sat amidst silky, tasseled surroundings. He posed like some fresh young androgynous offering at a night-town establishment, meeting the reader's gaze with an unnerving stare, innocent yet knowing. "Esoteric, New Orleans–born Truman Capote, 22, writes haunting short stories. His novel, 'Other Voices, Other Rooms,' will be out this fall," read the caption. Esoteric indeed—code for a young man who for that time and place dared to appear provokingly, unequivocally homosexual. Dick Simon saw the article and got on the phone to Bennett.

"How the hell do you get a full-page picture of an author in *Life* magazine before his first book comes out?" he demanded.

"Do you think that I'm going to tell you? Does Macy's tell Gimbel's?" came the reply. After the two hung up, Bennett called to Pauline:

"For God's sake, get me a copy of *Life*." He hadn't known about the article; it had been entirely his author's doing. Young Capote adored the camera, and the camera adored him.

William Styron was also struggling to be a writer. In those days before TV was well established, *Life*'s readership was vast, and he wondered how this fellow—about the same age—had landed in the public eye. When he read the stories, he was "knocked out . . . absolutely devastated"; they were "so brilliant." But although envious, Styron was also inspired: "If he could do it, maybe I could . . . too." Random congratulated itself: it had hooked Capote almost two years earlier.

Truman Streckfus Persons, born in New Orleans in 1924, had left the South of his early childhood to come north with his mercurial mother, Lillie Mae—who'd rechristened herself the far more elegant "Nina"—and Cuban stepfather, Joe Capote. For some years Truman shuttled back and forth between stays with beloved elderly relations in Alabama and periods in New York with Joe and Nina. At his Monroeville cousins' home, he became deeply attached to a tomboy named Nelle Harper Lee, who would turn him into "Dill" in her novel *To Kill a Mockingbird,* and whom he'd transform into "Idabel" in his first book. He felt predestined to be a writer, and in 1942—not yet eighteen, preternaturally pale, blond, and delicate (yet tough like one of Shakespeare's sprites)—he landed a copy-boy job at *The New Yorker.* Determined to be somebody, he soon spent evenings with well-known charmers whom *he* charmed, headline-grabbing glamour girls like Oona O'Neill.

At twenty, after a faux pas, he found himself fired by *The New Yorker* (he'd also tried and failed to have his own work published there). Happily, it was far from the only magazine serious about short fiction that paid well; other large-circulation weeklies and monthlies also had editors adept at spotting new talent. One was *Mademoiselle,* and in 1945, Capote placed "Miriam"—a precisely executed spine-tingler about a scary little girl who takes over the life and psyche of a spinster—in the June issue.

"What a fine story it is!" Bennett marveled.

More followed, in *Mademoiselle* and *Harper's Bazaar.* Rita Smith—assistant to *Mademoiselle*'s fiction editor—and her older sister, Carson McCullers, decided to help him. In 1941, then twenty-three-year-old McCullers had herself been hailed a sensation when Houghton Mifflin published *The Heart Is a Lonely Hunter.* Smith found Capote an agent, and

McCullers praised him to Linscott, whom she'd grown close to at Houghton.

On October 19, 1945, Bennett scribbled in his diary that RH "signed Capote." The contract specified an advance of $1,200—not vast, but more than twice the $500 that McCullers had received six years earlier from Houghton. It would be parceled out at a hundred dollars a month for the next year to keep him going, and to help Linscott maintain a degree of control. But as soon as Bennett met Capote at Random House, the potential for block-capital diary entries was clear: "Well, *that* was a day when Truman arrived," he later recalled. "He waltzed in . . . happy and absolutely assured. Everybody knew that somebody important had arrived upon the scene—particularly Truman!"

"Now you're going to be a writer and an artist," Bob Linscott proclaimed to his latest author, and both believed it. Linscott holds a curious place in RH lore; "an enigma" is what Capote called the New Englander, while Linscott's assistant said he was "very secretive." Some criticized him for buttering up authors, then turning on them if let down. Others saw him as a ladies' man. But Phyllis Cerf—a woman of iron-clad loyalties and dislikes—wasn't susceptible to his charm. In contrast to the generosity she found in most publishing people, she felt Linscott was "a chiseler" who did "nothing for love." Lew Miller told her of having to go to a meeting during a downpour, and asking to borrow Linscott's old raincoat. His response was to offer to sell it to Lew for twenty-five dollars.

True, RH editors, like those elsewhere, weren't paid princely salaries, and for years had had to moonlight. Saxe, Belle, and Linscott all compiled anthologies and received lump-sum payments or royalties in return; Saxe also taught a publishing course at Columbia. But Linscott devised a canny alternative: a rider inserted into many of his authors' contracts—the "Linscott clause"—specifying that once a sales target for that title had been met, he—in addition to the author—would earn a small royalty on sales.

Whatever others thought, Bennett had high regard for this long-experienced editor whom he'd lured from Boston when the firm was growing fast. Linscott projected a confidence foreign to highly strung Saxe—who recognized Capote's talent but was uneasy around him. Just as Saxe was right for Budd Schulberg, Linscott understood what Capote required: he could handle the justified cockiness *and* underlying neediness. As he'd done for a few other writers, Linscott provided a key to his apartment so that his newest charge could work there during the day. "We're going to support you, take care of you. You're like a racehorse," he told him.

In May 1947, Capote told Linscott about his ambition to write a beautiful book, "now more than ever because the world is so crazy and only art is sane and it has been proven time after time that after the ruins of a civilization are cleared away all that remains are the poems, the paintings, the sculpture, the books." He believed in his power to create art, and, as a craftsman, was a perfectionist. In July, apologizing for already being nine months late, he admitted: "Every word takes blood." Given his editor's Janus-like reputation, it was fortunate that Capote was such a good writer; both Linscott and Bennett were pleased with the results. Later, Bennett would characterize a finished book handed in by Capote as being "a polished gem, virtually perfect."

Like his publisher, when he wasn't sweating blood over his work, Capote played hard, often socializing with the Cerfs. Phyllis remembered meeting him early on. She was hastily putting together one of the at-home dinners for which she'd become famous, but it was proving problematic: an alarming number of guests had husbands who were away, so they'd be attending on their own. She "scrambled around," picking up a few stray men but not enough, so she called Bennett; he promised to invite a writer he'd just signed.

Among the unaccompanied ladies that evening was the formidable sixty-year-old Edna Ferber. When she arrived early, the highly precocious four-year-old Christopher, bathed, brushed, and properly attired in pajamas and robe, was summoned to entertain the grande literary dame before heading to bed. Ferber, in a good mood, assured Phyllis that she needn't worry; they would have a fine time without equal male representation. As more arrived and mingled noisily in the bar area upstairs, the bell rang. Ivor, the butler, opened the door. The guest seemed perhaps twelve years old: short, terribly slim, with enormous eyes and a very high voice. Ivor mounted the stairs in search of his mistress.

"Mrs. Cerf, are you expecting a child for dinner?" he discreetly enquired. Phyllis was puzzled, but Bennett overheard and responded, "Oh, that's Truman Capote."

Hours passed, and as the evening wound down, Ferber buttonholed

Phyllis to tell her she'd been silly to worry about the dinner being "uneven." Then the older woman added, "It is really quite horrible . . . to dress up your child and make him come down and sit at the dinner table." A number of drinks later, Ferber had evidently concluded that Capote was the same blond boy she'd met over her first cocktail.

Bennett would eventually "adopt" Truman, and he'd also grow to be Phyllis's "close friend." She found him "very amusing," but in the early years felt that the person whom she called "this extraordinary boy" was also very lonely. "I was . . . a security blanket for him to go to places," she recalled, so he "could be let in for sure." Capote liked to lunch at the Plaza Hotel, overlooking the park; he and Phyllis went there often. It was a time when un-closeted homosexuality was rare in America. Sure, those working in the arts were aware of the many gay writers, composers, and theater people in their midst. It was well known that Dick Rodgers's lyricist partner, Larry Hart, who'd died in 1943, was gay. So was Cole Porter, despite his marriage. On the RH list were Auden, Spender, Isherwood, and Gertrude. Yet if they lived with a certain degree of discretion above the waterline, the far greater population of homosexuals and bisexuals remained submerged underneath. Many even in the supposedly liberal artistic world were homophobic, and in the country at large, prejudice was omnipresent, socially acceptable, and could destroy even an established career. Many gay men and women refused to take any chances.

There had, for example, been persistent rumors about that *other* Hart, Bennett and Donald's friend Moss, who would spend years in psychoanalysis grappling with his particular torments. In August 1946, shortly after Moss's wedding to the actress Kitty Carlisle, Donald referred to his reputation in a letter to Bennett: "Were you surprised at Moss's marriage or did you know that he was going to take this step? That gal must be really full of sex if she is able to arouse any interest in our friend Mr. Hart."

Despite his closeness to Uncle Herbert and the profound influence Herbert had had on his life, Bennett wasn't above making remarks himself. Writing to the office from London a decade earlier, he'd declared that he wouldn't let designer and photographer Cecil Beaton get "within eight feet" of his pants, and described Auden as the "leading pansy" of the RH ranks. There were similar remarks about Noël Coward. The impulse to distance himself—literally—from Beaton (albeit conveyed as a joke), along with the other remarks, says something about Bennett's insecurities and a kind of guardedness. Yet in a world in which many Americans were profoundly ill at ease simply to be in the presence of a gay person, he was not. Others' homosexuality didn't rattle him, per se. "He was at home with it in Truman," Phyllis Cerf maintained categorically.

As well as organizing tête-à-têtes at the Plaza and often including Capote on the guest list at Sixty-Second Street, Phyllis brought him to one of her regular lunches at the St. Regis with the beautiful, influential women—with names like Paley and Astor—whom she'd met through her work at the Defense Recreation Committee. Such encounters opened doors to a world he longed to enter, dominated by women he'd later call "swans." Like most of them, Phyllis loved to gossip with Capote, recognizing that he had "the insight of an X-ray machine, coupled with the imagination of a Walter Mitty." Rightly, she often didn't believe his "flights of fancy," but he could surprise her, and they be true.

Many years later, Capote's lawyer Alan Schwartz recalled: "When Truman talked about people like Phyllis, he was this little boy talking about this big, strong woman. Phyllis is on the list of women he loved, but he didn't love her as much as he loved Babe Paley or Lee Radziwill or a few others." In other words, she was never a swan. As for her husband, Schwartz said, "Strangely enough, it was Bennett who was the quiet one in that threesome. Truman was an extremely critical person and not shy about expressing it, but he had a tremendous regard for Bennett. He really loved him."

. . .

"NOW A TRAVELER MUST make his way to Noon City by the best means he can."

With that first-line declaration in *Other Voices, Other Rooms,* the storyteller makes his way there—and the reader cannot help but follow, pulled into a place that envelops a visitor and does not let go. It is a Southern gothic world influenced by Faulkner, Welty, and others, but is also Capote's own: thick with heat and menace, dreams and regrets, innocence and perversion, but above all a desperate longing for love.

Joel Harrison Knox's mother is dead, and he's been living with an aunt in New Orleans. At thirteen, he's summoned to a dilapidated backwater estate called Skully's Landing by a father he does not know. The story is populated by people named "Jesus Fever," "Little Sunshine," and "Zoo," and by Joel's father, who turns out to be a helpless paralytic. Shortly after he arrives, Joel glances up to a window and sees a mysterious "queer lady" from another age, wearing a towering Madame de Pompadour wig. She stares, seeming to welcome him, then vanishes like an illusion he can't shake off. He also meets Cousin Randolph, a man oozing the acid sickly-sweetness of overripe fruit. In silk lounging pajamas, he's one with the place: solicitous and intriguing yet secretive; manipulative yet marked by an aura of pain. By the last page, Joel will know Randolph and the mysterious lady are one, and when he again appears in the silver pompadour and beckons, Joel answers the call, realizing the truth of Little Sunshine's words: if he tried to leave, "other voices, other rooms, voices lost and clouded" would ineluctably "strum his dreams." Any love "is natural and beautiful that lies within a person's nature." He leaves childhood behind, embracing his fate.

The novel can't be read without recognizing homosexuality as its underpinning. Later, in an introduction to a reprint edition, Capote acknowledged the work as an "unconscious" attempt to exorcise demons. But he insisted that, except for "a few incidents," he'd been unaware when he wrote it that the book was in any way autobiographical. Even so, as his biographer later declared, "rarely had a writer left himself so naked" in print. Joel's description in the book exactly matches Capote's image on the jacket, and what an image it was: among the most famous author photographs ever taken. He'd asked a friend to do the shoot, and his pose outdid even the *Life* picture. In a buttoned-up tattersall waistcoat, white shirt, and trousers, he reclined on a French sofa. The horizontal half-portrait is cropped on the left, just where the delicate fingers of his right hand hover over his crotch. Intensity resides on the right, in the flushed skin, full lips, fevered eyes of the blond-fringed face, daring the viewer to want him.

Many assumed RH had set the whole thing up, just as Dick Simon had thought Bennett responsible for the *Life* photo, but Capote, like Gertrude, sought out publicity. He'd posed as a lark, but also deliberately. The image caused tremendous talk and proved a windfall, garnering the attention he craved. Yet it was the work that, first and foremost, impressed Bennett. He wrote to Capote in December 1947 that he'd read the manuscript originally "in snatches," but read it again at one sitting on a train. "I want to tell you how much it thrilled me. It is an amazing piece of work. . . . I hope we will be your publishers forever and ever amen." He wired Don from the road: "Believe Capote novel will be a sensation strongly urge ten thousand minimum." The first printing was duly increased.

Having finished the book, Capote had been assigned by *Vogue* to go to L.A. for a fortnight to train his wide eyes on new territory: Hollywood. When he returned to New York, he told Bennett that he'd spent the first week staying with Garbo and the second with Chaplin. Being a fabricator himself, Bennett recognized the fabricator in Capote; after all, the bio he'd given for his dust jacket said, inter alia, that he'd "written speeches for a third-rate politician, danced on a riverboat, made a small fortune painting flowers on glass," and "studied fortunetelling with the celebrated Mrs. Acey Jones." Sympathetic to the youthful fakery (and jokes), Bennett printed the bio as written. However, starry-eyed Mr. Cerf also *wanted* Capote's tales to be true. As it turned out, he'd only lunched with Garbo; Charlie's wife, his friend Oona, had only thrown a party. Still—not a bad double coup for a twenty-three-year-old whose first novel had yet to appear.

With the new year, 1948, came publication. Capote and poet-anthologist Louis Untermeyer had been invited to speak at the sales conference early in January; worried that the list as a whole was only "fair," Bennett poured energy into this first novel. By month's end, an ad was splashed across full magazine pages; in it, the jacket photo took up half the space under the headline "THIS IS Truman Capote." Perhaps once a decade, it declared, an author comes along with "that magical quality" causing talk months before publication. It alluded to Saroyan, Faulkner, McCullers, the *Life* photo, and the rare fact then that a San Francisco bookseller had received twenty-three separate pre-orders; RH's rep hadn't even begun to sell the book. Notably, there was no mention of homosexuality. The ad concluded that Capote was more than "a young man of promise . . . he is the young man who has delivered on his promise." Both Bennett and Linscott believed it.

Reviews began to appear—"mostly raves," Bennett informed his diary. But that wasn't entirely true: some critics, including those of *Time, Newsweek,* and *The New York Times Book Review,* did not care for the novel. In *The Nation,* one of New York's most prominent public intellectuals, Diana Trilling, expressed a common ambivalence: not since the early Eudora Welty had she seen "such literary virtuosity," yet she felt "deeply antipathetic to the whole artistic-moral purpose." The *Herald Tribune* Sunday critic, on the other hand, judged it the "most exciting" first novel by a young American in years, while the daily *Times* reviewer Orville Prescott called it "positive proof of the arrival of a new writer of substantial talent." Surprisingly, many critics in other parts of the country, far from being shocked, were seduced by the writing. Bennett congratulated himself: "*Other Voices* looks like a sensation." The novel quickly went on the *Times* bestseller list, staying there nine weeks, and sold more than 26,000 copies—a feat, given its themes. The author photo migrated from reviews to ads to posters to anywhere connected with books, accompanied by the inevitable controversy. Soon, alarmed he wasn't being taken seriously, Capote said emphatically and ubiquitously that he hadn't initiated the shoot.

That fall, Truman took up with a new lover, Jack Dunphy, who'd be a presence for the rest of his life; and early in 1949 they sailed for Europe, where he'd work on his second novel. For ten years Capote would live mainly abroad. Subject to the isolation all writers crave, need, and hate, he hungered to hear from his publisher and editor, and be reassured about his work and essential place within RH. A chunk of manuscript and a typical letter, postmarked "Forio d'Ischia, Naples," arrived for Linscott in April 1949: "Are you satisfied or is it a disappointment? You can tell me truthfully."

"I'm happy, happy, happy to think of you ensconced there like an industrious cherub," Linscott replied. He regularly passed on the gossipy tidbits Truman loved, whether it was Philip Rahv's threat to sue Mary McCarthy, or the latest RH news. Even with Capote living so far away, his publishers were able to keep his name in front of reviewers and readers with two other books. The first was a story collection, *The Tree of Night,* and the other, *Local Color,* comprised travel pieces he'd written for women's magazines. But his second novel, *Summer Crossing*—a social comedy set in New York—proved unsatisfactory to him and to Linscott. He made the painful decision to put it aside and work on something new, inspired by his Alabama childhood and elderly cousins.

The fond, nostalgic story of *The Grass Harp*'s "five fools" who take shelter in the aerie of a tree house—protagonist and Capote stand-in Collin Fenwick; his elderly cousin Dolly; her best friend, Catherine; an older boy, Riley; and the retired Judge Cool—is told in flashback by Collin, now a lawyer. Its openness contrasts with *Other Voices*' claustrophobia. In September 1950, having received the first few chapters from Italy, Linscott cabled the "angel child" three words: "Wonderful wonderful wonderful." Bennett's telegram and letter agreed: everyone was "crazy" about the chapters.

"You are so good to me," Capote replied at once.

Three months later, during a grim week in the fighting playing out in Korea, Bennett wrote again in an almost fatherly fashion, fearing President Harry S. Truman might declare a national emergency. "I'd feel happier if you were home . . . but I take it for granted you're keeping an avenue of escape open in case worst comes to worst."

Just before the summer of 1951, the full manuscript arrived. Linscott, Bennett, and Bob Haas all found the ending unconvincing. Linscott conveyed that feeling, but left Capote to figure out what to do. Bennett, on the other hand, spelled out what he found wanting in each character's actions, concluding that Truman had gotten tired of the book and hurried to end what was now "little more than a novelette." Worried it would be hard to sell such a slim volume, Bennett still promised to publish even if it weren't reworked, but Capote was crushed, "stricken by such an overpowering trinity of opinion."

Since it had been announced for fall, the manuscript had already been set in type; proofs were en route to Europe. Capote wondered if publication should be postponed so he could revise the text to please them, but when he read the proofs he demurred, cabling that he preferred to publish the book "as is." If it was as his author wished, Bennett replied, it was "good enough" for him. Capote would inscribe Bennett's copy: "P & B did not like the end . . . but I did and do and I still love P & B." Later critics would judge the two Bobs and Bennett correct, but at the time of publication, many reviewers praised *The Grass Harp*. It sold half the number of copies of *Other Voices*—13,500—but that was still good, double *A Tree of Night* and triple *Local Color*. It also sold without benefit of the attention-grabbing photograph. Everybody came out well.

. . .

JOHN O'HARA, BORN IN 1905, was almost old enough to be Capote's father. The backdrop for many of his works would be "Gibbsville," his version of Pottsville, Pennsylvania, the gritty, suffocating town where he grew up. As in many small American cities then, a strict divide separated upper-crust WASPs from Irish Catholics—even ones like O'Hara's

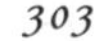

John O'Hara

doctor-father, who'd managed to secure respect in the community. Religious and class prejudice bred resentment, and O'Hara became a rebellious teen with a fondness for drink. After being thrown out of two schools, he was sent to one in Niagara, New York, where he thrived. Chosen as valedictorian, on the eve of the great day he got drunk, was barred from graduating, and humiliated his family. He'd dreamed of Yale and being a writer. Instead, his father died the next year and the family's fortunes plummeted.

Making his way to New York, he got a job at the *Herald Tribune* and soon published a first story in *The New Yorker*. By 1930, he'd worked at a handful of other papers, but drunkenness and truculence put a quick end to various jobs. Still, a handsome six-footer with thick dark hair, light eyes, and a broad chest, he was considered dashing. He'd also seen a bit of life: he'd worked as a waiter on an ocean liner and as a writer on a cruise ship; married his first wife at twenty-six and divorced at twenty-eight; toiled in the New York publicity mills of a few movie studios. Like William Faulkner, Nathanael West, and F. Scott Fitzgerald, he would also write scripts in Hollywood's dream factory itself.

In 1934, Harcourt published his first novel, *Appointment in Samarra*—tightly written, short, daring in its unvarnished portrait of class and mores. Considered ultra-frank and modern in its treatment of sex and use of language, it caused a sensation. Off-color words, snatches of colloquial dialogue, references to brands of cars and clothes and names of real public figures—these devices were innovative. O'Hara prided himself on the simple word, unencumbered by metaphor, and the meticulously checked fact.

Samarra unspooled over three days as its gentleman protagonist, Julian English, rushed toward suicide—drinking, brawling, betraying his wife. Even though there was no overriding reason for such a fate, he seemed predestined to self-destruct. Ernest Hemingway offered rare praise: *Samarra*'s author knew "exactly" what he was writing about and wrote it "marvelously well." O'Hara became friendly with Fitzgerald, whose work he admired, and roomed with the equally dashing and boozy Quent Reynolds.

Drinks, ladies, and words: O'Hara was fast with all three, producing as much as a chapter a week. He could stop in the middle of a sentence and resume days later—no matter the hangovers in between—without referring to where he'd left off. As Phyllis Cerf once said, he plotted an entire book in his mind before putting a word on paper. He'd written *Samarra* in a cheap hotel at night, sleeping during the day. Like Faulkner, he didn't drink when he wrote; that happened before and after.

A year later, Harcourt brought out *Butterfield 8,* a roman à clef about an upper-class Manhattan party girl who dies under questionable circumstances. The title and boxed epigraph on the title page—a 1930 ad from the New York Telephone Company explaining that a number would now be appended to each phone exchange name—were provocations: O'Hara was going to hold up the clearest mirror he could conjure to make readers take a hard look at their lives. He readily admitted that *Butterfield 8* was based on the actual story of Starr Faithfull, whose name, almost irresistibly, stood in stark contrast to the darkness and promiscuity of her very real life. Born into high society, as a child she'd been "seduced"—we'd now say abused—by a powerful family friend. She was twenty-five when her body washed up on a Long Island beach in the summer of '31.

Newspaper headline writers loved the lurid case: sales could be made as it played out day after day. Some stories found their way into Bennett's scrapbook, since it was in his apartment—at a crowded bon voyage party for his friend Miriam Hopkins—that Faithfull unknowingly had made her last goodbyes. She was never seen alive in public after that night, and Bennett had had to give testimony to the authorities.

Much of the praise reviewers had heaped on the author of *Appointment in Samarra* curdled with *Butterfield 8*. Still, the book sold, and readers understood from then on that when they picked up an O'Hara novel, one thing they'd get was sex. Two more books followed. In between, inspired by remorse he felt after a bad bender, O'Hara published a story in *The New Yorker* in the form of a letter from Joey Evans, a small-time nightclub emcee and big-time heel. "I wish I could take a vacation from myself," O'Hara had once told a friend. "I have, of course, taken quite a number of overnight vacations; getting so cockeyed drunk that twenty hours elapse before I recover." The magazine would publish more Joey "letters," and two years later, Richard Rodgers and Larry Hart put them to music on Broadway, with O'Hara writing the script. *Pal Joey*'s protagonist was no hero, but that didn't get in the way of the show's appeal. In the meantime, a group of Harcourt executives had started a new house, Duell, Sloan and Pearce, and O'Hara followed; in 1940, they published *Joey* to coincide with the musical.

The war came, bringing more rancor: the ulcers and bad teeth from drinking got him rejected by the military. Like Bennett, he felt left out. But unlike Bennett, who took every advantage of wartime opportunities, O'Hara drank more and produced less. Finally making it to the Pacific as a correspondent for *Liberty* in 1944, shipboard sobriety was good for him: on his return, his second wife, Belle, got pregnant, after seven barren years.

In March 1945, Duell, Sloan published *Pipe Night,* and on the front page of the *Times Book Review,* critic Lionel Trilling said of its stories that more than any other writer, O'Hara understood how people lived now, that "life's deepest emotions may be expressed by the angle at which a hat is worn. . . . For him customs and manners are morals." Still, a decade had elapsed since his last novel. When his editor, Sam Sloan, died suddenly, beneath the bluster O'Hara was shaken. Where would his career go now?

Phyllis liked O'Hara: she was the one who'd met him first, since his Hollywood stints had coincided with hers. Later, after she'd moved East, she and a date ran into him and Belle at Bleeck's, a watering hole favored by *Herald Tribune* reporters, and the two renewed their acquaintance. (Later, he'd take pleasure in needling his publisher that he'd known Phyllis before Bennett ever set eyes on her, "and so forth and so on.") O'Hara regularly made the rounds of bars, restaurants, and social gatherings, some the same parties that Bennett attended. One evening, he seized the opportunity to say that if O'Hara ever left his current house, RH would love to publish him. It wasn't until May 27, 1946, one week after moving into the Villard, that Bennett corralled him for lunch at the Stork. After getting back to the office, he dictated a letter, reiterating how very eager the firm was to have him. Without resorting to any "song and dance" about what RH could do—O'Hara knew the business as well as he did—Bennett promised that contractually, he could pretty much write his own ticket, and RH's performance would prove "the value we set on having your name on our list."

O'Hara rejected the overture, telling his diary that he'd never choose RH because Cerf "thinks he is somebody on his own." However, some months later, he agreed to another meeting, this time at a Hell's Kitchen tavern; by then, he'd realized that precisely because Bennett *was* "somebody on his own," he understood what the publisher's job was and wouldn't try to impose his ego on anyone's writing. As Bennett told the story, once O'Hara said that he'd come to RH, he flattered his catch, telling him it was a "great day," because O'Hara was "one of the great authors of America."

The response was immediate and sharp: "One of the great authors? Who else?"

"Well, Hemingway and Faulkner."

"I'll buy Faulkner," came the testy reply. He'd apparently soured on the man whose praise had helped him at the start.

To proclaim that everything O'Hara had published was now RH property, and assure a pipeline for the ML, Bennett was anxious to get control of his backlist. Rights to the earlier books resided with Duell, Sloan, apart from dramatic/movie rights to *Samarra* and *Pal Joey,* for which O'Hara had made other arrangements. Duell wanted $50,000, a serious sum. Bennett's custom was to haggle, but a deal was struck eventually.

In February 1947, Random House was made to understand the kind of diva they were now dealing with. Bob Haas wrote to a vacationing Bennett that Linscott had lunched with O'Hara, who, having signed on for a book of stories, was finally talking about publishing a novel after that. Although "99% vague," he demanded a $10,000 advance, and when Linscott suggested that they return to the office to talk further, he declined. Instead, a "nasty" letter arrived: clearly RH wasn't interested, O'Hara wrote, asking to be released from all obligations. Then he went on "a binge to end all binges."

Linscott sent a mollifying reply and some days later was rewarded with a phone call: O'Hara would drop by the next afternoon. He didn't. More calls, same response: he "couldn't be disturbed." The firm had to wait it out. In March, he sobered up and they were finally able to agree: $10,000 was advanced for a novel that took its title from Alexander Pope's "Epistle to a Lady": *A Rage to Live*. But that needed time; meanwhile, the story collection, *Hellbox*—the title referred to the container where printers threw discarded hot type—was O'Hara's first RH book. Published in August 1947, many of its tales were very brief, and only five hadn't first seen print in *The New Yorker.* A petty gangster on the lam and a showgirl who falls for the wrong guy; a new widow rekindling an impossible old flame; a world-weary producer who saves face rather than follow doctor's orders: discarded by life into its "hellbox," these were, as the *Times* reviewer would write, "rendered with pitiless precision" in stories "both appalling and splendid."

Although Linscott had briefly played go-between, Saxe had seen the book through the press: not an altogether smooth passage. Naturally, the printers had set the type based on the edited manuscript, and naturally the editing had corrected spellings and syntax to make them conform to standard English. Unfortunately, O'Hara wanted the type to spell and say things the way his characters would in life. He insisted the alterations be changed to his original. It had taken the *New Yorker* editors almost twenty years to learn how to deal with his copy, O'Hara told Bennett, and RH ought to benefit by their example.

In the summer of 1948, he again wanted Saxe to understand his place, warning: "You'd better get that surgical glint out of your eye," because far from cutting anything on the final manuscript of *A Rage to Live,* there'd be additions. Many of Saxe's writers welcomed his extensive revisions, but for artists like O'Neill and Faulkner, much of his role was to be the friend and handmaiden who catered to their personal needs and whims. With every author, Saxe looked for a certain intimacy. He was unprepared for O'Hara. As well as wanting to clean up his language, Saxe considered parts of the novel vulgar and obscene, and sought to cut one sexual liaison entirely. Quite apart from matters of taste, he feared the smut-hounds might wage a successful campaign against the book. When O'Hara came into the office one day, Saxe began to make his case. O'Hara's response was to pick up a paperweight and throw it at his editor.

Perhaps he was too drunk to throw straight, or aimed to one side; perhaps Saxe dodged in time—what exactly occurred was never clear. But although the paperweight didn't hit its target, the damage was done. O'Hara later sent a peace offering—a gold pencil with a note, "Still speaking, by God"—but Saxe could not overcome his wariness.

On Thanksgiving eve that year, O'Hara decided it was time to remind Bennett of his existence. There was no animus of the kind directed toward Saxe—he liked his new publisher—but the forget-me-not was typically sour-sweet: "Don't think I haven't noticed that only once, during the mating season, have you taken me to one of the haunts of . . . the expense accounts. . . . Nowadays I practically have to win (or lose) a football bet to get taken to the Ritz, the Colony, Voisin, 21. . . . Random never takes me to lunch." Without skipping a beat, he asked for an extra $10,000 to be paid before year's end, for the "income tax bite." He'd deliver *A Rage to Live* in that same time frame and was confident he'd hand in a much shorter novel, *The Farmers Hotel,* for 1950 publication.

Bennett's response was all business. "Sorry" that O'Hara was so pressed, RH would like to help, but could only manage an additional $2,500: "I must remind you that when the contract was signed . . . we gave in . . . on every single point. . . . What you are asking now is that the advance be doubled. That simply is more than the traffic will bear."

O'Hara denounced Bennett's "take-it-or-leave-it" reply. His tax payment was due in two weeks, and in order to finish his manuscript, he hadn't taken time out to make an appeal to the IRS. RH was "better positioned" to borrow $10,000 than he was. The situation was "very discouraging in itself, and even more so as an omen of the future."

Bennett let loose a page and a half of single-spaced venting. There was no cause for the "threatening" tone; without mutual understanding, the author-publisher relationship was impossible. Why did O'Hara take this "perverse delight" in discomfiting them? All RH had got for its work on *Hellbox* was a note that read "I am disappointed," and when Bennett had told him how much he'd liked the new novel, O'Hara hadn't even seemed pleased. "We are very proud to be your publishers," he said for the umpteenth time. "We don't intend, however, to be whipping boys. . . . This relationship means a great deal to me personally. I'd like to get it straight once and for all."

Always spoiling for a fight, O'Hara was not about to back down. Claiming that Bennett had failed to acknowledge his plan for another book, he replied: "If you are saying . . . get another publisher, please say it intelligibly and I'll . . . do exactly that."

Seeing that the game of attack and counterattack was getting nowhere, Bennett ceded ground. He enclosed a check for $2,500—cold cash had analgesic properties, even if less than requested—inside a letter that, despite expressing frustration, also attempted to answer O'Hara's underlying challenge and salve his amour propre: "Do we want you to stay . . . ? Damn it all, if we didn't want you very much indeed, do you think we'd be going through all this sturm and drang? If you think I like it, you're very wrong." But O'Hara, imagining other slights on other fronts, kept the rockets coming.

Thanksgiving and Christmas were past history. As the old year was expiring, Bennett released a final sally: "It seems impossible to please you. I don't suppose you can help the way you feel; by the same token we can't help resenting that feeling very deeply. Anyway, I wish you and Belle a Happy New Year and hope both for your sake and our own that your new novel will be a resounding success." He'd have to go through further lessons in the proper care and handling of O'Hara, and some success would help. But O'Hara had also learned that Bennett refused to be anybody's "whipping boy."

Six months later, more lessons had been learned. Bennett made sure to write to O'Hara just after he and Saxe had devoted a "full half hour" of sales conference to *A Rage to Live*. Cleaning up language that could have had the book banned had also required his personal intervention, and his letter expressly praised O'Hara for finally accepting that certain words and phrases had had to be altered to ensure publication and "eliminate any possible objections on the part of the squeamish."

But even then, the novel's protagonist, Grace Caldwell Tate—beautiful and a member of her Pennsylvania town's leading family—had proved too much for some. She loves her children and her husband, Sidney, and he loves her back—not just for her beauty, but for her "courage of the spirit." He conveys this appreciation while they're in bed, but with a typical O'Hara twist: Sidney has just told her they'll be getting a divorce, and rejected her sexual advances. Grace has had an affair for sex, thus contravening the rules by which her husband and society live. It is acceptable for Sidney to patronize a prostitute, but inconceivable for him to forgive his wife for her lover. Rules trump love for Sidney, whereas for Grace, life trumps rules. She moves to New York City. As Alexander

Pope wrote to the "lady" in the poem that gives the book its title: "You purchase Pain with all that Joy can give, / And die of nothing but a Rage to live."

Portraying female sexuality from a woman's perspective had been done but rarely by American male writers who took themselves seriously as creators of "literature"—Hawthorne and Dreiser come to mind. O'Hara joined them, but in *A Rage to Live* added a new element—his sex was unusually graphic. At one point Grace tells a rejected lover, "I'll never be able to wear *this* dress again," after she was forced to stand in his tight, unwanted embrace while he proceeded to climax against her. For this gimlet-eyed social chronicler, she was an Anna Karenina who chose not to go under the train but to take life as she found it, no matter the collateral damage.

However, Grace was no Anna and O'Hara no Tolstoy. Shorter forms like *Samarra* or the stories didn't require depth in a protagonist, but as O'Hara's novels got longer, the weakness in his characterizations would prove increasingly problematic. It was 1949, and the book was turned down by BOMC, whose judges decided that language such as Sidney's in the bedroom confrontation—"Do you think I have no balls for anybody but you, all these years? Do you think I never saw anybody I wanted to screw?"—had no place in "serious literature." Yet Bennett still managed to sell the book to the smaller Book Find Club, and did a condensation deal with *Omnibook*. He was "fantastic at promoting something that he loved, and he loved *A Rage to Live,*" Phyllis later said. He talked it up everywhere. Still, they braced themselves for publication.

Reviews were mixed. The *Times*' Orville Prescott, who'd praised Capote's *Other Voices,* panned O'Hara's "sensationalism." The *Herald Tribune* liked the book (the critic was a friend). But one review, by Brendan Gill in *The New Yorker,* stood alone, dividing O'Hara's career into "before" and "after." Already, his relationship with Harold Ross was difficult, and he was unhappy about past rejections and a negative review of *Butterfield 8:* resentment had been stoked, despite his having published more stories in *The New Yorker* than any other writer. Then Gill compared the novel to the recent *Kinsey Report* on male sexual behavior, calling it "Dr. O'Hara's handy guide to healthy sex practices," ending: "It is because of O'Hara's distinction that his failure here seems . . . a catastrophe."

He wouldn't publish another story in *The New Yorker* for a decade, but Random House took up the slack, O'Hara's association with Bennett becoming the paramount working relationship for the rest of the author's life. After the review appeared, he badgered Bennett into writing to Ross and demanding that Gill be fired. "You are incapable of ratiocination" and are "my natural enemy," Ross replied to a request both men knew was ridiculous. And yet the novel sold more than any of O'Hara's previous books by far. A month after publication, it was number one on the *Times* list with over 70,000 copies in print, and its sales velocity was amazing. "That damned O'Hara book can't be escaped in the length & breadth of this country; it's like a plague, a highly profitable one," the writer Irving Howe protested to Linscott. By year's end, 135,000 copies had been sold. Grosset & Dunlap would do a cheap reprint; Bantam published a paperback in 1951 that would go through thirty-three printings in twenty-five years.

Bennett had shown he'd be nobody's whipping boy, but also appreciated that at times he'd have to give in to certain demands and reward this thoroughbred with carrots of his own choosing. He no longer put in calls to O'Hara via Pauline, a habit that had invariably elicited an ugly earful. Now he picked up the phone himself. O'Hara had more than hinted that if the novel reached 100,000 copies, he'd like a silver cigarette box. "The problem is: do I say, 'I bludgeoned them into it,'" he mused to Bennett, "or do I just let our visitors think that the idea originated with you?" The box arrived, inscribed: "For John O'Hara from his grateful publishers Random House and the first hundred thousand purchasers of 'A Rage to Live' Christmas 1949." It struck exactly the right note. He came to expect a similar offering each time a book reached 100,000 in hardcover or a million in paperback, and counted five such by the end of his life. Bennett—with help from Don—had learned to play him "as skillfully as a master plays a Stradivarius," as one O'Hara biographer asserted, concluding: "There was nobody else who could have kept him."

Chapter 20

Friends and Enemies

THE MID-TO-LATE 1940S EXPANDED OPPORTUNITIES FOR MANY Americans, not least those at Random House. By fall 1946, however, the heady immediate postwar jubilation was giving way to dislocations of a rapidly changing society, and the chill of a "Cold War" creeping in. During the Depression, it had been common in big cities for artists, writers, intellectuals, and young people to look at all the empty-eyed suffering and see socialism as the solution. Some flirted with the allure of Communism as cure-all—as Bennett had, in the USSR—before snapping awake to its undesirable aspects and putting trust in FDR. Others remained sympathetic—fellow travelers, but not ready to commit. Still others joined openly or secretly, while some, like Budd Schulberg, joined and later left.

The U.S. House of Representatives had established a "Special Committee on Un-American Activities"—HUAC, for short—in 1938. Assailing "Communistic" tendencies and subversive, "anti-American" propaganda was a way for FDR's enemies to attack him, his policies, and organized labor. Like a malevolent genie, once created, it couldn't be put back into the bottle: HUAC proved too useful for grabbing attention, gaining leverage, and settling political scores. After the war, with fear of Communism spreading, efforts at requiring loyalty oaths to stem the "Red Menace" were being discussed not just in congressional committees but also in the Truman White House. People were being careful; liberals had cause to feel unease. Still, late in October 1946, Bennett brought home Eleanor Roosevelt—whom Truman had appointed to the new UN General Assembly, and who chaired its nascent Commission on Human Rights—to dine with thirty friends. Her topic was the Independent Citizens Committee of the Arts, Sciences and Professions, co-founded by her son James; it lobbied for internationalism, tolerance, and peaceful coexistence with the

Soviets. Conservatives viewed such groups as Communist fronts; talk that night turned "heated." John O'Hara, for one, had moved so far right that a few years later, he'd apply for a job with the CIA (and be turned down).

November brought Election Day. Bennett voted Democratic, but felt "lonely": the GOP swept into both House and Senate. With victory, the party rushed to achieve more visibility for HUAC, now chaired by New Jersey Republican representative J. Parnell Thomas, abetted by Mississippi Democrat John Rankin, a white supremacist antisemite. Also on the committee was an ambitious new California congressman intent on making his mark, Richard M. Nixon. The Thomas Committee, as HUAC was also called, would investigate Communist infiltration into unions and government, but for quick publicity it targeted Hollywood first. A subtext of "Jewish domination" of the industry would also play out. To be sure, Communist cells had existed there since the early 1930s, and the previous two years had seen strikes disrupt movie production. Studio bosses blamed labor troubles on the left, and detected a "pinkish" tinge on many scripts.

Bennett had soured on Hollywood as his marriage to Sylvia failed, but soon its magnetic pull proved irresistible, professionally and personally. Everyone knew his politics were liberal, but those of friends, family, authors, and business associates ran the gamut, some at the extremes. His talent for collecting and connecting conferred great advantages, but operating as a central switchboard also placed him in the middle of the divisions—leaving him open to sudden disruptions and unexpected tests.

To readers of *The Hollywood Reporter* back in 1942, he'd observed that the "paucity of Broadway product" during wartime had "forced Hollywood into the arms" of publishers. All at once, he'd written, studios had "discovered the magic possibilities of such phrases as 'Book-of-the-Month-Club Selection' and 'two hundred thousand copies in print,'" and if they'd studied their records, would have seen that "three out of four of the pictures that earned . . . sensational sums . . . were taken from books," not plays. If no agent were involved, it was his job to try to sell a book's movie rights and get a decent cut for RH. Editorial oversight he was happy to share with others, but the responsibility for dealing with Hollywood, like the task of overseeing advertising, he guarded for himself. Bennett had cultivated those connections and could speak the same language as studio tycoons, but whether a publisher benefited from a picture deal was decided anew with each contract; sometimes a house received nothing, even if big money was involved. In perhaps the most egregious example, John Steinbeck's *The Moon Is Down* had been a Viking success, but, adapted for the stage, it flopped. Yet it was the play's producer who pocketed 40 percent of the booty when film rights were sold for a record $300,000.

This was a state of affairs Bennett was set on changing, and how better than in person? High time to return to L.A.: he had booksellers, authors, and transplanted old friends to see as well as studio execs, and Phyllis was umbilically tied to Tinseltown. Ginger and Lela were there, as well as best friends Anne Shirley and Bubbles Schinasi. Three months after the war ended, Bubbles had married husband number two, movie producer Arthur Hornblow Jr., in a ceremony at the Cerfs'. She was twenty-five, he fifty-two—five years older than Bennett—and she had to resign herself to a West Coast life.

Anne, the former child star who'd given Phyllis a home when she'd needed one, was Chris's godmother. She and *her* new second husband, screenwriter and producer Adrian Scott, had spent several weeks staying with the Cerfs, welcoming 1946 together, and they'd come again that April for a much-appreciated second visit just after Jonathan was born. As a foursome, they got along splendidly. And so, rather than spending the worst winter weeks of 1947 in Florida or the Caribbean, there was all the more reason for Bennett and Phyllis to board the 20th Century Limited on January 29, heading west.

They made a few obligatory stops, calling on "poor old Uncle Al" Cerf in Chicago, and visiting Phyllis's mother in Oklahoma City. There, book signing involved both Cerfs: Phyllis had authored an RH kids' novelty book, *The Story of Dimples and Cocksure*. In Dallas, Bennett signed hundreds of *Anything for a Laugh* at Neiman Marcus, followed by dinner at Stanley Marcus's hacienda, and promised to devote a column to the fabulous store, a commerce in favors as natural to him as breathing. On February 9, they disembarked into the dark Deco welcome of Union Station and emerged into L.A.'s hard, bright sun. Again, Bennett ran around signing and giving talks, while every other waking hour the social merry-go-round spun full tilt. Hornblows, Scotts, Cousin Ginger, Frank Lloyd Wright's granddaughter—actress Anne Baxter, whom Bennett greatly fancied—and other glamorous names filled the diary. In one happy meeting, Jimmy Stewart related "wonderful things" about Don from their air force days in England.

A few days into the visit, after dinner at Chasen's famous watering hole, more serendipity: "THRUP MEETS SYLVIA S." Bennett had reprised his habit of sending Don, Bob, Saxe, and Jez epistolary renderings of his adventures; these now arrived under the rubric "Diary of an Idiot Boy in Hollywood." He couldn't resist sharing that, when they ran into Sylvia, Phyllis was "delightfully patronizing" while "Cerf, sophisticate and master of all situations, beat it for the gents' room." But at a party a couple nights later, Thrup was elsewhere in the crowded room when he chanced to meet the ex–Mrs. Cerf again. The "idiot boy" felt the old thrill. Though an "unmentionable" at home, she still had "something as far as I am concerned, goddamn it!" he could at least tell the gang.

During the trip, authors inevitably required attention. They met with Sinclair Lewis, who labored on scripts for extravagant pay but had railed against Hollywood self-censorship long before HUAC targeted the town. Yet although Bennett found him irritable, often drunk, and—equally hard for him to deal with—melancholy, he as well as Saxe had journeyed to Lewis's summer home to reassure Red of his importance. It was on one such visit the previous September that Bennett had finished reading the manuscript of *Kingsblood Royal,* Lewis's novel about an ostensibly white man who finds he has distant Black forebears. The story reaches a dramatic climax when war hero and pillar of the community Neil Kingsblood—who's come to know viscerally what it is to be a colored man in America—has to face down a mob set on evicting him.

Bennett enjoyed the book, just as he'd enjoyed Red's classics decades earlier, and was pleased to publish it. Lewis had based his protagonist loosely on Walter White, the blond, pale, blue-eyed Black who headed the NAACP, and on the experiences of friends to whom White had introduced him. However, Bennett recalled Red telling him that he didn't see the novel as simply about "the Negro problem." Instead he'd asked, "What is a Negro? There are Negroes who are whiter in appearance than many many whites. The fact is that they are Americans, and some of them are faced with special problems. But these problems are American problems, not Negro problems." Lewis had managed once again to tap into the moral fire that motivated his best work. It was a brave book, ahead of its time, and Bennett placed a provocative full-page ad in the *Times Book Review,* a single sentence writ large: "The story of a man who resigned from the white race." Although mainstream reviewers decried it as implausible, Black readers considered it unusually perceptive. *Ebony* named it best book of the year, and it was a major bestseller. Alas, it was a last hurrah: Lewis's next two books were sadly inadequate.

The Cerfs visited another West Coast author, this time accompanied by Bubbles, driving into the hills above La Jolla to Ted and Helen Geisel's home to discuss "brat books," as Ted called them, as well as the liberal politics that Bennett and the Geisels shared. Just a month earlier, he'd had to contact Ted about his underwater fantasy *McElligot's Pool,* which would be published that year. The only Seuss kids' book to have been created using watercolor, its production costs were too high, and RH was fenced in: if the retail price were too dear, people wouldn't buy it. Bennett persuaded Ted to accept less money at the outset, in favor of a royalty escalation later on.

The next day was memorialized in block capitals: the man in love with theater and movies, who would have given anything to have been an actor, was thrilled to go to MGM, walk onto a creditable "Random House" set patched together with the old Hollywood magic, and undergo a screen test. Arthur Hornblow had arranged what had begun, Bennett told the gang, as a joke to please him, but ended with the studio "getting serious (but not me, <u>honest</u>!)." Later, however, he did tell test director George Sidney that he hoped "something will come of it." A week later, the Cerfs and Hornblows returned to MGM to see the result. "Could have been worse!" was the verdict in Bennett's diary. Thinking back to that day a half century later, Leonora (Bubbles by then had grown into her given name) rendered careful judgment: "It was not an embarrassment."

The California trip included one more highlight, a destination that would become a fixture in Bennett's diary for years. As he'd write to Anne Shirley once back in New York, "Physically I am sitting at my desk at 457 Madison, but in my dreams I am still at La Quinta." In 1947, La Quinta was an oasis in California's desert, eight miles from a town called Indio in the Coachella Valley, not far from the strange spiky beauty of Joshua Tree National Monument. When it opened in 1926 with a black-tie party and glittering guests, the resort, absolutely in the middle of nowhere, had consisted of twenty *casitas,* a couple of hacienda-style wood-beamed tiled reception rooms, a dining hall dubbed "La Mirage," and a nine-hole golf course. Word got around discreetly, and more casitas and a pool followed. Small and personal, La Quinta could be highly social and shared with friends, but as Greta Garbo realized in the 1930s, it existed above all to be private.

At first, the fierce light outside Bennett and Phyllis's shuttered casita took getting used to, but at dusk the mountains became soft, shrouded, purple, blending finally into the dark immensity of the sky. No one could ask for a more romantic setting. He loved everything about La Quinta: acquiring his much-desired "burn" beside the pool, playing tennis with "the little woman" (she grew tan, too, to please her husband), going for long bike rides, being pampered with massages under the sun, dancing to live music beneath hacienda beams. Best of all, their close friends the Scotts and Hornblows were with them.

Adrian Scott had put together some of Hollywood's earliest noir films, as well as the Oscar-nominated *Crossfire*. Having opened even before *Gentleman's Agreement, Crossfire* was the first Hollywood movie to tackle antisemitism head-on. His intensity was tempered by a sweetness and sense of humor that made him good company, while his wife managed to be wry and genuinely funny. Even to her godson Chris, Anne seemed sexy, and the boy thought Adrian—thirteen years younger than Bennett—dashing. Arthur Hornblow, on the other hand, though very trim and dapper, was older than them all, and, with "British" mannerisms and a hairline that had receded many years before, seemed older still. On some evenings, the friends would take in a movie in Indio or dine beneath the stars. On the coolest nights, pleasantly tired from the day's exertions, they'd sit in the Cerfs' bungalow and submit to Bennett's jokes while tucking into a thick steak before the fire. Afterward, they played a game, or a hand of rummy.

At La Quinta, Bennett and Phyllis also found themselves socializing with tycoons and their pampered wives, and liked it. They spent many pleasant hours with Peggy and Howard Cullman: he was in tobacco, enjoyed the arts, and would eventually chair the giant Philip Morris company as well as New York's Port Authority. The Laskers were another favored couple; Mary's husband, Albert, was the advertising pioneer whose persuasive powers had given America its orange juice habit and, far less healthfully, encouraged its women to crave Lucky Strikes ("They would keep a lady slim!"). The Cerfs remained in touch with both couples. They'd vacationed with friends before, but this time was different: the desert rejuvenated Bennett as no other place could. "La Quinta won-

La Quinta, 1951 (clockwise) Bennett, Doris Vidor, Arthur Hornblow Jr., Phyllis, Bubbles, Charles Vidor

derful and that's all. Wonderful," he told his diary, amazement palpable, as he read Malcolm Lowry's *Under the Volcano*—for besides the swimming, tennis, and socializing, there was always the reading. To Stanley Marcus, who'd sung the resort's praises, he wrote: "La Quinta was everything you claimed for it and more."

In California, the "idiot boy" had written to the gang: "It's quite a life and if I told you I wasn't loving it, I'd be a colossal liar!" but added that he missed them all. He meant it. He'd write to Don about a recent call with Bob Haas, having felt "a real pang" on hearing that Don was in the room but hadn't said hello. "You must face the fact, Klopsky, that next to my little Thrup, you are the person I care most about . . . tho, God knows, I probably have a funny way of showing it. . . . I am a selfish and thoughtless bastard." After forty-six days away, on St. Patrick's Day (when the precinct surrounding the Villard and the city's Roman Catholic cathedral was at its busiest), Bennett came home to New York, his children, and Random House, picking up where he'd left off.

On the rushed day he'd left the city all those weeks ago, he'd squeezed in a chat with Frank Taylor, a young editor at Reynal & Hitchcock and husband of his *Books Are Bullets* radio colleague, Nan. Taylor had told him he was ready for a change, and on Bennett's first day back, returned to 457 Madison—with Albert Erskine, an ex–Reynal colleague, in tow—to talk about both coming to RH. Bennett saw the opportunities postwar America presented for growth, and instinctively liked these energetic fellows. The problem was money, and at the heart of it was the *American College Dictionary*.

Bennett had wanted, in his wife's words, to publish "the first dictionary of that time to reflect the American point of view," and to include new terminology, much of it coming from the war—like "atom bomb" and "existentialism." Donald and Bob had been much less keen, but Bennett's determination to get his way carried him along like a fair wind. "It was very smart," Phyllis recalled decades later. "Bennett had that vision," but after a moment, she added: "It almost broke Random House." The project's sheer scale was further complicated by his blithe underestimation of what it would entail. "We didn't have the faintest idea of what it would cost," he later admitted. He'd learn that making it would involve months of preliminary planning and three solid years of many people's work: temporary staff taken on for the task fluctuated between thirty and sixty people at any given time; the printing was complex; the paper requirement exceptional; and at first staff had to be accommodated offsite, in rented space. After RH moved into the Villard, the palazzo's cubbyhole attic offices were given over to the dictionary for the final push, but lacked the "air-cooling" of the floors below. Originally servants' quarters, in some ways in those early days they remained so: physically and psychologically separate, an exception to the way RH treated its employees.

Like many bosses, Bennett was an enormous egotist—but unlike many, he also wanted to be loved. In most ways, therefore, he was a generous and enlightened employer. Prodded by the union, he'd done a remarkable thing for the 1940s: hired a Black woman, Betty Lee March, as front-desk receptionist. She spoke with almost theatrical diction, and in 1952 would resign to sing in a production of *Porgy and Bess*.

Back in 1945, the partners had taken another step sufficiently unusual to have merited praise from *Publishers Weekly:* they'd compiled *An Introduction to Random House, Inc. for the New Employee*. "You probably want to know the kind of firm you're working for . . . and . . . things you can be glad about . . . as a member of our family group," the leaflet began, before detailing history and highlights; names and locations of staff; work conditions; union policy; benefits. Yet to some clerks scratching away on the 125,000 words defined in the dictionary, the conditions they labored under seemed Dickensian. The tiny offices were oven-like that first Villard summer, and when Bennett made his restless daily tour of the palazzo, he conspicuously omitted the attic from his rounds.

The partners had lured Clarence Barnhart, a well-known word wiz who'd already supervised the making of four dictionaries. However, as one RH executive attested years later, the chief turned out to be "a good lexicographer," but "dictatorial, pompous." Barnhart had assembled a full-time staff of seven, including his chubby, balding number two, managing editor Jess Stein. Many temporary staff had arrived straight from college; days researching a word's every possible variant spelling didn't constitute every young person's dream job, but for those whom it suited, the *ACD* would be a proving ground to form the backbone of a permanent RH dictionary/reference department.

Lists were contracted out to more than three hundred freelance "authorities," whose job was to put the *current* meaning of each word *first;* since other dictionaries did the reverse, it was seen as a selling point. The text would be embellished by 1,500 illustrations, with 300 maps, of which RH was inordinately proud, the whole squeezed into 1,472 pages, retailing for a substantial but affordable five dollars. Bob Haas had lamented in a letter to La Quinta that the dictionary was on schedule but costs were "jumping." However, any attempt to control them would bring delays, so better "to bang away at full speed and try to sell a lot . . . this year." He'd convened a luncheon with BOMC executives to persuade them to take the dictionary as a member premium, but they made no such commitment.

With the dictionary eating cash, it might have seemed crazy to add two trade editors to RH: they'd need salaries and money for acquisitions. Yet Bennett's instinct about Taylor and Erskine was so strong, he had to have them. In April, a release went out about both hires, talking up their experience: before Reynal, Taylor had worked at a Harper subsidiary and *The Saturday Review;* Erskine had helped found *The Southern Review,* and had had stints at New Directions, Doubleday, and *The Saturday Review.*

Erskine would participate in all activities of the RH/ML editorial department, while his friend would be a "roving editor." What the release didn't say was what made the hires possible: Hollywood. Taylor, with his star-power chiseled face, had been talking to MGM as well as RH, being just as interested in the movies as Bennett was. It had been decided that he'd divide his roving between RH and the studio, scoping out book projects with an eye for movie potential. For his part, Erskine—an intellectual, laconic, good-looking Southerner—would work as home backup for Taylor's scouting. After much legal wrangling, MGM had agreed to contribute $24,000 in salary for the two men—an ingenious, highly unorthodox solution to RH's limited cash. One other detail the release didn't mention: while at Reynal, Taylor had taken on a promising Black writer whom he'd bring to RH. His name was Ralph Ellison.

The plan was to publish the dictionary for the 1947 holiday season, but in May, Bennett's anxious diary noted: "postponed again. Barnhart's schedule berserk." Alas, more trouble waited, as other matters had also begun spinning out of control. A mid-June Monday began with him presiding over a "disturbing pow-wow" with Bob, Don, Manny, and controller Abe Friedman on the company's overexpansion and need for economies. They eliminated unnecessary advertising and, as publishers always do in a crunch, slashed titles—"sure losers and expensive gambles"—from the fall list. It wasn't enough. Should the partners cut their salaries? Trim the profit sharing with key staff?

By Friday, they'd each agreed to make a "special contribution" of $100,000 to the firm, and decided on the drastic step of trying to sell their part of the palazzo and rent it back. Then they came up with an equally radical possibility: sell the dictionary project to Harper, whom they'd already tapped to distribute it to schools and colleges. Harper's president, Cass Canfield, said no. Instead, ramrod-straight Bob went crawling to the bank, and in mid-July, new financing was in place. Bennett was able to leave for his Maine vacation. Unfortunately, Don soon reported that printing plates were going to cost $50,000 more than estimated, due to an "enormously high" number of author's alterations. It had been a problem, Barnhart later admitted to *The New York Times,* to get people to do the work "honestly and decently." What he meant was that some of his team had resorted to copying from other dictionaries. While not assigning any responsibility for the plagiarism to his own methods of oversight, Barnhart conceded that having to massage the purloined passages into acceptable copy at proof stage had been painfully expensive.

More money would somehow have to be found. On September 20, Bankers Trust came calling; the best they could offer was for the palazzo to be sold, then leased back to RH for twenty-one years, a prospect no one found appealing. The partners cast the net wider, and in due course appealed to Marine Midland Trust Company, to see if they could issue a bigger loan. Despite all the difficulties, on November 19 the first copies of the dictionary arrived. The cost had been estimated at $200,000; in reality, Bennett, Don, and Bob had invested about $550,000, and so publication two days before Thanksgiving, still in time for the holidays, was an enormous relief. But it wasn't until December that BOMC finally offered $30,000 for club rights, and Marine Midland tendered a $300,000 loan. Most remarkably, Merle Haas lent $100,000 of her own money to tide them over.

While RH echoed with hallelujahs, Barnhart told Jess Stein that the partners would keep only one of them to manage updates for new printings, sure that he himself would be the "keeper." But the consensus was that Barnhart didn't belong, and the partners were happy to see the back of him. Initially, they'd printed 50,000 dictionaries, but Bennett had told the *New York Journal-American* that RH would have to sell a minimum of 150,000 to cover costs. They did—and then some: a portion of the origination expense was amortized by using it as the base for two smaller dictionaries. Several decades later, Donald would tell an interviewer: "We sold well over a million [copies] of the *American College Dictionary.*" Yet because such projects cost so much to produce, he felt that a reliable author with steady popularity was generally a better bet.

. . .

BENNETT WAS STILL WORRYING about the dictionary when HUAC's Hollywood hearings on the Communist threat began on Monday, October 20, in Washington. J. Edgar Hoover's FBI had secretly funneled information to the Thomas Committee to help the conservatives' cause. The proceedings began with fanfare: a parade of twenty-four "friendly" witnesses, who were encouraged to make introductory remarks admitted as evidence even before questioning began. These witnesses included fiery Russian-born playwright, screenwriter, and novelist Ayn Rand; studio heads Jack Warner, Louis B. Mayer, and Walt Disney; actors Gary Cooper and Screen Actors Guild president Ronald Reagan; and Hoover's old pal (and beard), rabidly anti-Communist Lela Rogers, who enjoyed a bloodhound-like reputation for sniffing out anything remotely "red" in a script.

Smartly dressed with the trim figure and straight posture of a much younger woman, bottle-blond like her famous daughter, and with hair pulled back so severely into a coiled chignon that her eyes seemed to narrow into serpent slits, Lela was happy to tell the committee that as her daughter's business manager, she'd made sure Ginger had turned down the starring role in Theodore Dreiser's *Sister Carrie,* because the script was "open propaganda." Although she'd made a study of Communists' "devious" ways, Lela insisted that most of Hollywood "would not know a line of propaganda if they saw it," and was equally sure that a Communist, once hired, would try to recruit colleagues. She favored outlawing the Party entirely, as an agency of a foreign government.

Nineteen "unfriendly" witnesses—progressives and suspected Communists—were also scheduled to appear, among them Bennett and Phyllis's friend Adrian Scott. At a time of increasing racism against Blacks and Jews, the pathbreaking producer who'd trained a spotlight on anti-semitism in *Crossfire* almost inevitably found himself in the committee's crosshairs. That Friday, after listening to three friendly witnesses, Adrian boarded a train at Union Station and hightailed it out of Washington to New York, heading for the Cerf home and certain sympathy. He'd stay for the weekend, then return and be called to testify. On Sunday, talk about the investigation circled constantly like the tobacco smoke that accompanied it, seasoning their morning toast and shirred eggs, following them up and down the townhouse stairs, permeating everything.

Only eleven unfriendly witnesses were actually called, and *their* introductory statements were deemed inadmissible as evidence. Playwright Bertolt Brecht, who'd spent the war years in L.A., denied ever being a Communist, then swiftly fled to East Germany. When the others, including Adrian, were asked about Party membership, they refused to answer, citing the First Amendment, and were dubbed the "Hollywood Ten."

On the Tuesday that Adrian was testifying, Lela Rogers was in New York, and called on her niece. Phyllis was bound to "Aunt Lelee," her role model, in ways she wasn't bound even to her own mother, and while not as extreme as her aunt's, Phyllis's politics were considerably more conservative than her husband's. Nevertheless, life revolved around Bennett, and in these years she chose to be careful: she needed his approval, wanted to make him proud, and had learned very quickly not to upset him. She didn't express conservative opinions out loud. Lela arrived and immediately made clear how "really very upset" she was with this woman whom she and Ginger had practically created. How could Phyllis believe Scott was anything but a Red? Castigating her, however, was mere prologue to what Lela had in store for Bennett, once she discovered he was at home.

"In your publishing house you've got a cell of people working for you who are Communists. A whole cell!" she shouted. Worse, not only did he harbor Communists, he published "Communistic" manuscripts. With these words, she managed to attack the respect, affection, and pride in which he held his fanatically loyal staff, as well as the First Amendment freedoms that were at the heart of what he did.

When Bennett got very angry, his brown eyes truly flashed, and he emitted a strange humming sound, signs that an explosion was imminent. That followed now, its force propelling his surrogate mother-in-law down the stairs, out the door, out of sight.

"Lela Rogers here. Pfui! Fireworks!" he scribbled in his diary that night. The "Pfui!" may have included a showering of his wife's tears; she was very good at using them to deflect his storms and get her way. But this time, Bennett was adamant: Phyllis's aunt would not be welcome at Sixty-Second Street anytime soon.

Two days before Lela's unpardonable intrusion, the first of two successive thirty-minute Sunday night radio programs had aired on ABC affiliates nationwide under the rubric *Hollywood Fights Back*. Screenwriter/director John Huston, fellow director William Wyler, and fellow screenwriter Philip Dunne had been so rattled by HUAC's threats that they felt compelled to muster a communal response, and formed the "Committee for the First Amendment," with these Sunday broadcasts the result.

On October 26—the day the first program aired—a Hollywood contingent led by Humphrey Bogart had arrived in the capital on a chartered plane, with Huston as spokesman. The next day they demanded that HUAC be abolished. Many celebrities—including Bogart's wife, Lauren Bacall; Ira Gershwin; Gene Kelly; and Danny Kaye—would participate in the second broadcast. So would Bennett, who'd already spoken about the "Red probe" in a lecture the previous week. Now his would be one of forty-three marquee names on that second show. Judy Garland provided the introduction: "We're show business but also American citizens." Huston's wife, actress Evelyn Keyes, compared HUAC to the Ku Klux Klan. Naturally, a number of long-standing friends of Bennett were also involved. Moss Hart had written the screenplay for Laura Hobson's *Gentleman's Agreement,* which would win the 1948 Best Picture Oscar, but during the broadcast he argued that with HUAC's rise, a movie about antisemitism in America would be thrown out as "heresy." Wyler also declared that he couldn't have made the 1947 Oscar winner, *The Best Years of Our Lives,* in the present climate. Its screenplay, portraying the heartrending adjustments of three soldiers home from the war, had been written by Bennett's friend Robert Sherwood, who'd adapted it from a novella by MacKinlay Kantor, a newly signed RH author. Clifton Fadiman, an intellectual for all seasons who'd edited for S&S, reviewed for *The New Yorker,* judged for BOMC, and hosted the popular radio quiz show *Information Please,* also spoke. Bennett, juggling even more roles, was the only publisher to be involved in the broadcast.

The day after the first *Hollywood Fights Back* program, a huge ad ran in the *New York Herald Tribune,* paid for by Americans for Democratic Action, a newly formed liberal anti-Communist organization whose founders included Eleanor Roosevelt, John Kenneth Galbraith, and Arthur Schlesinger Jr. "We are against 'party-liners,'" declared the headline. "We are also against witch-hunts." Bennett had lent his name to the ad, this time joined by five fellow publishers, including Bob Haas and Harold Guinzburg. Most of the sixty-seven signers were authors, journalists, and theater people. The following Sunday, when the second anti-HUAC program aired, listeners heard Bennett caution that the investigation, if unopposed, would soon expand. While its ostensible purpose was to expose Hollywood's "domination" by Communists, what the committee had actually succeeded in doing was to give Americans "a graphic picture of Fascism in action." If Hollywood "can be bullied into producing only the kind of stories that fall in with this Committee's . . . prejudices, it seems obvious . . . publishers . . . will most certainly be next."

A Trade Winds column a few days later allowed him to expand his thoughts, taking on the behavior of committee members and friendly witnesses who "smeared reputations without fear of rebuttal." Added to that was "the obscene gloating of the worst newspapers." All of it had finally made even Hollywood's biggest magnates see that the committee's objective was not the censure of a handful of Communists, but a "brazen" attempt to dictate what movies could be made or shown. The freedom of everyone in the arts and journalism was at stake. As for the crowds jamming the committee room and "'cheering madly' every idiotic remark of the curious array of witnesses," they were there to gape at the stars, and "would have cheered just as madly anything these gods had had to say about the tapioca crop in Brazil."

It's almost inconceivable to think of a publisher today making such an open, impassioned political statement and having the platform to do so. Bennett's actions again echoed back to Horace Liveright and his journey to New York's state capital to oppose censorship. The big difference was that Bennett's broadcasting, lecturing, "columning," and book-writing careers had given him a voice that could be heard all over America. No other book publisher, before or since, has had that power. This time, his emotions had led him to a far different place than the one that had got him into trouble over Ezra Pound a year earlier. This time, head and heart had worked together.

What his immediate publishing family thought about it was made clear on a single sheet of paper. The top said "RANDOM HOUSE, INC," and was dated November 11, 1947. It politely demanded attention, for, unusually oversized, the sheet looked personal and yet clearly meant business. Someone had gone to the trouble of typing the company's name in those block capitals; ordinary printed letterhead paper couldn't have accommodated the one-paragraph message and two deep rows of firmly executed signatures below. "Dear Mr. Cerf," it began, then declared: "The courageous public stand which you have taken toward the House Committee on Un-American Activities has given us great pleasure. Your recent radio address and the 'Trade Winds' column have been greeted at Random House with heartfelt admiration. It is to us no small matter that our employer is a true liberal, in the best sense of the word."

Fifty-four employees had affixed their most legible John Hancocks. They came from every department, in positions high and low: Ray Freiman, head of production; Jess Stein, head of reference; Louise Bonino, in charge of juveniles; associate editor Belle Becker; newcomer Albert Erskine, a Republican who understood that HUAC was attacking freedom-loving citizens of every stripe; Jezebel's husband, accounting controller Abe Friedman; but also sales reps like Howard Treeger, and secretaries like Mary Barber, who typed for the big boss when Pauline was away. (Fully forty signatories were female, reflecting the prevalence of women on the middle and lower rungs of the business, even as the top remained stubbornly male.) Those closest to Bennett—Don and Bob, Saxe, Lew, and Jezebel—hadn't needed to sign: he knew how they felt. Given that the full-time staff probably didn't exceed seventy souls, the petition embodied an extraordinary show of loyalty, solidarity, and pride.

. . .

ANNE SHIRLEY HAD WANTED her husband to cooperate with HUAC, but like the rest of the "Ten," he'd refused. Adrian had assured Bennett and Phyllis that he was no Communist, and the Cerfs in turn had told their friends, asking them to rally to his cause. Yet like the other nine, Scott lost his job. Soon he was found guilty of contempt of Congress, fined, and sentenced to prison. Some months after Adrian's HUAC appearance, Anne phoned Phyllis: she wanted to talk, but not at the house. She suggested lunch at Schrafft's.

"I don't know how to tell you this," Anne began once they sat down. Then she confided to her best friend: "Adrian *is* a Communist." He'd joined the Party in 1944, before they'd married. She was "terribly upset" for herself, her marriage, and also for their friendship. Ten months after his appearance before the Thomas Committee, Anne Shirley divorced her husband. After he was blacklisted, he survived by writing TV scripts under an assumed name—for all-American *Lassie, The Adventures of Robin Hood,* and other shows.

Phyllis could never get over her sense of betrayal at having been "used so" by this man who'd lied to her. Anne married another screenwriter, Charles Lederer, at the Cerfs' home a year after divorcing Adrian. The friendship continued, but in the end, Phyllis broke with her, too, eventually finding a place for Anne on her personal blacklist.

All the while, the network of movieland connections grew, and threaded ever more intricately into the Cerfs' social life. "I began to look for my own friends, who became *our* friends," Phyllis later said, acknowledging that a wife is sometimes accused of "separating" her husband from "his great good friends." Bennett had always sought companions from the world of movies and theater, but once Phyllis settled securely into the marriage, publishing and literary folk like the Guinzburgs and Van Vechtens became much less present, while more and more of their inner circle were tied to Hollywood.

"I was deeply pleased to be remembered by you on my birthday. I see you seldom—but I love you both very dearly," Bennett wrote to Fania and Carl Van Vechten in 1948. Fourteen years later, he'd write to them again, with puzzlement: "My friendship with you . . . has been one of the highlights of my life, and I only regret that we seem to have drifted so far apart." Yet Phyllis was good at being Bennett's wife—for many years, superb. Given how busy he was, in most cases he probably barely noticed when friends like the Van Vechtens were edited out. The important thing was for the machinery of his unceasingly busy life to be smoothly serviced, while he was always surrounded by amusing, creative people. The important thing was never to be bored.

Still, Adrian and Bennett had liked each other and respected each other's work. At the end of September 1950, when he couldn't reach his old friend by phone, Adrian resorted to pen and paper to ask a favor before he was sentenced and went to jail. He tried to keep it light—perhaps from pride, perhaps judging what might work best with this particular friend. Now officially a pariah, he was a dangerous man to be associated with in an increasingly paranoid time. After serving one-third of the sentence, he'd be eligible for parole, and would need letters vouching for his character—"though not necessarily agreeing" with his politics, he explained—from "distinguished citizens," among whom "Chris, Jonny and I place you. We haven't won Phyllis over yet," he joked.

"When the time comes for you to request a parole, you can count upon me to help," Bennett assured him in the first sentence of his reply. Still, it was far easier to have taken a public stand in 1947 than it was to help a convicted member of the Hollywood Ten in 1950, by which point much of the liberal resistance to HUAC and its widening storm had been crushed or terrified into silence; Bennett took pains, therefore, to remove any doubt about his own position, not knowing who else might read the letter. But he also took pains to show something more—call it fairness, loyalty, decency, or perhaps grace: "I think your character is as admirable as your politics are deplorable. Wrong as Phyllis and I think you have been in this whole 'unfriendly ten' business, we cannot help but admire your courage in fighting for what you believe in, regardless of the costs. We consider you our good and life-long friend."

Chapter 21

Some Kind of Progress

On May 25, 1948, Bennett turned fifty. Don, Lew, Saxe, and Harry Maule celebrated and consoled him over lunch, while Phyllis and Herbert did the dinner honors. After taking in a picture at Radio City, he jotted his own appraisal into his diary: "50 years of some kind of progress!" Driven to be a winner and to surround himself with winners in a charmed circle, he could stop—for a moment—to indulge in a little self-congratulation. Nathan Wise's grandson had become Somebody, yet still retained the "lift and enthusiasm of a sophomore," as *The Saturday Review* said of its columnist. At the same time, the need for consolation was real. Fifty was uncompromisingly fifty then: an alarming number for a fellow who'd persisted in calling himself the "boy publisher" long after it ceased to be funny. Progress, yes, but he also regarded this particular birthday as "a crusher."

A few years earlier, the gentlemen of S&S had also congratulated themselves: they'd captured the best of Bennett-the-anthologist in *Try and Stop Me,* and sold more than a quarter million hardcover copies. The sequel they'd signed would be published as *Shake Well Before Using* in November, yet they wondered if his kind of humor book in peacetime would be as successful, and feared that the public might have been sated by *Anything for a Laugh,* which Bennett had insisted on bringing out with G&D and Bantam in 1946. He himself worried, knowing well the intense pressure a writer feels to repeat the success of a smash-hit debut. Working furiously to meet the April deadline, Bennett harbored doubts, having admitted to his diary that the first draft was "awful."

Just before going off on his winter jaunt, he'd focused on Gene O'Neill for one of *Shake Well*'s longer sketches, a five-page biographical profile peppered with anecdotes but also infused with veneration. O'Neill's primary interest in the theater was neither money, fame, nor critical approval. "He writes plays," Bennett declared, "because he cannot help it. They burn in his mind, and he pours them out on paper," regardless of length or commercial appeal. He finished by announcing that someday the world would know more about the great man's inner life, disclosing that O'Neill had told his family's story in a play called *Long Day's Journey into the Night* [*sic*]. Locked away in the RH safe, it would remain there, unopened, "until twenty-five years after [O'Neill's] death."

Bennett consistently tried to keep Gene's public flame alive; in a Trade Winds piece two years earlier, he'd reminded readers that O'Neill outsold all other American playwrights by a tremendous margin, noting *Strange Interlude*'s 125,000 copies, and the 80,000 of *Mourning Becomes Electra* (the average break-even sale for a published play was 4,000 copies). He also gave news of three works completed since O'Neill last lit up a Broadway marquee in 1934—*The Iceman Cometh, A Touch of the Poet,* and *A Moon for the Misbegotten*—and assured readers that *Iceman,* set in the waterfront saloons of Gene's youth, with Death playing the title role, was among his greatest. Yet it ran for just five months when produced on Broadway in October 1946; a year later, *Misbegotten* fared worse, closing even before it could open. Still, he stayed faithful and had been glad when the O'Neills returned to the city at the end of 1945 and settled into an East Side penthouse. Six weeks after *Iceman* opened, one of the great nights of Bennett's life had occurred, thanks to his friend Russel "Buck" Crouse, and very much involving O'Neill.

Crouse had been the Theatre Guild press agent for *Ah, Wilderness!* before writing plays and librettos himself, so his closeness to the O'Neills dated back more than a decade. He'd wanted to introduce Gene to another friend, Irving Berlin, whose songs O'Neill admired, and whose latest show, *Annie Get Your Gun,* was a current hit. That November Saturday, Buck and his wife, Anna, had invited Gene and Carlotta for dinner, and arranged for Irving and Ellin Berlin to join them afterward. The Berlins arrived, nervous about how the socializing would proceed, and having told their chauffeur to expect them again soon. Berlin sat at the piano and began to play his own and other Tin Pan Alley favorites. What he didn't know was that for years O'Neill had owned a white player piano covered with pictures of naked ladies that he'd bought from a New Orleans bordello and dubbed "Rosie." Indeed, when Bennett had visited the O'Neills at Tao House, Gene had brought him down into the cellar to "meet" Rosie, annoying Carlotta, who'd treated them like a couple of naughty boys.

As Berlin played and sang, O'Neill overcame his initial shyness and sang along. The genius of the American drama and the genius of the American musical were having a grand time together, and so were their wives. At some point the bell rang: the Berlins had forgotten about the chauffeur! But instead of winding the evening down, Crouse decided to open it up, and, though it was already late, phoned his writing partner Howard Lindsay and Lindsay's actress wife, Dorothy Stickney, as well as the Cerfs. Bennett and Phyllis had just returned from a party, but this was an invitation no one could refuse. The music continued until 3 A.M., and for Bennett—who often waltzed around the house singing popular tunes to himself—those hours were pure joy. That he could hardly carry a tune made no difference; his encyclopedic memory for lyrics never failed. Even Carlotta seemed pleased, sending a note saying that she thought him "wonderful."

He had to reciprocate; five days before Christmas, he hosted a party to honor O'Neill. The Crouses came, along with the O'Haras, Comminses, and others, among them popular bearded folk singer Burl Ives. The Cerfs had asked Ives to bring his guitar, and after a first round of songs Bennett turned to Gene. Knowing from the evening with Rosie that he loved to sing shanties from his seafaring days, Bennett asked if he cared to recall any now. Remember he did, and as Gene and Burl got going, the language grew saltier and saltier. Carlotta was not amused: this wasn't the image she'd cultivated of O'Neill the impenetrable great man. "We're going home, Gene," she announced.

"You go home without me!" he countered.

Bennett promised he'd get Gene safely home. Carlotta swept out as O'Neill kept singing. In Bennett's recounting, even the maids and five-year-old Chris took in some of the show, perched on the stairs one flight up—until he happened upon them. It was one of the last times Bennett felt Gene was himself, before a cascade of troubles overwhelmed him. Disappointment in the recent reception of his work had affected him, but his deteriorating health was worse. O'Neill's walking became less steady, his tremor more pronounced; the Crouses had invited the Berlins to arrive *after* dinner because Gene was embarrassed for any but the closest friends to see him eat. The next year, past problems resurfaced between him and Carlotta, arguments boiling over into scenes worthy of an actress and a dramatist. Obsessed with her husband, she became increasingly hostile, jealous of the pretty young actresses he still flirted with, suspicious of friends, angry at not being able to control his every moment. Wholly bound up in being "Mrs. Eugene O'Neill," Carlotta was also having to be an increasingly frail man's caretaker; pride and love mixed with resentment and frustration. For his part, Gene needed her but didn't seem to mind piquing her jealousy. As Anna Crouse observed, "Both adored and hated the other."

The very week in January 1948 when Bennett was devising his *Shake Well* portrait of O'Neill, the spouses' relationship approached a nadir, and Carlotta directed some of her animus at Saxe. He'd held a key to their safe deposit box for years, but now she made their lawyer insist he surrender it. Soon—after another blowup—she stormed out, took a hotel room, then moved to another and another, in touch with a few intimates but refusing to speak with her husband. Gene's tremor had become so bad he couldn't be alone, and a friend, Walter Casey, was enlisted to stay with him. However, on January 27, in the middle of the night, Gene staggered out of bed to use the bathroom, fell, and broke his left shoulder. Casey, having had a few drinks too many, was out cold while Gene moaned and later fainted; hours passed before Casey awoke and found him on the floor. O'Neill was taken to Doctors Hospital, where he'd remain for several months.

Manuscripts had been left in an unlocked drawer in Gene's desk. That Carlotta, in her state, might return and remove them preyed upon both Gene and Saxe, who decided that Casey should bring them to RH for safekeeping. A month after the accident, she came back to the penthouse, found the papers gone, and phoned Saxe. When he feigned ignorance, not wanting to say anything before speaking with Gene, she let loose a volley of epithets, declaring she had enough on him to send him to jail. From being the "loyal friend and charming companion," he'd become "a crook," "Jew bastard," and worse.

As soon as Carlotta slammed the receiver, a frantic Saxe wrote Gene, insisting that her language could only be explained by "a deep-seated illness." Soon he sought Bennett's help on what to do; Gene was miserable, and they had to do *something*. First Bennett phoned O'Neill, then overcame his reluctance to go anywhere near a hospital and spent a few hours at Gene's bedside. After seeing his shakes and shoulder, he was truly rattled.

Bennett wasn't alone among O'Neill's friends in hoping he might finally "shed" Carlotta, but Gene couldn't live without her. A reconciliation was effected, but her price was that they leave New York for seclusion elsewhere; she was reasserting control. After a brief stint in Boston, they found a house in Marblehead, along the Massachusetts coast. Bennett wouldn't see or properly correspond with O'Neill for three long years.

...

HIS OWN REVISIONS AND Saxe's help had improved *Shake Well* enough for a very relieved Bennett to hand in the manuscript on April 14. S&S's Albert Leventhal and Jack Goodman would further improve it. A while back, Bennett had agreed to have his portrait taken that same day by an up-and-coming Black photographer, Gordon Parks, who'd been breaking racial barriers and making money with fashion shoots for *Vogue* and others, and was about to join *Life*. In due course Parks would be acclaimed as a renaissance man—writer, filmmaker, musician, activist, as well as camera artist—but, at that moment, he was working on a how-to book for camera portraits, and Bennett was one of his subjects.

The morning of the shoot, Parks turned up at RH to find a "bleary-eyed, unshaven" fellow, whom he reckoned the worse for wear after having indulged too much on the social circuit the night before. He couldn't have known that Bennett had been stretching himself thin for weeks in order to deliver *Shake Well*. What's more, he often shaved in his private bathroom at work. Parks noticed a cast-off umbrella and trench coat as soon as he entered the office and wanted to use them as props, but Bennett swatted away the idea like a peevish child; using them would be "strictly out of character." And so, pose followed pose, a tedious ordeal for photographer and sitter alike, until Bennett had had enough and brought the session to a close. He'd underestimated his visitor, however—both as an artist and reader of people. As Parks was packing his equipment, he uttered a parting challenge: "I'm finished, you know, but not at all satisfied."

Bennett snapped to attention: "What's wrong?"

"The umbrella and the raincoat."

"Damned persistent fellow, aren't you?"

But the atmosphere shifted as Bennett's basic good humor and vanity came to the fore. He'd stand with the umbrella—if it remained unbuttoned. Parks watched him take the pose, and with it, "the ice melted and the fabulous Mr. Cerf became himself—super charged, tall, well-tailored and terrific": the man he'd imagined. He got the photo he'd come for, a portrait that a quarter century later would emerge as the archetypal image of Bennett-as-publisher, the one used on the cover of his posthumous memoir, *At Random*.

As Parks packed up a second time, Bennett inscribed a book for him. At home that evening, Parks opened it and read: "From your friend with an umbrella."

The archetypal image of "the fabulous Mr. Cerf"

If coverage from a growing corpus of newspaper and magazine articles agreed on anything, it was that the energy of Mr. Cerf *never* flagged, and that his wife kept up with him. "Try and Stop Them" headlined a July 12 *New York Post* weekend magazine profile. "Phyllis and Bennett Cerf make books an exciting career," read the caption under a big photo, where Bennett—pipe clenched, determination radiating from behind round tortoiseshell glasses—leaned over beautifully groomed Phyllis. A smaller photo captured the Cerfs holding hands in the garden, with—less happily for Bennett—a hint of the receding hairline he took pains to cover. The couple explained that Phyllis now used the small ground-floor extension as her cluttered workroom. Bennett willingly gave up the garden view for his orderly third-floor study, with its redwood bookshelves, file drawers, and hulk of a desk, designed to accommodate one person on each side.

Another profile, "Supercharged Cerf," in *The Saturday Evening Post,* revealed that in some drawers Bennett kept meticulously organized files, containing jokes scribbled down at parties or dinners, then typed on slips and arranged into subjects as disparate as "marriage" and "Wall Street": keys he used to unlock stories lodged in his steel-trap memory. When his sons were old enough, he'd enlist their services as "runners" in the serious game of sorting slips, an activity that took place in the bedroom. He'd map out category labels on his and Phyllis's beds, glance at each joke, and hand it to a boy, telling him which pile to put it in. Later, the piles migrated down the hall to the study.

Phyllis was the "perfect" mate for a writer, Bennett had boasted to the *Post,* insisting that his wife was one of the most serene people he'd ever met. When he blew up, she was always calm. He'd shout a bit, Phyllis conceded, but then quickly settle back to his wonderful self. Bennett didn't explain that a significant part of his wife's perfection lay in the sheer amount of book-work she put in behind the scenes.

His beloved Pauline had begun to feel the effects of keeping up with her boss's punishing pace, and the previous year had spoken of giving up the maid's quarters with its privileged personal bathroom, and leaving RH for a less stressful life. Bennett couldn't countenance such a loss: where would he be without Jezebel, the mythic, well-endowed, smart-talking helpmeet known to his authors and readers alike? Offering her a four-day week, he persuaded her to stay; but for after-hours and weekend work, Phyllis had to take up some of the slack. She continued to source and sort through jokes and type them onto slips, and to perform the important role of first reader. Phyllis also saw herself as the censor: if she thought a joke funny, it was; if she didn't, Bennett hummed a lot but listened.

Her work gave her a financial cut, but not the credit she craved. Already that year, she'd helped on *Shake Well,* and with a quickie Bantam paperback, *The Unexpected!,* whose cover proclaimed "twenty high tension stories that take you by surprise" but had only one byline: "Selected by Bennett Cerf." His publishers knew of her involvement in at least some books. Negotiating over *Anything for a Laugh,* Bernard Geis at Grosset insisted that Bennett be fair to Phyllis, arguing she deserved half the loot. And Dick Simon chided, "Every time I send your royalty checks, I feel that they should be addressed to Cerf and Serf. . . . Poor darling Phyllis."

The serf had rebelled a bit: she'd recently persuaded Bennett to split his fee for the daily TASM column fifty-fifty. At the same time, she recognized whom her world depended on, and the image to project when speaking to the press. In the newspaper profile she declared: "We have the same politics. We both like Scotch old-fashioneds. . . . We both stay up late at night. Bennett loves to sleep and I love to sleep; Bennett loves steak and I love steak. We have no problems." And yet she also let slip a detail that marred the idyll: when anything upset her, she'd said in passing, she could go silent for days. *That* hadn't changed. From under the controlled exterior, dark springs of frustration and rejection occasionally surfaced, chilling into icy bouts of withdrawal. Bennett could attempt to ignore her, but at his peril. On one memorable occasion, she took to her bed, and for days the language she spoke to her husband was silence. Her children, meanwhile, had to find their own ways of dealing with what pooled beneath their mother's serenity.

As for what lay beside Bennett's "supercharged" energy, the *Saturday Evening Post* writer, Jack Alexander, found the answer ultimately elusive. Bennett's friends said that although he made a "show of being superficial," he was really "deep and serious," but an unnamed author held that "the illusion of superficiality, if it is an illusion," was "convincing," and added: "I can't feel . . . any reality there," just "a flutter of shadows and reflections, and that is all."

. . .

BENNETT AND PHYLLIS HAD decided to spend as much of the long, hot New York summer away from the city as possible. Their La Quinta friends, the Cullmans, would be in Europe for the season's first half, and the Cerfs rented their large house in Westchester for a month. Phyllis and the kids relocated full-time to Purchase; Bennett commuted during the week, but played hooky whenever he could. He was masquerading as a millionaire, he joked to himself, and took full advantage of being near the Knopfs, Simons, and other friends who lived north of the city. In August, instead of going to Maine as they'd done before, Phyllis had arranged a rental in Provincetown, on Cape Cod. Bennett evangelized about his five-week family vacation there in Trade Winds: "You only live once . . . get all the time off you possibly can. . . . Three cheers for the lazy life!"

Lazy? Not exactly. He might lie in the sun a few hours, but would pack in so much else: tennis, games, picnics, swimming, walks—and plenty of New Yorkers to do them with. Add an orgy of reading: books by Albert Camus, Aldous Huxley, Dawn Powell, Graham Greene, and many more. He had to know what the competition was publishing, just as he had to know what was happening at the office. Letters traveled to and from the palazzo. He could never waste time.

Moss and Kitty Hart visited with their nine-month-old son Christopher, arriving in time to celebrate the other Chris's seventh birthday. Although the kid in Bennett enjoyed playing with his firstborn when moments could be found, fathering could also be a trifle exasperating. It had been obvious early that Chris was very bright, and equally obvious his parents' expectations were exceedingly high. Bennett might suddenly turn critical, and Phyllis demanded something close to perfection. That summer, she felt Chris was going through an "impossible" phase, becoming a Little Mr. Know-It-All, and enlisted Bennett "to prove our superiority" and dampen the "smart-aleck" in him. On the beach one day, he turned to his son with a history lesson—as fathers are wont to do even without spousal pressure. "Do you realize that this was where the Pilgrims landed?" Bennett asked. Most kids learned something else at school: the Pilgrims landed at Plymouth Rock. Chris told his dad that he was wrong.

"Wrong" was a word Bennett didn't like when applied to himself. He explained that the Pilgrims landed at Provincetown but remained only two weeks; after realizing the soil was poor, they crossed the bay to Plymouth. That, too, failed to convince. He was set on showing Chris his mistake, wanting him to get his facts right, but at such moments, others also saw something else, an unspoken double-edged message playing in the background. Chris was to make his dad proud, but never try to eclipse him.

"Damn it all," Bennett exclaimed, "we're going down to the bookstore and get you a book on this!" He knew every bookseller on the East Coast and that the store in Provincetown was first-rate, but they found no such children's book there for a very good reason: none existed. Back in the city, Bennett devoted a Trade Winds to Provincetown's history, and honor was satisfied. However, far more would come from the incident.

RH's juvenile editor Louise Bonino attended a conference the following spring, where an educator put in a plea for biographies for fifth and sixth graders. When Bennett heard about it, something clicked: he remembered Provincetown. But rather than discrete biographies, he thought in terms of a children's *series* centered on significant *events,* understanding the predictable income that a successful series could generate and the greater appeal that exciting episodes would have for young minds. The series could at once set the history straight; avoid the dry tone of a lot of school fare; and commission established authors of adult—not kids'—books, who were skilled at telling a good story.

Such a project would need investment: time to get the template right—reading level, writing style, design, illustrations, length, authors—as well as enough books launching simultaneously to make a splash and establish that the series was for the long term. Donald was enlisted to supervise production of "dummy" books—mock-ups with some text and images—and figure out prices and set sample pages. A list of potential subjects was drawn up. RH's reputation for children's books had been growing since the Smith & Haas merger brought Babar as well as Bonino: authors now included Walter Farley, Noel Streatfeild, Mae and Ira Freeman, Ruth Gannett, and Ted Geisel, whose combined efforts produced horse, ballet, science, and illustrated stories of all sorts.

The cheaper Wonder Books line that Bennett had been so keen to launch in 1946 to compete with S&S's Golden Books had amazed him by selling two million copies during its first six weeks, but by 1949 he, Don, and Bob were feeling overwhelmed: Bennett's appetite had been too indiscriminate. Distributed in five-and-dime stores, newsstands, and other non-bookstore venues, the line was in many respects a different, high-pressure business, more suited to magazine men or mass merchants. Forced to match Golden's twenty-five-cent price, the profit margin was terribly thin: everything depended on volume. When the history series idea developed to the point where it would become a reality, they'd already begun negotiating to sell Wonder to Grosset and Curtis Publishing; offloading it would create space for the new project, and the three partners and Lew Miller—the four owned Wonder jointly—would do very well from the deal, reaping about $750,000.

Bennett, as usual, came up with a winning title: "Landmarks." Bonino took Don's samples and toured libraries, schools, and stores to gauge reactions and refine plans. Fourteen months after Bennett's argument on the beach with Chris, the first ten topics were finalized, including the voyages of Columbus, story of Pocahontas, California Gold Rush, Pony Express, and, yes, the Pilgrim landing. They resolved that the first ten would land together at the start of the 1950 school year—and make their mark.

. . .

IN BENNETT'S *SHAKE WELL*, he'd included stories about William Faulkner as well as Gene O'Neill, but whether those particular incidents were real, apocryphal, or a combination is anyone's guess. One of the "harmless idiosyncrasies" he described involved Faulkner's habit of taking his shoes off. The story went that on a crowded subway express he removed them, and couldn't find either one when the train reached his stop. He "raised such a holler" that the motorman held the train until, crawling the length of the car on hands and knees, he "located the missing number nines at the other end." Another anecdote was part of a paean to Frank Case, manager of the Hotel Algonquin, the Mississippian's home away from home. After Faulkner arrived one evening looking "decidedly below par," Case asked what the problem was. "My stomach is bothering me," he replied. Case nodded: "Something you wrote, no doubt."

Despite these veiled allusions to his drinking, Faulkner's career was on the rise in 1948—although RH at that point had little to do with it. In Europe, his reputation was constant: writer Jean-Paul Sartre had said that for young French intellectuals, Faulkner was "a god" (a position Sartre rather fancied for himself). In America, however, Faulkner—like O'Neill—had fallen out of fashion. Not only was he always short of cash, his books were mostly out of print: of his thirteen novels, two story collections, and two volumes of verse, only the lurid *Sanctuary* was available—in the ML edition.

It's not in the first hardcover edition but in reprints that books live on. Before quality paperbacks, if a title disappeared from the ML or another hardcover reprint line that controlled the rights, it was effectively gone from store shelves, apart from the odd copy lurking among used books. The minimum sale by which ML titles lived or died had cast adrift not only works like Fitzgerald's *The Great Gatsby*—first published by

Scribner—but books originated by RH itself, Faulkner's among them. The partners recognized that he was one of the rarer jewels in their crown, but business was business: there was no demand for his backlist. As Bennett had appreciated at the outset, *Sanctuary* was a shocker that people would buy; what he, Don, and Bob failed to recognize was that, with consistent effort, it might be possible to *create* demand for his other books.

Enter poet-critic-historian Malcolm Cowley, who knew Faulkner and greatly appreciated the ambition and complexity of the Yoknapatawpha universe. Convinced that RH had badly neglected their author, Cowley was in a position to do something about it. During the war, Viking had introduced a new series of small-format albeit substantial anthologies called "Portables," and Cowley had been brought in as consulting editor. Having successfully handled *The Portable Hemingway,* he wanted to take on Faulkner.

Given the unpleasant memory of tussling with Bennett over Faulkner in 1940, as well as his uninspiring sales record, Viking was less than enthusiastic, so Cowley tried a different tack, suggesting to Hemingway's editor, Max Perkins, that Perkins poach him for Scribner. Unfortunately, Perkins was unequivocal: Faulkner was "finished." And so in a series of essays—for *The New York Times Book Review, Saturday Review,* and *Sewanee Review*—Cowley "revisited" Faulkner's works himself, and enthusiasm built surprisingly swiftly. Viking changed its mind and, with permission from RH, Cowley put together an anthology of extracts and stories. Publication of *The Portable Faulkner* in 1946 had forced a critical reevaluation: Robert Penn Warren's enthusiasm was typical when he declared, "The study of Faulkner is the most challenging single task in contemporary American literature for criticism to undertake."

In response to this flurry of interest, Bennett, Don, and Bob decided to correct errors and inconsistencies in earlier editions and reprint *The Sound and the Fury* and *As I Lay Dying* in a single ML volume, using a piece that Bill had written for the *Portable* as their introduction. They also committed to reprinting the other novels and a collection of short stories in due course. As Cowley poetically put it, the *Portable* was "a bayonet prick in the ass of Random House."

Earlier in the decade, needing to make money, Faulkner had signed with Warner to write movies. Among the screenplays he worked on were those for three iconic films: *To Have and Have Not, The Big Sleep,* and Jean Renoir's *The Southerner.* His agent Harold Ober and Bennett had used different connections (Bennett's was Jack Warner himself) to help get him released from the contract, so he could return to books.

Faulkner had long wrestled with what he thought would become his magnum opus, a novel in which he transposed the story of Christ and the Antichrist to the First World War. Describing it to Bob and Bennett, he'd confessed that he'd "grown up at last" as an artist and was "writing and rewriting, weighing every word." But a tax bill was looming, and he feared having to return to Hollywood to be able to pay it. Instead he wrote a short novel in three months, and on a late April evening in 1948, Bennett read the manuscript, finishing at 3 A.M. after a single sitting.

Faulkner had mentioned several titles, but was satisfied with none. Bennett, good at titles, wired a suggestion along with his congratulations. Since the novel was structured as a murder mystery and took place in part of a Mississippi county referred to as a "beat," why not call it *Beat Four*? Short, provocative, easily remembered, it *sounded* like a detective story. Bennett was so pleased with it, he asked Bill to wire his reaction collect. "Beat Four" would be like calling *Grand Hotel* "Floor Ten," Faulkner replied. It wasn't right, meant nothing, didn't please his ear. He'd make do with one of his own devising: *Intruder in the Dust*. A rebuke, it was similar to Gertrude's stingingly affectionate dictum that Bennett was "dumb": on a certain level, he didn't "get" who Stein or Faulkner was, or what each was about. But Bennett brushed it off: he had to.

The protagonist, Lucas Beauchamp, is an old, proud Black man who'd appeared in *Go Down, Moses* and is now in jail, accused of murdering a white farmer. Unless something happens fast, he'll be lynched. From jail, Lucas asks a white teen whom he once helped—"Chick" Mallison, whose uncle, Gavin Stevens, is a lawyer—to find the murderer. Agreeing, Chick enlists a Black lad, Aleck Sander, and an old white woman, Miss Habersham, to help, while Lucas directs the quest from his cell.

Faulkner, like Gertrude, had long enjoyed detective stories (at times supplied by Bennett), and well understood the genre's conventions, as his movie work had shown. In *Intruder,* crimes are investigated, bodies exhumed, and danger and suspense balanced with comic relief; but Faulkner also conveys thoughts on race, life, and history. While his sympathy for Black suffering is palpable, so is his unalterable tie to the South. As the book made its way through production, magazines showed no interest in serial sales. Faulkner feared he'd have to return to Hollywood and grub; the only other possible income source would be a sale to the movies. Happily, *that* was not the sort of thing Bennett overlooked.

Faulkner's relationship with RH predated Ober's entry onto the scene, and his contract gave Random hegemony over a book's dramatic, movie, radio, TV, and foreign rights, everything except pre-publication serialization. Ober thought that Warner had first dibs when the manuscript was ready to be shopped; Universal was also keen to see it, but to Ober's mortification, things didn't work out that way, courtesy of MGM. Frank Taylor, the editor Bennett had hired who was shared with MGM, had become more and more preoccupied by the movie half of his job (just before *Intruder*'s publication, he'd leave RH to work full-time for Hollywood). Ober assumed it was Taylor who'd given the studio the typescript, but when he complained, Bennett professed innocence: MGM had offered to buy the book "sight unseen," and in any event, he didn't understand how anyone could make a picture from such a racially charged story. (Ober himself, two months earlier, had expressed similar misgivings.) Nonetheless, Bennett asked the agent how much the rights might fetch. It was a detective story, and Faulkner was known in Hollywood, so "fifty thousand," came the reply. On July 9, Bennett closed a sale with MGM's New York agent for $50,000. Faulkner's contract gave RH a 20 percent cut: $10,000. Ober got nothing, yet still had to handle Warner's and Universal's displeasure.

RH—in the persons of Don and Linscott—had spent part of the previous year negotiating a model contract with the Authors Guild, the first such to be jointly written, and one that stood to benefit all publishers vis-à-vis movies. Whether or not a house had acted as agent, if it could establish within two years of publication that it had contributed to a book's "value" for a movie sale, it was entitled to up to 15 percent of the author's share. That figure went up to a maximum of 25 percent if it had actually agented the book. Ober nevertheless felt that Bennett had acted in bad faith, asking for his advice and then cutting him out. The incident rankled and the feeling lingered. He also considered RH's 20 percent too greedy. But Bennett, having grasped before many others did how essential the book-movie connection would be for a publisher's bottom line, had resolved that the firm would get its share. RH had acted as Faulkner's agent, and 20 percent was 5 percent less than it could have claimed if the sale had been made under the model agreement.

A decade later, Swifty Lazar, the legendary Hollywood dealmaker, offered his appraisal of Bennett's movie maneuvers: "You are the only publisher I know who really makes pretty damn good sales and us poor agents have to struggle around to keep up with you." Most important, whatever Faulkner thought of the dance between his agent and publisher, he didn't complain: the $40,000 he received brought security at last.

Intruder in the Dust was published on September 27, 1948. Primed by the *Portable,* the literary establishment paid more attention. *Time* judged that the novel could be taken as a detective story, a "humorous idyll (a kind of second cousin to *Huckleberry Finn*)," an "outraged exhortation," and a "parable of modern life." Above all, it was a "triumphant work of art." Most critics now see the book as minor, but one of Faulkner's more accessible novels. And yet even relatively accessible Faulkner isn't easy, as *Time* admitted. Would it sell? Faulkner was coming north to find out, after eight years away.

As light faded on Monday, October 18, Bennett and Phyllis drove out to LaGuardia Airport to welcome him back. In June, Faulkner had reminded Bennett that he'd not yet met his publisher's young wife, and had no direct knowledge of how Bennett fulfilled the role of husband, but then added: Random House "has been a good papa to me so maybe you are all right in that capacity." Bennett, ever the eager fan, wasn't only keen to do honor to his author, but also to show off his wife. When he wrote that he'd meet the plane, he told Faulkner to keep the evening clear to get acquainted with his "pleasant acquisition" of a bride. Phyllis had heard so many stories about their remarkable visitor that she felt more than a little intimidated. They were waiting at the gate when she saw a short, slim but well-built man wearing an old trench coat descend from the plane. The head under the battered slouch hat was not large, and the melancholy face had deep-set, hazel brown eyes and a beaky nose—a cross between a hawk's and a Roman's. Dark bushy brows were matched halfway down by the well-tended bristles of a mustache. Bill was becoming more handsome the older he got.

"Miss Phyllis," as their visitor called her, soon discovered he had no small talk, but her timidity evaporated when she saw that he was walking around with a huge hole in his sock. The take-charge young matron, whom Faulkner would later describe as "a kitten with steel claws underneath," insisted they go home to address this sartorial emergency. After making his feet respectable again, they ventured out to a cocktail party at Quent Reynolds's place in River House, the famous Deco building overlooking the East River. Returning home, they dined with Elliot Paul, the Manges, and a beautiful thirty-seven-year-old Mississippi native, Ruth Ford. Saxe joined them later.

Ford had met Faulkner years earlier, as a student at the University of Mississippi, before she moved to New York, modeled for magazines, and tried to become an actress. The two had grown better acquainted during his last Hollywood stint; by then, she was working in B pictures. Faulkner's Hollywood affair with Meta Carpenter had petered out, and at one point that evening at Bennett's, he turned to Ford and asked: "Ruth, I've been your gentleman friend for quite a while now. Ain't it time I was promoted?"

The desired promotion apparently did not take place.

He was at Random most of the next day, a crazy-busy one: Elliot Paul, Dick Simon and Max Schuster, and Sinclair Lewis—who was staying with the Cerfs and sailing for Europe the following morning—all made appearances. The chance overlap of Lewis and Faulkner (staying at the Algonquin) led to one of Bennett's favorite stories about the relationship between authors and publishers. As dinner was finishing at the Cerfs', Bob Haas phoned: he and Merle had been hosting a party at their apartment in Faulkner's honor, and wondered if Bennett, Phyllis, and Red would like to drop by. Bennett, sure his guest would be delighted, accepted instantly, then went to tell Lewis.

"This is *my* night," Red responded, taking him aback. "Haven't you been a publisher long enough to understand I don't want to share it with some other author?"

Bennett phoned Bob, begged off, and continued to chat with Red, who eventually said goodnight and went upstairs: he had to awaken early to make the boat.

Phyllis and Bennett were still talking in the living room when suddenly a voice called down the stairwell from two floors up: "Bennett! Bennett!"

Knowing how much Lewis had imbibed, and afraid something awful had happened, Bennett rushed to the stairs. "Red, what is it?"

"I just wanted to make sure you hadn't slipped out to see Faulkner."

But Lewis hadn't been the only one imbibing that night. At Bob's dinner, the party had proceeded with the old-fashioned graciousness of a bygone era. After the meal, Merle and the other women "withdrew," leaving the men to cigars and cognac—a good deal of cognac. Faulkner, Eric Devine (who'd helped him when he'd burned his back), and Hal Smith left at 2 A.M., only to continue drinking at Hal's apartment. "Mr. Faulkner went off the reservation as feared," Bennett told his diary after a report filtered back.

Ruth Ford phoned Faulkner the next day, inviting him to a party that night. He declined, and didn't sound right. Word reached Bennett that he was "out cold." The following day, a Thursday, she phoned again, and Bill sounded worse. On Friday morning, he didn't pick up. When Ford phoned Bennett in alarm, he told her that Faulkner was missing appointments. What had precipitated the crisis wasn't clear: was it the interviews he disliked, in which he often misspoke; the city, where so many wanted a piece of him; the difficulties he'd left at home; Ford's rejection; all of the above?

Malcolm Cowley came by the Algonquin that Friday for lunch, found him in terrible shape, and stepped out briefly, planning to return; in the interim, Ford and another friend, *New York Times* columnist Harvey Breit, arrived and gained access to the room, where Faulkner was semi-conscious. By the time Cowley returned, both Devine and Bob Haas had arrived. An ambulance was summoned and Cowley managed to get Faulkner into some clothes, so he could be taken to the Riverdale Sanitarium in the Bronx. Almost certainly Bob had made the arrangements, and RH was guarantor.

On Monday, Bennett lunched with Ford. She'd seen Faulkner at the sanitarium, highly agitated and shaking in withdrawal as well as desperate to leave. In the end, the doctor agreed to let Cowley take him home to Connecticut. Once in bed there, his speech was at first limited to begging Cowley's wife for a drink, but his powers of recovery were still remarkable. By the following Thursday, Bennett was relieved to tell his diary that Faulkner was "back on the beam after 5 days 'down under.'" That night, Ruth Ford even convened a small dinner party for him.

Friday was his last full day in the city, and calling at RH, he inscribed a copy of *Intruder* "For Bennett Cerf, from his old friend, Bill Faulkner." He lunched with Saxe and Cowley, in part to discuss a volume of collected stories, and was contemplating a play, something he'd never tried. Once back at Rowan Oak, he confided to Albert Erskine that he almost had a first act. It featured Temple Drake, the protagonist of *Sanctuary,* and in a hybrid form—a novel/drama in three acts—would be published in 1951 as *Requiem for a Nun*. Eight years later, Ruth Ford would play the lead role when it debuted on Broadway.

Before leaving New York, Faulkner purchased a corduroy riding jacket of the highest quality. In town, he liked to wear a pair of red suspenders presented to favored patrons of the Stork Club that Bennett had obtained. Such things mattered to him, as RH well knew: at times, Saxe, Bob, and soon Albert, too, acted as a personal shopping service for the gentleman from Mississippi. Indeed, Saxe had affectionately taken to referring to him as the velvet-suited children's book character "Little Lord Fauntleroy."

MGM's version of *Intruder in the Dust* was filmed partly on location in Oxford and premiered there in 1949. Faulkner didn't write the script but told Bennett privately that he'd helped without credit by rewriting and rearranging dialogue in the jail sequences, as well as in a scene in the sheriff's kitchen, and had coached the actor who played Lucas with his lines and inflection. He and Bennett both liked the picture.

Cowley had resurrected Faulkner with the *Portable,* but Bennett understood what a movie could do for a book, and for an author's security. The movie did it for Faulkner. During his lifetime, *Intruder in the Dust* sold almost 32,000 copies in its RH trade edition, four times more than *Absalom, Absalom!* and ten times more than *As I Lay Dying,* the novels that most critics regard as his greatest.

. . .

COMPLETE WITH TALES OF Faulkner and O'Neill, Bennett's *Shake Well* arrived in stores in November 1948. His foreword confidently predicted that the next decade would see American humor take a gentler turn based on character and situation, rather than persist in the wisecracks and rapier thrusts that had predominated in recent years (as he'd learn, Lenny Bruce, Dick Gregory, Mort Sahl, Woody Allen, and others would beg to differ). Nor was there anything gentle or naive about the way he used his position as master of Random House to aid and abet the sales of his outside projects. Just as Pauline helped with typing and Saxe with editing, he turned to Howard Treeger, the firm's vigorous New York salesman, to set up signings and accompany him to more than a dozen city stores.

Shake Well hit the bestseller list in mid-December, but there was a problem: S&S hadn't printed enough. Americans knew Bennett and saw the book as a perfect holiday gift. Major stores in big cities had sold out not just the first printing of 35,000, but also a second of 15,000 that was rushed through. The presiding geniuses of S&S put their heads together. Soon a release went to stores and was splashed across ads, headlined: "From Our Missing the Boat Department." It spoke of the superstition about second books but admitted, "We were wrong. Oh boy were we wrong." S&S had ordered another 20,000 copies and paper for more—a potential 100,000 books—and offered to pay most costs of retailers' ads for the next two months. Perhaps they could sell more of a second Cerf book than they'd sold of his first.

Wherever there were copies, *Shake Well* continued to sell, but it was no *TASM*. Most boats in the holiday flotilla had left without it: people don't present their nearest and dearest with an IOU. As other authors in similar situations have learned to their cost, it's hard, once momentum is suspended, to regain it, especially in winter doldrums. But perhaps the matter that he'd fretted over privately—quality—also came into play. At the end of his life, Bennett admitted that none of his other humor books achieved the richness of *TASM,* that first careful cull from stories he'd collected since youth.

Chapter 22

A Horse for a Long Race

ALTHOUGH UNCOMMONLY ADEPT AT INITIATING PROJECTS AND signing writers himself, Bennett—like every publisher—depended greatly on the talents, reputations, and contacts of his editors. He gave them more autonomy, trust, and affection than many heads of houses did, encouraging editors to take chances on writers. Now Saxe had an opportunity. On March 3, 1948, a Macmillan textbook editor had written him, apologizing for presuming upon their professional friendship "in a most grievous way." Forty-one-year-old James Michener badly needed advice. In a sense, he was calling in a chit; he'd been helpful to Saxe. It's not clear how they met, but Michener was already selling articles to magazines when he'd suggested that Saxe write for *Reader's Digest,* and even helped by critiquing Saxe's piece. Now he wanted to submit a novel, *The Homeward Journey,* declaring: "You know without my saying . . . I'd be proud to be one of your authors."

This was not his first effort, as Saxe was aware. A year earlier, Michener's own firm, Macmillan, had published his collection, *Tales of the South Pacific*. The chain of nineteen stories had conjured the players of the Pacific theater during World War II—sailors and officers, planters and Polynesians, misfits and dreamers—in all their fragile, flawed humanity. As one critic later wrote, Michener had managed, "in some incredible fashion," to convey "sensitive perceptions" about his characters, despite the prejudices then prevalent in the country and "the callous misery, boredom and slaughter of war."

Hardcover sales were strong, around the 25,000 mark, Michener revealed, but not the spectacular numbers that Margaret Mitchell's Southern epic *Gone with the Wind* or Kathleen Winsor's bodice ripper *Forever Amber* had made for the mighty Macmillan. He didn't have the appeal of a steel magnolia like Mitchell or the "glamour-girl" beauty of Winsor, whom Bennett had parodied in the ad for Gertrude and Alice. Bespectacled, balding, thin-lipped, bland, Michener once described himself as "tight" and "inhibited." In a crowd he wouldn't merit a second glance. Many major newspapers and magazines simply ignored *Tales of the South Pacific*. The *New York Times* critic Orville Prescott, however, did notice, even asserting that the stories would "make Mr. Michener famous." A few months later, in *The Yale Review,* Prescott pushed his advocacy further, calling him "one of the ablest and . . . most original writers to appear . . . for a long time."

James A. Michener

Michener had overcome the pacifist tenets of his Quaker faith to enlist in the Naval Reserve, and been called to active duty in 1943. Beginning as a seaman apprentice, he finished as a lieutenant commander. At war's end, helped by a friend in the right place, he managed to stay on as a naval "historical officer," island-hopping through the blue vastness of the South Pacific. Still, the stories seemed a strikingly odd undertaking given his thoroughly unremarkable demeanor. It was as if a mysterious surge from deep beneath the quiet surface of the man had risen up and exploded into exotic life, like the dozens of small volcanic islands shimmering above the waterline that he knew so well.

As is often the case, Michener's debut was not his first attempt at fiction. Before the war, he'd started the semi-autobiographical novel that became *The Homeward Journey* to try to make sense of his harrowing childhood. Now he'd completed it, and Macmillan had agreed to publish it, but he was uneasy about its reception. Perhaps it would be better to climb the ladder at Macmillan and publish elsewhere. "I obviously don't want you to take the book unless it's good," he wrote Saxe, but added: "If it is good, I feel that I may be a horse for a long race and . . . have other manuscripts in years to come."

James Albert Michener had started life with nothing. A self-described "foundling," he was led to believe that he was born in New York City—perhaps on February 3, 1907—and, at two weeks old, brought to Doylestown, Pennsylvania, and given to Mabel Michener, a widow who survived by sewing buttonholes and taking in other people's dirty laundry and abandoned children. She provided a name and a home, but one forever precarious: his childhood included two searing stints in the poorhouse and multiple evictions. He later recalled his mother "standing out in the road at dusk" wondering where they could sleep. "I have no idea who I am," he once said, and meant it, literally. As an adolescent, straitened circumstances spurred ambition but also produced restlessness, and later, a blurred accounting of several years. In his fourteenth summer, he began to "bum his way" around the country with a friend, and claimed the improbable feat of having visited all but three of the forty-eight states by the time he graduated high school. It was these "hobo-like experiences" that gave him "a fine appreciation" of his country and the kindness and friendliness of ordinary Americans, as well as a lifelong compulsion to lose himself in new vistas and cultures.

Part of that hunger arose from his earliest imaginings, in large part fired by books. Mabel had instilled a love of story, reading aloud to him from Dickens: balm to a boy grappling with a Dickensian childhood. At school, he showed himself to be a brilliant student, launching his intellectual life in his teens by reading *Père Goriot*. Later, he named Balzac—another workaholic who produced a vast oeuvre—a "prime mentor."

In *The Homeward Journey,* Michener's teenage stand-in, David, also feeds on stories and the dreams they inspire that can't be crushed: "His heart and mind were simply bursting. . . . Oh, the illimitable world that lay ahead! . . . How could a poorhouse or . . . barren rooms contain such a boy?" They didn't contain Michener. Swarthmore College gave him a scholarship, and he graduated summa cum laude in 1929. For a decade he moved around, correcting charts on a Mediterranean coal carrier; teaching at a boarding school; studying and teaching others how to teach at the University of Pennsylvania, Harvard's School of Education, and Colorado State College. Through this last—and a word from a textbook salesman—he'd made the Macmillan connection.

When Saxe responded encouragingly to his letter, Michener delivered the manuscript to RH by hand. He was impressed—not so much by the palazzo, which impressed everybody, but by the fact that the young woman greeting him at the front desk was pretty and, unexpectedly, Black. "I liked Saxe and . . . Random House had the guts to use a Negro girl as a receptionist," he'd recall decades later. "Whatever money Random . . . made from my writing is credited to those two facts."

His coming to RH was a little more complicated. Macmillan's president, George Brett, was looking for a successor to Michener's boss and had offered him the job, and Brett may have seen it as a stepping-stone to an even loftier position. At the same time, the company had contracted the novel and paid Michener a $1,000 advance. Brett, supposedly, was already feeling uncomfortable—too much mixing of church and state—about a second book from his promising editor. He'd also let his wife see it, and Mrs. Brett hadn't liked the book. *Why* is unclear, although the graphic poorhouse scenes and lurid elements in David's sexual awakening wouldn't have been to every woman's taste.

After *Tales of the South Pacific* appeared, Michener was pursued by the agent Carl Brandt. When Brandt read *The Homeward Journey,* however, he devastated its author by judging the novel hopeless. Michener wouldn't give up on it, but the notion of coercing his own employer into publishing it—or, worse, that Macmillan might reject the book as well—was excruciating. Saxe Commins, at least, had a reputation for kindness.

If Brett was giving him time to explore other options, then Michener's swearing Saxe to secrecy and insisting in his letter that while "Macmillan does not in any way want to get out of the contract . . . the president would agree to my publishing elsewhere" makes sense. Brett saw Michener as an editor who wrote on the side, but Michener was no longer sure he saw his future as an editor or publisher. After handing the manuscript to Saxe, he boarded a train for Colorado, promising to be back in a month.

On March 8—only five days after Michener wrote his query letter—Saxe wired: "Wildly enthusiastic," and asked him to phone, reversing the charges. A two-page letter followed. Saxe was excited by the book being utterly honest and "radiant with character." The storytelling was exciting, penetrating, compassionate. Saxe particularly praised scenes at the local pleasure ground, Paradise Park: a place of dreams, escape, and heartbreaking deception. "You have the Dickens feeling for people and story," he added, comfort to a man for whom Dickens was a touchstone, and ended with words that still remain a powerful predictor of success: "What is important now is the first glow of enthusiasm for the book. . . . That, above everything . . . helps to determine [its] fate . . . in a publishing house. I am, as I said in my telegram, wildly enthusiastic."

Michener wrote Brett that Saxe would "take a flier." He asked for his Macmillan contract to be voided and said he'd return the advance. "JIM MICHENER COMES TO RANDOM HOUSE," Bennett told his diary on March 19. The partners wanted to be sure there'd be no strain with Macmillan. Bob Haas knew Brett best and managed that. Michener would stay in his job, with two days off each week to write. If he made a go of it, Brett would let him resign amicably; otherwise, his career would be at Macmillan. He mentioned already having a partial manuscript for another novel, but confessed that this first book was dearest to his heart: "I want to shoot the works on this one, all my best thoughts, my best characters." He knew, though, that he required a lot of editing, and wanted Saxe's "most intimate" suggestions. Feeling that he could write to the standard of the current book "endlessly," he admitted, "I'm not sure I can do better."

Saxe's reply had the faith Michener needed: "I foresee one book after another, each . . . with great depth and meaning. My confidence is complete." In the letter enclosing the contracts, he added: "This is for life. I can't begin to tell you how happy I am about this grand association. Really great things will come of it for all of us."

The written agreement Saxe sent Michener had one odd feature: in the clause where the royalty advance should be, a line was typed through. Michener had returned the $1,000 to Macmillan, but no up-front money from RH was specified. In that first gushing letter to Colorado, Saxe had asked his new author if he wanted an advance, and also if he had an agent. Saxe preferred dealing without an intermediary, but Michener, a publishing insider, wanted an outside advocate. Soon, he knew the agent he wanted. Four years earlier, Helen Strauss, who'd worked in the movie business, had begun a new job at William Morris. The entertainment agency was taking a chance on her starting a literary division in their

Radio City offices. Like Bennett, they could see that the books-movie symbiosis would grow. Why not get a percentage from studio *and* publisher?

When she'd joined, the agency had staged a party at the swanky Pierre Hotel on Fifth Avenue to proclaim the seriousness of her arrival. Bill Morris Jr., the founder's son who, together with his friend Bennett, had saved a boy from drowning near Saranac Lake seven years earlier, told her that he had a "barometer" to gauge how good the party was—and more important, how good her prospects in the literary world looked to be.

"If Bennett Cerf showed up, I was in," she recalled decades later.

Bennett showed up.

Strauss and Michener had gone to dinner from time to time. His first marriage had ended, and he found her sophisticated and attractive, and decided that he liked her enough for "a warmly developing friendship" to blossom. But although not immune to romance, she was a career woman. Michener was moody, and life would have had to revolve around him. She soon eased the relationship into a "wholly professional" association. In due course, RH would send their new author a check not for $1,000—the sum he'd returned to Macmillan—but triple that amount: Strauss's doing. Over the next eighteen years, the association would turn into a rare creative/business friendship that helped to enable and define a life. In Michener's words, Strauss became "adviser, banker, critic, postman" as well as friend. A packager of ideas into sellable projects, she was also a savvy street fighter when necessary—quite capable of facing down Bennett Cerf.

. . .

DESPITE BEING DISAPPOINTED IN the review coverage of his *South Pacific* stories, Michener had attracted the attention of one particularly influential Hollywood reader. Donald Friede, who'd succeeded Bennett at Liveright and later partnered with Pat Covici, now worked in Hollywood and recommended the stories to MGM. The suggestion didn't fly, but an MGM story editor and actor, Kenneth MacKenna, brought up *Tales of the South Pacific* with Bennett's friends Dick Rodgers and Oscar Hammerstein, who'd recently enjoyed great success with *Oklahoma!* and *Carousel*. Together with two other Cerf buddies—Broadway director Josh Logan and agent/producer Leland Hayward—Rodgers and Hammerstein decided to purchase dramatic rights, at first offering Michener a lump sum. What none could have predicted—not even Bennett—was that a miracle of luck and timing would occur, in the form of a Pulitzer Prize.

Serendipitously, the Pulitzer board had changed the rules in 1947: now story collections, as well as novels, were eligible in the fiction category. A second piece of luck: Orville Prescott was one of a three-person jury that year, and lobbied for the newcomer. Eleven books were considered; no single title came up tops with all three. Indeed, although he advocated for it, *Tales of the South Pacific* ranked only third on Prescott's own list, and eighth and eleventh on those of the other judges. But Alice Roosevelt Longworth, Theodore Roosevelt's daughter, whispered in the ear of Arthur Krock, chairman of the Pulitzer advisory board, urging him to read Michener's stories. He obliged and was persuaded; at the board meeting on April 23, Krock won the day.

Michener was at work at Macmillan on May 3, 1948, when news came through that caused pandemonium—or what passed for it in a properly WASP establishment. The Pulitzer Prize for fiction had, for the first time, been awarded to a book of short stories, *Tales of the South Pacific.* Michener wouldn't be an editor much longer. As for the far-from-strict, far-from-proper, far-from-WASP master of 457 Madison Avenue, the reaction recorded in his diary was entirely predictable: "PULITZER PRIZES TO AUDEN FOR POETRY, BERT ANDREWS FOR JOURNALISM, MICHENER FOR NOVEL." Wystan Auden had won for *The Age of Anxiety.* Bert Andrews, who'd published one of the early books about the Red Scare—*Washington Witch Hunt*—with Random, had won for a series of articles in the *New York Herald Tribune.* And although Bennett hadn't yet published Michener, let alone his Pulitzer Prize–winning book, he could allow himself to be possessive. "BIG DAY FOR RANDOM!" he crowed.

The Pulitzer laurels reinforced the impression that Michener was a *literary* novelist—even a long-shot successor to Hemingway—at a time when critics were searching for new standard-bearers to lead American letters forward. Unfortunately, the first Michener book to bear the RH colophon wasn't meeting those expectations. *The Homeward Journey* had been renamed *The Fires of Spring,* a more evocative title. (Saxe had suggested the need for a change; Michener obliged; and Bennett, sensing more sales, deemed it "swell!") But then another problem arose. In July,

Saxe wrote Michener with urgency: he'd halted composition at the printer's because a Literary Guild executive, a story editor at Fox, and Bennett had all read the edited manuscript and issued the same criticism. David Harper wasn't emerging as a fully realized character—especially in his emotional and sexual relationships with women. Michener countered: he didn't like books parading a "bleeding heart," since he didn't think "real tough hearts bleed so much. They cover themselves with scar-tissue." It would be up to Saxe and Bennett to say how to put "a little blood" next to "a little scar tissue." But despite best efforts, when the novel was published in February 1949, the problem hadn't been resolved.

In reviewing *The Fires of Spring,* Michener's erstwhile champion Orville Prescott tried to be generous. He saw at once that it had been a maiden effort, and praised the poorhouse and amusement park scenes that had captivated Saxe. But although Michener was a "born writer," his novel "teetered" close to sentimentality. Prescott found the women less believable than many of the minor characters, and the book not nearly as fresh, gripping, or insightful as the *South Pacific* stories—and he was being kinder than most. In the Sunday *Times,* William DuBois found the novel "hot-headed" and "grimly-in-earnest." One "suffered" through Michener's monologues on literature, music, and art, and the sex passages had been written with a blunt instrument. The book was "a very bad novel," yet there was no denying "the drive, the gusto, the probing interest in life."

The strengths and weaknesses of Michener's writing were on clear display: narrative vigor versus slow, didactic discourse; "probing interest in life" versus stilted dialogue; the ability to find the exotic even in the local, versus weak characterization and a marked awkwardness writing about sex. A few days after the first reviews landed, Don, writing to "Cerfie" sunning himself at La Quinta, tried to make the best of it: "It's still too early to tell whether Michener is going to start rolling or just be another book."

A month earlier, the Cerfs—along with their friends Buck and Anna Crouse, *Good Housekeeping* editor Herb Mayes and his wife, Grace, and a few others—had gathered around the piano in Dick and Dorothy Rodgers's elegant apartment, listening to Dick play the score of *South Pacific.* Bennett was rapt, transported: everything about the theater that he so loved was embodied in that moment, in that music. Naturally, the recital took place several months before the show actually opened. The privilege of being among the privileged—insiders who could partake of the melodic beauty, emotional wallop, and sheer fun before everybody else—lent the experience an extra kick.

Opening night was Thursday, April 7. The Cerfs were guests at the packed party on the St. Regis Hotel roof just off Fifth Avenue, along with the Harts, Berlins, Quent and Ginny Reynolds, and, as Bennett noted, "God knows who else!" Jim Michener was proud and characteristically modest about his role, telling readers of the *Times* that Hammerstein, Rodgers, and Logan had improved his work "at almost every point." He had another reason to be grateful: on the evening of the opening, they'd said that for $4,500, they would let him buy a 1 percent stake in the show. He demurred at first, not having that kind of money, so they agreed to lend it to him, and take it out of his share as profits rolled in. "A magnificent musical drama" was *Times* critic Brooks Atkinson's verdict, noting the unprecedented participation of Metropolitan Opera star Ezio Pinza as hero, and "quicksilver" Mary Martin, with whom everyone was "more or less in love," as heroine. Reviews made clear that this popular musical theater piece was also a lasting work of art.

With the momentum of the Pulitzer, the hit Rodgers and Hammerstein show, and a blitz of advertisements, *The Fires of Spring* did roll: it even made the *Times* bestseller list. As for *Tales of the South Pacific,* S&S had displayed its usual eye for a reprint winner, having signed the book for Pocket early on. With the preferred lurid, pulpy mass-market cover, the paperback would sell two million copies. This particular horse was on his way to proving himself for a long and lucrative race indeed.

...

AS WELL AS UNDERSTANDING the symbiosis between books and movies, Helen Strauss was exceedingly talented at exploiting that between books and the many deep-pocketed magazines of the era that were angling for material. The musical's success enabled her to negotiate even more profitable work for Michener. That July, she brokered a seven-article contract with *Holiday* for $6,500—far larger than the advance many writers received for a novel. The series entailed revisiting some of those dots he'd connected on the Pacific: Polynesia, Australia, New Zealand, New

Guinea, and Guadalcanal. In October, *Holiday* commissioned a Fiji piece for another $1,500, as well as a short story for $2,500.

Although the roll call of magazine deals became continual, Strauss and her client hardly forgot Random House. An agreement had been finalized in April for a four-book deal; the novels were to be delivered starting in 1950, and bring $30,000 in advances with the royalty calculated as a straight 15 percent on the retail price of each hardcover sold. That represented a major change in Michener's favor from the typical graduated scale, where an author would receive 10 percent on the first "step," 12.5 percent on the next, and 15 percent only after reaching the third. For *The Fires of Spring,* the "steps" corresponded to the first 2,500 copies sold; the next 2,500; and, with 5,000 copies having been sold, 15 percent thereafter. It had taken authors like Faulkner quite a time to achieve a straight 15 percent royalty from the outset.

The contract specified that Michener would receive $5,000 on January 10 of each year, from 1951 through 1956, already outstripping the average American yearly income of about $3,200. If in any year the money RH owed Michener exceeded $5,000, he'd be paid the $5,000 plus the excess up to a total of $8,000—a ceiling that corresponded with the tax law. Anything left would be placed in an escrow account, in what was now referred to as a "deferred income plan"—the same kind of arrangement that had been negotiated with *The Snake Pit*'s Mary Jane Ward. The contract also gave RH 5 percent of the money from the sale of movie rights to any or all of the four novels.

Having finalized that agreement, Strauss wondered if the articles for *Holiday* might be repurposed to constitute yet another book for RH. Michener liked the idea, but wanted to intersperse short stories among the factual pieces, using the same settings. Strauss approached Bennett, who thought the proposal ridiculous. "To say that Bennett put me down was an understatement," she admitted years later. Telling her that she didn't know "the slightest bit" about publishing, he declared that no publisher would undertake such a project. Strauss stood her ground; having warmed to his subject, Bennett lost his temper. She did likewise, but in the heat of the moment, he ratcheted up the tension, calling her "an idiot." Impossible to know whether the contempt was greater, in that place and time, because she was a woman, but certainly he'd misjudged her: she wasn't some wide-eyed "girl." She'd sell that book and show him for the idiot *he* was. Strauss offered the project to Doubleday's Lee Barker, who was more than willing to take a flutter on this horse. There was no contractual obligation for her to go back to RH—the four-book deal was a separate matter—but she wanted to see Bennett squirm.

Like everyone in the business, he respected Barker and held Doubleday in a certain awe. It was unique: a well-oiled machine that controlled a multi-armed publishing house, retail bookstores, book clubs, and printing presses. It took Bennett less than a moment to realize that if Michener signed with Barker for one book, Doubleday would do everything in its power to keep him. Saxe had faith in this author, yet Bennett knew his damned temper and impetuousness had put RH at risk of losing him.

Strauss relished making him work to persuade her that RH should win the book; in the end, she relented and did the deal. They all knew it was better to have one home going forward, but she'd made her point. Bennett had learned to respect her as much as he would any tough man, but Strauss had also learned a lesson: each time she dealt with the head of the firm—and she'd represent Ralph Ellison, Robert Penn Warren, and many others—there was one key step she had to take in the author-agent-publisher dance: "To mention tactfully, as tactfully as I could, that Bennett was the 'star' of Random House."

The book, titled *Return to Paradise,* would be published in April 1951, and early in January, Don and Saxe cabled Michener in Hong Kong that it had been chosen by BOMC as its May selection. They were also excited by another project, wholly nonfiction, that Michener had suggested, arising from articles commissioned by *Life* and the *Herald Tribune*. Since he was already on the other side of the world, since travel made him even more energized, and since he'd developed a self-professed monomania about Asia, he'd decided to poke around a mere ten countries, from Japan to India, interview 120 individuals, and report it all to the folks back home. Work on the two books would overlap; the second would be titled *The Voice of Asia,* and be published that fall. Michener was fast and reliable; by the time he'd return to America and sign the contract in August, the book would already be in production.

Just after *Return to Paradise* came out, Bennett gleefully told his author that he'd sold reprint rights to Bantam for a "whopping" $12,500 advance, partly because the *Fires of Spring* paperback was "going like wildfire." He also reported that *Reader's Digest* would excerpt *Return to Paradise* in their fall condensed books, and the hardcover was number seven on the *Times* list. Foreign rights sales were negotiated in many countries, and Strauss had sold two of its stories to the movies. One picture, starring Gary Cooper, took the title of the book; the other, *Until They Sail,* starred a young Paul Newman.

Bantam's $8,000 advance bought reprint rights to *The Voice of Asia,* and book club rights were snapped up. With the Korean War raging, Michener had a lot to say to his fellow citizens about the other side of the world, and as a writer, he'd always inhabit three roles: teacher, reporter, storyteller. Much of his analysis remains prescient: "The destiny of the United States," Michener wrote, "will be determined in large part by decisions we make regarding our relations with Asia." He continued:

> To ignore such a continent, willfully to make it our implacable enemy, or stupidly to misunderstand the forces that motivate its nations would be extreme folly. . . . It is also possible . . . —probable if we continue to make basic mistakes—for the United States to become a museum relic like Greece, honored in memory for having brought . . . a fresh clean version of freedom; while Asia becomes the effective center. . . . Such a decline is not inevitable, but we can avert it only through intelligence, tolerance, and hard work.

He was telling those Americans who wanted to retreat from global responsibilities that the nation's coastlines and borders could not protect them: America was now and forever part of a larger world, and attention must be paid.

. . .

MICHENER'S COMMERCIAL STAR WAS rising high and fast, already showing auspicious signs of how essential he'd become to RH. He'd never draw from Bennett the emotional response that Stein, Capote, O'Neill, or O'Hara did, but they'd reached an understanding of their respective roles, one that would carry them through many years and more than a dozen books during Bennett's lifetime. "What it boils down to is this," Michener told him: "The better a publisher you are, the better for me. The better a writer I am, the better for you. Many things contribute to each status; many are a waste of time. We'd better concentrate on the contributors."

Bennett reciprocated with advice of his own, advice that Michener decades later acknowledged was well worth following: "Whenever you go into a strange town, stop at the bookstore. Tell the owner and especially the clerks how much you appreciate their support, because they're the ones who'll keep you alive."

"Now I see why the professionals are so fond of you," Michener recognized. "The only cost of courtesy is a little time." But there was more to the lesson.

"If they see you're really interested in books they'll ask you to autograph one or two, for their special customers," Bennett continued. "Always do it . . . autograph all the books of yours they have. Because then they can't ship the unsold copies back to us." Like many publishers then and now, he'd begun by selling books on the road. But unlike some, those were lessons Bennett never forgot.

Chapter 23

Midcentury

NINETEEN FORTY-NINE HAD BEEN GOOD TO RH AND TO THE CERFS—Bennett would pay tax on a personal income of $103,000 ($1.3 million today)—yet it was never enough. The war had made him into a public speaker, and with the tremendous success of *Try and Stop Me,* he'd joined a rarefied group, those paid to give talks, and signed with a lecture bureau to manage that new part of his life. Now he switched to another agency, which promised better venues, bigger audiences, more money; but although he hankered after dates at universities like Harvard and Princeton, the Ivy League would never provide most of his bookings. He was Phi Beta Kappa, but also a joke peddler.

Still, Bennett was flattered to speak before two thousand at Washington's most famous auditorium, Constitution Hall, the same place that a decade earlier notoriously had closed its doors to the marvelous Black contralto, Marian Anderson. (His contract had specified there would be no segregation.) But he was equally tickled to see his incandescent name on the marquee of Carson City's Tower Theater. In Chicago, he followed his agent's instructions to don dark suit, white shirt, black tie, and hold forth on "Changing Styles in American Humor" to seven hundred morticians, but also spoke on "Books the Public Is Reading" to three hundred members of Seattle's Washington Athletic Club.

By 1956, he'd earn more than $11,000 ($126,000 today) from his spring talks alone; the "seasoned trouper," as he loved to call himself, was by then a lecture circuit star. If five days of lecturing and store visits wore him out, a good twelve- or fourteen-hour Saturday night sleep—the kind a youth might indulge in—put him "back in the pink." Especially when talks coincided with a visit to the West Coast, Phyllis sometimes accompanied him, but as she got busier with her own projects, she went less often. Then the tours served an extra purpose: as an escape valve

Bright lights for the "seasoned trouper"

from the disciplines of his wife and marriage. Bennett's good friend Kitty Carlisle once observed that he had "many, many peccadilloes," and he looked forward to those breaks on the road.

The Cerf social system still lit up around the usual fixed stars and constellations. Phyllis had mastered the art of setting the scene and grouping many well-known figures and famous egos all at once. Her strategy was to cluster guests around one person—an author, composer, actor, politico—as the "star." The goal was for everyone to be relaxed, well fed, and never bored. At such parties, it was impossible not to notice the lugubrious thinness, basset-hound eyes, and six-feet-eight of Robert Sherwood, playwright, patriot, FDR speechwriter, and Algonquin Round Table alum. Bennett professed to have "fallen in love" with him when they met in the Liveright days, "and stayed in love . . . till the day [Sherwood] died." Having already won three Pulitzers for drama and an Oscar for the screenplay of *The Best Years of Our Lives,* in 1949 he added another Pulitzer, for a biography about Roosevelt and his adviser Harry Hopkins. Bennett was terribly pleased that a man so distinguished seemed to like his "feeble" jokes and puns.

Now Sherwood and his beautiful wife, Madeline Hurlock—who'd starred in Mack Sennett's silent comedies and was a year older than Bennett—became regulars at Sixty-Second Street, and the "Dowdy Duchess," as Bennett dubbed the always-elegant Mrs. Sherwood, took a particular interest in his boys. She'd become one of several special ladies whom Chris and Jon turned to for the undemanding attention that they craved. As for their father, he enjoyed engaging her in the usual naughty-boy banter he carried on with women who were not his wife. "Be sure to let me know the next time your knight is away from your bedside," Bennett, aka "Kingsie," wrote the Duchess. "I would like to do a little knight-work with you myself." The Duchess seemed happy to play along. However, as years progressed, it was Leonora Hornblow who'd assume the most special place among women in the Cerf universe, and in 1950 she was about to become an RH author. On January 3, Bennett and Phyllis hosted a grand evening to celebrate her newly minted status, a party that went on until 3 A.M.—no matter it was a workweek Tuesday.

Even with their so-close relationship, she hadn't secured the contract overnight. In 1943, Bennett had described the then twenty-three-year-old Bubbles as "the youngest literary glamour girl." The glamour was unassailable and the desire for literary success deep-rooted: the poor-little-rich-girl had spent a "miserable" childhood with her nose permanently escaping into a book. During the war, she'd presented Bennett with a first novel—a thinly disguised autobiography—that RH had gently rejected. When she later wrote Phyllis that she was working on a new book, Bennett appended a postscript to the reply: "Beloved, It being 2:23 a.m. . . . I naturally am in bed—a position in which my thoughts of you are warmest. . . . Do your novel, let us read it." By 1949, she'd written it.

Called *A Line from Eliot,* Hollywood and New York were its settings, furnished with rumpled sheets and whispered taboos involving extramarital affairs, impotence, frigidity, and a baby with Down syndrome who was relegated to an institution. Bob Linscott deemed the prose good and characters vivid, but felt Bubbles had *assembled* the novel rather than *written* it. Given her closeness to the master of the house, he was careful to provide a chapter-by-chapter analysis and pages of fixes. His boss agreed: "Bubbles has the ripe plums all right. What she needs is more of a tree on which to hang them!" But rather than wait for a second draft, he told Linscott to "give the kid a contract!" and ordered a $250 advance. *That* made it real, removing any whiff of vanity publishing.

Bubbles was elated, but also overwhelmed by the "drastic" changes Linscott wanted. Still, she worked at them, and when a new draft arrived, he wired that her work had paid off. (Linscott also knew he'd done as much as he could with the manuscript, and sent it on to production.) Re-christened *Memory and Desire,* part of the line from T. S. Eliot's *The*

Waste Land that she'd used as an epigraph, it now had a more obvious "selling" title, and instead of a photo, the jacket reproduced a painting of Bubbles done by her good friend Claudette Colbert. That, too, would generate talk.

Bennett had instructed his author to be her most seductive when appearing at sales conference the day after her book party. "Wiggle those hips," he urged, "then have lunch with us to prove to [the reps] that your wit and eloquence are just as irresistible as your exotic physical allure." She *was* exotic, and now bore a striking resemblance to the Sylvia of a decade earlier. The push for the book reached a climax in Los Angeles in early March, when three hundred guests ventured to the Beverly Hills Hotel to raise a glass to *Memory and Desire*. Everyone of importance in the book trade, stretching from San Francisco to San Diego, was on Bennett's two-hundred-person list, and he'd provided another two hundred invitations for Bubbles to send personally. "As long as we are doing all this, let's do it right," he told her, conjuring guests as though for a command performance.

Leonora Hornblow, all grown up

Booksellers, reviewers, and librarians downed cocktails, rubbing shoulders with Bogart, Bacall, and Jack Benny, metaphorically pinching themselves to be among such a glittering crowd. Bennett eased Bubs, in a little black dress, redder-than-red lipstick, and a glowing choker of pearls, around the room, introducing her to the critics and store owners, wanting her to charm them as she charmed him. In many respects, dark

Leonora and blue-eyed Phyllis made for a study in contrasts. While Thrup often had to diet, her friend stayed forever slim; while Bubbles's jet-black hair was piled high, Phyllis—having become too busy to fuss—had got herself shorn: practical, but rather matronly.

Reviews were respectable, and the book made a few bestseller lists. All that went into the publication of *Memory and Desire* was an outward affirmation of the closeness between these two couples. A private indication was the Cerfs' decision to designate the Hornblows as Chris and Jon's guardians, should the worst come to pass. In Leonora's long life, Bennett would be one of what she called her "sequoias," accomplished men who could be depended on when needed, appreciated her charms, and kept her amused. They in turn called on her good counsel, loyalty, and discretion. Also in this small forest were Ronald Reagan (she'd been a bridesmaid at his first wedding) and Frank Sinatra.

At one point, Leonora's relationship with "Blue," as she called Sinatra, tumbled beyond friendship into bed. Bennett, however, was the sequoia closest to her heart, and she was unique in his life. He loved her and could reveal himself to "Miss Twitter" (another pet name) as he did to no other woman—certainly not Phyllis. Leonora's son, Michael Hornblow, grew up to be a career diplomat, and chose his words carefully: if his mother hadn't been married to Arthur, and Bennett hadn't been married to Phyllis, Leonora and Bennett would in all probability have been married to each other. Yet somehow it all worked: Bennett's friendly relations with the older, dandyish Arthur Hornblow were seemingly never in doubt. That same March, he wrote Arthur—whom he nicknamed "Sir Tweedie" and "Tweedledum"—"You are the kind of friends a man dreams of having."

Occupied with his legions of friends, Bennett saw relatives on his own terms—for the most part, not often. Don had no such choice: he had responsibilities. When the nurse-companion who'd lived with his mentally ill sister for three decades retired, he had to move Elma to a Catholic facility in Westchester, where she'd live for the rest of her life. Don visited each week, year after year, just as he visited their mother almost daily. His and Marian's daughter, Lois, always looked to her father for help, and, as a young adult, very much needed his emotional support. His stepson, Tony Wimpfheimer, also depended on him. Tony, despite a warm heart and sense of humor, could be brusque and temperamental, in contrast to the stepfather he worshipped. He'd graduated from Williams and needed a start in the world. Don spoke to the Wolffs, longtime printers and binders of the ML, who agreed to grant a favor, but with no favoritism. Tony began at the bottom, worked hard, moved to Rutgers University Press, and would land in production at RH, where he'd remain for the rest of his career.

However, at this particular time, Don's family responsibilities extended further, to people he'd never met. In the late 1930s, the Salomons, middle-aged cousins of his mother, had like thousands of other Jews managed a last-ditch escape from Hitler's Germany to Shanghai, the only place that would take them. Now, a decade later, Dr. Salomon and his wife were caught in the end-stage Chinese Civil War. It fell to Don to help them come to America, and it wasn't easy. After Mao Zedong took power in October 1949, they and four hundred other Holocaust refugees spent ten weeks getting to a displaced persons camp in the Germany that they'd fled; if they wanted to go to North America, they had no other choice but to apply from there. Not until August 1951 was permission to emigrate granted, with the Klopfers as sponsors; the following month, Don stood at a New York dock, shepherding two strangers off a ship. Five years later, Dr. Salomon wrote again: now working at a hospital in New Jersey, he and his wife were about to become U.S. citizens. Yes, Donald replied, he'd be honored to be their witness.

. . .

IN 1949, THE RH partners had hired a new editor, handsome, thirty-one-year-old David McDowell, whom they viewed as something of a catch. His compass was, like Albert Erskine's, set in the South where he'd grown up. Just as Erskine had followed his professor Robert Penn Warren to several campuses, McDowell had followed his mentor, John Crowe Ransom—Warren's own teacher, as it happened—to Kenyon in Ohio. Like Warren, Ransom was a proponent of the Agrarian movement that idealized aspects of the antebellum South, and also a founder of the immensely influential "New Criticism" that argued for close reading of a text, unmediated by history or biography. McDowell had worked at the journal Ransom founded, the *Kenyon Review*—it had quickly become one of the leading "little" magazines—and had also published his own poetry and essays.

After wartime service and a stint in Europe, he'd returned to New York as U.S. editor of *transition,* the recently resurrected Paris-based avant-garde magazine of the 1920s and '30s. Like Erskine before him, he'd also joined New Directions, a small, cutting-edge publisher founded by steel-fortune scion James Laughlin. He arrived at RH having promised to bring William Carlos Williams and Paul Bowles from New Directions; Williams agreed to publish an autobiography at Random, followed by selected essays and two volumes of verse. Bowles's first novel, *The Sheltering Sky,* had made a literary and commercial splash for New Directions in 1949, and Bennett and McDowell met with Helen Strauss—Bowles was another client—and he came on board. In the next five years, Bowles published three books with RH, but went elsewhere after that; he'd later castigate Bennett as an architect of a "new sort of literary world" in which authors seeking success were supposed to sell themselves like carnival barkers. Having heard that on good authority from Truman Capote, Bowles pointed to him as a prime example of a writer who wasted time touting himself. He didn't seem to realize that Capote did so of his own accord, not requiring any push from his publisher.

Soon McDowell identified one more writer he wanted to sign, and in mid-April 1950, he and Bennett met with another powerful female agent, Bernice Baumgarten of Brandt & Brandt, who had the writer on her client list. "We have chance for WHITTAKER CHAMBERS autobiog," Bennett wrote in his diary, indicating that he knew this book could be big. Ten days elapsed, enough time to read sample material and, unusually, to seek opinions from a few friends. Later, Bennett recalled having asked Moss Hart, Robert Sherwood, and Laura Hobson to weigh in. When Chambers visited RH on April 24, Bennett discovered that he was also a Columbia man, three years younger; they had acquaintances in common. The diary recorded that RH would publish the book, *Witness,* followed the next day by another diary entry: "big excitement on Whittaker Chambers."

Politically, Chambers was a very controversial figure, and years later, when taping his oral history, Bennett put a dramatic spin on the visit that stood in stark contrast to the "big excitement" of the diary entry. When McDowell rose to fetch Chambers from reception and bring him up, Bennett recalled snapping at the editor, "Get that son of a bitch" out of the office. Soon he relented, and the meeting took place. The "drama" may have been an exaggerated or even false memory prompted by the tape recorder; however, even two decades later, the insecurity and ambivalence it revealed were true enough.

At that American moment, everyone knew who baggy-eyed, rumpled, heavyset Whittaker Chambers was. He'd been one of the best writer-editors on Henry Luce's *Time* magazine, but as a cooperating witness at the HUAC hearings in 1948—the first time that congressional hearings had been televised live—he admitted that he'd lied when previously denying he'd been a Communist and spy. The admission was prologue to denouncing his old friend Alger Hiss, a long-serving State Department mandarin who'd advised FDR, was a key figure in establishing the UN, and had recently left the government to preside over the Carnegie Endowment for International Peace. Now a deeply Christian conservative, Chambers had forfeited his career and standing to prove that his elegant friend, throughout his public service, had been a fellow Communist and spy. As evidence, he produced documents as well as microfilm that he'd briefly hidden inside a hollowed-out pumpkin on his farm in Maryland—the "Pumpkin Papers," they came to be called. Hiss claimed innocence and was tried, resulting in a hung jury. At a second trial, he was convicted in January 1950 of two counts of perjury. Three months later, Chambers walked into Bennett's office.

The imbroglio polarized the nation: many liberals believed that Hiss had been wrongfully convicted, and saw Chambers as radioactive, a Judas. Publicity from the hearings would later secure a Senate seat for HUAC committee member Richard Nixon, who'd pursued Hiss when others didn't want to believe Chambers. The ubiquitous coverage also emboldened the junior senator from Wisconsin, Joseph McCarthy, to seize his chance: waving a paper purportedly containing names of other Communists infesting the State Department, he hitched his fortune to rabid Red-hunting and a lawyer named Roy Cohn, and gave his name to one of the most shameful "isms" in American history.

Chambers's testimony and his own status as a perjurer had in many quarters made him a pariah. Through an autobiography, he hoped to explain his political and religious transformation to himself and his family, and offer it as a cautionary tale to the nation. He sought a mainstream house rather than one skewing right, understanding that it would lend a measure of credibility and help him reach as wide an audience as possible. Prior to Random, he'd shown material to Doubleday editor-in-chief Ken McCormick, who'd appreciated its power, but was firmly in the Hiss camp and couldn't stomach dealing with the author. Bennett had proclaimed his liberal bona fides in broadcasts, in columns, and in the books he published, but his new editor, McDowell, was a political conservative, and those circles were very interested in what Chambers had to say.

In a sense, the challenge Bennett faced in deciding whether to sign the book was a variation on the one he'd had over including Ezra Pound's poems in an anthology, but with a difference: after the sensational hearings and trials, and with Chambers's reputation as a writer, his book had a good shot at becoming a bestseller. Bennett later maintained that the friends who'd read the sample chapters had urged him to publish, but in the end, the decision was his. Baumgarten, the agent, had demanded a big advance—$15,000, since her client had lost his job—so it would be an expensive mistake if he got it wrong.

Chambers was a journalist used to tough deadlines, and to recoup the investment meant capitalizing on the trial publicity as soon as possible. The plan was for September delivery of the manuscript, only four months away. As soon as chapters came in, Don rushed them unedited to the typesetter; it would be more expensive, but McDowell would have to do his edits on the galley proofs. Justifying himself in a book took Chambers longer than anyone had anticipated, and it wasn't until right before Christmas 1951—more than a year later—that Bennett sat down to read the 627 galleys, and found himself utterly absorbed. Still, friends were giving him flak.

In mid-May 1952, he and Phyllis held a pre-publication dinner. Star attraction Chambers faced a star chamber of questioners, friends of Bennett like *Look* magazine publisher Mike Cowles and *This Week* editor Bill Nichols, but Hiss trial prosecutor Thomas Murphy was there to balance them out, and Bennett depended on Moss Hart's charm to overcome any awkwardness. He'd recall listening to Chambers and finally believed he was telling the truth. Decades later, when new documents surfaced, many historians agreed, but others still maintained that Hiss was innocent. The book was published in the kind of run reserved for John O'Hara: 100,000 copies. By then, *Witness* had been named BOMC's June selection, and Brandt & Brandt had auctioned first serial to *The Saturday Evening Post* for an amazing $75,000.

It didn't fail to deliver, as a bestseller and, as Chambers's biographer Sam Tanenhaus put it, "as the most heatedly debated" book of the era. Publication week, *The Saturday Review* splashed red ink against a cover drawing of Chambers as HUAC witness. Arthur M. Schlesinger Jr. wrote the review; John Dos Passos and Richard Nixon were among those furnishing commentary. "I don't think any book in recent history has gotten the critical attention accorded *Witness,*" Bennett told Chambers.

In June 1953, Bennett and Thrup climbed into their Cadillac convertible and set out on the six-hour drive to Westminster, Maryland, and the Chambers farm. Bennett wanted to see the famous pumpkin patch and talk about another book, provisionally titled *The Losing Side*. It was never finished; Chambers became so discouraged that he burned much of the manuscript. Bennett kept trying to cheer him along, but he'd never publish another book in his lifetime. His wife helped edit the posthumous collection *Cold Friday,* published in 1964 by Random House, three years after he died.

...

THE CENTURY'S MIDPOINT MARKED a milestone for Bennett and Don: twenty-five years since they'd bought the Modern Library and gone into business together. No matter it was two years before they began to publish new books "at random": the intention was there from the start, so 1950 was the year to celebrate their quarter century. Anniversaries are cause for reflection as well as jubilation, and the partners knew that to continue to flourish, RH, like any living organism, had to grow. Along with Lew Miller, they'd been scouting out acquisitions. Bennett tried to persuade Harold Guinzburg to sell him the Portable Library, a natural parallel to the ML; not surprisingly, Harold said no. They also talked with two fellows at Holt who wanted to start an RH college program in paperback; that didn't fly, either. Yet they needed a strategy to ensure the continued primacy of the ML, what *PW* called "the most reliable publishing property in the world." There were now 270 regular and 75 ML Giants; more than twenty million copies had been sold under their ownership. Among the top-ten regular bestsellers were Maugham's *Of Human Bondage,* Dostoyevsky's *The Brothers Karamazov,* Proust's *Swann's Way,* and two American novels, Lewis's *Arrowsmith* and Hemingway's *A Farewell to Arms*. Top-selling Giants included Tolstoy's *War and Peace,* Freud's *Basic Writings,* and Joyce's *Ulysses*. In the end, the partners chose to grow organically by creating Modern Library College Editions themselves: sixty-five-cent paperback versions of series books, starting with forty-one titles.

Just as important—if not more—was the publicity roll-out leading to a September launch for the new nonfiction children's series, Landmark Books, inspired by that argument Bennett had had with Chris. So much was riding on the would-be ML-for-the-nine-through-twelve-set. The American Booksellers Association had acknowledged his unique place within the industry by asking Bennett to emcee the ABA's own fiftieth anniversary party at their convention in June; he used the occasion to squeeze in a personal introduction to Landmarks. The crowd was enthusiastic, but no one had quite anticipated how the public would react: as soon as the series hit shelves at the start of the school year, parents rushed to buy all ten titles, and kids adored them. Boys, far more reluctant readers than girls, suddenly found true-life stories to fire their imaginations. By early October, virtually the entire 200,000-copy first run had been sold, and the series was being favorably reviewed all over the country. RH's campaign didn't let up.

"Gosh, it's exciting to be an American!" headlined a photo of a boy happily lost in the world of the Pony Express and other historical scenes in a *New York Times Book Review* ad. "As an antidote to the comics craze—as an incentive to learning—as sheer enjoyment," the ad promised, Landmark "should solve the problems" of parents and kids "wrestling with report cards." The logo planted the Washington Monument, a picket fence, and leafy trees beside the RH colophon. At a time when the country was worrying about the Korean War, the Cold War, and the Red Scare, could anything be more patriotic?

The Pony Express book by Samuel Hopkins Adams—Bennett had known him since the Liveright days, when Adams was a respectable novelist and, as "Warner Fabian," author of successful erotica—turned out to be one of the most popular titles. Given that Adams would turn eighty the next year, he'd chosen to take his payment as a lump sum up front. When Bennett saw how much more his old friend would have made had he opted for a royalty, he tore up the contract and gave him the percentage, even though it wasn't in RH's financial interest. Ultimately, it paid off for everyone: Adams would write two more Landmarks. Although Bennett had a deserved reputation for carefulness with money, and could even be money-mean, especially if he took against an author, as he had with Nathanael West—or in a few other glaring cases, like Sylvia Beach—he could also be impetuously generous, and believed in fair play. Rewriting Adams's deal was the right thing to do. All three partners shared that sense of decency and fair play: it was part of the glue holding these very different men, and the happy place they created, together.

The Landmark success went well beyond Bennett's or Louise Bonino's dreams. By 1951, rights to create recorded versions of the books for schools had been granted to a connection Bennett had made on his war bond tours, and filmstrips followed. Soon RH licensed rights for exclusive school versions, and Bonino began a parallel World Landmarks series. In 1953, BOMC started a "Young Readers of America" club with Landmarks as the exclusive selections; by 1956, it had sold more than two million copies. Certain Landmarks traveled onto foreign shores: Quent Reynolds's book about the Wright Brothers was translated into Hebrew, Japanese, Serbian, Vietnamese, Bengali, and other tongues. Ninety-seven titles had been published by 1956, and six million copies sold. Bonino credited Lew Miller as the "genius" who'd envisaged the scope of what could be done. The series also proved crucial to establishing RH as an innovative children's publisher, laying the groundwork for all that would follow once a mischievous cat appeared under Ted Geisel's hat in 1957, and changed children's publishing forever.

While the partners had been busy investing in series, they hadn't neglected the individual titles of the trade list: much of the anniversary publicity focused there. A release went out thanking editors, reviewers, and columnists for helping to make RH books known, and asserting that the latest group was the "most distinguished" ever, adding: "It is through his lists that a publisher speaks best." Most distinguished? It *was* a press release. But the list did include Robert Penn Warren's first RH novel, *World Enough and Time;* Budd Schulberg's *The Disenchanted,* a thinly veiled roman à clef about Scott Fitzgerald (a Book-of-the-Month); Pierre La Mure's *Moulin Rouge,* a fictionalized biography of Toulouse-Lautrec with film potential; MacKinlay Kantor's first RH novel, *Signal Thirty-Two;* and collections from Paul Bowles, Irwin Shaw, and William Faulkner.

In October, *PW* filled five pages with an RH anniversary retrospective. "It is sometimes hard for the uninformed to realize that there is more to Random House than Bennett Cerf," the magazine teased, adding that his myriad activities led some to conclude that he "neglected" his publishing work. "That is not true," *PW* countered. *The Saturday Review* also did right by its Trade Winds gadfly, inviting Dick Simon to be substitute columnist for a week, to take the measure of RH and its founders. In "Try and Stop Them," a witty four-page tribute, Dick declared that even after all these years, one of Bennett's charms was to have remained "a man of complete candor," while Don, once roving center in a book boys' football game, remained "the roving center" at Random. Both articles detailed similar touchstones: the ML; Meynell; O'Neill and the playwrights who followed; *Ulysses;* merging with Bob Haas; the dictionary; the editors; and the "mighty" Lew Miller, who "put things on a real business basis." Dick singled out bespectacled, bow-tied treasurer Manny Harper, "a man most people don't hear about," as key from the start, and revealed that Manny, Saxe, Miller, Linscott, Maule, Louise Bonino, and Ray Freiman together owned about 20 percent of the firm's common stock. RH was now one of the great houses, he concluded, made so by his friend and rival's "extraordinary ability and energy," but also by his genius in joining with others. Bennett couldn't have created better publicity if he'd written the pieces himself.

At year's end, egged on by their boy president, the gentlemen of RH agreed to try an innovative anniversary experiment: publication of Joseph Mankiewicz's film script for the hit movie *All About Eve,* along with a foreword from Mankiewicz. After watching a preview, Danny Kaye's wife, Sylvia, had hatched the idea and suggested it to Bennett. It was no big risk for a man who knew the economics of publishing plays. Besides, he saw it as a tribute to a brilliant cinematic dramatist and, not to be overlooked, friend. Nobody would get rich publishing it, but Bennett fancied growing "an aristocracy of screenwriters—not just the ones who get arty reviews . . . but the ones who write the smash hits." The notion of "aristocracy" might sit uneasily next to "smash hits," but he was speaking from instincts that made others liken him to a theater impresario or studio boss. Appreciating quality *and* popularity, he put great effort into *popularizing*. Decades later, a screenplay or shooting script occasionally makes its way onto a trade publisher's list.

. . .

THE ANNIVERSARY YEAR WAS winding down when on the first Friday in November, Bennett scribbled an exciting possibility in his diary: "Faulkner to get Nobel Prize?" Devourer of news that he was, he'd gotten wind of an Associated Press wire story out of Stockholm. Whispers joining the prize to the author's name had been in the air for a few years, as Faulkner well knew; he'd referenced them that February to Joan Williams, Memphis native and pretty Bard College student who'd won the *Mademoiselle* fiction contest the year before. Having engaged a reluctant Williams in a romance, he'd admitted to her that it would be a "gratuitous insult" to decline the Nobel, "but I don't want it."

The day after the AP story, United Press International followed suit. In 1949, the Swedish Academy had chosen not to award a literature Nobel. Now, UPI said, the Academy would make up for it by voting on two prizes, one for 1949, and one for 1950. Early on the morning of Friday, November 10, Faulkner received a call from New York–based Swedish journalist Sven Ahman, who told him that he'd won for 1949, for what the Academy cited as his "powerful and independent artistic contribution in America's new literature of the novel." British philosopher Bertrand Russell was to receive the 1950 award. However, when Ahman asked if he was looking forward to coming to Stockholm, Faulkner replied that there was too much work on the farm; he couldn't make the trip. In the early afternoon, once official word had finally arrived, long-distance lines were so jammed that Bob Haas couldn't get through on behalf of RH, and had to resort to a wire and letter. It was "absolutely the most heartwarming news . . . since God knows when," Bob wrote. Refusing to parrot banalities, he added: "I think you know well enough how I feel and . . . have felt ever since I read you and knew you."

For a man who hated intrusions into his routine, Faulkner found the unfamiliar spotlight exceedingly uncomfortable. After the news broke, he escaped by going hunting for six days, but pressure was building from family, friends, the State Department, and the Swedes to accept the prize and deliver the customary address in person. Once back at Rowan Oak, it became obvious that he was reacting to the pressure with a binge, soon compounded by a terrible cold that seemed close to pneumonia. In the long, strange, tragic symbiosis of William and Estelle Faulkner, both were frustrated, sensitive people who could neither bring each other happiness nor sunder the tie. Alcohol was an intermediary each used to get through life; Estelle often found it easier to deal with her husband when he was drunk. Now, seizing the moment and using seventeen-year-old daughter Jill as excuse—how could he deprive her of the chance to go to Europe with her Pappy?—Estelle overcame his reluctance. On November 27, he agreed that he and Jill would go to Stockholm.

Faulkner continued to drink and refuse to eat unless food was accompanied by alcohol, but Estelle spaced out the bourbon to effect a kind of withdrawal. He'd leave Mississippi for New York on December 6, a Wednesday, and depart for Europe on Friday. In the days between agreeing to go and going, practical matters had to be tackled, and naturally, the Faulkners turned to Random House. He needed white tie and tails for the ceremony; Estelle dictated his measurements to Saxe, who was to hire formal attire. The Haases would host a dinner on Wednesday, and the Cerfs on Thursday, both in celebration and as insurance policy: that way, they could keep an eye on his drinking.

Of far greater import, an acceptance speech had to be written. Joseph Blotner, the first Faulkner biographer, held that even in withdrawal and unable to hold a pencil or use a typewriter, Faulkner began dictating notes to his stepdaughter's husband. Yet according to Commins family lore, Saxe—either while Faulkner was in Mississippi, or during his stay in New York—helped on one of the most famous Nobel speeches ever given.

Saxe told his then eighteen-year-old son Eugene that he'd "ghost-written the first draft." Years later, Eugene's older sister, Frances, made the same assertion: "He did the first draft . . . [while] Faulkner was drying out." Betty Ballantine, widow of Saxe's nephew Ian and co-founder of Ballantine Books, agreed: Saxe "wrote that speech."

Under normal circumstances, he knew better than to attempt such a thing; Faulkner rarely brooked interference in his text. But circumstances weren't normal: the bingeing, the bad infection, the looming deadline. It's not unreasonable to believe that Saxe helped draft it. According to Blotner the speech evolved, changing considerably as it went through drafts, some written on Hotel Algonquin stationery and saved from the wastebasket by a butler at the American embassy in Stockholm, where Faulkner dictated the final version. As delivered, there are foreshortened but clear echoes of Gavin Stevens's philosophizing toward the end of *Intruder in the Dust,* as well as ideas linked to *A Fable,* the novel Faulkner had been struggling over for years. Better than anyone apart from their author, Saxe would have known both books. In this hour of need, he may well have plucked passages from each to assemble the skeleton of a speech.

On December 6, obviously unwell and unshaven, Faulkner flew to New York with Jill. The Haases met the plane and brought them to the Algonquin. Merle worried about how sick Faulkner looked, and he did nothing to allay concern by asking if she could get him antibiotics. She phoned her doctor, who said she could give the antibiotics so long as Faulkner did not drink. That evening, at the Haas family's Park Avenue home, Merle and her pilot daughter Betty, along with Dorothy Commins, made sure that Jill, who bore an uncanny likeness to her father, felt welcome. Bill's concession to doctor's orders was to mix Jack Daniels with water. Malcolm Cowley was among the guests and noticed how tense he appeared, screwing up inner reserves to survive the trip ahead. But though they got through the first night, the next morning Bob took one look when father and daughter arrived at RH and called Merle. Faulkner had a 102-degree fever. This time, he went to see Merle's doctor, who recognized a case of "la grippe" and another of nerves. He'd have to make do with as much rest as he could get and some penicillin.

That evening, the Cerfs had invited a crowd to Sixty-Second Street, among them the Haases, Klopfers, John O'Haras, critic Harvey Breit, Herbert and Glen, and Carol Brandt, story editor at MGM, who'd bought the film rights of *Intruder in the Dust* and made Faulkner financially stable. O'Hara was drinking heavily: the state in which he was most sensitive to any fancied slight, most capable of bullying, and most inclined to stick his chest out and assert his own primacy. Breit had known him to call Fitzgerald the greatest American writer in the past; only a few months earlier, O'Hara had transferred that title to Hemingway. Now he rose to address the crowd and make the grandest of grand gestures while the bile rumbled in his gut: Faulkner was "our only living genius," he proclaimed. It seemed to some in the room that he desperately wanted Faulkner to flatter him back, to call him equal in spite of the Nobel, but Faulkner didn't. In fact, Faulkner would later confide to a friend that O'Hara was a mere "Rutgers Scott Fitzgerald."

Coming to the end of his remarks, O'Hara—who set such store by expensive symbols—produced his own lighter, a gift from the father whom he'd had such a tortured relationship with, and offered it to the man who'd won the prize he coveted. Faulkner could not have known that the little lighter carried such meaning; nor could O'Hara have realized how unwell Faulkner was. The recipient of the gift uttered a simple "Thank you" and O'Hara's imagined moment of dramatic reciprocity fizzled into silence. Later, when Faulkner tried to use the gift, he couldn't get the damned thing to light; Breit had to show him how. O'Hara had simmered all the while, and now Donald saw his face flush as he called to Belle, told her they were going, and stormed out. Soon after, Faulkner left for the Algonquin. The next morning, Bennett, Don, and Saxe drove the Faulkners to Idlewild Airport. They'd fulfilled their charge—for the moment.

In Stockholm, Faulkner worked on the speech while he and Jill stayed at the American ambassador's residence. The other three U.S. laureates weren't looked after quite so carefully—they slept in hotels. There were interviews, sightseeing, dinners, and a meeting with Else Jonsson—widow of the journalist who four years earlier had predicted that one day he'd receive the Nobel.

On Sunday, December 10, King Gustaf Adolf presented the award. Faulkner looked the fine gentleman, terribly handsome in the tails that Saxe had rented, but when he got up to deliver the address, he stood too far from the microphone. That distance, compounded by his accent, quiet voice, and nerves, made him almost impossible to hear. Two days later he and Jill left for Paris, where, upended by the journey, the excitement, the demands and anxiety of caring for her father, Jill fell victim to the flu in turn. They traveled to London, then Ireland, the normal stopover, before they finally crossed the Atlantic and reached New York, where Saxe and Dorothy ministered to the girl.

Exactly one week after receiving his award, Faulkner and Jill, feeling better, went with Bennett, Phyllis, and Bubbles to Radio City to see the famous Christmas show, then backstage to admire the Rockettes, and later to Toots Shor's for a steak dinner. They ended the evening at the Algonquin, since Bennett was dying to inspect the Nobel "loot." One bit of loot that had traveled from New York to Sweden and back Bill planned to keep: the dress suit. But as Bob Linscott informed Truman Capote in a gossipy letter, the very particular Mr. Faulkner voiced a complaint: the trousers Saxe had rented had one satin stripe down the side of each leg; in Stockholm, he realized there should have been two. Faulkner would buy the monkey suit provided he got his money's worth: the tailor had to sew on a second set of stripes. (He did.)

Two days after Christmas, Faulkner wrote to Merle from Mississippi, saying that "Missy"—his name for Jill—was still trying to sift through all the experiences. Going to Stockholm, he realized, had been his only choice; not going would have been more than a mistake, it would have been in "bad taste," and therefore shameful. Instead, he'd tried to leave the Swedes with the "best taste possible" for his country and his publisher. In closing, he asked Merle to accept the seasonal wishes "which are not seasonal from me to you . . . they are constant." The courtly politeness, mix of genius-toughness-vulnerability, and the scope of his vision were recognized by all the RH partners and their wives. Bennett thought Faulkner "one of the most impressive men" he ever met. And despite ups and downs, Bill had declared to Bob a year earlier: "I have been so amazingly fortunate in publishers and agents."

In big display ads in *The New York Times* and *Herald Tribune,* RH announced Faulkner's Nobel win, noting the availability of his most recent book, the *Collected Stories,* and—in ML editions—*Sanctuary, Light in August,* and the single volume containing *The Sound and the Fury* and *As I Lay Dying* (the last three all back in print courtesy of attention generated by the *Portable* and *Intruder in the Dust*). All his other novels and collections were still unavailable. That would finally be corrected, thanks to the Nobel: indeed, *Absalom, Absalom!* would be recalled to active life in January. In March 1951, Donald also arranged for a chapbook of the Nobel address to be published in 3,500 copies, beautifully printed by the Spiral Press, for friends of Random and Spiral.

Although practically inaudible when spoken, as soon as the speech was printed in newspapers, it reverberated around the world. Faulkner began by insisting that the prize was not made to him as an individual, but to the life's work done "in the agony and sweat of the human spirit . . . to create . . . something which did not exist before." He conjured the overwhelming fear of the day, of nuclear annihilation and nothingness, but declared that it was the "problems of the human heart in conflict with itself" that alone were worth writing about. Insisting that he would not accept the end of man, he continued: "It is easy enough to say that man is immortal simply because he will endure. . . . I believe that man will not merely endure; he will prevail."

Nobel laureate

As readers of *Intruder* knew, he had chosen as one embodiment of that transcendent force an old Black man: Lucas Beauchamp had not only endured, but prevailed. The speech proclaimed it was the poet's duty—Faulkner, who began as a writer of poetry, essentially thought of his art as such—"to write about these things," because, finally, the poet's voice needn't merely record, but could be a "pillar" to help man "endure and prevail." With no small amount of practical help from the gentlemen of Random House, Bill Faulkner had done just that—and then some.

Chapter 24

What's *Not* His Line?

Bennett celebrated 1950 as Random House's quarter century, but, as he did most years now, lamented May 25 as "poor old Cerf's" (fifty-second) birthday. He didn't appreciate the thinning of his thatch or the acceleration in its color change; before parties, now, he sometimes asked Thrup to "mascara" his gray locks, and within a few years would undergo private hair treatments both at home and in the office. He also loathed getting "too damn much tummy," and on some days sacrificed lunch entirely. When the weather cooperated, he played hard at tennis and swimming to keep the silhouette trim.

For the summer, Phyllis decided to rent two contiguous Provincetown cottages. She brought the kids up in June, but unlike most wives, didn't stay. She'd explained to Bubbles years earlier that, faced with letting Bennett go on his own when she didn't feel like traveling, or accompanying him and putting up with it, she made the only choice she could: she went with. Now, because he had to remain at RH until August, she went back, leaving the boys with nanny Margaret. She'd make a few lightning visits to see them, but for weeks at a time would be in New York. Phyllis was well aware that her husband flirted with anything in a skirt, while Bennett understood that when she was near, he had to be careful around the ladies: his wife had "eyes in the back of her head." Yet she was fine about his solo trip that June: he'd been invited to the Joint Civilian Orientation Conference organized by the secretary of defense, a propaganda effort meant to ally opinion makers with the priorities of the American military. Never having seen active service, he was delighted by the prospect of hobnobbing with generals and CEOs.

The group convened on June 18 at the Pentagon and traveled to bases in Georgia and Florida, where Bennett was more supercharged than ever at the prospect of going up in a jet plane: commercial jet flights wouldn't begin for two years. Equally excited, he boarded the carrier *Midway* in Virginia, and it was at sea on the *Midway* that he awoke on June 26 to news that North Korea had attacked the South. Flown home in a military transport the next day, he headed straight for the office: part of the thrill of an experience lay in the telling of it. He soon discovered that all RH was frightened about the war.

Home meant back to routine: he had to produce a Trade Winds for July 15 in a hurry. "Hated every minute of it," he complained to his diary, an unusual sour note. Most years he'd go away for a month and easily resume the life he loved, but at that moment he felt "out of whack" writing a mere magazine piece, an echo of how he'd felt when Don marched off to war without him. Luckily, just after joining the family in Provincetown at the beginning of August, Bennett received a call that cheered him up.

William Ichabod "Bill" Nichols was editor of *This Week,* one of two color supplements—*Parade* was the other—that vied for syndication in the nation's Sunday papers. *This Week*'s circulation was nearly eleven million copies through twenty-eight papers, including the *New York Herald Tribune, Los Angeles Times,* and *San Francisco Chronicle.* To solve a production problem on one particular page, Nichols had to find a new weekly feature. It needed to be predictable and reliable, to complement certain kinds of ads, while also inviting readers' participation from time to time. Bennett's name had surfaced as a possible solution: with the authority of Random House and *The Saturday Review* behind him, he had entrée just about anywhere, and the joke books, Try and Stop Me column, radio stints, and lectures showed him to be friendly, funny, and popular.

Nichols offered a half-page column at $350 per week ($250 plus $100 maximum in expenses), an eye-popping amount. Several months earlier, Bennett had successfully argued Norman Cousins into raising his Trade Winds pay to $125 a week, increasing to $150 in 1951. Nichols promised more than twice that, and Bennett knew expenses were fungible. Phyllis was against taking it on: his perpetual motion already put everyone and everything into a constant spin. He, however, found the idea and the money irresistible, and spent the next weekend holed up, writing three sample columns. They passed muster, and in late September he signed to do thirteen trial weeks of what he called "Cerfboard," with a clause specifying automatic renewal if all went well. It would differ from Trade Winds in three ways: not being centered on the book business; focusing on a single theme each week, such as back-to-school or Christmas; and catering to a mass audience who often didn't put books near the center of their lives.

the Cerf board

GETTING OUT THE VOTE

To most Americans, Election Day provides a proof of the democratic system, an opportunity to feel we are playing an active role in the making of history. To one woman serving a life sentence in an upstate penitentiary, however, Election Day will always bring back rueful memories.

GUILTY! In 1948, about the hour poll experts were first beginning to interpret and laugh off President Truman's lead over Tom Dewey, the battered body of this woman's husband was discovered at the bottom of a steep flight of steps outside her apartment. Apprised of her loss, she affected shock and surprise, and said, "I begged him not to go back to that corner saloon but he paid no attention to me. When he came home drunk, I ordered him out. He must have tripped on the stairs, and the Lord have mercy on his soul."

Without hesitation, the investigating officer ordered, "Lock her up." What the pious lady had forgotten was that on every Election Day saloons are closed tight until the polls are closed.

FRAUD. The commissioner of elections in a town in the Deep South opened the ballot box at the close of the balloting and was flabbergasted to find a Republican vote near the top. It was an unprecedented situation, and he equivocated, "Hold this vote aside till we finish counting, boys. We'll decide what to do about it then." At the bottom of the box another Republican vote turned up. That made everything simple. "Some double-barreled crook in this town has voted twice," bellowed the commissioner. "Throw his two ballots out!"

INFLATION. William Jennings Bryan, who held a record for unsuccessful presidential tries that only Norman Thomas could shatter, made a ringing speech against the vested interests when he was a young man in Lincoln, Neb.

"It's a safe bet," he declared, "that any man who's piled up a million dollars or more for himself is probably an enemy of the people."

The years passed and Mr. Bryan prospered in his private affairs. He returned to Lincoln a man of means.

A reporter reminded him of his earlier speech and asked slyly, "Do you still feel the way you did about rich men?"

"Indeed I do," boomed Bryan. "As I said, any man who's piled up two million dollars or more for himself is probably an enemy of the people."

DOUBLE CROSS. In a hotly contested local election in Iowa, the Republican candidate ostentatiously refused to sling mud at his opponent. "Such tactics are beneath me," he proclaimed. "I will only say that he sailed from New York to Southampton and back last summer aboard the *America* and never washed once—which strikes me as the perfect example of a dirty double-crosser."

PROJECT. A Texas Democrat had successfully campaigned for a seat in the House of Representatives. To show his appreciation, he promptly introduced a bill to finance the widening of Trinity River back home. A Republican congressman from up north jumped to his feet in indignation.

"What can the government do for a piddling trickle like the Trinity?" he demanded. "Why, I can spit halfway across it." The Speaker of the House banged with his gavel and cried, "You're out of order." "You're damn right, I'm out of order," agreed the Republican. "If I was in order, I could spit all the way across it."

COURT JESTER. George E. Allen, the White House jester, has told a host of hilarious anecdotes about Washington bigwigs in his just-published "Presidents Who Have Known Me." Early in his career, Allen decided he'd rather be bright than be President. This policy has paid off. They do the worrying; he supplies the laughs.

LAST WORD. Allen says he but carries on the tradition of his father, who practiced law, politics and diplomacy in Booneville, Miss. One day a magistrate had the nerve to decide a case *against* Allen, senior. The latter waved a volume of Blackstone under the justice's nose in outrage. "Sit down," the judge shouted. "I know the law." "Of course you do," said Mr. Allen. "I just wanted to read this to show you what a damn fool Blackstone was."

Bennett Cerf

Mr. Cerf's column will appear regularly in future issues of THIS WEEK Magazine

The first "Cerfboard"

His debut was on November 5, with Election Day as the theme. Bennett covered the bases: a story about a woman who murdered her husband on polling day; a case of voting fraud in the Deep South; a humorous history lesson about a perennially unsuccessful presidential candidate. Most readers liked Cerfboard well enough. When a Phoenix newspaper executive complained that a column about Bennett's friend Stanley Marcus was a blatant plug for the Dallas department store, Nichols countered that Bennett brought such a rare mix of qualities, he wouldn't know where to look for a replacement. Besides, the "Starch rating"—measuring how much readers noticed ads on the page—had risen steadily.

Once established, Cerfboard's parameters became more flexible. For some issues, Bennett asked readers to send in jokes or puns; they loved seeing their names in print, as well as the ten dollars *This Week* paid for what he used. As for Bennett's own compensation, Nichols soon discovered what he politely described as his columnist's "very great diligence and carefulness" in money matters: he always wanted more. A year after Cerfboard's debut, the per-column fee increased to six hundred dollars and the expense ceiling to two hundred, more than doubling his pay. A half-page piece dashed off on part of a weekend earned more than most men made for a full workweek. Cerfboard, Trade Winds, the syndicated Try and Stop Me jokes—daily and weekly, columns upon columns bore his byline.

Over the next decade, Nichols came to know Bennett well, so well that when he deposited his papers at the Library of Congress in the late 1960s, he specified that this particular columnist was "so sensitive to comment of any kind" that documents related to Bennett had to be held in confidence and not released to any researcher without Nichols's express permission. Norman Cousins and others at *The Saturday Review* were acquainted with that same "sensitivity." Bennett had battled with the *SRL* concerning his copy so vociferously that it was finally agreed: if a staffer wanted to make a change and Bennett couldn't be found, it was "strictly" understood that his text was "to be printed . . . without any alteration"—this despite his occasionally needing to be saved from himself. As elsewhere, he could be too quick to spin a story rather than hew to facts, and the competitor in him wanted to be first with news, even if it meant blurting onto the page a tidbit he'd heard in confidence. At such times, he and his editors twisted uncomfortably over complaining letters that arrived singly or—after a really bad gaffe—in droves.

Like most people who worked closely with him, Nichols came to discover the childlike naivete and sentimentality that seemed so surprising from a man in Bennett's position, yet Nichols chose to emphasize the "incredible vitality" and "irrepresible [*sic*] good humor." Though the times might change, the value that Americans place on "laughter and optimism"—what Nichols identified as Bennett's "stock in trade"—does not waver. The ability to bring a smile and hope to fellow citizens made Bennett Cerf, in Nichols's estimation, "a uniquely American success story."

In early October, another interesting call came through. Mark Goodson, who along with Bill Todman produced television game shows, invited Bennett to lunch at his office on the seventh floor of the CBS Building, one block north of the palazzo. Goodson had heard that he was a good game player. When Bennett arrived, he was met by an immaculately groomed, beautifully dressed fellow in his mid-thirties, whose demeanor was Madison Avenue sleek, but serious and watchful. Goodson was short on time, and quickly got to the point: he and Todman needed a substitute for comedian Hal Block, one of the regular panelists on a show called *What's My Line?* The program would air live at 10:30 P.M. that Sunday night—only four days away. *What's My Line?* had been broadcast since February, but had moved to the Sunday night slot and gone weekly ten days earlier. Like television itself, the show was a new thing and had to prove its worth. Audience researchers had predicted that the timing was off: Who'd want to watch TV late on a Sunday night, with the workweek just ahead? The producers would soon find out.

Goodson, born poor in California, had a Berkeley Phi Beta Kappa key to match Bennett's from Columbia. In 1941, he'd begun collaborating with the equally well-tailored Todman in radio production, but in many ways they were opposites, the quick-tempered Californian a worrier and perfectionist workaholic, and Todman an extroverted New York native from a well-connected family, whose exuberance would more and more be fueled by alcohol. Goodson proceeded to outline for Bennett how *What's My Line?* was played. Each week, a series of contestants would appear before four panelists, who questioned them to guess each person's occupation; the contestant's role was to stump the panel. Besides Block, the man he'd substitute for, the team included actress Arlene Francis; Hearst syndicated columnist Dorothy Kilgallen, the *New York Journal-American*'s "Voice of Broadway"; and Louis Untermeyer, a poet, anthologist, critic, and, like Bennett, inveterate punster. Goodson and Todman had cast the show with "types," who had to complement and play off each other, their "chemistry" essential for success.

Arlene was the delightful, flirty, intuitive female, whose formidable brain and ambition lay disguised behind a warmth and charm as integral to her screen presence as the thick pancake makeup. Like Bennett, she made it all look so easy. The two would "hit it off perfectly": along with millions of Americans, Bennett would love Arlene.

Dorothy, at certain unflattering angles rather short on chin, was lace-curtain Irish, trailing the pedigree of a legendary Hearst newspaperman father. Cool and feline, she was carefully coiffed and dressed as the glamorous Park Avenue lady. Although Bennett would find that "personally, Dorothy was very nice," he knew she could be plenty "catty" in columns, as sharp-witted and -clawed as any woman scrabbling to succeed in a man's world. The kind of female some viewers loved to hate, popular for being unpopular, Dorothy played nakedly to win. Off camera, she diverged from most associates on the show in supporting HUAC's investigations—but then, she toed the Hearst political line.

Hal was the rubbery-faced comic, and Louis the witty egghead.

The other key on-screen presence was master of ceremonies John Charles Daly, a stickler for correct language who preferred to call himself "the moderator." Now in his mid-thirties, the Johannesburg-born newsman had covered the White House and been a foreign correspondent for CBS during the war. His had been the first radio voice to announce the news about the attack on Pearl Harbor and, four years later, about FDR's death. Once dubbed "the poor man's Edward R. Murrow," his talents were valuable enough that, within a few years, he'd simultaneously anchor the ABC-TV evening news, emcee *What's My Line?* for CBS, and appear on other programs as well. His distinctively accented, utterly clear diction projected an air of cultivation and control. Goodson and Todman had picked him for his dignity—but also because he could ad-lib. Yet Daly thought of himself first, last, and always as a newsman, just as five-lived Bennett would always be a publisher.

The show began with the panel seated; when viewers complained that they couldn't get a good look at the women's evening dresses, the routine changed: panelists walked in and then sat down. The game was structured so the studio and home audiences were, along with the emcee, privy to a contestant's occupation. Each round would begin with Daly providing a general hint—the person was salaried, or dealt in a service or product—and then he'd call on a panelist to ask the first question.

Has your product ever been alive? Could I hold it in my hand? Is it used by both sexes? Is it used in the house? Do you work in an office? Do people come to you? Do you make them look better? Only *yes* or *no* answers were allowed. One memorable night, comedian Steve Allen, a frequent guest panelist and the original host of the *Tonight Show,* posed a question to establish a product's size: *Is it bigger than a breadbox?* The question became a show standard, and soon entered the American lexicon.

If the contestant answered *yes,* that panelist would continue questioning until a *no* put an end to the privilege. With every *no,* the contestant won five dollars and the next panelist took over the interrogation. When a contestant accumulated ten negative replies, he or she would have gained fifty dollars—enough, say, to put a 20 percent deposit down on a TV set—and won the game. At that point, Daly revealed all to the panel. At times, play ended long before then with a panelist guessing triumphantly. Often someone guessed but got it wrong, and the mistake was played for laughs. In the eight months since the show's debut, they'd learned two things: the game must not lag, and laughter was its necessary corollary.

After two rounds of "regular" citizens—everyone from the hatcheck girl at the Stork, the very first contestant on the very first show, to a bank president, golf caddy, female (!) housepainter, or female (!!) bartender—the third round featured a "mystery guest" from radio, movies, theater, politics, sports, music, or even the literary world, who was paid for adding a frisson of star power. Indeed, one reason the program had moved to 10:30 P.M. Sunday was to allow a Broadway notable whose play ended around 10:00 to scurry over to the studio from the theater and put in a mystery appearance, plugging his or her show, of course. The plug was what made it worthwhile for the star, and what kept costs down for the game show producers. As the panelists donned blindfolds, Daly would summon the mystery guest by declaring: "Come and sign in, please"—later, "Enter" would replace "Come," and that phrase, like the breadbox question, would turn into a meme. To the sound of applause, the camera would zoom in on the guest scrawling his or her signature onto a chalkboard, and when play began and the guest replied using a disguised voice and often mugging for the camera, the audience loved it.

Everyone in the studio and at home looked forward to the mystery segment. Yet, with success and longevity, it was the regular panel and its moderator in their tuxedos and gowns who were the real draw. *They* were the "Sunday night royalty" of an idealized New York, a town of twinkling skyscrapers and Broadway marquees lit up against a darkening sky. Through the magic of a flickering black-and-white screen, they entered America's homes each week, as real and familiar as family but shining with celebrity's glow. The half hour at weekend's close would become part of America's routine, "a parlor game for the nation" that, as one TV executive described it, was also "the nation's Valium," a palliative for Sunday-night jitters as Americans faced the workweek ahead.

Of the regulars, the panelist whom Bennett would replace that week was in many ways odd man out. A Chicago comic, Hal Block was the sort of fellow who'd play dumb and tell a nun she was pretty, or "accidentally" let slip a risqué joke. He paid little heed to Daly, who could pull on his earlobe as much as he pleased—the emcee's sign that a panelist was straying into dangerous or vulgar territory. Untermeyer, Kilgallen, and Francis, by contrast, all conveyed an unmistakable air of Manhattan sophistication. They used four-syllable words, had excellent diction, processed information quickly, and gave it back fast in witty repartee—the signal characteristic of the show—appealing to the upper middle class and affluent who, in the early 1950s, owned most of America's TV sets.

Dorothy Kilgallen, Fred Allen, Arlene Francis,
John Daly (standing), and Bennett circa 1955
when Remington was a sponsor

Having passed his own midcentury, it was reassuring to Bennett that the regulars weren't especially handsome, beautiful, or young, and all looked their age: Block and Kilgallen both thirty-seven; Francis almost forty-three; Untermeyer an avuncular sixty-five. Daly, at thirty-six, was the baby, but also the authoritative fulcrum of the show. The aim of *What's My Line?* was to seem like a private game being played by an intimate group of worldly friends, but an audience *was* watching—and so was a sponsor, who wanted to get his money's worth. In 1950, networks had to fill a quota of hours whether there was sponsorship or not; it was in fact a mark of distinction to be a commercial program. In this case, the show had to satisfy the demands of Dr. Jules Montenier, a chemist whose patented "Stopette" underarm deodorant made the whole thing possible.

A courtly man, Montenier was shown in the opening commercial in lab coat amid test tubes, a chemist whose steaming potion was meant to address a universal human problem. By the third spot, at show's end, viewers knew the tag line: *Poof! There goes perspiration!* Bennett would later say, "He was a sweet man, but a bit of a fraud." No matter: for the next eight years, the audience learned to associate the well-dressed "class" of *What's My Line?* with body deodorant. However, when Hal Block quipped on air, "Make your armpit a charmpit!" the illusion was breeched, infuriating the others. In 1953, he'd be fired and replaced by the far more sophisticated, witty young writer-comedian-composer-pianist Steve Allen.

Personality, intelligence, and *how* you broke down a series of questions were what mattered. *What's My Line?* had to *look* light, but playing it well was surprisingly hard. Bennett adored any new gadget with the delight of a five-year-old; TV was no exception. He'd been introduced to the marvel at the World's Fair, and for Christmas 1948 brought home an RCA set, signaling to his diary its importance with block capitals. The next year, he'd installed one in his office. Gossip ran up and down the palazzo—*A TV?* He shrugged off any discomfiture. But of course, he didn't simply want to watch, he wanted to be on it. As early as 1946, when there were only six thousand sets in the United States, all in the New York area, he'd been on the CBS "tele-quiz" *See What You Know.*

Despite his elocution-teaching pop, Bennett didn't voice vowels and glottal stops in the anglicized, theatrical manner that many early television personalities—Francis and Kilgallen among them—adopted. In his mouth, words like "church" and "murder" were good old New York *choych* and *moydah.* The sound his voice produced was still lighter than what might have been expected from his robust frame, but the boyishness and good humor had already proved attractive on radio. Now he was figuring out how to adapt his personality to the small screen, and how his appearances there could bring added benefits to Random House. Already in March 1948, on *Author Meets Critic,* he'd given "a good account," *Variety* thought, when questioned about the *American College Dictionary.*

In September of that year, he'd emceed a CBS program with Gypsy Rose Lee, then in January 1949 hosted another, *We the People,* with *South*

Pacific and Metropolitan Opera star Ezio Pinza, and *Casablanca*'s Paul Henreid. Bennett had that useful talent of being able to talk with anyone. He'd met John Daly on a show called *Riddle Me This,* and engineered an appearance for himself and a deliriously happy Chris on *Howdy Doody*. The TV industry was developing fast, trying all kinds of things, making it up as it went along, a midcentury New York gold rush. Father and son were hardly alone in their enthusiasm: America had gone from six thousand to three million sets in three years.

That Sunday, October 15, 1950, when Bennett tried his hand at *What's My Line?,* there was no going out to dinner to see and be seen beforehand. He ate at home with Thrup, the kids, Herbert and Glen, then beetled twenty blocks south to the so-called world's largest studio. The CBS broadcast center, three stories high, was above Grand Central Terminal. Pigeons roosted nearby and occasionally made their presence known. (The show would soon move to a real theater, leaving winged interlopers behind.) Gil Fates was responsible for week-to-week production. One of his jobs was to arrange the warm-up; tall, gangly Fates and other staffers would impersonate contestants and put the panel through their paces. Engineers would check sound levels and camera shots. Fates would also warm up the studio audience. Bennett was introduced to prematurely gray, bow-tied, barrel-chested Franklin Heller, the show's director, whose college roommate had been none other than Herman Liveright—Horace's son. During the war he'd been executive producer in charge of USO plays for the troops, and as Goodson and Todman saw it, Heller was their resident intellectual and savior: only after he'd taken charge of cameras and figured out where to put people did Montenier sign on.

Another of Heller's jobs was to help the mystery guest find ways to hide his or her voice. When it seemed undisguisable (or a guest was too inebriated to disguise it), he had to implement a backup plan: send producer Mark Goodson on instead. Most famously, Judy Garland once turned up late, fortified by bottles of wine. It was not a reassuring backstage sight. However, just as Goodson was preparing to take her place, Garland emerged from the dressing room. *What's all the fucking rush?* she asked, before walking on and taking her seat beside Daly to thunderous applause. Since she couldn't be trusted to conceal the famous voice, she'd been given a crystal bell to signal *yes,* and a clicker to squeeze *no,* after each question posed by one of the masked panelists.

The third key member of the production team was Bob Bach, whose official role was to book mystery guests. The real reason for his presence was that *What's My Line?* was his brainchild. Martin Stone, the man behind *Howdy Doody,* had refined it with Goodson, but it was Bach's idea. They'd come to an "arrangement": Bach was given what was tantamount to a job for life, as long as he kept quiet about the show's origins.

Backstage: Arlene, Bennett, and Bob Bach, originator of the show

Now let's all play What's My Line?! Bennett heard announcer Johnny Olson declare, as he sat waiting. Usually, Olson would introduce the first panelist—*Miss Dorothy Kilgallen*—who would present the gentleman to her left, *Mr. Louis Untermeyer,* who'd introduce the lovely lady to his left, *Miss Arlene Francis*. Arlene would do the honors for *Mr. Hal Block,* and Block, finally, would announce *Mr. John Daly*. In those early years, introductions were brief, but later they became a vehicle for one-upmanship. By then, Bennett introduced Daly, and the audience had come to expect a witty thrust-and-parry. However, Daly maintained a tight protocol: although panelists were referred to by first names during the course of play, he'd begin by calling on *Miss Francis, Miss Kilgallen, Mr. Cerf,* and the formal conceit was reprised on a nameplate in front of each.

On Bennett's first night, early movie queen Gloria Swanson was the mystery guest, a woman who embodied more mystery than most. She sat, hair sheathed in a turban with a fine-meshed veil covering half her face, radiating an allure as sculpted, strange, and ageless as a sphinx. She'd just filmed her first picture in a very long time: Billy Wilder's *Sunset Boulevard*. In it, she played Norma Desmond, a deluded, washed-up version of her former self. Being on the show was good publicity, and as it turned out, the film would be considered one of Hollywood's greatest, and Swanson's crowning achievement. Afterward the diva, along with Bennett and Phyllis; Arlene and her husband, theater and radio actor Martin Gabel; Dorothy and her husband, former actor Dick Kollmar (together they broadcast a breakfast radio show from their Park Avenue apartment); Bach and his chic wife, Jean, who also worked in broadcasting; and other show staff repaired to the Waldorf, where they partied with a happy Dr. Montenier, at his expense.

Bennett had done fine. The show was fun and he wanted more of it.

It's likely that, when Bennett agreed to be a last-minute replacement, Goodson had dangled the prospect of future guest appearances on this or another show (G-T had launched *Beat the Clock* earlier that year). It would take six months, but in March, just back from a lecture tour and visit to La Quinta, Bennett was invited again as a *What's My Line?* panelist. However, this wasn't a casual summons: something had happened.

A group calling itself American Business Consultants Inc., funded by anti-Communists and staffed by former FBI agents, had issued a 215-page book, *Red Channels,* the previous June. Subtitled "The Report of Communist Influence in Radio and Television," it accused 151 people in broadcasting of being Communists or sympathizers. Many were cultural leaders and legends-in-the-making, including Orson Welles, Aaron Copland, Lena Horne, and Leonard Bernstein. At first, some entertainment insiders had looked on the badly printed book as a hoax. The cover illustration depicted a childishly drawn red hand, fingers splayed, about to clutch a black microphone. All that many listed in *Red Channels* were guilty of was supporting the New Deal or the fight against fascism; giving money and signing petitions to help Blacks, refugees, and unions; or opposing censorship. Yet although the research was riddled with errors, the timing was impeccable: the Korean War had begun less than a week after the broadside was issued, and fear of Communism clouded Americans' judgment. *Red Channels* was catnip to true believers in thrall to Senator Joe McCarthy, who was at his most powerful.

Bennett counted many named individuals as acquaintances or pals, some going back years: Lillian Hellman, Gypsy Rose Lee, Burl Ives, and Arlene Francis's husband, Marty Gabel, among them. Irwin Shaw was also on the list, and RH was scheduled to publish his second novel, *The Troubled Air*. Shaw's self-described subject—"Red-baiting in the radio world"—could not have been timelier, but like many named in *Red Channels,* he was blacklisted and fled to Europe, where he lived for the rest of his life.

Goodson and Todman had contacted Bennett this time because of another *Red Channels* name: Louis Untermeyer. It didn't matter that his anthologies were standard texts in schools and colleges. Nor did it matter that, in Bennett's words, he was "no more a Communist than J. Edgar Hoover." Alas, as Bennett also noted, Untermeyer was "a great signer." He'd lent his name to organizations that had made him "conspicuous."

The *What's My Line?* producing team—and even more unusually, the sponsor—tried to resist the pressure to drop Untermeyer, even though *Red Channels* encouraged boycotts of any show and product associated with someone on the list. When the trouble started, Dr. Montenier's attitude was, in effect, "We don't believe in pressure groups." Soon, however, came bags of letters protesting Untermeyer's presence, all written in similar language and obviously orchestrated. A group calling itself the Catholic War Veterans began stickering warnings on drugstore windows: STOP STOPETTE UNTIL STOPETTE STOPS UNTERMEYER. Pickets marched outside the studio. Goodson watched in dismay as *Red Channels* became "the bible of television," subscribed to by networks, sponsors, and ad agencies. Its premise, that Communists had infiltrated the medium, became doctrine. Witch hunts not only injected paranoia into creative industries, but also fomented cynical opportunism: people named names to get even for a job denied, a romance resisted, or to get out of debt by implicating those to whom they owed money. CBS demanded a loyalty oath from all employees. Gil Fates was forced to submit each prospective mystery guest's name for approval to a network vice president, and later to a "security man." Lists begat lists, and to be on one metastasized into being on them all. The pressure made people do things they were ashamed of. "It was a little bit like living through the Inquisition, or Mao's Cultural Revolution," Fates's widow recalled a half century later.

In the end Louis Untermeyer, "the great signer," bagged more trouble than the show cared to handle. If he'd wanted a chance at retaining his TV job, he would have needed to keep his head down, mouth shut, and pen in his pocket. Instead, on January 15, 1951, Untermeyer had appended his name to one cause too many: with sixteen others, he'd taken a large ad in *The New York Times* that pleaded with Americans to stand up for the First Amendment. In urging fellow citizens to read their own Constitution, his position had become untenable. CBS's chief attorney had informed him he had to quit.

Bennett, too, had signed things, been involved in broadcasts, and made speeches. Just a year before Untermeyer's plea in the *Times,* he—along with Bob Haas, S&S's Jack Goodman, and a slew of other publishers and prominent figures like Arthur Miller and Sid Perelman—had lent his name to a brief supporting First Amendment protections in connection with the Supreme Court appeal for two of the Hollywood Ten. Still, he'd learned to be wary. Only a month before Untermeyer's fateful ad, Bennett had told the *San Francisco Chronicle:* "Nowadays when any honest liberal opens his mouth, there's an organized group to start smearing him. You find yourself tearing up letters and wondering before you give to a charity. . . . At least book publishers are still able to publish without the permission of Senator McCarthy." Of course, as a publisher, he did seek advice on "loyalties and *Red Channels*" from lawyer Horace Manges, and the following year, along with Oscar Hammerstein and actress Judy Holliday (she'd been blacklisted by radio and TV, courtesy of *Red Channels*), took legal action against the Committee for the Negro in the Arts, an allegedly subversive group that had listed them as "initiating sponsors." Their names were removed from the committee's letterhead.

He did still publish without "permission" from McCarthy, however, whether it was Shaw's *The Troubled Air* that year, or a Landmark he commissioned from Shirley Jackson two years later on the Salem witch trials, specifically instructing her to "point out the moral of the tale (so applicable to the present day)." The network didn't regard Bennett as a liability like Untermeyer, but what neither he nor CBS realized was that Lela Rogers's good friend J. Edgar Hoover was keeping a file on him. (That discovery would come later.) Rather, the *What's My Line?* team saw him as "amiable," straightforward, with "no pretensions of being an egghead." They trusted his brow was high enough to show the great American public he was witty, but not an intellectual. They'd had enough of that with Untermeyer. Bennett was available and keen, so that Sunday, March 18, he and Phyllis dined with the Manges, and they all went to

CBS Studio 59 in the old Mansfield Theater on West Forty-Seventh Street, the show's new home. Untermeyer wasn't mentioned. Bennett was introduced as a "guest panelist," but was a regular from then on.

Mike Tomasco from Philadelphia—a young man with a bit of Sinatra about him—was the first contestant. In these early days, players didn't immediately settle in next to Daly; instead, they were invited to parade in front of the panel, the better to undergo close scrutiny—a kind of mock "perp walk" in HUAC times. Arlene asked to look inside Tomasco's suit jacket, and he willingly obliged. Then Daly gave each panelist a free guess about Tomasco's line before they really began. No wild card turned up true, but the guesses brought laughs. During the course of play, they managed to figure out that the product he dealt in was worn above the chest. It was Hal Block's turn, and Block called for help from the others. *Might it be something worn by a dog?* Bennett wondered aloud during the panel's brief on-air conference. However, new and not yet confident, he didn't assert himself. It was Block who played the suggestion for all it was worth, taking his time to go where Bennett had pointed: Tomasco's line was making dog collars.

He was followed by a Ritz-Carlton house detective who'd had close (benign, unremembered) encounters with several panelists. Then came the mystery guest: Estes Kefauver, a Tennessee senator who headed the government committee investigating organized crime. Its hearings were broadcast live, and just about anyone with a TV—Bennett included—had watched, riveted, learning a word many had never heard before: "Mafia." There wasn't much time for the fourth challenger, a bow-tied, middle-aged New Yorker named Alan Gerstel. But Dorothy asked to see his ring, and Bennett his American Legion button. Gerstel turned out to be a wine taster. As Bennett would learn, all life high and low passed before the privileged panelists and eager viewers of *What's My Line?*

Goodnight, Dorothy. Goodnight, Bennett. Goodnight, Arlene. Goodnight, Hal. Goodnight, John. Just like that, the week was over: Bennett could breathe easier. Again he'd done well, and a new Sunday pattern emerged. After the show, some habitually made straight for Grand Central and the suburbs, but Bennett and Phyllis would go out until the wee hours with panelists, Goodson, the mystery guest, or all of the above, often unwinding at more than one watering hole. It was all very public for a private drink-and-snack. That night, the evening ended at Toots Shor's. Some weeks, pals would come with the Cerfs to the studio—on May 27, it would be the Hornblows—and join them for a nightcap. Dick Rodgers had been the mystery guest, so they made quite a glamorous crowd. Other times, Bennett would invite an author. Special treatment included sitting in the control room as well as meeting all the panelists, Daly, and the production staff.

One time, Bennett took Bill Faulkner to a ringside table at the Copacabana after the show. Out came the Copa girls, but the spotlight also moved, training on "hot" tables like theirs. Faulkner walked out. It was hard for Bennett to understand not everyone loved the spotlight and hobnobbing with celebrities as he did, for he was utterly delighted by the turn his Sunday nights—for many, the loneliest night of the week—had taken.

He'd also come to see that this new third family—after those at Sixty-Second Street and the palazzo—had its own idiosyncrasies. Goodson's temper could flare over matters trivial or weighty. *What's My Line?* was played straight; it was never a crooked game, but even before the great unmasking of "fixed" quiz shows (most famously, in 1957, *Twenty-One*), the accusation was like a bad smell that hovered occasionally over all games. Goodson knew that if rumors weren't dispersed quickly, they could be the ruin of a show, so he'd instructed panelists *never* to leap to identify a mystery guest even if they had a strong suspicion who it was: better to pass and let others establish the celebrity's identity with a few questions before hazarding a guess. That is exactly what Bennett didn't do in June 1952 with jazzman Billy Eckstine: he guessed him at once. Goodson, "flabbergasted" by the risk Bennett had taken, wrote that he and Todman were "fond" of him and saw how he added to the show's "tone," but Bennett must make sure it never happened again.

Dorothy Kilgallen's marriage was troubled, despite the image she conveyed on screen, and on her breakfast radio program. Arlene Francis and Martin Gabel, whom viewers took to be the most devoted of couples, also fought once the cameras were off. Arlene, like Bennett, was an only child with an enormous need for adulation. Gabel, an intellectual stage actor, had trouble finding work post–*Red Channels*. Sometimes the Cerfs, Gabels, and Moss and Kitty Hart would go out together after the show. Kitty recalled that on certain evenings, "Marty would disappear, drinking all night." Still, for Bennett, the program brought a lot of fun both on and off the set.

Seriously competitive about any game he played, he became serious about this one, too. While Arlene never prepared, he, like Dorothy, *really* wanted to win, and worked at it. He'd sit in his office on a Friday afternoon with gossip columns, theater listings, and *Variety* spread before him, checking what was on, who was in, what was hot. Usually his door was open, and anyone was welcome to wander in to help whittle down likely mystery guests. When Sunday finally arrived and he was on-air, jokes and puns decreased markedly as soon as he took chase after an identity. He was paid well for the work he put in, work that he typically took care to make seem like no work at all. Each panelist negotiated his or her compensation, unaware what others earned, although it was suspected that Arlene, one of America's sweethearts, netted more than others. Seven months into his tenure, Bennett's *WML* "loot" was $250 per week. Four years later, the panelists' average pay was $500. At one point, salaries reached $1,000 per week. Bennett once said that when the show finally finished its broadcast tenure, panelists were clocking "scandalous amounts. . . . There has never been such easy money in the world."

It was also incredibly profitable for Goodson-Todman, since it was so cheap to make. Sure, employees worked hard: fans wrote in, suggesting contestants, and had to be answered; staff combed through newspapers nationwide, clipping candidates. But it was so successful that, in 1957, CBS bought the program and hired G-T to continue producing. Years later, when the show reached the end of its line, *TV Guide* estimated each episode had cost $40,000, half what was needed to produce most programs of similar length.

After Bennett assumed Untermeyer's seat in mid-March, he began to receive flattering mail and autograph requests. Recalling the humiliation that he'd felt with Sylvia, when fans pushed him aside to reach her, he savored the sweet revenge. The power of being a regular on a game show had an unusual feature: "You're playing yourself and the viewing audience loves you being you," Betsy Palmer, another longtime G-T panelist, explained. "You're as fallible and infallible as they are. You belong to them." So it was that a screenwriter/producer pal of the Cerfs, Charles Brackett, wrote to tell Bennett that he was with the Brackett family twice a day on Sundays: at breakfast while they perused Cerfboard, and in the evening on the show. Brackett wondered, tongue in cheek, if his family didn't devote more of their Sundays to Bennett Cerf than to their religious obligations. Joe Lesser, Knopf's longtime treasurer, communicated a variation on the theme: "I see you every Sunday night but, alas, you never notice me."

It was a marvelous feeling to be such a singular figure, straddling publishing and show business, and to be seen by show business insiders as "very, very unusual"—an insider himself. Yet this serendipitous celebrity and second career were two-sided. "Belonging to them"—even for a man who always wanted more love, more praise, more recognition—could at times be wearing. When it got to be too much, Bennett half-jokingly admitted, he would "mask [his] emotions under a frozen, desperate smile."

And if compiling joke books had already made him suspect, going on TV proved to a significant segment of the literary community that Bennett was an utter lightweight. It was unseemly or worse for a publisher with any claim to seriousness to play a game show. They said "cruel things" about him, just as they had about Untermeyer, judging such showmanship "low down on the food chain." Bennett "either had very low or very high self-esteem" to have done it, a novelist who was not unsympathetic concluded.

There was another danger, too, one that Bennett himself identified: "That feeling of fame is like a terrible drug," he admitted to a Wisconsin paper as early as 1953. "Recognition is a prop to the ego, and losing it is a desperately unhappy affair." However, on that front, for the moment, he had nothing to worry about: *What's My Line?* was fast becoming one of the most popular shows on TV.

Chapter 25

Gatsby in Paradise

More than two months of Sunday nights passed before it was announced that Bennett had replaced Louis Untermeyer on *What's My Line?* That same spring of 1951, the Red Scare impinged on his life in another way, when Budd Schulberg came calling in April.

Having been outed as a Communist in the HUAC hearings, Budd had offered to appear before the congressional committee as a friendly witness: a former Party member whose eyes had been opened a decade earlier to the darkness behind what had once seemed a beacon. He was to testify in May, and understood there were people who'd vilify him for it. Being blacklisted could destroy careers and lives, but cooperating could destroy friendships and souls. Not knowing how much screenwriting work he'd be able to get once he testified, he wanted reassurance that RH would continue to publish him.

Bennett had known from the start about Budd's enthusiasm for the Party: the Hollywood princeling had also visited the USSR in 1934. Then a boy of twenty, he was smitten with the system and returned a convinced Communist, having already lost all illusions about the dream factory where he'd grown up. Budd recalled how understanding Bennett had been—unlike others, his publisher "didn't jump" on him. But, unwittingly, he had played a part in Budd's original Party problem. After Bennett had encouraged the young man to turn his stories about Sammy Glick into a novel, Budd had asked the local Party boss, John Howard Lawson, for time off from politics to write. Lawson (later one of the Hollywood Ten) ordered him to submit an outline of the book for Party approval. "This was serious. It was 'Do it—or else,'" Budd recalled. "I chose 'Or else.'" He quit the Party.

After the surprise success of *What Makes Sammy Run?* Budd published *The Harder They Fall,* a fictional exposé of the boxing world. Then came

The Disenchanted, a rendering of F. Scott Fitzgerald's heyday and downfall, rooted in Budd's experience trying to co-author a screenplay with him in 1939, the year before Fitzgerald's death. Bennett had begun banging the drum early, announcing in Trade Winds in 1948 that it would be "a story of a fabulous writer of the Twenties and his equally fabulous wife." But after reading the manuscript at La Quinta in February 1950, his reaction in a letter to Saxe, far from being fabulous, echoed the book's title: "The more I think . . . the more disappointed I am . . . the pathos he's missed except in occasional fine scenes; the tie-up of Fitzgerald's crack-up with the end of an era has eluded him & the main figures are unsympathetic. . . . Maybe if you can hack 200 pages . . . it will come to life? . . . The story is too big for him!"

Nevertheless, a Trade Winds column just prior to publication gamely promoted *The Disenchanted,* describing Bennett's history with Schulberg and adding the usual anecdotal embroidery. Then he predicted that the novel was "headed for the heights," declaring that the prose was "explosive and direct," and the characters "three-dimensional and dynamic." Critics who'd scoffed that Budd could "only depict heels" would now encounter "the tragic and sympathy-compelling novelist who is the central character."

Whether Bennett was right privately or publicly (or whether Saxe managed to turn his blue pencil into a magic wand), BOMC took *The Disenchanted* as its main selection for November. Bill Faulkner, in a letter to Saxe, evinced a lack of enthusiasm, and Truman Capote, in a letter to Linscott, said he enjoyed the novel "rather half-heartedly." Still, *Times* critic Orville Prescott found it one of the "two or three most impressive" novels of the year, and the book was one of the top-ten fiction bestsellers. Budd had suddenly become a much more valuable property, and quite apart from their fifteen-year personal history and his own early sympathy for Russia and quick disillusion, Bennett was a businessman: keeping a winner was part of his job. A year after the publication of *The Disenchanted,* he bestowed canonical status on *What Makes Sammy Run?* by adding it to the ML, and in 1952 it would be among the series' top-twenty bestsellers.

Bennett told Budd not to worry about his relationship with RH, whether he went before HUAC as a friendly or hostile witness. That reassurance, Budd recalled a half century later, was "very decent of him at that time. He was more politically engaged than most of the Jewish publishers, very open-minded." Saxe also assured Budd that his "cause" wouldn't affect their work together. However, his decision to cooperate with HUAC and identify others as Communists would remain controversial for the rest of Budd's life.

. . .

EACH YEAR, BENNETT AND Phyllis, like many better-off New Yorkers, had the challenge of how and where to arrange a break from Gotham for the summer. Married more than a decade now, and with Chris almost ten, Jonathan five, and money flowing in from Bennett's ever-expanding tributaries, they knew it was long past time to stop being nomads. They needed another fixed point, not simply a line between work and home, but a perfect triangle: the house on Sixty-Second Street, the palazzo, and a bolt-hole beyond New York for the "perfect family" that they assured themselves and their sons they were.

The previous fall, Bennett had fancied buying two cottages in Provincetown, but it was not a convenient location for a New Yorker as busy as he. Now spring had arrived, so on the last Sunday in April the Cerfs set off in their new gray Cadillac convertible to see a house in Mt. Kisco; they'd liked one there when they first married. Unseasonably warm weather teased the city, letting them drive with the top down, as Bennett liked. Heading north, they crossed the Bronx and entered Westchester County, the land rising into towns and country that hadn't yet been parceled into suburbs. An hour or so after setting out, Hemlock Hill, the 1930s-era house they'd come to visit, was a moment away.

Several pleasant houses dotted both sides of Orchard Road. Soon they saw a longish drive with tall banks of hemlock on the left, and the reason for the house's name became obvious. They turned and proceeded up the drive. Years before, part of the land had been a nursery, and the evergreens had been left to age into a dense screen. The air smelled delightful to city noses; a pond glistened and old fruit trees were beginning to bloom. There was a garage and caretaker's cottage, a greenhouse, a red-clay tennis court, a semi–Olympic size pool, and a smaller pond that provided the water hazard for a two-hole golf course. The drive ended at a two-story white clapboard house whose side-wings elongated it into three parts. They parked and rang the bell at a small porch.

As soon as Maurice and Kitty Rosenfeld, the sellers, welcomed them in, the Cerfs saw that these Jewish owners had furnished the house in

WASP country style—simple, elegant, a bit playful. Robin's-egg-blue walls, sofas and armchairs in pink-and-green botanicals, a grand piano and bookcases, made for a lovely living room. A guest room, bath, and den were also on the ground floor, while a long dining room table seated ten even without leaves. The kitchen was dominated by a cast-iron stove and two fridges. A door led to a pantry, basement, servants' rooms. Upstairs was a master bedroom with a bath for each spouse, five smaller rooms and another bath, and an attic with cooling fans.

Back on the ground floor, they exited to a flagstone-covered portico with six white columns two stories high. Evidently they'd first entered at the *back,* and now were at the front. Looking up, the portico's light blue ceiling mimicked the sky. Looking down, a narrow, fast-moving river lay at the foot of a sloping lawn. Deciduous forest climbed the farther bank, and above it the cows of a working dairy grazed in the distance. A cascade of stone steps led from the side of the house to the pool, while white wrought-iron chairs and tables speckled the lawn. Birdsong flew through elm, oak, a rock garden, rose garden, flower and vegetable beds, and on to wisteria by the tennis court. Gracious, confident, yet unpretentious, this big house atop its hill was made to be filled with people.

The "wonderful" house in Mt. Kisco

The Rosenfelds were asking $155,000 ($2.07 million today) for Hemlock Hill and its forty-two acres, and were selling their home furnished. Something about them said to Bennett that they'd be generous. The estate was "wonderful," he told his diary after a storm had blown up, turning the dreamy, fugitive summer day into a cooler-headed city night. "If we only could!" The next week, he discussed the "improbable" deal with Rosenfeld and his son-in-law, and took a second "enchanted" look with Thrup. They returned to meet the agent with Bob Haas, a counterweight to Bennett's impetuousness. The house impressed Bob, but Bennett wouldn't budge past $120,000, and the sellers wouldn't accept less than $140,000. The sale was off, yet he couldn't forget the Eden; it lingered, exciting and disturbing him like a fever.

That late winter and spring, Bennett had been preoccupied with plotting a very different kind of escape, for one of his most beleaguered and beloved authors. Eugene O'Neill had been cut off from New York and Saxe by the vigilant Carlotta, but a crisis had arisen that Bennett hoped might allow O'Neill to find peace and companionship in the city once more. After fleeing Manhattan in 1948, the couple had renovated a secluded cottage in Marblehead, Massachusetts, where he could again live with the sound of the sea in his ears, but, closed in upon themselves during the frigid winters, he and Carlotta became more brittle in every way. Disagreements flared frequently. His son Shane, who'd spiraled from alcoholism to heroin use, was arrested for drug possession in 1948, and O'Neill declined to furnish bail. Two years later, Gene Jr.—who'd also succumbed to the family demons through drink—killed himself, adding to the despair O'Neill already felt over his own invalidism and inability to write. At the same time Carlotta, who'd taken bromide preparations to summon sleep for years, began medicating herself more; neither spouse realized that the buildup had turned toxic.

Saxe told the story to Bennett and Herbert: On the evening of February 5, after a dreadful quarrel, O'Neill stumbled out of the house without his stick. Thick snow lay on the ground. He tripped in the garden and, already weak, broke his right leg and could not get up. Carlotta, in a drug-induced fury, shut him out. At some point a doctor was called, and got O'Neill to a hospital. The next day a cop saw Carlotta wandering and incoherent, and she was taken to a psychiatric facility. Saxe and others hastened to Gene's side.

Bennett had been traveling when this occurred, but once back in March, he spoke with the Drama Guild's Lawrence Langner about Gene's "tragic predicament." Langner had brought in a consulting psychiatrist who'd suggested that Carlotta be declared insane and put under the temporary guardianship of a local lawyer; Gene reluctantly agreed. At the same time, Langner and O'Neill's New York lawyer urged him to come to the city by ambulance and train, where friends could look after him. Bennett hoped this would help both personally and professionally. He proposed to Bob Haas that RH might at last be able to publish *A Moon for the Misbegotten* and *A Touch of the Poet,* which had been languishing in the Villard safe. A decision hinged on O'Neill's health, and "the harpy he's married to," Bennett added. Carlotta "should have been committed ten years ago."

Gene did agree to come to New York. He arrived on March 30 and was taken to Doctors Hospital, weighing 107 pounds. But the day before he'd set out, physicians where Carlotta was being treated decided she'd overcome the bromide poisoning and released her. She went to court, charged her husband with cruelty, and asked for maintenance.

With Bennett's aversion to hospitals, he didn't visit O'Neill until April 19. Saxe more than made up for it, dropping in daily, and proposing that Gene live with him when discharged. Bennett and Langner devised a plan of their own: they'd consulted a lawyer to draw up divorce papers, conferred with doctors, and were looking to install Gene in an apartment in the city. They tried to persuade Russel Crouse of the rightness of their idea, given his closeness to O'Neill, but Crouse—the only friend in touch with Gene *and* Carlotta—wouldn't intervene: the O'Neills would soon be back together, he predicted.

Gene confided to Crouse on May 13 that he'd return to Boston on his wife's terms and live at the Hotel Shelton, across the street from a psychiatrist who'd been treating her and won her trust. He'd depart in four days. Two evenings later, Saxe and Dorothy visited and begged Gene to come to them. "I'd only be a burden, I can't even hold a cup of water," he replied. He put his arms around Saxe and said: "Goodbye, my brother." Bennett, however, persisted, and on May 16 arrived at the hospital to unveil his final plan to O'Neill, having delegated Phyllis to make the arrangements. She'd reserved a suite at the plush Carlyle Hotel on Madison Avenue, and engaged a male nurse to care for him. All was set; the nurse would transport him to the Carlyle the following morning. The great man of the theater listened with the quiet that had always impressed Bennett. They'd known each other almost twenty years, and O'Neill had formed an opinion as to what kind of man his publisher was. He couldn't help but notice the hero worship, but had also come to trust him in business, admire his enterprise, and enjoy his companionship. Yet he didn't share with Bennett the decision he'd signaled to Crouse and Saxe. When the nurse arrived the next morning, the patient had already gone.

Perhaps O'Neill had withheld the truth seeing that Bennett didn't grasp the depth of the bond between him and his wife. Perhaps he didn't have the strength to explain it, having to retain what little energy he had. Recounting the story years later, Bennett's memory was selective and faulty. In his version, Crouse signed on to his plan; Carlotta arrived at the hospital, "mesmerizing" Gene into returning; and O'Neill never told Saxe or Crouse of his decision to rejoin her. This, Bennett said, was because Gene was "ashamed to." More likely, Bennett was ashamed—or very hurt—for not having been taken into Gene's confidence as the others had been. Saxe, inconsolable, never saw his old friend again. But although Carlotta barred Saxe, she couldn't entirely sever her connection to his boss, O'Neill's publisher. When she wrote five days after their return that, having looked "ghastly," Gene looked "90% better," she closed by sending the "best of good wishes for you and Mme. Cerf." Replying, Bennett donned his own mask, hoping that "what lies ahead will be happy enough to make up for everything."

. . .

THAT THURSDAY WHEN O'NEILL'S surprise decision upended Bennett's plans, he found a way to console himself, as he always did. After dining with their friend Jack Benny, he and Thrup met Bubbles and Arthur at '21' and, over a long night of drinks and talk, Bennett revealed that he'd made a new offer for the Westchester house, and the owners were considering it. Their answer burst into his diary the following day: "BOUGHT MT. KISCO PROPERTY FOR 125M. DEAL TO BE CLOSED 6/30. ARE WE NUTS? PROBABLY!" The sellers had accepted a bid $30,000 below their asking price.

Sales conference and other necessary distractions intervened, but on Sunday, May 27, he drove Horace Manges and his son Jimmy up to the Mt. Kisco "folly." The next day, he took Donald and Jez for a "look-see." At fifty-three, it was still essential to gain the approval of those he loved and depended on: this was a great deal of money for a man who, despite his seeming extravagance, was careful about how he spent it. With Jez and Don beside him, he signed the contract, then talked to a local dealer about a second car—a station wagon for a country squire! At month's end, he found time to flip through old columns for inspiration: as a man who dealt in words, he'd truly possess the wonderful estate only after he'd renamed it. The clippings, however, did not yield an answer.

That Friday, June 1, was the turn of Saxe, advertising maven Aaron Sussman, and RH in-house promotion and publicity manager Allan Ullman to visit. Sussman was a talented photographer, and for Bennett—an important client and the friend who'd helped him start in business—he snapped plenty of pictures. Sussman also promised to help set up a darkroom for Phyllis, and teach her how to use it to good effect; soon RH covers would bear creditable author shots of Faulkner, O'Hara, and others taken by the boss's wife. Yet Saxe made the most crucial contribution that day, when he suggested calling the house "The Columns," pun very much intended. The name was perfect. Though Bennett converted $95,000 from stocks and bonds and took a $30,000 mortgage for the place, he never tired of saying that the dream house was bought not with RH takings, but with extracurricular earnings from lectures, books, TV—and, yes, columns. However, since more column inches always had to be filled, he conveniently ignored the name that couldn't be bettered long enough to orchestrate a Cerfboard house-naming contest. Hundreds of readers sent in suggestions like "The Road to Cerfdom." Three who were inspired to find the same solution as Saxe each received a dozen new books.

The closing took place early. On June 29, Thrup, Jon, and Vera the maid drove up in a new Plymouth station wagon. (Chris was at camp.) Bennett came later, with a married butler and cook who would live at The Columns. They inherited an Italian gardener from the Rosenfelds, and would also have a part-time maid. The previous owners *had* kept their promise: they left almost everything, even golf clubs. It was like stepping into someone else's barely worn, custom-made shoes: they might need a polish, but the fit and look were divine. You simply put them on and walked into another life.

The weather was foul that Saturday, but no matter. One of the first things Bennett did was to honor the gods who'd blessed him: he unpacked and carefully arranged a set of the ML on shelves in the den. Liveright and his Modern Library had been the first lucky dream to come true, the foundation for all that followed. Half a lifetime ago, he'd gone to the leafy Westchester town of New Rochelle to partake of Sunday lunch with Horace's family, a far cry from boyhood Sundays endured with his grandfather. Now *he* had the big, beautiful house to go with the pretty wife and clever kids, the exciting life, the famous pals. Not even Nathan Wise had owned a place like this. The sun shone on Sunday when Bob and Merle Haas arrived to baptize The Columns with friends.

On Monday morning, Bennett caught the 8:01 into Grand Central. He'd be commuting weekdays for most of the summer, and all the summers that followed. Bantam's John O'Connor provided companionship coming home, stretching the rules to introduce him to the comforts of the 4:50 Westchester club car. Ordinarily, Bennett would sit among the regular hot-and-sticky crowd of suits, for the exclusive air-conditioned club car was a private, members-only affair, attached weekdays to one morning train to the city and one evening train coming back. Determined to join the group, he reckoned the quickest way was to trade on his status as a columnist and appeal to the press office of the New York Central Railroad. The press manager approached the Wall Street banker who was the current arbiter of who got in. The club had accepted several new members recently, and there was no more space, the banker replied. Perhaps, the press manager suggested, Mr. Cerf could organize a club car of his own? All too clearly, Bennett understood that the real difficulty was not a lack of seats, but the same issue Phyllis had encountered searching for an apartment early in their marriage. Although O'Connor was Catholic, he'd somehow passed, but no one of the "Hebrew Persuasion" had ever been admitted. It took time and persistence, but Bennett became the first Jew to gain a seat in the car.

And yet, with this secular man who'd eschewed his roots and then had an epiphany in Jerusalem, religion still did not sit comfortably. On weekends, he and his Christian Science–inflected wife sent their boys to a Presbyterian Sunday school. In the city, after the Town School, Jonathan would follow Chris to the Quaker Friends Seminary for middle school, before heading to boarding school and college. It was a compromise whose strangeness was not lost on the boys, to raise them Presbyterian "with no one else of that religion" at home. In all other respects, life on Orchard Road had a wonderful completeness. Jonathan Cerf would think of it as "paradise." As for his dad, within weeks Bennett would confide to Nancy Wilson Ross, one of his newer authors, "I kind of think of myself there as the Great Gatsby of 1951," and soon expand upon that to a Chicago newspaperwoman: "like the Great Gatsby," Bennett wondered if it "all was really his."

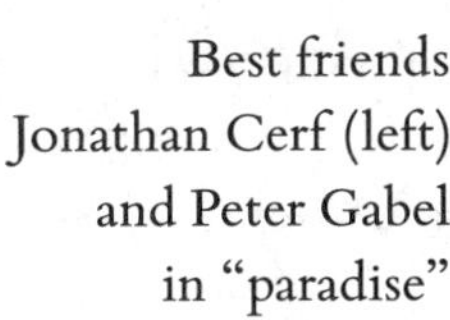

Best friends Jonathan Cerf (left) and Peter Gabel in "paradise"

Years earlier, he and Don had allowed the ML edition of Fitzgerald's novel to go out of print when sales had dwindled, before it had secured a hold within the literary canon. Nonetheless, they'd kept it on the list longer than sales had justified, because they saw *The Great Gatsby* as a great book, "the best business book ever written," as Donald wryly observed. Patently, Fitzgerald's protagonist remained in Bennett's mind, and in likening himself to Gatsby he was joking, yet it was a curious comparison. No one who has read the novel can forget that beneath Jay Gatsby's mystique—a dream of a life symbolized by an exquisite house—were self-inventions and deceptions that collapsed into tragedy. Bennett, the lucky man capable of taking his lecture audiences to "happyland," knew something about self-invention and deception. Yes, that frustrated RH author quoted in the *Saturday Evening Post* profile a few years back hadn't discerned any inner reality within his publisher, only that "flutter of shadows and reflections," but maybe Bennett had more in him than the author had supposed. He knew about Gatsby, and behind the joke, at this triumphant moment for the former playboy of the Western world now morphed into the man of property, lay a fear that no amount of joking could fully put to rest.

. . .

IN LATE MAY, BENNETT'S daydreams about The Columns had to pause long enough for him to entertain a visiting author. Thirteen years earlier, RH had published *The Tides of Mont St.-Michel,* a translation of Roger Vercel's Goncourt Prize–winning novel. Francophile Bob had championed the book, hoping for a *succès d'estime;* it surprised him and the others by becoming a genuine hit. Nobody had ever met the Frenchman, but recently Bob had waved a cable in front of Bennett: Vercel was coming to New York.

Bennett wasn't free for lunch on the appointed day, but was eager to do his bit by showing off the Villard. Vercel, bearded and formal in homburg, bow-tie, and gloves, went on the tour, uttering *"Formidable!"* at every turn. Smiling and chatting all the while, Bennett began to grow desperate: Vercel spoke practically no English. Eventually, his *"Formidable!"* gave way to *"Enchanté!"* in reply to his host's by-now-very-relieved *"Au revoir!"* Yet there was a *"je ne sais quoi"* about Vercel: a young woman in publicity was convinced that he reminded her of someone. Once upon a time Bob may have been fooled by Bennett's correspondence over the rare white salmon, but Bennett was utterly taken in by Lew Miller's impersonation of Monsieur Vercel, concocted by Lew and Bob with a little help from a makeup artist and a theatrical costumer. Once he'd recovered from his surprise, Bennett loved the prank, and within a few weeks, "Vercel's" visit found its way into the *Herald-Tribune Book Review:* just another day at Random House.

Later that year, Lew—universally recognized as the fourth member of the ruling quartet—would turn fifty, and there would be talk of selling him a large block of shares so he could become a partner. In the end, he couldn't afford them, and didn't want to borrow from the others. Yet in the crowded annals of practical jokes under the RH roof, the visit of Monsieur Vercel was the ultimate, definitely better than the parking meter that Tony Wimpfheimer stationed in Bennett's private bathroom one birthday—he *did* spend an inordinate amount of time on the phone there—which toppled over and broke Bennett's toe. It also bested the mystery sedan that hogged a coveted courtyard spot. With a Bible always on its passenger seat, everyone assumed it belonged to one of the cardinal's men—until early one morning Pat Knopf was seen slipping out of the car and over to his family's firm a block away. Somehow, the car never parked in the courtyard again.

. . .

THE COLUMNS CONSPIRED WITH *What's My Line?* to change Bennett's weekly rhythm. On Fridays, even if they indulged in a night on the town, he and Thrup would drive north, however late, arriving at one or two in the morning: he was that eager to get to the country. The kids would already be there with Margaret. Sundays the drive back had to accommodate his TV schedule. The question was whether he'd be able to work in the new place as efficiently as he did at Sixty-Second Street, but those worries vanished as soon as he wrote four weeks of Trade Winds in a day, closeted in his trim study wedged at the far end of the second floor. Like a captain on the prow of a ship, he commanded a bird's-eye view through windows on three sides; between bursts of writing, he'd pace, staring out at a sea of green. His boys knew not to disturb him, but he fulfilled his fatherly duty by telling Chris to watch ball games and fetch him when something big happened. Then they'd race down to the den and sit in front of the TV for a few minutes together. Jon, whom his parents nicknamed "the Monster," was usually out of doors. Phyllis wasn't happy when her sons wanted to watch TV, worried about the new medium's effects on kids. Often, she'd dream up activities with goals: they were to build whole towns of blocks, and write stories about them; when she and Bennett went on a trip, the boys might be told to devise a musical to perform on their return.

The journeys from Mt. Kisco to New York would become precious interludes for boys whose time with their father was so limited. Bennett would sing old-fashioned songs from his own childhood. He'd tell stories or jokes that he kept going for years, most notably about the Klutz family, who were responsible for each wrong move he made when driving. He also invented games. The water towers that rose on buildings once they hit the Bronx, if skinny and tall were "mushrooms," if fat and wide, "toadstools." Bennett counted mushrooms, and his sons toadstools; whoever counted the most won. One of his happiest car moments occurred when a truck packed with mushrooms passed them. Instantly, the "Count of Monte Kisco," as John Daly dubbed Bennett, gave himself two thousand points, for always in this and other games, he was referee. When the family dined together, each was given a certain number of votes in "democratic discussions," as he called them, but he had six, Phyllis three, and each boy one. Decades later, Chris recalled it as "a big joke, we could never win." Most of the time it was funny, "but not always."

New friends began to be collected at Mt. Kisco who had places in nearby towns, and old friends were invited on weekends. The Cerfs saw more of *Good Housekeeping* chief editor Herb Mayes, director Josh Logan, Frank Heller and Mark Goodson from TV, and the *Look* magazine Cowles. Albert Erskine, untangling himself from a second marriage, became the bachelor-on-call, partnering single females with excellent moves on the dance floor. The house also became a destination for favored authors. Less than a week after the Cerfs moved in, Bill Faulkner spent a night, accompanied by Saxe—just to be safe. The O'Haras, not to be outdone, arrived for two days in August. Quent and Ginny Reynolds came for meals. Truman Capote visited with Herbert Wise one night in September and would be singularly indulged during the next twenty years. Phyllis had a strict rule: no unmarried couples in the twin-bedded guest bedroom or the guest suite made from the gardener's cottage. Yet Truman was allowed to bring a boyfriend.

Weekend parties usually were no more than twenty people, but Phyllis would organize large gatherings on special occasions under a hired tent on the lawn. Though she might spend only a half hour each day in her big kitchen, she gave orders and menus to the servants, devised seating plans, and arranged cut flowers for every corner of the house. All was to be relaxed, but there was also some formality: finger bowls were used at dinner. The food was the fare that Bennett liked best: steak, chops, with corn on the cob and asparagus in season. Hamburgers and hotdogs were poolside favorites for lunch.

The one couple rarely seen at The Columns was Donald and Pat, although the Cerfs and Klopfers did mix at author gatherings and other publishers' parties. Very occasionally, Bennett and Phyllis put up at Don and Pat's farm if traveling south, or when a visitor like Faulkner was a guest there, but the Klopfers maintained their own orbit. The Crouses were much closer to them than to the Cerfs, as was Bennett's frat brother Oscar Hammerstein. Don had an enormous capacity for keeping friends, and women found him soulful and "a real charmer." The farmhouse had been modernized into quiet elegance; in summer, a guest might breakfast on cream and *fraises des bois* grown by Farmer Klopfer. During the cocktail hour at one early June party, the air suddenly grew chill; a rainbow of cashmere cardigans appeared on a garden table as if by magic. Pat and Phyllis may not have cared for each other, but each was superb at caring for their friends.

The Klopfers now went to Europe almost as often as the Cerfs to California, and Don began regularly making the rounds of London publishers. The last time RH had put real effort into cultivating the Brits had been in 1938, when Bennett visited England on the way to the Spanish Civil War. Most of RH's British authors were already under Don's purview: understatement suited them. And yet over the years, not every U.K. publisher had welcomed RH; in certain circles, a shadow lingered over its reputation. Dent, Cape, and especially Allen & Unwin had accused the firm of taking advantage of differences between U.S. and U.K. copyright law to "pirate" a dozen or so titles for the ML. The situation hadn't been resolved until 1948, when a mediator from the British Publishers Association met with Bob Haas (as opposed to "wild and volatile Cerf") to find a way forward. Honor was satisfied when Bob agreed to RH making retroactive payments. So it happened that in the spring of 1951, Don spent ten days in London calling on agents and publishers, following Bennett's "marching orders" (but ignoring his injunction to give Sir Stanley Unwin "one swift kick in the ass").

. . .

BETWEEN THEIR PUTTING DOWN the deposit and taking possession of the house, Phyllis did something unusual: she boarded a train for Oklahoma with the boys, to show her children to her ailing mother. Bennett thought this "infinitely better" than bringing her mother to New York; it was the only time the boys would meet their grandmother. Chris found her "a really nice lady," and he and Jonathan were introduced to their Aunt Jean's son, Phil, but it was clear even to a not-quite-ten-year-old that something "horrible" had happened between his mother and her sister. The week went by without meeting their aunt.

As for the Cerf side, Herbert and Glen came around often enough, and visits from "Poor Uncle Al" continued once or twice a year. On Bennett's West Coast trips, he made occasional sightings of his first crush, Cousin Del, and of Uncle Arthur and Aunt Ruby Wise. But at Christmas 1951, a voice from the past arrived via a card from Aunt Gert—Uncle Jerry Cerf's widow—long retired to the Adirondacks. "Tho you don't know it, you come to me often—and give me much joy. Where once, one had to spell out the name Cerf, now it's 'Are you related to Bennett Cerf—do you know him?'" *What's My Line?* and Cerfboard brought him everywhere. While pleased to receive her praise, he wasn't inspired to resume a relationship with her or other relatives, even for the sake of his sons.

As the year wound down, he could look back on a satisfactory twelve months. He'd put the distresses of dealing with O'Neill behind him. Schulberg would keep producing, and Whittaker Chambers continue to be big. Wanting to do something for authors whose success was less predictable, RH had commissioned *New Yorker* cartoonist Whitney Darrow Jr. to draw a small picture of a smiling messenger boy bearing a basket of roses labeled SUCCESS. The text read: "We are proud and pleased to greet you on publication day—RANDOM HOUSE." Every author, established or novice, would receive the card the day his or her book was officially born. Bennett had settled nicely into *What's My Line?* and was looking for more TV options: there'd been talk of a "Random House Television of the Air." He also saw that material from *WML* could freshen Trade Winds.

Greeting an author on publication day

In September, he and Thrup had celebrated their eleventh anniversary with their glittering new friends, Humphrey Bogart and Lauren Bacall, along with John and Belle O'Hara. In October, Alfred Hitchcock expressed interest in putting his cinematic stamp on a novel RH had recently published, David Dodge's *To Catch a Thief* (later, Bennett would boast that Hitch's film gave its star Grace Kelly the opportunity to meet a prince and become a princess). Halfway through November, Swede Pär

Lagerkvist, author of *Barabbas,* a novel Random had published in English translation in 1950, won the Nobel. Four days later, Louis B. Mayer offered $60,000 for picture rights. The news wasn't so good, however, the first week in December: Harold Ross, the pigeon serendipity had used to wing Phyllis to Bennett, died. Writing a reminiscence for *The Saturday Review,* Bennett didn't quite equal the obituaries he'd written for Liveright and Gershwin—he and Harold had become increasingly estranged, after all—but he did pretty well:

> *The New Yorker* . . . can and will prosper without Ross, but it will never be quite the same . . . the sparkle of the front section . . . the marvelous clarity and accuracy of its articles, and the originality, conciseness, and wit of its special features—these were the reflections of Harold Ross . . . and the amazing . . . temperamental, supersensitive, and persnickety geniuses whom first he discovered, then transformed into his dedicated slaves. For all his . . . idiosyncrasies, Ross was . . . the best damn magazine editor in the past fifty years.

Yet Bennett was too busy to dwell on what was past, what was lost, what was not to be: he'd never manage to get an article with his byline into that "damn magazine." A few weeks later, Christmas brought the usual excitement, but somehow it felt different. Instead of the city, they were in the country. Paradise wasn't limited to one season a year.

PART FOUR

1952–1959

"And the Mystery Guest Is . . ."

Cerf has managed . . . to convert the country into a . . . gigantic playpen for his energies.

—Bernard Kalb, 1953, in THE NEW YORK TIMES

It all reads like a love letter on the surface, but I have an uneasy feeling that underneath it rather cuts me down to size.

—Bennett Cerf, responding to a 1954 profile by his wife

. . . Bennett Cerf, the ideal publisher I had never expected to find.

—Ayn Rand, in an inscription written on August 22, 1957, in a copy of ATLAS SHRUGGED, *the Random House book she regarded as her masterpiece*

Chapter 26

What's New

Bennett, Phyllis, and Alicia Patterson Guggenheim (right) at "Falaise," Sands Point

PHYLLIS NEEDED SOMETHING ELSE TO DO. NINETEEN FIFTY-TWO WAS just beginning, and she'd turn thirty-six in April, a woman in her prime. Managing two boys and two houses, keeping up with her husband, doing good works, hobnobbing with high-profile pals—it wasn't enough. Being under the spotlight of Bennett's celebrity was fun, but she hungered for glory in her own right. Her friend Alicia Patterson Guggenheim had an idea: why not write for *Newsday,* the Long Island paper Alicia had founded and owned. In a weekly column called What's New, Phyllis would be the roving reporter, both wide-eyed Oklahoma girl and privileged Manhattan matron, who'd lead the paper's readers—young, middle-class colonizers of former potato fields—behind the high hedgerows guarding famous lives. The erstwhile movie magazine columnist now took her cue from Trade Winds, for as a reader confided to Bennett: "You make us feel that we know all these important authors and publishers that you write about personally, and it's a heady feeling." Saxe helped, too: as she spun stories, he taught her how to punctuate sentences.

Since her husband never allowed himself to waste time, absolutely nothing could be an idle activity for the rest of the household either, her sons had learned. Phyllis wrote the column on weekends and at night when Bennett was home working, her schedule still molded to his. Years later, she conceded that she'd had the choice of "being an angry wife, who had to look at that door that was closed" to her and the kids; of filling the house with people and leaving Bennett alone; or of joining him in his work. She'd done *that* for years, banking any resentment, but here was the chance for an ownership of her work and life. Full credit and full pay. "Bennett wanted me to work with him," she later recalled, "but had no real desire for me to go into the world . . . [and] get paid."

In ads, *Newsday* asked readers to laugh with Phyllis at "the latest doings of the intelligentsia," which for the paper included the family Cerf. One column might detail how a vacation gave rise to Landmark Books, while another described misadventures with Chip, their Boxer puppy. It had been decided that, to go with the country manor, they should have a dog. Rather than delegate naming to the boys, Bennett claimed that right, declaring him "a chip off the old block" (the pup's sire was a Westminster champion). He liked the idea of a pet, but naming was pretty much the extent of his participation. It fell to Margaret to be caregiver; the nanny wasn't particularly fond of animals.

Phyllis got a column, while the man who could reel off sixty letters a day got a new Dictaphone, and bestowed an endorsement on its maker. Soon his portrait appeared in ads in *Time* and *Newsweek*. "Successful men haven't got more time than anyone else but they do get more out of their time," ran the copy. It noted that the drawing depicted "a master user," but didn't give his name: *everyone* knew Bennett Cerf, who'd soon be associated with a panoply of products, from cocktail napkins to cigarettes. That year, he had to join the TV actors' union, another welcome sign of his bona fides.

Unwelcome was a publishing fracas at Grosset & Dunlap's paperback setup, Bantam. It had been eight years since RH led the charge to join with BOMC and three other publishers to buy G&D; since then, it had prospered, thanks mainly to Bantam. Saxe's nephew Ian Ballantine ran the subsidiary, reporting to G&D head (and Westchester club car member) John O'Connor. Like Bennett, Ian was an ambitious Columbia man, not short on ego. In 1939, at twenty-three, he'd convinced founder Allen Lane to let him and his wife, Betty, open a New York office for Penguin. After the war, he'd hoped RH would fund him to start a new company; instead, Bennett sent him to G&D. Ballantine hatched the Bantam rooster to compete with Pocket's kangaroo, and brought Penguin's New York chief editor and company secretary with him. Once paper became available postwar, paperbacks boomed like babies for Bantam, Pocket, and new players such as Fawcett and New American Library (NAL), as book-reading—not just the reading of magazines—crossed economic and social divides. In 1947, 95 million paperbacks were sold in the United States; by 1951, it was 231 million. Being the mass-market "home team" for its shareholder-publishers was an advantage, and Bantam benefited from the distribution reach into newsagents, five-and-dimes, and drugstores provided by another shareholder, magazine giant Curtis Publishing.

However, while Curtis wanted to concentrate on lucrative genres like romances and westerns, Ballantine was determined to put fine literature into the mix. On Bantam's first list was Twain's *Life on the Mississippi,* Steinbeck's *The Grapes of Wrath,* and the novel that Bennett and Don had so reluctantly put out of print in the ML—Fitzgerald's *The Great Gatsby.* Yet as time went on, that kind of personal enthusiasm was squeezed by corporate priorities, and there was also pressure to match the "selling" covers of rivals—bosomy blondes and provocative blurbs—that were transforming softcover racks into red-light districts. At the same time, the money was getting bigger and riskier: NAL had paid an unheard-of $35,000 to reprint Norman Mailer's *The Naked and the Dead.* Print runs ballooned, and unsold books—"returns"—came back to warehouses like yesterday's newspapers, with publishers having to swallow the losses. Bennett watched the paperback business getting "more cutthroat and competitive every day."

He, of course, was a Bantam director, providing general oversight while also protecting RH's stake and keeping an eye on possible threats to the ML. When O'Connor visited the Villard on a January Thursday with a tale to tell, and Ian Ballantine called at Sixty-Second Street with a different story that evening, Bennett faced a quandary. Muddling matters further, Bantam was due to reprint his own book, *Laughter Incorporated,* in July. O'Connor claimed that Bantam had become a factional battlefield, with the company secretary and chief editor who'd followed Ballantine complaining of unilateral decision-making. Ballantine countered that he was under huge pressure to sign the most competitive books, leaving little time for consultation. There was another complication: with roots in Penguin, he'd harbored a dream of spanning the Atlantic, and in 1951 had started a London subsidiary, Transworld. Ballantine used $26,000 of company money to set it up, but neglected to ask permission from the executive committee. With those under Ballantine spoiling to replace him, and those above him angry at his maverick flouting of rules, O'Connor had scheduled a "hearing," in effect calling for Ballantine's resignation.

Bennett saw something of himself in the dynamic idea man, a sympathy amplified by his allegiance to Saxe. Using $26,000 and a breach of protocol to justify Ian's ouster was absurd. The day before the "court-martial," as Bennett called it, he sent a two-page letter to O'Connor. "Ian Ballantine is Bantam, and Bantam is Ian Ballantine," he declared. Yes, Ian had admitted making mistakes, but Bantam had broken even its first year in business and made fantastic profits ever since. "Were I faced . . . with the choice of keeping Ian . . . or the entire rest of the organization," Bennett argued, "I would unhesitatingly let everybody [else] in the place walk out." He alone among the dozen directors supported Ballantine, who was soon fired. Without his leadership, Bantam quickly plunged into the red, and it would take two and a half years to find a talented businessman, Oscar Dystel, capable of leading the imprint back to health.

The Ballantine story didn't end with Ian's ouster. That fall, in Trade Winds, Bennett's alter ego, publisher "Anthony Bump," told of an encounter with a certain "Cosmo Heineken," who had a plan for "Revolutionizing the Publishing Industry." America's third most popular beer was Ballantine; *Saturday Review* readers would realize that, with "Heineken," Bennett was lampooning Ian Ballantine. Why? During the intervening months, Ian and his wife had founded their own company, Ballantine Books, with an idea that was indeed revolutionary. They would bring out new titles in hardcover and paperback *simultaneously,* changing the basic arithmetic of the business. The paperback royalty would double or quadruple to 8 percent and go entirely to the author, ending the prevailing fifty-fifty split with the originating publisher. Although Dr. Benjamin Spock's *The Common Sense Book of Baby and Child*

Care—published by Pocket and a huge seller—had been an early experiment along those lines, no one had thought to base a *company* on the concept. A few houses did cooperate, but most saw the plan as a threat, and Ian was forced to revert to the established system for much of his business. Except for a few such experiments, it would take more than a half century for new trade titles to debut simultaneously in multiple formats. That would happen courtesy of a digital revolution, but hardcovers still maintain an exclusive sales window before paperback reprints are published. Ballantine Books became a trailblazer, not as its founders had envisaged, but certainly through editorial genius. It would be the first paperback house to start a science fiction program, including books that not only transcended the genre, but were paperback originals. One, Ray Bradbury's *Fahrenheit 451,* was published their second year in business. The house also produced the first authorized paper editions of J. R. R. Tolkien's *The Hobbit* and *The Lord of the Rings,* bringing Middle Earth to millions.

...

THE FLIP SIDE OF lurid paperback covers—the kind Ballantine eschewed—was attention from censors, but sex was hardly alone in provoking scrutiny. The United States was fighting in Korea, and home-front assaults on civil liberties are never unusual during wartime. Add to the mix HUAC, along with local efforts by school, library, and parish groups, and the American Book Publishers Council's Committee on Censorship had its work cut out for it, defending the industry as well as individual houses against attempts at subverting free expression on moral, political, and ideological grounds. Donald was drafted to lead the committee. An obligation to publish the widest diversity of titles was being challenged by "do-gooders trying to impose conformity," he'd warned a Town Hall forum organized by the ACLU in spring 1951. The dangers publishers faced were made unnervingly clear that autumn, when Angus Cameron, chief editor and a director of Little, Brown, who'd had a hand in books from *The Joy of Cooking* to *The Catcher in the Rye,* was denounced as a Communist sympathizer. After "Counterattack," the newsletter behind *Red Channels,* declared that Little, Brown was a Communist front and listed thirty-one of Cameron's authors as fellow travelers, he was forced to resign and blacklisted. Bennett was disturbed enough to note LB's "commy troubles" in his diary, as well as talks he had with Horace

Manges on the subject. After all, Lela Rogers had thrown the same accusations at him.

In this freighted atmosphere, bookstore clerks were depicted as Red agents. Newsstand operators and tobacconists, with no say in what was on their racks (distributors chose the titles and put them in the stores), were denounced from pulpits as pornographers. Paperback reprints of novels by Steinbeck, Maugham, and O'Hara were on lists of objectionable books or banned outright. Don had to take on all comers: Catholic Church agents, police, vigilante groups. In June 1952, the newly created Gathings Committee was appointed by the House of Representatives with power to investigate "offensive and undesirable" books, magazines, and comics. Their report concluded that paperbacks largely appealed to "sensuality, immorality, filth, perversion, degeneracy." The army planned to establish a civilian committee to screen books going to soldiers. Don knew of units where officers and chaplains already censored a troop's books at will. Ten years earlier, the "old man" of forty had felt impelled to go to war for his country. Now he saw the current war being used to curtail freedoms he'd fought for. He wrote to the secretary of defense, and his quiet diplomacy, passionate and personal, proved effective. When his term was due to expire, the Book Publishers Council broke its rules in order to reelect him.

While Don was tangling with censors, Bennett was taking on Republicans. Nineteen fifty-two was an election year, and with an unpopular war, the Red Scare, and two decades of Democrats in the White House, people were restless. In Trade Winds a year earlier, he'd recognized that "confidence in President Truman seems to have hit a new low. . . . Like most other Americans I've met . . . I think the Democrats have been in the driver's seat long enough. It *is* 'time for a change.'" The lifelong Democrat seemed to be playing to his more conservative readers, but then lobbed a comeback: "I'm darned if I'm going to change from something to nothing!" However, the Republican presidential nominee turned out to be far from "nothing": at the convention, the World War II commander Dwight D. Eisenhower became the standard-bearer, with young Senator Richard M. Nixon of California his running mate.

Yet just as he'd fallen in love with FDR, Bennett fell again for the Democratic candidate: eloquent, witty Adlai Stevenson, the liberal governor of Illinois. Bennett met his man at a powerhouse dinner on September 21; that he was invited alongside media barons Luce, Hearst, and David Sarnoff (who controlled RCA and NBC) showed the multimedia reach he was now perceived to enjoy. He told favorable stories about Stevenson in Trade Winds, while Thrup repressed her native Republicanism (again) to jump on the bandwagon and work for him. "Volunteers for Stevenson" soon appealed to Bennett: Would RH publish an instant selection of the governor's speeches? The worshipful fan who'd once made (disastrous) multivolume obeisance to FDR felt exhilarated and flattered again: he loved being associated with a Great Man. The speeches, with an introduction by John Steinbeck, were rushed into an RH paperback for publication three weeks before the election, in no way publishing as usual. But although the book did well—the edition soon sold out—Bennett again paid dearly for the attention and proximity to greatness that he craved. On Sunday, September 28, the conservative *New York Journal-American* published a list of well-known Stevenson donors and how much each had contributed. All were in the thousands save for one. Bennett Cerf, the governor's publisher, had given ten whole bucks, a sum so incongruous, it earned him a headshot. Unlike Don and Bob, Bennett wasn't a great one for charity. The story was taken up nationwide.

The day after the revelation, Bennett was on a whirlwind trip to North Carolina, scheduled for a store visit, a TV appearance, and several speeches. Reporters dogged his every step, and Bennett admitted: "If I had had any idea they were going to print it, I would have made that $10 gift one of $1500. It looked so small." He tried to cast it merely as a token of appreciation tucked into a letter that thanked the governor for his willingness to wade into the muck of politics. How he *looked* to others, even more so now that he came through TV's big eye into their homes, counted for so much. Being perceived as a celebrity brought power and pleasure—"I was hot tonite!" his diary would gush after a winning streak and a few good jokes on the game show—but having that high profile could hurt. Nonetheless, the offending article went into a scrapbook, the compulsion to cherish anything bearing his name unalterable.

On Election Day, Ike trounced Adlai in a landslide, and Bennett's mind turned nervously elsewhere. Having always enjoyed spectacular health, at age fifty-four he had to check in to Doctors Hospital for his first-ever operation. Colleagues had joked about the boss's propensity for doing phone business in his bathroom. Now, five days as a patient offered an explanation: he spent so long in there because of hemorrhoids, and had developed a serious abscess. Three weeks later, having bounced back, he was in Illinois, flogging *Good for a Laugh* for the holidays, and visiting the governor's mansion. Though Stevenson had lost, publishers were vying to bring out his speeches in hardcover. By mid-December, RH had clinched the deal.

. . .

WHEN BENNETT WAS IN the hospital, Thrup had visited every day. "What would I do without her?" he'd asked his diary. William Faulkner could pose the same question about his editor and publishers: What would he do without them? A year earlier, he'd sent Bob Haas a formal request that in the event of his death, the firm continue to handle his work—already published and as yet unpublished. Saxe was to have final say as literary executor, continuing to edit anything he'd written. After a controversy blew up about Bill's winning the 1951 National Book Award for *Collected Stories*—a compilation of *previously* published fiction, some grumbled, shouldn't have been eligible—Bennett did his part, defending the win in Trade Winds. Then there were RH's *non*-literary responsibilities, everything from Saxe monitoring Bill's checking account and ordering whatever he needed, to Bob offering financial advice.

During these years, the difficulties in the Faulkners' marriage intensified, and Bill would travel to New York or Europe in part to see one of the young women who offered sexual and emotional release. With exceptional delicacy and loyalty, RH sometimes had a role in that. In the spring of 1951, Faulkner had instructed Saxe to tell his family he was in New York when in fact he was going to Paris to tryst with Else Jonsson, who'd caught his eye in Stockholm when he made the Nobel Prize visit. He asked Saxe to find a discreet hotel, and wanted to travel on a plane where Betty Haas was a stewardess, trusting Bob's daughter to keep his secret. Purposely or serendipitously, Bob gave the perfect cover by suggesting that Bill needed to revisit France to conjure scenes in *A Fable,* his long-gestating novel. All the while, the partners and Saxe worked to maintain cordiality with Estelle, who'd been a guest in all their homes. Faulkner didn't make it easy, insisting that however much she pleaded, the firm mustn't give her any money.

By the summer of 1952, unhappier than ever, Bill confessed to Saxe that he couldn't sleep or write, and was fantasizing about a break from his wife and all the other chains tying him down. He was trying to pick up the threads of *A Fable,* but his back had been plaguing him, made worse by falls from his horse. Alcohol assuaged the pain, but by October he was lost down the black hole of a binge, and his family couldn't cope. Estelle turned to Saxe, who dropped everything to travel to Oxford. He found Faulkner incoherent, in a stinking stupor, his hawk's face bruised and body battered from the drunken falls. At least Bill recognized him, but had no control over himself, and would have lain in his own filth had Saxe and a manservant not carried him again and again from bed to bathroom. The only thing he wanted was one more beer.

Saxe stayed up with him all night. Early in the morning, once Bill had fallen into a drowned sleep, Saxe wrote two letters to preserve his sanity: one to Dorothy, the other to Bennett and Bob (Don was in Paris). He feared this time it wasn't just alcohol's depredations, but a complete crack-up, and Estelle had made him responsible for what to do next. He arranged for Bill to stay in a Memphis hospital; the plan was that Faulkner later come to the Commins home, and then the Princeton Inn. Chain-smoking and hollow-eyed, Saxe began the long journey north later that day.

Bill did spend Thanksgiving with him and Dorothy, who to please their guest invited his young inamorata Joan Williams for the holiday. But within days another binge began and another collapse, leading to electroshock treatments in a Riverdale sanitarium. A place was found for him in New York when he was well enough, but most days he liked to work on *A Fable* in Saxe's office. He'd spend the odd night in the employees' lounge, or come to the office on a Saturday. Sometimes he'd skip the palazzo entirely and turn up at Saxe's home. Once, Budd Schulberg arrived early to work with Saxe in Princeton and found Faulkner sitting on a step, having waited who knows how long. Eventually, Bill returned to Oxford, but the pattern was set. The following February, it would be a well-known drying-out place—the Charles B. Towns private hospital on Central Park West—then a few days with the Haas family, a stay at the Algonquin, and back to Dorothy and Saxe. During one cycle, a young would-be novelist, working nights at the Towns switchboard, answered a call from a disoriented patient with a thick Southern accent. It took a moment for the operator to realize it was William Faulkner. When he looked at the room register to see who was responsible for his being there, he saw two names: Cerf and Klopfer.

"So I knew those names before I ever got published there," E. L. Doctorow mused, decades later.

Chapter 27

Bombshells and Whoppers

WHEN THE ANNOUNCEMENT WAS MADE ON JANUARY 8, 1953, THAT Ralph Ellison's *Invisible Man*—a debut novel that Random House had published the previous spring—had won the National Book Award for Fiction, it was the first surprise of a year that would see many. To capture the laurels, the book overcame the considerable advantages of Hemingway's *The Old Man and the Sea* and Steinbeck's *East of Eden,* and the considerable disadvantage, in that place and time, of having been written by an American who was Black. Thirty-eight, elegant, and soulfully handsome, Ellison had arrived at RH in 1947 along with Frank Taylor and Albert Erskine. Taylor had signed him at Reynal & Hitchcock, but both editors believed in Ellison and championed his book to Bennett, who agreed to a $2,000 advance. When Taylor moved full-time to Hollywood, Erskine took over. RH had shown care for a book that by nobody's measure would be an easy sell. Harlem Renaissance authors were largely passé. Ellison's friend Richard Wright's *Black Boy* had come out in 1945 (a blurb from Bennett had pronounced it beautifully written, "with the impact of a battleship"), but Wright was now an exile, and James Baldwin wouldn't arrive for another year.

The firm had tapped Ted McKnight Kauffer, whose association with RH went back to the Nonesuch 1920s, to design a brilliant cover: from a black background, a brown-and-white cubist face, one eye staring, emerges as though through window panes, or, perhaps, crosshairs. Albert wrote passionately to many contacts, promising a novel "of great richness and power—a book one can with complete confidence call important." As a Southerner, he knew "there will be people who . . . will not like it, but it is difficult to see how even they can ignore it." Bennett spent extra on advertising, and newly elevated (and, unusual for that era, female) publicity director Jean Ennis, puffing on her ever-present Gauloises through a long cigarette-holder, blanketed 1,300 opinion-makers with a press release. Recognizing the difficult, "anomalous position of the Negro" in a society where race prejudice was endemic, she affirmed the book's universality as "a valid . . . powerful interpretation" of the human condition. Reviews landed perfectly around publication in April. The Sunday *Times* saw "a resolutely honest, tormented, profoundly American book" defying color categorization, evoking Dante and Dostoyevsky, mapping a course "from the underground world into the light," and *Time* and the *Saturday Review* were enthusiastic. Ellison defended himself against critics by conjuring another RH author: "It is felt that there is something in the Negro experience that makes it not quite right for the novel. . . . [But] in this problem, as Faulkner [shows] . . . the American human conflict is at its most intense."

Ralph Ellison

By June, RH had sold more than 10,000 copies, "pretty darn good for a first novel by a young Negro in times like these," Bennett told a contact at Doubleday's book clubs. He was campaigning for *Invisible Man* to be offered as a premium: Black subscribers would be pleased by that rarity, "a Negro [author] listed" among all the others. After the National Book Award, Bennett took out more ads, and by the end of February orders had reached 18,000 copies. However, on the P&L statement, the book's gross profit vaporized once the customary subtraction for overheads—each title was supposed to contribute to general expenses—was factored in. By the end of 1955, 20,000 copies had been sold, but demand had dried up. With a nod from Lew Miller, who determined the size of print runs and whether a title stayed in stock, the production department remaindered what hardcovers were left; the paperback was still available.

Ellison wouldn't be the first author left in the dark when his publisher scrapped his book: he discovered almost by accident that it was out of stock. Feeling "a singular lack of respect"—RH should have allowed him to buy the copies—he complained to Erskine. Albert explained the math, then did an about-face. As "a matter of admitting and rectifying a mistake," they'd reprint. The firm felt in the wrong and had learned something: going forward, Erskine promised no remaindering would take place unless the editorial department was consulted.

Foreign publishers noticed *Invisible Man* early. British, Swedish, and Norwegian editions came out in 1953, and by the mid-1960s had been joined by a half dozen others. Slowly, Ellison's fellow citizens began to show more interest. His novel was excerpted in textbooks. The NAL paperback at first reaped disappointing sales, but reprinted in 1960 and again in 1963, the year the book was embraced by the ML. In 1965, it attained a kind of apotheosis: when the *New York Herald Tribune* asked two hundred authors, editors, and critics to name the most distinguished American novel of the previous twenty years—works by Faulkner, Bellow, Mailer, and others were in contention—*Invisible Man* topped the poll. RH brought out *Shadow and Act,* an essay collection, in 1964. Ellison long struggled with a second novel that would appear posthumously, but warm relations with Don and Albert continued. Indeed, in 1982, Ellison's wife, Fanny, wrote Don that she and Ralph "never lost our nostalgia" for the early RH days, of which "you and Pat, the Bennett Cerf's [*sic*] and Mr. Haas were so much a part."

. . .

BENNETT HEADED WEST A couple weeks after Ellison's firecracker win at the NBAs. He soon found himself dazzled by the glow emanating from a young woman lounging in Room 333 of the Beverly Hills Hotel, having delayed arriving at La Quinta in order to enjoy a tea date with Miss Marilyn Monroe. But while it gave him bragging rights, it was also work: he was profiling for *Esquire* the young actress generating so much talk. Her image, as it happened, graced his inner sanctum at the Villard. His La Quinta pal Bill Goetz—Louis B. Mayer's son-in-law—had sent him a calendar featuring nude pictures she'd posed for in the late 1940s, when needing cash. Bennett had mentioned the calendar in Trade Winds, and enjoyed how it tantalized colleagues. Now he was curious to meet "The Altogether Girl"—as the article was titled—in the flesh.

The commission was probably his idea: Bennett's internal radar pointed him toward every up-and-comer or VIP in America, and his connections usually helped gain at least an introduction. Monroe was working on a picture adapted from a book Bennett knew well from Liveright days: Anita Loos's *Gentlemen Prefer Blondes*. Two days earlier, he'd been on the Fox lot watching her and costar Jane Russell prance for a publicity shoot in black tights, high hats, "and not much else." Later, Bennett treasured a photo from that day, he in natty suit facing luminous Marilyn in her scanty costume. Sniffles had conveniently put her in bed for their second encounter.

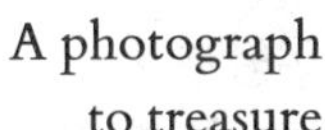

A photograph to treasure

"There's more to Marilyn Monroe than meets the eye," his opening gambit attested: "a generous nature, an IQ of adequate if not formidable proportions, and a fierce desire to become a first-rate actress and cultured . . . woman of the world." The IQ assessment was condescending, and Bennett winked and nudged his way through the rest, but the tone was sympathetic; not all gossip-masters feeding off her notoriety were so inclined. Even here, he turned to books. He told how her drama coach had encouraged her to buy the director Max Reinhardt's theater library at auction, outbidding UCLA and USC and causing such a flap that Reinhardt's son bought the books back. More surprising, Bennett described her sex appeal in terms of a book: she easily exuded "that certain something which the artist of the most lurid paperback jacket strives for in vain." He noted her bedside reading: Michael Chekhov's *To the Actor* (on stage technique) and the *Essays of Montaigne* (Montaigne *was* in the ML). The visit was unusual in another respect: at a certain point, Phyllis joined the tête-à-tête. Monroe had handlers, but so did he.

After the Cerfs arrived at La Quinta on February 1, forty-one-year-old Cousin Ginger swooped in briefly, counting on Bennett to give her away when she married husband number four, Jacques Bergerac, a stunning former French law student sixteen years younger, whom she'd "discovered" for the movies. In the desert, Bennett and Phyllis caught up with pals and made their first foray to Frank Sinatra's Palm Springs home, where Moss and Kitty were staying. The idyll was interrupted, however, by an update from Bob and Don about another blonde bombshell.

Two months earlier, the *New York Daily News* had set its front page ablaze with a story that spread everywhere: twenty-six-year-old Bronx-born ex-GI George Jorgensen Jr. had undergone injections and surgeries in Denmark to change sex, and emerged as "Christine." Although experimental operations of this kind had taken place in pre-war Germany, this was the first time most Americans had heard of the idea. The words "transsexual" and "transgender" had not been part of the national conversation at all, and most people were utterly shocked. Bennett realized that no news was bigger, and was all for signing young Jorgensen for a book. As he left for L.A., talks were underway, but now Bob signaled that he and Don were backing off.

"Damnit, Don, we must do this book," Bennett insisted as soon as he heard of the others' reluctance. "The interest . . . is enormous. . . . Fuck the difficulties (if not Christine herself) & get this lined up." Reacting to other RH news, he fumed in general: Faulkner was in Manhattan, "making an exhibition of himself." Novelist Nancy Mitford was raising a transatlantic fuss. Book clubs were ignoring RH. "What . . . are all our high-powered editors doing?" he thundered. "It's one thing to sit on their asses stewing over scripts that are put on their desks, it's another to

CREATE books. Have Linscott, Erskine . . . come up with ONE saleable idea in the past 6 months?"

It was exactly the kind of tempest Don and Bob had witnessed many times and knew to sit out—often the storm was as much a reaction to other matters in Bennett's life as to those at hand, but this time the back-and-forth continued. Harry Maule, who'd been assigned to the project, added his reservations. Jorgensen had refused a co-author, and Maule felt a self-written manuscript would be unpublishable. News of the project had spread in the trade, but the sales reps cautioned that booksellers refused to believe RH would back such a book, and Don's own fears were borne out: he'd taken "a riding from practically everyone." Many Americans in 1953 weren't ready to grapple with a work of art like *Invisible Man*. How, then, would they treat a memoir by an untested non-writer on the subject of a sex change? What would it mean to RH if accounts and readers saw it not as a courageous, groundbreaking story about a heartrending human dilemma, but as opportunistic sensationalism? And what if that turned out to be a bit too close to the truth?

Essential to both Don and Bob was a concept of dignity where sensationalism had no place, and this extended to RH, a projection of themselves. Bennett's relationship with dignity was different. He could feel shame: he'd complained about Faulkner sullying his image with public drunkenness, and the old Jesus Junior prissiness occasionally reared its head. But always more of a salesman than his partners, he'd also become a showman, and the pull of the spotlight was stronger; more than the others, he sensed where the zeitgeist was going, understood the power of celebrity, and was carried along by the prospect of publicity. Problems could be overcome later.

Outside RH, there were those who wondered at the partners' ability to work so well together, given such differences in temperament and personality. But like Ginger and Fred, they recognized that the joint dynamic was far greater than the sum of the parts. All three knew that Bennett's bold, instinctive action led the dance. And yet, at times the dance had to pause; at times Don and Bob had to counter his impetuous overreaching, and stop him when the firm threatened to get ahead of itself. On March 30, a lawyer-vetted release went out: RH wouldn't be associated with any book by Jorgensen. Not until 1967 was she able to publish her memoirs.

While weighing what to do about Christine, Don had been preoccupied with an author crisis of another sort, the "transatlantic fuss" Bennett had alluded to. Nancy Mitford, daughter of a lord and eldest sister in a brood that included Jessica, Debo, Unity, Pamela, and Diana, was a brilliant writer who'd reaped critical and commercial success, and was the firm's most important British novelist, author of four books before RH signed U.S. rights to *The Pursuit of Love* in 1945. It was Bennett who bestowed on her sixth, *Love in a Cold Climate,* its perfect title in 1949, and RH later published *The Blessing*. All chronicled manners and mores of the British upper class (and made forays into the French: Nancy lived in Paris). With witty sophistication she could make readers laugh out loud, yet beneath the brittle humor lay a serious inquiry into love.

As was usually the case, an option clause in her previous contract granted RH first refusal on her next book: it was to be a change of pace, a biography of Madame de Pompadour, mistress of Louis XV. On a recent trip to Paris, Donald had twice met with Mitford, so he was dumbfounded when her agent wrote to request an advance of $5,000, a better royalty ("stiff and unusual" for nonfiction, Don thought), and coolly advised that the biography would be her last RH book. When Bennett heard the news, he urged Don to fly to France as Bennett had once flown to Sea Island to court O'Neill, but Don preferred telephonic and epistolary diplomacy. After repeated (failed) entreaties, Mitford at last disclosed why she'd become disenchanted: "What I feel about Random House is that they have not much respect for books, & only care about sales."

It was a devastating rebuke. True, she was steeped in the condescension many of her class exhibited toward a nation that had eclipsed her own in the postwar pecking order, but she also had cause. The firm had "Americanized" certain sentences of *The Pursuit of Love* rather than leave the French phrases she'd sprinkled in, and nobody had consulted her—a breach of the compact between publisher and author, and the same complaint Gertrude Stein had made years before. After Mitford protested to Bennett, his breezy reply stressing the book's success had offended her. Then came another wrong move: RH hadn't sent proofs of *The Blessing* for her to okay.

Don made a final try. Yes, she had reason to be irritated. In the future he, Bennett, or Bob would gladly bring proofs to her personally. He'd hop on a plane *now* if she gave the word. Then he addressed the rebuke head-on: the partners prided themselves on their "distinguished authors," and he rattled off a long list. "That's sound and creative publishing, Nancy, not based on sales alone, but on quality. We don't publish plays and poetry . . . and first novels for sales; we publish because we love it and we have pride in a well-balanced list." "Flattered" he was so anxious to keep her, Mitford was also definite: *Pompadour* would be her last book with the firm. As it happened, she wasn't the only author to feel Random was becoming careless.

. . .

TWO YEARS EARLIER, James Michener had toured ten Asian countries and published his reportage, *The Voice of Asia,* as the Korean conflict raged. He'd summoned the courage to go to the war zone, where he stayed for weeks. Michener was "always in the right place at the right time," as Bennett noted. Embedded on the aircraft carriers *Essex* and *Valley Forge,* he'd seen bombing and reconnaissance missions from inside the fast new jets, and witnessed action on the ground, putting it all into a terse novel. The plot followed a World War II pilot recalled to active duty, who had to confront his trauma and ambivalence while on a bombing mission over North Korea.

In September 1952, *Life* had garnered huge attention by publishing Ernest Hemingway's novella *The Old Man and the Sea* in a single issue. Suddenly, after a ten-year sleep, Hemingway was the center of attention: the issue sold five million copies in two days, and was republished by Scribner as a short book. Michener had blurbed it for *Life,* and his canny agent had an idea: if the magazine gave such treatment to Hemingway, it could do the same for her client. After all, Michener had been called a possible inheritor of Hemingway's mantle, and the story couldn't be timelier. The magazine obliged, for a very considerable $30,000. Titled *The Bridges at Toko-Ri,* it was published the first week in July 1953 in *Life,* and also as a slim RH book.

Bennett sold rights to *Reader's Digest,* a Doubleday club, and Bantam for advances totaling another $30,000-plus. He happily informed his diary that Helen Strauss had negotiated a film sale to Paramount for $100,000—with 5 percent of Michener's net going to Random. This was real money, shared all around. The Korean armistice was signed at the end of July, just after the Paramount deal. In its first six months, the book sold more than 35,000 copies. Michener would refer to *The Bridges at Toko-Ri* as his experiment in "the well-crafted English novel" and called it his tightest, best-written book. He produced at such an incredible rate that even before the book was published, he'd finished a first draft of his *next* novel. This one explored interracial love, inspired by real-life stories he'd heard in Asia, and was infused with echoes of *Madame Butterfly* and *From Here to Eternity,* its two romances doomed by prevailing attitudes. Indeed, from *Tales of the South Pacific* on, Michener took a forceful stand against racial prejudice.

Both Strauss and her client had agreed that the draft of the new novel needed work, and were counting on Saxe's help: as Michener had readily admitted in the past, he was a fellow who required "a lot of editing." Back in 1951, he'd written Saxe: "It is impossible for me to tell you how much I appreciate my work with you." But the next thing Strauss heard about their current project was that Saxe was sending the marked manuscript to the printer, not seeing the need for a major edit. She sensed that without more work, the book would fail and harm Michener's reputation. Worse, she felt it was déjà vu: after all, Saxe had been forced to halt the presses and do more on *The Fires of Spring* when Bennett and others had judged it wanting.

And so, agent and author went to the palazzo. Strauss had decided that Saxe—who was the initial reason Michener had come to RH—must be taken off the book. Bennett was in California, so it was Donald she confronted. Strauss realized she was touching on "just about the most delicate nerve in publishing," the author-editor relationship, but wasn't arguing over just one book. Michener needed a different editor *going forward,* and from her experience representing Robert Penn Warren and Ralph Ellison, she knew the man she wanted: Albert Erskine. If she didn't get him, Strauss threatened to cancel the contract. Almost certainly Don would have phoned Bennett at La Quinta, and mulled it over with Bob, too. In such a situation, the partners generally agreed to do whatever it took to keep an author they valued, even if collateral damage was visited upon one as dear as Saxe. They ran a business, and painful choices had to be made.

The book's title, as with each of the novels Michener had published with RH thus far, had not come easily. Saxe had made the final decision in January, selecting from a list that Jim had supplied. Poignantly, he'd chosen *Sayonara*—the Japanese word for goodbye. Two months later, on March 1, 1953, Michener wrote to his new editor: "Klopfer was really fine the other morning and warmly fortified my own tentative conclusions. I would . . . be pleased if you would agree to work on my latest. . . . I think you know that as a man who wants to become an old pro I look forward to what you have to say." And so Erskine and Michener got to work, and the book got better. The popular magazine *McCall's* bested what *Life* had paid for *Toko-Ri:* $45,000 for early excerpts that would whet the public's appetite for publication in January 1954. Bennett's producer friend Bill Goetz and Warner Brothers would pay $250,000 for movie rights. The film, starring Marlon Brando, would be nominated for ten Oscars, and win four.

In 1951 and 1952, Michener had earned over $100,000 in royalties. In 1954, his accountant estimated his income for the previous year at $138,000, and he was also becoming well enough known to be sought out for endorsements, plugging beer, Pan American Airways, *The New York Times*—just like his busy publisher. The choice of Erskine would prove right: on one memorable and rare public occasion, Michener would turn to Albert and call him "my guru." As for RH, the foundling was on his way to becoming essential, a financial bulwark, an author whom Bennett would eventually describe in his oral history as "our instant gold mine."

Michener and Mitford weren't the only authors wanting a better fit. In Trade Winds, Bennett had declared that his most recent effort at humor between covers, *Good for a Laugh*—published the previous fall for the holiday season—was his best since *Try and Stop Me*. But like the Honorable Miss Mitford, he, too, had changed publishers. Almost from the start, friends and rivals Dick Simon and Bennett Cerf had walked a very fine line; Bennett could be acidic about Dick in his diary, and Dick was sometimes heard to mimic Bennett's speech inflections around S&S. After his second collection, *Shake Well Before Using,* had needed both Saxe and S&S's wunderkind Jack Goodman to whip it into shape, Goodman had come to RH with a book proposal of his own, which the partners first encouraged, but then turned down. Word then spread that when Bennett talked to him about a third joke book, Jack had asked: "What are you gonna call it—*The Bottom of the Barrel*?" Not long after, Bennett had moved to Doubleday.

He saw the change as a tonic, and by the end of 1953, 116,000 copies of *Good for a Laugh* were in print. Doubleday agreed to issue *Try and Stop Me* in a hardcover reprint, and also contracted a new book: a humor encyclopedia featuring jokes and anecdotes from well-known figures throughout American history, in which a maximum fifty pages would be Bennett's "own" material. The $24,000 advance he'd receive was more than what

Bennett offered most of his authors, and now he negotiated the kind of arrangement that RH top sellers like Michener had: Doubleday would hold his money and keep the interest it accrued for itself, paying him no more than $2,000 per year, so he'd avoid cripplingly high taxes.

As an author, he'd reached a milestone, and was careful to protect his position in other ways, too. Betty White had a daytime TV show, and began thinking about putting together a humor book to capitalize on her popularity. White's prospective co-author wrote to Bennett, seeking his counsel. "My honest advice . . . is to forget the whole damn business," he cautioned. "There is so little profit in books of this sort these days that it doesn't begin to be worth all the trouble. . . ."

His royalty statements begged to differ.

After *Good for a Laugh* had gotten off to a roaring start, Dick Simon wrote about an idea they'd discussed previously, a collection of Bennett's pieces on writers and the book trade. Dick thought a book of "greater stature" like that would be good for his old classmate's reputation among "litry" folk whose contempt for joke books was now well known, but Bennett had no desire to return to S&S. Doubleday editor-in-chief Ken McCormick had proposed something similar—a book of his "publishing recollections"—but Bennett would have none of it. Reflecting on the past, for a man like him, meant time away from living in the present: an old man's game.

Landmarks was another of his flourishing brainchildren. Bennett had prevailed upon a new crop of friends and notables, like Supreme Court Justice William O. Douglas and Buck Crouse, to author books for the children's series, and orchestrated a real coup by signing Quentin Reynolds for a Landmark about the FBI, with the bureau's cooperation and an introduction from J. Edgar Hoover. That deal had required strategy and toadying in equal measure: Quent had dispatched a letter to Hoover's deputy, Clyde Tolson, having met both men socially, noting that while he didn't expect "official blessing," he'd like to "submit to a very voluntary [unofficial] censorship," to catch "inadvertent" errors and convey the FBI's "real worth and spirit."

Quent was such a hearty fellow, so keen to be liked and to like in return, that bedrock concepts of journalistic independence did not get in his way. He told Tolson that he realized "the boss" would rather have a book recount the FBI story "without glorifying him," but no one could ignore that Hoover was "a very real hero to millions of kids." He also

Quentin Reynolds and Bennett

conveyed a message from his publisher: if the book could be titled *Hoover of the FBI,* it "would sell a million copies." The letter was "a masterpiece of diplomacy," Bennett assured Quent. Two weeks later, after getting an unofficial green light, the two repeated the necessary in a letter to Hoover: they were "only concerned" to do a book "of use to the Bureau and of interest to juvenile readers."

If journalistic ethics was no stumbling block to Quent, liberal politics proved no barrier to Bennett. Just as he'd been proud to sign *The Age of Suspicion*—a book by Jimmy Wechsler, the crusading editor of the *New York Post* who'd dared to take on McCarthy—he was happy to do business with Hoover, a man identified by Wechsler as underpinning McCarthyism. Perhaps dealing with Whit Chambers had paved the way, and anyway, nobody had a higher profile than the enigmatic "boss." Besides, Bennett had found it fun touring the FBI on his honeymoon, feeling the same excitement kids would experience vicariously in the Landmark. In June, a week after "cinching" the deal, the Red Scare reached a symbolic apex of immolation: the Rosenbergs had their date with the electric chair. Bennett noted it in his diary.

At summer's end, having already paid him to be dazzled by Miss Monroe in February, *Esquire* treated Bennett to another dose of all-

American pulchritude by asking him to cover the Miss America pageant in Atlantic City. He swam in the ocean, ogled the girls, and marveled at the famous horses diving off Steel Pier. *Esquire* editors loved the piece. (Evidently the pageant did, too: a few years later, he'd be invited to return as a judge.) That September, out of the blue, Cardinal Spellman offered to buy RH's wing of the palazzo for $800,000, almost twice what the partners had paid for it. They turned their neighbor down; still, how reassuring that if ever RH were in need, the palace that housed them had also become a rainy-day piggybank. One more bombshell would explode before the year was through, and it, too, involved Quent Reynolds. *Reader's Digest* had learned of cloak-and-dagger exploits in France by a Canadian wartime intelligence agent, George DuPre. It wanted to create a book from his story, which Quent would write. RH would publish the hardcover, and *RD* condense it for millions of subscribers.

DuPre, now a Calgary businessman, was a genuine grassroots phenomenon: after sharing his war experiences with neighbors, word spread; before long, he found himself invited to repeat the story to church groups, service clubs, Scout troops, and meetings all over Canada. Coached by the Allies to impersonate a man of very limited mental ability, he'd been dropped behind enemy lines to gather intelligence, and was captured and tortured, but kept his secrets and disguise. Everyone warmed to the modest sincerity of the "gentle spy," as he was called, and DuPre, a deeply religious father of two, wanted to donate his royalties to the Scouts. The book would be titled *The Man Who Wouldn't Talk*. Author and spy toiled together on the manuscript, and Reynolds also checked details on DuPre's background, interviewing Royal Canadian Air Force officials and even a government minister, and received final approval of the manuscript from its subject. RH published *The Man Who Wouldn't Talk* the third week in October to good sales and reviews, and the condensation appeared in the November *Reader's Digest*.

On Friday, November 13, 1953, Bennett received a wire that, given the date, he took to be a joke. Soon, though, he was on a phone call with the Calgary newsman who'd sent it and found that the joke was on him. The reporter, Douglas Collins, had been a prisoner during the war, and done some digging: DuPre had spent the war in Britain and Canada, not France. He'd started with a few exaggerations that grew bigger and bigger in an unacknowledged compact with his well-meaning listeners, until the lies had taken over his life. He'd wanted to be a hero, but became an impostor, and when Collins confronted him, DuPre crumpled.

Other calls quickly followed. On Sunday, *The New York Times* intended to put the story on page one. They'd all be tarred and feathered for fools, or worse: readers who'd paid good money for the book could cry *fraud*. Bennett had to come up with a plan, but couldn't stop time. Phyllis had organized a party for Saturday, and forty-four friends were coming, including a *Reader's Digest* executive, Ralph Henderson, as well as Quent. That evening, as guests began congregating, Henderson, Quent, and Bennett went off to speak in private. Henderson's boss had promised the *Times* that an explanation would appear in the January *Digest*. Bennett was, Henderson sympathized, not a perpetrator but a victim: he'd accepted the story for publication on the magazine's say-so. But damage was done, and Bennett desperately wondered what to do.

"I'll change the title," he suddenly said, thinking out loud. He'd call it "The Man Who Talked Too Much," the story of an incredible fake. "People will want to buy that," he laughed. The title, however, did not change, though he recycled the one-liner in interviews. On Monday, the *Times* reported that Random House "was still investigating." Later that day, Bennett dictated a press release and a letter to booksellers. The firm was authorizing stores to issue a refund to any customer who'd bought the book prior to November 14; RH would fully reimburse all retailers. He'd told papers to transfer the title—now showing up on bestseller lists—from nonfiction to fiction. Going forward, copies would include an account by Quent of the trickery.

Inspired damage control

"'The Man Who Wouldn't Talk' talked too much. Our apologies!" he concluded his letter. He also took big ads in the *Times, Herald Tribune,* and *Saturday Review,* with a bold "FACT" crossed out and "Fiction!" next to it. "The spy story that proved too good to be true" was the tagline. On November 24, he noted that more than a thousand orders had come in over the previous two days. People didn't seem to want their money back. *New York Post* editor Jimmy Wechsler congratulated him on a "brilliant" PR operation that had, alas, knocked mention of Wechsler's own book from the papers. Other publishers took their hats off, "for the quick and thoroughly fair manner with which you continue to give everyone their money's worth."

Chapter 28

Transitions and Home Truths

Though Bennett had survived the unmasking of George Dupre, the second half of 1953 and first days of 1954 brought troubles that couldn't be fixed with a few well-chosen words. Eugene O'Neill, cut off from the world, had willed himself to die on November 27. It was a death twinned with a close escape: three months earlier, in late August, they'd almost lost Saxe to a major heart attack. His decades of overwork and anxiety had called in their chit. Bennett and Don felt terribly worried about their old friend, but also had to be clear-eyed. A few months earlier, frustrated over the Jorgensen mess, Bennett had exploded about the trade department's seeming lack of energy. Linscott and Maule were old, McDowell proving an awkward match, Albert not signing enough talent, and Belle disadvantaged by being female in an industry where the only women who exercised clout were overwhelmingly agents or in children's books. Now "Saxie," the ever-present watcher in the morning and worrier in the evening, whose name they'd singled out to honor as EDITOR with theirs on letterhead, had shown his mortality. At sixty-plus, recovery was relative. They'd have to take a hard look at provisioning for the future.

A few days after the coronary, Bennett sat staring in the prow of his Mt. Kisco study, swirling pipe smoke commingling with the ripe perfume rising off the garden. He'd paused for a moment in composing a four-page letter to Saxe. A man who did everything fast, now he was taking exceptional care and writing in his best hand, like a youth addressing himself to a distant father; yet the letter made clear who was in charge.

Once Saxe returned, Bennett declared, he and Don would "brook no more . . . your shouldering everybody's responsibilities for them, or having your feelings hurt when any one of them proceeds to act the part of a typical author by making a complete bastard of himself." There'd be no more "seven-day-a-week nonsense." He finished on an unusual note of self-recognition, but Saxe was one of the few to whom Bennett allowed himself to open up a crack: "I've been playing the role of buffoon in print for so long now—and at such high rates, thank God!—that it's hard for me to stay serious long any more, but before I close I want to be sure you know that along with Phyllis, the kids, Donald, and Herbert, you are the guy I love most in the world. Random House IS Don, you, and myself."

Saxe Commins in the 1950s

Saxe cried when Dorothy read him the letter. The week before Christmas, he made his first trip to New York since being stricken, wanting to show his face at sales conference. Yet he was still so overwrought and tired, his smiles and hugs were predictably dampened by tears. Bennett and Don forced a compromise: for the present, he'd travel to town on Mondays and Thursdays and spend the other three mornings working from home in Princeton. Determined to accept the situation "with grace and always with silence," Saxe sat gray-faced in the strange familiarity of his office that first week of 1954, body and spirit chilled by a fatalistic melancholy. He'd been physically estranged from RH for four months and ten days—he'd counted each one. The new arrangement was "destined to bring . . . a gradual detachment and final separation," he reckoned. Still, there was work to be done, and for so long as he could, he would do it.

. . .

ON JANUARY 6, the firm got the good news that W. H. Auden's *The Shield of Achilles* had won the National Book Award for Poetry. Auden, his face all pouched eyes and dry riverbed of wrinkles, would sometimes be seen shuffling around the upstairs offices, a typical Englishman in scruffy carpet slippers, messy manuscript in hand. But he was, one editor remembered, "a very unusual author, highly principled in an assertive way. Auden never took an advance, but when he delivered a manuscript, he wanted his money." The divvying up of writers had made Don point man for most RH poets. Just as well: Auden would allude to Bennett as "a sixty-year-old giggling public man," a play on Yeats's line about "a sixty-year-old smiling public man" in *Among School Children*. Whether spurred by the Pound affair or from a more visceral instinct, he was said to be among those who saw Bennett as vulgar, one of God's gifts to anti-semites. Yet Bennett saw Auden as that rarity: a poet who brought not only glory, but profit.

The second week in January, news came of the sudden death of John O'Hara's beloved wife, Belle. The previous summer, O'Hara himself had almost died from a perforated ulcer brought on by boozing. With Belle's help, he'd stopped drinking. Now what would become of John and his motherless little girl? Added to all the somber news, New York's winter had turned brutal, and Bennett was impatient for California. But as he was wrapping up work at the office for six-plus weeks away, he had a date with the Geisels, who ironically had flown in from sun-blessed La Jolla. One reason was to deliver a promised manuscript, *Horton Hears a Who!*

RH had published the last major Seuss book, *If I Ran the Zoo,* in time for Christmas 1950, and the book had succeeded beyond expectations. But Ted had had to interrupt work on the next juvenile, *Scrambled Eggs Super!* when the siren song of a big Hollywood advance had lured him into scriptwriting a feature-length fantasy, *The 5000 Fingers of Dr. T.* For a man who liked control, this experience of the movie business—so different from his wartime work under the director Frank Capra—proved, in Ted's words, "a debaculous fiasco." By the time the eggs were scrambled, Christmas 1952 had passed, and they had to be served for spring.

Bennett had done well all those years before when he'd lured Ted from Vanguard by promising to publish anything he wrote. After a slow start, the books had sold well, reviews were good, and the pace of output would have pleased any publisher. He'd instinctively appreciated the originality of Ted's talent and the discipline underpinning it, while Ted had been impressed by Bennett's kinetic energy, determination, and savvy. The two tall, well-built men liked each other and enjoyed each other's company. And for one so extroverted and the other so shy, they shared important qualities: boyishness and whimsy; the use of humor and practical joking as shield and prod to navigate the world; a maverick's abhorrence of bureaucracy.

One of Bennett's great gifts was to intuit authors' needs, and he saw early that Ted would require special handling. When Saxe, in addition to Louise, was assigned to work with him, Ted was "terribly flattered" that Faulkner's helpmeet was also his, and judged Saxe "probably the only editor" from whom he ever learned, one who showed "great patience and understanding." "He never would tell you anything was wrong," Ted marveled. "He'd make you think, and you'd come around to your own conclusion. He'd spend an hour talking about three or four lines. . . . He helped me realize that a paragraph in a children's book is equal to a chapter in an adult book."

Before the Geisels left the Villard that wintry Friday, Louise summoned Saxe and Bennett to join Ted and Helen in her office to hear the good doctor read *Horton Hears a Who!* aloud. This was the first instance of what would become a tradition: henceforth Ted would do a command performance for each new book when he delivered it. Word inevitably spread, and for the lucky staff who could be there, the readings became a special perk of working at Random.

After the performance, both the Geisels and the Cerfs were soon heading west. Bennett lectured and signed his way through Tulsa, Dallas, Fort Worth, Topeka, and Denver, stopping off in Oklahoma City for a rare visit to Phyllis's mother, who threw a party for her famous son-in-law. Thrup met him in L.A., where they played with the usual crowd and also new friends: *It Happened One Night* star Claudette Colbert and her surgeon husband, Jack Pressman. Then it was on to La Quinta, where Phyllis's vacation was interrupted by good news: Bennett's pal Herb Mayes, the *Good Housekeeping* editor, gave her a leg up from *Newsday,* signing her to profile her husband for the June issue. She hurried home to start work, while Bennett remained in L.A. On March 4, a crystalline day, he flew to San Diego, where he, Ted Geisel, and Neil Morgan, a young columnist for the *San Diego Evening Tribune,* had been invited to visit Helicopter Squadron One and be lifted up in navy choppers. Like excited kids, they clutched HONORARY HELICOPTER PILOT IDs, grinning for photos in jackets and ties topped by huge military helmets, an almost Seussian incongruity. Privileged treatment was fast becoming the norm for Bennett.

In L.A., he'd made guest appearances on Bob Crosby's (Bing's baby brother) and Art Linkletter's TV shows, for he was increasingly in demand. Sponsors and networks dangled possibilities of developing a show around him, just as they'd done vis-à-vis radio. In March, ad agency J. Walter Thompson, acting for the Wine Growers of California, discussed a *Cerf at Random* show, and in April he visited ABC's New York studios to film pilots for *Live and Laugh with Bennett Cerf.* Viewing them later, he was disappointed. Neither came to anything.

The show that did glue Bennett and millions of Americans to their screens for several months in 1954 featured Joe McCarthy in the starring role. On Tuesday, March 9, crusading journalist Edward R. Murrow, on his CBS series *See It Now,* stood up to make the case against the junior senator from Wisconsin, mainly by using clips of McCarthy himself. Murrow's restraint made his argument all the more devastating. Two other Murrow shows were followed by televised Senate hearings on allegations that McCarthy and his chief counsel, Roy Cohn, had tried to undermine the military and hide their own corruption. It was a "losing battle" when Bennett tried to work, and so on a couple days in late April, much of RH crowded into the boss's office to watch the TV spectacle of McCarthy and Cohn grow more and more "repulsive."

The hearings lasted thirty-six days. Censorship and scare tactics wouldn't exactly vanish—many people were happy to continue persecuting others in the name of anti-Communism—but at that moment, America's eyes had opened more fully. In December, McCarthy would be censured by the Senate and become a pariah. A corner of the veil of fear that had hung over the country's creative industries would be lifted. Donald had been elected president of the American Book Publishers Council, and with his history of anti-censorship leadership, it felt like vindication.

However, for Bennett, that spring had brought a betrayal from an entirely unexpected source: the *Saturday Review*. His current contract was $6,000 for thirty columns; others supplied the fodder the rest of the year. *SRL*'s travel editor had been tapped to write the April 24 column, and co-opted Bennett's alter ego, Anthony Bump, for a parody of Trade

Winds' usual author. The piece had Bump, head of "Quondam House" and a money-grubbing, egotistical purveyor of used jokes, charming orders off of unsuspecting female store owners for titles they'd never sell.

Bennett was livid when he got hold of a proof. That damned chain of accusations about recycling jokes was rattling again, but this takedown had come from a magazine where he was a regular. The row with editor Norman Cousins ended only when Cousins killed the piece, and once more, Bennett couldn't help himself: he stashed away the offending proof. Two years later, it would be TV's turn to mock, when comedian Sid Caesar parodied *What's My Line?* on his weekly comedy show, reserving the sharpest takedown for Bennett's stand-in, one "Clifford Gelding," a "phony" with a peculiar voice who never shut up. The surname was particularly offensive, but might be explained by Bennett's own name: in old French slang, *cerf* was almost as insulting, since it meant "cuckold." Whatever Bennett thought at the time, all seemed cordial years later in front of the cameras when Caesar was mystery guest on *What's My Line?*

Phyllis's portrait of her spouse in the June *Good Housekeeping* went down much more easily. Editor Herb Mayes had given "My Husband Is No Joke to Live With" four prime pages plus parts of another five, and also a cover mention. That old saw about friends in high places had worked. "Is he the busiest man alive?" asked the sub-headline, then replied, "If not, he seems to be well on the way to getting there." As well as declaring her husband "just darling," but sometimes "more darling than others," Phyllis did, however, offer a few home truths.

Bennett was notoriously late to parties, finding it unbearable to be the first there, and she thought his inability to understand people who wasted time his most glaring fault. Then there was the "true confidential" part, about their honeymoon and marriage. After admitting her early resentment and disappointment, she generated a self-help catechism: "To be married does not mean ownership or bending one's will to the other's." She mustn't expect him to abandon interests she didn't share, and "under his tutelage" learned that if angry, you "shouted, perhaps, but . . . didn't sulk." RH, of course, took precedence over all. As for his children, they "fully understand him, and vice versa." What went unsaid was the daunting demand such expectations put on the boys to "fully understand" their super-octane dad, who could be competitive with them, as he'd been with Herbert. Toward the end, Phyllis admitted she was "constantly running, trying to keep up," but was sure of one thing: "No matter how fast I run, or how hard I try, Bennett will always win first prize." Still, she would never stop running, or trying.

. . .

THAT SPRING, LINSCOTT SHOWED his boss a comic novel about a country hick's service during the Korean War that had been rejected by several houses. Its author was a neophyte, Mac Hyman. Bennett took it home, found himself laughing out loud, and signed Hyman—with a proviso that the length be halved. He personally edited part of it; devised the perfect title, *No Time for Sergeants;* and took the step that he, uniquely among publishers, could do: blurbed the book. "I always thought I laughed til I cried was just a figure of speech until I read this," he wrote. "It's a fourstar, one hundred percent wowser." The novel hugged bestseller lists for months.

Another inspired pairing was to commission Shelby Foote, a respected if not big-selling Mississippi novelist, to produce an 800-page, 200,000-word history of the Civil War in time for the centenary in seven years. Although Foote had had no formal history training, his novels' sweep and attention to detail inspired confidence in his ability to do the job. However, Foote soon realized that the war would require *three* volumes, each stretching to a thousand pages, and the project would take *twenty* years. It would eventually help underpin Ken Burns's epic public TV series, getting a second, even stronger life then, selling hundreds of thousands of copies. Like Bennett's instinct about Hyman, his belief in Foote's trilogy paid off beyond anyone's imagining.

A British acquaintance suggested to Donald a different opportunity: that Penguin founder Allen Lane—now Sir Allen—might be open to a deal, since he was coming under increasing pressure from his British bankers. One idea was to buy the rights to incorporate selected Penguin classics into the ML, to fill lacunae and replace older versions of inferior quality. A second was to form a jointly owned enterprise for the whole classics line. Most intriguing was the third option: to buy out Lane's American subsidiary, and merge it into RH, the choice Bennett favored. Summer saw him lunching with the manager of Penguin U.S., run as a low-budget warehouse operation in Baltimore. It was the prologue to a series of exchanges between Lane and RH, with Don making the case to him in London in September.

Something had happened to render this kind of expansion not simply desirable but pressing. Jason Epstein, a brilliant twenty-four-year-old Columbia graduate and devotee of the Modern Library, had dreamed up a new kind of paperback series for his employer, Doubleday. Epstein's up-market, literary, larger-format Anchor Books debuted in April 1953, its first title Stendhal's *The Charterhouse of Parma,* a former jewel of the ML, now out of print. Within two weeks, *Charterhouse* and three other titles had sold 10,000 copies. Alfred and Blanche Knopf's son Pat had sniffed the future and persuaded his difficult parents to let him start Vintage, a series similar to Anchor that would reprint the firm's books. Later, Vintage would originate titles as well as reprint those bought from others. Harcourt, too, planned a "trade paperback" line.

With all those former GIs who'd acquired the reading habit; the young men and women heading to college; and the baby-boom children who'd follow, the potential was enormous. A strategic alliance with Penguin was exactly what RH needed to compete in this new age and defend the Modern Library, but negotiations with Lane dragged on, then tailed off. Since the partners knew they had to respond swiftly to the challenge, they initiated Modern Library Paperbacks to launch in January 1955. The first ten titles would be proven big sellers lifted directly from the regular ML, thus sure to lure readers into the new format, with the next half dozen coming from the RH backlist, books that were no longer available in hardcover.

Nevertheless, the most critical editorial problems remained: Linscott and Maule's age, and Saxe's health. Those worries played at the back of Bennett's mind at the end of April, as he tried to be especially charming during a lunch at Toots Shor's celebrity-and-sports hangout, seemingly an odd venue for his guest. Hiram Haydn was the intellectual, New York–based trade editor for Bobbs-Merrill, a venerable Indianapolis firm responsible for hits like Irma Rombauer's *The Joy of Cooking* and Ayn Rand's *The Fountainhead*. He'd previously been chief editor at Crown, but neither of those positions had earned him his intellectual bona fides. In fact, working at such middle-of-the-road houses indicated that he had the common touch so necessary to a general publisher. Rather, the egghead credentials came from his association with *The American Scholar,* the literary magazine of the Phi Beta Kappa Society, which Haydn had edited for the past ten years, and from his gig running the fiction-writing workshop at The New School for the past six. A bright light among his students there had been William Styron, a former Marine and McGraw-Hill editor. *Lie Down in Darkness,* Styron's debut novel, had attached to its author the tag of "one of the most promising of his generation," and reflected glory on the young man's mentor. To cap it all, Haydn had authored three novels; like Saxe and Linscott, he'd also had his byline on several anthologies and a series, but at forty-seven, was a generation younger.

Bennett courted him with the ardor of a man in love. May was French and expensive at Voisin; June more intimate, in Don's apartment with all three partners present; and on August 17, a sweltering Tuesday, Bennett popped the question in the pool at Mt. Kisco. His diary noted that he'd just about signed Haydn as chief editor, to begin January 1, 1955. Only formalities remained. The day before their happy splash, sensing how Haydn would jump, Bennett confided to Saxe the nature of their talks, so he'd hear it from him first. Saxe had never coveted the "chief editor" title. He told himself Hiram was "the most able man for the job in America." Yet when Bob phoned to say all was finalized, Saxe summed up his own prospects in a word: "clouded."

. . .

FOR A YEAR ALREADY, those unaccustomed clouds that had first announced themselves in Saxe's illness kept gathering anew. On Monday, June 14, Pauline did not show up for work. Rumor had it that an ambulance had rushed her to the hospital. Nobody knew exactly what had happened; all they heard was that something was terribly wrong. The smart, eager young working girl from Liveright had, over twenty-seven years, blossomed into a beloved pro, capable of keeping up with Bennett's quicksilver mind and punishing pace. From the roaring '20s to the buttoned-up '50s, she hadn't lost the twinkle in her eye or the indulgent heart that had put up with the practical jokes, the adolescent mindset, and her mythological transformation into Jezebel, she of the tight sweater, sassy lip, and curvy behind always ready for a "potch" or a dictation session perched on the boss's lap—at least in Bennett's telling.

Shared between him and Don, she'd been a participating witness to all the changes from Modern Library into Random House Inc., and had her own metamorphosis into a groomed and gracious executive secretary, married to equally long-serving Abraham Friedman, now the company controller. Along with Don and Saxe and Phyllis, Pauline had made Bennett's life possible. He couldn't have done the joke books without the evening and weekend hours she surrendered. She screened annoying calls, dealt with bores, understood his furies, laughed at his absurdities, made him smile. Only in February, the magazine *Today's Secretary* had celebrated her in a feature where she'd praised *him*. Now she was undergoing a full neurological workup.

"My Jez very sick indeed," Bennett anxiously scribbled in his diary on Tuesday. Meanwhile, for however long, Mary Barber would take over as his secretary.

For a man who hated anything related to illness, he was being buffeted by signs of it all around. That same June day, he had to wire Ted Geisel: Bennett had just heard that Helen had collapsed two weeks earlier with a rapidly spreading paralysis. It gripped her from the neck down, rendering swallowing and breathing almost impossible. She was headed for sudden death until a tracheotomy, iron lung, and feeding tube kept her precariously alive. The diagnosis was something most people had never heard of, Guillain-Barré syndrome. Bennett was well aware that Helen, older than her husband, was the practical one who negotiated the everyday, enabling Dr. Seuss's flights of fancy. In January, a question was asked about O'Hara that could now be posed about Ted: If his wife were to die, what would become of him?

Two days later, news about Pauline was "crushing." She'd developed a rare blood disorder, *thrombocytopenic purpura*. By the weekend, she was in a coma. Gloom settled over everything. One day, Bennett, Don, and Saxe sat in Saxe's office, wondering "when the team would be broken up," and who'd "go" first. Never before had they surrendered to such talk. A letter from Ted offered a moment of comfort. After three weeks under siege, the doctors said that Helen would live. She'd been removed from the iron lung, but they couldn't predict if she'd walk again. Bennett wanted to send books to help her recovery, but "I can't quite tell you how terribly I feel," was all he could write about Pauline. Trying to buck Bennett up, Ted replied that he'd keep rooting for Jezebel, "one of my favorite people," and that he and Helen "got a big kick out of seeing you and Arlene walk into [Helen's] hospital room tonight out of the television set."

For the next few weeks, Jez lay suspended in a living death. Though she rallied briefly in mid-July, regaining consciousness and sending a surge of hope through the office, she soon slipped back into a coma. On

Wednesday morning, August 4, the call came through: Jez had died at 5 A.M. Bennett had a golf date with Alfred Knopf. It was a "blessed relief" that the agony had ended, he told his diary, and a relief to have something to concentrate on to take his mind off the loss. Two days later, he was the only partner at the funeral: Bob and Don were away. Bennett closed the office from 12:30 to 3:00, so everyone could attend. It fell to him to give the eulogy.

Saxe wrote Don that Bennett had done "nobly," with "brief, simple and utterly sincere" words. When he read Saxe's note, Don wrote Bennett: "That must have been the most difficult talk you've ever given. I'm sure you said what all of us felt."

"This place will never be quite the same without her," Bennett replied. Then he pasted the obituaries into his clipping book and did something unusual: drew a rectangle on the page and wrote in block capitals, GOODBYE, JEZEBEL! followed by details of her passing. He who hated cemeteries and tombstones had made his own memorial to Pauline.

. . .

ON SUNDAY, JUNE 20, six days after Pauline had been hospitalized, Bennett was spending the day at home with Quent and Ginny Reynolds and Truman Capote, when unexpectedly he had to excuse himself for a long-distance call from Carlotta O'Neill. In 1952, a year after she and Gene had cloistered themselves in Massachusetts, Bennett had finally persuaded her to let him publish one of Gene's two plays left in the RH safe, *A Moon for the Misbegotten*. Alas, O'Neill's name hadn't blazed supremely incandescent over Broadway for years. The play wasn't theatrically produced, and sold so poorly, most copies had to be remaindered. He'd been eclipsed by two younger comets streaking across the Great White Way: Tennessee Williams and Arthur Miller.

Carlotta was phoning that Sunday about the one play still in the safe: *Long Day's Journey into Night*. At home, she also had a copy typed by Saxe, inscribed by Gene to his "beloved wife" and first reader. It was now seven months since he'd died, and she wanted Bennett to publish the "secret play" right away. She'd lived with knowledge of its cathartic power and explosive content for a dozen-plus years, long enough to decide to overlook her late husband's stipulation that it not see print till twenty-five years after his death.

This was a delicate, complex matter. Whatever Carlotta might think, given the agreement he'd signed with Gene about the twenty-five-year embargo, Bennett had to ascertain from Horace Manges if he could legally open the sealed package. After that, he had to talk it through with Don and Bob and Saxe. Once Horace gave the go-ahead, Bennett read the play on July 1, recording that fact in his diary in block capitals. The next day, he again spoke with Carlotta, but also phoned Saxe—who, of course, was apoplectic. How could she ignore Gene's wishes?

"Ever since I spoke to you . . . I have been pacing up and down worrying about *Long Day's Journey into Night,*" Bennett wrote in a long letter to Carlotta, dated July 6. He put his points into four numbered parts. First, although the play had some of O'Neill's most powerful writing, it gave "a simply horrifying portrait" of Gene's family. Bennett said that he kept asking himself, "What purpose will be served by publishing . . . now?" That Gene's mother, "through no fault of her own," became a morphine addict was a secret that had been kept from the world, but the play would "flaunt the fact." And worse, the portrait of his father was so awful, thousands of people would ask, "How could any man write that . . . about his own father?"

Second, he'd taken advice from Manges. Carlotta did have the legal right to overturn the quarter-century provision, but his own strong inclination was to abide by Gene's wishes. If she insisted on publishing now, he'd comply, but, to protect RH's good name, would require a statement that the play was issued on her order, and an explanation of why she felt it necessary to ignore Gene's wishes. He'd want her permission to give it to the press *and* print it in the book. On the phone, Carlotta had told him that she didn't care what people said, but Bennett "would resent very strongly any possible insinuation that we had published this play now either for purposes of getting publicity or making a profit." Third, she'd talked about donating revenue to a memorial fund. He encouraged her to explain how and where the money would be used.

Fourth, he held nothing back: "A certain part of my perturbation . . . stems . . . to a remark you made about 'leeches that hung around Gene for years . . .' Obviously you were referring to Saxe Commins, and I simply cannot let that . . . go unchallenged. [He] is one of the finest men I have ever met . . . the kind of friend to Gene that a man dreams of. . . . Saxe gave up his vacation to go out to California at his own expense and [type] . . . the very script . . . I . . . hold in my hands. . . ."

He finished by assuring her that he wouldn't respect himself if he hadn't told her exactly how he felt. In the end, she told him how *she* felt by authorizing the manuscript to be published by Yale University Press, who were happy to oblige in February 1956. She gave the script and publication rights, along with other papers, as a gift to Yale's library. Carlotta had forced Bennett's hand; rather than comply on her terms, RH had withdrawn from the field.

"In a funny way Carlotta was right," Anna Crouse, looking back a half century later and having known all the players, adjudicated. Yet she added: "But both Bennett and Donald had promised O'Neill." It involved matters of honor and loyalty to their author. In not wanting to "flaunt" Gene's family skeletons, Bennett had shown admirable concern, for that fearfulness had haunted and motivated Gene himself. Bennett was also a man of his time, subscribing to many of its proprieties. *Drug addict* was an unmentionable in the context of one's family. How could he sanction being the conduit through which the world would feed on the sensational story of the O'Neills? It would have required an enormous leap of faith and absolute conviction that he knew better than his author, to countermand Gene's wishes and trust in the power of the play and the public's ability to respond to it with understanding, rather than condemnation. There was also the matter of honor regarding Saxe, the editor who had come with O'Neill and devoted himself to the firm. To the partners' certain knowledge, he'd turned down far more lucrative offers in order to stay with Random House, and had been with them for twenty-one years.

After Bennett left the office that day, Saxe poured out his feelings to his diary, having read his boss's letter. It "was magnificent," he began, but "best of all was still more evidence of his loyalty to me and his innate sense of decency. I don't care what the others say, this is B at his best, devoted, just, and on the side of his friends through hell and high water. Whenever he is maligned, it would help to quote passages from this letter. But there's no point in defending him. He is quite able to take care of himself."

When *Long Day's Journey* opened on Broadway on November 7, 1956, Bennett and Phyllis Cerf were in the audience. Saxe, however, did not go to see the play.

Arguably, what Bennett did represents one of the finer moments in the history of publishers, authors, and editors. It was true emotionally—

to the love and respect he had for O'Neill (and also Saxe)—and true to how he viewed his professional responsibilities. Yet Carlotta's action recalled Gene's brilliance to life, once and for all reviving his body of work. *Long Day's Journey* posthumously won O'Neill a fourth Pulitzer Prize. It is the play, more than any other, that continues to draw new generations of audiences and readers.

. . .

A MONTH AFTER THE crisis over *Long Day's Journey,* and a fortnight after Pauline's death, a wedding would take place in Mississippi. Jill Faulkner was getting hitched to Paul Summers, a West Point graduate and Korean War veteran. Bill and Estelle were hosting the affair at Rowan Oak, and RH needed to be present. Don was in Europe. Bennett was holding a big company picnic at The Columns, and since Bob and Merle would be among the guests, no partner would be heading to Mississippi. Bennett did make sure to send a generous gift, one Jill cherished: a complete Modern Library. Invitations had been forwarded to Albert Erskine, Manny Harper, and Louise Bonino—those Bill knew best at RH. None would make it. That left Saxe and Dorothy. They'd go down for a week—it would be a vacation, they told themselves, the first they'd had together in years. Saxe tried not to think about the torrid weather and tempestuous relations between Bill and Estelle. Surely, for their daughter's wedding, they'd be on best behavior.

It was also an occasion to celebrate the publication of Bill's sixteenth novel, *A Fable,* the World War I story that had refused to be born for more than a decade and had required such intense emotional midwifery from its editor. It had officially emerged on August 2; Bennett had pronounced the book "superb," Bob thought it "tremendous," and Don assured its U.K. publisher that the novel was "powerful" and "wonderful." Bennett marked the publication with a steamroller of a push letter, claiming to reviewers that not only was it Faulkner's "most important" work, but the most important book of fiction "brought out in this country in the past 10 years. Possibly even this is an understatement, an accusation which I do not believe can often be leveled against a publisher." By the end of August, it was number five on the bestseller list and Bennett thought the firm would sell 35,000 to 40,000 copies—strong for Faulkner. A year later, *A Fable* would win both the Pulitzer Prize and the National Book Award.

At the same time, reviews came in *very* mixed. Carvel Collins in the *Times* wrote long and respectfully about this seeming "new departure" in subject, structure, and setting, Faulkner's "theological" novel with "formidable" difficulties, yet it was "one of the important works of our major novelist." Others begged to differ—most forcefully, once again, Brendan Gill in *The New Yorker*. "One would rather not say at all what must be said at once . . . that William Faulkner's 'A Fable' is a calamity," he began, eviscerating a decade's work. He spoke of a "bad small novel absurdly distended in scale," and a book subject to an underlying "vulgarity."

"Gill is an outrageous bastard," Bennett erupted to Don.

The novel wasn't the only hard labor Faulkner had put the extended RH family through during the past few years. There had been the caring for him, the drying out, and, as usual, the dealing with his secrets, most prominently the ending of the anguished affair with Joan Williams (she'd gotten married). During Saxe's recuperation, Bill had gone to Princeton to work with him on final changes to the manuscript, then had seen the Cerfs and Klopfers when he delivered it to the palazzo. Afterward he left for Europe, and then Egypt, to help his old friend Howard Hawks on a film. Saxe, of course, was primary secret-sharer, yet many secrets by this time were no secret to Estelle: she was fully aware of the affair with Joan. Often she, too, found succor in Saxe and Dorothy's kindness. In February, in a desperate state, she'd written to them that she was contemplating divorce. Life together had been misery for all three Faulkners.

What Estelle didn't know was that at the end of December 1953, while in Europe, Bill had met another young lady: a precocious, pale, dark-haired slip of a girl open to all things intellectual, rather uninhibited, and not averse to shocking her parents. He was infatuated and she in love with the greatest living American embodiment of literature, fifty-six to her nineteen. Her name was Jean Stein, and her father, Jules, had co-founded the talent agency MCA, and through it become an immensely rich Hollywood powerbroker.

But Saxe and Dorothy, in Oxford, now saw Bill, grave and handsome in his finery (they'd ordered it for him), give his virginal white-gowned daughter away. The heady scent of gardenias and roses permeated Rowan Oak, and the old house shone with silver, crystal, and the damp faces of servants who had made it gleam. Tables were laden with food and, of course, champagne and whiskey. They got through the wedding and the weekend. But in the days that followed, the flow of alcohol loosened Bill's tongue to the point where he was railing bitterly against Estelle. Saxe's only relief was to confide the litany to his diary:

> For hours [he] particularized about the armies committed against him and in general the charge was of theft of his money, extravagance and finally the abysmal ignorance around him. What he had to endure as an artist was his great cross. There was the tale of throwing the ms pages of *Light in August* out of the car window and his having to crawl on the roadside to pick up the scattered sheets. There was the time when pages of *A Fable* were thrown out the door. No one read what he wrote. . . . Money was wasted in charge accounts. He had to support her family.

By Wednesday, the cumulative drinking had put Bill into a "comatose state whining for liquor." "Thank God we persuaded them that we must leave tomorrow," Saxe added, but Thursday morning found Faulkner even deeper into a "stupor." At breakfast Estelle broached the matter of funds, and Saxe tried to change the subject. "I'll simply have to tell her that it's impossible to draw money from Random House without Bill's written authorization." Later, he accompanied Faulkner's stepson to the post office to collect the mail, and found a check for $5,000 from RH as well as a letter from Jean.

"There will be hell to pay on this score," he predicted, but when they returned, Bill was safe for the moment. Estelle, too, was "out cold." The Comminses were tremendously relieved to fly back to New York, the ending to a holiday that was anything but. On Friday, back in his light-filled home, Saxe confided to his journal: "The secret of Faulkner as writer is in Rowan Oak and in its accumulation of bitterness, hatred, degeneration, all transformed into the work that has brought Bill fame but has not purged that house of its evil. The sight of . . . Broadus helping the stark naked, tottering Nobel Prize winner to the toilet, making him drinks, wiping him, trying to placate him . . . all pride gone as the bottle dwindles."

Estelle phoned Princeton on Sunday: Faulkner was still unconscious. Saxe found it impossible to stop thinking about the hellish week he'd come through, and its implications for Bill. "*A Fable,* far from being the pinnacle of his career, as he was sure it would be, may topple him. But he will not be aware of the fall. . . . Such aloofness is a kind of armor and will save him from the arrows of criticism. But what will save him from being drowned in whiskey?"

Yet however shaky he was, Faulkner's remarkable powers of recovery put him back in New York in two weeks, sleeping at the Algonquin and spending days sitting in his editor's familiar green office with the maroon carpet, typing with two fingers.

Although Saxe had sometimes annoyed Bill (even if he couldn't make him change one word), Faulkner recognized the debt he owed this man, and made it public when he dedicated his next book, the story collection *Big Woods,* thus:

MEMO TO: Saxe Commins
FROM: Author
TO: Editor
We never always saw eye to eye
but we were always
looking at the same thing

It had been quite a year. They had all, to quote Faulkner, "endured."

Chapter 29
Energy

By the mid-1950s, Bennett had become "Mr. Publishing" to the ever-expanding millions of TV viewers. Americans' hearts opened to him as he came into their living rooms each Sunday, part of the routine of home; something about him inspired ease and trust. Silent film's "It Girl" Clara Bow gushed in a fan letter that he was the "kindest-looking man" she'd ever seen, whose love for people "overflows" the screen. His bounce seemed to inch a little higher whenever a group of men or women (pretty college girls preferred) spent the time and money to hear his sunny-side shtick on trends in humor or American letters. The lectures changed only superficially, according to location and the season's titles. Yet if the mail he amassed was to be believed, audiences were more than satisfied. He'd turn on the charm and sally forth, never mediated by notes. Goodwill and extraordinary memory were his supports. He fed on the fan-love that in turn opened him up to *them,* and never ceased to wonder that the fantastic life fate dealt him was his own.

Encountering that openness firsthand was skinny, Bronx-born Jules Feiffer, home from army service after the Korean draft and dreaming of a career as a cartoonist. Clutching his portfolio to show around, Feiffer was pounding shoe leather up Madison Avenue when he recognized the publisher from the game show walking near Saint Pat's. *What the hell,* he figured, and marched up: Would Bennett take a look at some cartoons? He didn't, or—in a rush—couldn't, but Bennett's manner was so friendly and his rejection of someone who felt like "the equivalent of a panhandler" so unexpectedly positive, that Feiffer was rather thrilled. In time, he found a slot at the new *Village Voice* and published a book with McGraw-Hill, but in 1960 the now-famous cartoonist moved over to, in Feiffer's words, "Broadway Bennett's" house.

Bennett also opened his heart to Stuart Brent, a well-known Chicago bookseller now teetering on the edge of insolvency, in arrears to the major houses. His wife had died, leaving him in a bad way, and with three kids to support. Bennett had come to know Brent during his lecture stops in the Windy City, and regarded him as a friend. He also appreciated the role Brent played in the community. He persuaded Alfred Knopf and several others to take a leap of faith and provide books and credit for an additional six months, no payment expected, no questions asked, Bennett's belief in Brent the only guarantor. The store survived.

As for his own books, so what if he massaged and repurposed many jokes from anthology to anthology? He certainly "slaved" in their collecting and organizing, as he frequently grumbled to his diary. He'd also learned to cover his back, by noting inside each new work—as he did in *The Vest Pocket Book of Jokes,* his first humor anthology for RH—that some stories had been in previous collections. Accusations of stealing continued from time to time, and the contempt of some in the literary world kept drizzling down, but the jack-o'-lantern grin swallowed it all.

Horace Manges thought Bennett wasn't insulted "unless he wanted to be." He seemed equipped with a second immune system that herded unpleasantness, like an invading organism, into a sealed-off space where it could be contained and detoxified, enabling him to get on with the important business of life. Saxe sensed something else: way below the surface, his boss was "embarrassed" about his simpler virtues, and had depths that "at first weren't apparent." No matter: the joke book that Bennett would publish on November 15, 1954, was neither simple nor remotely embarrassing. *An Encyclopedia of Modern American Humor,* prepared for Doubleday, was of a higher order than the usual stuff, a 688-page mammoth at the bargain price of $3.95. There hadn't been a humor treasury of such dimensions since before World War II.

The first funny tome to be classified according to region, it covered all parts of the country. Bennett had plucked parodies, verse, a wide variety of stories—and, unusually, excerpts from plays and radio shows—the whole representing a surprisingly large swath of America's better writers and humorists. Given that his previous yak-fest, *Good for a Laugh,* had sold nearly 90,000 copies, Doubleday was determined to go all out. This was major holiday fare, and critics obliged. John Hutchens's review in the *New York Herald Tribune* was typical. Bennett laughed at his own jokes, but was a "rare ranking storyteller" by being able to laugh at others'. His batting average was, say, ".783, not bad in any league, especially this one." Friends and authors congratulated him. Mac Hyman, whose *No Time for Sergeants* became a bestseller in no small part due to Bennett, was flattered to see an excerpt from his novel in the omnibus, but his thanks extended beyond flattery. "I have always been just a little bit ashamed of writing humor, but you have somehow made it all seem respectable, which makes me feel a lot better."

An Encyclopedia of Modern American Humor gets the full window treatment

It was Orville Prescott, chief daily book critic of *The New York Times,* who had the last word. His review began with an anecdote. Prescott had recently dined with one of America's finest historians. What, he asked the historian, did men like Jefferson, Hamilton, Washington, and Adams share that enabled them to accomplish so much?

"Energy," was the reply, "energy far beyond that of ordinary men."

"Few modern Americans possess this qualification for greatness in more abundance than the shy and diffident editor of the whacking big anthology which is up for our attention today," Prescott declared. "His name is Bennett Cerf."

At Columbia, they'd called him "Beans." With time, as Bennett donned more and more hats, the energy had become a steady source of comment and curiosity: even negative profiles referenced it. His wife and kids couldn't keep up with it. Friends gossiped about it. And Danny Kaye's wife, Sylvia, had immortalized "Vitamin B. Cerf" in a poem. As one of her verses asked: "So how did you get so energetic, so peripatetic? Your varied vocations, how have you planned 'em? And if, as I gather, they are well planned, the thing that is toughest to understand Is how do you also do so many things, at Random?"

That question had been posed for years, but no one had ever coupled what was behind the smile with anything so serious as had Mr. Prescott, tongue only half in cheek. Jefferson, Adams, Hamilton, *Cerf*? The question might also be asked: What if he hadn't expended so much of himself on jokes, columns, lectures, shows, and other ephemera? What *then* might he have done, favored with such a "qualification for greatness"? But had "the shy and diffident editor" craved less fame in the here and now, less of a good time, less attention, he wouldn't have been Bennett Cerf. And without Bennett Cerf—the whole package—there could have been no Random House.

. . .

A MONTH BEFORE BENNETT'S *Times* apotheosis, he was stewing over an especially hated task. The three partners decided they had to divorce editor David McDowell. Office gossip had it that too many of his books had failed financially, and weren't sufficiently well-received. Saxe dismissed the cocky younger editor as a man who favored "the first-person singular . . . without restraint or embarrassment," and McDowell's ardent conservatism had caused friction. To be fair, he had tried to hook big fish, courting Richard Nixon to do an autobiography, urging the now vice president "to keep careful notes, journals and files." Perhaps in doing so, in a small way, McDowell influenced the course of U.S. history. "Your idea of keeping careful notes of important happenings is very good, and I have started to do this," Nixon told his would-be editor. The note-keeping metastasized into incriminating tape recordings two decades later.

On the first Wednesday in October, McDowell was summoned into the boss's office. Bennett and Don had tossed a coin to decide who'd do the deed. Donald had lost, but insisted Bennett be present at the execution. Hiram Haydn was in that day—he wouldn't begin until January, but was turning up whenever time allowed, camping out in Saxe's office. The partners explained what was afoot, and Haydn saw they were discomforted. At the appointed hour, McDowell entered the big room that was usually so open, and the door closed behind him. No snatches of conversation could permeate its thick wood. After a time, Haydn looked at his watch: McDowell had been in there a good while. Eventually the door opened and closed again, after what seemed an hour. Footsteps retreated down the hall.

To allay his own anxiety, Haydn was desperate to hear what had happened, but the partners didn't emerge. He couldn't stop himself: he got up and knocked on the door. When it opened, he was dumbfounded: Bennett and Donald were laughing. McDowell, it turned out, had woman troubles, and needed money for the down payment on a house. Instead of firing him, Bennett and Don had felt sorry for him, and promised to help. When the meeting ended, they had two alternatives: yell at each other for being softhearted idiots instead of businessmen, or laugh at what they'd done. They chose laughter. Two days later, they lent McDowell $5,000.

They wanted the business to grow, and so were bringing in Haydn and also hiring a special projects editor, Paul Lapolla, from Doubleday. His brief was to develop nonfiction, often in conjunction with major corporations, brands, or magazines. Bertha "Bert" Krantz, a crackerjack copy editor who'd worked with Hiram, would also join, and other changes were in the offing. The palazzo was stuffed to capacity: what had once been a carefully constructed jigsaw of sitting rooms and bedrooms, dressing rooms and servants' quarters, could only be reconfigured so many ways. With 120 on staff, the firm had had to take space across town at 33 West Sixtieth Street to house functions like billing and auditing. There simply wasn't enough space—certainly not on the floor shared by the partners and senior editors. For Hiram to have a place worthy of his position and within earshot of them, he'd have to take over Saxe's sanctum. Already Saxe spent just two days in New York. His salary and hours for 1955 were set, but in 1956 and 1957 would be significantly curtailed, so it seemed reasonable. However, he'd have to move far away: up two flights. Bennett held off imparting the bad news as long as he could, until he finally had to tell Saxe, two days before Christmas.

Monday morning, January 3, 1955, Hiram stood on the threshold of that magic building. His official start was a day he'd never forget. Given the proximity of the archdiocese, some likened it to entering a literary cathedral; others, of the Hollywood persuasion, felt that any moment Fred and Ginger might glide down the stairs. Newcomers never failed to evince a wow, while regulars still asked: How do I deserve to be in such a place? Arriving early, Hiram was ushered toward Donald's office, but then lingered awkwardly outside Don's door. His new boss was absorbed in a phone call, and clearly distressed.

"No, no, Dorothy," Hiram heard him say. "You tell Saxe that noth-

Hiram Haydn

ing has changed, that we love him just as much as we always have." Saxe had ulcers that were making him miserable. He wasn't fit to come to the city. Anyway, his new office was still being prepared and wouldn't be ready for another week. When Donald finally re-cradled the receiver, it was as though he were surfacing from a deeply disturbing dream. A moment passed before the dark eyes in the long, sallow face took in the visitor, but then he focused, welcoming Hiram with a smile, and went to fetch Bob. Bennett, of course, wasn't in yet—Hiram would learn that he now rarely showed until ten or ten-thirty, given late nights and travels.

Hiram was puzzled why two partners were needed to walk him down the hall, but soon understood. A silent silver fox of a man had made his den in Saxe's office. Bob had known Bill Faulkner longest, and so been delegated to do the introductions. Hiram and Bill would be sharing the room for a week. Haydn was furious, embarrassed, intimidated. No hint had been given. He needed to start phoning agents and writers, but was terrified of disturbing Faulkner. Worse, he'd be blamed for displacing Saxe even though he'd told the partners he didn't feel right about taking his space. Agonized and impotent, he wasn't sure what to do.

The spell was broken by Bennett breezing in, but he came and went quickly. After what seemed an age, Faulkner finally turned with eyes that Haydn would always remember as "clear and kind." He assured the new editor that no amount of phone-calling would bother his ability to write, then addressed the more delicate matter.

"Are you troubled about being here in Saxe's office? You don't suppose that I think you wanted to take it away from him, do you? . . . No man in his right mind would want to come in and do that. . . . It's those great monopolists down the hall . . . they arranged it this way because they're sensible men. Now . . . do the things you're here for."

It was a benediction of sorts, a liberation. Hiram Haydn got to work.

Exactly one week later, Saxe Commins took the elevator straight to the fifth floor, to what seemed a small, newly painted closet of a room, with his books, furniture, and paraphernalia from many working years all set up. He couldn't help but feel sorrow over his "fallen estate." There was some comfort, however. Besides furnishings and books, one of his authors had made the move as well. Bill sat smoking and working in the old configuration. There'd be no change *there:* after all, it had been almost four years since Faulkner had conferred on Saxe the ultimate trust, appointing him his literary executor.

Later that morning, Jean Stein, Bill's young paramour, glided in. Bill may have felt obliged to show kindness and civility to Haydn the previous week, but to Jean he'd confided deep outrage at what had been done. A steady stream of awkward pilgrims rapped on the door to offer sheepish encouragement, including Bennett, Donald, and Bob, one by one. They came and went, to salve their own consciences, Saxe felt sure. Bill and Jean did the only thing they could: whisked him away, to distract him with a good lunch.

. . .

SAXE RETAINED OVERSIGHT FOR another longtime author, Budd Schulberg. After the success of *The Disenchanted,* RH had published a story collection, *Some Faces in the Crowd,* in 1953. (One tale would become the prescient 1957 film *A Face in the Crowd,* the story of a small-town redneck's meteoric TV rise and fall; a morality play about the manipulative power of the medium, with cameos by a dozen movers and shakers, including Bennett.) Budd had been incubating another novel, but was stuck. He put it aside to work on a screenplay for a fledgling movie producer, based on a 1948 Pulitzer Prize–winning newspaper exposé of the mob corruption and brutality endemic to New York City's docks. When the project went nowhere, he bought the rights from the would-be producer and teamed with the brilliant young director Elia Kazan to make *On the Waterfront,* for which Budd won the Academy Award for Best Original Screenplay.

Many assumed he and Kazan had used the film as a hindsight metaphor to justify their respective decisions to cooperate with HUAC. At one point the priest who helps longshoremen says that "there are ways of fighting back. . . . What's ratting to them is telling the truth for you." Yet in fact Budd had been working on the treatment long *before* he testified. He also wanted to expand the story into a novel, having spent months hanging out with the real-life dock handlers and the priest they looked to for guidance. Although it would have been ideal to debut film and book simultaneously, the novel needed too much work. *Waterfront* wasn't published until 1955, and was another innovation: the "novelization" of a screenplay was as uncommon then as was Bennett's decision to publish the film script of *All About Eve* a few years earlier.

Budd again had to work closely with Saxe, driving to Princeton and occupying the Comminses' weekends. To deal with proofing and fact-checking as fast as possible, one weekend he invited along "Brownie"—the dockworker who'd been key to bringing the screenplay and novel to life—to go over each line. The three worked until bedtime, when Dorothy put out the warm milk that ulcer-ridden Saxe was used to taking as a nightcap.

"I ain't drunk that since I been weaned," cackled Brownie, by then in silk lounging pajamas and robe. When he and Budd left a day and a half later, he assured the very proper Dorothy, "I'm gonna send you some French underwear when I get back, dear lady." Like his attire, they would have fallen off the back of a ship. Such were the perks of an editor's wife.

. . .

WHILE BILL FAULKNER WAS in town in January 1955, the Cerfs invited him and Jean to join them for an evening at the Copacabana, where Frank Sinatra was performing. Their other guests were John O'Hara and the woman who'd entered his life, Katharine Barnes Bryan. Known universally as "Sister," this handsome, elegant woman—a middle-aged divorcée with three children—had fallen in love with the impossible Irishman, who was deeply in love with her. Their relationship relieved Bennett and Don of fears about John again descending into booze. Instead, he and Sister would marry on the last day of the month, his fiftieth birthday. He'd just given her a gold cigarette case, sweetly engraved: "This belongs to Katharine Barnes O'Hara—and—So Do I."

Around the time O'Hara and Sister got hitched, Bennett and Phyllis took off for the West. Even though 1955 had just begun, he'd already whirled through several lecture tours. This time, they were to have a very special break. After a few days in L.A., they'd fly to Honolulu, where Bennett would lecture at the University of Hawaii and then relax. Hawaii was a very privileged destination, and Phyllis liked privilege. Just before they stepped inside the Pan Am clipper *Celestial* in L.A., their picture was snapped. She'd been dieting hard in the battle between her love of good food and drink, and the creeping figures on the scale. She looked terrific, thick hair short but now chic under a beret. With Bennett beside her in his light gray suit and tie, clutching fedora, trench coat, and the inevitable reading matter, her small gloved hand extended toward the sky in a victorious wave. Beneath California's sun it was hot in her full-length fur, not exactly necessary for the tropics, yet the statement was clear: they were VIPs, first-class all the way.

Except for the swooping flocks of mynahs that awakened them each dawn, the Royal Hawaiian Hotel was simply perfect. No trip for the Cerfs was complete, however, without a little business. In addition to lecturing, Bennett gave interviews to the local press, called on stores, and focused on another of those special authors who produced like clockwork and sold, with the potential to sell much more. Jim Michener's 1955 tax return pegged his professional income on a par with his publisher's—about $123,000 ($1.4 million today) from books and articles. That didn't include what he made from stocks. Already donating to colleges, libraries, and schools, that year Michener also gave $15,000 ($172,000) to the Honolulu Academy of Art.

He'd just bought a house overlooking the banyans and white beaches on the other side of Oahu, away from Honolulu's bustle. There, they hashed out his latest, *Rascals in Paradise,* a collection of ten nonfiction stories about South Seas adventurers that he'd co-write with Arthur Grove Day, a University of Hawaii professor. Jim also accompanied the Cerfs on a VIP tour of Pearl Harbor, and Bennett was pleased that his own national profile opened gates to the private paradises of big kahuna families. Afterward, however, he couldn't help but comment in Trade Winds on the tensions beneath the postcard perfection about the possibility of becoming a state.

Too many of the "nice," polite, entrenched landed gentry hobnobbing with him spoke in code, the kind that even the most secular Jew could decipher. Concerned about an increasingly "polyglot" population, they questioned the wisdom of granting statehood, fearing a loss of control and a "mongrel" takeover that could bring a Hawaiian with Japanese, Chinese, or Polynesian blood to Congress. The man who'd squired Anna May Wong saw his currency fall fast when he told them he viewed such a prospect as wonderful. Hawaii would become a state very soon, he assured his readers, and provide a living denial to the spread of authoritarianism across Asia, contributing to "the victory of the free world over the forces that endanger it."

Two years later, when *Rascals in Paradise* was published, Michener and his co-writer devoted an "Author's Note" to their publisher:

> Originally, eleven chapters of this book were submitted . . . but upon advice of counsel and after due consideration of the laws governing public decency, Chapter XI was suppressed. . . . [It] was entitled "Bennett Cerf, The Poor Man's Pepys" and contained . . . revealing items of reprobacy and nonfeasance by the subject . . . : backsliding, sowing of wild oats . . . robbing Peter to pay Paul . . . sybaritism . . . plagiarism, anthology, and assorted torts. Since Random House books sometimes find their way into family circles, and since the line of common decency must be drawn somewhere, this chapter has regretfully been destroyed, even though the authors considered it the most rascally . . . of the . . . volume.

How many publishers were teased in such a way by their authors? How many would be so delighted? Not the Knopfs or Guinzburg, nor Dick and Max, never mind the potentates at Harper, Doubleday, or straitlaced Scribner. The love letter was returned in kind: RH's colophon on the title page had mysteriously sprouted palm trees.

. . .

STARTING IN THE FALL of 1954 and continuing into the spring of 1955, Saxe and others at the palazzo found themselves subjected to interrogation by a tall, horn-rimmed journalist named Geoffrey T. Hellman. In August 1954, on a joyous, block-capital day, Bennett had gotten news that Hellman, a longtime *New Yorker* writer, had been given the go-ahead to profile him for the magazine. Others of his acquaintance—Alfred and Blanche, Max and Dick—had years earlier basked in a two- or three-part moment of *New Yorker* glory, all emerging with burnished egos. Until now, Bennett had been neglected—but not quite. Back in 1945, after the grand success of *Try and Stop Me,* the notion of a profile had been broached. That self-same Hellman had started collecting material, but Bennett's relationship with the magazine's editor, Harold Ross, had become sorely strained. Yes, Ross had introduced him to Phyllis, but partly as a sly joke on the Sylvia debacle. When Bennett, who'd very much wanted to see his byline in *The New Yorker,* submitted a piece to Ross during the war, the editor had rejected it. There'd be no second try.

Soon after Hellman had first begun work, Ross complained to a colleague about the "crassness" of the more "self-centered" book boys, and his target was obvious. The profile was put on hold. William Shawn, quiet and secretive where Ross had been loud and exuberant, took over as editor in 1951; like water and oil, he and Bennett had no relationship at all. Hellman, however, hadn't forgotten his initial efforts. Now, nine years later, the profile was back on.

Hellman shadowed Bennett at home, in the office, at Mt. Kisco, poking through diaries, scrapbooks, files, and bookshelves, all the surfaces and crevices of a crammed life. Incongruities jockeyed for space in his notebook. At Sixty-Second Street, the silver-set breakfast table saw its gray-haired fifty-six-year-old master repeatedly take delight in popping toast; yet the third-floor study spoke of a supremely organized, self-disciplined man, whose extensive home filing system was duplicated in the country. Closest to hand behind the kidney-shaped desk, Hellman noticed not high literature, but popular reference books with which Bennett plied his motley trades. It would take but a second to grab encyclopedia volumes; *Who's Who;* dictionaries, whether of synonyms, quotations, or biographical; and treasuries of anecdotes, epigrams, satires, and hoary jokes.

Books were everywhere in both houses—plenty bearing rivals' colophons. It seemed Bennett had read or at least knew them all: he could locate any title they talked about at once. In the study, on the highest shelf near the window, Hellman spied a discreet section devoted to sex. Kinsey's report was there, but most books were aphrodisiacal classics, like *The Satyricon, Fanny Hill,* and three volumes of *Poetica Erotica,* the majority "privately circulated," from the 1920s.

Hellman took in the airy impressiveness of Bennett's Villard office, its walls of books and the photos of Stein, O'Hara, and others with amusing, grateful inscriptions. In the prized bathroom, he tarried long enough to jot down the presence of the telephone, the dedication to Cloacina (goddess of sewage), the reading matter with jokey titles, and the toilet seat "For Juvenile Authors."

On the desk, he saw ordered piles of papers; pipes and good Dunhill tobacco; family photos; and small candy mountains, Hershey bars and sourballs enough for even the most insatiable boy's sweet tooth. His memory registered similar supplies at both houses. Along with Bennett's favored lunch of toasted bagel and peach ice-cream soda at the drugstore—consumed on days when he wasn't entertaining or being entertained at more august establishments—they evidenced surprisingly unsophisticated tastes for a guy whose forays into swanky nightclubs and hotels were well documented by gossips. But Bennett openly *adored* being spoiled. It could take the form of a standing order for New Orleans pralines, or coming first off a crowded plane; having baggage carried for him, or sitting at the best table. He never tired of getting a kick out of something the hoi polloi would dream about—if only it might happen to them!

There'd be plenty of material for this Boswell, who, although Jewish, cultivated an elite, WASP-like profile, and tended to argue over money with his editors; his current subject seemed to have enough of *that.* As well as trailing Bennett and quizzing palazzo denizens, he convened tête-à-têtes with Bennett's friends, competitors, and some who couldn't stand him. Leonard Lyons was on that list. Slowly the tiny pieces of the mosaic took shape. Moss Hart, whose childhood knew the hunger of Bronx and Brooklyn poverty rather than Harlem middle-class respectability, spoke of Bennett's "immaturity" paying off, of his friend living in "a lovely cocoon." Horace Manges recognized his sweetness and generosity, but also knew a man who in business could argue over pennies. Bob Haas spoke of a "quicksilver" fellow with an unusual gift for admitting his own mistakes, while Donald said that his friend's faults were "right on the surface." Being responsible for production, Don also had to deal with an image-conscious "gadfly," obsessed with the look of books, who wouldn't settle till he got the cover he wanted.

Phyllis generalized the point: her husband had "absolute nerve" going after *anything* he wanted. He charged through life believing he lived in a hotel, and it was up to her to make it first-class. Yet that, she asserted, was part of the confidence he generated: Bennett assumed competence in others. He trusted people to get the job done and left them to it. On the other hand, she didn't mind admitting that his damned punning and the silliness that went with it were tedious. And, over dinner at Lindy's with the Cerfs, Hellman heard her carp about Bennett's line in paid endorsements. He and Moss had recently donned black capes and swords, "dueling" over Heublein drinks for a magazine ad. She found it demeaning. Office equipment, coffee, tobacco—soon it would be Hertz rental cars and a deal with the American Motors Corporation, but as far as Bennett was concerned, the fees or payment-in-kind only got better. For "interviewing" AMC president George Romney in an ad that ran in *Life,* he'd be presented with an air-conditioned Rambler station wagon. Wouldn't that come in handy around Mt. Kisco, he wondered aloud.

"It's okay to do this sort of thing if you need the money," Phyllis responded, then turned to him. "You don't," she snapped.

There were times, though, when he had to admit: plugs could be tricky. A columnist in Ohio had criticized him for being introduced on *What's My Line?* as Random's publisher, and conspicuously mentioning titles and authors. Mark Goodson had cautioned all panelists to stop pushing friends' movies. And Alfred Knopf had sent a warning about gee-whiz boosterism: "Sometimes I think I ought to retire from publishing and try to protect you from your own better self," Knopf chided. It would be a fine pickle if readers assumed that anyone in New York thought Bennett wanted to be taken seriously. But unrepentant, Bennett would give himself the last word. In one of his columns a couple years later, he recognized that "being a celebrity today" had become "Big Business," and he was not in the business of making any apologies about it.

By Hellman's reckoning, in 1954 Bennett had earned $125,000 and claimed more than $40,000 in business expenses. RH's trade publishing sales were over $4 million, ranking fourth or fifth among all houses. As Horace Manges concluded, you couldn't help but admire how an "unimportant public school youngster" had lifted himself up to become a national figure. Hellman took note, but continued digging. The profile wasn't quite ready.

. . .

PUBLISHING WAS A WIN-SOME, lose-some gamble that required intuition, timing, nerve, and luck, and in the mid-1950s, triumphs were had and mistakes made, as a string of great-new-hopes and regrettably-nots moved in and out of RH editorial files. All the while, house authors had to be kept happy and working, requiring new energy from younger editors. When Belle Becker retired in May 1955, Bennett appointed Albert Erskine to her job as managing editor, giving him oversight of the editorial process from the production perspective. Deeply lettered, he'd proved a meticulous line and copy editor, and Bennett had also come to appreciate his acquisitions acumen. He'd turned to Albert for a quick verdict on a new British thriller a friend had told Bennett about: Macmillan was planning to publish it in the United States. Albert judged the novel "a superior product, smooth, fast, brutal, and as believable as such thrillers ever need to be." This was a first book, and he felt the writer's wartime experience would provide an exceptionally fecund seedbed for a series around the same protagonist. Bennett dashed off a letter to the author, stating that "your new book . . . is a gem of its kind"; he'd be "deeply interested" to hear of future plans. But though *Casino Royale*'s sales were lackluster, Macmillan kept with its author and he with them. A pity: James Bond's exploits were "just the sort of thing I think we could go to town with," Bennett had promised Ian Fleming.

November 1955 brought another potential transatlantic catch. Bennett launched a bid for Samuel Beckett's *Waiting for Godot,* being staged in London. The play had bored and baffled many, yet was judged brilliant and unbearably moving by others, a chasm so unbridgeable that the drama garnered a singular prize from the *Evening Standard*—never given before or since—as the "most controversial" play of the year. Bennett cabled David Higham, the British agent, saying how "very anxious" he was to buy rights before the U.S. premiere early in 1956. Priding himself on being the foremost trade publisher of plays in America, he regretted that marquee names like Tennessee Williams and Arthur Miller were now absent from the RH list. A play that had caused that much furor and been deemed that groundbreaking was something he wanted. Besides, there was a connection: Beckett had once worked as James Joyce's secretary.

Yet Bennett was left red-faced and laughing at himself, having been ignorant of one tiny detail: the play had been on sale in the United States since the previous year, having been brought out by a staggeringly confident young publisher named Barney Rosset, whose Grove Press sought to make big statements, march with the avant-garde, and stretch the boundaries of free expression. A year earlier, he'd asked Bennett to back his effort to publish an unexpurgated edition of the (still) banned *Lady Chatterley's Lover.* Who better to support him in a court case than the man who'd stood up for *Ulysses*? Surely Bennett must feel as he felt about the novel.

But surely, Bennett made clear, he didn't. He'd *met* Lawrence in Italy, and had tangled with his widow after her husband's death. Perhaps he couldn't stand Rosset daring to compare a fight for *Chatterley* to the fight for *Ulysses* (and capturing similar glory). Bennett dismissed the novel as "very silly," "deliberately pornographic," and ammunition for would-be banners. Any publisher mounting a case for *Chatterley,* he added atop his high horse, was "placing more than a little of his bet on getting some sensational publicity from the sale of a dirty book."

RH didn't have the connections on the ground or focused interest that Bob Haas had expended in the 1930s and Blanche Knopf still did when it came to foreign writers, but there was no slacking on the home front, with Faulkner, O'Hara, Penn Warren, Capote, and other leading Americans. Now the firm had great hopes for a cigar-chomping thirty-five-year-old new author, Mario Puzo. RH published his debut, *The Dark Arena,* in 1955, a gritty story about an ex-GI in postwar Germany. For a man whose idol was Dostoyevsky, and whose work looked on the dark side, he seemed very good-humored—at least that's what Hiram Haydn saw, since Puzo was part of his "farm team," as Bennett called the fiction workshop. RH would stick with him for *The Fortunate Pilgrim,* which would take a decade to percolate. Both were well reviewed, but like the vast majority of new fiction, each was a financial flop. Soon Puzo was broke and, given his sales history, getting no traction from RH or others when he mentioned a third novel. Putnam eventually took a chance, and in 1969, *they'd* be the fortunate publisher of *The Godfather.*

Along with Puzo's *Dark Arena,* RH had published work from another young writer, Leon Uris. His first book, *Battle Cry,* a World War II novel from Putnam, was a major bestseller. RH had paid dearly to lure him, but his second book, *The Angry Hills,* didn't perform as hoped. Still, Bennett stayed with him for his third, an epic exploring the history of Israel. Like Michener, Uris did extensive on-site research, and by fall 1956 was living there. When war broke out over Egypt's nationalization of the Suez Canal, he needed more money. Returning to New York, he called on his editor, Hiram. He'd already had $5,000 from RH and $5,000 from MGM, who'd bought film rights. Now Uris asked for a "gift" of

$8,000—a straight contribution—rather than an advance. Hiram was taken aback. He didn't care much for the tough, big ego, but agreed to go see if Bennett would stretch to a bit more. Uris had no chapters to show at all.

In Bennett's office, the boss's face progressed from amused to disbelieving to furious, eyes flashing in full-blown hurricane. The storm moved back across the hall to Hiram's, where the howling began. There wasn't any way Bennett Cerf would allow himself to be taken for a sucker. "Get out," he shouted at Uris. "Take your book anywhere you want. I'll cancel your contract, and I don't want any of the advance back. Keep it all. . . . Just don't come near here again." Exit Leon Uris and *Exodus,* to Doubleday. The novel would be a number-one bestseller, spawn a highly successful film, and be followed by a string of hits. In such circumstances, what does a publisher do? Everyone has writers whom they start with and drop—or lose—before they become part of the era's conversation. As Alfred Knopf once lamented, "In our business, the fellow who sows seldom reaps! The problem is to catch the author when he's really matured and ready for a success." It's hard to look on the ones who got away and not feel bad. In the many sessions Bennett taped for his oral history, names like Uris and Puzo did not come up. He liked to win and forget when he didn't. In those circumstances, the watchword was "never look back."

And so, he didn't linger on another marquee American missing from the RH ranks during his lifetime: the combatively charismatic young Norman Mailer. Bennett had given him plugs in Trade Winds for his celebrated debut, *The Naked and the Dead,* calling it a "fine" war book that got the success it deserved, despite complaints from some about his language (soldiers said "fug"—Mailer originally wrote "fuck"—but even the euphemism prompted an outcry). Although his next novel, *Barbary Shore,* got a much frostier critical and commercial reception, Mailer's publisher, Stanley Rinehart, had contracted a third, *The Deer Park.* The book was in galleys in the fall of 1954, scheduled for publication in February. Advertising and publicity had started to crank up, when the machine suddenly shuddered and stopped. Mailer had written a Hollywood story full of sex. Some—six lines about intercourse between a producer and a starlet, to be exact—wasn't palatable to Mr. Rinehart, who feared obscenity charges. "The Hollywood producer calls the girl in and it's clear oral sex is going on," Mailer summarized neatly, fifty years later.

At first, he agreed to alter a word here or there, but then thought better of it: he wouldn't change anything. Rinehart canceled the contract. Mailer mustered all the bravado he had to embark on the embarrassing odyssey of finding another publisher. Unusual circumstances demand unusual action: the custom was still for a book to be submitted exclusively to one firm at a time, and so *The Deer Park* journeyed sequentially to S&S, Harper, Scribner, and Harcourt, all of whom turned it down. Its next stop was the house of Knopf, where Blanche, always interested in attractive young literary men, had met Mailer and liked him, facilitating entrée. The Knopfs' lawyer had to get involved, and Alfred also read the novel. He saw that Mailer was "a highly intelligent and sophisticated writer—with considerable technical skill," but felt he was "just trying to tell a dirty story." Wriggling uncomfortably, Knopf managed to pass.

Hiram Haydn had heard about Mailer's dilemma from his best-known New School protégé, William Styron. In the New York hothouse of ambitious young men craning to catch the light of literary fame, Styron and Mailer had naturally met and grown friendly. Although Styron had read the manuscript and didn't care for it, he told Mailer he admired the effort, and Mailer asked him to put in a good word with Haydn. So the book came to Random, and Bennett spent Thanksgiving Day 1954 reading Mailer's manuscript. Though he found the novel "very dirty," he didn't dismiss it out of hand. On the contrary: he thought he might be willing to publish it. First, he wanted to hear what Hiram had to say. Haydn didn't like the book, finding it bleak and unengaging. He voted for rejection, not because of the questionable sex, but because he couldn't summon enthusiasm to get behind it. Bennett had hired Haydn to be chief editor. Given the blue material and the risk, what was the point of not following his advice? If you bring a man in to do a job, you must let him do it, or you undermine both him and yourself. Therefore, RH passed.

Mailer assumed the root of the rejection lay with Bennett. Big-mouthed Norman had heard on the grapevine that loose-lipped Bennett had quipped, "This book will set cock-sucking back twenty years." Whether that was true or not, what was undeniable was that after Mailer's book finally found a home at Putnam, its publisher, Walter Minton, was called by Bennett.

"You'll bring down the Iron Curtain of censorship on the industry if you publish that book," he warned.

Norman Mailer

Minton didn't know Bennett well, but his late father, Mel Minton, had never cared for his showboating. "That call seemed so unlike Cerf," the son recalled. "I suppose he was cautioning a young publisher, [forecasting] this would be bad." But once he was in, Walter Minton chose to make the most of his hot potato. "Some reviewers will dismiss Mailer as sex-obsessed," Putnam publicity declared, then made the case for the book and didn't back down. *The Deer Park* was published that fall of 1955, and by June 1956 had had a net hardcover sale of almost 50,000 copies, a fine showing. A year later, 560,000 paperback copies were in print. Haydn maintained to the end of his life that Bennett had been willing to publish. If that were the case, why warn Minton off? Was it that competitive instinct that normally drove him to accomplish so much? Having gone with Haydn's opinion, did a latent ambivalence, an *if I'm not publishing it, you're not publishing it* regret compel him to admonish Minton?

Whatever it was, Mailer heard about Bennett's warning to his publisher, and stewed. The men didn't cross paths for a year and a half, until both were invited to a party at the Connecticut home of Bill and Rose Styron. Mailer was his incorrigible macho self, wanting to arm-wrestle every man and prove he was the strongest in the room. He'd been drinking heavily, but so had most guests. Rose Styron began to feel a tension vibrating through the air that emanated from Norman and went beyond the usual posturing. He was looking at Bennett with open hostility.

Suddenly, Bill saw Norman barrel toward Bennett like a funnel cloud, and noticed how his publisher's face assumed a taut grin.

"I always wanted to meet you, Bennett," Mailer began, acid clarifying every syllable. Chewing him out, he called Bennett "stupid, arrogant, ignorant," but, strangled by rage, searched for more terrible words to spew. Bennett was scared: it was obvious that a well-muscled man a generation younger was in a mood to hit him. The surreal threat of impending violence in a gracious room full of partygoers was palpable. A minute later, Mailer spoke again. All he could see were the other man's teeth. "You're a dentist," he said at last, his words spitting contempt.

Bennett blanched, but kept smiling. Mailer turned on his heel and walked across the room. Later, Styron asked him to parse what he'd said.

"Every Jewish parent wants his son to become a doctor," Mailer explained. "If he becomes a dentist, he's second rate. Cerf understood me."

But the next day, in the cool light of morning, it was a night that neither Bennett Cerf nor Norman Mailer much wanted to remember.

Chapter 30

Families and Fieldtrips

Young children generally bored Bennett. Once his sons grew older, they became more interesting. It was fun to include them in weekend charades with Mt. Kisco guests; to join in sing-alongs when one of them sat at the piano; and to take in some of a Saturday afternoon ball game together—the boys soon emulated his ability to memorize every conceivable statistic. Yet even then there weren't many hours available for Chris and Jon. Lecture tours, business, and vacations with Phyllis took Bennett away for weeks at a time. He'd always acknowledged an exceptional closeness to his own pop as child and man; they "were together" until Bennett was forty-three. Yet he not only justified the breaks from his sons, he evangelized for them: an occasional separation is a "fine thing," he preached, illustrating the point to Cerfboard readers by reprising a story he'd told about Chris in Trade Winds six years earlier. The boy was only seven then, and his parents were leaving for six weeks on the West Coast. Chris was in a mood of "deep self-pity," and complained of a stomachache "the exact size of California."

"Better get it back to the size of school in New York," Bennett advised. It didn't occur to him how retelling the anecdote years after the fact might strike his now teenage son: that Chris could be embarrassed when friends or their parents came across it. Family, authors, friends were all fair game: stories were the basic pulp on which Bennett wrote his life. To be sure, Chris liked featuring in some—it was attention and connection—but other times, he wanted to disappear.

He could also be on the receiving end of his dad's lightning-quick "sensitivity." He'd been schooled from a very young age as to who in the family was number one. Phyllis had once made the boy compose a long apology for not paying "enough attention" to Daddy and not saying "thank you to everything" Daddy did for him. Even now, if Bennett came in and his son didn't say hello fast enough, feelings would be hurt, but God help him if Bennett was working and Chris disturbed him. Watchful Jonathan resolved *he* wouldn't be subjected to such attention.

As a motherless young man, Bennett had seen a great deal of Cerfs and Wises, but he'd shed many skins since then. His sons had no idea that their father had once been part of a large family circle, and Chris believed that his paternal grandmother had died when his father was two or three, so seldom was she mentioned. That's why it was exciting when their parents one spring Sunday announced that two relatives—Mary and Carrie Cerf—would come to meet them, before taking in a performance of *What's My Line?* Their dad seemed to have discovered them fully sprung, right in Manhattan. When they showed up at Sixty-Second Street, however, the pair weren't what the boys had expected. Of that indeterminate age that passes for "old" in a young person's eyes, Mary was angular, hawk-like, rather forbidding; Carrie shorter, roly-poly, friendlier. Both were dressed not for 1955, but for 1930, in suits and veiled hats. Their father seemed greatly amused.

The next morning, the sisters had transmogrified into anecdote material. They were recluses like the Collyer brothers, Bennett chuckled to his sons, and when they died, the Cerfs would inherit a great fortune. Lengthy riffs on the amazing riches to be found in their West End Avenue apartment followed, but it seemed a strange subject for jokes: the genteel Collyers had been hoarders who'd shut themselves up in their New York home until one died of starvation and the other was crushed under junk. In the eight years since the grisly find, they'd become legends.

Months later, when Carrie and Mary arrived for Thanksgiving, they committed a fatal error: they lost their novelty. The old girls' litany of aches and pains bored the paterfamilias, who skipped out for a solo walk in what was left of the afternoon, giving thanks that Phyllis could manage the guests. Having arrived so mysteriously in the life of Sixty-Second Street, the sisters exited the same way, leaving the boys to wonder if they really were related. But although rarely seen again, they continued to populate Bennett's conversation and columns—just like the Collyers.

Uncle Herbert, forever serious and frail, was a different story, occupying an unquestioned place in Bennett's heart. Although he'd remained too much the dilettante—Saxe had tried and failed to persuade him to become a disciplined writer—Herbert had always inspired enormous respect for his intellect. Now, however, Bennett confided to Saxe his worry that his uncle was reprising a pattern left behind decades earlier: despite sharing a home with Glen, Herbert was pursuing young men. A sickening premonition haunted Bennett: one day the phone would ring, and he'd hear that his uncle, now over sixty, had been beaten up. He took Herbert aside for a long talk at Mt. Kisco, but beyond the newly revived penchant for youth, Bennett was even more alarmed by another change: the brilliance had dulled. Herbert's memory was failing.

With so little extended family in their lives, it was friends who took up that space, and *they* were never in short supply. Moss and Kitty, Bubs and Arthur, remained closest of the close. But Arlene Francis and Marty Gabel, who already spent many a Sunday night sharing a late snack with Bennett and Phyllis after *What's My Line?,* were buying a hilltop acre at one end of the Mt. Kisco property, and the two families' lives would grow more entwined. Soon the Gabels' son Peter and Jonathan Cerf became best friends. Of Armenian Jewish stock—and, like Bennett, not recognized by many as a Jew—Arlene resembled him in other ways, too: utterly driven and juggling multiple careers, she cloaked ambition under irresistible charm.

Phyllis's friend Minnie Astor and her new husband, the painter James Whitney Fosburgh (Bennett insisted on spelling it "Fosberg," as though they were Jewish and not high-status WASPs), were on the scene, Minnie one of the famous Cushing sisters. *All About Eve*'s Joe Mankiewicz lived in nearby Bedford, and he and his wife and son Tom were regulars. Chris had developed a huge (unrequited) crush on a Botticelli-like teenager named Freddy Espy, who lived close by in Mt. Kisco and needed a family to escape to: her own was damaged by alcoholism and other problems. Bennett, as entranced as his son, "adopted" Freddy. In turn, she was charmed by how easy it was to talk to him, and by the undistracted attention he gave. He'd turn off the jokes and listen. Phyllis, however, didn't show much interest in this pixie who was looking for another mother—as Helen Brown, Phyllis-as-was, once did. Freddy, so comfortable with Bennett but wary about being alone with his wife, made sure it didn't happen too often.

. . .

AT THE PALAZZO, BUSINESS was going well, and Bennett was enjoying himself. The sums coming out of Hollywood were getting gratifyingly large, and would get larger still: "Red" Warren's *Band of Angels* sold for $200,000, and Irwin Shaw's *Lucy Crown* for more than $300,000. Mac Hyman's *No Time for Sergeants* had been adapted for TV and then for the stage by Ira Levin, a young writer whose thriller *A Kiss Before Dying* (published by S&S) had won the 1954 Edgar Award from the Mystery Writers of America for best first novel. Now Levin's version of Mac's story had become a hit on Broadway, and RH published it as a play. Promoting him in Trade Winds as "a brilliant technician," Bennett wondered if Levin could be persuaded to jump houses. He also had every hope that Mac would come through with a second success.

In the interim, he was able to capitalize on *No Time for Sergeants* readers and their appetite for military life writ "light" by signing a *Life* magazine staffer, William Brinkley, who'd come in with a series of stories about navy public relations officers on a Pacific island during World War II. Once Bennett convinced Brinkley that novels were easier to sell than stories, he agreed to "put pearls on a string," with help from Albert Erskine. Bennett once again bestowed the perfect title: *Don't Go Near the Water.* It became the bestselling novel of the year, and film rights were sold to MGM. It wasn't lost on him, Brinkley told his publisher, that interest in turning the book into a movie only started after Bennett had visited "the western Babylon."

Bennett the author

His own byline wasn't neglected, either. While putting together *The Vest Pocket Book of Jokes* for RH, he'd inked a far more consequential deal with Cass Canfield: in return for Bennett editing a *Reading for Pleasure* anthology for Harper, Canfield would sell him reprint rights to Aldous Huxley's *Brave New World* and James Thurber's *Carnival,* long desired for the ML. He'd found the process of combing through his previous books to cherry-pick stories for *Vest Pocket* a "helluva job," he'd complained to his diary, and for the Harper book swiftly hired an editor he knew at *This Week* to help find suitable selections, and followed Cass's advice by asking booksellers for suggestions. In between *Vest Pocket* and *Reading for Pleasure* would come *The Life of the Party,* which Doubleday would publish in October 1956. Saxe was ailing, so Bert Krantz joined the team, and would help out on Bennett's books going forward.

. . .

NINETEEN FIFTY-SIX HAD BEGUN with John O'Hara winning the National Book Award for *Ten North Frederick.* RH had captured the fiction prize two years running, following on Faulkner's win for *A Fable,* and the triumph was sweetly compounded by the book's being a big bestseller. For O'Hara, such recognition from the critical establishment had been a long time coming. John, who trusted no one, trusted his publisher, who'd helped through hard times to reach this place. For Bennett, the rejoicing was heartfelt: no question he thought O'Hara a great talent and loved him for it. He also thanked his stars for robust health, that luck having been brought home by what was happening to Dick Simon. At the end of November, he'd been rushed to New York Hospital with a heart "spasm," and Bennett had overcome his aversion in order to visit. January found Dick there again, and before 1956 was over he'd have another attack, his outlook dimming.

In late January, while Dick was pondering mortality, Bennett was in California with Phyllis and the Hornblows, boggled by Disneyland. The Cerfs were always up for the newest and latest, and the park had opened only six months earlier. Walt Disney had spent twenty-three years conjuring it, and before their visit, they lunched at the studio with the wizard himself. Different from any movie lot they'd ever seen, the buildings were all of a piece, and the young staff playing baseball and lolling on the lawns made it seem more like a college campus than a film factory. Disney the man struck them as distinct from other moguls: an empire-builder who seemed surprisingly unpretentious. "Absolutely great" was Bennett's verdict after a mad romp—riding, cruising, and flying along the map of Walt's fancies.

A few weeks after Bennett's return to New York, a major change occurred at Random House: Bob Haas, after two decades as a partner, retired. Meticulous Bob had broached the subject three years earlier, wanting to plan so his leaving wouldn't be too disruptive. They'd all met with the accountant J. K. Lasser, and it was settled that Bennett and Don would buy Haas out with $50,000 a year for ten years. Now he relinquished the vice presidency and his stock, but reassuringly would come to the palazzo several days a week to look after his authors, and remain a director. On Friday, March 16, while snow fell in the courtyard by way of benediction, Lew Miller threw a party for the firm's officers. Bennett had agreed that Don's stepson, Tony Wimpfheimer, would buy a chunk of Bob's shares and go on the board as secretary. Don took Bob's role as executive vice president; Lew continued as VP and director of sales; Manny Harper remained treasurer.

A month after the party, Hiram heard angry voices in the hall as Bennett and Don approached his office. Everyone had heard them yell at each other occasionally like the old professional married couple they were, but this was serious, and over a book. The manuscript of Englishwoman Honor Tracy's *The Straight and Narrow Path* had arrived, and they proceeded to outline very different views of it. Tracy's novel had started as dispatches for the London *Times* on life in an Irish village. Don found her lampooning of Hibernian habits amusing, and thought that beneath the satire lay a good deal of truth, but Bennett—that well-known humorist—felt it crouched uncomfortably on the backs of the Irish and their Catholicism. Tracy had converted to the faith, yet she'd shown that while the local priest lived high on the collection plate, villagers didn't have enough to eat. Both partners knew the backstory: the Church had sued the *Times* for libel after it printed episodes; the paper, leery of the Catholic establishment, had settled; Tracy then sued the *Times* and won. Bennett balked at going forward.

"Come on . . . you're just afraid that [Cardinal] Spellman will raise hell with you," Donald shouted, before launching the last catapult: "If you refuse to publish . . . don't ever call yourself a publisher to me again!"

It was Bennett who handled their eminent, very difficult, red-capped next-door neighbor, lunching with Spellman twice a year, and at times ambling up Madison Avenue with him, talking stocks and baseball. He'd arranged a mollifying meeting for himself, the cardinal, and John O'Hara after *A Rage to Live* had overheated the Legion of Decency. Taking a chance with one of their biggest authors was one thing; inviting trouble for this import, another. Yet he quieted down sufficiently to ask Hiram for a Solomonic reading.

A week later, Hiram felt a bit nervous announcing that he agreed with Don. "I predict we'll all be sorry," was Bennett's final word, but then calmly acceded to publication. What amazed Hiram was the unusual lack of rancor: to Bennett and Don's great credit, in this and other situations Hiram saw "no resentment, no reproach, no bickering." The book was a success with reviewers, stores, and readers, and the cardinal, as it happened, didn't give them any grief.

In early May, Bennett and Phyllis were on the move again, for a month and a half in Europe. Although Donald and Pat crossed the Atlantic every year, it had been an eighteen-year absence for Bennett. The last time he was there, Franco was bombing Barcelona and Hitler planning to pounce; now America feared the Soviets and their newly formed Warsaw Pact. Phyllis, just turned forty, had never left North America. Anxious to get on with sightseeing as soon as possible, the Cerfs opted to eschew the sea route and travel via Pan American Airlines first-class "*President*" service. The airline even sent a car to take them to Idlewild.

Eleven hours later, author Irwin Shaw and their *Snake Pit* director friend Tola Litvak met them for a reunion catch-up over breakfast at Orly Airport before heading into town. Bennett and Phyllis breathed in this pleasant companionship like the fresh spring air. Guiding them around gorgeous views of the Eiffel Tower, the Seine, etc., was fine and good, but what counted as much was that these were insiders who valued the Cerfs' place in their world and shielded them from anonymity. After a whirlwind day, they returned to the airport for a flight to Nice: even on vacation, there was no time to spare. From Nice they proceeded to Monte Carlo and lunch with the now aged Somerset Maugham in his beautiful gardens at Cap Ferrat. Bennett had done well by Maugham, and Maugham by him: at 297,000 copies, *Of Human Bondage* was an ML all-time bestseller. "First," Maugham assured him, "an author publishes for the money. . . . Later, if he's lucky, he can afford to do it for the prestige." Lunch was followed by dinner with Sam Behrman, who was on the Riviera helping Otto Preminger with the screenplay for *Bonjour Tristesse*. Bennett wanted to make sure Sam didn't forget the biography of Max Beerbohm he owed RH—a follow-up to his bestselling life of the art dealer Duveen.

Then it was Rome, followed by Venice, where as a young man thirty years earlier Bennett had pined for female companionship while Herbert cruised canal byways looking for boys. Here the magic of La Serenissima took over, as he and Phyllis were alone together for two whole days—a rarity in their married life. In a letter composed amid the old-fashioned luxury of the Gritti Palace Hotel, Bennett made a backhand acknowledgment that showed how unusual the idyll was: "You know, Saxe, she's a real nice gal! Have to get to know her better!" Peeking out from behind the irony was a hint of the wonder and shyness of a man not very comfortable with intimacy, and about as close to an intimate reflection as Bennett would allow himself to have.

"Have to get to know her better!"

In the same letter, he thanked Saxe for finding pieces for *Reading for Pleasure*. Bennett had to show Harper the anthology was progressing, for they were paying some of his expenses, ostensibly to gather European material. "This is one time when I really am going to need every last bit of help you can give," he admitted. "I want to make this book really *good*—and it will be so far out of my usual line that it is a definite challenge." The ML "*never* could have gotten" titles by Huxley and Thurber otherwise, and he had to deliver his end of the bargain! In the old days, the serious anthologies of plays and stories that went out under his byline had had a scholarly co-editor, and if they didn't, Herbert was in the prompter's box. Now his name was the selling point—it would carry the book on its own—and his sense of obligation about "the bargain" was such that the job *had* to be well done: it was a matter of honor. Yet beyond the time constraints imposed by his life, and beneath the veneer of impregnable confidence, lay the nagging doubt that he wasn't on an intellectual par with many authors and editors.

In Paris again, Bennett bemoaned his fifty-eighth birthday over a splendid dinner at the Ritz. Less successful was the after-dinner outing to the Folies Bergère, where the same disgust that he'd felt on the brothel crawl with loutish Uncle Leo during his first European trip rose up again. Finally they reached London, Bennett "delirious" to be there. How had he been away so long? Once more cocooned in the Savoy, he was interviewed by the *Express,* the *Standard,* the snooty *Telegraph*. Even in England, TV had made him somebody beyond books. When he turned up at King's Theatre in Hammersmith, West London, as a panelist on the U.K. *What's My Line?,* the autograph hounds were on to him, and he loved it. Still, he also enjoyed making the luncheon rounds with publishing potentates whom Don had dealt with through the years. To cap it all, Francis Meynell took him and Thrup to the quirky house where Mr. Nonesuch and Mr. Random had first met cute. But by mid-June, sitting at the captain's table on the super-smooth SS *United States*—the largest, fastest liner plying the Atlantic, befitting America's place in the world—they were more than ready for home.

There was bounce in Bennett's step six days later when, whisked off a special gangplank at eight in the morning on a West Side dock, their baggage already arrayed below, he and Thrup spied Chris, Jon, and Margaret, her young charges frantically waving hello. "There is probably no thrill in the world equal to seeing Paris, London, Rome and Venice for the first time," Phyllis told *Newsday* readers after she caught her breath. "But seeing New York's skyline after six weeks' absence is also . . . pretty wonderful."

Chapter 31

Feds and Nymphets

ONE EVENING BACK IN HIS EARLY MONTHS ON *WHAT'S MY LINE?*, Bennett had trooped over to Toots Shor's with Dorothy Kilgallen and was surprised to be joined by some of her right-wing cronies. These included his Columbia classmate George Sokolsky, who'd grown up to be one of Hearst's most powerful columnists and a devoted McCarthyite, lending a hand to many a blacklisting. Oddly, Bennett enjoyed their chat, but over the next few years became incensed (and worried, given the tenor of the times) whenever he ran into Sokolsky, who hailed him as "the Pinko Publisher." Eventually, in no uncertain terms, Bennett told him to study the RH list, since he'd taken a lot of liberal heat for *Witness*. The upshot was that the two had agreed to a lunch in June 1955. Bennett chose the Stork, making sure to reserve a table at the rear of the A-list Cub Room. Inevitably, Sokolsky arrived before ever-late Bennett, whom he greeted with a sardonic smile.

"I see that you got a table in the back . . . so nobody would see you with me."

"You're absolutely right, George. I'm not going to lie to you."

They crossed swords, but had a good time. As the meal wound down, Sokolsky faced him: "You say you'll publish books on the right. . . . If I ever come to you with [one] . . . good enough, will you publish it?" This was long before conservative imprints existed in trade houses.

"You're damned right I will," Bennett offered, wondering what he might be letting himself in for. In late September the phone rang. Sokolsky was shopping a book about the FBI, authorized and with an introduction by Hoover. Was it too "right" for Random House?

"George, are you kidding me? Every publisher in America would give his right arm for a book like that."

Sokolsky wasn't kidding, nor was Bennett. Unquestionably, much of

America had bought into the cult of the government crime-fighters and their seemingly invincible bulldog-faced leader. A meeting could be arranged with Lou Nichols, a top FBI man, for the next day at the Lotos Club. At first Bennett couldn't believe it—both the lucky call and the damned date. He'd wangled a ticket for the second game of the Yankees–Dodgers World Series for that afternoon. He gave away the ticket.

Whether he knew it or not, one reason the bureau was so cooperative was its fury at an earlier work written by Max Lowenthal, a lawyer and former adviser to Harry Truman, who made the first critical examination of Hoover and his creation. Lowenthal and his wife paid dearly by being smeared. Still, the book was so dry, it didn't make waves as the FBI had feared.

Nichols informed Bennett that the writer they'd cooperate with was Don Whitehead, who'd won two Pulitzers for the Associated Press and had recently published complimentary articles about Hoover. He'd gotten in touch with the bureau, wanting to do more features on "the fight against Communism." Now he'd be given a six-month release from his day job, having already been thoroughly vetted. RH would pay him what amounted to a half year's salary, as well as a royalty. The PR unit Nichols headed would give him an office, research staff, and source materials (some of which Whitehead mistakenly assumed were "raw" files).

He got to work, and on June 26, 1956, the FBI delivered the first twenty-four chapters two months late, but with Nichols's assurance that Whitehead had done multiple drafts, so the text was in good shape, and the rest would arrive the next day. Bennett quickly read the first batch, recording comments for Paul Lapolla, the recent hire he'd assigned to edit the book. (It seemed better to use a new man; publishing an FBI-themed Landmark for kids was one thing, but shining up to Hoover for a major trade title hadn't pleased some veteran staff.) What Bennett found, however, was "a mass of wonderful information" that, to put it politely, needed a great deal of editing—above all, "to temper the repeated adulatory paragraphs" about the chief, he told Lapolla. "Nobody admires Mr. Hoover more than I do, but by . . . repeating page after page, the reverse effect from what is intended is achieved." More "urgency and excitement" needed to be inserted, but "carefully." To Hoover, he dispatched a politic cable: "We are delighted with the book. With a very slight rearrangement . . . we will have . . . the most important book of the year."

With the manuscript delay, Bennett had thought it best to move publication to the spring, but the bureau insisted that copies be in stores for Christmas 1956. That meant the book, one way or another, had to be published on November 28. It was an insanely tight schedule: Lapolla would have eight days to tame the beast, and needed every second. The editor read the manuscript, dismayed at the extent to which it was "a naïve puff job." Clearly, despite those Pulitzers, one hand had been tied behind Whitehead's back. Bennett dispatched Lapolla to D.C. to revise with Nichols, telling him to "bring back the book the way it should be."

Although he hadn't been at RH long, Lapolla knew that if a project didn't work, Bennett would be embarrassed as much for himself as for the author, and an editor would hear about it, even more so in this case: no room for embarrassment with the FBI. Using Bennett's report on the initial batch as guide, Lapolla hashed it out with Whitehead and Nichols, and let them have a first go; he and Nichols then sat in a room and wrestled with the manuscript day and night. By July 5, the three had effected real improvement, and less than three weeks later, Lapolla sent the text to the designer. When he handed Bennett a list of Washington expenses to be reimbursed, Bennett glanced at the total, then doubled it: Lapolla had earned a bonus. Nichols was still waiting for clearance on some material, but all else was set. The attorney general had read and approved what was now called *The FBI Story: A Report to the People*.

At the end of October, Warner Brothers bought film rights for $140,000, and when reviews came in, they were generally good. *The New York Times Book Review* found the book "highly readable . . . the nearest thing extant to a sober and definitive history," written with "restraint and respect for facts." The paper's daily reviewer Charles Poore judged it "one of the most absorbing" crime and punishment narratives he'd read. Hoover declared himself appreciative, approving of Bennett's "personal interest," knowing he'd "push" the book "to the utmost"—and push he did. Even John Charles Daly was persuaded to put in a generous word on *WML* one Sunday. Bennett was also careful, making sure to send an advance photostat of the first big ad for the chief's scrutiny. A good thing, too, for on November 30, the day Hoover dictated his thank-you, the *Times* book page featured a disconcertingly eye-catching ad for *The FBI Story:* it was upside down, the only one on the page to be so, and unlikely to have been a mistake. Was a compositor settling a score with HUAC?

The flub didn't escape FBI notice, and Nichols complained to Bennett that it was the first such mess-up he'd ever seen.

In dealing with Hoover, Bennett mixed nervous respect—the man's overarching power inspired fear and awe in any sensible person—with calculation and genuine enthusiasm. Underneath the liberal politics and extrovert's bravado lurked the gee-whiz admiration for *anybody* talented or important. He enlisted Nichols to persuade the chief to autograph a copy, a volume that, without any awkwardness, Bennett would place on his shelves alongside books signed by FDR and Adlai Stevenson. A mid-December ad that appeared (right side up) above Bennett's own signature boasted, "Never, in the entire history of Random House, have we ever had a book that started so spectacularly." By Christmas, 175,000 copies were in print, and sales continued. *The FBI Story* would be the second-biggest nonfiction title of 1957.

Back in early July, while Lapolla and Nichols were sweating their task, Hoover had written to Bennett and signed himself "Edgar" for the first time. In December, Bennett felt sure enough to stop calling him "Mr. Hoover," although a slight shine of obsequiousness always hung about his letters. For one thing, on a visit to Lou Nichols's Alexandria home the previous fall, he'd learned that Hoover had a file on *him*. He'd done some "pretty silly things" when younger, like the trip to Spain, Nichols chided. There'd also been the 1945 National Campaign for Books for Russia, and the anti-HUAC *Hollywood Fights Back* broadcast. What he didn't say was that the file had been officially closed by orders of Washington HQ at the end of January 1951, despite the New York office's recommendation that Bennett be put on the Security Index.

Not long after *The FBI Story* was published, the chief sent him a small gift: a monograph titled *Communism Versus the Jewish People,* prepared for the bureau's agents. He noted that it emphasized the "fundamental differences" between Communism and the "ideas of the Jewish people. It establishes that the Communist movement is entirely incompatible with everything the Jewish people stand for traditionally." Whether Hoover was a virulent antisemite has been debated over the years, but whatever message he was sending through his gift, he didn't have to mention that Bennett was Jewish: that went without saying.

"It will be useful!" he assured "Edgar," and quickly changed the subject: that particular week, their book was "the #1 nonfiction bestseller in the U.S."

The Cerfs visiting J. Edgar Hoover in Washington two years after *The FBI Story* (from left: Clyde Tolson, Jonathan, Bennett, J. Edgar Hoover, Phyllis, Chris)

. . .

ONE EARLY NOVEMBER EVENING in 1956, Bennett put aside the newspaper coverage of Dwight Eisenhower's second presidential win, resigned himself to his man Adlai's second defeat, and turned to reading a novel that Bill Styron had passed along. It had been published abroad, and he took Styron's recommendation with the seriousness accorded a young man whom the literati saw as a possible heir to Faulkner. Styron was profoundly taken with the book, but knew some had found it unspeakable. For a minute, he'd even thought of publishing it privately himself (his wife Rose's family had money). In truth, he'd felt a few qualms about giving it to Bennett, noticing a doubtful nod of his new publisher's head and the unusually quiet acknowledgment: "Well, I don't know . . . dirty books," when he handed over Vladimir Nabokov's *Lolita*.

Bennett stayed up until 2 A.M., eyes darting fast as camera clicks, taking in the story of twelve-year-old Dolores Haze; her litterateur stepfather, Humbert Humbert, who was obsessed with her; and their American road trip into rape, incest, paranoia, banality, comedy, tragedy, madness, and death—all conveyed in exquisite prose that played sexual hide-and-seek. Donald read it as well, and they disagreed on whether to publish. Don, it seems, was hesitant; Bennett, willing. Although two years earlier he'd declined to support Barney Rosset over *Lady Chatterley,* he sensed in *Lolita* a link to the fight for *Ulysses*—or so Hiram Haydn thought. Certainly, the great majority of publishers in New York were by no means willing.

The émigré Russian aristocrat Nabokov taught literature at Cornell, and several years earlier had tried to interest publishers in the novel, but was rebuffed by Viking; New Directions; Farrar, Straus; and S&S, whose editors had called the manuscript "sheer pornography." *Lolita* was rejected at Doubleday as well, despite the enthusiasm evinced by young Jason Epstein; the firm's president, Douglas Black—a lawyer placed in that position by the squabbling Doubleday family—had been terrified by it. With all those houses, Nabokov had had dealings over previous books, or had friends who acted as intermediaries. He didn't approach RH, with whom he'd never had contact, although in 1944, four years after he arrived in the United States as a refugee, the nation's preeminent literary critic, Edmund Wilson, had told Linscott that Nabokov was the most brilliant man he'd ever met and one day would write a great novel.

Those who rejected *Lolita* had been worried it would land them in court. Therefore, like *Ulysses,* it was published in English in Paris. Maurice Girodias's Olympia Press brought it out in 1955 in two simple green volumes, reminiscent of Sylvia Beach's plain-blue *Ulysses*. Although *Lolita* had its detractors, it also had prominent defenders. As had happened with *Ulysses,* copies of the Olympia book began to trickle into America. Marboro Books, a mail-order operation that had been sourcing some titles from France, began to import the novel in greater numbers. Other "black marketers" did the same. Nabokov, who'd belatedly discovered the nature of the publisher he was dealing with (he hadn't known Olympia's reputation was based more on pornography than on its early publication of writers like Samuel Beckett), found himself in a copyright quagmire akin to the one faced by Joyce. United States law stipulated that if more than 1,500 copies were imported and sold in the country within five years of first publication abroad, and no homegrown edition had been published in that period registering American copyright, the author would lose the possibility of establishing copyright. *Lolita* would be in the public domain, and Nabokov stuck with Girodias.

And so, the novel was making a second go-round as 1956 gave way to

1957, being considered by a number of publishers. Bennett gave it to Hiram—whose daughter had been an admiring student of Nabokov's at Cornell—and asked whether to follow Donald's instinct or his own. Hiram's reaction was swift and definite: "nauseated" by the story, he found Nabokov's tone "sick," and was convinced any man who could write such a tale must be "cruel and sadistic." Styron was present to witness his editor's livid transformation. Hiram reminded Bill that he had a daughter the same age as Dolores-Lolita. Veins popping on his balding forehead, he shouted that perhaps when Bill's own daughter reached that age, he'd understand how truly "loathsome" the novel was. RH would publish the book over his "dead body."

Hiram's arrival had been accompanied by a subtle if basic change in structure, an indisputable shift in the power dynamic at Random House: Bennett had crowned him the firm's first editor-in-chief. A hierarchy, hardly perceptible but *there,* now operated in the Villard. Bennett understood that he had to pass on *Lolita* unless he wanted to undermine his own setup.

Across town, Epstein again tried to convince Doubleday to buy the novel and was making headway; so was a small, just-launched firm called McDowell, Obolensky. Bennett had been relieved to receive David McDowell's notice at the beginning of 1957. The problem of his uncomfortable fit had been solved without the partners having to engage in unpleasantness. Yet despite their willingness to risk a censorship trial, neither Doubleday nor McDowell, Obolensky would publish *Lolita*. Girodias's money demands were simply too outrageous, especially with the shadow of a court case looming. Enter a showgirl on the arm of Putnam's Walter Minton.

The young Putnam publisher had done business with Marboro Books, whose owner had mentioned *Lolita* and vouchsafed him a copy. But Minton didn't pay attention until Rosemary Ridgewell, a Latin Quarter nightclub dancer he was chasing, told him about it. The leggy (and well-read) brunette had seen excerpts in *The Anchor Review,* another of Jason Epstein's projects. *Then* Minton took notice. Reading through the night, he decided Girodias could go to the devil: he'd find a way to deal with him. Knowing the Marboro operation, Minton understood "it would not have been hard to establish that more than 1500 copies had been imported." Nabokov had to be getting desperate; Minton used that as leverage, and was also generous. Nabokov signed.

Minton had been willing to go where others feared to tread because, having assumed control of his father's company, he needed to build his own list, and needed the big sales that a ready-made controversy like *Deer Park* or *Lolita* would provide. As part of his campaign to hook books, he used scouts whom he rewarded with a commission for projects lured. Ridgewell had heard about this and was, as well as dating Minton, keeping company with a lawyer, Paul O'Dwyer, brother of a recent New York mayor. One day, Minton answered the phone to hear O'Dwyer tell him that their mutual showgirl was also a scout and had to be rewarded as such. A man of many connections, O'Dwyer didn't have to elaborate. She got her cut—the equivalent of a 10 percent author's royalty for the first year of sales, plus 10 percent of Putnam's share of subsidiary rights income for the first two years of publication. She also got her pretty picture in *Time*.

At RH, nobody was celebrating. After seeing his editor's volcanic fit, Bill Styron had fled down the hall to his publisher, and found him looking uncharacteristically forlorn. "That novel is a masterpiece," Bennett confided to the man who'd conveyed that verdict in the first place. Hiram had said he'd quit if anybody overruled him on this one. Styron heard his publisher sigh: "What a *wonderful* book!" Knowing *how* it had slipped from his grasp and *what* it might become, longing pressed into each word like strangled breath.

In his memoirs, Hiram recalled Bennett often "sadly" reminding him that he'd kept Random House from publishing *Lolita,* but he never budged. Quite the contrary, he insisted on making his opinion widely known. He considered himself very much the public intellectual, and was horrified to witness the novel becoming, as he saw it, "the toast of the literary world."

Never mind. He'd been busy incubating his own cause célèbre. An author who'd been at Bobbs-Merrill had written a new book and was looking for a new publisher. Hiram had first sat down to talk with Bennett about her the previous spring, six months before *Lolita* turned up. The lady's origins, like Nabokov's, were in St. Petersburg in the waning days of czarist Russia. (As it happened, her closest school friend had been Nabokov's younger sister.) In America, she'd cast aside her original identity as Alissa Rosenbaum in an act of determined reinvention.

Hiram had a problem with a pedophile and his nymphet, but Ayn Rand's Nietzschean capitalists were an entirely different matter.

Chapter 32

Ideal Publisher

IT WAS IN EARLY MARCH 1956 THAT HIRAM PLOPPED HIS LANKY FRAME into one of Bennett's guest chairs, stretched his legs, and began to talk about Ayn Rand and Jerome Weidman. An editorial conference at RH: how informal and flexible—no committee with agendas, just Bennett or Don or Donald-and-Bennett to chew over prospects and decide. Each author Hiram came to discuss trailed an impressive record. Weidman, New York born and bred, sang his songs in pitch-perfect Gothamese—tough, funny, but hardly pretty. "The first American street-smart novelist," he'd been called. He was twenty-four in 1937 when S&S published his debut, *I Can Get It for You Wholesale,* to high praise and sales. With it, Weidman forged a character template for later novels: abrasive, driven men who'd do anything for a buck, and the schlemiels they stepped on as they shoved their way up. New York's teeming life and ferocious energy was a character itself, akin to the London of Dickens—whom Weidman greatly admired.

From the beginning, he raised hackles: some fellow Jews accused him of being self-hating, of brazenly hanging out a particular line of dirty laundry as if it represented the entire New York Jewish experience. Weidman's defense was that he portrayed reality as he'd lived it growing up on the Lower East Side and in garment factories. Later he could point to others, like Budd Schulberg and Philip Roth, who came in for similar criticism. By 1956, he'd published ten novels, and moved from S&S to Harcourt, then Doubleday. Along the way, he'd exchanged the city for upscale Westport, a Connecticut town on Long Island Sound popular with families whose husbands commuted to jobs in advertising, TV, the arts, and the book trade. Albert Erskine would soon live there, and Hiram already did. That's how he and Weidman had met.

Bennett had first encountered "Jerry" twenty years earlier, and judged him "one of the most uneven writers" he knew. Yet as with O'Hara and Michener, his steady flow was a distinct asset, and enough books had sold for him to retain his value even as he moved from publisher to publisher. A deal wouldn't be brokered until May 1957, but the wait was worth it. The new novel, *The Enemy Camp,* was published in 1958 to raves and great sales (editorial suggestions from Hiram and Donald had helped). The next year, he'd co-write the book for the musical *Fiorello!,* which won the Pulitzer Prize for Drama and the Tony Award for Best Musical. Naturally, RH published it. The Cerfs grew close to Jerry and his Main Line Philadelphia WASP wife, Peggy, also a writer; they became frequent guests.

Literary luncheon with (from left) Helen Palmer Geisel, Ted Geisel, Donald Klopfer, William Styron, Jerry Weidman, Phyllis Cerf, Bennett, and Peggy Weidman

A few months after publishing *The Enemy Camp,* Bennett and Don put *I Can Get It for You Wholesale* into the ML. Weidman was moved to tell Bennett how it felt to be "a classic," as his thirteen-year-old son John, deeply impressed, now called him. As a young man, when Gimbel's and Macy's used to have one of their Depression price wars, Weidman would buy as many ML copies as he could, and dream that someday he'd have a book "in this wonderful series. I guess you never thought of yourself as being in the making dreams come true business, but so far as this household is concerned, you are." Peggy sensed something else in Bennett, a singularity: of all the people she'd ever known, "he liked living more than anybody," his life force was that distinctive. True, he loved being "somebody" among "a small world of somebodies," and in certain respects, she saw, that constituted his whole world. Yet well beyond those boundaries, he sought people out, being truly curious, genuinely interested.

. . .

NO QUESTION THAT THE second author on Hiram's mind that day of the office conference was a "somebody." The discussion about her was more urgent—and the gamble higher. Bennett knew Ayn Rand only by reputation. Her previous novel, *The Fountainhead,* with its Frank Lloyd Wright–like protagonist espousing unfettered egoism and the superiority of the creative, uncompromising individual, had grown into a word-of-mouth phenomenon, and, more unusual, had legs. Published thirteen years earlier, it steadily attracted new readers and earned for its author a growing circle of passionate acolytes. Hiram had a history with Rand from his days at Bobbs-Merrill. When he was newly installed as the Indianapolis firm's New York editor in 1950, the two forged an express connection: Hiram was told by his bosses that his most important task was "to keep Ayn Rand happy." They wanted to be sure they would publish her next moneymaker.

She wasn't happy, however. The company's president had disapproved of *The Fountainhead,* and Rand felt that Bobbs-Merrill had done little to spur sales. Her original editor—the person she liked and trusted—had been fired, and Hiram would have to work hard for any hope of securing her allegiance. He invited her to lunch and found himself opposite a short forty-five-year-old with midnight-black hair and huge jet eyes, transfixing in their focus and a camera for a remarkable X-ray mind. At certain angles, her face resembled Picasso's, with the same piercing intensity. She didn't suffer fools, made no apologies for being demanding, but demanded more of herself than anyone. Her new book had required an investment of more years—seven already—than even she had bargained for.

Their meetings continued. She had an intimidating talent for propounding ideas and squashing opposition with unswerving, coolly logical conviction. "What are your premises?" she'd interrogate in clear but accented English, relishing a fight. Hiram grew to enjoy the lunches, up to a point. When he left for RH, there was regret but also relief at saying goodbye. However, Rand's disenchantment with Bobbs-Merrill was terminal. She maneuvered to overthrow any claim they had to the new book, and after obtaining her release, she and her agent, Alan Collins, president of the powerful Curtis Brown firm, looked for a publisher. Given the track record of *The Fountainhead,* interest was widespread, but they decided to consider only four houses: Viking, where her old editor from Bobbs now worked; Knopf, where she had some early history; the well-funded McGraw-Hill; and Random, because of Hiram.

Yet she was dubious about RH. She had the impression—no doubt fomented by Lela Rogers, when she and Rand were friendly HUAC witnesses together—that Bennett Cerf and Donald Klopfer were Communists. Communism was something she could not abide: the visceral hatred went to Rand's core. "Collectivist" thinking, which in her universe included the safety net that FDR had stretched under Depression-era America, was anathema. Besides *The Fountainhead,* she'd published two earlier novels and written two plays that were produced. All emerged from the springboard of ideas—the purpose of language, plot, and characterization was to propel her philosophy of "Objectivism." Its essence, as Rand put it, was "the concept of man as a heroic being, with his own happiness as the moral purpose of his life, with productive achievement as his noblest activity and reason as his only absolute."

In fact, reason was far from absolute. The "heroic beings" of her novels enacted modern yet timeless melodramas marinated in myth and sexual fantasy. Isolated, handsome, creative, strong, and misunderstood, they were descendants of a Romanticism that Richard Wagner might have appreciated. Despite her exceptional intellect, there was an adolescent quality about Rand's storytelling. Someone or something was either good or evil, black or white. Grays didn't interest her. That certainty was what made her work so compelling. Rand's thinking was rooted in the searing childhood experience of seeing her family become unmoored and lose their cultured, bourgeois life to the chaos and degradations of the Bolshevik Revolution. The brilliant girl who came to America headed for Hollywood, mecca of reinvention, where through luck, pluck, drive, and will she went from "extra" to wardrobe department, then remade herself into a scriptwriter and finally a novelist. The movies taught her how to turn the pages—for herself and readers—and she learned the lessons well.

When Rand asserted to Haydn that Bennett and Don were Communists, he laughed so hard, she grew annoyed. For once he knew he'd win:

he reminded her that RH had published Whittaker Chambers's *Witness*. So it was that a lunch was set for the partners and Hiram to meet her and her agent on March 14 at the Ambassador Hotel, one of Bennett's usual watering holes, whose spaciousness and French atmosphere went down well with certain authors. She'd met other publishers, but only Pat Knopf had piqued her interest: he'd shown courage during the war, and was a persuasive salesman. Still, no one could match Bennett's profile, and though Rand already had some inkling of his status, the man sitting across from her had come as a surprise. In the flesh, he was well built, much better-looking than on screen, his face wonderfully mobile—and in no way intimidated. She challenged him almost immediately: Wouldn't he be frightened by her ideal society of unfettered capitalism, self-interest, and utterly open competition? On the contrary, he countered, he'd be only too pleased. Pushed to prove it, he provided a reason that delighted her: he was smarter than other publishers. He and Don had made RH into a great house *themselves*.

Hiram realized that Bennett attracted her. It was as if everything—the fleet mind, creative business sense, competitive spirit, intuition about people and books, appreciation for the absurd, incredible energy, charm, and still youthful ideals—conspired to make him the perfect foil for a woman regularly used to overawing most men. She saw that the man across the table was a *leader* who seemed to understand about happiness. He also understood Hollywood, where they had common connections. She liked the confidence that proposed an auction—let each house read and respond with comments by a set date, Bennett urged—then she could decide.

Rand also looked approvingly on warm, sophisticated Donald. When she summarized her novel's ideas, how it provided a moral defense of capitalism and a unique, anti-Left philosophy, his rejoinder was perceptive and on target: such a position, he said, would inevitably conflict with fundamental Judeo-Christian ethics.

After the lunch, she confided to Barbara Branden, one of her inner circle: "They spoke as I would want publishers to speak." Bennett and Donald were enthusiastic about her track record; their minds were open; they answered her questions and were straightforward about their own beliefs. This writer whose fiction dealt in archetypes was astonished and pleased to come face-to-face with the embodiments of what she'd dreamed of: they were her archetypal publishers.

Donald thought her "remarkable," but "wacky as a fruitcake."

Bennett hadn't expected to care for Rand, but found himself enjoying her company, savoring the "wonderful way" she "pinned" him to the wall, in effect challenging him to listen to himself, put his brain to work, and rein in the exaggerations. He wasn't afraid to tell her that he considered her philosophy of rational selfishness "abhorrent," but at the same time, he promised that if RH published her, "nobody" would be a censor. He liked this strong, self-invented, charismatic woman, just as decades earlier he'd liked Gertrude—and he hadn't much cared for Stein's politics, either. What went unacknowledged but could not be discounted was a subterranean commonality: Ayn Rand, like Gertrude and Bennett, was born Jewish.

A fortnight passed before late March winds whisked a short black cape and Napoleonic tricorne hat—only on Rand did they not look ridiculous—into the Villard. That night, Bennett recorded how things were developing: "Ayn Rand . . . picks Random House. Now [the] question is: do we pick Ayn?" Five boxes—a monster manuscript, not quite completed after thirteen years—had been forwarded by Alan Collins that day. The book's title was *Atlas Shrugged*.

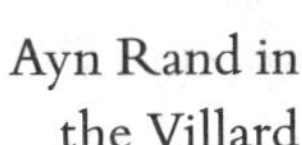

Ayn Rand in the Villard

The partners and Hiram would each take a turn getting through it. Bennett went last, devoting an April Sunday to the first six hundred pages of "endless" manuscript, judging the thick tranche "absurd, but compelling." At week's end he called for another conference with Rand and Collins: RH would be delighted to publish the novel *if* she got it down to a thousand pages. "It's a great book. Name your own terms," he added by way of encouragement.

Everyone understood, as Hiram put it, that Rand had "best seller stamped all over her." They also recognized she wouldn't come cheap. Rand and Collins had calculated exactly what they wanted: a $50,000 advance and a 15 percent royalty on all copies; a minimum $25,000 ad budget; a retail price not less than six dollars; a 75,000-copy first printing; the right to approve jacket design, back cover, and flap copy; consultation as to the timing of any reprint edition; and the very unusual right of refusal for any condensed version of the book, however lucrative. The advance would be paid in installments; with the tax laws as such, should the book sell for some years, Rand wanted a maximum $20,000 in any one year, the rest to be held by Random House. For their part, Bennett and Donald again insisted that the manuscript not exceed 600,000 words—still huge, but squeezable, with small type, into a single thousand-page volume.

The atmosphere grew gay and heady when everything was agreed, as though they'd been drinking flutes of champagne and, pleasantly tipsy, falling a little bit in love. Rand understood that Don and Bennett recognized the importance of her ideas even if they didn't agree with them, and she appreciated how Bennett relished the prospect of the book creating a little devilish fun with the Catholic hierarchy across the street. When she got back to her apartment that day, she felt buoyed on a wave of triumph: "This is life as it should be and ought to be—and, for once, is!"

Even after the contract was signed, there was still one subject to argue. Rand feared that the sexiest scenes and most extreme philosophical positions would be plucked out of context for advertisements, sensationalizing and misrepresenting the whole. Bobbs-Merrill had promoted *The Fountainhead* almost entirely as a sexy love story; even worse, by selectively slicing and dicing, its ads had patched together blurbs from reviewers who were actually Rand's intellectual enemies. She wanted none of that from RH. For major lines of advertising, she insisted that she be consulted. Advertising was, of course, Bennett's domain, and the final word came from him, but with Donald as his messenger. Yes, there'd be consultation—and quotes would be judiciously selected, Don promised—but "we are responsible for selling the book and . . . have to be the final judges." A line had been drawn: either she trusted her publisher or she didn't.

Bennett's charm campaign continued: he invited Rand and her husband, Frank O'Connor, to accompany him and Phyllis to the theater to watch *What's My Line?* and then to the Stork, followed by the Drake Room: Rand had gotten into night-owl habits, using amphetamines to work through the early hours on her magnum opus. Phyllis was worried about meeting this woman whom Bennett had chattered about, and then a "very peculiar" thing happened, as soon as the O'Connors walked through the townhouse door.

"We have met before," Rand said, after a glance.

Phyllis assured her that she must be mistaken.

"We have met before," Rand repeated.

"It's impossible. I certainly would remember if I had met you," Phyllis countered, truly disconcerted by this woman whose eyes fixed her to the spot.

The fierce face softened. "No, you wouldn't. Do you remember when you were . . . at RKO? I was working in the costume department."

Rand had dressed her.

Soon enough, the Cerfs would make the acquaintance of her young lover Nathaniel Branden (she was fifty, he twenty-five, and both their spouses knew of the affair). Disciples also included an ambitious young economist named Alan Greenspan, who at thirty-one was the most sophisticated, oldest acolyte, and whose investment advice Bennett happily solicited (decades later, Greenspan would bring Randian thinking to running the U.S. Federal Reserve). The Cerfs joined Rand's circle for dinners and reciprocated at Sixty-Second Street. Bennett loved to "trot her out" before those who'd sneered at his decision to sign her, and "invariably" he'd see a liberal friend fall hopelessly (if temporarily) under her spell. George Axelrod, screenwriter of *The Seven-Year Itch,* marveled that after five hours, Rand knew him better than his analyst did after five years.

As for the relationship between author and publisher, their lunches could extend to three hours, and he was tickled when she "graced" the palazzo with her "exciting" presence. Once upon a time Gertrude had said he was "sweet" but "dumb"; Rand, on the other hand, accorded him "a very good brain," but disapproved of how he used it. Bennett could tell she thought he "was wasting it all" on the "worthless" liberal causes he believed in. And yet, she was under *his* spell. One of Rand's friends would tell him, "You sound as wonderful as Ayn says you are. If I could only get it through my fool head that the man who writes the Cerfboard and publishes *AS* are one and the same, I'd probably fall for you." She was hardly alone in that conundrum.

At the same time, there was a novel to complete—Rand still hadn't finished—and publishing plans to set in motion. In September, Jean Ennis sent out a release trumpeting the association as one of the most "noteworthy" in RH history. By mid-February, Bennett began to strategize advertising. Don was "heartbroken" the manuscript was late (the plan had been to publish in early September), but with grim determination, working nonstop, Rand finished the third week in March. Publication was set for October 1957. Now it was up to Random House.

When Bennett had first turned the pages of *Atlas Shrugged* the previous April, he did so with the rapid riffle of the seasoned publisher who, under pressure from competitors, must decide whether to place a bet. A gut reaction and fast read of the financial auguries was required. Now a more measured and careful perusal was in order. At this stage, if he, Donald, and Hiram thought something didn't work, they would have to figure out how to persuade her to fix it. And so he devoted the last days of March to making his way through the mountain of 2,350 sheets stacked in neat piles before him. Bennett began on a Thursday evening, reading 348 pages; on Friday night he read until 2:30 A.M. All day Saturday he continued, completing 1,600 pages by bedtime, and at exactly 4 P.M. Sunday, finished: a considerable investment of time for a speed-reader.

Rand's heroine is heir to a great family railroad enterprise and endowed by her creator with beauty, energy, intelligence, and a name as unusual as her own: Dagny Taggart. The New York where Dagny lives, like the rest of America, is crumbling through an ever-deeper recession into a dirty, broken dystopia of venal incompetence and degradation, under a veneer of "collectivist" posturing and do-goodism (as opposed to profit-loving individualism). Her mission: to save Taggart Transcontinental from her brother Jim and his determined missteps and cronies. Dagny's first love, Francisco d'Anconia, a handsome prodigy, has gone bad, so no help there. Instead she joins forces with Hank Rearden, the nation's greatest steel magnate, but they're thwarted by bureaucracy-addicted drones and stunted souls like Jim, who, incapable of originality and hatefully jealous, want to crush creativity in others. Dagny and Rearden—with a wife as frightful as Jim—fall in love, and soon discover the incomplete remains of a marvelous motor able to convert atmospheric static electricity into focused power, just the thing for reanimating a railroad. Dagny sets out to find the motor's mysterious inventor.

At the same time, like a giant's set of falling dominoes, the vestiges of the country's remaining great enterprises are being abandoned as their leaders mysteriously disappear. Clues lead Dagny and Rearden to Galt's Gulch, a secret redoubt beyond a "ray-screen" in the Rockies, where they find John Galt, the motor's inventor, and all the missing industrialists living in a self-sufficient "Atlantis." Galt has gathered them to his last-chance cause: a strike on society that would stop "the motor of the world," and bring "moochers," "parasites," and "looters" to their knees. The makers have declared a showdown with the takers, to determine the course of history. Atlas has "shrugged" off the weight of the world, ultimately, perhaps, to save it.

Galt, it turns out, has led a parallel life as an anonymous worker on Dagny's rails, loving her from afar—and soon, from very near, as her third love (he's also best friend to her first love, D'Anconia, whose "badness" was a Galt-inspired beard). The great leader eventually alerts ordinary humans to what's going on via a national radio address, and as New York falls into darkness in a scene worthy of *Götterdämmerung,* Galt calls off the strike: time for the creative forces to emerge and remake their world. "What a book!" Bennett exhaled into his diary.

Rand had made clear to Hiram that she wasn't interested in being edited. He saw himself reduced to an expensive supernumerary, tinkering a bit, then handing the pages to Bert Krantz. At first scared by Rand, the copy editor was later able to develop a good working relationship with the grand inquisitor, sitting side by side going over commas and capitals, paragraphs and periods, in long sessions that extended over months rather than weeks. The extraordinary amount of money tied up in the book made every set of RH hands touching it nervous and careful. Unfortunately, they discovered a major problem: it was 45,000 words over the contracted limit, already at the extreme end of what could be stuffed between covers. Symptom and ultimate symbol of the problem was Galt's radio address, not finished when the novel was signed. Repeating over and over the philosophy explicit from the start, it would fill *sixty* printed book pages if left uncut. Hiram felt sure it would put readers off and needlessly swell costs, yet Rand wouldn't budge. This was an occasion when Bennett would have to act.

On Monday afternoon, the day after Bennett had finished reading her manuscript, Rand strode into the boss's office and sat down, wanting to hear the reaction from this publisher of whom she so approved, his having now had sufficient time to lose himself in the pages of her masterpiece. Likely he'd embroider upon his early estimation of its greatness. As he began to make the case for cuts, focusing on the Galt speech, she remained calm—even, perhaps, a bit amused—and heard him out. But Ayn Rand was not one to check her premises at the door. As she said in the biographical note she supplied for the book, her novels were more important than anything in her personal life. Their watchword was: *"And I mean it."*

When he finished, her response came as a question: "Would you cut the Bible?"

Bennett, confined to his chair, unable either to pace back and forth or worry at his handkerchief, understood that he'd more than met his match. In the end, though, he did make headway, by taking a different route. If Rand wouldn't cut the speech, she'd have to pay for it. An unusual amendment was inserted into the contract: the royalty would be 15 percent of the retail price, *less seven cents per copy*—the cost of extra paper, printing, and binding for extra length.

In the succeeding months, he met with Rand regularly. They consulted over the book's price: he would risk criticism and grumbling, and possibly antagonizing potential readers, to price it at a very expensive $6.95. He arranged a promotional deal involving mini-packs of cigarettes, specially imprinted with a gilt-toned dollar sign—the symbol dearest to Rand's heart—to be sent to influence-peddlers. She had placed a giant dollar sign, her answer to a crucifix or Star of David, watching over Galt's Gulch; she wore a gold brooch with it on her lapel; and her heroes smoked cigarettes bearing the symbol. Bennett would have the smokes wrapped in packages with questions like "What would happen if Atlas Shrugged?" and "Who is John Galt?" (the leitmotif challenge running through the novel), with the affirmation "They KNOW at Random House."

He arranged for her to speak to the reps at sales conference in May as a "special visitor," the fact of her presence underlining how crucial her doorstopper was to the immediate fortunes of the firm. Soon it was Thrup's turn to lend a hand, by taking pictures: she posed Rand in the Villard, capturing a flattering author shot that would occupy most of the back jacket. Two weeks later, a big ad appeared in *PW* reproducing a letter from Bennett: "I have just finished reading . . . Ayn Rand's new novel. . . . It will hit you with the force of a sledgehammer. Many people will be utterly dismayed by this astonishing book. Others will rate it one of the most important novels ever written. EVERYBODY will read it!" As word spread, signs began to appear of a possible backlash. The *Chicago Tribune* asked if Bennett would be "denounced as a reactionary" for publishing it, but he pressed on. On August 15, the first fat copies arrived. Their pages held together, all 1,168 of them. Rand swept into Bennett's office to be given the very first bound copy in triumph.

"EVERYBODY will read it!"

The following Sunday, Lew Miller dropped by the office to do some work, and on his desk found a beautifully wrapped package. The object, once liberated from the fancy paper and ribbon, turned out to be a copy of *Atlas Shrugged*. Everyone knew how much was riding on the tome. Was it a numbered-and-autographed copy, or had Bennett enclosed some special token to spur him on? As soon as Lew opened the book, anticipation turned to dismay: a rectangular hollow had been cut right through the center of all those pages, and two small yellow lemons inserted where the paper had been surgically removed. A card, bearing Rand's distinctive handwriting, more printed than cursive, declared: "Hope this doesn't turn into one of these."

He was truly flummoxed. A hollowed-out "shooting" book, equipped with a spring and a "cap" that went *BANG!* when it was opened, was a novelty item, the fate that awaited books so lifeless that even the remainder houses refused to take them, a destiny worse than the pulping mill. Lew wondered: Was Rand warning in high-handed fashion that he'd better sell the hell out of her book? Had something happened to upset her? Such a woman could find fault with *anything*. He phoned Bennett, who picked up Lew's anxiety like a disease.

Monday dawned: Bennett, Don, and Hiram all found similar packages on their desks. Nobody knew what to do. Failing a call from Rand, Bennett would have to bathe his voice in honey and phone her. Word soon reached production head Ray Freiman. He, too, had received a "gift," but was fully aware of its source. Sheepishly, he piped up: it was Tony Wimpfheimer's doing. Donald's stepson, who worked closely with Freiman, had decided that a major gamble deserved a good joke. He'd enlisted help from a pal at the bindery, and forged Rand's easy-to-mimic hand. He never thought anyone would take the prank seriously. Bennett hit the proverbial ceiling: Rand must never know what had happened. Three months later, Freiman arranged for a special leather-bound copy to be sent to her. There were no lemons in sight.

On Sunday, September 29, Bennett, both flattered and edgy, was substitute emcee for John Daly, and brought Albert Erskine, Cousin Ginger, and Rand and her husband as designated cheering squad to the show—a sign of how close they'd become. Eleven days later, every Villard vitrine facing Madison Avenue on the Random House side winked at passersby with the same book: a crisp copy of *Atlas Shrugged,* out that day. Bennett was diligent in sending Rand a photo, taking particular care in keeping her informed on everything being done to push the novel.

He'd personally sent copies to a vast mailing list of CEOs and other executives, judges, fellow publishers, and Hollywood types, anybody whose word-of-mouth could set off a chain reaction. The book was even a bridge to Aunt Lela Rogers: Bennett buttered up Rand's old comrade-in-anti-Communist-arms shamelessly. Some recipients admitted how cowed they were by the length and "arrogant egotism" of the author's self-written biography. Contrary to the normal custom, Bennett had inserted it within the body of the book, after the novel's end, rather than on the cover, where it would be lost the first time the jacket was removed. (Other publishers would take note and copy his innovation.) His counterparts at Scribner, Doubleday, and Harper congratulated him on "great skill and taste" in packaging Rand. Even Knopf acknowledged the feat, saying he didn't wonder that Atlas shrugged, "if you put a copy of this book on each of his shoulders." Still, he was grateful for his tome, "because I know you could have sold it." Nevertheless, the question lurked beneath Bennett's bright surface: How would critics and readers react? Would the grand bet pay off, or would Tony's "joke" turn out to be a premonition?

A week or so before official publication, copies began to appear in Manhattan. Howard Treeger, RH's New York salesman, accompanied Rand to major stores. On October 4, the USSR launched *Sputnik,* the first man-made satellite, into orbit above the Earth: the space age had begun. That the regime she hated had won this lap of the race didn't please her. Treeger heard Rand assure one account: "When *Sputnik* is forgotten, my books will still be selling."

Soon reviews began to roll in. Bennett judged the first ones "on the whole, better than expected." He and Donald had braced themselves for critical voices, which, in the weeks that followed, were not pretty. *The New York Times, New Yorker, Time, Washington Post,* and *Chicago Tribune* felt the novel sprang from "hate" and was "easy to hate"; one reviewer associated Rand's ideas with Hitler, and another with "an insane asylum." Adjectives like "crackbrained" and "grotesque" abounded. Harry Hansen, who'd often been helpful to Bennett with positive coverage, told him that this novel was "the bore of the century." Of course, there were breaks in the gloom: the *New York Herald Tribune* was positive, and Hearst's conservative *New York Daily Mirror* was over-the-top wonderful, judging Rand "the outstanding novelist and most profound philosopher of the twentieth century." It helped that the journalist making the pronouncement was her friend. Within the firm, distaste for her ideas was such that not everyone wished the book well. Linscott had retired, and oozed schadenfreude: "I must confess I was delighted that Random took a licking on *Atlas Shrugged,*" he told Saxe.

Although the critical licking was a fact of life—it would get worse in December, when Whittaker Chambers eviscerated Rand in *National*

Review—the book was selling. On November 4, it was number three on the *Herald Tribune* list and number five on the *Times*'. By Thanksgiving, 68,000 copies had been sold: respectable, "but no whirlwind," as Bennett admitted. Given how much energy and money had gone into it, the velocity and numbers should have been higher. In the end, *Atlas Shrugged* did sit on bestseller lists for seven months—no mean feat—but the real payoff was to come. Even more than *The Fountainhead,* it had strong, sturdy legs, well suited to competing in the publishing marathon. Five years after its debut, the novel had sold more than one million copies, and six-figure annual sales would continue unabated for decades.

Back in 1957—on August 22, one week after receiving her own first copies—Rand autographed two volumes for the man who'd turned her dream into reality. Presumably he wanted one for each house, or for Sixty-Second Street and the office, given the currency and importance he attached to this author. One reads as follows: "To Bennett—in the name of the best within you—Love—Ayn." The X-ray mind had come to apprehend something of what lay under the surface.

The second inscription is less intimate, more public, but a high compliment from one who dealt in archetypes: "To Bennett Cerf—the ideal publisher I had never expected to find—Ayn Rand."

Chapter 33

Party Cats and Cats in Hats

THE DAY AFTER BENNETT HAD FIRST MET AYN RAND, HE WAS IN extraordinary company again, this time theatrical. The Harts had invited a coterie including Rex Harrison, Alan Jay Lerner, and the Cerfs to a private room at '21' to wait out reviews after the opening of *My Fair Lady*. Such evenings were shot through with anxiety—as director, Moss's nerves were too strained to put up for long with the big first-night bash ten blocks away at Sardi's—but in this case, it was more a question of what level of rave the show would inspire, for they'd all felt that rare tingling and *knew* that the music, lyrics, and direction worked brilliantly. Bennett said it in a word: "Wonderful."

A new star had emerged in twenty-one-year-old English rose Julie Andrews, the soaring soprano Moss had had to coach to become Miss Eliza Doolittle. Andrews, a trouper since childhood, had been intimidated by the difficult, demanding Harrison and by George Bernard Shaw's famous play *Pygmalion,* the skeleton for Lerner's book and lyrics. She hadn't known how to do the role, but Moss understood what it was to be poor, wide-eyed, with nose pressed to the window—the hopes, frustrations, determination, and toil it took to copy the speech, style, manners of your "betters" to reinvent yourself. During one critical weekend he'd worked only with her, sympathizing with, teaching, inspiring, and bullying Andrews into becoming the flower girl–turned–lady. The autobiography he'd been struggling to write for RH would reveal that his own transformation had been no less dramatic, and loyal Bennett wanted to make sure his friend got his due, asking in Trade Winds "if it has been sufficiently emphasized" that the man who made *My Fair Lady*'s "parts fit so perfectly" was Moss Hart.

These would be fabulous party years for the *Life of the Party* boy, whether the gathering was intimate or grand, and the evenings that Phyllis organized at home were also at their peak. As Edna Ferber had declared, the Cerfs gave "the nicest dinner parties in all of New York City." In October 1956, six months after the evening with Moss, a huge group was gathered at Sixty-Second Street, jointly to honor Irwin Shaw, visiting from Europe—he'd been kind to them in Paris, and *Lucy Crown* had done so well—and Arthur and Leonora Hornblow, visiting from L.A. Leonora's second novel, *The Love Seekers,* would be published the following summer, bearing the gift of an alluring yet elegant author photo by Phyllis. With Linscott's retirement, Bubs now worked with Albert Erskine, whom Bennett was conspicuously touting as "the best goddam editor in the business." Boasting was part of his nature, yet this claim reflected Saxe's reduced state, and also was rooted in fact. The attention to each line and intellectual rigor Erskine brought was devoid of Saxe's anxiety and tendency to rewrite—and for some authors, better for it.

With seventy-one people, the Shaw-Hornblow soirée was a logistical challenge: the townhouse would be packed. Phyllis had, as usual, considered every detail that Lillian, the secretary she employed on the home front, would help her execute. The dining room furniture had been moved to the basement, replaced by small rented round tables and gold-toned ballroom chairs. She'd adopted the clever habit of inviting some guests for after-dinner socializing only, mitigating the squeeze a bit. Broadway performers would also come late, after their last curtain call. Just before ten, Bennett, Kilgallen, and Goodson would rush off to *What's My Line?,* and later race back. Although it started at 8 P.M., the party wouldn't end till 4 A.M. Monday morning.

That night, Phyllis managed to put a drink in each guest's hand and jam them in upstairs to mingle, yet through the happy buzz there remained a delayed expectation that continued as they made their way down and found their places at the small tables. Everyone wondered when the evening's *real* stars would show up—for, assuredly, the other guests had been alerted to the prospect of their coming. Finally, heads began to turn, eyes stared, and the glittering sea parted. The late-arriving couple were magnetic all right, but hardly dressed for such an elegant occasion.

Mike Todd, dark and burly like a prizefighter, had the swagger and insolent grin of the tough guy who has bet the house, lost it, bet again, and won. An immigrant rabbi's son, he'd started with nothing. Cunning, a willingness to do almost anything, outsize confidence, and sardonic charm had turned him into the Hollywood ringmaster of the moment. *Around the World in Eighty Days,* the expensive cinematic blockbuster Todd produced against all odds, had debuted at the Rivoli Theatre five days earlier. A smash hit, it would go on to win the Oscar for Best Picture. The Cerfs, Hornblows, and Harts had been among his guests at the premiere and at the "fabulous" supper party for several hundred. Bennett had brokered a deal with him, rushing through a 72-page one-dollar program to be sold at the Rivoli and also at bookstores, with a foreword by Todd (more likely his PR man), prologue by Edward R. Murrow, synopsis, and biographical sketches of the movie's forty-seven stars. *PW* asked if it was the start of a trend, "to take the souvenir program out of the theater . . . and into the bookstores," in another instance of Bennett's willingness to experiment. He'd also signed a biography of the impresario.

Todd's fiancée, Elizabeth Taylor, at twenty-four was twenty-three years his junior, stunning, saucy, and one of the two youngest at the party. Bennett had first met her in all her burgeoning glory two years earlier, as a mystery guest on *What's My Line?*

Kitty Hart found herself staring not at the exquisite face, but at the surprisingly nondescript gray shift the young woman was wearing. So carefully and beautifully dressed was Kitty (her clothes often selected by Moss) that she didn't understand how Taylor had come in *that,* not put together as the studios who already had charge of half her life might have wished. However, the relationship with Todd was one of the things freeing her from them. As the pair progressed through the room, they exuded sex and drink, perhaps a little too much of both. It was likely that they'd been fighting: there was a reputation for that, as well as for passionate lovemaking. Todd seemed to be dragging Taylor along on her heels, and grew louder, surly, abusive. Try as they might, no eyes could stray from the showman and his show.

Despite the presence of his own lovely wife, Rose, nearby, Bill Styron couldn't help but savor the other woman. Yet while he appreciated the "gorgeous" creature, she was "tending towards avoirdupois." Dick Rodgers, who these months was laboring over compositions for *Cinderella,* the maidenly TV musical he was writing for Julie Andrews, was sitting next to Styron, and turned to the younger man. "I'd like to fuck about ten pounds off that girl," Rodgers said, gimlet-eyed, unblinking. Styron was taken aback.

Finally, the sullen impresario and his flushed beauty collapsed into their chairs.

"It was unfortunate," Kitty felt. She was embarrassed for them.

"Todd did not treat Taylor well," Styron agreed, never witnessing another such "unruly incident" at the Cerfs'. Yet despite his twinge of discomfort, the evening, on balance, was terrific fun, the star power "bedazzling." It beat being chained to a desk, wriggling over a manuscript.

. . .

IF THE PARTIES WERE good, so was *What's My Line?*—its audience reached as high as thirty million viewers, more than one in six Americans. Mike Todd was the mystery guest one week, the same night Cousin Ginger turned up as a mystery bonus. Bennett had made his usual study of who was in town. It was his habit to stand in a dim corner of the studio just before the show started, squinting at a scribbled list of names he'd brought—so he knew that Mike and Liz were around and had recently tied the knot. There could be no bigger catch that week. He'd often been warned by Goodson and director Gil Fates not to go each time for a first guess if he was pretty sure he knew the mystery identity: they worried the show would look rigged. So, this night, he donned his best Cheshire cat smile.

"Would our guest be, by any chance, the man who is the producer of what will be the box office champion of this year and maybe all years?" Bennett enquired, then paused significantly. "Who I have in mind is the producer of *The Ten Commandments*."

The audience roared with laughter as John Daly moved the game on.

"I would like to remind our guest," Arlene Francis piped up, "that one of those commandments is 'Thou shalt not kill.' "

Todd pretended to cut Bennett dead without a handshake when exiting past the panel that night, knowing his "wrong" guess is what had made the segment memorable. Bennett's diary was modest: "Mistook Mike Todd for Cecil B. DeMille. Nailed Ginger."

Supreme Court Justice William O. Douglas; Jerry Lewis; Salvador Dali; the judge who'd married Marilyn Monroe and Arthur Miller—all made for good clean fun. Yet a shadow had descended a few months earlier, when panelist Fred Allen, the brilliant, beloved radio comic, keeled over from a heart attack on a Saturday night. Three years older than Bennett, he'd replaced Steve Allen (no relation) two years earlier. A true original, he'd influenced Groucho Marx and a young comedian named Johnny Carson. On Sunday afternoon, the show's grieving team met. They couldn't cancel: airtime had been bought by the sponsor, and Fred's widow wanted the show to go on. By a stroke of luck, Steve Allen was in town and took Fred's seat. Daly announced the death, then play proceeded, rather muted. In the final minutes, each panelist spoke about Fred. Bennett's puns and recycled jokes had proved irresistible to Fred's sense of the absurd: he'd skewered Bennett as "a tweed wastebasket." After all, Cerf *was* RH and now had the prestige of chairing the Peabody radio and TV awards, yet the jokes were so obsessive and the puns such groaners. The "wastebasket" was the first to admit that he'd "done rather well" by exploiting "a very small talent," and that night offered up fine words and feelings. The show met the challenge of Fred's death with "sweetness and guts," the *Hollywood Reporter* said. Most pleasing, another of Bennett's idols, Jack Benny—a close friend of Fred's—called to say how well he'd handled the goodbye. No steady panelist would fill Fred's seat; instead, a revolving roster would play alongside the regulars.

To be irreplaceable was the most eloquent memorial of all.

. . .

FOR SEVERAL YEARS NOW, on the lecture circuit and in column inches, Bennett was being asked to comment on how television affected children's book-reading. More often than not, he'd point to the fantastic success of S&S's Golden Books, or the sales that Landmarks enjoyed. Children's books were "cheaper" and "better" than ever. TV "isn't doing anything at all to good books," he'd conclude. "They're unassailable." But although many Americans were entranced with TV, not all adored it or thought its magic benign, and some didn't consider books "unassailable."

Despite her own guest spots on shows, Phyllis, for one, had been suspicious of the new medium, and strictly rationed viewing time for her sons. Among educators and intellectuals, fears about the effects of TV and that other menace, comic books, were spreading like worry lines across a mother's forehead. World War II had placed the United States at the pinnacle of power facing off against the Soviets, but the position brought both an overabundant confidence and a constant undertow of unease. In 1951, a meeting had been convened in Washington responding to the questions about kids and books, and a multi-authored essay collection followed, which aimed to push reading. Bennett's contribution, typically sunny, was titled "It's Fun to Read."

Yet while American fear and paranoia had been embodied by the name *McCarthy,* in 1957 it suddenly crystallized around a different name: *Sputnik.* Had the USSR beaten us to space because it was better at educating its children? The federal government decided to pour money into science and math in the struggle for supremacy over future brainpower, but even more fundamental was the notion that U.S. pupils lagged behind those in other nations by not learning to read early and well, and at a time when the baby boom showed no signs of abating.

Two writers had been especially good at sounding alarms. The first was Pulitzer Prize–winning author John Hersey in a May 1954 article across ten pages of *Life* entitled, "Why Do Students Bog Down on First R? A Local Committee Sheds Light on a National Problem: Reading." Hersey, who lived in tony Fairfield, Connecticut, had kids in school and a seat on that "local committee." Rudolf Flesch, the other writer, was a Viennese Jewish refugee with a doctorate in English from Columbia. A year after Hersey's fusillade, Harper released Flesch's tract-cum-self-help manual with a bombshell title: *Why Johnny Can't Read.* Flesch mainly directed his remarks at mothers, declaring that the teaching of reading was "too important to be left to the educators." His major salvo was aimed at toppling the current vogue for whole-word memorization or "sight reading," instead advocating for phonics, in which learners sound out letters. Flesch targeted other problems, too, such as the virtually omnipresent Dick-and-Jane school primers, which he characterized as "inane" and "vaguely feeble-minded." He also warned that the public schools' failure to prevent an illiterate underclass was a threat to democracy.

Hersey placed the problem, if anything, in an even wider philosophical context. "Goody-goody" primers, he argued, were not simply stunted in their word choice, repetition, and lack of imagination: their blandness was foreign to the reality of children's lives and taught pupils to conform rather than be individuals. It was essential that the teaching of reading be a vehicle for developing those "great American virtues of originality, individuality and independence." He noted the presence of much livelier books in stores, pointing to the Babar and Madeline series as good examples. With backing from school boards, publishers could do as well with primers. After all, why shouldn't kids have pictures that compete with TV images, and widen rather than narrow what the words mean—ones like those of the "wonderfully imaginative geniuses among children's illustrators, Tenniel, Howard Pyle, 'Dr. Seuss,' Walt Disney?"

Publishers took different tacks in responding to these urgent dispatches. RH concentrated on PR, sending out a volley of press releases. "RANDOM HOUSE SAYS JOHNNY CAN READ!" boasted one, echoing its bubbly president in undercutting the "gloomy predictions," and centering on the fifteen Landmarks to be published that fall. Another, devoted entirely to "Dr. Seuss, Doctor of Humane Letters," celebrated Ted Geisel's receiving an honorary doctorate from his alma mater, Dartmouth, alongside America's best-known living poet, Robert Frost. It also pushed his new book, *On Beyond Zebra!* Two others featured Walter Farley's *Black Stallion* books, as well as Davy Crockett titles—the coonskin-capped frontiersman was a big hit on TV. And yet, however much RH broadcast its record in securing the attention of older children, it was a trade house, not a textbook publisher, and skirted Hersey and Flesch's basic concerns about misguided pedagogy, boring first books that beginners struggled with, and their legacy of dealing with children who failed to become literate on schedule.

William Spaulding, the head of Houghton Mifflin's substantial education department, attempted a different response. Following Hersey's advice to the letter, he decided to publish a supplementary reader to complement his firm's elementary school program. Two of the four "illustrator-geniuses" that Hersey cited in his article were dead, and Disney otherwise engaged. That left Dr. Seuss. Spaulding approached Ted Geisel with the idea of creating for Houghton precisely the kind of early reader that Hersey and Flesch had advocated. He invited Geisel to Boston, dangling a challenge: write and illustrate a story that first graders couldn't put down. The book would be limited to a couple hundred words culled from the kinds of vocabulary lists Flesch had included at the back of his manual, directed at children who'd only just learned to read. First, though, a barrier had to be negotiated, one that neither man was sure could be surmounted. Geisel was an RH author, and Bennett well known for proprietary instincts. He wasn't in business to lend writers to others, especially if a potentially important project was involved.

There'd been the clash with Harold Guinzburg over Faulkner; Bennett would soon have a similarly unpleasant set-to with the ailing Dick Simon. Dick's friend, baseball great Jackie Robinson, had agreed to tell the story of his barrier-breaking life to journalist Carl Rowan. When Dick heard about it, he wanted S&S to publish the book. Alas, Rowan was an RH author.

Bennett was aware of the intimacy between the Simon and Robinson families, and a couple of times in the past had consented to RH authors writing books for Dick. He'd consider publishing the book jointly with S&S, but Dick thought the idea unworkable. When Bennett suggested that Robinson devote a dedication page to the Simons, Dick was offended: he wasn't interested in leveraging friendship for personal publicity, he just wanted to do the book. In the end, Bennett knew the project could be big, and Rowan was young and had a future. There was no question: the book would be published by RH or not at all. Eventually it was, in 1960.

Given how tough he could be, it was surprising—and a sign of his regard for Ted Geisel as well as Ted's capacity for holding his ground—that Bennett agreed to let the Houghton book go forward. Yet permission to "borrow" came with a proviso: Spaulding could publish the school edition, but RH reserved the right to market a trade version.

The good doctor first had to finish *If I Ran the Circus,* a follow-up Bennett had requested to *If I Ran the Zoo*. Ted eventually got to work on the reader, but, always the perfectionist, found the word restrictions maddening. Spaulding had given him three lists—the vocabulary from Houghton's own first-grade primer, and two others—a total of 348 words. His directions were to use no more than 230 of them. Ted knew the reading problem from the school's perspective, since his sister-in-law was a first-grade teacher, and he was acutely aware that his competition was TV, saying so in an essay for *The New York Times*. Yet his aim was to capitalize on the greater sophistication first graders had absorbed through the medium. He started to spin a story about a Queen Zebra before realizing that neither word was on a list. Out of sheer frustration, he decided the first two list words that rhymed would provide his title. They were "cat" and "hat."

Everything was a struggle: the rhyme and rhythm—writing in verse allowed for the repetition necessary to drill something into a kid's head; the humor—it *had* to have humor; and the plot—any book with his name on it needed a story that went beyond seeing Spot run. For months, nothing seemed good enough. Always second-guessing himself, he felt less confident than usual. Working late into the night, he'd fling hours of work toward the trash, only to have Helen retrieve it the next morning while he slept. She'd smooth the pages, read them, and quietly assure him in the afternoon that something was there. He'd avoid work for a day or two, then return, dragging on cigarette after cigarette, still doubting what he was doing was any good.

The pictures, too, were nerve-wracking, and technically unconventional. They had to illustrate but also extend the limited words: the Cat would be seen to juggle, but the word "juggle" could never appear. Geisel set black-and-white drawings against bright unmixed tones of red and blue, creating boldness and surprise but at the same time exerting definition and control. The idealized landscape of the conventional primer had been exchanged for assertive blocks of color. It took a year and a half to create text and pictures for a 64-page book that used only 220 different words, all but 21 from Spaulding's lists, with illustrations on every page. A restless man who like his publisher ranged and paced with a mercurial mind that always sought stimulation, he'd found making this book to be an almost "murderous" job.

The story begins with a boy and girl trapped indoors by rain, left behind to amuse themselves by a mother who's inexplicably absented herself for the day. Their only source of company is a single somnolent fish in a bowl. The Cat arrives, at once alluring and scary, knowing and unknowable and definitely uncontrollable—as felines (and children) often are. Chaos ensues. The fish, being a fish, is threatened by the Cat and everything he does, his small presence functioning as the voice of conscience and sense. Eventually order is restored as mysteriously as it was smashed. The book ends with the mother's beckoning arm and assertive leg entering the room (presumably followed by the rest of her), adult authority reestablishing itself. In the process she poses the logical question: What did they do while she was gone? Rather than answer, Geisel turns the tables, for the first time directly addressing the reader, using the second person. "You," the reader, must decide what the mother is going to be told.

The words and pictures of *The Cat in the Hat* reveal a world roiling with emotion and imagination, full of inexplicable forces—boredom, menace, anger, exuberance, wildness—that young children experience every day. Underlying the story's surface mischievousness, and that mischievous final lob to the reader, is a serious philosophical conundrum, for Ted Geisel was deeply concerned with the moral imperative of doing right. Do the children reveal the imaginative truth of what has gone on and show their world for what it is, or do they toe the Dick-and-Jane line and button up, affirming—depending on how you look at it—their right to their own private fantasies, or a rather precocious *mauvaise foi*? Tension lies just beneath the comic relief, which is what makes this book of the imagination so real.

In 1953, after his disastrous try at a Hollywood movie, Geisel had told his agent, Phyllis Jackson, that what he really wanted to do with the rest of his life was create books, but didn't know if he could make enough money doing it. He needed royalties of $5,000 a year at least. Three years later, Bennett wrote that Ted's six-month royalties would amount to about $17,500, with $13,000-plus coming from backlist, books out a year or longer. It was more than enough to underwrite a pleasant La Jolla life for a man with a wife and no kids. His pace of production, like O'Hara's and Michener's, had made him a steady asset. "If we had ten more authors like you . . . I could give up all my outside activities and sit on my can watching the grass grow," Bennett joked. "I hope you are as happy about the relationship as I am," he added, sending his love. However, on balance, Geisel's fame still probably rested more on the Flit ads than on books.

In February 1957, the month before *The Cat in the Hat* sprang onto store shelves, Bennett sent a congratulatory note, mentioning that he and Phyllis would come west in April. There was no sign something extraordinary might occur; then, suddenly, what publishers fantasize about began to happen. A run on the trade edition started almost as soon as books arrived in stores, even as Houghton Mifflin was finding unforeseen resistance to selling the unconventional reader into schools. Reviews were almost all raves. John Hersey declared it a "masterpiece," a "gift to the art of reading." Rudolf Flesch would eventually predict that "Dr. Seuss will emerge as one of the great classics of this area," and would call Geisel "a genius pure and simple."

His publishers agreed. In a joint interview Bennett and Don gave to *The New Yorker,* Bennett declared, "I consider him a genius. Nobody else has ever done books that have given American children such pleasure." Donald pointed out that Faulkner and Auden might be geniuses, too, but Bennett wasn't so sure. He stuck with Ted, asserting that his simplicity and modesty fit the classic pattern. Parents discovered *The Cat* and told other parents, while their kids told other kids. The magic circle of word-of-mouth grew larger and larger as reorders poured in. The book was, Bennett realized, "a sensation." Bill Spaulding was confounded: a sly New York publishing cat had seized momentum to wreak chaos on *his* expectations.

The last Wednesday in March, the Cerfs went to a small dinner party Bob and Merle Haas had organized for the Geisels at their apartment in town. As Babar's translator, Merle had a particular affection for children's books. Over coffee, the women—Merle's editor, Louise Bonino, was also there—sat by themselves, discussing children and books. Phyllis remembered how, after assuming Chris's reading precocity was normal, she'd worried about Jonathan not catching on fast enough. As the conversation continued, she began looking closely at Ted's new book—her first proper sighting—and as she turned the pages, Phyllis "went wild about it." Soon a notion came into her head. She wanted "to stir the pot" to see if she "couldn't get a better broth."

During the next few days, the idea took shape, bringing a universe of possibility with her at the center. It was deceptively simple: create a publishing house to produce a series of readers for young children, with *The Cat in the Hat* as presiding spirit, model, and emblem. It would be separate from RH—this was to be *hers,* not Bennett's—but it didn't preclude taking advantage of Random to do the operations work, or trawling the ocean of Bennett's authors in the way he'd encouraged Louise to do with Landmarks. She could even extend the net throughout their social circle. Of course, she wouldn't be entirely alone at the center: the idea was predicated on Ted becoming her partner in the company. When she confided it to her husband, the plan came as a surprise: he was preoccupied with Ayn Rand, work on his own *Reading for Pleasure,* and a dozen other things. Yet she knew him so well, and understood how to make the case. "Bennett let me do it," Phyllis would proudly recall, but RH would act as distributor.

A week later, she took Ted to lunch at Quo Vadis, a fashionable restaurant a block and a half's stroll from the townhouse. The red velvet opulence was hardly his native habitat, but Phyllis turned on the charm. Her conversation was lively with intelligence, energy, and a determination to convince. She worked hard to put him at ease, laying out the advantages of a series—mostly what it would mean for children—and how Ted would write some books, but that under his supervision others could also perfect the trick of opening the door to reading. Financial prospects were sound, and she assured him that this new project wouldn't get in the way of his regular "big books," as he soon came to call them. He was set to publish one that year, *How the Grinch Stole Christmas!,* that he hoped would bring people back to the true spirit of the holidays. One final push and she was done: to seize the opportunity *The Cat in the Hat* blew open, they'd have to start now, so as to stake their claim by publishing four or five books at once in fall 1958. She told Ted that *this* fall—1957—Harper was launching an "I Can Read" series with a book illustrated by a young man named Maurice Sendak. She didn't want to cede any ground.

He listened carefully and wondered what role Helen would play. They'd always been a team: he couldn't do his work without her. There was also the question of control. Advertising gigs had been more of a job, but the creative stuff was something else. Only once had he ceded control, on *The 5000 Fingers of Dr. T,* a bleak misery of an experience. The answer was for Helen to be a third partner. If problems arose, the Geisels would then have the upper hand.

Whatever it took, Phyllis was looking for a yes; when she heard that it would take Helen, she quickly acceded. Lunch finished, they shook hands, then walked to Random House and sat down with Bennett. On a sheet of plain paper, he sketched out a structure and two alternative share divisions for a company that Phyllis was calling Beginner Books. She and Ted having agreed on one set of figures, Bennett rewrote them, neatly, on two small sheets of memo paper bearing his name. This was Phyllis's baby, but it was constitutionally impossible for him not to want to be involved. Both sets of papers proclaimed the participation of a "Chief Consultant, Dr. Outgo Schmierkase," who was Bennett and Ted's alter ego. Such a zany linguistic contortion kept things light, deflecting the seriousness of the enterprise they were embarking on.

Who conjured Outgo isn't clear. Characters with similarly "German" or "Yiddish" names populated Bennett's letters, and he took gleeful satisfaction in dreaming them up. Ted was given to playing with *his* German heritage to concoct equally absurd avatars. What's undeniable is that the shared habit was a source of harmony: the two spoke the same language. In the future, a would-be author would get a soft letdown when a Beginner Books letter from Schmierkase rejected an unsolicited manuscript: in English, he was literally "Dr. Cheesespread." Legend has it that a fair number of friends of Ted and Helen, Bennett and Phyllis, qualified to receive them.

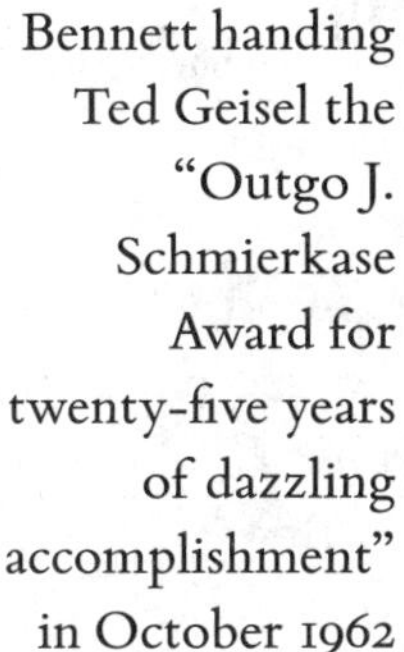

Bennett handing Ted Geisel the "Outgo J. Schmierkase Award for twenty-five years of dazzling accomplishment" in October 1962

That night, they toasted the new collaboration over cocktails at Sixty-Second Street. Two days later, Bennett sent Ted the carbon of a two-page memorandum headed for Horace Manges. "Beginner Books is to be an independent corporation, producing books for children who have just learned how to read . . . distributed exclusively through trade channels by Random House, Inc.," it began. The initial 100 shares would be valued at thirty dollars apiece. Ted and Helen would each receive 11; Bennett and Phyllis, 20 each; Don, 15, nephew Tony, 5; and Louise, Lew Miller, and production director Ray Freiman 6 each. Ted was to be president, Phyllis VP, Donald secretary-treasurer, and Ray art director. It helped that Ray was a fan and Ted respected him: art directors and artists aren't always harmonious, but Ted was open to direction from Ray.

Each book would have the same number of pages, format, and approximate word count as *The Cat in the Hat,* and retail at $1.95. RH would receive 20 percent of net proceeds for managing production, distribution, and bookkeeping, but at the outset would lend money to get the start-up going. Beginner would have a 10 percent share in movie, TV, and foreign rights, and the privilege of leasing printing plates to a textbook house—but only if Ted, Phyllis, and Don agreed. Lawyers are wont to wrangle and did, but even without signed papers, the fledgling firm's work began. However, a setback occurred almost at once: Helen had a small stroke, weakening her right side, leaving her depressed and shaky, and making Ted even more nervy. And yet, once home from the hospital, she still managed to be his sounding board, and forced herself to edit *The Grinch*.

A delicate situation required a seasoned go-between. It was Don who tried to persuade Ted that his lawyer's desire for, as Don put it, a "hard and fast irrevocable contract" revealed a basic misapprehension: Hadn't they decided Beginner was to be "informal and by mutual agreement and amongst friends?" If the lawyer insisted on business as usual, RH would have to negotiate a better deal for *itself.* It was advancing money to the start-up at less than the going interest rate, while having to pay higher interest on its own borrowing, and that wasn't the only disadvantage. The thing was predicated on goodwill and looking to the future. If it worked, in a few years they'd all make money, "possibly by even selling [Beginner] to Random House."

Yet Ted's lawyer argued sensibly and protectively: What if Donald and Bennett decided to sell and get out of the business? Bennett was nearly sixty, so this wasn't an idle thought. It took from April until August for the Geisels and their lawyer to overcome anxiety and sign. In the end, it circled back to Ted's original feeling about Bennett, that "this was a kind of star I wanted my wagon hitched to." The long, happy relationship had earned his trust many times over, and proved more persuasive than his lawyer's fears. During those months of back-and-forth, Ted had begun creating *The Cat in the Hat Comes Back* and would invite a college friend, Mike McClintock, to write *A Fly Went By*. Phyllis threw herself into dreaming up ideas and developing policies, a template, and word lists. An author would be handed a contract and glossy booklet explaining how to create a work of restricted vocabulary but unrestricted imagination.

"The six-year-old is your intellectual equal. He can understand almost anything you can, when . . . he sees it . . . on television. If you talk down . . . you lose him," was one of the booklet's commandments. Another stated that the reader must be able to "feel sympathy, love, dislike, admiration . . . for the people and animals you are writing about." A sense of humor was a "must."

Bennett would tell Helen Geisel that Phyllis was "eating, drinking and sleeping Beginner Books. . . . I've never seen her so completely enthralled." Her life had become a giddy maelstrom akin to the life he led, except that she didn't have a wife to depend on. House, kids, social life—even co-authoring a family puzzle book for RH—she was juggling it all, plus Beginner. Her mind galloped with notions about who could write for the series. Going through every contact in her head, she made a list.

Why not tap Broadway's Alan Jay Lerner to create stories for kids? What about Ray Bradbury for a book on spaceships? By early May, she'd convinced Truman Capote to write a Beginner that he'd titled *The Kite That Could Not Fly*.

Favorable winds generated by *The Cat in the Hat* pushed the enterprise forward. By Thanksgiving, 111,000 copies were in print, with the just-published *Grinch* also flying off shelves. Sales velocity grew. Bennett was thrilled to tell Helen *The Cat* was causing *all* Ted's books to sell "in incredible fashion. Let Russia have its Sputniks; we have our Dr. Seuss!"

But as time passed, the reality of very different personalities on two different coasts building a series and a company together began to set in. Ted's perfectionism impacted other writers and illustrators as well as his new partner, and some of his priorities as author/illustrator differed from the bottom-line notions of fellow shareholders. Phyllis's version of perfectionism also began to manifest itself, as did her penchant for getting her way. Although all tried to be on best behavior, misunderstandings occurred, patience was tested, and solutions had to be found, with Don being diplomat-in-chief. As Ted wrote him, it was "a hell of a job" trying to teach how to do something that only *The Cat in the Hat* had done thus far. "The job takes too much sweat and patience for the average writer, who is unwilling to do what I do . . . throw entire manuscripts away and start in fresh, five or six times," before being able to "marry the miserable word list with pictures." The few books they had from others needed "enormous work," he complained, and Helen soon lamented: "Writing is the worst job that anyone ever got into."

The first week in October, seven months after *The Cat in the Hat* had opened his bag of tricks and wreaked mischievous havoc with their lives, Ted and Helen visited Mt. Kisco for a few days. Beginner was "coming out of both ears" and Bennett fully expected "to dive into the now icy waters of the Kisco River" to escape, he joked in a note to Don, who was in London. Yet as he and Ted walked amid the just-turning crispness of the woods above the stream, they had a "long confab" about their new adventure, and the comfortable relationship built over many years came to the fore. Yes, there were growing pains, but it would all work out.

Optimism can be contagious. By Thanksgiving, despite the fact that "our authors' mortality rate is still high," Ted expressed greater confidence: "We are now beginning to see definite results," he told Bennett, "thanks, mainly, to the super-human efforts of your spouse and mine."

Five books were approved by all three partners to launch the series for fall 1958, among them *The Cat in the Hat Comes Back;* Mike McClintock's *A Fly Went By,* with illustrations by Fred Siebel; and *Sam and the Firefly,* by P. D. Eastman. At first, the Cerf and Geisel homes functioned as bicoastal HQs. Phyllis worked in the small shuttered office off the dining room, and it was Ray Freiman who persuaded Ted to build a dedicated cork-lined studio facing the Pacific; before then, he'd worked peripatetically around the house. Now Ted storyboarded projects on the workroom walls as though they were movies. Helen's office occupied a former garage, and soon would display a small needlepoint stitched by Phyllis of Ted's famous feline, with the legend: "This cat started a publishing house and 'no other cat can make this claim.' "

Early in May, Ted was needed in New York: the new business required more frequent, lengthier stays. Always suffering a crisis of confidence before a performance, he managed to do a small "public" reading of his *Cat* sequel, but a bigger hurdle awaited: sales conference at the Waldorf. On its second day, just before the meeting ended, Ted, Phyllis, and Bennett did a conjuring act, pulling the metaphorical curtain aside to reveal *The Cat in the Hat Comes Back* and the whole Beginner Books lineup. The salesmen, as one, got to their feet and cheered. By mid-July, the books had been put to bed: 60,000 copies of each were being printed, three times more than the usual run. A very considerable $200,000 loan from RH financed the start-up. "Ted and I don't think they are awfully good," Helen confided to her niece, "but they're as good as we can make them, and if they fail, WE don't have to take the loss!" Yet Ted was anxious about everything, even about charging coast-to-coast calls to the young company. He was to a certain extent afraid of money, and Bennett had to reassure him about this being their year of "getting our toes wet" and learning how "everybody gets a completely fair deal." Mistakes would be made, and disagreements arise, but they'd all be constantly learning. Bennett "deeply believed" that in an extremely short time, "we are going to have not only a very sound and profitable business, but one that runs as smoothly as silk. . . . Nothing is going to stop us!"

The five Beginner Books were widely reviewed, that fall of 1958. Not surprisingly, Ted's was singled out as superior, but the *Times, Herald Tribune,* and *Chicago Sunday Tribune* judged them generally "funny," "lively," even "wonderful." Just before Christmas, Helen could write to her niece that "after only 4 months of operation, we're in the black, and that is quite good for publishing." Her understatement was staggering. Beginner Books was managing to do what the Modern Library had done in the 1920s—only faster. Within three years, the first five books plus the original *Cat in the Hat* would have a total combined net sale of almost 1,225,000 copies.

The company was growing so fast that Phyllis was outgrowing her home office. Bennett would soon write to Helen and Ted about "tentative" plans to set aside space in the palazzo for Beginner, but was careful to say that nothing definite would be done until the Geisels approved it "in person." Soon they were in New York, and not only approved: they were delighted. The servants' quarters at the top of the house would be transformed into Beginner central. The elevator went as far as the floor below, so the brightly colored rooms were reachable only by the back stairs, a world unto themselves. Louise moved up, and a secretary was hired. The place was kitted out with a tiny kitchen, so Phyllis could fix herself a simple lunch and spend the whole day upstairs. When Bennett wasn't at some expensive beanery with an author or downing a bagel at the drugstore, he'd sometimes phone her secretary and ask if "the little woman" was in. He and Thrup would speak for a moment and then he'd be bounding up the stairs and she'd be in the kitchen, putting out crackers and heating canned soup. When he appeared, she'd throw her arms around his neck, lean in on tiptoe, and kiss him while waiting for the soup to warm.

Just as Phyllis had once occupied a desk at McCann-Erickson to which Ted could always lay claim, she now presided over a sky-blue fanciful kingdom that reached its apotheosis a half dozen weeks each year. Then the queen would step aside and the magic doctor appear, come to inspect and inspire the empire's eastern outpost. Phyllis's small stature was well suited to the dwarf windows, eaves, and odd half-doors of the old garret. Ted's height, on the other hand, made him look like a knobby-beaked fairy-tale giant when in residence. He loved the place and made hand-lettered signs that read "Small Books Editor," "Dr. Valerie Violet Vowel, D.V., Director of Consonants," and such. Dr. Schmierkase's presence was also noted.

Every new project bearing his name now started with a print run of at least 100,000 copies. By 1960, he'd be earning more than $150,000 a year in royalties from Beginner and RH—and that didn't include income from library, book club, and other licensing deals, which eventually brought in much more. But the matter of quality and its ally, control, kept rearing its head. Ted was distressed about a *Cat* toy: early runs of hundreds of thousands of them were manufactured badly, and the substandard workmanship reflected poorly on his good name and the prestige of the books. Yet it was with Phyllis that friction about control and quality would become almost a constant. They both had such strong feelings about every aspect of Beginner.

She complained to Bennett that she was the partner who had to find most of the talent, yet the expectations Ted placed upon authors and artists were untenable. She had to act as a buffer, even with people whose work he respected. Stan and Jan Berenstain, an established husband-wife team of magazine artists and book illustrators in Philadelphia, were among them. When their older son went crazy over Dr. Seuss, the Berenstains had asked their agent to try to get them on the Beginner bandwagon: they hankered to do a project for kids, and had an idea they thought worth pursuing. Phyllis was familiar with their magazine work and invited them to New York to meet with her and the Geisels. To begin with, the Berenstains were impressed that Phyllis was Ginger Rogers's cousin. They also liked how family-oriented she seemed, talking about Chris and Jon. In short order, they signed for a book called *Freddy Bear's Spanking*.

"Phyllis couldn't have been nicer," Stan Berenstain found, and it was clear that Ted "admired that we could really draw." But they quickly learned creating a Beginner wasn't as easy as it looked. Ted could be generous in how he helped, and was terrific on shaping structure, but the editing could be very difficult. "He wanted us to work along *his* lines," Stan recalled. "After the fourth version, Phyllis said, 'Ted, let Stan and Jan be Stan and Jan.' " She and Helen selected a small section of the story, about a honey hunt, and that became the book. Yet as the Berenstains would observe over many years, Ted tended to "brook no interference" about what a book should do. They sensed that, since he couldn't always get others to do it, "he would heavily rewrite," but some authors couldn't, wouldn't, be rewritten. Case in point: "It was not a happy day when Ted decided that Truman Capote's manuscript was awful." Phyllis, red-faced, had had to explain to Truman that his kite *really* couldn't fly. Her dream of recruiting big-name writers and bright-light friends soon shriveled under her partner's exacting gaze.

American kids adored TV westerns, and so a cowboy book was high on Phyllis's original wish list. In the summer and fall of 1958, frustration came to a head over *Cowboy Andy,* a book they'd contracted by Edna Walker Chandler, with illustrations by Everett Raymond Kinstler. Everyone agreed the story and pictures were problematic, but Phyllis worked relentlessly, determined to lasso the thing into shape. Helen couldn't help but admire that she managed to "put a story into a horrible conglomeration of pictures and made it interesting," but the book was still "all wrong." It would probably sell, but what would it say about their integrity?

Donald, yet again, reached for his white hat. Phyllis had "worked like a dog," he wrote Helen, and she and Ted had now accepted the text. They'd have to put up with the art. "This has developed into a moral question," he echoed Helen, but one Don viewed differently. They—the Cerfs, the Geisels, and Don himself—*were* Beginner, and had signed a contract. They had to go forward. Ted and Helen insisted on more revisions; the book was published. It sold well, whether they hated it or not.

Twenty-five years later, Ted had his likeness painted by the preeminent American society portraitist of the day: the same artist who'd drawn Cowboy Andy. "It was the worst book I ever illustrated," Ray Kinstler, who'd also paint Ronald Reagan, Bill Clinton, and five other presidents, admitted.

"It was the worst book *anybody* ever illustrated," Ted Geisel laughed. They both had traveled a long way.

In 1959, Bennett would publish a Beginner—*Bennett Cerf's Book of Laughs* (Phyllis did the actual writing, but his name would clinch the sales), followed a year later by *Bennett Cerf's Book of Riddles* (ditto), one that would bring smiles to generations of kids. Ted, in 1960, would publish *One Fish, Two Fish, Red Fish, Blue Fish* and *Green Eggs and Ham.* Work on their books could distract from the tensions for a while, but the wound would reopen a little deeper, a little wider with each fight, like the scabby knee of an awkward child who cannot help tripping and falling time and time again. Bennett would hear Phyllis and Ted on the phone for hours, arguing over a single word. Under it all was a puzzle: Phyllis, who'd grown up in the shadow of her cousin and spent her married life in the shadow of her husband, had placed herself in the shadow of a genius. Getting credit was paramount; over the years, she'd complain that if she did or said something new or amusing, more often than not it would be attributed to Bennett. Now she had Dr. Seuss to contend with, but wouldn't forgo what she considered her role, or her due.

Bennett also had to deal with his wife having far less time to cater to *him*. That wasn't convenient, but it was the growing strain between Phyllis and Ted that really drove him crazy. Sometimes it made him long for the days before Beginner.

Chapter 34

Hellos and Goodbyes

At the end of 1957, a new man arrived at Random House, and for a while he'd cushion some of the cracks developing in Phyllis's New York attic and Ted Geisel's La Jolla tower. Robert L. Bernstein stood out in a crowd. His athletic build, all six feet three inches, was animated by restless vigor topped by a thick shock of auburn hair. A scattershot explosion of freckles spattered across his large face, making him seem younger than his thirty-five years. Gangly, russet, spotted, he resembled nothing so much as a human Dalmatian. His brown eyes had that eager liquid canine brightness, yet the stare was unflickering, not soft. Bounding into the foreground, no tail-wagging follower, Bernstein ran to get ahead of the pack. S&S's Albert Leventhal had hired the Harvard graduate as a glorified office boy in 1946, after the army. He soon progressed to sales, throwing himself into the work. After three years, Leventhal awarded Bernstein an $8,000 bonus, a handsome sum given his base salary of $10,000. Third "S" Leon Shimkin, keeper of the purse, deemed it too much, too fast. He cut the bonus to $5,000.

Bernstein didn't lack for belief in himself. From that day on, a frost permeated the relationship between the towering Harvard boy and "little bookkeeper," a study in contrasts. The younger man's grandmothers had been born in America, and Bernstein was so thoroughly assimilated that, if not for the Jewish surname, he could easily have been taken for a WASP; Shimkin was the son of poor immigrant Russians and unmistakably ethnic. Despite the chill between them, Bernstein rose steadily. He became sales manager of the juvenile division, adept at merchandising Golden Books and Disney cartoon tie-ins, fantastic jackpots in a powerhouse division. A few years later, he was made a general sales manager. By 1956, Dick Simon's health had forced him to cede control of the firm to Shimkin. Jointly with Max Schuster, Shimkin was on the verge of buying back the company from Marshall Field, and purchasing Pocket Books entirely for himself. After that, change kept coming. Jack Goodman, who'd run much of S&S's day-to-day with Leventhal, died suddenly of a heart attack in July 1957. Shimkin used the upheaval to oust Bernstein. With a wife and three sons to support in suburban Scarsdale, he was given a week's severance for each of his eleven years at S&S, doled out one week at a time.

Despite the blow, Bernstein's head buzzed with entrepreneurial ideas about kids' books. He'd cultivated a good relationship with the extraordinary author-entertainer Kay Thompson, whose poor-little-rich-girl Eloise had gazed down from the "tippy-top" floor of the Plaza Hotel in 1955 to charm Manhattan and much of the rest of the country. Thompson had created a witty, beguiling story, playing off the mythic glamour of New York. Impressed with Bernstein, she made him vice president of Eloise Ltd., a firm they formed to sell subsidiary rights to her book. Around the same time, a close friend in the TV business threw him another lucrative lifeline. Michael Dann was on the production team for a series of prime-time fairy tales to be hosted and narrated by Shirley Temple, the beloved former movie moppet. They would air on NBC from January 1958 until Christmas. Bernstein immediately grasped the merchandising magic the Temple name and image could command. A large-format book, a cheaper line for five-and-dimes, and other variations: her fame would sell them all. Dann introduced Bernstein to Temple's lawyer, and he came away with a deal to exploit book rights to the shows.

Bennett heard about this go-getter from a friendly West Coast bookseller. Always on the lookout for talent, he was well aware that Lew Miller had been dropping hints about retiring. He tracked Bernstein down, arranged a meeting, and offered him a job as sales manager under "Gentleman Lew." Bernstein agreed, stipulating two conditions. First, he couldn't start for two months. He'd received four weeks of severance; seven more were due him, and Bernstein knew Shimkin would stop the money as soon as he joined RH. He refused to let his erstwhile nemesis avoid paying even a penny. Bennett thought for a moment, then tossed off a lesson Bernstein enjoyed reciting years later: "I'd like you to work seven weeks without pay, and at the end of that time, I will hire you and pay double salary for seven weeks. You should remember: there's always a way to screw a son-of-a-bitch." Next, Bernstein retrieved a paper from his pocket and handed it over. "The Demands of One Helen Bernstein" was written across the top. His wife knew the external layout of the Villard. She drove into the city often, but like many suburbanites, hated the hunt for parking. Her "demand" was to reserve a prized courtyard spot for herself.

"Bob, she's smarter than you," Bennett chortled.

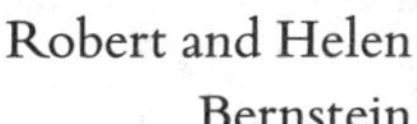

Robert and Helen Bernstein

He liked the flippant chutzpah of this plea masquerading as deal-breaker, and granted the wish: if the parking space were needed for a special author's use, she'd have to cede it, but otherwise it was hers. Bennett respected entrepreneurial talent, saw it in Helen's husband, and recognized it had to be rewarded. His own work habits were necessarily idiosyncratic, given all he packed into a day; he'd already proved flexible and open to unusual arrangements. Bennett hired Bernstein for a $25,000 salary and three-year contract as the new sales manager and Lew's heir presumptive—but also took him on in another capacity, one that Bernstein had suggested. A new subsidiary, Random House Enterprises, would be formed to handle the "exploitation and development" of commercial rights to book "properties" that lent themselves to such activity. They wouldn't be the usual rights sales, like reprints, movies, or book club deals. RHE was to *extend* the line of sales into new areas, such as toys and clothes. Half the stock would be held by RH, half by Bernstein, who would be president, and RHE would split profits fifty-fifty with each author.

The Shirley Temple franchise was a different matter, a project that Bernstein had *brought in*. He'd receive a commission of 5 percent of net profit on this and future titles that he hooked, akin to arrangements Linscott and others had negotiated. From the beginning, Bennett and Bernstein worked to make the most of Temple, since they were under tremendous time pressure—the TV shows would peter out at year's end. To announce the deal, they held a press conference at the Savoy Plaza, knowing that reporters would attend at the very least to bombard Temple, now almost thirty, with questions about a possible movie comeback. (Her answer was no.)

The Shirley Temple Storybook was rushed for October; by Christmas, it had sold more than 125,000 copies, and two related but cheaper books each sold nearly as much, and at a rate even faster than that of Dr. Seuss. So many fresh marketing ideas came into play: her old films were shown at book parties; the biggest department stores in major cities put look-alike mannequins in windows; "Shirley Temple"–licensed girls' dresses, handbags, and dolls were cross-promoted with books. When she deigned to make her only appearances at department stores near her home, "hysterical fans" in "mobs" of four thousand and six thousand crushed into the stores.

That first year, Bernstein made roughly $20,000 from the arrangement—almost doubling his salary. Bennett didn't begrudge it, as he was taken with how "strong" Bernstein was, smart, and with such hungry ambition. Another plus: Kay Thompson followed him, and RH would publish *Eloise at Christmastime*. For his part, Bernstein could hardly believe how very well-read Lew was, impressed that he, Bennett, and Don actually *read* most books they published. Lew worked closely with his acolyte, imparting a philosophy that became Bernstein's own: "The publishing house is the servant of the author." Of course, Bernstein knew authors mainly "didn't think of it that way." Were ever enough ads bought to satisfy a writer? Still, from Bennett and Don on down, he understood RH saw itself as a family devoted to its staff and authors.

Lew put him in charge of hiring new salesmen and imparted another lesson: "You have to buy the whole person." Once ensconced at RH, few wanted to leave. It was essential that a new man (they were all men) be the right "fit" as well as accepted for who he was. Bob couldn't wait to get to the office in the morning. Most days, he left Scarsdale without seeing his young sons wake up, and returned after they'd gone to bed. His mind was completely absorbed in the business. Blue-eyed, dark-haired, vivacious Helen managed everything else.

Both Cerfs liked the Bernsteins, who began to enjoy the perk of entrée into Bennett's other lives and worlds. On the first summons to a formal dinner at Sixty-Second Street, Bob maneuvered his big frame into a rented tuxedo. Try as he might, though, he couldn't wrangle the tie into a proper bow; neither could Helen. On the drive in from Scarsdale, they decided to stop at one of the swank Park Avenue buildings and find a friendly doorman to help. The first man didn't know how to do it; the second was too drunk to try. Mortified, Bob arrived at the townhouse with tie hanging undone. The bell was answered by a maid in black uniform, starched white cap, and apron, behind her Bennett rushing down the stairs. In a second, he perceived the problem, burst out laughing, ran back up, and returned holding a bag of pre-tied silk bows. Selecting one, he reached to put it on the younger man. Bennett was tall, but Bernstein three inches taller; he wasn't used to that. Still, Bennett's light touch quickly banished any embarrassment.

At the office, although the whole landscape of RH was there for Bernstein to roam in, his radar pointed naturally to the big juvenile authors, none bigger than Ted Geisel. "It's my feeling that Dr. Seuss can be huge and *The Cat in the Hat* alone can be a wonderful property," he gushed to Bennett. He had visions of licensing everything from "Cat's pajamas" to advertising rights (a big ice-cream company would be a cinch) to greeting cards, but Ted was wary, wanting to keep his work unsullied by potentially dodgy merchandise. Still, he was coaxed into doing a ten-day Boston-to-Chicago autograph tour. The cavalcade rolled through luncheons, TV appearances, school library and university events, and store signings. Bennett, reading Bob's dispatches, wired Ted in Detroit: "Reports indicate that you are even bigger than Brigitte Bardot. Congratulations and love to you and your hand maiden Bernstein." Never before had the business seen this scale of promotion for a children's author. It was a window on the future of marketing, branding, and the contribution top juvenile authors would bring to a publisher's bottom line.

Star turns before hordes of fans would stretch almost anyone who didn't have the unusual makeup of a Bennett Cerf, but touring was especially difficult for a shy person like Ted, whose fans would have been shocked by what challenged him most. He "wasn't a kids' person," Helen Geisel's niece Barbara had decided about her beloved aunt's husband.

"Ted had no idea how to deal with children," Helen Bernstein also realized, after observing him with her boys. The tour that Bob had organized proved hugely stressful for the amazing Dr. Seuss. Helen Geisel thought her husband would never do one again. (Eventually, however, he was persuaded.) The Geisels' bond with Bennett was deep, but as they got to know Bernstein, they found it good having him on the scene: his experience and interests aligned so neatly with the juvenile world. He began making regular trips to La Jolla; it was easier for him to fit them in than for Bennett.

Bernstein also had ideas about Babar, the little gray elephant who'd arrived from Paris twenty years earlier with Bob and Merle. Laurent de Brunhoff, the son of Babar's originator, had inherited his family's artistic talent. When he was thirteen, a year after his father, Jean, died, Laurent was asked to add color to the black-and-white drawings of his dad's last two stories (originally drawn for a newspaper), so they could be published as books. After the war, helped by two uncles in magazine publishing, he revived the series, with Merle continuing as translator. Within a month of Bernstein's arrival, a letter was crossing the Atlantic, introducing the new sales manager and conjuring visions of Babar wallpaper, fabric, and toys.

In 1964, Bernstein would invite Laurent de Brunhoff to come to America for a tour, and cooked up a plan for the elephant to cross the Atlantic with him. De Brunhoff, like the Geisels, would find Bernstein "energetic, helpful, and very appealing," and Bernstein would persuade him that it was in his best interest to reverse the established flow: originate new Babar books in English with RH, and *then* publish in French with de Brunhoff's longtime Paris house, Hachette. The family that Babar visited in the resulting story, *Babar Comes to America,* bore an uncanny resemblance to one with three boys in Scarsdale and parents named Helen and Bob. It wasn't quite the same as Gertrude putting Bennett and Don into *The Geographical History of America* or *Everybody's Autobiography,* but it wasn't entirely different, either.

Bernstein wasn't the only migrant from S&S. As with most businesses, ownership transitions tend to dislodge valuable staff, and in publishing, authors often follow. Bennett was good at capitalizing on such windows of opportunity. As soon as he heard that senior editor Lee Wright had also parted from the Esses, he tracked her down to convey "deep interest" in her future. She arrived at the Villard at the same time as her former colleague.

Wright's experience was long: she'd begun as Dick Simon's secretary in 1935, aged twenty-one. Two years later, she inaugurated the popular Inner Sanctum Mysteries, eventually publishing first books by Donald Westlake, Stanley Ellin, Gypsy Rose Lee, and Ira Levin. In addition to spotting mystery talent, she turned her hand to other kinds of books, too, including Laura Z. Hobson's bestseller *Gentleman's Agreement*. As well as publishing twenty books a year, for the past five years she'd also functioned as managing editor, akin to Albert Erskine. In adult trade publishing, a powerful female editor like Wright remained a rarity. Just the previous year, she'd initiated a series under the "brand" of Alfred Hitchcock, the rotund director of impeccably calculated box-office thrillers, who was now also fronting a weekly TV show and monthly mystery magazine. "Hitch" came along to RH for the ride. Wright also brought another money-in-the-bank property—an "annual" from the pseudonymous "Ellery Queen," whom more Americans associated with mysteries than any other author. Bennett had published a Queen ML Giant in 1941, and was delighted with the move. If it caused more friction with S&S, so be it.

...

WRIGHT JOINED ANOTHER NEW editor at RH. Early in 1957, the firm had welcomed soft-spoken Robert Loomis, whose voice was so quiet and uninflected that even Bennett was forced to cease jabbering and listen. Previously at Appleton and then Holt, he knew Hiram Haydn through William Styron, Loomis's best friend dating back to college. Sometimes Loomis sat in on Haydn's New School course, and rather than rush back to Westport on a late train, Haydn would spend the night on Loomis's Greenwich Village couch. Soon Hiram asked Bob to come see the boss. At an "interview" lasting all of ten minutes, Bennett met the pale-as-white-bread thirty-year-old with high hairline. His intention was to do Haydn's bidding and hire him; besides, he recognized the intellect underneath. Loomis wasn't showy or anxious; he was steady, which would suit many authors just fine. Bennett expressed "great hopes" for him, though somehow got it into his head that the young man's name was "George." When he encountered him in the hall, he made a point of hailing "George" and asking, "Are you happy?"—a concern that seemed altogether genuine. Loomis couldn't bring himself to correct the name. When his wife, Gloria, discovered she was pregnant, Bennett would drop hints—flippant but half serious—"If the baby's named Bennett, something's in it for you!"

Robert D. Loomis

Unfortunately, the couple's happiness was compromised by a typical Manhattan problem: their two rooms were too tiny to accommodate a child. They needed $8,000 to buy a co-op apartment, but couldn't scrape together the cash. One day Donald and Bennett called Loomis into Bennett's office. They'd heard about his dilemma, and Don handed over a check for $8,000.

"How will I pay this back?" Loomis wondered aloud, startled and elated.

"You'll pay it back," Don confidently replied, inspiring confidence in return. No legal document or note was exchanged or discussed, even though Loomis had been at the palazzo a total of six months. The question of the infant-naming worked itself out: nature made her a girl. Bennett understood that his suggestion, "Benita," wasn't every person's choice. He also came to appreciate that none of his editors was named "George."

The discussions that the partners had begun in 1954 with Penguin Books founder Sir Allen Lane, concerning a deal involving Lane's U.S. operation, had heated and cooled several times during the past few years. In July 1956, after returning with Phyllis from Europe, Bennett had sent Lane an important letter, spelling out "Notes for a possible basis whereby Random House could purchase Penguin Books for the American market." The document had guaranteed that should agreement be reached, RH would perpetuate the Penguin name in the United States, and Bennett and Don consider folding ML paperbacks into the imprint. However, with Lane, everything crept in slow motion. Bennett wouldn't give up. In September 1957, when Sir Allen visited New York, they talked again, and he took Lane and his daughter to *What's My Line?* Sessions with lawyers ensued, and Lane promised to send figures. The next month, Don—in London on his annual trip—continued the campaign. But later that month, Don wrote that everything "blew up." It would be some time before he and Bennett knew why.

All the while, they were aware of inroads being made by Anchor and Vintage into Modern Library sales, and tried to counter with more ads for the ML paperback line, but their problem couldn't be solved by advertising alone: it was more fundamental. Jess Stein had taken over responsibility for the series from the ailing Saxe, but Jess was a dictionary and reference man. The ML needed someone both more literary and entrepreneurial to stand up against the competition going forward. And so, in August 1958, Donald wrote to Lane again, offering to fly to London to resume talks. He was not alone, however. It turned out that Houghton Mifflin and Harper had also been courting Penguin, and Harper reckoned that they had a done deal.

A few weeks later, a different solution unexpectedly presented itself to Bennett and Don. Anchor's hugely ambitious, handsome enfant terrible, Jason Epstein, had been chafing at Doubleday, a house that he'd come to view through his dark-framed glasses as "an appendage of a mass market book club, run by a lawyer, not a publisher," and had quit. *Why not bring him in to rejuvenate the ML,* the partners asked themselves. A year earlier, unbeknown to them, Lane himself had tried to lure Epstein to run Penguin U.S. editorially. But Epstein, like Don, instinctively did not trust Lane, sensing the Penguin founder to be "a very slick character." By the time he quit Doubleday, however, Epstein had overcome his misgivings enough to hatch an alternative plan; he'd join with Grove Press's Barney Rosset to buy Penguin's U.S. operation. It would be, he thought, "the equivalent of Horace Liveright selling to Bennett Cerf."

The young men made the pilgrimage to England, confident that they could accomplish what their elders had not. It was a little like a French farce: while Bennett was trying to contact Epstein as an alternative to a Penguin deal, Epstein was already across the Atlantic, trying to forge a Penguin deal for himself. But he discovered what others would know soon enough: Lane couldn't dispose of Penguin because it was no longer his to sell. He'd borrowed too much, and the company was kept alive on an overdraft. His British bankers essentially owned it.

Bennett tracked his quarry down in London. When they spoke on the phone, Epstein insisted he didn't want to work for anyone. He'd create a new business, confident in his own resourcefulness. Nevertheless, he liked what he knew of the RH partners, and agreed to let them buy him lunch at home. And so, early in October, Donald and Bennett took him to Sardi's East. Epstein had met Don once, a few years earlier, and came away with the impression that this man "who looked and walked like a camel" was a "kind, lovely fellow." Bennett was "full of himself" but also a "gentle, decent man, a serious reader who knew a good writer from a bad one."

"Come be an editor," they urged. But having started a successful business at twenty-four, Epstein knew that being an RH editor would never be enough. Bennett wouldn't give up. Just as he'd accommodated Bernstein with Random House Enterprises, he again adapted the rules to get what he wanted and saw the firm needed. The ML was too important not to. "Come as an editor and we won't give you any other company responsibilities," he promised. That way, Epstein would also be able to start his own business. "And if it interests us and we'd like to invest in it," Bennett added, "all the better." On October 23, in block capitals, his diary recorded the hire. A heavyweight and "somebody" on the young intellectual scene, Epstein was a literary provocateur in touch with what was happening, who was in and who out, in a way that Bennett most certainly was not. He'd start the first Monday in November at the princely salary of $18,000.

Once he arrived, Epstein began poring over all things ML, and just before Christmas came to Bennett with a private business idea: a children's line of originals and reprints, the latter from well-loved British works like Frances Hodgson Burnett's *The Secret Garden* and Edwardian fairy-tale collections. Bennett encouraged him to start a company. Epstein did, calling his brainchild the Looking Glass Library, and published some fine reprints of British classics and one original that became a perennial: Norton Juster and Jules Feiffer's *The Phantom Tollbooth*. In 1960, Random bought the imprint, but financially it didn't really work, and soon fizzled out. In reaching for him, Bennett may have grabbed onto a shiny central ring on the merry-go-round of American literary culture, but Epstein was not an easy prize. Even before he arrived, word on the street was that along with the brilliance came an ego that could drive people crazy. In time, Bennett would call Jason "the cross I bear."

Refusing to be outdone, Epstein said that Bennett Cerf was "the bear I cross."

"Jason is Jason," Bennett would both laugh and sigh. "Brilliant . . . aggressive . . . absolutely unmanageable. He does things the way he pleases; and anybody who tries to tell him how to do something another way is wasting his breath." No one at Random ever seemed to disagree.

Jason Epstein and editor-to-be Nan Ahearn Talese having a good time among friends

. . .

IT WAS JUST AS well that these new faces were popping up around the Villard: the infusion of energy and distraction came as a long goodbye was reaching its end. Saxe Commins had never recovered his health after the 1953 heart attack, nor had he reconciled himself to the "twilight" of his career. Hiram Haydn's elevation flew in the face of Saxe's credo that the editor's job was to remain anonymous, "invisible." Still, he carried on as best he could, dividing his week between Princeton and the palazzo through the summer of 1957. Don tried to reassure him: "Never let me hear you say that you know what it is not to be wanted! . . . *very much* wanted," but Saxe was hospitalized again in November. The inevitable met the obvious: any work would be from home. He wrote to the partners, saying the only right option was to retire. Bennett countered in a call: he'd always be useful. The night before sales conference, Bennett phoned again to say how sorry he was that for the first time in thirty-three years, his old friend would be absent.

"What an enormous lift" the calls gave him, Saxe said.

In March he was well enough for Bill Faulkner to come to Princeton for two weeks to work on *The Mansion*. Saxe was also editing Edgar Snow's *Journey to the Beginning,* and hoping that his long-standing relationships with Irwin Shaw, Wystan Auden, and others would continue. In early July, he had another slight attack, but seemed to be recovering, and insisted on editing the last section of Snow's manuscript from his hospital bed. He put in the finishing touches on July 16. The following morning, a massive cerebral hemorrhage felled him. "SAXE COMMINS DEAD" was all Bennett could put in his diary for July 17, 1958.

Three days later, a small group of family and friends gathered in Princeton. Bennett was one of two speakers. The next night, dashing off a note to Dorothy, he unlocked his feelings: "I cannot get Saxe out of my thoughts—and RH will never be the same for me. I do hope that you are all right!" He and Don took it in turn to write to authors. "We all miss Saxe desperately, but . . . all of us had been reconciled to his loss . . . months ago," Bennett told *The Ox-Bow Incident*'s Walter Van Tilburg Clark. Don, closer to Faulkner, told him: "I know I won't take Saxe's place, but at least you can count on me." Albert Erskine would be Faulkner's new editor.

There were things Saxe did not do, and things he did too much, intervening too deeply for certain writers' taste, and being overly respectful of the texts of others. Hiram Haydn thought that Saxe became far too immersed in some of their lives, letting them absorb him and squeeze out the capacity for distance that every editor needs. O'Hara and Michener had parted company with him, although Michener wouldn't have come to Random but for Saxe; Ted Geisel said he was the only editor who ever taught him anything; to O'Neill and Faulkner, Schulberg and Lewis, he was in different ways a necessity. He also touched other RH writers without knowing it. Truman Capote's pen was barbed with acid-ink so often, yet when Capote learned about the death, he wrote Donald: "It made me very sad to hear of Saxe. He was a good sweet man."

. . .

WHILE BENNETT WAS SAYING hello and goodbye to new and old faces inside Random House, he was also absorbing changes elsewhere. *What's My Line?* had made him a star, and it was doing very nicely, thank you. In the summer of 1957, *Variety* declared it the third most popular show on TV, and a few months later went so far as to name it the top show in New York, ahead of favorites like *Gunsmoke* and *Nat King Cole*. Bennett demanded his pay be raised to $1,000 a week, and he'd also participate in a new Goodson-Todman profit-sharing scheme. His lecture fee was also now pegged at $1,000 (occasionally lowered for a venue he really wanted), and during these years he recorded annual income of around $20,500 from speaking. Royalties from Doubleday were "whopping": *The Life of the Party* had sold more than 85,000 copies, and was reprinted by Bantam. Doubleday had agreed to a $20,000 advance for *The Laugh's on Me,* and gave permission to reprint *The Encyclopedia of Modern American Humor* as a Modern Library Giant. Bennett Cerf Inc. was also branching into magazine sales. The *Vest Pocket Book of Jokes* was reprinted by a magazine company as a fifty-cent newsstand cheapie, *Bennett Cerf's Jokes of the Year.* The idea was to turn it into an annual. Then there was his relationship with another publisher, Harper, which had published *Reading for Pleasure,* the "serious" anthology for Christmas 1957. It was hard to keep up with the whirling dervish who'd come to enjoy, as the book's front flap copy put it, "a huge and loyal personal following."

TV had propelled the United States to embrace an age of celebrity, where people sought to parse their era through personalities rather than events or ideas. *What's My Line?* had turned Bennett into a celebrity on a scale he could hardly have imagined. Philippe Halsman, one of the preeminent midcentury portrait photographers, had invited him to "perform" for a series that became iconic. If Halsman photographed you leaping mid-air for his "Jump!" project, you'd truly arrived, whether your name was Richard Nixon, Audrey Hepburn, or Bennett Cerf. That fame could also travel: in an Italian newspaper series on "Heroes of American Television," Bennett was described, standing in for his country, as "a pagan worshiper of optimism" who, like can-do America, proceeded "according to a series of eliminations of complexities." However, Phyllis liked to bring her pagan-hero jumper back to earth. "My wife keeps my feet on the ground," Bennett averred. "When she thinks my head is getting too big . . . she lets me know that someday TV will end for me and I'll be just another book publisher." Yet it was hard to believe any such fate could await: it had been such a long time since he'd been only that.

Indeed, further proof of status had arrived in a new line he'd added: Loew's Incorporated, owner of MGM, appointed Bennett to its board. The invitation had come via old friend Howard Dietz, MGM's longtime vice president of publicity and the gifted lyricist for mutual pal Arthur Schwartz's songbook classics. There'd been a tough proxy fight for control; Louis B. Mayer disappeared from the company bearing his name, along with other directors. The new owners sought high-profile replacements, and Bennett was flying very high. Besides, chairman Joe Vogel thought he'd be a good sounding board about novels that might make profitable pictures.

Bennett loved the role. He may have taken pride in RH's harmony, but that didn't prevent him from enjoying a front-row seat on the power plays and bitchiness of Hollywood. The connection was also useful: he gleaned inside knowledge that no other publisher had, and could steer an RH "property" to MGM, as he'd do with E. M. Nathanson's *The Dirty Dozen,* Jean Kerr's *Please Don't Eat the Daisies,* and others. He could negotiate author difficulties with the studio, too. He had a good time going to premieres and knowing the inside dope, but also took his MGM responsibilities seriously. Some years later, he joined with a clutch of others to try to argue the company away from a disastrously expensive remake of *Mutiny on the Bounty* starring Marlon Brando, but the effort was thwarted. Nor did fellow directors take his advice when MGM was bleeding cash and he suggested they cut their own compensation: they "howled" him down. He'd also be overruled after trying to dissuade the studio from making an epic out of "the kind of book people bought but didn't always read" (though *he* had read it). And yet, in the end, he'd be glad he failed: the book was Boris Pasternak's *Doctor Zhivago,* and the movie became a classic.

In 1957, the man whom Swifty Lazar singled out as the only publisher good at making movie deals, had run an ad for RH books transferring to the screen during the next few years, heading it: "This must be love (because we feel so well!)," a clever inversion of "This Can't Be Love," a famously knowing Larry Hart lyric to a Dick Rodgers tune. The ad listed nineteen books-to-film, from *The FBI Story* and O'Hara's *Ten North Frederick* to Michener's *Sayonara* and Faulkner's *The Sound and the Fury*. Like Alfred Knopf, he'd always liked splashing his name on ads, forging a connection and feeling of trust on the part of the customer. He couldn't resist now, being better known than his company: "Movies <u>are</u> better than ever!" declared Bennett Cerf.

But as well as saying hello to new people and endeavors, he'd said goodbye to one of his lives. For fifteen years, he'd "conducted" Trade Winds, the column that had carried him into a second career fulfilling his youthful journalistic ambitions, and helped launch him into *What's My Line?* In 1957, he'd relinquished the influential perch on books and publishing that *Saturday Review* had provided, one that he'd extended into Broadway, Hollywood, and TV. Such a long stretch had inevitably generated moments of friction. He and *SRL*'s editor, Norman Cousins, had sparred regularly over jokes that Bennett insisted were harmless and Cousins feared were not. There was the one about author Fannie Hurst, who'd been dieting: "The same Hurst . . . but definitely <u>not</u> the same Fanny." That had provoked a bitter battle. Bennett won—and Cousins heard from offended readers. Accusations had sometimes flown about his being too glib or aggressive or self-serving, and occasionally he'd let slip an embarrassing mistake. From time to time the subject of the (too small) number of ads Random House took, or the (too few) editorial reviews RH books received, also stirred discontent. Then there was the money. He'd been receiving $8,000 a year for forty columns—$200 each—a higher rate, Cousins insisted, than any other writer's. Still, compared to some of his gainful pursuits, the effort churning them out was greater, the pay lower, and it niggled. *This Week* paid $800 plus expenses per Cerfboard.

At the end of 1956, his frustration had come to a head. Cousins had killed part of a column and slapped his wrist over a pun on "fornicate."

Then, when contract talks began, the magazine said he asked too much, and wouldn't bargain. Bennett had plenty to occupy him: he gave notice. "Jackie Robinson quits baseball just as BAC quit Trade Winds!" he told himself.

"I can tell you that no contributor . . . more consistently maintained a high standard . . . and, despite our little flare-ups, no contributor . . . was more fun to work with," Cousins declared, a last try at coaxing him to stay, but really a valedictory. *Saturday Review* gave him a fancy luncheon in a lovely high room with a view of the UN and the East River, where friends from myriad worlds, all plugged into the switchboard that was Bennett, sent him off. Surveying the scene, knowing there'd no longer be *quite* such pressure on his time, he felt slightly off, deflated.

"I can't be very funny today," he admitted to the gathering. "This is a sad occasion. It is dying a little bit and I'm not happy about it. But there are younger men who can get around and keep the department up to what Trade Winds ought to be. It is a terrible temptation to become a pompous ass when one gets older. We need young people . . . who will keep us from being too serious." He was pushing sixty; running as fast as he could, he couldn't run away from that.

Chapter 35

Everything Public

As BENNETT'S MILESTONE BIRTHDAY APPROACHED, TWO TELEVISION hosts—Edward R. Murrow, the most respected broadcast journalist of his generation, and Mike Wallace, a younger newsman on the rise—flattered him by recognizing his ubiquity. Murrow would devote half a program to him, and Wallace a full show, each remarking on his multiple identities. However, while hidebound distinctions separating high-brow, middle-brow, and popular culture were being eroded, they retained their power among an influential cadre of academics and writers, who disdained that multiplicity. Bennett's screen life canceled out his publishing life for them (if the joke books hadn't done so already). The young literature professor Matthew Bruccoli typified that view: "The guy on TV made me cringe. He was a clown, someone you wouldn't believe capable of reading a book." It wasn't until years later that Bruccoli, then the preeminent Fitzgerald scholar in America, became an RH author and saw another man, "the great, great publisher."

Bennett preferred to shrug off the dichotomy with an all-purpose "I'm a ham." And so when Wallace invited him to take the hot seat on his half-hour late-night program, he couldn't resist the urge to perform. A generation younger, Wallace was an aggressive interviewer. How could the head of Random House, an intellectual standard-bearer, lend himself to a television parlor game? Hadn't TV failed to fulfill its cultural promise? Worse, wasn't it replacing reading?

Bennett agreed that the networks did have a social responsibility beyond the purely commercial, just like book publishers. Unfortunately, it had become fashionable for the "snobbish egghead" to bash TV, and those who simply refused to watch he considered fools. *What's My Line?* wasn't meant to be "culture": it was a pastime. Being a panelist was fun, he liked the recognition, the show paid well, and viewers did gain edification: as a San Francisco cable car operator had told him, he watched in order to hear "good English."

Admitting that he tuned in most Sundays himself, Wallace suggested that perhaps Bennett was "the poor man's egghead." Still, wasn't TV responsible for the United States having the lowest proportion of book readers of any major English-speaking democracy? There were problems in the schools, Bennett acknowledged, but people who wanted to read good books were reading them. Vast numbers of others, if not watching TV, would still not read books.

In his lectures, he often railed against censorship, and the conversation pivoted to focus on the National Office for Decent Literature (NODL), an offshoot of the Catholic Bishops of America that compiled and circulated monthly lists of "objectionable" and "disapproved-for-youths" books, especially paperbacks. These lists inspired local parishes to organize boycotts of stores stocking novels—including some by Ernest Hemingway, Budd Schulberg, and of course John O'Hara—because the stories had four-letter words or a sex scene. The censorship issue was important, but delicate: no publisher wanted to alienate Catholics. Yet Wallace meant to stir controversy, and his guest's impulsiveness helped him do so. Too many Americans weren't satisfied to make rules just for themselves or their co-religionists, Bennett asserted. Thinking it would help them "get to heaven," they wanted to tell everyone what to do. But these "self-appointed snoop-hounds" weren't only selling short the public's ability to decide for itself; a group like the NODL was "overstepping the bounds of American liberty."

Wallace handed him a particularly lurid paperback. Bennett didn't want to read it, and said he wouldn't want his children to read it, but neither would he confiscate it and turn it into forbidden fruit. Once you let a censor tell you what to read, he explained, the censor starts telling you what to think and what to do. And remember: a publisher can only suggest changes. The *author* has the last word. If an author refuses to comply with advice, the publisher will have to accept the book "as is" or let the author take it elsewhere. Some angry Catholics wrote to the show after the interview aired, but a well-known poet and other viewers thanked Bennett. Praising himself on the "good sparring," he was relieved to put the grilling behind him.

Ed Murrow's fifteen-minute segment at home with the Cerfs four months later would have none of Wallace's combativeness, even though

Murrow's devotion to hard-hitting, issue-driven journalism was legend. CBS had insisted on a trade-off—Murrow's serious stuff had to be balanced by a popular show—and so, ironically, *Person to Person* interviews like this would set the template for friendly celebrity-focused TV of the future.

Dark and handsome, an omniscient wizard in a CBS studio, Murrow conducted the conversation remotely, peering at a huge screen where the exterior of the Cerf house magically appeared. "Bennett and Phyllis . . . hold down enough jobs to strain the time and talents of several people," he began. Then the scene dissolved to Bennett's study, where, sitting at his desk, the master of the house explained that the wall of books behind him consisted of the entire Modern Library plus the reference tomes he used for his columns, along with bound scrapbooks of clippings commemorating the headlines of his life. He descended the staircase to the living room, where Phyllis sat with their sons. "Bennett says that the boys can do anything they want, as long as they become publishers," she chuckled in tune with her husband. Jonathan had turned twelve the day before, and piped up that he was trying to write a Beginner Book. Bennett mentioned Chris's role in the birth of Landmarks, and that in a couple months, his sixteen-year-old would spend a second summer working at Random House. Despite her frequent refusal to let them watch TV when younger, Phyllis now told viewers that it had "encouraged" the boys to read, positioning herself as a defender of her husband and this new medium that had been so good to her family.

The kids were left behind as the camera followed their parents to the bar. Bookshelves there held RH's current bestsellers and the plays Bennett took such pride in publishing, as well as "the Cerf memorial shelf"—the volumes he'd authored himself. The tour ended in the library, floor-to-ceiling with more books. Bennett wanted to turn their home into a public library, Phyllis teased, but he interjected: books were the best decoration a house could have, making it "warm and cheerful." Beaming puppy-dog devotion toward her husband, she agreed: the book room was the "happy room" of their home. When Murrow asked about the publishing process, Bennett gave a verbal nod to Don. They read, on average, three manuscripts a week after much sifting by the editors. But it was the two of them, he emphasized, who still made the final decisions.

The Cerfs came across as well-heeled, establishment, middle-aged.

The hungry young publisher who'd chanced a fight on *Ulysses,* shown such passion for O'Neill, delighted in parrying with Stein, was not the man seen here. These shows were signifiers of having arrived. Another sign came soon after the Murrow show, when Bennett flew to Seattle to receive an honorary doctorate at the College of Puget Sound. Hardly on a par with Alfred Knopf's from Yale that same season, it nevertheless made Bennett happy, for he wasn't like Knopf. Interested in people from all walks of life, whether high or humble, he responded to them, and was genuinely grateful.

. . .

BY THE LATE 1950S it felt like Truman Capote had been around Random forever, although after his spectacular debut in 1948 and the quick succession of three more books, production between hard covers had slowed. For five years he'd written screenplays, magazine stories, and the book for a Broadway show based on one of them, *House of Flowers,* but though he'd promised Bennett a novella and enough stories for a volume, nothing materialized. In 1956, deep into the freeze of the Cold War, *The New Yorker* was responsible for a further delay: dangling an irresistible offer, it sent Capote to Moscow to cover the visit of a mainly Black American opera troupe performing Gershwin's *Porgy and Bess,* the first U.S. cultural mission to the USSR since the Bolshevik Revolution. *The Muses Are Heard* was published in two issues in October, a fresh, catty, I-am-a-camera account. With a novelist's gifts, Capote copied and extended an innovative narrative style that had been pioneered by *New Yorker* staff writer Lillian Ross, bringing fiction techniques to reportage, framing not just the singers and locale, but skewering the foibles of tour handlers and hangers-on. Inserting himself into the story, he favored the spirit of adventure over the letter of fact (a scene or two were almost certainly imagined). In the 1960s, this style would be known as the "New Journalism," and later come under the general rubric of "narrative nonfiction." Its enthusiastic masters would include Norman Mailer, Tom Wolfe, Joan Didion, and Gay Talese.

Bennett took advantage of the two-parter, republishing *Muses* as a slim book a few months after its *New Yorker* debut. To earn enough to live on, Capote depended on this dual-print life: appearing first in one of the glossies so fat with ads that their tastemaker editors could be generous with dollars and space, and a few months later as a Random House book. It wasn't until the spring of 1958 that Bennett, having advanced $7,500 for the fiction book years earlier, held the prize: three stories and a novella. Set in New York during the war, the novella was called *Breakfast at Tiffany's,* and he started reading it immediately. The animating spirit was a young woman named Holiday "Holly" Golightly, as bewitching a sprite as any that a word magician could conjure out of sharp contradictions and spare prose polished to a diamond-hard gleam. Intensely independent but strangely needy; not yet twenty, unsullied, yet the paid demimonde darling of rich older men; a shape-shifting self-inventor gliding gracefully on the surface of café society, Holly was irresistible. Everyone from Oona O'Neill Chaplin to RH author Carol Grace Saroyan to any number of Capote's other female friends couldn't resist fancying herself the inspiration. What was clear to anyone who knew him well was that a lot of Truman and his mother Lillie Mae–turned–Nina were in his heroine.

During much of the decade, he'd spent periods in Europe, and both Cerfs had checked in regularly, sending epistolary air-kisses alongside spicy slices of the gossip he craved, while in a low-key way asking how the writing was progressing. At times he revealed something of his struggle, having agonized over the novella's ending. Before Capote was satisfied, they'd read several versions. Initially, *Harper's Bazaar* had agreed to publish it, but when its editor was fired, her replacement balked at a few four-letter words and Holly's lifestyle. Capote, summering on the Greek island Paros, sought Bennett's assurance that he'd made the right decision placing it with *Esquire*. He was Truman's "Rock of Gibraltar," Phyllis later told Capote's biographer.

When Linscott retired, Bennett had thought that Hiram should work with Truman, but he'd proved an awkward match. "I really don't need an editor. I just need you," Phyllis once heard Capote say to her husband, and indeed, Bennett handled him "beautifully," Bert Krantz attested. At a certain point, Bennett asked Krantz to work with Capote, and she discovered that unlike Schulberg or Michener, "Truman didn't need much editing at all."

At the end of September, Capote wrote his publisher again, addressing him as "Beloved B," and explaining that he'd been summoned by the local Paros constabulary. They'd seized a large airmail package addressed to him that they suspected contained heroin. He was told to open it as they watched, and in these odd circumstances unwrapped the first finished copy of *Breakfast at Tiffany's*. "Nothing could detract from the pleasure it gave me," he assured Bennett, "for it *is* beautiful. . . . I am grateful to have such tasteful and considerate publishers."

By the fall of 1960, two years post-publication, the book had sold more than 30,000 copies: pretty good for Capote. Once Holly was embodied by Audrey Hepburn in a loosely based film version a year later—with her cigarette-holder, little black dress, and captivating grace—she entered American mythology, and the book went evergreen. As for RH's balance sheet, selling 30,000 copies of *Breakfast at Tiffany's* in two years was jam, a sweet extra. The basic foodstuff on which the firm thrived was still the Modern Library, but after *The Cat in the Hat,* Ted Geisel became a staple, too, and so was O'Hara, even if rather more difficult to swallow.

Indeed, in April 1958, six months before *Tiffany's* was due to be published, Bennett had dubbed August 1, 1958, "*our* Thanksgiving Day," the date O'Hara had promised to deliver *From the Terrace*. But again, he was being impossible. A contract hadn't yet been drawn up or signed (such slip-ups the flip side of RH's personal publishing style), and O'Hara was demanding that his novel debut on a more traditional Thanksgiving—the fourth Thursday in November, instead of early spring 1959. The manuscript would be *huge*—so big, it would make a 900-page book. To set, proof, correct, print, bind, then distribute such a monster to stores across the country for late November might push RH's production team as well as the manufacturers to their limit: it was, after all, the most crowded and critical publishing season of all.

Bennett and Don told him what they were facing, but he would only sign a contract if RH guaranteed Thanksgiving publication. "O'Hara is the most difficult author I have ever dealt with," Don almost screamed, when writing to the book's British publisher. While both he and Bennett had to deal with him, and each did so superbly, there was a difference in attitude. For Don, the trouble overshadowed everything. Yet Bennett forgave the infuriating weaknesses, respected the talent and discipline, and quite simply loved this author. He agreed to make that November 27 date, come what may, and was so confident about the prospects for *From the Terrace* that the first printing was pegged at 100,000. In the end, the firm would sell just about that number in hardcover, and O'Hara would receive his umpteenth engraved silver bauble from Bennett that year. The novel would rank fifth on the 1958 hardcover fiction bestseller list, and eventually be O'Hara's biggest-selling paperback.

. . .

THE DECADE WAS COMING to an end, and *The New Yorker* had taken a glacial time over its profile of Mr. Cerf. The idea had been floated in 1945; journalist Geoffrey Hellman did much of the legwork during 1954 and '55; and in 1957, Bennett had received word that the piece was "rising from the ashes." Nothing materialized. When he finally heard that the first installment of a two-part feature—Part I would extend across sections of twenty-five pages, Part II across sections of nineteen—was to be published in the May 9, 1959, issue, he hardly believed it.

On the opening page, the title "Publisher" and subtitle "Descent from Olympus" appeared above an artist's sketch: Bennett all receding hairline, slackening jaw, and dark horn-rims, curiously devoid of eyes. The first two and a half pages, although broken up by periods, had the effect of being one extremely extended sentence that had nothing to do with publishing, and seemingly nothing to do with Bennett. Instead, in a self-consciously baroque style, Hellman—a Yale alum and a fellow who liked hobnobbing with the "swell people," finding it indispensable to keep a copy of the *Social Register* beside his typewriter—listed the names and activities of successful professional men who chose to pursue "refined" cultural avocations in contrast to their less-than-inspiring but awfully lucrative day jobs. Only then did he introduce the subject of his profile as a "rare" reversal of the trend, whose lifework, "culturally speaking, leaves nothing to be desired," but whose other activities left "practically *everything* to be desired."

Inevitably, the takedown started with *What's My Line?* It was the same accusation that Mike Wallace had made, but Hellman went further. With one word—"purportedly"—he cast a looming question mark over the legitimacy of the enterprise at a time when so many game shows were mired in corruption and scandal. Then, on to a scathing portrait of the "lecture-platform jester," followed by the "endorser." Here, he noted that his subject ordinarily endorsed "without remuneration," but neglected to include the cases of booze or station wagon. He'd done some homework, though, describing how Phyllis's embarrassment had led her to conspire with her friend and *Newsday* patron Alicia Patterson in sending anonymous letters to Bennett condemning the plugs as unbefitting a man of his standing. He also said Alfred Knopf had blasted Bennett for the endorsements, and from earliest acquaintance had thought of him as a kid. But although Knopf had also told Hellman that Bennett was a "sweet guy" whose company he always enjoyed, and that RH published good books and published them well, no hint of that appeared.

The first five pages of Part I were merely a preamble. The remaining twenty were devoted to demolishing the "Cerf joke factory." As an "escapist from culture," everything else Bennett did was "eclipsed" by the "collector of humor," and here the "descent from Olympus" grew precipitous. Bennett's own expressed qualms about the effect the joke books might be having on his reputation were quoted, first from *Anything for a Laugh* in 1946, then from *The Life of the Party* ten years later. Advice he gave in *Laughter Incorporated*'s "How Not to Tell a Story" was highlighted: "Don't tell your story more than once to the same audience." Yet an avalanche of examples showing that through cutting and pasting, that was exactly what Bennett had done time and again, followed. As for the "odd" pinning of stories onto authors or friends, Hellman was "hard put to recognize Mr. Klopfer, a serious, dignified man," in a story about Farmer Klopfer and his mule, complete with hokey dialect. Many more examples followed.

If by chance his contempt hadn't fully penetrated, at the conclusion of Part I he used Bennett's own words to administer the coup de grâce. It was disarming that his subject refused to take life or himself very seriously, Hellman wrote, and then quoted Bennett: "I've exploited a small talent to the maximum . . . but come to think of it, for a publisher this is a mixed blessing. It's dangerous to go out to lunch with an author and be more important than he is." *How dare you?* Hellman seemed to ask. Yet in this long first half, *he* had also committed the deadly sin Bennett had cautioned against in "How Not to Tell a Story," by repeating himself ad nauseam.

A week later Part II appeared, subtitled "Big Day for Random," a quote from Bennett's diary made on the day three RH authors won Pulitzers. Above it was another sketch of the horn-rims sans eyes: readers could now appreciate the visual shorthand for the empty man described in Part I. Bennett was more of a "catalytic agent" than a reader of weighty books, Hellman declared (the effect being to cast doubt on whether he read at all), yet facts and figures about the Modern Library and Random House were offered that could only speak in a positive light. So did key members of the firm, whose words contrasted sharply with the devastating portrait Hellman had conjured. For Bob Haas, Bennett's outside activities were on balance helpful, publicizing the firm "in the right way."

Don attested that during their thirty-four years together, they'd never had "a serious disagreement about policy or anything else important." His partner did a lot of kidding, but "gets a lot of work done." Allowing Saxe to speak from the grave, Hellman quoted him saying that he had the highest regard for his boss both as man and publisher. Bennett had "sure instincts," plus the ability to be guided by those really in the know, and in Saxe's estimation, he was "the best publisher in the world."

Instead of Part I's jokes, in Part II Hellman piled up quotes from Bennett's all-action, no-reflection diaries, making no attempt to reconcile the jester and diary-keeper with the man his partners, longtime editor, and accomplishments described. The voices of authors, booksellers, and other interested parties were also missing, or at least not quoted or identified as such. The profile's two halves didn't fit into a coherent whole; the reader was left to form his or her own conclusions—if that were indeed possible, given the dissonance.

As for what Bennett—who'd waited so long for this supposed triumph—felt, seeing himself in the magazine's mirror this way, that was disclosed in stages. "FIRST HALF OF MY *NEW YORKER* PROFILE OUT . . . LENGTHY & DULL," he rationalized in his diary on May 7. About a week later, after his Broadway friend Howard Lindsay had called the piece "the most childish thing I have ever read," Bennett replied, referring to its author: "You can't get around that old adage, 'Once a pompous, humorless bore, always a pompous, humorless bore.'" When Part II was published, he confided to his diary a measure of relief: "much more flattering." Soon Dorothy Commins wrote to say how touched she and her children were to read what had been said about Saxe, reiterating how Saxe had loved him. Now raw feeling finally burst through.

"When I read the paragraphs about Saxe in that otherwise horrible *New Yorker* profile, tears sprang into my eyes," Bennett confessed. Saxe, one of the few people he could have unburdened himself to, was especially missed now.

For those who fully understood the subtext and did not favor its subject, the profile proved piquant, enjoyably sour. A journalist friend of Hellman's called it "a masterpiece of smiling assassination." Alfred Knopf, not above enjoying a little schadenfreude, told Hellman: "What a pleasure it is to read a profile in the old original *New Yorker* style. Blanche and I both got a great kick out of the first installment. . . . What a researcher you are." Others took another tack. Bennett had been quoted about his pride in being "literary midwife" to *Ulysses,* and now a letter arrived for Hellman from Robert Kastor, his friendship with Bennett of a quarter century earlier having cooled. Although admitting that Cerf had shown "initiative, energy, enterprise," it was he himself who'd done the "literary midwifery," Kastor asserted, and then asked: "Do you think that I might receive a few shares of Random House or better yet . . . credit?"

The day after Part I appeared, Victor Weybright, New American Library's head, proposed to Hellman that he extend the profile and turn it into a slim book. Together, they could create a "real best seller," probably a paperback original, but perhaps a joint publication with a hardcover house: After all, who hadn't heard of Bennett Cerf? Executives at Coward-McCann and Thomas Nelson had also contacted Hellman, wanting to make a book from the articles.

Three weeks later, however, Weybright abruptly rescinded the offer. Bennett wasn't only famous: he was a powerful publisher who was very angry and knew how to communicate both. Weybright now informed Hellman that "under no circumstances" did he want to annoy Bennett, who from the start had sold him rights to some of RH's best writers. He'd thought extending the profile would be "just a little bit of good clean fun," but noted that Bennett felt it "a disservice," and Weybright carefully copied him on the letter. A handwritten note from a Coward-McCann executive to Hellman followed suit and was far blunter. Bennett had promised to "do everything in his power" to prevent publication of a book. If that didn't work, he would do everything to stop it *after* publication. Nobody wanted an ugly lawsuit. Besides, he was refusing permission to reprint the jokes or the diary entries, and without those, the project was impossible.

No book was published, sparing Bennett another round of excruciating embarrassment. Nonetheless, the hurt ran deep: the dreamed-of *New Yorker* triumph had turned into a travesty. In length, detail, and prominence it was far worse than the "Barnaby Chirp" that S. J. Perelman had skewered him with in the magazine fifteen years earlier. But perhaps the deepest hurt didn't come via Hellman or any of the others who'd taken pleasure in Bennett's pain. Although Hiram Haydn was a defender and saw the profile as an injustice, complaining to Hellman about the "distorted interpretation" of Bennett's nature, he allowed that the journalist had been "a careful assembler of facts." It was the element of truth—the reality of the "joke factory" Bennett had created—that carried the sharpest sting. Bennett himself had given Hellman those weapons, despite recognizing the danger years before. Not once, but twice, in his own books, as Hellman had reminded him, he'd said he would stop, but didn't. His first anthology's title was all too apt.

In his own defense, it wasn't as though the books—both humorous and otherwise—had assembled themselves. He'd had help, but nobody could deny that he worked terribly hard at night and on weekends putting the collections together, doing the tedious "slaving" his diary complained about. But "Bennett Cerf" had become a brand. There was the iron discipline, the habit, the goal of another book with his name on it, and also the money: the Cerfs did not live in the style to which they'd become accustomed courtesy of what he drew from RH. And he had plenty of takers: sales never equaled the first great wartime success, but they got him onto bestseller lists and would have been the envy of most authors. People liked the books and kept buying.

Bennett was nearly sixty-one, and if anything, age intensifies the strongest and weakest characteristics of human nature. It was too late to change, nor did he want to. He'd played the joker for so long, he'd become a natural. RH remained more important than all the rest, yet he'd admitted to Hellman that it would be "an awful blow" when the show went off the air and he'd be "just a publisher again," as Phyllis was wont to remind him. TV, endorsements, lectures, and joke books were all of a piece. As long as he could, he'd stare straight ahead and hug that lucky multi-lane highway that had brought celebrity and wealth. Paying tolls was the cost of the ride.

. . .

HELLMAN HAD CONCLUDED THE profile by giving Donald the last word: "At our age, it's foolish to do anything except for the fun of it. The only way we can make a hell of a lot of money is to sell the firm. But then we'd be through." It seemed a curiously hasty wrap-up, and something of a non sequitur, given what had gone before. Yet Don was providing a clue to a very different scenario from the one Hellman had constructed out of jokes and condescension. It was 1959, and for the past year and a half, as the pipe smoke swirled around them, the two partners had grappled with that most basic question: What was the future of Random House and their place in it? They still had energy, but retiring was inevitable, even if it didn't happen on the day each turned sixty-five.

Despite Bennett's much-bruited belief that his boys *had* to become publishers, if they did so, it would be a long way off. Chris's stellar performance at Deerfield had won him an honorary scholarship to Harvard for the fall; he'd be there for four years. RH staff had liked him during his summers working at the firm, but he was very young, and Jonathan younger still. The two partners also knew (despite Pat Klopfer's wish to the contrary) that Donald's stepson, Tony Wimpfheimer, wasn't destined to lead the firm. Tony knew the entire publishing process and was very orderly and highly skilled at production, but along with the talent and good heart came a heavy hand. He hid his own sensitivity beneath pushiness. Lately, Bennett, Don, Albert, and Jess Stein had had to hash out how to deal with it. Eventually, Tony would be an excellent managing editor and company officer, but never its head.

Most of the money Donald and Bennett made they'd always plowed back into the firm. They didn't have an objective way of putting a value on what they'd built. If one died with no fixed valuation in place, would the surviving partner have enough cash to buy out the other's widow? Besides, the current inheritance-tax structure could exact too heavy a price on Phyllis or Pat. At the same time, Random's public image had never been higher, revenues never greater, and the country was changing. Although 1958 had seen a worldwide recession, at home there was that post-*Sputnik* drive and funding for education. Since 1945, the U.S. economy's curve had been up, up, up. Companies were getting bigger, and bigger was better, the culture insisted.

A publishing house with an outstanding trade list; a reference department anchored in dictionaries; established, trusted series like the Modern Library; and a flourishing juvenile division—with the rocket booster of the Beginner Books connection—could really go somewhere, if joined with far more investment capital, a larger educational and institutional framework, and more young, business-savvy human capital. Other publishers, wanting to grow, calculated what RH—ranked the eighth largest of the major houses by *PW*—could bring to them.

The first corporation to come calling was McGraw-Hill, already traded as a public stock. In February 1958, Donald McGraw and several top executives had proposed a deal, recognizing that they needed more heft for their general books division. Talks ensued. However, that summer, Bennett's old friend Charles R. Allen Jr. had also knocked at the door. Bennett and Charlie had met as young men working in the cashier's cage on Wall Street. Since then, helped by his brothers, Charlie had founded and built Allen & Company, an investment banking house that was discreet, select, successful, and influential well beyond its size. He had a finger in many pies and presented several scenarios for an RH future in which he could arrange the financing. A third knock had come from Cleveland-based World Publishing Company, publisher of *Webster's New World Dictionary,* Bibles, and the paperback line Tower Books. Although Bennett found it "fun" to contemplate, he didn't consider the World merger offer all that seriously.

It was still 1958 when Allen began being go-between for Henry Holt, nearly a century old and publisher of Robert Louis Stevenson, Robert Frost, and *Field and Stream* magazine. Like McGraw, World, Macmillan, Houghton, and a few others, Holt was riding a wave alongside the larger houses: it had issued public stock. The Texas oilman who controlled it saw educational publishing as his next big bonanza. The first week in December, Holt offered $2 million in cash and $2 million in stock to buy RH, with the partners keeping the palazzo. Bennett felt a rush of pleasurable excitement, but "They'll do better!" he told himself. After all, RH's revenue that year would fall just short of $9 million. He and Don sought Bob Haas's advice, and Bob agreed it was best to bide time. They declined the offer. Holt upped it to $6 million, and sweetened it with a stock option gimmick that would bring it to $6.5 million. The answer was still no.

Bennett and Don were well aware that conducting business was becoming costlier, and growth required cash. RH now comprised 165 souls. The extra space the firm leased across town near Columbus Circle was on the edge of slums (an area being depicted in *West Side Story* on Broadway), and staff there were unhappy about their exile from the palazzo to the "cruddy fringe." Inside the Villard, with space reconfigured for Beginner at the top, offices further down were being renovated. Copy editors had moved to the former dining room, now partitioned into cubicles, with Bert Krantz in charge. Each "gal" (all were young women) was pleased to have been able to choose the paint color of the door leading to her cubicle. The first time Bennett swung by to see the result, he quipped to Krantz that it looked like "a high-class brothel." Rather more diplomatically, it was dubbed "the Rabbit Penn Warren" (the name that stuck).

Early in 1959, Holt made another proposition, one recognizing Bennett's unique status in the world beyond publishing, guaranteed to appeal to his vanity: if the partners agreed to sell, Bennett would become president of the merged company. It was tempting, but his friend Charlie counseled against accepting: he had another idea. Allen & Co. wanted to engineer a public stock offering equal to a third of RH's value, essentially the portion that Bennett and Don had had to buy back from Bob Haas with loans and personal savings when Bob retired. Doing so, Allen estimated, would raise $2 to $2.5 million in cash for the pair. By spinning off this minority stake, they'd retain control; each would gain a swift payday, and the possibility of income growth from stock value increases; and RH would have a mechanism for raising more capital as needed. By the end of March, Allen had put the offer in writing, and two days before the first part of the *New Yorker* profile landed, Bennett and Charlie shook hands. It would require months to work through details, with lawyers and the Securities and Exchange Commission having their say.

RH's banker, George C. Textor, president of the Marine Midland Trust Company, had worked closely with Allen & Co., and would sit on the new board, as would Charlie. Bennett would be president; Donald, executive VP; and Tony, company secretary, with the three keeping a controlling stake of 63.4 percent of total outstanding shares after the offering was completed (Don would cede some equity to increase Tony's share). The two partners signed five-year contracts, agreeing to stay until July 31, 1964, just after Bennett turned sixty-six. He'd remain first among equals, with a salary of $60,000, versus Don's $53,000. Each man's annual allowance for travel and expenses was capped at $10,000. Lew Miller, Manny Harper, and Bob Haas would comprise the rest of the board. Bob Bernstein, Louise Bonino, Jason Epstein, Albert Erskine, Ray Freiman, and Jess Stein would have shares, and become RH vice presidents.

On October 1, 1959, a detailed prospectus was issued by Allen & Co., and the following day, 222,060 shares of common stock in Random House Inc. were put on sale to the public at $11.25 per share (totaling about eleven times company earnings for the fiscal year). In market terms the transaction was relatively small, and so for ease of initial issue, the stock would be traded "over the counter" rather than listed on the New

PROSPECTUS

222,060 Shares

Random House, Inc.

COMMON STOCK
(Par Value $1.00 Per Share)

The shares offered by this Prospectus are being sold by certain stockholders named under "Selling Stockholders". The Company will receive none of the proceeds.

THESE SECURITIES HAVE NOT BEEN APPROVED OR DISAPPROVED BY THE SECURITIES AND EXCHANGE COMMISSION NOR HAS THE COMMISSION PASSED UPON THE ACCURACY OR ADEQUACY OF THIS PROSPECTUS. ANY REPRESENTATION TO THE CONTRARY IS A CRIMINAL OFFENSE.

	Price to Public	Underwriting Discounts and Commissions(1)	Proceeds to Selling Stockholders(2)
Per Share	$11.25	$1.25	$10.00
Total	$2,498,175	$277,575	$2,220,600

(1) Arrangements have been made for indemnification of the Underwriter against certain liabilities and to reimburse the Underwriter in the amount of $10,000. for its expenses. Of the 222,060 shares being offered, 25,000 shares are first being offered to certain employees of the Company by the Underwriter at a price of $10. per share plus applicable stamp taxes and costs not to exceed 50¢ per share (See "Underwriting" herein).

(2) Before deduction of expenses of the Selling Stockholders in the estimated amount of $58,000.

These shares are being offered by the Underwriter named herein, subject to the approval of certain legal matters by Messrs. Holtzmann, Wise & Shepard, Counsel for the Underwriter and by Messrs. Weil, Gotshal & Manges, Counsel for the Selling Stockholders and the Company. It is expected that delivery of the shares to the Underwriter will take place in New York City on or about October 7, 1959, against payment therefor in New York funds.

ALLEN & COMPANY

Dated: October 1, 1959

York or American stock exchange. Future listing on one of the two Big Boards was a goal Bennett aspired to, harking back to his youth. Twenty-five thousand shares were withheld for offer at a discounted price, $10 per share, to RH employees. An option for 10 percent of those shares was granted to Lew Miller in recognition of his key service. Employees voted overwhelming confidence in the firm by subscribing more than twice the number of shares offered to them, so each subscription had to be halved.

Don immediately recouped about $950,000 from the sale; Tony, just under $200,000. The value of the chunk of stock Bennett sold rewarded him with a full seven figures, making him well and truly a millionaire from Random House alone. Pasting a photostat of the certified Allen & Co. check for $1,064,667.78 into his clipping book, he joked wonderingly, "BUT MONEY ISN'T EVERYTHING . . . !!!!" Nathan Wise, while no doubt approving of this development, would have expressed himself rather more seriously than his still-impertinent grandson.

It was essential that the creators of the intellectual property—the foundation for everything—be apprised of the new reality as swiftly as possible. "I like to think of you as a member of the inner Random House family," Bennett began a letter to RH authors, in which he described the reasons for a stock issue and enclosed the prospectus. The important thing was that he and Don would keep "complete control" of the firm. "We see no cloud whatever on the horizon," he ended, inviting them to get in touch. Walter Farley, creator of the *Black Stallion* series, had questions, since he wanted to buy stock: As one of the "family," could he do so at the employees' discount? Could he obtain an option to buy more later? Was he to buy through RH? This, too, was a vote of confidence, but naively, these were not questions that Bennett and Donald had anticipated.

"Good God, man, we didn't send you the prospectus . . . with the idea of your buying [stock]!" Donald told Farley, explaining it could only be bought through a broker. "Whether this would be a wise or a silly thing to do, I do not know," he added, carefully.

Everything about RH was so personal to the two men who'd founded it. Perhaps they hadn't fully foreseen the "big change," as Bennett put it, the feelings that would shadow them about the fluctuations inherent in other people's buying and selling stock in their firm. By law they were mandated to make periodic reports, and by their own sense of pride and code of decency and honor, they felt they owed their investors dividends and profits. "Instead of working for yourself and doing what you damn please, willing to risk a loss on something you want to do, if you're any kind of honest man, you feel a real responsibility to your stockholders," Bennett recognized. Suddenly, he and Don would be "publishing with one eye and watching our stock with the other." What would happen if people *lost* money by trusting and investing in them?

That didn't seem likely. As Bennett recorded in his diary (having followed stocks for years in his scribblings, he could no more refrain from chronicling RH's share price than not record baseball scores or how many columns he'd completed), the value just kept rising. What had started as $11.25 per share at the beginning of October closed at $20.50 on December 2.

They could hardly believe it, but before the year was out, they'd turn to Allen's services again. Warren Blaisdell, with a good track record editing science, math, and engineering texts for Boston's Addison-Wesley—a type of publishing they knew nothing about—wanted to set up a company. On December 30, Bennett shook hands with Blaisdell: RH would buy an 80 percent stake in his eponymous new firm. A "fantastic" year was ending with sales of $13.5 million. As *Variety* said, Wall Street had decided book publishers were "the new blue chips." Let *The New Yorker* make of Bennett what it would: people could judge for themselves. Everything was public now.

Chapter 36

Two Acts, One Finale

WALL STREET'S DALLIANCE WITH THE BOOK BUSINESS, SPURRED BY all those lovely federal education dollars, was only half responsible for pushing up RH's stock price. The other force driving demand was the high profile the firm was enjoying, helped by a fall 1959 list that Bennett and Don judged stellar. It included novels by William Faulkner, Robert Penn Warren, Irwin Shaw, and Harold L. "Doc" Humes (RH's answer to the Beat writers, Humes was also a founder of *The Paris Review*), as well as a debut that made Bennett proud: Lorraine Hansberry's *A Raisin in the Sun,* the first drama by an African American woman on Broadway. The day after seeing, along with Don and Bob Loomis, her urgent portrait of Black family life, he phoned the young writer and persuaded her to let him publish the "fine" play. There was money coming in from more Shirley Temple and a new Seuss, yet when Bennett reflected on the year, he singled out two books from two favored authors: James Michener's historically and paginally epic *Hawaii,* and Moss Hart's poignant yet antic autobiography, *Act One,* chronicling the struggle leading to first success.

For years Michener had desperately wanted to write a large-scale book about the islands, and in 1954 had outlined the novel, but two projects intervened. First was *Rascals in Paradise,* the collection of character portraits he wrote with his University of Hawaii co-author A. Grove Day. An entirely unexpected idea came next, born of a crisis that had erupted in October 1956, when Hungary rose up against the Soviets who'd controlled it since the end of World War II. The first serious attempt by an Eastern Bloc nation to reassert its independence, the revolt was crushed after only six days, and Michener, who'd never stop thinking of himself as a journalist as well as a novelist, felt impelled to act. He flew to Vienna and traveled to the Austria–Hungary border in mid-

November, stationing himself near a bridge where thousands were fleeing their homeland. For six weeks he interviewed hundreds of refugees, and the result was *The Bridge at Andau*. But instead of hewing strictly to fact, he melded reportage with fiction techniques, altering details and using composite portraits to protect identities. Shortly before the text arrived from Europe, Bennett praised Michener: he had an "uncanny genius" for being first out with a work on the most critical topic of the moment. Harking back to RH's all-hands-on-deck wartime days, he promised the firm would be as fast as its author, and ensure the book got the notice it deserved, to show the world the "true face" of Communism and demolish the "great Russian lie."

Back in New York in January, Michener worked intensively with Erskine and Krantz on the manuscript, and by early March 1957, *The Bridge at Andau* was in stores. Its appeal was instant and widespread: six European countries and Japan licensed rights, and the U.S. Information Agency, seeing useful Cold War propaganda, arranged for Korean, Chinese, and Arabic editions. That the text had very few errors and was far improved over his original was "a great tribute" to the entire RH staff, Michener declared, and dedicated the book to Erskine.

Now he could turn to the big one: *Hawaii*. It would be career-altering, and set the model for what readers would come to expect from "a Michener": a work of great breadth focused on a particular place, with layers of historical and on-site research underpinning an action-packed fictional framework, often across multiple generations. Michener placed great value on his time, and quickly enlisted A. Grove Day to find him a local researcher. This, too, would be part of the template: although he'd always experience firsthand the locales he depicted, he'd delegate some legwork to others. Michener's plan was for the novel to have five parts, ranging across the entirety of Hawaii's human story, plus a prelude about its natural history. Eighteen months later, in September 1958, he sent Erskine the first part, about the early Polynesians and *Haoles* (whites), and Albert liked what he read, seeing that Michener, by putting his imagination in control of the facts, had avoided being buried by "historical baggage."

The work of turning the mammoth 1,321-page typescript—with its many time frames, plotlines, and characters—into a polished book would fall to Erskine, closely assisted by Krantz. Both had read the draft, but would now burrow through, checking for consistency and coherence, and working with the author to ensure that characters weren't left dangling and narrative holes were repaired. With excitement cresting about Hawaii becoming the fiftieth state on August 21, 1959, Bennett aimed to publish in September, the schedule again very tight. Erskine cajoled Michener to make the long journey from Honolulu to collaborate over final revisions, promising that it would take six weeks maximum. He worried about having to peel away for a week to work with Bill Faulkner, who was due for a visit, but an unlucky break on Faulkner's part—thrown from a horse, he fractured his collarbone—kept him at home, and was a lucky break for *Hawaii*.

Michener never liked to linger in the city, and already knew that RH, in the person of Jean Ennis, would call on him again at publication to promote the book. Though some authors gobbled publicity opportunities like bonbons, Michener found the "exacting routine" of direct interaction with readers hard, and could only do so much. Nonetheless, he knew of too many talented writers tethered to houses not headed by a man like Bennett, with his drive and instinct for reaching the public. Although those standards might wear a writer thin, Michener had too often seen the alternative—a "desolation" other authors experienced elsewhere at being published "in absolute silence"—and so, professional that he was, did what he had to do.

When Bennett read the whole novel, he thought *Hawaii* "great!" Certainly, it was one of those charmed books where all fell into place—reprint rights, condensation, excerpts, feature stories. The big news was the "just about unprecedented" film deal agented by Helen Strauss, with a $600,000 guarantee against 10 percent of the profits. Flanked by film executives, Bennett announced a related agreement to the press: the studios would work with RH on a $100,000 joint campaign to keep the book in the public eye until the movie's release a few years later. And yet he observed with a tinge of regret that publishing was following a pattern set by movies and TV: while big books by well-known authors were bigger than ever, you couldn't give away a first novel, a situation that was "too bad for the culture of the country, but great for someone like Michener." Other publishers have occasionally acknowledged a similar ambivalence about the cultural space their biggest-selling authors take up (if not quite admitting to the sheer amount of investment they concentrate in that small circle), but few are willing to say it so openly. Luckily, Michener was an author who did care about those unknown novelists.

Despite being delayed until November to accommodate the Book-of-the-Month Club's schedule, *Hawaii* managed to be the third-biggest fiction bestseller of 1959, and would be the second biggest of 1960. *Time* pointed to one reason: though Michener's characters weren't deep, they moved fast, "through an incredible gauntlet" that included tidal waves, human sacrifices, volcanic eruptions, and more—enabling readers to get lost in the world he created while turning pages at a clip.

James Michener, Albert Erskine, and Bert Krantz at work

From *Hawaii* on, accepted practice would be broken, new molds set, and a relationship between writer, publisher, and very big money play out over forty-four books. Michener became the prototype of the brand-name author, and spent the rest of his productive years in service to books and travel. From *Hawaii* and successors like *The Source, Caravans, Centennial,* and more—bestsellers all—readers learned much history, most pretty accurate. It wasn't the high literature he'd aspired to, but no matter: to the job of storytelling, he brought a self-consciously strong code of civic responsibility, and the moral imperative of a former teacher to enlighten fellow citizens. He opened the eyes of countless Americans as well as others around the globe, at a time when fewer attended college, travel was beyond their means, and the internet didn't exist.

So long as tax-law ceilings meant that a large portion of Michener's earnings on any one book remained in an escrow account controlled by Random House, and RH could use the interest it generated, the firm's cash flow benefitted. He joined O'Hara and Geisel in a charmed trio whose sales were so predictably good that they could be counted on, along with the ML, to keep RH afloat in good seasons and bad. After only fifteen months, his earned royalty on *Hawaii* was more than $375,000, and RH's net profit $400,000-plus. Everyone had done fabulously well—and the film hadn't even been released. When it was, much delayed, in 1966, paperbacks had taken over, but the hardcover hadn't died. Bennett would later call Michener "the ideal author," who trusted RH and knew that the publisher "has his function, and he has his."

The deprivation of Michener's childhood had inspired a great carefulness and frugality that verged on tightfistedness, but at the same time a specific generosity. He had a strong business sense, and with the money earned from books and the income streams they fed, he incorporated tax-efficient companies, becoming, in effect, "Michener Inc." A portion of this money went to support children fathered by American servicemen in Asia, and to fund about 150 college scholarships, some for children of journalists who'd covered the Korean War. In an utterly unconventional arrangement, Erskine—whose knack for the stock market rivaled his talent for books—invested and managed the money that went into those scholarships, at one point almost $900,000. (Erskine received a cut.) Such openhandedness contrasted starkly with how emotionally closed Michener could be: he'd adopted a half Asian, half Caucasian orphaned baby with his second wife, but when they divorced and he married Mari, a Japanese American (this third marriage would last), the boy seemed to disappear from his life.

Assessments vary as to how much Michener would earn for himself and his publisher during his career, and how much he'd give away. In the 1990s, one estimate figured he'd already disbursed at least $100 million in charity. The lawyer who worked with him on estate planning at the end of his long life reckoned his philanthropy totaled "$175 million or more, and his giving was never tax-motivated." Grants to students, artists, poets, fiction writers, and writing programs (he wanted what became the Michener Center at the University of Texas *not* to be named after him), as well as museums, colleges, and universities, continued well beyond his death in 1997. James Michener exemplified how a writer could use the vast resources his popularity generated to change people's lives, individually and communally, for the better.

. . .

MICHENER MAY HAVE BEEN the "ideal author," but for Bennett, Moss Hart was rarer still. "I like people, but I seldom give my love very generously because I'm just too self-centered," Bennett acknowledged about himself. He recognized that, for the most part, he spent his days collecting acquaintances, far too many to foster intimacy. Only a few did he truly love, and among them he loved Moss with all his heart. Although insisting that Donald was the best friend he ever had, as time passed, the family saw a lot more of Moss than Don, and Kitty was one of Phyllis's closest friends, putting the Harts among a select few at the social center of the Cerfs' lives.

Kitty Carlisle Hart

It was through Kitty that Bennett came to judge the Miss America contest. With clothes mainly chosen for her by her husband, for years she'd decorated the country's "best-dressed" lists, and in 1956 had joined the panel of *To Tell the Truth,* a sister show to *What's My Line?* It wasn't surprising that in 1957 she was invited to judge the annual extravaganza, and the next year Moss, Bennett, and Phyllis conspired to join her among the judges in Atlantic City, all expenses paid by the pageant. As much a symbol of summer's end as Labor Day, the contestants paraded across TV screens into America's homes, a shared national ritual. The quartet had "a marvelous time," Kitty recalled, but the experience was rather more complicated.

One girl from the South, inspired by the prospect of statehood for Alaska and Hawaii, proposed that the United States could "solve" its problems by setting up another new state, sending "all the colored people there. That would make them happy and then we could all be happy." Phyllis hadn't wanted *that* girl to represent America to the world, she informed readers of her *Newsday* column, and judged accordingly. Then there was the *Time* magazine reporter who dropped by the Harts and Cerfs' cabana. The conversation, he reported, went like this: Phyllis lamenting no decent candidates; Kitty boasting that her legs were shapelier than the contestants'; Bennett wondering, "Do you think they're all certified virgins?" Letters flooded in: Bennett had insulted the candidates' chastity with a remark not befitting a man welcomed into the nation's homes. He had to apologize to officials and sponsors, but internally he seethed: private "badinage" had been leaked. The *Time* piece ended by quoting Moss, who'd thought the junket dubious from the start: "We're God's fools," he'd proclaimed, not knowing how right he was.

Indeed, Moss always seemed to deliver the precise bon mot, or be able to assess what was wrong in a situation and right it. Bennett's admiration knew no bounds: Within the vast net of extraordinary individuals who comprised his acquaintanceship, he felt Moss was in many ways "the most remarkable." With brilliance, charisma, a rags-to-riches story, he seemed the living, breathing embodiment of the theater, enacting a life Bennett might have wished for himself. If O'Neill stood atop the dramatic pantheon, Moss symbolized, as super-agent Swifty Lazar said, "the glamour, wit and charm of Broadway at its popular best." Donald would come to judge that Bennett "liked Moss better than any other person"; they shared "the same joy of living," a rare exuberance so foreign to Don's contemplative self. When Moss was up, no one was merrier, and RH staff, seeing Bennett and him laughing together, thought they "seemed like brothers." However, in certain respects they were an odd match. Moss could be acidly cutting, and Bennett had a thin skin. Bennett fled introspection, whereas for years Moss had been in analysis, preoccupied by his demons, and could slide into paralyzing depressions. That Moss had described Bennett to *The New Yorker*'s Hellman as having "no self-doubt" and as "God's happy man" wasn't surprising, given that the insecurities Bennett revealed to Bubbles Hornblow he'd never show to Moss; nor did Moss look deeply enough to perceive them.

But their shared traits counted for more: the drive to be someone and accomplish great things; an appetite for the work that would get them there, work that flowed into play; and a love for, and dedication to, the story—whether in trimming and recasting their own lives, or in the calling each pursued. One other commonality: rootedness in New York. "The only credential the city asked was the boldness to dream. For those who did, it unlocked its gates and treasures, not caring who they were or where they came from," Moss would write. Decades earlier, Bennett, the boy-man who'd sworn to Dick Simon that he'd become one of the important publishers in America, had pledged that credo just as viscerally. Kitty marveled that a man who'd started from circumstances so much less deprived than her husband's and their friends' should have burned with that same hunger. In the end, both (as well as Phyllis and Kitty) willed themselves to chance their luck and *be* lucky in the "Wonder City."

Moss Hart

Going back to the '30s, Moss had spun autobiographical tales in an almost "incantatory" fashion, reminding friends exactly how far he'd come—just as, from at least Columbia on, Bennett had broadcast anecdote after jokey anecdote to anyone who'd listen. For each, the practice seemed talismanic, a way to ward off anything bad. In 1941, Moss had talked of turning his stories into a book; later, of transforming them into a musical play. Nothing stuck. Then, in 1953, Kitty contracted meningitis, and the crisis seemed to push him into putting words on paper. A few months later, when the two couples celebrated the new year in Miami, he pulled out a sheaf of pages and read Bennett—"performed" is more accurate—the beginning of his autobiography. That summer, Moss had a heart attack. While recuperating, he worked on the book, and by the end of September gave Bennett four more chapters. A crisis of confidence and depression descended—he wanted to throw it out—but Kitty and the Cerfs wouldn't let him.

The distraction of *My Fair Lady* intervened. During winter and early spring tryouts, "readings" recommenced, delivered to cast members. More pages dribbled in, but depression descended again. Bennett kept encouragement coming, and Phyllis, who knew all about persistence, seemed able to tunnel through to Moss better than most. The two would have dinner and talk so intensely, they'd lose track of time. It was not for nothing that Bennett often used her as first reader. In January 1957, at Moss's most hopeless, she urged in a long letter that he "must go on," outlining specific suggestions for when he felt able to go into "the lonely room" to write the last third, as though punching her thoughts through the black ribbon onto paper would imprint them on his mind. So prone to doling out criticism, she could also be fiercely loyal, and insisted that his had "all the elements of the book that will live," a profound vote of confidence. "This book, dearest Phyl, owes a great deal to you," Moss would later acknowledge.

Soon Bennett persuaded him to hole up at Mt. Kisco, and writing resumed. Thanksgiving 1958 was less than a week away when Moss delivered a manuscript, and the Cerfs and Harts celebrated, dancing the night away at El Morocco. As the zebra-striped walls swirled around them, the four friends, intoxicated by friendship, the triumph of endurance, and oh yes, flutes of champagne, were sure that Moss had created something special. More revelry took place in Miami in February, and then at Round Hill in Jamaica, where the Hornblows joined them.

Once back in New York, Bennett planned the publishing campaign while Erskine and Krantz edited. Moss came in one day to work with Krantz, and at a certain point they were struggling to find the mot juste. Other copy editors toiling in the Rabbit Penn Warren overheard. Suddenly, a twenty-five-year-old new hire, Nan Ahearn, trilled "erstwhile!" over her cubicle wall and solved the problem. Moss was "enchanted" by the girl with the lovely voice—or so Bennett recalled. Certainly *he* was, and in a few years the now married, very talented Nan A. Talese would become the first female home-grown editor to achieve any kind of status at RH. In truth, given how important Moss was to Bennett, many staff touched the book en route to publication.

Reprising the tactic he'd used for Gertrude and a few others, the back cover was filled with a signed letter from Bennett promising readers that Moss's life "has had more zest and dazzle, more of the heartbreak of poverty and the glitter of success, than any of his work in the theatre." Publication took place mid-September, but the black-tie book party for the ages was held Friday, October 23, to coincide (just about) with Moss's birthday. Festivities began at seven sharp, with a screening in the MGM projection room (Bennett's board seat came in handy) of *Once in a Lifetime,* Moss's first success with George S. Kaufman. The party moved on to Leone's, the theater-district hangout, where red-checked tablecloths, Chianti, and dinner awaited. A hundred and fifty friends turned out, a banquet of Hollywood, Broadway, and the West End, from Sir John Gielgud and Marlene Dietrich to Ed Sullivan and Ethel Merman. Simone Signoret and Yves Montand added a *je ne sais quoi*. "If something had happened to the restaurant that night, the theater would have ended . . . because everybody . . . was at [the] party," Bennett chuckled. Moss had staged the evening, rehearsing to perfection like the drill sergeant he was.

Howard Dietz and Arthur Schwartz contributed a one-act play, *The Story of* <u>*Act One*</u>*;* Adolph Green and Betty Comden (*On the Town, Singin' in the Rain*) wrote a number, as did composer/lyricist Harold Rome. Mel Brooks and Mel Tolkin, young TV writers from Sid Caesar's already legendary *Your Show of Shows,* devised a routine in which Brooks played a world-famous Freudian analyst from the "Vienna School of Good Luck." His "luck" had brought him a fortune via his patient Moss. Shocking, the thoughts a "nice Jewish boy" came up with! Kitty, Phyllis, Arlene Francis, and Rome's wife, Florence, danced and sang "He's the top! He's a Lindy waiter. He's the top! He's a borscht potato," a parody written by Moss himself to Cole Porter's "You're the Top." Then Bennett, Arlene's husband Marty, Adolph Green, and Moss donned costumes reminiscent of *My Fair Lady*'s market women. Brandishing mops and pails, they became cleaning ladies servicing Random and other publishers while belting out "Oh, the Literary Life!," another Hart creation. Each chorus celebrated that night's "pickings" in the form of manuscripts that had been trashed. For the finale, they spun around and bowed, revealing white-aproned derrieres spelling out ACT ONE. The audience exploded in whoops and claps.

The Cerfs made it home at four in the morning. Letter after letter declared the gathering "the best party ever," certainly "bigger and better than any I'd ever gone to," Mel Brooks recalled. Two weeks later, sales had reached 87,000 copies, and most reviews were great.

"I know it seems absurd to . . . write you a formal letter," Moss began a note to his publisher. In all the "hullabaloo" surrounding the party, he'd neglected to thank Bennett for giving it. But even if he had, Moss declared, it wasn't a big enough acknowledgment, "because, certainly it was one of the great nights of my life." In one sense it was all part of the book's publication, but in another, he added, "it was not that at all, but an expression of your friendship, which as you know, I treasure." And it was even more than that. Moss profoundly believed in "the healing power of parties." Clearly, so did his publisher. The evening hadn't just been a celebration of Moss's life, but of life itself. More healing, alas, would soon be necessary.

That fall, Moss was already deep in discussions with Lerner and Loewe for a new show to follow *My Fair Lady,* well on its way to becoming the biggest Broadway musical ever. While Moss had added the success of *Act One,* Lerner and Loewe had put together the movie blockbuster *Gigi*. Expectations for *Camelot,* the trio's next collaboration—a musical retelling of the King Arthur–Guinevere–Lancelot love triangle, with Julie Andrews, Richard Burton, and a newcomer, Robert Goulet—couldn't have been higher.

Everything seemed to go wrong from the start. When the tryout opened in Toronto in the fall of 1960, the show proved to be a lumbering four and a half hours and in need of major surgery, but Lerner was rushed to the hospital with a nervous breakdown and bleeding ulcer, leaving Moss as sole script doctor. The stress proved too great: as Lerner was discharged, Moss was admitted to the hospital, after a second coronary. "MUCH FRANTIC PHONE CALLING," Bennett's diary said that mid-October day. A month later, a *Daily News* photographer caught Moss, gaunt and gray, at Grand Central Terminal being carried on a stretcher off a train from Canada. Bennett and Phyllis were the first friends to visit. Lerner, still shaky, had again taken charge, and when *Camelot* opened on December 3, reviews were not kind.

The Harts spent New Year's Eve with the Cerfs and Hornblows at Mt. Kisco. When Moss turned in *Act One,* Bennett had made one calculated change: at the book's close, he replaced his friend's words "The End" with "Intermission." Many critics and reporters had taken note, hoping along with Bennett that Moss would write a sequel, but in interviews he'd been coy, although once allowing: "I should write 'Act Two.' . . . There's a need for a book on the anatomy of success . . . particularly one that probes the mystery of human unhappiness—the unhappiness of a successful man." On that last night of December, looking back on what had happened and contemplating what might come, he told Bennett that he'd do the sequel. More urgently, in the new year he set about radically revising *Camelot*. Helped by a boost from Ed Sullivan, who featured a segment on his variety program in March, Moss saved it. Overnight, the show turned into a hit, but Moss still looked dreadful.

He'd enjoyed previous visits to Palm Springs, and, knowing how the desert had helped Fritz Loewe after his heart attack, Moss impulsively bought a house there—but not just for a vacation. In December, as soon as the private school term finished, the Harts upended their lives and moved west: they'd do anything to restore his health, even if it meant exile. They'd seen Bennett and Phyllis briefly at Thanksgiving, and the Cerfs consoled themselves by promising to spend their February break in California. Meanwhile, their busy days and nights took over.

On Wednesday, December 20, the RH switchboard operator buzzed Bennett: Mr. Hart was on the line. He was delighted, expecting the usual kibbitzing insult, but a few seconds later Bennett realized that he'd misunderstood: the voice was Kitty's.

"Moss just dropped dead," she announced, a quake reverberating across thousands of miles. He'd suffered a third coronary.

Scrambling to arrange tickets, the Cerfs boarded a jet for L.A. the next evening. When they landed, the city was shrouded in "fantastic" fog, the worst in a dozen years, conspiring with Bennett's emotions to render the whole thing surreal. A limousine deposited them in Palm Springs at 3 A.M. Swifty Lazar, Frank Sinatra, Harpo Marx, and others congregated at the house prior to the funeral at 1 P.M. In the afternoon, they talked over plans for a memorial to take place at the Music Box Theatre in Manhattan in January. When the Cerfs returned to New York on Christmas Eve, grief overwhelmed them. Back at the office, they went through the motions, not hiding their tears. *Act One* had touched everyone: everything stopped. RH cried with them.

Kitty came east to prepare for the memorial, and stayed at Sixty-Second Street; she'd do so again when organizing the move back from California. She lay low in a guest room, unable to face people, and "would wait up, then sit on the stairs" like a small girl when she heard Bennett and Phyllis return. They'd tell her about the parties and their friends. Kitty eventually wrote a will specifying that if anything happened to her, the Cerfs would be legal guardians of her children.

Bennett, among those chosen to speak at the memorial, told the packed crowd on January 9: "In my thirty-eight years in the publishing business, I never have seen an author derive such unalloyed delight from a bestseller. . . . To hear the relish with which he read his fan mail to me over the phone each morning was to understand what fun can be had in this life by a man who knows how to live it." But now Moss was dead at fifty-seven, and Bennett shaken to his core at sixty-three. No joke could shield him from the loss of one so dear, let alone his own mortality.

There would never be an *Act Two*.

PART FIVE

1960–1971

Real Business

Publishing . . . is both a profession and a business, and that is not unlike being a tortoise attempting to swim on land and walk on the water. . . . It is almost as difficult to practice as democracy.

—Hiram Haydn, in a talk to the Publishers' Ad Club, October 7, 1959

The publishing business has suddenly become real business.

—Bennett Cerf, on THE OPEN MIND, *NBC TV, November 13, 1960*

He loved doing the show, but publishing came first. It was his preoccupation, his vocation, his life.

—Stanley Kauffmann, recalling Bennett Cerf and a 1960 conversation

He was such a bright guy, how could he have done a thing like that to himself?

—Jerome Weidman in 1986, quoting Bennett Cerf in the late 1960s

Chapter 37

Knopfs

Alfred and Blanche Knopf and friends

THE MAN ACROSS THE TABLE FROM BENNETT AT THE AMBASSADOR Hotel was sixty-five years old, crowned with snow-white hair—what was left of it—and flushed with a wine lover's florid face. Below the balding pate, dark bushy brows and a big nose rose above a magnificent dapple-gray moustache. Alfred A. Knopf, no longer the "Persian prince" of youth, still cut an impressive figure, his barrel chest armored in the brightly colored shirt and tie that from the start demanded attention while also shielding shyness. In Bennett's eyes, Alfred was beyond question his better. Although he'd absorbed so much from Horace Liveright, whom Alfred had detested, he'd consciously chosen Knopf as model when he and Don began. Knopf's publishing never ceased to be an exemplar.

"He had taste, he knew books, and he had integrity," is how Bennett summed up the man he considered "probably the greatest publisher of our era." Alfred's insistence on excellence in design and manufacture was legend, and to early distinguished authors like Willa Cather and H. L. Mencken, the firm had added John Hersey, Raymond Chandler, Albert Camus, Jean-Paul Sartre, illustrious historians, et al. Long-dead Kahlil Gibran was an immortal source of cash flow, and rivals coveted Knopf's backlist for quality and solid (if less spectacular) sales.

Mr. Cerf and Mr. Knopf were at a familiar haunt on that last day of September 1957, meeting for one of their regular lunches. Bennett gabbed as usual on his subjects du jour: perhaps the incredibly productive Michener, or was it Moss Hart's struggle with writer's block? (Moss's psychiatrist, everyone knew, was Knopf's cousin.) But the talk from Alfred's end was far from ordinary. For two hours he served up sour fare about the curdled relations between his wife and son. Alfred's airing of troubles to a gossipy man who avoided emotional undertow wasn't as odd as it might seem. Bennett was able to put him at ease, and, when it counted, could be trusted to be a man of honor. Further, his sorry tale was hardly a shock: strains in that family were well known, and yet unburdening himself at such length showed how bad the situation had become.

Blanche had taken over nominal presidency of the firm, but most power rested absolutely with Alfred, as it had since they'd started in business forty-two years earlier. Whatever else was involved, a mutual fixation on books had sparked the early connection between the good-looking, standoffish youth and the smart girl with gray-green eyes. Trouble in the marriage had arrived early. Blanche would claim that her Austrian Jewish family hadn't favored the match, feeling themselves socially superior to the Polish Jewish Knopfs. Alfred Jr.—"Pat"—was born in 1918, but Blanche had no intention of staying home with a baby. In that place and time, it was highly unusual for a young married upper-middle-class Jewish woman with a child to lay claim to the outside life and career she desired. Through force of will she asserted herself, but it was not easy. Each workday, Blanche had to put up with Alfred's domineering father, Sam, the company treasurer. Until his demise in 1932, "S.K." was capable of "scaring to death" *male* staff, yet Alfred desperately wanted to please him. Later, he'd look back and say Blanche had "all the chutzpah in the world" and a fine "nose" for talent, but rules were stacked against her.

The problems went even deeper. Alfred's mother had killed herself when he was small, and he'd been raised by a stepmother with little warmth. Emotional and sexual incompatibility corroded his and Blanche's relationship, and she'd attempted suicide in 1921. Four years later, Blanche confessed to family friend Carl Van Vechten that she was "tired of sleeping" with her husband. One child was more than enough; dalliances would be pursued elsewhere. While they entertained together for bibulous weekend lunches at the "Hovel," the house where Alfred preferred to live in Westchester, Blanche's weeknights were spent at an elegant city apartment, useful for parties, intimate evenings, and, when he was a bachelor, reading with Bennett.

The Knopfs would do anything to advance the publishing house at the center of each of their lives, but their sense of partnership did not extend to their son. Neither parent knew how to give affection. Mostly Blanche was otherwise engaged. Although Pat worshipped Alfred as Alfred had worshipped S.K., the boy was bullied by him. Shunted to boarding school at seven, Pat would confess to an interviewer at fifty-three that Alfred had never told him "I love you."

In the summer of 1937, nineteen-year-old Pat failed to be admitted to Princeton, and was afraid to face his parents. He jumped on a train, ending up "barefoot, hungry, and broke" at a police station in Salt Lake City. The Knopfs were alerted and wired funds for him to return. Emotionally unable to deal with what had happened, Alfred years later downplayed the episode, declaring his son "none the worse" for it. Pat did graduate from Union College, but not the Ivy League his parents had expected. When war came, he joined the army air corps and was sent to Alabama for training before shipping abroad. One day he was surprised to be summoned to talk with his father. "Your mother wants to divorce me," Alfred, brusque as usual, informed him. (It transpired that Blanche had fallen hard for a German émigré.) Pat sensed his father was still in love with his mother, but had spent decades "scared to death of showing it." He "had a feeling" Alfred would agree to a divorce if he, Pat, favored it, but like countless children of unhappy marriages, he wanted his parents to stay together. In the end, Alfred offered to divorce Blanche if she left the firm, knowing it was the one thing she'd never do. The Knopfs remained yoked—*their* decision—however responsible Pat may have felt for it.

Bravely flying scores of bombing missions against terrible odds, he achieved the rank of captain, but credit remained thin at home. When Pat returned, he made a place for himself at the firm. He understood production, was a fine salesman, and had good instincts: he was the one to see the change Jason Epstein started with Anchor, and respond by creating Vintage. But one day he and Blanche disagreed over a design; their voices grew louder until it wasn't about a book. "You ruined my life once; you'll never get a chance to ruin it again!" his mother exploded.

It's likely those hard words detonated in 1952, a turning point. Pat, at thirty-four, wanted to settle down. He'd fallen in love with his secretary and proposed. Blanche, a secular Jew who'd mingled with all kinds, wasn't supportive. Alice was Catholic, but, more problematic, she was a policeman's daughter. Blanche had obscured her own father's rag-trade origins; Pat's intended, however much a lady, was hardly the socially prominent daughter-in-law she desired. At the wedding, Blanche wore black, and any embers of maternal warmth turned cold. She seemed to give up on Pat, and he on her. Donald Klopfer observed that after a few drinks, Pat confessed to anyone within earshot how much he hated his mother. As for Pat's father, Bennett told Alfred his son's chief handicap was how *closely* he patterned himself on the great Knopf. Alfred couldn't see it, and chose self-pity. For too long, he'd been "beaten" between Pat and Blanche. "We are a difficult lot," he admitted, but Pat should have "played for the biggest stakes."

Thus, Alfred unspooling his woes to Bennett over lunch, and Pat turning up at the palazzo seeking relief for his own soon after. He'd decided to quit the city and build a home in Westport for his growing family, but was in a financial bind and needed $5,000 fast. When Alfred learned that Don and Bennett had lent the money, he was furious.

A year passed, and Alfred and Bennett were lunching again, this time at the Stork. From Alfred's telling, relations with his son had further deteriorated. Later that September day, Pat hastened to RH to vent *his* side, grateful for the freedom of entry the partners gave: whenever the need arose, they made time for him. Pat liked both, yet felt a special fondness for Don, their chance encounter on that English airfield having forged an unspoken bond: Don became the ideal father figure. Pat also saw that while Alfred liked and respected Bennett, he could be irritated by him, but his regard for Don was absolute. For his part, Donald thought Pat full of bluster, but felt sorry for him. Alfred would give Pat authority one morning and rescind it the next, and the partners had heard how he'd belittle his son in front of staff. Don saw Alfred's selfishness as morally and socially offensive. Unlike Bennett, he wasn't overly fond of Knopf père.

The trouble this time stemmed from Pat's realizing that the firm needed new editorial energy, and wanting to provide it in the person of Simon Michael Bessie, a friend known to be a sophisticated, self-confident editor. During the war, Bessie had worked with Harold Guinzburg in Europe on government business, and when peace came, Guinzburg held out two offers: Bessie could work for him at Viking, or Guinzburg could speak to his friend Cass Canfield at Harper. "I think it's a good time for Harper to have a Jewish editor," he counseled. In the postwar world, it had become imperative for old-line houses to be livelier, more adept at creating bestsellers and building contemporary literary lists. Gingerly, doors opened. Nonetheless, a decade later, when Harper had to choose a new chief editor, Bessie lost out to a WASP rival, and his conviction that ethnicity had decided it chafed. What made the snub even more galling was that he'd turned down an offer from RH. Hiram had had Bennett's okay—Bennett agreed "Mike" Bessie was one of the best editors of his generation—but he'd stayed at Harper, only to see his hopes dashed.

Alfred A. Knopf Jr.—aka "Pat"

In the spring of 1958, Pat had seized on his friend's disappointment and asked him to join Knopf. Bessie would do so only if given the chance to become Pat's partner in the future of the firm. He wanted to join as a senior editor, and, when the older Knopfs retired, take over as chief editor and buy shares in the privately held firm. Pat told Mike that he thought he had Alfred's approval and a half-nod from Blanche, who was in Europe; it was a matter of negotiating details when she returned. Time passed, until one day Bessie received an envelope bearing the Knopf return address. "This is the hardest letter I've ever had to write," Pat began. His parents—both, but more Blanche than Alfred—had nixed the deal. Rather than seeing Bessie as a person with the intellect, languages, and experience to ensure that her most cherished authors—Jean-Paul Sartre, Albert Camus, Simone de Beauvoir—remained, Blanche saw a rival. Pat's hopes were crushed.

His flight in search of comfort at Random House created its own complication. Trying to bolster his cause, Pat had told Alfred of Hiram's attempt to lure Bessie to RH, and Alfred had raised the subject with Bennett at lunch. Whether Bennett had been evasive or actually denied it to his father, Pat would never know, but now, in front of Pat, Bennett demurred, summoning Hiram to back him up. Instead, Hiram accused his boss of lying to avoid friction with Alfred. The two began shouting in front of already-devastated Pat, until Hiram walked out, slamming the door: Bennett had behaved badly. Later he apologized—Hiram had felt sure his "unfailing honesty" would prevail—but the warring Knopfs were leaving casualties everywhere.

. . .

NINETEEN FIFTY-NINE WAS ALREADY almost two months underway, and Bennett and Donald hadn't divulged even to key staff their plans for the company to go public. Don took advantage of it being Washington's birthday, a holiday, to drop by the office for a quiet day's work, only to find Hiram there, plowing through his own. Given Haydn's position, Don felt it a good time to let him in on the secret. He began detailing the news, the added capital and projects it would mean, the stock options, when Hi, eyes oddly unsettled, stopped him, with something of his own to say.

He, too, had sworn secrecy about a deal in the works, but honor now dictated that he speak: he mustn't be privy to plans, because he'd be leaving RH. An irresistible opportunity—to partner in a new firm—had arisen. He was fifty-one and such a chance was unlikely to arise again. It had been a difficult decision, but he could say no more; he shouldn't have revealed that much. Left unmentioned was the fact that being chief editor hadn't turned out to be quite what he'd anticipated. Men like Harry Maule and Albert Erskine didn't subscribe to the hierarchy Hiram had envisaged—nor, for that matter, did Bennett or Donald. Nevertheless, he assured Don that he'd felt "happier at Random House than [in] . . . any other place" during his career.

"I think you're making a big mistake," Donald sighed. "You'll be giving up the editorial work you really like, and suffering all the headaches of trying to run a business—the headaches I know only too well." He wondered if they might persuade him to reconsider.

At the end of that week, Bennett returned from a Caribbean vacation and, hearing the news, metaphorically (and perhaps literally) paled beneath his tan, then flushed red. The following Monday, the three men discussed what he optimistically called Hi's "cloudy plans," but soon Bennett was uncomfortably aware that rumors were sweeping the trade. The storyline was clear: the Bessie imbroglio had brought Pat Knopf to an impasse so stark, it became a catalyst for action. Turning his back on his parents' firm, he'd join with Mike and Hiram to create a new house, and the trio had found generous backers. The reality of the parting put Bennett in a tailspin: he'd romanced Haydn and granted all he'd wanted; accepted the rejection of books like *Lolita* that he would have been willing to publish; and, to top it all, had signed a new contract with him in January. Had Haydn been plotting to leave while pledging loyalty?

Bennett marched into Hiram's office. The competitor in him throbbed with a possessive indignation lest he try to take authors and staff, too. Yet the tangle of emotions went deeper, knotted into his extreme sensitivity to rejection. RH was a family that he and Don headed. Now a member was abandoning the clan, and he could neither countenance nor cope with such betrayal. His parting sally—"To think . . . you'd rather work with [Pat and Mike] than with Donald and me!"—sounded like a kid shut out of a game that he thought he'd always referee.

The next days were hectic. Bennett had chats with a few key authors on their loyalties and intentions. Two of Hiram's biggest, Bill Styron and Jerry Weidman, seemed to assure him that they'd stay. Pat Knopf turned up, putting in a plea for understanding, yet sharing tidbits from deals he'd made for the firm that he and his partners had named Atheneum. Still, news remained *relatively* contained. That Saturday, the Styrons hosted a party at their country home; Hiram, a weekend guest, was lobbying for Bill to forget Bennett's blandishments and come with him. A buzzing throng turned up, including Doubleday publicity manager Pike Johnson. He soon called Pat and declared: "I know you're going to deny it, but the world is about to know it."

Hiram had talked. The story would make the front page of *The New York Times* the next morning. It was as if "the presidents of General Motors, Chrysler, and Ford left their jobs" to start a car company, the Sunday paper quoted a source. Such a thing didn't happen in the book business. The move had been precipitated, the paper was told, by the "particular challenge" posed by paperback growth. The new venture would publish hardcovers and trade paperbacks, including softcover originals. "In no case was there any question that any [of the partners] were dissatisfied with their jobs," an anonymous spokesman had insisted rather unconvincingly.

Bessie was distressed: he hadn't yet told Harper, since Cass Canfield had been abroad and was due back that Sunday. He scurried to wait in front of Canfield's home pending his arrival, to break the news. Blanche was also abroad, and Pat was advised by the loyal company treasurer, Joe Lesser, that he'd better exit the office before she returned, or the situation would be worse. That Monday, Knopf was in disarray: Pat had been sales manager, and several reps, plus the ad and production design managers, had decided to go with him. Others might follow.

At Random House, although Bennett would experience aftershocks of hurt and anger for weeks, he and Don got down to business. They set terms for divvying up Haydn's authors. If a writer they wanted to keep was under contract, RH wouldn't grant a release; but if the writer were merely under an *option* (agreements ordinarily specified that after a book was published, the house held an option for the *next* work, to be submitted on "terms to be arranged"), then the author would be considered a free agent. Haydn admitted that few would have made so generous an interpretation. The partners also affirmed that they'd honor the royalty they'd agreed to give him on "Haydn books" already contracted, both those published and the thirty-four not yet out.

Hiram assumed Bert Krantz would move with him—they'd been together at Crown, and his say-so had brought her to RH—but she promised Bennett she'd stay. That wasn't enough. Calling a meeting with Don, Bert, and Hiram, he fed her prompts, eager to hear her swear she'd "never think of leaving." She saw "that look in his eye" as "a 'you love me better' moment."

It was agreed that Haydn would leave on March 31. By then, a review of the figures had provided Bennett with consolation: it turned out that Hiram had spent too much cash collecting unproven authors. Good riddance to an "expensive luxury," he told himself. A few months later, he took Pat to lunch. "I've brought you a little present," Bennett said, handing over a sheaf of P&L statements for Haydn's books. "He lost $800,000 in five years," Bennett smirked. Pat was doubly shocked: by the amount, and by Bennett's vindictiveness. He'd never sensed him capable of such a mean gesture, one worthy of his parents.

What Pat couldn't guess was that what had transpired was a first act. When the curtain rose again, further exposition was necessary, but his decision had speeded the drama irrevocably.

. . .

THE TONE OF A workplace—especially one as relatively small and personal as a publishing house in those days—is set at the top. So it was with Random, and so it was with Knopf. While Bennett was wont to patrol the halls of 457 Madison Avenue cackling with his latest joke, asking staff from high to low, "Are you happy?," seeking reassurance it was so; and while Donald would listen to and comfort just about anyone, the customs a block and a half north at 501 Madison were rather different. There, the august establishment of Knopf occupied several floors of a Deco office tower, in contrast to Random's palazzo. But although the palace was lacking, it was the house of Knopf that Harding "Pete" Lemay—whose job as publicity manager encompassed a great deal more than publicity—would liken to a "royal court" of eighteenth-century Germany, complete with "tyrannical Emperor, devious Empress," and, while Pat had been in residence, "ebullient, if somewhat apprehensive, Crown Prince." There was nothing cozy or intimate about the kingdom. Young secretaries and assistants were to refrain from talking in the halls, and berated for idle chatter; nor were they to eat at their desks. Staff friendships were forged, but it wasn't made easy. As for friendships with authors, the Knopfs definitely discouraged those.

Around the time of Alfred's first confessional lunch with Bennett, the drawbridge had been lowered to admit Judith Jones, a sharp-cheekboned thirty-three-year-old with precise pageboy, proper suits, impeccable manners. She'd worked for Doubleday and Harold Ober's agency and had lived in France before joining the Knopf editorial department, hired primarily to assist with French writers. Blanche would never countenance a competitor like Mike Bessie, but this young woman posed no threat Mrs. Knopf couldn't handle.

While in Paris, Jones had pulled from the slush pile a manuscript that had been translated into French; she recommended it, setting in motion Doubleday's eventual publication of Anne Frank's diary. Yet she'd found Doubleday "very disappointing," always "cutting corners" on the physical quality of books. By contrast, she judged Knopf probably top of the top three houses (Viking and RH being the others). She'd looked forward to working there, but Jones soon found that Alfred was "an elitist snob, the kind who looked down on fellow Jews not of his class." (Like most people, she thought his father had been German Jewish rather than the Polish Jew he was—making the facade that much more essential to Alfred.) He was also capable of bullying anyone, including his wife. Now an elegant skeleton perfectly clad in Paris couture, heavy bangles, and purplish nail lacquer, Blanche's favored weapon was world-weary sarcasm.

The Knopfs competed with each other for the attention of staff, but Jones came to realize that people like her weren't especially valued: the couple couldn't do without their editors, yet mistrusted them. Blanche's ruined digestion wasn't all that was amiss physically; her eyesight was also bad, made worse by cataracts. Pride and will pushed her to wade out into the street courting physical peril, but inside Knopf, that pride orchestrated what another new editor, Stanley Kauffmann, called a "masquerade": a conspiracy of silence about her disability.

One of Jones's jobs was to read chapters and samples to Blanche that she could no longer easily read for herself, but if an author complained about Jones or a colleague, where Bennett and Don would have tried to get to the bottom of the dispute, the Knopfs *never* sided with an editor. Moreover, Blanche's attitude toward her own sex was generally far less warm than the feelings she exhibited toward men. It was hard for her to like and respect another woman, especially a younger one whom she needed. Jones would never forget the day when Anglo-Irish author Elizabeth Bowen, one of Blanche's favorites, visited, and she encountered Bowen in the coat closet. As Blanche's sight deteriorated, Jones wrote the editorial letters, albeit "filtered" by Blanche to make it seem as though

An inspirational orgy:
"beautiful" party, and sign
of much to come (p. 95)

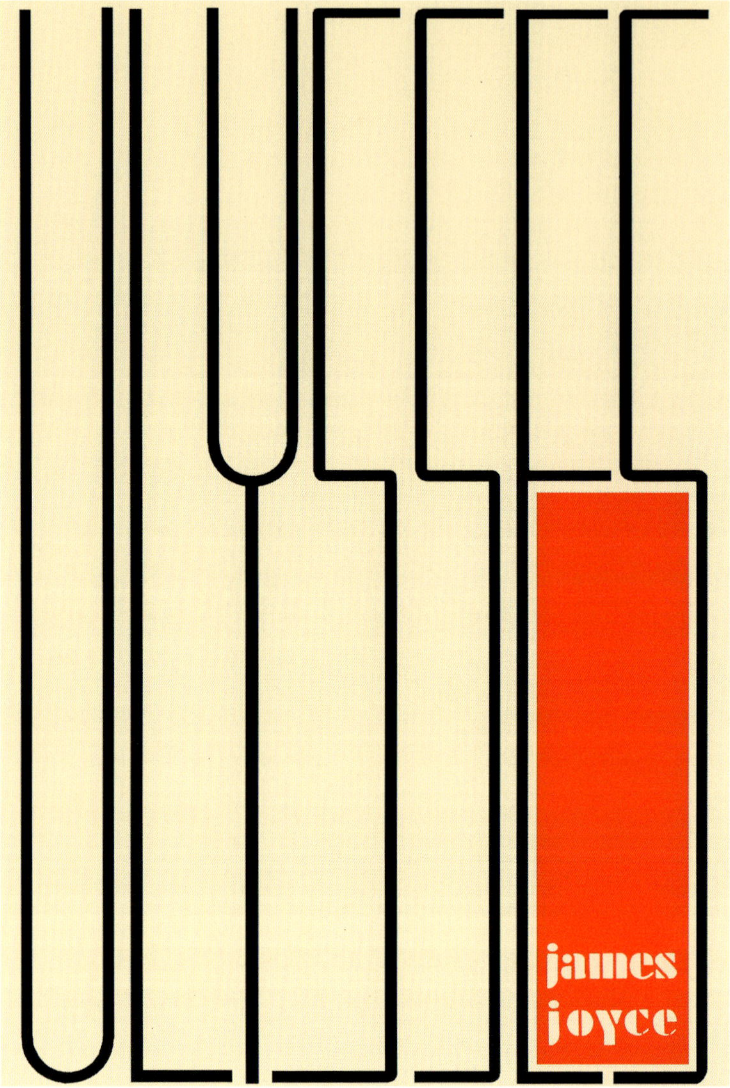

ULYSSES

james
joyce

A visionary cover by Ernst Reichl for a norm-shattering book (p. 139)

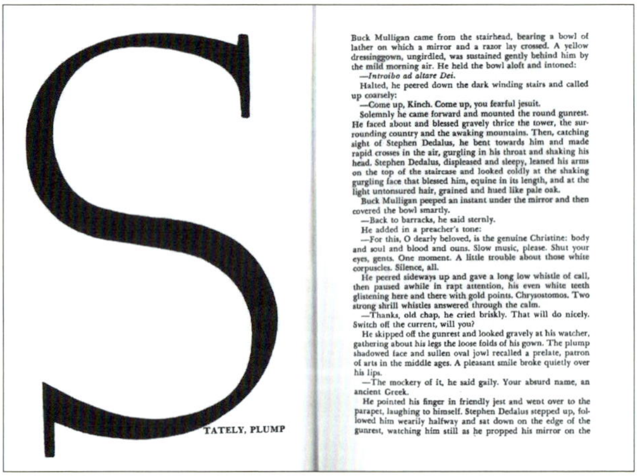

STATELY, PLUMP

Buck Mulligan came from the stairhead, bearing a bowl of lather on which a mirror and a razor lay crossed. A yellow dressinggown, ungirdled, was sustained gently behind him by the mild morning air. He held the bowl aloft and intoned:

—*Introibo ad altare Dei.*

Halted, he peered down the dark winding stairs and called up coarsely:

—Come up, Kinch. Come up, you fearful jesuit.

Solemnly he came forward and mounted the round gunrest. He faced about and blessed gravely thrice the tower, the surrounding country and the awaking mountains. Then, catching sight of Stephen Dedalus, he bent towards him and made rapid crosses in the air, gurgling in his throat and shaking his head. Stephen Dedalus, displeased and sleepy, leaned his arms on the top of the staircase and looked coldly at the shaking gurgling face that blessed him, equine in its length, and at the light untonsured hair, grained and hued like pale oak.

Buck Mulligan peeped an instant under the mirror and then covered the bowl smartly.

—Back to barracks, he said sternly.

He added in a preacher's tone:

—For this, O dearly beloved, is the genuine Christine: body and soul and blood and ouns. Slow music, please. Shut your eyes, gents. One moment. A little trouble about those white corpuscles. Silence, all.

He peered sideways up and gave a long low whistle of call, then paused awhile in rapt attention, his even white teeth glistening here and there with gold points. Chrysostomos. Two strong shrill whistles answered through the calm.

—Thanks, old chap, he cried briskly. That will do nicely. Switch off the current, will you?

He skipped off the gunrest and looked gravely at his watcher, gathering about his legs the loose folds of his gown. The plump shadowed face and sullen oval jowl recalled a prelate, patron of arts in the middle ages. A pleasant smile broke quietly over his lips.

—The mockery of it, he said gaily. Your absurd name, an ancient Greek.

He pointed his finger in friendly jest and went over to the parapet, laughing to himself. Stephen Dedalus stepped up, followed him wearily halfway and sat down on the edge of the gunrest, watching him still as he propped his mirror on the

The opening spread of *Ulysses:* the best-known book design Reichl ever made, and one of the best-known of all time (p. 138)

Try and Stop Me:
In 1944, Bennett Cerf became a #1 bestselling author. He was also a radio personality and columnist, and Random House was booming. Nothing could stop him now. (p. 258)

What Bennett saw from behind the palazzo's big desk (p. 283)

E. McKnight Kauffer's brilliant design for *Invisible Man,* Ralph Ellison's "profoundly American" book (p. 426)

When *The Cat in the Hat* sprang onto shelves, what publishers fantasize about began to happen. (p. 517)

Portnoy's
Complaint
Philip
Roth

Portnoy's Complaint: a major cultural event (p. 783)

Random House Annual Report 1960: bigger and public (pp. 609–610)

RANDOM HOUSE

Publishes the following

RANDOM HOUSE BOOKS
THE MODERN LIBRARY
MODERN LIBRARY PAPERBACKS
VINTAGE BOOKS
THE LIFETIME LIBRARY
ALLABOUT BOOKS
BEGINNER BOOKS
LANDMARK BOOKS
LEGACY BOOKS
RANDOM HOUSE TEXTBOOKS
THE AMERICAN COLLEGE DICTIONARY

Distributes the publications of the following

BERNARD GEIS ASSOCIATES
THE LOOKING GLASS LIBRARY

Divisions and Subsidiaries

ALFRED A. KNOPF, INC.
BLAISDELL PUBLISHING COMPANY
RANDOM HOUSE OF CANADA, LIMITED

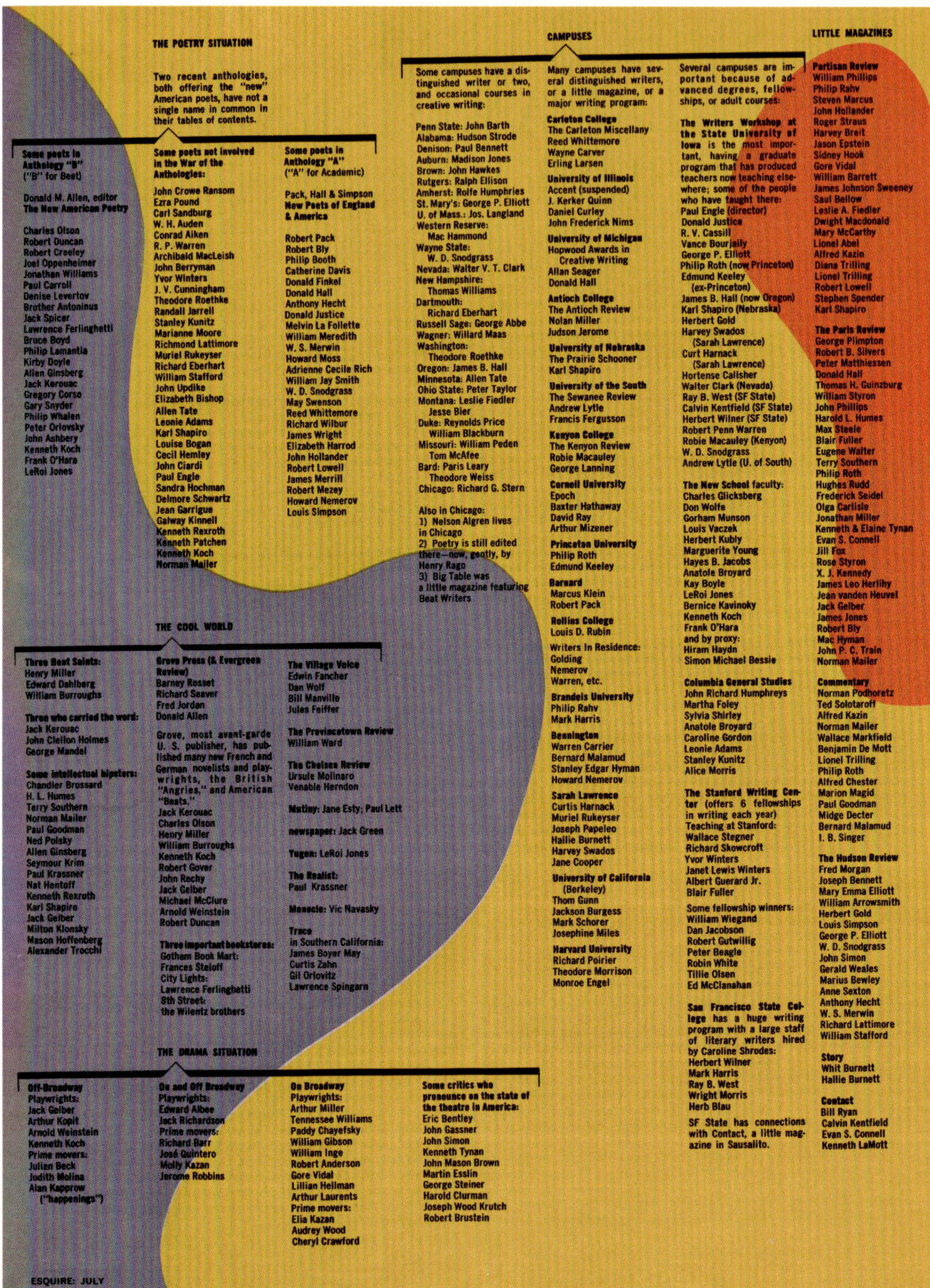

THE POETRY SITUATION

Two recent anthologies, both offering the "new" American poets, have not a single name in common in their tables of contents.

Some poets in Anthology "B" ("B" for Beat)

Donald M. Allen, editor
The New American Poetry

Charles Olson
Robert Duncan
Robert Creeley
Joel Oppenheimer
Jonathan Williams
Paul Carroll
Denise Levertov
Brother Antoninus
Jack Spicer
Lawrence Ferlinghetti
Bruce Boyd
Philip Lamantia
Kirby Doyle
Allen Ginsberg
Jack Kerouac
Gregory Corso
Gary Snyder
Philip Whalen
Peter Orlovsky
John Ashbery
Kenneth Koch
Frank O'Hara
LeRoi Jones

Some poets not involved in the War of the Anthologies:

John Crowe Ransom
Ezra Pound
Carl Sandburg
W. H. Auden
Conrad Aiken
R. P. Warren
Archibald MacLeish
John Berryman
Yvor Winters
J. V. Cunningham
Theodore Roethke
Randall Jarrell
Stanley Kunitz
Marianne Moore
Richmond Lattimore
Muriel Rukeyser
Richard Eberhart
William Stafford
John Updike
Elizabeth Bishop
Allen Tate
Leonie Adams
Karl Shapiro
Louise Bogan
Cecil Hemley
John Ciardi
Paul Engle
Sandra Hochman
Delmore Schwartz
Jean Garrigue
Galway Kinnell
Kenneth Rexroth
Kenneth Patchen
Kenneth Koch
Norman Mailer

Some poets in Anthology "A" ("A" for Academic)

Pack, Hall & Simpson
New Poets of England & America

Robert Pack
Robert Bly
Philip Booth
Catherine Davis
Donald Finkel
Donald Hall
Anthony Hecht
Donald Justice
Melvin La Follette
William Meredith
W. S. Merwin
Howard Moss
Adrienne Cecile Rich
William Jay Smith
W. D. Snodgrass
May Swenson
Reed Whittemore
Richard Wilbur
James Wright
Elizabeth Harrod
John Hollander
Robert Lowell
James Merrill
Robert Mezey
Howard Nemerov
Louis Simpson

THE COOL WORLD

Three Beat Saints:
Henry Miller
Edward Dahlberg
William Burroughs

Three who carried the word:
Jack Kerouac
John Clellon Holmes
George Mandel

Some intellectual hipsters:
Chandler Brossard
H. L. Humes
Terry Southern
Norman Mailer
Paul Goodman
Ned Polsky
Allen Ginsberg
Seymour Krim
Paul Krassner
Nat Hentoff
Kenneth Rexroth
Karl Shapiro
Jack Gelber
Milton Klonsky
Mason Hoffenberg
Alexander Trocchi

Grove Press (& Evergreen Review)
Barney Rosset
Richard Seaver
Fred Jordan
Donald Allen

Grove, most avant-garde U. S. publisher, has published many new French and German novelists and playwrights, the British "Angries," and American "Beats."
Jack Kerouac
Charles Olson
Henry Miller
William Burroughs
Kenneth Koch
Robert Gover
John Rechy
Jack Gelber
Michael McClure
Arnold Weinstein
Robert Duncan

Three important bookstores:
Gotham Book Mart:
Frances Steloff
City Lights:
Lawrence Ferlinghetti
8th Street:
the Wilentz brothers

The Village Voice
Edwin Fancher
Dan Wolf
Bill Manville
Jules Feiffer

The Provincetown Review
William Ward

The Chelsea Review
Ursule Molinaro
Venable Herndon

Mutiny: Jane Esty; Paul Lett

newspaper: Jack Green

Yugen: LeRoi Jones

The Realist:
Paul Krassner

Monocle: Vic Navasky

Trace
in Southern California:
James Boyer May
Curtis Zahn
Gil Orlovitz
Lawrence Spingarn

THE DRAMA SITUATION

Off-Broadway
Playwrights:
Jack Gelber
Arthur Kopit
Arnold Weinstein
Kenneth Koch
Prime movers:
Julian Beck
Judith Molina
Alan Kaprow
("happenings")

On and Off Broadway
Playwrights:
Edward Albee
Jack Richardson
Prime movers:
Richard Barr
José Quintero
Molly Kazan
Jerome Robbins

On Broadway
Playwrights:
Arthur Miller
Tennessee Williams
Paddy Chayefsky
William Gibson
William Inge
Robert Anderson
Gore Vidal
Lillian Hellman
Arthur Laurents
Prime movers:
Elia Kazan
Audrey Wood
Cheryl Crawford

Some critics who pronounce on the state of the theatre in America:
Eric Bentley
John Gassner
John Simon
Kenneth Tynan
John Mason Brown
Martin Esslin
George Steiner
Harold Clurman
Joseph Wood Krutch
Robert Brustein

CAMPUSES

Some campuses have a distinguished writer or two, and occasional courses in creative writing:

Penn State: John Barth
Alabama: Hudson Strode
Denison: Paul Bennett
Auburn: Madison Jones
Brown: John Hawkes
Rutgers: Ralph Ellison
Amherst: Rolfe Humphries
St. Mary's: George P. Elliott
U. of Mass.: Jos. Langland
Western Reserve:
Mac Hammond
Wayne State:
W. D. Snodgrass
Nevada: Walter V. T. Clark
New Hampshire:
Thomas Williams
Dartmouth:
Richard Eberhart
Russell Sage: George Abbe
Wagner: Willard Maas
Washington:
Theodore Roethke
Oregon: James B. Hall
Minnesota: Allen Tate
Ohio State: Peter Taylor
Montana: Leslie Fiedler
Jesse Bier
Duke: Reynolds Price
William Blackburn
Missouri: William Peden
Tom McAfee
Bard: Paris Leary
Theodore Weiss
Chicago: Richard G. Stern

Also in Chicago:
1) Nelson Algren lives in Chicago
2) Poetry is still edited there—now, gently, by Henry Rago
3) Big Table was a little magazine featuring Beat Writers

Many campuses have several distinguished writers, or a little magazine, or a major writing program:

Carleton College
The Carleton Miscellany
Reed Whittemore
Wayne Carver
Erling Larsen

University of Illinois
Accent (suspended)
J. Kerker Quinn
Daniel Curley
John Frederick Nims

University of Michigan
Hopwood Awards in Creative Writing
Allan Seager
Donald Hall

Antioch College
The Antioch Review
Nolan Miller
Judson Jerome

University of Nebraska
The Prairie Schooner
Karl Shapiro

University of the South
The Sewanee Review
Andrew Lytle
Francis Fergusson

Kenyon College
The Kenyon Review
Robie Macauley
George Lanning

Cornell University
Epoch
Baxter Hathaway
David Ray
Arthur Mizener

Princeton University
Philip Roth
Edmund Keeley

Barnard
Marcus Klein
Robert Pack

Rollins College
Louis D. Rubin

Writers In Residence:
Golding
Nemerov
Warren, etc.

Brandeis University
Philip Rahv
Mark Harris

Bennington
Warren Carrier
Bernard Malamud
Stanley Edgar Hyman
Howard Nemerov

Sarah Lawrence
Curtis Harnack
Muriel Rukeyser
Joseph Papeleo
Hallie Burnett
Harvey Swados
Jane Cooper

University of California (Berkeley)
Thom Gunn
Jackson Burgess
Mark Schorer
Josephine Miles

Harvard University
Richard Poirier
Theodore Morrison
Monroe Engel

Several campuses are important because of advanced degrees, fellowships, or adult courses:

The Writers Workshop at the State University of Iowa is the most important, having a graduate program that has produced teachers now teaching elsewhere; some of the people who have taught there:
Paul Engle (director)
Donald Justice
R. V. Cassill
Vance Bourjaily
George P. Elliott
Philip Roth (now Princeton)
Edmund Keeley (ex-Princeton)
James B. Hall (now Oregon)
Karl Shapiro (Nebraska)
Herbert Gold
Harvey Swados (Sarah Lawrence)
Curt Harnack (Sarah Lawrence)
Hortense Calisher
Walter Clark (Nevada)
Ray B. West (SF State)
Calvin Kentfield (SF State)
Herbert Wilner (SF State)
Robert Penn Warren
Robie Macauley (Kenyon)
W. D. Snodgrass
Andrew Lytle (U. of South)

The New School faculty:
Charles Glicksberg
Don Wolfe
Gorham Munson
Louis Vaczek
Herbert Kubly
Marguerite Young
Hayes B. Jacobs
Anatole Broyard
Kay Boyle
LeRoi Jones
Bernice Kavinoky
Kenneth Koch
Frank O'Hara
and by proxy:
Hiram Haydn
Simon Michael Bessie

Columbia General Studies
John Richard Humphreys
Martha Foley
Sylvia Shirley
Anatole Broyard
Caroline Gordon
Leonie Adams
Stanley Kunitz
Alice Morris

The Stanford Writing Center (offers 6 fellowships in writing each year)
Teaching at Stanford:
Wallace Stegner
Richard Skowcroft
Yvor Winters
Janet Lewis Winters
Albert Guerard Jr.
Blair Fuller

Some fellowship winners:
William Wiegand
Dan Jacobson
Robert Gutwillig
Peter Beagle
Robin White
Tillie Olsen
Ed McClanahan

San Francisco State College has a huge writing program with a large staff of literary writers hired by Caroline Shrodes:
Herbert Wilner
Mark Harris
Ray B. West
Wright Morris
Herb Blau

SF State has connections with Contact, a little magazine in Sausalito.

LITTLE MAGAZINES

Partisan Review
William Phillips
Philip Rahv
Steven Marcus
John Hollander
Roger Straus
Harvey Breit
Jason Epstein
Sidney Hook
Gore Vidal
William Barrett
James Johnson Sweeney
Saul Bellow
Leslie A. Fiedler
Dwight Macdonald
Mary McCarthy
Lionel Abel
Alfred Kazin
Diana Trilling
Lionel Trilling
Robert Lowell
Stephen Spender
Karl Shapiro

The Paris Review
George Plimpton
Robert B. Silvers
Peter Matthiessen
Donald Hall
Thomas H. Guinzburg
William Styron
John Phillips
Harold L. Humes
Max Steele
Blair Fuller
Eugene Walter
Terry Southern
Philip Roth
Hughes Rudd
Frederick Seidel
Olga Carlisle
Jonathan Miller
Kenneth & Elaine Tynan
Evan S. Connell
Jill Fox
Rose Styron
X. J. Kennedy
James Leo Herlihy
Jean vanden Heuvel
Jack Gelber
James Jones
Robert Bly
Mac Hyman
John P. C. Train
Norman Mailer

Commentary
Norman Podhoretz
Ted Solotaroff
Alfred Kazin
Norman Mailer
Wallace Markfield
Benjamin De Mott
Lionel Trilling
Philip Roth
Alfred Chester
Marion Magid
Paul Goodman
Midge Decter
Bernard Malamud
I. B. Singer

The Hudson Review
Fred Morgan
Joseph Bennett
Mary Emma Elliott
William Arrowsmith
Herbert Gold
Louis Simpson
George P. Elliott
W. D. Snodgrass
John Simon
Gerald Weales
Marius Bewley
Anne Sexton
Anthony Hecht
W. S. Merwin
Richard Lattimore
William Stafford

Story
Whit Burnett
Hallie Burnett

Contact
Bill Ryan
Calvin Kentfield
Evan S. Connell
Kenneth LaMott

ESQUIRE: JULY

Esquire's 1963 "Structure of the American Literary Establishment": Bennett Cerf's Random House was at the red-hot center. (p. 660)

IVORY TOWER

The Academic Critics

Shifting from their usual work on the classic texts for the learned journals, they frequently apply their techniques to contemporary writing.

John Crowe Ransom (Kenyon)
Harry Levin (Harvard)
Walter Bate (Harvard)
Cleanth Brooks (Yale)
Robert Penn Warren (Yale)
Henri Peyre (Yale)
Martin Price (Yale)
Louis Martz (Yale)
Leslie Fiedler (Montana)
Mark Schorer (Berkeley)
Richard Ellmann (Northwestern)
Leon Edel (NYU)
Lionel Trilling (Columbia)
Jacques Barzun (Columbia)
F. W. Dupee (Columbia)
Eric Bentley (Columbia)
Albert Guerard (Stanford)
Carlos Baker (Princeton)
Warren Beck (Lawrence)
Allen Tate (Minnesota)
Hugh Kenner (Berkeley)

The Theoreticians

Their conception of the nature of literary value ultimately shapes the structure of the literary establishment.

William K. Wimsatt (Yale)
Austin Warren (Michigan)
René Wellek (Yale)
Northrop Frye (Toronto)
Ronald Crane (Chicago)
I. A. Richards (Harvard)
Philip Wheelwright (Smith)
R. P. Blackmur (Princeton)
Mike Abrams (Cornell)
Yvor Winters (Stanford)
Kenneth Burke (Bennington)
Richard McKeon (Chicago)
Wayne C. Booth (Chicago)

The Working Critics

They frequently elevate book reviewing to the level of criticism.

Alfred Kazin
Granville Hicks
Robert Gorham Davis
Malcolm Cowley
Edmund Wilson
Anthony West
Paul Pickrel
Arthur Mizener
John Aldridge
Mary McCarthy
Elizabeth Hardwick
Steven Marcus
Norman Podhoretz
Ted Solotaroff
Dwight Macdonald
George Steiner
Ihab Hassan
Stanley Edgar Hyman
John Simon

Writers Who Get in Columns:
Gore Vidal
Paddy Chayefsky
Truman Capote
William Saroyan
Tennessee Williams
Edward Albee
Norman Mailer
Romain Gary
Carl Sandburg
James Jones
Joseph Heller
James Baldwin

BOOK PUBLISHERS

Random House (and Knopf and Pantheon)

With the acquisition of Knopf, Bennett Cerf secured Random's position as the most important literary publisher.

Random:
Jason Epstein*
Joseph Fox*

William Styron
John O'Hara
Robert Penn Warren
Dwight Macdonald
Anthony West
Ralph Ellison
Irwin Shaw
Philip Roth
George P. Elliott
Terry Southern
H. L. Humes
George Mandel
Calvin Kentfield
Truman Capote
W. H. Auden
Paul Goodman
Stanley Elkin
Richard Bankowsky
Burt Blechman

Knopf:
John Hersey
Shirley Ann Grau
John Updike
Kay Boyle
William Maxwell
Walker Percy
William Humphrey
George Steiner
W. D. Snodgrass
John Crowe Ransom

Viking

Thomas Guinzburg*
Malcolm Cowley*
Pascal Covici*
Helen Taylor*
Corlies Smith*
Catherine Carver*
Denver Lindley*

Arthur Miller
Saul Bellow
Jack Kerouac
Evan S. Connell Jr.
Wallace Stegner
Ken Kesey
Ivan Gold
H. E. F. Donohue
Oakley Hall
John Steinbeck
Hannah Arendt
Shirley Jackson

Houghton Mifflin

Dorothy de Santillana*
Robert Lescher*

Archibald MacLeish
John Kenneth Galbraith
Arthur Schlesinger Jr.
John Dos Passos
Louis Auchincloss
Carson McCullers
Maxwell Geismar
Arthur Mizener
Dorothy Baker
Clancy Sigal
Alan Marcus
Ellen Douglas
Charles Bell
Charles Bracelen Flood

Lippincott

Stewart Richardson*

With Keystone Books and a reactivated New World Writing Lippincott attracted some good new writers:
Tillie Olsen
Arno Karlen
Thomas Pynchon
Harper Lee
Barbara Solomon

Atheneum

Hiram Haydn*
Simon Michael Bessie*

Joan Williams
Edward Albee
Wright Morris
Reynolds Price
Gina Berriault
William Gibson
Randall Jarrell

Farrar, Straus

John Farrar*
Robert Giroux*
Cecil Hemley*

I. B. Singer
Bernard Malamud
James Purdy
Flannery O'Connor
Edmund Wilson
Robert Lowell
T. S. Eliot

G. P. Putnam's Sons

Walter Minton ("As a publisher he's a great general," says Norman Mailer) publishes strong literary books others won't do:
Norman Mailer
Vladimir Nabokov

Little, Brown

J. D. Salinger
Hortense Calisher
George Garrett
Peter de Vries
Nancy Hale
Edmund Keeley
Gore Vidal

Atlantic

Seymour Lawrence*
Peter Davison*

Edwin O'Connor
Brian Moore
Paul Adrian Brodeur
Ved Mehta
John Malcolm Brinnin
Dan Jacobson
Alfred Kazin
Katherine Anne Porter
Richard Yates

Macmillan

A. L. Hart*
Steve Zoll*

Mark Harris
Jack Gelber
Paul Goodman
A. J. Liebling
John Knowles
Albert Guerard

Simon and Schuster

Robert Gottlieb*

devoted to big-deal commercial books except for:

Joseph Heller
Bruce Jay Friedman
Lillian Ross
Niccolo Tucci
R. V. Cassill
S. J. Perelman
William Eastlake

Scribner's

Burroughs Mitchell*
Donald Hutter*
Harry Brague*

Still has a few tough writers:
James Jones
Davis Grubb
Bernard Wolfe
Michael Rumaker

McGraw-Hill

Robert Gutwillig*

Mark Schorer
Warren Miller
Richard G. Stern
Elizabeth Spencer
Allan Seager

Doubleday

Tim Seldes*
Sam Vaughan*

America's largest publishing house is not a factor in the structure of the literary establishment.

J. F. Powers

Harper & Row

Founded in 1817, Harper is now without a literary writer except for:
John Cheever

Holt, Rinehart & Winston

Founded in 1866, Holt is without a literary writer.

The Dial Press

James Silberman*

James Baldwin
Vance Bourjaily
Harold Brodkey
Thomas Berger
Herb Gold
Thomas Williams
Ed McClanahan

New Directions

James Laughlin used to do what Grove Press does today. Now N.D. publishes unsensational books by older writers:
Kenneth Patchen
Henry Miller
William Carlos Williams
Djuna Barnes
Lawrence Ferlinghetti
Kenneth Rexroth
Edward Dahlberg
Tennessee Williams
Vladimir Nabokov
Ezra Pound

Also new writers:
Gregory Corso
John Hawkes

World Publishing Company

Aaron Asher*

Harvey Swados
Stanley Edgar Hyman
Burton Bernstein
William Gaddis
Peter Feibleman
James Baker Hall
Harvey Breit

Harcourt, Brace & World

Dan Wickenden*
Margaret Marshall*

Eudora Welty
Richard Rovere
Jessamyn West
Mary McCarthy
James Gould Cozzens

Most active literary editors

COMMERCIAL MAGAZINES

The New Yorker

Editor: William Shawn
Fiction Editors:
Roger Angell
Robert Henderson
William Maxwell
Rachel McKenzie
plus innumerable checkers and "editors" (of copy) and staff writers and persons on "drawing account" and other sorts of semi-staff basis.

Some Old Hands:
Joe Mitchell
A. J. Liebling
E. J. Kahn
S. J. Perelman
Geoffrey Hellman
Lillian Ross
Dwight Macdonald
Robert Coates
Edmund Wilson
Anthony West
St. Clair McKelway
Brendan Gill
Philip Hamburger
Peter De Vries
J. D. Salinger
John Cheever
John Updike
Nancy Hale
Mavis Gallant
Sylvia Townsend Warner
Jessamyn West
Maeve Brennan

Some Newer Hands:
Paul Adrian Brodeur Jr.
Burton Bernstein
Tom Meehan
Anthony Bailey
Bernard Taper
Roy Bongartz
Harold Brodkey
Donald Malcolm
Ved Mehta

Ladies' fashion magazines:
Rita Smith (ex-Mlle)
Eleanor Perényi (ex-Mlle)
Cyrilly Abels (ex-Mlle)
Tracy Brigden (Mlle)
Alice Morris (Bazaar)
Allene Talmey (Vogue)

Harper's Magazine

John Fischer (editor)
Robert Silvers
Katherine Gauss Jackson
Eric Larrabee
Russell Lynes
David Boroff

THE HOT CENTER

AGENTS

McIntosh, McKee & Dodds

William Styron
Jackson Burgess
Curtis Harnack
Hiram Haydn
H. L. Humes
Russell Lynes
Warren Miller
Flannery O'Connor
Ed McClanahan
Evan S. Connell
Daniel Dodson
Cecil Hemley
Calvin Kentfield
Willard Motley
Clay Putnam

Harold Ober Associates

Ivan von Auw
Dorothy Olding

Edward Hoagland
Martin Russ
John Malcolm Brinnin
Dean Brelis
John Williams
Matthew Josephson
Marya Mannes
Paul Adrian Brodeur Jr.
Donald Ogden Stewart Jr.
Berton Roueché
J. D. Salinger
Robert Coates
Joseph Mitchell

Ashley Steiner

Alan Harrington
Arthur Miller
A. C. Spectorsky
Arthur Kopit
Martha Gellhorn
T. S. Mathews
Rona Jaffe
Grace Paley
Niccolò Tucci

Curtis Brown

Has many important English writers via Curtis Brown Ltd. but only one American literary figure:
John Knowles

Georges Borchardt

Ursule Molinaro
George Steiner

Russell and Volkening

Diarmuid Russell
Henry Volkening
Candida Donadio

Saul Bellow
Keith Botsford
Vance Bourjaily
George Plimpton
Blair Fuller
Peter Mathiesson
Richard Scowcroft
John R. Humphreys
Granville Hicks
Robie Macauley
Peter Davison
Bernard Malamud
Mavis Gallant
Eudora Welty
Jessamyn West
Wallace Markfield
Josephine Herbst
Reynolds Price
Tillie Olsen
Pati Hill
Dan Jacobson
Christine Weston
Philip Roth
Nelson Algren
Richard G. Stern
Chandler Brossard
Robt Gutwillig
Emile Capouya
R. V. Cassill
George P. Elliott
Brock Brower
Alfred Chester
William Gaddis
H. E. F. Donohue
Harvey Swados
Joseph Heller
Hayes B. Jacobs
Hughes Rudd
Sylvia Shirley
Elise Sanguinetti
George Garrett
Bruce Jay Friedman
Joyce Engelson
Thomas Meehan
Anthony Bailey
Burt Bernstein
George Mandel
Thomas Pynchon
E. L. Doctorow
Burt Raffel
Peter Sourian

Sterling Lord

Jack Kerouac
Terry Southern
George Bluestone
John Clellon Holmes
Hubert Selby
Aubrey Goodman
Robert O. Bowen
Arno Karlen
Ken Kesey
Edmund Keeley
LeRoi Jones
Donald Barthelme

James Brown

Louis Auchincloss
Leo Litwak
A. J. Liebling
Jean Stafford
Herbert Gold
Herbert Wilner

Brandt & Brandt

Harold Brodkey
Dawn Powell
Frank Rooney
Herbert Kubly
Wallace Stegner
Hortense Calisher
Shirley Ann Grau
Mark Schorer
James Gould Cozzens

Watkins Agency

Kay Boyle
Glendon Swarthout
Peter DeVries
Allan Seager

McIntosh & Otis

John Steinbeck
Walker Percy
Dennis Murphy
Ved Mehta
Erskine Caldwell
Peter Beagle
Marguerite Young

Harold Matson Co.

Bernard Wolfe
Richard Condon
Davis Grubb
William Eastlake
Ray Bradbury
Morley Callaghan

SQUARESVILLE

The NY Times Book Review editors:

Francis Brown
Ray Walters
Eliot Fremont-Smith
Lewis Nichols
Charles Simmons
William Du Bois

Some book reviewers:
Martin Levin
David Dempsey
William Peden
David Boroff
Wilbur Frohock
Harry T. Moore

Daily reviewers:
Charles Poore
Orville Prescott

Herald Tribune Book Review

Irita Van Doren
Maurice Dolbier

All "out of town" book page editors, featuring:

Lon Tinkle: Dallas News
Alice Bond: Boston Herald
Robt. Cromie: Chicago Trib
Hudson Grunewald: DC Star
Stan Peckham: Denver Post
Rex Barley: LA Mirror
Bill Hogan: SF Chronicle
John Hutchens: NY Tribune

The Saturday Review

Norman Cousins
John Ciardi

Editorial Board of Book of the Month Club:

John Mason Brown
Basil Davenport
Clifton Fadiman
Gilbert Highet

All Drama Critics

Brooks Atkinson (dean)
Howard Taubman (Times)
Walter Kerr (Tribune)
Richard Watts (Post)
Norman Nadel (Telegram)
John Chapman (News)
Robert Coleman (Mirror)
John McClain (Journal)

Independent Squares

Howard Mumford Jones
All the Fadiman Brothers
John Mason Brown
Bergen Evans
Maxwell Geismar

In a square by themselves:

J. Donald Adams
Whitney Balliett

All anthologists, featuring:

Oscar Williams
Louis Untermeyer

All writers' conferences, featuring:

Bread Loaf

All writers' magazines, featuring:

The Writer and Writer's Digest

Bennett Cerf's *The Sound of Laughter:* That sound was much needed those last few years.

esolved, that we, the Directors of Random House, Inc. hereby record our great sorrow on the occasion of the death of our fellow director Bennett Cerf on August 27, 1971.

ore than any other man, Bennett Cerf was the driving force which brought Random House from its modest beginnings to acknowledged preeminence in the field of publishing. His unique ability and his fresh and vital approach brought a whole new dimension to the business. His wit, friendliness, warm personality and unquestioned integrity constantly served to enlarge and enrich the lives of all those who were privileged to know him and to work with him.

The declaration of RH's directors: What makes a great publisher? (p. 828)

they'd originated with *her.* "You're the one who's been working on my books, aren't you?" Bowen whispered—so she knew.

Mrs. Knopf could be coquettish around men. Pete Lemay, treated with an interest absent from her dealings with son Pat, developed a warm filial relationship with Blanche, and for decades Bennett had enjoyed her company. He might have gossiped with Don about her affairs, but recognized how "gallant" Blanche could be: during the war, she'd gotten to Paris just behind the U.S. Army, and scooped up the best French authors. Bennett had reason to know she could be very "annoying," but also "such fun to fight with!," and considered her an "amazing" woman.

At heart, Lemay felt, Alfred was a businessman, a "procurer" of talent who loved books' physicality, rather than an editor. (Bennett's instincts for shaping a manuscript were arguably far sharper.) Although passionate about wine, national parks, photography, and classical music, he was no more a true intellectual than Mr. Cerf. Yet while Bennett reveled in attention and affection from the public, and Dick Simon proclaimed "Give the reader a break," Stanley Kauffmann once heard Alfred refer to people scurrying along Madison Avenue as "mutts."

Unable to reconcile his shyness and need for attention, Alfred's habits were calculated to keep others from getting too close. "A publisher should publish and let, perhaps, Bennett Cerf talk. . . . This is a bad business when a publisher starts talking," he advised a crowd of book people. In awe of academics, his literary range was more limited than Blanche's or Bennett's, whose scope was more popular and adventurous. Bennett had wanted to publish *Waiting for Godot,* but Knopf walked out of Beckett's *Endgame,* finding it "literally intolerable," and scorning its author as "crap." Although Knopf had sought distinguished foreign authors from the start, it was partly because translating and bringing their work to the United States was less costly than catching big fish at home. Kauffmann went so far as to deem Alfred's taste "severely limited," and by the late 1950s the firm was lagging in the competition for new American writers, the reason Kauffmann and another editor, Angus Cameron, had been hired. Although it took courage even in 1959 to engage Cameron—Little, Brown's former chief editor, who'd been blacklisted—Pat had told his father to hire him years earlier, and been rebuffed.

Alfred was also loath to listen to his son about the role that paperbacks would play, a shift Bennett understood early. And, seeing with a salesman's eyes, Pat had been stymied by his father's prudishness and fear of tainting Knopf's reputation even if a book had success written all over it. Knopf had published novels by Harold Robbins, but Alfred got "disillusioned" with his sexual explicitness. Those weren't "Knopf" books, he insisted. "Neither is *The Prophet,*" Pat snapped. The titles Alfred was most ashamed of made him the most money, Bennett knew.

In some situations, Alfred would initially appear jovial, but then veer into contempt. "My God! You haven't the brains of a cat!" he'd tell an employee in a meeting. At sales conference, he made a show of timing a nervous editor's presentation with his pocket watch, but if a rep spoke, he'd demand: "Who are you to be asking a question?" Even an author could become a target. One weekend at the Hovel, Bennett and Phyllis, the Bernsteins, Elizabeth Bowen, and a few others joined Alfred and Blanche for dinner. When wine was first being poured, Bowen said she'd prefer a Scotch. Alfred placed a glass of wine beside her. When Bowen again asked for Scotch, he berated her: one didn't spoil the palate for his fine dinner wine with whiskey.

"For God's sake, Alfred, give her a Scotch," came a rebuke from the other end of the table, only half couched in a laugh. It was Bennett. Bowen finally got her whiskey.

Blanche's sting also penetrated targets beyond family and staff. Novelist Shirley Hazzard never forgot lunching with her publisher shortly after Hazzard, in her early thirties, had married. As the conversation proceeded, Blanche, just back from England, described a meal she'd had with an author there. The author's husband had entered the London restaurant with "another woman" and sat down at a table nearby, Blanche recounted. Then she looked directly at Hazzard.

"One day your husband will do that to you," Blanche said.

Even to an artist of exquisite sensitivity like Hazzard, the "strange dichotomy" between the "barbaric cruelty" the Knopfs were each capable of, and their taste and literary ambition, was confounding, especially since Hazzard also knew another Blanche, a woman of "great spirit" who could be encouraging and kind. Indeed, most of those they hurt didn't waver in respect for the house, its list, and the standards the Knopfs set. As Jones realized, they had a genius for developing contacts with the right people at the right time—like "truffle dogs" able to sniff out where the treasure lay—but Alfred's limitation was that if he was put off by someone, he didn't publish him. Bennett more clearly saw a work's quality and prospects *apart* from the person. There is no way Alfred would have published John O'Hara. In this fairy-tale kingdom, by turns grim and blackly comic, where the blind were credited with sight while minions were rendered invisible, and the emperor's rudeness was legend, Jones, Lemay, and Kauffmann felt sorry for their employers, locked in a *No Exit*—as Blanche's author Jean-Paul Sartre might call it—of their own.

Bennett heard about the anxiety coursing through Knopf's corridors. Certainly, Alfred's judgment was cause for alarm. When a trusted commission salesman—who also sold books for RH—added Atheneum as a client, Alfred raged to the fellow that it was him or Pat. The salesman, looking to the future, chose Pat. Treasurer Joe Lesser and two other executives—Knopf's production head and the company secretary—were solicited by Alfred to buy the firm, so long as he and Blanche kept running it. The trio trooped off to the bank, but the finances wouldn't work. Fear increased that Pat's "defection" might cause the house to fall apart.

For years, a dream had danced around the edges of Bennett's brain, fantastic and far-fetched, yet impossibly tempting. Before World War II, he'd made a first move, proposing that he, Don, Bob Haas, Alfred, and Blanche develop a "joint imprint," to publish Knopf backlist under the auspices of the Modern Library. The books would be better served if allied to the ML machine, and there would be less hassle for Alfred. Knopf swatted away the suggestion at once. In the decades since, the idea would buzz back to life, with Bennett joking that if the Knopfs ever wanted to make a change, they could throw in their lot with Random. It was sure to get a rise—Alfred had come to expect such suggestions—and if he were in a good mood, the back-and-forth amused him. Bennett didn't dare hope, but lightly, persistently, set down his marker.

Nineteen sixty had hardly begun when another hammerblow descended upon the Knopfs, the absurd kind that an existentialist would point to as proof that the gods didn't exist. Albert Camus, forty-six and in the prime of life, had died in a crash on January 4. He'd been on a French country road in a car driven very fast by his Paris publisher, Michel Gallimard, and they'd hit a tree. Camus was a man whose importance to Blanche could not be overestimated—she'd pretty much invited questions from anybody every time she'd said his name—and no one had known how much what she'd insinuated was wishful or real. The call had come to Knopf from the French consulate. The message was meant for

Blanche, but luckily Alfred intercepted it and broke the news, gently. As she took in the death of her "cher ami" and began to sob, he put his arms around her, a fragile bird fluttering against his heart, both caught in a cage of their own devising. He knew she'd never fully recover from the loss. It was the only time Lemay, in all his years at Knopf, saw Alfred touch his wife.

Now, two months later, Alfred was lunching again with Bennett, and again bemoaning some conflict involving his son. As Bennett surveyed the busy scene at the Stork, he drew on some rarely tapped patience. He understood how deeply hurt his crusty friend was—Bennett *did* consider Knopf a friend. He listened and let Alfred talk. When a break finally came, he tossed off his familiar gambit: "It's a pity that we can't get together. . . ." But this time, both men knew the game was different. Bennett dared to be serious, and Alfred did not swat him away.

"Talk with Joe," he said quietly. Knopf was nothing if not proud. Better for preliminaries to be done at one remove. Joe Lesser, as treasurer, could handle it for him.

Others had also sensed an opportunity in the family bust-up. Macmillan president George Brett called to ask if Knopf was for sale. Alfred's answer was a decided "no." Representatives of the Blaustein family, who controlled the big oil concern Amoco, also showed interest, as part of an effort to diversify investments. Knopf's lawyer advised that by opening up their books, the couple would at least get an independent valuation of the company. They did, and the Blausteins made an offer of $1 million, then raised it to $1.25 million. In the end, Alfred decided that dealing with people who knew nothing about books would lead to unpleasantness. But strange things *were* happening. Before the month was out, New American Library was bought by the Chandler family, who owned the *L.A. Times*. The next day, March 29, Lesser met with Bennett and Don at the palazzo. A deal was "BARELY POSSIBLE," Bennett told his diary. He and Don decided to talk with Charlie Allen and his banking colleague Marvyn Carton.

On Friday, April 1, Lesser returned, carrying three years of financial statements. Bennett, Don, and Manny Harper pored over Knopf figures revealing 1959 after-tax profits of $175,000 on a gross of perhaps $4 million. They in turn provided Lesser with three years of RH financials—they'd grossed $12 million during the last fiscal year. Lesser let drop a number: $3 million. Bennett and Don sliced off a half million.

"COULD THIS BE?" Bennett asked himself, adding, "We are delirious at the prospect." It could hardly have been otherwise.

On Monday, April 11, as rumors began flying around Wall Street, RH's stock price jumped from $20.50 to $22. That afternoon, the partners visited Blanche and Alfred at 3 P.M. and stayed for an hour and a half. Carton had prepared preliminary figures showing that Knopf would account for about 17 percent of the assets of the combined businesses. Bennett had asked if his old friends wanted all cash, or partial payment in the form of RH stock. On that basis, valuing the stock conservatively at $20, they'd receive $2.7 million: 67,500 shares and $1,350,000 in cash. Soon, however, Bennett and Don thought again, and made a different proposal: since the RH share price was going up, it would be better for the Knopfs to take the whole price in stock.

Alfred sat in his lair next to Blanche, looking at the two men opposite, no longer boyish upstarts knocking on his door, seeking books for the Modern Library. He remembered being placed beside Bennett at a *Herald Tribune* author lunch when Cerf had spoken semi-publicly for perhaps the first time as a publisher. When he sat down, Alfred noticed sweat on the younger man's face and clothes. "Was it all right? Was it all right?" Bennett kept asking. Now those who didn't know him well only saw sleek TV shine. And Don—well, the war had aged him. These days the shadow of melancholy wreathed him as persistently as his pipe smoke.

He knew them, "probably the only people in the business who understood sufficiently what Knopf was about, to leave us alone." He could trust them to appreciate that if they let their people interfere with his editorial, manufacturing, or promotion policies, they'd destroy the very thing they wanted to buy. Knopf would become an RH division, and he and Blanche stay on. It would have gone against his nature if he hadn't had reservations: Alfred judged Bennett and Don "the smartest boys" in the business today, but also "somewhat schizophrenic." They did publish "some very bad, very cheap, very vulgar books," but then there were "very good ones." A chance for second thoughts had arisen only the day before: he'd convened a small Sunday lunch at the Hovel, and a guest passed on a message from bankers dealing with Macmillan and Crowell-Collier, in the midst of merging. Knopf could join them with absolute autonomy, the messenger promised. Alfred made no reply: he'd already taken his decision.

As the meeting with Don and Bennett wound down, Alfred felt terribly pleased and genuinely moved by their enthusiasm and disdain for bargaining. Nobody wanted to haggle. "Do you and Donald think that's a fair offer?" he'd demanded.

"If we didn't, we wouldn't be making it," Bennett said with complete conviction. "What do I care about how much money you get, when it all comes from Wall Street!"

Alfred took it: the plan seemed "so eminently . . . satisfactory." Despite his eruptions over endorsements and tedious hamming-it-up, it had never entered Alfred's—or Blanche's—mind that "tying in" with Bennett and Donald "would ever embarrass us." Yet after they'd toasted each other with champagne and the others had gone, Alfred admitted to a "let-down feeling, like you get when you finally get a rare book you've been looking for for years."

Bennett, on the contrary, was "DIZZY WITH EXCITEMENT!" He also felt relieved of that infuriating itch of Hiram's abandonment. Now he'd trumped anything his former chief editor had done to him or could do in the future. Four days later, Alfred and Blanche, Bennett and Don, and Charlie Allen met in Bennett's office at 10:30 A.M. and shook hands. It was done. That Bennett had made a lunch date with Pat at Sardi's East a few hours later was a fine serendipity: the news spilled across the table. Not a whisper had come from either parent.

"My mother's stock, you got that, too?" Pat wondered, incredulous.

"We told them it was all or nothing."

As the initial surprise wore off and the idea of Random owning his parents' firm took hold, Pat had an epiphany: Bennett had always wanted Knopf, and given the kind of man he was, would have found a way to get it even if Pat had stayed. The Knopf backlist and reputation was simply too great a temptation. The ML was Bennett's first baby: better than anyone, he'd understood what could be done with all those fine Knopf books.

Never prone to keeping news to himself, Bennett could hardly be expected to hold *this* in. Word began filtering through the palazzo and found its way to the Rabbit Penn Warren, where copy editor Nan Talese was shocked to hear it. RH buying Knopf: What was happening to high literary publishing? She brought her perplexity home that evening. It just so happened that her husband possessed the singularly perfect professional ear to receive it. Gay Talese was a reporter for *The New York*

Times, whose boss, Clifton Daniel, liked stories that interwove news with the social life of the city. Much of this gossip, Daniel believed, could be picked up around the quirky book business, in the handsome homes and long guest lists of men like Nelson Doubleday and Bennett Cerf. He wanted the *Times* to cover the business as a beat, and gave Talese the task.

Talese picked up the phone and called Bennett at home that evening. He was most cordial. The following morning, Talese walked around the corner: the Cerfs lived one block away. Bennett talked freely and proudly about the merger, and late that afternoon, Talese spoke to Alfred. It was clear that "Cerf was feeling better than Knopf." The next day, Easter Sunday, April 17, readers of *The New York Times* woke to photos of Bennett and Alfred, each above his respective colophon, and an italic headline centered across three columns at the top of the front page: "*Knopf, Random House in Publishing Merger,*" with a sub-headline that became legend: "*Deal Made on Handshake Over Luncheon.*" It would annoy Alfred that people thought the merger was closed during a lunch, but the story was given such play that it also took up most of a continuation page. He chuckled at the "fine obituaries" of himself and Bennett.

The New York T

NEW YORK, SUNDAY, APRIL 17, 1960.

Knopf, Random House in Publishing Merger

Deal Made on Handshake Over Luncheon —Cerf's Company to Buy Stock, but Knopf Will Stay on Job

By GAY TALESE

Alfred A. Knopf, for forty years a giant in American publishing whom H. L. Mencken called "the perfect publisher," will sell Alfred A. Knopf, Inc., to Random House, Inc., this week.

The move, unexpected in the publishing world, was confirmed yesterday by both Mr. Knopf and Random House's president, Bennett A. Cerf.

Random House will control all Knopf stock, but Mr. Knopf, and his wife, Blanche, with whom he founded the concern in 1915, will continue to run it under the Knopf name. They will retain their regular editors, writers and their long devotion to craftsmanship in printing and design.

The Knopfs will be paid in both Random House stock and cash, but the amounts will not be announced until later this week. Mr. and Mrs. Knopf will also serve on the Random House board of directors, but the two concerns will combine their bookkeeping, shipping and selling activities.

The decision, which was decided over a luncheon last week, will unite two of the nation's most celebrated publishers of quality writing.

What prompted the decision is debatable, but the merger follows a trend in the publishing field, as well as outside of it. Book publishers, forced to economize, are joining forces.

Also, Mr. Knopf, now 68 years old, was said to be deeply disappointed when his only son, Alfred Jr., quit the family concern last year. He started his own company, Athenaeum, with two other editors, Simon Michael Bessie, formerly of Harper Brothers, and Hiram Haydn, formerly of Random House.

It was a "gentleman's agreement," a mere handshake, that completed the deal this week between the two publishing houses, Mr. Cerf said.

Present at the luncheon, in

Continued on Page 76, Column 6

Bennett A. Cerf

Random House emblem

Alfred A. Knopf

Knopf emblem

"*COULD THIS BE?*" Bennett had asked himself.

Merging "was the logical thing to do," Knopf had told Talese, adding, "What prompted us to do it was . . . Mr. Cerf's great desire to have it come about. . . . We have no editorial compunction about being associated with Random House."

Talese had written a long piece under a tight deadline. He'd spoken to Alfred but not Blanche. Her role, she felt, had been diminished. *She* had brought in the French, Italian, and most of the British authors mentioned in the article. *She* had been honored as an "officier"—soon "chevalier"—of the Légion d'honneur. But Donald's role, too, had been underplayed. And Bennett had had to do damage control with Ayn Rand, whom Talese had left off the list of major authors. Still, the coverage—in the *Times* and elsewhere—was amazing. Two days later, a *Times* editorial, headlined "A Merger in Books," declared: "This is a good thing from the reader's point of view." A "significant" factor would be economies of scale—one book-keeping, one shipping, one sales department for both houses—that might keep prices down and "put good books more emphatically before our vast public, which reads so few . . . in proportion to its size." Everyone, including rivals, "will have good wishes for the Knopf-Cerf alliance." Certainly, the paper's owners, the Sulzbergers, who had long social ties to both parties, manifested such wishes.

On Wednesday, the Knopfs released a statement, explaining the essential condition of their retaining executive and editorial control and independence, even as they acknowledged the change in ownership and their joining the RH board. Bennett (but not Donald) would be elected to the Knopf board. They finished by stating: "We have the highest confidence in and respect for one another's taste, integrity, and competence. . . . It is because of this old relationship—it would not be too much to call it affection—that we were able to come to our agreement so quickly."

Nine days later, Alfred signed a five-year employment contract with the firm he'd founded. He was to be board chair, chief executive, and chair of the executive committee. His salary was pegged at $40,000, plus annual bonus and a stake in a profit-sharing plan, as well as various perquisites, including first-class tickets for business travel; a third of all expenses in maintaining "the corporate office" at his home; expenses for entertaining there; and, in addition, $10,000 annually for allowing the Hovel to be used for business. It was modeled on how Bennett treated himself. Blanche's salary was, like Donald's, a step lower: $33,000.

The purchase was completed on May 17, a day of delight for Bennett, but mixed emotion for the others. Donald's mother died that morning. Alfred, after lunching with his son, resigned himself: Pat "doesn't change." The best they could hope for was "a sort of cold peace."

Alfred approved the press release going out the following morning, which began by asserting that "publishing history was made," and concluded with a promise from the four principals that was classic Bennett: "By the time we are finished, Random House will be a completely rounded publishing company in the full 1960 sense of the word."

In counterpoint to the sunny publicity, Alfred couldn't ignore how sad Blanche and Joe Lesser seemed, and admitted to feeling low himself. But there was no use in it: they had to get on, and hope to heaven the vast pool of Random stock they were swimming in didn't go down the drain. Alfred held 53.4 percent of those 135,000 RH shares; Blanche, 25.2 percent; and just over 20 percent was divided among Lesser and three other Knopf men. In fact, RH stock just kept rising, and within a year, Alfred sold just under half his shares through Allen & Co. to an investment fund and the public for more than $1.3 million—almost what he'd got when he first sold the company.

Inside Knopf, the reaction to the merger varied greatly. Judith Jones had worried that with Pat gone, the firm might collapse, and found Random's purchase reassuring. They were just down the street, and once Bennett had introduced himself, she sensed that "he wanted to make us feel secure." Certainly he acted to allay any insecurity on Angus Cameron's part over his political history. As soon as the news hit the papers, Bennett called to say how pleased he and Donald were to be associated with a house where Cameron was an editor. "That's openers. Isn't that nice?" Cameron mused, having suffered through many moments that weren't, including banishment.

As time passed, Jones came to appreciate another distinct difference between Bennett and Alfred. Cerf followed his instincts, and trusted others to do the same. Knopf didn't share that kind of openness. When Jones wanted to publish a cookbook by two unknown Frenchwomen and an equally unknown American named Julia Child, Alfred confronted her: How could some woman from Smith College know about cooking? He ordered her to have the text "vetted." It was impossible for him to allow her simply to read it, appreciate it as one-of-a-kind, and go with her gut. When Jones saw Bennett in action at a joint sales conference, cracking jokes, kidding with reps, "a new world" opened up, "a democracy instead of the autocracy of Knopf."

Stanley Kauffmann, along with most Knopf staff, was a true believer that his firm was "the Acropolis of publishing," but RH a house that "frequently" did good books—there was a qualitative difference. He discovered what he'd thought was "not fact."

On the other hand, what Pete Lemay saw was a "brash, energetic" organization akin to a "1930s movie studio." He preferred Knopf's court intrigue to "the garish show-biz atmosphere" of RH. Lemay found Bennett's "patina" off-putting; he was too garrulous, masking nerves with talk, and always seemed to be playing a part. Yet Donald's irony and humor, his unassuming intelligence, were terribly appealing. Whatever Lemay may have thought of RH's partners, they appreciated his talent and ambition. Mergers, though, however genteel, bring collateral damage. Jean Ennis had managed to rise in a world where women were too often denied that opportunity. Now she had a rival, soon ascendant. A year after the merger, Lemay was tasked with running publicity for both houses, scooping up some of Ennis's staff in the process.

Publishing cronies, booksellers, academics, authors, and readers weighed in with opinions, often mingling congratulations with distress at the passing of an era, or concern lest standards be diluted. Others spoke of Bennett's stewardship of the ML as showing that he'd by no means destroy Knopf. John Hersey, one of Knopf's most prized authors, told Alfred that he'd stick with the firm as long as he was around, but go to Pat when Alfred retired. Hersey *liked* Bennett but didn't altogether respect him at that point, and dearly hoped that some of Alfred would "rub off" on him. Morris Ernst rattled a warning about the trend toward "gargantuan" in publishing, while Ben Huebsch saw a "fine solution" to the Knopf succession problem.

Bennett had surprised most publishers already, with RH's stock offering and its success. Old-line houses didn't think of Wall Street as a source of capital. Now he'd surprised them again: Alfred had always been judged such an individualist. Yet once he'd decided to sell, the buyer wasn't such a surprising choice. Knopf had been an innovator, and RH was an innovator, pioneering much in promotion, marketing, and the children's field that other houses imitated.

It wasn't long after the merger that Alfred blinked in disbelief at the contrast between how Knopf conducted itself and RH's operation. It was "astonishing." On the other hand, Stanley Kauffmann heard Bennett was "flabbergasted" at how poorly most Knopf books sold.

What did sell was Vintage, Pat's paperback line, and Bennett and Donald asked Jason Epstein to study the market and recommend what to do about reprints—Vintage, Modern Library paperbacks, and ML hardcovers—as a whole. Doubleday was making a major move combining all its paperback lines into one unit, with its own sales department and a dedicated fleet of book trucks, tailor-made to service paperback orders. Roger Straus and his partners had recently bought the Noonday Press, another trade paperback pioneer, and major university presses were becoming more active. To preserve the hardcover ML's market hegemony for as long as possible, Epstein suggested a vigorous new editorial program based on folding in available Knopf backlist with RH's own titles. Such a move would make the ML the single low-priced source of the major works of "perhaps 80% of the standard modern authors." The decision was also taken to merge the two existing paperback lines into one under Vintage rather than the Modern Library, but the books would bear the Random House colophon.

"We are really planning to do big things" with the combined line, Bennett declared to Alfred in August. Bob Bernstein wrote to the salesmen: he couldn't wait to execute the plan in January. However, when it was enacted, Alfred had a small meltdown: a Vintage ad spoke of RH's "acquisition" of Knopf. A friend had told him of Pat's brandishing the ad and squawking, "Look what they're doing to my father!" Alfred went to Don, and before day's end Bennett had phoned to say that Pete Lemay would henceforth be given approval over Vintage ads. The Knopf juvenile and mail-order departments moved to Random; RH's college and reference departments journeyed in the other direction. Knopf would adopt the general RH phone number. Not all were happy about the displacements, but in time a new equilibrium was established.

Five years post-merger, Don would speak elegantly to the reps about the Knopfs and their books at a sales conference. In a thank-you note, Alfred repeated what Don and Bennett "surely" knew: that the association of the quartet during those years was probably "unparalleled" in publishing history. ". . . Nice to realize, looking back, that we made our deal with the only publishers in the world with whom we could have made it. . . . Long may we wave."

What Bennett had envisioned had come to pass, and it would change publishing profoundly.

Chapter 38

Grow or Die

THE COMPANY WASN'T THE ONLY THING GROWING IN BENNETT'S LIFE. How could it be that in 1960, his boys turned nineteen and fourteen? Both had learned to play the piano from Herbert's partner, Glen Boles, showing passion as well as talent, even if it was for rock 'n' roll. Still, Bennett was pleased that Chris had put his passion to enterprising use in a combo barnstorming the city and suburbs. Impish, sweet, brainy (he'd matriculated at Harvard in the fall of 1959, and by spring was already on the dean's list), Chris seemed more anxious, and anxious to please, than ever, impelled to follow his famous father and desperate to succeed on his terms, be it in entertaining or collecting people. Some he collected were sons of his parents' successful friends, mingling in the city, around Westchester, and at Harvard; but his best friend came from outside the familiar circles.

Michael Frith had been a fellow boarder at Deerfield Academy, tall and loping, unlike the more compact Chris. The son of an upper-crust Bermudian family who owned some of the choicest views on an island renowned for them, he was magnetic and graceful, with that British pedigreed air that seemed to smooth any public wrinkles of self-doubt. Bennett and Phyllis liked him—his background met with her approval—and Bennett appreciated Michael's quick wit and talent for making funny drawings. He ended up being "adopted" by the Cerfs for holidays and weekends, when it wasn't easy to return to Bermuda.

At Harvard, Chris and Michael made a brilliant pair, complement and contrast, who together had rushed to join the editorial board of the humor magazine. With a father like Bennett, it was almost inevitable that Chris went all out for the *Lampoon*. He and Michael each wanted to be its editor, but Michael was the best cartoonist the magazine had seen in years, and not inclined to share the top spot. For Chris, the friendship trumped the position: unlike his dad, he settled for second-in-command.

That summer of 1960 he spent working nonstop with four other students, putting together and self-publishing a paperback, *The Ivy League Guide to New York,* to be distributed free at thirty-five East Coast colleges. The idea was to finance it profitably through advertising. Again, Bennett was pleased, and helped by providing connections.

That same summer Jonathan Cerf, shooting up lanky and dark-haired like his dad, had his first stint working at Random House. He continued to situate himself in the background, an observer of the forceful people around him and a careful chooser rather than a collector, who'd chosen to be twinned with Arlene Francis's son, Peter, as best-friend-for-life. Yet when Jon chose to flip an internal switch, he could be formidable, standing his ground intellectually or on the tennis court. Once, early in the season, Chris had defeated him in a match. The Columns soon resounded with the sustained *whump, whump, whump* of a lone racket smashing a ball for hours. In a rematch, Jon creamed Chris. That gene for winning, so essential to Bennett and Phyllis both, was in different ways present in each son, even the quiet one. Later, when it was Jon's turn at Harvard, he made sure to become the *Lampoon*'s chief editor.

. . .

IN THAT YEAR FOLLOWING RH's public offering, raising money to expand had become oh-so-easy. Wall Street was taking notice of an industry that, as one broker's report declared, had been "overlooked" as an investment medium. "No company" had been more aggressive in seeing growth possibilities than Random House, whose expansion, in the opinion of the Street's prognosticators, was solid, not just tied to economic cycles. Of course, Bennett hadn't begun to digest the changes that Knopf would entail, and had only just bought Warren Blaisdell's last stake in the start-up the former Addison-Wesley chief editor had retained when he and RH had joined forces a few months earlier. Although knowing nothing about the math and sciences side of the college text equation, Bennett had okayed a five-year capital commitment of $700,000, counting on Blaisdell to build RH into a market force. The numbers Blaisdell detailed about books he was signing—500,000 students per year taking college algebra courses by 1965!—were dazzling. For a two-volume calculus text by a Caltech mathematician, likely sales were 100,000 copies a year. Blaisdell, the ML, and Knopf's backlist would form a critical mass (Bennett had learned fully a quarter of Knopf revenues came from college sales). "In this direction lies the golden future of the book publishing business," he'd proclaimed at Blaisdell's purchase.

Charlie Allen, Marvyn Carton, and their young associate Alan Hirschfield would spend the coming months launching a flotilla of possible deals in his direction. When Jason Epstein mentioned L. W. Singer, an elementary and high school publisher, the partners found the idea appealing, and asked Carton to follow up, well aware that Seuss and Beginner were marching into schools, and Landmarks all over libraries. It made sense to cross-pollinate with a straight textbook firm, enabling RH to capture readers cradle-to-grave, in school and out, with text and trade. After all, who knew how the new decade would remake the future? Change was coming on many fronts, that was clear, and race was among the most visible. Four years earlier, in February 1956, the Supreme Court had overturned the high court of Alabama, which had tried to prevent a young Black woman, Autherine Lucy, from matriculating at that state's all-white university. After the ruling, Bill Faulkner and Robert Penn Warren had each made pronouncements in *Life* magazine on "the Negro situation"—with very mixed results.

Robert Penn Warren

"Red" Warren had left his Connecticut home and traveled back to his native South to talk with Blacks and whites, privileged as he was by the kind of entrée no son of the North could muster. In the July 1956 *Life* article and the RH volume expanding upon it—*Segregation: The Inner Conflict in the South*—he wanted to elucidate a range of thought and behavior, rather than recommend a course of action. In doing so, he broke with the more conservative views of fellow Southern Agrarian writers. Bennett was pleased that the book occasioned "an amazing amount of comment," yet Warren was accused by civil rights activists of being too much a "gradualist," and by white traditionalists of being a "traitor." Warren told his friend and editor Albert Erskine such name-calling was inevitable; luckily, Red was in Europe when the book came out that fall.

The rights struggle and supremacist backlash had been eating into Faulkner, too; he'd written Saxe a few months before the Supreme Court ruling in the Alabama case that Mississippi was "such an unhappy state to live in now" that he *had* to get lost in writing a book. In March, directly in response to the court's verdict, he published his *Life* essay, "A Letter to the North." Faulkner had worried that, with Miss Lucy being admitted under court order, violence could be done to her, and forced desegregation might start a more general conflagration. He tried to explain in his public letter that, while strongly against "the condition out of which this present evil . . . has grown," he opposed outside intervention by the law or police "to eradicate the evil overnight." Compulsory integration would be a disaster, he argued: if it occurred, he and fellow gradualists would "have to make a new choice." What that choice was, he left unsaid.

Just before the piece was to appear, Faulkner was in New York and had started on a bender. Drink removed the usual censors and sense. What went unsaid to *Life* degenerated into a woozy blurt to a London *Sunday Times* reporter come to interview him: if the "middle road" disappeared and it came to "fighting," he'd "fight for Mississippi against the United States even if it meant going out into the street and shooting Negroes." The *Life* and *Sunday Times* articles came out almost simultaneously. A few days later, manifestly inebriated, Faulkner was on Tex and Jinx Falkenberg's radio show, where he contradicted his previously stated sympathies to school integration, and asserted it might be better to continue segregated education. A firestorm erupted even as the inevitable collapse and confinement ensued. Two months later, he tried to distance himself from "statements which no sober man would make and, it seems to me, no sane man believe," but the words couldn't be erased. Much safer for him to be lost in a book.

More voices were being heard on race, more of them younger and more of them Black. Bennett had recently published Lorraine Hansberry and Carl Rowan, and found himself, at Rowan's invitation, speaking to a United Negro College Fund dinner. New ways of fighting the battle were emerging. A whites-only lunch counter at a five-and-dime in North Carolina would be desegregated in 1960 after six long months of student sit-ins, and help propel the start of a new organization, the Student Nonviolent Coordinating Committee, or SNCC. Before decade's end, RH would publish a manifesto by one of its leaders, Stokely Carmichael.

A new generation was changing the country's political profile as well. Much as he admired Adlai Stevenson, it was clear to Bennett and other liberal Democrats that the two-time nominee's day was done. Senator John F. Kennedy would, as Bennett put it, "whomp" all the competition and become an impossibly youthful standard-bearer that summer. Along with two-thirds of America's adults, Bennett watched the first televised presidential debate between Kennedy and his opponent, Vice President Richard Nixon.

Racial, political, social, sexual, cultural boundaries were shifting. The first birth control pill would gain FDA approval that spring, unleashing profound change in the lives of American women. But some things didn't change. The Cold War fueling those education dollars showed no sign of abating, and that's why Frances Singer of Syracuse flew to New York to talk about selling her family's textbook company to RH. Her late husband had begun publishing a year before Bennett and Don bought the ML; she'd run the company since his death in 1944.

One of Mrs. Singer's associate editors later had reason to describe her as "a very nice woman" and "a class act." A rarity for those times, the young editor was a person of color, named Toni Morrison. Coming to Syracuse from Ohio to find a place to live before taking up her job, Morrison encountered "housing problems." As a Black, divorced, single mother of two sons—a four-year-old and a baby—she wasn't having luck finding a rental. Her hopes rose about one building, only to see the application "delayed." Mrs. Singer heard about it. She never said anything to her new employee, but very quickly the "delay" ended, allowing Morrison to move in with her boys. When another problem required outside advice, Singer helped Morrison find a lawyer. Bennett, too, thought Frances Singer "a remarkable lady"; not many women headed companies of any kind in 1960 America. He was keen to do a deal.

Textbook sales had more than doubled in the previous seven years.

Since 1950, the nation's school population had grown from almost thirty million to nearly forty-three million children. Singer produced a financial summary showing that her firm was growing, but had fluctuated according to text adoption cycles. Bennett made an all-stock offer of RH shares worth $2.5 million. After a summer of negotiations, he signed a contract in Syracuse on September 28. By then, the stock had skyrocketed, bestowing a hugely increased payday—$4.5 million—on Mrs. Singer. Management would remain in place, and Bennett would serve as board chairman.

With all he was taking on, it seemed necessary to "curtail" some non-publishing activities—column-writing for *This Week* and some lecturing—since RH needed more of his time. But this latest deal also gave him a convenient excuse, for in truth, Cerfboard had run its course. Bennett had to think a bit differently these days: he had Wall Street to satisfy. Singer would have a "very favorable" effect upon RH earnings, he told *PW,* watching the stock obsessively. Yet in the privacy of his diary, he admitted some second thoughts, that it was climbing too high, too fast.

Cultural pundits scratched heads in semi-disbelief at how swiftly events were moving in the industry. In an article headlined "Publishers, Get on With It," the books editor of the *Dallas Times Herald* said that for the first time in its history, the United States was "on the verge of becoming a book buying country": a population that in large part had prided itself on anti-intellectualism suddenly seemed pro-reading. The editor asked if the newly enlarged houses would rise to their responsibilities, look at themselves, and cut the number of books they brought out, jettisoning the junk that had made statistics balloon to an unheard-of twelve thousand new titles the previous year. *Time* ran a highly critical piece on the business, and the *Saturday Review* commissioned a *Wall Street Journal* reporter, R. W. Apple Jr., to do a long feature, "The Gold Rush on Publishers' Row."

Apple frowned at the "incongruity" of names like Random House and Henry Holt being mentioned by brokers in the same breath as IBM and Texas Instruments, with the unexciting textbook, rather than the adventurous trade book, looming large as a vehicle for "foolproof" growth. With this new interest in publishing ascendant while the market as a whole had declined into a deep slump, he worried that the impact of "Wall Street money, men, and thinking" was bound to have greater influence on a creative endeavor than if the product had been, say, machine tools. Publishers were entrepreneurs, as interested in publishing good books as in making money, in a business that had acquired few trappings of modern capitalism—thus far.

Knopf's Angus Cameron had coined the term "non-book" for the kind of pre-digested, gimmicky trivia and ghosted celebrity-driven packages that had begun to clutter shelves. Apple figured that if quality publishing managed "to stand off the threat of excessive commercialism," its likely stronghold was the combined houses of Random and Knopf. Alfred had "steadfastly spurned the fool's gold" most publishers passed off as "the real thing," and RH, while less stringent, "seldom had a mediocre list." Bennett had told Apple that he'd "tried to compromise" between making money and publishing good books, and boasted that he knew how to handle shareholders. Yet Apple looked at the changing landscape and wondered, pointing to what had happened to TV, now overrun with banality, since CBS, ABC, and NBC's primary responsibility *was* "to make money." The article ended on a cloudy note, with a young banker anxious because he just couldn't see Wall Street evincing enthusiasm "for the kind of publisher who wants to put out a book because he thinks it has something to say regardless of commercial potential."

Bennett shrugged off the dark clouds. These days, he was frequently called upon to do so, whether in live forums or on television. For an episode of the Sunday current affairs show *The Open Mind,* he found himself debating "The State of American Book Publishing Today" and being referred to by the moderator, Princeton professor Eric Goldman, as "Mr. Octopus." As was often the case, in defending himself he went on the offensive, characterizing publishing as an industry slow to modernize that was at last joining the ranks of big boys like steel and cars, in seeking economies of scale through mergers. He took issue with Pocket Books' Freeman Lewis, another panelist, when Lewis contextualized it as "a very little business," producing total revenues of only "slightly over a billion dollars a year." The way Bennett saw it, because of textbooks, juveniles, and the population projections, books were "at that exploding point. The publishing business has suddenly become real business. . . . [It] is now being efficiently run." Yet he admitted: he expected to lose "considerable" money on fully *70 percent* of the new trade books he published. Any "good, decent publisher" operated with "two kinds of books in mind . . . the ones that he *knows* will lose money" but is "proud to publish" (poetry, first novels), and the "commercial" book, with paperback, movie, and condensation rights very much in mind.

It wasn't Wall Street, he added, but the tried-and-true RH team that attracted investors. If publishers—in their efforts to show profits—*did* get too big and commercial for their own creative interests and "stifled" young writers, he saw no shortage of graduates ready to start houses. It took very little money, just courage and nerve, to do so. As well as defending publishing, he also continued to defend TV and its effect on youth, and to justify his role in both. His trigger-quick remarks made for good copy, and, as usual, delivered self-inflicted wounds delighting his critics.

When a psychiatrist, a social worker, a CBS executive, and Bennett were invited to debate TV's responsibility to children in a forum up at Columbia, the CBS executive gave a nuanced response: "When we say the public does not want a serious program, what we're really saying is that we don't know how to do the program well enough to attract an audience." By contrast, Bennett charged ahead, asserting that "television is the greatest thing that's happened to kids since the discovery of mother's milk," claiming it whetted their appetite for information on subjects that in a pre-TV age they didn't know existed. "The sale of good children's books has multiplied ten-fold!" In the end, whatever pundits thought about his welcoming Wall Street and cozying up to television, he was too busy to let anything stop him, for as well as looking outside the company, he'd been growing it in other ways, from within.

. . .

AT THE SAME MEETING that okayed the Blaisdell deal, the RH directors had agreed to an expansion of the dictionary department. Lew Miller had floated the idea for a complete revision of the *American College Dictionary,* Bennett's grand project that had brought the company to the financial brink a dozen years earlier, before launching successfully and building into profitable small spinoffs and a backlist mainstay. Miller knew that a new edition of a much larger dictionary, the unabridged *Merriam-Webster,* was underway, and could threaten all others.

Random's *ACD* had 132,000 entries; he convinced Bennett and Don to do more than revise it, and produce their own unabridged with 185,000 entries. Lew saw it not as filling a publishing niche, but presenting a merchandising opportunity: it would be sold by stores, but, more crucial, could be sold by subscription, with work delegated to an outside operation to handle door-to-door and special sales (deals were struck with BOMC and *Time-Life*). The growing population (a 13 percent increase in the last seven years) and the new tract housing they inhabited opened up a sales vista. Ex-GIs who'd joined professions, started businesses, got union jobs, had dreams for their kids. What upwardly mobile family didn't need a dictionary?

Jess Stein headed both the college and reference departments, but the job of overseeing the project fell to Laurence Urdang, a lexicographer who'd been hired four years earlier to handle the regular reprints of the *ACD*. Long before he came to RH, Urdang walked along Madison Avenue and dreamed of working inside the palazzo. Once there, he judged his dream "hadn't been unfounded." Nevertheless, there were plenty of hassles. Miller soon decided that 185,000 entries "didn't sing," and told Urdang to include 200,000. A year later, 225,000 became the magic number. From time to time, Bennett, Donald, Lew, and Tony Wimpfheimer met with Urdang and Stein, to keep track of how work was going and hear them justify its great cost. Provoking particular discussion was Urdang's notion of using a computer to help in compilation. That had never been done before, anywhere. Urdang had naively thought that you "picked up the phone, called IBM," and they sent someone around who solved any problem. But the "problem" crystallized in the form of snowdrifts of confetti-like paper citation slips that could bury lexicographers who weren't careful. He hired a consultant, leased expensive giant mainframe time from IBM, and figured out what to do as they went along.

The dictionary: the largest investment in a single project under Bennett

By the time *The Random House Dictionary of the English Language* was published in 1966, it comprised 260,000-plus entries over 2,000-plus pages, and weighed more than nine pounds. It had also, like the first dictionary project, bewitched and bewildered RH into another "big mess" financially. The bank had had to come to the rescue to manage the well over $3 million required—the largest investment Bennett and Don had ever sunk into a single project. At publication, a sigh and a cheer were both in order, and since Bennett was away, Bob Bernstein presided over the celebratory lunch. "One time I went home and my wife asked, 'How was your day?' " Bernstein began his luncheon remarks, aping Bennett with an anecdote. "I can tell you that *fuck* is out and *shit* is in," he quoted himself telling Helen, beaming at his guests while the bashful color deepened beneath his freckles.

What was certainly in were pallets of dictionaries at the warehouse, each embodying a fraction of that huge investment. Now books had to be sold. Using a computer had been unusual; so was sending Urdang on a six-week radio/TV tour, with Bennett pitching in for appearances. A book signing by Bennett Cerf at, say, a local savings-and-loan was a major event in many towns. The bank would buy bulk copies and win new depositors, happy to line up, share a few words with a celebrity, and get a free signed dictionary in exchange for opening an account.

Yet although the dictionary was important, within the scope of Bennett's near vision lay a growth engine promising even greater rewards. Beginner Books, he told Frances Singer, had enjoyed sales of well over $900,000 in fiscal 1960 and was so darned profitable, it had earned about $100,000 after taxes. Such numbers were astounding to an adult trade publisher. The series was selling more units than the hardcover Modern Library and ML Giants combined. Pretty good for a company born on a cat's whisker! How could he not want it under his control? The first line of the founding agreement hammered out in 1957 had stipulated that Beginner was "to be an independent corporation." To alter that, he'd have to convince its three principals: Phyllis, who claimed it as her brainchild; Ted, the magician who'd sparked it into life; and Helen, wise counsel and organizer of her husband's days. Between "big" books and Beginners, Ted was earning a not-so-small fortune, at least $200,000 a year. Only A. A. Milne's Winnie-the-Pooh books touched his in sales. Rifling through a paper accordion of computer sales printout when E. J. Kahn came to interview him for a profile of Ted in *The New Yorker,* Bennett bragged that Geisel was "the most valuable literary property" in the United States. Five of the sixteen books on the *New York Times* children's bestseller list that spring had been authored by Dr. Seuss, and *The Cat in the Hat* had already sold more than a million copies.

The Tuesday after the Knopf deal had adorned the front page of the *Times,* Ted was to be found at 10 A.M. presiding over an eager audience in Louise Bonino's office, assembled to hear him read his fall Beginner Book. Knowing Ted's jitters all too intimately, Helen had urged Bennett not to call him "the Great Dr. Seuss." Such a fuss always made Ted feel that he had to sport "something extra, like horns or three ears." But this time, sans horns or third ear, he did come with something incredibly "extra." During the past year, the never daunted, ever driven Bennett had jokingly challenged his author to an impossible task: write a book using no more than fifty different words, wagering fifty dollars that he couldn't do it. Ted, never daunted and ever the perfectionist, took his publisher up on it, bringing the full intensity of his nervous genius to bear. As Helen told her niece, the work was "very hard," yet the book was "so cute and funny" that all his fans would love it. They did, beginning at Random House. *Green Eggs and Ham,* read by the Great Dr. Seuss in person, was such an astonishment that listeners insisted Ted at once read it again. As soon as he emerged from his state of wonder at what the relentless Sam-I-am could get up to within such verbal constraints, Bennett ceremoniously conceded that he'd lost the bet. The fifty-word book would become the most popular of all Seuss creations during his lifetime.

Something in Bennett knew how to play this man to perform to his utmost, just as he and Don played O'Hara. He could charm and joke, but wasn't afraid to be tough. When Ted began making autograph appearances for toys he'd licensed, Bennett insisted he hew to the contract: personal appearances in department and bookstores were "exclusively for Beginner" and RH. On the other hand, being in awe of his brilliance and accepting of his nature, if a deadline could not be met, he backed off. Ted's biographers judged Bennett "the ideal publisher" for Dr. Seuss.

Twelve days after the grand performance, the Geisels were guests at Mt. Kisco for Sunday lunch. Bennett braved his first cool April sunbath beside the pool, struck by how pretty the scene was, clouds of cherry and magnolia hovering above the lawn, everything alive again and new. Such spring loveliness was one of the rare advantages that Helen and Ted's native East Coast could claim over the steady warm magnificence of their chosen La Jolla. On Friday, Bennett had broached the notion of Random buying Beginner. The idea, like a change of weather, had to settle in: the ever-polite Geisels hardly seemed gung-ho. Financials really didn't interest Ted, yet like many who leave their money for others to manage, he was wary when such talks arose. He trusted Bennett, but he and Helen would have to speak to their attorney. Phyllis's smile was tight: *she* didn't want to sell. Ted's lawyer soon argued against a change, seeing unpleasant tax consequences, but Bennett's advisers found a way around the capital gains issue.

Two weeks later, when the Geisels again visited Mt. Kisco, Bennett continued the campaign. By the time they left for Manhattan late that Sunday (no rush, since *What's My Line?* had been taped), Ted and Helen had agreed, and Phyllis had had to give way. Bennett got what he wanted. All Beginner shares would be sold for 25,000 shares of RH stock, worth more than a half million dollars at that point. The Cerfs' forty shares and Ted and Helen's twenty-two comprised the biggest block. So long as the four agreed, the deal was done. Donald, Tony, Louise, Lew, and Ray Freiman fell into line. Together Helen and Ted would receive 5,500 shares of RH. Ted would be president of the subsidiary, Helen and Phyllis vice presidents.

Beginner wasn't a beginner anymore.

. . .

ON MONDAY, OCTOBER 17, 1960, Bennett was ready to do battle for hearts and minds, having been invited to address the New York Society of Security Analysts, the oracles who influenced the fate of U.S. stocks, a signal triumph for the former Wall Street whippersnapper. Although he'd once spoken to an audience of eleven thousand, his nerves were firing before this one of only four hundred, but he made sure not to show it: he delivered his remarks, as usual, without notes. Of course, he'd prepared carefully. Back in August he'd undergone a tryout, speaking to RH's first public general meeting of shareholders. Beforehand, he'd enlisted help from one of Horace Manges's young lawyers, to practice what (and what *not*) to say. Now, a personal phalanx—Phyllis, Don, Tony, Bob Haas, Bob Bernstein, Frances Singer—had joined him downtown. Publishing had become a "glamor" and "growth industry," he explained, "virtually depression-proof": even in the 1930s, people allowed themselves the luxury of a book. A second growth factor was the paperback revolution, a third the boom in textbooks and juveniles: many remained in print longer and were less costly to publish than adult books. It was becoming "Big Business."

He insisted that for him, being a publisher was nothing less than a matter of love: he'd have to be carried out of RH feetfirst. Yet he also put the business at a crossroads. "The cards are being dealt, and amalgamations and mergers" made that would play a decisive role for decades. "Within the next few years, some five or six great publishing combines will dominate," he predicted, the way a handful of companies held sway over the biggest manufacturing industries. RH, he determined, would be one: "not the biggest . . . but at least big enough so that nobody is going to kick us around." He was wrong in one respect—Random House, combined with Penguin, would indeed be the biggest—but he saw the future long before most others did.

After lunch, Bennett, Donald, and Frances visited the president of the stock exchange and were given a private tour. He could congratulate himself on a year of amazing success, but it wasn't enough. Within Bennett the desire for *new* and *more* lit up corners of his brain that demanded satisfaction. RH was destined for greatness, he'd assured the analysts, but wasn't through building yet. It was as though a key had been turned, a door opened, and *everybody* in the business was crowding around to peer inside, wondering what would come next, who would be next to stand beside the smiling Mr. Cerf, beckoning from the threshold of his grand palazzo.

Back in June, Bennett had already made an approach to William Jovanovich, Harcourt's remarkable young CEO. An immigrant coal miner's son whose ambition, toughness, and brilliance had catapulted him from textbook salesman to publishing president in seven years, Jovanovich had sent him packing, insisting there was "no possibility" of Harcourt merging with another firm. Behind the rejection lay Jovanovich's own empire dreams. Harcourt would merge with the World textbook company that year and do it by *his* playbook.

One prospect down, plenty to go. Six years earlier, Bennett had brushed aside Barney Rosset, the maverick force behind Grove Press, when Rosset had asked for backing to bring out an unexpurgated *Lady Chatterley's Lover.* But after Rosset fought the case and won, Bennett neatly turned face and bought reprint rights to Grove's edition for the ML. His action gave moral and cash support that mattered to the young publisher, for as soon as the case had been decided, others viewed the novel as no longer in copyright, and launched paperback editions without paying Grove a dime. The history between the two went back even further, to the early '50s. Rosset had just started when he took a Columbia night course taught by Saxe, through which he and a Grove staffer, Loly Eckert, were introduced to Bennett. Rosset's determination not to conform was on display: he'd appointed Eckert—a *woman* and a *German*—as his sales manager. Bennett wrote about her in Trade Winds, ink that Rosset believed "quite important" in establishing his fledgling firm's identity with the public.

Now, less than a week after being spurned by Jovanovich, Bennett and Jason Epstein were buying Barney lunch in full mating display, having been urged to do so by Charlie Allen, after Rosset had come knocking on Charlie's door. Grove hardcovers, its Evergreen paperback line, and the *Evergreen Review* were an exercise in hip, provocative, widely international publishing. They embraced neglected British and American classics (not just previously banned ones, although there were plenty of those); the leading edge at home; and the avant-garde abroad. Rosset signed what he liked, and he liked stirring things: alcoholic, social, sexual, political.

Bennett, never wanting to fall behind, always wanting to be at the moving center, had visions of joining Evergreen with Vintage. Allen & Co. crunched numbers, and Bennett made an offer to buy it for cash plus stock and options in RH. Rosset, chronically in need of capital, resembled Horace Liveright in that regard, but although "flattered," wasn't willing to part with control of *his* latter-day Modern Library, and nurtured overblown notions of Grove's worth. His counterproposal, involving Grove books as well as Evergreen, would allow RH to buy 5 percent of the paperback line initially, with an extremely expensive option to buy 25 percent more over the course of two years. Far from the clean purchase he'd envisaged, Bennett decided that Rosset wanted "too much." He'd bide his time, and if Grove's finances got even tighter, his quarry might be more reasonable. Everyone was friendly and the door stayed open, although Allen's young lieutenant Alan Hirschfield felt that, deep down, Bennett was "troubled" not just about the finances, but about what Barney might get up to and how it could reflect on RH.

The partners' dalliance with Bernard Geis was more concrete. He'd been in advertising and magazines before landing at Grosset & Dunlap with a helpful nod from Bennett, then sojourning at Prentice-Hall, and eventually forming his own firm, which became a distribution client of RH. Bennett and Don had learned that handling sales and warehousing for smaller operations could be lucrative. Slickly handsome and "finished" in an expensive Sulka silk tie, Geis was an extremely effective pitch man, capable of seducing men and women into buying almost anything, and endowed with canny instincts about the direction American culture was heading. Like Bennett, he loved being around the gloss and gossip of famous people, intuiting that the veneer of old proprieties was cracking in the Eisenhower '50s, and a world emerging where inhibitions would loosen beyond anyone's imagining, and klieg lights never be too bright. The financial backers of Bernard Geis Associates were a handful of TV heavyweights, like *What's My Line?*'s Goodson and Todman, as well as Art Linkletter and Groucho Marx.

While at Prentice-Hall, Geis had published Linkletter's book *Kids Say the Darndest Things,* based on amusing snippets of live conversation he'd had with cute small fry on his TV show. With Linkletter regularly promoting it on air in a seemingly offhand manner, the book became the number-one nonfiction bestseller of 1957, and remained so for 1958. Geis had his eureka moment: TV was the medium of promotion; and *promotability*—involving frequent, repeated exposure on-screen and anywhere else (author tours, column inches)—was key.

One of the first books to receive the Geis treatment was Marx's autobiography, *Groucho and Me,* published in the fall of 1959. Geis projects could be comic, vulgar, racy, light as air—but were always entirely commercial and sometimes genuinely innovative. They aimed for the appeal of mass-market paperbacks, but clothed between hard covers, sold at hardcover prices. In 1962, he'd bring out Helen Gurley Brown's *Sex and the Single Girl.* Her idea had been off-putting to some publishers, tackling the forbidden topics of female sexuality and female financial independence, but Geis saw an opportunity. He "underwrote her fearlessness: that was packaged and sold," recalled Letty Cottin Pogrebin, who, before co-founding *Ms.* magazine with Gloria Steinem, worked with Geis for a decade. Sell it did, for him and distributor Random House: it was the ninth-biggest nonfiction hardcover of the year. In paperback, millions more were sold.

One year later, Geis published a human-canine love story by an utterly driven woman with big black hair, long fake lashes, and thick pancake makeup, who took her adored poodle all over, the two of them often in matching outfits. *Every Night, Josephine!* was the first book by Jacqueline Susann. Having wanted and failed to be a show business star, Susann would only settle for being a star celebrity. As with Gurley Brown, other publishers had balked. This first success would pave the way for Susann's worldwide number-one bestseller, the sex-and-pills-fueled *Valley of the Dolls,* a "soap opera, show-business gossip, and tear-jerker" mélange. The trinity of Susann, her press-agent husband Irving, and Geis promoted it everywhere, whether on TV or on subways, with the discipline and inventiveness of a Hollywood studio.

Beside the distribution fees Geis paid RH, he brought the diversification of wholly and unabashedly commercial books for the reps to sell alongside the more usual mix; opened doors to some very good markets; and widened the universe of readers. In return, RH gave him a priceless respectability, and got his books into stores that might not otherwise have taken a look. But certain gimmicks—Geis routinely allocated $100,000 for Pogrebin to spend to push a title—were a bit too wild for tastes not aligned with more outré trends. Painting a tattoo on a live topless model perched high on a building above Times Square—against a billboard advertising a potboiler called *The Exhibitionist* (whose cover showed a woman with a tattoo on her back)—was not to everyone's taste. Still, Bennett recognized Geis's value to RH, so when the chance came to buy out his backers, he and Don took it seriously, and sought Lew Miller's advice.

Sure, Geis had whipped up bestsellers, kept useful contacts in politics, Hollywood, TV, and magazines, and it would be nice to prevent his books from landing in another publisher's lap; yet that kind of publishing, Lew cautioned, would never build into a backlist profitable in the long term. Geis was a circus ringmaster, and rather than burnish RH's reputation, bringing him inside would do the opposite. "Whenever a man in business goes into a proposition, he should go into it with great enthusiasm," Lew advised, "feeling that the new connection has a better chance for long range survival than not. . . . On the score of enthusiasm, I simply don't have it." The deal fizzled; RH continued to handle Geis only as a client—for a while.

Bennett and Don glanced at other possible betrothals: to American Heritage, Basic Books, even a medical publisher, but none were right. However, in the summer of 1960 things turned serious with Pantheon.

Formed in 1942 in a Greenwich Village apartment, its founders were the celebrated German Jewish publisher Kurt Wolff and his wife and colleague, Helen. Both were refugees, vestiges of a gloriously heterogeneous high-intellectual and cultural hothouse that had vanished amid Hitler's conflagration. Kyrill Schabert, the third founder, was an American whose stepfather was a professor of German literature at Yale. Despite Kurt's renown as the publisher of Kafka, Werfel, and others, it had been highly uncertain the firm could take root in wartime New York with only $7,500 in capital. Early on, Bennett had tried to help by welcoming Wolff "to the fraternity of American publishers" in Trade Winds. For those ignorant of the émigré's glories, the column offered bona fides for Wolff's "courage and good taste." Another Jewish exile, Russian-born French publisher Jacques Schiffrin, joined Pantheon its second year, and was seen as a fourth founder. In Paris, he'd established the similarly fine Bibliothèque de la Pléiade. Unfortunately, his tenure was cut short by his untimely death in 1950.

Starting with books by German and French authors (some published in English; others, like Camus, in their native language; still others in bilingual editions), the quartet branched out with foreign novelists little known in the United States, like Bernanos and Musil; nonfiction translations in art, history, theology, and psychology (notably Jung); and the scholarly Bollingen series, funded by the Mellons. By 1960, while not abandoning its high tone, Pantheon had initiated a profitable children's line and achieved a run of impressive adult commercial successes, starting with Anne Morrow Lindbergh's *Gift from the Sea;* a series of historical novels set in ancient Greece by Mary Renault; and *Born Free,* Joy Adamson's story of a lion named Elsa.

In 1958, it published an English translation of Boris Pasternak's modern Russian epic *Doctor Zhivago,* which had been quashed by government commissars in his homeland. (The manuscript was smuggled to Italy, and first saw print in Italian in 1957 via the new firm Feltrinelli, thence to Pantheon.) That same year, Pasternak won the Nobel Prize, but under intense political pressure was forced to repudiate the award. He became a cause célèbre and his novel a huge international bestseller: from publication in October to the end of December, Pantheon sold a half million copies, making *Zhivago* the number-one fiction title in America for 1958. Two years later, it published Giuseppe di Lampedusa's *The Leopard,* a sepia portrait of a nineteenth-century Sicilian nobleman and meditation on his fast-dying world, the third-biggest bestseller of 1960. By contrast, Knopf hadn't placed a title on the annual list since 1951.

The Wolffs had nurtured these flowers of exile but couldn't shake a longing for Europe; nor was the relationship with Schabert a happy one. In 1958 they'd moved to Switzerland, and in 1960 severed the Pantheon connection. As it happened, the chairman of Pantheon's board lived in Mt. Kisco, and like anyone in publishing, Nathan Levin had paid attention to the Knopf deal. One August afternoon, Bennett left his high hill, braving torrential rain to drive to Levin's home for what turned out to be a long talk. Nine months later, they shook hands.

The *Times* headline on May 14, 1961, bluntly named the engine driving the deal, a man rather than a company: "Cerf Set to Buy Pantheon Books." It was Bennett's fourth purchase in thirteen months (not including the tie with Blaisdell). He'd later claim that after David Lean's film of *Doctor Zhivago* was released at the end of 1965, the ML and paperback editions of the novel produced royalties equal to half what RH had paid for the company. The same promise of editorial independence made to Knopf was extended to Pantheon: Bennett and Don would advise when called upon, but never veto. He stressed that what the small house offered was its reputation for the European novel. Except for the ML, Random had neglected that territory for years.

Soon after the purchase was completed, the partners took a closer look. Schabert had come from sales, not editorial, and didn't possess that alchemy of business *and* book instincts. His vice president, Gerald Gross, specialized in production editing—the kind that gets a book polished and through the press, but not acquired in the first place. The momentum of the deal and the alluring scrim of fine bestsellers had obscured how much the company lost when the Wolffs left. For a year or so it could survive on backlist, rights income, and titles in the pipeline, but the staff rattled around amid echoes left by giants. An injection of authority, vision, and energy was needed if Pantheon were not, as one young editor put it, to wither into "an empty shell."

That editor had arrived in 1962, a year after the purchase, but was already more than familiar with the territory. Full-bearded, soft-spoken, twenty-seven-year-old André Schiffrin, son of Jacques, had worked summers at Pantheon before Yale and Cambridge. Intense, earnest, and unapologetically left-wing, he was a budding world citizen steeped in history, languages, and literature. It was, after all, his birthright: Schiffrin's literary opinion had been sought by his parents' friends—another émigré couple, the Reys—when he was five. As first reader of a picture story they hoped to publish, he clearly liked it. That story became *Curious George*.

Although unrelated as cause and consequence, not long after Schiffrin arrived, Schabert and Gross left. What to do? It was important the company stay separate rather than be absorbed into RH, not least because Knopf feared such a fate might befall his kingdom. Bennett and Don absolutely did not want to upset Alfred. André and the two other editors had a suggestion: Why not let them manage Pantheon? It would be an unusual gamble—more unusual than André, with a young man's confidence and naivete, realized—to place the little jewel of a house into the hands of a few unseasoned editors. Knopf would never have done so. Bennett and Don had to consider their financial responsibility to investors, and also make sure the company's name and reputation wouldn't be squandered. On the other hand, they'd been gambling in ways that Bennett had for years only dreamed of, and lately had been on a roll. Why not place another bet?

Making the case was a powerful intangible: emotional identification. Bennett and Donald peered back and forward, knowing what it was to be young, ambitious, and hungry to take on something substantial to build into one's own. They'd give André, who'd assume the lead, a chance. Don would be mentor, the authority of his signature appearing on new contracts for a while, and he persuaded Bob Haas to look in on the young people as well: "They need hand holding and fatherly advice!" Schiffrin saw how both Don and Bob identified with his situation, reminiscent of their younger days, the "interest in and link to Europe, the politics, the values." He appreciated Donald as a man who revealed his intellectual chops "not in what he said, but in how he listened," and felt Don recognized in him "the one real intellectual on the scene." Bennett was the talker, and given his schedule, less involved, but also less comfortable with a shy young man whose intellectual confidence could seem like arrogance. Nonetheless, André saw there was "much more" to him than the surface showed, "a performer, used to performing, who successfully concealed literary acumen." As for Bennett giving RH a public face, André was grateful for it, and for the entrée to high-profile figures no other head of house could match. In 1963, he'd be named chief editor.

Yet there were bumps, some early on. Mary Renault, an English lesbian who'd settled in South Africa, was in Bennett and Don's eyes Pantheon's single most important author. They understood the profit-making potential of a successful series, and her three novels set in ancient Greece, path-breaking in having homosexual underpinnings yet appealing widely to readers of historical fiction, were just the start of what promised to be a string of titles. The partners were concerned lest another house try to poach her, yet it soon became clear Renault was very far from Schiffrin's interests. Donald "gently remonstrated" with him when he confessed to not having read her latest. Whether it interested him or not, it was his job to do so.

. . .

WHILE BENNETT WAS COLLECTING companies and scaling heights, Dick Simon, the restless innovator responsible for his start in publishing and his most memorable success as an author, had been tumbling into a shadowy fall. The energizing spirit at S&S, just as Bennett was at RH, Dick had "made all the decisions," been the center of the action. The company had grown great by tapping his renaissance talents and instincts for what would interest Americans and what they would buy, whether it was crosswords, twenty-five-cent paperbacks, or affordable coffee-table books. But Dick didn't have a Donald or Bob; instead, obsessive, quivering-lipped Max was good at putting low- and middlebrow ideas into highbrow packages, and Leon Shimkin at counting numbers.

In retrospect, the slope had turned slippery starting in 1944, when Dick wanted capital for more big projects, and newspaper scion Marshall Field fancied getting into books. As ownership of S&S passed to the gentleman from Chicago, Dick's wife, Andrea, said it was like selling their firstborn. By the end of the decade, with Field in charge, Shimkin had slid into the lynchpin position, S&S no longer Dick's to run. From youth he'd suffered bouts of depression, and in 1944 had a stay in a hospital, and another in 1952. Quarrels between Simon and Schuster, and especially Simon and Shimkin, were constant. At the end of 1955, he was hospitalized again after a first heart attack, and a year later returned after a second. Bennett visited both times.

In 1957, when Shimkin bought Pocket from Field Enterprises and shunted Simon off the board, it had propelled Dick to contact Bennett about "needing some editorial companionship" to help with a memoir.

"I'd like to publish with a house where the man I know will take on the book, somewhat in the way that I took over in the publication of 'Try and Stop Me.' Do you feel you want to do this?" he beseeched Bennett, who hadn't followed up on an initial hint.

"It would be an honor and a pleasure to publish it," Bennett replied, pledging that when the time came, he'd personally oversee presentation and exploitation. He put Saxe on the job at once, despite his compromised health, knowing Saxe had ghostwritten many books, and was the man for dealing with emotional baggage.

Dick wasn't destitute, yet the situation eerily echoed a quarter century back, to when Horace Liveright had made a last-ditch plea to one of the brilliant young men whose careers he'd launched. Dick had given Horace a contract and advance. Now he was the needy one.

After he and Saxe met, Saxe wrote to Don, who was in England.

"What you say about Dick is quite sad," Don replied. "I hope he can make a book out of his life—I dunno!"

A few weeks later, after Max and Leon had bought S&S back from Field Enterprises, Simon officially left the employ of the firm he'd cofounded. Dick had badly lost out financially—he now owned no part of the company that bore his name. Was it to save face he told friends that Schuster and Shimkin had asked him to come in with them, but his doctor—who was also his brother-in-law—had nixed the idea? Certainly, his health was faltering: as well as the heart attacks, he shook a bit, and at times was sedated. There may have been mini-strokes. But the prospect of doing a book—with a secretary's help—seemed real. Dick had seen that "the once great Liveright . . . in a last flicker . . . tried to rehabilitate himself by writing his memoirs."

Horace Liveright had gotten to page 110; Dick Simon, alas, didn't get that far. He wrote an outline and one short, riveting chapter—about Liveright. After a third coronary on Friday, July 29, 1960, he died. Norman Cousins phoned Bennett, begging him to do an obituary for the *Saturday Review.* Bennett agreed, but felt uneasy and conflicted. Devoting a full weekend to it, he didn't get anywhere. Bennett confided to a friend that, against the image of the "glowingly alive" young man, the picture kept clouding with the "stark result after the early image was worn away" by decisions that he judged "so blindly selfish and self-centered" that they couldn't even be hinted at, lest the reader get a "distorted" picture. He'd devote another weekend to trying to make Dick "an authentic, if tarnished white knight," and if he didn't succeed, would phone to say he couldn't. In the end, the piece ran, but not until September 10.

"It will be a long time before the publishing world sees his like again," Bennett began. "It *has* been a long time, in fact, because the real Dick Simon, the man I mean to write about . . . began to die in spirit way back in 1944, when he sold the control of his business." He segued quickly into a present that was very much on his mind:

> For the publisher who cannot resist the fluttering of a certified check by a Wall Street banker, opportunity is knocking twice. . . . [But] to the men who must have autocratic control of their businesses to function at maximum efficiency . . . selling out or "moving under the umbrella of a large, liquid corporation" . . . spells utter disaster. . . . Dick . . . was a case in point. . . . When the decisions were no longer his to make . . . [he] was lost, lost.

Going back to the beginning, the "wonderfully attractive boy" he'd known was "irresistible," and grew into "a great publisher," whose "crowning contribution" was the successful development of the paperback, and who made S&S "a joyous and thrilling place to work." But later, "he sensed that the procession was passing him by. . . . His health began failing, and he retreated into a cheerless world of his own, pulling down the shades . . . and locking and relocking the doors. He had hit upon this method of shutting out death. It was an ingenious stratagem of a sorely troubled mind—but, alas, it didn't work."

Dick's brother Henry wrote, grateful for "that true-true-true snapshot." Albert Leventhal, one of Dick's brilliant protégés, thanked him for the "fine, honest and moving piece," especially since he'd been privy to Bennett's misgivings about taking it on. Bennett didn't mention the business of the memoir or how he felt about it—if he even knew how he really felt about it or about Dick. But two weekends' struggle for a fast writer—that showed something.

A strange denouement played out six months later. At a lunch with Horace Manges early in March 1961, Bennett discussed the "wild idea" of RH joining with Max Schuster to buy out Shimkin. In whose mind the idea hatched is uncertain. But as Max had learned, with Leon he'd signed on to "a partnership from hell." By the end of the month, Bennett was meeting with Max at home, trying not to get his hopes up. "Impossible but fun to hash over," he told himself. More talks followed, with Allen, Carton, Manges, and Max's lawyer. By the end of May, Bennett and Donald were scrutinizing S&S financials. But in early June, Bennett decided the outlook was "too dubious." It had all played out as a strange bookend to that long-ago attempt by Max and Dick to convince Bennett and Don to sell S&S the Modern Library. He'd wanted to do Dick justice. As for joining Max—what a crazy pipe dream, but exciting to have conjured it. Still, juggling all these dreams felt overwhelming, even for Bennett. "Deals, deals, deals!" he confided to the diary, head "swimming," "exhausted" by such talk.

Now the S&S dream was behind him: time to move on. He'd come uncomfortably close to confronting his own mortality—Dick was a year younger—and had to face that proximity again when Harold Guinzburg died of cancer in the fall of 1961, followed, of course, by Moss.

These past two years since the public offering, he'd gone from pacing out his particular patch, to climbing onto a fine steed and marveling at the faster, bigger world before him. He'd charged forward, thrilled with excitement. Yet however taut the reins, part of that compact of exhilaration was the unexpected. The rider might seem in control, but the animal had its own mind. Flying with the wind, impossible to know if a tumble might down you at the next turn.

Chapter 39

Appetites and Digestion

FROM THEIR EARLIEST DAYS IN BUSINESS, BENNETT RECOGNIZED DONALD as his balance. If Bennett's quick anger gathered into a tempest, Don's "Shut up!" took the wind out of the storm. When he fell in love with some "god-damned foolish idea," Donald *made* Bennett see sense. In their letters during the war, Don had worried about expansion: "Please don't let the damned thing get so big that we can't run it ourselves and get some fun out of it and still think we're contributing a little something to the future of America," he'd pleaded. Their contribution, he warned, was predicated upon being "intelligent" about how Random House grew. Bennett punted possible problems, confident that they could solve them, and forged ahead. Fifteen years had elapsed. Imagining and fearing what he did back then, Donald couldn't have foreseen the size of Random *now,* in the new year of 1961, with Beginner, Knopf, Singer, Blaisdell, and dictionaries added.

As the "inside" man, he, more than Bennett, had to wrestle with the day-to-day consequences of going public and getting so much bigger. With Bob Haas officially retired, the tasks of integration and liaison, of managing much of the larger staff and the off-site locations to accommodate them, fell to him. On the last Sunday in February 1961, Don arrived at Sixty-Second Street midafternoon, wanting to speak to Bennett. In the same room, the day before, Bernie Geis had sat in one of the overstuffed chairs. Bennett's brain was on a circular loop, prospects with Geis and other possible deals running round and round in his head, comprising his agenda. Don's discussion topic was quite different. He was thinking that the time had come for him to leave the firm. He'd had a big payday when they went public, and if he sold his remaining stock soon, the money could be converted into a diversified portfolio that would bring a comfortable retirement. The "bombshell" staggered Bennett.

How could he leave? They'd been partners for almost thirty-six years. Life would be chaos. *Everything* was predicated on Don being there. It simply would not be Random House without the two of them.

One month earlier, Donald had turned fifty-nine. Quite apart from everything going on at the office, he'd reached the age when a man looks toward the horizon, looks back, and takes stock of life. He'd been brooding a lot, and maybe Bennett had been too busy, even more self-centered than usual, to notice; signs had been there, and others had seen them. His whole adult life, Donald had endured the possessiveness of his mother. In May 1960, he'd been freed from that obligation when Stella died. But even before then, restlessness was evident when he strayed into a romantic entanglement with a very special author. At forty-four, Aline Saarinen was an associate art critic at *The New York Times,* quite a feat for a woman then. In 1959, RH had published her well-received book, *The Proud Possessors,* about America's great art collectors, men and women like J. P. Morgan, Isabella Stewart Gardner, and Gertrude and her Stein siblings, who amassed paintings and sculptures that came to underpin the nation's best museums.

Lovely and driven, she was born into a cultivated New York Jewish family. With her first husband she'd had two sons, now at Harvard and Yale. Her second husband was the celebrated architect and designer Eero Saarinen, whose sweeping visions included St. Louis's Gateway Arch and the TWA flight center in New York. At forty-one she'd given birth to his son. Having moved to Saarinen's home base near Detroit, she returned to New York monthly for her journalism.

Donald appreciated refinement and intellect, and Aline had both, with her pearls, silk foulard, and graduate degree. But although cool and ladylike, she was also sexually charged, a real-life Hitchcock blonde whose pageboy shone with golden highlights. She appealed to Bennett, too: he couldn't resist epistolary dallying. One of RH's "most beautiful" authors, she was also one of the "most talented." Having found her book "wonderful," there was "only one other thing" he could ask, "but being a discreet soul, I think I'd better tell it to you in person."

Donald's style suited her better, his attraction serious. Like many men in long, imperfect marriages, his eyes were open, and they opened wide when he met Aline, a daydream in a dry season. He and Pat had been married for more than twenty years. Unable to produce that desperately desired baby, they did not have a child to bind them together. Pat instead volunteered in organizations aiding mothers-to-be and their infants, and dabbled in interior design. Most well-off women at that time had no real career, and frustration bedeviled many. She had her admirers: Pat had shown sensitivity to Bill Faulkner. He'd confided unhappiness about the turn one of his love affairs had taken, and was grateful for her "wise kind and gentle and comforting" counsel. Donald felt sure that Bill had truly come to love Pat as a close friend. Some young authors found her welcoming and attractive. And she *was* elegant.

Yet the Cerfs weren't alone in disliking her. Jason Epstein's wife, Barbara, thought her "tiresome," "bossy." Bob Loomis winced at "boring" chatter. Many couldn't understand how a man as engaging as Donald could be married to her. Even in middle age, his craggy face, soft brown eyes, and inviting voice were attractive. He had charm; he had soul; he listened—qualities that appealed to women and men alike. In letters he addressed Aline not by name, but as "Beautiful." When he wrote about Hiram's departure, he vowed that to keep her, he'd edit her himself. The offer was consciously exaggerated, but unique. They'd agreed that her next book would be a biography of the architect Stanford White, whose firm had designed the Villard.

Toward the end of 1960, she wrote that once she finished a long piece for the *Times,* she would devote herself "body and soul" to Donald and Stanford, and wondered if the reason she hadn't received a promised parcel of Beginner Books for her boy was that Don's "subconscious rebel[led] against your female authors being mothers."

"My God, it was good to hear from you!" he replied immediately.

On September 1, 1961, Eero Saarinen died. He'd developed a brain tumor and went fast. It's unclear if before his death relations between author and publisher lay in the realm of fantasy or were consummated. At some point the intercourse almost certainly was carnal. Jason Epstein recalled the "famous affair." Bob Loomis heard about it. Don's daughter, Lois, knew of Aline. Yet although Donald and Lois's mother had divorced, he showed no sign of wanting to go through a second split. In the mysterious ways of marriage, he stayed tethered to Pat and in many respects devoted to her. Every morning, before leaving for the office, he'd bring her breakfast in bed.

A beloved father figure to men as opposite as Epstein and Schiffrin, elevated to "sainthood" by Loomis and Pat Knopf, Donald was a good man, but human, not a halo. He had appetites and limits. Being contemplative didn't preclude being restless; being the silent partner didn't mean business was everything. Far from it: he was a most cultured man. It had reached the point where carrying the practical burden of Bennett's relentless vision felt *too* burdensome.

The day after Don said he was considering retirement, Bennett rushed to convene a three-way meeting with Bob Haas and Lew Miller. They'd been with him and Donald since the mid-1930s and he could turn to them with complete trust and confidence. It was a long meeting.

There had been another recent weather-change in their normally steadfast friend: "Farmer Klopfer" had sold his beloved Blackberry Hill, the land and home near Flemington, New Jersey, that he'd originally bought with Bennett a quarter century earlier. To replace it, he and Pat purchased a property in Bedford, New York, ten miles from Mt. Kisco, six buildings in all, one dating to the eighteenth century. Early on, he had Bennett come look. The estate didn't have the same rich acreage as the farm, but it was beautiful and closer to Manhattan. Pat could play decorator, and in the summer Don could still grow tomatoes and bring them to the office for the staff to take home, just as he'd always done—that is, if he didn't retire.

By the end of June, four months had elapsed since the bombshell. During that interval, Donald and Bennett had decided to buy Pantheon and, more important, *not* to buy Geis or go for broke with Max Schuster. Brakes had been applied: Don had played his part. He *had* backed Bennett's wanting to launch a stock split to increase the number of RH shares, a prelude to satisfying the requirements for listing on the Big Board, the New York Stock Exchange. Trading over-the-counter wasn't good enough for Mr. Cerf. The Pantheon deal became a reality on the same day that arrangements were finalized for issuing the extra stock, a Thursday capping one hell of a busy week. Summer Fridays were wind-down days at RH, when Bennett often worked from The Columns. June 23 was one such day, and Don drove over from Bedford that afternoon. He'd had enough time to think things through, and told Bennett he'd decided not to retire yet. Having thrown in his lot with his friend long ago, whatever misgivings lurked at the back of his mind, he'd remain at his side in this new, different phase. They'd forge ahead as always, together.

. . .

BIGGER ENTAILED MORE PEOPLE, more authors, more books. Even before the deals really got rolling, the life cycle of growth and retirement meant that through the 1950s, a steady influx of men and women had taken up residence at Random House. As the '50s gave way to the '60s, others now joined them, and Joseph M. Fox was one who would leave his mark. Fired in 1955 by Alfred Knopf, he arrived at RH as an editor in September 1960, when his life *really* began. Priestly Saxe may have given everything to work and family, but other major editors at Random House combined an uncommon dedication to books and authors with at least one other passion. Linscott had had his farm; Erskine invested in stocks like a pro; Loomis piloted a plane any chance he got; Epstein started businesses. Joe Fox was the most eclectic and eccentric of all.

Joseph M. Fox

Bennett first met the big man from a blueblood Philadelphia family at a party the Styrons gave in 1956, the year Fox turned thirty. Rumpled and vaguely professorial, he was a mass of contradictions: curmudgeonly, sarcastic, yet warm; an adventurer who craved anonymity; a lovely sour wit with a penchant for staring into space in long, melancholy silences. At his desk he barricaded himself misanthropically behind yellowing towers of newsprint, yet to young female editors, agents, assistants, and writers, he often proved irresistible. Many years later Nora Ephron, after their love affair, would name the Tom Hanks character in *You've Got Mail* after him.

Desperate to work with young writers, Fox had obtained the Knopf job through Harper president Cass Canfield, his wife's stepfather. The connection made being fired by Alfred all the more crushing. Afterward, for almost a year, with a family to support, he earned his living by gambling, commuting each day from home—as it happened, in Bedford—to the exclusive New York Racquet Club, playing backgammon and poker for stakes. Rehearsing for months, he got on *The $64,000 Question*. After the TV quiz show scandal erupted, revealing that producers had "fixed" winners in advance, he sued the network for one dollar and a statement proving he hadn't cheated. He won the case. In July 1956, during his gambling year, he and a friend, the department store heir Peter Gimbel, survived the bends to be the first divers to photograph the Italian luxury liner *Andrea Doria* twenty-eight hours after she sank off the coast of Nantucket. It was the most newsworthy peacetime marine disaster since the *Titanic*.

Once at RH, it became clear that despite Knopf's opinion that Fox was "lazy," he was anything but. "Fox here . . . ," he'd announce when phoning an author, having acquired a reputation for paying attention to each word and every nuance in the writing. Fox had respected Alfred, but feared him. He respected and was fond of Bennett and Donald, appreciating Bennett's fine eye for books that the common reader would want. More than anything, he was grateful for the respect, confidence, and freedom they showed *him,* leaving him alone to choose the books he wanted to publish and fight for.

After Linscott retired, Truman Capote had told Bennett that he didn't need an editor so long as "Big Daddy" Cerf looked after him. Saxe wasn't the right fit, nor Hiram, nor anyone else. Bennett knew better.

Back in 1958, still on Paros and so grateful for his first sighting of the long-awaited finished copy of *Breakfast at Tiffany's,* Capote had confided that he was working on something new—a novel he was sure would become his "magnum opus." Unlike his other fiction, it would be "large." And yet, he had to be "very silent," so as not to alarm his "sitters." It wasn't until a lunch later that fall that Capote outlined the project to Bennett: the "sitters" were his beautiful society playmates, ladies like Babe Paley, Slim Hayward, and Gloria Vanderbilt. He already had a title: *Answered Prayers*. But writing fiction was lonely and *hard,* and transforming the lives of his friends into a great Proustian epic meant sustaining a long, perilous walk on the thinnest of high wires, knowing that eventually the wire-walk would be in full view of those friends, and it would be easy for him to fall to earth. Besides, he'd come to like the process, pace, and interaction that reporting and writing nonfiction like *The Muses Are Heard* entailed. In 1959, the gods—in the form of a newspaper article about a multiple murder in Kansas—answered his prayer for a story he did not have to veil in fiction. William Shawn, the *New Yorker* chief editor, had agreed to send him to the heartland to sniff around and cover the crime as a "journalist," and Capote was intent on it becoming his next book. He'd call it *In Cold Blood*. Bennett understood that Truman *had* to have a real editor—the right one—at RH. In Fox, he'd found him.

. . .

MEN LIKE FOX, BERNSTEIN, Dick Simon, and Bennett himself began their publishing careers in whole or in part as salesmen, migrating inside and up the ladder after an apprenticeship on the road or, perhaps, in the business office. Women in publishing didn't travel that route. They arrived as secretaries, publicity and advertising assistants, or junior copy editors. For them, "moving up" occurred in a very few areas. A woman might eventually become a publicity or promotion manager, a senior copy editor, or, like Louise Bonino, an editor in charge of juveniles. Early in 1962, Bennett formally created a "foreign rights department" to sell translation rights to overseas publishers and other clients, and put a woman in charge; rights became a female power preserve throughout the industry. However, a woman had to be very tough indeed to achieve the rank of full trade editor. Judith Jones would make it at Knopf. Lee Wright had made it at S&S and then RH, mainly through her talent for successful mysteries. But Belle Becker, after years working with authors and manuscripts at RH, had never achieved that status.

Still, a covey of bright-eyed, book-loving, college-educated "girls" cycled in and out of 457 Madison Avenue from the late '50s through the mid-'60s, with names like Alice Stewart (later an educator and essential muse to her writer husband, Calvin Trillin); Natalie Robins (poet and author-to-be); and Alice Mayhew (who would develop into the nonfiction colossus among editors at S&S). These were eager, sometimes brilliant women. Many were vaguer about careers than their male counterparts. But whether vague or ambitious, a young woman would soon grasp that her position in this clubby world was subsidiary, often subservient, and likely to remain so. Random was a man's place.

For some time, Lee Wright, alone of her sex, was privileged to use the executive bathroom, while all the other women had to troop downstairs. One day, Maxine Groffsky, a pert, sexy, highly literary redhead fresh out of Barnard, who was assigned to read the slush pile of unsolicited manuscripts, asked Wright if she, too, might use the more convenient facilities. "Why the hell not?" Wright responded a split-second later. The copy editors followed suit, "liberating" the bathroom. Bennett liked Groffsky, but also teased her in a daily ritual, one that someone with less grit might not have found so amusing. The routine involved a young author Bennett and Donald had just signed.

It was Donald who encountered Philip Roth while in Rome, and encouraged him to come to Random House. Roth had won the National Book Award for his first book, *Goodbye, Columbus,* a novella and short stories, at the beginning of 1960. Bennett did the courting of Roth's agent, Candida Donadio (the go-to agent for many hot young writers), and felt triumphant when Roth jumped ship from Houghton Mifflin. It soon became an open secret that Brenda Patimkin, the young woman in the title story of Roth's collection, was based on Groffsky.

"Hello, Columbus," Bennett would cheerfully call out to her on a daily stop en route to his office. "Goodbye, Columbus," he'd say when he left at night.

She put up with it, tossing her flaming hair and laughing with him. After a few years, Groffsky herself left, for twelve bohemian years in France, where, among other things, she ran the *Paris Review* office. Bennett, recognizing her literary instincts, gave her a note saying that she'd always be welcome to return to RH. Instead, once back in the United States, she became an agent.

Women like Bennett and Donald's Jezebel and Mary Barber, or Bob Bernstein's assistant Anne MarcoVecchio, were *essential:* these three men couldn't have managed without them. But the general male attitude toward the graduates from Barnard, Vassar, and other good schools was that they were temporary embellishments, husband-hunters who'd work for a few years, get married, get pregnant, and get out. If one made it to assistant editor and wanted to move up, often she left to become a literary agent or tried her luck elsewhere. Such were the game's rules. Nan Talese was an exception: even as her two daughters were born, she stayed, and slowly—slower than a man—began to climb the editorial ladder. Bennett and Don were aware that she and Gay needed the money her job brought. That she was beautiful and charmed them like a beloved daughter (ambition well camouflaged) no doubt helped.

Random House was a pleasanter place for smart women starting out than some firms. Sophia Duckworth had hated being an intern at Doubleday, spending days sharpening pencils, fetching coffee, and generally being "the slave." She applied to Random to be assistant to publicity director Jean Ennis. Her pedigree appealed to Bennett—Duckworth's stepfather was "King of Swing" Benny Goodman—and that helped land her the job. RH was livelier and more fun than Doubleday: everyone stayed for impromptu gatherings on Friday evenings. Sometimes, if a young woman didn't have enough work that afternoon, she'd go to the small kitchen and an hour later the sweet smell of a baking cake would funnel up the stairs, inviting everyone to the party.

Duckworth found herself being given interesting work. She was to help publicize Ayn Rand and keep her happy, fetching her out of an apartment that perpetually reeked of cat pee, to deposit her at elegant restaurants for interviews, with much talk along the way. She also worked hard on the campaign for a book Epstein published, Jane Jacobs's *The Death and Life of Great American Cities*. Jason knew the book was important, and made sure the staff did, too, working hard to create word-of-mouth. The success of Jacobs's cri de coeur for preserving the communities that gave heart, soul, and history to America's cities—Greenwich Village among them—against car-centric visions of planners like Robert Moses, impinged on them all.

Yet despite the rewarding work, Duckworth soon gathered that women like her were in large part treated as editors' "playthings." Flirting was endemic and infectious. Many book houses, like most advertising agencies, were located on or near Madison Avenue. Mad Men and their escapades had plenty of publishing peers. A sexualized atmosphere and sexism "came with the territory," as Rona Jaffe's bestselling novel *The Best of Everything* showed, even if women didn't consciously put a name to it. *That* would begin to happen in 1963, when Betty Friedan's *The Feminine Mystique* provided the starting shot for the second round of American feminism. A few years later, women got a boost from an unlikely source: the U.S. government. Publishers wanting to sell books to the government—whether education, military, or other dollars were involved—had to show that females were equitably employed. Suddenly, women were being promoted.

Long, three-martini lunches earned many an editor, not just Fox, the reputation for being a ladies' man. The label also stuck to Epstein, king of his own small autonomous RH kingdom, and his serial interest in (young) secretaries. Bennett once told Bob Bernstein's mother that Bob and Jason were "mass and class," and RH needed both, with Epstein's intellectual "class" proving invaluable. He edited Jacobs; was Auden's official editor (he needed no editing) after Saxe died; and would add Gore Vidal, E. L. Doctorow, Norman Mailer, and many others.

The presence of Phyllis in her attic lair—she could descend as swiftly as Hera upon Zeus without necessarily announcing it via interoffice telephone—acted, perhaps, as a check on Bennett's own roving eye. In these years they might argue, and she knew how to use tears, but Phyllis also knew how to toe the line, and made him that "very good wife" Donald spoke of. Although Sylvia Sidney remained the ultimate fantasy, other male staff gathered that Phyllis "made him a happy man." Bennett's penchant for outrageous flirting was, however, indulged within the halls of the palazzo as much as his appetite for punning. As he made the rounds, he could sometimes be seen with a girl giggling in his lap. Sexually, some staff thought of Bennett as a man who liked to play, but didn't act. Others made different assumptions. Pete Lemay was told never to phone before noon when Bennett was on the road, and assumed that not every morning was taken up with lecturing or media. Jason, subject of so many rumors himself, heard others about Bennett having "a bit on the side."

Certainly, at the Lotos Club one snowy sales conference morning, a young editor had an encounter with Bennett that she never forgot. After arriving, she sat down in a room adjoining the hall to pull off wet boots and put on pumps, and was delighted when, immaculately turned out as always, the big boss materialized and kindly offered to help. Bennett knelt down, and as he reached to grasp and tug at one boot, a hand climbed higher under her skirt, and touched her thigh. Although startled, she retained enough presence of mind to signal a definite lack of interest. The offending hand retreated; no further overture was ever made.

. . .

BENNETT AND DONALD HIRED one more senior employee during this period, a man they figured would be crucial to Random's future. Richard W. Kislik had gone to Harvard as well as its business school, and his training was like a new and foreign language injected into the palazzo's conversations. Slim, dark-haired, wearing a narrow tie, narrow lapels, a white shirt—a smart "IBM type"—he'd worked at Doubleday, rising to the position of controller, and briefly in magazines. Kislik was about to accept an offer from Grosset & Dunlap when his friend and former Doubleday colleague Jason suggested he come to meet Bennett and Don. Haas, Miller, and Bernstein interviewed him as well. From these talks Kislik gathered that they didn't know how to blend all the companies now comprising RH Inc.; no one had the requisite background in corporate scale or big-number crunching. Coming from the trade's reigning behemoth, Kislik was sure he did. Bennett, prepared to deal with Grosset's "outrage" at his poaching their recruit, offered a portfolio-without-title. He could call Kislik "administrator" or "coordinator," but it was a sign of how new the context was that he didn't know what to name the job, akin to today's "chief financial officer," helping to define and organize this greater RH for the future.

Bennett could be generous to friends and a gambler on deals, but in the course of regular business had always been cash-careful. He offered $20,000—only two-thirds Kislik's previous salary—but Kislik took it despite the cut. To him, Random had become *the* house. Of course, he was smart enough to extract a promise: in a year, if he proved his mettle, he'd recoup the lost third and then some. This man who dealt in numbers saw that salaries were kept low, but that Bennett was generous with expenses, and gave his people all kinds of perks. He was different from competitor Roger Straus, a showboat in a Rolls-Royce, and notoriously cheap with staff.

"You worked for Bennett because of the way he treated you. Ninety percent of the time, he was wonderful towards people," Kislik soon learned. He'd known that RH already had a controller, who'd been fine when the firm was smaller. With Kislik's arrival, a different company might have eased the older man out, but Bennett instructed him to ensure the fellow stayed. On the other hand, Kislik also witnessed "the other ten percent": when Bennett took a dislike to someone, he could be "terrible, unfair, wipe them out, and never change his mind."

Shortly after he arrived, Kislik helped arrange loans for capital-hungry Blaisdell, Singer, and the dictionary. He had to straighten out a major snafu between the billing and shipping departments: information wasn't being shared, publication dates had slipped, and complaints had been piling up from stores. Bennett took all this very personally: he was embarrassed as well as fearful that RH would tarnish its reputation, and with it, his own. Too many books had been coming out over budget as well as late. It was time to gather profit and loss statements for the past year on every title from every editor, and analyze them methodically—another of Kislik's tasks. However, while bosses in other houses used P&Ls as an instrument of fear, a means to make an editor feel that someone was always looking over his or her shoulder, Bennett and Don ensured that Kislik did no such thing. He was a symbol of change, but the tone was set by them.

He was also enlisted to act as buffer between Tony Wimpfheimer and staff who thought Donald's stepson too much the big shot. The more perceptive among them realized that beneath Tony's swagger was an uneasy truth and difficult situation: however capable he was, at base his position—he was now company secretary as well as a senior manager—was predicated on being Pat's son. Kislik, who was a friend of Tony's from the outside, could help defuse tensions.

Kislik's ambition was a given. He'd become the go-to man on Singer and Blaisdell as well as on organizational and space problems. He worked to make himself indispensable, a counterpoint and rival to Bernstein—all terribly friendly, of course. In other areas, his influence was more subtle or symbolic. Bennett's habit was to walk to the office each morning, even when he'd stayed up late with a manuscript. He liked the short stroll to midtown, enjoyed being recognized and greeted. A true New Yorker, he walked most places, since much of his world was so close. If he had to travel farther, he took the subway, rarely resorting to a cab. But his new financial man, in cahoots with Phyllis, worked on him to have a company car. Eventually, Bennett capitulated.

Kislik was too new to be in the party venturing downtown on September 20, 1961, a Wednesday that Bennett proclaimed one of the "red-letter" days of his life. It began, strangely, with a tiny twinge of sadness: at eight o'clock that morning, Chris, Jon, and Peter Gabel set off from the townhouse, Chris driving. He'd deposit the younger boys at Deerfield, then proceed to Harvard to begin his final year. It was the first time in two decades that the nest was empty. Bennett bruited it about that Phyllis had been close to tears for a week, but two hours after the boys' departure she was cheerfulness itself when the Cerfs, Klopfers, Knopfs, Bob Haas, Lew Miller, and Albert Erskine met Keith Funston, the president of the New York Stock Exchange, on the exchange's trading floor. At a time before algorithms took control, when buys and sells were done by madly gesticulating fellows, Random was number one on the ticker

(Bennett had made sure of that in advance), opening the day's trading under the symbol RH with eight hundred shares.

At the Stock Exchange: (from left) Tony Wimpfheimer, Lew Miller, Albert Erskine, Bennett, NYSE president G. Keith Funston, Alfred Knopf, unidentified, Donald Klopfer, Bob Haas

WELCOME TO THE NY STOCK EXCHANGE MRS. BENNETT CERF, the ticker declared, extending the formal courtesy of the era to the boss's wife. Bennett, so thrilled to have moved from over-the-counter to the Big Board, stashed the small piece of tape among his mementos. One day later, he dictated a "Letter to New Stockholders," welcoming them, appreciating the confidence they showed in the firm, and hoping they'd be pleased in the future with their investment. He encouraged every stockholder to be "an active participant in the affairs of the company," through favoring Random books, and by encouraging their local bookstores to display RH wares.

In dollar terms, amid the shadowy canyons of Wall Street, Random House—bulked up though it might be—was a rather small affair. However, very few companies, even the biggest, had a CEO with the public profile of Bennett Cerf. No publishing house, before or since, could be so instantly identified, so publicly, with one man.

Chapter 40

Go Down, Goodbye

Just over a year had passed since Donald decided to remain at Random House. Arriving at the Villard one fine summer morning, not too humid, not too hot, the kind New Yorkers pray for, the courtyard echoed faintly as St. Pat's tolled nine. The nation had marked its birthday two days earlier, rendering Midtown thin on the ground; Bennett was "idling" at Mt. Kisco, and a slow, easy Friday beckoned. Don had hardly settled at his desk when the call came. CBS News was on the line, wanting Bennett, saying it was urgent. The switchboard put it through immediately.

"I have bad news," the reporter began, as soon as Don picked up. Four small words banished all his plans. July 6, 1962, was less than two hours into its span of twenty-four when Bill Faulkner died, a couple months shy of his sixty-fifth birthday. His heart had given out in a Mississippi hospital. Two and a half weeks earlier, Faulkner had been thrown by a horse, an occurrence that had been happening fairly frequently. Some thought it was pure iron-willed recklessness for a man his age to ride like that, but as the word-fires grew harder to rekindle, he devoted less time to writing and more to horses. After the fall, the druggist's pills hadn't dulled the pain, so he turned to his all-purpose remedy. On July 5, Estelle had had to take him the usual route to Dr. Wright's sanitarium in Byhalia. It had seemed just another binge. Now he was dead.

The news came as a "great blow, great shock." This author whom Don had felt privileged to publish and liked to regard as a "very close" friend was gone. Nobody had seen it coming: Faulkner had seemed indestructible. Only two weeks before, Don had sent off the most recent in a string of cautionary letters replying to Bill's improvident notion of spending a couple hundred thousand dollars to buy a farm in Virginia, near his daughter Jill's family. He was now dividing his time between a house in Charlottesville that enabled him to see them and give talks at the University of Virginia, and his Oxford, Mississippi, "home place." Don and Pat had dined with him as recently as May, when he'd traveled to New York to be presented with the rare honor of the American Institute of Arts and Letters Gold Medal. At dinner he'd assured Bennett that Albert Erskine was "the best book editor alive today." Over these last years, he'd seen Erskine untangle inconsistencies running through his Snopes books in a way Saxe had not. Yet it was Don who'd become the trusted go-to man on sensitive matters after Bob retired and Saxe died.

As soon as he finished with CBS, Donald phoned The Columns, seeking solace in sharing the sad news, and wanting to alert Bennett that the press would call. *The New York Times* also found him in Mt. Kisco early. Bennett featured prominently in one of five Faulkner articles the paper carried the next day—remarkably generous coverage starting on page one, marking the passage of the man whom many had come to consider the finest American novelist of the century. One of his rivals for that garland, Ernest Hemingway, had died the year before and others, like Scott Fitzgerald, were long gone.

Bennett began by telling the *Times* interviewer, just as Donald had told CBS, how "terribly shocked" he felt.

Knowing Estelle's nerves from long experience, the partners decided it was best to phone Jill, but discovered that she'd already left for Mississippi, and no means of communication could put them in touch until she arrived. It didn't matter. Neither man had any question about what to do: they were going to the funeral. Arrangements had to be made, fast. Oxford was a small place, not a simple, straightforward journey from A to B. The reporters had told them that the service was set for the next afternoon at two. They'd try to reach Jill after landing in Memphis, before the drive to Oxford. They couldn't just turn up, unannounced. Yet surely the Faulkners would understand, they reckoned, and maybe take some solace from their coming.

That morning, Bill Styron, vacationing with his family on Martha's Vineyard, got a call from Ralph Graves, managing editor of *Life*. Graves had the inspired notion of dispatching him to cover the funeral. Like every writer, even more so one Southern-bred, Styron was shaken by the death. He was also ambitious. *Life*'s circulation was *huge*. After getting his brief from Graves, he called Bennett to find out what he knew and planned. He and Don might provide an introduction to the family. They decided to travel together. Styron was among those young authors whom RH most counted on for signs of greatness, a writer who might help fill the void that had opened that day. Both partners liked him; it would be a comfort to have him near.

Commercial jet travel in America had begun in 1958, but many routes, like the one they embarked on, were still serviced by turbo-props and multiple stops. Their path meandered from New York to Cincinnati, thence Nashville, before they finally landed in Memphis. As they made their way through the airport, Styron noticed a middle-aged woman headed in the opposite direction. She'd stopped and was staring hard: something had caught her eye. The "something" was Bennett, who, enervated and weary as they all were, was taking long drags on his pipe.

All of a sudden the woman changed course, drifted behind, then gained on them and let out a whoop. "Bennett Cerf! You're Bennett Cerf! Good Lord God, never thought I'd meet *you,*" the words spilled out. "What are you doin' here in Memphis?"

Her famous quarry spoke of a "sad occasion," then divulged the particulars, that he was on his way to William Faulkner's funeral.

"William *Who* . . . ?" she asked, eager and a little too loud.

For a fraction of a second the three men stood stuck, unable to extricate themselves from the excruciating incongruity. Styron could sense Bennett cringe, incredulous, the automatic smile in danger of slipping from his face. She was so aware of the big-shot TV celebrity, so unknowing of the man they mourned, a writer for the ages. They beat a retreat to the rental car and the Peabody Hotel, but the incident lingered, throbbing like a bruise beneath the skin of the next two days. It would show when Bennett excused himself and left Styron to mull it over with Don, who'd known him so long, and could speak of the paradox that was his friend. It would surface again in quiet talk between Bennett and Styron on the plane Saturday evening, flying home.

The woman's determined pursuit; his treasured role as a celebrity; her simple, unselfconscious ignorance of something far greater, had gotten to Bennett. Yes, he loved the limelight—and it had its usefulness in furthering RH interests—but part of him was painfully aware, Styron recognized, of "how cheap and meretricious" such fame could be. It was one of those fleeting moments when the conflict in Bennett's soul, so hard to reconcile and pin down—and almost always deeply hidden—hung naked and exposed, troubling to them all.

That night, while Bennett was busy giving interviews to the Memphis *Commercial Appeal* and other papers at the Peabody, Donald got through to Jill. *Of course,* come along to the family funeral in the house, tomorrow at noon, before the public ceremony.

The following morning, they piled into the Chevrolet to drive the eighty miles south-southeast to Oxford, the little town that was home both to William Faulkner and the state university, "Ole Miss." Bennett, who'd traversed America so often and so widely and been comfortable practically everywhere, had never been to rural Mississippi, deepest of the deep, the Ur-South in the mind of any Yankee. Although he'd enjoyed Dixie hospitality elsewhere, he'd later consider how "very odd" this journey felt. Partly, it was "heartbreak" (others might call it guilt or regret) that for so long, Faulkner had invited him to visit, and it was only now, with the man dead, that he was complying with the request. Yet he was honest enough to admit that he'd never been "very anxious" to go there: what he'd gleaned on his own and heard from Saxe had made him wary of a household that too often looked lifted from the pages of a gothic novel.

Retrospectively, it wasn't only grief that colored Bennett's memory. He would come to associate his unease with events that took place in Oxford three months later. On the last day of September, President Kennedy would order thousands of U.S. Army reserve troops down the same route the Chevy took. They'd be called upon to quell deadly riots when a young Black man named James Meredith faced the governor and a massed white mob from all over the state, converged to bar him from entering the university. Faulkner himself, in his last months, had taken an interest in Meredith's fight to enroll in Ole Miss.

But while many Southerners saw him as far too sympathetic to the Black man—he'd received hate mail, crank calls, and around Oxford certain businesses refused to serve such a "Negro-lover" (their term was far more abusive)—Bennett and Don had seen how he'd managed to alienate liberals as well. The poet Delmore Schwartz would later describe Faulkner as "a kind of victim of the social structure of the South." For Random's partners, his racial views presented a difficult conundrum. Bennett tried to deal with it publicly by telling people that Bill was "a liberal Mississippian, though some may call that a contradiction in terms." They'd had, he confessed, "many arguments about the colored man in the South."

James Baldwin had taken public issue with Faulkner's go-slow attitude, and Don, pressed by an interviewer, admitted, "I don't think that's completely unjustified on Mr. Baldwin's part." Yet he also defended Faulkner: "I do know that Bill had a deep love for the Negro, a real understanding for him, a deep sympathy for him, and just the sure knowledge within himself . . . that this [civil rights, desegregation] wasn't going to happen overnight." Lost in the turmoil was one of those small human ironies. It would be a point of pride for Jill, until the end of her days, that "Pappy" had paid the NAACP dues for a number of Black people who were part of his life.

. . .

WHEN THE THREE TRAVELERS reached Oxford, an odd feeling settled deep in them as they circled the town center. Peering through the car windows, everything was foreign and at the same time familiar: the white-columned courthouse on the little square; slit-mouthed white farmers in sun-bleached overalls, their wrinkles like dusty bird-tracks etched into aging skin; red-faced young fellows, short-sleeved and crew cut, clustered around the perimeter; quiet Black men under the trees, selling fruit they'd picked that morning. Bennett had seen this place in the film of *Intruder in the Dust*. All three knew it in their mind's eye as "Jefferson," in Faulkner's novels.

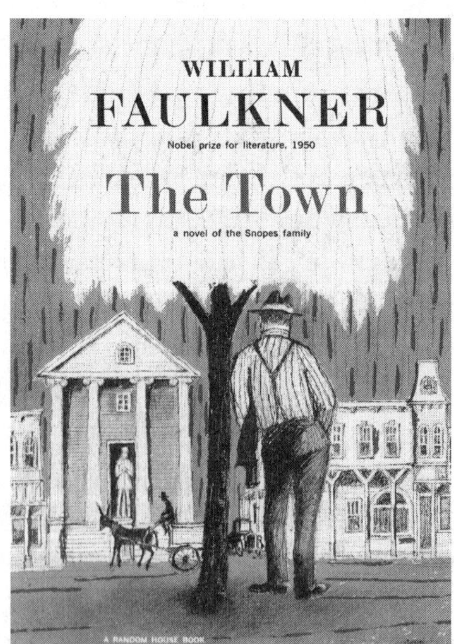

All three knew Oxford as "Jefferson" from the novels

Mrs. Nina Goolsby, editor and co-owner of the Oxford *Eagle,* was one of the newspaper people who'd been in touch the previous night. She said she had things to show Bennett and the others, and would be glad to take them for a tour of the town. They parked the Chevy and emerged from its cool cocoon, having paid extra for the luxury of air-conditioning. Outside, the heavy wet wallop of heat was stunning. They had anticipated the assault, but its intensity was overwhelming. The first fellow they asked to direct them to the *Eagle* stared. A second didn't answer, either. A third finally said, "I think it's over there." Bennett was sure all three knew its whereabouts, but their enmity to these Northern interlopers was as palpable as the heat.

Fat, bustling Mrs. Goolsby, friendly under a buzzing air-conditioner, had assembled a mess of back issues with articles by and about Faulkner. She wanted to prove that, whatever outsiders might think about the townspeople not caring for their local son, they did. Bennett remained far from convinced, but that *she* did care was unequivocal. Mrs. Goolsby had just returned from distributing handbills printed at her own expense—"In Memory of William Faulkner This Business Will Be Closed From 2:00 to 2:15 PM Today, July 7, 1962"—mounting a one-woman campaign to persuade store owners to place them in their windows and follow suit.

At half past eleven, the three men drove to Rowan Oak. As they walked down an arcade of tall canopied cedars toward the columned portico precisely centered at its end, they almost did a double-take: the man at the entrance could have been Bill. Up close, John Faulkner, one of his brothers, was thinner, his thatch a little whiter. Already he was a bit drunk and passing judgment on all who would enter. The whole extended clan had gathered. Bennett mused how most had never understood their famous relation; many didn't even like him. (The feeling was mutual.) Yet down the years, Bill had come through for them, and not a few had filled their bellies off his work. John Faulkner had been expecting his brother's publishers, but not any man from *Life.* He didn't want Styron snooping around, even if he was, as Bennett tried to persuade him, an admirer and fellow writer who'd do the great man justice. It was an uncomfortable replay of how Faulkner himself had fought off reporters whom Bennett had wanted him to meet.

Styron stayed outside. Inside, fans whirred, making it a degree or so cooler, but for two Yankees in suits, it was like wading through half-formed Jell-O. They paused for a moment at the parlor, where the body lay in a closed coffin perfectly devoid of flowers, then passed through the dining room, where a vast spread of offerings brought by relations—turkeys and hams, pies and puddings (as well as sweating pitchers of iced tea with which to down them)—awaited lunchtime. Finally they were shepherded upstairs to "Miss Estelle's" bedroom, where Jill joined them.

With help from AA, Estelle had stopped drinking a half dozen years before. Bennett saw her staring into space and suspected she'd taken something to calm her nerves. Don, looking at the same picture, saw a woman "composed and sensible" under the circumstances. She was vain, had been flirtatious in youth, and like Faulkner, coveted good clothes. All her life gardenia-pale, stick-thin, and cinched Scarlett O'Hara–tight, for this last public appearance she'd dressed the part. The twisting black edges of an oversized ruffle cascaded like tributaries down the front of her beige belted dress. A broad-brimmed black hat and elbow-length gloves rested nearby.

Don began to talk quietly about Bill. Estelle responded warmly. It wasn't simply the rules of decorum: a few years earlier, she'd been a guest at his farm, and as a younger woman who could be charming and open to being charmed, she'd enjoyed Bennett's company on rare visits to New York. Theirs was more than a quarter century of acquaintance. Donald later ventured that Faulkner's widow and daughter *were* genuinely glad to see them, even if the rest of the clan looked on with barely concealed hostility. Without question, Estelle and Jill thought *him* a true gentleman—a designation of particular significance within the code of the South. They were partial to his lady, "Miss Pat," as well. Thus, on his own account, he was right.

Yet Jill's feelings about Bennett were more ambivalent. Her father's daughter, she wasn't given to many words and had never felt quite comfortable when Bennett waltzed her into '21' or treated her to an evening at the theater. At times she tried to duck the boisterous voice intent on entertaining her, which seemed oblivious to her shy unease. Jill liked "Miss Phyllis" well enough, though, joining *her* conspiratorially in laughing at her spouse's undignified foolery behind his back. Bennett compounded Jill's discomfort by "showing her off" as she saw it, happily and pointedly introducing her as "William Faulkner's daughter," the same way he referenced his wife as "Ginger Rogers' cousin." The name-dropping was enough to make her squirm. Like Phyllis, Jill reaped the benefits of proximity to fame, but in her case had suffered its cost from earliest childhood. Once, when she was pleading with her father to stop drinking, Faulkner had lashed out: "Nobody remembers Shakespeare's children." The memory of that never left her. She was proud to be her father's daughter, but also struggled to be her own woman.

The way she felt about Bennett's displaying her like a badge of distinction wasn't unlike how Faulkner felt about Truman Capote trying to cozy up to him at Random House. When Jill visited New York with "Pappy," he'd send her into the palazzo, as scout and decoy, to avoid an encounter with Bennett's pet author. He desired no clinging attachment from a "fan boy."

Of course, Jill and Estelle felt the absence of the greatest comfort RH had given, and for "Mr. Saxe's" memory they retained only deep affection, gratitude, and the highest regard.

After a half hour with the two women, Donald and Bennett went downstairs, to the busy crowd tucking in to the sumptuous spread like a wake of hungry vultures. Were Bill Faulkner not dead in his box, he would have looked on, amused: six years earlier, he'd told Jean Stein that, if reincarnated, he wanted to come back as a buzzard.

Bennett left no trace of the Memphis airport encounter in his reminiscences; instead, he chose to remember another woman, one who sidled up while he and Don were milling around Faulkner's buzzard-filled parlor. *That* woman also asked if he wasn't "the fellow we see on Sunday night on *What's My Line?*" With his acknowledgment that yes, he was one and the same, the enmity he and Don had been experiencing from the room evaporated. To her, he became "one of the people who came to [her] house every week . . . an old friend." It was a comforting story layered on top of one not nearly so reassuring.

Later, when the extended kin and very few outsiders—Bennett; Donald; Faulkner's friend Shelby Foote (deep into writing his Civil War history for RH); Linton Massey, a devoted scholar and collector of all things Faulkner; and a couple of others—gathered in the parlor with the immediate family, Estelle recalled that Bennett had told her about Styron. She beckoned him, one more outsider, in. They listened as an Episcopalian minister slowly intoned a ten-minute service over the coffin: a few Bible selections, the Lord's Prayer, no eulogy, as simple as Bill would have wanted. Afterward, they got into the Chevy, part of a crocodile of cars behind the black-finned Cadillac hearse heading toward the square and then the cemetery.

Bennett looked at the battered old cars and could only sniff and shake his head at such a clapped-out cortege. Yet peering again from inside the blessed air-conditioning, he found himself jolted anew, the big city-slicker brought short by a sudden transformation in the queer hick town. It was as though a spell had been cast: nothing moved, every shop *was* closed, and the residents stood—about a third of the folk were Black—in the square or on balconies, silent, watching, erect, respectful. Police covered their hearts with their caps. All motion and sound ceased, except for the snap-and-flash of photographers' cameras and scratching of pens on reporters' pads; waiting on a knoll above the grave site, they had converged from all over, ants to a picnic.

Funerals "are a big thing around here," one laconic onlooker told Styron.

Bennett and Donald were more charitable. To Bennett's way of thinking, the town realized that "they had lost an important citizen. They hadn't read him. They didn't understand him. [Many] didn't pay much attention to him when alive." Some, Don thought, "hated" him; some "loved" him; many "couldn't quite cotton up to the fact that a man could scribble words on paper and make a decent living." But the people knew what they had to do *now*—just as Bennett and Donald had known—and they did it.

The mourners got to the cemetery. A tent had been erected on the side of a small hill, and under it a dozen or so chairs were placed for the closest family alongside the newly dug grave. The rest—still not a great crowd—stood as the minister reprised the same service he'd conducted at the house. The three men did not tarry. Styron had a deadline, and Donald wanted to return to New York if at all possible that night, however late. They said their goodbyes and made for Memphis.

A few days later, Bennett wrote to Shelby Foote. Curiosity had got the better of him: he wanted to know what transpired after they left. He hated not being in on action through to the end; it was like reading a story and stopping before the last chapter. He also expressed gratitude for the only consolation out of Oxford that day: Foote had reported good progress on his work.

"I think it will be one of the items on the Random House list of which I'll be most proud for the rest of my life," Bennett told him. There'd be no more pride in new works from Bill.

. . .

THE ROLE OF THE publisher does not end with an author's death. Originally, Bill had done Saxe the honor of naming him literary executor. Had that plan not been waylaid by Saxe's demise, RH would have exercised an extraordinary influence over Faulkner's literary afterlife. Instead, the task and privilege of ultimate control devolved to Jill. Still, there was much that RH, from apex to base, had to do. The job before them was "to make public" Faulkner's work in the widest sense. Not to take advantage of the coverage of his passing would have been to neglect that role. They'd continue to push hard for sales of his last novel, *The Reivers,* published only the previous month. Donald had predicted—correctly—that it would reach the bestseller list. But that was only one prong in the posthumous promotion plan.

A week after the death, Richard Krinsley, who'd become sales manager after Bob Bernstein was promoted, sent a memo to the salesmen: to capitalize on the interest in Faulkner, an announcement would go out to their very best accounts—about two hundred stores—offering a special promotion and physical display unit stocked with all of his works in print. Everything about the unit would be "very handsome . . . and infinitely more dignified and proper than anything we have ever done in this area." It was a distinct contrast to the way the firm had treated Bill for the first dozen or so years of their acquaintance. In those days, paltry sales hadn't justified keeping his backlist in print, so those titles had languished in limbo, cutting off any possibility of his earning money from them at a time when he was desperate for cash. Donald had come to feel "ashamed" about those decisions. Public taste is fickle, but perhaps *some* way could have been found to beat the drum and bring at least a modicum of his work back to life—what Malcolm Cowley accomplished under Viking's aegis with *The Portable Faulkner* in 1946—but they were plenty busy, and their resources limited. Now at least they'd make sure his books were available.

Yet publishing Faulkner had been a complicated business from the start, and if Donald was hard on himself because financials in the 1930s and '40s had trumped the responsibility to "make public," other obligations had been undertaken by RH in exemplary fashion. One had to do with his reputation, not just as a writer, but as a man. When the *New York Times* reporter telephoned him on the morning of the death, Bennett chose his words carefully: Of course, Faulkner's "literary impact" was "simply enormous," bringing him respect from "every type of author. Every other author in America looks upon [him] as one of our all-time greats." From the publisher's vantage point, he "was just about the ideal author," giving over his manuscript to RH and trusting them to do the right thing, never interfering or complaining. But beyond that—"besides being one of the greatest authors of our times"—Faulkner, Bennett stressed, was "about as fine a gentleman as I have ever met." He attested that he'd never seen him "do anything that wasn't gallant, fine and the mark of a perfect gentleman."

Yet he, Don, Bob, Saxe (and latterly, Albert) had during a quarter century seen plenty of behaviors that didn't fit into that description. They'd played a part in situations so far removed from business as usual, even publishing-business as usual, as to be almost inconceivable to outsiders. Whether it was arranging rescue from binges, exercising discretion over mistresses, purchasing pipes, clothes, etc.—even, on his instructions, denying Estelle the money she moaned for—they did what he asked, or what he needed them to do without even asking. The four suits in Saxe's office awaiting Bill's visits were the tiniest token of how much a part of RH he'd become.

To be sure, gossip about the drinking had gotten about—on one of his cultural goodwill missions for the U.S. government in the post-Nobel years, Faulkner had been photographed getting off a plane abroad, drunk and disheveled. Occasional inebriated and inflammatory assertions were of his own (un)doing. Yet for Bennett and Don, each deeply in love with words and books and publishing, what Faulkner had done with his pen rose high above anything self-destructive, pathetic, mean, or foolish that they'd witnessed, and that was what they were determined to project. Like his partner, Donald attested to an interviewer that Faulkner was "one of the greatest gentlemen that I've ever met." Oh yes, he was also "strange" and "involuted," but at the same time, Donald underlined, "a great, great human being."

If Mark Twain was arguably the foremost American prose writer of the nineteenth century, the one novelist who, in *Huckleberry Finn,* had dared to take on the forbidden subject of whites and Blacks that had torn the nation asunder—the subject that had to be addressed honestly if the country were ever to heal—Faulkner was Twain's twentieth-century white counterpart. In an entirely different but equally brilliant fashion, he'd taken up a similar challenge, and created a vast opus. That was the man Bennett and Don wanted the world to know they'd published, the man they wanted remembered—alongside a row of books that would, they felt sure, long endure.

Chapter 41

Heartburn and Heartache

BILL FAULKNER'S DEATH DELIVERED ANOTHER REMINDER OF BENNETT'S own mortality: at sixty-four, he was eight months younger than his author. While he usually took spectacular good health for granted, death's roll call had left shadows that he couldn't ignore. He'd always lived at a furious pace, yet time seemed to be fast-forwarding. How was it that seven months had elapsed since Moss had literally dropped dead? The magnitude of that loss had been intensified by one that barely preceded it: uncle Herbert Wise had died, aged sixty-eight, in October 1961. His influence had been greatest when young, but Herbert was still the closest family, aside from Phyllis and the boys, that Bennett had. Seeing such a brilliant man decline into a lost child was horrifying, and Bennett's diary entries grew ever more disbelieving. Grateful to leave the day-to-day to Herbert's partner, Glen, he pronounced it a "blessing" when death finally arrived.

Now he'd added Faulkner to his private necrology. He may not have understood the tortured workings of the man, but he'd been awed by him. Unfortunately, losing Bill wasn't the only bad news. The firm issued its 1962 Annual Report two weeks after Faulkner's death. For the year ending April 30, earnings were $1.06 per share on sales of $23,280,000, compared with the previous year's $1.09 on sales of $22,460,000: not what Wall Street wanted. At first glance, the downturn was hardly terrible, but once you deducted the capital gain from selling part of RH's Grosset & Dunlap holding—G&D's Bantam was booming—net earnings per share were sixty-three cents, a deep tumble. In a letter to shareholders introducing the report, Bennett reasoned that the hefty expense of expanding in the school, college, reference, library, and mail-order fields was essential, since the firm's future "so obviously" depended on them. "We have had no hesitancy in sacrificing current profits. . . . This is the way Random House was built when we were a private company," he argued, wanting shareholders to agree it was in the best interest of the public corporation to continue the same policy, and agree, too, that it was in the *individual's* best interest, even if not ideal for immediate return on investment. At the annual meeting on August 15, he was blunt in predicting it would be at least two years before RH paid dividends.

Bennett liked winning; he didn't like bearing unsatisfactory news, feeling pressured by the scale he'd so determinedly pursued, or facing the overwhelming challenge of lassoing it into shape. Though he resisted inserting layers of bureaucracy, fearful that old intimacies might disappear, even he had to admit his informal ways were no longer enough. The complexity of what he'd assembled from such disparate parts was catching up with him, and, always so decisive, he now wasn't sure what to do. Needing advice, he wanted it quickly from someone who could be objective, but also knew the firm inside out. Bernstein, Kislik, and others were hungry, with too much self-interest at stake, and he didn't want to risk unsettling Don or disturbing Lew.

Instead, the designated sage was Bob Haas, who'd remained an RH director after retiring as partner. He took up the challenge and, writing in longhand, drafted two memos for Bennett's eyes only. The first recognized that major decisions would require more information, more people to make them, and better-defined lines of responsibility, and so Bob floated the idea of an "Executive Committee." As well as Bennett, Don, Tony, Lew, Bob Bernstein, Dick Kislik, Jess Stein, Knopf's Joe Lesser, and Pantheon's Kyrill Schabert, he suggested that Warren Blaisdell and Albert Erskine be co-opted. Frances Singer could come from Syracuse every other time.

Bennett's "phobia" about meetings was well known: he'd enter a room but walk out if four people were huddled around a table. Anticipating his reaction, Bob couched the committee as a way to filter all important information up to him, but also fan it out to departments. Pressing for gathering on a fixed day every two weeks, he dangled hope that as the habit grew, once every four weeks might suffice. "Coordination & control" were the watchwords for this phase. "I know well of your allergy," Bob acknowledged, "but we *need* [a committee] now." To make the medicine go down, he played on Bennett's ego and identification with the firm: if he agreed to such a "systematic briefing," Bob had enough faith in his "energy & ability" to be sure that RH would "stage not only a successful comeback, but a brilliant one."

On July 17, 1962, the Executive Committee convened for the first time. From then on, it would be a permanent corporate fixture of Random House Inc., through rises and falls, ownership changes, and a new century. Not everyone on Bob's initial list was there that day, and by the next year the group would slim into a super-committee of six, comprising Bennett, Don, Tony, Lew, Bernstein, and Kislik. A larger editorial committee would form under it. However, that first meeting, one person in addition to the long original list had been added: Alfred Knopf.

Bennett opened the meeting by playing to character: The firm was "strong," its reputation "excellent." Present problems could be addressed by a budget that should be adhered to for each division and department within it; an accurate cash-flow report; and a general "tightening of the ship" on overheads and expenses. These were extraordinary notions, coming from the lips of Bennett Cerf. Until now, so much of the math had been scribbled inside his head. Alfred tried to help by recalling how in 1935, when his firm was buffeted by the Depression, it had been greatly strengthened by instituting a system of "correct" budgeting and forecasting. At RH, such a system didn't exist. Alfred insisted that what the company suffered from was "not an illness but a temporary 'indigestion,'" and suggested establishing levels of how many titles each division would be able to publish, according to how many the sales department and the stores they sold to could realistically handle. Ideally, they should concentrate on publishing fewer titles and selling more of each, a commercial consummation devoutly to be desired but rarely achieved in modern publishing. Talk circled around myriad issues: pricing structure, travel and expenses, whether the dictionary should be delayed. In the end, Alfred again made a simple, useful suggestion: that a real agenda rather than impromptu discussion be in place next time. Bennett may not have felt comfortable with the new world order, but he had to live in it.

Communication and reassurances about how RH was—and wasn't—changing needed to be conveyed within and outside the firm. The staff had to have a picture of where the company was heading; any one person could only apprehend the tip of an iceberg whose great mass had accreted in an astonishingly short time. Two days after the Executive Committee meeting, Don wrote to the salesmen, enclosing a copy of the just-printed Annual Report. He wanted to discuss the "disappointing showing." The reps were on the front lines, and might have to field questions from stores and shareholders. The "extraordinarily heavy" outlays on the Blaisdell math and science operation, the dictionary, and the college department would continue into the new year. At the same time, he admitted what Bennett hadn't been able to do overtly in the Annual Report: they hadn't controlled budgets or expenses nearly as well as they ought. That *would* change.

He chose to borrow Alfred's phrase, "We have a little indigestion at the present," then emphasized that the expansion "was a wise decision." Once the heartburn passed, "a beautifully rounded publishing business, able to earn excellent profits," would remain. Whether or not Don experienced any recurrence of his own doubts, he'd do his damnedest to make sure the staff felt secure. Yet indigestion continued to plague the body corporate. It was becoming increasingly obvious that something had to be done about Blaisdell eating hundreds of thousands of dollars in capital and giving "more headaches every day," as Bennett admitted to Helen Geisel.

He, Kislik, and Phyllis—who'd become his eyes and ears in the education field—held "grim" meetings that landed Bennett in an ever-deeper funk. They'd tried combining Blaisdell's sales force with those of RH and Knopf to cut costs, but college math and science texts didn't fit in the mix. Was it only a few years ago that he so rashly wanted in? Now everything in him wanted out. Amazingly, his luck held: Kislik, tasked with finding a buyer, found a deep-pocketed one. In July, the textbook firm Ginn & Co., a major player in the field, agreed to pay $600,000 for the unit. The sale effected an improvement in the balance sheet, although Bennett's relief was marred by Warren Blaisdell receiving an "outrageous" $100,000 cut.

The outward flow of capital to new and diverse investments continued. Like others, the firm had watched as a clutch of Western European nations signed the Treaty of Rome in 1957 to establish a common market. Six years on, the chance for U.S. publishers to compete with the Brits in selling export copies to Europe was growing. RH could reach the Continent's book buyers more easily from London than New York, so a small U.K. subsidiary was incorporated. To capture more school dollars at home, Bennett and Don bought a Chicago-based educational supplier, renaming it Random House School & Library Service Inc., and installed Lew Miller as president, overseeing it from the Villard. Within a year, the subsidiary had moved to New York.

Necessity and serendipity conspired to bring them to another investment, one of the most strategic and expensive that RH would ever make. For years, their warehousing and distribution arrangements had been less than efficient. By 1960, Modern Library and RH adult and juvenile books were stored in and distributed from industrial buildings in various parts of the city and New Jersey. With the absorption of new companies, even more locations were used, and different practices were in place in different divisions. Whether it was a simple matter, such as using messengers to deliver packages, or a complicated one like inventory, billing, and shipping management across divisions, the costs of doing business were multiplying, spawning unnecessary duplication. The company's health depended on addressing these issues.

In the autumn of 1963, Bennett accompanied Phyllis and a Singer executive to a "tea" RH convened in Baltimore for a large number of educators. With so many of them female, they might be a little more disposed to adopt Singer texts if that fellow they liked on TV charmed them in person. Maryland governor J. Millard Tawes and his wife, Avalynne, had invited the New York visitors to a dinner at the state mansion in Annapolis. By then, Bennett's fame had gained him entrée to statehouses all over the nation. Tawes had much of the rural politician about him, while Bennett was a big-city big shot. Yet his jokes, unpretentiousness, and ability to make a person feel the center of attention put Tawes at ease. They hit it off, gabbing away.

It happened that an ambitious Baltimore-based first cousin once removed of Bennett's beloved Gertrude—a man named Julian Stein, who'd come to know his celebrated relation partly through the triumphant American lecture tour Bennett had helped arrange—was Tawes's PR adviser. Back in 1958, the then-candidate had wanted to hand out a campaign souvenir to voters. Mrs. Tawes was a very good cook, and Stein dreamed up the idea of giving away her best recipes in a booklet. Thousands were distributed as Tawes barnstormed the state. Citizens liked the gesture, the recipes, and as it turned out, the candidate. The future governor's wife liked seeing her name in print. After becoming first lady, she determined to expand the object into a book.

Once Tawes was in office, he asked Stein to spearhead a Department of Economic Development, charged, among other tasks, with persuading out-of-state businesses to relocate or establish an offshoot in Maryland. During Bennett's "memorable night" with the governor, the subject of RH's warehouse and distribution needs floated to the surface. So did the first lady's bubbling desire to be a published author. Bennett was already familiar with one of the locales the governor wanted to develop: rural Carroll County was where he'd visited Whittaker Chambers, home to the pumpkin patch that had hidden his infamous papers. By December, the notion of building a warehouse just outside Westminster, the county seat, had become a serious discussion, with Kislik point man and "incentives," as Stein put it, under consideration. RH had also been exploring Pennsylvania locations, but in the end, dinner-table chitchat spawned a deal.

It would take until the summer of 1967 for Bennett to be able to return to Maryland and dedicate his "great new" state-of-the-art distribution center (and much longer—so long that he wouldn't live to see it—for the facility's many growing pains and glitches to be resolved). By the twenty-first century, Westminster would best all other publishers' distribution centers in efficiency. But far sooner, the governor's lady saw her part of the bargain consummated, when *My Favorite Maryland Recipes,* by Avalynne Tawes, was published by Random House in 1964.

. . .

THE SUMMER THAT FAULKNER DIED, so did Marilyn Monroe, whom Bennett had profiled as the "Altogether Girl." Oddly, when Phyllis recorded her oral history, she pointedly compared herself to the star. It was rather a leap for a woman who'd failed as an actress, but also, in some ways, understandable: she saw them both as having had difficult childhoods that led to Hollywood. "I survived, you see," she declared in the oral history. "It's Marilyn Monroe who . . . did not." It happened that in 1962, when the supernova flamed out, Phyllis was shining at her brightest.

Chance and luck had led her to Bennett; grit and intelligence had secured her there. She had husband, homes, social status, career—and two sons, along with every external proof of being a successful mother. In 1963, Chris would graduate cum laude from Harvard. The next year, Jon would matriculate. Exceptionally well-mannered, they were boys who usually posed where she placed them, in the picture she and Bennett wanted to present of the perfect family. Both were well aware that their mother intended for them to secure the family foothold atop the social

The Family Cerf: Phyllis was shining at her brightest.

ladder. Having been rejected by Freddy Espy, Chris saw other girls, but didn't appreciate his dad's curiosity about his dating and sex life—Bennett always wanted details. Luckily, with his mother, there was no such vicarious interest: *she* verged on the prudish.

Both Chris and Jon had done well, yet whatever either boy accomplished was never enough. Often quixotic, Phyllis's mood would turn to criticizing or goading. No matter that Chris's best friend, Michael Frith; Jon's best friend, Peter Gabel; or somebody else was present to hear the tongue-lashing. She saw it as doing her job—spurring them on—a job she did for herself *and* Bennett. At times, she prevailed upon *him* to do battle—mostly with their older son.

"*Why don't you start writing to your mother?*" Bennett would yell down the phone at Chris, after Phyllis had worked on him.

Always her husband's staunchest defender, she nonetheless was capable of doing an about-face, letting Bennett know how humiliated she was at his seeming lack of dignity in the pranks he perceived as playful. But she did have ways of getting back. One was called "Laugh Day." Indeed, when Bennett published his ninth humor book, it bore that as title. His wife, he explained in the introduction, had co-opted her closest pal, Leonora Hornblow, and occasionally their sons, for a ritual that showed what she thought of the jokes he let loose upon them. On such a day, as soon as he appeared downstairs, they'd laugh hysterically at anything he said or did, until he felt "ready to murder them." In real time,

Laugh Day lasted perhaps an hour, but for Bennett even fifteen minutes was an excruciating eternity.

Another date was also perennially awkward and painful, but from Phyllis's perspective. Despite the grades and successes Chris and Jon racked up, her mothering wasn't celebrated on Mother's Day, for the holiday didn't exist in the Cerf household. "Manufacturer's Day," Bennett called it, waving it off as a calculated invention of greeting card manufacturers, florists, and candy companies. That was not how Phyllis saw it. At Christmas, Bennett also failed her expectations. The holiday was hugely important to Phyllis beyond any usual significance, for it showed how far she'd come. She choreographed it with lavish decorations, a groaning table, and mountains of presents and overstuffed stockings, most chosen and bought by her with supreme care. Her three guys would each find anywhere from twenty to forty boxes under the tree.

Bennett complained to his diary about "hours & hours" opening expensive, useless gifts from dear ones. Each box wasn't just opened: its contents had to be displayed, *appreciated*. Yet year after year, his offering to her was found wanting. Bennett wasn't cheap; he was clueless. He loved giving her paperweights, while she didn't even like them. Whatever misguided token emerged from the box, her letdown was clear to her sons, if not to her husband. Bennett's getting a gift right—the sable coat that took months for the furrier to make, the pearls she loved—was so rare, it became etched in the boys' memories. Etched sharper still were Phyllis's disappointments, but the biggest wasn't associated with Mother's Day or Christmas. Instead, it was the flip side of her greatest triumph, Beginner Books.

Bennett had inflicted a deep wound in 1960 by slipping the thinnest of blades between her and the Geisels, persuading them to sell the company, and *then* informing Phyllis that it was so. Her immediate reaction had been to take to her bed for several days and refuse to speak. Waking up facing a cold, angry statue was almost more than he could bear. Eventually, the wound scarred over. Yes, he'd taken Beginner for Random, but Phyllis still ran the day-to-day. She had his ear. Everyone in the firm acknowledged it. She could be subtle and persistent—some called it "devious"—in getting what she wanted, gradually convincing Bennett that her idea for a book or an author was *his*. She would always be Thrup to him, yet in the past few years had acquired a second nickname. He would toss it off with a wink and nod behind her back. Bennett so loved wordplay, how could he resist elevating Phyllis, whose initials were "P.F.C." (as in "private first class"), into "The General"? After a while, others began referring to her that way. Later, Bennett, the boys, and a few friends came to tease her with it openly. One year, they hired a bugler and presented "The General" with four stars. She was not amused.

And yet, like most jokes, it wasn't entirely so. Bennett was well aware that his wife was "getting stronger and stronger," as he phrased it, more stubborn, opinionated, and domineering in her work. During the more than two decades that they'd lived together, she was careful to put him first. Now her office persona was spilling into their home life, and it was driving him crazy. He could not manage all the things *he* did if domestic waters were roiled, and Beginner was roiling them practically every day.

In his sixties, it was not as easy for Bennett to stay up late as it once had been. Phyllis was much younger, and a night person: some of her best ideas for new authors or new subjects came at two or three in the morning. Now, night after night, she repaired to the small office off the far end of the dining room, her wraparound Formica desk scattered with typescripts, word lists, and sketches. The dark quiet of the townhouse garden outside walled off the noisy city, as she smoked her ever-present Parliaments and argued points in long calls to La Jolla.

Phyllis had known Ted since his advertising days. The notion that he'd wanted to write the "Great Novel" and settled for kids' books remained in the back of her mind, and she was never afraid of critiquing him. After all, she saw herself as every author's close collaborator, at times rewriting half the text. Concepts, words, drawings—even a comma—would be debated for hours. Any and all Beginners, even Ted's, were fair game.

He was another night owl, perched high above the Pacific in his aerie. By the time they finished, Phyllis's ashtray would be full, and darkness blanketing *both* coasts. Bennett in the East and Helen in the West had long since given up and retired to bed. Gone were the mornings when Phyllis, still in peignoir, would see Bennett's suitcase in the hall and not want him to hit the road again. He wouldn't have to travel so often if she didn't spend so much money, he used to counter. Now, no matter how late she'd fallen into bed, Phyllis would rise early and rush back to the office after issuing orders to Lillian, her secretary at Sixty-Second Street.

Then it was on to orders for Elma, her secretary at the Villard. The punishing schedule was as overfull as Bennett's, but she thrived on it. *She* was the one responsible for generating plenty of the firm's cash.

Her shame at a lack of formal diplomas she made up for by dint of hard work. Phyllis believed her mission was to help millions of children learn to read. She'd gone through every elementary reading program and primer, taking them apart word-for-word; she'd consulted experts and attended conferences. Gradually, she became convinced that she was an expert, too. The word lists, guidelines, retyped manuscripts, and much of her personal correspondence were banged out on an IBM Selectric typewriter with an exceptionally large font, black and bold. What she wanted and who she was came through loud and clear in the big typeface. Beginner Books gave her power, identity, and independence. It made her the heroine of her own story. For her husband, however, the transformation was not so ideal.

Bennett's relationship with Ted remained constant: they trusted each other implicitly. At work, when he glanced up, Bennett saw Blue-Green Abelard, the Seussical sculpted animal Ted had made and given him, smiling quizzically, a beneficent, zany figurehead. To make 100 percent sure that Bennett was reading his "stuff," Ted continued to insert little jokes, as he'd done from the start, when he'd labeled the bucket of sap in *The Seven Lady Godivas* "Bennett Cerf." Thus, *Hop on Pop* had arrived in 1962 bearing the line "Con Tra Cep Tive, Kan Ga Roo." The pill may have been fomenting a revolution, but it wasn't the stuff of kiddies' books. Ted waited for the mock-irate call from New York informing him that he'd tried to pull a fast one. They would both cackle, then settle in for a good, long chat.

In December, by Ted's reckoning, everything was "going great" on what they were calling *The Dr. Seuss Dictionary*—a book that Bennett, Phyllis, and Bob Bernstein considered of the highest priority. Ted was working with another writer-illustrator, Phil Eastman, and Bernstein saw huge sales potential. However, by mid-January, after a "midnight telephone marathon" with Phyllis followed by a sleepless night, Ted wrote her that "at exactly 5:15 AM," he'd arrived upon a solution to what in six weeks had turned from "going great" into a "seemingly never-ending and exhausting problem." He was withdrawing the book from publication, since too much of his time and strength were being wasted. That wasn't all: he'd decided that any Dr. Seuss books he'd write for Beginner would now be delivered in finished form, as he'd always done for RH. "The only way I can possibly work effectively," he added, "is to make my own mistakes in my own personal, peculiar way. Last summer *Hop on Pop* was almost completely ruined when I tried to incorporate other people's mistakes into the concept." "Other people" meant Phyllis, and however much she considered herself the expert, there was no question who was the genius. Bennett had to step in to mollify his friend and author, but the rift between Ted and Phyllis had widened to the point where it was harder even for him to bridge the divide.

. . .

HIS SCHEDULE WAS AS crazy as ever, his appetite for living seemingly untouched, but in mid-March, with RH stock down, Bennett admitted to his diary that he didn't have "enough zing left" for the humor anthology Harper's Cass Canfield was urging him to compile. Beneath the smile, the perennial optimist felt agitated and enervated on many fronts—even at MGM board meetings, the conversation dwelled on big failures. All the while, he suffered through a "brouhaha" of headache-making meetings and phone calls as relations between La Jolla and Manhattan got worse. Often Ted refused to speak to Phyllis, wanting to deal with him or Bernstein. In frustration she'd weep, tears that Bennett hated.

The only really good news arrived on April 1. For the first time since early December, he went down to breakfast to be greeted by fresh newsprint. For 114 days, workers at the city's seven newspapers had been on strike over technology and jobs. Despite radio and TV, he'd felt cut off. Now the strike was finally over. Ironically, the ones who seemed to have benefited the most were Jason Epstein; his wife, Barbara; and their friend Robert Silvers.

The strike had presented a particular crisis for publishers: How would they attract readers' attention with no print reviews, feature stories, or ads? The Epsteins and Silvers had come up with a solution: start a critical mechanism of their own that would do the papers one better, publishing review essays of the first order, contributed by their friends. Thus, *The New York Review of Books* was born. The strike also helped give rise to one of Phyllis's more ambitious projects, as she and Jason set to work developing a kids' newspaper, to be circulated in schools. They aimed to compete with the incredibly successful *Weekly Reader,* published since the 1920s. (In the end, their project lasted only a couple of years.)

A few other sparks lightened the gloom: A lecture trip gave Bennett a break from home and office. Faulkner won a posthumous Pulitzer for *The Reivers.* And the Grolier Corporation sent a fat check—$180,000—for Beginner Book Club sales. That deal was a dream, one that Beginner author Stan Berenstain characterized as "digging oil in your own backyard." In less than three years, the book club had paid RH more than $1.2 million. But another reminder of how critical Beginner was to the bottom line arrived shortly after the check, and was cause for the greatest worry. Ted had decided to speak through an intermediary, his agent, Phyllis Jackson, who conveyed her message to Bernstein rather than to Bennett. Ted was *really* unhappy, and wanted free of Bennett's wife. Otherwise, he'd publish elsewhere. The threat was personal, shocking, unequivocal. Ted had thrown down the gauntlet, yet Phyllis Cerf was never one to give up.

The Executive Committee was to gather on May 1, and Beginner was high on the agenda. During the meeting, it was agreed that Ted should have "complete freedom" on all his books, whether Beginner or Random House, but would be "encouraged not to participate" in business matters handled in New York. Phyllis would have *her* projects. Bernstein was to prepare written discussion points to use with the Geisels, who were flying in from La Jolla a week later.

On May 9, a Thursday, Bennett took Ted and Helen for a meal at '21,' a place where they'd passed so many happy evenings. This night proved dyspeptic, "strained." Ted's agent phoned Bennett at home that Sunday. After *What's My Line?* the Cerfs stayed up late to plot "Geisels strategy." He so wanted to find a way to help, but, at the same time, to put an end to the turmoil: his loyalties were stretched to the limit in opposing interests of wife and author. Sales conference began at the Lotos Club the next morning, but at lunchtime he was closeted with Don and Bob Bernstein, mapping out a plan for what to do about Beginner.

It was pure coincidence that Stan and Jan Berenstain were at RH the day that the plan went into action. The couple had come up from Philadelphia to work with Ted and Phyllis, but strangely, the atmosphere in the cozy attic was "very different" from the usual: Phyllis was nowhere to be found. The Berenstains recognized that she could be tough but were grateful to her for it: she'd stood up to Ted when he interfered with their concepts and way of working. She'd always been nice to *them*. This morning, though, there was only Ted. They proceeded to storyboard their book onto the wall; suddenly, Donald entered. Never before had they seen him in the Beginner offices, and he'd brought with him, of all things, a large portfolio of cat pictures.

"Ted, I want you to see these," Stan distinctly heard Don say, all the while thinking to himself that Ted might have created the most famous children's cat in the world, but had no interest in others' feline renderings. Nonetheless, the two stationed themselves some distance away and flipped through the portfolio. As they did so, they talked quietly. Stan realized that they were discussing the future of Beginner. As the Berenstains came to understand, Beginner would henceforth be run by Ted and Helen from California, with Bob Bernstein and his assistant, Anne MarcoVecchio, heading the New York office. Louise Bonino and a young editor, Walter Retan, would help editorially. Phyllis had been frozen out, completely and permanently.

On May 21, Bennett recorded a "peaceful pow-wow" with the Geisels. The three even discussed his proposed animal riddle book for Beginner. He was eager to start—it had great potential—and he knew, too, that Phyllis would do most of the work, as she did on his other kids' books. But peace had come at a price. By the end of the month, the "enormity" of the change and "outrageous" Beginner "snafu" had "hit poor Thrup" and "K.O.d" her. "Woe, woe!" Bennett had sighed to his diary. However, not all had been entirely lost: a consolation was offered. Phyllis would be allowed to develop a new series—oriented toward schools but also sold into stores, for kids reading just beyond the Beginner level—that she'd call Step-Up Books.

Chris's friend Michael Frith, the talented cartoonist, had agreed to join RH after Harvard to help Ted and Bernstein, but, when he reported to the palazzo on his first day, was suddenly told that he'd be working with Mrs. Cerf. "Go up to the fifth floor," he was instructed. "And if you see Mr. and Mrs. Geisel in the elevator, don't talk to them." Chris, too, came to RH, receiving a warm welcome from Donald. He was also to help Phyllis, but the arrangement didn't last. Soon he moved over to the adult side.

Dick Kislik, RH's number-cruncher-in-chief, had been pushing a plan to prepare Chris for the long term: he should work for a year in

London at a friendly British publisher, followed by Harvard Business School and an MBA, and *then* join the company. Bennett wanted to do the right thing, and mentioned the idea to his son. But he was sixty-five, and didn't want to part with Chris for three long years. He wanted him in the firm, *now.* At year's end, he and Phyllis had a "big" talk with *both* sons about Random House, and the part they might play in its future.

They "REALLY want to be in RH," Bennett assured himself, but a hint of doubt remained. "I pray that they mean what they are telling me!"

Two months earlier, the Executive Committee had raised for discussion a novel topic: "the future ownership and direction of Random House." Contemplating what might come to pass, members saw three possibilities: ownership and management continuing with the present families (Chris, Jon, and Tony Wimpfheimer eventually taking over); merging with a complementary business, probably another publisher; selling Random House Inc. to "a firm whose management and policies would be acceptable to the present principals." All options would have to be discussed with Alfred Knopf and Francis Singer. In fact, there had already been expressions of interest from outside: Bennett's friend Herb Mayes, the editor of *McCall's* magazine, had broached the subject of a possible merger on behalf of his corporate masters. Philadelphia's Curtis Publishing, parent of *The Saturday Evening Post,* had also floated hints.

"Oy vay!" was all Bennett could say to his diary. Yet in taking the company public and expanding so rapidly, the genie had been let out of the bottle. It wasn't just him and Donald anymore. And thanks to his forcing Beginner into the Random fold, it wasn't just him, Thrup, Helen, Don, and Ted in control there, either. If it had been, the ultimate resolution of the "snafu" might have had a slight chance of being different. Bennett was president, but the Executive Committee was now in place, and ambitious younger men were wielding power through it. Phyllis, for one, had come to see Bob Bernstein in a very different light.

The Geisels felt liberated but sad, at least as far as Bennett was concerned. "What two birds while flying West will always remain close to two in the East. Answer: A brace of Geisels," they'd telegraphed Mt. Kisco on May 25, Bennett's sixty-fifth birthday.

"I think that due to you and all the others around here, we've got Beginner . . . back smoothly on the rails. From here on in, I pray that we'll be back on the old personal relationship that has meant so very,

very much to Phyllis and me," he responded, ever so carefully. But the truth was, hurt feelings were spread all around. Helen admitted to Bennett a couple months later that she'd been suffering a "cut-off feeling." Phyllis had wanted her legacy to be as primary creator of Beginner. Step-Up was successful—and she enjoyed bringing in friends like the Hornblows and Peggy Weidman as authors—but the series wasn't Beginner. The books, their impact, and their profits never came close, and she'd always feel a kind of diminishment. On the other hand, some maintained that although Beginner would continue to soar, the best of the books (as well as the worst) were produced during the time she and Ted worked together.

However "outrageous"—Bennett's word—he considered the "snafu" and the corner Thrup (and he himself) had been boxed into, he'd had a choice, albeit an impossible one. He could have supported his wife by falling on his sword, refusing to agree with the decision to force her out, and suffering the very great consequences. Instead, he chose his author and Random House.

This was the second time he'd betrayed her, after that first blow when he'd maneuvered for RH to take over Beginner. The marriage would continue. It would never be quite the same.

Chapter 42

Red Hot Fun

Esquire HAD BECOME THE HIPPEST, TREND-SPOTTING LARGE-circulation monthly in the nation, and in July 1963 published a special issue devoted to contemporary American literature. A string of first-rate writers, including Robert Penn Warren, Vladimir Nabokov, Flannery O'Connor, and Saul Bellow, contributed articles, as did Bob Linscott, who reminisced about his friendship with Bill Faulkner. The centerpiece of the issue, however, was a two-page map. As RH and other corporatizing publishers were adopting the organizational schema of big business, *Esquire* fiction editor L. Rust Hills intended the map to anatomize "the cultural-social-commercial situation" that produced, promoted, and evaluated *literary* writers. Titled "The Structure of the American Literary Establishment," it diagrammed what Hills termed "*a chart of power*."

In this new decade, the literary landscape was being reshaped by writers breaking more boundaries, paperbacks selling more copies, newer magazines exercising greater influence, and a fresh breed of agent—many of them female—blending higher receptivity to cultural risk-taking with a harder-nosed business sense. Names of editors, agents, critics, writers, as well as the magazines, newspapers, campuses, and publishers where they could be found, marched across the two-page spread in fourteen vertical columns, subdivided into dense blocks of type. Superimposed on the columns of black print set against a yolk-yellow background were three large, colored screen-tints, rising like continents from the sea of type, connecting discrete groupings one to another. The lavender "continent" on the left, the "Cool World," linked Beats and hipsters like Allen Ginsberg, Norman Mailer, and H. L. Humes to trailblazing off-Broadway playwrights like Edward Albee, young poets such as John Ashbery, alternative-newspapers-with-attitude like the *Village Voice,* store-cum-salons such as San Francisco's City Lights, and "the most avant-garde U.S. publisher," Grove Press.

No self-respecting habitué of the "Cool World" would be caught dead within the green-hued right-hand continent, "Squaresville." Here clustered the staff reviewers and editors of *The New York Times;* the drama critics of the city's other dailies; out-of-town book-page editors; Bennett's former stomping ground, the *Saturday Review;* and judges of the Book-of-the-Month Club, along with America's biggest publisher, Doubleday; the newly merged Holt, Rinehart & Winston; and old-line Harper. Squaresville exercised great power within middlebrow culture and the bestseller list, yet had "little consequence" on a writer's "real" reputation, Rust Hills insisted.

Between the "Cool World" and "Squaresville," a third continent straddled the map's middle: "The Hot Center." Colored fire-red, it boasted "little magazines" like *The Paris Review* that could launch a career; one commercial magazine, *The New Yorker,* that did the same; agents like Candida Donadio and Sterling Lord, trailing long lists of choice young writers; preeminent critics like Edmund Wilson, Dwight Macdonald, and Mary McCarthy; and "writers who get in columns"—Gore Vidal, James Baldwin, and Bennett's beloved Truman. Publishing houses here included the Viking Press, now led by Harold Guinzburg's son Tom; Farrar, Straus; Putnam; and a small independent, Dial Press. One single house occupied the nexus, the "red-hot" center. By adding Knopf and Pantheon to the already-strong mother list, "*Bennett Cerf secured Random's position as the most important literary publisher,*" Hills declared unequivocally. It was as though the teacher of a class of gifted students had stood up and announced in a ringing voice that a single clever child outshone the rest. Nothing could have pleased Bennett more. As a young man, he'd determined to become one of the leading American publishers, and was now anointed *the* leader. The unique distinction brought apotheosis and challenge: RH would have to keep up the reputation, while any envy the endorsement provoked needed to be offset.

Hills wanted to stir things, and succeeded. Letters poured in. The map was *Inspired! Indispensable! Infuriating!*—depending on if you were "in" or "out." One thing was sure: if you fancied yourself part of literary life, it couldn't be ignored. *Esquire* went so far as to put an asterisk next to names of editors who could "make or break" a career. At RH, Epstein and Fox got asterisks. "The point is, in the hot center . . . people know one another, and . . . are in a position to do something . . . [so] things get done," Hills declared. Bennett knew *that* from a tender age.

He pasted "The Structure of the American Literary Establishment" into his scrapbook, then took more consequential action. Always on the lookout for talent, he wanted to meet James Silberman, the "asterisked" Dial Press editor of James Baldwin, Herbert Gold, and other "hot" writers. Joe Fox had urged it: he knew Silberman from their Harvard days. On Monday, June 10 (*Esquire*'s July issue had of course debuted the month before), Bennett phoned Silberman, only to hear that he was about to take a job at McGraw-Hill. The man astride the red-hot center would not be deterred. "Before you make any other decision, I want you to talk to me in person. Are you free today for lunch?" Bennett inquired.

Silberman remembered spying him from a distance at parties, accepting as truth the gossip that he was "silly, not clever, more interested in TV than publishing." Yet something in the voice on the phone persuaded him to see the man up close. They met at the Four Seasons, which—almost as soon as it had opened in 1959 in the sleek Seagram Building—had become one of *the* lunch destinations for the powerful. What Silberman didn't know was that Bennett was on the hunt for a man to be groomed as *chief* editor. The house had entered a different stage; he and Don were older. While Bernstein and Kislik brought the sales, marketing, and administrative muscle this phase required, neither had the partners' editorial instincts. One was primarily a merchandiser and businessman, the other a businessman through and through.

What the Random House operation (distinct from Knopf or Pantheon) needed was a star editor who could also be a list-builder, cat-herder, number-cruncher, and diva-manager. In other words, a chief dedicated to writers and plugged into the zeitgeist, with exceptional common sense, skill, tact, and taste; someone capable of balancing corporate business imperatives against the separate interests of a whole covey of established, independent-minded editors, whose respect he'd have to earn, quickly. Bennett knew that Albert Erskine had no desire for such a role; his patience was for manuscripts, not necessarily for people. Jason was interested in his own favored authors and growing sidelines. Others were too young, too quiet, not right.

Bennett's ambitions had originally centered on Joe Fox. Almost as soon as Joe arrived, he became beloved by many. Although Bennett made jokes about Joe's workaholic ways, everyone recognized his devotion to authors. Yet Fox had disappointed him, refusing the offer: he didn't want to be bogged down in balance sheets. That meant bringing in someone who, unlike Hiram, would *fit* and *stay*. Jim Silberman, thirty-six, slight, dark-haired, horn-rimmed, intellectual, yet warm and with eyes and ears open to the wider culture, assured Bennett over lunch that he'd already made a commitment to McGraw-Hill. But the more Silberman said it, the more interested Bennett became. He'd seen the *Esquire* map, and was very keen.

"I'd like you to meet Don before you make a final decision," Bennett coaxed.

The guy others had snickered about wasn't the man sitting across from him, Silberman realized. He liked Bennett instantly, the energy, the enthusiasm. The next day, he met Donald at the palazzo. A day later, Fox took him for a drink at the Harvard Club. "Do it," he urged.

Silberman's wife, Leona Nevler, was a mother of two young children and, unusual for that time, also managing editor at a big paperback house, Fawcett. She'd proven her mettle in clubby male book publishing by spotting and freelance editing the explosive bestseller *Peyton Place*. Yet Nevler remained a self-confessed "snob" about TV, and saw Bennett as being of *that* world. Her vote was for McGraw. Silberman, suspended between two futures, phoned Bennett, who invited him to Mt. Kisco. They met at Grand Central, where he was blithely led past the crowds into the "private" car that Bennett had been the first Jew to integrate. They were picked up by the groundskeeper, Mackenzie, who drove to the big house on the hill. Silberman made the acquaintance of Phyllis and the boys over a splendid dinner, then was shown to a guest room, elegant but with as much thoughtful comfort as a person could desire.

In the middle of the night, the fairy tale took a dark turn: he awoke in a sweat. He didn't know these people. What was he doing? How would he ever find another author to satisfy them? But with morning, his head cleared and the clinging panic lifted, like fog burnt off by the sun. He went down to breakfast and on the table saw *two* copies of *The New York Times*. After coffee and eggs, Mackenzie drove them from the dream house through the storybook town to the station. As they stood awaiting the train to the city, he turned to his host, a man who had everything.

"What on earth do you need me for?" he wondered aloud.

Bennett fixed him in the eye, smiled, and spoke directly: "If you're as good as I think you are, you'll do very well at Random House."

There is nothing more intoxicating than an unequivocal vote of confidence from a very powerful man. The deal was closed, with no looking back, in that moment. James Silberman started at RH on July 1, entering as a senior editor, with an office near Phyllis in the attic—the palazzo was cramped to bursting. A year later, he became chief editor. He'd bring with him Herbert Gold and Vance Bourjaily, novelists judged "hot" by *Esquire,* but although Bennett worked with him to persuade James Baldwin, too—giving Baldwin the full treatment, including a dinner that Bennett judged one of the "best" he and Thrup ever held—Baldwin remained at Dial. Betty Friedan's *The Feminine Mystique* was published by Norton during the newspaper strike, but didn't take long to cause a sensation. Silberman quickly moved to acquire her next book. He'd go on to sign his Dial editorial successor, E. L. Doctorow, who'd publish *The Book of Daniel,* and all that came after it, with RH; and would also acquire *Future Shock* by Alvin Toffler; David Halberstam's *The Best and the Brightest;* and Muhammad Ali's autobiography, *The Greatest,* among many remarkable books. Bennett's bet more than paid off.

James Silberman and his author Muhammad Ali

. . .

EIGHT MONTHS AFTER SORTING out the structure of America's literary establishment, *Esquire* published "The Long Happy Life of Bennett Cerf," a five-and-a-half-page profile of the master of the house at its red-hot center, written by Thomas B. Morgan and illustrated by Diane Arbus with an unforgettable headshot. As soon as Bennett read it, he told his diary it was "VERY PLEASING!" Was that because his flaying by Geoffrey Hellman in *The New Yorker* five years earlier had shown him it could have been worse? Was there irony in the "very" and the block capitals? Or was it simply that the internal mechanism inoculating him against stings was doing its job again? Morgan, like Hellman, was not allergic to sarcasm: the profile's title, as well as its first line—"Bennett Alfred Cerf is perhaps the most *fun*-loving corporation president in America"—previewed the ironic tone that would follow. On the first page alone, Morgan used "fun" nine times, dredging up Hellman's *poking fun;* Bennett's being part of America's "*fun* capital"; his having *fun* courtesy of his place "in the bosom of the people"; his "love" of "*fun*"; and his "congenital aversion" to *fun*'s "opposites." Each repetition reinforced how unseemly it was for a man who wanted to be taken seriously as a publisher of literature to be seduced by *fun*.

As ever, Bennett appeared unfazed, allowing that he might be considered much more "distinguished" if he hadn't had "so much *fun* on the side." Morgan's litany resembled that of others who'd profiled him: Bennett avoided "any public inference" of having a profound or painful thought or taste for intellectual discourse; he preferred to discuss his *relationships* with authors rather than their work; his "blitheness," like "the sea-turtle's shell," was virtually "impregnable." He saw life through "horn-rimmed glasses" (a rose-colored echo was implicit). Yet the puzzle remained: *How* could a man seem all shiny shell, yet be the creative force behind RH and the ML, keeper of the keys to the most important literary sanctum in America?

Morgan couldn't know that when the spotlight singled him out, Bennett's default was to hide anxiety and put on a show, even though playing to type was in some ways serving him less and less well. Yet despite the generally disparaging tone, Morgan was unusual among journalists who'd profiled Cerf in that he did permit a few saving graces. He granted that Bennett listened well on any subject, and "in contrast to some other publishers," even read many of his authors' works. He was energetic, but also endearing. And although Morgan hated the show business terminology, he was unable to disagree when Bennett said that his role was, first, to spot "talent," and second, to keep the talent happy. RH wouldn't sit at the red-hot center if he hadn't done that.

Later, having experienced Bennett's punishing schedule firsthand, Morgan glimpsed behind the grin, seeing his subject sag, so tired, into a train compartment leaving Philadelphia to return home, weighted down even by the newspapers on his lap. The profile's last line spiraled back to that moment. Morgan had been with the Cerfs and Truman Capote—come to share chapters of *In Cold Blood*—and now watched as Capote drove away from The Columns, bidding farewell to his publisher, "Bennett Cerf, who is sixty-five years old." Sixty-five: the paradox lands like a blow. To be that age was to be *old,* yet the man who's been profiled, to all intents and purposes, comes across as a *boy*. A shadow of mortality lurks behind the burlesque.

Diane Arbus's accompanying photographic portrait also shocks: it is grotesque. She tried and tried, snapping *many* shots, all lined up on contact sheets, to get to the heart of the man, but couldn't get beyond the mask and surface show, the chatter and cackle, the crinkled-to-slits eyes and jack-o'-lantern face. The sitter frustrated her, as he'd frustrated Morgan. Depth eluded her. Renowned as an artist who could capture in her lens the poignant or freakish in any human being, Arbus didn't seem to care for Bennett Cerf at all. The mask became the face itself.

Many of those who worked with Bennett at RH day-to-day did have the time, patience, and inclination to peel back the mask. Silberman would learn that the "silly" fellow he'd heard about was, at heart, a "deeply hidden, very serious" publisher, for whom he'd develop lasting affection and respect. Silberman's wife also revised her estimate, and his author David Halberstam had *his* story to tell. Years later, already an RH author, Halberstam ran into Bennett in a hallway. They stood, having one conversation, when suddenly they went on to the next:

> He asked, "Who do you think I am?" as though we were playing a game. So, I told him: "A very shrewd guy, hidden behind a different persona . . . of a prankster and punster." It stopped him cold. I had thrown the dart a hundred yards and hit the bull's eye. He hadn't expected the answer. I hadn't expected to make it. You weren't supposed to say things like that. Nobody who really dealt with him found him a buffoon . . . an extraordinarily talented publisher, [he] knew what people to publish, and how to publish them.

A man of many parts, Bennett burst the seams of what it was permissible to be, and succeeded in getting so much of what he wanted from life, by—in the main—tolerating the contradictions in himself and in the multiple worlds he inhabited. He ran after celebrity, but was spurred on even more by a creative vision about books, perceiving how to build a business that went well beyond the confines of business-as-usual, to become part of the cultural fabric of the country. At times he was brought up short by his contradictions, forced to reflect for a moment rather than ceaselessly *do*. Bill Styron had seen one such pause on the way to Faulkner's funeral.

Leonora Hornblow, Bennett's confidante, had witnessed up close that "when he was sad, he was very, very sad," and felt "inadequate, insecure, that he never accomplished enough." He wasn't "the great" Knopf, or the Broadway dazzler of his deepest fantasies, a variation on his friend Moss. But such plummeting decrescendos didn't last long. He was too driven, too busy for that. Robert Bernstein had a few lines at the ready that he was apt to say, when explaining his boss to uncomprehending others: "If only you knew the whole man. It's like touching the elephant. Who Bennett is depends on which part you touch."

And so, man and boy, sixty-five years old, he donned those special spectacles, picked up *Esquire,* told himself the portrait was "VERY PLEASING," and raced on.

Chapter 43

Divorces and Disagreements

In 1963, WITH THE HINDSIGHT OF SIX YEARS, BENNETT COULD PROUDLY recall steering Ayn Rand's magnum opus to publication. Despite very negative reviews (and protests from other RH authors and friends), *Atlas Shrugged* had hugged the bestseller list for months. More important and rare, the stone-heavy tome had shown signs of remarkably buoyant long-term life. Like John Galt's marvelous motor, the word-of-mouth engine didn't flag: young people kept coming. They heard her or heard about her, and lost themselves in her book. Bennett understood the importance of catering to the appetites of fans, and so in 1959, RH had reissued *We the Living,* Rand's long-forgotten novel from 1936, and followed two years later with *For the New Intellectual,* a selection of the most "Objectivist" passages from her published novels. In 1962 came *Who Is Ayn Rand?,* an analysis by her young lover/acolyte Nathaniel Branden. However, Bennett longed to see her hypnotic eyes draw in readers from the dust jacket of a major new work, preferably a novel with the sales power of *Atlas Shrugged*.

Early in July 1963, publisher and author met for one of their tête-à-têtes, this time at the Hemisphere, a sleek, members-only executive lunch club atop the Time-Life Building, a recent addition to Rockefeller Center's western perimeter. The accordion-fold of wraparound windows with picture-perfect views, forty-eight stories above the streets where microscopic mortals scurried, seemed especially right for Rand. They spoke of various projects, mainly *Red Pawn,* a screen treatment she'd written three decades earlier, now languishing at Paramount. What if she updated and used it as basis for a film *and* a novel? Bennett drafted a letter to Paramount, then did something unusual: sent the signed, stamped, unsealed letter for her approval. If Rand objected to anything, her "arch angel friend," as he called himself, would redo it.

He was treading especially carefully. Bennett had put on the charm campaign from the start, but never pretended to be in her ideological camp—quite the contrary. Of course, he didn't share his bluntest views; his diary, not Rand, heard those. She took herself very seriously, and, used to absolute fealty from followers, increasingly expected it from others. Yet she'd always treated Don as an exception, respecting the fact that, at their first meeting, he'd not been afraid to say that her extreme moral defense of capitalism—"to the strong belong the spoils," as he saw it—went counter to Jewish and Christian ethics. Back before the publication dinner for *Atlas Shrugged,* an acolyte had announced that RH staff were expected to toast her, and their loyalty would be judged by what each said. Mr. Klopfer hadn't been required to do so, however: he was "a gentleman."

Seemingly Bennett, the man of action, didn't fall precisely within that category, and in the years since *Atlas,* she'd heard a little too often that he hadn't taken her side in conversations. That translated into Rand once declaring to an acquaintance that Bennett was "unloyal" and "a chicken." Nonetheless, in a letter about *Red Pawn,* she assured him: "Your attitude has been truly inspiring." Each needed the other and knew it. In late summer they spoke again, about a different project that soon took precedence: a collection of nonfiction pieces culled from her talks and articles. The country would go to the polls in a little over a year, either to reelect President Kennedy or repudiate his record. The lead-up presented opportunities for books of political ideas. Bennett assured Rand that one bearing her byline would be "a big seller." Her title essay for the collection, "The Fascist New Frontier," was a critique of JFK, his policies, and his initiatives. Rand had been especially incensed by the young president's injunction to "Ask not what your country can do for you . . ." and the infuriating fact of its being echoed everywhere.

Bennett, the staunch liberal, rattled off a letter brimming with delight at the prospect of a new book, and assured her he'd send word around RH that *The Fascist New Frontier* was slated for spring 1964. Surging with anticipation, his thoughts turned to sales, publicity, the sheer mesmerizing power of this author. He knew Walter Winchell had given the central essay a push when it was first published as a pamphlet: she inspired gallons of ink. He didn't pause to reflect on what the title portended or the pamphlet said; it's unclear if he read it fully, and if he did, he would have done so fast, as he read almost everything. This was RH's fifth book by or about Rand. It was publishing, not politics.

Her premise was that JFK's "New Frontier" ideology was fascistic (not vaguely socialistic, as many Americans supposed). She saw his economic policies, even his rhetoric, as akin to Adolf Hitler's, and went so far as to quote unattributed snippets of speeches by Hitler, Göring, and JFK, and ask the reader to guess who'd made them. As news about the book spread within the firm, voices rose even at the notion of such a title, "startling" Bennett by their vehemence. A week after he'd sent word to the staff, the drumbeat of editorial consternation was loud enough to be heard by the Executive Committee, who took up discussion of the "propriety" of the essay and whether its inflammatory title should be the collection's title as well. Thus far, it was the only material she'd submitted. Several committee members shared the editors' reservations, among them Donald, whose reaction had been "immediately against" it. Bennett, the worrier beneath the sunny surface, was worried now.

To cross Rand was to suffer consequences. With the sales history of *Atlas Shrugged,* such a move was not to be taken lightly. Bennett spoke with her toward the end of September, just before she was due to leave on a trip, conveying *something* of the dissent, and asked her to forward a dozen copies of the pamphlet for others' perusal. Given his early boosting and the mixed message delivered now, the chat rapidly deteriorated into angry words. In mid-October, when she returned to the city and phoned, what she heard was stunningly worse. Bennett himself now shared his colleagues' objections. He made his case; she made hers; they rehashed for a full hour. But however difficult Rand was, Bennett now felt pained: she was a remarkable person, and his admiration and affection were genuine. He flailed in a sea of anxiety.

The Executive Committee met again two mornings later and declared unequivocally: A book "under this title . . . cannot be published . . . improper comparisons, even if inadvertent, must be dropped." The essay had to be substantially cut or even deleted, and the title changed. Yet again Bennett was having to come to terms with the firm's altered power structure. The dynamics of a committee with assertive younger people meant more of them to please and less wiggle room. Had it been just Don and himself, perhaps they could have worked something out; as it was, they were the ones who had to face Rand that afternoon.

At three o'clock sharp she marched into his office, as he and Don rose to greet her. "You said when I came to you that you would publish anything I wrote," she charged, not altogether incorrectly, huge eyes burning. She saw bad faith on Bennett's part; she'd believed in *him,* the man who got things done, who made *Atlas Shrugged* come out right. Now he had betrayed her.

Behind the amiable mien, his eyes flashed a warning of their own, as he took up his theme: When he made that promise, they were talking about *Atlas Shrugged.* That was fiction. "You can say anything you want in a novel, but this . . . is something that I did not contemplate," he admitted. RH wasn't going to publish a *nonfiction* book that equated Kennedy with Hitler. JFK was the sitting president! However naive or careless he may have been at the beginning in whooping it up about the book, he was now, as RH staff were well aware, very angry. Was part of it anger not just at Rand, but at himself, for getting into this mess?

Donald took a turn, his voice calmer than Bennett's. She'd been impressed with how philosophical he was, and he'd pleased her at one point by admitting that despite his liberal credo, he accepted *one* of her ideas. She'd persuaded him that success in business depended on intelligence and ability, and so he had no cause to feel guilty about how well he'd done. Now he tried reasoning: It was one essay, one title. Plenty of alternatives could convey her meaning. He and Bennett had made a list: *America's Drift Toward Fascism; The Spread of Fascism in America; Whither America?; Where Is America Drifting?* Any would work.

She wasn't convinced, and circled time and again to their promise to publish whatever she wrote and not let politics interfere. Grueling hours passed—one, two, almost three—in a room that had become claustrophobic. Bennett fiddled as he always did, Donald seemed pinned to his chair, and Rand chain-smoked. Debate was her natural element: she could go on forever, but the partners could not. Don's eyes sought Bennett's; a moment later, he liberated himself from the chair's straitjacket, made his excuses, and left. Bennett continued alone.

Glazed with tiredness, he found his attention wandering. The October night was now well and truly dark. Bennett glanced at his watch. They'd been closeted there three hours and forty minutes. He and Thrup had an engagement that evening. He made a move to collect his things, saying that he must get home. Rand put on her cape but kept talking, eyes dangerous as black ice. As they left his office, walked down the stairs, and exited through the courtyard to Madison Avenue, the litany about his promise not to change her copy drilled into his head.

Relief came when he hailed a taxi near the corner of Fifty-First

Street, going uptown. As Bennett got in (Rand lived in the opposite direction), she launched a last salvo: "You're going to print every word I've written, or I won't let you publish the book."

"Get yourself another publisher!" he exploded, as the cab sped away.

The following morning, with a cooler head, he dictated a three-page letter before departing on a weekend trip. He left instructions for it not to be sent straightaway: he wanted to avoid another sin of haste. He'd review it when back, "to make it as perfect as possible" before dispatching it to its fate. In the end, he wrote three drafts. He reiterated that he'd "never try to censor" her ideas, but neither would he ever give up a publisher's "inalienable" right to ask for changes he deemed "necessary." He couldn't justify publishing a book that in his and Don's opinion resorted in its title and part of its text "to guilt by association and character assassination"—methods that he was sure Rand "would be the first to decry." He also mounted a self-defense. His about-face "in no sense means that I am not the head of my own publishing house. We have editors here whom I deeply respect, and any publisher who doesn't at least listen to the advice of his editors, is not my idea of a wise or judicious man. Furthermore, I have no respect for a man who cannot be convinced that he was wrong about something."

Rand's answer came ten days later. In a five-page response, brilliantly argued, she set out to demolish him. He'd assured her from the first that his editors' politics wouldn't interfere with *his* publishing; he wasn't fooling her, but himself, by believing this dispute was anything but that—it was entirely political. He'd "broken his word," but she wouldn't hold him to the contract.

In his reply, he said that she could title the book *Ayn Rand's Ideological Critique of the Kennedy Administration,* a phrase she'd used, and on the jacket say that the ideology was fascistic. Yet she must understand that after listening to their staff, he and Don had made *their* decision. The Hitler comparison had to go. "Nobody can be right all the time," he ended, "and I think that includes you, Ayn."

Three weeks later, the book's destiny was overtaken by that of the country. On Friday, November 22, Bennett returned from lunch to find Chris, André Schiffrin, and others gray-faced and desolate in front of his TV. JFK had been assassinated in Dallas. Like most Americans, they rushed home, and for a few days he was glued to the screen, in shocked disbelief and sorrow. RH closed on Monday, the day of the funeral, although he and Mary Barber called in at the palazzo to deal with pressing correspondence while also watching the coverage.

In a short note to Rand, he hoped she'd agree that the appalling events had rendered their discussion "academic." He was "anxious" for a reply to his previous letter, sent more than three weeks earlier, but perhaps Bennett already sensed what was happening. When he'd written after their stormy session, he told her he knew others would be willing to take up the book on her sales record alone. New American Library's Victor Weybright, her paperback house, did just that.

In December 1964, NAL published the collection as a paperback original, but rather than *The Fascist New Frontier,* it was titled *The Virtue of Selfishness,* and didn't include the disputed essay—JFK's assassination had made it old news. It sold well enough for NAL to release a hardcover later, and in March 1965, Rand's agent told Bennett that NAL would be her primary publisher going forward. In his diary, he expressed the anger he felt: she'd left "because I refused to publish her swill comparing Hitler to Jack Kennedy." There was no conscious recognition of his own missteps. But his letter to Rand on the same day could hardly have been more gracious. "Deeply, deeply sorry" she no longer wanted to publish with RH, he continued: "I wish you well. . . . You are one of the most wonderful people I ever have met . . . and this decision of yours will not change my feeling. . . . I acted in the way that my heart dictated and could not have done otherwise. You did the same. I hope I may continue to consider you my friend."

This time she answered. She would "always give credit" for the "many good actions" he'd taken on her behalf.

They would never communicate again.

. . .

IN-HOUSE PRESSURE HAD CONVINCED Bennett of the error of his ways vis-à-vis Rand's polemic. A year later, external pressure, in the form of JFK's widow and brother, tried to persuade him against another author's book on the late president. Dealing with pressure to prevent publication was part of the job: it could be subtle or overt, come from friends or a powerful figure, and at times be exerted by the government. The only constant was that handling it was never easy.

The author in question this time was Jim Bishop, a tough Irish American syndicated columnist possessed of an eighth-grade education, large ego, and ice-blue eyes. Book success had come to him in the mid-1950s with a staccato, you-are-there formula, where he telescoped major historical events into a mere twenty-four hours. At Harper he published *The Day Lincoln Was Shot; The Day Christ Died; The Day Christ Was Born.* In 1963, *Good Housekeeping* commissioned him to lend this technique to profiling the occupants of the White House. President Kennedy agreed to cooperate: he was facing a reelection campaign, and millions of women would read the article. Mrs. Kennedy was warier about the line between public and private, but had to go along with her husband. So it happened that for hours during October 21–24, Bishop trailed the most powerful man on earth and his lady around the White House.

He'd proposed to Harper that he expand the feature into a slim book, but editors there declined: it would be *too* slim. When Bob Loomis heard of the idea, he signed *A Day in the Life of President Kennedy* for RH. Disciplined by years of deadlines, Bishop wrote fast. Loomis was reading the manuscript on November 22, and when the news came from Dallas, he thought the book was as dead as the president. To his surprise, it proceeded. Two months later, the late president's press secretary, Pierre Salinger, phoned with sixty-odd corrections sought by Mrs. Kennedy; Bishop complied. Although other publishers were pumping out JFK books, *A Day in the Life of President Kennedy* was a godsend, RH's only title among the top annual bestsellers.

Even before 1963 had turned into 1964, Bishop put out feelers for a new project. Having detailed the first presidential assassination, he proposed to tackle the latest. Recognizing it was inevitable that writers would rush to the subject, he contacted Salinger, and also wrote to Robert Kennedy, proposing *The Day Kennedy Was Shot*. It would be in the family's interest to choose one respected author to work with, Bishop argued, as a way of offsetting the stampede of sensationalism sure to follow. The Kennedys evidently agreed, but that didn't extend to choosing him. Instead, they endorsed William Manchester and his proposal, *The Death of a President*. Bishop had intended to return to Harper, but Harper was handling Manchester, so he approached Random House and, in January, RH signed *The Day Kennedy Was Shot*. Bishop began work, but fairly quickly realized that people were refusing to talk to him.

Come May, Bennett was drawn into the problem firsthand. He, Phyllis, and Kitty Hart were attending a small weekend party hosted by agent/producer Leland Hayward, where Bennett was "enthralled" to find Jacqueline Kennedy his luncheon partner. At one point when chit-chat stalled around the table and no one knew quite how to restart it, being so careful around Mrs. Kennedy, Kitty proposed they play a game, where each person shared a daydream about living another life. In due course, Mrs. Kennedy's breathy voice confessed that she'd like to be a bird.

At the Haywards': (from left) Phyllis, Kitty Hart, Bennett, Jacqueline Kennedy, Pamela Hayward, Minnie Fosburgh

Later, she made it quietly clear to Bennett that she regretted the publication of the *Day in the Life* book, feeling that Bishop had taken advantage during his four days at the White House. Since she couldn't grow wings and fly away, she asked him, as a personal favor, not to publish the new book, her eyes filling as she spoke. He faltered, the moment absolutely excruciating, but then recovered and reiterated: he'd signed a contract. If he were to refuse to publish, another house would. He didn't need to state that Bishop had a track record, and the book would likely be a bestseller. He did assure her he'd do all he could to make sure Bishop understood her feelings.

Robert Kennedy was acquainted with Joe Fox, and by early August had conveyed the same request not to publish. RFK had also delivered the message to Bob Bernstein. By then, RH wasn't alone; Bishop had signed contracts with foreign houses. Yet the Kennedys were effective in closing doors: everyone was talking to Manchester, not to him. The only alternative was for Bishop to concentrate on another project temporarily, and continue to pry open doors if possible. He was keen to do a collection of his columns, and RH contracted that, as well as another book, *A Day in the Life of President Johnson*. Both looked to be quick and easy: for the columns, only a matter of choosing, cutting, and providing transitions; and as for Johnson, the country had rallied around him and would soon elect him in his own right by a landslide.

Neither book turned out to be easy. Bishop proved truculent and dilatory over the columns, even as everyone at RH recognized that such collections often don't sell. As for *A Day in the Life of President Johnson,* by the time it was published in 1967, the early goodwill toward him had been poisoned by Vietnam. In the end, Bennett told Jacqueline Kennedy that the person she had to appeal to if she wanted to stop publication of the assassination book was Jim Bishop, and Bishop refused her pleas. He'd begun to get some doors to open, even as relations with RH had become tense. Bishop blamed Bennett personally for the poor sales of the two latest books, and RH had grown weary of his demands. In the end, all it took was a little cleansing combustion at a party in Miami's Fontainebleau Hotel, when Bishop berated Bennett and Bennett gave as good as he got. The contract for the assassination book was canceled. Before then, Bennett had had several discussions with Jacqueline Kennedy about her editing a poetry anthology for RH. They came to nothing, but at least, after the Florida blowup, he no longer had the Kennedys on his back. Bishop found another publisher, and his book came out in 1968. It was not a bestseller.

. . .

TROUBLE WITH AUTHORS COMES in other forms as well. All publishers' records include written-off advances for projects never realized. Some are fatally misconceived; others prove too ambitious for would-be authors; yet others drag on so long that any timeliness is gone. Even with the best intentions, illness and crises can get in the way. Often, a publisher has limited recourse to recoup the advance, since litigation is expensive, time-consuming, and often fruitless, and taking an author to court isn't especially good for one's reputation. The aggregate for unrecoverable advances on manuscripts that never arrived or were terminally unpublishable can be scary to behold: in 1968, Bennett would venture that from its early days to then, RH had probably lost a million dollars.

Yet so *easy* it was for an editor to fall in love and a check to change hands. Bennett himself was far from immune, especially when a shimmering name was involved. Who'd never been seduced by the liquid eyes and melting voice of Judy Garland? In May 1959, she headlined a string of triumphant concerts at the Metropolitan Opera House and he was there on the first night: Bennett had always loved her. After cheering her on, he popped backstage, knowing Garland the way he knew every star, from multiple fleeting encounters. But as wasn't the case with other publishers, she knew *him*. Was it broached there and then, the usual gambit: Had she ever thought of telling her life story? He'd *love* to handle it. After all, Bennett would be publishing Moss Hart's autobiography that September, and for the past year had been cajoling Dick Rodgers to write his. Or was it Garland's husband and business manager, Sid Luft, who brought it up? What's sure is that six months later, a Garland autobiography was under serious discussion.

Luft flew to New York in November and met with Bennett and an old friend of Garland's named Freddie Finklehoffe, to plan *The Judy Garland Story*. She'd recount memories on tape, and Finklehoffe, a playwright/screenwriter who'd worked on a half dozen of her early movies like *For Me and My Gal* and *Meet Me in St. Louis,* would put them cohesively into print.

Bolstered by the huge response to *Act One,* it was easy for Bennett to envision an even greater pot of gold at the end of the rainbow for Garland. That gold was needed: despite the millions she'd made and fan loyalty she retained, she and Luft were perpetually broke. Pills and booze were the lady's main expenses, but her husband, a would-be tough guy and serially failing entrepreneur, liked nice things and horses, losing tens of thousands of dollars at the track.

The outlines of Garland's roller-coaster life were well known, and with his Hollywood connections, Bennett would have heard more. "One of the most tragic [women] in the world," he'd later say of her. And yet she was Judy Garland, ever the iconic Dorothy, and absolutely thrilling onstage. Her L.A. lawyer wanted a $75,000 advance, 20 percent royalty, and all subsidiary rights, but Bennett was having none of it. He was willing to pay $40,000—still large—a 15 percent royalty, and split subsidiary rights fifty-fifty. Just before Thanksgiving, he met again with Luft and Finklehoffe, and Garland was present. The venue was her room at Doctors Hospital, the Upper East Side medical mecca for the well-heeled wanting discretion and comfort, as well as a cure.

On the phone before the meeting, Garland had sounded "miserable."

Now he saw the puffy face, glassy eyes, smile straining under the show-must-go-on lipstick. The room exuded pain, the kind that made a visitor want to flee had the prize not been so great. Luft took Bennett aside: Garland was suffering from acute hepatitis, and the doctors were trying to drain fluid swelling every part of her body. What he didn't say was that her liver was failing, and if by some miracle she were to recover, her health would still be compromised, and performing unlikely to be part of the future. She was all of thirty-seven. Facing that scenario, a fat advance check was even more urgent and necessary: Luft was desperate for a deal.

On December 11, Bennett returned to the hospital room for dinner, reeling off jokes between mouthfuls of food and business talk. Garland picked at what she could. Ten days later, Santa came to Doctors Hospital early: a $50,000 contract was signed. Since the Lufts were worried about their bank balance *and* the tax man, they'd negotiated special terms. Rather than an advance, RH was immediately "giving" Garland a $20,000 "loan" up front, to be repaid out of royalties, unusual for that time. When Finklehoffe delivered the manuscript—the date was set for October, ten months away—Judy would receive another $10,000. The Lufts had insisted that Finklehoffe receive a $10,000 advance, paid in monthly installments, and $10,000 on delivery. It was a big throw of the dice to a dodgy patient and her inveterate gambler husband; not much security there. Finklehoffe seemed more of a sure bet, with all those movie credits behind him.

Garland's hospital stay lasted seven weeks, and she returned to L.A. by train in January. Once home, she took it slow and careful, and her much-abused body began to defy the grim prognosis. During the enforced rest, she told tales into a tape recorder. Bennett, meanwhile, got the word out. "A book for which publishers have been angling for years has been signed and sealed for Random House," the release boasted, while Garland declared: "There have been a lot of stories . . . about me . . . some . . . fantastically distorted. This . . . [will] set the record straight."

In July, Bennett lunched with an amazingly better Judy and told her he was anxious to see *something;* two weeks later he spoke with Finklehoffe, but still had nothing tangible. In August he checked in with the Lufts, now in London, via transatlantic call. He tried to keep the big bet from preying on his mind. In late October the manuscript was due, but

Finklehoffe delivered only sixty-odd pages. Nonetheless, a fabulous New Year's Day gathering at Betty Comden's, where Bennett and Phyllis heard Judy and Lena Horne wow the crowd, argued for optimism. So did the Cerfs' own bash in Garland's honor. Her "superb" singing brought a gusher of flattering phone calls: surely, he'd made the right investment. Alas, 1961 came and went. She was otherwise engaged; Finklehoffe disappeared. RH went through the motions of drafting a formal letter: if a full, acceptable manuscript didn't appear by mid-July 1963, his contract would be terminated, and Finklehoffe would have to repay the $10,000. Fat chance of that happening, they knew.

Luft had ceased being his wife's business manager, and Garland's new agent agreed with Bennett that they should try to find a new writer. Given the project's—and subject's—mercurial history, it wasn't easy. By now, Bennett was sweating the $30,000. Rescue came via his unparalleled social network. He and Phyllis had known Herb Mayes, now CEO of the McCall's corporation, forever. Big national women's monthlies like Herb's flagship magazine paid top dollar for book excerpts. Garland's name was a newsstand magnet, and RH controlled serial rights. The upshot, a two-parter cobbled together from the tapes and Finklehoffe's pages, ran in *McCall's* in 1964.

Bennett wrote to Garland that since he knew she'd been "just as worried" as he, she'd be happy that now, thanks to *McCall's,* the loan to her and advance to Finklehoffe was being earned back, then added: "I haven't given up hopes that one day we will still be able to do the really definitive story of your life. It will be a smash bestseller!" He sent his love. He'd recouped the financial loss for the company and mitigated his own embarrassment, while at the same time saving at least a little face for the sad lady herself. The weekly TV show she headlined had just been canceled, and Garland was in a bad way again. A few years later, a call came through and he heard the unmistakable voice, velvety and trembling, its brightness too bright, trying to convince him to take up the project again. Gently, he told her there would be no encore with RH. It was one of those books that got away.

Chapter 44

Backing Horses

Bennett was a businessman who liked to win, yet if winning were all, Random would have been a different place. He was also a dreamer, who chased his own dreams but also saw himself as a conduit for those of others. "You can get along fine . . . no matter what . . . if you work hard, think big, and most important, have a dream," he'd said in a speech to the Girls Clubs of America. However credulous such a statement might seem, he believed it and had the luck to live it, but feared that with age, we "begin to forget that dream we started out with." Still, he tried not to forget, and to find ways to use his position to boost writers' dreams as no other publisher could.

Nineteen sixty-four was a good year for his beloved Broadway. He cheered when a girl from Flatbush named Barbra Streisand became a star in *Funny Girl,* and loved *Hello Dolly,* croaking around the house to Louis Armstrong's hit cover of the title tune. But it was his reaction to a no-frills three-person play, *The Subject Was Roses*—about a New York soldier just home to his family from World War II—that showed how far the fan in him could go. The author, Frank Gilroy, worked as a scriptwriter on TV dramas. Although Gilroy's first staged play, mounted off-Broadway, had won an Obie in 1962, *Roses* was ignored when it made the rounds of producing offices. But Gilroy's neighbor, Edgar Lansbury, a TV art director from a theatrical family, read the script, believed in it, and agreed to produce it. Lansbury scraped together $37,357.27 from backers—a budget of skin and bones, with little flesh and no cushion if the show failed to take off. Opening in May, late in the season, that prospect seemed all too likely, especially with Broadway first-timers as producer, director, designer, and manager, and "virtual unknowns" for cast.

The theater gods bestowed good reviews, yet positive notices weren't sufficient: the house was only half full. Unless fortune turned quickly, there wouldn't be a big enough take to keep it going. Enter, stage left and right, angels bearing ink. On June 23, 1964, an unusual display ad ran in *The New York Times* alongside the conventional ads for theatrical offerings. It was printed in the form of a typed letter, paid for and signed by Bennett Cerf, that well-known panelist, columnist, first-nighter, and publisher of playwrights from Gene O'Neill to Moss Hart: "The other evening I saw a beautiful play, beautifully acted and directed, that gave me a wonderful evening. . . . The rest of the audience obviously enjoyed this comedy drama as thoroughly as I did. But there were too many empty seats. I urge YOU to go see it now. . . ."

No one had asked him to do it. Taking out the ad was an act of pure enthusiasm, backed by years of insight into the market and a conviction that he could help. This boost from a man welcomed into living rooms all over America, and perceived by so many as a trusted cultural arbiter, did what Bennett had hoped it would: made a difference at the box office.

A Madison Avenue ad man, Mark Lawrence, paid for a clever notice in *The New Yorker*. Others rallied, working to get the play *known*. One Wednesday at Sardi's, a suave, handsome Harry Belafonte charmed each lunching lady with a rose, by way of advertising *The Subject Was Roses*. With word-of-mouth started, *Roses* more than survived. It won the Pulitzer Prize and the Tony Award for best play, remained on Broadway for two years, and was made into a film. Bennett offered to publish the script, but, perhaps with the ghost of Moss urging him on, the project became bigger, something special. He placed the script within a nicely designed book about the play, including Gilroy's journal entries, reviews, and even the early balance sheet.

About Those Roses or How Not *To Do a Play and Succeed* was, like *Act One,* an insider's look and a celebration of the lows and highs of behind-the-scenes Broadway. It might also give heart to others. Bennett didn't publish *About Those Roses* to lose money, but whether it repaid its investment is an open question. There is no question that for him, it was a labor of love.

. . .

FOR GILROY, IT WAS a newspaper ad; for Rosanna Warren, Bennett's pitch for an audience came via a flap-copy letter, the same device he'd used for Gertrude Stein so many years earlier. He'd penned similar appeals for a few others, too, but never for an author only ten years old. The man who flirted with anything in a skirt from time to time developed a bond with the daughter of a friend or author. When Phyllis was pregnant the second time, he'd hoped for a girl; many of these friendships were a substitute for the daughter he never had. Girls like Pat Haas or Susanna Styron saw him as benevolent, playful, and most of all, *interested*—something he hadn't always been when his own sons were young boys. Of course, as Jill Faulkner's unease attested, not every girl found Bennett's personality appealing.

For Rosanna Warren, the daughter of two writers, Robert Penn Warren and Eleanor Clark, he'd been "a big figure" in her parents' lives as far back as she could remember. Her most vivid early memory of him came on a snowy Sunday in 1961, when she was eight. The occasion was her parents' annual holiday dinner-dance in their 300-year-old Connecticut barn–turned–home. The light-filled big room, three stories high, had a roaring fire, grand piano, and "glamorous grown-ups," friends like Bill and Rose Styron, Ralph and Fanny Ellison, and the Cerfs. The guests were sitting at table when, like Cinderella at the ball, Bennett saw his watch and realized that he needed to excuse himself to catch *What's My Line?* Sunday night wasn't Sunday night without the show, whether he was performing live or watching himself on tape. *How did I do?* he'd ask. The need for that pinch-me-it's-true reassurance had always been deep.

"Could you tell me where your television is?" he asked Eleanor, adding, "I have to see myself on the program." Bennett didn't realize the Warrens owned no TV, because Eleanor—who juggled the responsibilities of wife, mother, homemaker, hostess, and writer—disapproved of it. But the answer Rose Styron heard her give at the very idea of leaving the table to watch himself—they had all, of course, been drinking—was "That's disgusting." Rose saw Bennett shrink into the seat, his face a struggle, the party hubbub for the most part hiding his distress, although Rosanna, with a precocious child's antennae, was close enough to pick up *something*.

Soon, Eleanor relented: "If you must watch, people down the road have *two* sets."

By now, it was snowing hard. Bennett's warm smile was back in place, but his insides were shaky. He turned to Rose and asked if she'd accompany him. Rosanna watched as her mother wrapped them in layers, opened the door, then shut it—and the memory of any unpleasantness—

behind them. They tramped to the next house, owned by a family named Lee, and knocked; through the curtain Bennett and Rose saw a flickering screen and the outline of a husband and wife. Like many at that hour, they were tuned to *What's My Line?* Mrs. Lee appeared, wondering what two strangers were doing on her doorstep, but like the woman in Memphis, she underwent an epiphany. "It's Bennett Cerf! I'm watching you!" she laughed, both abashed and excited. Bennett introduced Rose. The Warrens' TV was "broken," he explained—the white lie made it simple, assuaging hurt feelings—and asked, "Can we watch with you?"

Quickly enough, they were settled on the sofa, while Mrs. Lee reached for her phone, to broadcast the news. By eleven o'clock, several carloads of suburbanites had braved the elements to come and watch Bennett Cerf watch Bennett Cerf. He was happy again, in his element. When they returned to the Warrens', everyone was dancing and gay. But Rose and Bennett—and Rosanna, too—would never forget that trip to the neighbors'.

No *Lassie, Bonanza,* no *Rocky and Bullwinkle* (and most certainly, no *What's My Line?*) entered Rosanna's life. When not in school, she mainly read, wrote, and drew. On another Sunday night—February 9, 1964—she wasn't one of millions going wild when four long-haired English lads made their American TV debut on Ed Sullivan's show. Bennett not only watched with the masses, but judged the Beatles "a riot!" Instead of television, from the age of seven, Rosanna had written and typed a family newspaper. By age ten, she felt grown up enough to try a novel; each summer, she'd watched her parents shut themselves away five hours a day to write, so why shouldn't she? They valued books above everything. She chose for her protagonist Joey, the more rambunctious of their two dogs, and soon began communing with a typewriter. Her parents were so taken with *The Joey Story* that at Christmas, Eleanor duplicated copies to give to friends. Bennett found *Joey* delicious, and decided to publish it. The little book was endearing, funny, extraordinarily well-written given its author's age, a recognizable slice of family life.

Red and Eleanor weren't so keen, worrying that *Joey* out in the world would spoil their daughter. Worse, it might make her into an object of curiosity. Yet they knew Bennett, and in the end trusted him *not* to do what came naturally. They specified that there were to be no personal interviews or "child prodigy" marketing. And so, as with Gilroy's play, he took up his pen and did what he could, this time in the form of the flap-copy letter. "We have not changed one word of her text and have preserved faithfully her own quaint ideas of spelling," he promised readers, adding that he wished "some of our older authors" had Rosanna's "verve and infectious love of life!" At sales conference he instructed the reps to tell booksellers that it was his personal project, and he packaged it well, with drawings by Roy McKie, who was good enough to work with Ted Geisel, and to illustrate many of Bennett's own books.

Rosanna was permitted a day off school, and in her best dress traveled with her parents from Connecticut for a terribly grown-up publication lunch with Bennett at '21.' Her toes did not touch the ground (figuratively, and perhaps literally). Later, he took them to the high-kicking "Rockets" (per Rosanna's "quaint" spelling) at Radio City. "The whole day was bursting with fun and happiness," she thanked him. *Joey* sold some copies despite the personal publicity ban, although not what Bennett had dreamed. Being unable to promote the book alongside its young author had made his vision of "huge" success unlikely from the start. Still, the Warrens were able to open a bank account in their daughter's name, and whenever the distinguished critic-professor-poet Rosanna Warren sells a new book to a publisher, or a poem to *The New Yorker,* she can't help but think of her first triumph. Money from her writing still goes into that special account, opened when Bennett Cerf, on a lark, published *Joey*.

. . .

HIS PROFOUND LOVE OF theater had forged the connection with Gilroy; boyish enthusiasm for the idea of publishing Rosanna led to *Joey*. Bennett also used his bully pulpit to advocate for new authors as a species—as he did in an editorial, "A Plea for the Unknown Writer," in *Variety*. Americans had a great propensity for "me-too-ism," he warned, tending to follow the herd to see the same movies and read the same books. But what about authors, "just as deserving and often more so," who haven't hit that "magic" circle? It seemed harder and harder for a new writer to be heard. For every *To Kill a Mockingbird; Goodbye, Columbus;* and *Catch-22,* there were at least a hundred "extremely good" first novels that weren't given even "a one-paragraph review," and that booksellers refused to stock. Yet so many great writers had recently died—Faulkner, Hemingway, and Thurber in the space of fifteen months—the only way to develop a new generation of greats, he editorialized, was to "let a clerk whom you trust persuade you to buy a book by somebody who has never had anything published before." Of course, he wasn't happy when a surfeit of unsold books by too many unknowns weighed down the balance sheet, but the mandate he and Don gave their editors to seek out fresh voices was emphatic and real.

Twenty-six-year-old Larry Bensky, the smart young associate editor who reported to Albert Erskine, made that clear in a talk to a group of Sarah Lawrence College writing students. Bensky put his own gloss on Bennett's words, assuring his listeners that "publishers will publish books knowing . . . they will not sell." Sometimes it took an investment of belief, patience, and enough money to see a writer through a second, third, even fourth book, before that author found the receptive moment and audience. On Bensky's desk at the Villard lay a manuscript that very much spoke to that kind of fervor. It had arrived addressed to "Fiction Editor Random House, Inc." in the spring of 1962, with a Tennessee return address. It had been sent there, its author would later say, because "they published the good authors." The cover letter—one page, double-spaced, typed—showed seriousness, pride, and a careful choice of words. The author noted that he'd received two grants for writing and had begun his novel three years earlier, but funds as much as struggle were an issue in how long it had taken to complete. Begging "indulgence in the matter" of typographical errors, the request itself conveyed a great deal.

Parcels of that ilk, known as "slush," regularly poured into the building, especially after one of Bennett's lecture tours. Like gumballs released from an old-fashioned vending machine, they came in many different "colors," yet essentially were all the same—utterly unremarkable and unpublishable. While some machines had prizes in small plastic capsules hidden among the gum, getting a manuscript worth reading was even rarer than a child seeing one of those longed-for capsules descend the gray metal shoot into his or her hand. Out of a sense of responsibility, decency, and the tiny chance that a prize might be claimed, RH took slush "very seriously." The order had come down that it was to be read, a task that routinely fell to one of the bright-eyed "girls." It was during Maxine Groffsky's tenure as keeper-of-the-slush that that particular manuscript arrived. She saw something and flagged it to Bensky. They'd come to RH at the same time; had Groffsky been male, she would have been doing the same job as he. Instead, she read slush and smiled when the big boss tossed off a hello or "Goodbye, Columbus."

Bensky was taken with the manuscript, too, and sent it, with a memo, to Erskine, calling it "a strange and, I think, beautiful novel in the Southern tradition," while admitting the book had "confused" him. "Neo-Faulknerian," it nonetheless was "not at all imitative." Centering on a young man, an old man, and a boy in rural East Tennessee forty years earlier, it needed another draft at least, lacking a final structure and coherence, yet the grasp of character, setting, and dialogue was impressive. It was "worth publishing." A few weeks later, after Erskine and others had read it, Bensky wrote to the author, twenty-eight-year-old Cormac McCarthy, expressing strong interest, yet falling short of promising a contract. Work had to be done, and approvals earned. He'd relate what he thought had to be worked on once he'd made a chart of character and time sequences, the craft he'd been learning in his apprenticeship to Albert. During the course of a year, he made suggestions and McCarthy took them; not every author is able to accept criticism. "This is a writer of real talent with an unlimited future," Bensky predicted.

The Brooklyn-born son of Jewish immigrants, Bensky was given to civil rights activism and demonstrating for peace. He and Erskine, the intellectual Southern WASP gentleman, had sometimes been at loggerheads. But Albert had plucked him from the "Rabbit Penn Warren," the first young man at Random House to have started at the bottom and been promoted on the editorial track from within, with an eye to grooming him quickly for full editor status. Along with Bennett and Don, Albert recognized that he could bridge the age and interest gap with younger writers. Chris and Michael Frith had also been put on that track; others would follow.

Bensky, however, entertained different plans, and decided to leave RH in the fall of 1963 for Europe. At a gathering in Bennett's townhouse, he'd met one of Chris's friends, George Plimpton, editor of *The Paris Review,* who'd offered the chance to be the magazine's Paris-based editor. Albert, Jason, Joe Fox, and Bennett each in turn tried to dissuade Bensky; he was adamant, but before he left, was able to offer McCarthy a contract and a $1,500 advance for what came to be titled *The Orchard Keeper.* With the Southern connection and Faulkner echoes, it made sense for Albert to assume responsibility for this author and his book going forward.

It was with Erskine's first editorial letter in mid-November that McCarthy grasped he was dealing with a higher order of editorial species. Albert began to tackle his stylistic homages to the Mississippi master, including peculiarities in punctuation straight out of Yoknapatawpha County. Trying not to inflict serious damage to a young man's confidence, but also to save the editorial team from the travails of "apostrophical eccentricities," he used the capital of having been Faulkner's editor to make the case for consistent punctuation. In a sustained back-and-forth through the mail, authorial prickles faced off against editorial prickles, each man feeling his way, probing, testing, getting to know the other. Gradually, trust grew as they continued to work, picking apart words and sentences. Both were Southern-bred, intellectual, intensely private, and did not suffer fools, yet exhibited a certain gregariousness in the right company. Each could be acidly funny or exquisitely polite, and wanted things *his* way. They suited each other.

As publication neared, Erskine was determined to do whatever he could to ensure *The Orchard Keeper* didn't get lost in the crowd like most of the novels whose fate Bennett had bemoaned. He wanted this distinctive voice to be noticed. And so he "scared up" endorsements from three of his most prestigious authors—Ralph Ellison, Robert Penn Warren, and James Michener—and from his friend Malcolm Cowley, who'd done so much to resurrect interest in Faulkner. The French, great Faulkner admirers, had bought foreign rights, as had the British. Most American reviews were good. Even Orville Prescott of *The New York Times,* whom many literati now disparaged for often getting things wrong, had to admit that this first novel, although at times "exasperating," was "impressive." Albert had already signed McCarthy for a second book, and raised the advance—to be doled out in installments to keep him working—to $4,500. Hardly huge, it was nevertheless recognition, three times the sum advanced for the first.

Despite the blurbs and reviews, *The Orchard Keeper* didn't make money for the firm. Nevertheless, Bensky's remarks at Sarah Lawrence were borne out: RH, in the person of an absolutely determined Albert Erskine, worked with this author, not just through a second book, but through three more, although none brought any real financial return, even as McCarthy developed a cult following and won a MacArthur "genius" grant. At one point Erskine found himself threatening to quit if he couldn't continue to publish McCarthy. It would not be until the debut of a sixth novel, *All the Pretty Horses,* in 1992, that the great promise he'd nurtured paid off in bestselling sales. By then, he was officially retired and ailing with cancer. It was the last McCarthy book on which he contributed some work.

Cormac McCarthy

"Albert was one of the best friends I ever had, an extraordinary man," McCarthy recalled. "Other than my brother, he was the best human being I've ever known, a person of honesty and rectitude." When the books weren't selling, "he tried to get me fellowships and foundation money and he did. He kept publishing me because he thought the books should be published, and Bennett Cerf thought if he said it, [then] they should. Cerf was a pretty bright guy, who loved books. When he realized who and what Albert was . . . he just turned him loose."

Chapter 45

Big Money, Different Equations

With the postwar march of suburbanization across America, shopping centers and strip malls had sprung up like weeds. Inside their supermarket aisles and bookstores, stand-alone racks and shelf space mushroomed with paperbacks, bringing books within easier, much cheaper reach of larger numbers of citizens. Now it became possible to sell way more copies in paperback than ever before, causing the financial balance and ground rules of trade publishing to shift. Rights sales became big money. Hollywood-style vocabulary and thinking crept into the business.

Irwin Shaw

Irwin Shaw was a writer who knew about that. RH had first published him in 1936 when Shaw was twenty-three, and stayed true to him after he was blacklisted and fled to Europe in 1951. A good writer, he'd also become a pleasure-seeker whose Swiss-and-Riviera lifestyle was predicated upon churning out movie screenplays. When he returned, post-McCarthy, for visits, he'd burrow into work with Saxe, whose help got him through ten books. He'd grieved, when Saxe died, at losing his "literary father." In the summer of 1964, after JFK's assassination and Rand's turning tail, RH was preparing to publish *two* Shaw manuscripts. He'd delivered a collection, *Love on a Dark Street,* scheduled for December. "Competent but slightly disappointed" was Bennett's verdict, most of the stories having appeared in magazines. The second book, *Voices of a Summer Day,* had just been copyedited by Nan Talese, who was about to put it into production.

Shaw had been assigned to Albert Erskine, but the two felt no real rapport. His last big book, *Two Weeks in Another Town,* published in 1960, had sold well, but when he examined his literary income, it couldn't compare with the movie lucre. He'd informed Bennett and Don that he wanted a bigger advance, and the paperback money split with RH to be sixty-forty in his favor.

Both partners, along with Albert and Joe Fox, had read *Voices of a Summer Day* and were surprised. Don called it "a short story . . . stretched out into a novella," and was right. Shaw had intended *Voices* to be in the *Love on a Dark Street* collection, but realized he could fulfill his second obligation to RH by separating it out as a novella. On his visit to RH that June, Bennett told him it was the slimmest "novel" he'd ever delivered. Shaw vented to Fox: "He called it *a little book!*" But Bennett had plenty to compare it with: Fox had wooed one of Shaw's pals, Peter Matthiessen, and Bennett had just finished his stunning *At Play in the Fields of the Lord.*

Contracts with house authors had often been less than formal. With his bruised feelings and expensive lifestyle, Shaw decided to get help from his movie agent, Swifty Lazar, fast becoming active on the literary front. Five foot two, utterly bald, and staring owl-like at his prey through round black spectacles, Lazar visited Bennett on June 23 with a shocking demand: Shaw wanted to control and collect *every cent* from *all* reprint rights going forward.

Splitting paperback rights income fifty-fifty with the writer was lifeblood to firms like RH, some years making the difference between profit and loss, even more so if a book were by a marquee name. Now, originating publishers weren't approaching just one reprint house; they had an auction with several, who at times threw down crazy-large sums to preempt hot "properties." Paperback rights to Michener's *Caravans* had sold for $200,000 the prior year. Lazar respected Cerf's Hollywood acumen; Cerf respected Lazar's shrewdness; each appreciated what the other had done to help their friend Moss. But Swifty's demand threatened a tenet of the trade. If Bennett agreed to RH not getting its cut on Shaw's books, *every* writer would have to have the same terms. How could RH survive? Grudgingly, he'd been willing to consider a higher advance and splitting the money sixty-forty in Shaw's favor, but that didn't fly. In the face-off between horn-rims and owl-rims, Lazar intimated none too subtly that others would be happy to sign Shaw.

Bennett had had enough. "We could publish the damn thing and tell him to go to hell, but no, we'll send you the manuscript back," he stormed. "You send us the check for the advance, and let's forget about Irwin Shaw!" Both books were being canceled. Although he could barely contain himself, Bennett attached no punitive conditions, but he did set one proviso: "I'll release him, but he's got to come in and ask me himself."

As Shaw eventually revealed in a letter to Don, Lazar had sensed the time was right to construct an amazing deal. He'd offered the two books as well as a third, as yet unwritten, to Dell and its sister company Delacorte Press, a hardcover line that Dell had recently established solely for the purpose of producing likely bestsellers. S&S had been allied with Pocket Books for a quarter century; within the next decade, other houses would see that being without a dedicated mass-market division put them at a disadvantage. Lazar sold Shaw as a novelist with literary credentials *and* brand recognition, the sort needed to jump-start a list. Locking in both "hard" and "soft" rights, Delacorte would later feed the reprint to Dell, where the big sales would be. The move translated into a huge $250,000 advance. On July 1, all was done. Bennett came into possession of a $15,000 check from Lazar for money advanced. In Shaw's letter to Don, he said the move had brought changes to his U.K. and French contracts, too; adding those, the total for the three-book deal was $350,000-plus. Impossible to turn down a fortune.

Even when the divorce was fresh, Don took it stoically, but Bennett reacted, as he later admitted, by being "childish." Nan Talese had worked carefully on *Voices*. After all, Shaw had been best man at her wedding. But before it was returned to Lazar, Bennett ordered Talese to erase all traces of her corrections. "He knew it was petty," she recalled a half century later. "He was deeply stung by the rejection. Very male, very silly. He really wasn't a petty person at all." Although Shaw published more books, some reaping great commercial success, critical opinion held that his best work had been done with RH. The author himself came to agree.

. . .

WITH RH PART-OWNER OF Bantam, Bennett was intimately aware of the profit a reprint house could make through a paperback hit, and a hardcover house reap by selling rights to that title. He also knew that while the big-name game could generate a jackpot from a single title, if the reprint house miscalculated, it—with hundreds of thousands of unsold paperbacks—would take a bath at the pulping mill. The hunt for the big book that played well as a paperback was not without peril.

Twenty years earlier, on a wartime Victory Bond selling tour, Bennett had made the acquaintance of Kathleen Winsor, a young woman instantly famous for her debut novel, *Forever Amber.* Its resourceful, bosomy, eponymous heroine traipsed through picaresque entanglements in Restoration England, such that the book was banned as pornographic in fourteen states. Naturally, it became a huge bestseller. Lonely home-front girls gobbled it up like that other rationed delicacy, chocolate. *Amber* sold a phenomenal 100,000 copies its first week and became *the* bestselling novel of the 1940s. More than any other title, it was responsible for popularizing the "bodice-ripper" among U.S. readers. RH's brilliant "Shucks, we've got glamour girls too!" advertisement in *PW,* depicting Gertrude and Alice for Stein's *Wars I Have Seen,* played off the Macmillan ad that had introduced the photogenic Miss Winsor and her book to the trade. Now, in the spring of 1964, Winsor was seeking a publisher for her fifth novel. Word came to Bennett that she'd be happy to let him peruse the 1,650 manuscript pages of *Wanderers Eastward, Wanderers West*. The pioneer saga was marbled with excess fat, but every book needs trimming, he told himself, perceiving "a damned good story" beneath the flab. Still, she wouldn't come cheap, and Bennett sought reassurance from Jim Silberman.

The younger man knew Winsor's saucy reputation, but it had been earned in the *1940s*. With her latest effort, Silberman ventured, the bedroom door tended to close too "discreetly" upon its occupants, and when it didn't, "it might better have." A string of First Amendment victories had given 1960s readers access to racier stuff. Even if an editor spent time and effort to improve the manuscript, it was still a long costume novel of a kind no longer in vogue. RH should pass.

Bennett considered his editor's warning, but his memory of *Forever Amber*'s sales spoke louder. In a three-page editorial letter to Winsor, he was encouraging. "It's a staggering and impressive job," he began. "And—regardless of all my criticism—I want to tell you . . . you have done a simply amazing job." In between the flattery and irony, he said she needed to cut a third out. But still believing she had a readership, he disregarded advice and signed the book. He wasn't alone in thinking her name retained resonance. A Literary Guild subsidiary took on *Wanderers,* as did the Book-of-the-Month Club. Those two rights sales and RH making a great pre-publication fuss of the novel were enough to attract interest from two big paperback houses. Bennett needed it: he'd taken the still-pretty Winsor to lunch and agreed to publish her next book. When he returned to the office and told Bob Bernstein what had occurred, Bernstein saw his boss was already worried: Bennett knew he'd been carried away.

It was a great relief when New American Library head Victor Weybright initially offered a $235,000 guaranty against a 15 percent royalty, and twenty-four hours later increased the bid to $250,000. Fawcett was also interested and came in at $260,000. Bennett felt very lucky. He was about to close on the Fawcett deal when John Budlong, a younger man just taking over the NAL helm from Weybright, phoned to say he needed to see him in person. Bennett asked Bernstein to sit in. After being ushered into Bennett's office, Budlong heard that NAL's bid had been topped by $10,000. "I'm not going to leave this room until you give me the Kathleen Winsor book," Budlong insisted. He then offered $500,000.

Bennett couldn't quite believe his ears. "Would you mind repeating that?"

Budlong did repeat it. New men always need to prove themselves, and he was no exception. A half million bucks, for Kathleen Winsor, incredible! After chatting briefly, Budlong rose, moving to leave, and they all shook hands. Bennett quickly joked, "John, can I walk you back to your office? I want to be sure nothing happens to you until you make out the contract."

Bernstein was appalled. It was apparent that Bennett thought the new man desperately foolish to tender such an offer, but why say so out loud? As soon as Budlong left, Bernstein asked his boss, "Why did you do that?"—a criticism, not a question.

He'd witnessed that kind of situation before, finding it problematic.

Bernstein had great respect for Bennett and what he'd built with Donald, and knew how serious he was beneath the jokes. He'd glimpsed the hurt in Bennett's face when people thought him a lightweight. He wasn't, as far as Bernstein was concerned, yet the Budlong interchange *was* an example of a troubling flaw: sometimes Bennett couldn't leave well enough alone. He didn't suffer fools gladly, that was part of it. Yet his childish urge to score that joke at Budlong's expense was too strong; had it been directed at his "sensitive" self, it would have hurt Bennett deeply. *Wanderers* would only sell about 30,000 hardcover copies, "clobbered" by reviews. NAL lost a fortune.

On the other hand, two weeks after the Winsor deal was negotiated, Fawcett agreed to pay even more—a $750,000 advance against a 25 percent royalty—for paperback rights to Michener's *The Source,* a sum that broke industry records. *Hawaii* having put Michener's value into the stratosphere, it was a pretty sure bet for the reprinter. Unlike Winsor's name, Michener's was current, a true magnet that would draw customers into stores. After reading the huge manuscript—bigger even than Winsor's *Wanderers*—Bennett knew that this one, retelling the story of Israel and the Jews from prehistoric times to the present, had "great" written all over it. Marketplace gold, it would make money for RH and Fawcett, too.

That same week came a third reprint deal, as Dell bought the rights to Betty Friedan's *Feminine Mystique* follow-up. The price tag was $125,000: very high for a nonfiction book that wasn't even written. In a mere fortnight, Winsor, Michener, and Friedan had brought Random House $1,325,000 in paperback guarantees. The money would be split with the authors, to be sure, but how many years of work had it taken for RH even to pass the million mark in turnover?

Now *reprint* sales were generating that kind of money. The publishing world was fast becoming a mad, wild place. Blink, and anything could happen.

Chapter 46

Big Business

Bennett blinked, and saw a "glorious" dream rise up before his eyes: a merger with Time-Life Incorporated. Senior people there had knocked on the door, and he and Don began secretly meeting with them late in January 1964. He told himself that joining forces had much to recommend it, but then yanked on his reins, insisting a consummation was "wildly improbable." He and Henry Luce, the magazine empire's legendary co-founder, were both born in 1898 and had started their companies within a few years of each other, but Luce was bowing out. Almost certainly, talks wouldn't have occurred otherwise: Luce had used his magazines as a personal megaphone for a conservative Republican agenda quite antithetical to Bennett's ideas.

The younger executives now in charge wanted to expand and diversify, having jumped on the synergy bandwagon rolling through corporate America. One new division especially lured Bennett. Time-Life Books repurposed magazine text and photos into big, illustrated volumes sold by mail order. Five years of rapid growth later, they were on coffee tables all over the country. Insert Random, Knopf, and Pantheon backlists, Modern Library, Vintage, and juveniles into the mail-order machine, and market reach could be fantastic. On top of that, the men on both sides got along beautifully, and Bennett allowed himself to hope.

He'd been there before. In the late '50s, McGraw, Holt, and even CBS's iron-willed boss William S. Paley had fancied RH as a plum worth picking and made approaches, but Charlie Allen's advice to go public had prevailed. Random was his and Don's; they'd intended to keep it that way. In the half decade since, however, Bennett had learned that the big check came with a price. While he and Don still retained control, they'd traded an exceedingly personal shop—where they did what they pleased and could risk a loss on something they wanted to try—for stock exchange regulations, answering to brokers, and quarter-on-quarter profit demands. Now there could only be more deals and complications in the incessant search for growth. As Charlie had said, "Once you lose your virginity, the next time is easier." Issuing stock in 1959 had seemed a way to *avoid* a sale, but going public had put them on a path to not owning their business.

Time-Life was a ubiquitous prestige brand with annual revenue approaching a half billion dollars, compared to Random's $30 million. The security of being part of a larger organization would be comforting after the market volatility RH had experienced, for having dreamed of seeing RH on the New York Stock Exchange, he hadn't expected the nightmares that would follow. After all those years hearing the starstruck refrain, *Hey, aren't you Bennett Cerf?,* a new variation was disturbing his ears: *Hey, what are you doing wrong with your company?* Those words had flown out at him for the first time in a theater. The man who spoke them had lost money on RH stock. More unpleasant encounters ensued. Many small investors had bought into Random because they "knew" Bennett, but the glamour stock was subject to the same fluctuations as any other. Worse, in the autumn of 1963, *Forbes* published a statistical chart analyzing how nineteen publishing stocks had fared from 1957 through 1962. It estimated figures for RH, rather than soliciting actual numbers. The result was "a pretty sick showing," Donald told the firm's bankers, annoyed about the estimates, but not denying the conclusion. Bennett became more rattled, even wary of going out, convinced he was letting people down who'd believed in him.

Seeking comfort, he opened up to Leonora. Don shouldered more of the day-to-day, but Bennett had always led the charge. Now he couldn't shake the feeling that he'd done something wrong, and worried everything would be taken from him—so odd, since he normally enjoyed the wonderful (and useful) quality of not blaming himself when things went bad. Leonora did her best to talk him back from a low she'd never seen him feel before. The depression seemed to lift, but unease hid in the background like a parasitical fever that could spike at any time.

Becoming part of Time-Life made sense in so many ways. He'd had to put aside the notion that one day his boys would run the firm. They were both too young. Chris now worked at RH, and other denizens of the palazzo appreciated his quickness, intelligence, and sweetness, but also recognized the insecurity that came from being Phyllis and Bennett's number-one son. Tony Wimpfheimer was capable in his way, a very good production man, but Pat Klopfer's dream that her son would take over was also pure fantasy. Too often Bennett reacted to Tony as a personal irritant, even when what he did was well meant, and Don showed no sign of judging his stepson right for the job; nor did Tony lobby for it. Bennett also knew that if he died and Phyllis came into control of a large block of shares, there was no way Donald would accept her as an active partner, a role she'd undoubtedly covet.

Negotiations with Time-Life continued for several months, before the lawyers on both sides sadly agreed that the Department of Justice would scotch a merger on antitrust grounds. In the government's eyes, it would concentrate too much market share in one corporation. Still, word had gotten out within the companies and on the street about the likely merger. On the strength of such gossip, RH shares had risen from $9.75 at the beginning of January to $14.75 four months later. As soon as the deal was dead, the stock started sliding again. The only consolation was that, thanks in large part to the Blaisdell sale and the delayed compensation agreements with authors like Michener and O'Hara, RH had two million dollars in the bank. On the other hand, the dictionary ate capital, and Syracuse-based Singer was underperforming and gulping money.

A half year passed. In October 1964, Dick Kislik—New York point man for Singer—delivered more bad news about its budget. The subsidiary had suffered a loss in the last fiscal year, and the situation wasn't improving. When RH bought her company, Bennett had counted on Frances Singer to continue running it. He trusted her; personal relationships were how he did business. Now, getting on in age and reeling from the losses, she admitted her oversight had become lax, her chief editor had been inadequate, and they'd been living on past successes and were being eclipsed by the competition. She had to rebuild the editorial team, and told Bennett that she needed Kislik to handle management. At the same time, battered pride and fear that a reshuffle would further erode morale impelled her to beg for a delay in announcing that shift.

Sensitive to her feelings, Bennett complied, yet frustration bubbled sourly inside him. Singer had already required a $2.5 million RH "loan." In his diary, he concentrated resentment onto Kislik, now dubbed the "joy-killer," even though the situation wasn't of Kislik's making. It was Bennett who'd barreled ahead without a clue about the basal text business, but it was easier to offload unpleasant feelings onto the messenger and number-cruncher who didn't fit in, than to face himself. Around Thanksgiving, a series of nosebleeds was bad enough to send Bennett to the hospital, and he was grateful to get through *What's My Line?* without a bleed on set. Sometimes, now, admitting to fatigue, he had to go home and lie down for an hour before rushing to evening activities. Still, most observers were unaware of any change at all.

Rumors that RH was in merger talks were pheromones to other suitors. Before the year ended, Don was fielding an inquiry from the Times-Mirror Corporation of Los Angeles, which owned newspapers, a TV station, and had begun to buy book publishers, including New American Library and World. Spring brought interest from even further afield, London. Paul Hamlyn was a brilliant British publisher who wanted to create an international "combine." Neither approach was taken very seriously, but soon others were. Felix Rohatyn, a canny partner in Wall Street investment bank Lazard Frères, arranged a lunch in May 1965 for Bennett and Don to meet Richard Prentice Ettinger, co-founder and president of Prentice-Hall, a dominant publisher in almost every sector of the U.S. text business. An RH–PH marriage could solve the Singer problem and do much more. However, it was common knowledge that Ettinger had almost sold Prentice to the Radio Corporation of America (RCA) only five months earlier. RCA had even announced the deal to the world, but then something went terribly wrong.

A *Fortune* Top 30 company and icon of American enterprise, RCA employed 92,000 people to design and supply equipment to NASA and the Pentagon; send cables around the world; manufacture the radios and TVs in many homes and cars; and control much of their programming via its NBC network. The RCA Victor records logo "His Master's Voice" was an icon in itself, and the subsidiary had won more Grammys than any other label in 1964, including for Bennett's current favorite, *Hello, Dolly!* But what had drawn RCA to Prentice was a new interest in the computer, data processing, and educational technology fields.

Since the late 1950s, "teaching machines" had been bruited as a way to solve seemingly insoluble problems in schools, and the government, with its vast pocketbook, was paying attention. RCA already made language labs, and had started a division to develop equipment and systems for handling print information. One proposal was to create facsimile machines that could deliver publications remotely. Others involved TV for classrooms, phones that connected listeners to recorded lectures, and "programmed" machines into which a student could plug answers and be graded automatically. RCA invested in hardware; it needed a publisher to supply "software." Prentice-Hall had seemed perfect, but its CEO less so—he was *too* smart. It turned out that if the deal had gone through, Ettinger would have held more shares in the merged company than David Sarnoff, the imperious CEO who'd spent his life building RCA. Once "General Sarnoff"—he'd acquired the rank of Brigadier General along the way—realized that, the deal was dead.

Now Lazard was searching for a new partner for Ettinger, but also hunting for one it could introduce to Sarnoff. RCA was also taking advice from a second bank, Lehman Brothers, and Bennett knew men there, too. So it was that the same week he lunched with Rohatyn and Ettinger, separate arrangements were made for him to meet with RCA. Through the summer of 1965, Bennett, Don, Kislik, and sometimes Bernstein conducted talks with Rohatyn and Prentice-Hall, but by early September, Random had concluded that a merger with PH would not happen.

For months, Bennett's diary was mum about further contact with RCA, yet the giant had been doing some homework. It had wooed away a Prentice senior executive to glean inside knowledge on the book business, and did research on Random, poking into publicly available financials and asking around. It had identified one RH author in particular—Pat Suppes, a professor whom Blaisdell had brought in—as a prize who could help advance teaching-machine dreams. RH knew very little about science and math, but Suppes's brilliance was so evident that when the Blaisdell imprint was sold off to Ginn, RH had insisted on keeping him.

Suppes directed Stanford's Institute for Mathematical Research in the Social Sciences. A pioneer of the "new math" in elementary schools, even more consequential was his vision of a future where children would access the personal services of a tutor in the form of a machine, in essence conjuring the personal computer a decade before its invention, and championing a democratic notion of education as philosophical underpinning to machine-assisted learning. Phyllis had discovered how influential he was, and made sure Bennett knew it, too. Besides, Suppes spent his childhood in Oklahoma, and was brought up on Christian Science, just like her.

The RCA Building

RCA was the largest tenant in the tallest tower of Rockefeller Center and so laid claim to it, with its three giant letters glowing big, red, and neon-bright atop what had come to be called the "RCA Building." From some of the palazzo windows, you could see it in the sky stretching above St. Pat's. Quietly in the distance it beckoned, an answer to Singer's drain on capital, stock fluctuations, the future. If he were going to cede his life's central work to anyone else, with RCA Bennett would at least hold out for something precious: a seat on its board. He'd been a director of MGM for years, and that was gossipy good fun, even if he thought some of the board's movie decisions woefully wrongheaded. But RCA was of an almost inconceivable magnitude. Bennett could look out and envisage Sarnoff on the fifty-third floor of *his* building, in a sleek boardroom. Imagine being seated at that big table alongside the General, weighing in on the future of one of the premier companies of the world.

In his sixty-seven years, the son of lovable, feckless Gus Cerf had scaled so many unexpected heights. Yet never were they good enough, and never could they satisfy that voice whispering *more*. Did it echo the demanding, dismissive voice of another self-made millionaire, his grandfather Nathan Wise, a hard man who hardly respected Bennett's father? The General in his tower lair: now Bennett had one more mountain to climb.

Chapter 47

Successor and Sale

Bob Haas's counsel might have come in handy now, but Bennett could no longer summon it. The previous July, Bob had been diagnosed with lung cancer, and died a few weeks later. Random teetered on the edge of major change, but there was no wise inside voice to counter the cacophony of bankers, lawyers, and ambitious younger men chittering their own agendas.

Once they went public and began expanding fast, something *had* changed in Don. Bennett had sensed it these past four years, ever since he was upended by that terrifying notion of Don's retiring. Was it then that they had had words? Late in life, Phyllis Cerf couldn't place the argument in time, but its effect was burned into her memory. Disagreements tumbled through Bennett and Donald's years together in business, but there was never a *fight,* wounding, scary, and personal—except for that one time. Details were hazy, but what she did recall was that afterward, Bennett looked terrible, really unwell. She was frightened, even worried he was going to die that night. How many people, after all, does anyone deeply love in a life? Bennett *really* loved Donald. The morning after the fight, both men awoke horribly depressed.

Time passed. After Don put aside the idea of retirement, things seemed to go on as before—but not quite. In his wartime letters, he'd feared bigness: get big, and it would upset their cozy intimacy. But big is what they'd become, and an inner cog in Donald had disengaged. Looking at the two partners, most others did not see it, but a chasm had opened between them.

Whether they proceeded to the altar with RCA was Bennett's decision to make. If he pushed, Don wouldn't stop him. Pros and cons sloshed around in his head, but one thought floated fast and clear to the surface: he didn't want to report to anyone. He'd have to arrange matters to stay above that—whatever happened, whoever owned them. Then it came to him: he would step aside from the presidency, but remain board chairman of RH. That was the way. *President:* it had been his title from the start. He'd still exercise primacy as chairman, he thought, but would have to appoint someone to the titular role. There were candidates, though none was perfect.

Companies, like people, tell stories about themselves. Their makers pinch, smooth, trim, ignore, and embroider, constructing narratives to seem sensible and inevitable. The actuality is more messily, poignantly human. Having to put aside the fantasy that his sons would run the business was hard for Bennett, for Phyllis, for Chris, for Jonathan—too hard to talk about, though it hung over them all. Now Kislik, all business, and Bernstein, all merchandising, were lining up, so ambitious, impatient, hitting their prime. Whatever influence Phyllis had on Bennett, it was clear she disliked Kislik. She didn't dislike Bernstein. He was useful to her publishing plans.

Although Bennett had mentally swatted Kislik the "joy-killer" off to one side, aspects of Bernstein, too, bothered him and others. Bob wasn't much of a reader—not of fiction, let alone literature with a capital "L." Politics was his bag. In some ways, he still seemed most at home devising smart sales campaigns for juveniles. Certain editors at that point didn't regard him as a "true book man," and felt that when he encountered serious disagreement, a chill could descend and stay. He also had a shy, square, puritanical streak: Bob not only looked like, but at times came across as, an unsophisticated big kid, not nearly as connected to the zeitgeist or as compelling a personality as the head of RH should be. He used to say to himself that Bennett was the top of the mountain, and knew he was no Bennett, lacking the mutable multiplicity and quick charm.

Take when Random published Richard Fariña's picaresque tale *Been Down So Long It Looks Like Up to Me,* a comic, contemporary riff on the *Odyssey* set in Ithaca, New York, and Cuba. Publication was celebrated at the Villard with a wild party—the way to go for a groovy novel by a brilliant young hipster. Fariña and his countercultural friends seemed not only to take over the palazzo, but to command the very center: Bennett's office. The ethereal yet fiery folk singer Joan Baez—sister to Fariña's wife, Mimi—had seated herself in Bennett's chair, long black tresses cascading down its back, and bare, dusty feet propped up on his clean, neat desk.

When Michael Frith wandered into the buzzing throng, Baez was glancing around the space, railing against porcine capitalists. He thought how lucky it was that Bennett wasn't there, but a moment later, who should saunter in but the capitalist himself, smooth and sharply dressed as always. The ragtag young people stared, essentially expecting—indeed, almost daring—Big Daddy-O to put his establishment-rooted feet very wrong. Frith, suddenly tense, was concerned lest they metaphorically tar and feather this man whom he regarded as family.

The master of the house only grinned. True, when he'd read Fariña's book in proofs, Bennett had judged it "weird." Yet the novel had received great blurbs, and he saw the appeal it had for his sons' generation: that was why they were all there. Within minutes of entering, he was seated on one of the overstuffed chairs, a pretty girl perched on each knee, letting Baez expatiate from her spot (his), everyone talking, drinking, laughing, any hint of rebellion gone. Making them feel he had no guard up and was utterly open had proved irresistible. He didn't lay claim to the room, but in just those few moments had succeeded in *owning* it: as simple and rare as a man walking in, expecting miracles, and getting them. A good time was had by all, not least Bennett. The contrast with the two stiffer, younger men vying for his job could not have been more stark.

He had, however, come to depend on both. A year earlier, he and Don had offered to sell Kislik and Bernstein 10 percent of their stock, along with an option on some of Alfred and Blanche's, as a way to keep them. Yet both could not fail to be aware, as Bernstein later said, that the editors were the princes, the real talent of the house. Mulling over who'd succeed him, Bennett looked long and hard at his editors, hoping that somehow he could settle on one with business pragmatism *and* literary instinct, in the mold set by Donald, Bob Haas, and himself.

Albert Erskine understood money all right, and "Alberto," as Bennett had taken to calling him after he'd married an Italian contessa, had the editorial talents and production expertise. But he was happiest nested at home with his wife and an author by his side. He made it clear he didn't want the job. Jason Epstein had carved out a prominent place in the intellectual and literary world and had a fine entrepreneurial head, but, self-centered and often difficult, Jason wasn't right. Bennett had to circle back to those who wanted the job.

Kislik sat at his elbow in every major transaction, and was closer to the financials than anyone. Bennett was aware that rumors of friction between them were spreading. That wasn't good, so he made a great show of taking Kislik to lunch at Sardi's East to quell negative gossip and put the quarrels behind them. Socially, he mingled more with Bob and Helen, and even used the Bernstein boys to help on a joke book. Bob's energy and eagerness echoed his own youthful ways, and Bob so clearly tried to emulate his joke-telling. He'd also benefited from the same on-the-road sales education that Bennett and Don had received and valued.

Even more, Bob had absorbed lessons from Lew, and latterly made a point of seeking management wisdom from Don over shared sandwiches in Don's office while Bennett was out gallivanting. Bernstein had assumed much of the responsibility for dealing with Ted and Helen, and managed to keep the Geisels happy while growing the Seuss business—no small feat. He'd also shown keen interest on the international front. In their early days, Bennett had loved leading the charge in Europe, but after the war, cocooned in the happy fame of *What's My Line?* and married to a woman with little tolerance for sightseeing, he'd remained stateside and left foreign relations to Don. The Frankfurt Book Fair had now become Bob's preserve.

The strange thing was, despite the rivalry, Kislik and Bernstein had come together once RCA entered the fray, to present a joint proposal: Why not sell control of the company to them? Approaching him like that was bold, harking back to what he and Don had done forty years earlier with Liveright—but Bennett was no desperate Horace. Besides, this was a whole different scale, and lining up financing would have been tricky. More to the point, Kislik and Bernstein were no marriage made in heaven. He and Donald wouldn't trust the future of the company to an uneasy, competitive pair. He could only marvel at what rare luck was his, that day he'd met his perfect complement in Don. If he sold, it would be to a major player, and the succession would already be in place. The timing would take everybody by surprise—including, perhaps, himself.

Four years earlier, in that happy era for Phyllis when she was running Beginner's New York operation, she'd written to Bernstein, whose responsibilities at S&S had included selling children's phonograph records based on Golden Books. She wanted advice: people were clamoring for Dr. Seuss records, and what interested her was arranging a joint venture.

"We do not want to be in the record business," she declared, "*but maybe RCA would like to be in the book business*. Do you think we could sell them on the idea of packaging a Seuss book and record for next Christmas?"

How strange to think of those words now. She'd never dreamed that one day Bennett would discuss RCA and a combo of a different sort. Phyllis wasn't happy: for her, control was paramount. Sell Random House? To RCA? She begged Bennett not to do it. As usual, being so busy all day cut down on moments for doubt to creep in, but he wasn't devoid of qualms. Despite the lovely image of a boardroom seat beside Sarnoff, at times Bennett felt shaky. Yet like an ocean liner mid-storm, he proved exceedingly hard to turn from the course he'd set.

Robert Todd Lang, a younger partner in Horace Manges's law firm, got a call to come over to the palazzo for an important meeting. When he arrived, Bennett, Donald, and Kislik greeted him with a question: If RH were to pursue a merger with RCA, would that affect their network of contracts with authors? They all knew that, like the strongest of silk filaments, it was the web of author agreements that underlay everything Random House was and did.

Yes, something undesirable could occur, Lang replied: under current law, a merger could trigger cancellation rights, and contracts become terminable. If an author didn't want publishing rights to a book to flow to RCA, he or she would be able to end the agreement. Bennett sat up, and charged Lang to go back, talk with his colleagues, and try to find a way around the problem. What the lawyers eventually proposed was a highly unusual deal of a sort Lang wasn't sure had ever been done before (if so, only once or twice in U.S. corporate history). They could organize a subsidiary of RCA, and have *it* merge into RH. RCA stock would be used to pay in an all-stock deal. A "subsidiary merger" was so far from the norm, they'd have to work to sell the idea.

Bennett, however, grasped Lang's explanation, and agreed pretty fast. He wasn't afraid to try something new. The lawyer was impressed with his mind, sense of purpose, and innate sense of proportion despite his fame. People who only knew the TV personality might judge him supercilious, but that would be a mistake: Bennett "saw things others didn't," Lang realized. Don had excellent judgment and was a hugely stabilizing force, but Bennett brought "more market value and the vision to be where change was, and understand it." After a lifetime of dealmaking, Lang concluded, "Never did the ball bounce bad with him, which is a pretty unique statement."

Among RCA's negotiators was Robert Sarnoff, the General's son and presumed heir, whom Lang and Bennett approached about the subsidiary merger. With "Bobby's" nod came the General's. Details and numbers would take time to work through.

. . .

OCTOBER 29, 1965, A Friday: Random House had scheduled a banquet to take place that evening. The gilded-age opulence of the Astor Hotel, stretching along a full block of Broadway from Forty-Fourth to Forty-Fifth Streets, seemed the perfect venue for the old-guard pair being honored. The hotel had held out against a newly aggressive seediness pervading Times Square, just as Alfred and Blanche Knopf, the honorees, symbolized a time of publisher-owners, fast giving way to corporatization.

The dinner commemorated publication of the first Borzoi book five decades earlier, and celebrated the lifework that went into what was often described as the most "distinguished" American imprint. Bennett and Don had marshaled 274 guests to raise a glass to Bennett's idol and his ever-chic wife. What guests didn't know was that Blanche, who'd always shown great physical courage, was again doing so now. She was suffering from advanced cancer, the latest, and most terrifying, in a chain of physical crises. Not enough nourishment had led to brittle bones, falls, a badly broken hip. She'd had a cataract operation, so wasn't as blind as before, but pain shadowed her constantly. One of the worst indignities for a woman in whom pride and vanity were intertwined was losing her hair to the treatments. Bennett, at one meeting, had been unable to stop himself from whispering to Alfred, "Is that a wig Blanche has on?"

In the years since the merger with RH and the almost simultaneous death of her *cher ami* Albert Camus, a kind of rapprochement had occurred between the Knopfs. Alfred had always loved Blanche in his gruff, deeply awkward way, and she'd come to need the companionship she'd rejected all those years earlier. He may have been slowing down—both Knopfs' contracts for the new year reflected this, with salary cuts linked to less responsibility—but Alfred remained as formidable as ever, and continued to bellow complaints. When RH tried an aggressive new mail-order scheme to sell first novels by soliciting readers' "advice" about the books (at the same time signing them up to buy a half dozen more first novels that year), Alfred exploded to Bennett that the plan was misleading and "poisonous." He was right (it ended).

Alfred's eruptions about RH's spendthrift ways were a different matter. When Bennett insisted that Blanche pay a $30,000 advance for two unseen novels by Muriel Spark, author of *The Prime of Miss Jean Brodie,* Alfred declared himself "ashamed" by such profligacy. But now it was Bennett's turn to be right: living too much on backlist, not enough fresh authorial blood was flowing, and Knopf was in danger of becoming sclerotic. He'd told Blanche to get some good new manuscripts, "whatever the price." Still, the association between the thunderbolt-wielding Olympian and the canny jokester with the common touch had worked out very well. "For Bennett, a wonderful boss" is how Alfred had inscribed a Christmas present a few years earlier.

That night at the Astor, all transgressions were forgiven, as a nonpareil crowd of friends, publishers, journalists, staff, and authors—from Langston Hughes to Julia Child—listened as speech after speech sang praises. Others were sung in a two-volume presentation set given to each guest. "A Salute," the testimonial bearing Bennett's byline, made clear that even now, he didn't see himself in the same league: "When I first met Alfred . . . I thought he was the finest and most important book publisher in America. Now, after over forty years of friendship . . . and . . . five . . . of the closest business relations—I feel even more strongly about his pre-eminent place. . . . I love him even for his faults! What more can a man say than that?"

Don's "A Tribute" explained that when he first read Alfred's pamphlet on Conrad, "I admired him. When I became a publisher . . . I loved the format of his books, and was enormously impressed with the vivid personality of a man who could assemble such a distinguished list." When they became partners, "I was frightened, but it has been great—at least . . . for me!" All was forgiven that night, but Don hadn't forgotten the man he knew. He'd chosen his words to be politic but not to lie, as he didn't share Bennett's fondness for the Knopfs. Alfred would always be, for him, as he'd later say, "a very arrogant, selfish man who never thought of anyone else."

Dick and Audrey Kislik were seated at Table 7; Bob and Helen Bernstein at Table 1, closest to the dais. To followers of protocol, that meant something, and they would have been right. Bernstein sat half listening, half preoccupied, next to department store magnate Stanley Marcus. Five years earlier, Bennett had persuaded his pal Stanley to include a full set of the ML as a unit in the famously fabulous Neiman-Marcus Christmas catalogue. Now it was obvious Marcus was wondering why, in such a glittering crowd, he'd been put next to a "nobody." Something in Bob was bursting to tell the old man and redress the balance, but he held his tongue. That was what he'd agreed to earlier that day, when Bennett walked into his office and, out of the blue, declared that in January, Bob would become Random's second president.

Of course, word began to leak. After the banquet, the Cerfs and Bernsteins were seen celebrating *something* at Sardi's. The news wasn't official until December 6, when Jean Ennis sent a release announcing a "realignment" of officers, as of January, with Bernstein as president; Bennett, chair and CEO; Don, vice chair; and Lewis Miller, chair of the Executive Committee. (Lew, having been superseded, had begun to negotiate for a comfortable retirement.) Bennett wanted "the top young people . . . to feel their oats" while their elders were still there. No time had shown a more obvious need for "young men with exciting new ideas and perspectives."

The company was enjoying its most prosperous year, he told Harry Gilroy, who was writing a story for the *Times*. Bennett predicted that sales for the fiscal year ending in March would be $34 million; when RH went public in 1959, revenues had been $12 million, with Knopf adding another $4 million in 1960. True to the character the public knew, he made a point of being lighthearted, showing Gilroy a copy of his new book, *Laugh Day,* inscribed for Bernstein: "To the prexy with fond regards from the man who is planning a comeback." Gilroy had heard other changes were afoot, and asked about a sale to CBS. Publishers might someday have to merge with the electronic companies, "or be left out of the field," was Bennett's last word.

Four days later, Carroll Newsom, the former Prentice-Hall president who'd decamped to RCA, was at RH "to prowl." By the week leading to Christmas, Bennett felt RCA was "moving in on us." On December 21, when Bennett was closeted with Don, Bob, and Kislik, Felix Rohatyn and his Lehman Brothers counterpart arrived. The General had become more involved in talks about price. RCA had offered half a share of its stock for one of RH's, and was willing to go up a bit, but Bennett wanted more. The time had come for him to go to the mountain, and see Sarnoff himself.

. . .

David Sarnoff

JUST AS AMERICANS "KNEW" *What's My Line?* panelist Bennett Cerf, they also "knew" General David Sarnoff. It was entirely typical of the man that during World War II, he'd maneuvered to get—and also earn—that status. Three hours hadn't passed after the attack on Pearl Harbor when he dispatched an RCA radiogram to President Roosevelt: "All our facilities and personnel are ready and at your instant service. . . ." Other industrialists also opened their doors, but Sarnoff was faster than most. In 1944, aged fifty-three, he was called to London by Supreme Allied Commander Dwight D. Eisenhower to take charge of coordinating radio communications for D-Day. If he messed up, consequences would be disastrous. He didn't, and became a general. No one who felt the power of his Akita-blue eyes thought of Sarnoff as the short man he was.

Born in a shtetl, he came to New York as a child and, with an eighth-grade education, started at the British-owned Marconi Wireless Telegraph Company of America. With a nose for engineering and communications technology also came an instinct for casting his contributions in the best possible light; like Bennett, he knew how to exaggerate. In April 1912, aged twenty-one, he was night manager of the Marconi telegraph station on the roof of Wanamaker's New York department store. Legend has it that he alone received the first wireless message that the *Titanic* was doomed, and stayed for seventy-two hours straight to give the developing news to the world. Far more likely is that after disaster struck, he and two others "kept a long vigil" to relay who was lost and who was saved. What's certain is that the *Titanic*'s sorry end jump-started his future.

In 1965, if you asked any American "Who founded RCA?," almost certainly the answer would have been "General Sarnoff." That was wrong. The company began in 1919, when the General Electric Corporation—with government backing, in the name of national security—forced a sale of Marconi's U.S. interests and put them under a subsidiary it called the Radio Corporation of America. But in another sense, there was truth in the misperception, for it was Sarnoff who envisioned and shaped what RCA would become. He'd had the foresight to understand before others did that through a "radio music box," the new wireless technology could be brought into American homes. Later, he took a risky bet on developing color TV when others scoffed. His drive to accomplish and capitalize on technological innovation smashed ceilings and bent competitors to his will; in some respects, he was the Steve Jobs or Elon Musk of his day, inspiring great loyalty, but also terrible fear. He'd crushed brilliant men who'd been his friends; a Cold War hawk, he'd supported McCarthy and blacklisting within RCA.

Bennett Cerf and David Sarnoff were different in so many ways. There was no charm, no boyishness, practically no humor in Sarnoff. Cerf's desperate desire to be loved was decidedly missing. So was the insecurity, the saving grace to Bennett's ego. But there were similarities: the drive and energy, the very good brain. Each excelled at taking over things started elsewhere, and capitalizing on them spectacularly. Bennett more often than not signed authors first published by others, but he was the one who knew how to give them what they wanted. He saw what could be done with the Modern Library. He understood the importance of linking books to other media. Sarnoff knew how to select partially developed ideas devised by genius inventors and turn them into things that could be made on a mass scale, and that America and the world would buy.

The General appreciated the power of brands, and Bennett, unique among book men, was one. RH by no means presented the best "software" for RCA's purposes, but it had Pat Suppes, and rival IBM was after him, too. If Sarnoff did a deal with Cerf, no question who'd be on top, no unpleasant surprise as with Prentice-Hall's Ettinger. RH would be a small province of RCA's empire, a tribute nation come to Rome, a phalanx among many advancing into a machine future.

All that remained was one last hurdle: to finalize the price.

Two days before Christmas, Bennett and Don "sneaked" into the RCA Building for a meeting with the General. Bobby Sarnoff was there, with Carroll Newsom and Felix Rohatyn. Sarnoff raised his offer to 0.6 of a share of RCA for one of RH, but Bennett had it in his head to settle for nothing less than 0.62—about $40 million, based on RCA's share price—and a seat on the board. The bankers were getting impatient, fearing he'd destroy the deal. At that point, RH was also speaking to another suitor, John Kluge, who controlled the Metromedia broadcasting empire. Bennett and Don left RCA to go to Metromedia and continue talking there. Maybe it was a way to forestall the reality of selling, playing one bidder against the other, making no decision at all.

The Cerfs celebrated Christmas with Cousin Ginger and Aunt Lela. The next day, a Sunday, Bennett was summoned to the General's home. He'd escaped into an NFL playoff game between the Baltimore Colts and Green Bay Packers on CBS, and resented having to go to Sarnoff's. When he arrived at the mansion on East Seventy-First Street, the General's French-born wife, Lizette, was watching the AFL playoffs on NBC. He told her she was watching the wrong game.

"I don't watch CBS," she replied. "The only thing that I watch on CBS is you on *What's My Line?*" Bennett felt that he'd gained an ally.

Again, Sarnoff offered 0.6 a share, and again Bennett refused, holding out for 0.62. The General wasn't used to this. He didn't like feeling frustrated.

"I'm not going back to my stockholders," he told Bennett. "I've been back twice. . . . You are either going to take sixty one-hundredths or the deal is off."

Bennett mustered all his cocky bravado. "Fine, let's watch the end of the football. . . . We're missing a very important game. . . . We'll still be able to catch the last quarter."

"You mean that you won't make the deal? . . . You know, we're very close to buying another business."

Bennett had heard that RCA was also investigating an educational publisher, but wouldn't give way.

Sarnoff was annoyed. Bobby and Rohatyn, in another room, had champagne chilling, ready to conclude. Calling them in, Sarnoff decided for all of them they'd talk again tomorrow.

"That's impossible," Bennett piped up, unable to suppress the grin of the boy who has found the golden ticket. He and Phyllis were leaving for Palm Springs, he announced, having been invited to spend the rest of the holidays with Frank Sinatra. They were flying out with Sinatra's new girl—a young actress named Mia Farrow—on the entertainer's private plane.

"With this deal hanging fire you're going off on vacation?" Sarnoff was incredulous.

"You're right I am," Bennett responded. "I'll be away eleven days."

"When you come back, my offer may be withdrawn."

"I've already turned down your offer. My proposition stands. When I come back, I will still make the deal at sixty-two one-hundredths," Bennett countered. Neither would budge, like two stubborn rhinos facing off against each other in the rarefied jungle of the Upper East Side.

Bennett, rather pleased with himself, thought he "had all the aces," but he wasn't the only player in this scene. Sarnoff, adept at theatrical flourishes, too, took an unexpected card from his pocket. If they did the deal, Bennett would have to step down from the MGM board and *What's My Line?* How could a director of RCA, owner of the National Broadcasting Corporation, appear week after week on a rival network? Sarnoff's reasoning was clear—at least to him.

For Bennett, it was "a shocker." Something like disbelief and fear fluttered through him. Leave *What's My Line?* That would require a wholesale readjustment of identity. *They knew him.* How could he give that up? How could Sarnoff demand such a thing? He looked at the General, solid, humorless, immovable. Bennett maintained the cocky scrim, but knew he had to get out of there. It was Sunday, winter, dark already. He walked the nine cold blocks home. His taped face would be there to reassure him later, when he tuned in to *What's My Line?*

Felix Rohatyn pondered. He was dealing with two men who, in the public eye, were on equal footing. The General was a legend, RCA big, but Random was a prestige name, and TV had made Bennett famous. Cerf added incalculable value. Rohatyn decided to work on Sarnoff.

"It's not the end of the world: You're big, they're small, why don't you make a show of generosity and elegance, and give Bennett what he wants?" Rohatyn cajoled.

Bennett went into the office that Monday earlier than usual, since he was leaving at noon for his trip. At 10:00 A.M. the switchboard buzzed: the General. He sounded in command as ever, but proceeded to raise his offer to 0.62! The business of *What's My Line?* hung in the air, but could hang a bit longer. At that moment, all Bennett could feel was a surge of triumph. They agreed that everything would be decided by January 10, when he would be back in New York.

Rumors and stock price started to soar almost at once, but Bennett's mind turned to the flying he would do that afternoon. He went home, told Thrup the news, and finished packing. Mia picked them up, and they proceeded to the jet at LaGuardia. Soon they were heading west, toward the sun Bennett craved—and to a man who'd become one of his new best friends.

Chapter 48

Sinatra

Bennett met Frank Sinatra for the first time in late autumn 1942, when he and Phyllis were party guests at the industrial designer Raymond Loewy's sleek offices. He saw an eager young man, nattily dressed, skinny as a scarecrow beneath the careful clothes, materialize next to the fellow playing the piano, and start singing. Most people were too busy chatting to pay attention. For them, music was background to the serious business of talk. However, with his deep feeling for the American songbook, Bennett did notice. He kept circling back to the piano, then finally lingered, asking for tune after tune. Sometimes—off-key though he was—he sang along. Sinatra took it in stride. By the end of the party, beguiled by the voice, Bennett had fallen a little bit in love. Already on his way, the crooner had been performing with Harry James and Tommy Dorsey, but wasn't a phenomenon yet. One month later, at the end of December, he'd stand front and center at the Paramount Theater. Bobby-soxers would go crazy, and a superstar be born.

In the 1950s, the two men's paths crossed again, through their mutual friend Mr. Hart. Sinatra loved *My Fair Lady,* identifying with Eliza Doolittle's metamorphosis, and had enormous respect for the "class" and talent of people like Moss. The Cerfs mingled with him at the Harts', and at homes of other friends, like "Hollywood princess" Edie Goetz, the daughter of MGM's Louis B. Mayer, and agent Leland Hayward. By 1957, Bennett and Phyllis were on a select list of forty whom Sinatra invited to the first formal dinner party at his new L.A. home. When Moss died so suddenly in 1961, a shared grief strengthened their bond.

The mid-1960s saw things changing for Sinatra. His was still the voice behind so many important moments, but the country, and he with it, was entering an uncertain time. The culture had begun to gyrate into something new. His grown-up music was challenged, often drowned out, by youthful sounds he didn't like. Nor was he pleased to be facing fifty. It was a good time to squire Mia Farrow, a dewy young bird, but also to cultivate an older crowd, burnished with esteem, whom he could admire. Both might distract from that half-century mark.

Bennett was in that older group, much more than a TV personality. At odd times, Sinatra liked improving himself by memorizing the dictionary. Bennett published them, and all those famous authors. To an autodidact ashamed of his lack of formal education, Bennett was about as intellectual as it got, a cultural force. "It wasn't easy for Frank to look up to people," Farrow observed, "but he did look up to Bennett." It helped that open, fun Bennett was anything but snooty or threatening, wearing accomplishments lightly, the self-discipline, drive, and work barely visible. His persona was not unlike how Sinatra sang: seeming so effortless at the mike. All those hours that went into breath control, phrasing—that was not allowed to show. Besides, Bennett seemed so comfortable in his skin, it put a moody man at ease. With him in the room, "it was like stepping into sunlight," Farrow recalled. Sinatra's younger daughter, Tina, saw "such a sweetness. When he laughed—and he laughed a lot—Bennett had a little boy's high giggle, and his shoulders went up and down." The corny jokes and fan-love were acceptable from him, not irritating but charming. He was so unashamed, so strangely innocent, yet a very successful man.

It wasn't hard to see why Bennett was eager to add Sinatra to his inner circle of friends. He loved showbiz as much as books, and Sinatra was at the pinnacle. Whatever bad-boy, mobbed-up gossip swirled around him, it couldn't touch his genius and magnetic center. And both men, at heart, were devoted to telling stories, each understanding the art and commerce of that work. Bennett also wanted to publish him. On April 23, in advance of his milestone birthday, *Life* magazine ran a sixteen-page cover story, "The Private World and Thoughts of Frank Sinatra," full of photos and perorations from the "Chairman of the Board." Bennett read it and picked up the phone. Sinatra answered. In the midst of shooting a movie, preparing for a documentary, and rehearsing a recording session, he made time to meet in May to discuss turning the *Life* feature into a book.

"I would be proud to publish you," Bennett had declared, a new kind of music to the singer's ears. He began discussing with Sinatra's PR man how to make it happen. In August, back in New York, Sinatra invited the Cerfs to dinner, where Bennett was delighted to meet Farrow. "A charming, beautiful nineteen she is!" his diary had gushed, making her one year younger than she was. The next month, Bennett's old friend Doris Vidor—another Hollywood princess, whose father, Harry Warner, had once hoped Bennett might marry her—organized a super-glittery soirée to celebrate the Cerfs' twenty-fifth anniversary. Frank and Mia were there. Now it was late December, and Sinatra was glad to have the Cerfs chaperone "his girl" west.

Two days after Christmas, Bennett, Phyllis, and their charge touched down at Palm Springs in Sinatra's jet. The man himself came to meet them. They drove to the two-and-a-half-acre compound on Wonder Palms Road, the place that, more than any other, he called home. Just a few thousand people lived in the town then; he'd chosen the spot both for privacy and space.

Bennett saw purple mountains rise in the distance, background to sun-bleached boulders, sand, and white pebbles that crunched underfoot. Tall palms, shorter citrus, and cactus—fantastic twisted fingers of saguaro, ocotillo, and low-lying succulents—dotted the property, with no attempt at lawn. Beside the pool, a gaily striped orange-and-white tent-pole awning stretched above matching loungers. Orange, Bennett soon realized, was a theme inside and out: orange sun, orange upholstery, orange short-sleeve shirts. The "happy" color, Sinatra called it. In due course, he'd decide that the Cerfs' Manhattan living room needed one of the orange-brown abstractions he liked painting. Unbidden, he arrived with it on their doorstep one weekend when Phyllis and Bennett were out. Let in by the maid who knew him well, he hung it himself, to give them a happy surprise. Modern art didn't speak to them, but that painting was deeply cherished.

Sinatra's Palm Springs compound comprised a main house whose dining room could seat two dozen; a restaurant-size kitchen; its master's very plain bedroom; the "Yul Brynner" room (a close pal and frequent visitor, the bald star with oversize charisma was away that holiday); and a "great hall" with bar, fireplace, piano, and projection area. Outside was a tennis court and guesthouses—ultimately five. The Cerfs shared a two-bedroom, four-bath cottage with their L.A. friends Ardie and Harriet Deutsch, whom Bennett favored as traveling companions after Moss died. Sinatra soon named it "Cerf Cottage," and Bennett and Phyllis would be welcomed back each year. "Hayward Cottage" was named for Leland Hayward, and there was "Hornblow Cottage" and "Christmas

Tree House," which often accommodated old-guard stars Rosalind Russell, Claudette Colbert, and husbands. Sinatra, "the Innkeeper," was embarrassingly generous, anticipating every whim of those he courted or cared for. Fly in stone crabs from the East Coast? Of course. Fill each set of baths in Cerf Cottage with luxuries? Easy. A careful "bathroom check" occurred before each arrived.

New Year's Eve found the compound's residents mingling with ninety or so non-staying guests come to see in the desert dawn. Frank, for a brief time, performed. Comedian Jack Benny, singer Dinah Shore, and composer Jimmy Van Heusen were among as stellar a group as any Bennett had known. He, unfortunately, had to slip away to bed at 2 A.M., to be awakened four hours later. The new mayor of New York, John Lindsay—the former congressman whom Bennett had for the past half dozen years befriended, and whose campaign biography he'd published—was to be ceremonially sworn in on the first day of January and had asked Bennett to emcee the inauguration. Tall, patrician, handsome, pro–civil rights, and anti-Goldwater, to many supporters Lindsay—the "fusion" candidate of the Liberal and Republican parties—exuded a whiff of Camelot and the promise of an optimistic future. Bennett was a true believer.

To get to New York on time, Sinatra's jet took him to L.A., where he caught a TWA flight bound east. When he landed at 3 P.M., Frank's New York "flunky" met him. A good thing, too: the city's subway and bus workers were on the first day of a first-ever transit strike, and a cab would have been hard to find. Lindsay, going on even less sleep than Bennett, eschewed wheels, instead striding purposefully downtown for four miles, from the Roosevelt Hotel to City Hall. "I still think it's a fun city," he told reporters, and during the tough years that followed, they didn't let him forget those words. But that day, all seemed charmed for Bennett. The weather was oddly warm, sixty degrees—he'd brought California with him. At 7 P.M., when he stood beside Lindsay on the eerily floodlit City Hall steps, twenty-five hundred people were gathered under a hazy moon, waiting.

"They said it would be a cold, wintry day when a Republican became mayor of New York," Bennett began. "We've got the winter, all right, but the cold has been dispelled by Mr. Quill," he quipped, referring to the fiery pronouncements of the transit union leader. People laughed. Between introductions and transitions, he sat next to Governor Nelson Rockefeller and his wife, Happy. When the new mayor finally spoke,

Lindsay seemed a shining embodiment of confidence, a beacon who gave the lie to rumblings of troubles gathering darkly on the horizon.

Later, Bennett looked in on the party at the Roosevelt and, just before 11 P.M., boarded a westbound jet. Sinatra's plane was waiting in L.A.: he was in Palm Springs twenty-one hours after he'd left it. Energy and adrenaline hadn't failed him. Up betimes at ten, he saw the Packers win the NFL title from the Browns. Pretty good for a fellow who'd soon turn sixty-eight.

. . .

SINATRA LIKED BESTOWING PET names, often affectionate, but sometimes with an edge. Bennett must have revealed his youthful nickname, for at first Farrow heard her beau call him "Beansy," but other monikers took over—"the Bookmaker," "Bennett the Bookie"—and those stuck. Sinatra enthusiastically adopted Bennett's nomenclature for Phyllis, but if you listened closely, there was an edge when he called her "The General," for he didn't take to her at first. Late at night, after she'd had a lot to drink, her acerbic humor became caustic, and she, difficult. Even during the day she was assertive, at times abrasively so, and could be very bossy, Farrow recalled.

Both Bennett and Sinatra were only children, each with a complicated relationship to his mother. They both knew the attendant loneliness and expectations, the push-pull of being a show-off mama's boy but also the little rebel, and living a great deal in their heads. Bennett rued the oversensitivity his mother had bequeathed, and sought reassurance from the crowd. Sinatra also needed it. He'd grown up terrified of his mother, who'd almost died giving birth, just as he'd almost died being born. Dolly Sinatra both spoiled and—literally—clubbed her son. He couldn't trust who she might be from hour to hour. As an adult, his mood swings, capacity for fierce loyalty, volcanic rage, and uncommon will, grit, and intelligence, mirrored hers.

Whatever Sinatra thought, Farrow liked Phyllis from the start, admiring that she wasn't "coy or retiring" and seemed to know who she was. But on some level, Phyllis also seemed "troubled," with many layers and "fierce things" inside her. For her part, knowing what it was to be attached to a powerful older man, Phyllis made a point of being kind to Farrow at a time when she needed it. Farrow felt awkward traveling with Sinatra, but the Cerfs made her comfortable.

She decided to "work" on Frank, to soften him toward Phyllis. Whether it was that, or greater exposure building immunity to her abrasive side, Sinatra did come around, especially after he began staying at Mt. Kisco and appreciated how she ran both houses so beautifully. Like him, she took such care of guests. In the end he found her smart, funny, exceptionally loyal, and, once he liked her well enough, also saw that she could be useful. Phyllis helped organize the compound crowd, and didn't mind being called "the General" when it came from him. One holiday, he presented her with a custom-made baseball cap, the word BOSS and five stars embroidered on it in gold. She clapped it on, and it rarely left her during that visit.

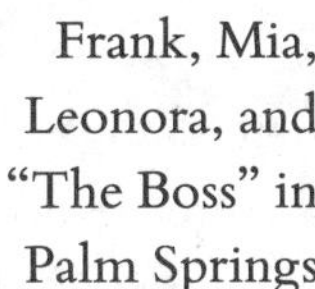
Frank, Mia, Leonora, and "The Boss" in Palm Springs

Back in New York, the Cerfs got into the habit of speaking with Sinatra on the phone every Sunday, "the day set aside for family," as Phyllis put it. Husband and wife were equally obsessed with him—as were many in that crowd. Sinatra was known for not only befriending the men, but bedding their wives—no hard feelings intended. Even her closest pals had no idea if Phyllis and Sinatra ever had an affair, but as to Leonora Hornblow and Frank—that was a different story. And Phyllis, so very competitive and jealous, knew it.

The way Frank occupied his waking hours was very different from how his older guests usually spent theirs. Playing innkeeper, he tried to arrange the day according to the way they lived in the world beyond the compound, yet much of the time, a formlessness reigned. Demands were not made. Some guests breakfasted together, but others could partake of breakfast anytime they wanted. They all knew Frank didn't rise until well after noon.

Bennett would tell jokes, while Phyllis would do needlepoint and play backgammon with Roz and Claudette. Everyone enjoyed charades. They'd lounge around the pool, some baring wrinkled bodies to the sun, while Farrow preferred to remain under the awning, all covered up. Later, they'd swim and have massages—one of Bennett's favorite ways to relax. Friends would jet in from L.A. or drive over from elsewhere in Palm Springs. A few times, Bennett and Frank peeled away to talk about the proposed book. In the evenings, Sinatra often screened movies.

At some point as a visit progressed, they'd fly to Las Vegas, to the Sands—operated by another Sinatra crony, Jack Entratter—where Frank often began a singing engagement. On their first such visit, the gig had him paired with Count Basie's orchestra. Bennett, Phyllis, and the others gambled with a purse provided by Frank. One year, in honor of Roz Russell, he gave each guest ten thousand silver dollars. Extreme generosity was one of the few ways he was able to express friendship, but it was also an assertion of power: he couldn't just be a buddy.

Many friends were uncomfortable with this imbalance in the relationship, but Farrow felt that Bennett was one of the few who dealt with it well. He seemed to treat their association more as one of equals. Perhaps it helped that he connected this aspect of Sinatra with Moss—both sharing the philosophy that "money is to be enjoyed" and spent. But even then, he clearly felt, consciously or otherwise, pressure to reciprocate any way he could. Sinatra was crazy about trains—he'd eventually add a converted caboose to the compound's buildings—and one year, Bennett gave his sons' train set to Frank, without consulting Chris or Jon. They never forgot it.

Las Vegas was where Sinatra's different worlds blurred. For a night or two, the "proper" New York and old Hollywood circles would mix with members of the "Rat Pack" and other less salubrious friends. For Christmas 1967, Sinatra would invite the Cerf boys to accompany their parents to Palm Springs. Farrow, four years younger than Chris and one year older than Jon, called them "the sons everyone would like to have." That time, Sinatra's friend Sammy Davis Jr. was headlining the Sands. Bennett and the boys piled into the jet for Vegas, leaving Phyllis and the other wives in Palm Springs. Davis, a generous soul like Sinatra, had arranged a special treat for Bennett's sons.

They were staying at Caesars Palace, and had returned to their room when a knock came at the door. Two pretty women, "presents" from Mr. Davis, had arrived to keep them company. Chris was twenty-six, Jon twenty-one, and neither had ever had an up-close-and-personal encounter with ladies of the night. Chris was "staggered." Jonathan, like his twenty-seven-year-old father in 1925, on his uncle Leo's guided tour of Paris brothels, was "horrified." The girls, however, turned out to be "nice," and well-versed in reading customers. The quartet spent an hour or so just talking. Still, the boys were glad to get on Sinatra's plane back to Palm Springs at 2 A.M. Ever the well-brought-up son, Jonathan wrote a thank-you note to Sammy. The "presents" had not been a surprise to Bennett. "Gals for the boys," he noted matter-of-factly in his diary.

Some of those who knew him well were discomfited by his dear friend Frank. "How can you be so close to him?" Bob Bernstein once asked, incredulous at the relationship.

Bennett shrugged off the younger man's disapproval, advising that "when you're past sixty, Bob, the most important thing in life is never to be bored. Frank Sinatra is *never* boring."

Bernstein would understand in due course. When he and Helen were invited to dinner parties at the Cerfs'—and as the new president of RH, they'd be invited often—Sinatra would sometimes turn up between the hours of eleven and midnight. He'd go to the piano—someone would play—and start singing. "It was a rare thing to be in that room," Bernstein realized.

. . .

WHEN BENNETT AND PHYLLIS flew back to New York after that first fabulous visit to Wonder Palms Road, it was as though they were emerging from one dream into another. That Sunday, January 9, he spent the day at home on the phone. He talked to the Hornblows about the trip, but, more important, he phoned Don, Tony Wimpfheimer, Horace Manges, and Bernstein, who'd been busy in his absence. Bennett had left the deal with RCA hanging in the balance. The next day, he had a date with General Sarnoff.

Chapter 49

Done Deal

It took less than ten minutes to walk from the Palazzo to the RCA Building. Curiously, for a gregarious man like Bennett, he went alone. Bob Bernstein, RH's new president, wasn't with him. No mention was made of Donald being there, either. Yet Bobby Sarnoff stood beside his father, witness to the betrothal. The deed was quickly done: the General and Bennett shook hands on an exchange of 0.62 of a share of RCA for each one of RH, what Bennett had held out for. RCA, a company with more than $2 billion in revenue and $100 million in profit in 1965, was paying more than $37.7 million, based on that day's market valuation.

The elder Sarnoff would turn seventy-five soon, and, like Bennett, had put his succession in place. On New Year's Day, RCA had elevated Bobby from head of NBC to president of the entire corporation. Bennett would let Bernstein handle Bobby and Elmer Engstrom, RCA's former president and new CEO, while he, as a member of the board—also confirmed by the handshake—would operate on a higher plane. In moving upstairs, the General assured his troops he'd continue to serve "actively" as board chair, the same title Bennett had retained at Random.

And so, a little after eleven o'clock in the morning on Monday, January 10, 1966, the future course of the firm that Bennett and Donald had nurtured for almost forty-one years was set. Working through details would require another three months, but the announcement of the agreement was on the Dow Jones ticker by lunchtime. It was, of course, subject to approval by the boards of each company, and the shareholders of Random House. RCA and RH sent out identical announcements with statements from the General and Bennett.

On news of the deal, RH stock surged, closing at $27, a far cry from the $9 it had tumbled to in the slump of 1963, when Bennett was afraid to leave the house. The self-doubt that gnawed at him had been vanquished, and newspapers began calling. The next day, a long story appeared in *The Wall Street Journal,* and two in *The New York Times*. The General spoke of a significant advance in joining "the oldest and the newest of the mass communication arts." In one *Times* piece, headlined "Cerf Welcomes Move," Bennett asserted that the merger fit with the expected "revolution" in education: RCA had the equipment, and Random the books. "We think we can work together to make a contribution to the educational development of the country."

It sounded great, but two years later, in his oral history, Bennett put a different spin on the story: "When RCA bought us, the thing that interested them most was the part . . . that interested me least . . . Singer." What meant far more was the promise, he told the *Times,* that RH would "continue to function as a separate entity with complete editorial autonomy in the hands of its own board, and no changes in its present personnel and management." Confiding to their lawyers, however, Bennett and Don feared losing control and freedom to do what they wanted, and instructed the attorneys to negotiate autonomy provisions in the contract. Both papers said that the Justice Department, via the Federal Trade Commission, wanted to review the deal to make sure it didn't violate antitrust law. (The agencies found no excessive concentration.)

While the plan to acquire Random led the headlines, it wasn't RCA's only announcement that day, and from a purely financial perspective, it was the less significant. The corporation also trumpeted it would budget a record $195 million to invest in its business, more than double the amount it had spent the prior year. More than half would expand production capacity for color TVs, while the rest would go into broadcasting, tape recorder and phonograph manufacturing, and computers. One of Bobby's big visions was to challenge IBM for dominance in that field.

Although Raytheon and Xerox had acquired text and academic publishers, the news about RCA and RH stunned the book world. Only six years earlier, when he bought Knopf, Bennett had declared to the *Saturday Review* that before he could ever be persuaded to sell Random House, "They'll have to carry me out in a wooden box." Yet he hadn't died, and knew it was crucial to cushion the shock and shape the news for RH authors, and do so at once. Along with the release, he sent each writer a personal letter, stressing that selling was "a great thing" for everyone, and wouldn't affect an author's relations with the company "in the slightest." Indeed, he hoped the merger would provide "possible increased earnings." If they had questions, he wanted them to phone him directly—an assurance that the personal touch was still in place.

However, many people remained puzzled, wondering how it would play out. The *Times*' book-beat reporter, Harry Gilroy, published a piece a week later that didn't welcome the entrance of companies like RCA into trade publishing. An electronics company wanting to succeed in the education market probably needed a book publisher, Gilroy wrote, and an educational book publisher might need an electronics connection, but "publishers who make a success of novels, whodunits, histories, biographies, essays and poetry without bothering with the educational market are happily free of this encroachment. Belles-lettres doesn't need electronics."

Gilroy's article happened to run alongside a giant advertisement. The big, bold headline read: "In business today . . . What you don't know can hurt you!" How much he didn't know about the corporation he was marrying, Bennett would soon find out.

Before January was out, the General, Bobby, and Engstrom had made their first official visit to Random House and broken bread at the Four Seasons with Bennett, Don, and Bob. Engstrom, Bobby, and two other RCA directors were to sit on the RH board, and Felix Rohatyn would join as well. David Sarnoff brooked no nonsense, and was known to shut people up if they went on too long. Bennett liked to talk, but things seemed to be going nicely between them. "Thank you with a cherry in it," Sarnoff had quaintly written, after the visit and lunch.

Yet Bennett's future on *What's My Line?* still dangled uncertainly. The General didn't see why the head of one of his divisions should appear on a rival network. Bennett had to admit to the *Times* that he might be required to leave the panel, and publicly tried to shrug it off as less than momentous: he was a grown-up, and all good things come to an end. Privately, he felt rattled, and *had* to find a way to persuade the General, so rarely swayed, to reverse himself.

It was ironic that Sarnoff had no understanding of the nexus between TV and celebrity. What spoke to him was engineering and technological brilliance, not entertainment and talent. In fact, he resented the notion of celebrity, hating the kind of social elite his archrival, CBS's Bill Paley, cultivated and belonged to, and loathing the more dubious public conduct of Hollywood.

Bennett turned to Michael Dann, Bob Bernstein's good friend in the television industry, whom he'd also known since the late 1950s. Could Dann make the General understand that his being on *What's My Line?* helped RH? Bernstein followed up with a call of his own, and Dann agreed to try. That it was the honeymoon period helped. Although Random would comprise only a tiny part of RCA—in 1966, 2 percent of sales—it was so well respected that Sarnoff considered it a plum. At the end of February, when Bennett met with Bobby and Engstrom to negotiate his salary—pegged at $80,000, plus a bonus of up to 50 percent, depending on company performance—he was told he'd be permitted to stay on *What's My Line?* for at least one more year. It was a huge relief, but by now he was also aware that a slide in the Nielsen ratings—long past the heights of the '50s—meant the show might not last much longer. Certainly, it was agreed that Bennett's salary would rise to $90,000 should it go off the air.

On March 4, the two boards rubber-stamped the plan whereby Random House Inc. would merge with RCA Publishing Company Inc., a wholly owned, newly constituted subsidiary of the Radio Corporation of America. At a special meeting lasting exactly twenty minutes on May 10, a formal vote of RH stockholders approved the sale. Nine days later, the name Random House went off the Big Board of the New York Stock Exchange, its final share price $31.25.

The closing took place at RCA. Neither Bennett nor the Sarnoffs were present; lawyers for both sides were, along with one director of RCA, and Donald representing the directors of RH. The certificate of merger was signed by Bob Bernstein and Bobby Sarnoff, as presidents of their respective companies. Bennett did not have to append his signature to a document that made Random House no longer his.

On the day of the closing, Bernstein and Bobby lunched together. Unlike his father, the younger Sarnoff was a man-about-town, very much "in" the world of Manhattan, and like many sons of remarkable men, he was not the General's equal in drive or vision. The meal was pleasant enough until Bobby let it be known that he didn't have bookshelves in his home.

"I don't believe in keeping books. You read, then get rid of them."

Bernstein felt unnerved. He'd consciously begun to grow into his new position, and some of the awe that Bennett and Don felt for books had rubbed off. They'd taught him the importance of placing capable people in key jobs, and letting them know their value was recognized. Yet with a throwaway line—literally and figuratively—Sarnoff seemed to be devaluing books, the deal, and Bernstein's worth, all at the same time. "It was a strange moment," he recalled. "I had enormous faith and joy in Random, but doubts about the future of its new corporate parent."

The coupling of RCA and Random House was a starting shot. Bankers and brokers, executives and publishers took note. A year later, CBS bought Holt, Rinehart & Winston. Xerox added another textbook publisher, Ginn, and then bought R. R. Bowker, the publisher of *Books in Print, Library Journal,* and *Publishers Weekly*. In 1967, International Telephone and Telegraph bought Bobbs-Merrill, but despite a large trade backlist of authors like Ayn Rand, the firm had turned exclusively to originating textbooks. Thereafter, mergers, acquisitions, and reshufflings never stopped. Although some smaller, privately controlled houses would remain, the old order of owner-publishers like Bennett and Don would give way to corporate or conglomerate control.

After the RCA merger, meetings of the RH board took place, but were mostly "very sleepy" affairs, Rohatyn observed. How could it be otherwise? "In a huge corporation, the board of a subsidiary is a meaningless thing," he well understood. Besides, he saw that the cultures of RH and RCA were "totally different." Bennett had been "overly spooked" by the roller-coaster of the stock price, and a bit overwhelmed by the too-rapid expansion into areas foreign to his expertise. Like many owners whom Rohatyn encountered during his long banking career, Bennett had rushed into the deal, never having thought through "what it would be like, all of a sudden, to be part of a giant corporation that ran on a completely different track."

Chapter 50

Blood Red and Black/White

THE RANDOM HOUSE SALE OPENED A DOOR TO THE UNKNOWN, BUT Bennett's days stayed grounded in the work he knew and loved. His diaries were full of Roth, O'Hara, Geisel, Michener, and Styron, but no author was more present than Truman Capote, whose latest book, *In Cold Blood,* was published a week after the RCA agreement was announced.

More than six years had passed since Capote, looking for a quick nonfiction project to earn some cash, had run across a wire-service story from Kansas while scanning the back pages of *The New York Times*. Dated November 16, 1959, the piece was headlined "Wealthy Farmer, 3 of Family Slain." He read that forty-eight-year-old Herbert W. Clutter, owner of a thousand acres, along with his wife and teenage son and daughter, had been bound, gagged, and killed at close range by shotgun blasts in their isolated farmhouse outside the town of Holcomb. The phone lines had been cut, yet nothing had been stolen. Two of the daughter's classmates had discovered the grisly mayhem; at the time of writing, no suspect had been identified.

Capote got the go-ahead from *The New Yorker*'s editor, William Shawn, to delineate the effects the murders were having on the small Kansas community. He'd have to travel to the flat, chilly prairie, sniff around, and absorb a place that was as alien to him as any he'd known during his sojourns abroad. Although at that time he didn't expect the article to stretch to book length, Capote hurried to tell Bennett, for he needed his help: he knew not a soul in Kansas, and Shawn, an extremely shy man, had no connections. "Big Daddy," on the other hand, had friends all over.

"You? In a west Kansas hamlet?" Bennett had chuckled, but then turned serious: Truman could count on his help. On a lecture trip five years earlier, he'd visited Kansas State College, where in addition to his official talk, he'd spent a day with English classes. As a celebrity, he'd also met the school's president, James McCain, and liked him well enough to give the college a nod in Trade Winds. McCain had told him to get in touch if he could be of service. Now he picked up the phone to renew the connection, and was in luck. McCain had known the Clutters, and was familiar with leading citizens of Garden City, the nearest big town to Holcomb. He'd write letters of introduction and make calls, but in return wanted Capote for an evening with the English department. New York writers didn't turn up in Manhattan (Kansas) every week.

Bennett accepted the invitation for Truman and, when McCain said that he and his family would be visiting New York that Christmas, hastened to invite them to lunch at '21.' It would be a thank-you, but also a chance to hear a firsthand report on Truman's activities, for beneath their lighthearted banter lay real affection between the older man and the "strange little boy" who'd grown up at Random. At times Bennett worried about him, and took it upon himself to prepare McCain—so McCain could prepare others—for the meeting. When people met Capote, Bennett admitted, they often were inclined "to laugh," but "don't let that first impression fool you."

Truman Capote in the late 1950s

Nonetheless, even armed with McCain's goodwill, Capote was well aware that a tense rural hamlet reeling from multiple murders might not take kindly to a high-pitched elfin outsider, looking much younger than his thirty-five years, nosing around. He wanted a friend with him to provide fellowship and help with legwork, so as not to linger long. The timing proved perfect for his childhood soulmate Nelle Harper Lee, who was delighted to play detective beside him: the adventure would distract from the itchy limbo of waiting for publication of her own novel, *To Kill a Mockingbird,* the next summer. Almost three years earlier, she'd had a chance to bring her writing to RH; Capote had spoken to Albert Erskine about her, and Erskine had asked to see Lee's work. She'd just given a few stories to a literary agent, soon followed by the first fifty pages of a novel. However, she told Erskine that what she had was already "in the market," politely rebuffing his approach; the agent had sent the pages to Lippincott. Bennett—who later judged *Mockingbird* one of the finest novels in recent years—was convinced Lee thought RH would take it "just to please Truman," and wanted "to make it on her own." But aiding Capote with *his* work was different. She was sorely needed: when they arrived the second week in December, first sightings of Capote raised eyebrows and suspicions.

McCain described to Bennett how Truman had waltzed in sporting pink velvet, saying, "I bet I'm the first man . . . to come to Manhattan, Kansas wearing a Dior jacket."

"I'll go you one better," he'd replied drily. "You're the first man or woman who ever came to Manhattan, Kansas, wearing a Dior jacket."

With Lee's help, Capote worked to tamp down misgivings. Alvin Dewey, the detective in charge for the Kansas Bureau of Investigation, began to tolerate him; later, Capote would charm Dewey's wife, Marie, and Dewey himself. With a bit more time, he'd morph into an "attraction" whose fascinating conversation opened doors to almost all the best homes.

On December 30, two suspects, Dick Hickock and Perry Smith, were seized in Las Vegas. They confessed, and Dewey brought them back to Kansas. Now Capote knew he had more than a *New Yorker* article facing him: he had the full tragic arc of a book. Although other detectives were also involved, he'd found a hero in handsome Al Dewey, and villains in the two men. He'd delve deep into what had formed them and motivated the killings, and what fate had in store, with his original plan of anatomizing the victims and their community layered beneath. In a sense, he'd be treading a time-honored path: novelists like Balzac and Dreiser had mined newspaper accounts as starting-off points. Where Capote diverged was in wanting to create a *nonfiction* narrative that in attention to style, character, atmosphere, voice, and pacing would display all the hallmarks of the finest fiction, while hewing to the facts. This was something new. Immensely excited, he quickly signed a contract with Bennett, and was soon visiting the killers in jail day after day, determined to win their trust, and stare into their very souls.

Dick Hickock was fair and twenty-eight, Perry Smith dark and thirty-one—close in age to their chronicler. While Capote's lack of height and high voice made him stand apart, something was physically "off" about each killer, too. Hickock had been in a car accident that left his eyes uneven and face a bit askew; having grown up poor on a small farm, he'd been twice divorced, committed crimes seeking easy money, and was mean, with a cruel streak, and knew it. Smith's face, with the smoke-black eyes and hair of his Cherokee mother, seemed to beg for sympathy. A motorbike crash had so damaged his legs, he was almost as short as Capote, but what truly set him apart were the dark sights *behind* his eyes: a neglectful, alcoholic mother who'd died young, a father who'd abandoned the family, a childhood of awful brutality in orphanages and "homes." Smith saw himself as kind, sensitive, well-meaning, highly intelligent, and fantasized about the life he might have led. Devoted to self-help books and word lists, he used fancy vocabulary to seem superior and worldly-wise. He'd killed two Clutters by his own admission, though Hickock said it was Smith who'd dispatched them all, and Capote would later agree. However, Smith mesmerized Capote, and in a deeply terrifying way. In him, Capote could recognize so much.

Truman's birth father, Arch Persons, was a con man who'd abandoned him during much of his childhood; his mother, Lillie Mae Faulk–turned–Nina Capote, was a narcissistic alcoholic who ultimately killed herself. Truman had been shunted off to relatives and marked as an outsider from the beginning. But where Smith believed unrealistically in talismanic lists and self-help books to redirect his life, Capote clung fiercely to his own brilliance and hard work.

Home from Kansas in late January 1960, he saw a lot of Bennett. In March, he and Lee returned to observe a quick, weeklong trial in which the outcome was obvious. Found guilty, Smith and Hickock were sentenced to hang on May 13, but Capote had no intention of making another pilgrimage to witness *that*. Once again back in New York, he intimated that the writing wouldn't take long—at least, that was Bennett's impression. Capote was returning to Europe to escape the social whirl, hunker down, and work. At the spring sales conference, Bennett couldn't help telling the reps about the book. Their "tongues [were] hanging out" and "pencils poised" to take orders, he wrote Truman, but it would be far longer than either imagined before they could do so: Smith and Hickock appealed the convictions, and the gears of justice turned with their own sense of time.

As Capote worked across the Atlantic, Bennett stayed in touch. RH had just gone public, and the Cerfs delightedly sent him a Christmas gift of five shares. Bennett knew enough not to press about the book. However, when Ernest Hemingway died in July 1961, prompting scrutiny of the American literary pecking order, he figured that Capote, three thousand miles away, would wonder about his place in it. Truman had been abroad almost a year and a half, and to assuage his own worry about progress, Bennett reminded him "how very, very much we miss you," adding: "Bill Styron listed you as one of the really important writers . . . today." Only then did he mention the book, admitting impatience, but knowing Capote would finish "when it satisfies the incredibly high standard you have set and maintained for yourself." But however delicately he'd finessed the reminder, a few months later, a "terribly upset" Truman cabled, demanding to know if RH intended to publish another Clutter book, by a certain "Mack Nations."

Bennett replied instantly that of course he'd "never do anything" like that, mystified where the devil Truman had picked up such an idea. But the Nations project, it turned out, did exist. A politically connected small-town Kansas reporter, Nations had interviewed Dick Hickock and several other inmates for a story on death row. While Capote was abroad, Hickock had decided that if anyone were to profit from a book about his life, *he* should. He signed a contract with a fifty-fifty split between himself and Nations, who interviewed him and that December placed an "abridgement" of his manuscript in *Male,* a pulpy adventure magazine. Capote was so anxious, he'd confided to the Deweys that the strain of the book made him sick to his stomach every morning. Soon, however, Bennett was the one seeking reassurance. A rumor that Capote was dallying with an offer from McGraw-Hill for more money began to circulate.

When repeated to the Cerfs at a dinner party, Phyllis exploded: "Truman Capote is going to be with Random House as long as he, Bennett and I are alive, and whoever told you that story is a goddam liar!"

Real comfort came a couple months later in Truman himself, who returned to New York briefly en route to Kansas, where he'd interview Smith's sister, and meet with the killers on death row. He'd heard they might be granted a new trial because of a ghastly legal mix-up, and was despondent about a delay. He stayed with the Cerfs for five days, secure in their affection and a sweetness he could tap into in Bennett. Years later, he'd tell his biographer how he could really talk to his publisher, who underneath the vast public surface was an "extremely sensitive" man. When they were together, Bennett was the listener. But in other ways, the visit proved hard. Capote felt alienated from friends clamoring to see him, who pressed in, expecting to be entertained by the antic butterfly they knew. Instead, he felt trapped in a bleak place so vivid, he was horrified by his dreams. Swallowed up by a relentless writing routine and his own perfectionism, *In Cold Blood* was all he could think of. He wanted to be rid of the goddamned book, but the only way was by writing the goddamned book. It had become his life.

He'd brought a precious gift to the Cerfs: two hundred manuscript pages. Only Bennett and Shawn were permitted to read them, and Bennett was overwhelmed by "how very much" Capote had grown as a writer. Wanting to share his feelings with someone who'd understand, he wrote to Jim McCain that *In Cold Blood* was destined to be "one of the greatest" American books this half century, and later reiterated to the British publisher Jamie Hamilton that it was "one of the most important" either firm "ever had the privilege" to print.

Capote returned to Europe, but despite the faith and encouragement from Bennett, he felt even worse, his emotions conflicted and churning. He'd grown dangerously fond of Smith, identifying far too closely with his dark doppelgänger. Moreover, he knew both men were counting on him to help them evade the noose. He'd tried to help, suggesting lawyers and so forth, but had also needed them to talk, so how could he discourage their fantasies? He'd told Bennett that he required at least another year to complete the book, but understood rather too clearly that the final chapter could be written only after there was a hanging.

Four years had passed since *Tiffany's* was published. To keep Capote's name in front of readers, Bennett thought it wise to assemble a collection from earlier material that had never appeared in a book. Truman would help choose the pieces: the distraction might do him good. When *Selected Writings* was published in 1963, it bore a dedication to Phyllis and Bennett. The volume was eventually reprinted in the ML—an accolade that greatly pleased its author. He finished the third part of *In Cold Blood* in February 1963 and kept working, but anxiety gripped him with word that Hickock and Smith had appealed in federal court for a new trial. If they got it, he feared he'd have a breakdown; already, he was drinking more. Finally, on February 20, 1965, more than five years after setting foot in Holcomb, he wrote Bennett, "Yesterday I finished . . . except for a few paragraphs," and said he would mail the manuscript to Joe Fox.

The court denied the latest appeal, but the lawyers got another stay of execution. Still, Capote felt sure that the killers' luck had run out. Back in March 1960, when they'd first been condemned, he hadn't felt a need to be present at the execution. Now his life had become too bound up in theirs. They each had the right to ask for a witness, and wanted *him*. Having become so entangled, he knew he had to finish by seeing them hang. He couldn't go alone. The circumstances made the role ill-suited to Bennett, and everyone knew that Shawn was beset by phobias. However, Bennett would not fail him: someone else at Random would go. Like Saxe summoned to cope with Bill Faulkner in the throes of his worst kind of binge, Joe Fox, as editor, would look after Capote. The two men were polar opposites, but Fox knew how to talk to him.

They arrived in Kansas City and holed up in the Muehlebach Hotel. Fox had to field repeated calls from the prison's assistant warden, phoning on behalf of Smith and Hickock, who desperately wanted to talk to Capote. He just couldn't. Nor could he sleep or leave the room; he sat and cried. He'd come all this way, but wasn't sure he could make it to the hanging. However, in a cold spring rain very late on April 13, he and Fox joined three Kansas detectives and headed for the prison, a half hour away. He and the detectives went in to see the condemned. Time passed, he reappeared, and motioned for Fox to follow, then introduced him to Hickock and Smith: awkward, thoughtless, but also understandable. He had no idea what he was doing. It was after midnight when the men were transferred to a warehouse where the gallows waited. Fox stayed outside, but Capote saw Dick Hickock hang. When it was Perry Smith's turn, he couldn't watch.

Sometime before boarding a plane in Kansas City, they called Bennett. Capote sobbed on the flight back to New York, tightly clutching Fox's hand. It was a long journey and felt longer still: the weeping did not stop. All Fox could do was cradle Truman's hand, stare straight ahead, summon a proud mournful dignity, and try to pretend that the people all around them did not exist.

. . .

WILLIAM SHAWN PUBLISHED *In Cold Blood* in four *New Yorker* installments during the fall of 1965, fueling a phenomenon: not since Charles Dickens were adult readers so driven to get hold of a serialized story. Swifty Lazar sold film rights for a half million dollars, while Bennett made a good book club deal and a paperback sale to NAL for another half million (RH would receive a third). Contracts were signed with fifteen foreign houses. Capote now had wealth as well as fame.

After years of blood, sweat, and tears

When Random published the hardcover in January, great care was taken. The austere dust jacket became an instant classic, with a funereal black border, large black and red letters, and the upper right corner diagonally pierced by a hatpin topped by a blood-colored bulb. Across from the title page, photos of Smith and Hickock's unnerving eyes, caged in red rectangles, stared out.

James Michener doubted that anyone else could have written *In Cold Blood* with such "severe control": using precisely the right vocabulary, managing the tension and horror, and telling a highly personal story "without allowing himself to become a central character." Harper Lee had already called her friend "the greatest craftsman we have going." And yet, despite having dedicated the book jointly to his longtime lover Jack Dunphy and to Lee, Capote left something out: he made no public acknowledgment of how much she'd helped, an omission that deeply wounded her and shocked those in the know. After *In Cold Blood* their friendship, like so much else, would never be the same.

That it would be a bestseller was a given, although everything was done to maximize potential. Capote understood the propulsive power of synchronicity—reviews, interviews, ads, appearances happening at once—and was a willing participant. The roll call was astonishing: covers of *Newsweek,* the *Saturday Review,* and Sunday book review and magazine sections across the country; eighteen pages in *Life*—the most ever about a book; the longest-ever interview in *The New York Times Book Review;* two TV programs; countless radio hours. RH sold 50,000 copies the first week, and the hardcover would be on the *Times* list for thirty-seven weeks, twelve as number one. But Bennett publicly and protectively worried the commercial success stoked prejudice about the book's "real value." Worse, some began attacking Capote as morally indefensible. British critic Kenneth Tynan claimed he'd used the killers rather than helped them; they might have avoided the gallows if he'd paid for more psychiatric testimony.

...

AFTER SO MUCH WORK and emotional turmoil, what Capote wanted more than anything was to put down his pen and party. If he gossiped and charmed and danced fast enough, the hubbub would drown out the dissonance and he might—for a time—ignore the trembling within. Friends like the Cerfs were happy to oblige. Three social gatherings were associated with *In Cold Blood:* two fabulous parties hosted by Bennett and Phyllis, while a third, given by Capote himself, was so grand, so minutely planned, so populated by the famous, rich, brilliant, and powerful (with others desolate at being left out), that it became almost performance art, and a legend.

The first took place in November, prior to publication, just after Bennett returned from a lightning visit to Missouri, where a small Baptist college bestowed an honorary degree. The Cerfs celebrated Truman and three upstanding Kansas citizens—the Deweys and the widow of the trial's presiding judge—welcoming to their townhouse a big crowd curious to meet them, from Dick Rodgers to Muriel Spark to Chris's friend George Plimpton. But the evening paled in comparison to a party the following summer, when Bennett and Phyllis erected a giant tricolor tent on The Columns lawn, to honor Independence Day and their dear friends Truman and Frank.

The special houseguests arrived Saturday noon, Sinatra with Mia Farrow. Tiny Truman made the self-conscious, five-foot-seven Frank look tall. They lounged by the pool as servants brought lunch down from the house, assisted by a wheelbarrow. (Ever generous, Frank soon made poolside fare faster and more fun by gifting the Cerfs with a rolling hot-dog cart, just like those in Central Park. They loved it, along with the pool-house beer on tap he also arranged.)

The evening would be one of Phyllis's "themed" parties. Bennett put on a red-white-blue cardigan and candy-striped tie, while small American flags fanned out from Phyllis's waist. To the strains of a five-piece band, eighty other guests materialized in a colorful blur, women in patriotic-hued dresses, and each man sporting a straw boater with a colored ribbon hatband, like those Bennett wore as a youth. Old friends and colleagues mingled with newer acquaintances, like Mr. and Mrs. Bobby Sarnoff and the *Today* show's Barbara Walters.

Thirty-six and supremely ambitious, Walters had arrived early with her husband, antennae primed. She and Bennett had met a half dozen times in recent months over flirty lunches at '21' and breakfasts at the Waldorf. She came to understand that he'd always liked a certain kind of wide, high-cheekboned look—what Bennett called a "little pussy-cat face"—like Sylvia's, Phyllis's, and hers, too. He had the power to open difficult doors to the likes of Sinatra and Capote, while she could push RH authors on breakfast TV. She was "thrilled" at this friendship with such "a very important and distinguished man." Several years later, she included Bennett with Sinatra, Kitty Hart, Arlene Francis, Coretta Scott King, and Richard Nixon as "among the most charming people anywhere." Another time, she'd rank Nixon, then at the height of his power, high in "warmth" and "sex appeal," and judge Sinatra and Bennett similarly "warm." (She would experience that "warmth" up close in Bennett's office: on one occasion, after his door closed, she didn't emerge for hours. RH tongues wagged, knowingly.) But when he introduced her to Truman at the party, Walters's boldness abandoned her; "overcome" with awkwardness, she peeped hello and rushed off, allowing others to step up.

It turned out to be a fantasy evening: When darkness fell, fireworks showered the night sky, their reflections shimmering along the Kisco River and rippling across the duck pond, where a model of Random House had taken up floating residence. Best of all, Sinatra, in a beautiful mood, sang a full hour with the band, while Capote, usually so jealous of attention paid to others, recognized it was a signal triumph to be feted alongside Frank.

Bobby Sarnoff reappeared at Mt. Kisco on Monday, the actual holiday. The previous November, NBC had aired a Sinatra special, *A Man and His Music;* now Bobby wanted, with Bennett's help, to sign another. Lunch was spent swaying Frank. (He agreed.) Sinatra also let slip that daughter Nancy fancied doing a book about him. Immediately, Bennett wrote to her. For a while, his life seemed all Sinatra, all the time: as soon as they were back in the city, Frank took the Cerfs to La Côte Basque for dinner with Mia, and, before the story broke, Bennett and Phyllis were privy to their engagement. When the Sinatras returned from their Las Vegas wedding, the Cerfs teamed up with Leland and Pamela Hayward to organize a caviar-and-champagne banquet at '21.' (Something called "arugella" salad was added at Frank's request.)

With Sinatra, anything could happen. After the meal, as the newlyweds were leaving, a photographer from the *New York Post* leaned in to snap a picture and Sinatra swung at him, providing copy for columns across the country. The next day, Mia's girlish hand hastened to assure "Darling Phyllis + Bennett" that she and her husband had had "such a good time!" Bennett even managed to persuade Francis Albert—as he was fond of calling Sinatra—to appear on *What's My Line?* with his bride the Sunday after Thanksgiving, though he, alas, had to recuse himself, knowing exactly who the mystery guests were.

. . .

WHILE THE CERFS WERE playing with Frank and Mia, Capote was preoccupied about whom to invite to a party, a masked ball, where *everyone* would effectively be a glamorous mystery guest. The where was a favorite haunt: the Plaza, the place Phyllis deemed his "security blanket," where she'd often accompanied the young Capote when he was nervous about being accepted.

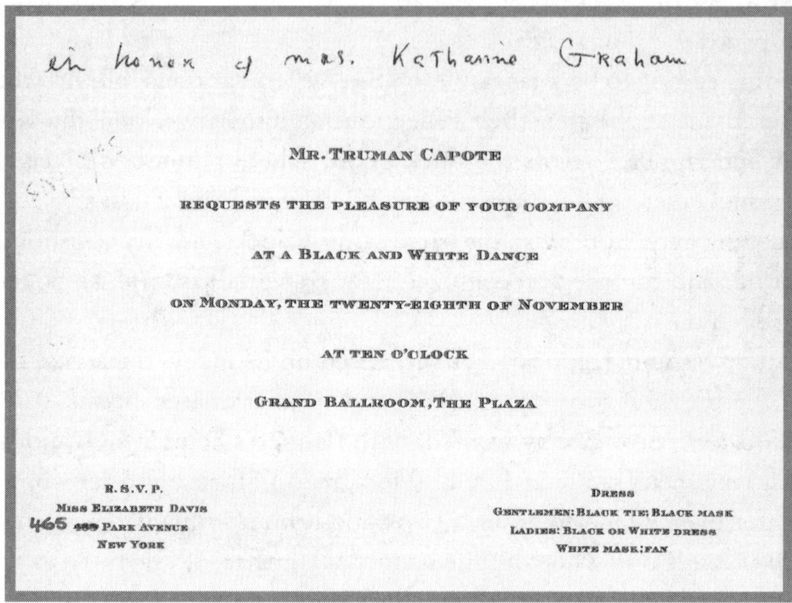
in honor of Mrs. Katharine Graham

MR. TRUMAN CAPOTE

REQUESTS THE PLEASURE OF YOUR COMPANY

AT A BLACK AND WHITE DANCE

ON MONDAY, THE TWENTY-EIGHTH OF NOVEMBER

AT TEN O'CLOCK

GRAND BALLROOM, THE PLAZA

R. S. V. P.
MISS ELIZABETH DAVIS
465 ~~465~~ PARK AVENUE
NEW YORK

DRESS
GENTLEMEN: BLACK TIE; BLACK MASK
LADIES: BLACK OR WHITE DRESS
WHITE MASK; FAN

"The party of the century"

Four hundred and eighty embossed invitations summoned guests to the Grand Ballroom at 10 P.M. on Monday, November 28, 1966, for a "Black and White Dance." Handwritten in blue ink was added, "In honor of Mrs. Katharine Graham." They went to denizens of vastly different worlds: Hollywood, Broadway, West End luminaries; artists, intellectuals, assorted close friends; media tycoons, titled aristocrats, and the simply super-rich. The crazy quilt of names included Brooke Astor, Sammy Davis Jr., Gloria Steinem, Mr. and Mrs. Alvin Dewey, the Maharaja of Jaipur, Rose Kennedy, and Andy Warhol. "What a cast!" Bennett marveled.

Capote had cleverly decided to hold the party in celebration of someone else, thereby reflecting well on himself. Graham, whose family owned *The Washington Post* and *Newsweek,* had been thrust into the publisher's seat by her husband's suicide three years earlier. She was capable but shy and, Capote thought, sad. He reckoned that through this event he could catapult her to the center of *le tout* New York. An inspired choice, she was also safe: had he singled out a Manhattan "swan" rather than a Washington widow, he would have set off a storm of envy. Fancying himself Professor Higgins to Graham's Eliza Doolittle, Capote was determined to set the scene just so: he borrowed the black-and-white theme (mandatory for both ladies' and gentlemen's attire) from his friend Cecil Beaton's brilliant Ascot races montage in the *My Fair Lady* movie. Through that color scheme, the book that had carried him to these heights also hovered. The fifty-three round tables were to be draped in red. Black, white, the color of blood, and glints of polished silver: the scene would be unforgettable.

As word spread about what would come to be called "the party of the century," woe betide those *not* on the list. Some lied and left town, telling friends they *had* been invited but couldn't make it; others begged or plotted to be added, and sixty succeeded. Capote had marshaled friends like the Paleys and Fosburghs to host pre-party dinners, and the Cerfs, with son Chris, supped at the Haywards' alongside the Sinatras, Hornblows, Claudette Colbert, and Stephen and Jean Kennedy Smith. Capote's magic list included many good friends of Bennett, along with a generous contingent from RH. Don, Bob Bernstein, Jason, Joe, Bobby Sarnoff (all with spouses), as well as Alfred Knopf, rubbed shoulders with house authors like Michener, Ellison, O'Hara, and Roth. Warren, Matthiessen, and Styron did the unthinkable: sent regrets.

It was raining when cars pulled in front of the Plaza, but that didn't stop photographers, journalists, and celebrity-mad civilians from crowding behind wooden barriers on both sides of the steps. Female guests vied to outdo one another in costumes, hair, masks. Leonora, a time-traveling marquise from Louis XIV's court, had had her long, piled locks painted white with liquid flour. The Bernsteins and Foxes arrived in a hired limousine and alighted onto the red carpet, as the line of guests inched toward the entrance. Everyone on the other side of the barriers seemed to have a camera, and flashes popped, dazzling them, as onlookers oohed, aahed, and called out familiar names. A young man with a camera eyed the Bernsteins, then said to the crowd: "They're nobody!" When it was his turn, Bennett, as usual, basked in being known.

But this was the end of 1966, and the nation's social and political tensions led some in the crowd to taunt these privileged few for being so self-satisfied and oblivious to the war escalating on the other side of the world, and the hungry, hurting, urgent reality right in the city. Unease did surface among some guests. Norman Mailer and McGeorge Bundy, a former adviser to John F. Kennedy and Lyndon Johnson, got into a shouting match over Vietnam. Sinatra was moody and not much for dancing, especially when Peter Duchin's band upped the tempo, but Mia wanted to groove. The problem was, she didn't know who anybody was behind the masks, and if she chose the wrong somebody to dance with, her husband would explode. She did know the Cerfs, so it was Chris—one of the few partygoers of her own generation—who ended up twisting with Mia, earning envious stares from others, but provoking no spontaneous combustion from Frank.

The revelry went on for twelve hours, until 10 A.M. Tuesday, although the Cerfs found themselves partied out when the clock reached four. "It was a good party as parties go," Phyllis said years later. "I mean, certainly the world was there, and you wouldn't have wanted to be left out of the world, so there we were." But she lived long enough to see beyond the twin triumphs of the book and its ultimate party. Steeped in the blood of six lives, Truman's ball was in one sense a bit like the Masque of the Red Death. He "never really recovered from that book," she'd tell his biographer. "That book started the unsettling of his life."

Chapter 51

Interventions

JUST AS RH WAS LAUNCHING *IN COLD BLOOD*, MARY WELSH HEMINGWAY tried to prevent the firm from publishing *Papa Hemingway,* A. E. Hotchner's memoir of friendship with her late husband. The project had started smoothly enough, when Hotchner—a wiry, bright-eyed fellow who'd done an unremarkable first novel with RH—strode into the palazzo in May 1964, pitching a book about a trip from Venice to Spain that he'd made with Hemingway some years earlier. Bennett got very excited, with good reason. He recalled the old days when he and Don felt such pride in the ML reprinting *The Sun Also Rises* and *A Farewell to Arms*. How thrilled he'd been when, out of the blue, the great Ernest Hemingway had turned up at the office! More pressingly, he thought of the past few weeks. Scribner had just published *A Moveable Feast,* Hemingway's posthumous remembrance of youth in a Paris long past. The memoir, authorized and edited by Mary, was generating enormous attention and fine sales. Hotchner would adopt it as a model: just as Hemingway had dished stories about Scott Fitzgerald, Bennett's beloved Gertrude, and others, he'd recount his adventures with Papa, weaving in stories he'd heard from his famous friend.

In fact, Hotchner knew *Feast* intimately, having helped it reach publication. Hemingway and "Hotch," two decades younger than Ernest, had been lunching at the Paris Ritz one day in 1956 when their meal was interrupted by news that a long-lost trunk had been found and retrieved from the hotel's *sous-sol*. It was Hemingway's, and its retrieval something to celebrate, for among its treasures were notebooks dating back thirty years. Hemingway began to stitch the resurrected stories together, entrusting his pal to deliver the result to Scribner in New York. Hotch also supplied the title, recalling that his famous friend had once called Paris "a moveable feast."

Hotchner's bona fides were impeccable, yet Bennett felt uneasy. He sensed that the memoir might end up "a rather mean book," a portrait that included Hemingway's uglier traits and showed the foolishness of his "Papa" routine. However, he persuaded himself that the meanness was "legitimate": *Feast,* after all, had been "very cruel" to Stein and Fitzgerald.

The book expanded in ways Bennett hadn't envisaged; four months for writing turned into a year, bringing more cause for concern but also keener anticipation. However, when he finally understood the complete narrative arc—perhaps only after reading the full first draft—Bennett knew he was holding a time bomb. After Hemingway died in 1961, Mary had told a clamoring press that he'd accidentally killed himself while cleaning a shotgun. Those who knew Hemingway well wondered and murmured, but for the world at large, Mary's word was fact. Now Hotchner revealed the truth: he'd intentionally put the weapon to his head, having spiraled into severe depression and delusion. The revelation of suicide would set off a sensation.

After reading the draft of *Mr. Papa,* Bennett shared his thoughts with Jim Silberman, Albert, and Don. "Morbidly fascinating," it could become a big seller, *but* several problems had to be overcome. The title was terrible. What about *Papa Hemingway*? The others agreed at once. A hundred pages or more had to be cut. Living people were involved, so the manuscript needed vetting for libel. Most important, Bennett wondered if Mary Hemingway had approved the text; if not, she could stir up trouble. He didn't want to have to tangle with her in court.

The gentlemen then invited Nan Talese, who'd risen within the Rabbit Penn Warren to the exalted role of associate editor, to read the text. A Roman Catholic, she'd be the acid test to determine if it was acceptable to reveal what had happened, since the Church usually viewed suicide as a sin. Once Talese assured them that the book should be published, they assigned her to be its editor, but it was Bennett who told Hotchner that, while cutting was necessary, the memoir also needed more of something: himself. "It's your story as much as Hemingway's," he urged, making the point that the friendship and Hotch's feelings for Papa would add immediacy and presence. Years later, grateful for Bennett's "innate good judgment and perspicacity," Hotchner agreed that the suggestion had made the story "much more meaningful."

Once the revised manuscript was set into type, galley proofs were sent to the widow. For four and a half years, the fourth Mrs. Hemingway, a former journalist now in her late fifties, had hidden the suicide from the world, and was trying not to face it herself. After reading the memoir, she expressed complete shock in a letter to Bennett, decrying Hotchner's "treachery" and invasion of her privacy for money, and adding that the text was full of errors. Tangling with the widow, the last thing he'd wanted, was exactly what Bennett had to do now. He called Horace Manges. RH had to recall galleys already sent to key early reviewers, the lawyer advised, but that, and other attempts to mollify Mrs. Hemingway, proved useless.

In January 1966, she went to court for an injunction to stop publication, based on four points. The book consisted of words mainly spoken by her husband in conversation; so much so, it was in effect *by* him, with Hotchner merely the "secretary" who'd jotted them down. It violated her rights, as heir, to his unpublished writings, as well as those of others she authorized (she'd hand-picked a biographer). It breached a confidential fiduciary relationship. And it infringed on her right to privacy. RH argued the suit was trying to suppress or distort the truth about Hemingway's suicide. The decision, a month later, rejected Mary's claims, finding that an author's words in conversation didn't constitute a work subject to copyright. (Bennett's suggestion that Hotchner expand his own presence in the book had taken on unexpected weight.) The judge also held that Mary's right to privacy was trumped by the competing doctrines of "the right of the public to know" and "the freedom of the press to inform."

The book debuted in April. In its first paragraph, Hotchner revealed how Papa had died, and a little later he justified himself by quoting his friend: the only way to account for anything was "to tell the whole truth . . . holding back nothing." Nan Talese had published her first bestseller. *Papa Hemingway* joined three other RH books on the list: Capote's *In Cold Blood,* Michener's *The Source,* and John Toland's World War II chronicle *The Last 100 Days*.

When Hotchner inscribed a copy for Bennett, he wrote: "For Papa Cerf, whose loyalty and judgment and good humor in the face of utter chaos I shall value for ever." Yet in spite of the court victory, good reviews, strong sales, and steady face he'd shown, Bennett continued to worry that the book was in questionable taste, after all. Mary's denunciation—that publishing it was "so far beneath" RH's "usual standards"—had managed to pierce his armor.

. . .

BENNETT HAD EMBRACED HAVING Bernard Geis's imprint as a client: distributing and selling the aggressively huckstered titles was lucrative, and readers didn't confuse Helen Gurley Brown's *Sex and the Single Girl* with Knopf, Pantheon, or Random books. But after RH began handling Jacqueline Susann's *Valley of the Dolls* in the spring of 1966, he did seem in two minds about a book he admitted he never read. When interviewed, Bennett might *tut-tut* about lurid depictions or the fact that characters were based on people he knew, like Judy Garland. Other times, he waved off criticism: the culture was changing, and people were abandoning former constraints. Besides, he was impressed with Susann's savvy and drive as a one-woman promotion machine.

However, that September, Geis crossed a line. First came an "intimate" memoir of Charlie Chaplin by Lita Grey, one of his former wives, a book RH refused to distribute. (Grove Press's Barney Rosset picked it up.) Then Geis commissioned Morton Cooper, Grey's co-author, to write *The King,* a steamy novel with major characters resembling Ronald Reagan and Bennett's friend Frank. Geis realized he'd better show the manuscript to his distributor.

"Scurrilous Sinatra novel!" Bennett erupted to his diary, finding himself in a bind. He had a business relationship with Geis. He was supposed to uphold free expression. But there was also the matter of Sinatra's privacy and readers' inability to differentiate fictional filth from fact. Even more, he knew that loyalty was supremely important to Frank, and the friendship meant too much not to intervene. However, Don and Bob reminded him: he had no leverage to stop Geis; all RH could do was refuse to distribute. Soon New American Library happily obliged. Bennett tried to persuade Sinatra not to sue, for that would only fuel publicity. He also tried to turn the situation to his advantage: time for Frank to publish his own story with RH, and Nancy to commit to her book about her father, so as to have the "real picture" fight such "swill."

The coup de grâce with Geis came in spring 1967, with *The Exhibitionist,* by "Henry Sutton" (aka David Slavitt), who based main characters on Henry and Jane Fonda. Slavitt was a poet and former *Newsweek* film critic, but quick commercial cash had proved irresistible. Bennett, fed up with dished-to-order scandal about those he knew, sent the "slimy" novel to Henry Fonda's press agent, to warn what was coming. RH had told Geis it would stop handling his new books come 1968, and Bennett invited the *Times*' Henry Raymont for an off-the-record chat about the breakup. Raymont's article quoted the man whom he noted had once freed *Ulysses:* "We don't want to be censors," but now "feel [we] should distribute and identify only with [our] own books."

The article, and situation, seemed to skew in Bennett's favor: *The King* was mentioned, but not his desire to protect—or fear to displease—Frank; and RH kept the right to handle Geis's profitable backlist. A year later, dictating his oral history, Bennett labeled *The King* a "failure," and took "pleasure" in that fact, but neglected to mention that in paperback it sold millions. He did find it hard not to win absolutely. He wasn't alone, however, in declining to link his name to such books. That September, five of Geis's thirteen backers voted with their bank accounts to sever support. Four years later, Bernard Geis Associates filed for bankruptcy.

. . .

DIFFERENT INTERVENTIONS WERE NEEDED for a project by Dorothy Kilgallen, grand inquisitor of *What's My Line?* and a woman Sinatra detested. They'd been friends before she wrote a few articles on him in the 1950s that he *really* didn't like. Later, he routinely savaged her looks in his nightclub act, and a dartboard in his Palm Springs home bore images of Kilgallen and two other columnists, Louella Parsons and Hedda Hopper.

While she was hardly Bennett's favorite colleague, he insisted, at least in public, that Dorothy could be "very nice" on a personal level. Certainly, as a Hearst columnist, she had power and a following, and in the summer of 1960 he'd signed her for a book, under the rubric *Murder One,* that would expand on her articles covering a dozen sensational trials. For a journalist used to churning out copy, it would be fast work and easy money: a $10,000 advance, with delivery in February. February came and went, and no manuscript arrived. The next few Februaries did, too. In May 1965, in the politest possible terms, Bennett tendered an ultimatum: six months to turn in a manuscript or refund the money. She'd deliver in December, Kilgallen assured him sweetly.

On Monday, November 8—having played *What's My Line?* with her the previous night—Bennett was stunned to learn that Dorothy had been found dead, aged fifty-two, in her East Side townhouse, her body propped up in bed. All of New York was abuzz. An autopsy found booze and barbiturates; rumors swirled about addiction. Soon, even stranger talk began to circulate: Kilgallen had covered the trial of Lee Harvey Oswald's assassin, Jack Ruby, and conspiracy theories abounded. Had she uncovered something and been murdered to shut her up?

It was easy to feel spooked. Just before 5:30 P.M. on the day after her death, in the full madness of a New York rush hour, the city—and much of the Northeast, stretching to Toronto—plunged into darkness. Eight hundred thousand straphangers were stuck in subways. Lights went out; cars crawled. People feared looting or worse, but miraculously, the kind of spirit that had buoyed the city during World War II took hold. At midtown intersections, New Yorkers stepped up spontaneously to direct traffic under a full moon. Bennett walked to Sardi's, where he dined by candlelight with Thrup, Cousin Ginger, and a Random contingent. Bob Bernstein could not get to Scarsdale, so spent the night at Sixty-Second Street. After thirteen dark hours, power returned.

A few days later, Bennett went to Kilgallen's home, where he and her husband, Dick Kollmar, saw heaps of clippings for *Murder One*. She'd told Bennett she was almost finished, but they found nothing like a full manuscript. What should he do? How would it look to ask Kollmar to return the advance? Better to find a way to stitch together what she'd left into a book.

Lee Wright, such a pro at editing thrillers, was persuaded to assemble it in exchange for 25 percent of publication royalties *after* the $10,000 had been earned back. RH wouldn't be out of pocket, and just possibly all the talk about Kilgallen's death might make the book—if they got it out fast—sell more than they'd initially reckoned on. Wright worked it over for four months, delivering a now adequately organized collection, but Bennett judged it terminally hobbled by the lack of any evidence that Dorothy had had a hand in writing it. He knew that her father, an old pro of a journalist, would "blow his top" at what RH proposed to publish under her name. Dismayed and angry, he had to find another way. Flipping through his mental Rolodex, he alighted upon the name Allan Ullman, RH's promotion director in the late '40s and early '50s, who'd also had stints at BOMC and the *Times*. A decade younger than Bennett, he'd grown up in the same Riverside Drive building. Ullman wrote slick copy and had done novelizations of movie and radio scripts. He'd also, on occasion, saved his wildly overcommitted RH boss by writing magazine book reviews as "Bennett Cerf." Scruples hadn't entered into it: so long as the magazines got what they wanted, the impersonation did no harm, Bennett had reasoned; it was like Thrup putting together kids' books for him. His was the name that sold with authority; they split the money, and it all worked out. Others might have viewed it very differently.

Ullman agreed to channel Dorothy—specifying that his own name never appear in print—and focused on six cases, each perfumed with the strong scent of scandalous sex. He wrote most of the introduction—"Dorothy Kilgallen to the Reader"—starting and ending with flattering words about her publisher, even adding a note, ascribed to "B.C.," on her death. While he generally liked to show his cleverness, he confided his authorship to just about no one. When he finally did acknowledge it in an oral history, Ullman labeled *Murder One* "a disgrace." "B.C.," though, ostensibly unfazed by any compunction, seemed satisfied with his solution. The book was published, and he sold paperback rights for $25,000—more than recouping RH's investment.

. . .

LEE WRIGHT HADN'T SOLVED the Kilgallen problem, but had earned her keep in large part by bringing over writers whose thrillers she'd handled in her previous life at S&S. One such was Ira Levin, whose *A Kiss Before Dying,* published in 1953, was not a huge seller, but had rewarded its young author with the Edgar Award for best first mystery. Levin concentrated on screenplays and stage plays for a while, but in 1966 delivered a second manuscript to Wright. Mixing thriller with horror, its trajectory would in no way be ordinary. *Rosemary's Baby* was one of those books—especially after it was adapted for film with Mia Farrow in the lead role—that not only contributed to defining an era, but outlasted it. The story of a young married woman who bears the devil's spawn while living in an old, gargoyle-encrusted New York apartment building, it carved its own peculiarly unforgettable niche in American culture.

Bennett spent a hot late-summer Saturday afternoon perusing the "strange witchcraft manuscript" by the pool at Mt. Kisco. Looking up, he could see the lovely scene all around, yet felt disturbed, and that feeling lingered. He was due to enter St. Luke's to undergo cataract removal, and per the usual protocol of the time, would be stuck there a whole week. Rushing to clear his desk at the palazzo on Wednesday, the day before being admitted, he made time to see Levin, since Bennett had a mission: he wanted him to change the ending.

Ira Levin liked his publisher. He'd met Bennett in the '50s, after he'd adapted Mac Hyman's bestseller *No Time for Sergeants* for the stage. At that time, Levin had confessed that he hoped, one day, to break free of the genre label. In his S&S days, the only person he'd ever dealt with was Lee Wright; at RH, Levin appreciated the fact that however busy Bennett was, he took pains to show him around and introduce him to others. He also liked the warmth and caring that pervaded the palazzo, emanating from the office of the man he was now meeting with his editor. Bennett suggested that perhaps Rosemary could be hit by a taxi, lose the baby, and not find out what it looked like. They talked it through, but neither Wright nor Levin thought it a good idea, and conveyed a lack of enthusiasm to the smiling, eager man on the other side of the desk.

As any reader of *Rosemary's Baby* knows, its denouement wasn't the one proposed by Bennett. Levin was grateful Cerf had given way: he knew other publishers might not have been so quick to accept it was the author's decision. However, in a speech six years earlier, Bennett had made that belief clear: "The author is the final arbiter of what goes into his book," he'd said, arguing that when a publisher suggests cuts, they often become the author's favorite parts. If he or she won't budge, a publisher has two choices: publish as the author wants, or reject the book. In the case of an important writer, both pride and excess verbiage are usually swallowed by the publisher, since "he damn well knows" that accommodating competitors will pounce at once. At that point, Levin's record hadn't put him in the category of "important writer," but Bennett intuited that *Rosemary* had the potential to be very successful. At sales conference early in December, he informed the reps that if they hadn't read the galleys, they should: "It's going to become a project of ours to push." The novel would sell 109,000 hardcover copies bearing Ira Levin's ending and a fantastic cover blurb from the now all-powerful Truman Capote. With the paperback sale and film, it was incredibly profitable for a book whose advance had been $2,500.

On Bennett's copy, Levin wrote: "To Bennett Cerf, Rosemary's Baby's godfather." Sometimes the best intervention was to listen, and not intervene at all.

Chapter 52

Turbulence

ROSEMARY'S BABY WOULD MAKE MIA FARROW'S CAREER, MARKING the passage from soap-opera ingénue to serious actress. It would also help destroy her marriage. Before then, Phyllis went to the trouble of remodeling the Mt. Kisco guest cottage especially for Mr. and Mrs. Sinatra, a surprise for their "honeymoon stay" in the summer of 1966. It was her job to make everything wonderful, totally comfortable for Frank, even ordering mirrors for the bathroom ceiling. (He was very conscious of the state of his hair.) Bennett, just a few years shy of seventy, also accommodated him, partying to ungodly hours, falling into bed at four or five in the morning.

Frank lounging by the pool at Mt. Kisco, doing the crossword

The Cerfs joined in the scene at swinging new venues with names like Maxwell's Plum in New York and The Daisy in L.A. Never one to be left behind, Bennett took cues from Mia and Frank, but also from his firstborn, Chris, very much tuned to his generation, and now editing adult titles, among them Andy Warhol's genre-bending coffee-table book, *Index*. Assembled in Japan, it featured cutting-edge pop-ups, a balloon, and a Velvet Underground 45 rpm disc. The night of Warhol's book party, the palazzo opened foil-festooned doors to the silver-wigged artist and his languorous druggy superstars, along with two hundred "flower children," as Bennett called them. His Cheshire-cat grin was simultaneously everywhere and nowhere, his office commandeered by young people yet again. In the end, he was relieved to go home and recover.

His visits with Sinatra to a bar called Jilly's involved a more comfortable kind of displacement. The hard-drinking Hell's Kitchen saloon, known to theater types, chorus girls, and Mafia men, was presided over by Jilly Rizzo, Frank's closest *paesan*. Hanging out with Sinatra and Jilly was like living a fairy tale, with a small voice inside murmuring, *Isn't this so much fun!* However, although he chose not to dwell on the tale's darker side, Bennett was aware it existed.

As spring turned to summer in 1967, Sinatra became increasingly irritable. He'd expected Mia to mold her days to his, but she wanted to advance her career. The age gap and chasm in interests began to weigh more heavily. Mia was making him feel old, rather than young and forever hip. Frank was set to star in a film called *The Detective;* Mia was to act alongside him. First, though, came *Rosemary's Baby*. When its director, Roman Polanski, went over schedule in L.A., Mia was unable to be in New York on time for Frank's picture. He forced a halt to work on *The Detective;* something primal could not be assuaged; and Sinatra's fury took the form of legal papers delivered to Mia's dressing room on the set of *Rosemary* the day before Thanksgiving. An application for a divorce was made out in her name. She signed what was in front of her. The day after Thanksgiving, news coverage spoke euphemistically of a "trial separation."

Christmas was less than two weeks away when Mia—in New York to finish outdoor scenes for *Rosemary*—turned up at the Cerfs' as they dined with Leonora Hornblow. Hysterical at the idea of losing Frank, she was desperate for solace and a way to make it come out right. In the end he recanted, allowing her to fly to Palm Springs with Phyllis for the holidays. Bennett would come later. A dubious reconciliation, Bennett told his diary, all the while projecting optimism to columnists knocking at his door for inside dope. But despite the brave face Mia put on, the marriage was over; eight months later, a quick Mexican divorce made it official.

Still, although he'd initiated the split, on some days Sinatra seemed most unhappy. A succession of beauties would render comfort soon enough, but on one occasion between the breakup and final divorce, he found himself in New York needing a date. Bennett and Phyllis, who'd do anything to make him happy, took it upon themselves to find one. Mia had been young, so they thought young: someone really special for the really special Francis Albert. They called Freddy Espy, the Botticelli-like girl for whom The Columns had been a haven when, as a teen, she'd needed to escape her unhappy home. She'd been very close to Bennett: he'd listened and helped her in many ways, had even given her an RH job. Of course, Chris had been madly in love with her, his first true love. And of course, she'd been going with a friend of Chris's, George Plimpton, for some years. Asking her was, Freddy would say forty years later, "not a nice thing to do." But they did, because it was for Frank; and she did, because the request came from Bennett. A few months later, she married Plimpton.

The Cerfs' love affair with Sinatra continued, apart from one memorable spat a few years later. They'd heard stories of bad behavior and witnessed what happened to Mia, but there was no adequate preparation for the moment when Frank turned on *them*. That night, Judy and Bill Green, an integral part of the Mt. Kisco scene, had hosted a dinner at their estate. By now, the Greens and Cerfs were pretty good friends. Bill, awfully rich and much older than his wife, was also a buddy of Sinatra's, and like Frank, fond of a drink. Judy, very smart, and with an Audrey Hepburn allure, had posed for Warhol, been taken up by Swifty Lazar as an aspiring writer, and was a magnet for every male. Phyllis worried that Judy was a little *too* close to Frank.

Sinatra was visiting the Cerfs, and accompanied them to the Greens', as did Chris and one of his more serious girlfriends, Helene Fagan. The dinner was extremely well lubricated, and it was very late when they piled into the Cadillac to drive home. Bennett, not a big drinker, was at the wheel, and they were well underway when Frank, on a whim, wanted to drop by Arlene and Marty Gabel's, to down one more for the road. Bennett was tired and could see that Sinatra had drunk far more than enough. He'd also heard the Gabels were away, and told Frank as much.

Sinatra ordered him to stop, insisting he'd walk to the Gabels' on his own, but the car kept going: the house would be a steep climb through dark woods, and Bennett worried about Frank's state.

Suddenly, Sinatra began screaming: he was getting out, he had to get out.

"Francis Albert, I won't let a friend of mine make a fool of himself," Bennett told the angry face in the rearview mirror.

"I won't let anybody tell me what to do," Sinatra shot back, following with a poisonous expletive-laced blast, entirely personal and crushing, directed at Bennett.

Phyllis swiveled and shook her fist: "No one's talking to my husband that way!"

Bennett turned pale. Chris and Helene, pinned in place, wanted to be anywhere but there.

When Bennett finally pulled into the drive, Sinatra went straight to the phone.

Early the next morning, a strange sound sliced through the country air. It was a helicopter, making for The Columns. It touched down on the lawn, Frank Sinatra got in, and the machine whirred up. He wasn't going to stay one more second than he had to.

He did, though, return soon enough. Bennett the Bookie and Phyllis the General welcomed him back. Whatever was said, no such scene played out again.

. . .

TWO CONSECUTIVE DEATHS EACH brought a different kind of disturbance. Blanche Knopf's health had become even more precarious. Extreme thinness and frailty hadn't been able to diminish her appetite for life, but in June 1966, cancer stopped it dead in her seventy-first year. To her author James M. Cain, Alfred would write that she went suddenly, "after immense suffering from an arthritic hip." Cancer was still unmentionably private. Three years earlier, doctors had debated whether to tell her. It was Alfred who insisted that they must.

Bennett found the funeral touching. He and Blanche had lunched à deux a few times the previous year, while Alfred was recovering from a heart attack. Bennett had long known she wasn't simply the cold spider people made her out to be; she well knew he was more than the jokester many took him for. What would happen to Alfred? Many at Knopf looked for signs.

What happened was that Alfred became reacquainted with Helen Hedrick, a poet and fiction writer whose only novel the firm had published in 1941. She was a widow, warm and outgoing. Ten months after Blanche's death, he and Mrs. Hedrick stunned their respective worlds by journeying to Rio and getting married. Donald counted himself among the utterly amazed, but Bennett, having hosted Alfred and his new lady friend at home one evening, accurately predicted that there might be nuptials. Helen brought Alfred happiness. His carapace softened. The great Knopf seemed more approachably human than he'd ever been before.

The second death came as a terrible surprise. Although Bob Bernstein had taken over primary responsibility for Dr. Seuss, Bennett cherished the Geisels' New York sojourns and looked forward to seeing them on his own jaunts west. Betweentimes, he and Ted rattled away happily on the phone, two punning boys knowing just how to spur each other on. Bennett always made sure to have a word with Helen, too.

Early in 1966, she asked a favor and Bennett happily complied. He made a star turn at a huge Seuss-themed charity ball in San Diego. The Cerfs dined with the Geisels and some younger friends, RH author Neil Morgan and his journalist wife Judith, and Ted's physician, Dr. Grey Dimond, and his pert wife Audrey, a former nurse. Eighteen months later, Bennett was at work when a call came through from Judith Morgan: Helen Geisel was dead. She'd killed herself. No one was to know that part, but Morgan, working against deadline for the *San Diego Union,* wanted a statement from Bennett for an obituary. Those first seconds, she heard shock on the silent line. Then he spoke, and Morgan heard sadness. She was one of the "most wonderful" women he'd ever met, Bennett began. He couldn't think of anyone he had a higher opinion of. As a worker, a creator, she was "the most unselfish person we've ever known." Almost always in pain, "you would never guess it. . . . She was a perfect sport." The obit said Helen was "found dead." Newspapers avoided the word *suicide*.

Bennett had been right about the pain, and Helen being a perfect sport. After her recovery from Guillain Barré, she was physically never again entirely well, but worked seven days a week to accommodate her husband and ran everything practical in their lives. She also pushed herself to be president of the local museum, active in the hospital, etc., etc. However, another kind of pain also plagued her. In February, she'd written to her niece that she "tiptoed" around, so as not to disturb Ted's work. Later, she confided to her sister-in-law that he had to be "patted on the back on the hour" or else he just slumped, convinced "that what he does is no good at all." In many ways, Helen had had to be mother as well as wife. She imposed a necessary discipline, but increasingly it wasn't well received, and her parlous health cast a pall.

Bob and Helen Bernstein had visited the tower house that summer, and Bob found Ted "strangely down and jumpy." He was amazed, after all this time, to hear Ted say how hard it was to work in his home studio high above the sea, and that perhaps he'd rent a place elsewhere. The Bernsteins wondered if there might be trouble in the marriage.

On October 23, 1967, when her body was found, there was a note for Ted. Helen wondered what had happened to them. Feeling herself "going down down down, into a black hole . . . too old and enmeshed in everything you do and are," she couldn't conceive of life without him. She knew her going would "leave quite a rumor," but that his reputation would "not be harmed." What Helen knew was that Ted and Audrey Dimond, his doctor's wife, had fallen in love. Helen had taken a large quantity of sleeping pills. Now the way was clear for a new Mrs. Geisel.

At first, Ted confided to a friend, "I didn't know whether to kill myself, burn the house down, or just go away and get lost," but in time, Audrey and her husband would divorce, paving the way for her to marry Ted. He was sixty-four; she was eighteen years younger, the same age gap as that between Bennett and Phyllis. Marrying Audrey—blonde, bubbly, and with eyes of a startling blue—was for Ted like drinking from Ponce de León's fountain. She was fond of bright colors and California casual (the better to show off a superb figure). He started to look different, growing a beard, perching fashionably big black spectacles atop his giant gin-blossomed nose, sporting turtlenecks and other youthful attire.

Audrey now bought all his clothes. "If he didn't like it, he didn't like it, but more and more, he liked everything," she proudly recalled. Mad about Ted, she determined to use her nurse's training to take the best care of him, undoubtedly prolonging his creative life. Yet the difference between Ted's wives was stark and, for Random House, presented a problem. Helen had been the first, best reader, editor, and mentor, able to stand up to Ted when necessary and exert substantial influence on the books; she was the pragmatic yet inspired organizer and liaison to the world beyond the tower, imbued with ideals, faculties, and standards in harmony with his. Her title had been "vice-president of Beginner Books," but she was far more: indispensable and irreplaceable. It was for Bennett and Bob to attend to the huge hole that had opened, and quickly. So much depended on the cash the imprint and Ted's other books generated. They could not endanger that flow.

Bernstein's assistant, Anne MarcoVecchio, had married. Now Anne Johnson, she became Beginner's administrative VP. Michael Frith took over as editor, working almost full-time with Ted. Walter Retan, who'd become RH's juvenile editor after Louise Bonino fell ill, handled his longer, non-Beginner titles. All three henceforth made frequent visits west, since Ted ventured less often to New York. In the autumn of 1968, however, he did make the trip, with Audrey in tow. Bennett thought her "nice," and the second Mrs. Geisel reciprocated the compliment.

"There weren't many . . . whom Ted could talk to, but he could talk to Bennett," she observed. "They both looked through the same end of the telescope. He gave Ted, so serious, a kind of brightness that he needed. The mix of the two together was delicious."

. . .

UNLIKE BEGINNER BOOKS, THE L. W. Singer Company did not change RH for the better. Great quantities of capital were invested—$750,000 in 1967 alone—in new Singer products, money that otherwise would have gone to RH profits; management teams were fired, new ones recruited, and the process repeated again. In 1967, the decision was made to relocate parts of the company from Syracuse to New York. Space was rented at 501 Madison Avenue—the office building housing Knopf. Because a significant portion of Knopf's revenue came from high school and college sales, it was thought the proximity might be beneficial. But the only positive long-lasting result of the move was the arrival in New York of Toni Morrison, who'd joined Singer three years earlier as associate editor for high school literature anthologies and texts.

The civil rights struggle, along with Vietnam, was saturating the nation's front pages. Reporters had begun to pay attention to a serious imbalance: America's schoolbook pictures and words were all about whites.

Officials making bulk educational purchases in cities like Detroit began to demand notice be paid to people of color. There was also the matter of representation—with the passage of the Civil Rights Act, big government contracts could no longer go to corporations whose staff did not include women and minorities—and RCA was very much in the government contract business. Being Black and female, Morrison fit the bill on both counts, a self-described "double-header," and more. In the late '60s she sported an Afro. She was the first woman to wear trousers to work in the textbook department. From time to time, she smoked a pipe like the boys. If you're regarded as "different" anyway, she reasoned, then why not?

Toni Morrison

Eventually, Morrison transferred to the trade department of Random House, where she would have a long, trailblazing, and distinguished editorial career, full of breakthroughs but also frustrations. As far as she was concerned, Bennett was all mask, one she didn't have occasion to penetrate. Donald, on the other hand, was "the man": elegant, a first-rate reader, with genuine insight. They talked a lot. Sometimes he'd mention his early childhood in Syracuse, or his wartime experiences, and ponder how it was possible to be a civilized person following all that.

From time to time, Morrison referred to financial difficulties—publishing salaries were far from generous—and one day Donald appeared bearing a $5,000 check from his personal account. She'd never asked for the loan, and tried not to accept it. He insisted: "There will always be more problems. Take it." She did. When it was time to buy a house, she phoned Bob Bernstein. He, too, had been "very nice . . . not patronizing, but supportive and forthright." Banks weren't in the business of issuing mortgages to divorced Black women with children. Bernstein called up the firm's banker. Morrison went in, filled out forms, and the mortgage came through.

Frances Singer, who'd set the template by helping Morrison rent a Syracuse apartment, resigned in March 1967 from the subsidiary that bore her husband's name. Series and titles would be sold off; others would be subsumed into a reorganized RH "Educational Division."

In his oral history, Bennett justified the purchase: wanting to be in textbooks, starting from scratch would have taken too long, so they bought a company that was "doing well." In the first two years, profits continued, "but we didn't realize the dry rot that was creeping in." Singer was a business he'd had no business getting into, but it had served to get him into RCA.

. . .

IN 1967, THE EDUCATIONAL side of RH's operation—not Singer, but the supply company now called RH School and Library Service—almost landed Lew Miller in jail. Lew had run the RH sales department like an emperor; after sales conferences, he'd go back and unilaterally decide what each title's print run would be, and his "automatic distribution" system was seen as revolutionary across the industry. He'd rejected a partnership when Bennett and Don had offered it, but being supplanted by Bob Bernstein couldn't have been easy for a man with Lew's pride. Still, having been given the subsidiary to build, he'd worked hard to grow revenues, recruiting a new force of seventy salesmen to sell selected trade titles, both kids' and adult, to the education market.

Early on, the growth rate was phenomenal—25 percent—and had "leveled off" to a still-impressive 15. Given the money the government was pumping into education, Lew told a reporter, "Five years from now I expect this to double our present sale of trade books." To avoid being undercut by jobbers slapping discounts on these specially bound school and library books, big publishers had established an informal net price system. When it came to the attention of the Department of Justice and a Senate subcommittee, the government brought suit against RH and seventeen other houses, charging price-fixing on wholesale books, a violation of the Sherman Antitrust Act. They claimed that publishers overcharged by 25 percent.

This was the kind of situation that RCA's attorneys found immensely alarming, since so much of the corporation's big-ticket defense work was bound up in government contracts. It was imperative that no whiff of impropriety foul the procurement pipeline. To the dismay of the other publishers, RCA didn't want to fight, but to settle, the sooner the better. Lew was in the hot seat, and, making everything worse, his wife had undergone two cancer operations. He decided it was time to get out. When Bennett heard, he wrote to his colleague of thirty years, whom he held in the highest regard and described as "one of my best friends in all this world."

Lew left in June. Bennett hosted a retirement luncheon at '21.' So strange to think of RH without him, and yet once he went, Lew Miller was well and truly gone, disappearing from the publishing scene and from his boss's diary. Did Bennett's web of connection stretch so thin, even Lew could fall through? Or was Lew's pride or disillusion so great, his wife's health so consuming, that he chose to leave it all behind?

The lawyers hammered out a consent decree that RH and the seventeen others signed, ending the practice of resale price maintenance and collusive bidding. It was an important moment. Bennett and other leading members of the clubby world of book publishing, who enjoyed nothing more than a friendly chat among friends, had to learn to be much more careful about what they said to one another from now on.

Chapter 53

Making It

IN JANUARY 1967, WHETHER TO SIGN *MAKING IT*, A CONTENTIOUS memoir by a thirty-six-year-old political provocateur named Norman Podhoretz, became Bennett's problem. The book had been submitted to Jim Silberman, who although interested, was also afraid. *Making It* had originally been signed by Farrar, Straus & Giroux, who'd published Podhoretz's first book. FSG saw him as a valuable addition to their list, but after reading the new book, backed off. Podhoretz was not unknown to RH: seven years earlier, when launching his now-defunct Looking Glass Library, Jason Epstein had briefly brought him in as an editor, and Podhoretz, who in 1960 had gone on to edit *Commentary,* the influential Jewish intellectual and political magazine, considered himself one of Jason's best friends. But Jason *hated* the latest manuscript, and wanted the firm to have nothing to do with it.

It was by peering beneath the shiny surface of his own success that Podhoretz had stirred up such a fuss; he'd dared to contemplate what "making it" in America means. Part passionate Rousseau-like confession, part cool analysis, it examined class, upward mobility, the desire for fame, power, money, and the price for grabbing the brass ring. While it was "impossible" to grow up without seeing success as life's goal, it was equally impossible not to believe that such success requires "a corruption of the spirit." Just as D. H. Lawrence had argued that sex was the "dirty little secret" of the Victorians, Podhoretz asserted that the desire for success was the dirty little secret that latter-day American intellectuals harbored beneath their high-minded facades.

The son of Jewish immigrants, he'd become a force within the New York chattering class, this parvenu up from hard-knocks Brownsville, Brooklyn, having been greatly helped by a high school teacher who taught him to smooth rough edges, and by becoming, at Columbia, protégé to Lionel Trilling, its doyen of lit crit. Roger Straus, notoriously money-mean, had agreed to what for FSG was a fabulous advance—$25,000—the kind that translated into selling a 50,000-copy first printing to break even. But after Podhoretz handed over the book, his editor, Robert Giroux, was appalled, as was Straus, and pressured him to withdraw from the contract.

What had set off alarms was that, while placing himself front and center under the microscope, Podhoretz had also scrutinized powerful pals, prominent figures like Norman Mailer, Mary McCarthy, James Baldwin, even his mentor, Trilling. Some might not take kindly to what he said or implied about their compromises, and could blunt the book's chances through mean-spirited reviews and negative word-of-mouth, or even sue for libel. Other publishers were also wary, but Silberman was eager to take it on, *if* he had Bennett's blessing. So often denigrated within the milieu Podhoretz inhabited, Bennett read the manuscript and didn't think in theoretical or political terms. What he saw was a fascinating tale, uncommonly candid and well told, with sales potential. In his usually decisive way, he told Silberman to offer $25,000.

RH released *Making It* quickly. It got off to a good start, and Bennett told Podhoretz it might even become a bestseller, but then controversy flared. Those who wrapped themselves in a cloak of moral exceptionalism were furious at being described as nakedly ambitious just like the rest of humanity, and resented Podhoretz's own quick climb to the top. Critic after critic attacked the book and its author, and the negative reviews discouraged readers from picking it up. Significant and thought-provoking though it was, *Making It* was left out to rot on the literary vine. Not until the late 1990s was it recognized as having been "positively prescient" about the conspicuous "acquisitive egotism" and vogue for "confessional" memoir that arrived so powerfully in the 1980s, and never left.

. . .

WHEN HE CHOSE TO publish Podhoretz, Bennett understood the story viscerally. As a young man, he'd also set out to "make it," and was unabashed about enjoying the success he'd reaped, needing the security of calling attention to it, wanting the approval of witnesses who patted him on the back, but also—and this made him unusual—wanting them to partake of great good fortune, too. It was rare for a man of such ego to encourage, rather than squelch, those nearby.

Few clearer signs of "making it" existed in America than seeing your face on the cover of *Time* magazine. Since the 1920s, *Time* had been telling the country who exercised power and who was rising to grasp it, where the new trends were and who were the tastemakers. You might disagree with *Time*'s politics, but in a pre-internet world, it was hard to ignore who adorned its covers. On December 16, 1966, Bennett received that honor. The year's motley lineup had included Robert F. Kennedy and Ronald Reagan; Saigon's Premier Ky and Hanoi's General Giap; Hendrik Verwoerd, iron-willed mastermind of South African apartheid, but also Robert C. Weaver, the first Black U.S. cabinet secretary. Artist Pietro Annigoni, with many *Time* covers behind him, captured Bennett looking tanned, furrowed, balding, with thin lips closed together in a faint, slightly lopsided smile. Shrewdness shone from dark beads of eyes staring straight at the reader behind huge spectacles. Painted in three-quarter perspective, he sat before a blue wash of books, a latter-day Medici posed in front of the treasure his lifetime of patronage had collected.

"BOOKS BY THE BILLION," proclaimed the diagonal banner running across the magazine's upper left corner.

One subject, more than any other, dominated *Time*'s portraits in 1966: the conflict in Vietnam, a war that *Time* supported, and Bennett, the father of two fighting-age sons, most definitely did not. "Viet Nam a real fuck-up," he told his diary that summer, the first time in a half century of diary-keeping that he'd used such strong language.

The emotions flaring from the war were on full display one evening when the Cerfs dined with Bennett's old acquaintance Averell "Ave" Harriman and his wife, Marie, at their Sands Point home. Other friends were there as well, along with the young society bandleader Peter Duchin, who'd been raised by the Harrimans after being orphaned. When the meal finished, they moved to the porch for coffee. Table talk inevitably turned to Vietnam: Harriman, who as a rich, long-powerful businessman, politician, and diplomat had had the ear of Democratic presidents from FDR to Johnson, was now a U.S. ambassador-at-large involved in negotiations about the war.

Phyllis's tongue, well primed, was ready to engage in a little political pugilism, but as remarks went back and forth, hers grew sharper, more pointedly personal. It was a time when differing views about the war fractured families and friendships. Why hadn't Harriman come out against U.S. involvement sooner, she demanded. He explained that he had walked a fine line to retain influence with those at the top, but Phyllis doubled down. "If you can't get this war to stop, you should!" she pressed, seeming to indict the ambassador himself for the continuing conflict. Suddenly, the sound of a slap resounded like a gunshot, followed by a silence that, if anything, seemed louder still. Harriman stared at his hand as though it belonged to someone else; Phyllis clutched at the face that had come into contact with that hand.

"Boy, Phyllis, you sure deserved that!" is what Duchin recalled Bennett saying next, an odd little grin crossing his face. That reaction shocked in its own right. Were his frustrations with Phyllis spilling out? Did astonishment, embarrassment, or insecurity push him to justify Harriman rather than support his wife? Or did Duchin, recalling the incident decades later, misremember words uttered in the past? Certainly, the grin was the kind those who knew Bennett could recognize. It had appeared when Norman Mailer threatened him, or a journalist asked a question he couldn't answer. It was his default when frightened or found wanting. It also appeared when Bennett did something wrong.

. . .

INCREASINGLY RIVEN AND PREOCCUPIED by the war, the country sought escape. It made sense to put Bennett on the cover of *Time:* everyone knew him, books were booming, and he'd embraced big business in the form of RCA. He learned of his impending glorification in mid-November, and despite the painful scrutiny he'd received in other profiles, was thrilled by the news. The lead reporter for the piece was twenty-six-year-old Christopher T. Cory. After a break-the-ice luncheon at '21,' Cory next met his subject ensconced behind his ten-foot desk at Random House. Sizing up his visitor, Bennett threw down the gauntlet: "Hello, Pest!"

For a moment the journalist was startled. But "Pest" soon yielded to "Boswell," said in such a way that Cory had no alternative but to reply, "Johnson!" In later sessions, Bennett often called for "Boswell," and Cory played along, that most welcome of listeners, a fresh audience.

This assignment was Cory's first big break, and he felt lucky in his subject. He got to wander through the palazzo, the townhouse, and The Columns; tag along to the Fontainebleau and *What's My Line?;* interview authors, publishers, friends. Boswell had to put up with Johnson's puns, of course, like the fellow named Kissinger who had his name changed so many times that soon all his friends were asking, "I wonder who's Kissinger now?" In the ceaseless accumulation, they could wax tedious. Yet Cory was entranced with Bennett as a wonderful raconteur, even if not quite the elegant conversationalist he'd envisaged in a publisher. (The "horribly nasal" voice also took some getting used to.) When Bennett bragged about pranks and practical jokes, about "enhancing" author stories to drum up word-of-mouth, it seemed part of a delightful game, and the journalist felt charmed, almost privileged, to be let in on it.

He did unearth information that Bennett hadn't rushed to volunteer. Cory calculated that from TV, lectures, syndicated columns, anthologies, and his RH salary and stock, Bennett was earning about $375,000 a year ($3.7 million today), big money compared to the earnings of vast numbers of Americans who claimed to know him. Apart from the celebrity conferred by TV, his byline had appeared on twenty-one joke and riddle books that together had sold more than five million copies. His columns reached fifteen million readers in 241 papers across the country.

How much did money factor into his publishing decisions, Cory wondered.

"Every publisher," Bennett maintained, "thinks of himself as an idealist, although the idealism is in the back of his head. . . . It's awfully hard to turn down a book that's going to make money. If I thought nobody else was going to publish it, it wouldn't matter. But the thought that if I don't, somebody else will—I can't stand that."

Others differed as to what mattered to him. Jason Epstein believed Bennett ran RH "as a conservative branch of show business, vulgar to a degree," yet what counted was "how important he feels it is to have Philip Roth and William Styron on the list. Some other publishers would know a thousand ways to get rich without having one author like that. Bennett Cerf doesn't."

Cory enjoyed his fortnight as Bennett's shadow, but *Time*'s practice was for reporters to hand their field notes to a staff writer, who'd stitch them into a story. Sending in the last file to his editor, Cory teased: "Can I quit now? My belly-laughing muscles are beginning to ache." Unlike others who'd profiled Bennett for major magazines, he wasn't all sarcasm. Nor was the tone of the feature based on his legwork. In *Time,* Bennett finally read a thoroughly pleasing profile that singled him out as a preeminent player in books. Calls and wires deluged RH.

Five decades later, Chris Cory rifled through his thick file of yellowing field notes with the kind of understanding a lifetime of experience imparts. Now what he saw, pulsing beneath the nicknames, bonhomie, and playful charm, were mechanisms to create distance, establish dominance, hide insecurity. He understood: charm could delight but also manipulate, and Bennett had been a pro at handling a young fellow still learning his craft. With hindsight, Cory could detect a man relentlessly ambitious for his business, with a highly competitive, combative edge. Unlike many men his age, Bennett wasn't cynical or bitter, but nor was he profound. A scrappy wheeler-dealer, he spent his time running hard, getting things done, trying not to plumb the depths—though he did appreciate, at times to the point of awe, depth in others. He perceived it in Don and Saxe. Most particularly, he knew its place at the core of his finest authors, and made their thoughts and insights accessible to a world of readers. Bennett, Cory recalled, was a perpetual "kid," "very smart," who'd set out to make it, and did. Along the way, he'd been able to use those "smarts" to do things "that he knew were both savvy and noble."

Chapter 54

Exits and Entrances

On a cold Monday afternoon in February 1967, the Cerfs were at JFK airport on their way to visit Claudette Colbert, who'd retired to Barbados. Bennett had been late to bed the night before, after playing two show episodes—one taped for the following week—then enjoying a nightcap at the St. Regis. Waiting in the Pan Am lounge, he heard his name paged: a *New York Times* reporter had tracked him down for a front-page story.

"Have you any statement . . . about the cancellation of *What's My Line?*" the fellow asked.

"What are you talking about?" Bennett blurted.

"Oh, you aren't going to be on next year."

"I have not heard that the program will be dropped," he replied, regaining composure, "but if it's true I am not disappointed. It's a miracle it's run [this long]. I enjoyed every minute."

He'd put a positive gloss on the news, but inside he was shaking. The previous night, no one had let slip even a whisper. He phoned Mark Goodson, who said this was the first *he'd* heard of any cancellation, and promised to find out what was going on. Goodson phoned back fast. The network had decided that *To Tell the Truth, I've Got a Secret,* and *What's My Line?* were "out." They weren't what a youthful prime-time audience wanted, and would run only until Labor Day.

When they landed in Barbados, who should the Cerfs run into at the airstrip but *WML*'s executive producer, Gil Fates, stopping on his way back to New York from Antigua. "I'm the first to give it to you: you've lost a show!" Bennett said breathlessly, needing to share the news. When he himself returned ten days later, it was to piles of stories chronicling *WML*'s demise. He'd admitted in an interview six years earlier that when Phyllis thought his head was getting too big, she reminded him that "someday television will end for me and I'll be just another book publisher." Yet the show had become so fused to who he was, it was almost impossible to believe it could die. *WML* had run longer than any other network evening show save for Ed Sullivan's, and had won Emmys in 1952, 1953, and 1958, and a Golden Globe in 1962. However, what had been the nation's fourth most popular program in 1955 was now seventy-ninth.

Everyone associated with the show protested the decision, but appeals to CBS were useless. It was a nice irony: the network executive who'd pulled the plug was Bob Bernstein's good friend Mike Dann, who'd earlier intervened on Bennett's behalf when General Sarnoff wanted him off the program. As Dann recalled with wry pragmatism: "There never was a good show with bad Nielsen ratings in commercial broadcasting." The zeitgeist had changed, youth was everything, and the pancaked faces of *WML*'s panelists hadn't been young from the start.

The final program, on September 3, featured Bennett, Steve Allen, Arlene, and Marty Gabel as panelists. The three contestants from the first 1950 show were welcomed back, clips were shown from years past, and John Daly was the mystery guest. Goodson hosted a farewell gathering at his home afterward, more wake than party, and the CBS president sent Cartier cigarette boxes to each principal player. "VERY SAD! ONLY 17-YEAR RUN! BOO-HOO," Bennett scribbled in his diary, summoning up his usual bravado. But *WML* had been far more than a show, as he well knew: it had been a way of life. Wherever he was, whatever he was doing, and whomever he was with, Sunday nights would be a lot lonelier from now on.

. . .

BENNETT AND DON HAD accomplished what other founders often failed to do: secured an heir for a future without them. With Bob Bernstein's elevation to the presidency, his rival Dick Kislik wasn't going to linger long. For Bennett, Kislik had come to symbolize the problems they were having with Singer, the new warehouse, and the computer facility—even if not of his making—and he wasn't unhappy when Kislik negotiated an exit early in 1968. The house of Knopf, on the other hand, hadn't managed to prepare for the future after the line of succession had ruptured with Pat's departure. In selling to Bennett and Don, Alfred and Blanche had secured sympathetic ownership, but made no provision for mortality. Now Blanche was dead, and Alfred easing off. The company was consistently, but marginally, in the black. Bills were paid by the backlist; that money machine *The Prophet;* and a few authors like John Hersey, Julia Child, and John Updike. Not many other fresh voices energized the list; without them, the future was uncertain.

The Knopfs had kept editors on the sidelines, fearful and lacking esteem. The idea of a successor springing from their midst was unthinkable. Two years before Blanche died, Bennett and Don had pressured them to bring in Seymour Lawrence, a well-regarded editor, to be groomed as editor-in-chief. He lasted six months. Among Knopf's longtime retainers, none had the commanding vitality and savvy to bring the house into the future. Pete Lemay, the publicity manager who essentially ran trade, sensed that Bernstein didn't like him, and the feeling was mutual. Within a year of Blanche's death, he'd gone. But as the question of who'd lead Knopf grew more urgent, a prospect emerged: Simon & Schuster's thirty-six-year-old editor-in-chief, Robert Gottlieb. The S&S where he'd made his career since starting as an editorial assistant in 1955, after Columbia and Cambridge, was now owned by that very odd pair, Max Schuster, who was incapable of running anything, and numbers-fixated Leon Shimkin, the "Silent S."

For most of Gottlieb's tenure, "the kids were running the store," as he saw it, and the sneaker-shod, black-spectacled, intense kid in charge of editorial had been left alone to publish a remarkable run of bestsellers: Joseph Heller's *Catch-22,* Chaim Potok's *The Chosen,* Jessica Mitford's *The American Way of Death,* Robert Crichton's *The Secret of Santa*

Robert Gottlieb

Vittoria, among others. By the middle of 1967, changes on the horizon threatened his autonomy. Marketing director Richard Snyder had barreled up the ranks; under the ruthlessly ambitious Snyder and Shimkin, S&S would become a very different house. Gottlieb confided to the agent Candida Donadio—both their careers had taken off when she'd sold him *Catch-22*—that he was thinking of moving, and Donadio advised that RH was the place to be. She called Joe Fox, who told Bernstein, and soon Gottlieb was in Bennett's diary as an "outside possibility."

On August 2, the two lunched at the Hemisphere Club to discuss what an astonished Gottlieb could only describe as "a fantasy." Though greatly tempted, he told Bennett that he'd consider coming only if Nina Bourne, a cherished colleague and renowned copywriter, came with him, the same kind of compact that O'Neill had extracted regarding Saxe so many years before. At fifty-one, Bourne was wallflower-plain, a cross between a favorite spinster aunt and a beloved child. Devoted to her work, she once described herself as "the demented governess who believes the baby is her own." She'd started at S&S fresh from Radcliffe in 1939 as a secretary, and soon had a crush on Dick Simon. Eventually rising to run advertising as the rare female vice president, her ad, catalogue, and jacket copy sparkled with the same wit that infused poems she published in *The New Yorker* when young. Bennett judged her "about the best in the business."

Nina Bourne, one of three bears from outer space

Gelatt

Gottlieb also proposed bringing someone else: S&S associate publisher Anthony Schulte. Blessed with an entrepreneurial streak and the dark, athletic good looks and prep-school veneer that made him publishing's answer to Cary Grant, Schulte had recently come to Gottlieb and Bourne with two proposals. One was for the three to start a firm—an idea Gottlieb rejected—but the other, to buy Dutton, an old house that was coming available, was intriguing. Gottlieb absolutely wouldn't move without Bourne; he wasn't as wedded to Schulte. While Schulte continued to explore Dutton, Gottlieb continued to talk with RH. No one wanted to attract attention, so early conversations between Gottlieb, Bennett, and Bernstein occurred at Bennett's home. Spurred by his history of bad blood with Shimkin, and needing to revitalize Knopf, Bernstein was determined to land him. Once Bourne and Schulte got involved, Bernstein met with all of them over lunches at the pied-à-terre Bennett had arranged for him to use when staying in the city: Claudette Colbert's apartment.

Over and over, Gottlieb would ask Bernstein the same question: With Alfred still there, and the old retainers in place, who would really be in charge? He wanted certainty that everyone, including Alfred, would accept him as arbiter of the future. At times, Bennett inserted himself into the talks: "They'll know," he promised Gottlieb, who nonetheless remained skittish. Bourne worried that "everybody at Knopf will wake up and feel like the three bears have landed in their beds, from outer space."

Anthony M. Schulte

Six months crawled by. It was nearly Christmas when Bob Loomis hosted a party at his Greenwich Village home, where the guests included Bernstein and Schulte. Drink in hand, Bernstein backed Schulte into a corner, looming over him with his height. "Are you coming, or aren't you?" he asked, alcohol making him even ruddier and younger-looking, but the ultimatum firm and clear. Schulte knew they had to stop stalling. "I'll sleep on it. You'll get an answer."

"Gottlieb Schulte Bourne deal looks on again," said Bennett's diary. One last assurance from Bernstein was needed: that if necessary, Gottlieb would have the authority to fire Alfred. Gottlieb got the answer he wanted. Soon, the trio agreed to come. On January 6, 1968, Tony Schulte was standing in line to board a ski lift in Vermont when a friend shouted, "You're in the newspaper!" *The New York Times* had reported that S&S was losing "three key executives" to Knopf. "Getting this champion team is a red-letter day," Bennett had bubbled to the paper. His diary carried the unfiltered version: "Delighted" at "pilfering . . . S&S nabobs." He'd sought Alfred's blessing over cocktails months earlier, but although Knopf told the *Times* he was "very glad indeed," he'd added that he'd not been involved in the negotiations, "don't know anything more than what I hear." Whispers circulated that he hadn't been consulted. Bennett dismissed such talk, insisting he'd fully briefed Alfred, but the old Olympian, having assumed he'd be head indefinitely, stayed "irritated." It fell to Don to inform him that he would have to adjust.

On his last day at S&S, Gottlieb stayed late to record details of all his projects, in order to phone authors and secure assurances they'd join him. In the end, he brought with him almost two dozen books under contract—including titles by Joseph Heller and Robert Crichton—a rare, astonishing infusion of fresh blood if ever there was one, and on unusually good money terms.

At the end of January, Bennett convened a cocktail party to fete the trio at the palazzo. One block north, the Knopf staff, for whom anxiety was a constant thrum they'd learned to live with, waited to know what the new regime would bring. Bernstein summoned at least one key Knopf editor and promised that if things didn't work out, there would be a job for him at RH. Employees would soon find that the rumpled kid who'd run the S&S list had his own taste and style: an intellectual, balletomane, and connoisseur of pop culture, Gottlieb preferred a sandwich in his office to lunch dates à la Bennett or Alfred. But despite his youth and seeming casualness, many came to feel that, like Alfred, he did not suffer challenges to his opinions, and was a "one-man show." Although a fellow no longer had to slick back his hair and straighten his tie when called in to see him, as those hauled before Alfred assuredly did, a Gottlieb summons could be equally worrying, and he could be just as condescending. With the arrival of the trio—all Jews—some employees felt that Knopf was becoming more "Jewish"; others saw only that Gottlieb liked to work in a tight circle, "with people who seemed extensions of himself." RH and Knopf had coexisted as two distinct houses under Bennett and Alfred, but soon after Gottlieb's arrival a territorial dispute flared over paperbacks. Pat Knopf had begun Vintage, now so successful; Gottlieb wanted to claw back a piece of it. Jason Epstein had no intention of ceding one bit of control. Although Gottlieb had to back down, rivalry simmered beneath the surface.

The transition manifested itself in various ways. Alfred complained about editors taking on too many books and spending too much, their judgment not being weighed by anyone in charge—though of course it was, by Gottlieb. He grew annoyed that "B.G." didn't want to publish what he, Alfred, judged an excellent history book. Time "for a showdown," he told his diary. "I don't think he knows what my kind of serious publishing in the field of history is."

The first book contracted by Gottlieb that Knopf published was Heller's *We Bombed in New Haven*. Bourne created an ad that Gottlieb considered wonderful, even though she forgot to insert the Borzoi colophon. Soon she found herself the recipient of one of Alfred's magenta memos, a thunderclap written with a rudeness that neither Bourne nor Gottlieb could quite believe. She sent it back with a message of her own: "Dear Alfred, I'm returning to you a note you just sent. I'm sure you wouldn't want an unintentionally rude note left around to be discovered in a file in the future. See you next week for lunch." Ten minutes later, he was at her door. "I didn't know my letter was rude," he told her. Before, no one had ever come right out and asked him not to behave that way. Nina had "debullied" Alfred.

On the day Gottlieb's appointment was announced, he'd written to Alfred, expressing hope that in a few years, the old lion wouldn't regret having accepted the change. "You could not have found an editor with a greater sense" of the firm's splendor, Gottlieb declared, "which of course doesn't mean that you will always like what I do. . . . But I hope you will." Alfred by no means always liked his successor's actions, but when he saw the house with his name on it flourishing, he came to tolerate them well enough. As for Bennett, getting Gottlieb, Schulte, and Bourne was "a miracle" that made him "very happy."

Chapter 55

Confessions and Controversies

WHILE KNOPF'S FUTURE WAS BEING SECURED, RANDOM HOUSE proper remained determinedly free-spirited. Bennett still poked his nose into manuscripts and offered opinions; Donald's wisdom was available to all; Bernstein weighed in on legal, financial, or merchandising matters, or when nonfiction piqued his political interests or a major children's author was involved. Jim Silberman recognized the strengths of his editors, but also that each was "odd": Jason Epstein, the law unto himself; Albert Erskine, aloof and old-fashioned; Joe Fox, the patrician gambler hidden behind his fortress of newsprint. One day, Silberman made Fox a proposition: a dime if he'd get rid of the piles fronting his desk. Fox pocketed the coin, tossed out the papers, then grew them back again. Bob Loomis alternately kept eyes down, all work, or up in the clouds, piloting his plane. Lee Wright, nobody's softie, was treated like a man. The "girls" in the boys' club—Nan Talese, Alice Mayhew, a few others—charmed or chafed. Bert Krantz, quite simply, married the job.

In the late 1960s, several of their older authors—John O'Hara, Robert Penn Warren, Jerry Weidman, Jim Michener—continued to be productive, if not always as good as their younger selves, with Michener's contribution to the balance sheet far outstripping them all. Yet it was to younger writers like Truman Capote, Peter Matthiessen, Bill Styron, and Philip Roth that the firm looked for its literary future. Truman, of course, stood apart: it felt like he'd been around forever, and he continued to bask (at times, insufferably) in the triumph of *In Cold Blood*.

Bill Styron loved being in the fold. Although Bobbs-Merrill had published *Lie Down in Darkness* to acclaim in 1951, it wasn't until he arrived at RH with Hiram Haydn that he felt like an *author,* rather than just another young man with a novel under his belt. He was captivated by the aura of that dream of a place, and played along when Bennett beckoned: "Boy writer! Boy writer!" As Styron told a friend, "I am great pals with not only old Ben Cerf but his pals, too: old Arlene Francis and old Buddy Schulberg and old Mossy Hart and swell old Colesy Porter and Dickie Rodgers . . . and I . . . call up old Joe Fox . . . and taunt him about the fun I'm having." Beneath the self-conscious sarcasm, he pinched himself. A writer's working hours are passed alone in silent struggle. Now a door had opened on another world, and he was treated like he belonged there. Bennett prized Bill's brilliance, warmth, and loyalty. Phyllis enjoyed their night-owl gossips. Rose was a published poet, but her easy affection stood in contrast to the chilly reception Bennett got from some literary ladies, and the Styron girls were special.

When *Set This House on Fire,* Styron's first work for RH, was published in 1960, Haydn had left for Atheneum, and Loomis had taken over as editor. Bennett had high hopes, promising that RH would *make* the book a bestseller. Of the 36,000-copy run, a third didn't sell, but that wasn't unusual. The movies didn't bite, nor did the novel get the same gushing notices as *Lie Down in Darkness.* Styron was let down, but told Bennett: "My spirit unbroken . . . all great work is damned so be of good cheer as I am." The book he was working on now—based on the life of Nat Turner, a slave who'd led a revolt in 1831—he'd wanted to begin before *Set This House on Fire.* Haydn had opposed it, thinking it would wound him with the stigma of "historical fiction," a label disdained by arbiters of "serious" literature. Unlike Haydn, Loomis understood this was the book his friend had to write. Styron's paternal grandmother had filled his head with tales of two slave girls whom she'd owned when only a girl herself. Nat Turner had lived and died thirty miles from the Virginia town where Styron grew up, and place always spoke to him.

Published accounts of Turner's life were rare and soon forgotten: a contemporaneous pamphlet made from a "confession" he dictated; a pro-slavery version in a 1900 history book; a mention in a 1943 Marxist text; a reference in Styron's schoolbook. The known facts were these: Turner had begun hearing voices and seeing visions urging him to lead his people out of bondage. Joined by a band of slaves heeding his call, he led the most effective and bloodiest uprising in the antebellum South. Fifty-seven white men, women, and children were killed during forty-eight hours of violence. In the end, he was caught, imprisoned, hanged, and flayed.

That so little was known of Turner, Styron thought, made him an ideal subject for fiction. Writing in the first person, his imagination could conjure his protagonist's mind, heart, and words for a "meditation on history." The book didn't come easily, but he was encouraged by his friend James Baldwin—who'd lived during the winter of 1961 in the Styrons' guesthouse—and of course by Loomis, who from time to time would appear in Roxbury to sit and listen, making suggestions or voicing appreciation as Styron read sections aloud. He also depended on Bennett. In 1962, Styron wanted to part company from his literary agent and told her, "My relationship with my publishers . . . has always been eminently satisfactory. . . . I simply do not need you to get $5000 more out of Bennett Cerf. He is all too happy to give it to me freely."

William Styron

At the end of 1964, he finally brought to the palazzo the first 220 pages. It was an important enough event for Bennett not only to note in his diary, but also to act on: three weeks later, he sold reprint rights for the half-completed book to NAL for $100,000. Impatient to share his excitement, the supreme networker knew how to reach Bill at the White House, where he was attending LBJ's "inaugural do." (Random had published the president's manifesto, *My Hope for America,* at the beginning of the year.) Summoned to the call, Styron was startled to hear who was on the line. All out of breath, Bennett whooped: "I've got great news!" It wasn't just that the amount seemed enormous, and Styron needed the money; he was amazed at the effort that had gone into finding him, and at the exuberance of his publisher. A few months later, Bennett confidently signed Styron's next book—whatever and whenever that would be.

"At long last!" he exhaled eighteen months later, in January 1967, after the full novel was delivered. Styron had dedicated the book to James Terry, an unlettered Southern-born Black man who was quite a presence in the family's life. He'd become caretaker of their Connecticut home; looked after the children when Rose and Bill were gone; and was godfather to their son. When Bennett finished reading, at 4:52 P.M. on a Sunday—he was careful to note the precise time in his diary, as though taking part in making history—he phoned to congratulate Styron on the "superb" work. BOMC seconded the opinion with a $150,000 guaranty. Loomis had solicited blurbs from "Red" Warren, Philip Roth, and others. In late September, Bennett confided to Styron what a thrill it was to be publishing "one of the great novels of the century!"

Producer David Wolper bought movie rights for a record $600,000; lined up Norman Jewison, who'd directed *In the Heat of the Night;* and approached Ossie Davis for the title role. When Davis turned it down, a young actor named James Earl Jones accepted. In October, *The Confessions of Nat Turner* was launched at '21' with ninety luminaries. The first printing was huge—125,000 copies—but even the fact sheet that had circulated in-house recognized that this "magnificent" novel might also carry "controversy." An obscure Black protagonist who'd killed whites had been plucked from history and recalled to life by a white writer with Southern roots. As if that weren't controversial enough, Styron's Nat was obsessed with a young white woman; was indecisive; and was not always heroic. However, Styron, Loomis, Bennett, and others agreed: No matter that aspects were historically debatable or wholly imagined. It was a *novel*.

A front-page piece by Wilfrid Sheed in *The New York Times Book Review* gave the first major critical response. Unfortunately, it picked apart the book as "windy" and "florid," judging it novelistically a failure. Worse, Sheed rejected the "meditation on history" motive, instead looking to the racially charged headlines of the day and finding Styron opportunistic. Thinking Sheed's criticism "outrageous," Bennett was mollified by positive reviews in *Time, Newsweek,* and *The New Yorker,* praising both the book and Styron's ambition and courage. Nevertheless, a drumbeat of reviews in *The Nation, The New Republic,* and elsewhere dissented. Despite the mixed response, *The Confessions of Nat Turner* sold very well, vying with Chaim Potok's *The Chosen* to be the second-biggest fiction bestseller of 1967, and in May 1968, Styron won the Pulitzer Prize. Alas, any pleasure from the award would prove short-lived.

After the nation's long history of racial oppression, Black consciousness had been rising, and the civil rights movement gaining ground. In 1963, Martin Luther King Jr. had shared his dream for a better tomorrow; the next year, LBJ signed the Civil Rights Act into law. But tension had continued to build. Unrest broke out in cities across America in 1967, and Detroit and Newark burned. A month before the Pulitzer announcement, King had been assassinated in Memphis. Although James Baldwin had told *Newsweek* that with *Nat Turner,* Styron had "begun the common history—*ours,*" other Black intellectuals were enraged by the novel. They accused its author of arrogantly, presumptuously co-opting their history and language for his own ends, and misrepresenting it. Hate mail arrived in Styron's mailbox. When speaking, he was heckled. Fear began to overwhelm him; he no longer wanted his kids to go out on their own.

Early one evening, Loomis was at home when the phone rang. Styron said he was at a hotel in the city, and asked if Loomis could come uptown right away, and bring a belt and pair of socks. Rose had traveled down to New York that morning. She had promised to check in with him, but hadn't; hours had dripped by without a call. He'd received a horrible letter a few days earlier, and become convinced that she'd been abducted. He'd driven to the city, to the hotel where Rose was supposed to spend the night, and forgotten to put on a belt and socks. Loomis brought what was needed, and Rose did eventually turn up, but the whirlwind continued.

In Hollywood, a Black Anti-Defamation Association was organized to stop the *Nat Turner* film from being made, and Ossie Davis became its spokesperson. The group's members wanted at the very least a significantly altered portrait of Turner, not the conflicted figure of the book. The film deal collapsed. For a long while, Styron recoiled from public life.

Bennett had predicted that *The Confessions of Nat Turner* would be used in history classes for the next fifty years, but hadn't factored in the tectonic changes of the 1960s. It would be the novels of Toni Morrison—still a textbook editor when Styron's book came out—that would become classroom staples. As publisher, RH came in for collateral criticism, but no one felt embarrassed to be associated with the book. Bennett himself continued to be "extremely proud" of it, and to look on Styron as one of RH's "proudest possessions."

. . .

BACK IN THE '50s, it had been Rose Styron, a reader for her friend George Plimpton's *Paris Review,* who'd come across a few unsolicited stories from a new voice, and recommended that Plimpton publish them. Thus, Philip Roth's *The Conversion of the Jews* had appeared in the spring 1958 issue, followed by more stories and the National Book Award–winning collection *Goodbye, Columbus*. While some saw his work as brilliant dissections of Jewish American life, others accused Roth of airing dirty laundry that made Jews look bad.

The Styrons and Roth had become friends, and when he grew dissatisfied with his book publisher, Houghton Mifflin, they urged him to come to RH. He was a very desirable catch. After Don charmed him over a fine dinner in Rome, Bennett finished the wooing at lunch in New York on the early September day that tall, dark, recognizably Jewish Roth and blonde, all-American Maggie (as Philip described his gentile wife) walked down the gangplank of the SS *France* after their European sojourn. To Roth, Bennett was very much "the impresario," with a charm, ease, and insouciance he coveted. But from the start, it was clear that Philip Roth wouldn't be the easiest of authors; for that matter, he was never the easiest man in the world. For that first RH contract in 1960, the partners agreed to a generous $21,000 advance, but Roth wanted control over more things than most authors—certainly most young ones—got. Bennett, writing to Roth's agent, Candida Donadio, in September, assured her that "every last detail" fulfilled her client's wishes, giving him final approval of jacket, flap copy, even of the advertising campaign.

Several weeks later, Roth gave Bennett three hundred pages of a novel about the crises facing two young Jewish men and their women. "Tremendously moving and magnificently written," was how Bennett found them, questioning only one scene, involving an abortion. He passed them to Bob Loomis—Don and the Styrons had thought he'd be a good match—who wrote Roth that the new work was even better than *Goodbye, Columbus*. In March, Bennett thought four hundred more pages were in places "almost unbearably heartbreaking," and told Roth the novel would be wonderful. Loomis found them "superb." That wasn't what Roth wanted to hear. Worried about certain aspects, he felt that he had to be challenged as well as praised, and informed Bennett that he wanted a different kind of editorial rapport.

He'd be able to meet and choose someone other than Loomis all in good time, Bennett promised, probably hoping that the relationship between the two would improve, but for Roth, the time was now. He wrote to Donald, who got Bennett to snap to attention and pick up the phone. He could try Jason, Joe, or another editor right away: of course, chemistry mattered. Soon Roth chose Fox. He liked his air of "audacity" coupled with "modesty," and the two grew personally as well as professionally close.

Bennett continued to pay attention. He urged Roth to meet Bob Bernstein, who arranged a rare opportunity to speak at sales conference about the novel, now called *Letting Go*. Both Bennett and Bernstein wanted to impress upon the reps that RH had the best of an important new generation of writers; they'd also discovered that Roth could be an enormously entertaining speaker. On June 15, 1962, Bennett wired, "Happy publication day and here's hoping for many more," having already sent a blue leather-bound copy to his author. But Roth kept complaining to the big boss that production and editorial mistakes had made him less than entirely happy.

Responding by expressing deep disappointment at "the little flies in the ointment" that had spoiled "complete pleasure," Bennett was at his most soothing, assuring him that corrections would appear in the next printing. On the day of an impending Roth visit, he went so far as to run downstairs to place copies of *Letting Go* in the palazzo's vitrines himself. It was clear that although still so young, Roth was nothing if not aware of the place he wanted in the pantheon: the competition he feared that season was from Faulkner, Nabokov, and Baldwin. Jean Ennis's publicity department, as well as Bennett, made sure attention didn't lack, but as with Styron's second book, reviews were mixed. Roth's promise was appreciated—the daily *Times* anointed him "probably the most talented novelist under thirty in America"—yet many agreed that the book was dreary, an estimable failure, albeit, as *Time* said, of a quality few could achieve. For all its weightiness, *Letting Go* briefly jumped onto the lower rungs of the bestseller list, outselling *Goodbye, Columbus,* but both author and publisher were disappointed.

There would be another book, but it would be long in the making: life was getting in the way. Roth's brief marriage had imploded. Maggie, to whom he'd dedicated *Letting Go,* now seemed a serial liar and deceitful stranger, whom he'd married when she claimed to be pregnant. She wasn't. Churning beneath the new novel—he'd call it *When She Was Good*—was a desire to understand how she'd become so destructive, tragic, cunning, and seductive enough to have trapped him. Ghostly variations on Maggie would hover at the edges of his fiction for decades. Early in June 1963, when he heard about the matrimonial problems, Bennett called up Horace Manges, who agreed to represent Roth in the divorce. It was summer, and Roth—who earned a living by college teaching—had fled to England. He wrote Fox, "shivering" with contrition when recalling some of his recent behavior. "I did . . . say an awful thing to you Joe," he admitted. The divorce negotiations were excruciating. Maggie claimed the right to a third of his ongoing income, as well as to furniture and Roth's *books;* and she insisted on being the beneficiary of his will.

"Absolutely monstrous," Fox sympathized. Just as Faulkner and O'Neill had so often called upon Saxe to do personal commissions, Roth turned to his editor. In time, Fox would lend him thousands of dollars. But Maggie, too, applied to Fox as a friend, placing him in a difficult position. She wondered if he might help her get work from RH that she could do from home.

When Fox mentioned it to Roth, Roth begged a favor: Could Fox send Maggie a letter innocently inquiring if she'd be interested in a *full-time* job at RH? Whatever she responded, it could help make the case that Roth didn't have to pay her so much.

They both knew what he was asking.

"I'm sorry, but my conscience just won't allow me," Fox replied. "I will do anything in the world I can to help you, save [for] this."

In the fall, Roth returned to America to teach. To welcome him back, Fox and Donadio organized a party at her apartment, with Bennett footing the bill. Roth would remember the warmth and kindness that his publisher showed during this stressful time, the invitations to the dazzling townhouse dinners and the occasional weekend forays to Mt. Kisco. So unlike his publisher in many ways, Roth did resemble him in at least one: he wanted to be *known*.

When She Was Good came out in March 1967. The $102,000 advance said a lot about Roth's opinion of himself and his desire for financial security—he wasn't yet divorced, but the legal separation did give Maggie much of his money—as well as about Bennett's belief in him: it was a huge leap from the $21,000 for *Letting Go*. Donadio also negotiated a rare paperback split in Roth's favor: he'd receive two-thirds, RH one-third, of the proceeds from any reprint sale, not the usual fifty-fifty. Like many authors faced with the high tax rates of the day, he'd agreed to let RH hold his money and pay him small set sums to keep what he owed the IRS down. Now, advised by a sharp lawyer, he demanded the firm pay him interest on what it held.

Bennett had his limits. Roth had better understand that they were publishers and not bankers; RH wouldn't pay interest "*under any circumstances*." As Donadio no doubt knew, that money was lifeblood to a publisher. Even more alarming, what Roth had asked would have put RH in legal jeopardy. If a publisher paid out more than the exact sum called for in one author's contract—and paying interest would do that—the IRS could disallow such clauses in *all* authors' contracts. The only legal alternative would be to terminate the agreement and sign a new one, with a larger set sum—on which Roth would have to pay more tax.

He backed down.

And yet, despite getting most of what he wanted, Roth seethed with frustration and vulnerability: so much was riding on the book, yet he wasn't in charge. He repeatedly asked about advertising, copy, jacket—everything—to the point where Fox had to make "heroic efforts" to shield colleagues from the calls. There was also the matter of the first printing. Roth had counted on 25,000 copies; Fox said others figured a more conservative 15,000, to start.

"Stupid sons of bitches don't know what they are holding," Roth fumed to him, and as he'd done five years earlier, he took the case to Don and Bennett, letting loose to Donadio in a single-spaced, two-and-a-half-page typed litany that she shared with his publishers. He'd grown disenchanted with Fox. It was his editor who wanted the smaller run; Bennett had earlier agreed to 25,000. Fox should have been on top of the advertising department, but ads had been taken in literary magazines instead of—rather than in addition to—the *Times*. Is this how RH advertised Capote or Styron? They'd better realize he'd scrutinize what they did for *Nat Turner*. Instructing Donadio to tell them he didn't "give a good shit" what others contributed to RH's bottom line, *his* concern was "stature": his books had to get "the big treatment," period.

Immediate damage control was needed. Fox and Bennett met with

Donadio, and Fox wrote an apology. He'd been "hurt" by Roth's letter, then "horrified," now felt "numb." He'd try to do better in every way. Roth could measure his distress: it had pushed Fox into therapy.

Mental and emotional fallout from the experience with Maggie had battered Roth's confidence as a writer. Allowing that he'd chosen Fox for the very qualities he now complained about, Roth said he was beyond "proving" himself, and a house had to be fully committed to go with him. Referring to a "subtle" conflict between him and his editor, he declared, "its future is the future." Fox was puzzled, not understanding what Roth meant. He would soon find out.

Roth had preceded his editor onto the analyst's couch years before, and writing *When She Was Good* served as a kind of "adjunct." Psychoanalysis sent him back to his Jewish roots, explored so fruitfully in *Goodbye, Columbus*. Opening up closed pathways enabled him—while laboring over *When She Was Good*—also to bring experiments of another sort to the page: stories, a play, infused with a what-the-hell energy, the kind he unleashed in riffs to friends.

Two other events liberated him. The first, Roth would always associate with the book party for *Nat Turner.* He felt unwell that night; his analyst said the cause was envy at Styron's star treatment. It soon transpired that the pain was totally physical: his appendix was about to burst. Roth very nearly died, and surviving that brush with mortality made him view life differently. The second occurred in 1968: Maggie was killed in a car crash. He still wasn't divorced—never would be—but the torture had ended.

At the same time, his writing experiments had coalesced around a character named Alex Portnoy. In April 1967, a month after *When She Was Good* was published, a story, "A Jewish Patient Begins His Analysis," in which Alex spilled all to a shrink, appeared in *Esquire,* generating a lot more excitement than Roth's novel. Another Alex story, "Whacking Off," in *Partisan Review,* was "instantly notorious." Two others appeared in *New American Review.* Roth saw Bennett that September to discuss plans. These tales of a protagonist pushed to extremes, trying to escape the confines of family and culture, were controversial, even more so than *Goodbye, Columbus*. They were also indelible. By mid-May 1968, *Time* was calling Roth's work "the most brilliant . . . radical humor in years."

Relations between author and editor seemed to have been patched up—sort of—but underneath, discontent ate at the bond. In January,

Philip Roth

Fox sent a letter; Roth's reply ended sourly, noting Fox had misspelled his name: "Philip with two l's. Come on, baby."

Fox exploded when he read it, scrawling at the bottom of Roth's note: "As to the 2 l's, I have a new secretary who didn't know any better. . . . This is childish! Why the fuck should I justify myself to you? . . . Go screw yourself, *baby!*"

Of course, Roth would never see it. Instead, Fox swallowed hard and went back to work. At the end of May, he sent a memo to Bennett, Bernstein, Ennis, and a few others, announcing an addition to the list: a novel, *Portnoy's Complaint,* of which the four magazine stories formed the major part. The rest would arrive in a week, and publication occur early in 1969. The advance would be "astronomical and worth every penny."

Fox knew Roth wanted $250,000, but was blindsided by a stipulation Roth made less than a fortnight later: Fox had to go. He would no longer be Roth's editor.

Business was business: if that was what Roth wanted, Bennett would have no option but to comply. What Fox could not understand was *how* he'd been told; the news came not from Roth, but via Donadio. "I'm sorry, for both our sakes, that you did not feel able to tell me yourself," was all he could write under the circumstances.

Roth quickly countered: he was "able" but "didn't want" to break the news personally. His confidence in their professional relationship was shot. He had to do what was "best" for him; if the collateral damage was a shattered friendship, so be it. Four years earlier, he'd kidded Fox that what he really needed was a Jewish editor, and Fox had wondered if Roth was only half joking. Now Jason Epstein would take over. Bennett met with Donadio to finalize the deal, and the next day was closeted with Roth and Jason, working through strategy for the paperback sale. In the end, *Portnoy's Complaint* was sold to Bantam for $350,000—the most they'd ever paid for a book. A few months earlier, Roth had repaid the outstanding money he owed Fox. The loan had been made in a different time, another life.

All of RH was ecstatic at the coup of getting the new book. "Roth's masterpiece," the in-house fact sheet anointed it, calling Alexander Portnoy "the Huck Finn of Newark." Echoing *Time*'s take on the excerpts, it described the work as "the most brilliant comic novel in years," but also an "unmistakably human cry of anguish," where "unappeasable sexuality" warred with the "iron grip" of a Jewish childhood and traditional morality.

In a February 1969 feature headlined "A Wild Blue Shocker and the American Novel of the Sixties," *Life* magazine hailed publication as "a major cultural event." Portnoy, "a savior and scapegoat," is "at the Christological age of 33 to take upon himself all the sins of sexually obsessed modern man and expiate them in a tragicomic crucifixion."

The excerpts and articles generated unstoppable momentum: *Portnoy* would have sold itself. RH's job was to distribute far and wide; to ensure that printers kept pace and all orders were filled; and to sell even more. It was also, if humanly possible, to draw a line between publicizing and sensationalizing. That job fell to Ennis, who had to try to separate Philip Roth, the man and author, from arch masturbator Alex Portnoy; to preserve a sense of the book as work of art and its author as artist. An incident involving Jacqueline Susann showed how hard that could be. Susann had published another novel, *The Love Machine,* that vied with *Portnoy* to be number one. Always the canny self-promoter, she went on *The Tonight Show* to flog her book. Telling Johnny Carson that she'd like to meet Roth, Susann added, "But I wouldn't want to shake his hand." Instantly, the put-down was notorious and ubiquitous.

RH received an avalanche of condemnation in the mail: "Disgusting!" "A disgrace!" "How dare you publish such filth!" "Never going to buy another Random House book again!" Letters accused Roth and the firm of "group defamation." The editors of *The New York Times* decried a decline in "standards of public decency" in the arts, in an editorial titled "Beyond the (Garbage) Pale," reserving special scorn for an unnamed but clearly identifiable bestseller. No matter that the paper's own critic had judged Roth's novel brilliant.

Like Styron, Roth had courted controversy and wasn't prepared for the actual fallout. That so many people thought he was Portnoy horrified him. As with Styron, the only option, at least for a while, was to withdraw from view. By the beginning of March, Jason wrote him that there were 450,000 copies in print. The Doubleday bookstore on Fifty-Seventh Street was averaging a copy sold every five minutes. A couple days later, it was Bennett's turn. He wrote Roth that RH had never experienced anything like it, and he didn't think any other publisher had, either, adding: "If you can find time to phone . . . I'd love just to say 'hello.' " He was awestruck, that much was obvious, but Bennett's thoughts about the novel itself were less clear. He'd read the excerpts, and after signing the contract in June 1968, quickly perused the manuscript. Unusually, he gave no reaction. He read the book a second time on publication—that, too, was unusual—and beyond mentioning the rereading, again left no opinion in his diary. Was it because even a secular, somewhat ambivalent Jew could feel uneasy about the portrayal of "Jewishness"?

Most people didn't realize Bennett was Jewish, nor was there anything overtly Jewish about RH, and he seemed satisfied with both situations. Pride in his heritage hadn't really awakened until that stay in Palestine when he was already a man of thirty-six. After World War II and Israel's founding, that feeling grew, and in 1965, when he'd briefly journeyed there again, he signed Jerusalem mayor Teddy Kollek for a book. After the 1967 Arab-Israeli War, he signed Moshe Dayan and Abba Eban for two more. So it was possible that "Jewishness" was a factor.

Or perhaps he was squeamish about *Portnoy*'s sex. At the start of the decade, in a talk on publishing before a room full of stock analysts, he'd said: "I believe that the public has had its fill of raw, oversexed books. . . . People today want cleaner stories . . . that show American life in a better light than did those so-called realistic novels . . . overpopulated with criminals, perverts, degenerates, and angry young men looking backwards, forwards and sideways."

Yet Bennett had fought to free *Ulysses* and been willing to take on *Lolita*. He was so proud of publishing John O'Hara. On the other hand, he'd lobbied against *Deer Park* and wouldn't help Barney Rosset with *Lady Chatterley*. Chris Cerf picked up hints from his dad that he was "a little nervous" about how "graphic" *Portnoy* was, but then he'd have that twinkle in his eye, so it was impossible to know what he really thought.

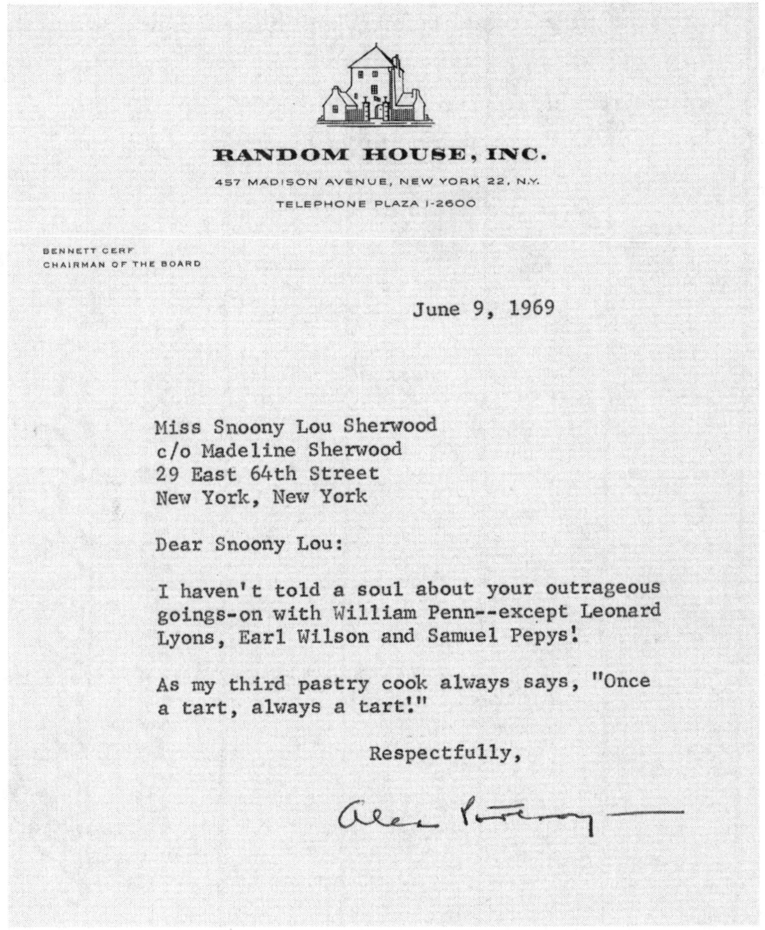

RANDOM HOUSE, INC.
457 MADISON AVENUE, NEW YORK 22, N.Y.
TELEPHONE PLAZA 1-2600

BENNETT CERF
CHAIRMAN OF THE BOARD

June 9, 1969

Miss Snoony Lou Sherwood
c/o Madeline Sherwood
29 East 64th Street
New York, New York

Dear Snoony Lou:

I haven't told a soul about your outrageous goings-on with William Penn--except Leonard Lyons, Earl Wilson and Samuel Pepys!

As my third pastry cook always says, "Once a tart, always a tart!"

Respectfully,

Bennett's own joking variation on
a *Portnoy* theme with good friend Madeline Sherwood

Michael Frith sensed a subterranean "unease" in the firm more generally, existing in tandem with all that proud excitement. Bob Bernstein's son Peter was aware of it in his father. Rebellion was ascendant in the 1960s for sure, but the shadow of the '50s hadn't vanished into nothingness. It was possible to feel both, and Bennett, unlike his author, did have to face the public. He wrote Roth after speaking to over a thousand Jewish ladies at a Pittsburgh synagogue. Each question was on *Portnoy:* "You would have laughed yourself sick at a couple [of them]."

A year later, when the novel was conspicuously ignored by the National Book Awards for the fiction prize—not even named as a finalist—Bennett felt the injustice keenly. He publicly refused to attend the ceremony, and ran a half-page ad for *Portnoy* in the *Times* on awards day. Again, Roth had cause to appreciate his publisher. Later, when he was traveling in Asia and came across a pirated Taiwanese paperback of *Portnoy,* he took the trouble to send it to RH, with an inscription: "To Bennett, the best publisher any man could have outside of Taiwan."

Chapter 56

Palace to Tower Block

WHILE NAT TURNER AND ALEX PORTNOY WERE EXPLODING ONTO the scene, demanding Bennett's attention, much else around him was changing and challenging the world he'd known. At the National Book Awards in March 1968, he listened as poetry winner Robert Bly used his speech to protest the Vietnam War, counseling draft resistance and donating his prize money to the anti-war movement. After an impassioned speech about inequality, nonfiction winner Jonathan Kozol promised *his* check to a ghetto leader. Not everyone approved. Cass Canfield—Bly's publisher—declared to a *New York Post* reporter that authors should focus on literature. Bennett disagreed. Kozol was electrifying, and anything to protest the war was legitimate. At a time of violence and crisis, he asked, "How can you avoid facing up? There is no ivory tower anymore."

He was appalled by the assassinations of Martin Luther King Jr. and Robert F. Kennedy, horrified by the "disgraceful" behavior of Chicago's police at the Democratic National Convention, and disheartened when that "schmo" Richard Nixon was elected president. He and Phyllis worked hard on behalf of their friend John Lindsay as the mayor struggled to deal with an increasingly troubled metropolis. Bennett tried to understand the unrest as he read *Black Power: The Politics of Liberation,* by SNCC founder Stokely Carmichael, and Black Panther leader Eldridge Cleaver's *Post-Prison Writings and Speeches,* both published by RH. "Terrifying" was his one-word reaction to Cleaver. Things had changed in the politics of his publishing life as well. However much he might have imagined doing business with David Sarnoff, his was but one voice at a long board table, where "yes" was the operative answer not only to the old overlord puffing on his big cigar, but to Bobby, who'd inherited the kingdom. Now, two years into the RCA era, the General was suddenly stricken with shingles, precursor to a catastrophic infection that devastated his nervous system, eliminating any counterweight to his son.

While his father had anchored the company in communications and electronics, the son was convinced that the future lay in diversification. Random kept awkward company with Hertz Rental Cars, Banquet Foods, Coronet Carpets, Arnold Palmer Enterprises, and other siblings often trailing debt. Since these divisions shared so little in common, economies of scale were nearly impossible. RCA's battle to achieve dominance in computers over IBM also generated losses. RH, holding funds for its authors, was that rare division with money in the bank.

Bennett had begun to feel lost and neglected—"sometimes I wonder if they know that they own us," he'd grumble—or bored by "dull as hell" proceedings that had nothing to do with RH. How to speak of frozen chicken dinners and the Modern Library in the same breath? He, Bernstein, and others at RH saw Sarnoff as totally ineffective, and Bobby didn't care for Bennett, either. At an RCA annual meeting in Indianapolis, Bobby expected to be the center of attention, but Bennett came with a local columnist in tow, and coverage was all about *him*.

After a lifetime closely monitoring his investments, he watched as RCA stock, under Bobby's leadership, went south. "From 65 to 47 in three months!" he groaned in February 1968. A year later, "RCA, that dog," was down to $43.875. By January 1970, the number furiously scribbled in Bennett's diary was "33½." He'd exchanged the old anxiety about RH being publicly traded for worry about shares and options his people now held in RCA. They'd gambled on a deal that he had brokered, using money they could ill afford to lose. Some, like Bernstein, were shrewd, made early gains, sold quickly; others held on and lost out. RCA mostly didn't try to interfere editorially, but Bennett could see no sense in the requisition forms in triplicate and other time-wasting bureaucracy; the insistence on five-year plans when publishing didn't lend itself to long-term projections; the accounting sleights-of-hand involving the timing of paper purchasing that caused headaches for the production department. RCA at one point even wanted to find a way to put a part number on every book.

There was extra cause for Bennett to mull over the changes he'd unleashed: Columbia was recording reminiscences from noteworthy alumni, and had invited him to tell the story of his life. In September 1967, it had dispatched a young woman, Robbin Hawkins, to Sixty-

Second Street, to prompt his memories. Closeted with Hawkins in his study, he didn't need much encouragement to talk. She was bright and attractive, although Phyllis's well-timed interruptions put paid to other impulses Hawkins felt sure he had. There was also another incentive for making the tapes: for years, publishing friends had urged him to write his memoirs, but he'd always been too busy living. Now he might manage to write, with the oral history as framework. Meeting with Hawkins twenty-one times, he unspooled adventures, triumphs, and jokes, until in one of the later sessions he grew more reflective. After conjuring "great days" when he, Don, and Bob Haas ran everything, Bennett shifted to the present: "You start getting bigger and you sacrifice many of those joys. . . . [Bigness is] the American dream, but I'm not certain it's a good one." What Donald had warned about during the Second World War had come to pass.

With his usual grace, Don seemed to accept the consequences of changes he'd never wanted, and be content playing the wise guru. Yet occasionally, when a staff member hurried by his office and glanced at him unawares, he was staring into space. Tony Wimpfheimer wondered if his stepfather wasn't a little depressed. Donald, so closed about his own feelings, such a patient listener, would once in a while blow up. The two book boys were seeing even less of each other. Lunches were rare, and evening socializing, already infrequent, rarer still. After almost fifty years, Bennett's diary now at times noted meetings with "Don K." or "Donald Klopfer," instead of plain "Don." In everyday matters, he saw much more of Bob Bernstein.

Bernstein freely acknowledged that he owed his good fortune to Bennett, Don, and Lew, but especially to Bennett, the man who'd sought him out and placed him at the top. He also knew that he was no Bennett Cerf. Driven, yes, but Bernstein was also shy and could be awkward or cool to the point of brusqueness. He saw his job as growing revenues, as well as keeping people from quitting and keeping RCA out of their hair. Asserting his own primacy meant, at times, ignoring his mentor. Bennett began to resent decisions Bob made without consulting him; giving up power was hard. Don saw that Bennett didn't want to do the day-to-day work of running the firm—now impossible anyway—yet kept dashing into Bob's office, "making a goddamn nuisance of himself." Chris Cerf, upset at changes happening to a place he'd loved his whole life, composed an eight-page letter in October 1968 lamenting a lack of "esprit de corps" and a sense that "big business" was taking over. He sent it to Bob Bernstein.

. . .

THE CENTER SEEMED TO shift: Bennett was spending more and more time being a celebrity. Claudette Colbert's husband had died, and she stayed at Sixty-Second Street for thirty-one weeks straight. Cousin Ginger visited on a regular basis, ten days at a time. The Cerfs jetted out to meet Francis Albert at the Fontainebleau and in Palm Springs more often.

What's My Line? returned, taped for daytime viewing, syndicated rather than nationally broadcast. It didn't have the old, live flair or the same cast, yet he was delighted to spend whole afternoons making multiple episodes, and be back in front of a camera, any camera. He was also pleased when invited for nighttime chitchat with Johnny Carson, Dick Cavett, or David Frost, and to add Johnny to his and Phyllis's circle. Persuaded by an interesting young producer named Roger Ailes, he occasionally ventured to Philadelphia to co-host Mike Douglas's daytime talk-and-variety show. Bennett's instincts, so good at spotting up-and-comers, recognized one in Ailes. Their meetings brought more invitations to appear on the show, and gave Ailes an influential New York connection. (Decades later, it was Ailes who would invent Fox News.)

On May 25, 1968, Bennett turned seventy. He didn't like the betrayals inflicted by age: liver spots speckling his hands, memory slips involving names and spelling, handwriting a bit trembly. Doing what he could with what remained of his hair, he carefully greased, combed, and tinted the gray strands a squirrelly red-brown. He'd always run so hard and lived so fully that now he admitted, "I'll probably never live to be eighty. If I do, it will be a miracle!"

Twice a year, for almost two decades, he'd lunched with RH's powerful neighbor Francis Cardinal Spellman, who ruled over New York's Roman Catholic archdiocese from administrative offices in the central and southern flanks of the palazzo. Often considered *the* most powerful New York cardinal ever, Spellman had backed Joseph McCarthy's witch hunt, and was extremely conservative in matters of free expression. When the two met, they talked about baseball and stocks—safe shared passions; books were a different matter. Among his complaints, Spellman often singled out the "gamier" aspects of John O'Hara's fiction.

"He's one of your own boys," Bennett had finally told him after one

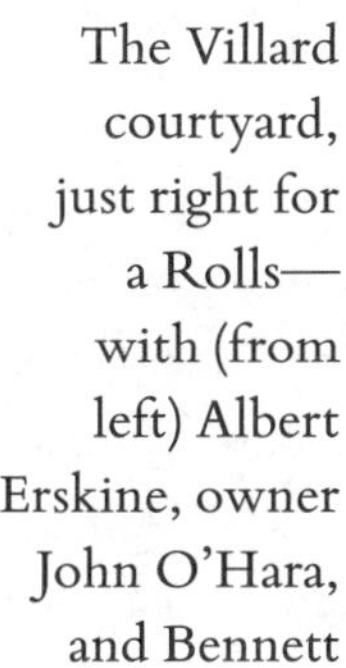

The Villard courtyard, just right for a Rolls—with (from left) Albert Erskine, owner John O'Hara, and Bennett

grumble too many. High time his Catholic author spoke up for himself. And so, on a bright April morning, O'Hara nosed his gleaming Rolls-Royce into the courtyard and stopped at the empty spot reserved for his visit. More than any mere car nearby, the stately Roller seemed at home. A head taller than the prelate and in full-bellied Savile Row three-piece, O'Hara bent low to kiss Spellman's ring, handed over a donation for the cardinal's favorite charity, and behaved impeccably.

On one topic, Bennett and His Eminence were in perfect accord: a shared love of the palazzo. Its beauty and profile within the cityscape fed both their considerable egos. Random's move into the north wing in 1946 predated by two years the Church's arrival in the more ornate south and central sections, but Bennett never forgot it was the Church that had helped him find RH a home. In the years since, developers had sniffed around like hungry dogs, dreaming of what they could do with this perfect location. Bennett occasionally met but more often rebuffed them, even as he joked of what they might offer. In 1955, after less than a decade there, he'd admitted that RH was already "hopelessly" overcrowded, and would be until the "happy day, perchance, when a [developer] offers . . . the Archdiocese and ourselves such a fabulous sum . . . we will have to conquer our edifice complex and move!" Instead, RH staff spilled into five other addresses—several on Madison Avenue, as well as south on Forty-Second Street, and northwest near Columbus Circle—causing chronic inefficiencies. Still, Bennett resisted leaving.

Four months into the RCA era, in the summer of 1966, had come a proposal from a commercial realty firm to move RH to a new building going up on Park Avenue. The developers had also approached the cardinal about the Church taking RH's wing, and word got around. The next summer, Bennett felt obliged to declare publicly that he and Spellman had preserved the mansions and weren't going anywhere, yet recognized that developers would probably tear down the complex "as soon as we're dead," and put up "one of those ugly . . . glass skyscrapers." However, that September, Bernstein made a major announcement: nearly all of RH's New York operations would be centralized in a black-aluminum and green-glass forty-story tower going up three avenues to the east, on the corner of Third Avenue and Fiftieth Street. The firm would take a twenty-five-year lease, its New York staff ranging over fourteen floors of what would be called the Random House Building. An exception was being made for the top executives and trade editors of the RH imprint; they'd remain in the palazzo so "closely identified" with the firm.

Yet a future there was far from certain. Postwar New York's prevailing notion of urban renewal, as the sad demise of the city's magnificent Pennsylvania Station—designed by the same architects as the palazzo—had shown two years earlier, was about demolition, development, and raking in dough. True, local activists like Jason's author Jane Jacobs were fighting back, and the city had established a Landmarks Preservation Commission, but it was all very new, and the laws rather weak. Cardinal Spellman died on December 2, 1967, only a couple months after RH had announced its intention to keep its part of the palazzo. Now Bennett felt very much "a loner," and two days later, his fears were borne out: "Agreed reluctantly to sell . . . 457 Madison within 2 years to combine entire operation at our . . . new building." The decision hadn't been his to make; it was his to go along with, and when speaking about it to authors, he was "rueful."

He and Don had been spending so little dedicated time together, but that day, they lunched. Tony Wimpfheimer was put in charge of the move; it would require more than a year, with Random's editors and executives going last. As for the fate of the palazzo, Bennett tried to hedge. Conceding to the press that it might well fall victim "to what we laughingly call progress," he said that RH "will *probably* sell," rather than admit to the certainty that it would.

The new address, 825 Third Avenue, was one to which little prestige accrued. From the early part of the century until the mid-1950s, Third

Avenue had been dominated by an elevated rail line, with trains screeching and clattering along its hulking superstructure day and night. When pressure to capitalize on the land proved too great, the entire "El" architecture was torn down, and big new buildings began to rise up. Yet in the minds of many New Yorkers, the location remained déclassé. Before he'd countenance going there, Bennett insisted on an address change: the building would be known by its cross street, "201 East 50th Street," rather than the more down-market 825 Third Avenue.

With the move, sensitivities awakened that had hardly factored in before. Something about a tower implies hierarchy, and people began to ask themselves what office size and placement would signify, and how best to jockey for better position. Even Bennett and Phyllis were not above it all. Phyllis had had the legs shortened on much of her furniture, to accommodate the lower ceilings in her attic offices. She felt unhappy about the standardized furniture she would now have to order, and also railed at her assistant being one in a row of secretaries. She insisted that Elma have an enclosure separating her from the rest.

In the palazzo, Bennett had prowled up and down from the most comfortably appointed, central room in the place. When Bernstein first became president, there had been no notion of Bennett ceding his quarters; the younger man moved into space that occupied the same footprint, but one floor higher. Power was centered there, but RH's heart remained below, while its soul stayed in Donald's green den. In the new tower, Bernstein would run the firm from "a most fantastic office," as one dazzled staffer described it: a separate suite occupied by the CEO and his key aide, Anne Johnson. It was "four times the size of Mr. Cerf's."

To make the move less painful, Wimpfheimer's team arranged for most of Bennett's things to be transported over a weekend. Before he took up residence at 201 East Fiftieth Street on the last day of June 1969, son Chris snapped a photograph in his father's old lair, where Bennett mugged for the camera in typical fashion. Held aloft and "carried out" by a quartet—Don and young editor John J. Simon, with RH marketer Bennett Sims and a visiting Roger Ailes assisting—he frowned dramatically, raising a fist in protest. Goodbye, Juliet balcony and private bathroom; goodbye, rosettes and ribbons in plaster and wood; goodbye, courtyard. No longer could Phyllis spy the Empire State Building's needle from her attic. The days of crowding into Bennett's office to watch a space launch or the World Series, and his taking Miss America all around

Bennett at center being carried out by (from left) John J. Simon, Bennett Sims, Donald, and Roger Ailes

the house, were gone. For Bill Styron, visiting the tower block would be akin to going to an insurance agency or law firm, "no personality whatsoever, no charm. It was utterly soulless." Bennett wasn't happy about having to wait for the elevator in the new place. Sure, his door had usually been open, but he'd also liked the palazzo's privacy, the ability to dash about, come and go, use the back stairs as he pleased. Phyllis's eyes and ears were ever on alert, and suddenly she seemed around him much more, often "being difficult."

That summer after the move, a storm blew up. New York is a windy city, and the tower seemed to sway with big gusts. Some staff felt panicky. Knopf's Judith Jones never forgot how Bennett unexpectedly appeared in the hall, reassuring them that the building was engineered that way for safety. He was making his rounds, feeling needed; old habits are hard to shake off. One morning during those early weeks, Michael Frith strode into the new three-story lobby and couldn't help thinking back to how he used to feel on entering the palazzo, when he'd open the massive door and see a warm prismatic light casting rainbows on the white marble. At Fiftieth Street, he was greeted by a huge modern blow-up of Rockwell Kent's RH logo, rendered in cool chrome. That day, under the blow-up with his back to the entrance, stood Bennett.

Thinking that his best friend's dad must be musing on all that he'd built during the past forty-five years, Frith approached, but stopped short when he got within earshot. Bennett was talking to himself. A string of swear words, then: "This is the only goddamn company to go from the major leagues to the bush leagues overnight, on purpose."

Chapter 57

Famous and Fading

IN MID-DECEMBER 1969, ONE OF BOB GOTTLIEB'S FAVORITE WRITERS, Jessica Mitford, paid Bennett a visit. Jessica, the sister of Donald's former author Nancy (who'd parted from RH on less than amicable terms), was another of the six aristocratic Mitford girls whose very public lives hardly typified those to the English manor born. Jessica's idiosyncrasies had included embracing Communism, running away to America, taking a leftist Jewish lawyer as second husband, and becoming a muckraking journalist. She was forty-seven in 1963 when Bob Gottlieb, at S&S, published *The American Way of Death,* her sharp—and bestselling—dive into the worst practices of the funeral industry. Now Oakland-based Jessica was delving into a mail-order writing school that Bennett had been associated with for years. Armed with research and other interviews—she'd saved him for last—she faced Bennett and began, in her plummy voice, to pepper him with thirty well-prepared questions. "Jessica Mitford out to crucify the Famous Writers School," he confided to his diary. What Bennett didn't know was how much damage might accrue to *him*.

The Famous Writers School (FWS) was an offshoot of the Famous Artists School (FAS), founded in 1947 by Albert Dorne, an ex-prizefighter and well-known commercial illustrator, to peddle mail-order art lessons. Dorne had recruited other high-profile artists—including Norman Rockwell and Stuart Davis—to lend their names and faces as "Guiding Faculty," and hired lesser mortals for the daily to-and-fro of corresponding with students about their art. So successful was FAS that Dorne and partners envisaged a similar enterprise for aspiring writers. Early in 1958, Mike Breslauer—an FAS founder and college friend of Bennett's—asked him to lunch with the school's director, Gordon Carroll, to hear plans for the Famous Writers School. Inviting him to be a founding member of the Guiding Faculty, they said that, like others, he'd be rewarded with a small percentage of the income from enrollment fees, as well as shares in the company.

In 1957, a three-year FAS course had cost a student $418; each Guiding Artist had received $8,000 in compensation, and Carroll expected that number to rise to $10,000 (about $114,000 today). He promised that a Guiding Writer's income would soon "equal or exceed" that of his artist brethren. In exchange, Bennett would permit his name and face to feature in FWS ads, help recruit faculty, contribute a short chapter about the mechanics of publishing to a home-study text the school would compile, and visit the headquarters in Westport, Connecticut, for morale-boosting chats with the staff instructors who actually dealt with students by mail.

The idea sounded great, but took longer than expected to gel. Not every famous writer whom Carroll approached shared Bennett's enthusiasm. (One skeptic, MacKinlay Kantor, a former RH author, likened it to joining a "little circle of confidence men.") Almost two years passed before a full cohort of Guiding Writers was assembled; when they were, they celebrated together at '21.' Along with Bennett were the TV writer Rod Serling, whose *Twilight Zone* had just debuted; Rudolf Flesch, author of *Why Johnny Can't Read;* novelist Faith Baldwin; Pulitzer Prize–winning historian Bruce Catton; English professor and TV host Bergen Evans; RH mystery writer Mignon Eberhart, "America's answer to Agatha Christie" (Bennett recruited her); and five others. Yet Bennett was singled out to pose with Dorne and Carroll for publicity shots.

FWS sent a long letter to prospective students, stating that the Guiding Faculty would "actively supervise" the program and had created the free sixteen-page test that would determine if they had the necessary talent. "If you want success, learn from successful people," it urged. Almost immediately, FWS took off. Students dreamed of improving their lives or getting rich quick through the latent talent the school assured them they had. (Fully 90 percent of respondents received such assurances after sending back tests.) Dorne wanted to add a photography school and grow in other ways, so in September 1961, the company used an initial public offering to raise capital. The stock, listed as FAS, boomed. Bennett followed it closely in his diary.

Years passed; both Breslauer and Dorne died. By 1969, the Famous Writers School had become a phenomenon, with 65,000 enrolled students and an 800-strong sales force. However, only fifty-five instructors were required to process student work, since the dropout rate was about 90 percent. The course price had risen to $785 ($900 on the popular installment plan), and even dropouts had to pay in full. Total revenue for the Famous Schools had reached $48 million (about $426 million today); Bennett's annual cut was $15,000 (about $133,000 today).

The inaugural Guiding Faculty of the Famous Writers School

He loved seeing his face gaze back from FWS advertisements. Any American opening a Sunday paper or major magazine couldn't miss them, the Famous Writers grouped around a table like prosperous Dutch burghers in an old master painting, sober, well-heeled, professional, yet welcoming and familiar. "Do you have a restless urge to write?" a smiling Bennett asked in one widely circulated ad. Another had him declaring, "If you want to write, my colleagues and I would like to test your writing aptitude." His priceless promotional value was easily engaged, as when he happily taped an FWS thirteen-week radio series, *Let's Talk About Writers,* involving sixty-five four-minute Monday-to-Friday daily "visits" to five hundred syndicated stations. The scripts were devised by a young would-be novelist named Mary Higgins Clark.

. . .

IT WAS JESSICA MITFORD's lawyer husband who'd drawn her attention to the FWS. A foreign-born widow, who'd signed up on the installment plan and soon regretted it, had come to him as a client. FWS had refused to cancel her contract and return the deposit until he sent a stiff letter, copied to the California Consumer Frauds Division, as well as to Bennett. Mitford also read a new book, *Writing Rackets,* where the FWS featured prominently. The morning she came by, Bennett welcomed her with his usual cordiality, and proceeded to describe his role. He visited Westport HQ just once or twice a year, often bringing along an editor like Jim Silberman or Bob Loomis to talk to the staff. (Instructors eagerly followed up by sending their own manuscripts; RH editors weren't nearly so eager to receive them.) Bennett stressed that professors, lawyers, businesspeople also took the course, not to become authors, but to learn to write intelligibly. At times, he had to "raise hell" about advertising overreach, but took it for granted that FWS executives were honest—he liked them—and he knew nothing about the business arrangements. "I can't put that too strongly." The instructors were "very good people," well paid, and FWS ran "a happy shop."

How many books by its students had RH published? Mitford asked.

"Oh now Jessica, you're pulling my leg," the answer tumbled out. "You don't think a sophisticated person, capable of writing a book, would take a mail-order writing course?"

The game of thirty questions continued: Wasn't the sales method a bit dubious?

Mail order had deficiencies, he conceded, its crux a hard pitch, but that was the case with lots of enterprises. RH was publishing *Up the Organization,* an exposé of big business. "Only the very gullible would take a mail-order writing course," he repeated. "*Please* don't quote me!"

Their little chat now almost done, Mitford saw no reason to hold back, and took a parting shot: How could he lend his name to this "fraudulent" enterprise?

With the broad grin came the signature answer given to so many questioners over so many years: "Frankly, I'm an awful ham." He added that he loved seeing his name in the papers.

The feature had been commissioned by the West Coast editor of *The Atlantic,* but Mitford was soon informed that the big guns in Boston were killing it: the FWS had spent thousands on advertising in the magazine. She contacted *McCall's,* where an editor was enthusiastic. Her high spirits restored, Mitford sent them the article, and took a photocopy to show a friend (almost certainly Gottlieb) at Knopf. Bennett, whose office in the new building was on the twelfth floor, happened to make an appearance on the twenty-first—the Knopf floor—just as she was visiting. Mitford was doubly taken aback, first to see him there, then to find him genial as ever, joking to her: "Ah! There is the arch-villain. I hope you're not going to murder us!"

Bennett had a *McCall's* connection of his own: the former *Life* columnist Shana Alexander had recently arrived there as editor-in-chief, and she was the journalist he'd tried to pair with Sinatra for his autobiography. Although the deal with Frank had fallen through, Bennett and Alexander had seen each other often these past few years, and the link went back further. He'd dated her mother, Cecelia, when they were young, and after his divorce from Sylvia, the two got reacquainted. Shana was a teenager then, and Bennett went to her parents' apartment a couple times a week for about a year, ostensibly to take Shana and her sister bowling. But thirty years on, in a book he inscribed to her, he wrote: "For Cecelia's lovely daughter who, if memory serves, may possibly be my own."

Suddenly, over her editor's objections, Alexander rejected the FWS feature as "not very good." At the same time, she paid Mitford an unusually high "kill" fee—the same amount she'd have received had *McCall's* published the piece. Surmising that Bennett was behind the rejection, Mitford felt like "slaughtering" him. She determined to find a new home for it, revise the text to expunge any kindness she might have shown, and use it to "destroy the brute."

Life agreed to take the feature, then backed out. However, it was generating so much talk in the industry that *The Atlantic*'s chief editor changed his mind, and scheduled Mitford's "Let Us Now Appraise Famous Writers" as its cover story for July 1970. "There is probably nothing illegal in the FWS operation," she'd stated, not wanting to be sued. Yet the piece was a takedown as powerful as any she'd written. Her "appraisal" pointed to Bennett at every turn, and quote him she did, his request to go off the record be damned: he'd hanged himself with his own words. But in her anger, she also strayed from strict facts, citing him as a founder and as FWS's chief mover and shaker, neither of which was true. The issue enjoyed the largest newsstand sale of any in *The Atlantic*'s history to that date. The article was picked up by newspapers, talk shows, and college classes, and reprinted in England and West Germany, where the FWS had outposts.

Shana Alexander was quoted by *Time* as saying that she'd tried to get Bennett to resign from the school, but he'd refused. In fact, others, years before, had already attempted to change his mind. Even in FWS's first year, Bennett had received a complaint from a couple in Florida, passed it to school director Gordon Carroll, and been assured that the "tiny minority" of complainers were "unreasonable" or "irascible." Yet that was nothing compared to a five-page certified letter sent to him and other Guiding Faculty in 1964. Written by a former West Virginia magistrate and city police judge who'd resigned after a half year as an FWS salesman, it was far more damning than anything Mitford had said. The writer had appealed to them, hoping they were unaware of what was being done in their names, and wanting a display of "honor" to remove the "tarnish."

Bill Styron saw FWS as another indication of Bennett's "dichotomy," the "almost promiscuous unawareness of certain proprieties past which you don't allow yourself to go. The very name is suspect." Chris Cerf figured that his dad had "convinced" himself that the school was really helpful. He thought people loved it, was proud of the textbook they made for students. It took him "longer to be embarrassed than anyone thought it should: I never heard him say he wished he hadn't done it. He was furious with Mitford." Still others saw Bennett's involvement as a sign of his constant willingness to trust others, an almost refreshing gullibility.

Bennett pasted the article in his scrapbook with a caption: "Hatchet job on FWS by Jessica Mitford." In March 1971, in a postscript to his oral history, he insisted she'd distorted his comments, and ignored the school's good features: "We are still hearing repercussions, but I hope they will soon die down." He wasn't entirely alone in asserting that some students had benefited. Mary Higgins Clark had seen a friend's assignments and the critiques she'd received, and judged the assignments "excellent," and the critiques "very well done." But the brouhaha didn't die down. The Famous Schools filed for bankruptcy protection in 1972. The company had expanded too quickly, the share price plummeted, and Mitford supplied the coup de grace.

Years later, Jonathan Cerf, wanting to buy a house in Connecticut, visited a real estate agent. The man, hearing his unusual surname, stared with a stoniness bordering on hatred. "Your family ruined my life. Other lives, too," he said. He'd worked for the Famous Writers School.

. . .

PHYLLIS HAD BECOME DEVOTED to a half-hour exercise regime devised by the physical therapist heading the body beautiful department at Elizabeth Arden. Marjorie Craig lived near Mt. Kisco, and was persuaded to come to The Columns every Saturday to put both Cerfs through their paces. Having seen the children's book future with *The Cat in the Hat,* Phyllis had another eureka moment: there might be a book in the fitness routine. She offered Craig a $750 advance, and, acting as coach to her coach, helped plan the text and step-by-step instructions for each exercise.

When *Miss Craig's 21-Day Shape-Up Program for Men and Women* debuted in October 1968, the Cerfs and their guru were totally gung-ho, even demonstrating exercises on TV. The book rocketed to the bestseller list, stayed thirty-two weeks, and with such a small advance, was incredibly profitable. Feeling powerful in a way she hadn't since her exile from Beginner, Phyllis's thoughts turned to series-building. She signed Craig for a wrinkle-prevention book, with a kids' fitness guide to follow. Craig's advance also rocketed, to $15,000 for the wrinkle book, but Phyllis decided that she, too, deserved a reward. She'd been an equity partner in Beginner; got a small cut for work on Bennett's books; and knew that Linscott, Saxe, and others had been given a percentage on successful titles they'd edited. Craig's name was on the cover, but *she, Phyllis,* had made the books happen. Mid-October 1970, with *Miss Craig's Face-Saving Exercises* six weeks from publication, she went to Bob Bernstein to work out a deal.

"I can't start giving royalties to editors on authors' books—that would be giving away ownership of the company," he informed her, suggesting she speak to Craig to see if she'd forfeit a few points of her own cut. Even better: look beyond wrinkles and convince Craig to let her "package" future projects. If Phyllis did that—took care of everything except final printing, marketing, sales, and distribution—he'd be able to make some arrangement. Phyllis was incredulous. Bob seemed to have forgotten that, once upon a time, Bennett had given *him* a cut, when he brought in Shirley Temple and her storybook. With all they'd done for him, this was his reply? Anger pushed an unthinkable idea to the surface: if he didn't relent, she would resign.

Only a week earlier, Bennett had reached a crossroads of his own. He'd been feuding ever more frequently with Bobby Sarnoff over RCA's retirement rules. Sarnoff had notified him that, at seventy-two, he was overdue to step down as RH board chair. Andy Conrad, a book-loving executive whom Bennett and others liked, now acted as blessed interface between RH and RCA. Conrad tried to cushion the blow over a gourmet lunch at the Toque Blanche, urging Bennett to remain, with a "Senior Editor" title. "Should I stay or walk out?" he tortured himself, then asked Thrup, Don, and Bob. Deciding to try on the diminished title, he confided to his diary, "I do hate the thought of leaving my own creation, Random House." But now Thrup's threat to resign had forced the issue anew. "Maybe I should quit with her?" he wondered.

Bernstein soon summoned him to his office suite: they had to talk. Wanting Bennett to hear it from him, Bob said, "I can't give your wife a royalty. What do you think I should do?"

Feeling besieged on all sides, Bennett found only one answer: "Don't ask my advice. You have to do what you think is right." Bernstein tried to placate Phyllis, but it was too late.

"What am I to do?" Bennett, who used to be so sure, agonized again, but Phyllis knew exactly what she'd do: escape to Paris for a week with her young friend Charlotte Ford. Another face-off with Bernstein followed her return. "Looks like we'll both quit," Bennett's diary now said. The next day, November 10, Bob came to his office, not only to discuss his future at RH, but also that notion, raised repeatedly over the years, of an autobiography. Bob was keen for Bennett to do one, and for RH to publish it. After more weeks of back-and-forth, they at least settled on Don becoming RH chair, and Bennett a senior editor, until May 25, 1973—his seventy-fifth birthday. The last day of November, *Miss Craig's Face-Saving Exercises* was published. It sold well—more than 50,000 copies—though far less than the first collaboration. At the end of January, Phyllis resigned. She never spoke to Bernstein again.

Negotiations over terms for the autobiography dragged on. Bennett's friend Cass Canfield wanted the book for Harper, promising a $100,000 advance—more money if necessary—since with Bennett on board as promoter-in-chief, the memoir was sure to succeed. Not until July 1971 did Bennett agree to publish what he now called *At Random* with his own firm, rather than with Harper. Bernstein had upped the advance to $125,000. Bennett wanted either Albert or Nan as editor. Yet even with the contract settled, a degree of uncertainty persisted: "When, as, and if" he actually finished the book was a phrase Bennett used on more than one occasion.

. . .

RH AND ITS EDITORS were buzzing. Established authors like Michener continued producing, and new talent kept coming. Bob Loomis had challenged a friend of James Baldwin's to write the story of her life, and so served as midwife to Maya Angelou and *I Know Why the Caged Bird Sings*. Eudora Welty had signed with Albert for her first novel in fifteen years. Alvin Toffler gave Jim Silberman a huge bestseller in *Future Shock*. Nan Talese had signed a wistful self-published poet-songwriter-actor named Rod McKuen and tapped into a phenomenon.

Sometimes, when there were problems, Bennett's help would be sought, but often, now, he'd plunk himself down in a busy editor's guest chair and begin, "I hope I'm not interrupting you." Bert Krantz was pained to hear it: the words felt wrong. Here was a man she knew as head of house, wandering around as though he had nothing important to do. Jason Epstein noticed, too: the jack-o'-lantern grin seemed to be fading, its owner disappearing like the Cheshire cat.

Partly, it was his health. As recently as 1966, when Bennett had checked in for an overnight stay at Lenox Hill Hospital for the very first physical of his adult life, he was judged to be "in good shape for a poop my age." But he'd developed a slight tremor that those closest to him noticed; the tiny writing in his diary sometimes showed it, too. As part of that physical, he'd had a proctology exam, a follow-up to the hemorrhoid operation fourteen years earlier, but his physician, Dr. Jensen, said all was well. Still, in 1969 the doctor made him undergo the unpleasant procedure again, and only a year later repeat it. This time, Jensen found evidence of a polyp, and special X-rays revealed not one, but three growths. Although he thought them "almost certainly benign," it was best to remove them, but opening Bennett up, unfortunately, would be no small matter.

He entered Lenox Hill Hospital on December 14, 1970. The stay began with more tests, as well as inhalation exercises that were meant to improve the lung power of longtime smokers like him. A week later, he spent four hours on the operating table. A day or so after that, Bennett developed an intestinal blockage: he'd been given food too soon. A tube extended out from his lower abdomen, but another had to be inserted through his right nostril, snaking into his stomach to provide nourishment. Fevered and delirious, he yanked it out. Jensen and his colleagues managed to insert a new feeding tube through his left nostril, but for four days he lay, a very sick man. A few more went by before the crisis passed, but good news triumphed: he was told the polyps were benign. Slowly he started to improve, but couldn't help noting that 1971 was "inauspiciously" ushered in at Lenox Hill.

Friday, January 8, saw blessed release after three long weeks. The night before Bennett's discharge, Mayor Lindsay and his wife, Mary, found time to visit; earlier in the week, still stuck with tubes, Bennett had been amazed to see Senator Javits and his wife, Marion, at his side. As word spread about his health, calls and letters had streamed in. "I really thought you were too tough and too resilient to let anything make you put up with a hospital," wrote former New York governor Tom Dewey, then added: "We all know you are human after all."

In the end, nothing was better than crossing the threshold of 132 East Sixty-Second Street, and feeling his body resume something akin to normal functioning. Don accompanied him a few days later for his first expedition outside, a terribly exciting walk around the block. How many years had it been since that other stroll, the long one that had cemented their friendship and decided so much about the course of both their lives! Yet how little he'd seen Don lately. . . . At week's end, Dr. Jensen said he could resume a regular routine—he just had to take it steadily—and ordered flesh to be put back on: he'd lost thirteen pounds, and was the lightest he'd been in decades.

He was glad when February came, and he and Thrup escaped to Barbados and Claudette Colbert's guest cottage at Belle Rive. Phyllis had just resigned from RH, and a month under the sun with a passel of friends and privacy when they wanted it would do them good. Bennett had brought along the transcript of his Columbia oral history—a pile of more than a thousand pages—and, sheltering under the pagoda midway down the lawn, with the soothing murmur of the sea beyond, finally had time to correct mistakes that had crept in when the transcript was typed. Nevertheless, once they returned to New York, he still couldn't start on the autobiography, having to compile an anthology of anecdotes, puns, and tales—*Stories to Make You Feel Better*—that he'd promised Bernstein, the twenty-fourth humor book to bear his byline.

The world was a wonderful place: Bennett had evaded cancer; America had twice put men on the moon; and in March he sat among the elect—some astronauts, as well as Walter Cronkite, Deborah Kerr, and others lucky enough to have tickets—to watch Joe Frazier triumph over RH's author Muhammad Ali at Madison Square Garden. It was also a terrible place: the Vietnam quagmire deepened; New York, visibly, was on the skids and running out of cash; and Bennett's diary recorded a steady stream of friends dying. Among them was John O'Hara, who'd gone suddenly, a heart attack in Princeton, aged sixty-five. At a memorial held at RH for the "persnickety," moody man whom he'd admired and "truly loved" in spite of (and because of) their frequent jousting, Bennett eulogized him, calling O'Hara "the most generally unappreciated author in American literary history." As always, he wanted to make the case for greatness.

Nixon was in the White House, and in April and early May, while vacationing at Sinatra's desert retreat, Bennett and Phyllis made the acquaintance of Henry Kissinger, the Harvard professor now become the president's national security adviser. Kissinger didn't stay at Sinatra's, but turned up there, or at nearby friends of Frank, for five or six nights, and they chatted. The conversation continued in June, when the Cerfs met him again in Washington.

Kissinger counted himself a "naïve" in New York society, where he wasn't recognized as a particularly great trophy. With their history of taking people in hand, Bennett and Phyllis invited him to Mt. Kisco, organizing the first weekend in August for the visit. But before then, in mid-July, he stunned the world when he returned from a secret mission to Communist China, where the United States had had no diplomatic relations since Mao Zedong took power in 1949. His trip was prelude to an even bigger bombshell: the president would visit Peking the following year. The geopolitical map—along with Kissinger's life—was about to be redrawn.

A secure line had to be installed in the guest cottage so he could talk to Nixon, and other weekend companions had to be carefully chosen. Among them were close friends like the Hornblows; TV's Mary Healy and Angie Dickinson, lively, pretty ladies both; *Times* publisher "Punch" Sulzberger; Senator Javits; and Lally Weymouth, whose family owned

The Washington Post and *Newsweek*. Neither Cerf was well: Phyllis had contracted shingles, and Bennett, whose right leg pained him, had just been diagnosed with phlebitis, a vein inflammation. Yet in hosting Kissinger, they knew they'd drawn a prize card: many in their circle didn't care for Nixon, but were mighty excited about China.

Bennett had lent his name, and occasionally time, to anti-war efforts, but his guest found him "very friendly, courtly, and thoughtful." Most conversations for Kissinger during that era dwelled compulsively on Vietnam, so he found it a relief to talk with someone "who could discuss international problems without my being beaten to death." He also liked Phyllis. Although she had a "bossy demeanor," and her husband called her "The General," Kissinger found her a lot of fun, and Bennett seemed to appreciate that. At the back of Bennett's mind, Kissinger reckoned, was eventually signing him as an author. He'd written books in the past, of course—academic books. An entrée into the New York establishment, and possibly a book deal, would be of mutual benefit. No major publisher had approached him until Bennett did—and that was before China.

Soon, they were lining up.

. . .

JONATHAN CERF HAD PARTICIPATED in the Kissinger weekend—along with his young wife. Bennett and Phyllis had blinked, and their boys had grown up. Jon, wry and thoughtful, with Phyllis's cornflower eyes and Bennett's dark hair and height, had bested his older brother at Harvard by being editor of the *Lampoon,* and was now the first to marry. It was a time when bright young men, rather than worry about what they'd do with their lives, worried how to stay alive and out of Vietnam. When in the fall of 1968 Jon went to teach at an inner-city school, he'd met Rosanne Novick, an art teacher from a Jewish family in New Jersey, and fell in love. By the summer of 1969, Bennett was describing her as "Jon's Rosanne." He made her feel welcome, at home; with Phyllis, there was the sense of being "looked over." A year later, on a Wednesday night in mid-August, the couple came to Sixty-Second Street to announce that they'd marry. The wedding took place only a fortnight later, on the terrace at Mt. Kisco, with a judge presiding and assorted Novicks, Bennett, Phyllis, Chris, best friend Peter Gabel, and nanny Margaret Brennan the entire party.

Chris had had a succession of girls, in whom his father continued to take an interest: it seemed as though his private life could never be entirely his own. One summer, Bennett kept pestering him about a friend, Susan Cooke—broadcaster Alistair's daughter—wanting them to be a couple, and Chris decided to play a joke to put an end to the prodding. He and Susan rented fancy gear and had Polaroids taken of their "wedding." They then invited Bennett to lunch at '21' to show and tell him the great news. As he was such a tease and prankster himself, they thought he'd see through the ploy and laugh it off at once, but Bennett blanched, hardly holding back tears: he truly believed they'd eloped. It was ironic: when his jokes stung, he'd dismiss the pain and tell Chris, "Just get over it." Now it required agonized apologies for him to get over this.

By 1970, two of Chris's friends were clearly special: Helene Fagan, descended from well-off Hawaiian planters, and Genevieve Charbin, whose family were French transplants to Montreal and owners of a silk and velvet factory. Genevieve (or "Velvet," as Bennett called her, not entirely to her liking) was brainy and fiercely independent, a creative thinker who'd dropped out of college, but was now back studying physics and astronomy. She ran with Andy Warhol's Factory crowd, and in 1965 had starred in *My Hustler,* one of his films. For Phyllis, who'd envisaged Chris marrying someone like Charlotte Ford, great-granddaughter of the Ford Motor Company's founder—a match that would secure the Cerfs a future in high society—Genevieve was "too interesting by half." She set out to convince Bennett that the young woman wasn't ideal; soon both parents were giving off negative signals, though in Bennett's case it was more because he saw Helene as "darling." Yet she was more friend than passion; Chris was crazy about Genevieve.

Whatever he did, Chris felt he was always "Bennett Cerf's son," required to do nothing that could possibly upset his dad. He was supposed to become a somebody, make his parents proud, but the message also seemed to be: *Make a bit less money, be a bit less famous.* Yet if his father upset him, Chris was to say nothing. He'd bought a townhouse one block farther east along Sixty-Second Street, but he and Jon were expected often at 132, and to attend parental outings with and without their "passions," as Bennett called the young women.

One day, Chris was in Joe Fox's office, trying to impress an author, when his father breezed by and announced, "If you want laundry done, you'd better bring it along tonight." He was mortified, and during the summer of 1970, when Jon established independence by marrying, Chris did it by leaving RH. He'd received a call from Joan Ganz Cooney, a friend of Jason Epstein's. Cooney had turned to Jason for help, wanting to develop books and related products to support a new TV program she was producing called *Sesame Street*. She and Jason had worked up a business plan, but Cooney needed an editor to carry it out. Jason suggested Chris.

As it happened, in 1964, after college, he'd been in the Army National Guard with Jeff Moss, the show's head writer. Joe Raposo, the genius responsible for its music, had been a friend at Harvard. When Chris arrived to be interviewed, Cooney saw "energy, creativity, and sweetness—the sweetness of someone in touch with his inner child." She offered him the job; he'd have accepted whatever it paid, but in fact it came with more money than he'd been making at Random. Bennett hadn't wanted people to think he was paying his son too much.

There was only one problem: Chris dreaded telling his dad, fearful of hurting those famously sensitive feelings. Donald provided the reassurance that Chris needed: "This is a good move," Don insisted, in fatherly fashion. However upset Bennett was, Chris had to do it, and Don promised that if the new job didn't work out, there'd always be a place for him at RH. September 1970 had begun with Jon's wedding, and ended with Chris's departure.

The next summer, three weeks before Henry Kissinger's visit, Jerry and Peggy Weidman came to The Columns for a farewell weekend: they were moving to Florida, and visits to Mt. Kisco would be a lot less frequent. Having awakened just after sunrise that quiet Sunday, Jerry decided to slip out for a swim while the others slept. The air was full of birdsong, but a different sound stopped him cold as he approached the scrim of trees and vines shielding the pool. Through the greenery, he made out someone in pajamas and a robe sitting on a chair, sobbing. Jerry tried to turn back, but just as he'd heard and seen, Jerry had been seen and heard, too.

"It's okay," Bennett croaked, wiping his eyes, "Come on in, the water's fine." The statement was followed by a laugh, but not the usual kind. Jerry walked forward and plunged into the pool for a few laps, giving Bennett time to regain some composure. Afterward, dripping wet, he pulled up another chair, and they talked, these two who'd known each other for thirty-five years. What it came down to was Bennett wondering why he and Don had sold Random to RCA. As Bennett himself had once said to Jerry about Dick Simon setting in motion the process that would lose him S&S, how could such a bright guy have done a thing like that to himself?

Fifteen years later, in his autobiography, Weidman would conjure that moment, but so long after the fact that details were muddled. Still, the conclusion was clear. "Bennett liked winners," Weidman wrote, then elaborated: what he *really* liked was being in the ambience of the winners' circle. The shock of seeing it from the outside was bewildering, alien. He felt lost.

Jon and Rosanne—now established in an apartment on the Upper East Side—were looking forward to celebrating their first anniversary three weeks after Kissinger's visit. Chris was sharing a rented seaside house in Amagansett, on Long Island, with his good friend George Plimpton, and George's wife, Freddy Espy. They all managed to get along, despite Freddy and Chris's history. Genevieve usually accompanied him.

Phyllis's shingles had begun to improve, but Bennett's phlebitis didn't. People noticed: he walked with a bit of a limp, and had to prop up the leg while sitting. Marjorie Craig's best efforts at helping him with exercise weren't working. He never talked about his health, but one day let slip to Bill Styron, who could see Bennett felt down, that he had a problem. Suddenly, with enormous feeling, he confided: "Bill, I want to live."

"Damn leg no better," he wrote on Sunday, August 15, along with the fact that Truman Capote had stayed for the weekend; the Fosburghs and Greens had joined them for lunch; and the Yanks had lost the game. There would be no diary entry the next day or in the days that followed. Scar tissue had formed adhesions inside his gut, and another blockage occurred. He returned to Lenox Hill, where the surgeons had to slice him open. As they wheeled Bennett into the OR, he told Jon, "Look after your mother." He'd never said that before.

He was in the hospital for ten days or so, and once the initial scare was over, had begun dictating letters, and saw a few friends. But he didn't look good. The weight he'd put back after the first operation melted away, and his skin seemed gray and slack. Suddenly, he looked old. Capote visited and felt odd: it was almost as if Bennett were saying goodbye. Phyllis responded as she always did when nervous: by taking charge. Convinced Bennett would be better off at The Columns, she urged the doctors to let him convalesce there. It wasn't unreasonable, and in the end, they acquiesced. On Thursday, August 26, Bennett dictated and signed a letter to Alfred and Helen Knopf, thanking them for a note they'd sent, closing like his old jokey self: "The food is proving too wonderful and rich for my system . . . and I've gotten permission to go home to Mount Kisco tomorrow. . . . I do hope we can all get together there very soon again."

Chris was in Long Island with Genevieve. Jon and Rosanne accompanied Phyllis to Lenox Hill on Friday, to help ease Bennett into the car so he could go home. He told them how wonderful they were being, and that he'd never forget. Bennett and Phyllis got to Mt. Kisco, and the servants helped settle him in. They ate dinner, went upstairs, prepared for the night, and were together in their two beds pushed side by side, when something happened.

Phyllis immediately phoned Jonathan, and told him that Bennett had had a heart attack. It took a few moments for him to process what his mother was really trying to say. The phlebitis that Bennett had complained about was dangerous: clots formed, and they could travel to the lung or heart. No one had thought he was going to die, not from that. Tropical storm Doria had barreled up the East Coast and was drenching the city, but Jon and Rosanne stood in the street, instantly soaked, and hailed a taxi. He offered the driver a wad of cash. They had to get to Westchester, and soon. Rain drummed on the roof and hood; wings of spray flew up in their wake as they left the lights of the metropolis behind, heading north through the dark hills.

The weather was equally bad in Amagansett. The Plimptons and Chris and Genevieve were ending their evening by playing round after round of the dictionary game. As soon as Jonathan got off the call with his mother, he phoned Chris. The phone lines were down in some places; he was lucky to get through. "You're not going to believe this: Dad has died."

"What? Not a chance."

Phyllis didn't want Chris to come that night: he was too far, the weather too terrible. But Genevieve put him in the passenger seat, then drove them the hundred and thirty miles to Westchester. At one point they veered off the road, but she kept her head and traveled on. Even bypassing the city, it took many hours. Rosanne and Jon had arrived long before.

"I have to wash the sheets. There's blood. I have to wash them," Phyllis told Rosanne, leading her into the bathroom. Rosanne took the soiled linen and began to scrub, wondering why she was doing so.

Phyllis phoned Donald—it was very late. He promised to come in the morning.

"I know Bennett has left me instructions on what to do. All I have to do is find the right drawer." Like a prayer, over and over, Phyllis repeated it.

In the hours and days that followed, she kept looking.

Epilogue

Revolving Doors

AFTER THE "FUN FUNERAL" AT COLUMBIA, MOURNERS DISPERSED across the city. Staff from every corner of the company remained in shock. It was a beautiful, shining day, and the Styrons and Philip Roth went together to lunch. A group from Knopf and RH walked to Riverside Park and lingered, looking out at ships plying the shimmering Hudson. Many of the closest friends and colleagues went to the house: Phyllis had made sure plenty of food and drink was on hand. Bennett's secretary, Mary Barber, wanting to help, downed a few drinks and waded through the crowd. "I won't leave you," she swore, unsteadily hugging Phyllis. Mary's voice rose: "The only way I'll go is if they carry my body out of this house!"

"That can be arranged," muttered Frank Sinatra, standing nearby, a thin smile breaking across his face. His sidekick Jilly Rizzo was also paying respects, but left abruptly, apologizing that a family friend in Philadelphia had become "deeply and unexpectedly sick." Phyllis and the boys understood what "family" he was referring to, and that the "friend" had been killed by the Mafia. Nevertheless, they were grateful for a moment's distraction.

Phyllis's face, taut and set like a Greek mask, was terribly wan. Bert Krantz suggested they slip away for a breath of air in the park. They sat on a bench holding hands, quietly weeping. Then Bert walked Phyllis back to Sixty-Second Street, said goodbye, and took the bus home.

People underestimated how expensive it was to be Bennett Cerf, reckoning him a lot richer than he actually was. Life at The Columns and in the townhouse hadn't come cheap: running expenses surpassed $100,000 annually (about $779,000 today). His will was dated August 15, 1968, three years before he died, and not written with a view to disappearing anytime soon. When it was probated in Surrogate's Court two days after the funeral, aside from certain assets like the houses, the total gross cash estate amounted to just under $6.5 million ($50 million today). He settled a $5,000 legacy plus life annuity on Margaret Brennan, the nanny who'd loved his sons. A year's salary plus $3,000 went to "my friend and gardener" Robert Mackenzie, who'd made Mt. Kisco so beautiful. Thousand-dollar tokens of "love and affection" went to a string of friends with names like Sinatra, Colbert, Klopfer, Bernstein, and Hart. These high-profile bequests were much covered in the press; to the end, Bennett was his own best publicist.

Chris, bereft after his father died, gradually began to come into his own in a way he couldn't while Bennett lived. In 1972, he married Genevieve Charbin. Three years later, *People* asked if they were the "trendiest couple" in America, and also, in these liberated times, whether the marriage would last. When Genevieve became pregnant, the prospect of progeny made Phyllis suddenly solicitous, crossing Lexington Avenue to visit her daughter-in-law so frequently, it seemed almost daily. A difficult miscarriage put an end to the solicitude, as well as to any idea of posterity. Over the years, the marriage evolved into friendship and separate lives. Eventually they divorced, and in 2015, Chris married the writer Katherine Vaz. His contribution to the Children's Television Workshop went far beyond books, toys, and games: he wrote many of the songs that kids (and parents) loved, like "Count It Higher" and "The Letter B." He collaborated on several non-*Sesame* TV specials and book projects with sitcom star Marlo Thomas, like *Free to Be . . . You and Me*. After leaving *Sesame Street,* he co-created with Michael Frith *Between the Lions,* a children's reading program for public TV. Like Bennett, Chris compiled anthologies; his were mainly satiric and political. His three Grammys and seven Emmys are displayed at his home, as is Ted Geisel's Blue-Green Abelard, the sculpted head that once adorned Bennett's office. His social network is vast.

Jonathan chose a different path. For a while, he worked on a math textbook series, and in 1980 became world champion of the two-player strategy game Othello. But rather than inhabit a grand public stage, he removed himself from any spotlight, leading a determinedly private life, working as a computer programmer and occasionally playing in a band with old pals. Close to his wife's family, he keeps a small circle of friends, and he and Rosanne remain in the apartment where they began in 1970.

Neither Chris nor Jonathan had children.

As for Phyllis, just after Bennett's death her public poise was exemplary, eliciting praise even from Pat Klopfer. In spite of her grief, Phyllis "said all the right things, and did all the right things," Pat observed. Yet soon she began lashing out at the servants and at her sons. On the boys' birthdays, she'd instituted a tradition: they had to give *her* presents. Now nothing was enough to fill the void. Friends remained loyal: Kitty, Leonora. Francis Albert Sinatra, especially, helped: they talked every Sunday. He made sure she had some fun.

"That silly man," Phyllis had complained when embarrassed by Bennett's puns or pranks, yet he'd been the center of her life, source of the influence she wielded, and the only person able to keep her in check. It had hurt more than she cared to admit when the obituary in *Variety* excavated "Helen Nichols," "Ginger Rogers's cousin," and the *L.A. Times* ran a photo of him with Sylvia. James Michener wanted to fund a library in Bennett's honor, but Phyllis refused the offer, for reasons known only to herself. Now she needed another powerful man as organizing principle. Chris and Jon counted themselves lucky when, a bit more than three years after their father died, Phyllis married Robert F. Wagner, who'd been New York's Democratic mayor from 1954 to 1965.

He moved into the townhouse and The Columns, bringing a more political tone to her parties. After becoming Mrs. Wagner, she was one of four can-do ladies behind the Women's Committee for Central Park, feeding into a new conservancy dedicated to bringing the ravaged oasis back from the crime and decay that had befallen it. She returned to paid work, too, her new husband having introduced her to Mary Wells Lawrence, the most famous woman in advertising. Wells assigned her to accounts like New York City and New York State, both sorely in need of an image makeover. It was Phyllis who persuaded Sinatra, Carol Channing, and other friends to do TV spots proclaiming "I Love New York," to try to dispel would-be tourists' fears. Robert F. Wagner died in 1991 of cancer and heart failure. There would be no third husband.

Phyllis boasted of being the woman behind two powerful men, and in many ways she'd made the grand life Bennett lived possible. In later years, though, she grew unable or unwilling to recognize boundaries between his accomplishments and hers. She didn't like being alone or getting older, and, always the impatient perfectionist, grew more so, exacerbated by a fondness for alcohol. The eyes that *The New York Times* once noted could "sparkle, smile, chill and sometimes freeze," froze more readily, even with friends like Leonora. In the end, her mind deteriorated, as did everything. Servants clustered below, hearing her, a restless ghost haunting her own home, calling out to other ghosts, three in particular: the mother who'd neglected her; the sister who'd made her jealous; and Bennett, who'd given her the chance at another life, and loved her, in his fashion. Helen Maurine Brown Nichols, who made herself Phyllis Fraser Cerf Wagner, died on November 25, 2006, aged ninety, having outlived Bennett by thirty-five years.

Donald continued at RH, the graceful elder statesman. Once a month, new hires would gather in a conference room to be welcomed by him. For them he was a living, breathing talisman of past glories, as well as of their own hopes for the future. However, officially he'd stepped down as RH chairman, and RCA policy was for retired executives to disappear. Pressed by the company, Bob Bernstein went to see him, to ascertain his thoughts on the future. Don was a man without hobbies, other than books and travel, and needed a place to come each morning. All he wanted was to offer advice when asked; a small office where he could do so; and a $7,500 expense account to take people to lunch. Bernstein told RCA he would not countenance forcing Don to leave, and no one else was to raise the subject again as long as he remained president.

The corporation backed down.

Donald and Bob

At the end of 1975 or start of 1976, when Don was seventy-three, a letter arrived at RH out of the blue, from Communist Czechoslovakia, resurrecting a vivid ghost from his and Bennett's past: Martha Dodd. After America's fear of Communism had metastasized into witch hunts in the late 1940s and early '50s, Martha and her husband, Alfred Stern, had fled New York for Mexico, then Prague, where they settled; and Martha worked editing English-language books. In the 1960s, after a brief stay in Castro's Cuba, they tried to be forgiven their political sins and return to the United States, but were told they'd be prosecuted as traitors if they did. And so Martha wrote from Prague, evoking their former acquaintance, and asking Don to get a book for her, in the way he and Bennett had in the old days. It wasn't an RH title, but one written by a Russian dissident living in the United States, grandson of foreign minister Maxim Litvinov—the man whose wife and daughter had entertained Bennett in Moscow.

Donald was delighted to hear from her, and for a decade they corresponded. His letters are those of an older man talking about the past, and about the intervening half century and what was happening now to him and to RH. They're warm and wistful. Most of hers are gone—for of course Don's exist only because she kept them, as she'd kept his two 1935 love letters, through all her many moves. However, in Martha Dodd's papers, there are no letters from Bennett.

Don and Pat continued to take long vacations in Europe, although an increasingly painful back at times forced her to remain in their hotel room while he went out. Her closest friend, now widowed, often accompanied them, staying in an adjoining room. On one trip to Italy, Pat found Donald caressing her friend. The friendship didn't survive, but the marriage did. A year or so later, when Pat became really ill, the marriage also survived a suicide attempt: depressed and wanting to avoid the indignities of a failing body, she swallowed pills. He rushed back from sales conference in Florida, and was quite solicitous after that. Pat died of heart failure in 1979.

Two years later, Don married Katie Louchheim, a widow and very much a somebody. A native New Yorker, she'd spent most of her life in Washington, in the corridors of power, working with the UN; as vice chair of the Democratic National Committee; and as a State Department official under JFK and LBJ. She'd also published poetry and several books. When young, she'd moved in the same circles as Don and Bennett, and had briefly dated Bennett during his Liveright days. She moved to New York, into the home Don and Pat had shared in the elegant Beekman. Don had lost or grown bored with many old pals, and liked the idea that Katie would bring a new world of interesting friends. Yet having lived in D.C. so long, she found herself, in her late seventies, in New York, inhabiting another woman's apartment, and felt lost. The marriage didn't work out as either spouse had hoped.

Donald continued to walk to RH most days, but the last week in May 1986, he had a cerebral hemorrhage and died on May 30, aged eighty-four. The graveside funeral in Brooklyn was quiet, with just his stepson, Tony, speaking. Veterans who'd served with him read Don's *Times* obituary and sent letters. He'd been a father figure to so many, as he'd been to Random House staff. In a later eulogy, Ralph Ellison wrote that Donald had "affirmed the ideals of democracy fully as much as he fulfilled the highest standards of publishing."

He never found what he was searching for with any of his wives. At times, he seemed to have feigned happiness. Don's partnership with Bennett was another matter. Pat Klopfer, writing to Phyllis after Bennett's death, admitted that the men's relationship had become "one of nostalgia . . . they were on different channels." Bennett had neglected and hurt Don in the final decade, yet "in a strange masculine way they loved each other deeply," Pat attested. Don's daughter, Lois, agreed: "My father felt closer to Bennett than to any other man." They'd shared a dream, trusted each other, and for far longer than many pairings, enjoyed the other's company. They'd liked most authors they published, and the men and women who worked for them, and kept many a very long time. To a *Times* reporter who interviewed him on his eightieth birthday, Donald declared: "I've worked with wonderful authors and colleagues. I've had the best of it."

. . .

THAT UNUSUAL PLAYFULNESS AND *need* for his people to be happy and to love him were Bennett's uniquely; Bob Bernstein was cooler, strong-willed, but with a loose management style dependent on a few key executives. Although RCA had installed financial people with little understanding of publishing (the exception being Alexander MacGregor III, RH's new CFO, whom Bernstein judged "terrific"), Bernstein and his lieutenants quickly learned to shield staff from their more egregious inroads, and the imprints kept their personalities. RH stayed a good place to work, and the basic feeling of freedom remained. Jim Silberman continued to run Random adult trade; André Schiffrin was in charge of Pantheon; and Bob Gottlieb, who once said he reported only to God, ran Knopf. Bernstein was well aware that RCA's conservative board weren't pleased by the left-wing books some editors were acquiring, but they continued to sign them anyway.

In 1967, fearing Federal Trade Commission scrutiny into monopolistic behavior, RCA had forced RH to give up its part-ownership of Bantam, putting Random at a disadvantage: it lost the inside track for reprinting its own bestsellers. Bernstein wasn't allowed to buy another paperback house until 1973, a sickly one. Ballantine Books, the brainchild of Saxe Commins's nephew Ian Ballantine, had been drowning in red ink and wouldn't attract government attention, but would cost years to turn around. By now, RCA was also ailing. The computer division, having constantly gobbled capital, had to be shuttered. It left RCA with the largest corporate write-off up to that point in American history. In November 1975, the board rebelled against Bobby Sarnoff and his conglomerate mishmash, setting in motion Sarnoff's departure.

Bernstein, like Bennett, was perpetually restless. He was growing RH Inc., that was clear, but by the late 1970s, much of his time was being siphoned off, not for money-making "lines" as Bennett's had been, but for a cause. In the 1930s, his grandfather had helped sixty-eight Jews flee his hometown in Germany, an act that had made a deep impression on the boy. While on a U.S. publishing mission to Moscow in 1970, Bernstein had seen the persecution Soviet writers endured. Memories stirred, and he found a calling: soon he pushed for the Association of American Publishers to form an International Freedom to Publish Committee with him as chair. In 1978, he and two others went further, starting Helsinki Watch—later renamed Human Rights Watch—to support dissidents behind the Iron Curtain, some of whom Bernstein published.

Rumors had begun to circulate that RCA wanted to offload Random House. LBJ's Great Society money had dried up, synergy had proved a pipe dream, and the profit margins in trade publishing were not high. The Times Mirror Corporation again knocked at the door, as it had done back in 1964, and in February 1977, RH was almost sold to it for $60 million, but the deal fell through. For a minute, Bernstein dreamed of joining with investors to buy Random himself, but that went nowhere. Early in September 1979, the RCA board gave him all of a half hour's notice before a corporate release went out that Random House and Banquet Foods—the books and chickens operations—were being put on the block. Bernstein had to scramble to tell staff, authors, and agents before newspapers did.

Investment bankers Lazard Frères and Lehman Brothers were engaged to reel in buyers; it soon came down to Hearst and Advance Publications, and then Hearst balked at the price. Advance was prepared to pay $75 million, and a deal nearly finalized, but then Ballantine was walloped by losses again. No way would Advance go ahead. A private, family-owned New York company, it had been founded by Sam Newhouse and was now run by his sons, Si and Donald. They had newspaper, radio, and cable assets, and, under the Condé Nast banner, twenty magazines, including *Mademoiselle, Glamour,* and the prestige glossy *Vogue*. That year, the family enterprise was estimated to have made more than $100 million in profit. Si ran the magazines, and was the brother interested in this prestige book publisher. RCA had called a final conference to try to salvage the deal, and the story goes that Si walked in, but remained silent. The memory of the $75 million that Ballantine's bad results had hexed hung in the air, when an RCA executive offered Advance a $10 million loan, interest-free, for a period of five or ten years. Si accepted. An agreement in principle was announced in February 1980. RCA had bought RH in 1966 for $38 million, and added Ballantine for another $6.4 million. The leading papers reported that the Newhouses were paying $65–$70 million to buy their new bauble.

For an hour and fifteen minutes one day each week, Si Newhouse and Bob Bernstein met to discuss business in the Four Seasons Grill Room, plush with Midtown's power elite. They had plenty to discuss, for Si wanted RH Inc. to grow, and it did. Not only had it bought Fawcett, a financially sound paperback house that, joined with Ballantine, finally made the numbers work, it had also added other companies, as well as distribution clients, and started an innovative division to do books and videos on cassette tape.

Back in 1976, Bernstein had clashed with Jim Silberman, who left to set up his own imprint, Summit Books, at S&S, adding to the tally of those who shuttled between RH and its old rival. Jim had fulfilled Bennett's hopes for what a chief editor/publisher could be. After his departure, Jason Epstein took over the editorial reins at Random, but, always mainly interested in his own projects, didn't suit the job. Disorganization and discord seeped in. The Modern Library, so championed by the young Jason, began to be neglected.

With Bernstein often tied up in human rights activities, Si was taking more turns at the RH tiller, adding executives and becoming increasingly confident about his own book instincts. A shy, plain man, Newhouse loved the glittery social scene and liked the idea of splashy celebrity titles, envisioning a profitable symbiosis between his magazine and book properties. In 1985, he saw one such opportunity. *GQ* ran a cover story on Donald Trump, then little-known outside New York, and it generated such an increase in newsstand sales, Si picked up the phone, called Trump, and proposed he do a book with RH (a talented ghost did the hard work of actually conceptualizing and writing it). *The Art of the Deal,* published in 1987, changed Trump's life.

Newhouse fancied international stature, and bought a group of London publishers in order to have it. A quarter century earlier, Don had suggested to his friend Billy Collins that RH and Collins create a jointly owned "super-corporation" straddling the Atlantic. Don had seen strength in an alliance with a U.K. house that he and Bennett knew well. Si didn't have that long-standing link, and his new purchases trailed problems. And then, in the summer of 1988, the urge to buy one of the last New York book groups of any scale still in private hands proved irresistible.

Started as the Outlet Books remainder operation in 1933, the company came to be called Crown, after the trade publishing imprint it founded. Later, Crown added other imprints, book clubs, and a direct-mail business. Newhouse wanted the deal sewn up fast. He saw mail order as a good way to sell books across all imprints, and he thought Outlet would help RH handle remainders more efficiently. And it was the *boom-boom* '80s, and the pizzazz of Crown's bestselling front-list—authors like Judith Krantz and Martha Stewart and the lavish parties they inspired—spoke to him. Announced in mid-August, the rushed deal was completed before the end of September.

It turned out that Outlet and the direct-mail operation were losing a fortune, and the only part of the mail business that was making money was one RH had had no knowledge of—a sideline in pornographic videocassettes (shut down soon enough). But Si wasn't given to blaming himself for the problems unleashed by his latest buy. On November 1, 1989, when indigestion once again lay heavily upon the RH Inc. body corporate, Newhouse called senior staff from all New York divisions—sixty people or so—to the Fiftieth Street boardroom. He uttered platitudes, then announced that Bob Bernstein, towering above him, was retiring, and ceded the floor. Two minutes into his speech, Bob couldn't go on: his voice cracked and eyes glistened. He looked out at Helen, who'd accompanied him. Forcing a few more words, he apologized and said he'd be back, then left the room. During the ten long minutes that followed, not a word was spoken. When Bob returned, he got on with it. He was sixty-six, and had always said he wanted to work until he was seventy. Bennett had placed him at the helm twenty-three years earlier.

It seems to happen every single time to the people who found or build publishing houses, when a sale or a merger occurs, or doesn't go well. They think nothing will happen to *them,* that this time will be different, but it never is. They're always kicked up—like Bennett—or kicked out, like Bob. During his tenure, revenues had gone from $40 million to $800–$900 million. True, overheads were high, profits thin—some said that, toward the end, they'd vanished, thanks to Crown; and Bernstein's hands-off style and good works—for his human rights pursuits were estimably that—had allowed certain matters to go unattended. But the finale was brutal.

He'd left no designated successor, no plan. Newhouse appointed an outsider, Alberto Vitale, who'd earned a doctorate in economics in his native Italy, and a Wharton MBA. Vitale had joined Bantam in 1975, which by then had an Italian owner, but soon a family-controlled German media conglomerate, Bertelsmann, bought Bantam, and in 1986 added Doubleday and Dell. Vitale became CEO of the combined Bantam, Doubleday, and Dell, known as BDD. Having executed that integration for Bertelsmann, Newhouse pegged him as the man to tackle the Crown mess at Random House Inc. After Bernstein's ouster, the big CEO suite was painted white: Vitale's style would be Italian modern. Bernstein had taken his personal files, but much was left behind, and some of it discarded. "Look what I rescued from the trash heap!" a fellow said to RH's librarian. It was a large photograph of Bennett and Donald.

Vitale, like Newhouse, was interested in big books and big authors that would sell, sell, sell. One of the first things he did at RH was demand better numbers and substantial cost-cutting from Pantheon, which still published literary fiction—often in translation—as well as high-concept, frequently controversial history, sociology, and politics, oriented left. Titles like Art Spiegelman's *Maus* and Studs Terkel's *The Good War* reaped financial success, but many others sold very modestly at best. Bernstein had effectively exempted Pantheon from paying its share of the large corporate overheads apportioned among divisions; with overheads factored in, it had lost money in recent years. Newhouse had wanted Bernstein to "correct" the situation, but he hadn't; now Vitale had been brought in to pull on the reins. Intellectual, international André Schiffrin had run Pantheon for so long, and his position was unique, given that his father had been one of its founders. He insisted the division was being "unfairly" asked to shoulder costs not of its making, and rejected Vitale's economies. Immovable object had met irresistible force. Schiffrin was fired; his editors resigned in protest. The situation escalated into a vitriolic, full-scale cause célèbre, and a bitter aftertaste lingered for years.

On the other hand, also at Newhouse's urging, Vitale hired Harry Evans to run the RH division in the fall of 1990. A famously crusading, brilliant London newspaper editor, Evans was married to one of Newhouse's imported British magazine stars, Tina Brown. Rather clueless about book publishing, he could learn. A slight, charismatic man, who like Bennett charmed effortlessly and did not sit still, Evans saw that the division—now known as "Little Random"—had lost luster, and tried to restore it. Appreciating the importance of history and PR, he asked Chris Cerf to lunch, feeling that Bennett's ghost should be coaxed into the light, and put to use.

For years the ML had languished, and was now in a sadly reduced state. Titles had been cut, and rights to others reclaimed by originating publishers. There was even talk of remaindering some at Outlet and transplanting viable ones into a series at Knopf. Like many bantamweights, Harry relished a good fight. For him, the ML's fate symbolized the rise or fall of Little Random, but it was also personal. As a graduate student in the 1950s, he'd thought of it as *his* library. He had no intention of letting the ML move anywhere. Relaunching, under Little Random, became his priority. In 1992, on the ML's seventy-fifth anniversary, he did so with fanfare and panache—redesigns, a grand editorial board, inspired promotion—and succeeded in recalling it to life.

For the trade list, he spent lavishly on big books and big names, not always wisely. He also supported serious titles for modest advances that sometimes succeeded very well. Most important, he revived not just the ML, but Random House's public profile. With fabulous parties, book breakfasts, glossy newsletters, and Harry's overall flair, RH hadn't been so talked about since Bennett's day. But Evans's talents didn't extend to close managing of day-to-day business and balance sheets, and he was "nudged" back to magazines and newspapers in 1997.

That November, Si Newhouse had a significant birthday: he turned seventy. On that very day, he was approached by Thomas Middelhoff, the hard-charging strategy head at Bertelsmann. Middelhoff was visiting from Germany to scout another big American buy to add to Bantam, Doubleday, Dell, and had met with the heads of News Corporation, Viacom, and Disney. Quality spoke strongly to German pride, and getting Random House would be, for the Mohn family who controlled Bertelsmann, winning first prize. When Middelhoff asked Si if Advance would ever sell RH, it was the same sort of dream that Bennett had entertained about Knopf. And, like Bennett, Middelhoff was surprised by the answer: Newhouse wanted a week to think about it. After all, RH was costing his family a constant stream of capital for a return more rooted in prestige than profit. There seemed no end in sight for the sky-high advances agents were demanding for big books, or the retail pressures squeezing margins ever thinner.

On March 23, 1998, the acquisition was announced by Middelhoff and Peter Olson, the CEO of Bertelsmann's North American Book Group, to the staff of BDD, who applauded; when the two men, along with Newhouse, informed executives at Random House, there was stunned silence. Estimates of the price were pegged at around $1.2 billion. Olson, an American, would be the new CEO of a combined BDD–RH, to be known as Random House Inc. Vitale had been judged too slow in integrating Crown with RH, and his services were no longer required. The next year, New York became Bertelsmann's global book-publishing headquarters; the BDD imprints remained in their old offices, but RH had to move to two temporary locations, making the staff feel like nomads. The reason? Newhouse, who now held the base lease on the tower that Bennett had hated, could double the rent by finding new tenants. Eventually, RH and the former BDD moved to space leased by Bertelsmann in a new, fifty-two-story mixed-use residential/office building at 1745 Broadway, between Fifty-Fifth and Fifty-Sixth Streets.

A series of presidents, publishers, and chief editors of various divisions under the Random House Inc. roof had come and gone, but the revolving doors kept spinning. Peter Olson, found wanting in the BDD integration and other matters, lost the confidence of his corporate masters. In May 2008, Bertelsmann plucked Markus Dohle, a young, highly energetic executive from its printing unit in Germany, to replace him and restructure RH. By now, the publishing world was starkly divided into a large constellation of very small companies; a shrinking cluster of medium-size houses; and a handful of giant combines: HarperCollins, S&S, Macmillan, Hachette, Penguin, and RH. But as well as competing among themselves, the giants faced a new technological world whose behemoths—Amazon, Google, Apple, Facebook—were remaking the rules. The big houses thought they needed to get bigger to survive.

In the fall of 2012, Random House shocked the book world by announcing that it and Penguin, owned by the British-based Pearson, would merge. Penguin, ranked second behind RH in U.S. market share and third in the U.K., had a larger global presence, with established subsidiaries in Australia, New Zealand, and many current and former Commonwealth countries in Africa and Asia. At first, Bertelsmann controlled 53 percent of the merged entity, but by April 2020 it owned all of what was now called Penguin Random House.

Two years earlier, Bertelsmann had elevated an American, Madeline McIntosh—who for two decades had climbed the RH ladder (apart from a brief but useful sojourn at Amazon)—to be CEO of Penguin Random House U.S. Dohle had previously held executive responsibility for both the global business and the American flagship; now, he'd focus on corporate acquisitions and international, while McIntosh supervised the integration of Penguin. No surprise that six months into her watch, a new round of restructuring occurred, and the next year, more. Penguin had been downtown, but early in 2019, its staff completed a migration to RH's midtown tower.

It is hard to increase market share by originating individual titles; much easier to increase it through acquiring more imprints and companies from the outside. In 2020, when Simon & Schuster's corporate parent, Paramount, decided that despite it being a healthy, profitable division, S&S no longer fit strategically into Paramount's plans, PRH jumped at the chance to buy it, and was the determined bidder, offering $2.17 billion—far more than its competitors, Hachette and HarperCollins. So odd to think back to Dick Simon and Max Schuster proposing to take over the rock on which Bennett and Don's foundation was built—the Modern Library—almost a century earlier. Odd, too, to think back to Max desperately discussing with Bennett whether RH could save him from that "partnership from hell" with Shimkin. How entangled the stories of the two firms had been, and remained: the current CEO of S&S, Jonathan Karp, had for years been the bright young man at RH, who some had thought might top the ladder there.

The U.S. Department of Justice reckoned that the deal would have allowed PRH to control just under half the market for rights to top-selling trade books in America. PRH disagreed. However, having allowed the Penguin merger and many other book business consolidations to occur—Amazon is generally estimated to command at least 50 percent of retail book sales in the country—the government decided it was time to say enough is enough. It fought the deal in court, and in a stunning turnaround, won. S&S went under the control of a private global investment firm.

Markus Dohle almost immediately suffered the same fate that predecessors had when something big went wrong. As part of PRH's bid, it had promised to pay Paramount a $200 million fee—a painful amount—should the deal not be consummated. Dohle had been tasked with growing the company, but unhappily for him, the Justice Department of Joseph Biden turned out to be far less consolidation-friendly than those of his two presidential predecessors. Dohle was the loser, and was gone in December 2022. On the last day of January 2023, his resignation was followed by that of McIntosh.

The dominant partner usually determines the nature of the combine forged in a merger; when RH was bought by RCA, that didn't quite happen. What the founders had built was so strong and personal, and Bob Bernstein had acted to preserve what he could. However, with so many turns and spins since, Random House—and Penguin as well—had been repeatedly remade and corporatized on both sides of the Atlantic. After the Penguin and Random House merger, the question of what the logo would be was raised. Would it depict a penguin inside a house? A house inside a penguin? The two symbols next to each other? For more than a decade, only the stylized words "Penguin Random House" were used. But in 2024, under current CEO Nihar Malaviya, it was decided that the black-and-white penguin in its orange oval carried great brand recognition—much greater than the image of Random's house. Now it stands alone, alongside the words "Penguin Random House," as corporate logo.

Madeline McIntosh, who'd started out wanting to be an editor, said during her CEO stint that the lesson she'd taken from Amazon was that while publishing had been "a culture of talk and people, opinions and emotions, where debate and discussion" drove decisions, "Amazon removed the personal and political . . . and figured out how to boil [decisions] down to math problems." Although Bennett, Don, and their ilk were businessmen "with computers in their heads," it's a long way from that to the algorithms and decisions of today.

No one now in publishing can say with any certainty what will happen to the business in a digital age where old models are being fundamentally disrupted by forces like Amazon, social media, and the effects of screens on the habit of reading itself; where self-publishing generates hundreds of thousands of titles a year in the United States alone, making discovery of any individual book that much more difficult, and artificial intelligence promises to kick-start an even larger title avalanche; where long-trusted review mechanisms that enabled book discovery have given way to a plethora of influencers; where political polarization and attempts at censorship are spreading like wildfire, and where AI will change publishing houses from within, and the landscape for books from without, in ways we cannot yet imagine.

. . .

AS LONG AS THEY COULD, the editors whom Bennett and Donald had assembled kept editing. Joe Fox continued to do so until November 1995, when he was felled by a massive heart attack at his RH desk. A few years after Bennett's death, Nan Talese felt she had to leave Random to get to the top; she went—where else?—to S&S. Later she moved to Houghton, then Doubleday, and was given her own imprint there, which became one of the most distinguished in publishing. After a sixty-year career, Talese retired in 2020. Toni Morrison was a trailblazer, helpmeet to and advocate for Black writers across America, until the success of her own writing enabled her to devote herself to it full-time. By her death in 2019, she'd long been acknowledged an American—and universal—

master. Albert Erskine continued at RH, devotedly and meticulously working with authors until his retirement in 1987, and then edited part-time until his death six years later.

After his ouster, André Schiffrin started the New Press, a not-for-profit house that has continued beyond his death in 2013. Bob Gottlieb left Knopf in 1987 to edit Si Newhouse's *New Yorker* for five years, and later wrote books of his own, while continuing to work with a few Knopf authors. Post-Gottlieb, a well-known London editor/publisher, Sonny Mehta, was imported to run Knopf, and eventually added Pantheon, Vintage, and Doubleday to his portfolio. Until his death in 2019, he was widely regarded as the most brilliant publisher of his era. Bob Loomis remained at RH for fifty-four years, until officially retiring in 2011, long enough for him to have acquired this book in the autumn of 2002. In his retirement, he saw its author through many drafts before he died, in 2020, aged ninety-three. It was the last book on which he worked.

. . .

IN THE ARCHIVE OF Bennett's papers at Columbia is a sheet of fine paper, done in the style of an illuminated manuscript, its initial capitals and borders a rainbow of colors. In part, it reads:

> At a meeting of the board of directors of Random House, Inc. held at the RCA Building on the morning of Wednesday, September 1, 1971, and with regard to the death of Bennett Cerf the following resolutions were . . . unanimously adopted:
>
> More than any other man, [he] was the driving force which brought Random House from its modest beginnings to acknowledged preeminence. . . . His unique ability and his fresh and vital approach brought a whole new dimension to the business. . . .

It was signed "Donald S. Klopfer, Chairman of the Board." Dictating his own oral history four years later, Don elaborated: "If I'd been running Random House completely, we would not be the publishing house we are today. We wouldn't be as big and we wouldn't be as good . . . because I had the feeling that you are only judged by the books that you publish. . . . Bennett was much smarter . . . [he] knew that you need the publicity . . . the ability to sell the books [and] all the appurtenances that go with it. . . . He has never been given the real credit for being as good a publisher as he was. He was a damned good publisher . . . much better at that than he was on television or on the lecture tour. . . . He was supposed to be very good at those things, too."

A literary agent once said that inevitably, every publisher tends to be something of an autocrat and something of a Don Juan. But what constitutes a great one?

Ask an author, and the answer will be someone who intuits—or at least hires others who have that understanding, and the freedom and finances to act on it—what the author is trying to do, and what he or she needs to do it; and who understands how the work, once done, can be made known, so there's a fair chance the book may be bought, the author heard, and the publisher stay in business. Loving and caring about books, respecting the sweat and magic that go into writing them, and possessing wide and varied interests and a computer in the head: these also help.

Ask a bookseller, and the answer will be someone who understands the thin margins and constraints under which stores operate; who knows that without the bookseller's partnership, a publisher is nothing; who knows, too, what it takes to help one book stand out from the vast tide of titles that flow on and off the shelves each season, and doesn't tire of doing it again and again.

Ask a reader, and the answer will be someone who has an eye, an ear, a feel for the zeitgeist, but also for the past and future; an appreciation for mass as well as class; and, in Dick Simon's words, knows the importance of "giving the reader a break."

Bennett Cerf, while not without his critics, was all these things, and more.

A few years after his death, Jason Epstein and Bert Krantz were waiting for an elevator at Random House. They were chatting, and kept talking when it arrived and they got in; somehow, Bennett's name came up. A younger employee heard them, turned, and asked, "Who's Bennett?"

Bert felt as though a knife had gone through her. She and Jason looked at each other. The door opened and they got out. "*Sic transit gloria mundi,*" she thought. "There it was."

Who today, outside a narrow band of devotees, knows the name of any individual publisher, living or dead? Ours is a period marked by the obliteration of publisher identity, where individuals and imprints have been rendered increasingly faceless. Bennett wanted so much during his life to be *known,* but as Norman Cousins, the longtime editor of the *Saturday Review,* recognized, his very "style, splendor and swoosh" might have worked to obscure his "main aim and achievement": his publishing. As a young man, when Bennett memorialized his mentor, Horace Liveright, for *PW,* he described their last meeting. Liveright had skimmed over "the really noteworthy events" of his life, and dwelled instead on episodes that were "better left unmentioned." Bennett had done something similar. He'd allowed that light, bright scrim of celebrity to define so much of his own life. After he died and it went dark, he was quickly relegated to the ephemeral. But some things last longer, as he well knew. Random House, albeit utterly changed, still exists. So does the Modern Library. The books remain.

Acknowledgments

DURING ITS EXTENDED GESTATION, MANY PEOPLE CONTRIBUTED TO this book. They did so by bringing it to life in generous hours of interviews; through patient help at the libraries and archives where they work; by lending papers, images, recordings, and books; by assisting with research or administrative tasks; through sharing publishing expertise and wisdom; by serving as references for fellowships and residencies; in providing financial assistance; by reading all or parts of the manuscript; weighing in on titles, jackets, and photographs; offering comments, criticism, good counsel, and moral support. Their enthusiasm, encouragement, and belief in the book helped to sustain me for twenty-three years. Some are no longer here to see their faith and trust fulfilled, but through the publication of this book, at least some of their essence will live on, for what are books, if not the links that define the long chain of human memory.

In an already very long volume, there isn't room to acknowledge every single person. To those named, and those unnamed but part of a larger group, you have my profound thanks.

For interviews: Jean Bach, DeWitt Clinton "Bud" Baker, Betty Ballantine, Richard Baron, Otto Barz, Barbara Palmer Bayler, Frances Commins Bennett, Lawrence Bensky, Laurel Bentley, Jan Berenstain, Stan Berenstain, Anne Bernays, Helen Bernstein, Peter W. Bernstein, Robert L. Bernstein, Simon Michael Bessie, Helene Fagan Bidwell, Alexandra Mayes Birnbaum, Lucienne S. Bloch, Priscilla "Pat" Merle Haas Blum, Glen Boles (via Steven Bach), Nina Bourne, George Braziller, Stuart Brent, Mel Brooks, Debbie Brothers, Helen Gurley Brown, Matthew J. Bruccoli, Eleanor Carlucci, Joanne Carson, Dick Cavett, Christopher Cerf, Jonathan Cerf, Rosanne Cerf, Vinton Cerf, Mary Higgins Clark (via Lisl Cade), Gerald Clarke, Robert Cohen, Betty Comden, Eugene Commins, Don Congdon, Joan Ganz Cooney, Christopher T. Cory, Anna Crouse, Annette Danek, Michael Dann, Laurent de Brunhoff (via Phyllis Rose), Armand Deutsch, Harrriet Deutsch, E. L. Doctorow, Peter Duchin, Ulla Dydo, Oscar Dystel, Barbara Epstein, Jason Epstein, Marisa Erskine, Silvia Erskine, Harold Evans, Mia Farrow, Carol Fass, Faye Fates, Jules Feiffer, Dr. Stanley Fisher, Isabel W. "Jill" Fuller Fox, Harry Frankfurt, Jane Friedman, Michael K. Frith, Wendy Frith, Dr. William A. Frosch, Peter Gabel, Jonathan Galassi, Jack Gambatese, Lydia Gasman, Bibi Gaston, Audrey Geisel, Arthur Gelb, Robert Giroux, Edward Goldberg, Howard Goldstein, Michael Goodkin, Robert A. Gottlieb, Ashbel Green, Maxine Groffsky, Richard Grossman, Thomas Guinzburg, David Halberstam, Catherine Hart, Christopher Hart, Kitty Carlisle Hart, Joyce Hartman, Mary Robbin Reynolds Hawkins, Shirley Hazzard, Alan Hirschfield, Leonora Hornblow, Michael Hornblow, A. E. Hotchner, Elinor Green Hunter, Fritz Jacobi, Mark Jaffe, Morton Janklow, Judith Jones, Howard Kaminsky, Carla Kaplan, Justin Kaplan, John Kastor, Mae Kastor, Stanley Kauffmann, Everett Raymond Kinstler, Sanford Kirschenbaum, Richard W. Kislik (via Mike Shatzkin), Henry A. Kissinger, Alfred A. Knopf Jr., Michael Korda, Albert C. Kosow, Bertha Krantz, Richard Krinsley, John Lahr, Robert Todd Lang, Edgar Lansbury, Paul Lapolla, Owen Laster, Paula Lawrence, Christopher Lehmann-Haupt, Harding Lemay, Sharon Lerner, J. P. Leventhal, Ira Levin, Martin P. Levin, Lois Klopfer Levy, Toinette Lippe, Gloria Loomis, Robert D. Loomis, Sterling Lord, Jeffrey Lyons, Alexander MacGregor III, Norman Mailer, Peter Mayer, Charlotte Mayerson, Cormac McCarthy, Jayne Meadows, Aileen Mehle (aka Suzy Knickerbocker), Ved Mehta, Alan Merkin, Michael Mewshaw, Walter Minton, Kate Monaghan, Sandra Koodin Paul Money, Judith Morgan, Toni Morrison, Ann Mudge, Leona Nevler, Phyllis Newman, Betsy Palmer, Betty Haas Pfister, Freddy Espy Plimpton, Norman Podhoretz, Letty Cottin Pogrebin, Betty S. Prashker, John Richardson, Natalie Robins, Felix Rohatyn, Barney Rosset, Philip Roth (replied to questions by mail), Enid Kastor Rubin, Regina Ryan, C. Stephen Saunders, Sophia Duckworth Schachter, André Schiffrin, Herbert S. Schlosser, Herbert K. Schnall, Anne Kaufman Schneider, Budd Schulberg, Anthony M. Schulte, Alan U. Schwartz, Timothy Seldes, Selma Shapiro, James H. Silberman, Al Silverman, Joanna Simon, John J. Simon, Lucy Simon, Tina Sinatra, Peter Stansky,

Jean Stein, Julian Stein, Rose Styron, Susanna Styron, William Styron, Cathy Summers, Paul Summers, Gay Talese, Nan A. Talese, Arthur Thornhill Jr., John Thornton, Howard Treeger, Seymour Turk, Laurence Urdang, Pamela Usdan, Marina Vaizey, Samuel Vaughan, Alberto Vitale, Phyllis Cerf Wagner, Barbara Walters, Rosanna Warren, John Weidman, Peggy Weidman, Elma Merz Otto Westney, Lucy Liveright Koch Wilson, Charles A. (Tony) Wimpfheimer, Andrew Frank Winning, Harry Wolff, Boris Wolfson.

To libraries, archives, institutions: The Columbia University Rare Book and Manuscript Library functioned as keystone in the archival building blocks of this biography. Without the Random House Records, Bennett Cerf Papers, and the Bennett Cerf and Donald S. Klopfer oral histories housed there, this book could not have been written. Columbia's other publishing oral histories and archives; the Barnard College archives; and the Watson Library also provided source material.

Thanks, too, to the Academy of Motion Picture Arts and Sciences Margaret Herrick Library; Boston University Howard Gotlieb Archival Research Center Collections; The British Library Sound Archives; Dartmouth College Rauner Special Collections Library; the Library of Congress Special Collections; the Massachusetts Historical Society; the New York City Department of Records and Kenneth R. Cobb; New-York Historical Patricia D. Klingenstein Library; New York Public Library Manuscripts and Archives Division, Berg Collection, General Research Division, Photography Division, and the Library for the Performing Arts Billy Rose Theater Division; the New York Society Library and the New York Society Library Special Collections; New York University Fales Library Special Collections; W.W. Norton (and Drake McFeeley) for access to early files of Horace Liveright, Inc., and Norton's Donald Lamm for information on William Faulkner; Ohio State University Libraries Special Collections; the Paley Center, New York and Jane Klain; Pennsylvania State University Eberly Family Special Collections Library; Princeton University Library Special Collections; the Random House oral histories and archives held by Penguin Random House, with thanks to Mimi Bowling; the Ransom Center, University of Texas at Austin, with thanks to Richard Oram and Richard Workman; the Franklin Delano Roosevelt Presidential Library; Southeast Missouri State University Center for Faulkner Studies; Stanford University Special Collections; UCLA Library Special Collections; UC San Diego Library Seuss Collection; the University of Pennsylvania Kislak Center for Special Collections and Nancy Shawcross; The University of Reading British Publishing and Printing Archives; USC Cinema Library and the late Ned Comstock; the Albert and Shirley Small Special Collections Library, University of Virginia, with thanks to Hoke Perkins and Heather Moore Riser; William Morris Endeavor and Eric Simonoff and Eric Zohn for access to WME's James A. Michener papers; Special Collections, Williams College, thanks to Wayne Hammond, Ruth Quattlebaum, and Robert Voltz; Wisconsin Historical Society; Yale University Beinecke Rare Book and Manuscript Library.

Thanks to former *Publishers Weekly* librarian Gary Ink for access to the *PW* archives (now in Columbia's RBML); to Christi Cassidy and Carl Pritzkat for help in accessing *PW* material today; to George W. Slowik Jr., *PW*'s impresario and my friend; to Jim Milliot; and to *PW*'s late chief editor John F. Baker, who set me on the path to becoming a writer.

Most of this book was written at four libraries. I would like to extend special thanks to the following: Michael T. Ryan for his sustained interest and help, as well as Courtney Chartier, Mary Marshall Clark, Tara Craig, Susan B. Hamson, Jennifer B. Lee, Tom McCutchon, Melina Moe, Kevin O'Connor, Jane Rodgers Siegel, Jocelyn K. Wilk at Columbia's RBML; David Smith, Melanie Locay, Rebecca Federman, and Miriam Gianni for allowing me to be part of the Allen Room at the New York Public Library, and to the General Research librarians who have been so helpful while I've been there. Thanks to Catherine Creedon for welcoming me to the John Jermain Memorial Library, Sag Harbor, and to its staff, past and present. The New York Society Library's late head librarian Mark Piel and late deputy head Jane Goldstein encouraged me for years with their kindness and interest; Susan Chan, Katie Fricas, Sayer Holliday, Janet Howard, MariaLuisa Monda, Patrick Rayner, Rafael Rodriguez, Linnea Savapoulas, the late Harriet Shapiro, and Diane Srebnick helped turn the library into my home away from home; Steve McGuirl discovered books that would prove useful to this one. Thanks to former head Mark Bartlett, current head Carolyn Waters, and the entire NYSL staff.

For lending, giving, suggesting, or facilitating the use of photographs, papers, books, videos, information: Christopher and Jonathan

Cerf and Lois Klopfer Levy were extraordinarily generous with materials that illuminated their fathers' lives. Many thanks also to: Peter Amby; Victoria Arthur; Patryk Babiracki; Frances Commins Bennett; Peter W. Bernstein; Robert L. Bernstein; Louis Daniel Brodsky; Ellen F. Brown; The Century Association (Brynn White, Russell Flinchum, Celestina Cuadrado); Tracy Conrad; Christopher T. Cory; Bonnie Crosby; Elizabeth Darhansoff; Bruno de Harak; Vivian Ducat; Carlton Ealy; Charles Egleston; Kay Eldredge; Marisa and Silvia Erskine; Gary Giddins; Lizzie Gottlieb; Arlene Harris, Esq.; Erinn Hartman and Alfred A. Knopf, Inc.; Caroline and Michael Hornblow; Anne Isaak; Nicholas Latimer; Diana Loomis; Hilary Loomis; Robert D. Loomis; Caleb Marcus; Helen Marcus; Marion Meade; Anne Prescott; Gail Regina; Adam Rothberg; Enid Kastor Rubin; Selma Shapiro; Gay Talese; Walter Weintz; Ann Wimpfheimer.

Editing, research assistance, legal advice, reading, funding: I signed a contract with Robert Loomis at Random House in the fall of 2002 for what Bob thought would be a "celebration" of Bennett Cerf, and I thought would be a biography. Bob had been hired by Bennett in 1957. We both learned that I had taken on far more than either of us had imagined. Bennett's life had "a vast surface," Jonathan Cerf told me, and he was right. I had not only to traverse that expanse, but to explore what lay beneath. After a few years, while continuing to research, I started to draft chapters. Bob read them. "Just keep writing," he'd say. Nine years passed; Bob retired. By then, the injunction had changed: "Just keep writing, but it's going to be too long." I was nowhere near done.

Jonathan Jao, a talented young editor, took over, but soon moved to a bigger job at another house. The book, in publishing parlance, was "orphaned." Bob got in touch and suggested that he start reading, and we start meeting, again, but sotto voce—he'd retired, after all. We worked together until he died in the spring of 2020. He was ninety-three and I was his last author. I am grateful for his steady encouragement, elegant lessons, and dedication to the book. By the time the full draft was completed, it was far too long for one volume; Bob and I began cutting. When he died, a lot more cutting was needed. I was helped by Alice Truax, a deft hand with a phrase, and especially by Paul Golob, who persisted, wielding both scalpel and axe. Along the way, the book that you are reading lost at least five hundred pages—probably more. Although I did most picture research myself, thanks go to Carol Poticny for help in tracking down very hard-to-find photographs, and for her dedicated work in clearing permissions.

In the early years of this book, Laurele Riippa was invaluable in helping to organize my files. Several sets of young hands were involved at various junctures. Through the good offices of now-retired Columbia professor Patricia O'Toole, Quinn Latimer was awarded a Hertog Fellowship to be my research assistant for a semester. Many years later, Anabel Graff's services were suggested to me by novelist Ben Fountain, and she proved terrific at finding the impossible. Joannlee Lebron cheerfully saved me from many a computer glitch, and probably saved my sanity when helping to revise the endnotes and more.

I would like to thank the entire Random House team, past and present, whose work has in one way or another touched this book. The following—including the essential freelancers who in Bennett Cerf's day would have been on staff—were involved in the latter stages of bringing it to publication: Barbara Bachman, Rebecca Berlant, Mark Birkey, Monica Brown, Melissa Churchill, Richard Elman, Matthew Martin, Pam Rehm, Matthew Schneider, and Molly Turpin. A special shout-out to Lawrence Krauser, whose thoughtful enthusiasm helped keep me going.

Stephen Baister, Diana Howard, Deborah Lesser, David Reid, Professor David Richman, and Jonathan Segal read all or a substantial part of the manuscript. For the many hours put in and suggestions made, I am in their debt. I am equally grateful to Kai Bird, Heather Clark, Molly Haskell, Joseph Kanon, James Kaplan, and Amanda Vaill for reading and blurbing the book. It means much to me that Jonathan Cerf read the entire galley proof and gave a thumbs-up. Nicholas Latimer has been extraordinarily kind and helped in so many ways, not least through Michael Lionstar and the fine author photos he made. Esther Margolis, over many conversations, shared publishing wisdom. Laura Bleiberg, Vickie M. Feldman, Linda Fentiman, Bette-Lee Fox, and Daisy Maryles provided moral support. Andy and Beth McKillop and Pat Knopf gave early encouragement. James McGrath Morris started Biographers International Organization and encouraged me to be a founding director. Thanks to Jamie and BIO for lessons learned. The late Kenneth Silverman welcomed me into the NYU Biography Seminar (now the NYU-CUNY seminar), and its members have helped educate and sustain a neophyte; so, too, did the members of the Gotham Biography Group, now, alas, disbanded.

My thanks to the Pew Charitable Trusts, the late Michael Janeway, and Andras Szanto for their parts in awarding me a National Arts Journalism Program research fellowship at the Columbia Journalism School for 2001–2002, when the idea for this book germinated. I am grateful to the National Endowment for the Humanities for granting me a Public Scholar Award for 2016–2017, a vote of confidence at a crucial time. The Ransom Center at the University of Texas at Austin provided a four-week research fellowship. The Ragdale Foundation in Lake Forest, Illinois, granted me five writers' residencies. The Women's Media Group provided a grant toward improving my website. Fellowships and residencies do not arise on their own. Thanks to the following who provided references: James Atlas, E. L. Doctorow, Amanda Foreman, Jonathan Galassi, Michael Janeway, Frances Kiernan, Megan Marshall, Sonny Mehta, Peter Osnos, Patricia O'Toole, Susan Ralston, Amanda Vaill.

Ellis Levine and Mary Rasenberger, CEO of the Authors Guild, were helpful on legal matters. My agent, Eric Simonoff, has offered sage advice, support, and rare commitment: after switching agencies, he continued to represent me for sixteen years, without, for the most part, being paid for it. I am very grateful. Thanks, too, to his colleague Sian-Ashleigh Edwards.

The expense involved in a biography like this is enormous, and an advance, fellowships, and income from freelance work only go so far. My husband, David Reid, has been unstinting in his support of the project, financially and otherwise. It has been a very long road. My family, immediate and extended, has had to live with this book living in me these many years. I am grateful for their forbearance.

For two-thirds of my son's life, the book grew up alongside him. Ben got used to hearing me remark whenever a person, place, or thing we came across was related to my subject's life. He would respond, "The Bennett Connection!" It became a habit, a half-teasing, half-serious call-and-response, loving, hilarious, reassuring. I have dedicated this book to certain members of my family who have passed on, but have written it with Ben's generation, and the generations that follow, also in mind. In a world changing at such breakneck speed, acknowledging the past and our connections to it seems ever more valuable—and necessary.

Key to Abbreviations

INDIVIDUALS

AAK—Alfred A. Knopf
AAK Jr.—Alfred A. Knopf Jr.
AE—Albert Erskine
AP—Anne Prescott
AR—Ayn Rand
BAC—Bennett Alfred Cerf (aka Bennett Cerf)
BH—Ben Huebsch
BK—Bertha Krantz
BPB—Barbara Palmer Bayler
BWK—Blanche Wolf Knopf
BWS—Budd Schulberg
CBC—Christopher Bennett Cerf
CM—Cormac McCarthy
CMON—Carlotta Monterey O'Neill
CVV—Carl Van Vechten
CW—Charles A. "Tony" Wimpfheimer
DSK—Donald Simon Klopfer
EKR—Enid Kastor Rubin
EON—Eugene O'Neill
FCB—Frances Commins Bennett
FDR—Franklin Delano Roosevelt
FEP—Freddy Espy Plimpton
FM—Francis Meynell
FS—Frank Sinatra
GB—Glen Boles
GS—Gertrude Stein
GTH—Geoffrey T. Hellman
HAW—Herbert Alvin Wise
HBL—Horace Brisbin Liveright
HPG—Helen Palmer Geisel (aka Mrs. Ted Geisel)
JAM—James A. Michener
JE—Jason Epstein
JFC—Jonathan Fraser Cerf
JHS—James H. Silberman
JJ—James Joyce
JMF—Joseph M. Fox
JOH—John O'Hara
KCH—Kitty Carlisle Hart
LH—Leonora Hornblow
LKL—Lois Klopfer Levy
LM—Lewis Miller
ME—Morris Ernst
MH—Moss Hart
MJW—Mary Jane Ward
MKF—Michael K. Frith
MLS—Max Lincoln Schuster
NB—Nina Bourne
PC—Phyllis Cerf (aka Phyllis Cerf Wagner, Phyllis Fraser, Helen Brown, Helen Nichols)
PR—Philip Roth
RDL—Robert Duane Loomis
RE—Ralph Ellison
RK—Robert Kastor
RKH—Robert K. Haas
RLB—Robert L. Bernstein
RLS—Richard Leo Simon
RNL—Robert N. Linscott
SC—Saxe Commins
SS—Sylvia Sidney
TC—Truman Capote
TSG—Theodor Seuss Geisel (aka Dr. Seuss)
TW—Tennessee Williams
WF—William Faulkner
WS—William Styron

ARCHIVES, INSTITUTIONS, PUBLICATIONS

AAKR—Alfred A. Knopf Inc. Records, Harry Ransom Center, University of Texas at Austin

AEP—Albert Erskine Papers, MSS 13497, University of Virginia (including certain papers of William Faulkner and James A. Michener)

Age of the Great Depression—Dixon Wecter, *The Age of the Great Depression,* vol. 13, *A History of American Life* (New York: Franklin Watts, 1975)

ALHP—Arthur and Leonora Hornblow Papers, Margaret Herrick Library, AMPAS

AMPAS—Academy of Motion Picture Arts and Sciences Margaret Herrick Library Special Collections

AP—Anne Prescott Papers from her late husband, Peter Prescott; these have now been donated to the Knopf Records at the Ransom Center

AR—Bennett Cerf, *At Random: The Reminiscences of Bennett Cerf* (New York: Random House, 1977)

B&L—Boni and Liveright

BAC OH—Bennett A. Cerf Oral History, Oral History Collection, Rare Book and Manuscript Library, Columbia University

BOMC—Book-of-the-Month Club

BWSP—Budd Wilson Schulberg Papers, MS-978, Dartmouth College

CBC OH—Christopher Cerf Oral History, Random House Inc. Oral History Project

CEFC—Charles E. Feinberg Collection at the Morris Library, Southern Illinois University at Carbondale

Chodes interview—DSK Oral History interview by Stephen Chodes, Oral History Collection, Rare Book and Manuscript Library, Columbia University

COBIW—Council on Books in Wartime

CP—Cerf Papers, Rare Book and Manuscript Library, Columbia University

CPCC—Cerf Papers Catalogued Correspondence, Rare Book and Manuscript Library, Columbia University

DDDB—Bennett Cerf and Donald Klopfer, *Dear Donald, Dear Bennett: The Wartime Correspondence of Bennett Cerf and Donald Klopfer* (New York: Random House, 2002)

DSK OH—Donald Simon Klopfer Oral History, Rare Book and Manuscript Library, Columbia University

DSKP—Donald Simon Klopfer Papers, Chapin Library, Williams College (DSK's books do not form a collection, having been donated individually as a bequest to Williams)

DSK/RLB Papers—DSK Random House papers preserved by RLB

FWS—The Famous Writers School

Golden Age—John Tebbel, *A History of Book Publishing in the United States,* vol. 3, *The Golden Age Between Two Wars, 1920–1940* (New York: R. R. Bowker, 1978)

Great Change—John Tebbel, *A History of Book Publishing in the United States,* vol. 4, *The Great Change, 1940–1980* (New York: R. R. Bowker, 1981)

GSP—Gertrude Stein Papers, YCAL MS 76 Beinecke Rare Book and Manuscript Library, Yale

GTHP—Geoffrey T. Hellman Papers MSS.050, Fales Library, New York University

House of B&L—*Dictionary of Literary Biography,* vol. 288, *The House of Boni and Liveright, 1917–1933: A Documentary Volume,* ed. Charles Egleston (Farmington Hills, Mich.: Bruccoli Clark Layman-Gale, 2004)

JAMP—James A. Michener Papers, Library of Congress

JJRC—James Joyce Collection, Ransom Center

KP—Komroff Papers, Rare Book and Manuscript Library, Columbia University

LDJIN—*Long Day's Journey into Night*

LG—Literary Guild

LoC—Library of Congress

M&L—Michael Moscato and Leslie LeBlanc, eds., with an introduction by Richard Ellmann, *The United States of America v. One Book Entitled Ulysses by James Joyce, Documents and Commentary—A 50-Year Retrospective* (Maryland: University Publications of America, 1984)

MDP—Martha Dodd Papers, Library of Congress
MGM—Metro-Goldwyn-Mayer
MH/KCHP—Moss Hart and Kitty Carlisle Hart Papers, Wisconsin Historical Society
MJWC—Mary Jane Ward Collection, Howard Gotlieb Library, Boston University
ML—Modern Library
MLEP—Morris Leopold Ernst Papers, Ransom Center
NAL—New American Library
NYPL—New York Public Library
NYT—The New York Times
NYTBR—The New York Times Book Review
OCC—Dorothy Commins, *"Love and Admiration and Respect": The O'Neill-Commins Correspondence* (Durham: Duke University Press, 1986)
OH—Oral History
OP—Ober Papers, MSS 16807, University of Virginia
P&L—profit and loss
PC OH—The Reminiscences of Phyllis Cerf Wagner, 1978, Oral History Collection, Rare Book and Manuscript Library, Columbia University
PRP—Philip Roth Papers, Library of Congress
PW—Publishers Weekly clippings files; these have now been donated to the RBML, Columbia
RBML—Rare Book and Manuscript Library, Columbia University
RC—Harry Ransom Center, University of Texas at Austin
REP—Ralph Ellison Papers, Library of Congress
RH—Random House
RHCC—Random House Catalogued Correspondence, Rare Book and Manuscript Library, Columbia University
RHR—Random House Records, Rare Book and Manuscript Library, Columbia University
RLSP—Richard Leo Simon Papers, Rare Book and Manuscript Library, Columbia University
RMHP—Robert and Merle Haas Papers, Manuscripts Division, New York Public Library
S&S—Simon & Schuster
SCP—Saxe Commins Papers, Manuscripts Division, Princeton University Library
Seuss Collection—Dr. Seuss Collection, University of California at San Diego
SP—William Saroyan Papers, Special Collections, Stanford University
SRL—The Saturday Review of Literature
TASM—Try and Stop Me
TBAT—Too Brief a Treat: The Letters of Truman Capote, ed. Gerald Clarke (New York: Random House, 2004)
TNY—The New Yorker
TWIMH—James A. Michener, *The World Is My Home* (New York: Random House, 1992)
UCLA—University of California at Los Angeles
USCCL—University of Southern California Cinema Library
WFC—William Faulkner Collection, University of Virginia
WME—William Morris Endeavor Agency
WML—What's My Line?
WSJ—The Wall Street Journal

Notes

vii **"Life on earth":** Wall caption from "Mummy: The Inside Story" exhibition, British Museum, 2004.

vii **"And identity is funny":** Gertrude Stein (hereafter GS), *Everybody's Autobiography* (New York: Random House [hereafter RH], 1937), 68.

vii **"There are so many":** Picasso to Kahnweiler, wall caption from *Picasso Portraits* exhibition, National Portrait Gallery, London, Oct. 6, 2016–Feb. 5, 2017.

TO THE READER

xiii **"because [out] of everybody":** Cormac McCarthy (hereafter CM) to author, Mar. 12, 2008.

xiii **"Bennett Cerf [had] secured":** L. Rust Hills, "The Structure of the American Literary Establishment," *Esquire,* July 1963, 41–43.

xiv **fixated on "fun":** Thomas B. Morgan, "The Long Happy Life of Bennett Cerf," *Esquire,* Mar. 1964.

xv **"Stepping into sunlight":** Mia Farrow to author, Mar. 3, 2003.

xv **Extraordinary energy:** Orville Prescott, "Books of the Times," *New York Times* (hereafter *NYT*), Nov. 17, 1954, Box 68, Bennett Cerf Papers (hereafter CP), Rare Book and Manuscript Library, Columbia University Library (hereafter RBML).

xv **"Was I okay?":** Otto Barz to author, Jan. 9, 2006. Barz, a former RH production manager, quotes Bennett Cerf's (hereafter BAC) question to him. Others cited similar experiences.

xv **"play toy":** Elmer Adler to BAC, Aug. 28, 1928, Cerf Papers Catalogued Correspondence, RBML (hereafter CPCC).

xvi **"within ten years":** BAC quoted in Richard L. Simon (hereafter RLS), Trade Winds, *Saturday Review of Literature* (hereafter *SRL*), Dec. 23, 1950, 4.

PROLOGUE: AUGUST 31, 1971 "THEY CAN'T TAKE THAT AWAY FROM ME"

xxxi **"They can't take that away from me":** 1937 song title and lyrics by Ira Gershwin. Also, lyrics on xxxviii: "The way you wear your hat" and "No, no, they can't take that away from me."

xxxi **a fun funeral:** Howard Treeger to author, July 1, 2003. Treeger was a longtime RH sales rep.

xxxi **to send Cerf off:** Funeral details per Christopher Bennett Cerf (hereafter CBC) to author, Dec. 18, 2002. See also Henry Raymont, "Cerf Rites Draw Friends of Two 'Worlds,'" *NYT,* Sept. 1, 1971.

xxxi **"the friendliest, smilingest":** Helen Gurley Brown to Phyllis Cerf (hereafter PC), Oct. 26, 1971, Box 8, CP.

xxxi **looking out on the lady chapel:** Details of the view are from E. B. White, "Answers to Hard Questions," *The New Yorker* (hereafter *TNY*), May 4, 1957, Box 69, CP.

xxxii ***They know me:*** Armand Deutsch to author, June 2, 2003, quoting a phrase BAC often said.

xxxii **"Hey, aren't you":** Bertha "Bert" Krantz (hereafter BK), longtime RH copy chief, to author, Nov. 4, 2002.

xxxii **"I'd know you anywhere":** Morgan, "Long Happy Life of Bennett Cerf."

xxxii **sleek and smiling:** Michael K. Frith, Cerf family friend, RH editor (hereafter MKF), to author, Aug. 13, 2003.

xxxii **loved being "known":** James H. Silberman, former RH chief editor (hereafter JHS), to author, Feb. 5, 2003.

xxxii **five minutes into Saturday:** Mt. Kisco Vital Records Death Certificate. See also the obituaries in *The New York Post,* Aug. 28, 1971, as well as *The Los Angeles Times* and *The Washington Post,* Aug. 29, 1971 (both front page).

xxxii **no one had thought:** Rosanne Cerf, BAC's daughter-in-law, to author, Feb. 18, 2004.

xxxii **Nobody knew what his health was:** Leonora Hornblow (hereafter LH) to author, Nov. 17, 2002.

xxxii **never quite the same:** Jonathan Fraser Cerf (hereafter JFC) to author, Mar. 4, 2003.

xxxiii **"Poor old Cerf":** BAC 1971 diary, Box 12, CP.

xxxiii **gathered for birthday commiserations:** *Variety,* May 26, 1971, Box 73, CP.

xxxiii **"Trouble, trouble!":** BAC 1971 diary, Box 12, CP.

xxxiii **"Damn leg no better":** BAC 1971 diary, Box 12, CP.

xxxiii **believed in being good:** Reminiscences of BAC, Columbia University Oral History Collection (hereafter BAC OH), 1021.

xxxiii **"I can't":** Donald Simon Klopfer (hereafter DSK), quoted by PC in her Reminiscences, Columbia University Oral History Collection (hereafter PC OH). "Donald refused, saying it would be hypocritical." LH to author, Mar. 5, 2003.

xxxiii **songs would be by:** Fact sheet compiled at time of funeral, CBC to author.

xxxiv **"Is she out of her mind?":** Quotation as well as the details of the arrangements come from Robert L. Bernstein (hereafter RLB) to author, Feb. 25, 2003. Friendly suggested contacting Columbia's president; the go-ahead came from the president's secretary, who wired him in Rome. Telegram, correspondence in BAC file, Columbiana Collection, Columbia University.

xxxiv **"a tragic loss":** John V. Lindsay statement, Office of the Mayor, Aug. 28, 1971, Box 2, CP.

xxxiv **William Faulkner's widow:** Estelle Faulkner to Mrs. B. Cerf, telegram, Aug. 28, 1971, Box 1, CP.

xxxiv **"very great gift":** Robert Penn Warren to PC, Sept. 15, 1971, Box 2, CP.

xxxiv **"I can't possibly imagine":** Alistair Cooke to PC, Sept. 4, 1971, Box 1, CP.

xxxiv **city was going down a precipitous road:** State of the city and nation from headlines in *NYT,* Aug. 27, Sept. 1, 1971.

xxxv **Italian Renaissance grandeur:** Andrew S. Dolkart, *History and Architecture of St. Paul's,* church brochure.

xxxv **who had played the wise father:** Alan U. Schwartz, lawyer of Truman Capote (hereafter TC), to author, June 2, 2003.

xxxv **Others in the cadre:** Courtesy CBC.

xxxv **white roses and a note:** Florist's receipt of TC order: Box 1, CP.

xxxv **white roses covered the foot:** Rosanne Cerf to author, Feb. 18, 2004.

xxxv **his introduction and the authors' eulogies:** Texts courtesy CBC.

xxxvi **quavering voice:** Canfield on funeral audio recording, courtesy CBC.

xxxvi **glistened with tears:** BK to author, Nov. 4, 2002.

xxxvii **"a little bit in love":** Liz Carpenter to PC, Aug. 29, 1971, Box 8, CP.

xxxvii **wanted more of everything:** LH to author, Nov. 17, 2002.

xxxvii **"You will never have this outpouring":** Nan A. Talese to author, Jan. 7, 2003.

xxxviii **"strange dichotomy":** William Styron (hereafter WS) to author, Mar. 3, 2002.

xxxviii **"fathered the Modern Library":** Philip Roth (hereafter PR) to author, Oct. 29, 2004.

PART ONE, 1898–1919: A RATHER UNUSUAL SPECIMEN

CHAPTER I: INHERITANCE

3 **phalanx of towers:** The public housing Masaryk Towers date to 1963.

3 **"I'm rather an unusual specimen":** BAC OH, 1.

3 **The death certificate specified:** New York City Department of Records and Information Services, Municipal Archives. To make matters even more confusing, on the certificate, Gustave's father's birthplace is given as "France." Whether the clerk made a mistake in transcribing the information; whether Bennett made a mistake in giving it; whether Bennett discovered in his father's papers after the death the true birthplace of his grandfather is impossible to determine.

4 **"Cerf Family" tree:** Handwritten by BAC, dated Oct. 6, 1941, on RH/BAC letterhead paper. PC, CBC, and JFC added later, and BAC's death noted in PC's hand. Courtesy CBC and JFC.

4 **he was Benoît:** Gustave's father, Benoît, appears on Fredericka Wise/Gustave Cerf City of New York Marriage Certificate #17519, filed Nov. 13, 1896. In the July 1870 census Benoît Cerf is listed as thirty-six years old. His birth date was Feb. 4, 1834, per https://www.findagrave.com/memorial/178878618/benoit-cerf; a passport has it as 1835; "Cerf Family" pedigree has it Feb. 14, 1834. His mother, Caroline, in the 1850 census (roll M432-546) was

born in France in 1809; age in 1850 given as forty. On the internet her birth year is given as 1797 and her date of death July 3, 1887, per https://www.findagrave.com/memorial/178880399/caroline-cerf. Findagrave.com has Benoît born in Eddyville, New York.

4 **officially "Benoît":** Birth certificate, State of New York, #27689.

4 **His grandfather had died:** Bennett's grandfather was sixty years old when he died on Feb. 8, 1895, Kings County, New York; NY Death Index, #2635, Soundex C610.

4 **one being Lazarus Cerf:** See John Doggett Jr., *The New-York City and Co-Partnership Directory for 1842 & 1843* (New York, 1843), 62. The NY state census population estimate of 371,223 for 1845 can be found in Robert Ernst, *Immigrant Life in New York City 1825–1863* (Syracuse: Syracuse University Press, 1994), 192.

4 **A year later, Caroline:** Caroline Cerf listed in Doggett, *The New-York City and Co-Partnership Directory for 1844 & 1845* (New York, 1845), 68.

4 **had come to America:** Paula E. Hyman, *The Jews of Modern France* (Berkeley: University of California Press, 1998), 13–14; Esther Benbassa, *The Jews of France* (Princeton: Princeton University Press, 1999), 66–67.

4 **Their surname:** *Cerf, Hart,* and *Hirsch* all derive from the Hebrew "Naftali" or "Naphtali," one of the twelve sons of Jacob. The patriarch blessed him as "a hind let loose: he giveth goodly words"—not a bad thing for a publisher. The name literally means "deer," but there are implied meanings: presumed lustiness or a cuckold's horns. See Patrick Hanks and Flavia Hodges, *A Dictionary of Surnames* (Oxford: Oxford University Press, 1988), 101, 242, 257, 382.

4 **listed as a clockmaker:** Charles R. Rode, *Rode's New York City Directory 1850–51* (New York, 1850), 91. As watchmakers, see *The New York City Directory 1851–2* (New York: Doggett & Rode), 103. Benoît's brother Adolph Maurice is listed as two years older, his dates 1832–97. https://www.findagrave.com/memorial/178880356/adolph-maurice-cerf.

4 **Once the Civil War broke out:** Benoît served three months in the 6th Regiment, H Company, NY State Militia, http://www.nps.gov/civilwar/search/soldiers-detail.htm?soldierId=3A7A3EBC-DC7A-DF11-BF36-B8AC6F5D926A.

4 **expanded into jewelry:** *Trow's,* May 1, 1862, 148.

4 **he'd married Bavarian-born Mathilda Newwitter:** It was sometimes rendered "Newitter." BAC's handwritten family tree says Mathilda born in Bavaria; other sources cite Prussia.

4 **fathered four children:** New York State Census, July 1870.

4 **amassed real estate:** This also included a $4,000 Brooklyn property from father-in-law Manasses Newwitter. See "Real Estate Transfers," *Brooklyn Eagle,* May 19, 1875, 3; *Trow's,* May 1, 1881, 250.

4 **fifth of nine children:** I have determined the number of Wise children from the 1880 and 1900 censuses, and from Wise family burial records at Mt. Neboh Cemetery. Three children presumably died young; in his OH, 2, BAC refers to six adult children. According to the NYC Death Index Soundex W200, Delphine died on Jan. 4, 1893, at the age of forty-four. Herbert Alvin Wise's (hereafter HAW) birth certificate gives his date of birth as Dec. 6, 1892.

4 **Grandmother Delphine was born:** Fredericka's death certificate specifies that her mother was born in Germany; her brother HAW's birth certificate specifies that their mother was born in Luxembourg. Birth certificate 156-52-637527, NYC Municipal Archives, delayed registration, filed June 24, 1952.

5 **"like the Smith brothers":** BAC OH, 6.

5 **But Nathan was no WASP:** In the 1880 and 1900 censuses, Nathan Wise's origin is Germany. According to his 1905 passport application, he was born Sept. 22, 1842, in Lengsfeld, Saxony.

5 **"Cerf was a great exaggerator":** Arthur Gelb to author, May 2005.

5 **anything about the maternal side:** CBC and JFC to author, multiple interviews.

5 **and his death in 1908:** Date courtesy Mt. Neboh Cemetery, New York.

6 **ancestral amnesia and Americanized names:** Like their friend Bennett, Herbert Mayes (né Meyersheim), who edited *Good Housekeeping, McCall's,* and *Cosmopolitan,* and Herbert Bayard Swope (his father was born Schwab), editor of Pulitzer's newspaper the *New York World,* pursued trappings of high WASP society and weren't known by most people as Jews. Alexandra Mayes Birnbaum to author, Nov. 2, 2004. See also E. J. Kahn, *The World of Swope* (New York: Simon & Schuster [hereafter S&S], 1965), 84.

6 **Germans predominated, Jews among them:** Moses Rischin, *The Promised City: New York's Jews, 1870–1914* (Cambridge: Harvard University Press, 1962), 68–69.

6 **"Nathan Wise, tobacco":** The address was 170 Rivington Street. See *Trow's New*

York City Directory for year ending May 1, 1874 (New York: Trow Directory, Printing and Bookbinding Company), 1410. Big nose and long face: Nathan Wise passport applications, May 6, 1884, and June 6, 1905. Per his 1905 application, he arrived in New York in Nov. 1863.

6 **Wholesale Tobacco Association:** *Brooklyn Eagle* announcement, "Albany," May 30, 1880, 4; see also "Wise & Bendheim: Nathan Wise Dead," *The Tobacco Leaf* (New York), vol. 45, July 23, 1908, 1. For Wise household details, see 1880 Manhattan Census: Roll T-9_895, page 470B, enumeration district 585, image 0342.

6 **James Buchanan Duke arrived:** John K. Winkler, *Tobacco Tycoon: The Story of James Buchanan Duke* (New York: RH, 1942), 9–60.

6 **using independent competitors:** Winkler, *Tobacco Tycoon,* 125–29.

6 **Metropolitan Tobacco:** "Big New Tobacco Concern," *NYT,* Jan. 22, 1899, 3; "A New Tobacco Company," *Wall Street Journal* (hereafter *WSJ*), Jan. 23, 1899, 4.

6 **rebuked Metropolitan:** "Method of Distribution," *Brooklyn Eagle,* Jan. 31, 1899, 1; Winkler, *Tobacco Tycoon,* 235–36.

6 **"conservative":** BAC OH, 1.

7 **"hydra-headed trust":** BAC, Trade Winds, *SRL,* Apr. 22, 1944.

7 **"being good":** BAC OH, 1021.

7 **New York City was incorporated:** David C. Hammack, "Consolidation," *The Encyclopedia of New York City,* edited by Kenneth T. Jackson (New Haven: Yale University Press, 1995), 277–78. See also Lloyd Ultan and Gary Hermaly, *The Birth of the Bronx* (New York: Bronx County Historical Society, 2000); Stephen Jenkins, *The Story of the Bronx* (New York: G.P. Putnam's Sons, 1912).

7 **trading in dimensions:** For a typical deal, see entry under Nathan Wise in "The Real Estate Market," *NYT,* Oct. 14, 1886, 7.

7 **pioneer of building loans:** See "Follow the Lead of the 'Leaders'!!" ad, *New York Tribune,* Sept. 25, 1919, 23, http://chroniclingamerica.loc.gov/lccn/sn83030214/1919-09-25/ed-1/seq-23/.

7 **"daughter of Mr. Nathan Wise":** *NYT,* Nov. 12, 1896.

7 **his most spectacular coup:** "Real Estate Men May Upset Plans for Tunnel," *Chicago Daily Tribune,* Jan. 25, 1902, 4. See also *NYT,* Jan. 25, 1902.

7 **"a consideration of $140,000":** *Brooklyn Eagle,* Mar. 4, 1902, 20.

7 **"kow-towed":** BAC OH, 6.

8 **"with a marvelous backhand":** BAC OH, 6.

8 **"was loaded with charm":** BAC OH, 1, 3.

8 **Polo Grounds:** Howard Dietz to PC, Sept. 8, 1971, Box 8, CP. Dietz said that Gustave attended 154 games a year and marveled that he had the time.

8 **"just about made a living":** BAC OH, 33.

8 **"absolutely adored him":** BAC OH, 3.

9 **"the creative body":** Kitty Carlisle Hart (hereafter KCH) to author, Dec. 14, 2002.

9 **laid to rest:** Cemetery details courtesy Mt. Neboh Cemetery, Glendale, New York.

9 **"If you can leave people":** BAC OH, 1021.

10 **"Nobody can be that happy":** Barbara Epstein, co-founder of *The New York Review of Books,* to author, Oct. 29, 2004. Epstein's former husband, Jason Epstein (hereafter JE), was a longtime RH editor.

CHAPTER 2: A PRETTY SMART KID

11 **synagogues sprouted up:** On Harlem synagogues, including the one on BAC's block, see David W. Dunlap, *From Abyssinian to Zion: A Guide to Manhattan's Houses of Worship* (New York: Columbia University Press, 2004), 26.

11 **"outrage":** BAC OH, 3; exact wording was "to the outrage of my grandfather." See Cerf/Wise marriage certificate City of New York #17519; for the wedding details, see *NYT,* Nov. 12, 1896. In the notice, Fredericka is "Freda," but in the 1908 probate papers attached to Nathan Wise's will at NYC Surrogate's Court, she is referred to—and signs as—"Frieda." Similarly, documentation exists for "Gustav" and "Gustave." To avoid confusion, I use Frieda and Gustave throughout. Wedding was at "Tuxedo Hall" in midtown and was presided over by Rabbi Harris of Temple Israel. Re Temple Israel, see also Michael Henry Adams, *Harlem Lost and Found* (New York: Monacelli Press, 2002), 202.

11 **nearly died:** CBC to author (date not noted).

11 **ketchup, cigarettes, and the like:** According to BAC OH, 3, Gustave designed labels for Blue Label ketchup and Murad, the leading brand of Turkish tobacco. BAC told Christopher Cory, who reported *Time*'s cover story on BAC in the Dec. 16, 1966, issue, that the company his father worked for was Rhode & Brand; Cory to author. In the 1900 and 1910 Censuses, Gustave is listed as "lithographer."

11 **Cerfs lived with:** For details on 118th Street, see twelfth census of the U.S., 1900, NY Borough of Manhattan.

11 **brand-new, six-story:** Thirteenth census of the U.S., 1910, NY Borough of Manhattan.

11 **"very handsome, charming, wonderful":** BAC OH, 2. Gustave still referred to BAC as "Sonny" in his letters from the 1930s.
12 **but Frieda doesn't smile:** BAC and mother photo in Box 34, CP.
12 **"a very happy family":** BAC OH, 4–5.
12 **"very easily hurt":** BAC OH, 4–5.
12 **"not being able to hit Big League":** BAC OH, 2.
12 **Buster Brown collar:** BAC OH, 8.
13 **"tough little kids":** BAC OH, 10.
13 **stepped Dutch roofs:** In his OH, 8, BAC says PS 10 was in such bad shape, it "should have been torn down." It may have been in bad shape when he recorded his OH, but when he was a student, the school was quite new. On PS 10, see NYC Department of Education Property Schedules, 1908.
13 **"real life began":** BAC OH, 4.
13 **"absolutely middle class":** BAC OH, 12.
13 **"nasty little boys":** BAC OH, 15.
13 **"a pretty smart kid":** BAC OH, 10.
13 **would almost photographically imprint:** JFC to author, July 9, 2003.
13 **The experience "soured" him:** BAC OH, 12.
13 **wouldn't let Frieda ask her father:** BAC OH, 10, 9.
13 **"soft touch of the world":** BAC OH, 27.
13 **nor did work as a hosiery salesman:** BAC OH, 33–34. In the 1915 NY census and 1920 Federal census, Gustave's work is listed as "hosiery."
13 **Soon he was smitten with sports and adventure magazines:** BAC OH, 11.
14 **Nathan Wise had signed a will:** Surrogate's Court, County of New York. Filed Sept. 29, 1908; petition and proofs, Oct. 8, 1908. Date and place of death in probate documents.
14 **$10,000 was common shorthand:** Thirteen years after Nathan's death, his Metropolitan Tobacco associate Adolph D. Bendheim died, and the *NYT* recorded an estate worth $2.5 million (more than $45 million today). See "Bendheim Left $2,529,679," *NYT,* Jan. 4, 1923, 13.
15 **"the largest and most up-to-date":** Background on Riviera (and Sound Realty, the company Nathan Wise founded), from the Audubon Park Historic District Committee, *Audubon Park: Request for Evaluation for Historic District Status,* report submitted to the New York Landmarks Preservation Commission, Mar. 2003, 17, 18.
15 **on the twelfth floor:** The Cerf family lived in 12H per BAC diary, Sept. 13, 1918, Box 11, CP. See also Andrew Alpern, *New York's Fabulous Luxury Apartments* (New York: Dover, 1975). Riviera ads reproduced in Audubon Park Historic District Committee report.
15 **"Wonderful":** BAC OH, 23.
15 **"Back into the bustle":** Text of *St. Nicholas* story, Box 36 and Box 72, CP.
15 **"real life":** BAC OH, 17.
16 **Townsend Harris Hall:** Now known as Townsend Harris High School (THHS), see Townsend Harris Alumni website, https://thaa.org/thhs-history/. Background and BAC's transcript courtesy Pamela Delvecchio, Susan Rodriguez, and Elizabeth Betgilan, THHS. Townsend Harris Hall grew out of a preparatory program at City College; some say it started in 1904, others 1905. It predated today's most famous NYC academically competitive high schools, Stuyvesant and Bronx Science. Closed in the 1940s, Townsend Harris reopened in the 1980s. Now associated with Queens College, it remains one of the best NYC public schools.
16 **"The dropouts were fantastic":** BAC OH, 17.
16 **earning grades in the 70s and 80s:** First year transcript, fall/spring semesters: French 80/72; English 78/78; math 88/78; history 87/78; drawing 73/69.
16 **His grades improved:** Second year transcript, fall/spring semesters: French 78/87; English 83/87; math 73/66; history 89/80; drawing 68/69; German 67/67.
16 **Packard Commercial School:** BAC OH, 31, 28.
16 **"was going to make money":** BAC OH, 31, 28.
16 **Frieda Cerf came under a physician's care:** Frieda Cerf New York City Death Certificate 16887, filed May 24, 1914.
16 **Frieda had been "desperately anxious":** BAC OH, 5.
16 **"weakened my mother":** Both infants, the unnamed boy and a girl named Dorothy May, are on Bennett's entry on findagrave.com. He does not mention the first baby, who according to Findagrave died in 1903. Bennett says the girl's birth and death were less than a year before Frieda's own; if Findagrave is correct, the year it happened was 1911, when he was thirteen, three years prior to Frieda's death.
16 **"It was the day before":** BAC OH, 5.
17 **Bennett began keeping a diary:** There is no evidence that he kept one before January 1915.
17 **"Barring May 24":** Sept. 18, 1918, Box 11, CP. The reason for his disappointment was rejection for officer training during World War I because of his eyesight. He was later able to join up with glasses.
17 **"The important thing":** BAC OH, 2.

BAC and his father lived together at the Riviera. When he first moved to the Navarro, his father may have shared the apartment; certainly, Gustave later had a separate apartment upstairs.

17 **Wises and Cerfs:** Since BAC always refers to relations by first names, it's impossible to determine who are Wises and who are Cerfs. His diary entry for Sept. 27, 1918, may provide the best clue: "Whole Cerf family here for supper. Uncles Jerry, Morris, Max, Leo, Aunts Gert and Celia, and Alfred."

CHAPTER 3: COLUMBIA

19 **"knew everything":** BAC OH, 6–7, 28. In his OH, BAC claimed HAW was weak because his mother was fifty-one when he was born (6); on HAW's birth certificate her age is listed as forty-four. For HAW's experiences at Horace Mann and failure to graduate college, see transcripts, Columbiana file on HAW. It contains a death notice (presumably information from BAC or HAW's partner of several decades, Glen Boles [hereafter GB]) that mentions chess team; so does HAW's obituary, *NY Herald Tribune,* Oct. 4, 1961. The OH says he had punctured a lung. Hunchback: GB to author, Jan. 20, 2005; also, CBC; JFC; Peter Stansky and Marina Vaizey to author, July 23, 2009.

19 **Herbert's bouts with tuberculosis:** BAC diaries.

19 **Bennett fiercely wanted to win:** See Jerome Weidman, *Praying for Rain* (New York: Harper & Row, 1986), 362.

19 **"never terribly strong":** BAC OH, 6. The tennis scores are in BAC diaries, Box 11, CP.

19 **Founded in 1754:** For Columbia history, see James Boylan, *Pulitzer's School: Columbia University's School of Journalism, 1903–2003* (New York: Columbia University Press, 2003), chs. 2 & 3; Robert A. McCaughey, *Stand Columbia: A History of Columbia University in the City of New York* (New York: Columbia University Press, 2003).

20 **"suitable candidates":** Boylan, *Pulitzer's School,* 14.

20 **one of 176 male:** Journalism School population in *Annual Report of the President and the Treasurer to the Trustees with Accompanying Documents for the Year Ending June 30, 1917* (New York: Columbia University, 1920), 131, Columbiana Collection.

20 **An "imperious chief executive":** Boylan, *Pulitzer's School,* 12.

20 **"Hebrews" now comprised:** For graduating NYC high schools, see McCaughey, *Stand Columbia,* 261.

20 **including some Jewish students:** On the war and Jews, see McCaughey, *Stand Columbia,* 257, 268. After the war, the proportion of Jews hovered around 25 percent, although Jewish undergraduates at Columbia College declined to between 8 and 10 percent. By way of comparison, in the 1920s, 15 percent of students at Harvard as a whole, and less than 10 percent of Harvard undergraduates, were Jews; 10 percent of Yale undergraduates were Jews; and only 5 percent at Princeton. For a fuller discussion of Jews at Columbia, see McCaughey, *Stand Columbia,* chapter 9, from which these statistics have been taken.

20 **"All Columbia students are Jews":** *Vanity Fair* article quoted in McCaughey, *Stand Columbia,* 257.

20 **Bennett Alfred Cerf:** BAC, about to publish a book with Harper, confirmed to Harper's Beulah Hagen on Aug. 6, 1957, that "my full legal name is Bennett Cerf." Box 10, Harper & Row Papers, Columbia University.

20 **He was six feet tall:** BAC discharge papers specify his height as 5'10"; passports say 6'0". It's conceivable—he was young enough when discharged—that he grew two inches in his early twenties, but impossible to know, given his predilection for exaggeration. He was always described as tall.

20 **accepted into a fraternity:** BAC OH, 33.

20 **"You're born wanting":** BAC OH, 31.

20 **"A good editor":** BAC OH, 1015.

20 **Before classes started, he'd approached the college paper:** BAC diary, Sept. 26, 1916.

21 **organizing committee:** On Nov. 15, 1916, BAC wrote in his diary that he was elected class secretary; in the OH, 36, he claimed to have been vice president.

21 **miniature bowling:** BAC diary, Feb. 21, 1918, Box 11, CP; **parlor golf:** BAC diary, Jan. 5, 1918, Box 11, CP; **speculative discussions:** BAC diary, Feb. 18, 1917, Box 11, CP.

21 **Herbert described himself as a "writer":** Census of Block #4, election district 45, State of New York, June 1, 1915.

21 **friend and supporter of poets like Hart Crane:** GB to author, Jan. 20, 2005.

21 **friend who was a broker:** The brokerage house was Sartorius. On "valued customer," see BAC OH, 62–63.

21 **his first cousin Delphine:** BAC diary, Jan. 20, 1917, and other dates.

21 **Marie Mayer entered:** BAC OH, 39. OH and his diary showed that fifty years later they remained friends.

21 **"tag" his initials:** BAC diary, Jan. 2, 1917.

21 **imaginary "interviews":** BAC diary, Feb. 26, Mar. 30, 1917.

21 **even Herbert:** BAC diary, May 14, 1917, Box 11, CP.

21 **"because I'm blankety blanked":** Apr. 11, 1917, BAC, Box 11, CP.

21 **editor-in-chief:** BAC diary, Jan. 9, 1918.

21 **"like a burlesque show":** BAC OH, 41.

22 **"All I can say is":** BAC OH, 45.

22 **Any more vulgarity:** BAC OH, 1029.

22 **"I want to congratulate you":** Dean's letter in Box 36, CP. BAC notes it in his diary, Mar. 5, 1918.

22 **"cold . . . unapproachable maverick":** BAC, "The Great Tradition," *Spectator,* July 7, 1919, Box 36, CP.

23 **"for one stick of dynamite":** BAC *Spectator* clipping, Box 36, CP.

23 **had to cancel classes:** BAC diary, Jan. 18, 1918. Columbia canceled classes on Mondays for ten weeks to save coal.

23 **liberal inclinations:** BAC OH, 12–13. For an example of a sports story showing BAC's liberal inclinations, see *Spectator* clipping, Jan. 15, 1917, Box 36, CP.

23 **about thirty thousand city lives:** Francesco Aimone, "The 1918 Influenza Epidemic in New York City: A Review of the Public Health Response," *Public Health Reports* 125, Suppl. 3 (2010): 71–79.

23 **"good [officer] material":** BAC diary, Aug. 7, 1918.

23 **"riff-raff":** BAC diary, Aug. 8, 1918.

23 **something wrong with his heart:** BAC diary, Sept. 18, 1918, which he called the "bitterest day" in his life since his mother died. The next day, by "judicious manipulation," BAC passed the eye test and reversed the decision.

23 **an honorable discharge:** Honorable Discharge #5139279, in Box 35, CP.

23 **At once Bennett signed up:** BAC OH, 43.

23 **physics:** BAC diary, Sept. 11, 1919.

23 **joint degree:** BAC diary, Sept. 11, 1919.

23 **Phi Beta Kappa:** May 28, 1920, Box 36, CP. BAC's first-term grades were English A−; History A; Politics B; Philosophy A; Journalism B+; French A−; Phys Ed C; Hygiene B. BAC diary, Feb. 3, 1917. Later, he received straight A's in academic subjects and a B in military training.

24 **"not to clutter":** BAC OH, 59.

24 **"Spent the day":** BAC diary, Feb. 3, 1917.

24 **"Read first two books":** BAC diary, Feb. 20, 1918.

24 **"Herbert went over":** BAC diary, Apr. 3, 1918.

24 **changing his life:** BAC OH, 53.

24 **Through Steeves:** BAC OH, 54–60. BAC repaid his help by publishing a "dreadful detective story" he wrote: BAC OH, 60.

24 **Weaver's comparative literature class:** BAC OH, 54–60.

24 **"became a very close friend":** BAC OH, 60.

25 **"irregular life":** All quotes from this section in BAC OH, 29–30. Also, GB, JFC, and CBC as well as Peter Stansky and Marina Vaizey, who both knew HAW as young people, discussed his homosexuality with the author.

26 **"Bennett was somebody":** HAW analyzed by student of Freud's; GB to author, Jan. 20, 2005. GB, an actor–turned–PhD psychoanalyst who specialized in gay patients, had many occasions to observe BAC.

26 **"with Eddie Klopfer":** BAC diary, Feb. 11, 1919, Box 11, CP.

26 **they clicked:** On this early rapport, see Donald Simon Klopfer Oral History, RBML, 6 (hereafter DSK OH).

26 **welcomed their second child:** DSK birth certificate, Bureau of Records Borough of Manhattan #5234. Also, Lois Klopfer Levy (hereafter LKL) to author, Nov. 19, 2003; Klopfer family tree courtesy LKL. Stella Danziger Klopfer Jacobson's dates were Sept. 27, 1871–May 17, 1960, courtesy Mt. Neboh Cemetery.

27 **"very unsuccessful":** DSK OH, Feb. 14, 1975, 2; LKL to author.

27 **"really hard up":** DSK OH, 2. Simon was born on July 16, 1860, and died on Aug. 23, 1912, dates courtesy Mt. Neboh Cemetery.

27 **took in a boarder:** LKL to author, Nov. 9, 2003.

27 **old flame:** DSK OH, 2.

27 **a certain affluence:** DSK OH, 2. When Manny died in 1922, he left $615,927. "Estates Appraised. Jacobson, Emanuel," *NYT,* Jan. 24, 1923, 38. See also "Emanuel Jacobson's Will," *NYT,* July 7, 1922, 2. See also article on Emanuel's brother Henry's will: "Wills for Probate," *NYT,* Jan. 20, 1923, 22.

27 **"taken sick":** DSK OH, 3. If DSK's dating is correct, that would have been 1920, when he was eighteen. However, his dating is not entirely reliable. For example, in his OH, DSK says, "I graduated DeWitt Clinton when I was about 14 or something." He was fifteen when he left Clinton.

28 **places like Andover:** "Andover was still pretty actively Calvinist in those days. There wasn't really a quota—but there was." Ruth Quattlebaum, Phillips Academy, Andover, to author, May 20, 2005. Of 164 senior boys in the 1918 yearbook, only six had recognizably Jewish surnames.

28 **an attentive, attractive listener:** Robert Duane Loomis (hereafter RDL) to author, Dec. 10, 2003; Charles Wimpfheimer (hereafter CW) to author, Dec. 26, 2002; Alfred A. Knopf Jr. (hereafter AAK Jr.) to author, Dec. 16, 2002.

28 **enrolled at Columbia:** DSK in 1932 Alumni Register and 1918–19 Student Directory, courtesy Columbiana Collection.

28 **dispute with his stepfather:** See essay on DSK by Richmond Dean Williams, 1950, in Williams College Archives. LKL (on Nov. 19, 2003) and Robert Volz, Williams librarian (Aug. 6, 2007), each said that DSK also attended Princeton very briefly; Volz said DSK left because of antisemitism. There is no record of DSK at Yale or Princeton. In his OH, DSK said that at Williams, he decided to be an engineer, and wanted to finish at Williams and then go to MIT. His stepfather told him to go to Yale's specialized Sheffield scientific school instead, but DSK disagreed and quit school.

28 **$125,000 inheritance:** BAC OH, 27.

28 **"already stronger":** BAC OH, 27.

PART TWO, 1920–1940: FROM PLAYBOY OF THE WESTERN WORLD TO MAN OF PROPERTY

29 **"The transition from the playboy":** BAC to GS, Sept. 17, 1941, CPCC.

CHAPTER 4: LOVE WRONG

31 **"All Wall Street":** BAC diary, Sept. 15, 1919, Box 11, CP.

31 **its biggest client:** BAC diary, Oct. 7, 1919. Sartorius & Einstein was later called Sartorius, Smith & Loewi.

31 **His salary:** BAC diary, Sept. 19, 1919.

31 **"decent living":** Average worker's earnings: Ann Douglas, *Terrible Honesty: Mongrel Manhattan in the 1920s* (New York: Farrar, Straus & Giroux, 1995), 18.

31 **good moment to arrive:** Gordon Thomas and Max Morgan-Witts, *The Day the Bubble Burst* (Garden City: Doubleday, 1979).

31 **"lit up":** BAC diary, Nov. 3, 1919.

31 **often with Howard Dietz:** BAC OH, 21.

31 **free tickets:** BAC OH, 46.

31 **"the fellow opening":** BAC OH, 18.

31 **"electrified":** BAC, "Where Are the Shows of Yesterday?" *Variety,* Jan. 9, 1957, Box 69, CP.

31 **"Empire to see":** BAC diary, Nov. 5, 1919, Box 11, CP.

32 **drawn to the wider world:** BAC OH, 66, 67.

32 **home to more than:** In 1910 the population of Manhattan was 2,331,542. In 2020 it was 1,694,251. See U.S. Census. http://www.census.gov.

32 **influx of Russian and Eastern European Jews:** Judith Ramsey Ehrlich and Barry J. Rehfeld, *The New Crowd* (Boston: Little, Brown & Co., 1989). More than 2.5 million Russian and Eastern European Jews arrived in America between 1880 and 1925, and a good proportion sojourned at least for a time in NYC.

32 **"It wasn't all that easy":** KCH to author, Dec. 14, 2002.

32 **"the biggest anti-Semite":** BAC diary, May 7, 1919.

32 **"to the German Jew":** BAC OH, 16.

32 **"The Hebrew hypocrites":** BAC diary, Sept. 26 & 27, Oct. 4, 1919, Box 11, CP.

32 **"Bennett would have preferred":** KCH to author, Dec. 14, 2002.

32 **bought an interest in Sartorius:** BAC diary, June 1, 1921.

32 **His byline appeared:** It was in the *Ceres Union Monthly* and *Daily Garment News.* Box 36, CP.

33 **"Buy Liberty Bonds":** The *New York Tribune* story, BAC OH, 64–66.

33 **His last *Tribune* piece:** *Tribune* clips, Mar.–May, 1922, Box 36, CP.

33 **"an inveterate flirt":** Barbara Walters to author, Oct. 15, 2004.

33 **"wormed" an extra quarter:** BAC OH, 20.

33 **"That's the first time":** BAC OH, 25–26.

33 **"Marie is a peach":** BAC diary, Feb. 16, 1919.

33 **attached to his watch chain:** BAC diary, Feb. 19, 1919, Box 11, CP.

33 **"Interesting developments":** BAC diary, Mar. 6, 1919, Box 11, CP.

34 **"absolutely beautiful young girl":** BAC OH, 130–35.

34 **very wealthy, country-clubbing:** Ansbacher background per LKL to author, Nov. 19, 2003.

34 **"amusing":** BAC OH, 131.

34 **he crossed the Hudson:** DSK OH, 4, 6.

34 **"When we finished that":** BAC OH, 132. The word BAC used in his OH was "trip" rather than "walk."

34 **"Our interests were identical":** DSK OH, 6.

36 **Elberon and Deal:** Marjorie Edelson and Kay Zimmerer, *An Historic Perspective of the Township of Ocean* (Township of Ocean, New Jersey, 1974); Marie A. Sylvester, *Around Deal Lake* (both Dover, N.H.: Arcadia Publishing, 1998); Randall Gabrielan, *Long Branch People and Places* (Dover, N.H.: Arcadia Publishing, 1998). Courtesy LKL.

36 **"The Bookleggers":** The Bookleggers calling card courtesy LKL.

36 **he'd hold club memberships:** See Box 36, CP.

36 **"Bennett gave in":** BAC diary, Nov. 8, 1921, Box 11, CP.

37 **"I have not kept":** BAC diary, Jan. 2, 1923, Box 11, CP.

37 **"Marian and I get along":** BAC diary, Jan. 5, 1923. *Merton of the Movies,* by Harry Leon Wilson, published originally in 1922 and from which BAC took the "low-comedy face" quote, is now available courtesy of Project Gutenberg. Plot details courtesy IMDb; George S. Kaufman and Marc Connelly wrote the source 1922 play.

37 **"something electric":** BAC diary, Mar. 23, 1923, Box 11, CP.

37 **beautiful girl:** BAC diary, Mar. 27, 1923.

37 **"Helen came down":** BAC diary, Apr. 4, 1923, Box 11.

37 **finally got married:** LKL provided wedding details and a video of a home movie snippet of the wedding. LKL to author, Nov. 19, 2003.

CHAPTER 5: LIVERIGHT

38 **a tiny bit annoyed:** BAC OH, 69–70.

38 **urging of fellow alum Max Schuster:** *Dictionary of Literary Biography,* vol. 288, *The House of Boni and Liveright, 1917–1933: A Documentary Volume,* edited by Charles Egleston (Farmington Hills, Mich.: Bruccoli Clark Layman-Gale, 2004), 46 (hereafter *House of B&L*).

38 **A lunch was arranged:** BAC OH, 70. The date of the meeting is in BAC's diary, Box 11, CP.

38 **awed by the powerful, theatrical charisma:** For background on Liveright (hereafter HBL) and his firm, see BAC OH; Walker Gilmer, *Horace Liveright: Publisher of the Twenties* (New York: David Lewis, 1970); John Tebbel, *A History of Book Publishing in the United States,* vol. 3, *The Golden Age Between Two Wars, 1920–1940* (New York: R. R. Bowker, 1978) (hereafter *Golden Age*); Tom Dardis, *Firebrand: The Life of Horace Liveright, The Man Who Changed American Publishing* (New York: RH, 1995); Egleston, *House of B&L;* Charles A. Madison, *Book Publishing in America* (New York: McGraw-Hill, 1966).

38 **Horace Brisbin Liveright:** There is some disagreement about HBL's middle name. According to Dardis, it is "Brisbane," but Gilmer and Egleston use "Brisbin." See Dardis, *Firebrand,* 30; Gilmer, *Horace Liveright,* vii; Egleston, *House of B&L,* 20.

39 **Liveright was often eviscerated:** Margaret Case Harriman, *The Vicious Circle* (New York: Rinehart & Co., 1951), 14. Round tablers themselves called their "club" the Vicious Circle.

39 **"We're a very individual firm":** HBL quoted in BAC OH, 72.

39 **"a dour and sulky bastard":** BAC OH, 73. There's no mention of the Dreiser baseball episode in BAC's diary, which is highly unusual. Encounters with famous people were always recorded. BAC went on to say in his OH that he immediately decided to join Liveright and phoned the brokerage firm after lunch to give in his notice. However, as mentioned, further discussion did occur before he joined.

39 **More meetings:** Meeting with HBL. BAC diary, Oct. 2, 1923, Box 11, CP.

39 **He'd lend the company:** The amount BAC actually appears to have lent was $24,000 rather than $25,000. See next note.

40 **"OK for Mr. Liveright":** Employment details from copy of BAC's contract. It, along with a contract for the sale of the Modern Library (hereafter ML), is in a "Cerf" file embedded among author files of the Liveright Publishing Corporation, now a subsidiary of W. W. Norton & Co. The contract was to run until the end of 1926. The file has copies of two financial notes dated Feb. 6 and Mar. 24, 1924, each recording a $12,000 loan by BAC to HBL. Both were paid off on Sept. 1, 1925, with ML sale.

40 **Uncle Herbert was consulted:** BAC OH, 73.

40 **"Jazz Age in microcosm":** Edith W. Stern, "The Man Who Was Unafraid," *SRL,* June 28, 1941, 10.

40 **"I walked in and met":** BAC OH, 73.

40 **"A man can stand":** B. W. Huebsch (hereafter BH), quoted in "B. W. Huebsch, Publisher, Dead," *NYT,* Aug. 8, 1964.

40 **"was mostly in the hands":** BAC OH, 89.

40 **made it increasingly urban:** In 1910, 45.7% lived in cities; by 1920, more than half did, and the percentage kept growing. See Tebbel, *Golden Age,* 4.

41 **At twenty-three:** On HBL's early stock market history, see Manuel Komroff, "The Liveright Story," in *A Story-Teller's World,* circa 1968, Box 20A, 7, Komroff Papers, Columbia University (hereafter KP).

42 **"Little Leather Library":** Tebbel, *Golden Age,* 6; Egleston, *House of B&L,* 20; Dardis, *Firebrand,* 47–48.

42 **Liveright borrowed cash:** backing for ML also came from a friend of Mr. Elsas: Egleston, *House of B&L,* 5.

42 **a debt to Everyman's Library:** See generally Jay Satterfield, *"The World's Best Books":*

Taste, Culture, and the Modern Library (Amherst: University of Massachusetts Press, 2002), 25–30.

42 **first dozen Modern Library (ML) titles:** Gilmer, *Horace Liveright,* 11. Maurice Maeterlinck and Anatole France were the other two inaugural authors.

42 **response from the reading public:** Gilmer, *Horace Liveright,* 11.

42 **literary adviser and vice president:** On Seltzer's participation, see Egleston, *House of B&L,* 5, 7.

42 **"gallop to the nearest store":** *Publishers Weekly* (hereafter *PW*) ad, Aug. 18, 1917, quoted in Egleston, *House of B&L.*

42 **"hungry for what was sophisticated":** Louis Kronenberger, "Gambler in Publishing: Horace Liveright," *The Atlantic Monthly,* Jan. 1965, 95.

43 **romantic reverence:** Lucy Liveright Koch Wilson, HBL's daughter, to author, Jan. 10, 2008. HBL came from a family of book-lovers. Older sister Ada F. Liveright was librarian of the School District of Philadelphia's central Pedagogical Library. *Library Journal,* Apr. 1909, vol. 34, 160. His first cousins Addie and Babette owned the Liveright Book Shop in NYC from 1924 to 1952. "Nostalgic Twins," *TNY,* Mar. 2, 1963, 24–26. BAC was a patron.

43 **fresh, vital:** Stern, "Man Who Was Unafraid," 14.

43 **sell syndication rights:** Komroff, "Liveright Story," 37. $7,000 in 1917 is equivalent to $190,000 in 2025. Trotsky returned to Russia after the Feb. 1917 revolution.

43 **With the toss of a coin:** Boni & Liveright (hereafter B&L) would change its name in 1928 to Horace Liveright, Inc., and in 1931 to Liveright, Inc. In 1933 it would become Liveright Publishing Corporation, Inc.

43 **he read manuscripts:** Lucy Liveright Koch Wilson to author, Jan. 10, 2008.

44 **make many decisions himself:** Donald Friede, *The Mechanical Angel* (New York: Alfred A. Knopf, 1948), 26.

44 **"shit":** See Gilmer, *Horace Liveright,* 60 and chapter 4, "John Sumner's Vice Society."

44 **"At least this man":** Sherwood Anderson, *Memoirs: A Critical Edition,* edited by Ray Lewis White (Chapel Hill: University of North Carolina Press, 1969), 517–18.

44 **"I don't think he's got":** BAC OH, 83, 91.

44 **gambling losses:** See Komroff, *Intimate Portraits,* Faulkner chapter, 41 (unpublished), Box 20A, KP.

44 **"no truck with nonentities":** Stern, "Man Who Was Unafraid," 10 & 14.

44 **future publishers:** The group also included Leon Shimkin, Donald Friede, Manuel Siwek, and Julian Messner.

44 **Would-be novelist:** Komroff's novels were later published by B&L, Coward McCann, Harper, and FSG.

44 **after an illegal abortion:** Lillian Hellman, *An Unfinished Woman* (Boston: Little, Brown, 1969), 39–40. It took place after BAC had left B&L; his replacement Donald Friede provided the name of the abortionist.

45 **"Even the stenographers":** Hellman, *Unfinished Woman,* 38.

45 **Liveright could publish:** Egleston, *House of B&L,* 7, 9, 11, 188–89.

45 **Seventeen others:** Stern, "Man Who Was Unafraid," 14.

45 **"more than most publishers":** Edward L. Bernays, *Biography of an Idea* (New York: S&S, 1965), 253. On Bernays's brother-in-law Fleischman, 277. See also Egleston, *House of B&L,* 7.

45 **If you understood:** Bernays figured out how to persuade too well; he helped convince American women to smoke.

45 **weekly newsletters:** Bernays, *Biography of an Idea,* 284.

45 **"invoked the American weakness":** See Catherine Turner, *Marketing Modernism Between the Two World Wars* (Amherst: University of Massachusetts Press, 2003), 43.

45 **"exciting" world of books:** HBL's commitment to making books was known to involve imagination, innovation, and considerable cash. During the 1920s, he spent more than $1 million to promote his books in print. See Gilmer, *Horace Liveright,* 90.

46 **Thanks to him:** Gilmer, *Horace Liveright,* 60. Chapter 4, "John Sumner's Vice Society," gives a full portrait of censorship activities and the anti-censorship fight. For a chronology of banned books, see Egleston, *House of B&L,* 7–9.

46 **"those cheap little publishers":** Komroff, "Liveright Story," 218.

46 **he lamented:** Told on background to the author.

46 **"No woman was ever":** On the fight against the Clean Books Bill, see Gilmer, *Horace Liveright,* 60–80.

46 **There's no better initiation:** BAC OH, 84–85; RLS, Trade Winds, *SRL,* Sept. 21, 1946, Box 19, Richard Leo Simon Papers, Rare Book and Manuscript Library, Columbia (hereafter RLSP).

47 **"the one playwright":** On the marketing of O'Neill and *Strange Interlude,* see Dardis, *Firebrand,* 60.

47 **"a book by a negro":** *New York Times Book Review* (hereafter *NYTBR*), Aug. 12, 1923.

47 **known antisemite:** Pound agreement memorandum, Jan. 4, 1922, Pell Papers, courtesy Gary Giddins. The contract was

for two years, paying Pound a minimum of $500 per year as an advance whether or not B&L published his translations. HBL did bring out Pound's translation of Edouard Estaunie's *The Call of the Road* in 1923.

47 **Pound had taken him:** Dardis, *Firebrand,* 87.

47 **now numbering:** In the RBML collection at Columbia University, Gabriele D'Annunzio's *The Triumph of Death* translated by Arthur Hornblow appears in a "First Impression" in 1923. The book contains a complete list of ML titles, and the D'Annunzio book is listed as #112. However, according to a June 1924 ad, the number then was 108. Titles were sometimes dropped. See Egleston, *House of B&L.*

47 **"the city of the Good Time":** Ford Madox Ford, *New York Is Not America* (New York: Albert & Charles Boni, 1927), 49.

47 **"Mr. Liveright is":** "With the Makers of Books in America: XVI The House of Boni & Liveright," *The Literary Digest International Book Review,* 1924, courtesy *PW* file on Liveright.

47 **switchboard "girl":** Kronenberger, "Gambler in Publishing," 95.

48 **scarlet-walled:** Kronenberger, "Gambler in Publishing," 98. Stern describes the decoration, but Gilmer says embellishments were actually on panels concealing the entrance. Stern, "Man Who Was Unafraid," 14; Gilmer, *Horace Liveright,* 84.

48 **showers in Central Park:** Stern, "Man Who Was Unafraid," 14.

48 **Doubling as a bookcase:** see Dardis, *Firebrand,* 135.

49 **coral, jade, and mauve:** Stern, "Man Who Was Unafraid," 14.

49 **surrounding trees:** The trees were mainly acacias. For a description of B&L's office, see *PW,* Aug. 18, 1923.

49 **three-piece jazz band:** Komroff, "Liveright Story," 196.

49 **Variety was welcome:** Gilmer, *Horace Liveright,* 84.

49 **so many in evidence:** Kronenberger, "Gambler in Publishing," 99.

49 **"respectable, high-class chatty":** Hellman, *Unfinished Woman,* 36.

49 **"went right through":** BAC OH, 120.

49 **Guests progressed:** HBL, in "Insert X" to his unfinished autobiography, *The Turbulent Years,* Box 2, KP.

49 **casually fondled:** BAC OH, 102.

49 **"a little necking":** BAC OH, 104.

49 **"What must you think of me?":** BAC OH, 104.

50 **"never entirely 'respectable'":** See "With the Makers of Books in America: XVI The House of Boni & Liveright."

50 **"beneath contempt":** Louis Kronenberger, "Gambler in Publishing," 97.

50 **"Jesus Junior":** BAC OH, 110; Gilmer, *Horace Liveright,* 91.

50 **"I was the wide-eyed kid":** BAC OH, 78.

50 **unsuccessful mine owner:** Komroff, "Liveright Story," 4.

50 **"very rigid and stern":** Lucy Liveright Koch Wilson to author, May 14, 2010. (HBL's mother was a Fleisher, a well-known Philadelphia Jewish family.)

50 **Bennett would sometimes:** Lucy Liveright Koch Wilson to author, Jan. 10, 2008, and May 14, 2010. Lucy was born in 1915.

50 **slightly peculiar, effeminate:** Lucy Liveright Koch Wilson, Jan. 10, 2008. Many interviewees used similar terms in describing BAC's speech.

50 **basement shipping room:** Komroff, "Liveright Story," 186.

50 **didn't flaunt:** Komroff, "Liveright Story," 186.

50 **"sleek and dark":** Edward Weeks, *Writers and Friends* (Boston: Little, Brown, 1982), 189, 309.

51 **shrewder judge:** Weeks, *Writers and Friends,* 189.

51 **"keen quality":** Komroff, "Liveright Story," 186.

51 **a B&L catalogue:** Box 111.8, W. W. Norton Records, Columbia University.

51 **Bennett's first blurbs:** Scrapbook, Box 36, CP.

52 **"attention, undivided attention":** Gilmer, *Horace Liveright,* 24.

52 **"if an editor felt":** BAC OH, 101–2.

52 **the title parade:** 1924–25 notable Liveright publications from Egleston, *House of B&L.*

52 **alone among the staff:** Friede, *Mechanical Angel,* 18.

52 **lost out on each copy:** Friede, *Mechanical Angel,* 18; Gilmer, *Horace Liveright,* 105.

52 **auditor's account:** Friede, *Mechanical Angel,* 27.

52 **Modern Library sale:** BAC OH, 124–30.

52 **popular speakeasy:** Jack and Charlie's later became the '21' Club.

53 **"Why the Modern Library Is Worth $250,000":** When DSK died, RLB, then the president, transferred DSK's early financial history papers (up to the merger with Smith & Haas in 1936) to his own files (hereafter DSK/RLB Papers). RLB showed these to me. This document, which comes from these papers, shows that in 1918, retailing for 60 cents each, the ML had sold 122,450 copies with gross earnings

of $16,393; in 1924, the retail price was 95 cents and 260,115 copies were sold, for earnings of $63,885.

53 **furious literary agent:** The agent, identified by Komroff to Edward Weeks on Sept. 19, 1971, was Carl Brandt. See KP.

53 **just seemed to spur:** BAC OH, 124.

54 **"the wild day":** Komroff to Weeks, Sept. 19, 1971, KP.

54 **"was going to try":** DSK OH, 10–11.

54 **The only signatures:** Presumably Lucile Liveright (via her father) owned the vast majority of stock, and HBL and Pell, as officers of the corporation, were empowered in that capacity to sign. It's unclear who all the stockholders were. On the signing page is a scribble: "OK—Donald S. Friede." Most likely HBL had already sold shares (i.e., borrowed from) BAC's successor as vice president, Friede. Pell almost certainly had shares; he eventually bought the company. BAC file is in Liveright Publishing Corporation author contracts at W. W. Norton & Co. See also Dardis, *Firebrand,* 76. A letter from BAC indicates that the day before the sale, he had lent HBL an additional $3,500. The sale document includes a provision for HBL to pay back that $3,500, along with another $2,000 also lent, beyond the sums of BAC's original employment contract.

In HBL's unpublished memoir, he describes "several weeks" of discussions with a tableful of participants re sale. Komroff also indicates a large meeting, but calls it the *closing*. See Komroff, "Liveright Story," 205. Presumably, the meetings HBL referred to took place between BAC's return from Europe and the final, amended agreement. However, given BAC's penchant for exaggeration, and the reference in his diary on May 20, 1925, to "a whirlwind conference," it is entirely possible that more people were involved on May 19, as HBL recalled in "Insert Y," 2, from *The Turbulent Years,* in Komroff, Box 2.

54 **closing would take place:** Liveright had demanded an "advisory counsel" clause in the sale contract of May 19, 1925 (held in the file at W. W. Norton), whereby he'd receive $3,000 per year for five years for services that were not wanted and probably would never be provided. It's not in an amendment dated June 30, 1925. However, in "Highlights in the History of the Modern Library and Random House," written in 1936 when RH merged with Smith & Haas, it is stated that BAC and DSK instead bought him off with a lump sum of $10,000. See "Highlights," Box 4, CP.

CHAPTER 6: THE BOOK BOYS

55 **"I don't like Jews":** Ford, *New York Is Not America,* 126. The Boni brothers' company was incorporated in 1923.

55 **and one girl:** A second "girl," Evelyn Shrifte, would join Vanguard Press in 1928 and eventually become president of the company.

55 **Century Association and other social bastions:** BAC and Alfred A. Knopf (hereafter AAK) both applied for membership in the Century and were rejected. On BAC's application, see official minutes of the Century Association Committee on Admissions, Oct. 9, 1957, and Dec. 11, 1957, courtesy Dr. Russell A. Flinchum, former Century archivist; Dr. Flinchum to author, Oct. 23, 2012; and BAC 1957 diary. On AAK's application, see Box 1, Folder 4, series 1, Thayer Hobson Papers, Harry Ransom Center, University of Texas (hereafter RC).

55 **Harry Scherman and Robert Haas:** A third founder, Maxwell Sackheim, soon left the company and New York.

55 **The prejudice they encountered:** To get a sense of the ugly, shocking prejudice the Jewish book boys faced, see Ben Hecht, *A Jew in Love* (New York: Covici Friede, 1931), 3. Hecht's protagonist is said to be partly based on Liveright, and partly on theatrical agent Jed Harris.

56 **sartorial splendor:** For full sources on AAK's background, see Chapter 37, "Knopfs." On the clothing and facial hair, see Lurton Blassingame, "The Trinity—and a Dog," *TNY,* Aug. 21, 1926, 15–17.

56 **"determined to be a publisher":** AAK, "Some Random Recollections," *Typophile Chapbook XXII* (New York: The Typophiles, 1949), 9.

56 **became the first Jew:** Charles A. Madison, *Jewish Publishing in America* (New York: Sanhedrin Press, 1976), 254. On the connection between AAK's father and Doubleday job via Long Island Railroad contact, see "Some Random Recollections," 10.

57 **"extremely generous":** "Some Random Recollections," 12–17.

57 **colors not dissimilar:** From Geoffrey Hellman (hereafter GTH), "Profiles: Alfred A. Knopf Publisher Part I: A Very Dignified Pavane," *TNY,* Nov. 20, 1948, 46. Other parts of three-part profile, "Flair Is the Word" and "The Pleasures, Prides, and Cream," published in the Nov. 27 and Dec. 4 issues.

57 **wouldn't be generous:** Blassingame, "The Trinity—and a Dog," 16.

58 **Persian prince:** The comparison comes from Carl Van Vechten (hereafter CVV). See GTH, "A Very Dignified Pavane," 44.

58 **"fortnightly Friday soirees":** GTH, "The Pleasures, Prides, and Cream," 42.

58 **flapper-thin:** AAK Jr. discussed the weight issues of Blanche Wolf Knopf (hereafter BWK) in an interview with Susan Sheehan, Feb. 3, 1975, courtesy Anne Prescott (hereafter AP). Sheehan did this and other interviews for a biography of AAK that she later abandoned. Her interviews went to Peter Prescott, who died before he could complete his biography of AAK. Prescott's widow, AP, kindly allowed me to see his materials. These materials are now at the RC. Laura Claridge attributed BWK's thinness and lack of appetite to other factors as well, including painful adhesions from endometriosis. See Claridge, *The Lady with the Borzoi: Blanche Knopf Literary Tastemaker Extraordinaire* (New York: Farrar, Straus and Giroux, 2016), 52, 68.

58 **If a man wanted a new suit:** Stanley Kauffmann to author, Apr. 20, 2012.

58 **"Mr. Alfred A. Knopf":** quoted in GTH, "A Very Dignified Pavane."

58 **"Young, exotic, and charming":** See Blassingame, "The Trinity—and a Dog." "Exotic" was a code word for "Jewish."

59 **bringing in sales:** Gayle Feldman, "The Borzoi Three-Quarterly: Knopf's Seventy-Five-Year History," *PW,* Oct. 26, 1990. Statistic from *PW* internal file on Alfred A. Knopf, Inc.

59 **Publishers' Lunch Club:** Tebbel, *Golden Age,* 130.

59 **"the Spinoza sense":** On Schuster's childhood, see Max Lincoln Schuster (hereafter MLS) OH, 2–3, 5–6, 184, Columbia University.

59 **grew up in a house:** for RLS childhood and family, see Marie Brenner, "I Never Sang for My Mother," *Vanity Fair,* Aug. 1995, 132–46. See also GTH, "How to Win Profits and Influence Literature," *TNY,* part 1, Sept. 20, 1939. The next two parts were published in the Oct. 7 and 14 issues. Joanna Simon to author, Nov. 9, 2005.

59 **"who knew if":** Nina Bourne (hereafter NB) to author, Nov. 15, 2006. NB started in publishing in 1939 as RLS's secretary.

59 **"democratizing":** MLS OH, 53–54, 57–58.

59 **"only good books":** The manifesto is dated May 20, 1923. See Herbert S. Mitgang, "Simon & Schuster History on Display," *NYT,* May 21, 1982.

59 **Pegging their own salaries:** Albert R. Leventhal, "The 20s: Ah, Those Were the Publishing Days," *PW,* Oct. 14, 1974, 36–38. For the amount each partner and family contributed, see GTH, "How to Win Profits and Influence Literature," part 2.

60 **third-largest stake:** On his father, Thomas Guinzburg to author, Feb. 11, 2003. See also Harold Guinzburg's Columbia OH, 15–16.

60 **Guinzburg's grandfather:** Ancestry information from Thomas Guinzburg to author, Feb. 11 & 28, 2003. Harold Guinzburg's maternal grandfather owned Kleinert Rubber. His father was a banker/real estate investor.

60 **"We had no answer":** MLS OH, 68–69.

60 **a suitable book:** MLS OH, 61–62. Crosswords had made their first appearances in newspapers a decade earlier.

60 **the trio responsible:** The crossword trio were Margaret Petherbridge, Prosper Buranelli, and F. Gregory Hartswick. Petherbridge was later married to publisher John Farrar, a founder of Farrar, Straus & Giroux.

60 **"Practically every":** RLS to Fred Melcher, *PW* editor, July 27, 1932, *PW* S&S files.

60 **novelty element:** Leventhal, "The 20s."

60 **$1.35 per copy:** *Simon & Schuster: The First Seventy-Five Years* (New York: S&S, 1999), 12.

61 **take a one-inch ad:** Peter Schwed, *Turning the Pages* (New York: Macmillan, 1984), 2.

61 **"a little unliterary":** MLS OH, 63–64. Plaza name from telephone exchange: Schwed, 2.

61 **first "real" books:** *PW,* May 31, 1924.

61 **a very useful one:** Shimkin's coming to B&L, then S&S: John Tebbel, "Leon Shimkin: The Businessman as Publisher," *SRL,* Sept. 10, 1966, 74–75, 80. See also "The Story of Simon and Schuster," *Book Production Magazine,* Mar. 1964; *Simon & Schuster: The First Seventy-Five Years,* 23–24.

61 **they persuaded:** "Take a Bow Harold Guinzburg," *PW,* Feb. 3, 1945, 636.

61 **"vulgarians":** Justin Kaplan to author, May 3, 2004. Kaplan had worked for MLS as a young man.

61 **"the bad boys":** Tebbel, *Golden Age,* 554.

61 **"He had his own brilliance":** NB to author, Nov. 15, 2006.

62 **founded by E. Haldeman-Julius:** Abraham Blinderman, "Haldeman-Julius and the 'Little Blue Books,'" *AB Bookman's Weekly,* Oct. 16, 1978; Tebbel, *Golden Age,* 203–9; Madison, *Book Publishing in America,* 396–98; "Socialist, Scorned by Banker Father-in-law, Wins Fortune," *The World,* Mar. 18, 1928; Harry Gilroy, "Durants' History Reaches Its End," *NYT,* Sept. 19,

1967, 44; Walter Clemons, "Ten Little Pocket Books and How They Grew," *NYT,* June 15, 1969, BR8.

62 **who would become a mainstay:** Durant had a co-author for the S&S books: his wife, Ariel.

62 ***Trader Horn:*** GTH, "How to Win Profits and Influence Literature," part 2, 29.

62 **Dick had a breakdown:** GTH, "How to Win Profits and Influence Literature," part 3, 26.

62 **"Inner Sanctum":** RLS, "The Truth about *The Inner Sanctum*—Well, 95 Per Cent of It," *The Atlantic Bookshelf,* 67–70, clipping, n.d.

62 **"very mysterious":** NB to author, Nov. 15, 2006.

CHAPTER 7: EMBARKATIONS

64 **"Dick Simon and I sat up":** BAC 1925 travel journal in Box 11, CP. Unless otherwise specified, this is the source for all BAC quotes in the chapter.

64 **"remote future":** RLS to MLS, June 5, 1925, Box 250, MLS Papers, Columbia University.

65 **reserved at the Waldorf:** The rivalry between RH and S&S deepened over the decades. BAC stated that RLS had reserved a room "in some dump I wouldn't be seen dead in." BAC OH, 151. But as BAC's diary shows, RLS had reserved in advance at the Waldorf—very far from a dump.

65 **National Gallery:** In his diary, BAC wrote "Royal Gallery." There isn't a "Royal Gallery" and so he would have meant either the National Gallery; the Royal Academy; or the Gallery in Buckingham Palace. Given the proximity of Trafalgar Square, it was likely the National.

66 **the B&L treasurer:** DSK said of Pell that "he was constantly falsifying the daily card of cash balance . . . he would never let Horace know there was money in the bank. . . . And I suspect that some of the money that was loaned to [B&L] in those days at 12%, which was unheard of then . . . was probably some of Pell's." DSK OH, 41–42. The sale contract dated May 19 in Liveright files at W. W. Norton confirms Sept. 1 date.

66 **lawyer Edwin Falk:** Unclear why BAC used his friend Edwin Falk on the ML transaction, instead of fraternity brother Horace Manges, who would become the RH corporate lawyer and remain so for decades.

67 **incorporated in New York:** A search by the New York County Clerk Business Archives Dept. did not turn up the original incorporation document. However, a "Certificate of Change of Name of Modern Library, Inc. to Random House, Inc.," dated Mar. 23, 1936, in their files, provides the original incorporation date. In 1936 Gustave was company secretary; likely he was from the beginning.

67 **across the street:** "Modern Library Celebrates a Tenth Anniversary," *PW,* Sept. 7, 1935, 730–31.

67 **"everything was to be":** BAC OH, 147.

67 **These papers:** I have inserted dollar signs into the two columns for clarity.

68 **"News!":** The ad ran Aug. 1, 1925. Box 36, CP.

68 **"impossible":** "Plan New Modern Library Program," *PW,* July 25, 1925.

69 **more than half the books:** Statistics on title mix and dead vs. living authors from Gordon Barrick Neavill, *The Modern Library Series,* PhD dissertation, University of Chicago, Aug. 7, 1984, 84. Neavill provides much detailed analysis.

69 **Five new reprints:** Per Fall 1925 Modern Library catalogue, Box 167, Random House Records, Columbia (hereafter RHR).

69 **The Joyce wasn't out:** Per "The Modern Library: A Complete List of the 126 Titles Including Additional Numbers to be Published," Autumn 1926, Box 118, RHR.

69 **Bennett managed:** In BAC's figures dating from Aug. 1, 1925, he provides per-week salary estimates: BAC, $85.00; DSK, $65.00; Manny Harper, $30.00; Helen, $25.00; Abe, $20.00. The June 25 memo has BAC at $90.00; DSK, $65.00; Bookkeep, $40.00; Stenog & phone, $35.00; Shipping, $40.00. Per DSK/RLB Papers. DSK recalled that in addition to Helen Berlin there was another girl. This may have been Pauline Kreiswirth, who certainly migrated from B&L early on. See DSK OH, 12.

70 **"They stank to high heaven":** DSK OH, 12.

70 **binding would be cloth:** BAC and DSK experimented with different kinds of cloth, only settling on "balloon" cloth two and a half years later. See *PW,* Feb. 9, 1929, 657.

70 **Established "book travelers":** For instance, James Crowder in Chicago, Desmond Fitzgerald on the West Coast.

70 **They hit the road:** On the sales trips, see DSK OH, 12–13.

70 **Boston in a blizzard:** BAC diary, Feb. 4, 1926, Box 11, CP.

70 **constantly consulting:** DSK OH, 20.

70 **would quickly show results:** In 1928, RLS and MLS, proposing to buy the ML from

BAC and DSK, compiled a prospectus to that effect; it contained the series' sales figures from inception through that year, per prospectus, DSK/RLB Papers. Turnover was $225,000 in 1926; $270,000 in 1927; and $300,000 (estimated) for 1928. In 1936, at the time of the merger with Smith & Haas, sales were adjusted slightly to, respectively, $218,467; $260,496; $295,007. In 1926, the first full year under BAC and DSK, 386,000 units sold, an increase of 35.5%. For the figure of nearly half a million copies in 1927, see *PW,* Mar. 10, 1928, 1028.

70 **recouped their initial investment:** BAC OH, 140.

70 **"an institution":** *PW,* Feb. 9, 1929, 657. The number of ML titles is taken from ML catalogues. Box 167, RHR.

70 **"absolutely no deadwood":** Form letter, Jan. 6, 1927, Box 167, RHR.

71 **"final sale":** The practice of "returns" is generally believed to have been started by S&S during the Depression to try to help struggling booksellers stay in business.

71 **policy of advertising:** Satterfield, *"The World's Best Books,"* esp. 43–46. Satterfield, like Neavill, provides much detailed ML information.

71 **"The Worst Sellers":** *TNY* ad, Feb. 13, 1926, Box 36, CP. The "overlooked" titles were Andrea Latzko's *Men in War,* Ouida's *In a Winter City, Marjorie Fleming's Book,* and Maeterlinck's *A Miracle of St. Anthony.* Knopf's ads used a similar "worst-seller, best-seller" appeal.

71 **field had become crowded:** On rivals and the role of introductions, see Satterfield, *"The World's Best Books,"* 75, 83–84.

72 **Deciding to be strategic:** See AAK–BAC letters on *Green Mansions,* Box 125, RHR.

72 **"Yours always, Alfred":** See, for example, correspondence on *The American Mercury,* Box 133, RHR.

72 **jokey telegram:** "Lodovici Klopfer and Magillovitch Cerf" to AAK, Nov. 13, 1936, Box 133, RHR.

72 **"prize package":** BAC's second travel diary is in Box 11, CP.

72 **ML's European scout:** BAC to Manuel Komroff, Aug. 25, 1926, RH Catalogued Correspondence (hereafter RHCC).

73 **Eisenach:** The city is famous in Germany as the place where Bach became musically active and where Martin Luther produced the first German vernacular translations of the Bible.

73 ***"mishpocha":*** Word for "family" in Yiddish. BAC spelled it "*mashpocha.*"

74 **"*aus-gekissed*"; "*aus-gefressed*":** "Kissed" and "fed" in BAC's bastardized German!

74 **Nonesuch's founder:** The other two founding partners of Nonesuch were Francis Meynell's wife, Vera Mendel, and David Garnett, author of *Lady into Fox* and *Aspects of Love* and a member of the Bloomsbury set.

74 **presiding genius:** On Meynell (hereafter FM), see John Dreyfus, *A History of the Nonesuch Press, with an Introduction by Geoffrey Keynes and a Descriptive Catalogue by David McKitterick, Simon Rendall, and John Dreyfus* (London: Nonesuch Press, 1981).

74 **close friend of Dickens:** FM, *My Lives* (New York: RH, 1971), 11.

74 **"fine prices":** See FM in *PW,* Sept. 13, 1971.

74 **"brisk young man":** FM, *My Lives,* 177.

CHAPTER 8: "THE RANDOM HOUSE"

75 **their ninth-floor loft:** 1926 catalogue, BAC 1926 diary, and RH incorporation papers all give 71 W. 45th St. as ML address. "Plan New Modern Library Program," *PW,* July 25, 1925, has it as 75 W. 45th Street; *PW,* Jan. 29, 1927, has it as 73 West 45th Street. Presumably the building covered all three numbers.

75 **backgammon or bridge:** BAC OH, 172.

75 **card-tossing competitions:** FM, *My Lives,* 177.

75 **anthologist who hadn't bathed:** BAC OH, 190–91.

75 **wine-making machine:** BAC OH, 189.

75 **"so discontentedly":** BAC to Manuel Komroff, Aug. 25, 1926, RHCC.

75 **Enter Elmer Adler:** In his OH, BAC says Adler became a partner at the end of 1927, when Pynson printed *Candide* (actually printed 1928). Incorporation documents show he was a partner from the start. BAC OH, 198.

75 **"country-squirish":** "Elmer Adler, Bibliophile, Dies; Expert Printer and Collector, 77," *NYT,* Jan. 12, 1962; see also obituary, *PW,* Jan. 22, 1962.

75 **he'd been thrown out:** David Pankow, "Elmer Adler," in *Grolier 2000,* edited by Claudia Funke (New York: The Grolier Club, 2000), 1–4.

76 **"exacting":** *PW,* Jan. 22, 1962; **"unbending":** *PW,* Mar. 7, 1931.

76 **Adler introduced Alfred to W. A. Dwiggins:** See AAK OH, 69, Columbia.

77 **the ML's "flying girl" torchbearer colophon:** BAC OH, 144. Most people thought the torchbearer was androgynous; later, it appeared decidedly male.

77 **"un-commercial":** Frederick B. Adams Jr., "Elmer Adler, Apostle of Good Taste," *PW,* Apr. 5, 1941.

77 ***three* partners:** RH incorporation documents are in the NY State Business Archives. The new company had two hundred shares "without par value," i.e., without a specified nominal value, and each man held one share to satisfy minimum filing requirements.

78 **"books of typographical excellence":** Press release on RH birth, Box 36, Book #3, CP.

78 **Luckily, a partner:** The partner was a Mr. Heimerdinger.

78 **dispatched a letter and contract:** Box 171, RHR.

78 **"We will certainly":** BAC to FM, Dec. 10, 1926, Box 171, RHR.

78 **"I've got the name":** On BAC's account of the eureka moment, see BAC OH, 195. He says he left the Kent meeting to go to the bathroom and dreamt up the name while there. It's impossible to know whether BAC added that element as embroidery or if it occurred that way. When RH was at 457 Madison Avenue and BAC had his own bathroom with phone, he was known to spend time in there making calls. In Box 118, RHR, on a list of 1927 financial calculations in BAC's hand, there is also a list of discussion items. Significantly, it included "our name."

79 **"deeply religious":** MLS OH, 2.

79 **an eccentric old house:** LKL, claiming that her parents' country house in Deal was Kent's model for the colophon, showed photos to author to support the premise. LKL, May 4, 2005. Since Marian and Donald didn't marry until Sept. 1927, the dating doesn't work, but DSK *later* referred to the summer house as "a real Random House."

79 ***Benito Cereno:*** Holiday list of price quotations, Oct. 1928, Box 134, RHR. Samples of *Cereno* and other Nonesuch titles in A. J. A. Symons, Desmond Flower, and FM, *The Nonesuch Century: An Appraisal, a Personal Note, and a Bibliography of the First 100 Books Issued by the Press, 1923–34* (London: Nonesuch Press, 1936).

79 **priced at $46.00:** RH bought books from Nonesuch at a discount of 40% off the U.K. published price and sold them at prices equivalent to the U.K. retail price, with five cents' wiggle room for currency fluctuation. RH was entitled to sell to stores at a discount up to 40%. It would pay transport, customs fees, and half of the insurance costs.

In our time, the internet has thrown into question the feasibility of territorial exclusivity. Amazon is agent and symbol of far more fluid borders, presenting big challenges to a copyright system based on old technology.

79 **greater financial rewards:** BAC's 1927 handwritten calculations are in Box 118, RHR. (The list of discussion items that included "our name" is here.)

80 **"the inveterate reader-out-loud":** BAC promotional copy for *The Week-end Book:* Box 171, RHR.

80 **"No self-respecting":** *NY Herald Tribune,* quoted in proof copy of RH ad, Box 133, RHR. *The Week-end Book,* republished by Duckworth in London in 2005, noted that the book had had thirty-four printings. A 1934 Nonesuch catalogue said 120,000-plus copies had already been sold. Box 166, RHR.

80 **far more devoted:** DSK donated some papers (hereafter DSKP) and his books (DSK Bequest) to Williams College, which made a printed inventory shown to the author. Many, but not all, of BAC's books went to Columbia. DSK was a lifelong collector of rare books; for BAC, it was a phase.

80 **"first crack":** DSK to BAC, May 12, 1927, Box 171, RHR.

80 **ambitious project:** The Great Depression would reduce the scale of the Shakespeare project from twenty-six volumes to seven.

80 **"bored" by contract details:** For contract details, see BAC to FM, Dec. 10, 1926, Box 71, RHR.

80 **"joint venture":** BAC to DSK, May 12, 1927, Box 171, RHR. See also Dreyfus, *History of the Nonesuch Press,* 39–40.

80 **"That's the most goddamned":** BAC OH, 178.

80 **"Here indeed we pledge":** FM to BAC, May 27, 1927, Box 171, RHR.

80 **it was time to move:** See "Highlights in the History of the Modern Library and Random House," prepared for the 1936 merger with Smith & Haas, RH file, *PW* Records.

81 **Deco modernity:** *PW,* Feb. 9, 1929, 657.

81 **"You step off":** "Modern Quarters for Modern Enterprises," *PW,* June 16, 1928, 2442–44.

81 **large print from Kent:** BAC to Kent, Dec. 12, 1927, Box 165, RHR.

81 **"a modern work of art":** For a description of the offices, see First Reader column, "Modernizing the Modern," *The World,* July 23, 1927, loose clipping inserted into BAC's 1926 (*sic*) travel journal, Box 11, CP.

82 **Thousands of prospectuses:** Elmer Adler to BAC, Nov. 3, 1927, Box 165, RHR. See also Adler to RH, Feb. 15, 1928, RHCC.

82 **oversubscribed:** BAC to Kent, Dec. 22, 1927, Box 165, RHR.

82 **book was priced:** BAC to John K. Hutchens, *NY Herald Tribune,* Sept. 10, 1950, and DSK, in his OH, mistakenly recalled the *Candide* selling price as $15. On *Candide,* see "Rockwell Kent pictures in new edition of *Candide,*" RH press release, Sept. 1929, Box 18, Pynson Printers Records, New York Public Library (hereafter NYPL).

82 **often bore little relation:** Obituary of Elmer Adler, *NYT,* Jan. 12, 1962.

82 **more than he'd reckoned:** BAC to Pynson Printers, Dec. 26, 1927, Box 165, RHR; Adler to BAC, Apr. 25, 1928. The original estimate was $12,400; the actual bill was $16,800. Kent would receive $4,250 of the $16,800.

82 **"the greatest contribution":** Elmer Adler to Charles Dreifus Jr., Sept. 21, 1928, Box 165, RHR. Stanley Morrison was the expert quoted. Morrison also quoted in Adler to DSK, May 20, 1928, RHCC.

82 **"deluged":** Per ML release, June 10, 1929, Box 133, RHR. The first run of the inexpensive version was 5,000 copies.

82 **offering book club rights:** BAC to Robert K. Haas (hereafter RKH), July 29, 1929; Literary Guild (hereafter LG) to BAC, Oct. 2, 1929, Box 165, RHR.

82 **"controversial":** Sutliff, vice president of LG, to BAC, Dec. 23, 1929, Box 165, RHR.

82 **"Dear Beans":** Elmer Adler to BAC, July 13, 1928, RHCC.

82 **grousing about not getting his due:** The original plan had "made it entirely unnecessary for me to assume any financial obligation." See Elmer Adler to BAC, Oct. 5, 1928, RHCC.

83 **"the Random House" was merely "a play toy":** Elmer Adler to BAC, Aug. 28, 1928, RHCC.

83 **"very little of the spirit . . . withdraw entirely":** Adler to BAC, Sept. 5, 1928, RHCC.

83 **fancy accounting:** Alterations to financial structure in letter dated Sept. 28, 1928, Box 64, RHR. It twice states that arrangements "will be begun as of January 1st, 1928," in effect backdating changes in the agreement. The capital stock was increased from three to fifteen shares of $1,000 par—i.e., nominal—value each, with five going to each partner. BAC predicted that within a few years, the salaries would be "but a minor . . . share of profits" from RH. In the Sept. 28 letter, the salaries were listed as $100 (BAC); $87.50 (DSK); $62.50 (Elmer Adler). Certificates "aggregating five shares" to Adler mentioned in BAC to Adler, Oct. 24, 1928, Box 64, RHR. Charles Edmund Merrill Jr. was also on the RH Inc. board, per the dedications on Merrill's copy of *Candide.* Call no. PG2082 C3 E5 1928, RC. Merrill also provided the book's "Bibliographical Note."

83 **soon Bennett invested:** Elmer Adler to BAC, Mar. 20, 1929, Box 18, Pynson Printers Records.

83 **an unexpected development:** Nine-page prospectus from S&S, n.d. (1928), DSK/RLB Papers. On the S&S offer, see BAC OH, 150.

83 **"Messrs. Cerf and Klopfer":** MLS listed a third inducement, "c) development of the typographical magazine now pending." This was *The Colophon,* Elmer Adler's idea of a magazine for bibliophiles.

84 **wait until "Beans" was home:** RLS to MLS, June 5, 1925, Box 250, MLS Papers.

84 **"Within ten years":** BAC quoted in RLS, Trade Winds, *SRL,* Dec. 23, 1950, 4.

84 **"more prominent":** See "Book Notes," May 1926, Box 36, CP.

84 **plowing most profits:** Estimated net profit for 1926 was $27,150. For 1927 the figure was $32,530.

84 **held real estate jointly:** For correspondence on their joint investments via a syndicate, see Box 3, CP. BAC also invested for his Uncle Al and also for Julian Messner. BAC to Albert M. Cerf, Dec. 27, 1926, Box 71, RHR. Messner to BAC, Nov. 21, 1929; BAC to Messner, Nov. 29, 1929, Box 3, CP.

84 **at a time when 40 percent:** Dixon Wecter, *The Age of the Great Depression,* vol. 13, *A History of American Life* (New York: Franklin Watts, 1975), 10 (hereafter *Age of the Great Depression*).

84 **just-finished Navarro:** The Navarro building still stands. It became a Ritz-Carlton; an Intercontinental; luxury co-ops.

84 **soon paying $5,600 per year:** See BAC to Sam Minskoff, Dec. 7, 1931, Box 3, CP. His bills at the hotel's restaurant averaged $100–$200 per month. By contrast, 25 cents could buy a sirloin dinner in a modest eatery. *This Fabulous Century: 1930–1940* (New York: Time-Life Books, 1969), 14.

84 **four-room flat:** BAC OH, 445. It's not clear when Gustave Cerf moved upstairs or whether his rent was included in the $5,600.

84 **modern, masculine:** PC descriptions quoted by JFC to author, Feb. 14, 2007.

84 **Bennett had commissioned:** BAC to Stewart Hecht, Dec. 5, 1927; BAC to Earl Bock, Dec. 12, 1927, Box 71, RHR. The music player cost a pricey $750.

85 **1929 Cadillac:** Isadore Fried Insurance to BAC, Oct. 25, 1928, Box 71, RHR.

85 **he boarded the Clevelander:** 1928 diary, CP.

85 **Covering far more territory:** Box 171, RHR.

85 **Mesmerized:** For Angelo's description of BAC's reaction, see Paul A. Bennett, "The Grabhorns: Their Methods and 'Best' Books," *PW,* undated clipping. This first Grabhorn book taken by RH, *The Voiage and Traveile of Sir John Maundeville,* was among the fifty books of the year commended by the American Institute of Graphic Arts. See Will Ransom, *Private Presses and Their Books* (1929; repr. New York: AMS Press, 1976), 302. RH also published a Grabhorn edition of Hawthorne's *The Scarlet Letter;* it was also named a book of the year.

85 **"a knockout":** BAC to DSK, May 7, 1929, Box 65, RHR. The production cost to RH would be $40 per copy. In 1930, RH reprinted the book in a trade edition but left Melville's name off the cover! The error was soon corrected. BAC OH, 200.

85 **"with the most distinct understanding":** BAC to Harold Mason, Jan. 12, 1929, Box 3, CP.

85 **"going to be one of the great authors":** BAC OH, 326. HBL had published Faulkner's (hereafter WF) first two novels, *Soldier's Pay* and *Mosquitoes,* after BAC left B&L. BAC says the novel Mason told him about was *Sanctuary,* WF's "third," which was published by Harcourt Brace. But WF's third novel was *Sartoris,* published in 1929 by Harcourt. *Sanctuary* was actually WF's sixth; Cape and Smith published *The Sound and the Fury, As I Lay Dying,* and *Sanctuary,* in 1929, '30, and '31, respectively.

Four decades later, BAC either misremembered the book Mason spoke of or got publisher and chronology wrong. Since he called it "shocking," the editors of *At Random* opted for *Sanctuary*. BAC, *At Random: The Reminiscences of Bennett Cerf* (1977; repr. New York: RH, 2002), 129 (hereafter *AR*).

BAC first published WF in the ML in 1932: *Sanctuary,* with an introduction by the author. A special limited edition of *The Sound and the Fury* was advertised in 1933–34—an announcement appeared on the endpapers of Robinson Jeffers's *Give Your Heart to the Hawks*—but it was never realized.

86 **third jaunt abroad:** For the itinerary, see BAC 1928 diary, Box 11, CP.

86 **"Let's keep at the top":** BAC to DSK, n.d., Box 171, RHR.

86 **"Naples on a melancholy day":** BAC wrote that in his scrapbook next to a birthday cable from his dad. Box 36, CP.

86 ***South Wind:*** "Chart of Modern Library Titles in Order of Sales Popularity, Jan–June 1928," Box 765, RHR. Sixth on the list, it had sold 4,586 copies. The leader, *The Romance of Leonardo Da Vinci,* had sold 12,264 copies.

86 **story of this visit:** BAC OH, 225–29. BAC repurposed it in a Trade Winds, *SRL,* Mar. 29, 1952. Frieda Lawrence, not amused, wrote to the editor and to BAC personally on Apr. 7, 1952, pointing out small factual and date errors in his "despicable" story. Frieda Lawrence Collection, RC. But clearly it was the story itself rather than the small errors that bothered her (one can hardly define Frieda and Lawrence's relationship through her housekeeping). BAC made a partial correction in Trade Winds on May 10, 1952, but years later reprised the story in his OH. This is another "simple" story where it's impossible to untangle how much was fabricated.

87 ***My Skirmish with Jolly Roger:*** Preface first appeared as part of "popular" *Lady Chatterley* version published by Edward Titus in Paris. HAW was RH's go-between. Titus to BAC, July 30, 1929, Box 164, RHR.

87 **deputized his uncle:** HAW and FM: BAC to FM, July 5, 1929, Box 171, RHR. On booksellers and HAW, see J. G. Wilson to BAC, Sept. 27, 1929, Box 119, RHR. On HAW and foreign publishers, see BAC to HAW, Nov. 27, 1933, Box 82, RHR.

87 **gentle fixture:** See for example BAC to Vera Meynell, n.d., 1927 (1) folder, Box 171, RHR.

87 **"a family":** BAC quoted by RDL to the author. RDL quoted it innumerable times.

87 **"a roaring good time":** BAC to Vera Meynell, Dec. 6, 1928, Box 171, RHR.

87 **"What a . . . lucky":** FM, *My Lives,* 178.

87 **"the gamble":** FM, *My Lives,* 177.

87 **broker on the floor below:** DSK, *TNY,* May 16, 1959; FM, *My Lives,* 177–78.

88 **"My dear friends":** FM to BAC, DSK, and Elmer Adler, Feb. 9, 1929, Box 171, RHR.

CHAPTER 9: THEY FLOAT

89 **Since 1922:** Depression background and statistics, https://www.fdic.gov/history/1920-1929 and https://www.fdic.gov/history/1930-1939. See also Wecter, *Age of the Great Depression*.

89 **"Suffice it to say":** BAC to FM, Oct. 30, 1929, Box 171, RHR.

89 **$15 billion in market value:** Wecter, *Age of the Great Depression,* 12.

89 **hopeful and painfully ironic:** See Wecter, *Age of the Great Depression,* 13, 17, 19.

89 **$50,000 "call loan":** For correspondence on the principal and interest paid, see Sartorius to ML, Jan. 14, Feb. 24, Apr. 17, 1930, Box 766, RHR. The definition of the term "call loan" has changed over the decades, but Edward Goldberg (professor of business, NYU and Baruch College) read the correspondence and confirmed to the author on Dec. 10, 2017, that in this case it was a loan to Sartorius.

90 **a grand country house:** DSK to FM, Apr. 14, 1930, Box 171, RHR. In the city, DSK lived at 1112 Park Ave.

90 **a difficult delivery:** LKL to author, May 4, 2005. DSK mentioned "obstetrical unpleasantness" in a letter to FM, Aug. 8, 1929, Box 171, RHR.

90 **urge booksellers to substitute:** BAC told Theodore Dreiser that one of the main reasons the ML remained so popular was pruning and allowing booksellers to return for full credit. Apr. 10, 1939, RHCC.

90 **sold a million:** On sales and culling, see BAC, "To our customers," letter, Jan. 6, Dec. 29, 1930, Box 167, RHR.

90 **Scott Fitzgerald was delighted:** On the *Great Gatsby* ML reprint, Matthew J. Bruccoli to author, Dec. 11, 2005. See also Matthew J. Bruccoli, *Some Sort of Epic Grandeur: The Life of F. Scott Fitzgerald* (New York: Harcourt Brace Jovanovich, 1981), 392. The rights remained with Scribner and its later corporate owners until the book entered the public domain in 2021.

90 **suddenly willing to negotiate:** BAC to J. G. Wilson, June 10, 1931, Box 119, RHR.

90 **Sun Dial Library:** Contract draft, with press release, Apr. 4, 1930, Box 764, RHR. See also BAC to Floyd H. Nourse, Box 765, RHR. ML paid Doubleday $24,000.

91 **International Apple Shippers:** Wecter, *Age of the Great Depression*. See Wecter for soup kitchens, Empire State Building, etc.

91 **"Hooverville" shantytown:** Roy Rosenzweig and Elizabeth Blackmar, *The Park and the People: A History of Central Park* (Ithaca: Cornell University Press, 1992), 440.

91 **"absolutely imperative":** BAC to Sam Minskoff, Dec. 7, 1931; Leonard Gans to BAC, Aug. 19, 1932; BAC to Mr. Kashin, Aug. 19, 1932; BAC to Mr. Rachmied, Oct. 22, 1932; BAC to Minskoff, Apr. 17, 1933, all Box 3, CP.

91 **£2,000 loan:** FM to BAC, July 16, 1930, Box 172, RHR.

91 **further market collapse:** BAC to FM, Aug. 4, 1930, Box 172, RHR.

91 **agreed to pay Bert Wolff:** Wolff to BAC, July 3, 1931, Box 160, RHR.

91 **"Need any money?":** BAC to Edwin Grabhorn, Oct. 2, 1929, RHCC.

91 **$3,000 on account:** BAC to Edwin Grabhorn, Nov. 26, 1929, Box 165, RHR.

91 **upped his price:** Edwin Grabhorn to BAC, Aug. 27, 1930, RHCC.

91 **the book was prized:** DSK OH, 15.

92 **precious first editions:** Edwin Grabhorn to BAC, n.d.; BAC to Edwin Grabhorn, June 22, 1931, RHCC.

92 **bill RH directly:** BAC to Edwin Grabhorn, Aug. 27, 1931, RHCC.

92 **"practically uncollectible":** Edwin Grabhorn to BAC, July 10, 1932, RHCC.

92 **"a jug of gin":** BAC to Edwin Grabhorn, July 21, 1932, RHCC.

92 **"I guess you thank God":** Edwin Grabhorn to BAC, July 10, 1932, RHCC.

92 **loss leader:** For the Macy's-Gimbel's price wars discussion, see Satterfield, *"The World's Best Books,"* 1.

92 **22 percent of the workforce:** Richard Sutch and Susan B. Carter, eds., *Historical Statistics of the U.S. Millennial Edition,* vol. 2 (New York: Cambridge University Press, 2006) and https://www.fdic.gov/history/1930-1939.

92 **sixteen-page insert:** May 18, 1932, Box 36, CP.

93 **"They float!":** *PW,* May 14, 1932, 2015. On the ad, see Satterfield, *"The World's Best Books,"* 78.

93 **all sorts of ways:** On the ML Book a Month Plan and Multiple Commission plan, see Box 167, RHR. BAC stated to FM that RH was subsumed into ML Inc.; however, New York State business records indicate that the corporate name was briefly changed from Random House Inc. to Publishers' Products Corporation, which was the entity behind the multiple-commission chain-selling operation. Certificate filed in NY State Business Archives, Mar. 11, 1933. PPC dissolved May 4, 1935. For a critical take on the operation, see *PW,* Apr. 1, 1933, 1126.

94 **"had lost their heads":** See ML Giants publicity leaflet. Box 167, RHR.

94 **"most creative":** On Sally Ball, see Satterfield, *"The World's Best Books,"* 73–74.

95 **devoted to her:** Donald remained in touch with Ball for decades. She was greatly saddened that as Bennett's profile rose meteorically after World War II, he became much less attentive. She was sent a monthly check by RH throughout old age. For the 1950s correspondence between DSK and Ball, see Boxes 29, 36, RHR.

95 **Twelve Against the Gods:** References to this club pepper DSK and BAC correspondence during this period. See also Satterfield, *"The World's Best Books,"* 136–37.

95 **"Thanatopsis":** Tom Guinzburg to author, Feb. 28, 2003; see Margaret Case Harriman, *The Vicious Circle* (New York: Rinehart, 1951), 233–49.

95 **"a so-called tea":** Invitation, Box 36, CP. The image was recycled in 1992 by Harold Evans and the "spiritual heirs of BAC and DSK" for a party celebrating the ML's seventy-fifth anniversary and relaunching.

95 **"beautiful":** Rockwell Kent to DSK, Feb. 2, 1930, RHCC.

96 **One list later that year:** Undated, Box 3, CP. The party would have taken place in 1930, since Ginger Rogers's invitation was sent to the theater where she was appearing in *Girl Crazy*.

96 **"a very, very special":** BAC to FM, Aug. 23, 1929, Box 171, RHR.

96 **"something from heaven":** BAC on his father and Hopkins, in BAC OH, 230, 235.

96 **"I fell":** BAC OH, 123, 193.

96 **"Desolate at not":** BAC to Hopkins, July 14, 1932, Box 3, CP.

96 **a number of dates:** BAC diaries, Box 11, CP.

96 **magnificent daughter:** On Wong, see www.imdb.com/name/nm0938923/bio.

96 **Mixing was easier:** Miscegenation laws stayed on the books in many states, e.g., in California until 1947.

96 **Rosamond Pinchot:** Pinchot's diary entries as well as her father's antisemitism and attitude to BAC per Patricia Gaston, Pinchot's biographer and granddaughter, to author, Mar. 11, 2007.

97 **"For my dear Lamb-boy":** On the dates with BAC and the visit to the family seat, see BAC diaries, Box 11, CP. From April through Dec. 1933, twenty-one dates are recorded; only three in 1934.

97 **Broadway producer:** This was Jed Harris, who, with Horace Liveright, was the inspiration for Ben Hecht's protagonist in *A Jew in Love*.

97 **"our minimum requirements":** BAC to Carol Quimby, Dec. 6, 1932, Box 3, CP.

97 **"She disliked the country":** BAC OH, 916.

97 **"an exquisite figure":** FM to DSK, Oct. 11, 1929, Box 171, RHR.

97 **just before Thanksgiving:** Letters between BWK and BAC, Nov. 17–22, 1933, Box 125, RHR.

97 **"first cousin of Mr. Dashiell Hammett":** BWK's author Dashiell Hammett created the detective Sam Spade, portrayed by Humphrey Bogart in *The Maltese Falcon*.

98 **"Not as cold":** BAC OH, 916.

98 **companion aboard the SS *Van Dam*:** In Feb. 1932, the Havana trip with Gershwin made the Cuban papers. For clippings, see Box 36, CP.

98 **signed edition of sixteen works:** Box 151, RHR.

98 **"banged out":** BAC, "In Memory of George Gershwin," Trade Winds, *SRL*, July 17, 1943; see also BAC OH, 597.

99 **a little rhumba:** BAC, *SRL*, July 17, 1943. See also BAC 1932 diary, Box 11, CP.

99 **"wondrous":** BAC, *SRL*, July 17, 1943.

99 **home movies showed:** LKL kindly allowed me to see the early home movies.

99 **"Marian is once more":** DSK to FM, Aug. 8, 1929, Box 171, RHR.

100 **"the most beautiful woman":** Jane Grabhorn to DSK, July 1936, RHCC.

100 **"she wasn't in the least bit cold":** DSK to Jane Grabhorn, July 7, 1936.

100 **"had to have everything her way":** LKL to author, May 24, 2005.

100 **Telegrams tell:** Telegrams between Marian, BAC, and DSK, Box 3, CP.

100 **Skippy:** LKL to author, Nov. 19, 2003. LKL recalled BAC being there.

100 **then flew home:** BAC to FM, July 28, 1933, Box 172, RHR.

100 **"I think [Bennett] always carried":** LKL to author, May 24, 2005.

101 **the slightest intention:** BAC to Elmer Adler, July 22, 1930, Box 18, Pynson Printers Records.

101 **"reorganized":** *PW*, June 4, 1932. Elmer Adler remained bitter. See Adler to BAC, Nov. 15, 1937, RHCC.

101 **Modern Library took over:** BAC to FM, July 28, 1933, Box 172, RHR.

101 **contract stipulated:** Box 18, Pynson Printers Records.

101 **To Rockwell Kent, Pa complained:** Elmer Adler to Kent, June 1, 1932, Box 11, Pynson Printers Records.

101 **"compelled . . . for one third":** Elmer Adler to Kent, July 8, 1932, Box 11, Pynson Printers Records.

101 **"heavily overspent":** FM to BAC, July 13, 1933, Box 172, RHR.

101 **surplus money:** BAC to FM, July 24, 1933, Box 172, RHR.

101 **"Judged from any angle":** BAC to FM, July 8, 1935, Box 172, RHR.

102 **"much mental castigation":** HBL to Komroff, Box 1A, KP.

102 **he'd been squeezed out:** On HBL's last days, see Komroff, "Liveright Story"; Kronenberger, "Gambler in Publishing"; Gilmer, *Horace Liveright;* Dardis, *Firebrand,* chapter 5 notes; BAC OH, 69–72; see also BAC, "Horace Liveright, An Unedited Obituary," *PW,* Oct. 7, 1933, 1229–30; HBL obituary, *PW,* Sept. 30, 1933, 1141;

"Horace Liveright Dies of Pneumonia," *NYT,* Sept. 25, 1933, 15.

102 **He went to Hollywood:** Obituary, *PW,* Sept. 30, 1933.

102 **sordid affair:** BAC OH, 170.

102 **"Horace, I don't think":** Kronenberger, "Gambler in Publishing," 104.

102 **cheap apartment-hotel:** See Komroff, "Liveright Story," 262, 269, Box 20A, KP.

102 **"I always feared":** HBL quoted in Komroff, "Liveright Story," 122.

102 **gave him a contract:** *NYT* obituary, Sept. 25, 1933, 15.

103 **$2,000 as an advance:** Komroff, "Liveright Story," 262.

103 **turbulence ended:** *NYT* obituary, Sept. 25, 1933, 15.

103 **"great pains":** BAC OH, 171.

103 **Alfred Harcourt and Theodore Dreiser:** Harcourt wrote to BAC: "I think it [BAC's obituary of HBL] was a fine thing for you to do, and you've done it beautifully": Oct. 9, 1933, courtesy CBC.

103 **many former theatrical and literary associates:** "Sinclair Eulogizes Horace Liveright," *NYT,* Sept. 27, 1933, 21.

103 **"amazing faculty":** BAC's Liveright obituary is in *AR,* 80–81.

103 **tried to persuade a bookbinder:** BAC to Van Rees bindery, Apr. 25, 1933, Box 125, RHR.

103 **another publisher:** The publisher was Tom Coward of Coward, McCann. Salop was the remainder broker. See Box 125, RHR.

103 **the firm owed:** "To the Creditors of Liveright, Inc." letter, June 9, 1933, RHR, specifies $100,000.

103 **dummy company:** Dardis, *Firebrand,* 355.

104 **a first printing of 20,000 copies:** "Liveright, Inc., Put Into Bankruptcy," *NYT,* May 5, 1933, 16. W. W. Norton bought what was left of Liveright in 1974 and relaunched it in 2012.

CHAPTER 10: DENTIST, PATIENT—AND PUBLISHER

105 **collapsing house of Liveright:** On the life of O'Neill (hereafter EON), see Louis Sheaffer's two-volume biography, *O'Neill: Son and Playwright* (Boston: Little, Brown, 1968) and *O'Neill: Son and Artist* (Boston: Little, Brown, 1973); Arthur and Barbara Gelb, *O'Neill* (New York: Harper & Row, 1973); the Gelbs' *O'Neill: Life with Monte Cristo* (New York: Applause Books, 2002); the Gelbs' updated biography *By Women Possessed: A Life of Eugene O'Neill* (New York: Putnam, 2016); Dorothy Commins, *"Love and Admiration and Respect": The O'Neill-Commins Correspondence* (Durham: Duke University Press, 1986) (hereafter OCC); Dorothy Commins, *What Is an Editor? Saxe Commins at Work* (Chicago: University of Chicago Press, 1978); Robert M. Dowling, *Eugene O'Neill: A Life in Four Acts* (New Haven: Yale University Press, 2014); and from eOneill.com.

105 **Even Eugene O'Neill's failures:** Sheaffer, *O'Neill: Son and Artist,* 416.

105 **"Situation too confused":** EON to Smith, Apr. 21, 1933, RHCC.

105 **Bennett soon wired O'Neill:** BAC to EON, May 23, 1933, RHCC.

105 **fly down:** BAC diary, May 29, 1933, Box 11, CP.

106 **"an artist or nothing":** EON to George Pierce Baker, in Sheaffer, *O'Neill: Son and Playwright,* 293.

106 **"the handsomest, most arresting":** BAC OH, 94, 210.

107 **"frightfully dilapidated teeth":** EON to Saxe Commins (hereafter SC), Mar. 12, 1921, in Sheaffer, *O'Neill: Son and Artist,* 54.

107 **Dr. Saxe Commins:** Born 1892, per Frances Commins Bennett (hereafter FCB), SC's daughter, to author, May 29, 2007. Different sources give original name as Cominsky and Comminsky.

107 **Stella married E. J. "Teddy" Ballantine:** Stella and Teddy Ballantine's son Ian would grow up to be a brilliant publisher: first manager of Penguin Books in the United States; founding editor of Bantam Books; founder of the imprint that bears his name, now part of Penguin Random House. SC was instrumental in helping his nephew start in book publishing.

107 **"coarser equipment":** Emma Goldman, *Living My Life,* vol. 1 (New York: Dover, 1970), 291. The anarchist who assassinated McKinley was Leon Czolgosz; Goldman had met with him.

107 **"tense":** Commins, *What Is an Editor?* 1.

107 **police often searched:** Goldman, *Living My Life,* vol. 1, 314. In his early years, SC was often taunted that his aunt was a "murderess."

108 **he was loyal:** Goldman, *Living My Life,* vol. 1, 314.

108 **greatly admired:** FCB to author, May 29, 2007. In 1913, SC, Stella, and Teddy lived with Goldman. Candace Falk, *Love, Anarchy, and Emma Goldman* (New York: Holt, 1984), 191, 195, 197; Goldman, *Living My Life,* vol. 2, 515; Alice Wexler, *Emma Goldman: An Intimate Life* (New York: Pantheon, 1984), 216.

108 **helped on her anarchist magazine:** Falk, *Love, Anarchy, and Emma Goldman,* 229.

108 **Emma had visited:** Goldman, *Living My Life,* vol. 2, 582.

108 **wild man:** BAC OH, 212.

108 **literature and philosophy:** Commins, *OCC,* 13.

108 **good listener:** Commins, *What Is an Editor?* 2.

108 **"polish up":** EON to SC, Mar. 12, 1921, quoted in Sheaffer, *O'Neill: Son and Artist,* 54.

108 **"the closest of friends":** Sheaffer, *O'Neill: Son and Playwright,* 376–77.

108 **Liveright had published O'Neill's first:** Even before Liveright published EON, *Bound East for Cardiff* saw publication with two other plays in pamphlet form, as *The Provincetown Plays, First Series* edited by Frank Shay, Nov. 1916. EON had also published an earlier play privately.

108 **visited the O'Neills:** On that trip and EON's life during this period generally, see Commins, *What Is an Editor?* 3–11.

109 **120,000 copies:** The number sold by Jan. 1932. Furthermore, EON's books had sold in aggregate 700,000 copies, including *Mourning Becomes Electra,* 60,000. Arthur and Barbara Gelb, *By Women Possessed,* 418. 110,000 sold is specified for *Interlude* by Commins, *What Is an Editor?* 18.

109 **with $600 borrowed:** EON to SC, May 22, 1932, private collection. Travis Bogard and Jackson R. Bryer, eds., *Selected Letters of Eugene O'Neill* (New Haven: Yale University Press, 1988), 396.

110 **called a meeting:** Details of Liveright bankruptcy based on SC's notes. The firm owed unpaid royalties in excess of $150,000. See Commins, *What Is an Editor?* 15–20. A letter from the period specifies $100,000. June 9, 1933, RHR.

110 **what a handsome couple:** BAC had met Carlotta Monterey O'Neill (hereafter CMON) before, with her then-husband Ralph Barton, he of the too-expensive catalogue illustrations. She either had forgotten or pretended not to know him, and he took his cue from her. BAC OH, 214.

110 **"Cerf just arrived":** CMON to SC, May 29, 1933, in Commins, *OCC,* 157. There are several explanations for SC not accompanying BAC. In CMON's telegram to SC she says "manuscript arrived" at the same time BAC did. Probably EON had not wanted SC to be distracted from his editorial work. Also, the suggestion that SC accompany BAC might have come from SC rather than BAC. In the handwritten draft of a telegram to EON, he originally wrote, "Saxe would like to come with me and I will bring him unless you would rather see me alone." It was changed to "I would like to bring Saxe." BAC draft, May 23, 1933, RHR. This way BAC could be the actor—his preferred mode—rather than the acted upon.

111 **revealing that Robinson Jeffers:** RH contract terms included 15% royalty, $2,500 advance for *Give My Heart to the Hawks,* and the optioned books. For guarantees of back royalties due him by Liveright, see Jeffers to BAC, telegram, May 10, 1933, RHCC; BAC to FM, July 28, 1933, RHR. BAC also promised to negotiate to buy printing plates and copies of Jeffers's books. BAC to Mrs. Robinson Jeffers, Aug. 10, 1933, Box 86, RHR.

111 **"miles at a stretch":** BAC specified "six miles at a stretch." BAC OH, 211.

111 **Bennett looks younger:** Photo in scrapbook in CP.

111 **"the only man I ever":** BAC OH, 211.

111 **"Cerf is a *very clever*":** CMON to SC, May 30, 1933, in Commins, *OCC,* 157–58.

112 **"and then some":** In a letter to EON on June 2, 1933, BAC gave year-by-year sales for *Moon of the Caribbees* and *The Emperor Jones,* both having been published in ML editions by Liveright and continued by BAC and DSK, so EON knew the value of the ML connection. The first sold in aggregate more than 23,000 copies from 1923–32; the second, more than 12,000 copies from 1928–32. RHCC.

112 **unusual stipulation:** On the SC job, see EON to George Jean Nathan, May 31, 1933, in Bogard and Bryer, eds., *Selected Letters,* 413–14.

112 **"drive and enthusiasm":** EON to SC, June 5 (?), 1933, quoted in Commins, *OCC,* 159–60.

112 **"in an exceptionally sound position":** EON to George Jean Nathan, May 31, 1933, in Bogard and Bryer, eds., *Selected Letters,* 414.

112 **Saxe took the credo:** "Random House Celebrates Its Twenty-Fifth Birthday," *PW,* Oct. 21, 1950, 1848.

112 **"almost more important":** Sheaffer, *O'Neill: Son and Artist,* 417.

112 **"the potential of an imaginative":** Commins, *What Is an Editor?* 26.

113 **the advance "all wrong":** EON to BAC, June 4, 1933, RHCC. In that letter, EON writes, "the advance as applied to three . . . is one thousand less than I would have received from Liveright. . . ." Probably a day later, EON also mentions the advance: "as applied to three plays it would amount to less advance per play than I would have got from Liveright. So I'm asking . . . five on

each. . . ." EON to SC, June 5 (?), 1933, *OCC*. It appears that Liveright would have paid $2,000 per play.

113 **other favorable terms:** Draft and unsigned final contract, RHCC. BAC also agreed to compensate EON for royalties and a book club advance lost to the bankruptcy and also to make good 70% of the revenue from sales of club rights to new plays.

113 **"tuck them away":** BAC to EON, June 30, 1933, RHR.

113 **"Cerf is inclined":** CMON to SC, June 10, 1933, quoted in Bogard and Bryer, eds., *Selected Letters,* 161.

113 **"Mr. O'Neill":** BAC to CMON, July 13, 1933, RHCC.

113 **O'Neill's exclusive publisher:** BAC to Sophus Keith Winther, author of *A Critical Study of Eugene O'Neill,* Sept. 5, 1933, Box 97a, RHR. The advance was $200.

113 **"put rather severe strain":** BAC to FM, July 28, 1933, RHR.

113 **the dilemma of man:** See analysis in Bogard and Bryer, eds., *Selected Letters,* 384. CMON put her own slant on *Days Without End,* seeing it as a story about a wife's "all-consuming" love for her husband. CMON to SC, July 9 (?), 1933, in Sheaffer, *O'Neill: Son and Artist,* 417.

114 **seven drafts:** Bogard and Bryer, eds., *Selected Letters,* 384.

114 **"A gamble, of course":** EON to BAC, Aug. 10, 1933, courtesy CBC and JFC. BAC, first among fans, folded this letter into his copy of *Ah, Wilderness!* Along with two photos of himself and EON, it remained on a bookshelf in his New York townhouse until his widow's death, when CBC and JFC asked me to go through the books there. BAC would often slip such a letter—from WF, Albert Einstein, et al.—into a related book.

114 **"Mr. Stay-at-home":** CMON to BAC, Oct. 11, 1933, RHCC. RH also reprised the steamship/setting sun, seagull/cresting wave Liveright endpaper designs in order to maintain continuity for fans.

114 **By month's end . . . on most bestseller lists:** BAC to CMON, Oct. 27, 1933, RHCC.

114 **second only to:** Sheaffer, *O'Neill: Son and Artist,* 421.

114 **"No, I *certainly cannot consent*":** EON to BAC, Nov. 6, 1933, RHCC.

115 **"soul-stirring triumph":** BAC to EON, Nov. 9, 1933, RHR.

115 **"didn't have the nerve":** BAC to EON, Jan. 17, 1934, RHCC.

115 **"And replying to yours":** Inscription on *Days Without End,* courtesy CBC and JFC.

115 **keep them active:** BAC to EON, Feb. 26, 1934, RHR.

115 **"up against one":** EON to BAC, Feb. 28, 1934, RHCC.

115 **"With you, one forgets":** CMON to BAC and DSK, Aug. 9, 1934, RHCC.

116 **"the greatest failure":** Sheaffer, *O'Neill: Son and Artist,* 442.

116 **"which, for plays":** EON to BAC, Apr. 22, 1935, RHR. The combined sale of all EON's plays by Jan. 1932 was even higher: 700,000 copies. See Arthur and Barbara Gelb, *By Women Possessed,* 418.

116 **resettle in Seattle:** Sheaffer, *O'Neill: Son and Artist,* 456–58.

116 **Bennett wired at once**: The three telegrams of Dec. 9, 1936, and BAC's apologetic letter to EON, Dec. 10, 1936, are all in RHR.

CHAPTER II: ONE-BOOK ODYSSEY

118 **Censorship plagued Joyce:** On Joyce (hereafter JJ) and the publication of *Ulysses,* see RHR (especially the special "James Joyce" Box) and CP at Columbia; BAC, DSK, and BH OHs at Columbia; Ernst Reichl Papers at Columbia; Sylvia Beach Papers at Princeton; Morris Leopold Ernst Papers and JJ Collection, both at RC (hereafter MLEP and JJC, respectively); Charles E. Feinberg Collection at the Morris Library, Southern Illinois University at Carbondale (hereafter CEFC); *AR;* and *Ulysses* (ML edition, 1946). Most will later be noted for direct quotation or specific attribution. Tom Dardis's and Walker Gilmer's biographies of Horace Liveright (see previous chapters) were helpful vis-à-vis HBL's early offer to publish *Ulysses* and the marriages of Leon and Helen Fleischman and of Helen and Giorgio Joyce. Carol Shloss's biography, *Lucia Joyce: To Dance in the Wake* (New York: Farrar, Straus & Giroux, 2003), was helpful on JJ's family. I interviewed Simon Michael Bessie and Alan U. Schwartz about Morris Ernst (hereafter ME); Enid Kastor Rubin (hereafter EKR) about her father Robert Kastor (hereafter RK); John Kastor and his wife Mae on the Kastor family.

More sources: Richard Ellmann, *James Joyce* (New York: Oxford University Press, 1982); Stuart Gilbert, editor, *Letters of James Joyce* (New York: Viking Press, 1957); Richard Ellmann, ed., *Letters of James Joyce,* vol. 3 (New York: Viking Press, 1966); Michael Moscato and Leslie LeBlanc, eds., with an introduction by Richard Ellmann, *The United States of America v. One Book Entitled* Ulysses *by*

James Joyce, Documents and Commentary—A 50-Year Retrospective (Maryland: University Publications of America, 1984) (hereafter M&L); Paul Vanderham, *James Joyce and Censorship* (New York: NYU Press, 1998); Turner, *Marketing Modernism Between the Two World Wars;* Noel Riley Fitch, *Sylvia Beach and the Lost Generation* (New York: W. W. Norton, 1983); Edward de Grazia, *Girls Lean Back Everywhere: The Law on Obscenity and the Assault on Genius* (New York: RH, 1992); Paul S. Boyer, *Purity in Print* (New York: Scribner, 1968); Hugh Ford, *Published in Paris* (New York: Macmillan, 1975); Margaret Anderson, *My Thirty Years' War* (New York: Covici, Friede, 1930); ME and Alexander Lindey, eds., *The Censor Marches On* (Garden City, N.Y.: Doubleday, Doran, 1940); Brenda Maddox, *Nora* (London, Hamish Hamilton, 1988); Robert Spoo, "Copyright Protectionism and Its Discontents: The Case of James Joyce's *Ulysses* in America," *Yale Law Journal* 108, no. 3 (Dec. 1998): 633–67; and last but not least, Joseph M. Hassett, *The Ulysses Trials: Beauty and Truth Meet the Law* (Dublin: Lilliput Press, 2016) provided much useful background and source material. Kevin Birmingham, *The Most Dangerous Book: The Battle for James Joyce's Ulysses* (New York: Penguin Press, 2014), provides background on JJ but is not illuminating re BAC and DSK.

118 **nine years of setbacks:** JJ sent *Dubliners* to Grant Richards in London in 1905. Richards contracted it in 1906, but fearing obscenity prosecution, rejected it later that year; rejections by others followed. Once *The Egoist* began publishing JJ, Richards signed it again in 1913 and published it in 1914. See Sean Hutchinson, "The Long and Difficult Publication History of James Joyce's Dubliners," in *Mental Floss,* June 24, 2014, https//mentalfloss.com/article57437/long-and-difficult-publication-history-james-joyces-dubliners.

118 **use of swear words:** On *Portrait* swear words and excising from serialization, see Ed Mulhall, "The Story of James Joyce's 'Tiresome Book'—and It Ain't Ulysses!" *Century Ireland, RTÉ,* n.d., https://www.rte.ie/centuryireland/index.php/articles/publishing-the-artists-portrait-james-joyce-and-his-tiresome-book.

118 **twelve printers refused:** De Grazia, *Girls Lean Back Everywhere,* 18. The *Egoist* printer had already made changes without JJ knowing.

119 **insights from Freud:** Freud's influence on JJ has been grist for scholarly disputation. In *Finnegans Wake,* JJ poked fun at the good doctor; some scholars assert that JJ denied any influence at all. But given the reach of Freud's theories in intellectual circles by the second decade of the twentieth century, JJ could hardly have escaped unscathed.

119 **Ulysses-Odysseus:** Ulysses is the Roman version of the Greek name Odysseus.

120 ***Little Review:*** *The Little Review* was first published in Chicago before moving to New York in 1925.

120 **boldly displayed the credo:** Per DSK's copies of the *Ulysses* issues of *The Little Review,* which I was able to see courtesy of the DSK bequest, Williams College.

120 **copyright notice in Anderson's name:** For a discussion of the ramifications, see Spoo, "Copyright Protectionism and Its Discontents"; Bruce Arnold, *The Scandal of "Ulysses": The Sensational Life of a Twentieth-Century Masterpiece* (New York: St. Martin's Press, 1991), ch. 4.

120 **"unmailable":** Anderson editorializing in June 1919 issue of *The Little Review.*

120 **"strong hard filth":** John Quinn letter to Shane Leslie, June 21, 1922, John Quinn Papers, NYPL, quoted in Vanderham, *James Joyce and Censorship,* 9.

120 **the women were fined:** Weaver serialized parts of *Ulysses* in *The Egoist,* drawing similar objections to those resulting in Anderson and Heap's fine; she told JJ that no U.K. printer would set the book. Ford, *Published in Paris,* 5.

120 **He approached Huebsch:** BH published JJ's poem-songs *Chamber Music* and his play *Exiles* in 1918. For Quinn and BH's discussions on *Ulysses,* see Turner, *Marketing Modernism Between the Two World Wars,* 178; Gilbert, ed., *Letters of James Joyce,* 155–57.

120 **"slightly draped":** John Quinn to HBL, May 11, 1922, quoted in B. L. Reid, *The Man from New York: John Quinn and His Friends* (New York: Oxford University Press, 1968), 484.

120 **He told Liveright:** On HBL and Quinn, see Reid, *Man from New York,* 485. See also Turner, *Marketing Modernism Between the Two World Wars,* 179. HBL's offer was a $1,000 advance for a limited-edition *Ulysses* and trade editions of JJ's next three novels.

120 **French lover Adrienne Monnier:** De Grazia, *Girls Lean Back Everywhere,* 21 (footnote). In the same note de Grazia says that Riley Fitch and Maddox support JJ having suggested to Beach that she publish the book. For the opposite perspective, see Hassett, *Ulysses Trials,* 108.

121 **Joyce revised much:** For alterations from

The Little Review to Shakespeare version, see Spoo, "Copyright Protectionism and Its Discontents," 639–40.

121 **spiderweb of corrections:** For photos of two specimen galley pages (without page numbers), see Anderson, *My Thirty Years' War.*

121 **Beach proved efficient:** On Beach, see Helen Joyce, "Portrait of the Artist by His Daughter-in-Law," unpublished manuscript, Box 7, Folder 3, JJC.

121 **One thousand numbered copies:** The first 100 were signed and numbered on fine Dutch paper; the next 150 on Verge d'Arches paper; the rest on handmade paper of an unspecified kind. From copy #168, given to RK and Margaret Kastor, Mar. 8, 1931, courtesy EKR.

121 **One found its way:** DSK's copy of the seventh edition is in his bequest to the Chapin Library, Williams College.

121 **pirated fourteen episodes:** The novel had eighteen in total.

122 **Instead, he sought an injunction:** On the Roth imbroglio, see Spoo, "Copyright Protectionism and Its Discontents," 640. There is controversy surrounding JJ's relationship with Roth. See, for example, Arnold, *Scandal of "Ulysses."* To establish copyright on first publication, Anderson would have had to register and deposit at the Library of Congress (hereafter LoC) each episode in *The Little Review* within the legally specified period. This not having happened, there was no U.S. copyright on much of the material.

122 **organize a petition:** Ellmann, *James Joyce,* 587.

122 **ninth printing:** see Vanderham, *James Joyce and Censorship,* 83.

122 **he'd come to resent:** On JJ's changing attitude toward Beach, see Riley Fitch, *Sylvia Beach and the Lost Generation,* 308–9.

122 **formalize their arrangement:** Riley Fitch, *Sylvia Beach and the Lost Generation,* 307–8. Hassett ascribes JJ drawing up the Beach contract as his "cynical attempt" to convince his lawyers in the Roth case that he didn't have to pay them. Hassett, *Ulysses Trials,* 126.

122 **sent it to Beach and Joyce:** Quinn had died in 1924.

122 **pay legal fees:** BH to Beach, May 16, 1931, Box 1, Folder 7, CEFC. The offer comprised a £200 advance and 10% royalties. Riley Fitch, *Sylvia Beach and the Lost Generation,* 322.

122 **a bid from Claude Kendall:** Brad Bigelow, "Classic Covers from Claude Kendall Books," *The Neglected Books Page,* July 14, 2013, https://neglectedbooks.com/?p=2027; "Publisher Slain, Autopsy Shows," *NYT,* Nov. 27, 1937, https://www.nytimes.com/1937/11/27/archives/publisher-slain-autopsy-shows-claude-h-kendall-beaten-to-death-in-h.html. Kendall's offer also specified a 10% royalty on the first 3,000 copies sold, escalating to 15% thereafter. For Kendall's offer, see Curtis Brown, cable from NY office, June 25, 1931, Box 1, Folder 7, CEFC.

123 **$25,000 for her:** Sylvia Beach to James B. Pinker & Son, July 4, 1931, Box 1, Folder 7, CEFC.

123 **"rough-around-the-edges":** Alan U. Schwartz to author, June 2, 2003. Schwartz worked with Ernst from 1958 to 1976.

123 ***To the Pure:*** The book was published in 1928.

123 **"This would be":** Lindey memo to ME, Aug. 6, 1931, MLEP, reprinted in M&L, 77.

123 **However, Huebsch and Ernst still met:** ME to BH, Oct. 21, 1931, MLEP, reprinted in M&L, 98–99.

123 **license reprint rights:** BH to BAC, Nov. 6, 1931, RHR, reprinted in Turner, *Marketing Modernism Between the Two World Wars,* 194. In Turner's interpretation, BAC's only interest in *Ulysses* at this point was for the ML, but BH's subsequent statement "you graciously stood aside for us" strongly indicates otherwise. BH to BAC, Dec. 17, 1931, MLEP, reprinted in M&L, 100. So do BAC's October meetings with RK (these meetings are noted below).

123 **Pinker brothers:** Ellmann, ed., JJ letters, 65 (note). There were three Pinkers: founder James, who died in 1922, and his sons Ralph and Eric, who acted interchangeably for JJ. Both sons later served prison terms for embezzling clients' funds, as is explained in Northwestern University's helpful biographical sketch, https://findingaids.library.northwestern.edu/agents/people/2254.

123 **"to take a portion":** BH quoted in Riley Fitch, *Sylvia Beach and the Lost Generation,* 321.

123 **talks with Huebsch:** In his OH, BH said Viking's business manager scotched the deal.

123 **already dropped out:** Turner, *Marketing Modernism Between the Two World Wars,* 193.

123 **"hopeless to try":** BH to BAC, Dec. 17, 1931, MLEP, reprinted in M&L, 100.

124 **"The only thing":** ME to BAC, Dec. 21, 1931, JJ Box.

124 **"what we can do":** BAC to ME, Dec. 22, 1931, JJ Box.

124 **"You are standing":** Colum quoted in Riley Fitch, *Sylvia Beach and the Lost Generation,* 323.

124 **Helen Kastor Fleischman:** On first marriage and background, see Shloss, *Lucia Joyce,* 92–94, 165–70.

124 **Her mother's mental illness:** On the Kastor family, EKR, daughter of RK, to author, Sept. 5, Oct. 22, 2007; Dr. John Kastor, RK's nephew, and John's wife, Mae Kastor, to author, Oct. 21, 2007.

124 **"volunteer":** For Helen's and others' impressions of her relationship with JJ, see Shloss, *Lucia Joyce,* 166–69.

124 **her friend Paul Léon:** Shloss, *Lucia Joyce,* 94.

124 **another answer:** Beach to BAC, letter regarding a review of *Dubliners,* Feb. 3, 1927, Box 18, RHR. According to DSK, "Both of us actually had met Joyce in Paris." DSK OH, 16.

125 **a connection with Bennett:** RK to PC, Aug. 29, 1971, Box 8, CP.

125 **"High up":** BAC, "Publishing *Ulysses,*" *Contempo,* vol. 3, no. 13, Feb. 15, 1934, 1–2, in scrapbook, Box 37, CP.

125 **"comfortable":** EKR to author, Sept. 5, 2007.

125 **"gregarious," "stentorian," and remarkable:** John and Mae Kastor to author, Oct. 21, 2007. Additionally, BAC flirted with RK's wife, Margaret. BAC to Margaret Kastor, Aug. 4, 1931, JJ Box.

125 **his long relationship with the Sartorius firm:** On the first recorded meeting between BAC and RK, see BAC diary, Oct. 3, 1931, Box 11, CP. On RK's lawyer, EKR to author, Sept. 5, 2007.

125 **Harcourt, Vanguard, and Morrow:** RK apologized to James Henle of Vanguard Press for an approach Sartorius had made. RK to Henle, Mar. 18, 1932, JJ Box. Writing to T. S. Eliot, JJ mentions possible offers from Harcourt Brace and another publisher and says an offer had come from Morrow that was similar to RH's but with "conditions." JJ to Eliot, Mar. 4, 1932, reprinted in Gilbert, ed., *Letters of James Joyce,* 316.

125 **"No copyright":** BAC to RK, Dec. 30, 1931, JJ Box.

125 **Add the 15 percent royalty the firm would give:** The offer comprised a 15% trade royalty; 10% royalty on a ML reprint; and $2,500 advance; BAC offer per Dec. 30 letter to RK.

126 **Huebsch had at least:** On Beach, JJ, and royalty, see Riley Fitch, *Sylvia Beach and the Lost Generation,* 318–23.

126 **she'd relinquish her rights:** See Riley Fitch, *Sylvia Beach and the Lost Generation.*

126 **"considerable influence":** RK to BAC, Dec. 31, 1931, JJ Box.

126 **perilous pregnancy:** Helen Joyce, "Portrait of the Artist by His Daughter-in-Law," Box 7, Folder 3, JJC.

126 **her brother hand-delivered:** For the date Feb. 21, 1932, see JJ to T. S. Eliot, Feb. 13, 1932, in Gilbert, ed., *Letters of James Joyce.* Maddox writes, "Five days [after the birth of Stephen James Joyce] Bennett Cerf arrived in Paris. . . . At first he offered . . . a miserly two-hundred-dollar advance on *Ulysses.* Robert Kastor . . . shamed him into quintupling it." Maddox, *Nora,* 367. Maddox credits RK's sister, Ellen Bentley, now deceased, as source. I have found no corroborating evidence. BAC diary makes clear he was not in Paris.

126 **rival proposal:** Eric Pinker to Ralph Pinker, Feb. 16, 1932, courtesy EKR. Morrow offered a 10% royalty to run until the difference between 10% and 15% paid legalization costs. The royalty would then rise to 15% and ultimately 20% after the first 25,000 copies sold.

126 **pay $250 on signing:** Mar. 7, 1932, to Paul Léon, presumably from Eric Pinker (letter unsigned), but the purple and red type are identical to his letter of Feb. 16, 1932, courtesy EKR. The Pinkers' predilection for Morrow no doubt reflected the fact that the bid came through them and involved an extra $250; however, it may also have reflected BAC being Jewish and Morrow's Thayer Hobson being a WASP. JJ parted from the Pinkers five years later.

126 **"Have received full":** RK via Leonard S. Herzig to DSK, Mar. 8, 1932, courtesy EKR.

126 **"Pinker Colum":** RK to Giorgio Joyce, telegram, Mar. 17, 1932, courtesy EKR.

127 **$1,000 signing advance:** JJ to RK, telegram, Mar. 19, 1932, courtesy EKR.

127 **it had to be now:** Ernst's warning came via the Gotham Book Mart. JJ to RK, telegram, Mar. 19, 1932, courtesy EKR. Both this and previous cable are signed simply "Joyce."

127 **"unable" to contact Morrow:** RK to Giorgio Joyce, Mar. 21, 1932, courtesy EKR. RK here expresses confusion over whether the telegrams are being sent by JJ or Giorgio. RK assumes Giorgio; more likely, even if Giorgio was the literal sender, they came from JJ.

127 **"totally disinterested angle":** RK to Giorgio Joyce, Mar. 21, 1932, courtesy EKR.

127 **Bennett met with:** The dates for meetings with ME and RK are in his diary, Box 11, CP.

127 **Morrow's offer . . . stalled at $250:** RK to Mr. and Mrs. Giorgio Joyce, Mar. 24, 1932, courtesy EKR.

127 **"not less than three hundred words":** RK to Mr. and Mrs. Giorgio Joyce, Mar. 23, 1932, JJ Box. In the address, RK's letter says it is going via the SS *Bremen*.

127 **The $1,500 balance:** The royalty was tweaked on the contract, so 15% would rise to 20% after 25,000 sold.

127 **most important proviso:** JJ's royalty on the ML edition was 10% (lower than on the trade). Copy of contract document is in JJ Box.

128 **"a very bitter fight":** BAC to RK, Dec. 30, 1931, JJ Box. ME got 25 cents on every copy of *The Well of Loneliness* sold. De Grazia, *Girls Lean Back Everywhere,* 197. See also ME to BH, Oct. 21, 1931, MLEP, reprinted in M&L, 98–99.

128 **If they won:** For the financial terms pertaining to ME, see BAC to ME, Mar. 23, 1932, JJ Box; Lindey to BAC, Mar. 24, 1932, Box 269, MLEP, reprinted in M&L, 109. Several books assert that ME received the higher royalty only on the first 10,000 hardcover copies sold, but I've found no documentary proof. RH attorney Laura Goldin on Oct. 1, 2007, confirmed that the arrangement was 5% hardcover royalty and 2% reprint royalty, encompassing ML edition and, referencing later documents, Vintage paperback. $50 per diem. BAC to Lindey, Box 269, MLEP.

128 **"the chances are":** BAC to Marion Dodd, Hampshire Bookshop, June 21, 1932, JJ Box.

128 **"10 to 1":** BAC to Roy L. Howard, Apr. 6, 1932, JJ Box.

128 **"a 50–50 chance":** DSK to Margaret Anderson, May 10, 1932, JJ Box. The main purpose of DSK's letter was to ascertain the copyright situation vis-à-vis *Ulysses* episodes in *The Little Review.*

128 **several hundred thousand dollars:** Alden Whitman, "Morris Ernst, 'Ulysses' Case Lawyer, Dies," *NYT,* May 23, 1976. By 1964, all U.S. editions had sold "close to a half-million copies." ME and Alan U. Schwartz, "Four-Letter Words and the Unconscious," reprinted in M&L, 35.

128 **had had more faith:** Alan U. Schwartz to author, email, Sept. 11, 2007.

128 **reading *Ulysses*:** BAC diary, Apr. 20, 1932, Box 11, CP.

128 **"There are several dull":** BAC to Dr. John Watson, J. Walter Thompson Co., May 31, 1932, JJ Box.

129 **national repute:** Lindey to BAC, Mar. 24, 1932, MLEP, reprinted in M&L, 109.

129 **he told Léon:** For the instructions on the sending of *Ulysses,* see BAC to Léon, Apr. 19, 1932, JJ Box.

129 **"frank opinions":** The "letter and questionnaire to librarians" and "letter to prominent people" are in JJ Box, as are earlier versions. BAC drafted original versions of the letters; Lindey suggested they'd get a bigger response from librarians if they didn't have to draft letters but instead fill out a questionnaire.

129 **mailed a questionnaire:** "Between 800 and 900 letters went out to librarians alone." BAC to Lindey, May 9, 1932, reprinted in M&L, 137–38. For ME's instructions on "100 libraries," see ME to Lindey, memo, Apr. 20, 1932, MLEP, reprinted in M&L, 20.

129 **"To read [*Ulysses*]":** Dreiser to BAC, May 13, 1932, Theodore Dreiser Collection, University of Pennsylvania.

129 **authorization letter:** JJ to BAC, Apr. 2, 1932, RHR.

129 **Into the precious book:** List of enclosures, MLEP, reprinted in M&L, 130. The actual book over which the case was fought now resides in Columbia University's rare books collection. It is housed in a box consisting of three volumes. One is *Ulysses* itself. The second is a small red limited-edition booklet comprising ME's brief, ME's memorandum, and ME's brief for the Court of Appeals. The third volume has the pasted-in items that had been housed within the book for the court case. These don't entirely match the list Léon specified.

130 **"official scrutiny":** Lindey to Collector of Customs, May 2, 1932, MLEP, reprinted in M&L, 133–34.

130 **"one of the hottest days":** For BAC's account of the seizure at the docks, see BAC OH, 266. The facts are: the *Bremen* docked May 3, 1932, on a pleasant spring day in the sixties, not one of the hottest days; who was there to carry off the book or receive it went unrecorded. On the *Bremen*'s arrival, see "Shipping and Mails," *NYT,* May 3, 1932, 43. On the weather for May 3, 1932, see "The Weather," *NYT,* May 4, 1932, 41.

130 **"unscathed":** DSK spoke of the test volume twice. In his OH, he echoes BAC. DSK OH, 16. Later, on Sept. 14, 1983, he stated, "We mailed a copy," as quoted in M&L, 73.

130 **"I had to redeliver":** ME, "Reflections on the *Ulysses* Trial and Censorship," *The James Joyce Quarterly,* Fall 1965, reprinted in M&L, 44–52.

130 **"The book in question":** H. C. Stewart to Lindey, May 13, 1932, MLEP, reprinted in M&L, 142. Stewart added that *Ulysses* had been excluded as obscene in a 1928 Customs decision pertaining to an attempt to import books that also included

The Strangest Voluptuousness and *The Vice of Women*. Lindey said these were "technical works" on "unnatural passion." *Ulysses* was different. Lindey to Stewart, May 17, 1932, MLEP, reprinted in M&L, 146.

130 **forfeiture, confiscation:** H. C. Stewart to Lindey, May 24, 1932, MLEP, reprinted in M&L, 149.

131 **"cordial and cooperative":** Lindey to ME, June 14, 1932, MLEP, reprinted in M&L, 154.

131 **"masterpiece":** Coleman quoted by Lindey to ME, July 30, 1932, MLEP, reprinted in M&L, 157.

131 **no ordinary book:** Lindey to ME, Aug. 12, 1932, MLEP, reprinted in M&L, 158.

131 **"a vicious and unpardonable affair":** BAC to RK, Aug. 4, 1932, JJ Box.

131 **interest would wane:** Lindey to ME, Sept. 20, 1932, MLEP, reprinted in M&L, 159.

131 **new pirate rise:** BAC to ME, Oct. 20, 1932, RHR.

131 **reading the whole book aloud:** ME to BAC, Nov. 11, 1932, MLEP, reprinted in M&L, 164.

131 **"in his discretion":** Lindey to Stewart, May 5, 1933, MLEP, reprinted in M&L, 177.

132 **"of sufficient literary merit":** Frank Dow, Acting Commissioner of Customs in Washington, to the Collector of Customs, New York, June 16, 1933, MLEP, reprinted in M&L, 203–4.

132 **"dirty words":** BAC to Léon, Aug. 30, 1933, RHR.

132 **by motion of a single judge:** United States District Court record, in MLEP, reprinted in M&L, 179–80.

132 **almost from the start:** ME first mentions Woolsey to Lindey, Aug. 12, 1932, MLEP, reprinted in M&L, 158.

132 **"fond of old furniture":** Richard Ellmann, in his introduction to M&L.

132 **Coleman's appreciation:** On Coleman not prosecuting before Judge Patterson, see Lindey to ME, MLEP, reprinted in M&L, 212.

132 **After three trial postponements:** BAC to Léon, July 26, 1933, RHR.

132 **exchange briefs:** Dates in letter from lawyers to BAC, Aug. 30, 1933, MLEP, reprinted in M&L, 219.

132 **Its five parts:** Copies of original brief at Columbia and in DSKP, reprinted in M&L.

133 **"swell":** BAC to Lindey, n.d. (after Sept. 16, 1933), MLEP, reprinted in M&L, 231.

133 **"Hicklin" test:** De Grazia, *Girls Lean Back Everywhere*, xi.

134 **"very thrilling":** DSK OH, 17.

134 **a midtown building:** The City Bar Association building still stands, but the Byrne Room was demolished long ago.

134 **a bench of justice:** *NY Herald Tribune*, Nov. 26, 1933, BAC scrapbook, Box 37, CP.

134 **gravelly-voiced:** Alan Schwartz to author, Sept. 7, 2001.

134 **"horrid, torrid":** On the trial, see ME, "Reflections on the *Ulysses* Trial and Censorship," *The James Joyce Quarterly*, Fall 1965, reprinted in M&L, 44–52. For a different ME account, see ME and Lindey, eds., *The Censor Marches On*, reprinted in M&L, 21–23. The quotes about his wife are from the latter.

134 **heavy-lidded:** "Woolsey, J.," *TNY*, Jan. 8, 1944, 16.

134 **"a puritanical censor":** *NY Herald Tribune*, Nov. 26, 1933.

134 **"dare" attack:** Coleman quoted in *NYT*, Nov. 26, 1933.

135 **follow the people's will:** *NY Herald Tribune*, Nov. 26, 1933.

135 **"ought to take":** *NYT*, Nov. 26, 1933.

135 **marginal "X":** The "X" marks and brackets are still visible in the government's copy of *Ulysses*, held at Columbia. It appears at some point an attempt was made to erase markings. The two passages were on 486 and 714, respectively.

135 **"to plant":** ME and Lindey, *The Censor Marches On*.

135 **"shocking surprise":** *NY Herald Tribune*, Nov. 26, 1933, Box 37, CP.

135 **"bothered, stirred":** *NY Herald Tribune*, Nov. 26, 1933, Box 37, CP.

135 **"really read":** *NY Herald Tribune*, Nov. 26, 1933, Box 37, CP.

136 **"That's the book":** On the interplay between ME and Woolsey, see *NYT*, Nov. 26, 1933.

136 **"Random House has signed":** Catalogue in JJ Box.

136 **"unbelievable":** *NY Herald Tribune*, Nov. 26, 1933, in Box 37, CP.

136 **"straight in the mirror":** Woolsey quoted in "Woolsey, J.," 17.

137 **checked with two friends:** The two friends were Henry Seidel Canby and Charles E. Merrill Jr. BAC knew both men. See Lindey to Ernst memo, Dec. 7, 1933, in MLEP, reprinted in M&L, 316–17.

On Apr. 21, 1932, only a month after sending the contract to JJ, BAC's diary reveals he met with Canby, editor of the *SRL*, to discuss *Ulysses* and seek his support. Canby provided one of the letters ME used in the case. Charles Edmund Merrill Jr. was a textbook publisher and had been "first friend" to, that is, investor in, Elmer Adler's Pynson Printers. He was a director of RH Inc. when *Candide* was published and wrote the bibliographical note, where he is thanked by Adler and BAC. Box 40, Elmer Adler Papers, Princeton University.

137 **who congratulated and thanked:** JJ to BAC, Dec. 7, 1933. Cable is in JJ Box.

137 **"My admiration":** AAK to BAC, Dec. 8, 1933, RHR.

138 **Bennett rushed releases:** Telegrams to NY newspapers, Dec. 6, 1933, JJ Box. BAC and DSK sent out typewritten copy of Woolsey's decision, which was later printed in a special booklet.

138 **could finally link:** "News from RH," Dec. 8, 1933, RHR.

138 **"a week of wonders":** Harry Hansen, "The First Reader," *NY World-Telegram,* Dec. 7, 1933, Box 37, CP.

138 **It was Don who'd give:** For DSK's instructions to printers, see letters between DSK and Peck, Dec. 8 & 12, 1933; DSK and Bert Wolff, Dec. 15 & 19, 1933, both JJ Box. The exact run was 10,300. Martha Scotford, "Ulysses: Fast Track to 1934 Best Seller," *Design Observer,* Dec. 2, 2009, https://media.designobserver.com/feature/feature/12067.

138 **"Go ahead":** For Reichl's description of the DSK call, see Harry Hansen, *NY World-Telegram,* Jan. 25, 1934. Other versions have BAC making the call. Since DSK ran production, I favor Hansen's account. There's been a contentious history of corrections to *Ulysses.* The Rosenbach Museum in Philadelphia houses JJ's original manuscript (bought from Quinn's estate) and has issued a useful booklet on the controversy.

138 **already-announced publication date:** The date is mentioned in BAC to Léon, letter, Dec. 7, 1933, JJ Box.

138 **"The New Deal":** ME, "Foreword," *Ulysses,* ML edition, 1946. The date of the foreword's composition is given as Dec. 11, 1933, the date that Lindey sent the draft to ME. Alexander Lindey to ME, Box 270, MLEP.

138 **"the best-known":** Reichl on *Ulysses,* on his production card for the book, Box 4, Ernst Reichl Papers, Columbia University. Production information also on a card inserted into BAC's own copy of the book, RHR.

139 **thin black verticals:** In original cover design and first edition, Reichl included his name in small black letters alongside the scarlet box, but it was deleted in later editions. See *Ulysses* card, Box 4, Ernst Reichl Papers.

139 **filled her entire window:** "News from Random House," Feb. 1934, Box 37, CP.

139 **"I thought I'd make":** On Williams and his sheet, see BAC OH, 269–70.

140 **"Naturally we would like":** BAC to Léon, Jan. 17, 1934, JJ Box.

140 **wouldn't be ready until February:** According to Ellmann, "the first one hundred copies were published to secure copyright in January 1934, and the rest followed in February." Ellmann, introduction to M&L, xxi.

140 **advance sale of 13,000 copies:** "News from Random House," press release, Feb. 1934, Box 37, CP.

140 **Three cardinal rules:** George Stevens, *Lincoln's Doctor's Dog and Other Famous Bestsellers* (Philadelphia: J. B. Lippincott, 1939), 29.

140 **book sales in general would improve:** For a comparison of sales from 1933 and 1934, see Tebbel, *Golden Age,* 446.

141 **handle RH advertising for decades:** Sussman's agency would later be called Sussman & Sugar.

141 **"the novel America":** Ad in *SRL,* Jan. 20, 1934, reprinted in Turner, *Marketing Modernism Between the Two World Wars,* 202.

141 **25,000 orders:** Turner, *Marketing Modernism Between the Two World Wars,* 210.

141 **"How to enjoy":** Ad is in Box 37, CP. According to Turner, it ran in *SRL* on Feb. 10, 1934.

141 **puzzle-and-epic-loving:** The public currently adored Hervey Allen's 1,200-page Napoleonic saga, *Anthony Adverse,* which was the best-selling novel in the United States for the calendar years 1933 and 1934. Alice Payne Hackett and James Henry Burke, *80 Years of Best Sellers, 1895–1975* (New York: R. R. Bowker Company, 1977), 115, 117.

142 **"If you . . . have so little":** BAC to Paul Léon, Nov. 22, 1933, RHR, reprinted in M&L, 281. The chart was made by JJ biographer Herbert Gorman.

142 **stores asked for reprints:** "Statesmanship in Advertising," *PW,* Apr. 14, 1934.

142 **a pious Catholic:** Conboy had replaced Coleman and Atlas's former boss George Medalie.

142 **35,000 copies in print:** JJ to Carola Giedion-Welcker, Apr. 25, 1934, in Ellmann, ed., *Letters of James Joyce,* vol. 3, 302; RH ad, "James Joyce's *Ulysses* remains on sale!" which ran after Conboy's appeal of the decision in Mar. 1934. Ad in JJ Box.

142 **over lunch in Paris:** BAC diary, CP. JJ refers to BAC's visit in several letters, including one to Carola Giedion-Welcker, Apr. 25, 1934, in Gilbert, ed., *Letters of James Joyce,* 302.

142 **"overwhelming public approval":** On the brief, see "Random House Files Reply in *Ulysses* Case," *NY Herald Tribune,* May 3, 1934, reprinted in M&L, 440.

142 **"blushing, stammering, rocking nervously":** "*Ulysses,* 'Unchaste and Lustful,' No Lunchtime Story for 3 Judges," *New York World-Telegram,* May 16, 1934, reprinted in M&L, 443.

142 **read aloud twenty-five passages:** "Is Conboy's Face Red as He Reads *Ulysses* in Court," *NY Daily News,* May 17, 1934, reprinted in M&L, 444.

142 **"Two little girlies":** *New York Daily News,* May 18, 1934, reprinted in M&L, 449.

142 **"Art certainly cannot":** Appeals Court judgment quoted in "*Ulysses* Wins in U.S. Appeal on 2 to 1 Vote," *New York World-Telegram,* Aug. 7, 1934, reprinted in M&L, 463–64.

143 **has been invoked in obscenity cases:** See David Margolick, "Judge's *Ulysses* Ruling Still a Landmark 50 Years Later," *NYT,* Dec. 6, 1983. I have paraphrased remarks made by lawyer Martin Garbus.

143 **"the finest hour":** DSK OH, 19.

143 **"imposing":** BAC to JJ, Feb. 23, 1940, Box 63, Eugène and Maria Jolas Papers, Yale University.

143 **"the greatest difficulty":** JJ to BAC, Dec. 8, 1939, JJ Box.

143 **license to cable funds:** BAC to JJ, Aug. 27, 1940, Box 63, Eugène and Maria Jolas Papers.

143 **"very happy":** BAC to JJ, Oct. 1, 1940, Box 63, Eugène and Maria Jolas Papers.

143 **Joyce died:** Shloss, *Lucia Joyce,* 407.

143 **desperate for Helen Joyce:** Shloss, *Lucia Joyce,* 384–85.

143 **they found him:** Shloss, *Lucia Joyce,* 24.

144 **we've still not heard:** See Stacey Herbert, "A Draft for '*Ulysses* in Print: the Family Tree,' an Installation for the Exhibition James Joyce and *Ulysses* at the National Library Ireland" in *Genetic Joyce Studies,* issue 4, Spring 2004, Center for Manuscript Genetics, University of Antwerp. In addition, see E. Christian Kopff, "Publishers and Sinners," *Chronicles,* Jan. 1989, 16–18; and Albert Erskine (hereafter AE) note on *Ulysses* print history, both Albert Erskine Papers, University of Virginia (hereafter AEP).

144 **After the ruling:** Lindey to BAC, Oct. 25, Nov. 2, 1934, MLEP; BAC to Lindey, Nov. 1, 1934, RHR, all reprinted in M&L, 474–75. *NY Herald Tribune* re donation, Oct. 13, 1934, Box 37, CP.

144 **Bennett presented it:** Court case copy and BAC's copy at the RBML.

144 **"a very favored friend":** BAC OH, 274. BAC always addressed JJ as "Mr. Joyce" in his letters.

144 **"Someday I'm going to write":** BAC OH, 273–74.

144 **got the inscription right:** Contrast JJ's inscription to Ernst (curiously, in the UK Bodley Head edition): "valiant and victorious defender . . . in respectful recognition." Volume is in the University of Texas at Austin library, cited in Hassett, *Ulysses Trials,* 200.

CHAPTER 12: DARING YOUNG MEN

145 **"young prima donna":** BAC Travel Record Book, Box 11, CP. On the trip, also see 1934 diary; BAC OH, 288–312. I've favored the diaries; the OH is full of exaggerations and episodes BAC later admitted inventing. There were many more trip stops than I've been able to include.

146 **"secret love":** BAC OH, 243–45. If a play sold 1,500 or 2,000 copies, RH would just about break even.

146 **"that biggest pigeon":** BAC OH, 289–90. He inflated the amount in the OH; his diary has the actual amount (off by $1) but fails to mention it was *Guinzburg* who had won the money; the balance won was $339. For the actual amounts won and lost, see BAC to Harold Ross, Aug. 3, 1934, Box 17, *TNY* records, NYPL.

146 **celebrated seven-book translation:** Moncrieff's title, *Remembrance of Things Past,* taken from Shakespeare's Sonnet 30, was later supplanted by the more literal *In Search of Lost Time.* The Bonis' uncle, Thomas Seltzer, had been the first American to publish the early volumes of Moncrieff's translation; when he left the business, the rights passed to his nephews, who issued the remaining parts. Proust died in 1922, before the last three volumes (of seven) were published in French. Gallimard had, to its own later regret, originally rejected the first volume. Proust paid Grasset to publish it, in a vanity arrangement. Proust also wrote false blurbs for his work. See Russell Smith, *The Globe and Mail,* Oct. 3, 2017. Gallimard soon became Proust's publisher. Moncrieff died before he could finish translating the last volume; the job was later completed by others. For BAC's views on Proust, see BAC OH, 262, 466–68.

146 **"one of the most":** RH catalogue copy for 1941, as quoted in *AR.*

146 **two friends:** Eugène Jolas—expatriate Franco-American publisher of the avant-garde literary magazine *transition*—and his wife, Maria. See BAC's diary.

147 **four hundred currently:** BAC's travel record. I have not been able to confirm this as the number of students enrolled.

147 **Another such moment:** BAC OH, 293.

148 **he promised himself:** In 1965, BAC made good on the promise, returning to Israel.

148 **"Oh, the Jews":** *Jews in America* (New York: RH and Time-Fortune, 1936), 38.

148 **"squelched":** For the promo letter for *Jews in America,* see Cerf to Berkowitz, Apr. 8, 1936, Box 145, RHR.

148 **Minna Vinner:** BAC mentions Minna (also Mina) Vinner in his travel diary but speaks of her at length in the OH, where he emphasizes the romance. The only hint in his diary comes in a car, trying to get to the airport after two hours' sleep: "We traveled with Minna curled up in most un-Intourist-like fashion in my lap."

148 **a terrible famine:** The Ukraine famine was man-made and killed millions in 1932 and 1933. The *NYT* Moscow correspondent, Walter Duranty, was famously one of those who denied that it was happening.

149 **CERFURA SUNOVABICH:** DSK to BAC, June 4, 1934, courtesy CBC.

149 **sized up the situation:** BAC OH, 309.

149 **"a unique authority":** BAC, "The Book Business in Russia," *PW,* July 28, 1934.

149 **his male secretary:** BAC identifies the secretary as "Mr. Soumarakoff"; the correct spelling was "Sumarokov."

150 **who'd received free tickets:** On Tairov, the politics of theaters, and their audiences, Professor Boris Wolfson of Amherst College, an expert on Russian theater, supplied details to author, June 20, 2018.

151 **cadre of readers:** RHR Boxes 201, 202, Editorial Reports 1934–40. The readers included Joseph Krutch, Kit Buckles, Micaela Welch, Peggy Packard, Harriette McLain, Leane Zugsmith, and Maitland Edey.

151 **"string together":** Maitland Edey report on John Cheever, Apr. 1, 1935, Box 201, RHR.

151 **John Cheever posed:** Cheever would have a later, protracted, ultimately negative go-round with RH editor Robert N. Linscott (hereafter RNL).

151 **rejection file:** Boxes 201 & 202, RHR.

152 **"more talent":** Maitland Edey was again the reader on Isherwood. That crucial third reader was RKH, who in 1936 merged his firm into RH and became a partner, as we shall see.

152 **"We could do more":** BAC to Strachey, Nov. 1, 1933, Box 107, RHR. Strachey's wife, Celia, briefly functioned as RH's London scout.

152 **Whit Burnett and his wife:** Burnett was a newspaperman. He began by mimeographing sheets in Vienna, then moved to Mallorca. "Harry Hansen's Radio Review," Nov. 5, 1934, RHCC.

152 **twenty-five-year-old:** See John Leggett, *A Daring Young Man: A Biography of William Saroyan* (New York: Alfred A. Knopf, 2002).

153 **he'd rather have:** Saroyan to BAC, Mar. 25, 1934, RHCC.

153 **rushed a contract:** Included in BAC to Saroyan, Apr. 13, 1934, Saroyan Papers, Stanford University (hereafter SP).

153 **"no good at all":** BAC to Saroyan, Mar. 29, 1934, Box 90, SP.

154 **expensively reset:** SC to Saroyan, July 9, 1934, RHCC.

154 **author's primary responsibility:** DSK to Saroyan, Apr. 17, 1934, RHCC.

154 **promised to make:** Leggett, *Daring Young Man,* 31. The cover was by Ernst Reichl, designer of *Ulysses*.

154 **bestseller list in New York:** BAC to Saroyan, Oct. 30, 1934, SP.

154 **"What a publisher":** Saroyan to BAC, Oct. 16, 1934, RHCC.

154 **one of the happiest:** BAC to Saroyan, Oct. 30, 1934, SP.

154 **"one more important":** BAC to Saroyan, Nov. 23, 1934, SP.

154 **desperately wanted:** JFC to author, Feb. 8, 2006.

154 **capable of dictating:** BAC letter-writing prowess comes from Christopher Cory, notes dated Nov. 30, 1966, "The Man," VII, 2, for *Time* cover story on BAC, Dec. 16, 1966.

154 **"Jezebel":** Many BAC letters, columns, and his OH (101), refer to Kreiswirth as "Jezebel." The character was played by BAC's friend Miriam Hopkins in the eponymous play in 1933–34, and by Bette Davis in the 1938 film.

154 **6,700 copies:** BAC to Saroyan, Feb. 6, 1935, SP.

155 **600-plus review copies:** BAC to Saroyan, Feb. 6, 1935, SP.

155 **"getting by with murder":** Saroyan to BAC, Oct. 22, 1934, RHCC.

155 **"in an amusing":** In his OH, BAC recounts the ferry anecdote and other stories he says he planted to push the book. BAC OH, 376. I have not found corroborating evidence of such stories circulating.

155 **decided to sell:** *Time,* Aug. 26, 1935, Box 36, CP. The buyer was Dr. Kurt Simon, a German Jewish refugee married to a rich American. His family had controlled the *Frankfurter Zeitung* before the rise of Hitler.

155 **"amazing":** BAC OH, 375–76.

156 **"I am a great writer":** Saroyan to BAC, Dec. 19, 1935, RHCC.

156 **"wild" man:** BAC OH, 375–76.

156 **"wholly alive":** Saroyan, *Daring Young Man,* preface.

156 **"To hell with this":** BAC to Saroyan, Dec. 31, 1935, SP.

156 **too-strong wine:** BAC to Saroyan, Mar. 5, 1936, SP.

156 **the book RH had declined:** AAK to WS, copied to BAC, Apr. 13, 1936, Box 125, RHR. On AAK, see BAC to Saroyan, Apr. 13, 1936; BAC to Saroyan, Aug. 11, 1936, SP.

156 **had already been rejected:** BAC to Saroyan, Apr. 8, 1936, SP.

156 **"When I think":** BAC to Saroyan, Sept. 15, 1936, SP.

156 **one was from Bennett:** Leggett, *Daring Young Man,* 140. In 1955, BAC published a pseudonymous first novel, *The Secret in the Daisy,* by "Carol Grace," knowing that it was by Saroyan's ex-wife (Saroyan had helped her with the manuscript). In 1968 and '69, CBC, while at RH, published two books by their son, Aram.

156 **Impressed by it:** BAC to Tillie Lerner, July 30, 1934, Box 19, Tillie Olsen Papers, Stanford.

156 **check her out:** BAC to Saroyan, Aug. 10, 23, & 31, Sept. 5, 14, & 18, 1934, SP; Saroyan to BAC, Aug. 21, Sept. 12, 1934, RHCC.

156 **It turned out:** Lerner to BAC, Aug. 6, 1934, Box 89, RHR. Lerner was born in Nebraska to a socialist father. Teresa Landale was her pen name. Saroyan to BAC, Aug. 17, 1934, Box 38, RHCC.

156 **"the main book factor":** Lerner to BAC, Aug. 6, 1934, Box 19, Tillie Olsen Papers.

157 **"an advance on a contract":** On Macmillan history, see Lerner to BAC, Sept. 10, 1934, Box 89, RHR.

157 **"conservatism":** BAC to Lerner, Sept. 14, 1934, Box 89, RHR.

157 **"the colossus of American publishing":** NYPL biographical information, Macmillan Co. records, archives.nypl.org/mss/1830.

157 **"hammer and tongs":** BAC to Lerner, Oct. 5, 1934, Box 19, Tillie Olsen Papers.

157 **"unashamedly Communistic":** BAC to Lerner, Oct. 25, 1934, Box 19, Tillie Olsen Papers.

157 **she needed more:** BAC to Lerner, Jan. 18, 1935, Box 19, Tillie Olsen Papers. BAC to Sanora Babb, June 4, 1935; BAC to Lerner, June 18, 1935, both Box 89, RHR.

157 **"too lousy":** Lerner to BAC, undated; BAC to Lerner, Jan. 14, 1936, Box 89, RHR.

157 **remained unfinished:** The title of Olsen's unfinished novel is *Yonnondio: From the Thirties.* In *Silences,* a collection of essays, she discusses, among other subjects, writer's block. See Olsen, *Silences* (New York: Delacorte, 1978).

CHAPTER 13: GLAMOUR GIRLS

159 **failed to place work:** On GS and *Atlantic* history, see Christopher Schmidt, *JSTOR Daily,* Oct. 1, 2014, https://daily.jstor.org/gertrude-stein-and-the-atlantic-monthly/.

159 **shock to fury:** For reactions to the *Autobiography,* see Janet Hobhouse, *Everybody Who Was Anybody: A Biography of Gertrude Stein* (New York: Putnam, 1975), 166–68.

159 **not exactly "true":** Hobhouse, *Everybody Who Was Anybody,* 162.

159 **man-about-town:** CVV had caused an uproar with his best-known novel, *Nigger Heaven,* published by Knopf in 1926 (he was a friend of BWK's). In 1929, the ML reprinted his novel *Peter Whiffle.* On the friendship between GS and CVV, see Edward White, "The Making of an American," *The Paris Review,* May 14, 2014, https://www.theparisreview.org/blog/2014/05/14/the-making-of-an-american/.

159 **defining duality:** CVV photos of BAC, Box 2, CP.

159 ***Three Lives:*** Publication letters are in the RHR and Box 139, Gertrude Stein and Alice B. Toklas Papers, Yale (hereafter GSP). The advance was $300, but an extra payment to GS for the right to use the old plates made it $400 in total. See BAC to William Bradley, June 16, 1933, Box 105, RHR.

159 **"Miss Stein":** BAC to Bradley, June 16, 1933, Box 105, RHR. From the 1920s to the 1970s, expat American William Bradley and later his French wife, Jenny, were the preeminent go-betweens in Franco-American deals. In 1934, GS severed the connection. BAC to GS, Sept. 13, 1934, Box 101, GSP.

160 **"tremendous success":** BAC to GS, Oct. 23, 1933, RHCC. More than a quarter of the initial sales were from Macy's.

160 **too soon:** BAC to GS, Nov. 21, 1933 (and GS's reply), Film 1155, Box 100, GSP.

160 **"the imprint just used":** BAC to GS, Feb. 1, 1934, Box 139, GSP.

160 **"Gertrude Stein's strange":** Cover blurb, *Four Saints,* first edition, Box 97a, RHR.

161 **"very pleasant and very voluble":** On the visit to GS in Paris, see BAC 1934 travel diary, Box 11, CP.

161 **"the Mama of Dada":** The phrase was

coined by Clifton Fadiman. Hobhouse, *Everybody Who Was Anybody,* 173. Just after signing *Three Lives,* BAC presciently asked GS on July 13, 1933, if there were "any chance" she could come to the United States. BAC to GS, July 13, 1933, GSP.

161 **soon dropped him:** On Bradley's failure with the lectures, see William Rice, "Gertrude Stein's American Lecture Tour," in *Letters of Gertrude Stein and Thornton Wilder,* edited by Burns and Dydo with Rice, 333–34. CVV and Sherwood Anderson lobbied for a tour. James Mellow, *Charmed Circle: Gertrude Stein and Company* (New York: Praeger, 1974), 355.

161 **managed to cajole her:** See Hobhouse, *Everybody Who Was Anybody,* 173–74. In his OH, BAC suggests he was responsible for GS's return. However crucial his role as publisher and publicist was, the others were far more responsible. BAC OH, 278.

161 **"How happy we would":** BAC to GS, July 26, 1934, Film 1155, Box 100, GSP. (Relieving her of her Plain Edition problem is also in this letter.)

162 **wouldn't be delivered to RH in time:** BAC to GS, Jan. 8, 1935, Film 1155, Box 100, GSP.

162 **collection of word portraits:** BAC to GS, cable, Aug. 22, 1934, and letter from BAC to GS, Aug. 27, 1934, Film 1155, Box 100, GSP. In this correspondence was talk of another autobiography at CVV's suggestion.

162 **absolutely imperative:** BAC to GS, Aug. 27, 1934, Box 100, GSP.

162 **"I know I can trust":** Two letters, GS to BAC, both Sept. 6, 1934, RHCC.

162 **"I am full of anticipation":** GS to BAC, circa Sept. 30, 1934, RHCC.

162 **On a fine, clear:** GS docked on Oct. 24, 1934. "Shipping and Mails," *NYT,* Oct. 24, 1934, 43; see also *NYT,* Oct. 25, 1934, 46.

162 **pencils ready:** See clippings in GSP; BAC clipping books in CP; W. G. Rogers, *When This You See Remember Me: Gertrude Stein in Person* (New York: Harcourt, 1948), 120–23; BAC OH, 278.

162 **"Robin Hood" cap:** Many newspaper descriptions and photos re clothing.

162 **thin gray mouse:** Evelyn Seeley, "Alice Toklas Hides in Shadows of Stein," *New York World-Telegram,* Oct. 25, 1934.

162 **"raptly":** "Gertrude Stein Arrives and Baffles Reporters by Making Herself Clear," *NYT,* Oct. 25, 1934.

162 **"to tell very plainly":** *NYT,* Oct. 25, 1934, 25.

162 **"Why don't you write":** *NYT,* Oct. 25, 1934, 25.

162 **"beautiful eyes":** See Ernest Hemingway, *A Moveable Feast* (New York: Scribner Classics, 1996), 21.

163 **voice imbued:** "Valentine to Sherwood Anderson," sound recording, 1CD0214488, 1935, Sound Archives, British Library.

163 **"secretary":** Rogers, *When This You See Remember Me,* 123.

163 **"is to be exciting":** Rogers, *When This You See Remember Me,* 123.

163 **"parry and riposte":** *NYT,* Oct. 25, 1934, 25.

163 **As her dark eyes:** For GS's reaction on first seeing New York, see Hobhouse, *Everybody Who Was Anybody,* 177.

163 **"Gertrude Stein Arrives":** Mellow, *Charmed Circle,* 381.

163 **three-room suite:** Alice B. Toklas, *What Is Remembered* (New York: Holt, Rinehart & Winston, 1963), 143–44.

163 **"literally [falling] in love":** BAC, interviewed about GS for Perry Miller Adato's 1970 TV documentary "When This You See, Remember Me," courtesy Paley Center, New York.

163 **profile judged Stein:** "Facts About Faces: VI. Gertrude Stein," *The New Republic,* Mar. 13, 1935, 120, GSP. For some—like Hemingway—GS's charisma exuded an element of "unexpected sexual magnetism." See Janet Malcolm, *Two Lives: Gertrude and Alice* (New Haven: Yale University Press, 2007).

164 **"As if we did not know it":** For an account of the walk and the electric sign, see Toklas, *What Is Remembered,* 144.

164 **"They all know me":** GS manuscript of "I Came Here and I Am," article written for *Cosmopolitan,* Feb. 1935, courtesy CBC and JFC. On the $1,700 fee for article, see Harry Hansen, "The First Reader," *New York World-Telegram,* Jan. 10, 1935, courtesy CBC and JFC.

164 **"For Bennett":** GS manuscript of "I Came Here and I Am," courtesy CBC and JFC.

164 **Swedish Maids Employment Bureau:** BAC OH, 281. A typed page dated 1934 seems to be BAC's text for the anecdote, and indicates it is to be used for a column in the May 1935 issue of *Story* magazine. Box 143, GSP. I have been unable to locate that issue. The anecdote did appear in print; see *The Washington Post,* May 19, 1935. Lise Jaillant, "Shucks! We've Got Glamour Girls Too! Gertrude Stein, Bennett Cerf, and the Culture of Celebrity," *Journal of Modern Literature* 39, no. 1 (Fall 2015): 162.

164 **"the Sybil of Montparnasse":** Frequent description of GS, origin unknown.

164 **Hopkins thought her wonderful:** BAC

OH; BAC interview by Patricia Meyrowits, BBC, sound recording, ILP0195374, Jan. 1, 1968, Sound Archives, British Library.

164 **Stein was soon amused:** BAC OH, 282.

164 **disarmed them:** BAC OH, 281.

164 **enjoy life more:** BAC interview by Patricia Meyrowits.

164 **"Shucks":** *PW,* Sept. 9, Oct. 28, 1944.

164 **"Mr. Woollcott":** BAC OH, 281. Diary has lunch taking place Nov. 2, 1934.

165 **happy camaraderie:** For dates of these gatherings, see BAC diary, Box 11, CP.

165 **"Miss Stein [was] a Wow":** *New York Sun,* Nov. 1, 1934, GSP; Joseph W. Alsop Jr., "Gertrude Stein Likes to Look at Paintings . . . ," *NY Herald Tribune,* Nov. 2, 1934, GSP.

166 **"rather pitying":** BAC to GS, Dec. 17, 1935, Film 1155, Box 100, GSP. GS's exact words, quoted by BAC in the letter, were: "Bennett, you're a very sweet boy, but you're dumb!"

166 **Traveling to thirty universities:** For the trip chronology, see Burns and Dydo with William Rice, eds., *Letters of Gertrude Stein and Thornton Wilder,* 339–51. For details on the social gatherings, see BAC diary.

166 **"nicest of editors":** GS (and Toklas PS) to BAC, circa Dec. 15, 1934, RHCC.

166 **"I hope you are remembering":** BAC to GS, Dec. 19, 1934, RHCC.

166 **The last day of 1934:** On BAC's first meeting with Sylvia Sidney (hereafter SS), see BAC diary.

167 **"cleaned up":** *Bad Girl* ran from Oct. 2, 1930, to Dec. 1930, Internet Broadway Database. https://www.ibdb.com/broadway-production/bad-girl-11153. SS discussed *Bad Girl* in a profile. See Arthur Bell, "Sylvia's Souvenirs," *NYT,* Dec. 17, 1972, clippings files, University of Southern California Cinema Library (hereafter USCCL).

167 **The moment she walked:** BAC OH, 231.

167 **"Mr. Cerf":** The first meeting between BAC and SS is in BAC's diary. He elaborates in his OH (232–34), from which I have quoted (and edited) dialogue.

167 **Five female stars:** On SS, see *American National Biography Online,* http://www.anb.org/articles/18/18-03561-article.html; Fandango, http://www.fandango.com/sylviasidney/filmography/p65554; IMDb, http://us.imdb.com/name/nm0796662/bio; "Silvia Sidney, 30's Film Heroine, Dies at 88," *NYT,* July 2, 1999; David Thomson, *New Biographical Dictionary of Film* (New York: Knopf, 2004), 807–8; Budd Schulberg (hereafter BWS), *Moving Pictures: Memories of a Hollywood Prince* (New York: Stein and Day, 1981); Albert C. Kosow, SS's half brother, to author, May 20, 2008; BWS to author, Oct. 14, 2003, and Jan. 15, 2008. In 1935, SS would earn an impressive $110,000 salary. Katherine Albert, "Sylvia Sidney Plays Truth," *Modern Screen* 13, no. 1 (June 1936): 104, courtesy USCCL.

167 **marred by a dark fleck:** NIE, "When Sylvia Came Back," *St. Louis Post-Dispatch,* Sept. 20, 1931, SS biography file, Margaret Herrick Library, Academy of Motion Picture Arts and Sciences (hereafter AMPAS).

167 **only major female star:** Theda Bara was of the silent era; Luise Rainer didn't make her U.S. debut until 1935; Hedy Lamarr achieved U.S. stardom in the late 1930s; Paulette Goddard was not a major star at this time.

168 **signed with Fox:** On SS's early career, see James Robert Parish, *The Paramount Pretties* (New Rochelle, N.Y.: Arlington House, 1972), 261–93. Titles included *Broadway Nights* (1927) and *Thru Different Eyes* (1929).

168 **urged B.P.:** According to BWS, the Schulbergs saw SS in *Strictly Dishonorable.* See BWS, *Moving Pictures,* 353. Parish, however, says that they saw her in *Bad Girl.* See Parish, *Paramount Pretties.*

168 **approved of her performance:** Parish, *Paramount Pretties,* 268.

169 **"little Kike hoor":** BWS to author, Oct. 14, 2003.

169 **scotch highball:** BWS, *Moving Pictures,* 383.

169 **"Goddammit":** BWS to author, Oct. 14, 2003.

169 **"No, I am not":** SS quoted in unsourced clipping, Aug. 19, 1933, SS microfiche file, AMPAS.

169 **was forced out:** B.P.'s slide discussed by former brother-in-law Sam Jaffe, Jaffe OH, 143, AMPAS.

169 **B.P. informed:** See Parish, *Paramount Pretties,* 272.

169 **hundreds and hundreds:** Elizabeth Wilson, "I Do as I Darn Please!" *Silver Screen,* Nov. 1935, AMPAS. Photos of SS standing in front of her books also at AMPAS.

169 **revamp his bedroom:** BAC chose Bob Heller, a leading proponent of streamline design, for the job. On the redecoration, see 1935 diary, Box 11, CP.

169 **That Sunday:** Dates for meetings with SS in BAC diary, Box 11, CP.

169 **impressed by a student's lead story:** BAC OH, 641–42.

170 **"Incest?":** 1935 diary, Box 11, CP.

170 **energetic friendliness:** BWS to author, Oct. 14, 2003, and Jan. 15, 2008.

170 **linked to Proust:** BAC OH, 261. In the OH, BAC says he was "happy as a clam at

high tide." He often used clichés, but the metaphor is especially jarring given Proust and the circumstance. He recorded the statement thirty years after the fact, when he probably had an early-stage Parkinson-like condition, per CBC and JFC. One effect can be to "loosen" frontal-lobe "censors."

170 **stream of wires west:** There are no copies of wires to SS in the CP. BAC's letters had been scrutinized by PC after his death (PC left occasional notes in the archives). But it was said that he won her by "wires she received continually." See "Dan Cupid," "Sylvia Sidney's Romance," *Screen Play,* Dec. 1935, Box 37, CP.

170 **they drove for hours:** BAC diary, May 25, 1935.

170 **suite at the Essex House:** SS moved to Lombardy Hotel on Monday, May 27, 1935. BAC diary.

170 **hoi polloi:** BAC diary.

170 **Thick fog closed:** BAC diary.

171 **blue funk:** BAC diary, July 25, 1935.

171 **paradise was regained:** Sexual matters of a different sort occupied his workdays, as BAC negotiated to buy trade distribution rights to British psychologist Havelock Ellis's landmark seven-volume *Studies in the Psychology of Sex.* Though dry and technical, sex did sell, exceeding BAC and DSK's "fondest expectations." BAC OH, 248.

171 **"very moot":** BAC to GS, Aug. 16, 1935, Film 1155, Box 100, GSP.

171 **careful, polite, driven:** On Pop's contrasting attitudes to Sylvia and Miriam, "Sylvia Sidney to Wed Young Publisher, Gotham Gossips Say," unsourced, Sept. 8, 1935, Box 39, CP; BAC OH, 235.

171 **come into vogue:** John Scott, "Runaway Marriages Popular in Hollywood," Feb. 28, 1937, *LAT,* C1, USCCL.

171 **an absolute crisis:** BAC to GS, Sept. 17, 1935, Film 1155, Box 100, GSP.

172 **bad weather forced:** On SS's flight, ceremony, return to Los Angeles, see "Sylvia Sidney and Cerf Wed Amid Plane Trouble," Oct. 2, 1935, *LAT,* A1, USCCL clipping file.

172 **one perfect day:** BAC diary.

172 **trips between London and L.A.:** BAC in *The Film Daily,* Nov. 11, 1935, Box 37, CP.

172 ***The Trail of the Lonesome Pine:*** "Trail of the Lonesome Pine" was GS's favorite song. GS, *The Autobiography of Alice B. Toklas* (New York: Harcourt, 1933), 293–95; see also Edward Burns, ed., *Staying on Alone: Letters of Alice B. Toklas* (New York: Liveright, 1973), 10–11.

172 **a very altered reality:** BAC OH, 239–41. BAC's diary shows lunch with Wanger two days after the wedding. The OH outlines an elaborate scene; I have generally followed it here.

172 **however hurt:** BAC told Una Jeffers that he was "bitterly hurt." BAC to Jeffers, Jan. 24, 1936, Robinson Jeffers Collection, RC.

172 **one of the loneliest times:** BAC diary, Oct. 25, 1935, Box 11, CP.

172 **"one of the three":** Alma Whitaker, "Marriages Win Over Divorces in 1935," *LAT,* Jan. 5, 1936, B1, courtesy USCCL clipping file. The ceremonies of Claudette Colbert and Joan Crawford were the other two.

173 **"Having shaken":** BAC to GS, Nov. 11, 1935, Film 1155, Box 100, GSP. When he wrote to Saroyan, BAC used the term "putrid dust."

173 **"At any rate":** BAC to GS, Film 1155, Box 100, GSP.

173 **"fragile happiness":** SS appeared in German director Fritz Lang's first three American films (1936, '37, '38). According to David Thomson, "In all of these [outstanding films], she caught exactly the fragile happiness allowed in Lang's world." Thomson, *New Biographical Dictionary of Film,* 808.

173 **"It will be nice":** GS to BAC, Jan. 1936, RHCC.

174 **You must be possessed:** BAC to GS, Jan. 9, 1936, Box 106A, RHR. BAC would send a similar letter to Una Jeffers, whom he had found sympathetic when they met in Carmel. BAC to Jeffers, Jan. 24, 1936, Jeffers Collection, RC. On BAC denials, see, for example, Reed Kendall, "Around and About in Hollywood," *LAT,* Jan. 20, 1936, 13, courtesy USCCL.

174 **"There is no other man":** "Decide to Call It Quits," *LAT,* Jan. 22, 1936, A1, USCCL.

174 **"Dapper and unperturbed":** James B. Reston, "Marriage to Sylvia Sidney Tags Cerf," *Dallas News* (Associated Press), Jan. 27, 1936, Box 37, CP.

174 **"hadn't a chance to click":** Sheilah Graham, "Sylvia Sidney Admits Repenting at Leisure," *LAT,* Feb. 15, 1936, 7, USCCL.

174 **"I like going to bed":** Julie Lang Hunt, "Sylvia Sidney Thinks Popularity Can Be a Handicap," *Movie Mirror,* May 1935, AMPAS.

174 **hated parties:** Elizabeth Wilson, "I Do as I Darn Please!" *Silver Screen,* Nov. 1935, AMPAS.

174 **interlocutory judgment of divorce:** L.A. County Court Records Center, file D141, 848.

175 **"A wish and hope":** SS to Ben (B.P.) Schulberg, May 27, 1936, Budd Schulberg

Papers, MS-978, Dartmouth College (hereafter BWSP).

175 **"a tie that nobody":** BWS to author, Oct. 14, 2003.

175 **"bad part":** BAC OH, 236.

175 **"One should never":** Parish, *Paramount Pretties,* 272.

175 **The drawer was full:** JFC and his mother and brother found them after BAC's death. JFC to author, Feb. 8, 2006.

175 **honey blonde:** Self-description by Martha Dodd quoted in Shareen Blair Brysac, *Resisting Hitler: Mildred Harnack and the Red Orchestra* (New York: Oxford University Press, 2000), 139. One page earlier, Brysac notes that Dodd had already abandoned her first marriage to a New York banker.

175 **"slightly anti-Semitic":** Martha Dodd, *Through Embassy Eyes* (New York: Harcourt Brace, 1939), 5.

175 **Central Park Casino:** See Martha Dodd Stern to DSK, Mar. 12, 1976, Box 5, Martha Dodd Papers, LoC (hereafter MDP).

176 **"particularly enthusiastic":** BAC to FM, May 22, 1935, Box 172, RHR.

176 **"Darling":** DSK to Martha Dodd, June 10, 1935, Box 5, MDP.

176 **"red flames licking":** DSK to Martha Dodd, June 1935, Box 5, MDP.

176 **couldn't change his booking:** Dodd felt that his going south after the USSR instead of heading back to Berlin had "proved fatal" to their affair. Dodd to DSK, Mar. 12, 1976, Box 5, MDP.

177 **both men had fancied:** For Pinchot, one date with DSK sufficed. Bibi Gaston, Pinchot's granddaughter, to author.

177 **"the old boy":** BAC to RH (unnamed recipients), May 27, 1936, Box 4, CP.

177 **would have an option:** BAC to RH, May 29, 1936, Box 4, CP.

177 **"tremendously":** DSK to BAC, June 5, 1936, Box 4, CP.

177 **"Ostriches":** DSK to BAC, June 2, 1936, Box 4, CP.

177 **Bennett viewed:** BAC to RH, May 20, 1936, Box 4, CP.

177 **"No bloodshed":** BAC to RH, May 25, 1936, Box 4, CP. Letter mentions Hopkins's Stein paintings.

177 **"My next":** BAC to RH, June 8, 1936, Box 4, CP.

177 **Nuremberg citizenship laws:** See "Rise of the Nazis and Beginning of Persecution," Yad Vashem website, https://www.yadvashem.org/holocaust/about/nazi-germany-1933-39/beginning-of-persecution.html.

178 **"Mr Klopfer's little Martha":** BAC to RH, June 8, 1936, Box 4, CP.

178 **Martha thought it "hilariously" funny:** BAC OH, 317–18. In the OH, BAC also tells of a picnic the day of the boat trip presided over by no less than Hitler's number two, Hermann Goering. Although BAC recorded the boat trip in his diary, he made no mention of Goering. It was extremely rare for him to omit a famous encounter, but wasn't atypical of him to embroider a story for dramatic effect.

178 **"You are a strange":** Martha Dodd to BAC, Apr. 24, 1937, Box 4, CP.

178 **"we . . . who enjoy it":** Martha Dodd to BAC, Sept. 21, 1937, Box 4, CP.

178 **"trying to be mother":** BAC to Martha Dodd, May 5, 1937, Box 4, CP.

178 **Donald had married:** DSK married Selwyn on Wednesday, June 30, 1937. BAC diary, Box 11, CP. See also BAC to Martha Dodd, Aug. 24, 1937, Box 4, CP.

179 **recruit her as a spy:** FBI counterintelligence and McCarthy-era congressional investigations revealed some of the story, but more was revealed after the fall of the USSR and the publication of its intelligence files. On Dodd's spying, affair with Vinogradov, and marriage to Stern, see Allen Weinstein and Alexander Vassiliev, *The Haunted Wood* (New York: RH, 1999), 50–71. On Vinogradov and Dodd's affair with Luftwaffe official, see Herbert Romerstein, *The Venona Secrets: Exposing Soviet Espionage and America's Traitors* (Washington, D.C.: Regnery Publishing, 2000), 375–78.

179 **"What in the world":** Martha Dodd to BAC, Sept. 21, 1937, Box 4, CP.

179 **purged and killed:** Vinogradov's death was kept from Dodd. See Weinstein and Vassiliev, *Haunted Wood.*

179 **the gossip wasn't true:** On the Winchell broadcast, see BAC diary, Jan. 17, 1938, Box 11, CP.

179 **"book peddler":** For Winchell's column, see undated clipping, Box 37, CP.

179 **peppered Bennett's diary:** Dodd is mentioned on Feb. 5, Mar. 7, 10, & 13, Apr. 15 & 22, May 2, 1938, Box 11, CP.

CHAPTER 14: READY FOR THE BIG THINGS

181 **"for just this book":** James Saxon Childers, "Scanning the Bookshelf," *The Birmingham News Age Herald,* Mar. 1, 1936, Box 37, CP.

181 **"ready for the Big Things":** BAC to GS, Jan. 27, 1936, Box 106A, RHR.

181 **a great step forward:** BAC to Alice Toklas, Jan. 31, 1936, RHCC.

181 **Knopf had had to survive:** John Thornton, AAK biographer, to author, Aug. 12, 2008.

181 **doing better than many:** Data on ML/RH finances and merger per DSK/RLB Papers. ML sales reached $378,000 in 1931—one of the worst years of the Depression—and fell from 1932 to 1934. $330,000 in 1935 was an increase over 1934. As a comparison, RH sales in 1934 reached approx. $169,000.

181 **quickest way to grow:** DSK OH, 47.

181 **"K.M.V.":** Box 145, RHR.

182 **merger talks:** meeting in BAC 1935 diary, CP.

182 **entangled in debt:** BAC to John Strachey, RHR. Covici-Friede declared bankruptcy in 1937. In July 1938, Covici asked RH for a $1,000 loan. RH wanted first drafts of Steinbeck's *In Dubious Battle, Pastures of Heaven,* and *Tortilla Flat* as security. RH document, July 20, 1938, Box 1, Folder 5, Pascal Covici Correspondence, RC. Within a month, Covici joined Viking as a senior editor.

182 **"the real dirty work":** Scherman OH, 32, 38, Columbia.

182 **Robert Haas had had stints:** On his involvement with the Little Leather Library and the Book-of-the-Month Club (hereafter BOMC), see Charles Lee, *The Hidden Public: The Story of the Book-of-the-Month Club* (Garden City: Doubleday, 1958), 22–30; Janice A. Radway, *A Feeling for Books* (Chapel Hill: University of North Carolina Press, 1997), 191.

182 **New York branch:** Tebbel, *Golden Age,* 171; Priscilla Haas Blum to author, Feb. 7, 2003.

182 **ML reprint of *Sanctuary:*** DSK to RKH, June 5, 1933, and ML invoice to Smith & Haas, July 19, 1933, Box 18, RHR.

182 **"absent-minded":** Alden Whitman, "Harrison Smith of the *Saturday Review* Is Dead," *NYT,* Jan. 9, 1971.

182 **Quiet, angular:** Martin Levin to author, Apr. 21, 2004. Levin knew BAC, RKH, et al. He joined Grosset & Dunlap in 1950; ultimately ran Times-Mirror's book companies; and became an attorney specializing in publishing mergers and acquisitions.

182 **impeccably tailored:** "Robert Haas, 74, Publisher, Dead," *NYT,* Aug. 13, 1964, 29.

183 **"Everybody was being":** On *Moby-Dick* and BOMC, see BAC OH, 201–2. I haven't found documentary evidence.

183 **merger was agreed:** Box 5, Robert Kalman Haas and Merle Simon Haas Papers, Manuscripts Division, NYPL (hereafter RMHP).

183 **Bob's initial contribution:** $175,000, per DSK/RLB Papers. The exact amount RKH paid may have changed before the deal was finalized. On Dec. 24, 1937, BAC's accountant, Martin Podoll, wrote to the Income Tax Bureau in Albany mentioning the 25 shares of the ML sold to RKH, on which BAC made "$62,500." If DSK was paid an equal amount, RKH would have paid $125,000. Box 4, CP.

184 **unbelievably smart:** Ulla Dydo, distinguished GS scholar, to author, Feb. 15, 2008. Dydo said that BAC "suited GS to perfection."

184 **"in the right way":** GS to BAC, Feb. 1936, RHCC.

184 **"Always and always":** GS to BAC, Aug. 1938, RHR.

184 **"we can feel proud of":** BAC to Alice B. Toklas, Jan. 31, 1936, RHCC.

184 **three S&H editors:** Weil, Gotshal & Manges to Emanuel Harper, Apr. 23, 1936, Box 147, RHR. S&H had had three female directors, including Bonino.

184 **recruited Lewis Miller:** Background, "Random House Celebrates Its Twenty-Fifth Birthday," *PW,* Oct. 21, 1950, 1848.

184 **best book salesman *ever:*** Martin Levin to author, Apr. 21, 2004.

184 **better job:** DSK OH, 47.

184 **"Carlton House":** "Random House Launches New Merchandising Plan," *PW,* Jan. 16, 1937, 225. The Carlton House contract is mentioned in BAC's 1936 diary, Box 11, CP.

184 **"bargains":** Ray Healy to BAC, Aug. 16, 1936, RHR.

184 **"of the greatest integrity":** DSK quoted in Gordon Barrick Neavill in *The Modern Library Series,* Ph.D. dissertation, University of Chicago, Aug. 7, 1984, 181.

184 **"I like my new":** RKH to Robert Haas Jr., Box 5, RMHP.

185 **smelled something fishy:** BAC OH, 362–65. In OH, the aquarium head is Mr. Schneider, but in *AR,* the name was changed to Grady. The letter paper is in BAC archive. RKH confirmed episode to GTH, who recorded it in his interview notes, Series 2, Box 12, Folder 12, Geoffrey T. Hellman Papers, MSS 050, Fales Library, NYU (hereafter GTHP).

185 **already taken issue:** Merle Haas said to her son that RKH was "relieved" to have "two young and able men to work with." Merle Haas to Robert Haas Jr., Jan. 15, 1936, Box 5, RMHP.

185 **"amusing but irritating":** BAC OH, 318–19.

185 **"exceedingly":** BAC diary, Dec. 14, 1936, Box 11, CP.

185 **"the plastic historian":** "Davidson, Sculptor, Dies in France at 68," *NYT,* Jan. 3, 1952. A casting of his bust of GS is on a pedestal in Bryant Park, just behind the main branch of the NYPL.

185 **hoped to cajole:** RH would reject Davidson's book. See 1937–38 correspondence between BAC and Davidson, RHR.
185 **"fantastic":** BAC diary.
185 **"rich":** Jo Davidson, *Between Sittings* (New York: Dial Press, 1951).
185 **astray four times:** BAC diary, Box 11, CP.
185 **bad plumbing:** Picasso biographer John Richardson noted that bathroom and other arrangements at Bilignin were not geared to the comfort of guests. Richardson to author, Oct. 2, 2008.
186 **fill his walls with books:** On BAC's attitude to possessions, JFC to author many times.
186 **"Go home and paint":** BAC tells Picasso story in British Library Sound Archives 1LP0195374; see also "When This You See, Remember Me" documentary.
186 **"not poetry":** John Richardson, "Picasso and Gertrude Stein: Mano a Mano, Tête-à-Tête," *NYT,* Feb. 10, 1991.
186 **most likely apocryphal:** Albert Erskine, knowing well his boss's penchant for fabrication, did not include the Picasso story in *AR*. "One cannot say for sure" whether it happened, per Picasso poetry expert Lydia Gasman to author, Oct. 15, 2008.
186 **but nervous:** "I only hope that I will understand it." BAC to GS, June 26, 1935, Film 155, Box 100, GSP; see also BAC to GS, Oct. 15, 1936, Box 106a, RHR.
186 **"I do not know what":** Flap copy and review slip in DSK copy of *The Geographical History,* DSK Bequest, Williams College.
187 **"I am I":** GS, *The Geographical History of America or the Relation of Human Nature to the Human Mind* (New York: RH, 1936), 71.
187 **"listened" to "the human mind":** GS, *Geographical History,* 44. On what GS meant by "human nature" and "the human mind," see Dydo and Burns with Rice, eds., *Letters of Gertrude Stein and Thornton Wilder,* xix, 54, 68. Also Dydo to author, Feb. 15, 2008.
187 **"made to be happy":** BAC worried that GS made HAW seem "a much better person" than himself. BAC to GS, Dec. 17, 1935, Box 100, Film 155, GSP. What she meant was that HAW was more intellectual and sophisticated.
187 ***Everybody's Autobiography:*** The year before *Everybody's Autobiography* was published, BAC bought the rights to *The Autobiography of Alice B. Toklas* from Harcourt, to ensure that RH published all GS's trade books. BAC to GS, Aug. 13, 1936, Box 106A, RHR.
187 **"I always want":** GS, *Everybody's Autobiography,* 295.
187 **"tall and pleasant":** GS, *Everybody's Autobiography,* 204.
187 **"Bennett Cerf had a father":** See in Dydo and Burns with Rice, eds., *Letters of Gertrude Stein and Thornton Wilder,* 117, note 2.
187 **"Bennett Cerf has a father":** Dydo and Burns with Rice, eds., *Letters of Gertrude Stein and Thornton Wilder,* 133.
187 **"misinterpretation":** BAC to GS, Sept. 8, 1937, RHCC.
188 **"to hell with them":** BAC to GS, Jan. 14, 1938, RHCC.
188 **compiling and editing:** Given the number of changes, it's likely Rosenman wrote or rewrote many notes.
188 **"profound":** BAC to Samuel I. Rosenman, Mar. 3, 1937, Box 102, RHR.
188 **Roosevelt chose RH:** BAC diary, May 20, 1937, Box 11, CP.
188 **In the contract:** Letters with terms sent May 3, 24, & 25, 1937, from BAC to Rosenman; contract draft dated "June," all Box 102, RHR.
188 **motored with:** "Roosevelt's State Papers to Be Issued by Random House," *PW,* July 10, 1937, 113–14.
188 **a pricey fifteen:** The 2025 value of $15 in 1938 dollars is about $319.
188 **Bob's turn would come:** On Franklin Delano Roosevelt (hereafter FDR) visits, see BAC diary; on the visit with DSK, see "News from RH," Dec. 15, 1937, Box 19, CP. Rosenman was at the White House during the BAC/DSK trip, and another project was hatched by the three men on the return journey: a limited edition, fine-press book to be made from a set of drawings FDR had shown them. FDR lined up Captain Dudley Knox, head of the Naval Records Library, to supply the text; FDR supplied the introduction; and BAC/DSK engaged Edwin Grabhorn to design and print *Naval Sketches of the War in California: Reproducing Twenty-eight Drawings Made in 1846–7,* which RH published in 1939. BAC to FDR, Dec. 13, 1937; FDR to BAC, Dec. 20, 1937, President's Secretary's Files 158, FDR Presidential Library, Hyde Park.
188 **most important project:** BAC to GS, Apr. 1938, GSP.
188 **two pre-publication deals:** George T. Bye, FDR's literary agent, to FDR, Feb. 8, 1938; George Carlin to Bye, Feb. 3, 1938, President's Secretary's Files, 158.
189 **had been budgeted:** "An Approximate Estimate of the Cost Per Volume of the Public Papers and Addresses of FDR," undated, Box 102, RHR. The exact number of the run was 3,616. Rosenman to FDR, Mar. 24, 1938, Box 102, RHR.
189 **15,000 sets:** As late as January, BAC planned a run of 10,000. See BAC to Rosenman, Jan. 28, 1938, Box 102, RHR.

189 **Special paper and leather:** Haddon Craftsmen to Cahn, Jan. 12, 1939, Box 102, RHR.

189 **"Roosevelt Recession":** For 1937–38 recession, see https://www.fdrlibrary.org/budget.

189 **"to a useful public purpose":** For the statement, see Feb. 28 and Mar. 1, 1938, Box 158, President's Secretary's Files.

189 **"They are feeling very low":** Rosenman to FDR, Mar. 24, 1938, Box 102, RHR. RH's cut of the *Liberty* deal—$6,750—was to have been used for publicity; FDR agreed the money could be used toward paying the manufacturing bills, but the firm had to promise to spend an extra $3,500 on publicity.

189 **"Barring some miracle":** BAC to Rosenman, Apr. 18, 1938, Box 102, RHR.

190 **deluged with complaints:** Joseph Mitchell, "Roosevelt's Publisher Lays 'Sabotage' to Booksellers Says Some Keep Only Set or Two of President's Papers in Stock," *New York World Telegram,* May 6, 1938, Box 37, CP. BAC also referred to the complaints in vivid terms. See BAC OH, 380–92.

190 **sign a pledge:** Memo to Lew Miller (unsigned from BAC or DSK), Apr. 27, 1938, Box 102, RHR. It is unclear if the pledge was for regular salesmen or door-to-door canvassers. DSK to Cyrus Wood, Apr. 4, 1938, Box 102, RHR. Subsequently, RH did use "several" door-to-door salesmen, to no success. BAC to Rosenman, Sept. 13, 1938, Box 102, RHR.

190 **without completely losing face:** BAC to Rosenman, Apr. 18, 1938, Box 102, RHR.

190 **the *next* four books:** RKH to BAC and DSK, July 8, 1938; BAC to Rosenman, July 21, 1938, Box 102, RHR.

190 **"Not a single word":** BAC to Rosenman, Aug. 12, 1938, Box 102, RHR.

190 **door-to-door salesmen:** BAC to Rosenman, Sept. 13, 1938, Box 102, RHR.

190 **misguided from the start:** BAC's only consolation was the authors' responsibility to cover excess alterations. Rosenman's large number of insertions and corrections had cost $5,872.97. The printer reduced the cost to $5,000. Ironically, in the letter acknowledging receipt of the checks for author's alterations, RH actually *sent* Rosenman two checks, one for him, one for FDR, $1,751 each, representing the first three months' royalties from the books. Herbert R. Cahn to Rosenman, Sept. 13, Dec. 8, 1938, and Dec. 19, 1943, all Box 102, RHR.

190 **clogging space:** The original print run was 8,000 (many sheets were left unbound); 2,532 ordinary and 95 special sets were sold. See handwritten figures on "Saxe Commins" notepaper, Box 13, Folder 13, GTHP. BAC said, "2600 sold at regular price, 3000 remaindered, rest destroyed." Per GTH's interview notes.

190 **offered to sell:** Most of the 600-plus bound books and 5,000-plus sets of sheets were offered to Rosenman and FDR. BAC to Rosenman, Apr. 17, 1939, Box 102, RHR.

191 **defended the industry:** BAC, "Books on Our Table," *The New York Post,* Sept. 6, 1938, Box 37, CP.

191 **Don crossed to and from:** DSK to BAC, Oct. 11, 1938, Box 71, RHR; DSK OH, 21. OH mistakenly said Strachey was on the island only three days.

191 **illegal:** See "Strachey Winner in Fight on Ban," *NYT,* Jan. 24, 1939, 42.

192 **terrifying and depressing:** BAC to GS, Mar. 17, 1938, GSP.

192 **helped organize a luncheon:** BAC diary; *New York Tribune,* Apr. 1, 1938, Box 37, CP.

192 **"the hell with tomorrow":** BAC to GS, Sept. 8, 1937, GSP.

192 **won more American friends:** Paul's book "had a big influence on a lot of people, including me." BAC OH, 395.

192 **led a squadron:** Judith Thurman, "Rules of Engagement: Writing, Fighting, and André Malraux," *TNY,* May 2, 2005, 102.

192 **cri de coeur:** In Mar. 1937, Malraux spoke in NYC to raise money for the Loyalists. RKH, "assisted by Ernest Hemingway," translated the speech and persuaded ML printers H. Wolff to do a 350-copy signed, limited edition, at no cost. RH donated the proceeds from their sale. RKH to BAC, Mar. 3, 1937, Box 4, CP.

193 **probably crazy:** BAC to Edwin Grabhorn, Sept. 7, 1938, Box 102, RHR.

194 **"swell girl":** BAC diary, Aug. 14, 1938.

194 **"quivered with emotion":** BAC OH, 403. The RH union branch only lasted until the Book and Magazine Guild joined with the department store workers' union.

194 **accompany him to Barcelona:** BAC diary; Box 37, CP; BAC OH, 406–13.

194 **"practically impossible":** BAC to Passport Division, Sept. 8, 1938, Box 4, CP.

194 **respectfully denied:** John J. Scanlan to BAC, Sept. 10, 1938, Box 4, CP.

194 **phoned FDR's secretary:** Telegram from M. A. Le Hand to BAC, Sept. 10, 1938, Box 4, CP.

194 **"rage, disgust, despair":** BAC to RKH, Oct. 1938, Box 71, RHR.

194 **he and Fred Thompson dined:** Fred *was* a party member. See Harvey Klehr, John Earl Haynes, and Fridrikh Firsov, *The Se-*

cret World of American Communism (New Haven: Yale University Press, 1991), 304.

194 **a "sound anti-Fascist":** Ralph Bates to Don Fernando de los Rios, Sept. 8, 1938, Box 4, CP.

195 **"La Pasionaria":** Davidson, *Between Sittings,* 311. The book also mentions de la Mora and del Vayo.

195 **"*No pasarán!*":** Paul Hofmann, "Dolores Ibarruri, 'La Pasionaria' of Spanish Civil War, Dies at 93," *NYT,* Nov. 13, 1989. On La Pasionaria, Malraux, and the war, see Peter Wyden, *The Passionate War* (New York: S&S, 1983).

195 **ESTA ES LA OBRA:** BAC diary, Oct. 14, 1938, CP.

195 **furious, not frightened:** BAC, "They Are Still Selling Books in Spain," *PW,* Nov. 26, 1938, 1893–1896.

195 **The bookstore:** BAC, "They Are Still Selling Books in Spain."

196 **million-throated roar:** BAC, "They Are Still Selling Books in Spain"; BAC diary; BAC OH. I've followed the contemporary accounts unless indicated. In his OH, BAC says sarcastically and self-critically he was a "hero" until it was suggested he go to the front. He also says Spain's president and prime minister gave him messages for FDR. BAC OH, 413. I have found no independent documentation for the latter.

196 **witnessed how fast life could be lost:** "Skater Drowns, Chum Saved by New Yorkers," *New York Tribune,* Jan. 2, 1937, Box 37, CP.

196 **good-luck charm:** CBC and JFC to author.

196 **he'd wet himself:** BAC OH, 410. In his diary he simply wrote, "exhausted by excitement." BAC diary, Oct. 14, 1938.

196 **gaunt men in rubble:** Photos, Box 37, CP.

197 **read into the night:** The book was Frank Jellinek, *The Civil War in Spain* (London: Gollancz/Left Book Club, 1938).

197 **hyperkinetic, chain-smoking:** BAC OH, 412.

197 **"deserve everything":** BAC to GS, Oct. 23, 1938, RHR.

197 **selling even faster:** "News from Random House," autumn 1938, Box 37, CP.

197 **"Nazi bastards":** BAC diary, Nov. 13, 1938.

198 **footing the printing bill:** Davidson, *Between Sittings,* 316.

198 **all heard tales of persecution:** American Jewish Joint Distribution Committee letter from BAC to eighteen publishers, Apr. 7, 1937, Box 4, CP.

198 **writing at the behest:** Buck learned she won the Nobel on Nov. 10, 1938, just after the Polzer episode.

199 **Bennett stepped up:** Richard Walsh to DSK, Oct. 25, 1938, Box 141, RHR. For the remaining Polzer correspondence, see Box 4, CP.

199 **"Owing to your generosity":** Annie Polzer to BAC, Oct. 12, 1938, Box 4, CP.

199 **their rare name:** Cerf was not the only one to write BAC. A Hungarian couple, the Reisses, had fled to Shanghai but couldn't tolerate the climate. BAC met with Dr. Frederick Reiss on Nov. 25, 1938, and agreed to sponsor them. There is no indication if the couple arrived or who brokered the introduction. The Angeluscheff family, naturalized Germans, had fled to Paris and wanted sponsorship. Correspondence, Box 4, CP.

199 **"The only immigrants sponsored":** BAC to Reiss, Jan. 8, 1940, Box 4, CP.

199 **absolute silence:** Max Oestreicher to BAC, Jan. 6, 1940; BAC to Max Oestreicher, Jan. 11, 1940, Box 4, CP.

200 **a certain Miss Dodd:** BAC diary. The book was Dodd, *Through Embassy Eyes* (New York: Harcourt, 1939).

200 **volatile:** On the affair, see BAC's diary entries.

200 **take everything he wrote:** BAC to Theodor Seuss Geisel (hereafter TSG), Feb. 28, 1939, Box 82, RHR. See text of *Pentellic Bilge,* Box 19, Dr. Seuss Collection, University of California at San Diego (hereafter Seuss Collection). "Pentellic" is presumably an invented corruption of "pentelic," the marble of the Parthenon.

201 **let soft living:** BAC OH, 414. A Finnish woman in Nassau helped BAC forget Helen by becoming a "newly acquired, temporary wife." See DSK to BAC, Mar. 21, 1939, Box 4, CP. BAC makes a reference to "my little Finn went home yesterday." BAC to DSK, notes, n.d., Box 4, CP.

201 **One Saturday in July:** BAC diary.

CHAPTER 15: FOR LOVE OR MONEY

202 **"god damned kid cousin":** BAC OH, 429. In BAC's OH, he says Ginger Rogers was also present that weekend. His diary on July 15, 1939, mentions only Ross, Lela, and Phyllis. I have followed the diary.

202 **"to bring B.P. Schulberg":** PC OH, dictated to Barbaralee Diamonstein, Columbia, 100.

203 **"I was a virgin":** PC to author, Jan. 23, 2003. She emphasized her virginity repeatedly during the interview.

203 **Phyllis entered the world:** Helen Brown's birth certificate 20742, State of Missouri, courtesy JFC. According to the certificate,

Helen's parents Albert Percy and Verda Virginia Brown resided in Kansas City.

203 **four girls:** The Owens sisters' full names were Verda Virginia, Lela Emogene, Jean, and Wilma. Their parents were Walter and Saphrona.

203 **gas explosion:** Brown was killed and "his daughter fatally injured." *Oil and Gas Journal,* vol. 15, Feb. 1, 1917. Whether there was another daughter, or whether this is incorrect and refers to Emogene's injuries, is impossible to know. In PC OH transcript, sister is Jean; other sources say Gene.

203 **the days before movies talked:** On Lela and Ginger Rogers, see Gladys Hall, "Ginger Rogers' True Life Story," *Modern Screen,* Mar. 1937, 69–84, courtesy USCCL; Ginger Rogers, *Ginger: My Story* (New York: HarperCollins, 1991); John Springer and Jack Hamilton, *They Had Faces Then* (Secaucus, N.J.: Citadel Press, 1974), 325–66; Thomson, *New Biographical Dictionary of Film,* 749–50.

203 **"walking, living doll":** Rogers, *Ginger,* 16.

203 **"Jinja":** Rogers, *Ginger,* 16.

203 **worked on scripts:** At Fox, Lela worked under the pen name Lela Leibrand.

203 **"darnedest drum-beater":** "What's New . . . by Phyllis Cerf," *Newsday,* Feb. 13, 1958, courtesy CBC and JFC.

204 **wrote publicity for the Corps:** By chance, Lela worked with Max Schuster in the Liberty Bonds office.

204 **"In those days":** PC to author, Jan. 23, 2003; other interviews were on Jan. 29, Feb. 13, and Dec. 23 of the same year. See also PC OH.

204 **her sister's brain:** PC to author, Jan. 23, 2003. PC was a very unreliable narrator, claiming in her OH, for example, that Ginger's father was the son of the governor of Kansas, patently untrue. She also said her sister "hated" her. PC OH, 6. Yet in the last months of her life, sliding into dementia, servants heard her call for three people: Bennett, her mother, and Gene.

204 **"became my mother, really":** The Black domestic was Clara Willingham. In her OH, PC veers from emphasizing how "very important" Willingham was, to then calling her "a servant." Presumably she was both. PC OH, 18.

204 **brief untethering:** Ginger's first husband was Jack Culpepper; they were known as "Ginger and Pepper," per PC. According to Ginger's autobiography, during her elopement with Culpepper, her mother's marriage to Rogers broke up. Culpepper had been the beau of Virginia and Lela's sister, Jean. Like most families, this one had patterns: multiple marriages; names across generations; Hollywood. Jilted Aunt Jean went on to marry an actor, Vinton Hayworth, whose niece would become 1940s sex goddess Rita. See Rogers, *Ginger.* Rogers married and divorced five times.

204 **"the little things":** PC OH, 135.

204 **wanted to be like her aunt:** PC to author, Jan. 23, 2003.

205 **for alliteration:** Rogers, *Ginger,* 107–8.

205 **"a disaster":** PC OH, 24.

205 **became Helen Nichols again:** In the Hollywood part of PC's OH, her memories are unreliable. Her dates do not cohere with attendance records held at the Oklahoma City schools. Given that there is no transcript for 1932–33 and that she appears as a newcomer in fan magazines (*The New Movie Magazine, Motion Picture, Photoplay*) starting Aug. 1932, I assume that is the year she first went to Hollywood. She was in school in Oklahoma for the 1933–34 year. There is no evidence of a graduation from Classen High School.

206 **made magic together:** Some sources put *Flying Down to Rio* as Ginger's nineteenth picture. Astaire was born "Frederick Austerlitz" to an Austrian immigrant father whose Jewish parents had converted to Catholicism; his U.S. mother was Lutheran.

206 **highest-paid star:** The claim comes from www.reelclassics.com. Ginger and Fred Astaire as box-office champions of the Depression: see *This Fabulous Century, 1930–1940* (New York: Time-Life Books, 1969), 188; also, "Ginger Rogers," Reel Classics, www.reelclassics.com/Actresses/Ginger/ginger-bio.htm.

206 **Ginger opened the door:** PC OH, 34.

206 **she got a contract:** PC OH, 34, 58.

206 **it wasn't funny:** PC OH, 34, 58.

206 **bit parts:** After RKO, PC worked at Universal, Fox, Republic—wherever she could.

206 **assistant to RKO's production head:** Later, Lela ran her own school, famously championing a showgirl she spotted in one of Ginger's pictures: Lucille Ball. See "What's New . . . by Phyllis Cerf," *Newsday,* Feb. 13, 1958, courtesy CBC and JFC.

207 **They huddled:** Priscilla Haas Blum to author, Feb. 7, 2003.

207 **to court Lewis:** BAC diary, Sept. 1 & 3, 1939; BAC OH.

207 **heard FDR announce:** BAC diary, Sept. 1 & 3, 1939; BAC OH.

207 **"with colors flying":** BAC to GS, Sept. 8, 1939, RHCC.

207 **sheepish:** BAC OH, 434.

207 **"small and quiet and darling":** BAC OH, 438.
208 **an item:** BAC diary, Nov. 26, 1939.
208 **"deeply thrilled":** BAC diary, Feb. 24, 1940.
208 **"something there":** BAC diary, Jan. 28, 1940.
209 **heading to Nassau:** PC OH, 179; see also BAC diary.
209 **won $346:** BAC diary.
209 **"Allied Ball":** BAC diary. Progression of the war regularly noted in diary.
210 **"going to hell in a hack":** BAC diary, May 21, 1940.
210 **"Might as well have fun":** BAC diary, May 23, 1940. The Buick convertible mentioned in diary entry, also in PC OH, 202; BAC to Phyllis Fraser, June 19, 1940, courtesy CBC and JFC.
210 **"futile":** BAC diary, June 13, 1940.
210 **"unique, invaluable":** BAC to Phyllis Fraser, June 13, 1940, courtesy CBC and JFC.
210 **"haunted!!!":** BAC to Phyllis Fraser, May 29, 1940, courtesy CBC and JFC.
210 **"Overwhelmed":** BAC to Phyllis Fraser, June 10, 1940, courtesy CBC and JFC.
210 **"Never knew":** BAC to Phyllis Fraser, June 7, 1940, courtesy CBC and JFC.
210 **"cute":** Phyllis Fraser to BAC, spring (?) 1940, courtesy CBC and JFC.
210 **"cagey":** Phyllis Fraser to BAC, June 11, 1940, courtesy CBC and JFC.
210 **"YOU AND I":** BAC to Phyllis Fraser, June 25, 1940, courtesy CBC and JFC.
211 **serene day:** BAC diary, Aug. 10, 1940.
211 **he was tense:** BAC OH, 443.
211 **"daughter":** PC OH, 181.
211 **Bennett was a Jew:** GB to author, Jan. 20, 2005.
212 **the essential connection:** Wedding items in *NYT* and *NY Herald Tribune,* Sept. 4, 1940, courtesy Columbiana Collection.
212 **an old pal:** The wedding eve party was organized by BAC's Columbia friend Mike Breslauer, who would later introduce him to the Famous Writers School (see chapter 57; hereafter FWS).
212 **"summer city hall":** BAC diary; BAC scrapbooks; BAC OH.
212 **"Even if he told":** WF to RKH, Oct. 5, 1940, in Joseph Blotner, ed., *Selected Letters of William Faulkner* (New York: RH, 1977), 136.
212 **"porterhouse steak and domesticity":** RKH to WF, Oct. 9, 1940, 13497, AEP. AE, who was WF's last editor at RH, photocopied much of the correspondence between WF and RH. There is original correspondence in 16807, the William Faulkner Collection, University of Virginia (hereafter WFC).
212 **only American to stand:** On WF's place among the great modernists, see Frederick R. Karl, *William Faulkner: American Writer* (New York: Weidenfeld & Nicolson, 1989), 582.
213 **"get a great kick":** BAC to WF, Apr. 8, 1940, AEP.
213 **back income tax:** WF to RKH (and BAC), Apr. 22, 1940, WFC.
214 **mortgaging mules:** WF to RKH, Apr. 28, 1940, in Blotner, ed., *Selected Letters of William Faulkner,* 122.
214 **"a pretty substantial endowment":** RKH to WF, May 1, 1940, AEP.
214 **"any moral compass whatsoever":** WF to RKH, "Friday" (May 3, 1940), received May 6, 1940, in Blotner, ed., *Selected Letters of William Faulkner,* 122–23.
214 **"good friends":** WF to RKH, June 1, 1940, in Blotner, ed., *Selected Letters of William Faulkner,* 126.
214 **"You know how deeply":** RKH to WF, June 10, 1940, AEP.
215 **RH had its own woes:** In a letter to DSK on Dec. 31, 1943, BAC refers to their having been on their knees to the bank "three years ago." In an earlier letter to DSK, written June 26, 1942, BAC refers to "notes payable of $66,000. The latter figure includes $35,000 to the bank, $15,000 to ourselves and $16,000 in trade acceptances." On Sept. 3, 1942, DSK tells BAC, "I'm disturbed at our owing the bank 55 grand, but I hope we can pay it off this year. . . ." The first two letters are reproduced in *Dear Donald, Dear Bennett: The Wartime Correspondence of Bennett Cerf and Donald Klopfer* (New York: RH, 2002) (hereafter *DDDB*); the third is in Box 5, CP.
215 **unnamed novel:** WF to RKH, "Wednesday" (June 12, 1940), received June 14, 1940, in Blotner, ed., *Selected Letters of William Faulkner,* 129–30.
215 **confirmed in a telegram:** WF to RH, June 18, 1940, in Blotner, ed., *Selected Letters of William Faulkner,* 130.
215 **"Please do nothing further":** BAC to WF, June 19, 1940, AEP.
215 **heartsick:** The exact phrase was "sick at heart." BAC to WF, June 19, 1940, AEP.
216 **"fast and loose":** WF to BAC, "Thursday" (June 20, 1940), in Blotner, ed., *Selected Letters of William Faulkner,* 130–31.
216 **"you likewise understand ours":** BAC to WF, June 24, 1940, AEP.
216 **"Faulkner probably lost to us":** BAC diary, June 24, 1940.
216 **Horace Liveright brought out:** The two Liveright novels followed WF's first published book, *The Marble Faun* (1924), a collection of pastoral verse whose publication

was subsidized by his Mississippi friend and mentor, Phil Stone.

216 **"Well, I'm going":** WF to Mrs. Walter B. McLean, Oct. 1928, in Blotner, ed., *Selected Letters of William Faulkner,* 41.

216 **Estelle Faulkner became pregnant:** The baby, named Alabama, was born in Jan. 1931 and died nine days later, a continuing sorrow.

216 **"the intrusion of Greek tragedy":** Malraux wrote a preface to *Sanctuary.* The quote is in Malcolm Cowley, "Faulkner Was Wrong About *Sanctuary,*" *NYT,* Feb. 22, 1981.

217 **Joyce and Dostoyevsky:** WF to BAC, Apr. 15, 1931, Box 2, CP. WF spelled the name "Dostoyefsky."

217 **"queer fish":** BAC to Edwin Grabhorn, Dec. 7, 1932, Box 2, WFC.

217 **"five to one":** BAC to Milton Abernethy, Nov. 19, 1931, *Contempo* Collection, RC.

217 ***Idyll in the Desert:*** According to Judith L. Sensibar, Estelle Faulkner was the real author of *Idyll in the Desert.* See Sensibar, *Faulkner and Love: The Women Who Shaped His Art* (New Haven: Yale University Press, 2010), 241.

217 **solely for money:** WF's claim has generally been seen as bravado, not truth.

217 **being in such demand:** See WF to Estelle Faulkner, Nov. 12, 1931, quoted in Blotner, *Faulkner: A Biography* (New York: RH, 1974), 737, vol. 1.

217 **all his nerve endings:** Blotner, *Faulkner,* 719, vol. 1.

217 **the oblivion of drink:** Blotner, *Faulkner,* 717–21, vol. 1.

218 **"Mrs. Knopf has been very nice":** On the '21' lunch and the Knopf party, see Blotner, *Faulkner,* 741–42, vol. 1. See also AAK one-page reminiscence, dictated July 7, 1962, just after WF's death, courtesy AP.

218 **They made the rounds:** Blotner, *Faulkner,* 745, vol. 1.

218 **slender, vivid woman:** Marshall Smith quoted in Blotner, *Faulkner,* 745, vol. 1.

218 **he charmed her:** Blotner, *Faulkner,* 748–49, vol. 1.

218 **"courtesies":** Ben Wasson to BAC, Dec. 8, 1931, AEP.

218 **also liked the books he made:** WF thanked BAC for *Idyll* on Dec. 27, 1931, CPCC.

218 **publishing four books:** The titles were *Light in August; A Green Bough; Doctor Martino and Other Stories;* and *Pylon.* S&H also agreed to RH doing a limited edition of *The Sound and the Fury.* BAC, certain that connoisseurs with cash would buy it, lined up the Grabhorns to make the book in an unusual way. The novel uses stream-of-consciousness by unreliable narrators to tell the story of the Compsons; most challenging is the first part, where the tale is literally "told by an idiot," Benjy Compson. Each paragraph was to be printed in one of three colors, so the reader would know if it was set in childhood, adolescence, or manhood. As BAC counseled Edwin Grabhorn: "the book must be read all the way through . . . and then all the mystifying portions clarify [into] a beautiful whole." BAC to Grabhorn, Dec. 7, 1932. WF color-coded the text. But between the Grabhorns and RH, it went missing. For years, BAC and the Grabhorns exchanged letters. Box 2, Mss 10280, WFC. BAC blamed the Grabhorns; they blamed him. The marked text has never been found.

219 **"Why in hell not?":** WF's comments on galley proofs of *Light in August* (galleys 109 & 138), RC.

219 **"selling" title:** Karl, *William Faulkner,* 617. On the changes to *Absalom, Absalom!* see Louis Mayeux, "Noel Polk: William Faulkner 'Continues to Amaze,'" *Southern Bookman,* July 27, 2010, https://louismayeux.typepad.com/southern_bookman/2010/07/noel-polk-william-faulkner-continues-to-amaze.html.

219 **"more interesting than any book":** DSK to BAC, Mar. 21, 1939, CP.

219 **"a con man":** Stephen Longstreet interview, June 12, 1965, in Joseph Blotner Papers, Southeast Missouri State University, quoted in Carl Rollyson, *The Life of William Faulkner,* Vol. 2 (Charlottesville: University of Virginia Press, 2020), 207.

219 **"anxious":** BAC to WF, Oct. 29, 1937, Box 3, Folder 38, WFC.

219 **a burn:** Blotner, *Faulkner,* 974–75, vol. 2; Karl, *William Faulkner,* 598.

220 **was given $350:** Box 3, Folder 38, WFC.

220 **"domestic situation":** Box 2, AEP.

220 **"Bennett, it was *my* vacation":** BAC OH, 329.

220 **had to bow out:** Harold Guinzburg to WF, July 3, 1940, AEP.

220 **"for all time":** BAC to WF, July 8, 1940, AEP.

221 **"dull":** WF to BAC, July 24, 1940, in Blotner, ed., *Selected Letters of William Faulkner,* 134.

221 **"I have not approached":** WF to BAC, July 28, 1940, in Blotner, ed., *Selected Letters of William Faulkner,* 135.

221 **"So a seven-hour drive":** PC OH, 206.

222 **"I don't want to go":** PC OH, 232.

222 **or find a way:** BAC's diary has a honeymoon itinerary, which notes "tour of town (alone!)" in Williamsburg, Oct. 22, 1940. But on that same date, he writes, "Happy

sunburned approve of marriage!"—utterly contradicting PC's OH (231–37) detailing arguments and power struggle. I have paraphrased 277–78 of her OH on BAC, "my mother, my father, my mentor." On the honeymoon and broader topics like anger vs. sulking, see PC, "My Husband Is No Joke to Live With," *Good Housekeeping*, June 1954.

222 **"She made him":** DSK OH, 71.

223 **person who'd forwarded:** PC OH, 300–301.

223 **placed a small cradle:** BAC OH, 445–46.

224 **"Pulsifer":** I have been unable to ascertain why BAC chose this name. One possible meaning is "seed carrier" or "pea carrier," just as Lucifer is "light carrier." PC admitted that BAC was "frightened" of "the thought of fatherhood." PC OH, 302.

224 **"Why don't you look at houses?":** PC OH, 246–49. For the house file, see Box 5, CP. On Oct. 27, 1941, Robert Heller gave BAC total expenditures as $22,914.71, more than doubling the price of the house. Max Schuster's wife, Rae, did the garden. BAC to Rae Schuster, Oct. 17, 1941.

224 **"an anguished hour":** On Pop's illness and death, see BAC diary, Sept. 22–Oct. 2, 1941.

225 **"Darling":** BAC to PC, Aug. 27, 1941, courtesy CBC and JFC.

225 **"The transition":** BAC to GS, Sept. 17, 1941, CPCC.

PART THREE, 1941–1951: TRY AND STOP ME

227 **"Our business":** BAC to DSK, Nov. 14, 1944, in *DDDB* (New York: RH, 2002), 185.

227 **"No one underrates":** Unattributed but probably Jack Goodman, "Note About the Author," in BAC, *Try and Stop Me* (New York: S&S, 1944), 380 (hereafter *TASM*).

CHAPTER 16: PATRIOTISM AND PROFIT

229 **seed of encouragement:** BWS to author, Oct. 14, 2003. Contrast $250 advance with $1,500 per movie script as cited in Eric Homberger, "Budd Schulberg: Novelist and Oscar-Winning Screenwriter Who Testified at the HUAC Hearings," *The Guardian*, Aug. 6, 2009.

229 **"being brought into a family":** BWS to author, Oct. 14, 2003. *What Made*—not *Makes*—*Sammy Run?* was the title used in letters from BAC to BWS, Mar. 29, July 9 & 10, 1940, MS-978 (68), BWSP.

229 **7,000 copies:** BAC to BWS, Mar. 25, 1941, MS-978 (68), BWSP.

229 **"utterly fearless":** F. Scott Fitzgerald to BAC, Dec. 13. 1940, reprinted in Matthew Bruccoli with Judith S. Baughman, *F. Scott Fitzgerald on Authorship* (Columbia: University of South Carolina Press, 1996).

230 **"That horrible book":** BWS quoting Goldwyn to author, Jan. 15, 2008.

230 **became a critical success:** The novel was also dramatized twice for TV and made into a Broadway musical. It was never made into a Hollywood movie.

230 **save only the happy things:** BWS to author, Oct. 14, 2003.

230 **about thirty new trade titles:** These did not include new ML reprints.

230 **demand for nonfiction:** See John Tebbel, *A History of Book Publishing in the United States*, Vol. IV, *The Great Change, 1940–1980* (New York: R. R. Bowker, 1981), 2, 3 (hereafter *Great Change*).

230 **The firm brought out:** RH Spring Catalogue, 1941, Box 166, RHR.

230 **"standing on a summit":** BAC, *TASM*, 363.

231 ***London Can Take It:*** The fifteen thousand theaters were in the United States, Canada, and Latin America. The British still consider it a movie of considerable significance. See: https://media.nationalarchives.gov.uk/index.php/london-can-take-it/.

231 **"heartwarming":** BAC, Trade Winds, *SRL*, Sept. 11, 1943.

231 **"There is so darn much":** Elliot Paul to SC, quoted in Commins, *What Is an Editor?* 37.

231 **"I should name you":** DSK OH, 38.

231 **$500 bonus:** BAC to DSK, Sept. 4, 1942, in *DDDB*, 32.

231 **seventh movie deal:** "Signs of a Promising Spring," *PW*, Apr. 11, 1942. The film that was eventually made was entirely different from Paul's book; the only similarity was the title. BAC had also sold film rights to *The Ox-Bow Incident* and to a book by Sally Benson; she had titled it "35 Kensington Street," but BAC suggested *Meet Me in St. Louis*. The film version included one of Judy Garland's most beloved performances.

231 **number-one bestseller:** RH and BOMC editions of *The Last Time I Saw Paris* sold 170,000 copies.

231 **who banned it:** BAC Trade Winds, *SRL*, Sept. 11, 1943. BAC wrote about Paul's idiosyncratic "antics" that he exploited. For instance, in one story Paul brings a cage of carrier pigeons to the office so that RH could communicate with him at his Connecticut farm. See BAC, *TASM*, 116. See also Commins, *What Is an Editor?*; FCB to author, Nov. 30, 2002. Another story: Paul

was a boogie-woogie player. BAC had a piano hoisted through the office window so he could play at his book launch.

231 **squabbling over points:** *AR,* 160–61.

231 **a stiff walk in the cold:** BAC diary, Dec. 7, 1941, Box 11, CP.

232 **crackled with the startling news:** CW told how they learned of Pearl Harbor in *Donald S. Klopfer: An Appreciation* (New York: RH, 1987), a memorial book privately published.

232 **"I can't get it out":** DSK to BAC, Mar. 21, 1939, Box 4, CP.

232 **national epiphany:** Allan Nevins, "How We Felt About the War," in *While You Were Gone: A Report on Wartime Life in the United States,* edited by Jack Goodman (New York: S&S, 1946). BAC noted war developments in his diary.

232 **"kind of funny":** BAC to EON and CMON, Dec. 9, 1941, RHCC.

232 **he tracked him:** BAC diary, Box 11, CP.

233 **would be an immediate bestseller:** BAC OH, 779.

233 **received his classification:** BAC diary, Box 11, CP.

233 **wasn't much of a provider:** LKL to author, Nov. 19, 2003.

233 **miscarried several times:** In a letter to Martha Dodd, DSK mentioned that Pat had six miscarriages. DSK to Dodd, Feb. 11, 1981, MDP. On the hospitalizations, BAC wrote, "Pat just home from hospital" (Jan. 14, 1941) and "Pat who has had another mishap" (May 10, 1941). BAC diary, Box 11, CP.

233 **formally asking:** BAC diary.

233 **"STUNNED":** BAC diary, Box 11, CP.

233 **Midafternoon Saturday:** BAC diary, Box 11, CP.

234 **"BAC bet Donald":** Box 5, CP. BAC-DSK wartime letters in boxes 5 and 6; most are reprinted in *DDDB.*

234 **felt lonely:** See BAC diary, June 1, 9, & 10, 1942, Box 11, CP.

234 **"too seldom":** DSK to the "Gang," June 2, 1942, Box 5, CP.

234 **"usually dead":** DSK to BAC, June 9, 1942, in *DDDB,* 8.

234 **"We all envy you":** BAC to DSK, June 9, 1942, in *DDDB,* 5.

234 **lonesome for the life:** DSK to BAC, June 23, 1942, in *DDDB,* 17.

234 **"wet-nursing":** DSK to BAC, June 23, 1942, in *DDDB,* 17.

235 **take advantage of the farm:** Aug. 31, 1942, in *DDDB,* 29.

235 **churning out anthologies:** Story collections in translation were also published by RH, but compiled by other editors, not BAC.

235 **twenty-five dollars a column:** This was not mere change; the government estimated a "sound minimum standard of living" for an average family requiring a yearly income of $1,675. See Nevins, "How We Felt About the War," 19.

235 **"pretty careful":** BAC, Trade Winds, *SRL,* Feb. 28, 1942. Mr. Carlton Ealy kindly allowed me to photocopy his collection of BAC's *SRL* columns for this book. They are also in BAC's scrapbooks at Columbia.

235 **creating government war propaganda:** He was at the C.O.I., forerunner of the O.S.S., which spawned the C.I.A. Robert O. Ballou, *A History of the Council on Books in Wartime, 1942–46* (New York: Country Life Press, 1946), 84 (hereafter *History of the Council*). Guinzburg was chief of the domestic publications division and eventually became director of the London-based Publications Division of the Office of War Information.

235 **"stopping passers-by in their tracks":** BAC, Trade Winds, *SRL,* Apr. 11, 1942.

235 **welcome news to every publisher:** BAC, Trade Winds, *SRL,* Aug. 1, 1942. He misspelled Trautman as "Troutman."

235 **such a hit:** Sept. 17, 1942, BAC to Norman Cousins, Box 5, CP.

235 **began to excerpt:** BAC diary, Oct. 9, 1942. By 1947, this contributed $2,400 to his annual income. See Ralph Henderson to BAC, June 25, 1947, Box 6, RHR. The *Chicago Tribune* had wanted to reprint columns for $25 each, but BAC said "too little." See BAC diary, Oct. 8, 1942. *Reader's Digest* monthly circulation was eight million. Eric Hodgins, "The Magazines," in *While You Were Gone,* ed. Goodman, 405. However, BAC says circulation "jumped to 9,200,000." BAC to DSK, Jan. 29, 1943, in *DDDB,* 67.

236 **The first "Literary Crypt":** PC OH, 263. The cryptograms began on June 26, 1943.

236 **"intriguing new":** BAC, Trade Winds, *SRL,* July 10, 1943.

236 **ten-millionth copy:** ML, "Book Notes," *NY Herald Tribune,* May 26, 1941.

236 **five-month PR campaign:** "Modern Library Tries Out Movie Publicity Technique," *PW,* Sept. 27, 1941.

237 **It was Dick:** The 25-cent price was RLS's idea; the distribution was Shimkin's. Seymour Turk to author, Dec. 5, 2005. Turk was Shimkin's protégé. Book prices hadn't been this low since the Civil War, apart from the Little Blue Books.

237 **"fold in three months":** BAC, quoted in Wallis E. Howe, "The First Half Billion," *Bestsellers,* Sept. 1962, quoted in Tebbel, *Great Change,* 367.

237 **in 1936 . . . he'd written Don:** BAC to DSK, May 20, 1936, Box 4, CP.

237 **23 million copies sold:** On Pocket Books, see Tebbel, *Great Change,* 366–67.

237 **could sell half a million:** BAC to DSK, Aug. 31, 1942, in *DDDB,* 29.

237 **"present obsession":** BAC diary, Sept. 21, 1942, Box 11, CP.

238 **"up to their asses":** BAC diary, Feb. 16–23, 1942, Box 11, CP.

238 **"for purposes of identification":** BAC to Terry Turner, Apr. 22, 1941, Box 5, CP.

238 **"just in case":** BAC diary, Sept. 20, 1942, Box 11, CP.

238 **an addendum specified:** One-page memo by RKH for RH Inc., signed by BAC, PFC, and Pauline K. Friedman, July 28, 1942, Box 5, CP.

238 **no new typewriters:** BAC diary, Mar. 8, 1942, Box 11, CP.

238 **"hot and crowded":** BAC to DSK, June 15, 1943, in *DDDB,* 78.

238 **"just like that":** Paul Gallico, "What We Talked About," in *While You Were Gone,* ed. Goodman, 30–37.

238 **what was happening in Britain:** BAC, Trade Winds, *SRL,* Aug. 29, 1942.

238 **if Saxe was killing himself:** DSK to BAC, Sept. 26, 1942, in *DDDB,* 38.

238 **"slaving":** BAC to DSK, Sept. 29, 1942, in *DDDB,* 40–41.

239 **crowded his diary:** On BAC's involvement with the Red Cross, Navy relief, and the Treasury, see BAC diary, Apr. 20, 1942.

239 **ranked only fifteenth:** See Tebbel, *Great Change,* 17. If all subsidiaries were included in the accounting, Doubleday was first. Even without its affiliates, it soon overtook Macmillan. Others producing more titles than RH at war's start included Oxford University Press; McGraw-Hill; Dutton; Dodd, Mead; Blue Ribbon; Scribner; Harcourt; Farrar & Rinehart; Appleton-Century; and Houghton Mifflin. Knopf was seventeenth.

239 **"given less other entertainment":** BAC, "War and the Book Business," *PW,* Mar. 28, 1942, Box 38, CP.

239 **haunt the industry:** Tebbel, *Great Change,* 23.

239 **"Victory Book Campaign":** Tebbel, *Great Change,* 23. BAC pointed out that the campaign had received only tepid support and tried to rally publishers; that became moot with ASEs. BAC, Trade Winds, *SRL,* Apr. 10, 1943.

239 **umbrella organization:** Tebbel, *Great Change,* 24–55; Ballou, *History of the Council;* BAC, Trade Winds, *SRL,* Nov. 28, 1942, Mar. 6, June 12, 1943, Nov. 11, 1944; dedicated CBW folder, Box 137, RHR.

239 **"Books Are Weapons in the War of Ideas":** BAC wrongly attributed the slogan to FDR. BAC, Trade Winds, *SRL,* Nov. 28, 1942. Many others did, too. It seems highly unlikely that BAC was not aware that Norton had originated it. After the FDR public papers imbroglio, however, he did have reason to flatter the president.

239 **joined the effort:** Key early figures included Clarence Boutell of Putnam and George Oakes of the *NYT.* The American Booksellers Association (ABA), the American Library Association (ALA), and PEN America were allied organizations. The industry also gave rise to other patriotic initiatives. For instance, the Book and Magazine Guild, Helen Thompson's union, had a Book Mobilization Committee.

239 ***They Burned the Books:*** See Box 38, CP.

240 **"Through books, we have":** FDR to W. W. Norton, Dec. 1, 1942, reproduced in Ballou, *History of the Council.*

240 ***Books Are Bullets:*** The Council on Books in Wartime (hereafter COBIW) also sponsored "Fighting Words," a chat between an author and a publisher, on another station, featuring Doubleday's Ken McCormick and others as the host. See Ballou, *History of the Council,* 34.

240 **"try-out":** BAC diary, Oct. 7, 1942. A rehearsal had taken place on Oct. 5.

240 **"to ad lib":** Nan Taylor, quoted in Donald Porter Geddes, guest Trade Winds columnist, *SRL,* Mar. 6, 1943. The remarks about Mussolini's syphilis are also from Geddes.

240 **"all confidence":** John Farrar to BAC, May 10, 1943, Box 2, CP.

241 **"pestered":** BAC to DSK, Oct. 16, 1942, Box 5, CP.

241 **a contract with him personally:** BAC to Robert de Graff, Dec. 2, 1942, Box 5, CP.

241 **"new life":** Janet Lumb to BAC, n.d., with Oct. 21, 1942, letter from BAC, Box 137, RHR.

241 **only six Imperatives:** W. L. White, *They Were Expendable* (Harcourt); John Hersey, *Into the Valley* and *A Bell for Adano* (Knopf); Wendell Willkie, *One World* (S&S); Walter Lippmann, *U.S. Foreign Policy* (Little, Brown); and Edgar Snow, *People on Our Side* (RH).

241 **forced to return:** BAC to DSK, Sept. 29, 1942, 41; DSK to BAC, Oct. 16, 1942, in *DDDB,* 45.

241 **"end her trouble":** BAC to DSK, Feb. 10, 1943, Box 5, CP.

241 **six miscarriages:** DSK mentions them to Martha Dodd, Feb. 11, 1981, MDP.

242 **wouldn't let her lead:** PC OH, 278–79.

242 **$500 household allowance:** KCH to au-

thor, several times. She said that when she married Moss Hart (hereafter MH), she'd asked PC what BAC gave her as a housekeeping allowance.

242 **"Honeymoon Inc.":** See *Variety,* May 27, 1942, Box 38, CP.

242 **Under the pseudonym "Phyllis Morris":** Though divorced, Leonora had been Mrs. Wayne Morris.

242 **"One Man's Honeymoon":** *Liberty,* May 22, 1943, Box 65, CP.

242 **Defense Recreation Committee:** PC OH, 279–81.

242 **several pampered weeks:** On Patterson/Guggenheim visits, see BAC diaries.

243 **20,000 copies:** BAC diary; BAC to DSK, July 12, 1944, in *DDDB,* 168.

243 **pay off the bank loan:** BAC to DSK, Oct. 30, 1942, in *DDDB,* 47.

244 **kept a diary:** BAC OH, 479–80. While stranded in the New Hebrides awaiting transport back to Pearl Harbor, Tregaskis turned the diary into a book.

244 ***"Guadalcanal Diary":*** BAC to newspapers, Nov. 13, 1942, Box 110, RHR.

244 **as a main selection:** BAC to DSK, Nov. 16, 1942, in *DDDB,* 55–56.

244 **novel publicity plan:** Greene to BAC, Nov. 19, 1942; BAC reply, Nov. 20, Box 10, RHR.

244 **"done with complete simplicity":** BAC to DSK, Dec. 15, 1942, in *DDDB,* 57–58.

245 **"suspended animation":** BAC to DSK, July 20, 1943, in *DDDB,* 93.

245 **if the lucky publisher:** RLS to BAC, July 13, 1943, Box 2, CPCC.

246 **"restlessness and futility":** DSK to BAC, July 11, 1943, in *DDDB,* 91.

246 **"Don't let the business":** DSK to BAC, July 22, 1943, in *DDDB,* 96.

246 **censorship delay:** BAC to DSK, Aug. 20, 1943, in *DDDB,* 103.

246 **would never return home:** Priscilla Haas Blum to author, July 8, 2009. RKH had written to his son about the nature of a good publisher. It involved being a polymath, with "catholic tastes," "literary ideals," etc., who brought "ideas, energy, and a certain keenness for the marketplace" and was "a good mixer," finding book ideas in all sorts, from "duchesses to ditch-diggers." A timeless description of what is ideal in a publisher, it was dated Feb. 14, 1940, and is in Box 5, RMHP. See also Feb. 27, 1940, letter from Merle Haas concerning RKH Jr. following in his father's footsteps, Box 5, RMHP.

246 **"I was as proud":** DSK to RKH and Merle Haas, June 3, 1943, Box 5, RMHP.

246 **"Bob has been wonderful":** BAC to DSK, June 15, 1943, in *DDDB,* 78. Betty, one of Haas's two daughters, had taken flying lessons in college; having volunteered for the Women Air Force Service Pilots, she was in basic training when the news about her brother came. Her role would be to pilot bombers across the United States to free men up to fight overseas. It would be dangerous work, involving planes that had hardly been tested. Many families might have insisted that she ask for a compassionate discharge; the Haas family did not. Betty served, one of just over a thousand female volunteer pilots, for the rest of the war. She said that her brother's death "almost killed both my parents." Betty Haas Pfister to author, May 12, 2005.

246 **"Bob, dear boy":** WF to RKH, "Thursday" (July 1, 1943), in Blotner, ed., *Selected Letters of William Faulkner,* 175. The original is in Box 5, RMHP.

246 **"much nicer":** WF to Mrs. Walter B. McLean, Oct. 1928, in Blotner, ed., *Selected Letters of William Faulkner,* 41.

247 **tremor threatening his ability:** EON had been given a diagnosis of Parkinson's, but it was erroneous, and the medicines he was given often worsened his symptoms. After his death, an autopsy showed he had a rare disease afflicting cells of the cerebellum. Arthur and Barbara Gelb, *By Women Possessed,* 572.

247 **come East:** BAC to CMON, Aug. 31, 1943, RHCC.

247 **"Bennett dear":** CMON to BAC, May 11, 1942, RHCC.

247 **"a tempest in a teapot":** BAC to CMON, May 15, 1942, RHCC.

247 **"nauseating":** BAC to CMON, June 29, 1943, RHCC.

248 **400,000 copies:** "Boy Publishing Wonder," *Beacon Journal* (Akron), May 5, 1943.

248 **700,000 copies:** *PW,* Nov. 20, 1943.

248 **"phenomenal":** BAC quoted in *Of Men and Books,* Jan. 16, 1943, vol. 2, no. 16, Northwestern University on the Air, Box 38, CP. The net profit on June 30, 1943, would be $285,000.

248 **sixty-one employees:** Fact sheet, Aug. 26, 1943, Box 147, RHR. RH took a second floor on Feb. 19, 1943, and a third on Nov. 19, 1943. BAC diary, Box 11, CP.

248 **$300,000 order:** BAC to DSK, May 11, 1943, in *DDDB,* 71. In another letter to DSK, BAC describes the complicated deal with Duplaix. May 28, 1943, in *DDDB,* 75.

249 **"Those bastards":** BAC to DSK, Aug. 20, 1943, in *DDDB,* 104.

249 **Phyllis would author:** PC's Little Golden Books were *This Little Piggy and Other Counting Rhymes* and *Mother Goose.*

249 **Illustrated Modern Library:** BAC to DSK,

June 22, 1943; DSK to BAC, June 26, 1943; BAC to DSK, June 30, 1943; BAC to DSK, July 9, 1943, in *DDDB,* 80–85, 89–90.

249 **"Now all we need":** *DDDB,* 84–85.

249 **What about entering:** DSK to BAC, June 26, 1943, in *DDDB,* 83.

249 **step down as publicity director:** Warder Norton to BAC, Aug. 19, 1943, Box 137, RHR.

249 **"Armed Services Editions":** Malcolm "Pike" Johnson of Doubleday first broached the idea of the COBIW acting as a copyright pool to supply the government with new books to be printed on special plates unlike others previously made. Minutes, Executive Committee meeting, Feb. 10, 1943, Box 137, RHR.

250 **which is how Bennett was asked:** Philip Van Doren Stern to BAC, Nov. 5, 1943, Box 137, RHR.

250 **155,000-plus copies:** In addition to ASEs, a separate program—Overseas Editions—would send 3.5 million specially printed books in English, French, German, Italian for sale to inhabitants of recently freed, now Allied-occupied territories in Europe, North Africa, the Middle East, and Asia. Ballou, *History of the Council,* 83–94.

250 **"boys reading as they":** Ballou, *History of the Council,* 83.

251 **"It would be the most":** DSK to BAC, Aug. 23, 1943, in *DDDB,* 105.

251 **"agog":** BAC diary, Box 11, CP.

251 **"Don't ever worry":** DSK to BAC, Sept. 17, 1943, in *DDDB,* 109.

252 **"You win the war":** BAC to DSK, Sept. 20, 1943, Box 5, CP.

252 **"I almost froze":** DSK to BAC, Nov. 7, 1943, in *DDDB,* 114.

252 **"curves" and "angles":** Fritz Jacobi to author, Aug. 7, 2003. For the work of the 445th Bomber Group, I am indebted to Jacobi. In 1943, he was twenty-two with two years at Harvard behind him. Immediately after the war, DSK gave him a job at RH.

253 **"from the vast loneliness":** DSK to BAC, Nov. 5, 1943, in *DDDB,* 113.

253 **"eating out my insides":** BAC to DSK, Nov. 5, 1943, Box 5, CP.

253 **"Business couldn't be better":** BAC to DSK, Nov. 5, 1943, Box 5, CP.

253 **add a senior editor:** BAC to DSK, Mar. 11, 1944, in *DDDB,* 134–35.

253 **"Nothing, of course":** BAC to DSK, Feb. 21, 1944, in *DDDB,* 139, 138.

253 **"Random House of Canada":** BAC diary, Mar. 21, 1943, Box 11, CP.

254 **just bought 60,000:** BAC to DSK, Dec. 10, 1943, in *DDDB,* 120.

254 **"sales conference halted":** BAC to DSK, Jan. 11, 1944, in *DDDB,* 128.

254 **"too good to be true":** Jan. 12, 1944, in *DDDB,* 130–31.

254 **"Jesus, I'll have to learn":** DSK to BAC, Feb. 8, 1944, in *DDDB,* 133.

254 **"I won't have the dough":** DSK to BAC, Mar. 11, 1944, in *DDDB,* 144.

254 **"gay and mad":** DSK to BAC, Feb. 8, 1944, in *DDDB,* 133–34.

254 **"Don't be a God damned fool":** DSK to BAC, Mar. 3, 1944, in *DDDB,* 142–43.

255 **"That's quite an organization":** DSK to BAC, Mar. 3, 1944, in *DDDB,* 142.

255 **"small-time operator":** DSK to BAC, Mar. 11, 1944, in *DDDB,* 144.

255 **"no possibility":** BAC to DSK, Mar. 21, 1944, in *DDDB,* 145–50.

255 **"Please don't let the damned thing":** DSK to BAC, Apr. 13, 1944, in *DDDB,* 153.

256 **It all began with Marshall Field:** On the Grosset & Dunlap purchase, Marshall Field's purchase of controlling stake in S&S and Pocket, and the decision to start Bantam, see BAC letters to DSK in Box 6 CP; Tebbel, *Great Change,* 70–72, 202; BAC Box 65, CP; BAC diary, Box 11, CP.

256 **making it much harder:** BAC to DSK, Oct. 10, 1944, Box 6, CP.

256 **rocked the publishing world:** BAC diary, Sept. 28, 1944.

257 **"smarty pantses":** BAC to DSK, Oct. 2, 1944, Box 6, CP.

257 **"utmost confidence":** DSK to BAC, Oct. 30, 1944, Box 6, CP.

257 **"We bought Grosset!":** AAK Jr. to author, Dec. 6, 2002.

257 **an unusual mix:** BAC to DSK, Oct. 10, 1944, Box 6, CP.

257 **be paid to manage:** RKH to Harry Scherman, Nov. 20, 1944; G&D board of directors meeting minutes, Dec. 6, 1944, Box 6, CP. Of the other staff, Lew Miller and Ray Freiman made $4,000 each; Manny Harper $1,200; SC, Maule, and RNL $600 each; Bonino (being a woman) $500; Abe Friedman $500. Writing to the G&D board of directors, RKH notes that O'Connor has been so efficient as to make it appropriate to lower the final payments made to himself, BAC, and DSK due on Nov. 26, 1945, to a total of $8,000 divided among the three of them, and that for the second year the compensation for themselves and other RH employees be revised downward. RKH to G&D board, Aug. 29, 1945.

257 **"real 'Big Business'":** "Publisher-Author-Columnist-Critic-Raconteur Bennett Cerf Spills the Dirt on Genial Robber Barons of Book Industry," *The New York Post,* Nov. 30, 1944, Box 65, CP.

258 **"drunk with dreams":** BAC to DSK, Oct. 2, 1944, in *DDDB,* 177.

258 **"Silver Gertrudes":** Box 65, CP. The other three authors were Dale Carnegie (*How to Win Friends and Influence People*), James Hilton (*Lost Horizon*), and Marion Hargrove (*See Here, Private Hargrove*).

258 **didn't have enough paper:** Elinor Green Hunter—a former S&S employee—to author, June 11, 2010.

258 **A $1,000 advance and 15 percent royalty:** See BAC diary, June 1 & 12, 1944, Box 11, CP, for *TASM* contract details. (RLS, in an unpublished fragment of autobiography [29], described the origin of the title. Courtesy S&S.)

258 **full-page ad:** Nov. 5, 1944, Box 65, CP.

259 **shy high school boys:** One of the self-described shy high school boys was Princeton professor Harry Frankfurt. Frankfurt to author, Nov. 7, 2005.

259 **"I . . . must tell you":** John M. Woolsey to BAC, Mar. 7, 1945, Box 65, CP.

259 **in print:** For sales figures on *TASM,* see BAC diary. S&S appears to have overprinted toward the end, because in a Feb. 21, 1946, letter from Elinor Green of S&S to BAC, Green states that actual sales had reached 248,645 copies. Box 2, RHR. GTH quotes a figure of 160,000 copies for the Armed Services Edition from a 1945 Columbia *Jester* article. Box 12, NYU.

259 **"Bennett Cerf: Publisher of Classics":** Eugene Kinkead, profile, *Life,* Dec. 3, 1945.

260 **"Finale":** BAC diary, Aug. 13, 1945.

260 **"display some outward":** Lew Miller to BAC.

260 **He'd also merited:** DSK to BAC, May 3, 1945, Box 6, CP.

260 **"the happiest of my entire life":** BAC to DSK, Aug. 18, 1944, in *DDDB,* 172.

260 **"You know full well":** DSK to BAC, Apr. 13, 1944, in *DDDB,* 154.

260 **"An officer, home":** BAC, *TASM,* 371.

CHAPTER 17: MR. CHIRP IN THE LYONS DEN

262 **"COME TO OUR":** PC to Mr. and Mrs. Arthur Schwartz et al., Dec. 26, 1945, Box 6, CP. The misplaced apostrophe in "Cerf's" may be PC's doing rather than the telegraph operator's. Her spelling and punctuation were unreliable but improved under SC's tutelage.

262 **new clipping book:** The photo of the three Cerfs is also in a clipping book, CP.

263 **by over a hundred papers:** On Leonard Lyons, his son Jeffrey Lyons, who became a prominent movie critic, to author, Nov. 3, 2009; Alden Whitman, "Leonard Lyons Dies; Columnist 40 Years," *NYT,* Oct. 8, 1976; "The Press: Celebrity Chronicler," *Time,* May 25, 1959.

263 **"an oasis":** BAC to DSK, Apr. 13, 1943, CP.

263 **"good personal friend":** BAC to ME, Feb. 7, 1945, RHR.

264 **"column conductors":** BAC, *TASM,* ix–x.

264 **loved to pin them on:** BAC to Abel Green, Feb. 13, 1946, Box 2, RHR.

264 **first accusation of many:** On Jan. 23, 1946, BAC compiled six accusations from Lyons's columns into "The Collected Writings of Leonard Lyons," a typewritten sheet dated in BAC's handwriting, Box 2, RHR.

264 **"poring over these columns":** Leonard Lyons, "Lyons Den," *The New York Post,* May 8, 1945, Box 65, CP. BAC's scribbled comment is below the clipping.

264 **gotten his facts wrong:** I have not found the *TASM* contract among BAC's papers, but the terms for the war humor book specified 60% to BAC, 30% to PC, and 10% to Pauline. However, in an undated letter to LH, PC says she is receiving 40% of the royalty on the war humor book, the cartoon book, "and another book that he has just contracted to do of anecdotes," although PC, like her husband, often exaggerated. If she received 40%, did Pauline receive 10% and BAC 50%? In a letter from Mar. 1946, Bernard Geis of Grosset & Dunlap tried to persuade BAC to give PC 50% of the royalty on a joke book, apparently without success; however, in a June 1947 letter from King Features, PC was given 50% of the royalty for the syndicated joke column. See Boxes 2, 6, RHR.

264 **"I have been bitter":** BAC to ME, Feb. 7, 1945, Box 2, RHR.

264 **"long distant past":** ME to BAC, Feb. 1, 1945, Box 2, RHR.

264 **claimed to have a contract:** In the letter to ME dated Feb. 7, 1945, BAC speaks of Lyons' contract; in the letter to BAC dated Feb. 1, 1945, ME states: "several of the columnists, to my knowledge and no doubt yours, have considered doing a book of consolidated stories clipped out of their own columns." In the OH he reiterates: "It turned out [Lyons] had a contract . . . for a book of stories, which he has never done." BAC OH, 574.

265 **"informally":** ME to BAC, Feb. 1, 1945.

265 **"some kind":** ME to BAC, Feb. 8, 1945.

265 **"taking bread":** PC OH, 404.

265 **"put in a class":** BAC to Walter Winchell, July 3, 1945, Box 2, RHR.

265 **"barroom babble":** "The Press: Try and Stop Him," *Time,* Apr. 1, 1946.

265 **"who owns the ocean":** Malcom Bingay, *Detroit Free Press;* BAC reply, Apr. 26, 1946, both Box 2, RHR.

265 **"intimate incidents":** John William Rogers, "Of Books and People: A Consideration of Bennett Cerf's Vastly Popular *Try and Stop Me," Dallas Times Herald,* May 13, 1945, Box 65, CP.

265 **"the poison barb":** T. O. Thackrey to BAC, Nov. 25, 1946, Box 2, RHR.

266 **"disgusting":** BAC to Thackrey, Nov. 27, 1946, Box 2, RHR.

266 **"I have very few enemies":** BAC OH, 573.

266 **"cherishing":** On the persistent nature of the Lyons-Cerf feud, Jeffrey Lyons to author, Nov. 3, 2009; CBC to author many times. Columnist Edith Gwynne of *The Hollywood Reporter* also accused BAC of stealing jokes. See letters between BAC and H. R. Wilkerson, *The Hollywood Reporter,* May 7 & 12, 1947, Box 2, RHR.

266 **"dashingest":** Mary Morris, "Try and Stop Bennett Cerf," *PM,* Apr. 7, 1945, Box 39, CP.

267 **"Today Cerf":** Eugene Kinkead, "Bennett Cerf: Publisher of Classics and Best Sellers, He Is Now the Nation's No. 1 Peddler of Jokes," *Life,* Dec. 3, 1945, Box 39, CP.

267 **"not too bad!"** BAC diary, Nov. 28, 1945, Box 11, CP.

267 **"I've sat in Saxe Commins' office":** Joe Jackson, *The San Francisco Chronicle,* Dec. 5, 1945, Box 65, CP.

267 **"because of the things he said":** PC to LH, Feb. 12, 1945, courtesy Michael Hornblow.

267 **written without his knowledge:** BAC to Elmer Adler, Jan. 18, 1944, Elmer Adler Papers.

268 **official income for 1944:** BAC to State of New York, Mar. 4, 1946, Box 2, RHR. Early in 1946, the tax department of New York state queried BAC's income and expense deductions. His $58,000 income was almost $19,000 more than in 1943. BAC knocked off $8,000 in business expenses (home library maintenance).

268 **flattering publicity:** For instance, he was mentioned as a "distinguished" policy owner. Eric Johnson, Penn Mutual Life, to BAC, Sept. 5, 1946; BAC to Johnson, Sept. 11, 1946, both Box 2, RHR.

268 **"in the grind":** Virginia Lattman to BAC, Oct. 7, 1946; BAC to Lattman, Oct. 9, Box 2, RHR.

268 **"presumptuous":** BAC to P. A. Staples, president of Hershey, Oct. 3, 1946; see also correspondence between BAC and other Hershey executives, Oct. 8 & 10, Dec. 5, 1946, all Box 2, RHR.

269 **liked Bennett's humor:** S. J. Perelman to BAC, July 23, 1937, in Prudence Crowther, ed., *Don't Tread on Me: The Selected Letters of S. J. Perelman* (New York: Viking, 1987), 13.

269 **bestseller:** Dorothy Herrmann, *S. J. Perelman: A Life* (New York: G.P. Putnam's, 1986), 166. See also Crowther, ed., *Don't Tread on Me.* Marion Meade, biographer of Nathanael West, kindly provided background on BAC's relationship with West and lent me her copies of letters.

269 **lost an additional $600:** For the general balance sheet of *The Day of the Locust,* see BAC to Nathanael West, Feb. 23, 1940, courtesy Marion Meade.

269 **Later that year:** Perelman's claim that BAC asked for return of West's advance is mentioned by Crowther in her introduction to Perelman's letters. Crowther, ed., *Don't Tread on Me,* xx. Neither West biographer Meade nor I found correspondence confirming this claim.

270 **Christmas telegram:** Herrmann, *S. J. Perelman,* 172.

270 **"America's Sweetheart":** S. J. Perelman to James Thurber, Mar. 5, 1946, in Crowther, ed., *Don't Tread on Me,* 67–68.

270 **several years not speaking:** On the Perelman-Klopfer denouement, see Herrmann, *S. J. Perelman,* 172–73.

270 **"Undoubtedly, you will":** BAC to Evelyn Scott, Aug. 17, 1936, Box 16, Scott Collection, RC.

271 **"a twister":** Peter Parker, *Isherwood: A Life Revealed* (New York: RH, 2004), 376.

271 **"that incomparable ass":** Christopher Isherwood, *Lost Years: A Memoir, 1945–1951* (New York: HarperCollins, 2000), 119.

271 **"a book publisher by choice":** BAC, *Anything for a Laugh* (New York: Bantam Books, 1946), 6–8.

271 **"objected to printing":** BAC to the *NY Herald Tribune,* Jan. 22, 1946. His column concerning Pound and his appeal to readers appeared on Feb. 9, 1946. Readers' letters and BAC's notice were published in *SRL* on Mar. 16. Materials are in the Bennett Cerf Correspondence Regarding the Ezra Pound Controversy Collection, Princeton University. Unless otherwise noted, BAC, Gannett comments from there. See also Auden to BAC, Jan. 29, 1946.

272 **a traitor, period:** Howard Treeger to author, July 1, 2003. Treeger had joined RH as a salesman in Feb. 1944, after serving in the war. He said BAC was "adamant we wouldn't have Pound in the anthology."

273 **Bennett was offended:** BAC to Jean G. Rogers, Mar. 21, 1946, Box 4, RHR.

274 **"After the publishers":** On the negotia-

tion with Pound's representative, see Box 1, Julien Cornell Papers, Yale University.

274 **stuck in his gorge:** A quarter century later, when dictating his OH, BAC recanted his decision to include the poems, saying: "I still in my heart don't think that I was wrong." BAC OH, 650.

274 **"very stupid":** DSK OH, 35.

274 **send Saxe the manuscript:** SC's response re *The Age of Anxiety,* see SC to Auden, Jan. 28, 1947, Box 1, Saxe Commins Papers, Princeton University (hereafter SCP).

274 **mixed messages about Bennett:** Shortly after extricating himself from the Pound muddle, BAC fought censors who were trying to ban an RH book, Vincent McHugh's *The Blue Hen's Chickens,* over "erotic" poems and provided friendly testimony in Macmillan's censorship fight over their bestselling bodice-ripper, Kathleen Winsor's *Forever Amber.*

274 **might make a trip:** BAC to GS, Mar. 12, 1946, RHR.

274 **"come through the holocaust":** BAC to GS, May 13, 1940, Film 1155, Box 100, GSP.

274 **ninety thousand residing:** www.holocaustchronicle.org, appendices.

274 **they owed their survival:** For an account of GS's wartime life and the role of Faÿ, see Janet Malcolm, *Two Lives: Gertrude and Alice* (New Haven: Yale University Press, 2007).

275 **"the German Romanticist":** Eric Sevareid, *Not So Wild a Dream,* quoted in Malcolm, *Two Lives,* 103.

275 **"liberate":** Burns and Dydo with Rice, eds., *Letters of Gertrude Stein and Thornton Wilder,* 314, note 1; Rogers, *When This You See Remember Me,* 241.

275 **leader of the group:** Sevareid would enjoy a distinguished career as a CBS newsman.

275 **"terribly happy":** BAC to GS, Sept. 5, 1944, Box 106a, RHR.

275 **"aware of her indomitable courage":** *Wars I Have Seen* with intact dust jacket copy by BAC in DSK's copy, DSK Bequest.

276 **made his feelings known:** SC's reader's report, Oct. 3, 1944, SC Papers.

277 **"For the records":** BAC on GS, "Introduction to the speeches of Marshal Pétain," RHCC.

277 **all got a great laugh:** BAC to GS, Mar. 12, 1946, RHR.

277 **her Pétain apologia:** In recent years, scholars have tried to parse away some of her confounding views, pointing to shadings within *Wars I Have Seen* that may reveal a kind of political epiphany. "I used not to understand but I am beginning to now," she said toward the book's end. After the U.S. soldiers arrived in Culoz, she recalled, "I began to have what you might call a posthumous fear . . . hearing what had been happening to others, of course one knew it but now one had time to feel it and so I was quite frightened." GS quoted in Malcolm, *Two Lives,* 104, 106.

277 **"pretty darn good":** BAC to GS, May 14, 1945, RHCC.

277 **"Book received":** I have been unable to find original correspondence, but BAC used story in "News from Random House" circular, undated, Box 12, Folder 11, GTHP. See also "Transatlantic Nonsense," *The Chicago Sun,* June 24, 1945, Box 65, CP; Eugene Kinkead, profile, *Life,* Dec. 3, 1945.

CHAPTER 18: GOLDEN ERA FOR A BROWNSTONE PALACE

278 **The notice arrived:** BAC 1946 diary, Box 11, CP.

278 **"asked in a friendly way":** BAC to Eva Cerf, Feb. 21, 1946, Box 2, RHR.

278 **every Jesuit school:** For the story of buying 457 Madison Avenue, see BAC OH, 487–95.

279 **row houses:** After BAC bought his townhouse, its brownstone cladding was painted gray and "streamlined" in the Deco style. After PC's death, the brownstone façade was restored stylistically to look late nineteenth century.

279 **"the richest and handsomest":** Brendan Gill, undated, "Notes on the Villard Houses," RH clipping file, *PW.*

280 **The families who'd lived:** Christopher Gray, "A Landmark 6-Home Complex in Dark Brownstone," *NYT,* Dec. 21, 2003. Details of Villard history are taken from this article; from a tour given by Francis Moroni for the Municipal Art Society, which for a time had its headquarters at 457 Madison Avenue; press release from the Landmarks Preservation Commission, Sept. 30, 1968, Number 2, LP-0269, concerning designation of the buildings as landmarks; William Robbins, "Random House Will Leave Mansion for a Skyscraper," *NYT,* Aug. 19, 1968; "Random House Moves Into an Old Mansion," *PW,* July 13, 1946, 173–76; RH publicity sheet dated 1956, AEP.

280 **three-year lease:** On the signing, see BAC diary, Box 11, CP.

280 **"wonderful rooms":** "Random House to

Move in April," *PW,* Feb. 9, 1946, RH clipping file, *PW.*

280 **his natural caution:** For an amusing sketch by a certain "Pierre Andrezel Horatio Nostalgia" (a.k.a. RKH) on buying the Villard from Kennedy, see "Remembrance of Things Past," RMHP.

280 **"had any business":** DSK OH, 62.

280 **Twenty years later:** Robbins, "Random House Will Leave Mansion for a Skyscraper."

280 **"very imaginative":** Robert Giroux to author, Dec. 16, 2005.

280 **Part Hollywood, part Madison Avenue:** JE to author, Dec. 9, 2003.

281 **"we truly are entering":** BAC, "Publishing Today," lecture given Oct. 10, 1946, RHR.

281 **"It was an old-fashioned elegance":** WS to author, Mar. 3, 2003.

281 **"rattling around":** Harry Hansen, *New York Telegram,* June 6, 1946, Box 65, CP.

282 **"air-cooling":** On the office, see "Random House Moves Into an Old Mansion," *PW,* July 13, 1946.

282 **"I knew":** BAC quoted in "Random House Moves Into an Old Mansion."

283 **"Every God damned":** BAC to Mrs. Joseph Merriam, Nov. 4, 1946, Box 2, RHR.

283 **The room could only be:** RH decoration: Lillian Schary Waldman to RKH, Mar. 21, 1946, Box 6, RHR.

284 **"DELIGHTED WITH MY OFFICE":** BAC diary, May 19 & 20, 1946, Box 11, CP.

285 **new role of promotion manager:** On the hiring of Ullman, see Box 65, CP.

285 **very tricky subject:** On the publication of *The Snake Pit,* see BAC OH, 560–64. Irene James is identified as go-between in correspondence in Mary Jane Ward Collection, Boston University (hereafter MJWC). Nowhere in the correspondence is James's novel identified as being about incest; I have taken that from BAC.

285 **her agent refused:** James to RNL, May 11, 1945.

285 **"Do you hear voices?":** Mary Jane Ward (hereafter MJW), *The Snake Pit* (New York: RH, 1946), 3.

285 **within the illness:** DSK knew of such situations better than most, having been responsible for his sister's care for so long. Two years after publishing *The Snake Pit,* DSK was forced to find a new home for Elma when her caregiver retired; he ended up placing her in an asylum run by nuns. For correspondence about Elma Klopfer, see Box 24.

285 **Bennett had worried:** RNL to Mrs. Edward Quayle (a.k.a. MJW), July 2, 1945, MJWC.

286 **Omens were good:** On *The Snake Pit* as it relates to book club, *Reader's Digest,* and movie sales as well as MJW's visit, see BAC diary, Box 11, CP. The movie sale was for $40,000; *Reader's Digest* paid $10,000 to abridge the novel. Much of what BAC said about *The Snake Pit* in his OH is unreliable or contradicted by the MJWC.

286 **"exciting":** MJW to BAC, Jan. 17, 1946, MJWC.

286 **"just people":** MJW to BAC, Feb. 5, 1946, MJWC.

286 **"Put your faith":** BAC to MJW, 1946, Box 4, RHR.

286 **"real artists in hospitality":** MJW to BAC, Oct. 31, 1946, MJWC.

286 **"why the publishing business":** BAC OH, 561.

287 **"Proceed with our blessings":** BAC to MJW, Mar. 7, 1946; see also payment schedule request from MJW to BAC, Mar. 4, 1946. On the "100,000 mark," see RNL to MJW, Sept. 10, 1946, all Box 4, RHR.

287 **broke twenty years of attendance records:** See *NY Herald Tribune,* June 12, 1949, in MJW's scrapbook, MJWC. The article noted that a UK nurses' organization had protested the film for not reflecting British mental institutions and also that it was too frightening.

287 **"apologize for their Jewishness":** Fritz Jacobi to RNL, July 25, 1947, Box 234, RHR.

287 **"lost track of":** The OH session in which BAC discussed *The Snake Pit* was Jan. 12, 1968.

288 **Ward got letters:** MJW to RNL, Nov. 4, 1946, MJWC.

288 **no reason to share:** On Jonathan Cerf's birth, see PC OH, 302–3.

288 **"If it's a girl":** BAC to GS, Sept. 4, 1945, GSP.

288 **"For a guy whose motto":** BAC to GS, Mar. 27, 1946, GSP.

288 **"highly presumptuous":** BAC quoted in SC to unknown recipient (Whitney Oates?), Apr. 4, 1946, Box 17, SCP.

288 **"in a mood of bitter disillusionment":** BAC to Edgar Snow, Apr. 12, 1946, Box 4, RHR.

289 **"These have been years":** RKH to BAC, Apr. 1, 1946, Box 65, CP. Although RKH's hopes for Bob Jr. had been dashed, his sister, "the Brat," would join the RH publicity department in 1947 and stay until she had children.

289 **granted a royalty revision:** BAC to GS, June 18, 1945, MSS 76, Box 101, GSP.

290 **"impossible":** BAC to GS, Nov. 20, 1945, RHR.

290 **"wildly favorable":** BAC to GS, Dec. 13, 1945, RHR.
290 **her feeling of loss:** MJW to BAC, Aug. 2, 1946, MJWC.
291 **died holding a copy:** Rogers, *When This You See Remember Me,* 247.
291 **memorial displays:** Rogers, *When This You See Remember Me,* 10.
291 **"They asked me":** GS, *Reflection on the Atomic Bomb: The Previously Uncollected Writings* (Boston: David R. Godine, 1975).
291 **"I only wanted":** Alice B. Toklas to BAC, Aug. 4, 1946, RHCC.
291 **"[He] said he would print":** GS, quoted in *AR,* 108.

CHAPTER 19: A NEW VOICE, ANOTHER HOME

292 **"Big Daddy":** BAC OH, 702; PC OH, 390. TC began to call BAC "Big Daddy" after seeing Tennessee Williams's (TW) 1955 play, *Cat on a Hot Tin Roof.* The ironic comparison was with a character who was an overbearing southern patriarch. TC had also called BAC "Great White Father."
293 **"How the hell":** For the RLS story, see BAC OH, 689. Pauline isn't specified, but she would have been the person to whom he cried out.
294 **his author's doing:** *Life* photo, TC to RNL, May 1947, in Gerald Clarke, ed., *Too Brief a Treat: The Letters of Truman Capote* (New York: RH, 2004), 46 (hereafter *TBAT*).
294 **"knocked out":** WS, quoted in George Plimpton, *Truman Capote: In Which Various Friends, Enemies, Acquaintances, and Detractors Recall His Turbulent Career* (New York: Nan A. Talese/Doubleday, 1997), 240.
294 **had left the South:** On TC's background, see Gerald Clarke, *Capote: A Biography* (New York: S&S, 1988).
294 **"What a fine story it is!":** BAC OH, 688.
295 **"signed Capote":** BAC diary, Box 11, CP.
295 **"Well, *that* was a day":** BAC OH, 688.
295 **"Now you're going to be a writer":** RNL to TC, in Clarke, *Capote,* 98.
295 **"an enigma":** TC to Newton Arvin, June 27, 1962, in Clarke, ed., *TBAT,* 353.
295 **"very secretive":** Naomi Bliven, RNL's editorial assistant, to Gerald Clarke, n.d., courtesy Clarke.
295 **buttering up:** see Clarke, *Capote,* 136.
295 **ladies' man:** Jean Stein, WF's young companion in the early 1950s, was among those taken with RNL. Stein to author, July 7, 2003.
295 **"a chiseler":** On PC's attitude toward RNL, see PC to Gerald Clarke (undated), courtesy Clarke.
295 **Saxe also taught:** The Columbia course began in 1947 and, in rather different form, still exists.
295 **"Linscott clause":** See RKH to BAC, Feb. 17, 1948, Box 9, RHR; the topic was author Martha Albrand. Her agency, Brandt & Brandt, said that "if she signs it, they won't handle her anymore." This suggests, given her agents' reaction, that RNL's cut may have affected the author's royalties.
295 **was uneasy around him:** Relationship between SC and TC per FCB to author, Feb. 22, 2009; Eugene Commins to author, Apr. 9, 2009.
295 **key to his apartment:** Clarke, *Capote,* 135.
296 **"We're going to support you":** RNL to TC, in Clarke, *Capote,* 98.
296 **"now more than ever":** TC to RNL, May 1947 (?), in Clarke, ed., *TBAT,* 45–46.
296 **"Every word takes blood":** TC to RNL, late July 1947, in Clarke, ed., *TBAT,* 48.
296 **"a polished gem":** BAC OH, 694.
296 **"scrambled around":** PC OH, 382–84.
297 **"adopt":** PC OH, 385. PC's actual words were "surely let in." I have changed to "let in for sure" for grammatical correctness.
297 **"Were you surprised":** DSK to BAC, Aug. 14, 1946, Box 2, RHR. HAW's lover, GB, told Hart biographer Steven Bach that he'd had a fling with MH. Bach, *Dazzler* (Boston: Da Capo, 2002), 158. GB repeated this assertion to the author, Jan. 20, 2005.
297 **"within eight feet":** BAC to RH, May 27, 1936, Box 4, CP.
298 **"He was at home":** PC to author, Jan. 29, 2003.
298 **Such encounters opened doors:** PC introduced TC to society ladies. PC OH, 390–91. TC achieved lightning success at a very young age. Everyone in certain New York circles would have wanted to meet him. It is probable, given PC's proclivity for taking credit, that hers was not the only introduction he received to his future "swans."
298 **"the insight of an X-ray machine":** PC, "What's New . . . by Phyllis Cerf," *Newsday,* May 5, 1955.
298 **"When Truman talked":** Alan U. Schwartz to author, June 2, 2003.
298 **"Now a traveler":** TC, *Other Voices, Other Rooms,* 20th anniversary edition (New York: RH, 1968).
299 **"strum his dreams":** TC, *Other Voices, Other Rooms,* 100.
299 **"is natural and beautiful":** TC, *Other Voices, Other Rooms,* 147.
299 **"unconscious":** TC, *Other Voices, Other Rooms,* ix.
299 **"rarely had a writer":** Clarke, *Capote,* 154.

The friend who took the photograph was Harold Halma.

299 **"in snatches":** BAC to TC, Dec. 9, 1947, Box 6, RHR.

299 **"Believe Capote novel will be":** BAC to DSK, Dec. 1, 1947, Box 6, RHR.

300 **only lunched with Garbo:** BAC tells the story of TC's first Hollywood foray in his OH; see *AR,* 225. The facts are related in Clarke, *Capote,* 149.

300 **"fair":** BAC diary, Jan. 8, 1948, Box 11, CP.

300 **"a young man of promise":** Box 66, CP.

300 **"such literary virtuosity":** Diana Trilling quoted in Plimpton, *Truman Capote,* 78.

301 **seduced by the writing:** On the critical reception of *Other Voices,* see Clarke, *Capote,* 155–56.

301 **"*Other Voices* looks":** BAC diary, Jan. 22, 1948, Box 11, CP.

301 **emphatically and ubiquitously:** For TC's denials about the shoot, see Clarke, *Capote,* 159.

301 **"Are you satisfied":** TC to RNL, Apr. 1, 1949, RHCC.

301 **"I'm happy, happy, happy":** RNL to TC, Apr. 6, 1949, RHCC.

301 **"Wonderful wonderful wonderful":** RNL to TC, Sept. 15, 1950, Box 295, RHR.

302 **"crazy":** BAC to TC, Sept. 28, 1950, RHCC.

302 **"You are so good to me":** TC to BAC, Sept. 22, 1950, RHCC.

302 **"I'd feel happier":** BAC to TC, Dec. 12, 1950, RHCC.

302 **ending unconvincing:** RNL to TC, n.d., in Clarke, ed., *TBAT,* 179.

302 **"little more than a novelette":** BAC to TC, in Clarke, *Capote,* 222.

302 **"stricken by such":** TC to RNL, June 27, 1951, RHCC.

302 **"as is":** TC to BAC, July 9, 1951, RHCC.

302 **"good enough":** BAC to TC, July 10, 1951, RHCC.

302 **inscribe Bennett's copy:** Courtesy CBC and JFC.

302 **that was still good:** Clarke, *Capote,* 224.

302 **almost old enough:** For John O'Hara (hereafter JOH) chronology, see Matthew J. Bruccoli, ed., *Selected Letters of John O'Hara* (New York: RH, 1978), xv–xxi. See also Matthew J. Bruccoli, *The O'Hara Concern* (New York: RH, 1975); Geoffrey Wolff, *The Art of Burning Bridges: A Life of John O'Hara* (New York: Alfred A. Knopf, 2003); Frank MacShane, *The Life of John O'Hara* (New York: Dutton, 1980); Robert Emmet Long, *John O'Hara* (New York: Frederick Ungar, 1983); Finis Farr, *O'Hara: A Biography* (Boston: Little, Brown, 1973).

304 **"exactly":** Hemingway quoted in John Updike, introduction to *Appointment in Samarra* (New York: Vintage Books, 2003), xii.

304 **plotted an entire book:** "What's New . . . by Phyllis Cerf," *Newsday,* Sept. 22, 1955.

304 **Starr Faithfull:** Clippings, Box 36, CP. On Faithfull, see Frederick Lewis Allen, *Since Yesterday: The 1930s in America* (New York: Harper Brothers, 1940), 45.

305 **inspired by remorse:** On *Pal Joey,* see Bruccoli, *O'Hara Concern,* 150.

305 **"I wish I could":** JOH to Robert Simmonds, quoted in Updike, introduction to *Appointment in Samara,* xiii.

305 **"life's deepest emotions":** Lionel Trilling quoted in Bruccoli, *O'Hara Concern,* 177.

305 **"and so forth and so on":** PC OH, 333; see generally 330–38, 498–500, 503–4.

305 **would love to publish him:** PC OH, 334.

305 **corralled him for lunch:** For dates of JOH meetings, see BAC 1946 diary, Box 11, CP.

306 **"thinks he is somebody":** JOH quoted in Bruccoli, *O'Hara Concern,* 182.

306 **understood what the publisher's job:** Bruccoli, *O'Hara Concern,* 182.

306 **"great day":** BAC OH, 803.

306 **Duell wanted:** Charles Duell to BAC, Oct. 31, 1946; BAC reply, Nov. 11, 1946, both Box 6, RHR.

306 **Bennett's custom:** I have not managed to unearth how the "haggling" was resolved.

306 **"99% vague":** RKH to BAC, Feb. 26, 1947, Box 6, RHR.

307 **"rendered with pitiless precision":** Richard Sullivan, *NYT,* Aug. 17, 1947.

307 **alterations be changed:** JOH to BAC, n.d., in John O'Hara Papers, Pennsylvania State University.

307 **"You'd better get":** JOH to SC, n.d., in Bruccoli, *O'Hara Concern,* 187.

308 **"Don't think I haven't":** JOH to BAC, Nov. 24, 1948, RHCC.

308 **"I must remind you":** BAC to JOH, Nov. 26, 1948, RHCC.

308 **"take-it-or-leave-it":** JOH to BAC, Nov. 27, 1948, RHCC.

308 **"threatening":** BAC to JOH, Nov. 29, 1948, RHCC.

308 **"If you are saying":** JOH to BAC, Nov. 30, 1948, RHCC.

309 **"Do we want you":** BAC to JOH, Dec. 1, 1948, RHCC.

309 **"It seems impossible":** BAC to JOH, Dec. 30, 1948, RHCC.

309 **"full half hour":** BAC to JOH, June 7, 1949, RHCC. When the script of JOH's next novel, *The Farmers Hotel,* came in, BAC tried to convince JOH to omit the word "fuck," fearing that the book might be banned. JOH would not budge; the book

was printed as written and published in 1951; when Bantam brought the paperback out in 1952, Detroit, then the U.S.'s fifth-largest city, banned it. PC OH, 498–99. According to PC, BAC was even more outraged when a later JOH manuscript came in with the term "mother fucker." Once again BAC lobbied for deletion. "I'll tell you what I'll do for you, Bennett. I'll take out *mother,*" replied JOH. PC OH, 499.

309 **"courage of the spirit":** JOH, *A Rage to Live* (New York: RH, 1949), 244.

309 **"You purchase Pain":** Pope's poem is on the title page of *A Rage to Live.*

310 **"I'll never be able":** JOH, *A Rage to Live,* 425.

310 **an Anna Karenina who chose:** Bruccoli, *O'Hara Concern,* 196.

310 **"Do you think I have no balls":** JOH, *A Rage to Live,* 245.

310 **"Dr. O'Hara's handy guide":** Brendan Gill, "The O'Hare Report and the Wit of Miss McCarthy," *TNY,* Aug. 12, 1949.

311 **"You are incapable of ratiocination":** Thomas Kunkel, *Genius in Disguise: Harold Ross of the New Yorker* (New York: RH, 1995), 284. Kunkel takes the story from Brendan Gill's memoir *Here at the New Yorker* (New York: RH, 1975), 272. I have not been able to locate BAC's letter to Ross or Ross's to BAC in *TNY* records at the NYPL or RH records at Columbia University.

311 **sales velocity was amazing:** For JOH numbers, see BAC diary, Sept. 12, 1949.

311 **"That damned O'Hara book":** Irving Howe to RNL, Oct. 16, 1949, Box 25, AEP.

311 **135,000 copies:** Hackett and Burke, *80 Years of Best Sellers, 1895–1975,* 150.

311 **"The problem is":** JOH to BAC, Dec. 15, 1949, RHCC. The inscription is quoted in another letter, Apr. 17, 1956, RHCC. The latter also indicates that JOH reciprocated with presents occasionally, like a Mark Cross passport case for PC's first trip abroad. On the cigarette box, see Bruccoli, *O'Hara Concern,* 192.

311 **"as skillfully as a master":** Bruccoli to author, Dec. 11, 2005.

CHAPTER 20: FRIENDS AND ENEMIES

312 **U.S. House of Representatives had established:** Ellen Schrecker, *Many Are the Crimes: McCarthyism in America* (New York: Little, Brown, 1998), 90–91. On HUAC, see Richard Schwartz, *Cold War Culture* (New York: Facts on File, 2000); Richard M. Fried, *Nightmare in Red: The McCarthy Era in Perspective* (New York: Oxford University Press, 1990); Ted Morgan, *Reds: McCarthyism in Twentieth-Century America* (New York: RH, 2003).

313 **"heated":** BAC diary, Oct. 27, 1946, Box 11, CP.

313 **John O'Hara, for one:** See Herbert Mitgang, *Dangerous Dossiers: Exposing the Secret War Against America's Greatest Authors* (New York: Donald I. Fine, 1988), 108–12.

313 **"lonely":** BAC diary, Nov. 5, 1946.

313 **"Jewish domination":** See Jennifer E. Langdon, *Caught in the Crossfire: Adrian Scott and the Politics of Americanism in 1940s Hollywood* (New York: Columbia University Press, 2008), ch. 9. Much of the background for the later discussion of HUAC and Adrian Scott is based on Langdon.

313 **"paucity of Broadway product":** BAC, "Galleys West?" *The Hollywood Reporter,* Nov. 1, 1942, Box 66, CP.

314 **was set on changing:** DSK and RNL negotiated a model contract with the Authors Guild, the first jointly written benefitting all houses. If a publisher acted as agent or not, if it could establish within two years of publication that it had contributed to a book's "value" for a movie sale, it was entitled to monies "not to exceed 15% of the author's share." It got an extra 10% for agenting. See *Variety,* Nov. 12, 1947, Box 66, CP; "Authors Guild and Random House Sign Model Contract Form," *PW,* Nov. 29, 1947.

314 **in a ceremony at the Cerfs':** BAC diary.

314 **much-appreciated second visit:** BAC diary.

314 **visiting Phyllis's mother:** See *Daily Oklahoman,* Feb. 3, 1947, Box 66, CP; BAC to Frances Merriam, Dec. 26, 1946, Box 2, RHR. After Oklahoma, they met up with Walter Owens, PC's "inventor" grandfather, in California. BAC called him a "remarkable old guy!" BAC diary, Feb. 23, 1947.

314 **an RH kids' novelty book:** *The Story of Dimples and Cocksure* is a draw-it-yourself book for RH in which an elephant's trunk begins to shrink and a clever bird helps restore it to size. PC was deeply dimpled; was BAC cocksure!?! (A psychologist might weigh in.)

314 **promised to devote a column to the fabulous store:** BAC to Stanley Marcus, Mar. 26, 1947, Box 2, RHR.

314 **"wonderful things":** BAC to DSK et al., "Diary of an Idiot Boy," circa Feb. 15, 1947, Box 6, RHR.

315 **"delightfully patronizing":** BAC to DSK et al., "Diary of an Idiot Boy."

315 **"something as far as":** BAC to DSK et al., "Diary of an Idiot Boy."

315 **"unmentionable":** CBC to author, June 9, 2003.

315 **had journeyed to Lewis's:** SC, rather than Maule, did much editing work. See Box 5, SCP. Referencing Mark Schorer's Lewis biography, DSK told Dorothy Commins, "Certainly give Saxe credit for the time and devotion and editorial work he did with Red." DSK to Dorothy Commins, Mar. 11, 1971.

315 **Bennett enjoyed the book:** BAC diary, Sept. 2, 1946.

315 **Lewis had based his protagonist:** On *Kingsblood Royal,* see Brent Staples, "When the Bard of *Main Street* Turned the Kingsbloods Black," *NYT,* Aug. 18, 2002.

315 **Instead he'd asked:** See A. C. Spectorsky, "In New York," *Chicago Sun,* Jan. 19, 1947.

315 **provocative full-page ad:** *NYTBR,* May 25, 1947, Box 66, CP.

315 **mainstream reviewers:** For both judgments, see Staples, "When the Bard of *Main Street* Turned the Kingsbloods Black."

316 **major bestseller:** *Kingsblood Royal* ranked #8 on *PW*'s annual list. The Literary Guild printed just under 100,000 copies. BAC diary, May 20, 1947. The RH trade version sale was about 100,000. *AR,* 146.

316 **The Cerfs visited another West Coast author:** BAC to DSK et al., "Diary of an Idiot Boy."

316 **"brat books":** TSG to BAC, Dec. 10, 1947, Box 6, RHR.

316 **undergo a screen test:** BAC to DSK et al., circa Feb. 15, 1947, Box 6, RHR; BAC diary, Feb. 15, 1947.

316 **"something will come of it":** BAC to George Sidney, Mar. 31, 1947, Box 2, RHR.

316 **"Could have been worse!":** BAC diary, Feb. 22, 1947.

316 **"It was not an embarrassment":** LH to author, Nov. 17, 2002.

316 **"Physically I am sitting":** BAC to Mrs. Adrian Scott, Apr. 1, 1947, Box 2, RHR.

316 **La Quinta:** *Quinta* in Spanish means a country estate or inn.

316 **Small and personal:** Today, La Quinta is a much larger resort.

317 **socializing with tycoons:** Cullmans and Laskers in BAC diary, Feb.–Mar. 1947. On BAC and PC's typical La Quinta activities, see subsequent BAC diaries.

318 **"La Quinta was everything":** BAC to Stanley Marcus, Mar. 26, 1947, Box 2, RHR.

318 **"It's quite a life":** BAC to DSK et al., circa Feb. 15, 1947, Box 6, RHR.

318 **"a real pang":** BAC to DSK, "Washington's Bday," 1947, Box 6, RHR.

318 **a chat with Frank Taylor:** Discussions (also with AE) took place on Jan. 29, Mar. 18, 19, 20, 21, 24, 25, 26, & 31, Apr. 9 & 18, BAC diary.

319 **"the first dictionary of that time":** PC OH, 514. See Bob Considine, "On the Line," *Baltimore News-Post,* Nov. 21, 1947, Box 66, CP.

319 **"It was very smart":** PC to author, Feb. 13, 2003.

319 **"We didn't have the faintest":** See BAC interview in Roy Newquist, ed., *Counterpoint* (Chicago: Rand McNally, 1964), 101.

319 **hired a Black woman:** TC biographer Gerald Clarke's interview notes with former RH staffer Naomi Bliven mention a "Negro" receptionist, whom Bliven calls Elga. She describes the union's role in her hiring and her move to *Porgy and Bess* on Broadway. However, a July 13, 1946, *PW* article about the Villard shows a receptionist who appears to be Black identified as Betty Lee March. Conceivably, more than one receptionist was Black. However, I have not found a performer with either name in the cast for the opera's 1953 revival.

319 **"You probably want to know":** See 1945 version of the pamphlet. That and 1948 version, *PW* RH files.

320 **seemed Dickensian:** Justin Kaplan to author, May 3, 2004. He worked there as "Joseph Kaplan."

320 **"a good lexicographer":** Laurence Urdang to author, Nov. 24, 2003.

320 **backbone of a permanent:** Leonore Fleischer, "A Woman of Many Words," profile of Lenore Hauck Crary, *PW,* Aug. 16, 1991. Crary came to the *ACD* in the 1940s and retired many years later as managing editor of dictionaries.

320 **"authorities":** Croswell Bowen, *PM,* Dec. 7, 1947, Box 66, CP.

320 **1,500 illustrations:** There are significant discrepancies in the press descriptions of the dictionary. Contrast statistics from *PM* and *NYT,* Nov. 25, 1947, Box 66, CP, with those of *PW,* Oct. 11, 1947. 125,000 entries; 1,500 illustrations incl. 300 maps; 324 authorities, according to *PW;* 132,000 entries, according to *NYT;* 26,000 illustrations, 1,800 maps, per Croswell Bowen, *PM. PW* states that the dictionary took three years plus planning; others say six. Having seen the *ACD,* the one thing I can say is that the embedded maps are tiny, frequent, simple, and clear.

320 **"jumping":** RKH to BAC, Feb. 26, 1947, Box 6, RHR.

320 **luncheon with BOMC executives:** RKH to BAC, Feb. 12, 1947, Box 6, RHR.

320 **"roving editor":** Taylor/AE press release, Apr. 10, 1947, Box 66, CP.
321 **MGM had agreed to contribute:** BAC diary, Mar. 21, 1947.
321 **"postponed again":** BAC diary, May 19, 1947.
321 **"special contribution":** BAC diary, June 17, 18, 20, 25, 27, & 30, 1947.
321 **"enormously high":** DSK to BAC, Aug. 7, 1947, Box 6, RHR.
321 **Bankers Trust came calling:** BAC diary, Sept. 20, 1947.
322 **first copies of the dictionary:** BAC diary.
322 **BOMC finally offered . . . Marine Midland tendered:** BAC diary, Dec. 10 & 11, 1947.
322 **Merle Haas lent:** DSK to George Textor, Marine Midland, Dec. 23, 1948, Box 10, RHR.
322 **"keeper":** Laurence Urdang to author, Nov. 24, 2003.
322 **see the back of him:** RKH to BAC, Feb. 25, 1948, Box 9, RHR.
322 **a minimum of 150,000:** Sobol, *New York Journal,* Nov. 28, 1947, Box 66, CP.
322 **"We sold well over":** DSK OH, 37.
323 **"would not know a line":** For Lela Rogers HUAC testimony, see *Hearings Regarding the Communist Infiltration of the Motion Picture Industry,*" Eightieth Congress, First Session (Washington, D.C.: USGPO, 1947), 229–37, USCCL.
323 **shirred eggs:** BAC's daily breakfast per CBC to author, June 9, 2003.
323 **didn't express conservative opinions:** CBC to author, June 9, 2003.
324 **"In your publishing house":** PC OH, 226–28. Also CBC to author, June 9, 2003. Typically, in her OH, PC placed herself at the center of the argument with Lela.
324 **an explosion was imminent:** BAC diary, Oct. 28, 1947. BAC's humming was mentioned in CBC to author, June 9, 2003. On his flashing eyes, see Hiram Haydn, *Words and Faces* (New York, Harcourt Brace Jovanovich, 1974), 7.
324 **very good at using them:** JE to author, Dec. 9, 2003.
324 ***Hollywood Fights Back:*** Oct. 26, Nov. 2, 1947, available at Paley Center for Media, NYC.
324 **"Red probe":** "Bennett Cerf at Woodmere Hits Red Probe," *Nassau Star,* Oct. 23, 1947, Box 66, CP.
325 **"We are against 'party-liners'":** On BAC's participation in anti-HUAC protests, see Box 66, CP. Chester Kerr, George Macy, and Thomas Coward were the other publishers.
325 **"smeared reputations":** BAC, Trade Winds, *SRL,* Nov. 8, 1947.
326 **politely demanded attention:** Memo/petition to BAC, Nov. 11, 1947, Box 7, CP.
327 **"I don't know how":** PC OH.
327 **her personal blacklist:** CBC described the break to author, June 9, 2003.
327 **"I began to look for my own friends":** PC OH, 215.
328 **"I was deeply pleased":** BAC to Fania and CVV, May 25, 1948, Van Vechten Papers, Yale University.
328 **"My friendship with you":** BAC to CVV, Nov. 13, 1962, Van Vechten Papers.
328 **"though not necessarily agreeing":** Adrian Scott to BAC, "Sunday" [Sept./Oct. 1950], Box 14, RHR.
328 **"When the time comes":** BAC to Adrian Scott, Oct. 3, 1950, Box 14, RHR.

CHAPTER 21: SOME KIND OF PROGRESS

329 **"50 years of some kind":** BAC diary, Box 11, CP.
329 **"lift and enthusiasm":** Lee Rogow, guest Trade Winds columnist, *SRL,* Dec. 4, 1948.
329 **"a crusher":** BAC, Trade Winds, *SRL,* Oct. 23, 1948.
329 **"awful":** BAC diary, Dec. 31, 1947.
330 **"He writes plays":** See BAC, *Shake Well Before Using* (New York: S&S, 1948), 50–54. BAC noted in his diary that he was writing the piece. BAC diary, Jan. 25, 1948. On the secrecy surrounding *Long Day's Journey into Night* (hereafter *LDJIN*), what BAC and DSK knew of the play at this time was probably conveyed by SC. BAC's diary does not record his reading the script until July 1, 1954.
330 **average break-even sale:** Robert Coleman, "The Theatre," *New York Sunday Mirror,* Apr. 8, 1951, Box 67, CP. He says *Strange Interlude* sold 100,000 copies, whereas BAC's figure was 125,000, and the Gelbs said 120,000. BAC, Trade Winds, *SRL,* Feb. 23, 1946; Arthur and Barbara Gelb, *By Woman Possessed: A Life of Eugene O'Neill,* 418. Coleman notes that from publication in 1946 until 1951, *Iceman* sold a not inconsiderable 40,000 copies.
331 **"meet" Rosie:** BAC OH, 217. Also Anna Crouse to author, June 14, 2007.
331 **decided to open it up:** Details of this party per Anna Crouse to author, June 14, 2007. For BAC's reaction, see BAC diary, Nov. 23, 1946.
331 **those hours were pure joy:** In his OH, BAC misremembered, claiming to have taken EON to the Crouses for dinner. He also claimed that CMON was angry; others did not recall anger. He clearly conflated her reaction to the later party with this one. BAC OH, 220.

331 **"wonderful":** CMON to BAC, Nov. 24 or 25, 1946, RHR. BAC responded Nov. 26.

331 **hosted a party:** BAC OH, 221–22; "What's New . . . by Phyllis Cerf," *Newsday,* Nov. 8, 1956, courtesy CBC and JFC. See also Arthur and Barbara Gelb, *O'Neill;* Sheaffer, *O'Neill: Son and Artist.*

331 **"We're going home":** BAC OH, 222.

331 **arguments boiling over:** Bogard and Bryer, eds., *Selected Letters,* 573.

332 **"Both adored and hated":** Anna Crouse to author, June 14, 2007.

332 **made their lawyer insist:** SC to Melville Cane, Jan. 19, 1948; Melville Cane to SC, January 21, 1948, SCP.

332 **after another blow-up:** For series of disastrous events, see Arthur and Barbara Gelb, *O'Neill,* 889–94; Sheaffer, *O'Neill: Son and Artist,* 605–12.

332 **"loyal friend":** CMON to SC, Feb. 1940 (inscribed on a photograph in Box 11), SCP.

332 **"a crook," "Jew bastard":** See Sheaffer.

332 **"a deep-seated illness":** SC to EON, Feb. 26, 1948, SCP.

333 **"shed" Carlotta:** BAC diary, Mar. 25, 1948.

333 **"I'm finished, you know":** Gordon Parks, *Camera Portraits: The Techniques and Principles of Documentary Portraiture* (New York: Franklin Watts, 1948), 20.

334 **"Try and Stop Them":** Mary Braggiotti, *New York Post,* July 12, 1948, Box 66, CP.

335 **meticulously organized files:** Jack Alexander, "Supercharged Cerf," *Saturday Evening Post,* Dec. 18, 1947, Box 66, CP.

335 **"runners":** JFC to author, Nov. 4, 2003.

335 **where would he be without Jezebel:** BAC diary, Apr. 4 & 18, 1947.

335 **Phyllis also saw herself:** PC to author, Feb. 13, 2003.

336 **"Every time I send":** RLS to BAC, Aug. 1, 1952, Box 21, RHR. On the royalty split, see also Bernard Geis to BAC, Mar. 26, 1946, Box 2, RHR. In early 1953 BAC specified 60% to himself, 30% to PC, and 10% to Pauline; he also made a point of removing Pauline from royalties on reprint editions. See BAC to Charles Marshall of Garden City Publishing, Mar. 6, 1953, Box 22, RHR. BAC did ask SC for help with his books. See BAC diary, Apr. 7, 1948, "Saxe took over *Shake Well* manuscript." The previous day's entry said it needed cutting.

336 **fifty-fifty:** A. E. Pfrommer, King Features, to BAC, June 27, 1947, Box 6, RHR.

336 **for days:** CBC and JFC to author, several times.

336 **"show of being superficial":** Alexander, "Supercharged Cerf."

336 **masquerading as a millionaire:** BAC diary, June 25, 1948.

336 **"You only live once":** BAC, Trade Winds, *SRL,* Sept. 25, 1948.

337 **never waste time:** JFC to author, July 9, 2003.

337 **something close to perfection:** JFC to author, July 9, 2003.

337 **"smart-aleck":** BAC OH, 453.

337 **"Do you realize":** On Landmarks, see BAC OH, 453–57. BAC said he left Provincetown with the idea and the first ten titles fully formed. Diary and correspondence indicate otherwise.

In an article later that year, PC says *she* discovered that the Pilgrims landed in Provincetown, and "loyal" Bennett suggested they go to the bookstore. It's here she says CBC was an "impossible" know-it-all and speaks of "bombarding" him with information "to prove our superiority." PC, *Newsday,* Nov. 12, 1953.

337 **unspoken double-edged message:** JFC to author, July 9, 2003.

337 **honor was satisfied:** BAC, Trade Winds, *SRL,* Sept. 18, 1948.

338 **list of potential subjects:** Landmark story told in a 1956 *PW* feature, 460–63 (month and date obscured), courtesy *PW* RH clippings file.

338 **the four owned Wonder jointly:** To be clear, Wonder was *personally* owned by the partners and Miller, not by RH: See *Variety,* June 1, 1949, Box 66, CP. The $750,000 was paid in a lump sum and royalties over fifteen years. See also BAC diary, Apr. 1 and 14, 1949.

339 **topics were finalized:** Landmark authors would include Quent Reynolds, Dorothy Canfield Fisher, MacKinlay Kantor, and Samuel Hopkins Adams.

339 **"harmless idiosyncrasies":** BAC, *Shake Well,* 108, 273.

339 **"a god":** Sartre quoted in Robert W. Hamblin and Louis Daniel Brodsky, *Selections from the William Faulkner Collection of Louis Daniel Brodsky: A Descriptive Catalogue* (Charlottesville: University Press of Virginia for Southeast Missouri State University and the Bibliographical Society of the University of Virginia, 1979), 99.

340 **wanted to take on Faulkner:** On *The Portable Faulkner,* see Hamblin and Brodsky, *Selections from the William Faulkner Collection of Louis Daniel Brodsky.*

340 **Faulkner was "finished":** Perkins quoted by Malcolm Cowley to WF, July 22, 1944, in Malcolm Cowley, *The Faulkner-Cowley*

File Letters and Memories 1944–62 (New York: Viking Press, 1966), 8–9.

340 **"The study of Faulkner":** Robert Penn Warren, in *Faulkner-Cowley File,* 93.

340 **"a bayonet prick":** Malcolm Cowley to WF, Aug. 9, 1945, Cowley, *Faulkner-Cowley File,* 22.

340 **to help get him released:** Karl, *William Faulkner,* 741.

341 **"grown up at last":** WF to BAC and RKH, Jan. 10, 1945, AEP.

341 **finishing at 3 A.M.:** In his diary, BAC writes, "read whole of new Faulkner novel, in today, suggested title Beat Four," but three days later writes, "First new Faulkner ms in ten years in. Sat up until 3am finishing it at single stretch. Title: Intruder in the Dust. Typical Faulkner!" BAC diary, Apr. 26 & 29, 1948.

341 **would be like calling:** WF to BAC, undated, 10280A, Box 2, AEP.

341 **Lucas directs the quest:** The first mention of a plot is in WF to RKH, June 7, 1940, in Karl, *William Faulkner,* 766.

342 **contract gave Random hegemony:** Ober to WF, Oct. 26, 1949, Box 1, MSS 16807 (previously 8969), Ober Papers, University of Virginia (hereafter OP).

342 **leave RH to work:** BAC to Metro-Goldwyn-Mayer (hereafter MGM), Sept. 8, 1948, Box 10, RHR.

342 **had expressed similar misgivings:** Harold Ober to H. N. Swanson, May 10, 1948, OP.

342 **"fifty thousand":** Harold Ober to H. N. Swanson, July 13, 1948, OP.

342 **Ober got nothing:** On Sept. 24, 1948, BAC also sold *Intruder* to *Omnibook* for $2,000. BAC diary.

342 **benefit all publishers:** See *Variety,* Nov. 12, 1947, Box 66, CP; "Authors Guild and Random House Sign Model Contract Form," *PW,* Nov. 29, 1947.

342 **"You are the only publisher":** Irving Paul "Swifty" Lazar to BAC, Apr. 2, 1957, Box 34, RHR.

343 **"triumphant work of art":** *Time* review of *Intruder,* Oct. 4, 1948.

343 **"has been a good papa":** WF to BAC, May or early June 1948, MSS 16807 (previously 10280A), WFC.

343 **"pleasant acquisition":** BAC to WF, Oct. 13, 1948, MSS 16807 (previously 10280A), WFC.

343 **becoming more handsome:** DSK OH, 89.

343 **her timidity evaporated:** "What's New . . . by Phyllis Cerf," *Newsday,* Aug. 12, 1954, courtesy CBC and JFC.

343 **"a kitten with steel claws underneath":** WF to Jean Stein, Folder 5, Box 242, Jean Stein Papers, NYPL.

343 **ventured out to a cocktail party:** BAC diary, Oct. 18, 1948, Box 11, CP.

344 **Ford had met Faulkner:** Dennis Hevesi, "Ruth Ford, Film and Stage Actress, Dies at 98," *NYT,* Aug. 14, 2009.

344 **"Ain't it time":** Blotner, *Faulkner,* vol. 2, 1265.

344 **"This is *my* night":** *AR,* 146–47.

344 **a good deal of cognac:** Cowley, *Faulkner-Cowley File,* 103.

345 **"out cold":** BAC diary, Oct. 20, 1948. Jay Parini posits Ford's rejection as the reason for the binge. See Parini, *One Matchless Time* (New York: HarperCollins, 2004), 300.

345 **ambulance was summoned:** Blotner says WF was taken to the Fieldstone Sanitarium on 250th Street. No such place existed. Bennett speaks of WF being at "Riverdale Sanitorium." BAC diary, Oct. 23, 1948. Riverdale Sanitarium is at 252nd Street, near Broadway, in the Bronx. Blotner claims Cowley, Ford, Harvey Breit, Eric Devine, Ward Morehouse, RKH were all in WF's Algonquin room at the time. Blotner, *Faulkner,* vol. 2, 1267.

345 **begging Cowley's wife:** Parini, *One Matchless Time,* 300.

345 **he inscribed a copy:** WF also put place and date. The volume is at the RBML.

345 **almost had a first act:** WF to AE, Nov. 1, 1948, 13497, AEP. The play's start has heretofore been dated to Feb. 11, 1949.

346 **red suspenders:** BAC OH, 335.

346 **"Little Lord Fauntleroy":** Louis Sheaffer to DSK, DSK OH, 89.

346 **both liked the picture:** Undated WF letter to BAC removed from a copy of the book, now in CPCC.

346 **sold almost 32,000:** Ledger page listing "Total Sales—William Faulkner as of March 31, 1963," "General Files," AEP. I have assumed this represents complete cumulative trade sales of RH editions (as opposed to ML) across all years since publication until 1963. The only titles that had sold more copies than *Intruder,* per this, were the *Collected Stories* (37,740), *A Fable* (40,549), and *The Reivers* (66,271).

346 **turned to Howard Treeger:** Treeger to author, July 1, 2003.

346 **S&S hadn't printed enough:** When *Shake Well* came out in Britain a year later, the publisher Hammond & Hammond had to ration printing because it, too, was over-subscribed. *The Bookseller,* London, Nov. 4, 1950, Box 67, CP.

347 **"From Our Missing the Boat Department":** S&S ad, Dec. 15, 1948, Box 66, CP.

347 **none of his other humor books:** BAC

OH, 485. BAC would publish *Laughter, Inc.* in 1950 followed by *Good for a Laugh* in 1952 and *The Encyclopedia of Modern American Humor* in 1954, all from Doubleday or a Doubleday subsidiary. He never published with S&S again.

CHAPTER 22: A HORSE FOR A LONG RACE

348 **"in a most grievous way":** James A. Michener (hereafter JAM) to SC, Mar. 3, 1948, AEP.

348 **write for *Reader's Digest*:** JAM to SC, June 2, 1947; SC to JAM, June 5, 1947, Box 6, SCP.

348 **"You know without my saying":** JAM to SC, Mar. 3, 1948, AEP.

348 **"in some incredible fashion":** Brooks Atkinson, "At the Theatre," *NYT,* Apr. 8, 1949, 30. Atkinson—the paper's chief drama critic—was reviewing the musical, but these comments were about JAM's stories.

348 **around the 25,000 mark:** "People Who Read and Write," *NYT,* May 16, 1948.

349 **"tight" and "inhibited":** JAM quoted in Caryn James, "The Michener Phenomenon," *NYT Magazine,* Sept. 8, 1985. I have composed my portrait of JAM's character in this and later chapters primarily from JAM's memoir, *The World Is My Home* (New York: RH, 1992; hereafter *TWIMH*), and from interviews with BK, Marisa and Silvia Erskine, JE, Owen Laster, RLB, and Debbie Brothers.

349 **simply ignored *Tales*:** Helen M. Strauss, *A Talent for Luck* (New York: RH, 1979), 100.

349 **"make Mr. Michener famous":** Orville Prescott, *NYT,* Feb. 3, 1947.

349 **"one of the ablest":** Prescott, *Yale Review,* Apr. 13, 1947.

349 **"historical officer":** Lawrence Grobel, "Playboy Interview: James A. Michener," *Playboy,* Sept. 1981; see also RH publicity sheet "About the Author," undated, circa 1953, AEP. On this sheet, the information that JAM was "later . . . Senior Historical Officer for the South Pacific district" has been crossed out. According to JAM, a fellow lieutenant, impersonating an admiral, typed and signed fake orders that enabled him to travel the South Pacific on "tours of inspection," and that later the position became more or less official. JAM, *TWIMH,* 20.

350 **"I obviously don't want":** JAM to SC, Mar. 3, 1948, Box 14, AEP.

350 **perhaps on February 3, 1907:** Stephen J. May, *Michener: A Writer's Journey* (Norman: University of Oklahoma Press, 2005), 7. Some have speculated Mabel Michener was JAM's birth mother.

350 **who survived by:** In many interviews, in his official RH biography, and in *TWIMH,* JAM referred to his impoverished childhood. Most sources refer to Mabel Michener's taking in laundry and children. In his *Playboy* interview, JAM mentioned work in a sweatshop. Grobel, "Playboy Interview."

350 **"standing out":** JAM quoted in May, *Michener,* 11.

350 **"I have no idea":** JAM quoted in James, "Michener Phenomenon."

350 **"bum his way":** RH "About the Author" circa 1953, AEP.

350 **"prime mentor":** JAM, "A Faithful Remembrance," *Testimony* (Honolulu: White Knight Press, 1983), 5. This was a 200-copy chapbook, courtesy William Morris Endeavor Agency (hereafter WME), JAM files.

350 **"His heart and mind":** JAM, *The Fires of Spring* (New York: RH, 1949), 10.

350 **summa cum laude:** Swarthmore record and JAM background from summary biographies prepared by RH in 1978 and 1982, AEP, and one dated Mar. 29, 1991, courtesy WME.

351 **"I liked Saxe":** JAM to Dorothy Commins, Mar. 11, 1970, Box 6, SCP.

351 **stepping-stone:** JAM to SC, Mar. 16, 1948, Box 14, AEP. On the search for a successor to JAM's immediate boss, see JAM to Brett, Mar. 12, 1948, and Brett to JAM, Mar. 18, 1948, quoted in May, *Michener,* 81.

351 **Mrs. Brett hadn't liked:** JAM, *TWIMH,* 456.

351 **he devastated its author:** JAM, *TWIMH,* 284. JAM doesn't give the agent's name, but May says it was Brandt. May, *Michener,* 79.

351 **"Macmillan does not in any way":** JAM to SC, Mar. 3, 1948, Box 14, AEP.

351 **back in a month:** JAM to SC, n.d., Box 14, AEP.

351 **"Wildly enthusiastic":** SC to JAM, Mar. 8, 1948, Box 14, AEP.

352 **"What is important":** SC to JAM, Mar. 9, 1948, Box 14, AEP.

352 **"take a flier":** JAM quotes his letter to Brett, in JAM to SC, Mar. 16, 1948, Box 14, AEP.

352 **"JIM MICHENER COMES":** BAC diary, Mar. 19, 1948, Box 11, CP.

352 **Bob Haas knew Brett best:** RKH to Brett, Mar. 19, 1948, Box 14, AEP.

352 **Brett would let him resign:** JAM to SC, "Wednesday," Box 14, AEP.

352 **"I want to shoot the works":** JAM to SC, "Wednesday."

352 **"I foresee one book":** SC to JAM, Mar. 31, 1948, AEP.

352 **"This is for life":** SC to JAM, Apr. 22, 1948, AEP.

352 **no up-front money:** JAM's copy of *Fires of Spring* contract, courtesy WME.

353 **"barometer":** Strauss, *Talent for Luck,* 46.

353 **"a warmly developing friendship":** Strauss, *Talent for Luck,* 103.

353 **triple that amount:** DSK to JAM, Dec. 21, 1948, Box 14, AEP.

353 **"adviser, banker":** JAM to Strauss, Sept. 9, 1949, Box 17, AEP.

354 **a lump sum:** In one account, JAM was first offered a $500 lump sum by Hayward and Logan (presumably jointly with Rodgers and Hammerstein) for dramatic rights to *Tales of the South Pacific*. JAM rejected the lump sum in favor of 1% "future royalties." See May, *Michener,* 78. May does not provide a source, and I have been unable to corroborate his information.

354 **Krock won the day:** Accounts of JAM winning the Pulitzer differ. For his version, see JAM, *TWIMH,* 287. However, a different picture emerges in Larry Swindell, "An Epic Hero," *Fort Worth Star-Telegram,* Oct. 16, 1997. I have relied on John Hohenberg, *The Pulitzer Prizes* (New York: Columbia University Press, 1974), 200–201 and "Pulitzer Fiction Report," report by the fiction jury to the advisory board, internal document, Mar. 23, 1948, courtesy then-deputy administrator Edward M. Kliment. Hohenberg was the longtime Pulitzer administrator.

354 **"PULITZER PRIZES":** BAC diary, May 3, 1948, Box 11, CP.

354 **"swell!":** BAC pencil note on JAM to SC, Aug. 7, 1948, AEP.

355 **with urgency:** SC to JAM, July 26, 1948, AEP.

355 **"bleeding heart":** JAM to SC, July 29, 1948, AEP.

355 **"born writer":** Orville Prescott, "Books of the Times," *NYT,* Feb. 7, 1949.

355 **"hot-headed":** William Du Bois, "Young Man Comes of Age, Grimly," *NYT,* Feb. 6, 1949.

355 **It's still too early":** DSK to BAC, Feb. 10, 1949, Box 12, RHR.

355 **gathered around the piano:** BAC diary, Jan. 22, 1949, Box 11, CP. "La Perfecta" was BAC's nickname for Dorothy Rodgers, whom he had dated a few times in his youth.

356 **"God knows who else!":** On the *South Pacific* opening, see BAC diary, Apr. 7 & 8, 1949, Box 11, CP.

356 **"at almost every point":** JAM, "Happy Talk," *NYT,* July 3, 1949.

356 **1 percent stake:** Grobel, "Playboy Interview." On the $4,500 offer, see Laurence Maslon, *The South Pacific Companion* (New York: Touchstone, 2008), courtesy Ted Chapin, Rodgers & Hammerstein Organization. While May speaks of an initial rejected "lump sum" offer and accepted 1% "royalty," (see note **"a lump sum"** above), Grobel, Maslon, and Todd Purdum's R&H biography *Something Wonderful* all speak of JAM accepting a 1% stake in the show and paying for it with profits as they rolled in. I have been unable to find further corroboration of Grobel as to the offer being made on opening night. See May, *Michener,* 78; Grobel, "Playboy Interview"; Maslon, *South Pacific Companion;* Purdum, *Something Wonderful: Rodgers and Hammerstein's Broadway Revolution* (New York: Henry Holt, 2018).

356 **"A magnificent musical drama":** Brooks Atkinson, "At the Theatre," *NYT,* Apr. 8, 1949, 30.

356 **blitz of advertisements:** Jan. 15, 1949, Box 60, CP.

356 **bestseller list:** *NYT,* May 22, 1949.

356 **the paperback would sell:** Albin Krebs, "James Michener, Author of Novels That Sweep Through the History of Places, Is Dead," *NYT,* Oct. 17, 1997.

357 **four-book deal:** The contract is dated Apr. 1, 1949, on an internal 1993 cumulative abstract tallied by William Morris from all contracts made for its client JAM. However, in the contract files, the actual document, signed by JAM and RKH, is dated July 6, 1949, and gives the Sept. 1, 1950, rather than Apr. 1, 1950, delivery date for the first novel. The contract was amended Jan. 29, 1951, and Jan. 9, 1953; delivery and payment dates had to be altered due to subsequent contracts JAM had with RH for projects in intervening years. Abstracts and contracts courtesy WME.

357 **average American yearly income:** 1950 income from www.thepeoplehistory.com.

357 **"deferred income plan":** The arrangements with JAM, JOH, and others were eventually referred to by this term. Leona Nevler to Lee Wright, July 17, 1963, Box 55, RHR.

357 **"To say that Bennett":** Strauss, *Talent for Luck,* 104.

358 **"To mention tactfully":** Strauss, *Talent for Luck,* 104.

358 **They were also excited:** DSK and SC to JAM, Jan. 5, 1951, Box 17, AEP.

358 **monomania about Asia:** JAM, *The Voice of Asia* (New York: RH, 1951), 8.

358 **the second would be titled:** The contract is dated Aug. 8, 1951, per WME, but DSK

letter to Strauss six months earlier says contract attached and specifies $6,000 advance. DSK to Strauss, Feb. 13, 1951, Box 20, AEP.

358 **hardcover was number seven:** Records show that 26,031 copies sold. *Return to Paradise* royalty statement, Oct. 31, 1951, James A. Michener Papers, LoC (hereafter JAMP).

359 **sold two of its stories:** Strauss, *Talent for Luck,* 105.

359 **book club rights:** *Voice of Asia* club sale, Sept. 7, 1951; paperback sale, Oct. 1, 1951. BAC diary, Box 12, CP.

359 **"The destiny of the United States":** JAM, *Voice of Asia,* 332, 337, 338.

359 **"What it boils down to":** JAM to BAC, July 11, 1951, Box 17, AEP.

360 **"Whenever you go into":** JAM, *My Lost Mexico* (Austin, Tex.: State House Press, 1992), 62–63.

CHAPTER 23: MIDCENTURY

361 **personal income:** BAC diary, Dec. 31, 1949, Box 12, CP.

361 **rarefied group:** BAC lecture schedules, topics, financial details, correspondence in Box 31, CP. On lecture commissions, see "What's New . . . by Phyllis Cerf," *Newsday,* Nov. 19, 1953. His first lecture agent was Colston Leigh; later it was the Lee Keedick Agency, where he was handled by Elizabeth Schenk for years.

361 **there would be no segregation:** Box 31, CP. The date of the Constitution Hall lecture was Dec. 5, 1949.

361 **name on the marquee:** BAC diary, Mar. 9, 1949, Box 12, CP.

361 **"seasoned trouper":** BAC, Trade Winds, *SRL,* Jan. 29, 1949.

361 **"back in the pink":** BAC diary, Mar. 6, 1949. Earlier he recorded that he had "slept clear through to 1:40pm!" BAC diary, Jan. 30, 1949. He regularly noted such sleeps.

362 **"many, many peccadilloes":** KCH to author, Dec. 14, 2002, and Dec. 17, 2004.

362 **breaks on the road:** KCH to author, Feb. 4, 2006.

362 **strategy was to cluster guests:** PC to author, Dec. 23, 2003.

362 **"fallen in love" with him:** BAC OH, 97–98.

363 **"Be sure to let me know":** BAC (a.k.a. Kingsie) to Madeline Sherwood, Oct. 18, 1955, Box 2, CP.

363 **party that went on:** BAC diary, Jan. 3, 1950, Box 12, CP.

363 **"the youngest literary glamour girl":** BAC, Trade Winds, *SRL,* Apr. 10, 1943.

363 **"miserable" childhood:** Stephen Miller, "Leonora Hornblow, Obituary," *The New York Sun,* Nov. 10, 2005. LH information per Michael Hornblow to author, Feb. 12, 2006. Also useful was Steven M. L. Aronson, "Legendary Lives 2: Memory and Desire Leonora Hornblow," *Town and Country,* July 1993. On LH's childhood, see "Mrs. Salmon Bride of Leon Schinasi," *NYT,* Sept. 3, 1926; "Aim of Suit to Keep Love of His Child," *NYT,* Oct. 3, 1926; "$60,000 a Year Spent on Schinasi Children," *NYT,* Aug. 17, 1935.

363 **"Beloved":** BAC to Bubbles Schinasi, Feb. 12, 1945, courtesy Michael Hornblow. Many letters that Michael Hornblow allowed me to see are now housed at AMPAS (see following note).

363 **Bob Linscott deemed the prose:** For the 1949 report, BAC's memo, and the Hornblow contract, see Arthur and Leonora Hornblow Papers, Margaret Herrick Library, AMPAS (hereafter ALHP). An undated letter in the Hornblow papers from LH to BAC indicates his part in renaming the novel; the notion that Arthur Hornblow and George Oppenheimer had suggested the title appeared in a Louella Parsons column, Nov. 16, 1949, Box 67, CP.

364 **"Wiggle those hips":** BAC to LH, Dec. 22, 1949, ALHP.

364 **"As long as we are doing":** BAC to LH, Jan. 20, 1950, courtesy Michael Hornblow.

365 **Thrup often had to diet:** PC to LH, Mar. 13, 1952, courtesy Michael Hornblow. For PC's hair, I looked at *Newsday* headshots.

365 **designate the Hornblows:** BAC diary, Dec. 21, 1950, Box 12, CP.

365 **tumbled beyond friendship:** LH's affair with Sinatra per KCH to author, Feb. 4, 2006.

365 **if his mother hadn't been married:** Michael Hornblow to author, Feb. 12, 2006.

365 **"You are the kind of friends":** BAC to Arthur Hornblow, Mar. 10, 1950, ALHP.

365 **had to move Elma:** DSK to Lester Degenstein, Nov. 8, 1948; DSK to Sister Fidelia, May 12, 1949, Box 10, RHR.

366 **Tony began at the bottom:** DSK to Harold Wimpfheimer, Jan. 20, 1949; DSK to Harold Hunger, Sept. 26, 1949, both Box 13, RHR.

366 **It fell to Don:** For letters between Stella Klopfer Jacobson, DSK, and Paul and Tina Salomon as well as background and correspondence with officials and organizations, see Boxes 10, 13, 14, 17, 30, RHR.

366 **something of a catch:** BAC diary, Jan. 6, 1950, Box 12, CP.

366 **where he'd grown up:** However, McDowell had been born in Minneapolis, not the South. In his OH, BAC refers to him as "Davy." In *AR,* AE and PC refer to him as "Dave."

367 **joined New Directions:** On McDowell, see Louise Davis, *The Nashville Tennessean Magazine,* Apr. 17, 1949, Box 39, AEP.

367 **"new sort of literary world":** Paul Bowles to Wendy Lesser, Oct. 25, 1980, in Jeffrey Miller, ed., *In Touch: The Letters of Paul Bowles* (London: HarperCollins, 1995), 502, 518.

367 **"big excitement on Whittaker Chambers":** A contract for *Duveen,* Sam Behrman's biography of the art dealer—it started as a profile in *TNY* and ended as an RH bestseller—was issued at the same time as the Chambers contract. Diary, Box 12, CP.

367 **"Get that son of a bitch":** BAC OH, 850–61.

368 **secure a Senate seat:** Dictating his OH in 1968 with a lifetime of liberal politics behind him and Nixon's election victory in front of him, BAC said that Nixon on personal acquaintance was "very nice . . . very sincere . . . [and would] make a good President." He added, "He's so anxious to win that he's sacrificed many of his scruples and he'll do anything . . . That's what's made him 'Tricky Dicky,' but . . . this is a man who knows his job and . . . works like a fool." BAC OH, 852. However, in the diary meant for his own eyes several months later, BAC would call Nixon a "schmo": BAC diary, Aug. 8, 1968. Even more curious, Spiro Agnew was a cherished contact, but perhaps the Maryland connection—before becoming vice president, Agnew was governor of the state where RH's new warehouse was located—helps explain it.

368 **shown material to Doubleday:** On the rejection and Chambers coming to RH, see Sam Tanenhaus, *Whittaker Chambers: A Biography* (New York: Modern Library, 1998), 446–47; *AR.*

369 **edits on the galley proofs:** "Dave McDowell to edit Chambers." BAC diary, Jan. 4, 1952, Box 12, CP.

369 **found himself utterly absorbed:** BAC (and PC) read Chambers proofs and discussed them on Dec. 22, 28, and 29, 1951. Box 12, CP.

369 **pre-publication dinner:** BAC OH, 857.

369 **believed he was telling:** BAC OH, 858–59.

369 ***Saturday Review* splashed red ink:** Issue of May 24, 1952, Box 68, CP.

369 **"I don't think any book":** BAC to Chambers, June 10, 1952, RHR, quoted in Tanenhaus, *Whittaker Chambers.* Tanenhaus also provides helpful information on the advance and print run of *Witness* as well as the *Saturday Evening Post*'s $75,000 bid for the serial rights. Tanenhaus, *Whittaker Chambers,* 463, 448.

370 **sell him the Portable Library:** For the BAC offer on Portables, see BAC diary, Sept. 23, 1949, Box 12, CP.

370 **talked with two fellows at Holt:** BAC diary.

370 **"the most reliable":** "Random House Celebrates Its Twenty-Fifth Birthday," *PW,* Oct. 21, 1950. Sales statistics from this article. Maugham, 220,000 copies; Dostoyevsky, 170,000; Proust, 130,000; Lewis, 101,000; Hemingway, 87,000: Tolstoy, 236,000; Freud, 203,000; Joyce, 127,000.

370 **grow organically:** BAC diary, Nov. 30, Dec. 2, 1949, and Jan. 5, 1950.

371 ***"Gosh, it's exciting":*** Landmark ad, *NYTBR,* Nov. 19, 1950.

372 **Rewriting Adams's deal:** GTH interview with PC for *TNY* profile, GTHP.

373 **"It is through his lists":** Twenty-fifth anniversary press release, Box 67, CP.

373 **"That is not true":** RH twenty-fifth anniversary story, *PW,* Oct. 21, 1950.

374 ***All About Eve:*** Judith Crist, "First a Movie, Now a Book," *NY Herald Tribune,* Dec. 3, 1950, Box 67, CP.

374 **"Faulkner to get Nobel Prize?":** BAC diary, Nov. 3, 1950, Box 12, CP.

374 **Whispers joining the prize:** Blotner, *Faulkner: A Biography,* vol. 2, 1207.

374 **"gratuitous insult":** WF to Joan Williams, Feb. 22, 1950, in Blotner, ed., *Selected Letters of William Faulkner,* 299.

375 **"absolutely the most heartwarming news":** RKH (?) to WF, Nov. 10, 1950, MSS 16807, WFC. The letter is unsigned but almost certainly from RKH.

375 **For a man who hated intrusions:** Unless otherwise noted, my sources for the Nobel Prize story are Karl, *William Faulkner,* 806–18; Blotner, *Faulkner,* vol. 2, 1337–1371; BAC OH.

375 **Estelle dictated his measurements:** Blotner's sources are Estelle Faulkner and Dorothy Commins. Blotner, *Faulkner,* vol. 2, 1351. In an interview with the author on Nov. 30, 2002, Dorothy's daughter, FCB, stated that her father asked her mother to deal with Estelle on the phone. Typically, BAC spun the story differently, that he talked with WF about measurements and WF insisted that BAC "treat" him to it. BAC OH, 332–33.

375 **"ghostwritten the first draft":** Eugene Commins to author, Apr. 9, 2009; FCB to author, Nov. 30, 2002, and Feb. 22, 2009.

376 **"wrote that speech":** Betty Ballantine to author, Nov. 26, 2002.

376 **It's not unreasonable:** BAC spoke of SC as a frustrated writer. SC's story *Confessions of a Ghost* was about a ghostwriter who ghosted so much he could no longer find his own voice. Courtesy Eugene Commins.

376 **saved from the wastebasket:** Blotner describes how he obtained copies of drafts from the butler and talks about WF's Nobel address in "Writing William Faulkner's Biography," typescript of an undated speech Blotner gave. The typescript is housed in the Brodsky Collection, Southeast Missouri State University, published June 10, 2011, https://semo.edu/faulkner-studies/teaching-faulkner/writing-biography.html.

377 **"Rutgers Scott Fitzgerald":** WF to Jean Stein, Folder 5, Box 242, Jean Stein Papers.

377 **saw his face flush:** DSK OH, 90. Per DSK, the lighter had been given to JOH by playwright Philip Barry, but Blotner said that WF told him the lighter had belonged to JOH's father. Blotner, *Faulkner,* vol. 2, 1356.

377 **drove the Faulkners to Idlewild:** BAC says he drove with WF, Jill, DSK, and SC. BAC diary, Dec. 8, 1950. Another account has the Haases, the Cerfs, and Harold Ober accompanying the Faulkners. See Blotner, *Faulkner,* vol. 2, 1356.

377 **a meeting with Else Jonsson:** Jonsson was another young woman whom WF's publishers helped hide from Estelle.

378 **dying to inspect:** BAC diary, Dec. 17, 1950. Blotner says Jill Faulkner was ill; BAC doesn't mention it. The diary entry implies that Jill came along for the evening. Blotner, *Faulkner,* vol. 2, 1369.

378 **second set of stripes:** RNL to TC, Dec. 20, 1950, RHCC.

378 **in "bad taste":** WF to Merle Haas, Dec. 27, 1950, MSS 13497, Faulkner Papers, AEP.

378 **"one of the most impressive men":** *AR,* 130.

378 **"I have been so amazingly":** WF to RKH, received Nov. 9, 1949, MSS 13497, Faulkner Papers, AEP.

379 **Lucas Beauchamp had not only:** WF, *Intruder in the Dust* (New York: RH, 1948), 149, 193, 204.

379 **"pillar":** "William Faulkner's Speech of Acceptance upon the Award of the Nobel Prize for Literature," *The Faulkner Reader* (New York: RH, 1954), 3–4.

CHAPTER 24: WHAT'S *NOT* HIS LINE?

380 **"poor old Cerf's":** BAC diary, May 25, 1950, Box 12, CP.

380 **"mascara":** BAC diary, June 3, 1950, Box 12, CP.

380 **private hair treatments:** BAC diary, June 2, July 1 & 21, Aug. 10, 1953, Box 12, CP.

380 **"too damn much tummy":** BAC diary, Apr. 26, 1951, Box 12, CP.

380 **made the only choice:** PC to LH, Feb. 12, 1945, courtesy Michael Hornblow.

380 **"eyes in the back of her head":** BAC OH, 453.

380 **Joint Civilian Orientation Conference:** It still takes place.

381 **"Hated every minute":** BAC diary, June 28, 1950, Box 12, CP.

381 **Bennett's name had surfaced:** On BAC's appeal, see William Nichols to Harry Montgomery, associate publisher of the *Phoenix Republic and Gazette,* Dec. 16, 1952, Box 58, William Ichabod Nichols Papers, LoC.

381 **Bennett had successfully argued:** Apr. 6 & 7, 1950, diary, Box 12, CP.

381 **expenses were fungible:** For instance, BAC's home study air-conditioner was paid for by *SRL.* See Lillian Schary Small to Norman Cousins, Mar. 24, 1947, Box 94, Norman Cousins Papers, University of California at Los Angeles (hereafter UCLA).

381 **Phyllis was against taking it on:** On Cerfboard generally, see BAC OH, 506–7, 753–56.

381 **thirteen trial weeks:** For the contract, see Box 34, William Ichabod Nichols Papers; correspondence is in Box 58.

382 **His debut:** Box 67, CP. The perennially unsuccessful candidate was William Jennings Bryan.

382 **"Starch rating":** Nichols to Montgomery, Dec. 16, 1952, Box 58, William Ichabod Nichols Papers. Starch ratings were instituted by Dr. Daniel Starch, a former Harvard professor who was one of the founders of modern market research.

383 **"very great diligence and carefulness":** Nichols's general note re BAC, Oct. 28, 1969, Folder 131, Box 34, William Ichabod Nichols Papers. In Jan. 1956 the basic fee was increased to $700 ($900 with expenses). When his rate was raised to a combined $1,000 per week in Jan. 1958, it was for forty-six columns a year. BAC no longer wanted to do extra columns for vacations.

383 **columns upon columns:** Nichols's *This Week* contract specified certain quid pro quos regarding personal appearances representing the magazine as well as mentions of *This Week* in lectures and media appearances. BAC did Cerfboard for a full de-

cade; his parting with the magazine was amicable enough. The times had changed.

383 **"strictly":** BAC to Eloise Hazard, Nov. 16 or 18, 1948, RHR.

383 **twisted uncomfortably over complaining letters:** *SRL* editor Cousins published one such, from Putnam president Melville Minton, on Dec. 30, 1950. BAC put it in his clipping book, Box 67, CP.

383 **"incredible vitality":** See Nichols's general note above re BAC, Oct. 28, 1969.

383 **good game player:** Goodson quoted in BAC OH. On *What's My Line?* (hereafter *WML?*), see BAC OH, 730–52. See also Gil Fates, *What's My Line? The Inside History of TV's Most Famous Panel Show* (Englewood Cliffs, N.J.: Prentice-Hall, 1978). Also invaluable were my interviews with Gil Fates's widow, Faye Fates; Bob Bach's widow, Jean Bach; former TV executive Michael Dann; Arlene Francis's son, Peter Gabel; Jayne Meadows, guest panelist and wife of sometime regular Steve Allen; Mark Goodson's last assistant, Pamela Usdan; *WML?* guest panelist Betsy Palmer; and KCH, who, like Meadows and Palmer, was a regular on other Goodson-Todman shows.

384 **Madison Avenue sleek:** On Mark Goodson and Bill Todman, see Cynthia Lindsay, "Goodson and Todman: The Ether Empire," *Show,* Mar. 1965, 48–51, 92–93, courtesy former G-T casting director Helen Marcus. Lindsay quotes PC calling Goodson "a worrier." See also James Poling, "Programs Packaged to Go," *Collier's,* May 24, 1952, Box 36, CP.

384 **fueled by alcohol:** KCH to author, Dec. 14, 2002; Pamela Usdan to author, Aug. 16, 2011.

384 **"chemistry":** Betsy Palmer to author, Oct. 24, 2005.

384 **"hit it off perfectly":** BAC OH, 732.

384 **"personally, Dorothy":** BAC OH, 732.

385 **popular for being unpopular:** Peter Gabel to author, July 16, 2005.

385 **"the poor man's Edward R. Murrow":** Tom Link, "Great Shows: What's My Line?" *Emmy Magazine,* vol. 4, no. 4, 1982, 58, courtesy USCCL.

385 **picked him for his dignity:** Richard K. Doan, "End of the Line," *TV Guide,* June 17, 1967, Box 39, CP.

385 **the women's evening dresses:** Francis's dresses were borrowed from the chic store Bonwit Teller and returned each week. Jean Bach to author, May 20, 2003. Jayne Meadows's gowns for *I've Got a Secret* were borrowed from Bergdorf's and then another supplier; afterward, they were sold as having been worn by Meadows on TV. Similar arrangements were negotiated with jewelers. Jayne Meadows to author, May 16, 2005.

385 ***Has your product ever been alive?:*** Fates, *What's My Line?* 98–99.

385 ***Is it bigger than a breadbox?:*** Fates, *What's My Line?* 29.

385 **would have gained fifty dollars:** Whether they stumped the panel or not, contestants took home $50. See Franklin Heller interviewed by Loring Mandel in a Studio One Video History, Paley Center, New York, T87: 0384.

386 **"mystery guest":** The fee for a mystery guest in the show's early days also appears to have been $50. At least, that is the amount that John Daly stated Senator Estes Kefauver was receiving in the segment that aired Mar. 18, 1951. Fates mentions a $500 fee, which appears to have been applicable for much of the program's run. See Fates, *What's My Line?* 44. Usdan, who worked for the successor company to G-T, said the collection of old contract files was destroyed—and the history of such things with it.

386 **"Sunday night royalty":** Peter Gabel to author, July 16, 2005.

386 **"a parlor game":** Michael Dann, TV executive, to author, Feb. 4, 2003.

387 **appealing to the upper middle class:** On the relationship between the quality of TV and the "quality" of the audience, see Heller, Studio One interview.

387 **authoritative fulcrum:** Jean Bach to author, May 20, 2003.

387 **mark of distinction:** Heller, Studio One interview.

388 ***Poof!:*** Advertisement, *Chicago Tribune,* Oct. 23, 1951, Box 68, CP. The commercials changed over time. The ones mentioned were used when BAC first went on.

388 **"He was a sweet man":** BAC OH, 731.

388 **well-dressed "class":** When the show started, men wore suits and ties, and the suits were not necessarily dark; for a brief time they wore tuxedo jackets and silk bow ties; later, they kept the bow ties but wore dark suit jackets instead of tuxedos (many viewers thought they were tuxedos).

388 **"Make your armpit":** Fates, *What's My Line?* 15. G-T was delighted with Montenier's sponsorship. Yet as the show's popularity grew, Montenier's ad agency refused to pay for the time slot in TV markets where his products weren't sold, including Tallahassee, Savannah, and Memphis. BAC claimed *WML?* "ruined the poor man" because it became so expensive to sponsor,

and that ultimately, he was forced to sell to the Helene Curtis Company, which took over sponsorship. But BAC also said Montenier refused to share the program with another sponsor, which was patently wrong: in the pre-Curtis years, sponsorship alternated between Stopette and Remington Rand. Later sponsors included Sunbeam and Kellogg, all iconic brands. BAC OH.

388 **he'd be fired:** Fates, who had to tell Block, attributes the firing to his vulgarity and not fitting in. See Fates, *What's My Line?* 14–15. Heller claims Block was fired because he cheated; he claims that Block had someone signaling to him in the audience. See Heller, Studio One interview.

388 ***how* you broke down:** Jayne Meadows to author, May 16, 2005.

388 **surprisingly hard:** Peter Gabel to author, July 16, 2005.

388 ***See What You Know:*** *Variety,* Feb. 20, 1946, in *Variety Television Reviews,* vol. 3, 1923–1950 (New York: Garland Publishing, 1989). *Whom* he knew had been crucial; the show's director was Dick Rodgers's brother-in-law. More appearances with Dick and wife Dorothy followed.

388 **lighter than what might have been expected:** Betsy Palmer to author, Oct. 24, 2005.

388 **"a good account":** *Variety,* Mar. 31, 1948.

388 **In September of that year:** On the dates of BAC's early TV appearances and the purchases of his TV sets, see BAC diaries, Boxes 11, 12, CP.

389 **six thousand to three million sets:** Laurence Bergreen, *Look Now, Pay Later: The Rise of Network Broadcasting* (Garden City: Doubleday, 1980), 142–43.

389 **Pigeons roosted nearby:** Fates, *What's My Line?* 7. On the Mansfield Theater, see James Saxon Childers, "Is What's My Line on the Up-and-Up?" *Atlanta Journal-Constitution* magazine, Jan. 1956, Box 69, CP. Childers's article is the earliest I found explaining the behind-the-scenes production of the show. Later articles indicate that as time went on, the panel hardly rehearsed or didn't rehearse at all.

389 **Gil Fates was responsible:** Fates first met BAC on *See What You Know.* Fates quoted in Jeff Kisseloff, *The Box: An Oral History of Television, 1920–1961* (New York: Viking, 1995), 469.

389 **whose college roommate had been:** Lucy Liveright Koch Wilson to author, Jan. 10, 2008.

389 **their resident intellectual:** Michael Dann to author, Feb. 4, 2003. On Heller's contribution to the show, see Bob Stewart and Franklin Heller quoted in Kisseloff, *The Box,* 470.

389 ***What's all the fucking rush?:*** Garland quoted in Fates, *What's My Line?* 41. The show aired on Mar. 5, 1967. Despite the mechanical help, having heard a brief snatch of "disguised" voice, BAC guessed her.

390 **real reason for his presence:** Faye Fates to author, May 14, 2003; Jean Bach to author, May 20, 2003; Heller quoted in Kisseloff, *The Box,* 470.

391 **repaired to the Waldorf:** BAC diary.

392 **publish his second novel:** "Irwin Shaw, The Art of Fiction," interview by George Plimpton and John Phillips, *The Paris Review,* Winter 1953, no. 4. Shaw says an editor at a "minor" book club made his publisher swear Shaw was not a Communist in order to consider the book.

392 **contacted Bennett this time:** See Fates, *What's My Line?*; Eric Burns, *Invasion of the Mind Snatchers: Television's Conquest of America in the Fifties* (Philadelphia: Temple University Press, 2010), 166–74; Bergreen, *Look Now, Pay Later;* Erik Barnouw, *The Golden Web: A History of Broadcasting in the United States,* vol. 2, 1933–53 (New York: Oxford University Press, 1968), 265–67.

392 **"no more a Communist than J. Edgar Hoover":** BAC OH, 732.

392 **"We don't believe in pressure groups":** Montenier paraphrased by Jean Bach to author, May 20, 2003. Daly obliquely referred to this five years later, in episode #297, after the Red Scare had abated. Montenier was "the first spot," meaning, a guest who was not a mystery guest but someone known to the panel and for whom they had to don their blindfolds. Daly said that unlike the situation with other shows he could name, Montenier had never tried to "interfere" with *WML?* Fates insisted the producing team at first tried to resist the pressure to fire Untermeyer. See Fates, *What's My Line?* 9.

392 **"the bible of television":** Mark Goodson, "'If I Stood Up Earlier . . . ,'" *NYT,* Jan. 13, 1991. Goodson's extraordinary essay was effectively a confession re the uneasy history of the collaboration between shows, networks, and sponsors during the McCarthy era. He detailed the Untermeyer episode but also episodes involving Henry Morgan and Anna Lee on two other shows, when he did offer real resistance.

392 **named names to get even:** Frank Taylor, then living in Hollywood and working in the movies, wrote a letter to AE in which he discusses people getting even and getting rid of debts. See Frank Taylor to AE, Sept. 17, 1951, Box 41, 13497, AEP.

392 **forced to submit:** On the blacklist and

Untermeyer's departure from the show, see Fates, *What's My Line?* 9–12.

392 **"It was a little bit like":** Faye Fates to author, May 14, 2003. Some cultural critics consider the whole setup of these game shows—the friendly interrogations and secret identities; the masking of panelists; the unmasking of mystery guests; the reassuring, prize-giving capitalism—to be a metaphor for the McCarthy era.

393 **taken a large ad:** "What Are You Doing Out There?" in *NYT,* Jan. 15, 1951.

393 **lent his name to a brief:** The Hollywood Ten brief was filed Feb. 24, 1950. See Herrmann, *S. J. Perelman,* 197. For the publishers' names, see *The New York Compass,* Mar. 1, 1950, Box 67, CP.

393 **"Nowadays when any honest liberal":** *San Francisco Chronicle,* Feb. 26, 1951, Box 67, CP.

393 **"initiating sponsors":** BAC diary, May 11, 1951, Box 12, CP.

393 **Their names were removed:** On BAC and Hammerstein and Holliday's legal action regarding the CNA, see Frederick Woltman, "Commies Lurk Behind Shifty Fronts," *New York World-Telegram,* Oct. 27, 1952, Box 68, CP. Untermeyer's fate would doubtless have been on BAC's mind when he wanted to have his name removed from the CNA letterhead.

393 **"point out the moral":** BAC to Shirley Jackson, Apr. 15, 1953, Shirley Jackson Papers, LoC.

393 **"amiable":** Jean Bach to author, May 20, 2003.

394 **"perp walk":** After a few years it disappeared from the show.

394 **a free guess:** The free guess was later eliminated.

394 **Then came the mystery guest:** This episode with Senator Kefauver aired Mar. 18, 1951. The hearings were also noted in BAC diary, Apr. 15, 1951.

394 **but Bennett and Phyllis would go out:** Faye Fates to author, May 14, 2003.

395 **ringside table at the Copacabana:** Jean Bach to author, May 20, 2003.

395 **"flabbergasted":** Mark Goodson to BAC, June 9, 1952, CP.

395 **marriage was troubled:** Kilgallen info per Jean Bach to author, May 20, 2003.

395 **enormous need for adulation:** Richard Gehman, "The Amazing Armenian," Part 1, *TV Guide,* June 23, 1962, 20–21.

395 **"Marty would disappear":** KCH to author, Dec. 14, 2002. Martin Gabel and Francis-Gabel marriage per Jean Bach to author, May 20, 2003. Bach produced Francis's radio show.

395 ***really* wanted to win:** Faye Fates to author, May 14, 2003.

396 **jokes and puns decreased markedly:** Faye Fates to author, May 14, 2003.

396 **"loot":** BAC diary, Oct. 22, 1951, Box 12, CP.

396 **Four years later:** "How to Be a Panelist," *Time,* Apr. 4, 1955, Box 39, CP.

396 **$1,000 per week:** According to Fates, regular panelists were under contract to G-T and "paid much more," but he does not specify how much; later he states that panelists got $1,000. See Fates, *What's My Line?* 44, 111. In 1954 *Newsweek* asserted that Arlene Francis was paid $1,000 per performance. "Arlene Francis: The Quick Queen of Television," *Newsweek,* July 19, 1954.

396 **"scandalous amounts":** BAC OH, 733.

396 **each episode had cost $40,000:** Doan, "End of the Line."

396 **Recalling the humiliation:** BAC OH, 735.

396 **"You're playing yourself":** Betsy Palmer to author, Oct. 24, 2005.

396 **he was with the Brackett family:** Charles Brackett to BAC, Nov. 2, 1959, Margaret Herrick Library, AMPAS.

396 **"I see you every Sunday night":** Joseph C. Lesser to BAC, May 5, 1952, Box 20, RHR.

397 **"very, very unusual":** Jayne Meadows to author, May 16, 2005. Meadows said this in the context of knowing many people in publishing, because her husband, Steve Allen, had published many books.

397 **"mask [his] emotions":** BAC said this in a piece for the *SRL* reprinted in the *Saturday Evening Post,* Mar. 6, 1948, Box 66, CP. The comment was made in the context of the joke books, having to deal with people telling him the same joke he'd heard before, but the frozen smile appeared in other contexts, too.

397 **"cruel things":** Anne Bernays to author, May 3, 2004.

397 **"That feeling of fame":** BAC quoted in Havens Wilber, "Educators Should Fight McCarthyism, Cerf Says Here," *Capitol Times* (Madison, Wisc.), Jan. 24, 1953, Box 68, CP.

397 **one of the most popular shows:** By May 1952, G-T would have six shows seen by 34 million Americans, one-fifth of the population. *What's My Line?* drew the biggest audience, almost 10 million. See Poling, "Programs Packaged to Go."

CHAPTER 25: GATSBY IN PARADISE

398 **Bennett had replaced Louis Untermeyer:** "Untermeyer Out. Cerf, Others Hit Allegations," *Broadcasting Washington,* June 11, 1951, Box 67, CP.

398 **Budd Schulberg came calling:** BAC diary, Apr. 20, 1951, Box 12, CP.

398 **"didn't jump":** BWS to author, Jan. 15, 2008.

398 **"This was serious":** BWS to author, Apr. 19, 2004.

399 **"a story of a fabulous writer":** BAC, Trade Winds, *SRL,* July 17, 1948.

399 **"The more I think":** BAC to SC, Feb. 24, 1950, Box 2, SCP.

399 **"headed for the heights":** BAC, Trade Winds, *SRL,* Nov. 14, 1950.

399 **BOMC took *The Disenchanted:*** On BOMC, BAC told SC that he would "derive a certain satisfaction." BAC to SC, June 13, 1950, Box 2, SCP. See also BAC diary, Aug. 25, 1950.

399 **a lack of enthusiasm:** On BWS's novel, WF writes in letter possibly dated Oct. 16, 1950, no. 729, in Louis Daniel Brodsky and Robert Hamblin, eds., *Faulkner: A Comprehensive Guide to the Brodsky Collection* Vol. I, *The Biobibliography* (Jackson: University Press of Mississippi, 1982).

399 **"rather half-heartedly":** TC to RNL, Feb. 28, 1951, in Clarke, ed., *TBAT,* 160.

399 **"two or three most impressive":** Prescott quoted in clipping, Box 67, CP.

399 **top-twenty bestsellers:** *What Makes Sammy Run?* sold 6,605 copies from Nov. 1951 to Oct. 1952, making it number 19 in ML Top 100. Box 166, RHR.

399 **"very decent of him":** BWS to author, Jan. 15, 2008. On his decision to cooperate, see Victor S. Navasky, *Naming Names* (New York: Viking, 1980), 73, 239–46, 306–13.

400 **would remain controversial:** All but one of the people BWS named—BAC's former author Tillie Lerner Olsen—were already known as Communists. Navasky, *Naming Names,* 283.

400 **"perfect family":** CBC to author, Aug. 7, 2003. He added, "Real, deep problems were not discussed in our perfect family."

400 **fancied buying two cottages:** BAC to Ossie Ball, Sept. 12, 1950, Box 14, RHR.

400 **house in Mt. Kisco:** JFC generously accompanied the author on Oct. 22, 2003, to visit the country house where he grew up. Jane and Bill Lewis, the then-owners, graciously welcomed us to tour the premises. The description of the car is from BAC's diary and JFC. The elements of the house and grounds in the early years and catalogue of furniture is from JFC. He supplied further information on Mt. Kisco, Mar. 11, 2003, and Oct. 26 & 27, 2011. On the weather, see *NYT,* Apr. 30, 1951.

401 **asking $155,000:** According to Dollar Times, in 2025 dollars, the asking price would have been about $1.9 million. For the asking price and acreage, see *NY Herald Tribune,* June 10, 1951, Box 67, CP.

401 **"wonderful":** BAC diary, Apr. 29, 1951, Box 12, CP.

402 **"improbable" deal:** BAC diary, May 4, 1951.

402 **"enchanted":** BAC diary, May 6, 1951.

402 **"tragic predicament":** BAC diary, Mar. 11, 1951.

403 **languishing in the Villard safe:** Wanting to seize the moment, a letter was drafted as though from EON to BAC and SC granting permission to publish *A Moon for the Misbegotten* and *A Touch of the Poet,* Mar. 17, 1951, SCP (unsigned). Unclear if drafted by BAC or SC or ever sent.

403 **"the harpy he's married to":** BAC to RKH, Mar. 20, 1951, Box 17, RHR.

403 **107 pounds:** EON's weight, SC to Kenneth Macgowan, Apr. 2, 1951, Macgowan Papers, UCLA.

403 **asked for maintenance:** On EON's 1951 crisis, see Sheaffer, *O'Neill: Son and Artist,* 636–56; Arthur and Barbara Gelb, *O'Neill,* 908–32.

403 **didn't visit O'Neill:** There is no mention of a visit in the BAC diary before this. Usually, BAC would mention the first of anything in his diary, so it's not very likely there were earlier visits. Five of the days between Mar. 30 and Apr. 19 BAC was in Washington. His visit on the eve of EON's departure isn't in the diary, but then, he was unaware that EON planned to leave.

403 **O'Neills would soon be back together:** Russel "Buck" Crouse role per Anna Crouse to author, June 14, 2007.

403 **listened with the quiet:** "Gene has the most amazing effect upon me; there is something so restful about sitting in that cool house of yours and hearing him speak in that calm and deliberate way." BAC to CMON, Sept. 8, 1942, RHR. BAC said EON was the one man who could make him shut up.

404 **"mesmerizing":** On EON's crisis, see BAC OH, 218–20.

404 **not having been taken into Gene's confidence:** In his OH, BAC speaks of being "furious" at EON's departure.

404 **"ghastly":** CMON to BAC, May 22, 1951.

404 **"what lies ahead":** BAC to CMON, May 23, 1951, RHCC.

405 **taken by the boss's wife:** Sussman teaching Phyllis photography per CBC to author, Feb. 18, 2002.

405 **$30,000 mortgage:** BAC diary, June 14, 1951.

405 **Cerfboard house-naming contest:** BAC, "The Pun House," Cerfboard, *This Week,* Dec. 9, 1951, Box 67, CP.

405 **Vera the maid:** At this time the servants included Margaret, Ivar, Vera, a cook, and a live-out laundress and handyman. For a list of the 62nd St. servants, see BAC to F. H. Link, Jan. 19, 1951, Box 16, RHR.

406 **baptize The Columns:** On the first few days at Mt. Kisco, see BAC diary, June 29 & 30, July 1, 1951, Box 12, CP.

406 **organize a club car:** July 2, 1951, BAC diary; Harold T. White to Raymond Blosser, press manager of New York Central, July 31, 1951; Blosser to BAC (attaching White's letter), Aug. 1, 1951, Box 16, RHR.

406 **the same issue Phyllis had encountered:** BAC's feelings about prejudice per JFC to author, Mar. 11, 2003.

406 **became the first Jew:** JFC to author, Mar. 11, 2003; Richard Baron, former co-owner of the Dial Press, to author, Sept. 3, 2004.

406 **"with no one else of that religion":** JFC to author, Mar. 11, 2003.

406 **"paradise":** JFC to author, Oct. 22, 2003.

406 **"the Great Gatsby of 1951":** BAC to Nancy Wilson Ross, Aug. 21, 1951, Box 21, RHR. **"like the Great Gatsby":** BAC quoted in Fanny Butcher, *Chicago Tribune,* Sept. 16, 1951, Box 67, CP.

407 **"the best business book ever written":** DSK OH, 39.

408 **just another day at Random House:** For the Vercel story, see BAC OH, 513–15; John Hutchens, *Herald-Tribune Book Review,* June 17, 1951, Box 67, CP. Additionally, CW recounted it to author, May 16, 2007. In some details BAC's and CW's versions differ from Hutchens; I have followed Hutchens.

408 **large block of shares:** On deal for LM, see BAC diary, Nov. 1, 1951.

408 **In the end:** CW to author, Feb. 26, 2002.

408 **toppled over and broke:** RDL, CW, et al. to author.

408 **With a Bible always:** RDL, CW, et al. to author.

409 **four weeks of Trade Winds in a day:** BAC diary, July 11, 1951.

409 **watch ball games and fetch:** CBC to author, July 31, 2003.

409 **"the Monster":** CBC to author, Dec. 18, 2002.

409 **devise a musical:** CBC to author, Dec. 18, 2002.

409 **Klutz family:** CBC to author, July 31, 2003.

409 **"mushrooms":** CBC to author, Dec. 18, 2002.

409 **"a big joke, we could never win":** CBC to author, Dec. 18, 2002.

410 **"a real charmer":** Joyce Hartman to author, Sept. 12, 2004. Hartman, a New York editor for Houghton Mifflin, was married to the Klopfers' personal physician.

410 **rainbow of cashmere cardigans:** "Pat's Nifty at Fifty" party took place on June 2, 1956; BAC and PC were in London. The guest list mentions RKH and Merle, the Fadimans, the Hammersteins, among sixty-plus attending, DSKP. The cashmere was recalled by Hartman, who also remembered the *fraises des bois*.

410 **The Klopfers now went to Europe:** DSK trips noted in BAC diaries.

411 **"wild and volatile Cerf":** Mediator C. J. Greenwood to Sir Stanley Unwin, June 24, 1947 (Greenwood miswrote the date as June 24, 1945, but a date stamp shows it was received in June 1947), George Allen & Unwin Records, the University of Reading. Papers in A&U and Cape collections at Reading detail the dispute. With the advent of digital publishing, territorial rights are again very much in the air.

411 **"marching orders":** BAC to DSK, Mar. 27, 1951, Box 17, RHR.

411 **"one swift kick":** BAC to DSK, Mar. 20, 1951, Box 17, RHR.

411 **"infinitely better":** BAC to Mignon Eberhart, mystery author, May 29, 1951, Box 17, RHR.

411 **without meeting their aunt:** Oklahoma visit per CBC to author, Jan. 21, June 9, 2003. It appears that Phil (James Phillip Clendenin, born 1935), whom the boys met, was the son of Phyllis's mother, whose last marriage was to Austin Courtney Clendenin, and therefore Phyllis's half brother, but CBC and JFC recalled him being introduced as their cousin. See okcremation .com/obituaries/James-Clendenin.

411 **"Tho you don't":** Card from Gertrude Cerf to BAC, n.d., and his reply, Dec. 27, 1951, Box 16, RHR.

412 **"We are proud":** Publication card mentioned in Trade Winds, *SRL,* Mar. 3, 1951, The card itself is in Box 67, CP.

412 **later, Bennett would boast:** BAC OH, 976. See also BAC diary, Oct. 10, 1951.

412 **won the Nobel:** BAC diary, Nov. 15, 1951, Box 12, CP.

413 **$60,000 for picture rights:** BAC diary, Nov. 19, 1951, Box 12, CP.

413 **"*The New Yorker* . . . can and will":** Ross obituary, Trade Winds, *SRL,* Dec. 29, 1951.

PART FOUR, 1952–1959: "AND THE MYSTERY GUEST IS . . ."

415 **"And the Mystery Guest Is . . .":** The phrase was uttered each week by John Charles Daly, the *What's My Line?* moderator.

415 **"Cerf has managed":** Bernard Kalb, "Bennett Cerf: He Also Works in Video," *NYT,* Aug. 2, 1953.

415 **"It all reads":** BAC, Trade Winds, *SRL,* May 15, 1954; PC profile of BAC, *Good Housekeeping,* June 1954.

415 **". . . Bennett Cerf, the ideal publisher":** Ayn Rand to BAC, RBML, Columbia.

CHAPTER 26: WHAT'S NEW

417 **doing good works:** PC was on the boards of the National Urban League and the Play Schools Association. *The Pittsburgh Courier,* Nov. 25, 1950, Box 67, CP.

417 **"You make us feel":** Mrs. Margaret McKim quoted in BAC, Trade Winds, *SRL,* Nov. 10, 1951.

417 **Saxe helped, too:** PC OH, 106.

418 **absolutely nothing could be:** CBC to author, Feb. 25, 2005.

418 **"being an angry wife":** PC OH, 297–98.

418 **"Bennett wanted me":** PC OH, 278.

418 **"the latest doings of the intelligentsia":** "What's New . . . by Phyllis Cerf" ad, *Newsday,* July 23, 1954, among others.

418 **"a chip off the old block":** BAC diary, Mar. 8, 1952, Box 12, CP; "What's New . . . by Phyllis Cerf," *Newsday,* Sept. 6, 1956.

418 **wasn't particularly fond:** JFC to author, Mar. 11, 2003.

418 **got a new Dictaphone:** Jan. 3, 1952, BAC diary, Box 12, CP.

418 **panoply of products:** See advertisements, Box 68, CP; BAC diary, Sept. 16, 1951.

418 **TV actors' union:** BAC diary, Jan. 10, 1952.

418 **publishing fracas:** BAC diary, Dec. 12, 1952, Box 12, CP.

418 **not short on ego:** FCB, Ballantine's cousin, to author, Oct. 22, 2011.

419 **Ballantine hatched the Bantam rooster:** Betty Ballantine to author, Nov. 26, 2002, and Nov. 10, 2010. See also Kenneth C. Davis, *Two-Bit Culture* (Boston: Houghton Mifflin, 1984), 51, 54, 102–3, 107–9, 160–62. Ian's senior thesis re ML distribution weaknesses had helped get him the Penguin job. Betty Ballantine to author, Nov. 26, 2002.

419 **New York chief editor and company secretary:** They were Walter Pitkin Jr. and Sidney Kramer, respectively.

419 **In 1947, 95 million:** Douglas M. Black, president of the American Book Publishers Council, to H. Ralph Burton, General Counsel, House Select Committee, Oct. 13, 1952, Box 19, RHR.

419 **NAL had paid:** Carl F. Kaestle and Janice Radway, *A History of the Book in America, Vol. 4* (Chapel Hill: University of North Carolina Press, 2009), 85.

419 **Print runs ballooned:** Davis, *Two-Bit Culture.* Paperbacks background also from Black to Burton, Box 19, RHR, Oct. 13, 1952.

419 **"more cutthroat":** BAC to John O'Connor, Jan. 17, 1952, Box 20, RHR.

419 **When O'Connor visited:** The date for both visits was Jan. 10, 1952. BAC diary, Box 12, CP.

420 **under huge pressure:** On the Ballantine firing, see BAC OH, 611–12; Davis, *Two-Bit Culture,* 160–61; Boxes 19 & 20, RHR, where BAC speaks of a "Pitkin faction." According to Betty Ballantine, Ian "mismanaged emotional relationships" with staff and ascribed a motivating "animosity" to Kramer. Ballantine to author, Nov. 10, 2010; Kramer declined to comment to author.

420 **allegiance to Saxe:** Ballantine saw SC as his emotional father figure. SC taught Betty Ballantine how to edit. Betty Ballantine to author, Nov. 10, 2010.

420 **"court-martial":** BAC diary, Jan. 18, 1952.

420 **made fantastic profits:** Kramer predicted an after-tax profit of $223,000. See Kramer to Bantam board, memo, Dec. 24, 1952, Box 20, RHR. Financial success under Ballantine per Betty Ballantine to author, Nov. 26, 2002. BAC told O'Connor that "the annual profit and loss statement speaks for itself." BAC to O'Connor, Jan. 17, 1952, Box 20, RHR.

420 **"Were I faced":** BAC to John O'Connor, Jan. 17, 1952, Box 20, RHR.

420 **He alone among the dozen:** Betty Ballantine to author, Nov. 26, 2002. Minutes of meeting, Feb. 5, 1952, Box 20, RHR.

420 **plunged into the red:** Davis, *Two-Bit Culture,* 250.

420 **a certain "Cosmo Heineken":** BAC, Trade Winds, *SRL,* Oct. 4, 1952. BAC criticized the "dynamic if sometimes rash" Ballantine without the veil of parody in print, but they remained friendly. BAC, Trade Winds, *SRL,* May 16, 1954; Betty Ballantine to author, Nov. 26, 2002.

420 **changing the basic arithmetic:** Ballantine's concept of "simulprint" editions was analyzed in a report by O'Connor, June 30, 1952, Box 20, RHR. See also Davis, *Two-Bit Culture,* 160–62. Ballantine's radical idea was a precursor to changes wrought by Amazon's Kindle.

421 **Ray Bradbury's *Fahrenheit 451:*** Davis, *Two-Bit Culture,* 167.

421 **American Book Publishers Council's:** This was the forerunner to today's Association of American Publishers.

421 **"do-gooders trying":** DSK quoted in ACLU release, May 8, 1951, Box 17, RHR.

421 **he was forced to resign:** On Cameron, per Arthur Thornhill Jr., to author, Dec. 15, 2004. Thornhill Jr. was young, working at Little, Brown when this took place; his father was board chairman. Corroboration per editor John Simon to author, Dec. 1, 2002. Simon worked with Cameron at Knopf. LB author Arthur Schlesinger Jr., upset that his publisher Cameron had declined George Orwell's anti-Communist *Animal Farm,* publicly excoriated Cameron as pro-Stalin and left for a different house. See Douglas Martin, "Angus Cameron, 93, Editor Forced Out in McCarthy Era," *NYT,* Nov. 23, 2002.

421 **"commy troubles":** BAC diary, Sept. 13 & 15, 1951.

422 **lists of objectionable books:** On the censorship dilemma, see Davis, *Two-Bit Culture,* 217–41. For letters and memos and other office collateral detailing many fronts of the censorship battle and DSK's role, see Boxes 17, 19, 22, 24, RHR.

422 **"sensuality, immorality":** Quoted in Davis, *Two-Bit Culture,* 235.

422 **civilian committee to screen:** Victor Weybright to DSK, Mar. 12, 1952, Box 19, RHR.

422 **wrote to the secretary of defense:** DSK to Hon. Robert Lovett, Jan. 9, 1953, Box 24, RHR.

422 **broke its rules:** Douglas M. Black, American Book Publishers Council, to DSK, June 23, 1952, Box 19, RHR.

422 **"confidence in President Truman":** BAC, Trade Winds, *SRL,* Apr. 7, 1951.

422 **Bennett fell again:** On the Stevenson nomination, see BAC diary, July 25. BAC disapproved of the nomination of segregationist Alabama senator John Sparkman for vice president. See BAC diary, July 26, 1952, Box 12, CP.

422 **Bennett met his man:** BAC diary, Sept. 21, 22, 23, & 24, 1952.

423 **the edition soon sold out:** *PW,* Nov. 29, 1942.

423 **"If I had had any idea":** BAC quoted in *Greensboro Record,* Sept. 30, 1952.

423 **"I was hot tonite!":** BAC diary, Jan. 20, 1952.

423 **a serious abscess:** BAC diary, Nov. 10–14, 1952.

424 **RH had clinched the deal:** The date was Dec. 16, 1952. The visit to Stevenson was on Dec. 6. Both BAC diary.

424 **Saxe was to have final say:** WF to RKH, Apr. 13, 1951, MSS 16807, previously 10280A, Box 2, WFC.

424 **defending the win:** BAC, Trade Winds, *SRL,* Apr. 28, 1951.

424 **going to Paris to tryst:** WF to SC, probably mid-Feb. 1951; WF to SC, early Apr. 1951, in Louis D. Brodsky and Robert W. Hamblin, eds., *Faulkner: A Comprehensive Guide to the Brodsky Collection:* Vol. II: *The Letters* (Jackson: University of Mississippi Press, 1984), 62 and 66, respectively.

424 **to keep his secret:** On the role of Betty Haas, see Brodsky and Hamblin, eds., *Faulkner,* vol. 2, 62. WF mentions RKH's suggestion in undated letter to SC, Mar. 1951, 65.

424 **mustn't give her any money:** WF to SC, early May 1952, Brodsky and Hamblin, eds., *Faulkner,* vol. 2, 75.

424 **fantasizing about a break:** WF to SC, postmarked July 30, 1952, Brodsky and Hamblin, eds., *Faulkner,* vol. 2, 80.

425 **Saxe wrote two letters:** See SC to BAC and RKH, SC to Dorothy Commins, both Oct. 8, 1952, in Brodsky and Hamblin, eds., *Faulkner,* vol. 2, 89–91. In Princeton and NYC: Blotner, *Faulkner,* vol. 2, 1439–42.

425 **who knows how long:** BWS's exact words to the author were "I don't know how long," Oct. 4, 2003.

425 **"So I knew":** E. L. Doctorow to author, July 4, 2005.

CHAPTER 27: BOMBSHELLS AND WHOPPERS

426 **To capture the laurels:** On the National Book Awards odds, see BAC, Trade Winds, *SRL,* Feb. 7, 1953. The fiction judges were Saul Bellow, Martha Foley, Irving Howe, Harvard professor Howard Mumford Jones, and Alfred Kazin, according to an NBA ad, *NYT,* Feb. 1, 1953. The newspaper's "In and Out of Books" column that day states the vote was four to one on the first ballot. Jones opted for Hemingway; see Arnold Rampersad's *Ralph Ellison: A Biography* (New York: Alfred A. Knopf, 2007), 269. Hemingway's reemergence had made him the clear front-runner.

426 **agreed to a $2,000 advance:** In contract July 18, 1947, Box 154, Ralph Ellison Papers, LoC (hereafter REP). The agent was Diarmid Russell. The contract does not mention repayment to Reynal & Hitchcock. See also Rampersad, *Ralph Ellison,* 211.

426 **When Taylor moved:** By 1952, the publication year for *Invisible Man,* Taylor had returned to books as editor-in-chief of Dell. He'd later be publisher of Avon and editor-in-chief of McGraw-Hill trade and also produce *The Misfits,* directed by John Huston.

426 **"with the impact of a battleship":** BAC blurb for Wright, Box 65, CP.

426 **"there will be people":** AE to Ralph Ellison (hereafter RE) et al., Mar. 19, 1952, Box 154, REP.

427 **"anomalous position":** RH press release, Mar. 25, 1952, Box 154, REP.

427 **"a resolutely honest":** Wright Morris, "The World Below," *NYT,* Apr. 13, 1952. Orville Prescott called it the "most impressive" fiction by any Black American author that he'd read. See Prescott, "Books of the Times," *NYT,* Apr. 16, 1952.

427 **"It is felt that":** RE quoted in Harvey Breit, "Talk with Ralph Ellison," *NYT,* May 4, 1952.

427 **"pretty darn good":** BAC to Milton Runyon, June 10, 1952, Box 20, RHR.

427 **gross profit vaporized:** *Invisible Man* had net sales of $36,162. It cost $17,740 to manufacture; $6,598 was spent on promotion and ads. Total costs, including the royalty, were $33,693. Gross profit was $5,857. Once $10,849 (the 30% of sales charged as overhead) was subtracted, the book showed a deficit of $4,992. From profit and loss (P&L) report covering Apr. 14, 1952 (publication date), to Feb. 28, 1953, AEP.

428 **remaindered what hardcovers were left:** AE to RE, Dec. 6, 1955, Box 65, REP. The New American Library (hereafter NAL) had bought reprint rights for a $7,500 advance predicated on a sale of 300,000 copies. By mid-1955, 165,000 copies had been sold. But BAC criticized NAL distribution as "ineffectual." Unattributed note, Oct. 23, 1963, Box 154, REP.

428 **"a singular lack of respect":** RE to AE, Nov. 22, 1955, Box 65, REP.

428 **"a matter of admitting":** AE to RE, Dec. 6, 1955, Box 65, REP.

428 **Foreign publishers noticed:** Royalty statements for foreign sales, dated June 2, 1966, compiled for AE, Box 154, REP.

428 **attained a kind of apotheosis:** On the *NY Herald Tribune* poll, see Herbert Mitgang, "'Invisible Man,' as Vivid Today as in 1952," *NYT,* Mar. 1, 1982. In 1998, when RH president Harold Evans relaunched the ML and, as part of the marketing effort, drew up a list of the 100 best novels ever written, RE's book wasn't first but was on the list.

428 **"never lost our nostalgia":** Fanny Ellison and RE to DSK, Feb. 1, 1982, Box 65, REP.

429 **calendar featuring nude pictures:** BAC diary, Mar. 17, 1952, Box 12, CP; BAC, "Trade Winds," Apr. 18, 1952.

429 ***Gentlemen Prefer Blondes:*** This was the film where Monroe made the "dumb blonde" role a touchstone.

429 **"and not much else":** BAC, "The 'Altogether' Girl," *Esquire,* July 1953, Box 68, CP.

430 **Phyllis joined the tête-à-tête:** BAC quoted on PC's insistence that she be there in Havens Wilber, "Educators Should Fight Mccarthyism, [*sic*] Cerf Says Here," *Capitol Times* (Madison, Wisc.), Jan. 24, 1953. In the *Esquire* piece BAC says he summoned PC by phone late in the interview; this is repeated in his OH. In PC's "What's New" column of Jan. 21, 1954—the week Marilyn Monroe and Joe DiMaggio wed—PC implies she was there the whole time; that Monroe could quote the acting book by heart; and that Monroe read and liked Montaigne. (If so, then the exclamation point inserted in parentheses after "Montaigne" in BAC's article is a bit of a put-down playing to the stereotypical attitudes of many *Esquire* readers.)

430 **made their first foray:** The visit was Feb. 15, 1953. BAC diary, Box 12, CP.

430 **emerged as "Christine":** Jorgensen was not the first medically assisted transsexual but was the first widely known in America, and the first to use both hormones and surgery. See John T. McQuiston, "Christine Jorgensen of Sex-Change Fame Dies at 62," *NYT,* May 4, 1989. I could not determine how the deal was initiated, if RH met Jorgensen or read anything, or if an intent to publish was put in writing.

430 **"Damnit, Don":** BAC to DSK, Feb. 19, 1953, Box 22, RHR.

431 **sales reps cautioned:** DSK to BAC, Feb. 20, 1953, Box 22; **"a riding":** DSK to BAC, Feb. 24, 1953, Box 24, RHR.

431 **lawyer-vetted release:** Box 22, RHR.

432 **firm's most important British novelist:** The three novels published by RH are generally regarded as Mitford's finest. Apart from two early books, her U.K. publisher was Hamish Hamilton.

432 **"stiff and unusual":** DSK to Mrs. Peter Rodd (Mitford's married name), Feb. 5, 1953, Box 24, RHR.

432 **"What I feel about Random House":** Nancy Rodd to DSK, Feb. 11, 1953, Box 24, RHR.

432 **"That's sound and creative":** DSK to Mrs. Peter Rodd, Mar. 12, 1953, Box 24, RHR.

433 **"Flattered":** Nancy Rodd to DSK, Mar. 16, 1953, Box 24, RHR.

433 **He'd summoned the courage:** JAM, *TWIMH,* 364–68. See also Warren E. Thompson, "The Reality Behind Toko-Ri," *Military Officer Magazine,* June 2003, Box 12, AEP.

433 **"always in the right place":** BAC OH, 537.

433 **his canny agent had an idea:** from Strauss, *Talent for Luck,* 106.

433 **Bennett sold rights to *Reader's Digest:*** Ralph E. Henderson to BAC, June 12, 1953, WME; to Doubleday club: Milton Runyon to BAC, Sept. 20, 1953, WME; to Bantam: contract, Sept. 14, 1953, WME.

433 **film sale to Paramount:** July 13, 1953, BAC diary, Box 12, CP.

433 **more than 35,000 copies:** RH P&L report, Feb. 28, 1954, AEP.

433 **"the well-crafted English novel":** Grobel, "Playboy Interview" per Grobel, *Talking with Michener* (Jackson: University Press of Mississippi, 1999).

434 **"It is impossible":** JAM to SC, Jan. 23, 1951, Box 17, AEP.

434 **it was Donald she confronted:** Strauss's account of the blow-up has BAC "hitting the ceiling," but it was DSK whom she confronted. BAC diary; see also Strauss, *Talent for Luck,* 108–9.

434 **she knew the man she wanted:** In his OH, BAC offered an alternative reason for Michener wanting a new editor: Saxe was "a frustrated writer and he would always try to rewrite," so an "annoyed" Michener "couldn't work with him any longer." BAC OH, 1015. But BAC's memory was unreliable here; rewriting was not the problem.

434 **Saxe had made the final decision:** SC to JAM, Jan. 5, 1953, Box 17, AEP.

434 **"Klopfer was really fine":** JAM to Erskine, Mar. 1, 1953, Box 17, AEP.

435 **The popular magazine *McCall's:*** Contract, June 15, 1953, JAMP.

435 **would pay $250,000:** See Carl Goldstein, representing Julius Lefkowitz & Co. CPA to JAM, Mar. 1, 1957, JAMP.

435 **earned over $100,000 in royalties:** May, *Michener,* 107.

435 **estimated his income:** Allen A. Kaufman of Julius Lefkowitz and Co. to JAM, Aug. 20, 1954, JAMP.

435 **sought out for endorsements:** They are listed in contract abstracts. WME.

435 **"my guru":** JAM quoted by Marisa Erskine to author, Apr. 25, 2008.

435 **"our instant gold mine":** BAC OH, 537.

435 **his best since *Try and Stop Me:*** BAC, Trade Winds, *SRL,* Dec. 27, 1952.

435 **"What are you gonna call it":** Elinor Green Hunter to author, June 11, 2010. Green (as she then was), hired by Jack Goodman, worked at S&S from 1940 to 1953. BAC himself had looked on his first draft as "awful." BAC diary, Dec. 31, 1947, CP.

435 **116,000 copies:** BAC diary, Dec. 9, 1953, Box 12, CP. These were gross sales; the net, after returns, would have been less. The figures of 66,000, 75,000, and 90,000 were mentioned in various places. See Doubleday's Ferris Mack to BAC, July 30, 1953, Box 23, RHR; Doubleday's John Sargent to BAC, Nov. 27, 1953, Box 23, RHR; press release, Hanover House, May 1954, Box 68, CP, respectively.

435 **The $24,000 advance:** BAC diary, Oct. 13, 1953, Box 12, CP.

436 **no more than $2,000:** Box 23, RHR.

436 **"My honest advice":** BAC to Mrs. Dick Cathcart, Oct. 22, 1954, Box 26, RHR.

436 **"greater stature":** RLS to BAC, Nov. 25, 1952, Box 21, RHR.

436 **"publishing recollections":** Ken McCormick to BAC, Feb. 23, 1951; BAC to McCormick, Mar. 12, 1951, Box 17, RHR.

436 **hearty fellow:** BAC OH, 782.

437 **"would sell a million copies":** Quentin Reynolds to Clyde Tolson, May 28, 1953, Box 24, RHR.

437 **"a masterpiece of diplomacy":** BAC to Quentin Reynolds, June 1, 1953, Box 24, RHR.

437 **"only concerned":** Quentin Reynolds and BAC to J. Edgar Hoover, June 11, 1953, Box 23, RHR.

437 **underpinning McCarthyism:** Wechsler's book received a major *NYTBR* ad on Nov. 22, 1953, that BAC saved. Box 68, CP.

437 **"cinching":** BAC diary, June 11, 1953, Box 12, CP.

437 **date with the electric chair:** June 19, 1953, Box 12, CP.

438 **cover the Miss America pageant:** BAC diary, Sept. 14, 1953.

438 ***Esquire* editors loved:** BAC diary, Dec. 7, 1953.

438 **buy RH's wing:** BAC diary, Sept. 14, 1953.

438 **cloak-and-dagger exploits:** BAC OH, 781–84. Ralph Henderson recounts the party conversation with BAC and Reynolds in his Columbia OH, 212–19. See also Douglas Dales, " 'Hero' of War Book Admits Exploits as Cloak-Dagger Spy Were a Hoax," *NYT,* Nov. 15, 1953; BAC diary, Nov. 13, 14, 16, 18, & 24, 1953. BAC letter to booksellers, Nov. 16, 1953; the article by Douglas Collins, and many other newspaper and magazine clips about the hoax are in Box 68, CP. *PW* report, Nov. 21, 1953, courtesy *PW.* See also BAC, Trade Winds, *SRL,* Nov. 28, 1953.

440 **"brilliant":** James Wechsler to BAC, Nov. 19, 1953, Box 24, RHR.

440 **"for the quick":** Victor Weybright to BAC, Nov. 25, 1953, Box 24, RHR.

CHAPTER 28: TRANSITIONS AND HOME TRUTHS

441 **"Saxie":** DSK to SC, Aug. 24, 1953, Box 24, RHR.
441 **"brook no more":** BAC to SC, Aug. 27, 1953, SCP.
442 **Saxe cried:** Dorothy Commins to BAC, Sept. 2, 1953, Box 22, RHR.
442 **Yet he was still:** BAC to Irwin Shaw, Dec. 23, 1953, Box 24, RHR. Shaw had wanted SC to come to Europe to work on a manuscript.
442 **the other three mornings:** For SC work schedule, see SC to WF, Jan. 18, 1954, Box 2, AEP.
442 **counted each one:** Jan. 4, 1954, SC diary, courtesy FCB.
442 **"destined to bring":** SC diary, Jan. 5, 1954.
443 **"a very unusual author":** JE to author, Dec. 9, 2003.
443 **"a sixty-year-old smiling public man":** JE to author, Dec. 9, 2003.
443 **saw Bennett as vulgar:** Confided to the author by an anonymous source.
443 **Yet Bennett saw Auden:** BAC told Auden that his books did indeed turn a profit. See BAC to Auden, Feb. 23, 1954, Box 29, RHR.
443 **had almost died:** Bruccoli, *O'Hara Concern,* 215.
443 ***If I Ran the Zoo:*** See Judith Morgan and Neil Morgan, *Dr. Seuss and Mr. Geisel: A Biography* (New York: RH, 1995), 132.
443 **"a debaculous fiasco":** TSG quoted in Morgan and Morgan, *Dr. Seuss and Mr. Geisel,* 138.
444 **"terribly flattered":** TSG to Dorothy Commins, Mar. 19, 1970, Box 5, SCP.
444 **"He never would tell":** Interview with TSG quoted in Morgan and Morgan, *Dr. Seuss and Mr. Geisel,* 138.
444 **to hear the good doctor:** Morgan and Morgan, *Dr. Seuss and Mr. Geisel,* 145.
444 **who threw a party:** On the Oklahoma City party, see BAC diary.
445 **Helicopter Squadron One:** BAC diary, Mar. 4, 1954; "Bennett Cerf Acquires New Line" article (unsourced) in Box 68, CP. TSG arranged the outing, Morgan and Morgan, *Dr. Seuss and Mr. Geisel,* 184.
445 **his CBS series:** Letter from BAC to Murrow expressing admiration is mentioned in BAC diary, Mar. 9–10, 1954.
445 **"losing battle":** Apr. 27 & 28, 1954, BAC diary.
446 **row with editor Norman Cousins:** On the dispute over the parody and killing of the piece, see BAC diary, Apr. 13, 1954. The dead article is in CP.
446 **when comedian Sid Caesar:** The episode aired Dec. 1, 1956; it is viewable T83:0351 at the Paley Center, New York.
446 **Phyllis's portrait:** Mrs. Bennett Cerf, "My Husband Is No Joke to Live With," *Good Housekeeping,* June 1954, 56–59, 222–26, CP.
447 **personally edited part:** BAC diary, May 19. BAC also devised the perfect title, per his diary, Apr. 21, 1954.
447 **I always thought:** BAC OH, 548–49.
447 **hugged bestseller lists:** BAC to Mac Hyman, Dec. 13, 1954, Box 28, RHR.
447 **to commission Shelby Foote:** BAC diary, Aug. 2 & 3, 1954.
447 **pressure from his British bankers:** JE to author, Dec. 9, 2003.
447 **low-budget warehouse operation:** JE to author, Dec. 9, 2003. Harry Paroissien was the manager who ran Penguin's U.S. operation.
448 **with Don making the case:** Per Peter Mayer, who had a long stint as Penguin CEO, Lane periodically carried on these sorts of talks with many publishers. Mayer to author, Oct. 27, 2006. For the 1954 Penguin letters, see Box 28, RHR.
448 **a series similar to Anchor:** Tebbel, *Great Change,* 192.
448 **Modern Library Paperbacks:** BAC to Mrs. Edward Quayle, Nov. 11, 1954, Box 28, RHR. *The Snake Pit* was one of the first.
448 **egghead credentials:** "You Meet Such Interesting PEOPLE," *PW,* Dec. 4, 1954, clipping book, Box 68, CP. See also *PW,* July 30, 1956.
449 **"the most able man":** SC diary, Aug. 16, 1954.
449 **"clouded":** SC diary, Aug. 18, 1954.
449 **Rumor had it:** SC diary, June 14, 1954. The progression of the illness is noted in both SC and BAC's diaries. For Pauline's obituaries, see *PW,* Aug. 21, 1954; *NYT* and *NY Herald Tribune,* Aug. 5, 1954, all in Box 68, CP.
450 **Only in February:** *Today's Secretary,* Feb. 1954, Box 68, CP.
450 **had to wire Ted Geisel:** BAC to TSG, June 15, 1954, Box 27, RHR.
450 **"crushing":** BAC diary, June 17, 1954.
450 ***thrombocytopenic purpura:*** BAC diary has Pauline's illness as *thrombopenic purpura*. The proper term is *thrombocytopenic purpura*. He also said it was "always fatal," but that is no longer the case, with steroid treatment. I have been unable to determine how commonly patients died of the disease in 1954.
450 **"when the team":** SC diary, June 24, 1954.
450 **"I can't quite tell you":** BAC to TSG, June 22, 1954, Box 27, RHR.

450 **"one of my favorite people":** TSG to BAC, July 4, 1954, Box 27, RHR.

451 **"blessed relief":** BAC diary, Aug. 4, 1954.

451 **"That must have been":** DSK to BAC, Aug. 15, 1954, Box 26, RHR.

451 **"This place will never":** BAC to Pat Klopfer and DSK, Aug. 6, 1954, Box 26, RHR.

451 **GOODBYE:** BAC clipping book, Box 68, CP.

451 **sold so poorly:** Sheaffer, *O'Neill: Son and Artist,* 664.

451 **"beloved wife":** Sheaffer, *O'Neill: Son and Artist,* 663. CMON was born on Dec. 28, 1888.

451 **publish the "secret play":** The phone calls with CMON are noted in BAC's diary. BAC refers to *LDJIN* as EON's "secret play" in July 1, 1954, entry. Among other justifications for publishing, CMON would later say it was Gene Jr. who had requested the delay; with Gene Jr.'s death, there was no reason not to publish. Sheaffer, *O'Neill: Son and Artist,* 634; see also Commins, *What Is an Editor?* 57–61.

452 **"Ever since I spoke":** BAC to CMON, July 6, 1954, RHCC.

453 **"In a funny way":** Anna Crouse to author, June 14, 2007.

453 **"was magnificent":** SC diary, July 6, 1954, courtesy FCB. Copies of BAC's letter exist in the RHR and in the SCP. Small differences—keystroke mistakes, for example—exist in the two: clearly, they were typed separately.

At Princeton are two other papers: a handwritten copy of the paragraph re SC in SC's own hand and a typewritten copy of the same paragraph. In each, the paragraph is numbered "five" instead of "four," either a mistake or an indication that a paragraph BAC originally dictated as part of the letter was deleted before it was finalized and sent. On each copy of the paragraph Dorothy Commins has appended a note: the typed sheet says "S. Commins's transcription of a letter written by Bennett Cerf to CMON, July 6, 1954," and on the handwritten paper, "Copy of Bennett Cerf's letter to Carlotta."

However, at the bottom of the handwritten copy, in BAC's unmistakable hand, is written "OK!" and signed "Bennett." Why BAC would write that on SC's copy is unclear. It would seem strange for him to want to cast an eye over SC's copy simply to ensure he'd copied it correctly. Had BAC discussed the paragraph with SC, given it to him to look over, *before* sending the final version to CMON? Like the multiple Chinese colophons that must be deciphered to appreciate the history of a scroll painting, this requires pondering—and isn't fully deciphered yet!

453 **were in the audience:** BAC diary.

454 **Invitations had been forwarded:** WF had asked SC to forward invitations to home addresses for him. Box 1, AEP.

454 **"superb":** BAC diary, Nov. 26, 1953.

454 **"tremendous":** RKH to SC, Oct. 26, 1953, in Brodsky and Hamblin, eds., *Faulkner,* vol. 2, 122.

454 **"powerful":** DSK to Harold Raymond, Nov. 30, 1953, Box 22, RHR.

454 **"most important":** BAC to "Dear Bookseller," Box 68, CP.

454 **Bennett thought the firm:** BAC to DSK, Aug. 27, 1954, Box 26, RHR.

455 **"new departure":** Carvel Collins, "War and Peace and Mr. Faulkner," *NYTBR,* Aug. 1, 1954.

455 **"One would rather not say":** Brendan Gill, "Fifth Gospel," *TNY,* Aug. 28, 1954.

455 **"Gill is an outrageous bastard":** BAC to DSK, Aug. 27, 1954, Box 26, RHR.

455 **found succor in Saxe:** Karl, *William Faulkner,* 873–74.

455 **Her name was Jean Stein:** Karl, *William Faulkner,* 874–75.

455 **handsome in his finery:** SC to WF, July 29, 1954, Box 1, AEP.

456 **"For hours [he] particularized":** This is the first time any parts of SC's 1954 diary entries have been reproduced. These date from Wednesday, Aug. 25, through Sunday, Aug. 29. I have cut to avoid repetition and extraneous detail. Courtesy FCB.

457 **familiar green office:** "Doom," in "The Talk of the Town," *TNY,* Feb. 28, 1953, 18.

457 **"Memo to: Saxe Commins":** WF, *Big Woods: The Hunting Stories of William Faulkner* (New York: RH, 1955), dedication.

CHAPTER 29: ENERGY

458 **"kindest-looking man":** Clara Bow to BAC, Jan. 1, 1959, RHCC.

458 **never mediated by notes:** BAC to Anne Parker, Nov. 23, 1954, Box 27, RHR.

458 **"the equivalent of a panhandler":** Jules Feiffer to author, Jan. 6, 2004.

459 **The store survived:** Stuart Brent to author, May 5, 2005. It remained into the 1990s.

459 **"unless he wanted to be":** Horace Manges to Geoffrey T. Hellman, Series 2, Box 12, GTHP.

459 **"embarrassed":** SC to GTH, Series 2, Box 12, GTHP.

459 **nearly 90,000 copies:** Hanover House press release, May 1954, Box 68, CP.

459 **"rare ranking storyteller":** John Hutchens, *NY Herald Tribune,* n.d., Box 68, CP.

460 **"I have always been":** Mac Hyman to BAC, Dec. 3, 1954, Box 28, RHR.

460 **"Energy":** Orville Prescott, "Books of the Times," *NYT,* Nov. 17, 1954, Box 68, CP.

460 **"Vitamin B. Cerf":** Sylvia Fine Kaye, "Intravenous Observed," poem. Quoted in BAC, Trade Winds, *SRL,* Mar. 22, 1952.

461 **tongue only half in cheek:** A year after the *Encyclopedia of Modern American Humor* review, RH published a memoir about the critic's role, *The Five Dollar Gold Piece,* by one Orville Prescott. See Box 69, CP. Publishing, like most businesses, is often greased by quid pro quo.

461 **Office gossip had it:** Haydn, *Words & Faces,* 89.

461 **"the first-person singular":** SC diary, Dec. 14, 1954, courtesy FCB.

461 **"to keep careful notes":** David McDowell to Richard M. Nixon, Mar. 6, 1953, Box 1559, RHR.

461 **"Your idea of keeping":** Richard M. Nixon to David McDowell, Mar. 14, 1953, Box 1559, RHR.

461 **McDowell was summoned:** We have two accounts of McDowell's dismissal. See BAC OH, 878–79; Haydn, *Words and Faces,* 89–90. Haydn does not identify the editor in question, mentioning only BAC and DSK; BAC's recollection features all three partners.

462 **Two days later, they lent:** Haydn and BAC both describe McDowell incident happening on one day; BAC's diary speaks of a "big confab on his new house & future status" on Oct. 6 and helping him "solve his real estate problem" on Oct. 8. On Jan. 23, 1957, when McDowell informed BAC he was resigning to form his own firm, BAC reacted in one word: "Hooray!" Box 12, CP.

462 **His brief was to develop:** Paul Lapolla to author, May 29, 2003.

462 **With 120 on staff:** BAC to GTH. New building: DSK to GTH, Series 2, Box 12, GTHP.

462 **significantly curtailed:** SC diary, Dec. 23, 1954, courtesy FCB.

462 **finally had to tell Saxe:** BAC diary, Dec. 23, 1954, CP.

462 **How do I deserve to be:** Jules Feiffer to author, Jan. 6, 2004. Many former RH staff and authors reported similar reactions, and I felt likewise, on touring the building three times.

462 **His new boss was absorbed:** Haydn, *Words and Faces,* 81–83. I have followed his storyline but the words are my own, unless quoted. Some of his memories are not exact. For instance, he states that he shared an office with WF for two weeks; as BAC's diary makes clear, it was one week.

464 **small, newly painted closet:** Jean Stein to author, July 7, 2003.

464 **"fallen estate":** SC diary, Jan. 10, 1955, courtesy FCB.

464 **his literary executor:** Apr. 13, 1951, in Brodsky and Hamblin, eds., *Faulkner,* vol. 2, xvii.

464 **deep outrage:** Jean Stein to author, July 7, 2003.

465 **"there are ways of fighting":** Tim Weiner, "Budd Schulberg, 'On the Waterfront' Writer, Dies at 95," *NYT,* Aug. 6, 2009.

465 **Yet in fact:** On the history of *On the Waterfront,* see BWS, introduction, *On the Waterfront* (New York: Donald I. Fine, 1987). See also James T. Fisher, *On the Irish Waterfront: The Crusader, the Movie, and the Soul of the Port of New York* (Ithaca: Cornell University Press, 2009).

465 **fallen off the back of a ship:** SC, "Story of On the Waterfront," Box 12, SCP; FCB to author, Nov. 30, 2002; Commins, *What Is an Editor?* 110–14.

465 **"Sister":** Bruccoli, *O'Hara Concern,* 222–23.

465 **gold cigarette case:** PC, "These I Remember: Some Holiday Reminiscences," *Good Housekeeping,* Dec. 1, 1955, courtesy CBC and JFC.

466 **first-class all the way:** For Hawaii photos, see Box 69, CP. See "What's New . . . by Phyllis Cerf," *Newsday,* Mar. 10, 1955; BAC, Trade Winds, *SRL,* Apr. 9, 1955. Hawaii became a state in Aug. 1959.

466 **about $123,000:** See Allen A. Kaufman to JAM, Jan. 17, 1956, JAMP.

466 **"nice," polite, entrenched:** BAC, Trade Winds, *SRL,* Apr. 9, 1955.

467 **"Originally, eleven chapters":** JAM and A. Grove Day, *Rascals in Paradise* (New York: RH, 1957).

468 **There'd be no second try:** BAC submitted piece on Oct. 25, 1943, and Ross rejected it on Nov. 1, 1943. Ross wrote to a colleague about it. Harold Ross to Gus Lobrano, late 1943, Box 31, *TNY* records, NYPL.

468 **"crassness":** Harold Ross to Mr. (Hawley) Truax, Nov. 19, 1945, Box 31, *TNY* records, NYPL. Ross instructed his secretary to copy BAC on the letter to Truax, but actually to send only the copy to BAC, not the original to Truax.

468 **the profile was back on:** BAC diary, Aug. 19, 1954. For Aug. 1945 correspondence with Frances Merriam, RH publicity director, see GTHP. On Nov. 20, 1945,

BAC wrote to GTH, "I will be ready to get to work on the profile whenever you are." It is unclear why the idea was shelved for nine years.

468 **"privately circulated":** GTH mentions the "sex books." In a visit to BAC's house after PC's death, I viewed the shelf: the *Satyricon* and *Poetica Erotica* are from my notes, not GTH's.

469 **cultivated an elite:** On GTH, see Gill, *Here at the New Yorker,* 355–66; also Ved Mehta to author, Feb. 1, 2013. Mehta was a staff writer at *TNY* and a colleague of GTH's.

469 **"right on the surface":** For interview notes from which quotations and attributions in this section are taken, see Series 2, Box 12, GTHP.

470 **"dueling":** Dec. 21, 1954, BAC diary, Box 12, CP; PC's reaction per GTH notes and also PC OH, Columbia.

470 **"interviewing":** Mar. 12, 1956, Box 69, CP.

470 **"It's okay":** Exchange from GTH.

470 **plugs could be tricky:** Robert Connors, "Cerf Tries to Defend Plug," *Columbus Dispatch,* Dec. 30, 1955, Box 69, CP; Mark Goodson to BAC, June 30, 1954, Box 26, RHR.

470 **"Sometimes I think":** AAK to BAC, Dec. 16, 1954, Box 27, RHR. The note references BAC, Trade Winds, *SRL,* Dec. 18, 1954.

470 **"being a celebrity today":** BAC, "Endorsements, Inc.," Trade Winds, *SRL,* June 16, 1956. BAC appeared on George Gobel's NBC comedy show on Jan. 28, 1956, per BAC diary; he played a publisher, i.e., himself, and was rewarded by NBC owner RCA with an expensive TV set. David P. O'Malley to BAC, Jan. 30, 1956, Box 69, CP.

471 **"a superior product":** AE to BAC, Apr. 1, 1954, Box 27, RHR.

471 **"your new book":** BAC to Ian Fleming, Apr. 2, 1954, Box 27, RHR.

471 **"very anxious":** BAC to David Higham, Nov. 11, 1955, Box 23, RHR.

471 **marquee names:** In 1940 BAC had negotiated a contract to publish Tennessee Williams's first play, *Battle of Angels*, but the play was a failure and never published. When TW's next play, *The Glass Menagerie,* was staged in 1944, it was a smash hit, but by that time Williams very much wanted to be published by his close friend James Laughlin, the founder of New Directions. BAC insisted on exercising the option in the contract for *Battle of Angels* regarding TW's next play (that is, *Glass Menagerie*), so RH published *Menagerie* in 1945, but agreed that New Directions would publish all of TW's future work. However, BAC did eventually accede to TW's desire for *Menagerie* to be handled by his friend, and in 1949, New Directions reissued the play and has published it ever since. BAC to TW, Sept. 4, 1940, BAC to TW, Apr. 2, 1945, both RHCC; and Ellen F. Brown to author, May 22, 2019. Brown is writing a biography of TW.

472 **"very silly":** BAC to Barney Rosset, June 24, 1954, Grove Press Records, Syracuse University, courtesy A. D. Goff.

472 **"farm team":** BAC quoted in Haydn, *Words & Faces,* 16; see also 240.

472 ***they'd* be the fortunate publisher:** For the story of *The Godfather*'s publication, see William Targ, *Indecent Pleasures* (New York: Macmillan, 1975), 112. Between his second RH novel and *The Godfather,* Puzo published a children's book and a pulpy revenge thriller under a pseudonym.

472 **major bestseller:** On *Battle Cry,* see Hackett and Burke, *80 Years of Best Sellers, 1895–1975,* 160.

473 **"Get out":** Haydn, *Words & Faces,* 255–56. The editor claimed Uris wanted the money to offset the loss of a house bought in Israel; he also claimed Uris had to flee when war broke out, although Uris's obituaries mention his working as a correspondent in Israel for several years. Haydn has Uris requesting $12,000, but he likely misremembered. In 1957 BAC had it as $8,000. BAC to James Russell, Jan. 10, 1957, Box 35, RHR. In his diary for Jan. 7, 1957, AAK notes BAC also told him $8,000. Per AAK, Uris wanted the money to reimburse half his expenses. For the figures for the original advance from RH and MGM, see AAK diary, Box 632, Alfred A. Knopf Inc. Records, RC, University of Texas at Austin (hereafter AAKR).

473 **"In our business":** AAK diary, Apr. 20, 1954, Box 632, AAKR.

473 **"The Hollywood producer":** Norman Mailer to author, May 28, 2004.

474 **embark on the embarrassing odyssey:** In *Advertisements for Myself,* Mailer recounts his version of *The Deer Park* publication story. The woman is described as a "call girl"; to the author Mailer described her as a "starlet." Mailer, *Advertisements for Myself* (New York: Perigee Books, 1981), 198–201; see also Haydn, *Words and Faces,* 100, 263–64.

474 **"a highly intelligent":** Dec. 16, 1954, Box 632, AAKR. From the entry, it is unclear exactly how BWK and Pat viewed the manuscript; AAK speaks of BWK blaming Pat. However, elsewhere AAK says

that "Blanche was eager for us to take it over." See AAK's unpublished memoirs, 1093, AAKR. He also talks about a cocktail party BWK gave to which Mailer and his wife were invited, after the book had been sold to Putnam. Mailer offered to bet Knopf the book would sell over 100,000 copies; Knopf said he declined to take him up on the wager. However, two letters from Mailer inserted into the Knopf memoir make it clear that Mailer thought he had agreed to it. Mailer to AAK, Oct. 8, 1955, 1095; Mailer to BWK, Oct. 10, 1955, 1094, AAKR.

The order in which the manuscript made the rounds of publishers is not exactly clear. I have assumed, given the Styron-Mailer connection, that it came to RH before circulating among the others. From the dating of the AAK and BAC diary entries, it *is* clear it went to BAC before it went to BWK.

474 **put in a good word:** On Styron interceding, see Mailer, *Advertisements for Myself,* 199.

474 **"very dirty":** BAC diary, Nov. 25, 1954, Box 12, CP.

474 **"This book will set":** Norman Mailer to author, May 28, 2004. Lee Mortimer reported that BAC predicted that "it would have government censors over the book industry again." Mortimer added: "Another famous old line publisher's comment was 'it will set back the art of love-making 2,000 years.'" In the muddy world of off-the-record remarks, it is entirely possible that "another publisher" was also BAC. The pronouncement seems too close to the remark Mailer attributed to BAC to be coincidental. See Lee Mortimer, "New York Confidential," *The Mirror,* Sept. 2, 1955, Box 69, CP.

474 **"You'll bring down":** Walter Minton to author, Oct. 23, 2006.

475 **"Some reviewers":** See Lee Mortimer, "New York Confidential," *The Mirror,* Sept. 2, 1955, Box 69, CP.

475 **50,000 copies:** Cy Rembar to Norman Mailer, May 31, 1956, and May 2, 1957, Box 740.7-9, Norman Mailer Papers, RC.

475 **with open hostility:** Rose Styron to author, Nov. 12, 2003.

476 **"I always wanted":** Mailer quoted by WS to author, Mar. 3, 2003.

476 **"You're a dentist":** Norman Mailer to author, May 28, 2004. Much of this passage quotes Mailer's words directly, albeit in the third person.

476 **"Every Jewish parent":** Mailer quoted by WS to author, Mar. 3, 2003. Hiram Haydn's version differs in interesting details. Haydn remembered Mailer goading BAC all evening with "aspersions on his manhood," calling him "Sally Cerf," and finally daring him to "step outside." Despite the difference in age, BAC walked to the front door and stood outside, willing to fight. Mailer didn't follow, content with having humiliated BAC. Haydn, *Words & Faces,* 100. Interviewed by the author, Mailer explosively denied calling BAC "Sally" or challenging him to fight. William Styron did not recall the "Sally" insult or BAC going outside, but it is possible Haydn's memory was less clouded by alcohol than those of the others.

CHAPTER 30: FAMILIES AND FIELDTRIPS

477 **Young children:** Horace Manges to Geoffrey T. Hellman, Series 2, Box 12, GTHP.

477 **"were together":** BAC OH, 2.

477 **"fine thing":** Cerfboard, "The Kids Come Back," Aug. 21, 1955, Box 69, CP; BAC, Trade Winds, *SRL,* Apr. 9, 1949.

477 **Chris liked featuring:** CBC to author, Dec. 18, 2002.

477 **"enough attention":** CBC to BAC, n.d. (1947–early 1950s), Box 7, CP.

478 **didn't say hello fast enough:** CBC to author, Dec. 18, 2002.

478 **resolved *he* wouldn't be:** JFC to author, Jan. 19, 2005.

478 **so seldom was she mentioned:** CBC to author, June 9, 2003.

478 **would come to meet:** CBC to author, June 9, July 31, 2003, and Feb. 25, 2005; see also BAC diary, Mar. 29, Apr. 17, Nov. 24, 1955; Mary and Carrie to BAC, June 17, 1957; BAC to Mary and Carrie, June 18, 1957, Box 33, RHR. When BAC was young, Mary and Carrie were not in his diaries.

479 **Herbert was pursuing:** SC diary, May 24, 1955, courtesy FCB.

479 **long talk at Mt. Kisco:** BAC diary, July 4, 1955.

479 **became best friends:** JFC and Peter Gabel to author.

479 **"Fosberg":** e.g., BAC diary, Mar. 29, 1956.

479 **needed a family to escape to:** Freddy Espy Plimpton (hereafter FEP) to author, Jan. 20, 2008; also, CBC to author, numerous times.

480 **more than $300,000:** Jan. 13, 1956, BAC diary.

480 **"a brilliant technician":** BAC, Trade Winds, *SRL,* Oct. 1, 1955.

480 **"put pearls on a string":** *AR,* 221.

480 **bestselling novel of the year, and film rights:** Hackett and Burke, *80 Years of Best*

Sellers, 1895–1975, 170; Feb 21 & 28, 1956, BAC diary.

480 **It wasn't lost on him:** William Brinkley to BAC, Feb. 26, 1956, Box 29, RHR.

480 **far more consequential deal:** Jan. 6, 1956, BAC diary.

481 **"helluva job":** BAC diary, July 29, 1955.

481 **swiftly hired an editor:** BAC to Joe Geiss, Feb. 20, Apr. 30, 1956, and Geiss to BAC, Apr. 23, 1956, Box 29, RHR.

481 **followed Cass's advice:** Cass Canfield to BAC, Aug. 10, 1956; BAC to Stanley Hunnewell, Oct. 11, 1956; BAC to Canfield, Mar. 9, 1956, all Box 29, RHR.

481 **would help out on Bennett's books:** On the role of BK, see BAC diary, Apr. 10, 1956.

481 **who trusted no one:** PC to author, Dec. 23, 2003.

481 **"spasm":** Nov. 30, 1955, and Jan. 9, Nov. 9, 1956, BAC diary, Box 12, CP.

481 **Walt Disney had spent:** "What's New . . . by Phyllis Cerf," *Newsday,* Feb. 23, Mar. 1, 1956, courtesy CBC and JFC.

481 **"Absolutely great":** Jan. 24, 1956, BAC diary.

482 **met with the accountant:** BAC diary, Apr. 20 & 21, June 22 & 24, 1953.

482 **the firm's officers:** *PW,* Mar. 24, 1956.

482 ***The Straight and Narrow Path* had arrived:** BAC OH, 499–500; BAC diary, Apr. 1956; Haydn, *Words & Faces,* 95–96. The quotes come from Haydn, the backstory from BAC.

482 **outline very different views:** BAC claims to have "screamed with laughter," then "got scared" at the last minute; Haydn says BAC thought the book a "cheap and vulgar attack."

482 **It was Bennett who handled:** BAC OH, 496–98.

483 **Anxious to get on:** BAC, Trade Winds, *SRL,* Oct. 6, 1956.

483 **After a whirlwind day:** On BAC's European activities, see BAC diary, May 9–June 19, 1956, and separate travel journal, Box 12, CP.

483 **297,000 copies:** For ML statistics, see "The Modern Library Bestsellers" list, Box 382, RHR.

483 **"First":** Maugham quoted in BAC, "Trade Winds," *SRL,* Oct. 6, 1956.

484 **"You know, Saxe":** BAC to SC, May 18, 1956, SCP.

484 **paying some of his expenses:** BAC to Cass Canfield, Mar. 9, 1956, Box 29, RHR. The sum was $3,750.

485 **nagging doubt:** Rose Styron confirmed this to me: "Despite Bennett's being a man of such gregariousness and accomplishment . . . he didn't feel himself on an equal footing intellectually with some of his authors. . . . He was never confident of his own intellect." Rose Styron to author, Nov. 12, 2003.

485 **"There is probably no thrill":** "What's New . . . by Phyllis Cerf," *Newsday,* June 28, 1956, courtesy CBC and JFC.

CHAPTER 31: FEDS AND NYMPHETS

486 **"the Pinko Publisher":** BAC OH, 417. Sokolsky friendship and story behind *The FBI Story:* BAC OH, 416–23, 862–65.

486 **Bennett chose the Stork:** The lunch took place on June 8, 1955, the Lotos Club meeting on Sept. 29, 1955. BAC diary, Box 12, CP.

487 **it didn't make waves:** Lowenthal's book *The Federal Bureau of Investigation* was published by William Sloan Assoc. See Curt Gentry, *J. Edgar Hoover: The Man and His Secrets* (New York: W. W. Norton, 1991), 386–87.

487 **"the fight against Communism":** FBI files quoted in Athan G. Theoharis and John Stuart Cox, *The Boss: J. Edgar Hoover and the Great American Inquisition* (Philadelphia: Temple University Press, 1988), 310.

487 **thoroughly vetted:** Gentry, *J. Edgar Hoover,* 446. In a memo to Clyde Tolson on May 2, 1956, filed in 62-102693-38 and obtained as part of the author's FOIA search of BAC's 100-369422 FBI file, Nichols notes that BAC was to pay Whitehead for six months, but payment for up to one more month was necessary to finish the project. The memo discusses the publication timeframe and gives Nichols's reassurance as to the manuscript's "shape." Whitehead joined the *NY Herald Tribune* rather than return to the Associated Press; after the success of the book, he went freelance.

487 **the FBI delivered:** BAC diary, Box 12, CP.

487 **hadn't pleased:** Paul Lapolla to author, May 29, 2003.

487 **"a mass of wonderful information":** BAC, "Notes After Reading 310 Pages of THE F.B.I. ADVENTURE," June 27, 1956, Box 30, RHR. The title was later changed.

487 **"We are delighted":** BAC to J. Edgar Hoover, June 28, 1956, Box 30, RHR.

488 **"a naïve puff job":** Lapolla to author, May 29, 2003.

488 **Bennett would be embarrassed:** Lapolla to author, May 29, 2003

488 **Using Bennett's report:** Lapolla to author, May 29, 2003.

488 **earned a bonus:** Lapolla to author, May 29, 2003.

488 **The attorney general had read:** Paul Lapolla to BAC and DSK, memo, July 25, 1956, Box 30, RHR.

488 **Warner Brothers bought film rights:** BAC diary, Oct. 26, 1956. There was a second deal on Nov. 28, 1956. See also J. Edgar Hoover to BAC, Dec. 3, 1956, RHCC. The second deal Bennett arranged involved Schenley Distillers whiskey baron Lewis Rosenstiel buying 25,000 copies to give to public libraries. Nichols subsequently left the FBI to work for Rosenstiel.

488 **"highly readable":** Cabell Phillips, "Meet Mr. Hoover's Men," *NYTBR,* Dec. 16, 1956.

488 **"one of the most absorbing":** Charles Poore, "Books of the Times," *NYT,* Dec. 11, 1956.

488 **"personal interest":** J. Edgar Hoover to BAC, Nov. 30, 1956, RHCC. On John Charles Daly, see J. Edgar Hoover to BAC, Dec. 3, 1956, RHCC.

488 **disconcertingly eye-catching:** Photostat of *NYT* books page with wrongly impositioned ad is in BAC's FBI file, as is letter from Nichols to BAC, Dec. 4, 1956.

489 **"Never, in the entire history":** ad in *NYT,* Dec. 15, 1956, Box 69, CP.

489 **second-biggest nonfiction title:** Hackett and Burke, *80 Years of Best Sellers, 1895–1975,* p. 172. On the same page, a sale of 173,000 copies is mentioned; BAC says 175,000 copies were in print. BAC diary, Dec. 19, 1956.

489 **"pretty silly things":** On revelation of FBI file, see BAC OH, 422. Per BAC diary, the visit to Nichols took place Nov. 2, 1955, a year before publication; in the OH BAC says it happened just prior to publication.

489 **file had been officially closed:** A. M. Jones to Mr. Nichols, FBI office memorandum, May 14, 1957. One can speculate as to why HQ overruled the N.Y. office: Might it be linked to Lela Rogers and Hoover?

On the second page of BAC's file, after his parents, education, and two wives are listed, is a redacted box before his career is profiled. One can assume the space would have been occupied by the name of a relative, e.g., Lela or Ginger Rogers, or the name of a lover. On page 14, the section marked "Relatives" lists "Wife—PHYLLIS FRASER"; then there is a redacted box; then "Former Wife—SYLVIA SIDNEY." My inclination is to assume Lela's name was redacted. On page 15 of the file, discussing BAC's marriage, it is stated that "[Confidential] informant advised that FRASER is the cousin of GINGER ROGERS." A line has been drawn through the latter.

In Apr. 1957, BAC's name reappears in FBI files when permission was granted to interview him in connection with the Bureau's investigation into Alfred Stern—husband of a redacted but unforgettable Martha Dodd. FBI internal memo, Apr. 25, 1957, "cc 100369422 (Cerf)."

489 **"fundamental differences":** J. Edgar Hoover to BAC, Mar. 1, 1957, RHCC.

489 **Whether Hoover was:** Anthony Summers maintains that Hoover was an antsemite; Richard Gid Powers maintains that he was not. See Summers, *Official and Confidential: The Secret Life of J. Edgar Hoover* (New York: Putnam, 1993), 55–56; Powers, *J. Edgar Hoover: The Life and the Power* (New York: Free Press, 1987), 521–22.

489 **"It will be useful!":** BAC to J. Edgar Hoover, Mar. 5, 1957, RHCC.

490 **"Well, I don't know":** On *Lolita*'s passage through RH, see William Styron, "The Book on Lolita," *TNY,* Sept. 4, 1995, 33.

490 **Bennett stayed up:** *Lolita* reading recorded in BAC diary. Despite the aid of several capable librarians in the RBML at Columbia, I was unable to decipher BAC's one-word reaction to the book noted in the diary.

491 **or so Hiram Haydn:** Walter Minton, the eventual publisher of *Lolita,* told me his part of the story on Oct. 23, 2006. Haydn writes, "Either Donald or Bennett was in favor of taking it, the other opposed. I think . . . Bennett . . . was positive." See Haydn, *Words & Faces,* 264–66. I have found no mention of the book in BAC's OH or papers.

491 **"sheer pornography":** Brian Boyd, *Vladimir Nabokov: The American Years* (Princeton: Princeton University Press, 1991), 262. The book contains an excellent account of the trials and tribulations of *Lolita,* including the publishers who turned it down (264).

491 **had been terrified by it:** Boyd, *Vladimir Nabokov,* 299.

491 **He didn't approach RH:** "I have never had any dealings with them." Nabokov to JE, Mar. 5, 1957, in Matthew J. Bruccoli and Dmitri Nabokov, eds., *Vladimir Nabokov: Selected Letters, 1940–1977* (New York: Harcourt Brace Jovanovich, 1989), 206.

491 **had told Linscott:** See Boyd, *Vladimir Nabokov,* 40, note 16.

491 **Marboro Books:** Minton to author, Oct. 23, 2006.

492 **"nauseated":** Haydn, *Words & Faces,* 264 (his exact words were "revolted to the point of nausea").

492 **"loathsome":** Haydn quoted in Styron, "Book on Lolita."

492 **"it would not have been hard":** Minton to author, Oct. 23, 2006.

493 **her pretty picture in *Time:*** "The *Lolita* Case," *Time,* Nov. 17, 1958, 102.

493 **Hiram had first sat down to talk:** BAC diary, Box 12, CP.

493 **her closest school friend:** Anne C. Heller, *Ayn Rand and the World She Made* (New York: Nan A. Talese/Doubleday, 2009), 26.

493 **an act of determined reinvention:** For Ayn Rand background, see biographical note, Ayn Rand Papers, LoC, 2.

CHAPTER 32: IDEAL PUBLISHER

494 **talk about Ayn Rand:** On the AR/Weidman discussion, see Mar. 7, 1956, BAC diary, Box 12, CP.

494 **pitch-perfect Gothamese:** For Jerry Weidman background, John Weidman to author, Oct. 30, 2006; see also Weidman, *Praying for Rain;* Mel Gussow, "Jerome Weidman Dies at 85; Author of Novels and Plays," *NYT,* Oct. 7, 1998.

494 **"The first American street-smart novelist":** Alistair Cooke, "Letter from America," BBC broadcast, Oct. 1998, http://news.bbc.co.uk/2/hi/programmes/letter_from_america_/3208004.stm.

494 ***I Can Get It for You Wholesale:*** Weidman's debut was made into a hit musical a quarter century later; it featured the Broadway debut of another ambitious young New Yorker: Barbra Streisand.

494 **moved from S&S:** While writing his second novel, Weidman worked as Max Schuster's assistant.

494 **how he and Weidman had met:** Haydn, *Words & Faces,* 103.

495 **"one of the most uneven writers":** BAC OH, 978.

495 **the wait was worth it:** On the Weidman deal, see May 1, 1957, BAC diary, Box 12, CP.

495 **raves and great sales:** BAC diary, June 13, 1958. For Haydn's and DSK's thoughts on the final revision of the manuscript, see Haydn to Weidman, July 3, 1957, Box 13, Folder 3, Jerome Weidman Collection, RC. BAC is not referenced.

495 **thirteen-year-old son John:** John Weidman would become a librettist/writer, collaborating with Stephen Sondheim and Susan Stroman on major Broadway shows; mentor to Lin-Manuel Miranda.

495 **"in this wonderful series":** Jerome Weidman to BAC, Jan. 8, 1959, Box 7, Folder 5, Weidman Collection,.

495 **"he liked living":** Peggy Weidman to author, Oct. 3, 2003.

496 **word-of-mouth phenomenon:** Hiram Haydn to Ross Baker, May 27, 1957; Baker to Haydn, May 28, 1957, Box 436, RHR. *The Fountainhead* was signed by Knopf, but they cancelled the contract after Rand missed two deadlines. Heller, *Ayn Rand and the World She Made,* 106, 122.

496 **"to keep Ayn Rand happy":** Haydn, *Words & Faces,* 256.

496 **piercing intensity:** Haydn, *Words & Faces,* 257.

496 **"What are your premises?":** Haydn, *Words & Faces,* 257.

497 **"the concept of man":** Wolfgang Saxon, "Ayn Rand, 'Fountainhead' Author, Dies," *NYT,* Mar. 7, 1982, 36.

497 **Grays didn't interest her:** "The Life and Views of Ayn Rand, Capitalism's Martyred Hero," *The Economist,* Oct. 24, 2009, 95.

497 **she learned the lessons well:** On Rand and her philosophy, I consulted Haydn, *Words & Faces,* 256–62; BAC OH, 944–52; DSK OH, 79; Heller, *Ayn Rand and the World She Made;* Saxon, "Ayn Rand, 'Fountainhead' Author, Dies"; as well as Michael S. Berliner, ed., *Letters of Ayn Rand* (New York: Dutton, 1995); Edward Rothstein, "Considering the Last Romantic, Ayn Rand, at 100," *NYT,* Feb. 2, 2005; Harriet Rubin, "The Literature of Capitalism: Ayn Rand's Defense of Success Influenced Greenspan and Others," *NYT,* Sept. 15, 2007, C1, C8; "The Life and Views of Ayn Rand, Capitalism's Martyred Hero," *Economist,* 95–96; Thomas Mallon, "Life and Letters: Possessed: Did Ayn Rand's Cult Outstrip Her Canon?" *TNY,* Nov. 9, 2009, 61–67; and Charles Murray, "Who Is Ayn Rand?" *Claremont Review of Books,* June 1, 2010.

498 **She liked the confidence:** Heller, *Ayn Rand and the World She Made,* 273.

498 **perceptive and on target:** Heller, *Ayn Rand and the World She Made,* 273.

498 **"They spoke as I would":** Barbara Branden quoted in Heller, *Ayn Rand and the World She Made,* 273.

499 **"remarkable":** DSK OH, 79.

499 **"wonderful way":** BAC OH, 945.

499 **a short black cape:** Haydn, *Words & Faces,* 257.

499 **"Ayn Rand . . . picks Random House":** BAC diary, Mar. 29, 1956, Box 12, CP.

499 **Five boxes:** Alan Collins to Hiram Haydn, Mar. 29, 1956, Box 436, RHR.

499 **"endless":** BAC diary, Apr. 22, 1956.

500 **down to a thousand pages:** BAC diary, Apr. 27, 1956.

500 **"best seller stamped":** Haydn, *Words & Faces,* 261.
500 **calculated exactly what they wanted:** Alan Collins to BAC, May 2, 1956, Box 29, RHR.
500 **maximum $20,000:** Alan Collins to BAC, May 2, 1956, Box 29, RHR.
500 **recognized the importance:** Barbara Branden quoted in Heller, *Ayn Rand and the World She Made,* 274.
500 **"This is life":** Nathaniel Branden, *Judgment Day,* quoted in Heller, *Ayn Rand and the World She Made,* 274. It is unclear which date this reflects: on Apr. 27, 1956, BAC speaks of Rand in the office and the firm being willing to publish if the book is no more than 1,000 pages; on May 4, 1956, BAC writes, "Signed Ayn Rand for Atlas Shrugged" but there is no indication that she was actually in the office. The "signing" could indicate agreement over the phone. See BAC diary.
500 **insisted that she be consulted:** Alan Collins to DSK, July 25, 1956; DSK to Collins, July 27, 1956, Box 29, RHR.
501 **"very peculiar":** On the meeting of AR and PC, see BAC OH, 948.
501 **Alan Greenspan:** Alan Greenspan to BAC, Nov. 15, 1957; BAC to Greenspan, Nov. 20, 1957, Box 33, RHR.
501 **Rand's circle for dinners:** See, e.g., Nov. 11, 1957, and Oct. 6, 1958, BAC diaries, Box 12, CP.
501 **"trot her out":** BAC OH, 946.
501 **lunches could extend:** See, e.g., BAC diary, Aug. 22, 1956.
501 **"exciting" presence:** BAC to AR, Sept. 10, 1957, Box 35, RHR.
501 **"a very good brain":** BAC OH, 947.
502 **"You sound as wonderful":** Ruth Alexander to BAC, Sept. 16, 1957, Box 32, RHR.
502 **"noteworthy":** RH press release, Sept. 7, 1956, Box 69, CP.
503 **"What a book!":** BAC diary, Mar. 28–31, 1957, Box 12, CP.
504 **would put readers off:** BAC OH, 950.
504 **Rand strode in:** Apr 1, 1957, BAC diary.
504 **"*And I mean it*":** AR, *Atlas Shrugged* (New York: RH, 1957), n.p. (penultimate printed page).
504 ***less seven cents per copy:*** BAC to Rand, May 9, June 4, 1957, Box 35, RHR.
504 **arranged a promotional deal:** Ruth Hill to BAC, Sept. 6, 1957, Box 32, RHR. The deal was arranged on May 10, 1957. On agreeing a price with AR, see BAC diary, May 3, 1957, Box 12, CP.
505 **"denounced as a reactionary":** *Chicago Tribune,* May 5, 1957, Box 69, CP.
505 **given the very first bound copy:** BAC diary, Aug. 15, 1957, Box 12, CP.
505 **two small yellow lemons:** CW to author, May 15, 2007; Box 35, RHR.
506 **special leather-bound:** BAC to AR, Nov. 15, 1957, Box 35, RHR.
506 **Bennett buttered up:** BAC to Lela E. Rogers, Sept. 16, 1957, Box 32, RHR.
506 **"arrogant egotism":** Ralph C. Champlin, vice president of Pennsylvania Railroad, to BAC, Oct. 2, 1957, Box 32, RHR.
507 **copy his innovation:** Ken McCormick, editor-in-chief of Doubleday, to BAC, Sept. 5, 1957, Box 32, RHR.
507 **"great skill and taste":** Charles Scribner Jr. to BAC, Aug. 30, 1957, Box 32, RHR.
507 **"if you put a copy":** AAK to BAC, Aug. 30, 1957, Box 32, RHR.
507 **grand bet pay off:** Haydn arrived just when RH was recalibrating its financials to provide a truer P&L. In 1955, Linscott devised a new formula for determining the overhead contribution each book was to make to the bottom line. Previously it was calculated at 30% of sales per title. In the new arrangement, a flat charge of $1,000 per book plus a smaller percentage calculated in relation to RH sales as a whole was instituted. See RNL to SC et al., memo, Mar. 29, 1955, AEP.
507 **"When *Sputnik* is forgotten":** AR quoted by Howard Treeger to author, July 1, 2003.
507 **"on the whole":** BAC diary, Oct. 11, 1957.
507 **"crackbrained":** See Heller, *Ayn Rand and the World She Made,* 283.
507 **"the bore of the century":** Harry Hansen to BAC, Sept. 20, 1957, Box 32, RHR.
507 **"I must confess":** RNL to SC, Jan. 1, 1958, Box 5, SCP.
507 **"but no whirlwind":** BAC diary, Nov. 4, 1957. On Thanksgiving week BAC told AR that sales through Nov. 22 were approximately 68,348 copies. See BAC to AR, Nov. 25, 1957, Box 35, RHR. An ad that ran in Dec. 1957 claimed 125,000 copies in print and another 35,000 on order at the printer. Box 70, CP. Publishers are notorious for inflating these sorts of figures; "in print" does not mean "sold."
508 **sold more than one million:** Heller, *Ayn Rand and the World She Made,* 286.
508 **"To Bennett Cerf":** For the two inscribed volumes from AR to BAC, see RBML, Columbia.

CHAPTER 33: PARTY CATS AND CATS IN HATS

509 **the opening of *My Fair Lady:*** It opened Mar. 15, 1956. On the party, see "What's New . . . by Phyllis Cerf," *Newsday,* Nov. 20, 1958.

509 **"Wonderful":** BAC diary, Mar. 15, 1956, Box 12, CP.

509 **worked only with her:** See Bach, *Dazzler,* esp. 350–65; Jared Brown, *Moss Hart: A Prince of the Theatre* (New York: Back Stage Books, 2006), esp. 344–51. See generally MH, *Act One* (New York: RH, 1959). Brown notes the much larger opening night party at Sardi's. See also Academy of Achievement Julie Andrews interview, June 10, 2004, www.achievement.org/autodoc/page/andoint-4.

509 **"if it has been":** BAC, Trade Winds, *SRL,* May 5, 1956.

510 **"the nicest dinner parties":** Edna Ferber to PC, Jan. 21, 1950, CPCC.

510 **a huge group:** BAC diary, Oct. 21, 1956.

510 **"the best goddam":** BAC, quoted by Quentin Reynolds to AE, Apr. 11, 1956, RHCC.

510 **Lillian, the secretary:** Lillian Winning's role per JFC to author, Feb. 22, 2013.

510 **dining room furniture:** JFC to author, Feb. 22, 2013.

510 **adopted the clever habit:** PC to author, Feb. 13, 2003.

511 **"fabulous":** Radie Harris, "Broadway Ballyhoo," *The Hollywood Reporter,* Oct. 23, 1956, Box 69, CP. The premiere had taken place on Oct. 17, per BAC diary.

511 **"to take the souvenir":** *PW,* Oct. 29, 1956, Box 69, CP.

511 **signed a biography:** The book was being written with Todd's cooperation by screenwriter Art Cohn; both were killed in a plane crash in spring 1958. The book was published posthumously.

511 **one of the two youngest:** Not clear if Taylor or Goodson's wife, Virginia, was the youngest.

511 **Bennett had first met her:** On the *What's My Line?* appearance, see BAC diary, Nov. 14, 1954.

511 **surprisingly nondescript gray shift:** KCH to author, Dec. 14, 2002.

511 **there was a reputation:** J. Randy Taraborrelli, *Elizabeth* (New York: Warner Books, 2006), 129; William J. Mann, *How to Be a Movie Star* (New York: Houghton Mifflin Harcourt, 2009), 184–85.

511 **dragging Taylor:** KCH to author, Dec. 14, 2002.

511 **"tending towards avoirdupois":** WS to author, Mar. 3, 2003.

511 **"I'd like to fuck":** Richard Rodgers to WS per WS to author, Mar. 3, 2003.

512 **"Todd did not treat Taylor well":** WS to author, Mar. 3, 2003.

512 **thirty million viewers:** On *What's My Line?* appearances and comments, see BAC diary. On the ratings, BAC's pre-show ritual, and Todd's gust appearance, see Fates, *What's My Line?* 13, 58–59. On Todd, see BAC diary, Feb. 17, 1957.

513 **grieving team met:** BAC OH, 741–42; on Allen's death, see BAC diary, Mar. 17, 18, & 19, 1956.

513 **"tweed wastebasket":** Dick Cavett quoting Allen to author, Feb. 26, 2013. Another Goodson-Todman panelist, Henry Morgan, in *Here's Morgan!* (Fort Lee: Barricade Books, 1994), also recalled Allen skewering BAC that way.

513 **chairing the Peabody radio and TV awards:** BAC served on the board from 1946 to 1967 and from 1970 to 1971.

513 **"a very small talent":** BAC quoted in Cedric Adams, "In This Corner," *Minneapolis Star,* Apr. 27, 1956, Box 69, CP.

513 **"sweetness and guts":** *Hollywood Reporter,* Mar. 18, 1956, Box 69, CP.

513 **Jack Benny:** BAC diary, Mar. 19, 1956.

513 **"They're unassailable":** For text of speech to Columbia alumni, see BAC, "Trends in Publishing," *Library Service News,* May 1953, 1–3, Columbia School of Library Service, Columbiana Collection.

513 **strictly rationed:** CBC to author, Dec. 18, 2002.

514 **"It's Fun to Read":** Alfred Stefferud, ed., *The Wonderful World of Books* (New York: New American Library, 1953), also published simultaneously in hardcover by Houghton Mifflin. See Danny Heitman, "Don't Just Read for Fun," *Christian Science Monitor,* Jan. 11, 2008, https://www.csmonitor.com/Commentary/Opinion/2008/0111/p09s02-coop.html.

514 ***Sputnik:*** nssdc.gfsc.nasa.gov/nmc/spacecraft display.do?id=1957001B.

514 **"Why Do Students Bog Down":** Hersey, "Why Do Students Bog Down on First R?" *Life,* May 24, 1954, 136–40, 142, 144, 147–48, 150.

514 **bombshell title:** Rudolf Flesch, *Why Johnny Can't Read and What You Can Do About It* (1955; repr. New York: Perennial Library, 1986) .

514 **"inane":** Flesch, *Why Johnny Can't Read and What You Can Do About It,* 84.

514 **"Goody-goody":** Hersey, "Why Do Students Bog Down on First R?" 137.

514 **"great American virtues":** Hersey, "Why Do Students Bog Down on First R?" 140.

514 **publishers could do as well:** Hersey, "Why Do Students Bog Down on First R?" 137.

515 **"wonderfully imaginative geniuses":** Hersey, "Why Do Students Bog Down on First R?" 148.

515 **volley of press releases:** RHR.

515 **That left Dr. Seuss:** On *The Cat in the Hat* publishing story, I generally follow Morgan and Morgan, *Dr. Seuss and Mr. Geisel,* 147–68. See also Donald E. Pease, *Theodor Seuss Geisel* (New York: Oxford University Press, Lives and Legacies Series, 2010), 101–15.

516 **Rowan was an RH author:** For Jackie Robinson book correspondence, see Box 35, RHR. The Robinson-Rowan book, *Wait Till Next Year,* was published by RH in Nov. 1960.

516 **since his sister-in-law:** Barbara Palmer Bayler (hereafter BPB), niece of Helen Palmer Geisel (hereafter HPG), to author, May 22, 2012.

516 **his competition was TV:** Dr. Seuss, "How Orlo Got His Book," *NYT,* Nov. 17, 1957.

516 **greater sophistication:** David Dempsey, "The Significance of Dr. Seuss," *NYTBR,* May 11, 1958.

516 **first two list words:** Morgan and Morgan, *Dr. Seuss and Mr. Geisel,* 154.

516 **fling hours of work:** TSG described the difficulty of writing the *Cat* to E. J. Kahn for Kahn's *TNY* profile "Children's Friend," Dec. 17, 1960, Box 37, E. J. Kahn Papers, NYPL. HPG's description of rescuing pages quoted in "What's New . . . by Phyllis Cerf," *Newsday,* Mar. 31, 1955, courtesy CBC and JFC.

517 **technically unconventional:** Morgan and Morgan, *Dr. Seuss and Mr. Geisel,* 155.

517 **only 220 different words:** For an analysis of *The Cat in the Hat,* see William E. Spaulding to Theodore Strauss, Sept. 19, 1956, Box 37, E. J. Kahn Papers.

517 **restless man:** BPB to author, May 22, 2012. She added: "If Ted were young today, people might say he had ADHD."

517 **"murderous":** Dr. Seuss, "Making Children Want to Read," *Book Chat,* Fall 1958, Seuss Collection.

518 **Tension lies just beneath:** Louis Menand perceptively says that "transgression and hypocrisy" are the keys to *The Cat in the Hat*. See Menand, "Cat People: What Dr. Seuss Really Taught Us," *TNY,* Dec. 23–30, 2002, 148–54. Pease has a different take, referencing Bruno Bettelheim. Certainly despite its success, the book did not appeal to every child; some preferred the predictable safety of Dick and Jane. See Pease, *Theodor Seuss Geisel*.

518 **$5,000 a year at least:** Morgan and Morgan, *Dr. Seuss and Mr. Geisel,* 140.

518 **"If we had ten more":** BAC to TSG, Jan. 4, 1956, Box 30, RHR.

518 **congratulatory note:** BAC to TSG, Feb. 12, 1957, Box 33, RHR.

518 **unforeseen resistance:** Pease, *Theodor Seuss Geisel,* 101.

518 **"masterpiece":** Hersey quoted in Morgan and Morgan, *Dr. Seuss and Mr. Geisel,* 156.

518 **"Dr. Seuss will emerge":** Dr. Rudolf Flesch quoted on jacket copy of TSG, *The Sneetches and Other Stories* (New York: RH, 1961).

518 **the classic pattern:** BAC and DSK to E. J. Kahn, Box 37, E. J. Kahn Papers.

519 **"a sensation":** BAC diary, Apr. 29, 1957, Box 12, CP.

519 **a sly New York publishing cat:** The Beginner Book *Cat in the Hat* total net sales up to June 23, 1961, were 409,829 copies, per sales report, Box 605, RHR. One source states that the Houghton school edition sold 40,000 copies compared to Beginner's "million copy sale." See G. M. Fenellosa, Houghton Mifflin, to Phyllis Jackson, June 2, 1960, Box 45, RHR. Presumably he was including book club and library sales.

519 **"went wild about it":** PC quoted in Morgan and Morgan, *Dr. Seuss and Mr. Geisel,* 156.

519 **"to stir the pot":** PC to author, Jan. 29, 2003.

519 **"Bennett let me do it":** PC to author, Jan. 29, 2003. According to PC, her difficulty in finding books for Jonathan made her suggest first-grade readers to BAC, who spoke to Bonino, and then Bonino spoke to TSG, who then started *The Cat in the Hat*—and Houghton came to RH to ask if it could do a school version of RH's book. PC OH, 322–23. But the opposite had occurred: *Houghton* had approached TSG.

520 **"I Can Read" series:** See Leonard S. Marcus, *Minders of Make Believe* (Boston: Houghton Mifflin, 2008), 207–8.

520 **couldn't do his work without her:** HPG was in some ways like a mother. BPB to author, May 22, 2012. Early in the marriage, HPG had to have her ovaries removed. TSG invented an imaginary child, "Chrysanthemum-Pearl," a device for hiding the pain of their not being able to conceive. Pease quotes from a note HPG sent to fellow Wellesley alumnae that reveals the pathos of the situation. BPB felt "it was because she didn't have children that in some ways he was like her child." See Morgan and Morgan, *Dr. Seuss and Mr. Geisel,* 90–91; Pease, *Theodor Seuss Geisel,* 114.

520 **Bennett rewrote them:** Handwritten calculations, Box 32, RHR. The first set of figures specifies 100 shares, with TSG and HPG each having 11; Phyllis, Donald, and BAC each holding 20; Louise Bonino, pro-

duction head Ray Freiman, and sales director Lew Miller each holding 6. The alternative division had HPG and TSG each getting 11¼ shares; Phyllis, Donald, and BAC 22½ each; Louise and Ray 5 each; Lew 2. The author's royalty was calculated at 10 cents per copy, with the artist receiving a flat fee of $1,000 for the job. If artist and writer were the same person, payment was to be 12½ cents per book, total. In the early 1970s, when Walter Retan headed RH children's books, Stan and Jan Berenstain complained the cents-per-copy system instead of a percentage was unfair, and it was changed.

520 **soft letdown:** CBC to author, Jan. 26, 2006.

520 **"Dr. Cheesespread":** Schmierkase translation courtesy Stephen Baister and MKF.

521 **"Beginner Books is to be":** Unsigned memo, Apr. 5, 1957, Box 32, RHR.

521 **open to direction from Ray:** Stan Berenstain to author, July 3, 2003. See also Morgan and Morgan, *Dr. Seuss and Mr. Geisel,* 123.

521 **retail at $1.95:** BAC had first suggested $2.00. The author would receive an advance of $1,000 when a "complete and satisfactory" manuscript was delivered, plus 10 cents per copy. The maximum fee to each artist would be $1,000 flat. However, a combined author/illustrator got a $1,000 advance plus 12½ cent per copy royalty. DSK to HSG, July 21, 1958, RHCC.

521 **would lend money:** RH put in about $200,000 for the first Beginner Books.

521 **Lawyers are wont:** See TSG's initialed comment on letter from Frank J. Kockritz Jr., May 18, 1957, Box 32, RHR.

521 **Helen had a small stroke:** Morgan and Morgan, *Dr. Seuss and Mr. Geisel,* 157.

522 **"hard and fast irrevocable contract":** DSK to TSG, May 23, 1957, Box 32, RHR.

522 **"this was a kind of star":** E. J. Kahn interview with TSG, Nov. 21, 1959, Box 37, Kahn Papers, NYPL.

522 **"The six-year-old":** Box 870, RHR.

522 **"eating, drinking":** BAC to HSG, Aug. 19, 1957, Box 32, RHR.

522 **she was juggling it all:** PC was also working on *The Complete Family Fun Book,* with her magazine cryptogram co-author Edith Young, for publication by RH in Nov. 1957.

523 **she made a list:** "Possible People to Approach for Beginner Books," Box 32, RHR.

523 ***The Kite That Could Not Fly:*** For lunch with TC in which this Beginner was discussed, see BAC diary, May 1, 1957, Box 12, CP. The book was to have been illustrated by Hilary Knight, the artist of S&S's great success, *Eloise*. BAC diary, July 31, 1957. On the book's title, see DSK to TC, July 11, 1957, Box 32, RHR. TC received a $1,000 advance per DSK to TC, July 17, 1957. In undated letter to DSK, presumably summer 1957, PC says the TC manuscript is in Louise Bonino's hands. Box 34, RHR. TC spoke of "re-doing the children's book" but had a different story in mind. TC to BAC, July 23, 1959. By that time, he was well into the travails of the Clutters. In the interim, TC, having also received an advance for a book on Sinbad for another RH children's series, wrote to BAC on Sept. 29, 1958, to say he couldn't do such a "boring" project. RHCC.

523 **111,000 copies:** For *Cat* and *Grinch* figures, see BAC to TSG, Nov. 25, 1957, Box 33, RHR.

523 **"in incredible fashion":** BAC to HPG, Nov. 18, 1957, Box 33, RHR.

523 **"a hell of a job":** TSG to DSK, Aug. 10, 1957, Box 33, RHR.

523 **"writing is the worst":** HPG to BPB, Mar. 19, 1958, courtesy BPB.

523 **"coming out of both ears":** BAC to DSK, Oct. 4, 1957, Box 34, RHR.

523 **"long confab":** BAC diary, Oct. 5, 1957.

523 **"our authors' mortality rate":** TSG to DSK, Aug. 10, 1957, Box 33, RHR.

524 **Five books were approved:** The other two were *The Big Jump and Other Stories* by Benjamin Elkin with illustrations by Katherine Evans, and *A Big Ball of String* by Marion Holland.

524 **cork-lined studio:** Kahn, "Children's Friend," 80.

524 **a small needlepoint:** Morgan and Morgan, *Dr. Seuss and Mr. Geisel,* 159; Kahn, "Children's Friend."

524 **got to their feet and cheered:** BAC diary, May 14, 1957.

524 **$200,000 loan:** HPG to BPB, July 17, 1958, courtesy BPB.

524 **"getting our toes wet":** BAC to TSG, Aug. 13, 1958, Box 32, RHR.

524 **widely reviewed:** Ellen Lewis Buell, "A Few New Books for All the New Readers," *NYT,* Oct. 5, 1958; unattributed in *NY Herald Tribune,* Nov. 2, 1958; unattributed in *The Chicago Sunday Tribune,* Nov. 2, 1958, all courtesy *PW.*

525 **"after only 4 months":** HPG to BPB, Dec. 14, 1958, courtesy BPB.

525 **1,225,000 copies:** The exact total net sale as of June 23, 1961, for the first five Beginners plus *The Cat in the Hat* was 1,224,648. Box 605, RHR.

525 **"in person":** BAC to HPG and TSG, Mar. 3, 1959, Box 40, RHR.

525 **waiting for the soup:** BAC lunch visits, Elma Merz Otto Westney to author, July 21, 2003. As Elma Merz she became PC's secretary in 1962, worked with her until 1971, and left RH in 1984.
525 **He loved the place:** Michael Frith to author, Aug. 13, 2003; Elma Merz Otto Westney to author, July 21, 2003.
525 **at least 100,000 copies:** Kahn, "Children's Friend," 47.
525 **earning more than $150,000:** E. J. Kahn interview with TSG, Nov. 21, 1959, Box 37, E. J. Kahn Papers.
526 **distressed about a *Cat* toy:** TSG to Phyllis Jackson, Dec. 22, 1959, Box 45, RHR.
526 **act as a buffer:** PC complained to Bennett about TSG. See Morgan and Morgan, *Dr. Seuss and Mr. Geisel,* 166.
526 ***Freddy Bear's Spanking:*** About 240 more books would be based on that family of bears before Stan Berenstain's death in 2005. By that time, after many management changes at RH, the family (the two Berenstain sons had joined their parents in creating the books) moved to HarperCollins. See Sterling Lord, *Lord of Publishing: A Memoir* (New York: Open Road, 2013), 208–27.
526 **"Phyllis couldn't have":** Stan Berenstain to author, July 3, 2003.
527 **"put a story":** HPG to PC, Aug. 4, 1958, RHR.
527 **"worked like a dog":** DSK to HPG, Oct. 9, 1958.
527 **"It was the worst book":** Everett Raymond Kinstler to author, Apr. 9, 2013.
527 **Phyllis did the actual writing:** CBC and JFC to author, multiple times.
527 **arguing over a single word:** BAC OH, 462.
528 **Getting credit was paramount:** PC OH, 396.
528 **long for the days:** BAC OH, 462.

CHAPTER 34: HELLOS AND GOODBYES

529 **He cut the bonus:** Robert L. Bernstein (RLB) to author, May 5, 2003.
529 **Bernstein rose steadily:** RLB background and arrival at RH per RLB to author, Feb. 25, Apr. 1, May 5, 2003, Dec. 7, 2006, and Apr. 16, 2013; Peter Bernstein, RLB's son, to author, Apr. 10 & 11, 2013; Helen Bernstein to author, Oct. 26, 2005; Michael Dann to author, Feb. 4, 2003. RLB interview with John F. Baker, Mar. 20, 2001, RH OH project, courtesy RH Inc. See also *PW,* Dec. 16, 1957, and Dec. 30, 1967.
530 **beguiling story:** On *Eloise,* see BAC, Trade Winds, *SRL,* Mar. 31, 1956.
530 **Eloise Ltd.:** *PW,* Dec. 16, 1957.
530 **"Gentleman Lew":** Gloria Loomis to author, Nov. 3, 2004.
530 **"I'd like you to work":** BAC quoted by RLB to author, Feb. 25, 2003.
531 **Random House Enterprises:** DSK to RLB, Dec. 26, 1957, Box 32, RHR. BAC, DSK, and LM were the other officers of RHE.
531 **split profits fifty-fifty:** RLB to DSK, Feb. 27, 1958, Box 37, RHR.
532 **commission of 5 percent:** DSK to RLB, Dec. 20, 1957, Box 32, RHR.
532 **press conference:** BAC diary, Mar. 18, 1958, CP, Box 12; *New York Film Daily,* Mar. 19, 1958, Box 70, CP.
532 **"hysterical fans":** "Bookstores Benefit From New Career of Shirley Temple," *PW,* Dec. 29, 1958.
532 **almost doubling his salary:** Edward A. Fogel to DSK, Dec. 4, 1957, Box 32, RHR.
532 **"strong":** BAC OH, 888.
532 **actually *read:*** RLB to author, Apr. 1, 2003.
532 **"The publishing house is the servant":** RLB quoting LM to author, May 5, 2003.
532 **"You have to buy":** RLB to author, Apr. 1, 2003.
532 **Bob couldn't wait:** RLB to author, Feb. 25, 2003.
533 **completely absorbed:** Helen Bernstein to author, Oct. 26, 2005.
533 **couldn't wrangle the tie:** RLB to author, Feb. 25, 2003; Helen Bernstein to author, Oct. 26, 2005.
533 **"It's my feeling":** RLB to BAC, Mar. 5, 1958, Box 37, RHR.
533 **visions of licensing:** RLB to DSK, Feb. 6, 1958, Box 37, RHR. On RLS's early enthusiasm for TSG, see Morgan and Morgan, *Dr. Seuss and Mr. Geisel,* 160–61.
533 **"Reports indicate":** BAC to TSG, Nov. 5, 1958, Box 37, RHR.
533 **Never before had:** See Morgan and Morgan, *Dr. Seuss and Mr. Geisel,* 160–61.
533 **"wasn't a kids' person":** BPB to author, May 22, 2012.
534 **"Ted had no idea":** Helen Bernstein to author, Oct. 26, 2005.
534 **never do one again:** HPG to BPB, Nov. 3 (presumably 1958), courtesy BPB.
534 **asked to add color:** Babar background per Laurent de Brunhoff and Phyllis Rose (Madame de Brunhoff) to author, June 7, 2013.
534 **letter was crossing the Atlantic:** Emanuel Harper to Laurent de Brunhoff, Jan. 30, 1958, Box 37, RHR.
534 **"energetic, helpful":** Laurent de Brunhoff and Phyllis Rose to author, June 7, 2013.
534 **parents named Helen and Bob:** Helen

Bernstein to author, Oct. 26, 2005. *Babar Comes to America* was published in 1965.

534 **"deep interest":** BAC to Lee Wright, Nov. 7, 1957, Box 35, RHR.

535 **"Ellery Queen":** Ellery Queen was both a fictional detective and the nom de plume of the Brooklyn-born cousins who conjured him. They were Frederic Dannay (real name Daniel Nathan) and Manfred Bennington Lee (real name Emanuel Lepofsky); Queen was associated with a radio show, magazine, movies, comics, and books.

535 **delighted with the move:** BAC to Manfred B. Lee and Fred Dannay, Dec. 30, 1957, Box 35, RHR.

535 **"great hopes":** BAC to Bruce Bliven Jr., Feb. 12, 1957, Box 32, RHR.

535 **"George":** RDL to author, Mar. 16, 2003, and Feb. 12, 2009.

536 **handed over a check:** RDL to author, Mar. 16, 2003, and Feb. 12, 2009.

537 **"Notes for a possible basis":** Box 7, CP.

537 **Lane promised to send figures:** For Penguin discussions, see BAC diary, Sept. 4, 8, & 18, Oct. 16, 1957, Box 12, CP.

537 **"blew up":** DSK to Allen Lane, Aug. 28, 1958, Box 38, RHR.

537 **aware of inroads:** See large ad for ML Paperbacks in *NYTBR,* Oct. 27, 1957, Box 70, CP.

537 **"an appendage":** JE to author, Dec. 9, 2003.

538 **"a very slick character":** JE to author, Mar. 11, 2010.

538 **"the equivalent of":** JE to author, Dec. 9, 2003.

538 **young men made the pilgrimage:** JE and Rosset's attempt per JE to author, Mar. 11, 2010.

538 **Lane couldn't dispose of Penguin:** JE to author, Jan. 3, 2013. The chronology is as follows: Sept. 8, 1958, BAC learns JE is out of Doubleday; Sept. 19, BAC speaks to JE in London; Oct. 6, first lunch in New York; Oct. 10, Jess Stein tries to prevent hiring of JE; Oct. 21, Stein dissents again; Oct. 22, second lunch; Oct. 23, JE is hired. BAC diary, Box 12, CP.

538 **"Come as an editor":** BAC quoted by JE to author, Dec. 9, 2003. JE also related vivid characterizations of DSK and BAC.

538 **poring over all things ML:** JE to BAC, Dec. 9, 1958, and six pages of sales, Box 538, RHR.

539 **Looking Glass Library:** JE to author, Dec. 9, 2003.

539 **financially it didn't really work:** RDL to author, June 25, 2013.

539 **"the cross I bear":** BAC OH, 622. "the bear I cross": *AR,* 202.

539 **"absolutely unmanageable":** BAC sought the opinion of Douglas Black, Doubleday president (and the lawyer whom JE disparaged), the day after his first lunch with JE. Black said, "Epstein will drive you crazy." After a decade together, BAC himself pronounced JE "absolutely unmanageable." BAC OH, 622.

540 **"twilight":** SC diary, July 18, 1956, courtesy FCB and Eugene Commins. The passage is as follows: "This morning's *Times* carried the announcement that Hiram has been appointed editor-in-chief . . . there were assurances given that this post must not be created. . . . this is merely a public declaration of a fact that has been tacitly accepted for over two years and is more evidence of the twilight of my career. . . . What was obvious to me . . . is now publicly known and I must not let myself care."

540 **"invisible":** SC declared this belief several times. After his death he was quoted as saying, "the role of the editor is to be invisible." See "Saxe Commins Dies, Senior Editor at Random House," *NY Herald Tribune,* July 17, 1958, Box 70, CP. He once declined to appear on a TV show because of a desire "to maintain anonymity." See SC to Beverly Garry, NBC TV, Apr. 15, 1957, Box 382, RHR.

540 **"Never let me hear":** DSK to SC, Sept. 22, 1957, Box 5, SCP.

540 **the only right option:** SC to BAC and DSK, Dec. 1, 1957, Box 33, RHR.

540 **"What an enormous lift":** SC to BAC, Dec. 14, 1957, Box 35, RHR.

540 **to come to Princeton:** The date was Mar. 1958. See *The Daily Princetonian,* Mar. 19, 1958, Box 37, RHR.

540 **last section of Snow's manuscript:** BAC to Edgar Snow, Sept. 17, 1958; Snow to BAC, Sept. 21, 1958, Box 39, RHR.

540 **cerebral hemorrhage:** BAC to Irwin Shaw, July 21, 1958, Box 39, RHR. The other eulogist was Whitney J. "Mike" Oates, co-editor with Eugene O'Neill Jr. of the Greek drama collection published by RH.

540 **"I cannot get Saxe":** BAC to Dorothy Berliner Commins, July 21, 1958, Box 1, SCP.

540 **"We all miss Saxe desperately":** BAC to Walter Van Tilburg Clark, Sept. 8, 1958, Box 36, RHR.

540 **"I know I won't take":** DSK to WF, Aug. 21, 1958, Box 37, RHR.

541 **capacity for distance:** Haydn, *Words & Faces,* 91.

541 **"It made me very sad":** TC to DSK, Aug. 1958, RHCC.

541 **third most popular show:** *Variety,* June 19, 1957, Box 69, CP.

541 **top show in New York:** *Variety,* Aug. 28, 1957, Box 69, CP. According to the Nielsen ratings and rankings, the show was in the top 30 from 1952–54, 1956–57, 1959–61, and 1962–64. A. C. Nielsen Jr. himself was a contestant on the show—and BAC guessed him.

541 **$1,000 a week:** BAC to Mark Goodson, July 17, 1957, Box 33, RHR, and BAC diary, Aug. 29, 1957, Box 12, CP; **profit-sharing:** William S. Todman to BAC, Oct. 15, 1957, Box 33, RHR.

541 **his lecture fee:** Mary Barber to Elizabeth Schenk, n.d., Box 34, RHR; **$20,500 from speaking:** BAC to Elizabeth Schenk, Feb. 25, 1958, Box 38, RHR.

541 **"whopping":** BAC diary, July 23, 1957, Box 12, CP; **85,000 copies:** John T. Sargent to BAC, Mar. 15, 1957, Box 33, RHR. *Life of the Party* sold 102,927 copies by Mar. 1, 1959, in the Doubleday edition. "Bennett Cerf Properity [*sic*]," memo, Box 35, CP.

541 ***Bennett Cerf's Jokes of the Year:*** Jerry Mason to BAC, Feb. 12, 1957, Box 32, RHR. The book went on sale in June 1957; by Apr. 25, 1958, it had earned BAC more than $2,300 (2½ cents per copy). Memo from Art Levy, Box 32, RHR.

541 **"a huge and loyal personal following":** *Reading for Pleasure* cover, Box 70, CP.

542 **"a pagan worshiper of optimism":** See Yvon de Begnac, "The Optimism of the United States Lies in Bennett Cerf's Voice," newspaper clipping dated likely early 1958, translated from the Italian, Box 70, CP. De Begnac was Mussolini's biographer and wrote for several of Italy's major papers.

542 **"My wife keeps my feet":** BAC quoted in "Human Dynamo Cerf Publisher TV Star Has Numerous Irons on Fire," *Columbia Dispatch,* June 13, 1957, Box 69, CP.

542 **invitation had come:** BAC diary, July 22, 1957, Box 12, CP. On BAC's role at MGM, see BAC OH, 256–57.

542 **good sounding board:** Board minutes, May 21, 1958, Box 37, RHR.

542 **"howled":** BAC diary, Aug. 8, 1963, Box 12, CP.

543 **only publisher good at making movie deals:** Irving Lazar to BAC, Apr. 2, 1957, Box 34, RHR.

543 **"Movies are better than ever!":** See books into movies ad, Box 34, RHR.

543 **"The same Hurst":** Typescript 3–4 of Jessyca Russell, "Bennett Cerf," *Magazine Digest,* Series 2, Box 12, Folder 11, GTHP.

543 **$8,000 a year:** BAC to Norman Cousins, Jan. 4, 1956. See Cousins to BAC, Nov. 29, 1954, for arguments over pay. Both Box 33, RHR.

543 ***This Week* paid $800 plus expenses:** William I. Nichols to BAC, June 14, 1957, William Ichabod Nichols Papers, LoC.

543 **"fornicate":** The woman in the anecdote was named "Forney Kate." *SRL* dead slug (the rejected matter that had been set into type) for Oct. 13, 1956, and Norman Cousins to BAC, Sept. 28, 1956, Norman Cousins Papers, UCLA.

544 **he asked too much:** Norman Cousins to BAC, Dec. 19, 1956, Cousins Papers, UCLA.

544 **"Jackie Robinson quits baseball":** BAC diary, Jan. 7, 1957, Box 12, CP.

544 **"I can tell you":** Cousins to BAC, Dec. 19, 1956, Cousins Papers, UCLA.

544 **"I can't be very funny today":** BAC quoted in "Cerf Leaves *SR,*" *PW,* Apr. 1, 1957.

CHAPTER 35: EVERYTHING PUBLIC

545 **Murrow would devote:** *The Mike Wallace Interview* ran on Nov. 30, 1957, *Person-to-Person* on Apr. 4, 1958, both live. *The Mike Wallace Interview* is available online via the RC. *Person-to-Person* is available via CD from CBS TV Archives.

545 **"the guy on TV":** Matthew J. Bruccoli to author, Dec. 11, 2005.

545 **"I'm a ham":** e.g., BAC OH, 734, 940.

546 **often railed against censorship:** DSK was more knowledgeable given his activities on behalf of the industry. See, for example, Peter S. Jennison to Sidney J. Gans (copy to DSK), Dec. 17, 1957, and DSK to New Jersey governor Robert Meyner, Apr. 24, 1957, Box 32, RHR.

546 **Some angry Catholics wrote:** Letters are in *The Mike Wallace Interview Collection,* RC. Supporting letter from poet Richard Armour to BAC, Dec. 24, 1957, Box 33, RHR.

546 **"good sparring":** BAC diary, Nov. 30, 1957, Box 12, CP.

548 **honorary doctorate:** BAC diary, May 30, 1958, Box 12, CP. The College of Puget Sound is now the University of Puget Sound, part of Seattle University. BAC also received honorary doctorates from William Jewell College (Nov. 11, 1965), Western Maryland College (June 6, 1966), and Pace College in Westchester (now Pace University; June 7, 1971), Box 35, CP.

548 ***The Muses Are Heard:*** Clarke, *Capote,* 290–306.

549 **having advanced $7,500:** P&L, Box 612, RHR.

549 ***Breakfast at Tiffany's:*** BAC read it on May 4, 1958, BAC diary.
549 **they'd read several versions:** PC in Clarke, *Capote,* 307.
549 **sought Bennett's assurance:** TC to BAC, June 1958, in Clarke, ed., *TBAT,* 250–51.
549 **Truman's "Rock of Gibraltar":** PC to Gerald Clarke, interview transcript, 23, Jan. 17, 1978, courtesy Clarke.
549 **"I really don't need":** PC to Gerald Clarke, interview transcript, 23, Jan. 17, 1978, courtesy Clarke.
549 **"beautifully":** BK to author, Nov. 4, 2002.
549 **"Truman didn't need":** BK to author, Nov. 4, 2002.
550 **"nothing could detract":** TC to BAC, Sept. 29, 1958, in Clarke, ed., *TBAT,* 257–58.
550 **sold more than 30,000 copies:** *Breakfast at Tiffany's* P&L statement from publication, Oct. 28, 1958, until Nov. 30, 1960, Box 612, RHR. The exact number sold was 31,684. The book was on the bestseller list for ten weeks, per Christopher Bram, *Eminent Outlaws: The Gay Writers Who Changed America* (New York: Twelve, 2012), 67.
550 **"*our* Thanksgiving Day":** BAC diary, Apr. 21, 1958, Box 12, CP.
550 **"O'Hara is the most difficult author":** DSK to Dennis Cohen, Sept. 15, 1958, Box 36, RHR.
550 **loved this author:** BAC, "Portrait of a Pro," *SRL,* June 11, 1955.
550 **O'Hara's biggest-selling paperback:** Bruccoli, *O'Hara Concern,* 247.
551 **"rising from the ashes":** BAC to GTH, Mar. 15, 1957, Box 13, GTHP.
551 **two-part feature:** GTH, "Profiles: Publisher I—Descent from Olympus," *TNY,* May 9, 1959, 48–92; GTH, "Profiles: Publisher II—Big Day for Random," *TNY,* May 16, 1959, 49–84. Note that some of the twenty-five pages had ads on them.
551 **"swell people":** Ved Mehta to author, Feb. 1, 2013.
551 **copy of the *Social Register:*** Gill, *Here at the New Yorker,* 355–66.
551 **"purportedly":** GTH profile, Part I, 52.
552 **"Cerf joke factory":** GTH profile, Part I, 54.
552 **"odd" pinning of stories:** GTH profile, Part I, 76.
552 **"I've exploited a small talent":** GTH profile, Part I, 92.
552 **empty man described in Part I:** Some of GTH's facts are incorrect. For instance, GTH asserts that at sixteen, BAC "graduated second in a class of three hundred and was salutatorian" of Townsend Harris; in fact BAC dropped out. In his OH, he claimed to have been salutatorian of his grammar school. See GTH, Part II, 49.
552 **"catalytic agent":** GTH profile, Part II, 62.
552 **"in the right way":** RKH quoted in GTH profile, Part II, 80.
553 **"a serious disagreement":** DSK quoted in GTH profile, Part II, 80.
553 **"the best publisher in the world":** SC quoted in GTH profile, Part II, 55.
553 **"FIRST HALF":** BAC diary, May 7, 1959. On May 4, three days earlier, the diary states: "Checked proofs of my New Yorker profile with Ward." It is puzzling—why did BAC not express horror, object to *TNY,* consult his lawyer? Possibly he was only given quotes/facts to check over the phone, or selected proof pages. In a letter from Coward-McCann's Jack Geoghegan to GTH on June 4, 1959, Box 13, F15, GTHP, NYU, Geoghegan claimed BAC told him part of the profile was "completely" (Geoghegan's underlining) rewritten, the implication being he was deliberately misled. Geoghegan to GTH, June 4, 1959, Box 13, F15, GTHP.
553 **"the most childish thing":** Howard Lindsay to BAC, "Monday" (May 11, 1959); BAC to Lindsay, May 13, 1959, Box 41, RHR.
553 **"much more flattering":** BAC diary, May 14, 1959, Box 12, CP.
553 **Soon Dorothy Commins wrote:** Dorothy Commins to BAC, May 19, 1959, Box 40, RHR.
553 **"When I read the paragraphs":** BAC to Dorothy Commins, May 20, 1959, Box 40, RHR.
553 **"a masterpiece of smiling assassination":** Eve Auchincloss, editor at *Harper's Bazaar,* to GTH, "Tuesday," Box 13, Folder 15, GTHP.
553 **"What a pleasure":** AAK to GTH, May 12, 1959, Box 13, Folder 15, GTHP.
554 **"Do you think that I might receive":** RK to GTH, May 18, 1959, Box 3, Folder 15, GTHP. Twelve years later, after BAC's death, RK's condolence letter to PC mentioned other feelings: "shock" that a man of "eternal youth" had died. RK to PC, Aug. 29, 1971, Box 8, CP.
554 **"real best seller":** Victor Weybright to GTH, May 8, 1959, Box 13, Folder 15, GTHP.
554 **Coward-McCann and Thomas Nelson:** John J. Geoghegan, vice president of Coward-McCann, to GTH, May 20, 1959; John Lowell Pratt, Thomas Nelson & Sons, to GTH, Sept. 19, 1960, Box 13, Folder 15, GTHP.
554 **"just a little bit of good clean fun":** Vic-

tor Weybright to GTH, June 1, 1959, Box 13, Folder 15, GTHP.

554 **"do everything in his power":** Jack Geoghegan to GTH, June 4, 1959, Box 13, Folder 15, GTHP. A subsequent letter from Pratt to Geoghegan dated Aug. 12, 1959, raises the likelihood that if *TNY* material were reprinted verbatim in a book, the magazine, as well as the book publisher, would be legally liable should BAC sue and win.

554 **"distorted interpretation . . . a careful assembler":** Hiram Haydn to GTH, Aug. 10, 1959, Box 13, Folder 15, GTHP. Haydn, writing about an error GTH had made concerning him, was being ironic in "careful assembler."

555 **"an awful blow":** BAC to GTH, from interview notes, Box 12, Folder 12, GTHP.

555 **"At our age":** GTH, Part II, 84.

556 **honorary scholarship to Harvard:** May 15, 1959, BAC diary, Box 12, CP.

556 **hid his own sensitivity:** JHS to author, Feb. 5, 2003.

556 **hash out how to deal with it:** BAC diary, Nov. 10, 1959, Box 12, CP.

556 **ranked the eighth largest:** Allen & Co./RH prospectus, Box 54, RHR. The prospectus lists inventory figures as of June 30, 1959, and they speak volumes. Just under a million dollars was tied up in ML inventory (all editions) and just over $900,000 in juveniles (unclear if Beginner Books inventory included, since Beginner Books was at that point separate but *distributed* by RH. Only $300,000 in "other trade" inventory. No line is given for dictionaries; perhaps they were included in $500,000-plus "other paper and cloth."

556 **Talks ensued:** BAC diary, Feb. 4, June 17, 1958, Box 12, CP.

557 **didn't consider the World merger offer:** BAC diary, Aug. 26, 1958, Box 12, CP.

557 **"They'll do better!":** BAC diary, Dec. 5, 1958. For further Holt developments, see BAC diary, Dec. 12, 15, 16, & 18, 1958, and Jan. 7, 1959.

557 **RH's revenue that year:** BAC diary, Dec. 30, 1958.

557 **comprised 165 souls:** Allen & Co./RH prospectus.

557 **"cruddy fringe":** Stan Lipton to DSK, Jan. 16, 1959, Box 41, RHR. Lipton complained on behalf of his fellow employees. DSK's reply of Jan. 19, 1959, assured him rather sharply that the slums would give way to what New York now knows as Lincoln Center. The exact address was 30 West 60th Street.

557 **"a high-class brothel":** BK to author, Nov. 4, 2002.

557 **"the Rabbit Penn Warren":** BK to author, Nov. 4, 2002.

558 **engineer a public stock offering:** For the initial proposal, see BAC diary, May 28, 1959. After loans and preferred stock were retired, DSK and BAC would each keep about 200,000 shares; Allen have 75,000; 25,000 be reserved for staff; and Allen offer 100,000 to the public at $11.50 per share.

558 **raising more capital:** BAC couldn't resist flirting, and Goldman Sachs was also interested in underwriting a public offering. Gustave L. Levy to BAC, Mar. 2, 1959, Box 41, RHR. See also *Variety,* Apr. 22, 1959, Box 70, CP.

558 **shook hands:** Allen's colleague Marvyn Carton was often point man in the talks.

558 **five-year contracts:** Courtesy of a company search by Arlene Harris Esq., Kaye, Scholer.

558 **RH vice presidencies:** BAC diary, Aug. 20, 1959, Box 12, CP.

558 **$11.25 per share:** Allen & Co./RH prospectus; *NYT* and *New York Journal American,* Oct. 2, 1959, Box 70, CP.

559 **had to be halved:** *Variety,* Oct. 7, 1959, Box 70, CP.

559 **recouped about $950,000:** The exact figures were DSK, $949,062.18; CW, $199,320, courtesy company search by Arlene Harris.

559 **well and truly a millionaire:** After the initial offering, BAC retained 200,000 shares, or 31.7% of outstanding common stock; DSK 160,000 shares, and CW, 40,000 shares, per the prospectus.

559 **"I like to think":** BAC to Ralph Ellison (et al.), Oct. 12, 1959, REP.

560 **Could he obtain:** See Walter Farley to BAC, Dec. 19, 1959; DSK to Farley, Oct. 26, 1959, Box 40, RHR.

560 **"Instead of working for yourself":** BAC OH, 870.

560 **closed at $20.50:** BAC diary, Dec. 2, 1959, Box 12, CP.

560 **"fantastic":** BAC diary, Dec. 30, 1959, Box 12, CP.

560 **"the new blue chips":** *Variety,* Dec. 16, 1959, Box 70, CP.

CHAPTER 36: TWO ACTS, ONE FINALE

562 **lovely federal education dollars:** The National Defense Education Act was passed by Congress in 1958.

562 **fall 1959 list:** The fall 1959 list extended from June through Thanksgiving.

562 ***A Raisin in the Sun:*** Hansberry's classic play went on to win the New York Drama Critics Circle award for best play. BAC invited Hansberry to lunch along with Phyl-

lis and Kitty, Apr. 1, 1959, and up to Mt. Kisco with her husband on July 4, 1959. BAC diary, Box 12, CP. The fall list included another significant African American debut: Paule Marshall's *Brown Girl, Brownstones*.

562 **phoned the young writer . . . "fine" play:** BAC diary, Mar. 23 & 24, 1959.

562 **in 1954 had outlined:** JAM to A. Grove Day, Mar. 22, 1957, AEP.

562 **felt impelled to act:** See Foreword, flap copy, and "About the Author" text in JAM, *The Bridge at Andau* (New York: RH, 1957). An ML selection of JAM's writing was also published in 1957.

563 **"uncanny genius":** BAC to JAM, Dec. 12, 1956, Box 12, AEP.

563 **"true face":** BAC to JAM, Dec. 12, 1956, AEP. Also cover and flap copy of *The Bridge at Andau*.

563 **instant and widespread:** For rights sales, see WME JAM files, courtesy Eric Simonoff.

563 **"a great tribute":** JAM to BAC, Mar. 27, 1957, Box 34, RHR.

563 **find him a local researcher:** JAM to A. Grove Day, Mar. 22, 1957. "Outside experts" are also referred to: JAM to AE, Dec. 14, 1958, AEP.

563 **novel to have five parts:** JAM to A. Grove Day, Mar. 22, 1957, AEP.

563 **"historical baggage":** AE to JAM, Sept. 22, 1958, AEP. The "baggage" grew more burdensome, and AE and BK even more crucial to JAM. On BK's importance, see JAM to BK (cc BAC, AE), Nov. 24, 1965, Box 62, RHR.

564 **six weeks maximum:** AE to JAM, Mar. 27, 1959; AE to RA Freiman, Apr. 9, 1959, AEP.

564 **"exacting routine":** JAM to A. Grove Day, Mar. 22, 1957, AEP.

564 **"great!":** BAC diary, May 28, 1959, CP.

564 **"just about unprecedented":** Box 103, JAMP. See also *San Francisco Chronicle*, Sept. 27, 1959; "3-Prong Promo to Keep Michener's 'Hawaii' Stewing," *Variety*, Sept. 23, 1959, Box 70, CP.

564 **"too bad for the culture":** BAC quoted in *Variety*, Sept. 23, 1959, Box 70, CP.

565 **third-biggest fiction bestseller:** Hackett and Burke, *80 Years of Best Sellers, 1895–1975*, 177, 178, 180.

565 **"through an incredible gauntlet":** *Time*, Nov. 23, 1959, 107–10.

566 **more than $375,000:** JAMP.

566 **"the ideal author":** BAC OH, 537.

566 **tightfistedness:** Marisa Erskine, AE's widow, to author, Apr. 25, 2008.

566 **children fathered by American:** See Larry Swindell, "An Epic Hero," *Fort Worth Star-Telegram*, Oct. 16, 1997, courtesy WME.

566 **fund about 150 college scholarships:** Marie Arana-Ward, "James Michener," *Washington Post* Book World, Oct. 3, 1993, courtesy WME. On JAM's largesse, see JAM to Alden Whitman, July 4, 1980, AEP, in which, he defends the money he accumulated from writing by saying how he uses it to help others.

566 **almost $900,000:** Marisa Erskine to author, Apr. 25, 2008. For a balance sheet for stock investments by AE, see AEP. In a one-page accounting on Jan. 10, 1970, JAM states: "Albert Erskine supervises a stock account for me. . . . For this service, Erskine receives an agreed-upon fee." JAMP.

566 **disappear from his life:** Marisa Erskine to author, Apr. 25, 2008. With his second wife, Vange, he'd also taken in a second child from a similarly mixed background but returned the toddler to the orphanage before the adoption was final. On JAM's marriages and children, see Stephen J. May, *Michener: A Writer's Journey* (Norman: University of Oklahoma Press, 2005); Grobel, "Playboy Interview." In his own memoir, *TWIMH*, JAM barely mentions his first two marriages.

566 **$100 million:** The Associated Press, quoted in JAM's obituary by Alvin Krebs, *NYT*, Oct. 17, 1997. Susan Gray provides a figure of $117 million. Gray, "Epic Gifts by a Writer of Bestsellers," *Chronicle of Philanthropy*, Jan. 9, 1997.

566 **"$175 million or more":** C. Stephen Saunders to author, Aug. 12, 2024.

567 **with all his heart:** BAC OH, 672.

567 **With clothes mainly chosen:** KCH to author, Dec. 14, 2002.

567 **"best-dressed":** "Here They Are Girls: 12 Best Dressed in U.S.," *Chicago Herald-Examiner*, Mar. 19, 1939, KCH scrapbook, Moss Hart and Kitty Carlisle Hart Papers, Wisconsin Historical Society (hereafter MH/KCHP).

567 **"a marvelous time":** KCH to author, Dec. 14, 2002.

568 **"all the colored people there":** Contestant quoted in PC, "Here's a Choice View of Beauty Pageant," *Newsday*, Sept. 18, 1958, courtesy CBC and JFC.

568 **"Do you think":** Serrell Hillman, "Summit," *Time*, Sept. 15, 1958, 46.

568 **"badinage":** For the pageant story, see BAC OH, 971–72. He and PC judged again in 1960.

568 **"the most remarkable":** BAC OH, 672, 679.

568 **"the glamour, wit and charm":** Lazar quoted in Richard Goldstein, *Helluva Town* (New York: Free Press, 2010), 161.

568 **"liked Moss better":** DSK OH, 76.

568 **"seemed like brothers":** Nan Talese to author, Jan. 7, 2003.

568 **Moss had been in analysis:** His analyst, Dr. Lawrence Kubie, who was one of Manhattan's best-known practitioners, was AAK's cousin.

568 **"God's happy man":** GTH interview notes with MH, Box 12, GTHP.

569 **"The only credential":** MH, *Act One,* 436.

569 **"incantatory":** Bach, *Dazzler,* 367. Bach provides the fullest background on MH.

569 **turning his stories into a book:** Bach, *Dazzler,* 326.

569 **meningitis:** BAC diary speaks of "polio," but Dr. Catherine Hart says her mother contracted meningitis. Catherine Hart to author, Oct. 10, 2013.

570 **pulled out a sheaf:** BAC diary, Jan. 2, 1954, Box 12, CP.

570 **four more chapters:** BAC diary, Sept. 23, 1954, Box 12, CP.

570 **The two would have dinner:** MH 1954 diary, May 5, Oct. 28, Nov. 11, 1954, MH/KCHP.

570 **"must go on":** PC to MH, Jan. 22, 1957, MH/KCHP.

570 **"This book, dearest Phyl":** Handwritten in book, July 1959, courtesy CBC and JFC.

570 **flutes of champagne:** BAC diary, Nov. 21, 1958, Box 12, CP.

570 **Round Hill:** BAC, Cerfboard, *This Week,* Apr. 26, 1959, Box 70, CP. A famous photo of the six friends at Round Hill, taken by Richard Avedon, is reproduced in *AR,* 266–67.

570 **"enchanted":** BAC OH, 681. Lee Wright had arrived after a long career at S&S. Talese was "home-grown," although in the end, had to leave "home" to gain the recognition she sought. Later, she was given her own imprint at Doubleday, which became a part of Penguin Random House, so it all came full circle.

571 **"has had more zest and dazzle":** BAC's original back jacket copy used in ads in many newspapers, autumn 1959, MH/KCHP.

571 **to coincide (just about):** The party actually took place the day before MH's 55th birthday. A copy of telegram invitations sent by BAC and DSK is in MH/KCHP.

571 **"If something had happened":** BAC OH, 681–82; BAC diary, Oct. 23, 1959; *The Roman American,* Nov. 8–9, 1959, 7, MH/KCHP; Cholly Knickerbocker's gossip column, *New York Journal-American,* Oct. 25, 1959, MH/KCHP; *PW,* Nov. 9, 1959; Bach, *Dazzler,* 370–71; KCH to author, Dec. 14, 2002. The thank-you notes BAC received are in Box 41, RHR.

571 **from the "Vienna School of Good Luck":** Mel Brooks to author, Nov. 20, 2013.

572 **"bigger and better":** Mel Brooks to author, Nov. 20, 2013.

572 **87,000 copies:** *PW,* Nov. 9, 1959.

572 **"I know it seems absurd":** MH to BAC, Box 1, CP.

572 **"the healing power of parties":** Paula Lawrence, Lincoln Center public tribute to MH, Oct. 19, 2004. Lawrence had been a self-described "flame" of MH's in the latter's early years.

572 **biggest Broadway musical:** Advertisement for *My Fair Lady,* dated July 12, 1961, MH/KCHP.

572 **after a second coronary:** Bach, *Dazzler,* 371–79.

572 **"MUCH FRANTIC PHONE CALLING":** BAC diary, Oct. 14, 1960, Box 12, CP.

572 **carried on a stretcher:** Photo of MH at Grand Central, Nov. 14, 1960, MH/KCHP.

572 **first friends to visit:** BAC diary, Nov. 21, 1960, Box 12, CP.

573 **"I should write":** Cecil Smith, "Next: 'Act Two' from the Pen of Moss Hart," n.d., MH/KCHP.

573 **he'd do the sequel:** BAC diary, Dec. 31, 1960.

573 **Moss saved it:** Bach, *Dazzler,* 378–80.

573 **"Moss just dropped dead":** BAC OH, 684. For the KCH phone call, see BAC diary, Dec. 20, 1961, Box 12, CP.

573 **"fantastic":** BAC diary.

573 **RH cried with them:** BK to author, Nov. 4, 2002.

574 **"would wait up, then sit":** KCH to author, Feb. 4, 2006.

574 **legal guardians of her children:** KCH to author, Dec. 14, 2002.

574 **told the packed crowd:** Howard Lindsay was the emcee; the speakers, in addition to BAC, were Brooks Atkinson, Alan Jay Lerner, Edna Ferber, and Dore Schary. Memorial booklet BAC had printed at RH, courtesy CBC and JFC.

PART FIVE, 1960–1971: REAL BUSINESS

575 **"Publishing . . . is both":** Haydn, Oct. 7, 1959, Box 41, RHR.

575 **"The publishing business has":** BAC quoted in *Open Mind* transcript, Box 7, CP. *The Open Mind* was a current affairs program on NBC's New York affiliate that later moved to PBS. BAC appeared on the program on Nov. 13, 1960.

575 **"He loved doing the show":** Stanley Kauffmann to author, Apr. 20, 2012.

575 **"He was such a bright guy":** Weidman, *Praying for Rain,* 360.

CHAPTER 37: KNOPFS

577 **"Persian prince":** Comparison made by CVV, repeated by Geoffrey T. Hellman in his three-part *TNY* AAK profile, Nov. 20, 27, Dec. 4, 1948.

577 **chosen Knopf as model:** See BAC, Trade Winds, *SRL,* Apr. 8, 1950.

578 **"He had taste":** BAC OH, 906.

578 **one of their regular lunches:** BAC diary, Sept. 30, 1957, Box 12, CP.

578 **family hadn't favored the match:** Harding Lemay to author, May 6, 2003.

Source material for this chapter is primarily from my interviews with AAK Jr., Harding Lemay, Judith Jones, NB, Simon Michael Bessie, Stanley Kauffmann, Ashbel Green, and Regina Ryan; GTH's *TNY* profile; BAC OH, DSK OH, AAK OH, all Columbia; AAKR, RC; and interviews and material collected by Susan Sheehan and Peter Prescott, including a fragment of a biography of AAK by Prescott that he did not live to complete, supplied to me by Anne Prescott (AP). These papers are now at the RC.

578 **"scaring to death":** Clifton Fadiman to Peter Prescott, Sept. 4, 1987, courtesy AP.

578 **"all the chutzpah":** AAK quoted in Linda Kuehl, "Talk with Mr. Knopf," *NYT,* Feb. 24, 1974.

579 **Alfred's mother had killed herself:** This appears in Peter Prescott's unpublished AAK biography, courtesy AP. See also Claridge, *Lady with the Borzoi,* 20–23.

579 **stepmother with little warmth:** AAK OH, 4.

579 **she'd attempted suicide:** Desmond Flower, *Fellows in Foolscap: Memoirs of a Publisher* (London: Robert Hale, 1991), 23, cited in Claridge, *Lady with the Borzoi,* 69.

579 **"tired of sleeping":** CVV to Fania Marinoff, Feb. 19, 1925, in Bruce Kellner, ed., *Letters of Carl Van Vechten* (New Haven: Yale University Press, 1987), 75.

579 **dalliances would be pursued:** Charles Dellheim tells of finding a memoir fragment in File 6, Box 686, AAKR; the text detailed BWK's story of the marriage during what Dellheim characterized as "a moment of bitter reflection." In Dellheim's reading, BWK hated AAK's father Samuel, resented AAK inviting Samuel to be treasurer of the firm in 1921, and responded by having the first of her "escapes," that is, an affair. She also spoke, he says, of sexual incompatibility. The fragment is no longer directly available to researchers. See Dellheim, "A Fragment of a Heart in the Knopf Archives," *Chronicle of Higher Education,* July 19, 1999, B4.

579 **Pat worshipped Alfred:** Georgia Colin to Susan Sheehan, Jan. 29, 1975, courtesy AP.

579 **never told him:** AAK Jr. to Susan Sheehan, Feb. 3, 1975, courtesy AP.

579 **afraid to face his parents:** AAK Jr. to Susan Sheehan, Feb. 3, 1975, courtesy AP.

579 **jumped on a train:** AAK Jr. to author, Dec. 6, 2002; AAK Jr. to Susan Sheehan, Feb. 3, 1975, courtesy AP.

579 **"barefoot, hungry, and broke":** *Time,* Mar. 23, 1959, Box 70, CP.

579 **"none the worse":** AAK, unpublished memoirs, Box 610.3, 414, AAKR.

579 **"scared to death":** AAK Jr. to Susan Sheehan, Feb. 3, 1975. AAK Jr. told me that his parents came to see him in person; twenty-seven years earlier, his interview with Sheehan seemed to indicate the divorce conversation took place on the phone. AAK Jr. to author, Dec. 6, 2002.

580 **"You ruined my life":** BWK quoted by AAK Jr. to author, Dec. 6, 2002.

580 **Blanche wore black:** Georgia Colin to Susan Sheehan, Feb. 25, 1975, courtesy AP. The dress was by Balenciaga.

580 **give up on Pat:** "When I got married my mother gave up on me." AAK Jr. to author, Dec. 6, 2002. AAK said BWK was "broken-hearted" by AAK Jr.'s marriage. AAK OH, 1.

580 **hated his mother:** DSK to Susan Sheehan, Jan. 29, 1975, courtesy AP.

580 **how *closely* he patterned himself:** AAK diary, July 1, 1954, Box 632, AAKR.

580 **"played for the biggest stakes":** AAK diary, Apr. 30, 1957, Box 632, AAKR.

580 **financial bind and needed $5,000 fast:** Respectively, AAK Jr. and DSK, Nov. 23 & 28, Dec. 14 & 15, 1960, Box 42, RHR; AAK Jr. to Peter Prescott, Nov. 20, 1995, courtesy AP.

580 **he was furious:** AAK Jr. to Peter Prescott, Nov. 20, 1995, courtesy AP.

580 **this time at the Stork:** AAK Jr. meeting, BAC diary, Sept. 23, 1958, Box 12, CP. Further discussions took place on Sept. 24 & 26.

580 **freedom of entry:** AAK Jr. to author, Dec. 6, 2002.

580 **ideal father figure:** AAK Jr. to author, Dec. 6, 2002.

580 **felt sorry for him:** DSK to Susan Sheehan, Jan. 29, 1975, courtesy AP.

581 **belittle his son:** BAC OH, 905.

581 **"I think it's a good time":** Guinzburg's statement quoted by Simon Michael Bessie to author, Apr. 23, 2004.

581 **agreed "Mike" Bessie:** BAC OH, 907.

582 **nixed the deal:** Simon Michael Bessie to author, Apr. 23, 2004.

582 **"unfailing honesty":** On the entire contretemps, see Haydn, *Words & Faces,* 111–13.

583 **didn't subscribe to the hierarchy:** Haydn, *Words & Faces,* 85–87.

583 **"happier at Random House":** Haydn to BAC and Irita van Doren, June 23, 1959, Box 41, RHR.

583 **"I think you're making":** DSK quoted in Haydn, *Words & Faces,* 101; on the founding of Atheneum, see 100–103.

583 **"cloudy plans":** BAC diary, Mar. 9, 1959, Box 12, CP.

583 **rumors were sweeping:** BAC diary, Mar. 11, 1959, Box 12, CP.

583 **generous backers:** Richard Ernst, a former Knopf salesman, was a cousin of Bessie's then wife (lawyer ME's daughter) and married to a Bloomingdale. *Time,* Mar. 23, 1959, Box 70, CP. He was brought in by AAK Jr. Haydn brought in Marc Friedlaender, William Roth, and Trumbull Huntington. Haydn, *Words & Faces,* 114, 116, 123.

583 **plotting to leave:** Haydn maintained that, when AAK Jr. and Bessie approached him between Christmas and New Year, he expressed doubt about joining them and signed the RH contract in good faith; only at the end of January, when approached by one of the backers, did he take the offer seriously. Haydn to BAC and Irita van Doren, June 23, 1959.

583 **"To think . . . you'd rather":** Haydn, *Words & Faces,* 102.

584 **"I know you're going":** Johnson quoted by AAK Jr. to author, Dec. 6, 2002. AAK Jr. claimed that Haydn divulged the secret; Bessie, in an interview with Peter Prescott on Mar. 17, 1990 or 1991, asserted it was BAC who leaked the news, which given BAC's diary entries, seems unlikely. Courtesy AP.

584 **would make the front page:** Robert Conley, "3 Book Executives Forming Own Firm," *NYT,* Mar. 15, 1959, 1, 46.

584 **scurried to wait:** AAK Jr. to author, Dec. 6, 2002.

584 **he'd better exit:** AAK Jr. to Susan Sheehan, Feb. 3, 1975, courtesy AP.

584 **in disarray:** Harding Lemay, *Inside, Looking Out* (New York: Harper & Row, 1971), 247.

584 **few would have made:** Haydn, *Words & Faces,* 103.

584 **"Haydn books":** A proviso was that should the author of an unpublished "Haydn" book ever want his services—even after he left for Atheneum—Haydn had to comply in order to receive the royalty. RH Inc. to Haydn, Mar. 31, 1959, Box 41, RHR.

584 **"a 'you love me better' moment":** BK to author, Nov. 4, 2002.

585 **"expensive luxury":** BAC diary, Mar. 12, 1959.

585 **"I've brought you":** AAK Jr. to Susan Sheehan, Feb. 21, 1975, courtesy AP.

585 **"royal court":** Lemay, *Inside, Looking Out,* 231. Others echoed Lemay's metaphor. He "felt like a courtier of a queen," according to Stanley Kauffmann, "Album of the Knopfs," *Albums of a Life* (Riverdale-on-Hudson, N.Y.: Sheep Meadow Press, 2007), 260. Judith Jones spoke of Lemay being a "grand vizier." Judith Jones to author, Feb. 21, 2003.

585 **Young secretaries and assistants:** Regina Ryan to author, Feb. 11, 2011.

585 **definitely discouraged those:** Lemay, *Inside, Looking Out,* 235.

586 **"very disappointing":** Judith Jones to author, Feb. 21, 2003.

586 **"an elitist snob":** Judith Jones to author, Feb. 21, 2003. Instances of AAK's discomfort toward his religion abound in his diary and memoirs. He often talks of Jews as though they were of a different ethnicity from himself, e.g., "my taxi driver was one of those friendly and talkative fellows of the Jewish persuasion." On Mar. 4, 1961, he speaks of being amazed that an author like Robert Nathan would be willing to do "this sort of goo under his own name, but money—my dear sir—money for the Sephardic Jew always." AAK Diary, Boxes 611.4, 633.

586 **world-weary sarcasm:** Lemay, *Inside, Looking Out,* 232.

586 **competed with each other:** Lemay, *Inside, Looking Out,* 239.

586 **"masquerade":** Kauffmann, "Album of the Knopfs," 260. Kauffmann arrived the summer of 1959, a few months after AAK Jr.'s departure. Stanley Kauffmann to author, Apr. 20, 2012.

586 **"You're the one who's been":** Judith Jones quoting Elizabeth Bowen to author, Feb. 21, 2003.

587 **coquettish around men:** Judith Jones to author, Feb. 21, 2003.

587 **"gallant":** BAC OH, 914.

587 **"procurer":** Lemay to author, May 6, 2003.

587 **"mutts":** Kauffmann, "Album of the Knopfs," 264.

587 **"A publisher should publish":** AAK, "On Making a Few Books," *The New Colophon,* Oct. 24, 1949, Box 666.3, AAKR.

587 **"literally intolerable":** AAK diary, Apr. 3, 1958, Box 632, AAKR.

587 **"severely limited":** Kauffmann, "Album of the Knopfs," 259. A year into his tenure at Knopf, just after the RH-Knopf merger, BAC suggested to AAK that Kauffmann

move to RH. AAK refused. Three months later, AAK would decide that Kauffmann wasn't earning his keep and fire him. At that point, BAC again tried to help, taking Kauffmann to lunch and suggesting various jobs, but Kauffmann decided that he had had enough of publishing and joined *The New Republic,* where he would be one of the nation's foremost film critics for more than a half century. While at Knopf, Kauffmann had signed Walker Percy, a writer whom others didn't have much faith in. *The Moviegoer* was published with little fanfare. It won the National Book Award for fiction.

587 **been rebuffed:** AAK Jr.'s attempt to hire Cameron per Harding Lemay to Susan Sheehan, Feb. 1, 1975, courtesy AP.

587 **the role that paperbacks would play:** Irving Wallace to Peter Prescott, Feb. 16, 1988, courtesy AP. Wallace claims to have been the first author to sell paperback rights to a book—his biography of P. T. Barnum, *The Fabulous Showman,* to NAL—prior to selling hardcover rights. Judith Jones described AAK as set in his ways and not moving with the times. Judith Jones to author, Feb. 21, 2003.

587 **"disillusioned":** On dropping Robbins, see AAK unpublished memoirs, 1110, Box 611.3, AAKR. On the comparison of Robbins and Gibran, AAK Jr. made the remark in a talk attended by the author at the Small Press Center in New York, Feb. 26, 2004. He also said he couldn't buy Robbins's books for Atheneum, since all three partners had to agree on acquisitions. Haydn nixed Robbins and also Puzo's *The Godfather.*

588 **The titles Alfred was most ashamed of:** BAC OH, 911–12. Irving Wallace speaks of AAK finding his novel *The Chapman Report* "disgusting and obscene," adding that he didn't want his agent to send the manuscript to AAK. When the agent sent it anyway, AAK not only wouldn't publish it, he tried to prevent others from doing so. Wallace to Peter Prescott, Feb. 16, 1988.

588 **"My God! You haven't":** AAK quoted in GTH profile, Part 1, 50.

588 **with his pocket watch:** Lemay, *Inside, Looking Out,* 240.

588 **"Who are you to be asking":** AAK quoted by Judith Jones to author, Feb. 21, 2003.

588 **"For God's sake, Alfred":** BAC quoted by RLB to author, Dec. 18, 2013. Shirley Hazzard also recounted how AAK could offend, in describing the first encounter between him and her husband, Francis Steegmuller. As a student at Columbia, Steegmuller had written a biography of Ben Jonson under a pseudonym, sent it to Knopf, and received a letter of acceptance. The Knopfs invited him to lunch. When they saw how young he was, AAK said to BWK, "This makes it easy. We don't have to go to a restaurant. We can just have something here." Hazzard to author, Dec. 17, 2003.

588 **"One day your husband":** Shirley Hazzard to author, Dec. 17, 2003.

588 **"great spirit":** Hazzard to AAK after BWK's death, reprinted in *The Borzoi Quarterly,* vol. 15, no. 3, memorial issue. In the introduction, AAK spoke of his and BWK's "long and happy life together." Courtesy Nicholas Latimer.

588 **"truffle dogs":** Judith Jones to author, Feb. 21, 2003.

588 **Bennett more clearly saw:** John Hersey to Peter Prescott, July 21, 1988, courtesy AP.

589 **it was him or Pat:** The commission salesman was Joseph Consolino. Consolino to BAC, Dec. 3, 1959, Box 40, RHR.

589 **"defection":** Judith Jones to author, Feb. 21, 2003.

589 **"joint imprint":** BAC to AAK, Feb. 15, 1939, Box 125, RHR.

589 **"cher ami":** BWK, in the later years of their correspondence, addressed Camus this way (literally, "dear friend"). See, e.g., BWK to Camus, Apr. 12, 1957, in *The Dictionary of Literary Biography,* vol. 355, *The House of Knopf, 1915–1960,* edited by Cathy Henderson and Richard W. Oram (Detroit: Gale Cengage, 2010), 149.

590 **she'd never fully recover:** AAK unpublished memoirs, Box 612.3, AAKR.

590 **saw Alfred touch his wife:** Harding Lemay to Susan Sheehan, Feb. 1, 1975, courtesy AP.

590 **how deeply hurt:** BAC diary, Mar. 24, 1959, Box 12, CP.

590 **"It's a pity that we can't":** BAC quoted in AAK to Susan Sheehan, July 2, 1974, courtesy AP.

590 **Bennett dared to be serious:** BAC diary, Mar. 9, 1960, Box 12, CP.

590 **"Talk with Joe":** AAK claims to have said, "Why don't you work out something? Show us what you have in mind." AAK OH, 271. I here follow Joseph Lesser's slightly different narrative in Peter Prescott's notes, courtesy AP.

590 **Macmillan president George Brett:** After the publication of *AR,* AAK wanted to establish his version of the RH-AAK deal, so wrote to Louis Starr, head of the Columbia OH Research Collection, on Oct. 7, 1977, concerning Brett and the Blausteins. Courtesy Columbia. In the same letter, AAK states, "How much Pat had discussed

his troubles with Bennett Cerf I do not know. But the only outsider who knew at all times what the relationships were within the firm was Ralph F. Colin"—his lawyer—"and most decidedly not Bennett Cerf." BAC clearly didn't have the same access as Colin; on the other hand, his diary entries make clear he'd heard quite a lot from AAK.

590 **He and Don decided:** Unclear from BAC diary and RH and Knopf records exactly when Allen and Carton were brought in and if they'd advised RH's initial bid of $2.5 million; when the offer was changed from cash and stock to all stock; what was and wasn't done in the final negotiations. I requested but was unable to obtain records of the deal from Allen & Co.

I have followed the timeline in BAC's diary. Joseph Lesser's timeline, recalled in an interview years later among Peter Prescott's notes, is as follows: an exchange of financials occurred; Bennett gave the AAK information to Allen; a week later, BAC called Lesser and made a proposal; Lesser met with BAC and DSK again, and at that point BAC made an offer; Lesser conveyed the offer to AAK and BWK, with AAK not keen to bargain, but Lesser feeling AAK should do better; Lesser returned to BAC, who had decided with DSK to better the Allen recommendation, believing it was the right thing to do. Lesser never revealed his counter-figure, which happened to be less than the new figure offered by BAC. In Lesser's presence, BAC then phoned AAK saying Lesser was satisfied; according to Lesser, AAK agreed it was a deal without knowing what the final price was.

590 **on a gross:** Gay Talese, "Random House Will Buy Knopf in Merger," *NYT,* Jan. 17, 1960. The Talese article pegs the RH gross at $12 million; a *WSJ* article published the next day says $13–14 million. On Sept. 5, 1960, *PW* reported on RH's first annual report since one-third of its stock went public. The company had done a record volume of $11,931,388 for the year ending Apr. 30, 1960. Consolidated earnings statement revealed $1,751,962 earned before federal taxes; net income of $845,634; and earnings per share of $1.34. Figures for the previous year were, respectively, $9,242,739 in volume; $1,281,639 pre-tax income; $642,818 net income; earnings per share $1.02.

591 **the partners visited Blanche and Alfred:** AAK diary, Apr. 11, 1960, Box 633, AAKR.

591 **take the whole price in stock:** AAK OH, 274.

591 **"Was it all right?":** AAK quoting BAC to Susan Sheehan, July 2, 1974, courtesy AP.

591 **"probably the only people":** AAK OH, 279.

591 **"the smartest boys":** AAK OH, 269.

591 **a guest passed on:** AAK diary, Apr. 10, 1960, Box 633, AAKR.

592 **"Do you and Donald think":** BAC OH, 910.

592 **"If we didn't":** BAC quoted in AAK diary, Apr. 11, 1960, Box 633, AAKR.

592 **"so eminently . . . satisfactory":** AAK OH, 273.

592 **"tying in":** AAK quoted in Linda Kuehl, "Talk With Mr. Knopf," *NYT,* Feb. 24, 1974.

592 **"let-down feeling":** AAK diary, Apr. 11, 1960, Box 633, AAKR.

592 **"DIZZY":** BAC diary, Apr. 11, 1960.

592 **he'd trumped anything:** Nan Talese to author, Jan. 7, 2003.

592 **would have found a way:** AAK Jr. to author, Dec. 6, 2002.

592 **She brought her perplexity home:** Nan Talese to author, Jan. 7, 2003, and Feb. 24, 2005; Gay Talese to author, Dec. 1, 2004.

593 **"*Deal Made on Handshake*":** The full *NYT* deck read: *"Deal Made on Handshake Over Luncheon—Cerf's Company to Buy Stock, but Knopf Will Stay on Job."* The deck was changed for the later edition, deleting luncheon handshake. In his OH, BAC feeds the legend, saying AAK agreed to the merger over lunch. BAC OH, 910.

593 **"fine obituaries":** AAK diary, Apr. 15, 1960, Box 633, AAKR.

594 **Her role, she felt:** British friend Ian Parsons of Chatto & Windus, who was staying at the Hovel the weekend Talese's story ran, assured BWK that although it "didn't nearly do justice" to her—or DSK's—contribution, fellow publishers and authors "know it well enough." See Parsons to BWK, Apr. 27, 1960, Box 693.2, AAKR.

594 **"significant":** "A Merger in Books," editorial, *NYT,* Apr. 19, 1960, 36.

594 **Bennett (but not Donald):** Press release, May 18, 1960, AAKR.

594 **"We have the highest confidence":** *Borzoi Quarterly,* vol. 9, no. 3, 1960.

594 **five-year employment contract:** Peter Prescott notes, courtesy AP. Prescott calculated BWK's salary per her known salary in 1965 when the contract was renewed.

594 **"doesn't change":** AAK diary, May 17, 1960, Box 633, AAKR.

595 **"publishing history was made":** Press release, May 18, 1960, AAKR.

595 **feeling low:** AAK diary, May 17, 1960.

595 **Alfred held 53.4 percent:** Joseph Lesser, memo, May 18, 1960, AAKR; also Wil-

liam A. Koshland to Peter Prescott, Sept. 12, 1988 (figures re Dec. 1960 and Mar. 1961 stock sales as well), courtesy AP. AAK held 72,089 shares, or $1,441,800, BWK 34,039 shares, or $680,400.

595 **"he wanted to make us feel secure":** Judith Jones to author, Feb. 21, 2003.

595 **"That's openers":** Angus Cameron OH, 572, Columbia. Cameron's recollection was that BAC and DSK invited him to lunch the next day; according to BAC's diary, a lunch didn't occur until Nov. 18, 1960. On Sept. 21, 1960, BAC received a letter from Edward C. Krauss threatening no future purchases of RH books if Cameron was employed. Krauss said he had dispatched a similar letter to AAK when Cameron was hired. BAC replied on Sept. 27, 1960, calling Cameron "one of the finest editors," adding, "What books you buy . . . or do not buy is a question that concerns you and nobody else." Box 45, RHR.

595 **"vetted":** Judith Jones to author, Feb. 21, 2003.

595 **"a new world":** Judith Jones to author, Feb. 21, 2003.

596 **"not fact":** Stanley Kauffmann to author, Apr. 20, 2012.

596 **"brash, energetic":** Lemay, *Inside, Looking Out,* 247.

596 **"patina":** Lemay to author, May 6, 2003.

596 **running publicity for both houses:** Press release, June 26, 1961, Box 71, CP. Rivalry and women denied opportunity to rise: Sophia Duckworth Schachter to author, Apr. 6, 2009. Schachter was hired by Ennis as a publicity assistant in 1959 because her stepfather was bandleader Benny Goodman, and Ennis thought BAC "would like that." After the merger, Schachter reported to Lemay.

596 **"rub off":** AAK diary, Apr. 19, 1960, Box 633, AAKR.

596 **"fine solution":** BH to AAK, Apr. 19, 1960, Box 578.1, AAKR.

596 **that other houses imitated:** Arthur Thornhill Jr., a former Little, Brown director, to author, Dec. 15, 2004.

596 **"astonishing":** AAK OH, 275.

596 **what to do about reprints:** *PW,* July 11, 1960.

597 **"perhaps 80%":** JE to BAC and DSK, July 8, 1960, Box 44, RHR.

597 **under Vintage rather than:** BAC to S. N. Behrman, June 24, 1960, S. N. Behrman Papers, RC. After the merger, Morris Philipson, the Knopf editor who had supervised Vintage after Pat's departure, moved to Villard, reporting to JE.

597 **"We are really planning":** BAC to AAK, Aug. 30, 1960, Box 45, RHR.

597 **"Look what they're doing":** AAK quoting his son in his diary, Jan. 17, 1961, AAKR.

597 **a new equilibrium:** Changes noted in BAC 1960 diary entries, Box 12, CP.

597 **"unparalleled":** AAK to DSK, May 12, 1965, Box 517.9, AAKR.

CHAPTER 38: GROW OR DIE

598 **"combo barnstorming":** BAC diary, June 18, 1959, Box 12, CP. Information on CBC and JFC from many author interviews with them, as well as with MKF and Peter Gabel.

598 **dean's list:** BAC diary, Mar. 18, 1960, Box 12, CP.

598 **all out for the *Lampoon:*** Chris maneuvered for BAC to be elected an "honorary editor" of the *Lampoon,* greatly pleasing him. CBC to author multiple times.

599 ***The Ivy League Guide:*** Bernie Bookbinder, "4 Harvards, 1 Yale Man Collaborators—on Book," *Newsday,* July 1, 1960, Box 70, CP.

599 **Jon creamed Chris:** MKF to author, Mar. 26, 2012.

599 **the *Lampoon*'s chief editor:** Peter Gabel didn't run, so as not to challenge JFC. Gabel to author, July 16, 2005.

599 **"overlooked":** "Special Report" by Thomson & McKinnon stockbrokers, Feb. 23, 1960; see also "The Many Rooms of Random House," a report by A.G. Edwards & Sons, Mar. 23, 1960, Box 70, CP.

599 **Warren Blaisdell's last stake:** On the first 80% purchased, see DSK to Arthur Kamm, Jan. 22, 1960, Box 44, RHR; the remaining 20%, see BAC diary, Apr. 16, 1960, Box 12, CP.

599 **capital commitment of $700,000:** May 2, 1960, Box 42, RHR.

599 **likely sales were 100,000:** Warren Blaisdell to BAC, July 29, Oct. 17, 1960, Box 42, RHR; see also BAC diary, May 16, 1960, Box 12, CP. The author was Tom Apostol, whose text became a standard. BAC spelled Apostol "Apostle." 100,000 in "Remarks made by Bennett Cerf President of Random House Inc. to the New York Society of Security Analysts," Oct. 17, 1960, 9, Box 42, RHR.

600 **"In this direction":** "Blaisdell Textbook Division Formed by Random House," RH release, Box 44, RHR.

600 **mentioned L. W. Singer:** JE to author, Mar. 15, 2014; DSK to Marvyn Carton, May 11, 1960, Box 42, RHR.

600 **"Red" Warren had left:** See RPW, "Divided South Searches Its Soul," *Life,* July 9, 1956.

601 **"an amazing amount":** BAC to RPW, Oct. 9, 1956, RHCC.

601 **"traitor":** RPW to AE, Oct. 2, 1956, courtesy Marisa and Silvia Erskine. In 1965, RPW would come out passionately for integration in an RH book, *Who Speaks for the Negro?* in which he interviewed leaders like Malcolm X and Martin Luther King Jr.

601 **"such an unhappy state":** WF to SC, undated but probably Dec. 1955, in Louis Brodsky and Hamblin, eds., *Faulkner,* vol. 2, 187.

601 **"A Letter to the North":** *Life,* Mar. 5, 1956.

601 **violence could be done:** Riots did break out on campus after Lucy was admitted; she was suspended for her own safety and later expelled by the trustees on a trumped-up technicality. In 1989 she was finally able to enroll and received an M.A. in 1992. In 2022 a campus building was renamed in her honor.

601 **"fight for Mississippi":** The *Sunday Times* interview was republished eventually in a New York political magazine, *The Reporter.*

601 **"statements which no sober man":** See generally Louis Daniel Brodsky, "Faulkner and the Racial Crisis, 1956," *Southern Review* 23 (Autumn 1988): 791–802, quotation 797.

602 **United Negro College Fund dinner:** BAC diary, May 5, 1960, Box 12, CP.

602 **"whomp":** BAC diary, May 10, 1960, Box 12, CP.

602 **watched the first televised presidential debate:** BAC diary, Sept. 26, 1960, Box 12, CP.

602 **first birth control pill:** Allen & Co. invested in Syntex, a Mexican company that had synthesized the pill in the early 1950s. However, Searle was first to get FDA approval in 1960; Syntex's pill came on the U.S. market two years later. Alan Hirschfield to author, Jan. 14, 2003.

602 **selling her family's textbook company:** BAC to Mrs. L. W. Singer, June 10, 1960, Box 46, RHR.

602 **"a very nice woman":** Toni Morrison to author, Jan. 11, 2006 (also **"class act"; "housing problems"; "delayed"**). Morrison was not an employee at the time RH bought Singer; she arrived a few years later, in 1965. She was thirty-four when she started, having answered an ad in *The New York Review of Books,* and was brought in as an associate editor to work on literature textbooks. With the infusion of federal money and civil rights legislation, textbooks suddenly had to be more representative.

602 **"a remarkable lady":** "Remarks made by Bennett Cerf . . . to the New York Society of Security Analysts," Oct. 17, 1960, 11, Box 42, RHR.

602 **Textbook sales had more than doubled:** See Hornblower & Weeks market analysis, Aug. 1, 1960, Box 44, RHR.

603 **thirty to nearly forty-three million:** Frances Singer answering a question at the New York Society of Security Analysts meeting, Oct. 17, 1960.

603 **but had fluctuated:** Singer net sales/income summary 1951–60, Box 46, RHR. The figures for 1959–60 were $226,000 after-tax income on sales of $4.3 million. Figures for 1950–51 were net after-tax income $102,000 and net sales $1.7 million and $15,000 and $1.9 million, respectively, for 1955–56. Mrs. Singer also controlled the real estate concern owning the property that her publishing company rented. See Edwin H. Adams & Co to BAC, June 22, 1960, Box 46, RHR.

603 **all-stock offer:** See BAC diary, July 8, Aug. 27, Sept. 26 & 28, Oct. 31, Nov. 25, 1960, Box 12, CP.

603 **"curtail":** "Random House Buys L.W. Singer Company," *PW,* Oct. 10, 1960, courtesy *PW* files.

603 **"on the verge of becoming":** Decherd Turner, "Publishers, Please Get on With It!" May 5, 1960, *Dallas Times-Herald,* AAKR. In the twenty-first century, despite frequent calls by publishers to slim their lists, U.S. book production has ballooned beyond all recognition. With the advent of self-publishing, the number of titles is staggering; at the same time, the decimation of print review sections and other traditional print gatekeepers has made it harder for readers to discover many new books.

603 **twelve thousand new titles:** By comparison, in 2021, 571,606 print and ebooks were "traditionally" published, and 2,300,336 self-published in the United States (all these books have an ISBN), statistics courtesy of Beat Barblan and Andrew Kovacs at Bowker.

603 **"The Gold Rush on Publishers' Row":** R. W. Apple Jr., "The Gold Rush on Publishers' Row," *SRL,* Oct. 8, 1960, courtesy AAKR. "Johnny" Apple would go on to enjoy a long career at the *NYT.*

604 **"Mr. Octopus":** *The Open Mind,* originated and moderated for decades by Richard Heffner, was hosted for several years by Eric Goldman, a Princeton history professor. The program with BAC aired Nov. 13, 1960, when the show was on NBC's New York affiliate. It eventually moved to PBS. Transcript, Box 7, CP.

605 **"television is the greatest thing":** BAC and others quoted in Martin Tolchin, "Publisher Defends TV as Intellectual 'Tonic,'" *NYT,* Apr. 30, 1960, Columbiana Collection.

605 **expansion of the dictionary department:** BAC diary, Jan. 22, 1960. According to longtime RH lexicographer Laurence Urdang, anywhere from 50 to 150 people worked at any one time, and hundreds of outside experts were consulted. Urdang to author, Nov. 24, 2003.

606 **The growing population:** Hornblower & Weeks market analysis, Aug. 1, 1960, Box 44, RHR. Lew Miller's role and reasoning for what would become the *Random House Dictionary of the English Language* and its development per Laurence Urdang to author, Nov. 24, 2003; see also Bruce Weber, "Laurence Urdang, Language Expert Who Edited Dictionaries, Dies at 81," *NYT,* Aug. 26, 2008. I have generally accepted Urdang's view that Jess Stein's work was more executive in nature than lexicographical. Stein received a percentage on sales. In addition to his $20,000 salary, his rate was "1% on the annual sale of textbooks over $200,000, and 1% on the annual sale of reference books over $800,000." See DSK to Stein, Feb. 5, 1960, Box 46, RHR.

606 **handle the regular reprints:** This was painstaking work. Entries had to be updated, removed, or corrected within the constraints of discrete slugs of hot metal type and an already-determined number of pages.

606 **"hadn't been unfounded":** Urdang to author, Nov. 24, 2003.

606 **185,000 entries:** In dictionary-speak, an "entry" is not the same as a "word." Entries, according to Urdang, include headwords and inflected forms where there is a spelling change or different form or change in part of speech, as in *take, taking, took,* and so on. Urdang to author, Nov. 24, 2003.

607 **"big mess":** JE to author, Dec. 9, 2003.

607 **"*fuck* is out":** Otto Barz, former RH production manager, quoting RLB to author, Jan. 9, 2006.

607 **book signing by Bennett Cerf:** For an example, see poster for appearance at Columbia Savings and Loan, Box 56, CP.

607 **over $900,000:** BAC to Frances Singer, June 10, 1960, Box 46, RHR. The published RH Annual Report dated July 1960 for fiscal year ending Apr. 30, 1960, listed sales volume for Beginner Books of $928,120 and net after-tax profit of $104,530. Overall RH sales volume was $11,931,388 and net profit $845,634. Earnings after provisions for taxes equaled $1.34 per share for 630,460 shares outstanding. This was *prior* to the acquisition of Knopf, Singer, and Beginner. Annual Report, courtesy *PW* files.

RH after-tax profits as a whole for 1959 were $737,539 or 10.4%, according to a "Board of Directors Meeting Comparison of Net Profit" for all years, Dec. 20, 1960, Box 42, RHR. The estimated figure for 1960 was $857,000, or 10.5%. I have been unable to find an explanation for the disparity in figures between the published annual report $845,634 and this figure of $857,000.

607 **numbers were astounding:** An undated memo in Box 612, RHR from RLB to A. L. Friedman showed net sales for seven months ending Nov. 30, 1959, compared to seven months ending Nov. 30, 1960. Regular ML, ML Giants, and Beginner Books in 1959 respectively sold 787,405; 198,079; and 672,339 copies; for 1960, the figures were 651,453; 196,576; 902,761. An arrangement for direct mail-order sales to schools via Grolier was negotiated. In 1960, Beginners sold twice the number of copies of Landmarks. Adult trade, by comparison, sold 1,227,085 copies. The performance of Beginner was, to quote BAC, "phenomenal."

607 **under his control:** There was also the problem of Houghton Mifflin's having school rights (the books had special library and class bindings) to three Seuss titles. The Geisels were frustrated by HM's approach versus RH's. In a letter to her sister-in-law, HPG was "so disgusted with the slowness of Houghton-Mifflin that I'd just as soon Ted didn't get too involved with them. . . . We've just turned down Random House for a deal on a Reader, & I think maybe it was a big mistake. . . ." HPG to Gladys Palmer, "August 15" (year n.d. between 1957 and 1960), courtesy BPB.

In May/June 1960, TSG's agent Phyllis Jackson and RH would together pressure Houghton Mifflin president William Spaulding to relinquish HM's exclusive textbook rights to the school market for *The Cat in the Hat, The Cat Comes Back,* and *Yertle the Turtle*. HM's edition had "underperformed," having been trounced by the trade edition. HM agreed to declare the schools an "open market" and moving forward was paid a 10-cent royalty by RH for every copy of each of these three titles sold in that market. HM saved face; RH gained control. For Spaulding, Jackson, BAC, DSK correspondence, see Box 45, RHR.

607 **"to be an independent corporation":** Agreement, Apr. 5, 1957, Box 32, RHR.

607 **at least $200,000 a year:** RLB to E. J. Kahn. On Dr. Seuss and Milne, see Lew Miller to E. J. Kahn, Box 37, E. J. Kahn Papers, n.d. 1959.

608 **"the most valuable literary property":** BAC to E. J. Kahn, n.d. 1959, Box 37, E. J. Kahn Papers. For the profile, see Kahn, "Children's Friend," *TNY,* Dec. 17, 1960. Even HPG was pleased with it.

608 **Five of the sixteen books:** Folder 17, Box 36, Seuss Collection.

608 **more than a million copies:** RH press release on Beginner Books sale, July 28, 1960, Box 70, CP.

608 **presiding over an eager audience:** BAC diary, Apr. 19, 1960, Box 12, CP.

608 **"something extra":** HPG to BAC, Mar. 20, 1960, quoted in Morgan and Morgan, *Dr. Seuss and Mr. Geisel,* 169.

608 **"very hard":** HPG to BPB, Mar. 30, 1960, courtesy BPB.

608 **"exclusively for Beginner":** BAC to TSG, June 1, 1960, Box 44, RHR.

608 **"the ideal publisher":** Morgan and Morgan, *Dr. Seuss and Mr. Geisel,* 171. TSG maintained that BAC never paid up the bet (170).

608 **cherry and magnolia:** BAC diary, Apr. 30, 1960.

609 **didn't want to sell:** *AR,* 154–55.

609 **25,000 shares of RH:** BAC diary, May 15, 1960, Box 12, CP; "RH's Acquisition," *Variety,* Aug. 8, 1960, Box 70, CP. See also RH press release, July 28, 1960, Box 70, CP. The deal would be signed by the principals and ratified by RH shareholders at the AGM in August.

609 **Helen and Ted would receive:** PC to HPG and TSG, June 10, 1960, Box 45, RHR. HPG would function in DSK's previous capacity as secretary/treasurer. DSK to PC, Aug. 25, 1960, Box 42, RHR.

609 **do battle for hearts and minds:** BAC diary, Oct. 17, 1960, Box 12, CP.

609 **without notes:** "Remarks made by Bennett Cerf President of Random House Inc. to The New York Society of Security Analysts on October 17, 1960," 24-page chapbook, courtesy *PW* files. The chapbook, whose back cover lists the eight divisions of Random House Inc. (Random House Books, the ML, Beginner Books, *American College Dictionary,* Vintage Books, Alfred A. Knopf, Blaisdell, Singer), was presumably published by RH. Page 12 of the chapbook makes clear BAC's remarks were "extemporaneous."

609 **"virtually depression-proof":** BAC's opinion on page 4 was colored by the experience of publishing the ML. The Knopfs almost went under, and others did.

610 **"Big Business":** BAC to NYSSA, 17.

610 **"The cards are being dealt":** BAC to NYSSA, 8, 9.

610 **"no possibility":** William Jovanovich to BAC, June 15, 1960, Box 44, RHR.

610 **the World textbook company:** This firm and the "World" that Allen & Co. suggested to RH were two different companies. On Jovanovich, see Emily Eakin, "William Jovanovich, 81, Longtime Publishing Chief, Dies," *NYT,* Dec. 6, 2001. Jovanovich would turn Harcourt (renamed by shareholders in 1970 as Harcourt, Brace Jovanovich) into a textbook powerhouse while continuing to publish trade books. He would diversify beyond publishing, buying Sea World and developing that franchise, growing Harcourt from an $8 million business in 1954 to a $1.3 billion business when he left in 1990. However, in fending off a hostile takeover bid from British newspaper and publishing tycoon Robert Maxwell, Jovanovich weakened HBJ by assuming too much debt. The company was forced to sell itself to Houghton Mifflin a year after Jovanovich left; Houghton Mifflin Harcourt was later subsumed into HarperCollins.

610 **plenty to go:** BAC and DSK were approached for backing in 1960 by Henry Carlisle, a former Knopf editor who started his own short-lived house. They turned him down, DSK averring: "we are going through a process of considerable confusion at the present time." DSK to Carlisle, Dec. 6, 1960, Box 42, RHR.

610 **unexpurgated:** BAC had tangled unpleasantly with D. H. Lawrence's widow, Frieda, which, according to JE, would have influenced his opinion of the book. JE to author, Apr. 3, 2014.

610 **moral and cash support:** Barney Rosset to author, Dec. 12, 2005. Reprint rights were bought on Aug. 5, 1959. BAC diary, Box 12, CP. There were already paperback editions on sale of the bowdlerized text that had been published by Knopf when several paperback publishers rushed new editions to press after the court decision. Given the still-canonical nature of the ML, BAC's decision to pay was critical to Rosset.

611 **"quite important":** Barney Rosset to author, Dec. 12, 2005. Eckert, who was German, would become Rosset's second wife.

611 **urged to do so:** Alan Hirschfield to author, Jan. 14, 2003.

611 **joining Evergreen with Vintage:** AAK diary, July 12, 1960, AAKR.

611 **Bennett made an offer:** The offer from BAC is referenced in Barney Rosset to BAC, July 6, 1960, Box 44, RHR, and in BAC to Barney Rosset, July 26, 1960, Box 44, RHR. I have been unable to find BAC's original offer (prior to July 6), but the July 26 letter from BAC makes clear that the "original idea" was "buying Evergreen completely for cash, plus stock and options in Random House."

611 **overblown notions of Grove's worth:** Rosset estimated the "present worth" of Grove to be $1,000,000–$2,000,000. Rosset to BAC, July 6, 1960, Box 44, RHR. JE said that figure was "far more than it [Grove] was worth." JE to author, Apr. 3, 2014.

611 **His counterproposal:** Rosset submitted to BAC "Revised Proposals for Agreement with Grove Press," July 21, 1960, Box 44, RHR. Rosset wanted RH to take over back-end operations for all of Grove Press except for sales and advertising in exchange for 20% of net sales; RH would have an option on all hardcover books developed by Grove, including ones that might come from arrangements already made with overseas publishers; on any book thus taken, Grove could participate on a 50/50 basis. The 5% of Evergreen would cost RH $25,000 cash. The 25% Evergreen option was for two years; RH would have to pay $10,000 for each percent bought. Rosset would get an option to buy a number of RH shares. RH would get a seat on the Evergreen board.

611 **"too much":** BAC diary, July 21, 1960, Box 12, CP. Talks with Rosset had begun on June 20, 1960; continued, either with Rosset or with Allen & Co., through mid-July. BAC diary, June 24, 27, & 30, July 11 & 13. Talks ended when both sides agreed not to proceed: BAC to Barney Rosset, July 26, 1960, and Barney Rosset to BAC, July 26, 1960, Box 44, RHR. Rosset financed Grove by selling off parcels of land he owned in the Hamptons, per *Obscene,* a 2008 biographical documentary on him by Daniel O'Connor and Neil Ortenberg.

611 **Bennett was "troubled":** Rosset later branched into film distribution, and in the summer of 1971 fought a ban on the Swedish film *I Am Curious (Yellow)* all the way up to the Supreme Court. It was expensive, and Rosset recalled that "open door." An agreement was hammered out whereby RH would handle everything for Grove except editorial and share equally in profits—and losses. An immediate cash infusion from RH kept Rosset publishing. Seventeen months later, in a 17-page affidavit, with accusations flying, Rosset sued to dissolve the deal. He couldn't have things any way but his. For 1963 notes approving a possible purchase of Evergreen, see Box 650, RHR. On the 1971 arrangement, see Box 1558, RHR. See also *PW,* Aug. 2, 1971, and Nov. 27, 1972.

612 **with a helpful nod:** As Geis recognized, "You are the man who got me into the book publishing business." See Bernard Geis to BAC, July 9, 1959, Box 40, RHR.

612 **Slickly handsome:** On Bernard Geis, see Riva D. Atlas, "Bernard Geis, Celebrity Publisher, Dies at 91," *NYT,* Jan. 10, 2001; also Letty Cottin Pogrebin to author, Aug. 12, 2013. In 1960 Geis hired Pogrebin, aged twenty-one, to do the publicity for his books. She left a vice-president.

612 **financial backers:** In "TV's Big Boys Turn to Books," *L.A. Herald Examiner,* Mar. 15, 1959, Box 70, CP, Goodson and Todman aren't mentioned, but they are in Geis's *NYT* obituary (see last note), and recalled by Pogrebin, who also remembers *Look* publisher Gardner Cowles—a BAC friend—as another backer. According to an RH internal memo, Apr. 3, 1961, Box 608 RHR, Geis's backers were *Esquire, Look,* Linkletter, Goodson-Todman, Marx, the *Queen for a Day* TV operation, Ralph Edwards of *This Is Your Life,* and two early investors in Diners' Club.

612 **ninth-biggest nonfiction hardcover:** Hackett and Burke, *80 Years of Best Sellers, 1895–1975,* 186.

613 **"soap opera":** Michael Korda, *Another Life* (New York: RH, 1999), 248. See also 245–49.

613 **"Whenever a man":** Lew Miller to BAC, DSK and RLB, Apr. 6, 1961, Box 608, RHR.

613 **only as a client:** BAC diary, Feb. 25, Apr. 7 & 10, 1961. A "manufacturing agreement" whereby RH would take over all production for Geis was mooted. R. W. Kislik to RLB, Sept. 14, 1961, Box 608, RHR.

613 **other possible betrothals:** Talks with Basic founder Arthur Rosenthal occurred on Sept. 11, 1961; further developments Sept. 22 and Oct. 4, 1961. BAC diary, Box 12, CP. On American Heritage, see BAC diary, May 3, 1961. DSK spoke of medical publisher Grune and Stratton. See DSK to Martin Podoll, Feb. 24, 1961, Box 49, RHR. In addition, they experimented with making and selling science kits for elementary schoolchildren in conjunction with a New Jersey company. RH Inc. annual general meeting minutes, Box 50, RHR.

613 **things turned serious:** "Pantheon Books: The Years Since 1941," Pantheon's 25th anniversary catalogue, Dec. 1966, *PW* files.

614 **"to the fraternity":** BAC, "Trade Winds," *SRL,* Oct. 30, 1943.

614 **impressive adult commercial successes:** Lindbergh's book came out in 1955; Renault's in 1956, 1958; Adamson's in 1960.

614 **his novel a huge international bestseller:** See Hackett and Burke, *80 Years of Best Sellers, 1895–1975.*

615 **third-biggest bestseller:** *The Leopard* was first published in Italy by Feltrinelli; that house had also first published *Dr. Zhivago,* making clear the increasing importance of cultivating rights relationships with foreign houses.

615 **severed the Pantheon connection:** A year later, William Jovanovich lured the Wolffs to Harcourt (though physically, they remained in Switzerland for as long as Kurt was alive), by creating the first-ever personal trade imprint within a large publishing house, Helen and Kurt Wolff Books. On the textbook front, Bennett's agreement with Blaisdell was similarly innovative.

615 **braving torrential rain:** Meeting happened on Aug. 19, 1960. That day had record-breaking rain and floods in the Bronx and Westchester. Weather report, *NYT,* Aug. 20, 1960. BAC met with Schabert on Aug. 30, 1960; again with Levin on Apr. 21 and May 1, 1961; and discussed with DSK, RLB, and Lew Miller on May 3, 1961. BAC diaries, Box 12, CP.

615 **produced royalties:** On the *Dr. Zhivago* movie, see BAC OH, 915.

615 **editorial independence:** Pantheon Books Inc., press release, May 22, 1961, Box 52, *PW* Records, Columbia.

615 **reputation for the European:** Morris Kaplan, "Cerf Set to Buy Pantheon Books," *NYT,* May 14, 1961.

615 **"an empty shell":** André Schiffrin to author, Dec. 1, 2005. For further background on Pantheon, see André Schiffrin, *The Business of Books* (New York: Verso, 2000), 34–37; "Kurt Wolff, Publisher, 76, Dies; Issued Books Here and Abroad," *NYT,* Oct. 23, 1963; "Kurt Wolff, Publisher of Notables' Works," *NY Herald Tribune,* Oct. 23, 1963; Sarah Crichton, "André Schiffrin of Pantheon Talks About . . . ," *PW,* Mar. 19, 1982; brief note about the Wolffs' departure, *PW,* Aug. 15, 1960.

616 **two other editors:** They were Paula Van Doren and Morris Philipson. André Schiffrin to author, Dec. 1, 2005.

616 **"They need hand holding":** DSK to RKH, Aug. 30, 1962, Box 52, RHR.

616 **"interest in and link to":** Schiffrin to author, Dec. 1, 2005.

617 **single most important author:** DSK to Mary Renault, Aug. 17, 1962, Box 53, RHR. Renault was the pen name of Eileen Mary Challans.

617 **"gently remonstrated":** Schiffrin, *Business of Books,* 37. In the end, Pantheon published five more Renault novels.

617 **"made all the decisions":** NB, who had started as RLS's secretary in 1939 and worked at S&S until moving to Knopf in 1968, to author, Feb. 21, 2003. Jerome Weidman's novel *The Center of the Action* (New York: RH, 1969) is in part a thinly veiled portrait of S&S, where Weidman had once worked.

617 **twenty-five-cent paperbacks:** Shimkin assured his protégé Seymour Turk that it was RLS and no one else who "deserved credit" for the workable 25-cent paperback concept. Turk to author, Dec. 5, 2005. According to Turk, Shimkin's contribution was distributing via magazine wholesalers.

617 **quivering-lipped:** Richard Grossman to author, Dec. 19, 2006. Grossman had worked at S&S, then published successfully, founding his own eponymous company, before becoming a psychotherapist.

617 **like selling their firstborn:** Joanna Simon to author, Nov. 9, 2005.

617 **bouts of depression:** Lucy Simon, RLS's daughter, to author, Apr. 23, 2014. On RLS's early hospital stints, see Box 3, RLSP; Marie Brenner, "I Never Sang for My Mother," *Vanity Fair,* Aug. 1995; Sheila Weller, *Girls Like Us* (New York: Atria Books, 2008).

617 **Quarrels:** Shimkin pushing RLS aside per J. P. Leventhal, son of Albert Leventhal, to author, Nov. 11, 2005; Richard Grossman to author, Dec. 18, 2006. See also Leon Shimkin to RLS, Aug. 9, 1952, Box 37, RLSP.

617 **Bennett visited both times:** Visits on Nov. 30, 1955, and Dec. 5, 1956, BAC diary, Box 12, CP. On Jan. 9, 1956, as well as on Nov. 9, 1956, BAC also noted in his diary that RLS was in the hospital.

617 **shunted Simon off:** On the sale of Pocket and the departure of RLS from the board, see RLS to George Young, June 24, 1957, Box 6, RLSP. Of Leon Shimkin, Joanna Simon said: "Shimkin turned out to be a traitor. He really betrayed my father at the end." Joanna Simon to author, Nov. 9, 2005. Her sister Lucy said: "Shimkin set out to get my father out, and Max Schuster sided with Shimkin." Lucy Simon to author, Apr. 23, 2014.

617 **"needing some editorial companion-**

ship": RLS to BAC, Aug. 28, 1957, Box 35, RHR.

618 **"It would be an honor"**: BAC to RLS, Sept. 11, 1957, Box 35, RHR. There is also an undated two-page outline in Box 37, RLSP.

618 **"What you say about Dick"**: DSK to SC, Sept. 22, 1957, Box 5, SC Papers.

618 **officially left the employ**: As of Oct. 1, 1957, according to a letter RLS sent to lawyer John F. Wharton. Mar. 8, 1958, Box 6, RLSP.

618 **health was faltering**: "sedated" per RLS to lawyer John F. Wharton, Mar. 8, 1958, Box 6, RLSP; "shook" per J. P. Leventhal to author, Nov. 11, 2005; "mini-strokes" per Joanna Simon to author, Nov. 9, 2005.

618 **"the once great"**: From RLS's typescript chapter with manuscript corrections, "The Unpredictable Horace Liveright." Box 7, Columbia, dated "November 21" with no year, RLSP.

619 **"an authentic, if tarnished"**: BAC to his friend Bernardine Scherman, Aug. 15, 1960, Box 46, RHR.

619 **"that true-true-true snapshot"**: Henry Simon to BAC, Sept. 2, 1960; Albert Leventhal to BAC, Sept. 2, 1960, Box 71, CP. According to Joanna Simon, her mother reacted differently: she was "furious" and found the last part of the eulogy "so offensive." Joanna Simon to author, Nov. 9, 2005.

619 **"wild idea"**: BAC diary, Mar. 3, 1961, Box 12, CP.

620 **"a partnership from hell"**: Shimkin-Schuster relationship per NB to author, Nov. 9, 2005.

620 **"Impossible but fun"**: BAC diary, Mar. 25, 1961, Box 12, CP.

620 **"too dubious"**: BAC diary, June 5, 1961. In Jan. 1966, Max Schuster announced that he would sell his half of S&S to Leon Shimkin. Shimkin, who already controlled Pocket Books, would merge the two companies, controlling everything. *PW,* Jan. 31, Feb. 14, 1966, courtesy *PW* files.

620 **"Deals, deals, deals!"**: BAC diary, Mar. 9 & 18, 1961, Box 12, CP.

620 **Harold Guinzburg died**: BAC diary, Oct. 18, 1961, Box 12, CP.

CHAPTER 39: APPETITES AND DIGESTION

621 **"Shut up!"**: DSK's ability to handle BAC: BAC OH, 147–48.

621 **"Please don't let"**: DSK to BAC, Apr. 13, 1944, in *DDDB,* 153.

621 **"bombshell"**: BAC diary, Feb. 26, 1961, Box 12, CP.

622 **brooding a lot**: Lucienne S. Bloch to author, June 16, 2008. Bloch worked at RH from Sept. 1960 through Aug. 1962.

622 ***The Proud Possessors:*** The profit was $22,000 before overheads. Box 58, CP.

622 **pearls, silk foulard**: I have based my description of Aline Saarinen on the *Proud Possessors* jacket photograph by RDL; on the author's note in the book; and on Cathleen McGuigan, "Aline Saarinen: '50s Wonder Woman," *Newsweek,* Nov. 5, 2009.

622 **"most beautiful"**: BAC to Aline Saarinen, Oct. 22, 1958, Box 39, RHR.

622 **did not have a child to bind them**: Pat Klopfer was a president of the Maternity Center Association in New York and a founding trustee of the Family Centered Maternity Program at Lenox Hill Hospital. "Florence S. Klopfer Dead at 73," *NYT,* Dec. 22, 1979. After her death on Dec. 20, 1979, Lenox Hill renamed the unit the Florence Selwyn Klopfer Maternity Care Unit. A hole at the center of Pat's life was her inability to have a child with DSK. The unit that operates in her name delivers 4,500 babies a year. Lenox Hill Hospital website.

623 **"wise kind"**: WF to Pat Klopfer, Dec. 7, 1953, DSKP. The letter concerned WF's affair with Joan Williams.

623 **love Pat as a close friend**: Stephen Chodes interview of DSK, July 19, 1962, 9, Columbia OH Collection, RBML (hereafter Chodes interview).

623 **welcoming and attractive**: writer Michael Mewshaw to author, May 15, 2014.

623 **"tiresome"**: Barbara Epstein to author, Oct. 29, 2004.

623 **"boring"**: RDL to author, May 20, 2014.

623 **craggy face**: Joyce Hartman, Houghton-Mifflin editor, friend of the Klopfers, and wife of DSK's physician, to author, Sept. 12, 2004. Hartman spoke of his charm and appeal to women.

623 **he had soul**: Barbara Epstein to author, Oct. 29, 2004.

623 **"Beautiful"**: DSK to Aline B. Saarinen, Jan. 27, 1959, Box 41, RHR; also "Beautiful One": Mar. 24, 1959, Box 41, RHR.

623 **edit her himself**: DSK to Mrs. Eero Saarinen, Mar. 16, 1959, Box 41, RHR. Among the many letters I have read from DSK in this period, the offer was unique.

623 **"subconscious"**: Aline B. Saarinen to DSK, Nov. 2, 1960, Box 46, RHR.

623 **"My God, it was good"**: DSK to Mrs. Eero Saarinen, Nov. 7, 1960, Box 46, RHR.

623 **"famous affair"**: JE to author, Dec. 9, 2003. Also RDL to author, May 20, 2015;

LKL to author, May 4, 2005. The White biography didn't happen. Saarinen became a contributor to the *Today* show in 1963, and in 1964 became only the third female staff reporter for NBC. In 1972, she died of a brain tumor, as her husband had a decade earlier.

623 **breakfast in bed:** Richard W. Kislik to author, Nov. 11, 2002.

624 **convene a three-way meeting:** BAC diary, Feb. 27, 1961, Box 12, CP.

624 **his beloved Blackberry Hill:** DSK to Dorothy Commins, Sept. 13, 1960, Box 43, RHR.

624 **had Bennett come look:** On the Bedford visit (BAC calls it Pound Ridge, which is close to Bedford), see BAC diary, Mar. 4, 1961, Box 12, CP. The six buildings included a five-room eighteenth-century custodian's cottage that DSK and Pat lent for years to the Hartmans as a weekend cottage. On the estate's buildings, see DSK to Samuel Metzger Jr., Jan. 25, 1962, Box 52, RHR.

624 **could still grow tomatoes:** Maxine Groffsky to author, Jan. 10, 2005.

624 **not to retire yet:** DSK "abandoned all ideas of retiring." BAC diary, June 23, 1961, Box 12, CP.

625 **Fired in 1955:** AAK had fired Fox (hereafter JMF) because he thought he wasn't pulling his weight; when JMF showed him a list of books he'd signed, AAK tried to rescind the termination, but it was too late. JMF would not work for a man "who didn't know what his editor was doing." RLB to author, Dec. 18, 2013.

625 **when his life *really* began:** Isabel W. "Jill" Fuller Fox, Joe's first wife, married from 1950 to 1969, to author, July 7, 2003. She provided background for this section.

625 **blueblood:** One JMF ancestor was James Logan, who arrived in Pennsylvania in 1699. Jill Fuller Fox to author, July 7, 2003. For physical description, see Mary B. W. Tabor, "Joseph M. Fox, a Senior Editor at Random House, Dies at 69," *NYT,* Nov. 30, 1995. BAC met JMF on Jan. 21, 1956; see BAC diary.

625 **a mass of contradictions:** "warm," "sarcastic," "curmudgeonly": John Irving, "Fox Here . . . ," *TNY,* Dec. 25, 1995; "lovely sour wit," "staring," "melancholy silences": Timothy Seldes to author, Nov. 29, 2004.

625 **after their love affair:** Jesse Kornbluth, "Scenes from a Marriage," *New York,* Mar. 14, 1983.

626 **most newsworthy peacetime marine disaster:** from Tabor, "Joseph M. Fox, a Senior Editor at Random House, Dies at 69."

626 **Fox was "lazy":** On Aug. 4, 1954, a year before JMF was fired, AAK wrote to BWK that left to his own devices in the office, JMF was "lazy," but added that "his taste is pretty good." AAKR.

626 **"Fox here . . .":** John Irving, "Fox Here . . ." Irving, as well as Peter Matthiessen and Martin Cruz Smith, numbered among JMF's many distinguished authors.

626 ***Answered Prayers:*** TC to BAC, Sept. 29, 1958, in Clarke, ed., *TBAT,* 258. In his diary, BAC noted, "Truman tells of new major novel." BAC diary, Nov. 3, 1958.

627 **Women in publishing didn't:** The exception to the absence of female book travelers was Sarah "Sally" Ball in the 1930s.

627 **"foreign rights department":** BAC to TC, Mar. 21, 1962, Box 51, RHR.

627 **"girls":** I use the word "girl" advisedly. This is how these women were talked about at the time.

627 **executive bathroom:** Maxine Groffsky to author, Jan. 10, 2005.

628 **felt triumphant:** BAC makes a half dozen references to wanting to get PR in his 1960 diary.

628 **Anne MarcoVecchio:** In 1965, Anne MarcoVecchio would marry and become Anne Johnson.

628 **left to become a literary agent:** One of the RH secretaries who made a successful transition to agenting was Berenice Hoffman.

629 **sharpening pencils:** Sophia Duckworth Schachter to author, Apr. 6, 2009. When Schachter married and decided to leave, BAC tried to keep her, offering to put her on the editorial track, which she ascribed to her pedigree. She left anyway.

629 **inviting everyone to the party:** Maxine Groffsky to author, Jan. 10, 2005.

629 **cat pee:** Schachter to author, Apr. 6, 2009.

629 **knew the book was important:** Schachter to author, Apr. 6, 2009.

629 **"playthings":** Schachter to author, Apr. 6, 2009.

629 **"came with the territory":** Lucienne S. Bloch to author, June 16, 2008. Rona Jaffe, a Radcliffe graduate who had worked at Fawcett, a mass market/magazine house, published *The Best of Everything* with S&S in 1958.

629 **being promoted:** Information on government contracts and women in publishing per Betty S. Prashker to author, Feb. 8, 2006. Prashker was a pioneer among women editors in publishing; she started as a reader at Doubleday in 1945 and after various incarnations in various places became a VP there and later at Crown.

629 **small autonomous RH kingdom:** Larry Bensky to author, Nov. 26, 2003. Bensky was a young editor at RH.

629 **serial interest in (young) secretaries:** Schachter to author, Apr. 6, 2009; Harding Lemay to author, May 6, 2003. Others also made the same observation about JE.

630 **"mass and class":** RLB to author, Apr. 1, 2003.

630 **knew how to use tears:** JE to author, Dec. 9, 2003. RLB and others have also testified to this.

630 **"made him a happy man":** Richard W. Kislik to author, Nov. 11, 2002.

630 **girl giggling in his lap:** Schachter to author, Apr. 6, 2009. She went on to say it was "oddly innocent."

630 **never to phone before noon:** Harding Lemay to author, May 6, 2003.

630 **"a bit on the side":** JE to author, Dec. 9, 2003.

630 **The offending hand retreated:** The story about the boot was related to the author by the boot's owner in confidence.

630 **"IBM type":** Laurence Urdang to author, Nov. 24, 2003.

630 **about to accept an offer from Grosset:** Richard W. Kislik to author, Nov. 11, 2002. Grosset, of course, was partly owned by RH. Urged by Bennett, the company had also gone public. The value of RH's investment in G&D had increased from $311,000 to $4 million. See BAC to G&D head John O'Connor, Nov. 11, 1960, Box 44, RHR; BAC diary, May 12, 1961, Box 12, CP.

631 **"outrage":** BAC diary, July 14, 1961, Box 12, CP.

631 **"administrator":** BAC diary, July 14, 1961, Box 12, CP.

631 **notoriously cheap with staff:** On Roger Straus, Richard W. Kislik to author, Nov. 11, 2002. See also Boris Kachka, *Hothouse* (New York: S&S, 2013).

631 **ensure the fellow stayed:** Kislik to author, Nov. 11, 2002. The controller was Morris Berkowitz.

632 **another of Kislik's tasks:** BAC to Dick Kislik, Aug. 21, 1961, Box 49, RHR.

632 **"red-letter":** BAC to Philip L. West, NYSE, Sept. 15, 1961, Box 50, RHR.

632 **number one on the ticker:** BAC to Edward C. Gray, NYSE, Aug. 18, 1961, Box 50, RHR.

633 **stashed the small piece of tape:** Ticker tape, Box 35, CP.

633 **"Letter to New Stockholders":** Box 50, RHR.

CHAPTER 40: GO DOWN, GOODBYE

634 **St. Pat's tolled nine:** The cathedral bells had been automated in 1942, but still tolled the hour and were audible from the courtyard. Kate Monaghan, St. Patrick's communications dept., to author, July 10, 2014.

634 **"I have bad news":** Chodes interview, 1. This interview, which took place less than two weeks after WF's death, was specifically about WF's death and funeral.

634 **heart had given out:** "William Faulkner Is Dead in Mississippi Home Town," UPI, *NYT,* July 7, 1962.

634 **and more to horses:** Chodes interview, 8.

634 **Now he was dead:** For the background, see Hughes Rudd, "The Death of William Faulkner," *The Saturday Evening Post,* July 13, 1963, 32–35; Blotner, *Faulkner;* Karl, *William Faulkner;* Chodes interview, 9. DSK does not mention the drinking or drying out, saying only that WF's family reported him to have been in "bad shape" after the fall. Rudd's view was that the family preferred to "massage" the circumstances surrounding his death, and presumably DSK chose discretion. Hard to imagine that, after so many years, he did not know what a visit to Byhalia meant.

634 **"great blow, great shock":** Chodes interview.

635 **"home place":** WF to DSK, June 7, 1962, AEP.

635 **"the best book editor alive today":** BAC OH, 338. According to OH transcript, BAC followed up by asking WF if he'd told AE as much, whereupon WF replied: "When I've got a horse running good, I don't stop to give him a piece of sugar."

635 **untangle inconsistencies:** AE to WF, Feb. 6, 1959, AEP; BAC to Brooks Atkinson, June 21, 1962, Box 51, RHR.

635 **"terribly shocked":** Five years after WF's death, on Nov. 7, 1967, BAC said that news of the death had come via a call from the *NYT.* It is not clear if DSK or the *NYT* got to him first. BAC OH, 337–49, quotation 341; BAC quoted in "Kennedy Leads Nation's Tributes to 'Great Creator,'" *NYT,* July 7, 1962.

635 **introduction to the family:** WS to author, Mar. 3, 2003. See also WS, "As He Lay Dead, a Bitter Grief," *Life,* July 20, 1962; reprinted in WS, *This Quiet Dust* (New York: Vintage, 1993), 279–85.

636 **travel together:** DSK stated, "We got to Memphis and picked up Bill." Chodes interview, 2. However, in BAC OH and in my interview with WS, BAC and WS both stated that WS traveled with them from New York. In DSK's general OH, done much later, he states ambiguously, "I went down to the funeral with Bennett and Bill." Given how close to the event Chodes spoke to DSK and the fact of WS having to do the extra leg from Martha's Vineyard,

it's entirely possible they met at the airport in Memphis.

636 **Their path meandered:** WS to author, Mar. 3, 2003. Undoubtedly it was a complicated, multiple-stop route, but speaking to me forty years after the fact, WS may have misremembered particulars. In a letter to William Blackburn a few days after the funeral, he writes of a plane travel "ordeal" involving several charter flights; he was coming from Martha's Vineyard and returning to Roxbury, Connecticut. He also mentions an "endless" return flight via "Nashville, Cincinnati, and Pittsburgh" that presumably began in Memphis. See WS to William Blackburn, July 11, 1962, in Rose Styron and R. Blakeslee Gilpin, eds., *Selected Letters of William Styron* (New York: RH, 2012), 336.

636 **troubling to them all:** WS to author, Mar. 3, 2003.

637 **"very odd":** BAC OH, 342.

637 **"heartbreak":** BAC OH, 341.

637 **taken an interest in Meredith's fight:** Karl, *William Faulkner,* 1037.

637 **hate mail, crank calls:** "The Curse and the Hope," *Time,* July 17, 1964, 44–48.

637 **"a kind of victim":** Delmore Schwartz quoted in "William Faulkner Is Dead in Mississippi Home Town," *NYT,* July 7, 1962, 7.

637 **"a liberal Mississippian":** BAC OH, 341.

637 **"many arguments":** BAC OH, 340.

638 **"I don't think":** Chodes interview, 7.

638 **NAACP dues:** Cathy Summers, WF's granddaughter, to author, May 19, 2011.

639 **enmity:** BAC OH, 343.

639 **a bit drunk:** WS to author, Mar. 3, 2003.

639 **feeling was mutual:** BAC OH, 345.

640 **a closed coffin:** In his OH, 345, BAC states that the coffin was open and that he and DSK suggested it be closed. This contradicts every other account, all of which state that it was closed.

640 **help from AA:** Estelle Faulkner to SC, Nov. 5, 1956, in Brodsky and Hamblin, eds., *Faulkner,* vol. 2, 199.

640 **suspected she'd taken something:** BAC OH, 347. Although Estelle had relinquished alcohol, she had a long history of drug abuse.

640 **"composed and sensible":** Chodes interview, 3.

640 **true gentleman:** Paul Summers, Jill Faulkner's husband, to author, Oct. 17, 2008; Cathy Summers to author, May 19, 2011.

640 **"Miss Phyllis":** Paul Summers to author, Oct. 17, 2008.

640 **"showing her off":** Jill Faulkner Summers died before I was able to interview her, but both Paul Summers and Cathy Summers described, in similar terms, her attitude to BAC. TC story per Cathy Summers to author, May 19, 2011.

641 **"Nobody remembers":** Cathy Summers's mother, Jill, quoted by Cathy Summers to author, May 19, 2011.

641 **struggled to be her own woman:** Cathy Summers to author, May 19, 2011.

641 **"fan boy":** Cathy Summers to author, May 19, 2011. TC, for his part, described a scene to his biographer, Gerald Clarke, that, if WF remembered it, would have been highly embarrassing and further cause for avoidance. TC let himself into the Villard one evening in 1958, and hearing dreadful weeping, encountered a very drunk WF in the room where he sometimes slept on a couch. He was inconsolable; Jean Stein had informed him that she was getting married and their affair was over. TC claimed to have stayed with WF a couple hours and also claimed that when WF died four years later, "it was really of a broken heart." TC quoted in Clarke, *Capote,* 208.

641 **the highest regard:** Estelle and Jill's affection and respect for SC, per Paul Summers and Cathy Summers to author.

641 **buzzard:** "Interviews, William Faulkner, the Art of Fiction," WF interviewed by Jean Stein in *The Paris Review,* no. 12, Spring 1956.

641 **"the fellow we see":** BAC OH, 347. Unquestionably, BAC would have been recognized by most people familiar with *What's My Line?* at that wake. However, given his propensity for confabulation, one must wonder if the story of the woman at the funeral is a transposition of the painful earlier encounter.

641 **and a couple of others:** Although BAC, DSK, and WS don't mention his presence, WF's first biographer, Joseph Blotner, indicates that he, too, was at the funeral, having come down from Charlottesville, where he was a young scholar at UVa, with Jill Faulkner Summers. See Blotner, *Faulkner,* vol. 2, 1840.

641 **Bible selections:** Psalms 20 and 46; lines from Job and Paul's Epistle to the Romans.

642 **"are a big thing":** WS, "As He Lay Dead, a Bitter Grief."

642 **"they had lost":** BAC OH, 348.

642 **"hated":** Chodes interview, 7–8.

642 **good progress on his work:** BAC OH, 347. BAC also mentions another consolation: finding the 1957 Harper anthology that he had edited, *Reading for Pleasure,* in WF's bedroom. It is impossible to verify that this was the case. WS told the author

that he found a copy of *Lie Down in Darkness* in WF's library, and various accounts have both WF and Estelle having read it.

642 **"I think it will be":** BAC to Shelby Foote, July 12, 1962, Box 52, RHR.

643 **reach the bestseller list:** It was an unusual feat for a WF book, but DSK had predicted to WF that *The Reivers* would become "a big bestseller" as soon as he read the manuscript, calling it "one of the funniest books I have ever read." DSK to WF, Oct. 23, 1961, AEP. Its popular potential was recognized by BOMC, which made it a selection. BAC diary, Oct. 30, 1961, Box 12, CP. According to a P&L report of sales from publication covering June 4, 1962, to Mar. 31, 1964, it sold over 68,000 copies during that period. This compares to a P&L report for *The Mansion* from publication on Oct. 13, 1959, to Jan. 31, 1961, indicating that it had sold about 26,000 copies. AEP.

643 **"very handsome":** Richard Krinsley to RH salesmen, July 13, 1962, Folder 33, Box 3, WFC (10280).

643 **"ashamed":** DSK OH, 28.

643 **"literary impact":** "BAC quoted in "Kennedy Leads Nation's Tributes to 'Great Creator,'" *NYT,* July 7, 1962. The trust between author and publishers had been such that several years earlier, *The Mansion* was already in production when BAC and DSK realized that they had forgotten to issue a contract for the book. They issued one—fast. DSK to WF, July 29, 1959, Box 40, RHR. The novel was published that November.

644 **"besides being":** DSK OH, 26–27.

CHAPTER 41: HEARTBURN AND HEARTACHE

645 **spectacular good health:** JFC to author, Dec. 18, 2002.

645 **since Moss had literally dropped dead:** BAC worries about dying per CBC to author, Dec. 18, 2002.

645 **"blessing":** BAC to LH, Oct. 20, 1961, Box 58, RHR. Herbert died on Oct. 3, 1961, probably of Alzheimer's disease. For the previous five years, BAC's diary had many anguished entries about his decline.

645 **not what Wall Street wanted:** Annual Report, Random House, Inc., 1962, AAKR.

646 **at least two years:** *PW,* Sept. 3, 1962.

646 **for Bennett's eyes only:** RKH's handwritten memos are addressed solely to BAC. Perhaps BAC, recognizing he was the one who had bitten off more than RH could easily chew, went to RKH in strictest confidence; perhaps DSK also encouraged RKH to persuade BAC about necessary changes.

646 **"phobia":** RDL to author, Oct. 25, 2014.

646 **"I know well":** RKH, memos, July 3 & 5, 1962, Box 7, CP. Erskine, Blaisdell, Miller, and Schabert were not at the first meeting.

647 **for the first time:** "Confidential Minutes of the Executive Committee Meeting," July 17, 1962, Box 650, RHR.

648 **"We have a little indigestion":** DSK to Richard H. Liebermann, July 19, 1962, Box 53, RHR.

648 **indigestion continued:** For the nine months ending Jan. 31, 1963, RH reported net earnings of 46 cents per share, compared to 74 cents (plus an extra 43 cents from the sale of G&D stock) during the comparable period in 1961. See *PW,* Apr. 1, 1963. By fall 1963, RH's financial year ended Mar. 31, making it difficult to gauge comparable figures. *PW,* Sept. 2, 1963.

648 **eating hundreds of thousands of dollars:** Richard Kislik to author, Nov. 11, 2002.

648 **"more headaches every day":** BAC to Mrs. Theodor Geisel, Aug. 1, 1963, Box 56, RHR.

648 **"grim" meetings:** BAC diary, Feb. 26, 1963, Box 12, CP.

648 **They'd tried combining:** "Random, Knopf, Blaisdell Combine College Sales," *PW,* Mar. 4, 1963.

648 **pay $600,000:** *PW,* Aug. 5, 1963. A lower sum, $345,000, is mentioned in *PW,* July 6, 1964.

648 **"outrageous":** BAC diary, July 18, 1963, Box 12, CP.

648 **U.K. subsidiary:** RH 1962 Annual Report; see also Dennis Hart, "Random Harvest," *British Books,* June 1963, reprinted from *The Guardian,* courtesy *PW* files.

649 **They hit it off:** Julian Stein to author, July 10, 2003. See also BAC diary, Oct. 17, 1963, Box 12, CP.

649 **expand the object into a book:** Julian Stein to author. On Stein, see Frederick M. Rasmussen, "Julian Samuel Stein, Jr., PR Executive," *Baltimore Sun,* June 30, 2012.

650 **"great new":** BAC diary, June 14, 1967, Box 12, CP.

650 **growing pains and glitches:** RDL to author, Oct. 24, 2014; Former RH CEO Alberto Vitale to author, July 20, 2003; Jack Gambatese to author, Nov. 17, 2014. Per former CEO Vitale, Gambatese figured out how to fix the problems and ran the warehouse for many years.

650 **"I survived, you see":** PC OH, 83.

651 **rejected by Freddy Espy:** CBC to author, July 31, 2003; JFC to author, Sept. 30, 2014.

651 **always wanted details:** CBC to author, June 9, 2003.

651 **verged on the prudish:** JFC to author, Jan. 19, 2005.

651 **quixotic:** Elma Merz Otto Westney, PC's secretary at RH, to author, July 21, 2003.

651 **hear the tongue-lashing:** MKF to author, Dec. 14, 2006. Many RH staff also bore witness.

651 ***"Why don't you":*** AAK Jr. to author, Dec. 6, 2002. He witnessed this scene.

651 **"ready to murder them":** BAC, *Laugh Day* (New York: Doubleday, 1966).

652 **excruciating eternity:** CBC to author, July 31, 2003; JFC to author, Sept. 30, 2014.

652 **"Manufacturer's Day":** PC OH, 110. In the OH, PC is clearly hurt that Mother's Day was not celebrated. JFC confirmed his father's attitude. JFC to author, Sept. 30, 2014.

652 **twenty to forty boxes:** JFC to author, Sept. 30, 2014.

652 **"hours & hours":** BAC diary, Dec. 25, 1960.

652 **giving her paperweights:** JFC to author, Sept. 30, 2014.

652 **persuading them to sell:** For the first mention of talking with the Geisels about RH buying Beginner, see BAC diary, Apr. 29, 1960. There is no mention in diary or correspondence of broaching the topic with PC. JFC thinks his father may have talked with the Geisels before PC. JFC to author, Sept. 30, 2014.

652 **take to her bed:** CBC and JFC remembering it, concluded by process of elimination that it happened when BAC bought Beginner. Other instances of anger had PC sequestering herself for a briefer time.

652 **She had his ear:** PC to author, Jan. 29, 2003.

652 **Everyone in the firm:** Per JE to author, Dec. 9, 2003, "She thought she could do whatever she wanted with BAC on her side."

652 **"devious":** Richard Kislik to author, Nov. 11, 2002.

652 **gradually convincing Bennett:** JFC to author, Mar. 11, 2003.

653 **"The General":** BAC OH, 463. Many people recalled the nickname "The General," including Helen Bernstein to author, June 8, 2012; MKF to author, May 31, 2012.

653 **hired a bugler:** BAC OH, 463.

653 **"getting stronger":** BAC OH, 462.

653 **driving him crazy:** CBC to author, June 9, 2003.

653 **if domestic waters were roiled:** Elma Merz Otto Westney to author, July 21, 2003.

653 **not as easy:** JFC to author, Sept. 30, 2014.

653 **"Great Novel":** PC to author, Jan. 23, 2003.

653 **wouldn't have to travel so often:** AAK Jr. quoting PC to author, Dec. 6, 2002.

654 **Her shame at a lack:** JFC to author, Sept. 30, 2014.

654 **convinced that she was an expert:** JFC to author, Sept. 30, 2014.

654 **exceptionally large font:** JFC to author, Sept. 30, 2014. The typeface size in PC's letters matched that used in the books.

654 **"Con Tra Cep Tive":** Morgan and Morgan, *Dr. Seuss & Mr. Geisel,* 178–79.

654 **"going great":** TSG to PC, Dec. 5, 1962, RHCC.

654 **"midnight telephone marathon":** TSG to PC, Jan. 16, 1963, Box 56, RHR.

655 **to mollify his friend:** BAC diary, Jan. 18, 1963, Box 12, CP. The retitled *Cat in the Hat Beginner Book Dictionary* by P. D. Eastman and "the Cat himself" was published in 1964.

655 **"enough zing left":** BAC diary, Mar. 8, 1963, Box 12, CP.

655 **big failures:** On MGM's losses, see BAC diary, Apr. 23, 1963, Box 12, CP.

655 **"brouhaha":** BAC diary, Mar. 13, 1963, Box 12, CP.

655 **Often Ted refused:** Richard Kislik to author, Nov. 11, 2002.

655 **greeted by fresh newsprint:** The long-term effect of the strike was to sound the death knell for several New York City newspapers.

656 **kids' newspaper:** Executive Committee agenda, July 24, 1963, Box 650, RHR. The plan was to publish separate editions for five grade levels, with content superior to the corresponding editions of the *Weekly Reader.* PC and JE's project enlisted the cooperation of the NYC public school system; working with the head of the curriculum division proved to be a stumbling block. JE to author, Dec. 9, 2003.

656 **posthumous Pulitzer:** BAC diary, May 6, 1963, Box 12, CP.

656 **fat check:** BAC diary, Apr. 25, 1963, Box 12, CP.

656 **"digging oil":** Stan Berenstain to author, July 3, 2003.

656 **more than $1.2 million:** See E. S. Howell to RLB, Oct. 28, 1963, Box 650, RHR.

656 **his agent, Phyllis Jackson:** "I felt the same way about Phyllis Jackson that I felt about Bennett . . . they should be entitled to go on forever." TSG to DSK, Mar. 31, 1977, RHCC.

656 **wanted free of Bennett's wife:** RLB to author, Jan. 18, 2006. I have followed RLB's narrative, but there is no way to know the exact sequence and when and

how BAC was told TSG wanted to split. With the permission of TSG's widow, I asked to see Jackson's files through the agency she worked for, but my request was denied. Much between BAC, PC, and TSG was conducted by phone, not necessarily written down.

656 **"complete freedom":** Executive Committee Minutes for May 1, 1963, Box 650, RHR. A 3-page memo in the back of the folder has no indication of who wrote it or was to receive it; presumably these are RLB's discussion points.

656 **"strained":** BAC diary, May 9, 1963. This was the first talk on reorganization for Beginner Books.

656 **plot "Geisels strategy":** BAC diary, May 12, 1963, Box 12, CP.

656 **closeted with Don and Bob:** BAC diary, May 13, 1963, Box 12, CP.

657 **"Ted, I want you to":** DSK quoted by Stan Berenstain to author, July 3, 2003. Berenstain also described Beginner offices the day TSG was told of PC's forced departure.

657 **"peaceful pow-wow":** BAC diary, May 21, 1963.

657 **do most of the work:** JFC to author, Sept. 30, 2014.

657 **"enormity . . . Woe":** BAC diary, May 28 & 29, 1963, Box 12, CP.

657 **"Go up to the fifth":** MKF to author, Dec. 4, 2006.

657 **warm welcome from Donald:** DSK to CBC, Western Union telegram, June 12, 1963, Box 56, RHR.

657 **also to help Phyllis:** BAC to "Mrs. Ted Geisel," Aug. 1, 1963, Box 56, RHR.

658 **Harvard Business School:** BAC to "Mrs. Ted Geisel," Aug. 1, 1963, Box 56, RHR; also CBC to author, Aug. 7, 2003.

658 **"REALLY want":** BAC diary, Dec. 22, 1963, Box 12, CP.

658 **expressions of interest:** BAC diary, Oct. 31, 1963, Box 12, CP.

658 **"Oy vay!":** BAC diary, Dec. 16, 1963, Box 12, CP.

658 **"What two birds":** Unsigned telegram, May 25, 1963.

658 **"I think that due to you":** BAC to HPG and TSG, May 27, 1963, Box 56, RHR.

659 **"cut-off feeling":** HPG to BAC, July 30, 1963, Box 56, RHR.

659 **Phyllis had wanted her legacy:** MKF to author, Dec. 4, 2006.

659 **a kind of diminishment:** MKF to author, May 31, 2012.

659 **betrayed her:** JFC to author, July 9, 2003.

659 **never be quite the same:** Judith Morgan to author, Mar. 10, 2012. Others offered the same view.

CHAPTER 42: RED HOT FUN

660 **hippest, trend-spotting:** Bruce Weber, "L. Rust Hills, Fiction Editor at *Esquire,* Dies at 83," *NYT,* Aug. 13, 2008.

660 **"*a chart of power*":** L. Rust Hills, "The Structure of the American Literary Establishment," *Esquire,* July 1963, 41–43, Box 71, CP. Italics added. Many of the editors and publishers interviewed for this book remembered it.

661 **"*Bennett Cerf secured*":** Italics added.

661 **Letters poured in:** These were printed in the Sept. and Oct. issues of the magazine.

661 **Epstein and Fox got asterisks:** JMF and JE were the only editors in all of RH Inc. to receive an asterisk.

662 **"Before you make":** JHS reconstructed events in an interview with the author, Feb. 5, 2003.

663 **Fox had disappointed him:** Jill Fuller Fox to author, July 7, 2003. JMF felt a slight "cooling" from BAC after saying no.

663 **the more Silberman said it:** JHS to author, Feb. 5, 2003.

663 **self-confessed "snob":** Leona Nevler to author, Dec. 2, 2005.

663 **been the first Jew:** JHS's boss, Richard Baron, then co-owner of Dial Press, told the author that BAC was first to break the unofficial ban on Jews in the club car. CBC and JFC confirmed it.

664 **one of the "best":** BAC diary, Oct. 1, 1963. The diners were BAC and PC; Baldwin; broadcaster Alistair Cooke and his wife, Jane; Dick and Dorothy Rodgers; CBC.

664 **acquire her next book:** Friedan's *It Changed My Life: Writings on the Women's Movement* would not be published until 1976.

664 **many remarkable books:** Toffler's uncredited (at the time) co-author was his wife, Heidi. The Ali book was written with Richard Durham and sustained criticism as to factual accuracy and the role the Nation of Islam played in reading (and presumably critiquing) the manuscript as it was being written. Toni Morrison was the editor on the book.

664 **more than paid off:** BAC died in 1971. JHS left RH in 1975 to start Summit Books, his own imprint at S&S, after a personal disagreement with BAC's successor, RLB.

664 **written by Thomas B. Morgan:** Morgan, "The Long Happy Life of Bennett Cerf," *Esquire,* Mar. 1964. RH editor Nan Talese's husband, Gay, a frequent *Esquire* contributor who for a period wrote full-time for the magazine, characterized Morgan as "very much around," "eyes open," "ears

alert." Talese quoted in Douglas Martin, "Thomas B. Morgan, Writer, Editor and Lindsay Press Aide, Dies at 87," *NYT,* June 18, 2014. Morgan was press aide to Adlai Stevenson during his 1960 presidential bid; a feature writer for *Look, Life, Harper's;* editor of the *Village Voice;* president of NYC's public radio and TV corporation; and press secretary to John V. Lindsay during Lindsay's second term.

665 **"VERY PLEASING!":** The capital letters and underlining are both from BAC in his diary, Feb. 14, 1964, Box 12, CP.

665 **"Bennett Alfred Cerf is perhaps":** Italics in quotes from Morgan's profile are mine, not Morgan's, apart from GTH "*poking fun*" at BAC.

665 **"so much *fun* on the side":** Ironically, RDL asserted that BAC did not use the word "fun" frequently. He said, "I never heard him say he was having fun. What I remember far better is his often tugging at his hankie in consternation at some problem that had to be solved." RDL to author, Dec. 20, 2014.

666 **mask became the face:** See Anthony W. Lee and John Pultz, *Diane Arbus: Family Albums* (New Haven: Yale University Press, 2003), 10–12; Patricia Bosworth, *Diane Arbus: A Biography* (New York: W.W. Norton, 1984), 304. The Arbus estate would not grant permission for the photograph to be reproduced unless the author removed certain words from the description.

666 **"deeply hidden":** JHS to author, Feb. 5, 2003.

666 **"He asked, 'Who do you think I am?'":** David Halberstam to author, Nov. 24, 2003.

667 **"when he was sad":** LH to author, Nov. 17, 2002.

667 **"If only you knew":** RLB to author, Sept. 23, 2003.

CHAPTER 43: DIVORCES AND DISAGREEMENTS

668 **protests from other RH authors and friends:** One letter came from author Hildegarde Dolson, who was especially upset about an RH ad in the *NYT* implying that RH supported Rand's novel as "the great Truth." Dolson to BAC, Dec. 11, 1957, Box 33, RHR.

668 ***We the Living:*** The book was published by Cassell in London in 1935 and by Macmillan in the United States in 1936.

668 **the Hemisphere:** The lunch was on July 2, 1963. BAC diary, Box 12, CP.

668 ***Red Pawn:*** On the deal, see BAC to Alvin G. Manuel, Aug. 30, 1963, Box 57, RHR. Writing to BAC on July 29, 1963, AR enclosed a synopsis of the story along with its Hollywood history. See Michael S. Berliner, ed., *Letters of Ayn Rand* (New York: Dutton, 1995), 610–11.

668 **"arch angel friend":** BAC to AR, July 30, 1963, Box 57, RHR.

669 **"to the strong":** DSK OH, 80. Re DSK and AR philosophy, see also Barbara Branden, *The Passion of Ayn Rand* (New York: Doubleday, 1986), 286.

669 **"a gentleman":** Loyalty toast story per RDL to author, Dec. 20, 2014. RDL was not present but was told by staff who were.

669 **"unloyal":** See Heller, *Ayn Rand and the World She Made,* 334. AR made the remarks to agent Perry Knowlton, per Heller.

669 **"Your attitude has been":** AR to BAC, July 29, 1963, in Michael S. Berliner, ed., *Letters of Ayn Rand* (New York: Dutton, 1995), 610–11.

669 **collection of nonfiction pieces:** BAC diary, Aug. 28, 1963, Box 12, CP.

669 **"a big seller":** AR to BAC, Oct. 30, 1963, RHCC, reprinted in Berliner, ed., *Letters of Ayn Rand,* 617–21.

669 **"Ask not what your country":** Jennifer Burns, *Goddess of the Market: Ayn Rand and the American Right* (New York: Oxford University Press, 2009), 210.

669 **he'd send word around:** BAC to AR, Aug. 28, 1963, Box 57, RHR.

669 **Walter Winchell had given:** AR to BAC, Oct. 30, 1963, RHCC, reprinted in Berliner, ed., *Letters of Ayn Rand,* 617–21.

669 **didn't pause to reflect:** It is not clear if BAC read the pamphlet immediately or only after his editors began to object to the title. For a copy of *The Fascist New Frontier* pamphlet, see Box 57, RHR.

670 **"startling":** BAC to AR, Oct. 18, 1963, Box 57 (also 649), RHR. Most probably JMF was an early reader. BAC discussed the project when JMF came to Mt. Kisco on Labor Day, Sept. 2, 1963. He discussed again with JMF and JHS on Sept. 24 over lunch. BAC diary, Box 12, CP.

670 **"propriety":** Executive Committee meeting minutes, Sept. 11, 1963; see also minutes, Sept. 18, 1963. Box 650, RHR.

670 **"immediately against":** BAC to AR, Oct. 18, 1963, Box 57 (also 649), RHR.

670 **forward a dozen copies:** The sequence of events—in particular, when AR supplied the extra copies and when RH editors and executives actually read the text—I have had to reconstruct from her letter and BAC's letter and diary entries, but reconstruction is an imperfect science.

670 **angry words:** BAC diary, Sept. 24, 1963, Box 12, CP.
670 **rehashed for a full hour:** BAC diary, Oct. 14, 1963, Box 12, CP.
670 **"under this title":** Executive Committee meeting minutes, Oct. 16, 1963, Box 650, RHR.
670 **"you would publish anything":** AR quoted by BAC in BAC OH, 950. I have followed the OH for much of the story.
670 **huge eyes burning:** DSK's exact words were "fire in her eyes." DSK OH, 80.
671 **"You can say anything":** BAC OH, 950.
671 **very angry:** BK to author, Nov. 4, 2002.
671 **no cause to feel guilty:** Branden, *Passion of Ayn Rand,* 288.
671 **Grueling hours passed:** BAC diary, Oct. 16, 1963, Box 12, CP.
671 **Bennett continued alone:** BAC diary makes clear that DSK was present only part of the time.
671 **three hours and forty minutes:** BAC diary, Oct. 16, 1963, Box 12, CP.
672 **"to make it as perfect":** BAC diary, Oct. 19, 1963, Box 12, CP.
672 **"never try to censor":** BAC to AR, final version of letter dated Oct. 18, 1963.
672 **"broken his word":** AR to BAC, Oct. 30, 1963, RHCC, reprinted in Berliner, ed., *Letters of Ayn Rand.*
672 **"Nobody can be right":** Two typed drafts, with emendations in BAC's hand as well as someone else's, both undated, are in Box 57, RHR. There is no carbon of a final version. Berliner states that in AR's letters, there is "no record of a response from Cerf." However, in his diary on Oct. 31, 1963, BAC states "received 5-page letter from Ayn Rand on her proposed polit book and answered in 3 pages." See Berliner, ed., *Letters of Ayn Rand,* 621. In a letter to AR dated Nov. 26, 1963, BAC refers to his letter of Nov. 1, presumably the final version of the two drafts that strangely is missing from both RH and AR files.
672 **glued to the screen:** BAC diary, Nov. 22, 1963, Box 12, CP.
673 **"academic":** BAC to AR, Nov. 26, 1963, Box 57, RHR.
673 ***The Virtue of Selfishness:*** Heller, *Ayn Rand and the World She Made,* 336–37.
673 **her primary publisher:** BAC diary, Mar. 29, 1965, Box 12, CP.
673 **"because I refused":** BAC diary, Mar. 29, 1965, Box 12, CP.
673 **"Deeply, deeply sorry":** BAC to AR, Mar. 29, 1965, RHCC.
673 **"always give credit":** AR to BAC, Apr. 5, 1965, RHCC.
674 **staccato, you-are-there:** Background on Bishop and the project per RDL to author, Apr. 12, 2015. See also Jim Bishop, *A Bishop's Confession* (Boston: Little, Brown, 1981); James Barron, "Jim Bishop, a Columnist, Dies: Popular Author of 21 Books," *NYT,* July 28, 1987. Bill O'Reilly would reprise Bishop's winning formula a half century later in his own books. There is copyright in words, but not in ideas.
674 **Bishop trailed:** For the exact dates Bishop spent with JFK and Jacqueline Kennedy, see Jim Bishop, *A Day in the Life of President Kennedy* (New York: RH, 1964), viii.
674 **sixty-odd corrections:** Jim Bishop, *The Day Kennedy Was Shot* (New York: Funk & Wagnalls, 1968), xiv.
674 **only title among the top:** Hackett and Burke, *80 Years of Best Sellers, 1895–1975,* 192–93. The hardcover sold 139,000 copies in 1964.
674 **in January, RH signed:** BAC to Robert F. Kennedy, Aug. 10, 1964, Box 59, RHR.
674 **"enthralled":** BAC diary, May 17, 1964. For the lunch with Jacqueline Kennedy, see BAC OH, 837.
675 **she'd like to be a bird:** KCH to author, Dec. 17, 2004.
675 **Bishop had taken advantage:** On Kennedy's unhappiness over earlier book, see BAC OH, 836. Bishop speaks of incidents that she did not like. See Bishop, *Bishop's Confession,* 386.
675 **not to publish:** BAC to Robert F. Kennedy, Aug. 10, 1964, Box 59, RHR.
676 **contract for the assassination book:** BAC OH, 838–39; Bishop, *Day Kennedy Was Shot,* xiv.
676 **poetry anthology:** BAC diary, Sept. 12, 17, 1964, Box 12, CP.
676 **lost a million dollars:** BAC OH, 522.
677 **had always loved her:** BAC OH, 523.
677 **he popped backstage:** The backstage visit to see Garland was May 11, 1959. BAC diary, Box 12, CP.
677 **cajoling Dick Rodgers:** Discussions with Rodgers several times in 1958. BAC diary. Nothing came of them. In 1971, discussions were rekindled; there are several references in BAC's diary to a $25,000 advance. BAC died later that year, Rodgers in 1977. No book was published.
677 **"One of the most tragic":** BAC OH, 523.
677 **having none of it:** $75,000 advance: Marvin Meyer to BAC, Nov. 20, 1959; BAC to Meyer, Nov. 23, 1959, Box 56, RHR.
677 **Garland was present:** BAC diary, Nov. 13, 1959, Box 12, CP.
677 **"miserable":** BAC OH, 523.
678 **acute hepatitis:** BAC diary, Nov. 24, 1959; BAC OH. On Garland, see Gerald Clarke, *Get Happy: The Life of Judy Garland* (New

York: RH, 2000), esp. 347, 391–92 on the illness and the autobiography attempt. On Luft, see Mark Steyn, "Post Mortem: The Least Worst Man: Sidney Luft (1915–2005)," *The Atlantic Monthly,* Dec. 2005, courtesy AAK Jr.

678 **still be compromised:** Finklehoffe would later assert that Luft had been told it was cirrhosis of the liver. See Randy L. Schmidt, "Op-Ed: Judy Garland's Final Effort to Tell Her Own Story," Advocate .com, Aug. 14, 2014.

678 **$50,000 contract:** BAC diary, Dec. 21, 1959, Box 12, CP.

678 **The Lufts had insisted:** Draft contract and a letter, BAC to David Begelman, Garland's then-agent reprising the terms, June 10, 1963, Box 56, RHR. Between the two hospital visits and after, until the contract was set, were telephone calls. BAC mentions a $50,000 advance being superseded by $30,000, of which $20,000 would be a "loan." See BAC to Jacob F. Raskin, an attorney at RH lawyers Weil, Gotshal and Manges, Nov. 16, 1959, Box 56, RHR.

678 **"There have been a lot":** PR release, Jan. 4, 1960, Box 70, CP.

679 **delivered only sixty-odd pages:** Meetings and calls with Garland, Luft, and Finklehoffe, BAC diary, July 13, Aug. 1, 8, & 21, Nov. 23, 1960, Box 12, CP.

679 **"superb":** BAC diary, Jan. 27, 1961, Box 12, CP.

679 **went through the motions:** An undated carbon of the letter to Finklehoffe is in Box 56, RHR.

679 **"just as worried":** BAC to Judy Garland, Feb. 10, 1964, Box 59, RHR.

679 **heard the unmistakable voice:** On Garland's 1966 approach to BAC, see Schmidt, "Op-Ed."

CHAPTER 44: BACKING HORSES

680 **"You can get along fine":** BAC typescript speech, Mar. 1963, Box 57, RHR. It is likely that this aphorism originated with comedian/philosopher Will Rogers.

680 **a theatrical family:** Lansbury's mother had acted on the London stage, and his older sister, Angela, was already known in theater and film. His twin brother, Bruce, soon became a producer on TV serials.

680 **"virtual unknowns":** Frank D. Gilroy, *About Those Roses, or How* Not *To Do a Play and Succeed* (New York: RH, 1965), 4 (Gilroy's exact words were "virtually unknown"). Also, Edgar Lansbury to author, Feb. 14, 2015. The returned soldier was played by an actor who would *become* a star, Martin Sheen; his parents were played by Irene Dailey and Jack Albertson, who would win a Tony Award.

681 **"The other evening I saw":** *The Subject Was Roses* ad, clipping book, Box 72, CP. In the ad, BAC called this very serious play a "comedy drama"—presumably he thought that would entice more theatergoers to an important drama by an unknown.

681 **A Madison Avenue ad man:** Lawrence ad per Edgar Lansbury to author, Feb. 14, 2015.

681 **One Wednesday at Sardi's:** Louis Calta, "A Long Shot Play and How It Won," *NYT,* July 2, 1964, Box 72, CP.

682 **"a big figure":** Rosanna Warren to author, May 16, 2003. All of her subsequent quotes are from this interview.

682 **"That's disgusting":** Eleanor Clark quoted by Rose Styron to author, Nov. 12, 2003. Both Rosanna Warren and Rose Styron recounted the TV story. Warren noted BAC's "distress" but didn't mention a remark from her mother as cause.

683 **tramped to the next house:** BAC identified the neighbors as the Lees. See BAC diary, Dec. 31, 1961, Box 12, CP.

683 **"a riot!":** BAC diary, Feb. 9, 1964, Box 12, CP.

683 **"child prodigy":** Rosanna Warren to author, May 16, 2003.

684 **"We have not changed":** BAC on the flap copy of Rosanna Phelps Warren, *The Joey Story* (New York: RH, 1964), courtesy Rosanna Warren.

684 **his personal project:** BAC to Mrs. Robert Penn Warren, May 27, 1964, Box 60, RHR.

684 **"The whole day":** Rosanna Warren to BAC, Nov. 2, 1964, courtesy JFC.

684 **"huge" success unlikely:** BAC OH, 556.

684 **"just as deserving":** BAC, "A Plea for the Unknown Writer," *Variety,* Jan. 9, 1963, Box 649, RHR.

685 **"publishers will publish":** "Random House Associate Discusses Role of Publisher," Larry Bensky (presumably from Sarah Lawrence College) quoted in unsourced clipping, Box 528, RHR.

685 **"they published the good authors":** CM to author, Mar. 12, 2008.

685 **"indulgence in the matter":** CM to RH, undated (likely Apr. 1962), AEP. On the letter is a handwritten note: "MG 5/3 Larry Bensky." Groffsky recalled passing CM to Bensky. Groffsky to author, Jan. 10, 2005.

685 **"very seriously":** Larry Bensky to author, Nov. 26, 2003.

685 **had Groffsky been male:** Her ability and the sexist unfairness behind her not being

promoted per Larry Bensky to author, Nov. 26, 2003.

686 **"a strange and, I think, beautiful":** Larry Bensky to AE, May 21, 1962, AEP.

686 **expressing strong interest:** Larry Bensky to CM, June 12, 1962, AEP. CM was born on July 20, 1933, so he was about to turn twenty-nine when he heard from Bensky.

686 **"This is a writer of real talent":** Larry Bensky to AE, July 9, 1963, AEP.

686 **at loggerheads:** See AE to Larry Bensky, Jan. 19, 1962; Larry Bensky to AE, Jan. 20, 1962, Box 527, RHR.

686 **$1,500 advance:** "One of the owners of the company" had read and "liked" the manuscript. See Larry Bensky to CM, Aug. 6, 1963, AEP. Almost certainly this was DSK, since BAC read the galleys more than a year later. BAC diary, Dec. 30, 1964.

687 **"apostrophical eccentricities":** AE to CM, Nov. 14, 1963, AEP.

687 **Southern-bred:** CM was born in Rhode Island but moved to Tennessee at the age of four, as per his bio on *The Orchard Keeper.*

687 **"scared up":** AE to CM, Apr. 3, 1964, AEP.

687 **"exasperating":** Orville Prescott, "Still Another Disciple of William Faulkner," "Books of the Times," *NYT,* May 12, 1965.

687 **raised the advance:** CM to AE, received Dec. 4, 1964, AEP; on the increased advance, see AE to CM, Dec. 30, 1964, AEP.

687 **didn't make money:** An internal report declared a negative "contribution/gross profit" of $765. See P&L report covering May 5, 1965–Nov. 30, 1966, period, June 29, 1967, AEP.

687 **threatening to quit:** RLB to author, Dec. 18, 2013.

688 **the last McCarthy book:** AE worked on the book, but with his health declining, CM got an agent who moved him from the RH imprint to Knopf, where the novel was published. He remained there until he died.

688 **"Albert was one of the best":** CM to author, Mar. 12, 2008.

CHAPTER 45: BIG MONEY, DIFFERENT EQUATIONS

690 **"literary father":** Irwin Shaw to Dorothy Commins, July 20, 1958, Box 13, SCP.

690 ***Love on a Dark Street:*** BAC to Irwin Shaw, Jan. 30, 1964, RHCC.

690 **"Competent but slightly disappointed":** BAC diary, Mar. 29, 1964, Box 12, CP.

690 **couldn't compare with the movie lucre:** *Two Weeks in Another Town* sales 38,375 regular and 4,158 "special" copies. P&L report covering Jan. 1960–Jan. 31, 1961, AEP.

690 **wanted a bigger advance:** In Aug. 1962 Shaw went to BAC and DSK, threatening to leave if they didn't pay a higher advance. They agreed to $55,000—an enormous sum—by the end of the year as an advance on a full-length novel to be delivered Sept. 1, 1963, and to adjust the usual reprint terms to 60/40 in Shaw's favor. Shaw would be referred to in the contract as an RH employee, which would allow them to pay him through foreign channels so he wouldn't have to pay tax. See Michael Shnayerson, *Irwin Shaw* (New York: Putnam, 1989), 281–82. I have not seen independent corroboration for any of this. I did find the check Lazar sent to RH as payment (in full) for Irwin Shaw's obligation in the amount of $15,000—the sum RH sent to Irwin Shaw on Dec. 28, 1962. BAC to Lazar, July 1, 1964, Box 59, RHR.

690 **"a short story":** DSK OH, 54–55.

690 **"He called it":** Shnayerson, *Irwin Shaw,* 293.

690 **had just finished:** See BAC diary, June 20, 1964, Box 12, CP.

690 **a shocking demand:** BAC diary, June 23, 1964, Box 12, CP.

690 **had sold for:** JAM sale in BAC diary, July 10, 1963, and July 24, 1963, Box 12, CP.

691 **threatened a tenet:** BAC to Irwin Shaw, Dec. 26, 1961, RHCC.

691 **How could RH survive?:** In his OH, 55, DSK said: "We couldn't survive . . ."

691 **"We could publish the damn thing":** BAC OH, 667.

691 **"I'll release him":** DSK OH, 55. DSK has BAC saying this but there are competing versions of the story: one told by BAC in his OH; one from DSK, to which presumably Schnayerson had no access; one in Schnayerson's biography, taken partly from BAC OH and partly from correspondence. The key evidence is BAC to Lazar, July 1, 1964; DSK to Irwin Shaw, July 17, 1964. Shaw says he "had told Erskine and Bennett" and owed DSK a letter because he "should have come in to talk to [him]."

691 **huge $250,000 advance:** DSK OH, 56.

691 **all was done:** In BAC's account of the move, he mistakenly references "Dell and Dial," but Dial had been bought by Dell. BAC diary, July 1, 1964; see also BAC to Irving Paul Lazar, July 1, 1964, Box 59, RHR.

691 **$350,000-plus:** Irwin Shaw to DSK, July 17, 1964, RHCC.

691 **"childish":** BAC OH, 670.

691 **"He knew it was petty":** Nan Talese to author, Jan. 7, 2003.

692 **came to agree:** Shnayerson, *Irwin Shaw,* 294.

692 **phenomenal 100,000 copies:** For *Forever Amber* sales data, see Peter Guttridge, "Kathleen Winsor, Author of the Racy Bestseller 'Forever Amber,'" *The Independent,* May 29, 2003.

692 **1,650 manuscript pages:** BAC notes 1,900 pages at first, but the night he finishes, notes 1,650 pages. BAC diary, May 15 & 19, 1964, Box 12, CP.

692 **"a damned good story":** BAC OH, 582.

692 **"discreetly":** JHS to BAC, May 15, 1964, Box 60, RHR.

693 **"It's a staggering":** BAC to Kathleen Winsor, May 21, 1964, Box 60, RHR.

693 **knew he'd been carried away:** RLB to author, Apr. 1, 2003.

693 **"John, can I walk":** BAC OH; RLB to author, Apr. 1, 2003. In his OH, BAC makes Budlong look even more foolish. I have only used those statements that RLB recalled BAC making.

694 **as far as Bernstein:** RLB to author, May 5, 2003.

694 **didn't suffer fools gladly:** Larry Bensky to author, Nov. 26, 2003.

694 **30,000 hardcover copies:** BAC OH, 582.

694 **"clobbered":** BAC diary, May 2, 1965, Box 12, CP.

694 **NAL lost a fortune:** BAC OH, 584.

694 **$750,000 advance:** BAC diary, Feb. 12, 1965, Box 12, CP.

694 **"great":** On BAC reading *The Source,* see BAC diary, Aug. 2 & 5, 1964, Box 12, CP.

694 **wasn't even written:** On the Friedan sale, see BAC diary, Feb. 24, 1965, Box 12, CP. Friedan's book would not be written for a long time and also would not be the book originally contracted. In Sept. 1974 she signed an agreement with RH to replace the book she had not delivered with *It Changed My Life,* a cut-and-paste job based on articles and speeches. If she didn't deliver by year's end, she'd have to return the $30,750 she had received. The new book—with Friedan getting an extra $25,000 sweetener—was published in June 1976, twelve-plus years after the original contract. It failed. See Judith Hennessee, *Betty Friedan: Her Life* (New York, RH, 1999), 217–21.

CHAPTER 46: BIG BUSINESS

695 **"glorious" dream:** BAC OH, 889.

695 **"wildly improbable":** BAC diary, Jan. 28, 1964, Box 12, CP. For meetings with Time-Life CEO Andrew Heiskell and VP and head of direct mail Jerome Hardy, see BAC diary, Jan.–Apr.

695 **conservative Republican agenda:** Luce founded his company in 1923, the year BAC started at Liveright. Heiskell became CEO in 1960, but Luce didn't give up as editor-in-chief at *all* Time-Life magazines until 1964. He also remained the largest single shareholder. See Alden Whitman, "Henry Luce, 68, Dies in Phoenix," *NYT,* Mar. 1, 1967, 1, 33.

695 **could be fantastic:** BAC OH, 890.

695 **got along beautifully:** BAC OH, 889.

695 **William S. Paley:** Mentioned by DSK in John F. Baker, "Fifty Years of Publishing At Random," *PW,* Aug. 4, 1975. Per DSK, when Paley saw RH's figures, he decided it was too small to be of interest.

696 **"Once you lose":** Charles Allen quoted by CW to author, June 12, 2015.

696 **not owning their business:** BAC OH, 870.

696 **approaching a half billion dollars:** For the Time-Life annual revenue for 1966 ($503) million, see Whitman, "Henry Luce, 68, Dies in Phoenix." RH audited net sales for the year ending Mar. 31, 1964, were $29,619,000. See Certificate of Merger of RH Inc. into RCA Publishing Co. Inc. For the financial year ending Mar. 31, 1965, RH audited net sales were $31,831,000. *Unaudited* net sales for the calendar year ending Dec. 31, 1965, were $36,149,000.

696 ***Hey, what are you doing:*** BAC OH, 875–76. Variation on this story per CBC multiple times to author. He recalls it taking place on the street outside the theater where BAC had just finished appearing on *WML?*

696 **statistical chart:** DSK to George Textor, RH board member and president of Marine Midland Bank, Oct. 22, 1963, Box 643, RHR.

696 **letting people down:** CBC in RH OH, 10.

696 **feeling that he'd done:** LH to author, Nov. 17, 2002.

697 **a role she'd undoubtedly covet:** For discussion about widows coming into the business, see BAC OH, 867.

697 **scotch a merger:** BAC diary, Apr. 21, 1964.

697 **shares had risen:** See BAC diary, Jan. 2, Apr. 22, June 15, 1964, Box 12, CP.

697 **oversight had become lax:** AAK OH, July 2, 1974, courtesy AP.

697 **needed Kislik to handle:** Frances Singer to BAC, Nov. 7, 1964, Box 60, RHR.

697 **$2.5 million RH "loan":** BAC diary, June 15, 1964, Box 12, CP.

697 **"joy-killer":** BAC diary, Oct. 23, 1964, Box 12, CP.

698 **series of nosebleeds:** See BAC diary, Nov. 25, 26, 29, & 30, 1964, Box 12, CP.

698 **fielding an inquiry:** BAC diary, Dec. 5, 1964, Box 12, CP.

698 **"combine":** BAC diary, Apr. 12, 1965, Box 12, CP.
698 **meet Richard Prentice Ettinger:** BAC diary, May 17, 1965, Box 12, CP.
698 **RH–PH marriage:** PH reported $5.4 million in earnings on sales of $63.7 million in 1964, a very healthy ratio for book publishing. Robert Metz, "Personality: Law Clerk Turned Publisher," *NYT,* July 11, 1965.
698 **had won more Grammys:** RCA 1964 Annual Report, 7.
698 **systems for handling print information:** See Harry Gilroy, "R.C.A. Joins Electronics and Books," *NYT,* Jan. 16, 1966.
699 **the deal was dead:** "Notes to Financial Statements," RCA Annual Report for 1964, Proquest Historical Annual Reports, courtesy Watson Library, Columbia.
699 **separate arrangements were made:** RCA meeting, BAC diary, May 20, 1965, Box 12, CP.
699 **doing some homework:** BAC OH, 882.
699 **Pat Suppes:** John Markoff, "Patrick Suppes, 92, Pioneer in Computerized Learning," *NYT,* Dec. 3, 2014; BAC OH, 891–94.
700 **"RCA Building":** It would later be called the GE Building and then the Comcast Building. In the twenty-first century, it is familiarly known as "30 Rock."
700 **weighing in on the future:** BAC's ambition to be on RCA board per Ashbel Green to author, Nov. 13, 2002. Green was a legendary Knopf editor.

CHAPTER 47: SUCCESSOR AND SALE

701 **died a few weeks later:** RKH died on Aug. 12, 1964.
701 **had had words:** PC to author, Jan. 23, 2003.
701 ***really* loved Donald:** LH to author, Nov. 17, 2002.
702 **she disliked Kislik:** CBC to author, June 9, 2003.
702 **"true book man":** Judith Jones to author, Feb. 21, 2003. She noted that he later "proved to be much better than anyone had anticipated."
702 **square, puritanical streak:** CBC to author, June 9, 2003.
702 **top of the mountain:** RLB to Peter Prescott, Dec. 24, 1991, courtesy AP.
702 **a wild party:** BAC diary, Mar. 21, 1966, Box 12, CP.
703 **suddenly tense, was concerned:** MKF to author, Aug. 13, 2003.
703 **"weird":** BAC diary, Feb. 13, 1966, Box 12, CP. Five weeks after the party, Fariña died in a motorcycle crash.
703 **had no guard up:** MKF to author, Aug. 13, 2003.
703 **10 percent of their stock:** BAC diary, Feb. 4 & 14, 1964, Box 12, CP.
703 **the editors were the princes:** RLB to author, Apr. 1, 2003.
703 **"Alberto":** After Erskine married Marisa Bisi, who was from Italy, BAC often referred to him that way.
703 **didn't want the job:** BAC's desire for Erskine to take over per LH to author, Nov. 17, 2002.
703 **Kislik sat at his elbow:** Sterling Lord to author, Nov. 12, 2004.
704 **rumors of friction:** BAC diary, Apr. 19, 1965, Box 12, CP.
704 **management wisdom from Don:** Unpublished RLB OH, 68.
704 **joint proposal:** RWK to author, Nov. 11, 2002. When asked about it, RLB at first said: "I didn't get along with Dick Kislik. He was very aware of running for president." Later he said on the subject of a purchase, "I don't remember. It's very possible, though." RLB to author, Apr. 1, 2003.
704 **wouldn't trust the future:** RWK to author, Nov. 11, 2002.
704 **"We do not want to be":** Handwritten memo from PC to RLB, n.d., emphasis added; RLB to PC, Dec. 27, 1961 (reply), Box 629, RHR.
705 **She begged Bennett not to:** PC OH, 428.
705 **cut down on moments for doubt:** LH to author, Nov. 17, 2002.
705 **"subsidiary merger":** Robert Todd Lang to author, May 5, 2004.
705 **"saw things others didn't":** Robert Todd Lang to author, May 2, 2004.
706 **advanced cancer:** AAK diary, Sept. 11, 1963, Box 612.3, 1539, AAKR.
706 **badly broken hip:** AAK diary, Nov. 4, 1961, Box 637, AAKR.
706 **"Is that a wig":** BAC quoted by AAK to Susan Sheehan, tape 5, courtesy AP.
706 **salary cuts linked to less responsibility:** DSK to AAK, BWK, Apr. 12, 1965, Box 62, RHR.
707 **"poisonous":** AAK to BAC, June 13, 1961, AAKR. The scheme AAK objected to was called the "Corresponding Readers" plan. Two versions of a 1961 form letter from the "Corresponding Readers Office," undated from 1961, are in his papers. GTH stingingly criticized the initiative. See GTH, "Help!" *TNY,* Sept. 2, 1961.
707 **"ashamed":** AAK diary, Jan. 8, 1963, Box 637, AAKR.
707 **"For Bennett":** AAK to BAC, Christmas 1963, Box 35, CP.
707 **nonpareil crowd:** Guest list for Knopf banquet, courtesy AP.

707 **"A Salute":** This and "A Tribute" reprinted in: *Portrait of a Publisher 1915–1965,* vol. 2, *Alfred A. Knopf and the Borzoi Imprint: Recollections and Appreciations,* introduction by Paul A. Bennett (New York: The Typophiles, 1965), 257, 262.

707 **"a very arrogant, selfish man":** DSK to Susan Sheehan, Jan. 29, 1975, courtesy AP.

708 **a full set of the ML:** BAC diary, May 13, 1960, Box 12, CP.

708 **he held his tongue:** RLB to author, Feb. 25, Apr. 1, 2003, June 13, 2012.

708 **celebrating *something* at Sardi's:** BAC diary, Oct. 29, 1965, Box 12, CP.

708 **"realignment":** Box 72, CP.

708 **"To the prexy":** Harry Gilroy, "Cerf to Be Chairman at Random House," *NYT,* Dec. 7, 1965.

708 **"to prowl":** BAC diary, Dec. 10, 1965, Box 12, CP.

708 **"moving in on us":** BAC diary, Dec. 20, 1965, Box 12, CP.

708 **become more involved:** Felix Rohatyn to author, June 8, 2005. BAC consistently misspelled Rohatyn's name in his diary, as "Rowayton" (a town in Connecticut).

709 **"All our facilities":** Sarnoff wire quoted in Thomas S. W. Lewis, *Empire of the Air: The Men Who Made Radio* (New York: HarperCollins, 1991), 279. For Sarnoff and WWII: see Lewis, 279–97.

710 **"kept a long vigil":** Donald L. Miller, *Supreme City: How Jazz Age Manhattan Gave Birth to Modern America* (New York: S&S, 2014), 300–301.

710 **"radio music box":** Lewis, *Empire of the Air,* 115–16; on Sarnoff and RCA, see Miller, *Supreme City,* 295–318; Kenneth Bilby, *The General: David Sarnoff and the Rise of the Communications Industry* (New York: Harper & Row, 1986); Eugene Lyons, *David Sarnoff* (New York: Harper & Row, 1966).

710 **bent competitors to his will:** Herbert S. Schlosser to author, Feb. 16, 2014. Schlosser was a senior executive at NBC for many years.

710 **supported McCarthy:** See "About Sarnoff," background information for "Big Dream Small Screen," *American Experience,* PBS, aired Feb. 10, 1997, http://www.pbs.org/wgbh/amex/technology/bigdream/masarnoff.html.

710 **how to select partially developed ideas:** Miller, *Supreme City,* 307.

711 **"sneaked":** BAC diary, Dec. 23, 1965; on the meeting and call, see Dec. 26 & 27, Box 12, CP.

711 **bankers were getting impatient:** BAC OH, 882. Except where indicated, I have followed BAC's account of the sale in his OH, 882–85. It was told with his usual brio—and, presumably, his usual embroidery. Where it conflicts with his diary entries or the accounts of others, like Rohatyn, who were directly involved, I have gone with the facts as I see them. For instance, the OH claims the price wasn't resolved until after the vacation, but it was the next morning on the phone, before BAC left for Palm Springs, that Sarnoff agreed to the price, according to his diary. The OH makes no reference to Sarnoff's stipulation re *WML?* at the Sunday meeting, but again, it is noted in the diary.

711 **Metromedia:** Its stations would form the core for what became the Fox Broadcasting Company.

712 **champagne chilling:** BAC refers to Bobby and "a banker" also there. BAC OH. I assume this was Rohatyn, who said he persuaded Sarnoff to increase the price by Monday morning. Rohatyn to author, June 8, 2005.

712 **"a shocker":** BAC diary, Dec. 26, 1965.

712 **"It's not the end of the world":** Felix Rohatyn to author, June 8, 2005.

713 **the switchboard buzzed:** BAC diary, Dec. 27, 1965.

CHAPTER 48: SINATRA

714 **Bennett met Frank Sinatra:** BAC, "Trade Winds," *SRL,* Jan. 15, 1944.

714 **in love:** PC OH, 162–66.

714 **identifying with Eliza Doolittle's:** Sam Kashner, "The Loneliest Guy in the World," *GQ,* Nov. 1999, 350–58, courtesy Margaret Herrick Library clipping files, AMPAS. Kashner was referencing the film version of *My Fair Lady.*

714 **mingled with him:** At Sinatra's (hereafter FS) house rented by the Harts, Feb. 15, 1953; at MH's, Dec. 18, 1954; at Goetz's party for the Cerfs, Dec. 5, 1957, all BAC diary, Box 12, CP.

714 **select list of forty:** "What's New . . . by Phyllis Cerf," *Newsday,* May 2, 1957, courtesy CBC and JFC.

714 **voice behind so many:** Mia Farrow to author, Mar. 3, 2003.

715 **cultivate an older crowd:** BAC and PC's relationship with FS, and FS generally, per author interviews with Tina Sinatra, June 10, 2008; Mia Farrow, Mar. 3, 2003; Armand and Harriet Deutsch, June 2, 2003; Leonora Hornblow, Nov. 17, 2002; Helene Fagan Bidwell, May 25, 2005; and James Kaplan, Mar. 24, 2015. James Kaplan kindly shared advance sections of the second volume of his Sinatra biography, *The*

Chairman (New York: Doubleday, 2015). I have also relied on multiple interviews with CBC, JFC, PC, KCH, and RLB. Quotes are from interviews unless otherwise specified. On Sinatra generally, see Tina Sinatra, *My Father's Daughter: A Memoir* (New York: S&S, 2000); James Kaplan, *Frank: The Voice* (New York: Doubleday, 2010); Kitty Kelley, *His Way: The Unauthorized Biography of Frank Sinatra* (New York: Bantam Books, 1986); George Jacobs and William Stadiem, *Mr. S: My Life with Frank Sinatra* (New York: HarperCollins, 2003); Armand Deutsch, *Me and Bogie* (New York: Putnam, 1991); Pete Hamill, *Why Sinatra Matters* (New York: Little, Brown, 1998); John Lahr, *Sinatra: The Artist and the Man* (New York: RH, 1997); Earl Wilson, *Sinatra: An Unauthorized Biography* (New York: Macmillan, 1976); Gay Talese, "Frank Sinatra Has a Cold," *Esquire,* Apr. 1966; "Eighty-Two Very Good Years," in "The Talk of the Town," *TNY,* May 25, 1998.

715 **"such a sweetness":** Tina Sinatra to author.

715 **"I would be proud":** BAC to FS, May 3, 1965, Box 63, RHR.

715 **discussing with Sinatra's PR man:** This was Jim Mahoney. BAC diary, May 14, 1965, Box 12, CP.

715 **"A charming, beautiful":** BAC diary, Aug. 15, 1965, Box 12, CP. Farrow was twenty, not nineteen.

716 **"his girl":** *AR,* 287.

716 **The man himself:** BAC diary, Dec. 27, 1965, Box 12, CP.

716 **both for privacy and space:** See David McClintick, "*AD* Revisits Frank Sinatra's Palm Springs Compound," *Architectural Digest,* Nov. 30, 1998, www.architecturaldigest.com/celebrity-homes/1998/frank-sinatra-palm-springs-california-house-article; "Sinatra's Palm Springs," *Inside Palm Springs,* www.palmspringsusa.com/newsletter/index. Wonder Palms is now "Frank Sinatra Drive."

716 **deeply cherished:** On the FS painting, see "Eighty-Two Very Good Years"; the author viewed the painting on multiple visits to 62nd St.

716 **Sinatra's Palm Springs compound:** See Aileen Mehle, "Suzy Says," *Chicago Tribune,* Jan. 9, 1969, Proquest Historical Newspapers.

717 **"bathroom check":** Farrow to author, Mar. 3, 2003.

717 **emcee the inauguration:** On BAC's relationship with Lindsay, see correspondence between BAC and JVL, Jan. 13 & 26, 1961, Oct. 11, 1963, RHCC, RHR; see also BAC to Cass Canfield, Aug. 26, 1965, Box 62, RHR. PC was also actively involved in supporting Lindsay, according to Elma Merz Otto Westney, PC's secretary, to author, July 21, 2003; Daniel E. Button's *Lindsay, A Man for Tomorrow* was included in an RH ad in *PW,* June 14, 1965. On the inauguration, see "The Talk of the Town," in *TNY,* Jan. 8, 1966.

717 **"I still think it's a fun city":** Dick Schapp first quoted Lindsay saying it in the *NY Herald Tribune;* it's been used ironically many times since. See, for example, Editorial, "When Fun City Wasn't," *NYT,* May 27, 2010.

718 **twenty-one hours after:** BAC diary, Jan. 1, 1966.

718 **"Beansy":** Farrow to author, Mar. 3, 2003.

718 **didn't take to her at first:** Farrow to author, Mar. 3, 2003.

718 **she'd had a lot:** Farrow to author, Mar. 3, 2003.

718 **"coy or retiring":** Farrow to author, Mar. 3, 2003.

719 **organize the compound crowd:** Farrow to author, Mar. 3, 2003.

719 **BOSS and five stars:** Photographs in Sinatra Christmas Album, Box 75, CP.

719 **that was a different story:** LH's affair with FS per KCH to author, Dec. 17, 2004. Tina Sinatra and Mia Farrow each recounted having "heard" that after BAC's death, PC had an affair with FS. "Phyllis got alarmingly attached to my father, from things I would hear," Tina Sinatra recalled to the author.

719 **Phyllis, so very competitive:** CBC to author, Aug. 7, 2003.

720 **Everyone enjoyed charades:** Farrow to author, Mar. 3, 2003.

720 **all covered up:** Photographs in Sinatra Christmas Album, Box 75, CP.

720 **couldn't just be a buddy:** see Lahr, *Sinatra,* 60–61.

720 **"money is to be enjoyed":** BAC OH, 1018–19.

720 **gave his sons' train set:** CBC to author, Oct. 30, 2003.

721 **The "presents" had not been a surprise:** JFC to author, Oct. 8, 2014.

721 **"Gals for the boys":** BAC diary, Dec. 27, 1967; also CBC to James Kaplan, June 21, 2006, courtesy James Kaplan.

721 **"How can you be":** RLB to author, Sept. 23, 2003.

CHAPTER 49: DONE DEAL

722 **he went alone:** Every news account pointedly mentions the presence of Robert Sarnoff as a witness without mentioning

anyone else. RLB confirmed to the author on Oct. 1, 2015, that he was not there. BAC's diary makes no mention of DSK.

722 **the General and Bennett shook hands:** BAC diary, Jan. 10, 1966, Box 12, CP. For details of stock prices and valuations in this chapter and announcement on the ticker, see "RCA Announces Plans to Acquire Random House," *WSJ,* Jan. 11, 1966.

722 **"actively" as board chair:** RCA 1966 Annual Report, 3, via Proquest Historical Annual Reports.

723 **self-doubt that gnawed:** Alan Hirschfield to author, Jan. 14, 2003.

723 **"When RCA bought us":** BAC OH, 894. He said this on Feb. 5, 1968, only two years after the merger.

723 **"continue to function":** Harry Gilroy, "Cerf Welcomes Move," *NYT,* Jan. 11, 1966.

723 **autonomy provisions:** Robert Todd Lang, Weil, Gotschal partner, to author, May 5, 2004.

723 **"They'll have to carry":** BAC quoted in "Trade Winds," *SRL,* May 7, 1960, Box 70, CP.

723 **"a great thing":** RCA press release, Jan. 10, 1966, AAKR; RH release and letter from BAC, Box 51, MacKinlay Kantor Papers, LoC.

724 **"publishers who make a success":** Harry Gilroy, "R.C.A. Joins Electronics and Books," *NYT,* January 16, 1966.

724 **made their first official visit:** See BAC diary, Jan. 24 & 31, 1966, Box 12, CP. The other RCA directors who would go on the RH board were Paul Mazur and Carroll Newsom, the latter ex-Prentice-Hall. Merger offering document, Apr. 7, 1966, AAKR.

724 **brooked no nonsense:** Herbert S. Schlosser to author, Feb. 16, 2014; characterization of Sarnoff per Felix Rohatyn to author, June 8, 2005.

724 **"Thank you":** David Sarnoff to BAC, Jan. 27, 1966, courtesy CBC and JFC.

724 **had no understanding:** Michael Dann to author, Feb. 4, 2003.

725 **2 percent of sales:** RCA 1966 Annual Report, 32, Proquest.

725 **pegged at $80,000:** BAC diary, Feb. 23 & 28, 1966, Box 12, CP. His salary at RH pre-RCA was $54,000 plus $6,000 in deferred compensation. He also received $20,334 in retirement benefits between Apr. 1 and Aug. 31, 1965. Merger offering document, Apr. 7, 1966, AAKR.

725 **a formal vote:** Attorney files of Arthur P. Jacobs, Weil, Gotschal and Manges, 00001-0015-7-imo-17, 34.

725 **Donald representing the directors:** "Persons Present at Closing" document courtesy of company search by Arlene Harris, Esq.

725 **not the General's equal:** Robert Sarnoff characterization per Herbert S. Schlosser to author, Feb. 16, 2014; DeWitt Clinton Baker to author, Nov. 17, 2003; Alexander MacGregor III to author, Oct. 29, 2003.

726 **"It was a strange":** RLB unpublished OH, 96.

726 **starting shot:** Rohatyn to author, June 8, 2005.

726 **mergers, acquisitions, and reshufflings:** Thomas Whiteside, *The Blockbuster Complex* (Middletown, Conn.: Wesleyan University Press, 1980).

726 **"very sleepy":** Rohatyn to author, June 8, 2005.

CHAPTER 50: BLOOD RED AND BLACK/WHITE

727 **no author was more present:** On *In Cold Blood,* see Clarke, *Capote,* 318–403. I have closely followed Clarke's chronology and analysis. See also Clarke, ed., *TBAT;* Plimpton, *Truman Capote;* Bram, *Eminent Outlaws;* Charles J. Shields, *Mockingbird: A Portrait of Harper Lee* (New York: Henry Holt, 2006).

727 **wire-service story:** "Wealthy Farmer, 3 of Family Slain," *NYT* (UPI), Nov. 16, 1959.

727 **go-ahead from *The New Yorker*'s editor:** According to Michael Edelson, a retired professor of humanities at Stony Brook University, TC was offered a choice of assignments by *TNY:* the Clutter story or one on the "invisible" women who cleaned apartments. TC's friend Slim Keith voted for the "easy" story on Kansas. Edelson insisted that the usual account—TC seeing the article in the *NYT*—was "not accurate." Edelson quoted in Michelle Trauring, "Exploring Capote and His Kansas Nightmare," *The Sag Harbor Express,* Jan. 19, 2017.

727 **"You? In a west Kansas":** BAC OH, 695.

728 **Kansas State College:** The name was later changed to Kansas State University.

728 **a nod in Trade Winds:** *SRL,* July 24, 1954.

728 **letters of introduction:** BAC OH, 695–96.

728 **lunch at '21':** BAC diary, Dec. 28, 1959, Box 12, CP.

728 **"strange little boy":** Alan U. Schwartz, TC's attorney from 1969 on, as well as his literary executor, to author, June 2, 2003. Schwartz witnessed TC's attitude toward BAC many times. He also heard PC talk about how BAC "really loved" TC. Armand Deutsch spoke of BAC "watching

over Truman like a mother hen." Deutsch to author, June 2, 2003. And in an unpublished interview Gerald Clarke conducted with PC, she spoke of BAC "worrying" about TC. Unpublished interview transcript, 15–16, courtesy Clarke.

728 **"to laugh":** BAC OH, 696.

729 **He wanted a friend:** TC first asked Andrew Lyndon to accompany him, but Lyndon demurred.

729 **asked to see Lee's work:** AE to Nelle Harper Lee, Jan. 14, 1957; Nelle Harper Lee to AE, Jan. 20, 1957, RHCC. See also Shields, *Mockingbird,* 114–15. According to Shields, the pages were from *Go Set a Watchman.*

729 **"just to please Truman":** BAC OH, 705. BAC added: "As a matter of fact, if she had brought it to us, it may not have turned out as well as it did. It would have depended on who became the editor." By that time, he had met Lee and liked her. Despite BAC's enormous regard for Erskine, the conservative Southerner might not have suited Lee. Perhaps, by then, BAC had also heard about the exceptional amount of work Lippincott editor Tay Hohoff had put into the book.

729 **"I bet I'm the first":** BAC OH, 697.

729 **"attraction":** Dolores Hope quoted in Clarke, *Capote,* 323.

730 **something new:** Not many well-known books had used fictional techniques to craft a nonfiction narrative before *In Cold Blood.* One was Lillian Ross's *Picture,* published in 1952. Ross wrote for *TNY.* John Hersey had also done so in *Hiroshima,* which took up a whole issue of *TNY* in 1946, before being published by Knopf as a book. Nan Talese's husband, Gay, would apply the techniques to articles beginning in the early 1960s. Tom Wolfe and Norman Mailer would follow.

TC said that he did not tape his interlocutors or take notes in front of them, so as to put them at ease, and instead compiled notes after an interview. He always insisted that he had been factually scrupulous, but in the intervening years it has become clear that TC's desire to write a compelling narrative was more powerful than his commitment to facts.

730 **quickly signed a contract:** Unusually, there are *four* contracts between RH and TC for *In Cold Blood;* the contractual history supplies its own mystery in the publication saga. For the contracts, see files of Alan U. Schwartz.

The narrative is as follows. The first signed contract had a $3,000 advance. BAC to TC, Jan. 21, 1960, Box 42, RHR. It was crossed out and superseded by a new contract in 1962 between Verluisant S.A., a Lichtenstein company that would own the copyright on TC's behalf, and RH. TC, domiciled in Switzerland, did this for tax reasons. Then the advance jumped to $15,000. See BAC to TC, Feb. 1, Mar. 9, 1962, Box 51, RHR; TC to BAC, Feb. 14, 1962, in Clarke, ed., *TBAT,* 338. Then TC thought better of the tax dodge and also decided that he wanted no advance. See TC to BAC, Apr. 5, 1962, in Clarke, ed., *TBAT,* 345. Finally, Schwartz has *two* contracts between TC and RH, both dated Apr. 11, 1962. One is a single book contract with no advance; the other is a three-book contract, for *In Cold Blood* and two untitled books. Handwritten on it is a note stating that, as regards books two and three, it is superseded by a contract signed May 21, 1969.

Concerned about TC not taking any advance, BAC insisted on putting in writing that "if the need should arise," funds would be available "at any time." BAC to TC, Apr. 10, 1962, RHCC. In Jan. 1963, TC requested $12,000 and got it. TC to BAC, Jan. 14; BAC to TC, Jan. 18, 1963, RHCC.

730 **Capote would later agree:** Smith at first confessed to murdering the men and said that Hickock killed the women; later, he said that he killed the women as well. The issue has never been resolved.

730 **killed herself:** Nina Capote committed suicide in 1954, when TC was twenty-nine.

731 **couldn't help telling:** BAC to TC, May 10, 1960, RHCC.

731 **"how very, very much":** BAC to TC, July 14, 1961, RHCC.

731 **"terribly upset":** TC to BAC, Oct. 9, 1961, Box 47, RHR.

731 **"never do anything":** BAC to TC, Oct. 10, 1961, Box 47, RHR.

731 **But the Nations project . . . did exist:** See www.kshs.org/archives/229182; also Erin McCarthy, "Details from the In Cold Blood Killers' Case Files," *Mental Floss,* June 6, 2013, http://mentalfloss.com/article/50958/15-details-cold-blood-killers-case-files. Supposedly Nations did produce a longer manuscript that vanished with his death in 1968.

731 **sick to his stomach:** TC to Alvin and Marie Dewey, Dec. 9, 1961, in Clarke, ed., *TBAT,* 335.

732 **"Truman Capote is going":** PC quoted in BAC to TC, Nov. 28, 1961, Box 47, RHR.

732 **despondent about a delay:** TC to BAC, Dec. 4, 1961, in Clarke, ed., *TBAT,* 334.

732 **sweetness he could tap into:** TC to BAC, Feb. 14, 1962, in Clarke, ed., *TBAT,* 337.

732 **"extremely sensitive":** TC to Gerald Clarke in Clarke interview notes, 11 (there is also a handwritten number, *362,* at the top of the page), courtesy Clarke to author.

732 **Bennett was the quiet one:** Schwartz to author, June 2, 2003.

732 **horrified by his dreams:** TC quoted in Clarke, ed., *TBAT,* 273.

732 **"how very much":** BAC to Newquist in Roy Newquist, *Counterpoint* (Chicago: Rand McNally, 1964), 102.

732 **"one of the greatest":** BAC to James A. McCain, Jan. 16, 1962, Box 52, RHR.

732 **"one of the most important":** BAC to Jamie Hamilton, Dec. 20, 1963, Box 56, RHR.

732 **encouragement from Bennett:** TC to BAC, Feb. 14, 1962, in Clarke, ed., *TBAT,* 338–39.

732 **doppelgänger:** TC's editor, Joe Fox, quoted in Plimpton, *Truman Capote,* 174.

732 **suggesting lawyers:** Fox, quoted in Plimpton, *Truman Capote,* 179.

733 **dedication to Phyllis and Bennett:** For *Selected Writings* it reads "For Phyllis and Bennett." TC to BAC, June 25, 1962, RHCC. In BAC and PC's personal copy, TC added, "My dearest ones, from an always loving TC." Courtesy CBC and JFC.

733 **reprinted in the ML:** *Selected Writings* was published at the beginning of 1965.

733 **he'd have a breakdown:** TC's phrase was "a complete breakdown." See TC to Cecil Beaton, Sept. 17, 1963, in Clarke, ed., *TBAT,* 389.

733 **"Yesterday I finished":** TC to BAC, Feb. 20, 1965.

733 **polar opposites:** Alan Schwartz to author, June 2, 2003.

733 **they called Bennett:** BAC diary, Apr. 13, 1965. BAC confused the date (writing the diary after the fact, he sometimes did so). The hanging took place on Apr. 14.

734 **the weeping did not stop:** For Fox's account of the hanging and the flight, see Plimpton, *Truman Capote,* 179, 183, 184, 190, 191.

734 **not since Charles Dickens:** Clarke mentions the frantic anticipation in California for Dickens's *Old Curiosity Shop.* See Clarke, *Capote,* 360.

734 **paperback sale:** See BAC to *The New Republic,* May 11, 1966, Box 1559, RHR. Richard Brooks would direct a Columbia Pictures film production. The book club rights were sold to BOMC.

734 **fifteen foreign houses:** Harry Gilroy, "A Book in a New Form Earns $2-Million for Truman Capote," *NYT,* Dec. 31, 1965.

734 **austere dust jacket:** The cover was designed by S. Neil Fujita. BAC noted that he gave final jacket approval on Oct. 24, 1965. See also William Grimes, "S. Neil Fujita, Innovative Graphic Designer, Dies at 89," *NYT,* Oct. 27, 2010.

735 **"severe control":** JAM, foreword to Lawrence Grobel, *Conversations with Capote* (New York: New American Library, 1985), 10.

735 **"the greatest craftsman":** Nelle Harper Lee quoted in Shields, *Mockingbird,* 240.

735 **50,000 copies:** BAC to Edward Chase, Jan. 26, 1966, Box 1559, RHR. From publication to the end of Sept. 1967, all hardcover editions, including the U.S., U.K., and foreign-language editions, had sold in aggregate 310,676 copies, a massive number for a literary work at that time. Jean Ennis to Anne Graham Bell, Oct. 2, 1967, Box 971, RHR. On the bestseller ranking, see Bram, *Eminent Outlaws,* 94.

735 **"real value":** BAC quoted in William D. Smith, "Advertising: A Success Money Didn't Buy," *NYT,* Feb. 20, 1966.

735 **used the killers:** Anthony Lewis, "British Acclaim 'In Cold Blood' but Tynan Criticizes Capote for Not Helping Killers," *NYT,* Mar. 15, 1966. Cynthia Ozick famously accused TC of "esthetic manipulation" where "style" is prized over "deed" and "narcissism" masquerades as "objectivity." See Ozick, "Reconsideration," *New Republic,* Jan. 27, 1973. After the turn of the millennium, long-buried Clutter case files were unearthed and the drumbeat of criticism that TC had not hewed to fact and had skewed the point of view to favor Dewey as hero became deafening. See for example Kevin Helliker, "Capote Classic 'In Cold Blood' Tainted by Long-Lost Files," *WSJ,* Feb. 9–10, 2013.

736 **an honorary degree:** William Jewell College awarded BAC doctor of letters on Nov. 11, 1965. BAC diary, Box 12, CP.

736 **The Cerfs celebrated Truman:** BAC diary, Nov. 13, 1965, Box 12, CP. The presiding judge in the Clutter trial had been Roland Tate.

736 **rolling hot-dog cart:** CBC and JFC to author, numerous times.

736 **"themed":** On the red-white-and-blue dinner, see *McCall's,* July 1967 (referencing the 1966 party), BAC clipping book, Box 72, CP.

736 **flirty lunches at '21':** BAC 1966 diary mentions meetings with Walters on Feb. 15, Mar. 1, Apr. 11, May 3, June 13, July 2, Sept. 22, Dec. 3 & 19, Box 12, CP.

736 **"little pussy-cat face":** Barbara Walters to author, Oct. 15, 2004.

736 **she could push RH authors:** Walters provoked FS's ire a few years later when she phoned him, at the behest of NBC, to check on a rumor that he was marrying Pamela Hayward. FS was furious; Walters asked BAC to pass along her letter of apology to FS, which he did. Barbara Walters to author, Oct. 15, 2004. Cover letter, Barbara Walters to BAC, May 18 (year not specified), courtesy JFC.

736 **"thrilled":** Barbara Walters to author, Oct. 15, 2004. "I was fond of him," she added.

736 **"among the most":** Barbara Walters, *McCall's,* Nov. 1970, in BAC scrapbook, CP, also in Barbara Walters, *How to Talk with Practically Anybody About Practically Anything* (New York: Doubleday, 1970), 113.

736 **"warmth":** *Philadelphia Inquirer,* Oct. 5, 1970, in BAC scrapbook, CP.

737 **RH tongues wagged:** John J. Simon, an RH editor from 1966 to 1973 whose office was near Bennett's, recalled Walters's long, "closed door" visit to BAC. The implication was clear. Simon to author, Nov. 18, 2002.

737 **"overcome":** Walters, *How to Talk with Practically Anybody About Practically Anything,* xiii.

737 **in a beautiful mood:** BAC diary, July 3, 1966.

737 **swaying Frank:** BAC diary, July 4, 1966. Two months after the Sarnoff-Sinatra meeting at Mt. Kisco, BAC, FS, and his lawyer Mickey Rudin, along with Felix Rohatyn and his boss Andre Meyer, met in Meyer's apartment to discuss RCA buying Reprise, FS's label. BAC was proving useful to RCA. BAC diary, Sept. 4, Nov. 20, 1966, Box 12, CP.

737 **"arugella":** *Arugula* was the intended word. Earl Wilson's "It Happened One Night" column, c. 1966, Margaret Herrick Library, AMPAS Sinatra clipping files.

737 **Sinatra swung at him:** Kaplan, *The Chairman.*

737 **"Darling Phyllis + Bennett":** Mia Farrow to PC and BAC, July 27, 1966, Box 1560, RHR.

737 **mystery guests:** By contrast, on *WML?* the panelists donned masks to prevent them from seeing the identity of the MG.

738 **"security blanket":** PC in Plimpton, *Truman Capote,* 248.

738 **embossed invitations:** CPCC.

738 **"What a cast!":** BAC diary, Nov. 28, 1966.

738 **reflecting well on himself:** On the ball, see Clarke, *Capote,* 369–85; Plimpton, *Truman Capote,* 247–56; Bram, *Eminent Outlaws,* 95–96; Deborah Davis, *Party of the Century* (Hoboken: John Wiley, 2006); Amy Fine Collins, "A Night to Remember," *Vanity Fair,* July 1996, https://archive.vanityfair.com/article/1996/7/a-night-to-remember; Sarah Jane Rodman, "Party of the Century: Truman Capote's Black and White Ball," 2014, PhD dissertation, Harvard University, http://nrs.harvard.edu/urn-3:HUL.InstRepos:13041037.

739 **draped in red:** TC was aided in choosing the decorations and color scheme by Evie Backer, wife of *New York Post* editor George Backer and a friend of the Cerfs and many in their circle.

739 **liquid flour:** LH quoted in Plimpton, *Truman Capote,* 263.

739 **"They're nobody!":** RLB unpublished OH, 101.

740 **didn't know who anybody:** Farrow quoted in Plimpton, *Truman Capote,* 259.

740 **ended up twisting:** CBC to author.

740 **"It was a good":** PC quoted in Plimpton, *Truman Capote,* 256.

740 **"never really recovered":** PC quoted in Clarke, *Capote,* 397.

CHAPTER 51: INTERVENTIONS

741 **unremarkable first novel:** see A. E. Hotchner, *Choice People: The Greats, Near-Greats, and Ingrates I Have Known* (New York: Morrow, 1984), 358; and BAC OH, 994. Erskine edited the book. Mutual friend George Axelrod, screenwriter for *Breakfast at Tiffany's,* introduced BAC to Hotchner. As a twenty-eight-year-old *Cosmopolitan* editor, he was sent to Havana in 1948 to persuade forty-nine-year-old Hemingway to write an essay on "the future of literature." Friendship blossomed. A. E. Hotchner, *Papa Hemingway* (New York: RH, 1966), 3. He had qualified to practice as a lawyer but didn't do so. A. E. Hotchner to author, Apr. 15, 2004.

741 **very excited:** BAC to A. E. Hotchner, May 28, 1964, Box 59, RHR.

741 **How thrilled he'd been:** BAC OH, 530. However, according to Leonard J. Leff, Hemingway liked neither the jacket nor the introduction to the ML edition of *The Sun Also Rises*. See Leff, *Hemingway and His Conspirators* (New York: Rowman & Littlefield, 1997), 132.

741 ***A Moveable Feast:*** A. E. Hotchner, "Don't Touch 'A Moveable Feast,'" *NYT,* July 19, 2009.

742 **"a rather mean book":** BAC OH, 994.

742 **The book expanded:** BAC OH, 531. Hotchner mentions a book that would only retrace the path of the trip. See A. E. Hotchner to BAC, June 4, 1964, Box 59

RHR. He reiterated that original intention to me in an interview on Apr. 15, 2004.

742 **"Morbidly fascinating":** BAC, editorial report, June 2, 1965, Box 61, RHR.

742 **acid test:** Nan A. Talese to author, Jan. 7, 2003.

742 **"It's your story":** A. E. Hotchner to author, Apr. 15, 2004.

742 **"innate good judgment":** A. E. Hotchner to author, Apr. 15, 2004.

743 **After reading the memoir:** On the court case, see Lewis Nichols, "In and Out of Books," *NYT,* Apr. 3, 1966; *PW,* Jan. 24, Mar. 7 & 28, 1966; *NYT,* Jan. 15, 28, & 29, Feb. 22, Mar. 1 & 18, July 23, Aug. 23, 1966.

743 **hidden the suicide:** "Hemingway Dead of Shotgun Wound; Wife Says He Was Cleaning Weapon," *NYT,* July 3, 1961.

743 **trying not to face it:** Harry Gilroy, "Widow Believes Hemingway Committed Suicide," *NYT,* Aug. 23, 1966.

743 **"treachery":** Mary Hemingway to BAC, Dec. 10, 1965, RHCC.

743 **suppress or distort:** Robert E. Tomasson, "'Papa Hemingway' Brought to Court," *NYT,* Jan. 29, 1966.

743 **"the right of the public":** "Mrs. Hemingway Denied Injunction on Memoirs," *PW,* Mar. 7, 1966. Mary Hemingway appealed, and the appeal was also rejected.

743 **"to tell the whole":** Hotchner, *Papa Hemingway,* x.

743 **her first bestseller:** Within six months, there were 115,000 copies in print. See RH ad, *NYT,* Oct. 10, 1966, 38. In addition, about thirty foreign editions were published. A. E. Hotchner to author, Apr. 15, 2004.

743 ***Papa Hemingway* joined:** Jacqueline Susann's *The Valley of the Dolls,* published by Bernard Geis Associates but distributed by RH, was also very much on the list.

743 **"For Papa Cerf":** BAC's copy courtesy CBC and JFC.

744 **in questionable taste:** BAC OH, 995.

744 **"so far beneath":** Mary Hemingway to BAC, Dec. 25, 1965, RHCC. During the summer of 1966, Mrs. Hemingway finally admitted to the journalist Oriana Fallaci that her husband had killed himself. She was being interviewed for an article that appeared in Italian in the magazine *Europa,* and in a somewhat different form in English "An Interview with Mary Hemingway: 'My Husband, Ernest Hemingway,'" in *Look,* Sept. 6, 1966. However, she vowed to persist in her fight against Hotchner. See also Harry Gilroy, "Widow Believes Hemingway Committed Suicide . . . Assails Hotchner Book," *NYT,* Aug. 23, 1966. That summer, Mary won the right to a jury trial, but only on the grounds that the book had violated her right to privacy. See "Hemingway's Widow Allowed Jury Trial," *NYT,* July 23, 1966. I have not been able to find any record of a jury trial. A N.Y. Supreme Court ruling favoring A. E. Hotchner and RH was issued in 1968.

744 **savvy and drive:** BAC OH, 1002–1004.

744 **"Scurrilous Sinatra novel!":** BAC diary, Nov. 3, 1966, Box 12, CP. BAC tells the story in his OH, 1003–1006.

744 **friendship meant too much:** BAC spoke of a need to "squelch" Geis's "Sinatra foul play." See BAC diary, Nov. 4, 1966, Box 12, CP.

744 **"real picture":** BAC to Nancy Sinatra, Nov. 14, 1966, Box 1560, RHR.

745 **"slimy":** BAC diary, Mar. 14, 1967, Box 12, CP. *The Exhibitionist* was distributed by Crown.

745 **"We don't want":** BAC quoted in Henry Raymont, "Random House to Stop Distributing Geis Books," *NYT,* Apr. 7, 1967.

745 **Geis's profitable backlist:** Raymont, "Random House to Stop Distributing Geis Books."

745 **labeled *The King* a "failure":** BAC OH, 1005.

745 **sold millions:** Christopher Hawtree, "Morton Cooper: Dime Novelist and Author of *The King,*" *The Independent,* June 22, 2004. The book sold three million copies.

745 **five of Geis's thirteen:** Harry Gilroy, "Partners Lost by Bernard Geis," *NYT,* Sept. 7, 1967.

745 **bankruptcy:** Riva D. Atlas, "Bernard Geis, Celebrity Publisher, Dies at 91," *NYT,* Jan. 10, 2001.

745 **dartboard in his Palm Springs home:** Armand Deutsch, *Me and Bogie* (New York: Putnam, 1991), 115.

745 **"very nice":** BAC OH, 732.

745 **tendered an ultimatum:** BAC to Dorothy Kilgallen, May 7, 1965; Dorothy Kilgallen to BAC, May 12, 1965, Box 62, RHR.

746 **abuzz:** BAC's phrase is "buzzing with news." See BAC diary, Nov. 9, 1965, Box 12, CP.

746 **Bennett walked to Sardi's:** BAC diary, Nov. 9, 1965, Box 12, CP.

746 **heaps of clippings:** BAC diary, Nov. 19, 1965, Box 12, CP.

746 **almost finished:** BAC to DSK, Sept. 13, 1965, Box 61, RHR.

746 **"blow his top":** BAC, editorial report, *Murder One,* Mar. 10, 1966, RHR, Box 1559. BAC records reading "Lee Wright's inadequate substitute job on Kilgallen book," in his diary, Mar. 7, 1966, Box 12, CP.

747 **on occasion:** Alan Ullman OH, Columbia, 48–49, 79.
747 **"Dorothy Kilgallen to the Reader":** Ullman OH, 153. See Dorothy Kilgallen, *Murder One* (New York: RH, 1967), ix–xi.
747 **"a disgrace":** Ullman OH, 153.
747 **sold paperback rights:** Ullman OH, 155.
747 **was not a huge seller:** Ira Levin to author, May 12, 2003.
747 **"strange witchcraft manuscript":** BAC recorded reading *Rosemary's Baby* on Aug. 6, 1966. The office meeting between Levin and BAC took place on Aug. 10, 1966. BAC diary, Box 12, CP.
747 **undergo cataract removal:** BAC diary, Box 12, CP.
748 **Bennett suggested:** Ira Levin to author, May 12, 2003.
748 **"The author is the final arbiter":** BAC quoted in Christopher T. Cory, typed notes dated Nov. 30, 1966, for *Time* cover profile of BAC, Dec. 16, 1966, courtesy Cory to author.
748 **"It's going to become":** BAC quoted in Cory notes.
748 **"To Bennett Cerf":** Book courtesy CBC and JFC.

CHAPTER 52: TURBULENCE

749 **remodeling:** JFC to author, Oct. 22, 2003.
749 **"honeymoon stay":** Their real honeymoon took place at Claudette Colbert's home in Barbados. Farrow to author, Mar. 3, 2003.
749 **It was her job:** MKF to author, Aug. 13, 2003.
749 **ordering mirrors:** JFC to author, Oct. 22, 2003.
750 **"flower children":** BAC diary, Dec. 14, 1967, Box 12, CP. See Sally Kempton and Ross Wetzsteon, "Andy Warhol's Book Party: Put-On, Pop-Out, Blow-Up," *Village Voice,* Dec. 21, 1967.
750 **go home and recover:** BAC diary, Dec. 14, 1967, Box 12, CP.
750 **closest *paesan:*** On Jilly, see Talese, "Frank Sinatra Has a Cold"; George Jacobs and William Stadiem, *Mr. S.: My Life with Frank Sinatra* (New York: HarperCollins, 2003), 210.
750 **living a fairy tale:** CBC to author, Aug. 7, 2003.
750 **making him feel old:** James Kaplan, *Sinatra: The Chairman* (New York: Doubleday, 2015), 733–37.
750 **Hysterical at the idea:** BAC diary, Dec. 13, 1967, Box 12, CP.
750 **Bennett would come later:** This was the visit when Chris and Jon were presented with Sammy Davis Jr.'s "gift" of two call girls.
750 **dubious reconciliation:** BAC diary, Dec. 14, 1967, Box 12, CP. Projecting optimism per Earl Wilson: *Sinatra: An Unauthorized Biography* (New York: Macmillan, 1976), 226.
751 **quick Mexican divorce:** It was granted on Aug. 19, 1968. Wilson, *Sinatra,* 228.
751 **seemed most unhappy:** FEP on FS's emotional state to author, Jan. 20, 2008.
751 **"not a nice thing to do":** FEP to author, Jan. 20, 2008. FEP said there were several dates. Most likely they took place toward the end of January 1968, when FS was in New York per BAC's diary. However, the diary does not mention FEP.
751 **one memorable spat:** The episode was recounted by Helene Fagan Bidwell to author, May 25, 2005; CBC to author, Aug. 7, 2003.
751 **was a magnet for every male:** Judy Green background per CBC to author, Aug. 7, 2003; Helene Fagan Bidwell to author, May 25, 2005; David Patrick Columbia, https://www.newyorksocialdiary.com/turning-back-the-clock/.
751 ***too* close to Frank:** CBC to author, Aug. 7, 2003.
752 **cancer stopped it dead:** On BWK's death, see BAC diary, June 4, 1966; "Mrs. Blanche Wolf Knopf of Publishing Firm Dies," *NYT,* June 5, 1966, 86.
752 **"after immense suffering":** AAK to James M. Cain, June 8, 1966, Box 522.6, AAKR.
752 **insisted that they must:** AAK diary, Sept. 11 & 13, 1963, Box 612.3, AAKR.
752 **touching:** BAC diary, June 7, 1966, Box 12, CP.
752 **cold spider:** Laurence Urdang quoting Knopf staff members to author, Nov. 24, 2003.
753 **looked for signs:** Betsey Hutchins, Alfred A. Knopf Inc., to BAC, June 24, 1966, Box 1559, RHR.
753 **accurately predicted:** DSK to AAK, Mar. 15, 1967, Box 1559, RHR.
753 **more approachably human:** Judith Jones to author, Feb. 21, 2003.
753 **made a star turn:** Mss 230, Box 18, Seuss Collection.
753 **dined with the Geisels:** BAC diary, Feb. 4 & 6, 1966.
753 **Helen Geisel was dead:** Morgan and Morgan, *Dr. Seuss & Mr. Geisel,* 185, 194–203.
753 **wanted a statement from Bennett:** In BAC diary, Helen Geisel's death is recorded as having occurred on Oct. 25, 1967. Occasionally, BAC didn't record activities for several days and then got dates mixed up when he filled in the blanks. That clearly happened here, for HPG died on Oct. 23, which is when Judith Morgan

phoned BAC. Morgan to author, Mar. 10, 2012.

753 **"most wonderful":** BAC quoted by Judith Morgan to author, Mar. 10, 2012.

753 **"found dead":** "Helen Palmer, Children's Writer and Wife of Dr. Seuss, Is Dead," *NYT,* Oct. 24, 1967.

754 **"tiptoed":** HPG to BPB, Feb. 14, 1967, courtesy BPB.

754 **"patted on the back":** HPG to Gladys Palmer, Apr. 5, 1967, courtesy BPB.

754 **"strangely down and jumpy":** RLB quoted in Morgan and Morgan, *Dr. Seuss & Mr. Geisel,* 193.

754 **"going down down down":** For HPG's suicide note, see Morgan and Morgan, *Dr. Seuss & Mr. Geisel,* 195–96.

754 **"I didn't know whether":** TSG to Stanley Willis, quoted in Morgan and Morgan, *Dr. Seuss & Mr. Geisel,* 195.

754 **giant gin-blossomed nose:** MKF to author, May 31, 2012.

754 **"If he didn't like it":** Audrey Geisel to author, July 6, 2006.

754 **undoubtedly prolonging:** Audrey told MKF she was studying gerontology to that end. MKF to author, Dec. 4, 2006.

754 **difference between Ted's wives:** MKF to author, Dec. 4, 2006.

755 **indispensable and irreplaceable:** Within HPG's family it was "known" that HPG supplied some of the prose in TSG's early books, like *The King's Stilts.* BPB to author, May 22, 2012.

755 **Bennett thought her "nice":** BAC diary, Oct. 7, 1968, Box 12, CP.

755 **"There weren't many":** Audrey Geisel to author, July 6, 2006.

755 **$750,000 in 1967 alone:** Memo (no sender or recipient specified, but likely from either BAC or RLB), July 31, 1967, Box 58, CP.

755 **management teams were fired:** "One man claimed to have been in the CIA . . . they lied about their CV's." Toni Morrison to author, Jan. 11, 2006.

755 **relocate parts of the company:** BAC diary, June 1, 1967, Box 12, CP.

756 **"double-header" . . . "different":** Toni Morrison to author, Jan. 11, 2006.

756 **"the man":** Toni Morrison to author, Jan. 11, 2006.

757 **bearing a $5,000 check:** Toni Morrison to author, Jan. 11, 2006.

757 **"very nice . . . not patronizing"; called up the firm's banker:** Toni Morrison to author, Jan. 11, 2006.

757 **resigned in March 1967:** BAC diary, Mar. 31, 1967, Box 12, CP.

757 **"Educational Division":** "Singer we closed down. It just didn't belong. We sold a number of the series." DeWitt Clinton "Bud" Baker to author, Nov. 17, 2003. Bud Baker was a top executive at RH at the time. See also John F. Baker, "Fifty Years of Publishing At Random," *PW,* Aug. 4, 1975.

757 **"doing well":** BAC OH, 846, recorded Feb. 1, 1968.

757 **like an emperor:** RDL to author, Mar. 1, 2016.

757 **Lew's pride:** RLB unpublished OH, 69, courtesy RLB.

757 **seventy salesmen:** Cory notes.

757 **"leveled off":** Cory notes.

758 **brought suit:** BAC OH, 630–31; BAC diary, Feb. 8 & 9, Oct. 18, 1967, Box 12, CP.

758 **publishers overcharged:** "State Fights Decree on Book Price Fixes," *Chicago Tribune,* Nov. 3, 1967. The "price-fixing" accusations were concentrated in Chicago and Philadelphia. See memo (no sender or recipient specified, but likely from BAC or RLB), July 31, 1967, Box 58, CP.

758 **To the dismay:** Bud Baker to author, Nov. 17, 2003.

758 **two cancer operations:** Lew Miller to BAC, Feb. 1, 1967; BAC to Miller, Feb. 18, 1967, Box 1559, RHR.

758 **"one of my best friends":** BAC to Lewis Miller, Feb. 28, 1967, Box 1559, RHR.

758 **consent decree:** Memorandum from Joseph N. Kraft, counsel, to BAC, DSK et al. Re Settlement of Government's Civil Antitrust Suit in Chicago, Dec. 5, 1967, AAKR; BAC OH, 630–31; Defendants' draft, Sept. 8, 1967, Box 1559, RHR; Bud Baker to author, Nov. 17, 2003.

CHAPTER 53: MAKING IT

759 **seven years earlier:** Norman Podhoretz to author, July 9, 2013.

759 ***hated:*** Norman Podhoretz to author, July 9, 2013.

759 **"a corruption of the spirit":** Norman Podhoretz to his first agent Lynn Nesbit, quoted in Thomas L. Jeffers, *Norman Podhoretz: A Biography* (New York: Cambridge University Press, 2010), 107. Additional background from Podhoretz to author, July 9, 2013, and Jeffers.

759 **"dirty little secret":** See Norman Podhoretz, *Making It* (New York: RH, 1967), xvi–xvii.

760 **appalled:** Podhoretz to author, July 9, 2013. Podhoretz's agent, Lynn Nesbit, was involved, and he and she quickly parted. Podhoretz then signed with agent Candida Donadio, who liked the book and did the deal with RH.

760 **fascinating:** *Making It* flap copy. BAC's

characterization of the book: per Podhoretz to author, July 9, 2013.

760 **to offer $25,000:** BAC diary, Jan. 19, 1967, Box 12, CP. BAC told Podhoretz, "I'm crazy about it. It talks about all the smart young people in the intellectual establishment, and I think it's going to be a great success." BAC to Podhoretz, Feb. 24, 1967, quoted in Jeffers, *Norman Podhoretz,* 107.

760 **discouraged readers:** Podhoretz to author, July 9, 2013. Podhoretz thought that potential readers felt they knew enough about the book from reviews.

760 **"positively prescient":** Daphne Merkin quoted in Jeffers, *Norman Podhoretz,* 108.

761 **rather than squelch:** RLB told Cory that BAC was the only man he knew of large ego "who didn't squelch anybody else around him." Cory notes.

761 **motley lineup:** *Time* 1966 covers cited: RFK (Sept. 16), Reagan (Oct. 7), Ky (Feb. 18), Giap (June 17), Verwoerd (Aug. 26), Weaver (Mar. 4).

761 **"Viet Nam a real fuck-up":** BAC diary, Aug. 27, 1966, Box 12, CP. I have read all BAC's diaries, and have not seen another occasion of his using "fuck" in a diary. A few weeks earlier, he had referred to the "Viet Nam mess."

762 **"If you can't get":** Peter Duchin to author, May 22, 2003. This is Duchin's characterization of PC and BAC statements, made almost forty years after the fact (he thought it occurred in 1967). The incident also appears in Duchin (written with Charles Michener), *Ghost of a Chance* (New York: RH, 1996), 96–97.

762 **It also appeared:** RLB to author, May 16, 2016.

762 **the news:** BAC diary, Nov. 19, 1966.

762 **break-the-ice luncheon:** BAC diary, Nov. 23, 1966.

762 **"Hello, Pest!":** BAC quoted by Cory, Dec. 6, 1966, in telex to *Time* re Cory's cover story, courtesy Cory to author. The rest of Cory's characterizations per Cory to author, May 29, 2005. Unless otherwise stated, Cory's file notes and interview with the author provided all background for section.

763 **interview authors, publishers, friends:** Cory's files do not have a complete list of interviewees, but he did speak to at least one who was never a favorite of BAC: S&S's Leon Shimkin.

763 **"I wonder":** "Publishing: A Cerfit of Riches," *Time,* Dec. 16, 1966, 102. Other puns are in Cory's notes.

763 **"horribly nasal":** Cory notes, Nov. 30, 1966.

763 **information that Bennett hadn't rushed:** "Publishing," 100.

763 **His columns reached:** Cory notes, Nov. 30, 1966.

763 **"Every publisher":** "Publishing," 101–2.

763 **"as a conservative branch":** "Publishing," 107.

764 **mechanisms to create distance:** Observations and quotations throughout this paragraph are from Cory to author, May 29, 2005.

CHAPTER 54: EXITS AND ENTRANCES

765 **cold Monday afternoon:** For activities on Sunday, Feb. 12, and Monday, Feb. 13, see BAC 1967 diary, Box 12, CP; BAC OH, 750–51.

765 **"Have you any statement":** BAC quoted in Robert E. Dallos, "'What's My Line?' Leaving TV in Fall," *NYT,* Feb. 14, 1967.

765 **"I'm the first":** BAC quoted by Faye Fates, widow of Gil Fates, to author, May 14, 2003.

765 **piles of stories:** BAC diary, Feb. 27, 1967, Box 12, CP.

765 **"someday television will end":** "Bennett Cerf: Colossus with Horn-Rimmed Glasses," June 26, 1962, clipping courtesy USC Cinema Library.

766 **fourth most popular . . . was now seventy-ninth:** See Mark Goodson to BAC, Dec. 21, 1955, Box 2; *TV Guide,* June 17, 1967, Box 39, both CP.

766 **"There never was a good show":** Michael Dann to author, Feb. 4, 2003. On the demise of *WML?* see Fates, *What's My Line?* 119.

766 **"VERY SAD!":** On the final night of *WML?* see BAC diary, Sept. 3, 1967, Box 12, CP.

766 **a way of life:** Arlene Francis and Florence Rome, *Arlene Francis: An Autobiography* (New York: S&S, 1978), 91.

766 **negotiated an exit:** BAC diary, Feb. 1, 1968, Box 12, CP.

766 **consistently, but marginally:** Ashbel Green to author, Nov. 13, 2002.

766 **Bills were paid:** Anthony M. Schulte to author, Nov. 7, 2006.

767 **He lasted six months:** Ashbel Green to author, Nov. 13, 2002.

767 **essentially ran trade:** Judith Jones to author, Feb. 21, 2003.

767 **sensed that Bernstein didn't like:** Harding Lemay to author, May 6, 2003.

767 **that very odd pair:** RLS, MLS, and Shimkin had sold to Marshall Field; when Field died, MLS and Shimkin bought the company back, paying a settlement to RLS but cutting him out of ownership.

767 **"the kids were running":** Robert A. Gottlieb interviewed by Larissa MacFar-

quahar, "The Art of Editing No. 1," *The Paris Review,* no. 132, fall 1994.

768 **changes on the horizon:** Toinette Lippe, Robert A. Gottlieb's former assistant, to author, Mar. 28, 2016.

768 **the place to be:** Donadio's advice per Robert A. Gottlieb to author, Aug. 3, 2005.

768 **"outside possibility":** BAC diary, July 26, 1967.

768 **"a fantasy":** Robert A. Gottlieb to author, Aug. 3, 2005; see also BAC diary. It is unclear if RLB was with BAC and Robert A. Gottlieb. According to Toinette Lippe, Robert A. Gottlieb had long entertained dreams about Knopf. Lippe to author, Mar. 28, 2016.

768 **"the demented governess":** NB quoted by Robert A. Gottlieb at NB's memorial service, May 19, 2010.

768 **crush on Dick Simon:** NB to author, Nov. 15, 2006.

768 **"about the best":** BAC OH, 919.

769 **wasn't as wedded to Schulte:** Robert A. Gottlieb to author, Aug. 3, 2005.

769 **pied-à-terre:** When business kept RLB in the city late at night or when he had to entertain "at home" in the city, he had use of Colbert's apartment, since she had retired to her estate, Belle Rive, in Barbados. On the rare occasions during the year when she needed to spend time in New York, the apartment was hers to use. She became an honorary aunt to RLB's three sons.

769 **who would really be:** Robert A. Gottlieb to author, Aug. 3, 2005.

769 **"They'll know":** BAC quoted by Robert A. Gottlieb to author, Aug. 3, 2005.

769 **"everybody at Knopf":** NB paraphrased by Robert A. Gottlieb to author, Aug. 3, 2005.

770 **"I'll sleep on it":** Anthony M. Schulte recalling the scene to author, May 22, 2003. Gottlieb, meanwhile, had decided he didn't want to take on Dutton. Robert A. Gottlieb to author, Aug. 3, 2005.

770 **"Gottlieb Schulte Bourne deal":** BAC diary, Dec. 19, 1967, Box 12, CP.

770 **authority to fire Alfred:** Peter Prescott book proposal for AAK biography, 11–12, based on Robert A. Gottlieb interview with Susan Sheehan, courtesy AP.

770 **"Getting this champion":** BAC quoted in Henry Raymont, "Knopf Hires 3 Top Aides of Simon and Schuster," *NYT,* Jan. 6, 1968.

770 **"pilfering . . . S&S nabobs":** BAC diary, Jan. 8, 1968, Box 12, CP.

770 **sought Alfred's blessing:** BAC diary, Oct. 2, 1967, Box 12, CP.

770 **"very glad indeed":** AAK quoted in Raymont, "Knopf Hires 3 Top Aides of Simon and Schuster."

770 **hadn't been consulted:** Robbin Hawkins, BAC's OH interviewer, clearly interpreted it that way after hearing BAC speak about it, per her questions in BAC OH, 658.

770 **insisting he'd fully briefed:** BAC OH, 658.

770 **"irritated":** Henry Raymont, "Book Trade Upset by Changes in Ownership, Size and Staff," *NYT,* Mar. 4, 1968.

770 **It fell to Don:** Notes on DSK interview with Susan Sheehan, Jan. 29, 1975, courtesy AP. I have assumed DSK is speaking about the arrival of Robert A. Gottlieb, Anthony M. Schulte, and NB; however, he could be referring to a period several years later, when RCA was pressing for AAK to retire fully.

770 **secure assurances:** Lippe to author, Mar. 28, 2016.

770 **unusually good money terms:** RH would reimburse S&S for whatever it had advanced these writers, but S&S didn't insist on reimbursement for interest on the money already paid out. Anthony M. Schulte to author, Apr. 28, 2006. Almost certainly Gottlieb wouldn't be able to bring that kind of number now.

770 **convened a cocktail party:** Anthony M. Schulte to author, May 22, 2003.

770 **at least one key Knopf editor:** That editor was Ashbel Green. Green to author, Nov. 13, 2002.

770 **"one-man show":** Judith Jones to Peter Prescott, Feb. 17, 1990, courtesy AP.

771 **could be just as condescending:** Regina Ryan to author, Feb. 11, 2011. Fear of Robert A. Gottlieb per Anthony M. Schulte to author, May 22, 2003; Regina Ryan to author, Feb. 11, 2011. Others spoke similarly. The difference between working under BAC and AAK per Eleanor Carlucci to author, Sept. 11, 2003. Carlucci was AAK's last secretary and, like Judith Jones, said that the gruff, forbidding exterior hid shyness, and if one got beyond that wall, "he could be wonderful."

771 **"Jewish":** Judith Jones to author, Feb. 21, 2003.

771 **"with people who seemed":** Regina Ryan to author, Feb. 11, 2011.

771 **territorial dispute:** John J. Simon to author, Nov. 18, 2002. Simon was Epstein's second-in-command at Vintage and an acquiring editor in his own right, whose authors included Abbie Hoffman and Stokely Carmichael.

771 **Alfred complained about editors:** For instance, AAK to Mr. Gottlieb, Nov. 24, 1969; Robert A. Gottlieb to AAK, Nov. 24, 1969, courtesy AP.

771 **"for a showdown":** AAK diary, "Xmas" (1969), Box 637, AAKR.

771 **"Dear Alfred, I'm returning":** NB quoted by Robert A. Gottlieb to author, Aug. 3, 2005.

771 **"You could not have found":** Robert A. Gottlieb to "Mr. Knopf," Jan. 7, 1968, Box 650, AAKR.

771 **"a miracle":** BAC OH, 920. Robert A. Gottlieb remained at AAK until 1987, when he began a five-year stint as *TNY* editor. Even after leaving Knopf, he edited select titles until his death in 2023, aged 92. His publishing encompassed Robert Caro's *The Power Broker* and Caro's still-unfinished multi-volume biography *The Years of Lyndon Johnson;* Lauren Bacall's memoirs; Bill Clinton's memoirs; and Toni Morrison's novels.

In the mid-1970s, RLB elevated Anthony M. Schulte to be the second-highest corporate executive at RH Inc.; many regarded him as the heir apparent. Instead, Schulte left the corporation in 1986 to become a publishing dealmaker and consultant. He died in 2012.

NB died at age 93 in 2010. She worked at Knopf almost until the end.

CHAPTER 55: CONFESSIONS AND CONTROVERSIES

772 **Jim Silberman recognized:** Characterizations of JE, AE, JMF, and RDL per JHS to author, Feb. 5, 2003.

772 **Bill Styron loved:** WS to John P. Marquand Jr., July 4, 1956, in Rose Styron with R. Blakeslee Gilpin, eds., *Selected Letters of William Styron,* 220.

772 **felt like an *author:*** See WS to William Blackburn, Apr. 20, 1955, in Rose Styron with Gilpin, eds., *Selected Letters of William Styron,* 213.

772 **"Boy writer!":** Alexandra Styron, *Reading My Father* (New York: Scribner, 2011), 135.

773 **"I am great pals":** WS to Marquand, in Rose Styron with Gilpin, eds., *Selected Letters of William Styron,* 220–21. Fox was not yet an RH editor.

773 **Styron girls were special:** Susanna Styron to author, Nov. 18, 2003.

773 ***make* the book a bestseller:** BAC to Jerry Wald, Apr. 26, 1960, Box 46, RHR.

773 **36,000-copy run:** P&L report for *Set This House on Fire,* July 31, 1961, Box 612, RHR.

773 **nor did the novel:** BAC OH, 982. The first WS work published by BAC, DSK, and RKH was an ML reprint of *The Long March,* published in 1952, when WS was still a Bobbs-Merrill author.

773 **"My spirit unbroken":** WS to BAC, June 1960, Box 46, RHR.

773 **"historical fiction":** RDL to author, Apr. 30, 2016.

773 **tales of two slave girls:** WS to Robert Penn Warren, June 20, 1967, in Rose Styron with Gilpin, eds., *Selected Letters of William Styron,* 419.

773 **Published accounts:** A Baltimore lawyer, Thomas Gray, was responsible for the pamphlet; *The Southampton Insurrection* (1900) was by William S. Drewry; *American Negro Slave Revolts* (1943) was by Herbert Aptheker. They are discussed in WS, *This Quiet Dust and Other Writings* (New York: Vintage International, 1993), 15–16, 4–5, as is WS's school book, 9–10.

773 **the most effective:** Certainly as WS saw it.

774 **"meditation on history":** WS quoted in Michiko Kakutani, "Styron Visible: Naming the Evils That Humans Do," *NYT,* Nov. 3, 2006.

774 **didn't come easily:** WS to Leon Edwards, Feb. 5, 1962, in Rose Styron with Gilpin, eds., *Selected Letters of William Styron,* 314.

774 **encouraged by his friend:** Rose Styron with Gilpin, eds., *Selected Letters of William Styron,* 325 (note).

774 **"My relationship with my publishers":** WS to agent Elizabeth McKee, in Rose Styron with Gilpin, eds., *Selected Letters of William Styron,* 330. WS did later engage Don Congdon as his agent; he had a separate agent who looked after foreign rights.

774 **the first 220 pages:** BAC diary, Dec. 16, 1964.

774 **to NAL for $100,000:** Jan. 19, 1965, Box 12, CP.

774 **"inaugural do":** WS to Hope Leresche, Jan. 21, 1965, in Rose Styron with Gilpin, eds., *Selected Letters of William Styron,* 336–37.

774 **"I've got great news!":** BAC quoted by WS to author, Mar. 3, 2003.

774 **amazed at the effort:** WS to author, Mar. 3, 2003.

775 **signed Styron's next book:** BAC diary, May 6, 1965, Box 12, CP.

775 **"At long last!":** BAC diary, Jan. 20, 1967, Box 12, CP.

775 **quite a presence:** Rose Styron to author, June 9, 2016.

775 **"superb" work:** BAC diary, Jan. 29, 1967, Box 12, CP.

775 **$150,000 guaranty:** BAC diary, Feb. 20, 1967, Box 12, CP.

775 **Loomis had solicited blurbs:** RDL to author, Apr. 30, 2016.

775 **In late September:** BAC to WS, Sept. 25, 1967, Box 1560, RHR.

775 **bought movie rights:** BAC diary, Oct. 14, 1967, Box 12, CP; WS to William Blackburn, Nov. 29, 1967, in Rose Styron with

Gilpin, eds., *Selected Letters of William Styron,* 429.

775 **lined up Norman Jewison:** Sam Tanenhaus, "The Nat Turner Wars," *Vanity Fair,* Sept. 2016, 267.

775 **young actor named James Earl Jones:** Rose Styron with Gilpin, eds., *Selected Letters of William Styron,* xii.

775 **125,000 copies:** James L. W. West III, *William Styron, A Life* (New York: RH, 1998), 376.

775 **"magnificent" novel might also carry "controversy":** RH Fact Sheet, Sept. 1967, Box 811, RHR.

775 **obscure Black protagonist:** WS claimed Nat Turner was not well known even to Blacks, per *This Quiet Dust,* 4. Tanenhaus claims that Turner's history was alive in Black history and folklore, per "Nat Turner Wars," 267.

775 **picked apart the book:** Wilfrid Sheed, "The Slave Who Became a Man," *NYTBR,* Oct. 8, 1967.

775 **"outrageous":** BAC diary, Sept. 29, 1967, Box 12, CP.

775 **drumbeat of reviews:** see West, *William Styron, A Life,* 376–77; Styron, *Reading My Father,* 25; Christopher Lehmann-Haupt, "William Styron, 81, Novelist Who Transcended Roots, Dies," *NYT,* Nov. 2, 2006.

776 **second-biggest:** Hackett and Burke, *80 Years of Best Sellers, 1895–1975,* 201–2. Excluding the book club edition, the novel sold 170,000 hardcovers per West, *William Styron, A Life,* 395.

776 **James Baldwin had told:** West, *William Styron, A Life,* 335–36. In 1968, highly critical views were collected and published by historian John Henrik Clarke in an essay collection, *William Styron's Nat Turner: Ten Black Writers Respond,* published by Beacon Press, per West, *William Styron, A Life,* 385. WS considered the book "damning": WS to PR, Apr. 30, 1968, Box 33, Philip Roth Papers, LoC (hereafter PRP).

776 **he no longer wanted:** Rose Styron to author, June 9, 2016.

776 **Loomis was at home:** RDL to author, Apr. 30, 2016; Rose Styron to author, June 9, 2016. See also West, *William Styron, A Life,* 381–82; Alexandra Styron, *Reading My Father.*

776 **film deal collapsed:** West, *William Styron, A Life,* 381; see also Tanenhaus, "Nat Turner Wars," 267.

776 **Styron recoiled:** WS, *This Quiet Dust,* 5.

776 **Bennett had predicted:** BAC OH, 983.

776 **collateral criticism:** RDL to author, Apr. 30, 2016. Toni Morrison would later criticize the book in a *Paris Review* interview, all the while noting that WS had "a right to write about whatever he wants." "Toni Morrison, The Art of Fiction No. 134," *Paris Review,* Issue 128, Fall 1993, https://www.theparisreview.org/interviews/1888/the-art-of-fiction-no-134-toni-morrison.

777 **"extremely proud":** BAC's pride per CBC to author, June 7, 2016.

777 **"proudest possessions":** BAC OH, 982.

777 **Back in the '50s:** Rose Styron to author, June 9, 2016.

777 **followed by more stories:** The early publication in *TNY* generated much controversy. See David Remnick, "Into the Clear: Philip Roth Puts Turbulence in Its Place," *TNY,* May 8, 2000.

777 **After Don charmed him:** On arranging the first lunch, see PR to BAC, Aug. 18, 1960; BAC to PR, Aug. 22, 1960, RHCC. They met on Sept. 6. BAC diary, Box 12, CP.

777 **blonde, all-American Maggie:** PR, *The Facts: A Novelist's Autobiography* (New York: Farrar, Straus and Giroux, 1988), 81. In the book she is called "Josie."

777 **"the impresario":** PR to author, Oct. 29, 2004.

777 **he was never the easiest man in the world:** Ann Mudge speaking of PR to author, June 8, 2016. Mudge was one of the loves of PR's life.

777 **first RH contract:** Handwritten internal RH note, n.d., Box 45, RHR.

777 **"every last detail":** BAC to Candida Donadio, Sept. 20, 1960, Box 45, RHR.

777 **"Tremendously moving":** BAC to PR, Sept. 26, 1960, Box 45, RHR.

777 **passed them to Bob Loomis:** RDL to PR, Oct. 4, 1960, Box 850, RHR.

777 **four hundred more pages:** BAC to PR, Apr. 3, 1961, Box 50, RHR.

777 **"superb":** RDL to PR, Mar. 10, 1961, Box 850, RHR.

777 **Worried about certain aspects:** See RDL to PR, Apr. 3, 1961, Box 850, RHR.

778 **who got Bennett to snap:** PR to DSK, Apr. 21, 1961, RHCC.

778 **chemistry mattered:** PR to DSK, Apr. 21, 1961; note added to PR's Apr. 21 letter in BAC's hand, Apr. 26, 1961; DSK to PR, Apr. 28, 1961, RHCC.

778 **Roth chose Fox:** PR to BAC, June 19, 1961, RHCC.

778 **"audacity" coupled with "modesty":** PR to BAC, Sept. 21, 1961, RHCC.

778 **urged Roth to meet:** BAC to PR, June 21, 1961, RHCC.

778 **Bennett and Bernstein wanted to impress:** JMF to PR, Dec. 5, 1961, Box 850, RHA.

778 **enormously entertaining:** RDL to author, Aug. 11, 2016.

778 **"Happy publication day":** BAC to PR, June 15, 1962, Box 5, PRP.

778 **blue leather-bound copy:** BAC to PR, May 29, 1962, Box 53, RHR.

778 **Roth kept complaining:** PR to JMF, Apr. 20, 1962, RHCC.

778 **expressing deep disappointment:** BAC to PR, Apr. 23, 1962, RHCC.

778 **impending Roth visit:** Regina Ryan to author, Feb. 11, 2011. Ryan, who worked at Knopf, heard the vitrines story from then-RH editor Berenice Hoffman.

778 **nothing if not aware:** PR to JMF, Apr. 20, 1962.

778 **"probably the most talented":** Orville Prescott, "Books of the Times," *NYT,* June 15, 1962.

778 **of a quality few could achieve:** "Books: The Grey Plague," *Time,* June 15, 1962.

778 **For all its weightiness:** PR to BAC, July 12, 1962, RHCC. *Goodbye, Columbus* sold 20,000 copies. RH editorial fact sheet, June 15, 1962, Box 850, RHR. Claudia Roth Pierpont believes the correct figure to be 12,000 copies. See Claudia Roth Pierpont, *Roth Unbound: A Writer and His Books* (New York: Farrar, Straus and Giroux, 2013), 60. The tallies for *Letting Go* are 27,817 copies sold at $3.25 (another 3,000 were in a $1.20 edition). See *Letting Go* P&L, Mar. 31, 1964, Box 850, RHR.

778 **both author and publisher were disappointed:** Roth Pierpont, *Roth Unbound,* 34.

779 **serial liar and deceitful stranger:** Margaret "Maggie" Martinson was almost five years older than PR and had had two children from her first marriage. Her eleven-year-old daughter lived with PR and Martinson during their brief marriage. She paid a pregnant woman to provide a urine specimen that she got tested and presented to PR as her own. See Roth Pierpont, *Roth Unbound,* 40–43.

779 **heard about the matrimonial problems:** BAC diary, June 11, 1963, Box 12, CP; see also PR to JMF, Aug. 3, 1963, RHCC.

779 **"shivering":** PR to JMF, July 14, 1963, RHCC.

779 **divorce negotiations:** PR to JMF, Aug. 3, 1963, RHCC. The word "books" is underlined.

779 **"Absolutely monstrous":** JMF to PR, Aug. 7, 1963, RHCC.

779 **help her get work:** Maggie Roth to JMF, July 2, 1963, Box 850, RHR.

779 **Whatever she responded:** PR to JMF, Aug. 3, 1963, RHCC.

779 **"I will do anything":** JMF to PR, Aug. 7, 1963, RHCC. I have inserted a comma between "you" and "save" to make Fox's meaning clear to the reader. Here "save" means "except for."

779 **organized a party:** JMF to BAC, Sept. 10, 1963, Box 850, RHR.

779 **remember the warmth:** Roth Pierpont, *Roth Unbound,* 45; Blake Bailey, PR biographer, to author, May 25, 2016.

779 **So unlike his publisher:** PR to JMF, July 14, 1963, RHCC.

779 **The $102,000 advance:** On the contract terms, see Candida Donadio to JMF, July 28, 1966, Box 850, RHR.

780 ***"under any circumstances"*****:** BAC to Candida Donadio, Aug. 1, 1966, Box 1560 RHR. See also Donadio to JMF, July 28, 1966, Box 1560, RHR; PR to JMF, Aug. 5, 1967, RHCC.

780 **"heroic efforts":** JMF to Bill Ryan, Mar. 7, 1967, Box 850, RHR.

780 **"Stupid sons of bitches":** PR to JMF, n.d., Box 850, RHR.

780 **"give a good shit":** PR to Donadio, July 28, 1967, Box 10, PRP.

781 **He'd been "hurt":** JMF to PR, Aug. 1, 1967, Box 850, RHR.

781 **a "subtle" conflict:** PR to JMF, Aug. 5, 1967, RHCC.

781 **Fox was puzzled:** JMF to PR, Aug. 9, 1967, Box 850, RHR.

781 **Roth had preceded his editor:** Roth Pierpont, *Roth Unbound,* 54.

781 **Roth very nearly died:** see Roth Pierpont, *Roth Unbound,* 50.

781 **"instantly notorious":** Roth Pierpont, *Roth Unbound,* 51.

781 **Roth saw Bennett:** BAC diary, Sept. 21, 1967, Box 12, CP.

781 **"the most brilliant":** *Time* quoted in Howard Junker, "Will This Finally Be Philip Roth's Year?" *New York,* Jan. 13, 1969; reprinted in George J. Searles, ed., *Conversations with Philip Roth* (Jackson: University Press of Mississippi, 1992), 16.

782 **"Philip with two l's":** PR to JMF, Jan. 10, 1968; JMF reaction, n.d., RHCC.

782 **"astronomical and worth":** JMF to BAC et al., May 29, 1968, Box 850, RHR.

782 **"I'm sorry, for both":** JMF to PR, circa June 10, 1968, Box 10, PRP. JMF refers to the day he was informed of PR's leaving him as a Monday. The most likely date is June 10, 1968. See JMF to PR, Aug. 28, 1968, Box 850, RHR.

783 **"able" but "didn't want":** PR to JMF, June 13, 1968, Box 10, PRP.

783 **he'd kidded Fox:** JMF to PR, Aug. 17, 1964, Box 850, RHR.

783 **sold to Bantam:** On the Bantam deal, see BAC diary, June 11 & 12, 1968, Box 12, CP.

Diary says Bantam agreed to $400,000, but the contract, dated June 17, 1968, specifies $350,000. Box 1115, RHR.

783 **Roth had repaid:** PR to JMF, Feb. 29, 1968, RHCC.

783 **RH was ecstatic:** RDL to author, Apr. 30, 2016.

783 **"Roth's masterpiece":** RH fact sheet on *Portnoy's Complaint,* Box 1080, RHR.

783 **"a major cultural event":** Albert Goldman, "*Portnoy's Complaint* by Philip Roth Looms as a Wild Blue Shocker and the American Novel of the Sixties," *Life,* Feb. 7, 1969.

783 **That job fell to Ennis:** When she died suddenly eighteen months after *Portnoy* was published, PR made sure to attend her funeral. BAC to PR, Oct. 22, 1970, Box 5, PRP.

784 **"But I wouldn't want":** Roth Pierpont, *Roth Unbound,* 64; Remnick, "Into the Clear."

784 **RH received an avalanche:** Words and phrases are taken from reader letters. Boxes 1379 & 1172, RHR.

784 **editors of *The New York Times:*** Editorial, *NYT,* Apr. 1, 1969, 46.

784 **450,000 copies in print:** See JE to PR, Mar. 3, 1969, Box 1080, RHR. Of those, fully 250,000 had already been sold. Doubleday bookstore rate of sale in same letter.

784 **"If you can find time":** BAC to PR, Mar. 7, 1969, Box 5, PRP.

784 **he gave no reaction:** On BAC finishing the book, see BAC diary, June 19, 1968, Box 12, CP.

784 **read the book a second time:** BAC diary, Feb. 9, 1969, Box 12, CP.

784 **for two more:** BAC diary, June 27, July 12, 1967. BAC also responded to a personal appeal from Kollek for contributions to repair damage from the Six Day War, sending a check for $25,000. BAC to Teddy Kollek, June 27, 1967, Box 1559, RHR.

784 **"I believe that the public":** "Remarks Made by Bennett Cerf President of Random House, Inc. to the New York Society of Security Analysts, 10/17/1960," courtesy RH file, *PW* Records.

785 **"a little nervous":** CBC to author, June 17, 2016.

785 **subterranean "unease":** MKF to author, June 9, 2016.

785 **Bob Bernstein's son:** Peter Bernstein to author, Mar. 28, 2012.

786 **"You would have laughed":** BAC to PR, Mar. 19, 1969, Box 5, PRP.

786 **publicly refused to attend:** BAC to PR, Mar. 5, 1970, Box 5, PRP.

786 **"To Bennett":** Book and inscription courtesy CBC and JFC.

In 1971, RH published PR's savage satire on President Richard Nixon, *Our Gang.* Shortly before he died, BAC read it and judged it "tasteless." BAC diary, Aug. 3, 1971, Box 12, CP. When it came time to negotiate PR's next two works—a novella, *The Breast,* and a full-length fiction, *The Great American Novel*—PR used a lawyer instead of Donadio: billable hours were cheaper than 10% of his advance and royalties. A $450,000 advance was agreed, but now PR refused to share paperback income with RH. Neither RH nor PR would budge, and PR went to Holt, although wrote notes to DSK, RLB, and JE stating that his association with RH had not only been "successful" but "in almost all respects a happy one." See, e.g., PR to RLB, May 20, 1972, Box 1115, RHR. DSK replied, "I hope you will . . . write many more good books and not become too bewitched by the money." DSK to PR, June 27, 1972.

CHAPTER 56: PALACE TO TOWER BLOCK

787 **"How can you avoid":** BAC quoted in untitled clipping by Martha MacGregor, *New York Post,* Mar. 9, 1968, Box 73, CP.

787 **"disgraceful":** BAC diary, Aug. 29, 1968, Box 12, CP.

787 **"schmo":** BAC diary, Aug. 8, 1968, Box 12, CP.

787 **Bennett tried to understand:** BAC recorded reading Carmichael on Aug. 2, 1967. BAC diary, Box 12, CP.

787 **"Terrifying":** BAC recorded reading Cleaver on Mar. 7, 1969. See BAC diary, Box 12, CP. *Ramparts* magazine/McGraw-Hill had published Cleaver's first book, the celebrated memoir *Soul on Ice.*

787 **However much:** PC referenced David Sarnoff being BAC's "friend and a person that he could talk to," adding, "Random House was such a minor part of the big picture of RCA that unless you had a close relationship with them, you were lost." "Friend" was clearly an exaggeration, but the point stands. PC OH, 430.

788 **stricken with shingles:** On Sarnoff's illness, see Thomas S. W. Lewis, *Empire of the Air: the Men Who Made Radio* (New York: HarperCollins, 1991), 354–55. Sarnoff would die on Dec. 12, 1971, blind, deaf, and barely able to speak.

788 **the future lay in diversification:** See generally Bilby, *The General,* 277–78.

788 **begun to feel lost:** Around this time BAC referenced "neglect by Sarnoff." BAC diary, Feb. 2, 1968, Box 12, CP. It is un-

clear which Sarnoff he meant; the elder was still active.

788 **"sometimes I wonder":** BAC OH, 896.

788 **"dull as hell":** BAC diary, Oct. 2, 1968. Bobby was fully in charge.

788 **totally ineffective:** DeWitt Clinton Baker to author, Nov. 17, 2003. Baker was RH VP for Administration and Finance, hired by RLB to take over Richard Kislik's role at RH.

788 **RCA annual meeting:** RLB to author, June 13, 2012. It likely happened in 1968, when BAC was being accompanied by Marge Silberman, who wrote for *The Jewish Post*. BAC diary, May 6 & 7, 1968, Box 12, CP.

788 **"From 65 to 47":** Feb. 2, 1968; 43⅞: Jan. 30, 1969; 33½: Jan. 6, 1970; all BAC diaries, Box 12, CP.

788 **others held on and lost out:** RDL to author, June 29, 2016; RLB to author, Apr. 11, 2012.

788 **RCA mostly didn't try:** BAC OH, 921.

788 **five-year plans:** CW to author, May 8, 2003.

788 **reminiscences from noteworthy alumni:** Columbia was also hoping to tee up more material legacies. BAC's papers were left to the university, as were the RH papers. It hoped for a large financial contribution as well.

789 **bright and attractive:** BAC implied he'd like to do more than flirt. Robbin Reynolds Hawkins to author, July 10, 2003.

789 **"You start getting bigger":** BAC OH, 866–67.

789 **he was staring into space:** BK to author, Nov. 4, 2002.

789 **Tony Wimpfheimer wondered:** CW to author, May 8, 2003.

789 **Bernstein freely acknowledged:** In many interviews with the author, RLB expressed his debt to BAC.

789 **He saw his job as:** RLB's mindset per JE to author, Mar. 11, 2010.

789 **Bennett began to resent decisions:** BAC OH, 1020.

789 **"making a goddamn nuisance":** DSK to Susan Sheehan, Jan. 29, 1975, courtesy AP.

789 **"esprit de corps":** CBC to RLB, Oct. 15, 1968, Box 870, RHR.

790 **Claudette Colbert's husband had died:** BAC diary, June 12, 1969, Box 12, CP.

790 **interesting young producer:** Ailes, the founder of Fox News, makes several appearances in BAC's diaries. Ailes's FBI file revealed that BAC had invested $5,000 in Ailes's production company during this era. Ailes can be glimpsed in the photograph where BAC is being "carried out" of the Villard. See Danielle Wiener-Bronner, "What's Inside the FBI File on Roger Ailes," CNN, Jan. 27, 2018, https://money.cnn.com/2018/01/27/media/roger-ailes-fbi-file/index.html.

790 **didn't like the betrayals:** In his last years, the spelling and recall for names was less good in BAC's diary. For instance, SC's widow became "Dorothy Cummings." Feb. 7, 1968, Box 12, CP.

790 **squirrelly red-brown:** The dyed hair and liver spots are visible in photographs of BAC from the late 1960s and early 1970s, including one on the cover of his book *The Sound of Laughter* (New York: RH, 1970).

790 **"I'll probably never live":** BAC OH, 880.

790 **Twice a year:** Spellman also had offices in his residence across Madison Avenue abutting St. Patrick's. It was in the residence that the lunch took place.

790 **Often considered *the* most powerful:** See John Cooney, *The American Pope: The Life and Times of Francis Cardinal Spellman* (New York: Times Books, 1984). Although BAC described Spellman as a "very decent man," (BAC OH, 497–98), Cooney's book revealed the Cardinal to be a hypocrite.

790 **"He's one of your":** BAC OH, 497–98.

791 **on a bright April:** Photograph featuring BAC, Spellman, JOH, Apr. 23, 1965, Box 72, CP.

791 **"happy day, perchance":** BAC to unnamed multiple recipients, Jan. 3, 1955, Box 69, CP.

791 **Instead, RH staff spilled:** Inefficiencies per RDL to author several times.

791 **Still, Bennett resisted:** See, e.g., "big meeting on moving plans. I'm very much against selling 457 now." BAC diary, Nov. 20, 1961, Box 12, CP.

791 **Four months into the RCA era:** John J. Reynolds to BAC, proposal on Park Avenue, Aug. 11, 1966, Box 1560, RHR.

792 **The developers had also approached:** Harry L. Langer to Francis Cardinal Spellman, attached letter, July 7, 1966, Box 1560, RHR.

792 **"as soon as we're dead":** BAC quoted in William Robbins, "Random House Will Leave Mansion for a Skyscraper," *NYT,* Aug. 19, 1968, 74, BAC file, Columbiana Collection. It is stated that BAC made the remark "a little over a year ago," therefore placing it in the summer of '67.

792 **An exception was being made:** On the construction of 825 Third Avenue, see undated RH release, Box 1559, RHR. It speaks of nine floors, *spread among* fourteen, being occupied by RH. All other accounts speak of fourteen. See "RCA Family Newsletter Fall 1968," Box 73, CP. Additionally, it was stated that the man-

sion would be retained. See "News of Realty: A Publisher Move," *NYT*, Sept. 14, 1967.

792 **future there was far from certain:** On BAC's public remarks on the trajectory of the mansions' fate, see Ada Louise Huxtable, "How to Impoverish a City at $400 a Square Foot," *NYT*, Sept. 29, 1968, courtesy *PW* clipping files. BAC made remarks similar to those attributed to him by Huxtable in his OH, 494–95. Although he speaks of the "likelihood" of selling the building and its being pulled down, he in fact had known for a month that the building was being put up for sale. Contrast BAC diary, Dec. 4, 1967, cited below, with the date of OH recording, Jan. 8, 1968.

792 **"a loner":** BAC OH, 495.

792 **"Agreed reluctantly to sell":** BAC diary, Dec. 4, 1967, Box 12, CP.

792 **"rueful":** WS to author, Mar. 3, 2003.

792 **He and Don had been spending:** Also lunching with BAC and DSK was Manny Harper, who had been with them longer than anyone.

792 **"to what we laughingly":** BAC quoted in Robbins, "Random House Will Leave Mansion for a Skyscraper."

792 **"will *probably* sell":** BAC quoted in Huxtable, "How to Impoverish a City at $400 a Square Foot."

RLB asserted that he tried and failed to convince Robert Sarnoff to turn the mansion into New York's "most spectacular" bookstore. Unpublished RLB OH, 118. On Apr. 1, 2003, RLB told the author that he had not wanted to sell and put the blame for what happened on BAC. Had BAC, RLB said, faced up to the problem early enough, they might have moved to a new building closer to the palazzo and kept it. See also RLB with Doug Merlino, *Speaking Freely: My Life in Publishing and Human Rights* (New York: The New Press, 2016), 92. RLB writes of a building going up next to the Villard Houses; presumably that is the building currently on the southeast corner of 50th and Madison. Such an arrangement would have had to be made *before* RCA bought the firm. However, the only building possibility that I could find mentioned in the RH archives was the one at 59th and Park.

On the subsequent history, see Steven R. Weisman, "Villard Houses, City Landmark, Are Purchased by Archdiocese," *NYT*, Mar. 12, 1971; Edward B. Fiske, "21-Million First Ave. Complex to House Archdiocesan Offices," *NYT*, Aug. 12, 1971; Carter B. Horsley, "Archdiocese Is Negotiating to Lease Villard Houses for Hotel Air Rights," *NYT*, Mar. 15, 1974; and Paul Goldberger, "Villard Houses: Option for the Future," Dec. 9, 1974. In Mar. 1971, the Archdiocese bought the northern wing from RCA. Five months later, the Church announced it was moving to a new tower on First Avenue. After it moved, the palazzo was empty and in limbo. Finally, a developer, Harry Helmsley, agreed to lease air rights and preserve much of it (partially demolishing rear sections), to build a fifty-story hotel behind it. Thus it stands today.

793 **Bennett insisted:** Address change to 201 E. 50th per Alan Merkin to author, Nov. 25, 2003. Merkin was the nephew of Nat Wartels, founder of Crown. Also Howard Goldstein to author, May 16, 2003. Goldstein worked in production at RH. Fashions change, and at this writing, the building, which had been developed by the Durst family, is known as 825 Third Ave.

793 **sensitivities awakened:** CW to author, Dec. 26, 2002.

793 **unhappy about the standardized furniture:** Sandra Koodin Paul Money to author, June 16, 2008. Money was a staff member involved in carrying out the move to 201 E. 50th St.

793 **"a most fantastic office":** Howard Goldstein to author, May 16, 2003.

793 **make the move less painful:** Sandra Koodin Paul Money to author, June 16, 2008.

793 **No longer could Phyllis spy:** CBC to author, Oct. 30, 2003.

793 **crowding into Bennett's office:** Lucienne S. Bloch to author, June 16, 2008; BK to author, Nov. 4, 2002.

794 **"no personality whatsoever":** WS to author, Mar. 3, 2003.

794 **Bennett wasn't happy:** Sandra Koodin Paul Money to author, June 16, 2008.

794 **"being difficult":** JE to author, Mar. 11, 2010.

794 **making his rounds:** Judith Jones to author, Feb. 21, 2003.

795 **"This is the only goddamn company":** BAC in lobby quoted by MKF to author, Aug. 13, 2003.

CHAPTER 57: FAMOUS AND FADING

796 **mid-December 1969:** Mitford visit, BAC diary, Dec. 19, 1969, Box 12, CP.

796 **Jessica's idiosyncrasies:** Background on the Mitford family per Carla Kaplan, biographer of Jessica, to author, Oct. 30, Nov. 4, 2016; Laura Thompson, *The Six: The Lives of the Mitford Sisters* (New York: St. Martin's Press, 2016).

796 **she'd saved him for last:** Jessica Mitford, *Poison Penmanship: The Gentle Art of Muckraking* (New York: Alfred A. Knopf, 1979), 174.

796 **thirty well-prepared questions:** For Mitford's handwritten list of questions, see Box 100, Folder 879, Jessica Mitford Papers, Ohio State University. BAC granted Mitford the lengthy interview because she was under contract to Knopf for her next book. BAC OH, 1027.

796 **"Jessica Mitford out to crucify":** BAC diary, Dec. 19, 1969, Box 12, CP.

796 **an offshoot:** See Randy Kennedy, "The Draw of a Mail-Order Art School," *NYT,* Mar. 23, 2014.

796 **Early in 1958:** Breslauer had organized BAC's wedding-eve dinner when he married PC. BAC diary. BAC always called him "Mike." See "Milton K. Breslauer, 67, Dies; Aide of Famous Artists School," *NYT,* Nov. 12, 1968. Breslauer was FAS company secretary. The lunch took place on Mar. 19, 1958. BAC diary, Box 12, CP.

796 **he'd be rewarded:** BAC would receive .1666%. Gilbert K. Granet, Famous Schools, to BAC, Nov. 2, 1964, Box 59, RHR. The original pitch letter specified that each of the twelve "Guiding Faculty" would share equally in a total pot of 2% of the gross cash income. See the full set of Guiding Faculty documents, Box 24, MacKinlay Kantor Papers.

797 **"equal or exceed":** Guiding Faculty documents. Kantor rejected the offer. Kantor to Carroll, July 5, 1958. Box 24, Kantor Papers.

797 **"little circle of confidence men":** Kantor to Carroll, July 5, 1958, Box 24, Kantor Papers.

797 **celebrated together at '21':** BAC diary, Dec. 3, 1959, Box 12, CP.

797 **Bennett recruited her:** See, e.g., BAC to Mignon Eberhart, July 10, 1961, Box 48, RHR. Three more Guiding Faculty would join later: longtime director of the University of Iowa Writers' Workshop Paul Engle; poet and children's author Phyllis McGinley; and editor, anthologist, radio/TV personality, and talking head Clifton Fadiman.

797 **Bennett was singled out:** Publicity shots, BAC diary, Aug. 10, 1960, Box 12, CP.

797 **"If you want success":** N.d., Kantor Papers.

797 **90 percent of respondents:** Jessica Mitford, "Let Us Now Appraise Famous Writers," *The Atlantic,* July 1970.

798 **Bennett's annual cut:** In the front of BAC's 1971 diary he notes: "FAS 1307.82 x 12," presumably meaning a monthly amount, which would work out to $15,693.84. In 1964, per Granet to BAC, he received $7,731.71. Other statistics from Mitford.

798 **"Do you have a restless":** Ad text from Mitford; *Life* magazine, Feb. 21, 1969, BAC scrapbooks.

798 ***Let's Talk About Writers:*** BAC diary, Mar. 19, 1969, Box 12, CP.

798 **The scripts were devised:** Mary Higgins Clark to author, Jan. 21, 2008.

799 **Mitford also read:** Robert Byrne, *Writing Rackets* (New York: Lyle Stuart, Inc., 1969).

799 **He visited Westport HQ:** One visit was with RDL and another with JHS. BAC diary, June 13, 1965, and Aug. 24, 1967, respectively.

799 **sending their own manuscripts:** RDL to author, Apr. 30, 2016.

799 **"Oh now Jessica":** Jessica Mitford Papers. This account differs somewhat from BAC's quotes in the final article. Unless noted, quotes are from the notes, which I assume are closest to what he said.

799 **feature had been commissioned:** West Coast editor William Abrahams was a well-known editor/writer.

799 **contacted *McCall's:*** The editor was Vivian Cadden.

800 **"Ah! There is the":** "Queen of Muckrakers," *Time,* July 20, 1970. For a longer description of the Knopf encounter with BAC (but published nine years after the fact), see Mitford, *Poison Penmanship,* 175. Curiously, the "friend" she was visiting at Knopf is unnamed. Presumably it is Gottlieb, who published *Poison Penmanship*. She describes them "giggling" over the article when BAC walks in. She says that he asked who was publishing it (odd that he had not ascertained the publisher when she interviewed him). When she said *McCall's,* she quotes him exclaiming: "They're out of their mind if they think they can get away with this." Gottlieb, when asked by the author on Dec. 13, 2016, if he recalled the incident, said he did not at all.

800 **Bennett had a *McCall's* connection:** "Talked to Shana Alexander to . . . clinch her for Frank Sinatra autobiography." BAC diary, June 30, 1967.

800 **ostensibly to take:** Shana Alexander, *Happy Days: My Mother, My Father, My Sister, and Me* (New York: Doubleday, 1995), 176; family relationship per Laurel Bentley, Alexander's sister, to author, May 21, 2012. A letter from sculptor Jo Davidson to BAC mentions "your little friend, Miss Celia Ager." Jo Davidson to BAC, Aug. 26, 1936, RHCC. BAC put the inscription on *Papa Hemingway.*

800 **"For Cecelia's lovely daughter":** Alexander, *Happy Days,* 262.

800 **over her editor's objections:** On the *McCall's* rejection, see Barbara Blakemore to Mitford, n.d. (presumably Feb. 1970) and Feb. 18, 1970, Box 100, Folder 886, Jessica Mitford Papers.

800 **"not very good":** Shana Alexander quoted in undated article from BAC scrapbook, Box 73, CP. In Feb. 1970 Vivian Cadden (the *McCall's* editor who had wanted to publish Mitford's article) quoted Shana Alexander to Jessica Mitford, about Alexander fearing to make "an enemy" of BAC. See Peter Y. Sussman, ed., *Decca: The Letters of Jessica Mitford* (New York: Knopf, 2006), 412–13, note 132.

800 **"destroy the brute":** Jessica Mitford to Barbara Kahn, Feb. 17, 1970, in Sussman, ed., *Decca,* 412–13.

800 **largest newsstand sale:** Mitford, *Poison Penmanship,* 177.

801 **FWS's first year:** Gordon Carroll to BAC, Oct. 9, 1961, Box 48, RHR.

801 **writer had appealed:** William C. Lawson to BAC, postmarked Mar. 2, 1964, Box 59, RHR.

801 **Bennett's "dichotomy":** WS to author, Mar. 3, 2003.

801 **It took him "longer to be embarrassed":** CBC to author, Aug. 7, 2003, Mar. 30, 2016.

801 **willingness to trust others:** Dr. J. S. Rice to PC, Aug. 29, 1971, Box 10, CP.

801 **"Hatchet job":** Scrapbook, Box 73, CP.

801 **"We are still hearing":** BAC OH, 1027.

801 **Mary Higgins Clark had seen:** Mary Higgins Clark to author, Jan. 21, 2008.

801 **filed for bankruptcy:** Kennedy, "Draw of a Mail-Order Art School." The FTC also investigated the FWS. The school, however, refused to die completely. Like a worm that regenerates after being sliced in two, later entities were organized under the same name. Among internet-age heirs in spirit, if not in name, are a number of companies associated with self-publishing programs, as well as lawsuits, and a certain online university that settled with plaintiffs for $25 million after the election of 2016.

802 **"Your family ruined":** Quoted by JFC to author, Sept. 30, 2014. When BAC dictated his OH, he discussed the FWS. Some was included in the first draft of *AR,* but the material was later deleted by PC and AE, who edited the manuscript. For the deleted pages, see Box 21, CP.

802 **Even demonstrating exercises on TV:** BAC diary, Nov. 12 & 27, 1968, Box 12, CP.

802 **The book rocketed:** Publication of Miss Craig exercise book: Hackett and Burke, *80 Years of Best Sellers, 1895–1975,* 205–6; see also BAC OH, 1024. According to a P&L statement for sales up to Mar. 31, 1972, *Shape-Up* sold from publication to that date 212,937 copies of 221,128 printed (excluding book clubs), a very "clean" sale. Box 1054, RHR.

802 **She signed Craig:** RH published *Miss Craig's Growing-Up Exercises to Help Children Grow Up to Be Healthy Adults* in 1973.

802 **Craig's advance also rocketed:** The sum was $15,000. Book's P&L statement, Box 1054, RHR.

802 **"I can't start giving":** RLB quoting himself to author, Apr. 11, 2012.

802 **let her "package":** RLB to author, Feb. 25, 2003, Oct. 26, 2006.

802 **Bob seemed to have forgotten:** BAC gave RLB a 2% royalty on sales of the Shirley Temple book. RLB to author, Sept. 23, 2003.

803 **"Should I stay":** BAC diary, Oct. 7, 1970, Box 12, CP.

803 **"Maybe I should quit":** BAC diary, Oct. 15, 1970, Box 12, CP.

803 **"I can't give your wife":** Full exchange per RLB to author, Feb. 25, 2003.

803 **"What am I to do?":** BAC diary, Oct. 16, 1970, Box 12, CP.

803 **"Looks like we'll both quit":** BAC diary, Nov. 9, 1970, Box 12, CP.

803 **more weeks of back-and-forth:** On the new titles for DSK and BAC, see BAC diary, Nov. 25, 1970, Box 12, CP.

803 **It sold well:** Out of 70,000 printed, *Face-Saving* sold 54,000 copies. See P&L statement for sales up to Mar. 31, 1972, Box 1054, RHR.

803 **Phyllis resigned:** BAC diary, Jan. 28, 1971, Box 12, CP.

803 **She never spoke:** RLB to author, Feb. 25, 2003.

803 **Negotiations over terms:** BAC records Canfield's bid for the book on June 10, 1971. By contrast, BAC had offered a "reluctant" $25,000 to Dick Rodgers for his memoir. BAC diary, June 10 & 2, 1971, Box 12, CP.

804 **wanted either Albert or Nan:** BAC to JHS, July 20, 1971, Box 23, CP.

804 **"When, as, and if":** See, e.g., BAC to JHS, July 20, 1971, Box 23, CP.

804 **"I hope I'm not":** BK to author, Nov. 14, 2002.

804 **disappearing like the Cheshire cat:** JE to author, Dec. 9, 2003.

804 **"in good shape":** BAC diary, Mar. 9, 1966.

804 **"almost certainly benign":** BAC diary, Dec. 15, 1970. This was no small matter. Laparoscopic techniques were not yet common, making the surgery much more complicated than today.

804 **Lenox Hill Hospital:** See generally BAC diary, Dec. 15–31, 1970, Box 12, CP.
805 **"inauspiciously":** BAC diary, Jan. 1, 1971, Box 12, CP.
805 **Mayor Lindsay:** BAC diary, Jan. 7, 1971.
805 **amazed to see Senator Javits:** BAC diary, Jan. 3, 1971.
805 **"I really thought":** Thomas E. Dewey to BAC, Dec. 24, 1970, CPCC.
805 **At week's end:** BAC's weight had dropped from 171 to 158 pounds. BAC diary, Jan. 15, 1971, Box 12, CP.
805 **glad when February came:** On the *Belle Rive* visit, see BAC diary, Feb. 1–Mar. 1, 1971, Box 12, CP.
806 **"persnickety":** BAC OH, 1027.
806 **"the most generally unappreciated":** BAC quoted in *Random House Bulletin,* Summer 1970, Box 73, CP. JOH had died on Apr. 11, 1970; BAC was in Los Angeles, co-emceeing a USC benefit dedicated to MH. Having missed JOH funeral, BAC arranged the memorial service at RH.
806 **Kissinger didn't stay at Sinatra's:** Henry Kissinger is mentioned in BAC's diary quite a bit during this period. See BAC diary, Apr. 29 & 30, May 2, 3, & 4, June 29, 1971, Box 12, CP. Kissinger told me during an interview on June 29, 2004, that he did not actually stay at Sinatra's.
806 **a "naïve" in New York society:** Kissinger to author, June 29, 2004.
806 **secure line:** BAC diary, Aug. 4, 1971, Box 12, CP.
806 **other weekend companions:** BAC diary, Aug. 6, 7, & 8, 1971, Box 12, CP.
807 **Neither Cerf was well:** See BAC diary, Aug. 2 & 6, 1971, Box 12, CP.
807 **"very friendly":** Kissinger to author, June 29, 2004. The other quotes in this paragraph also come from this interview.
807 **they were lining up:** Kissinger to author, June 29, 2004.
807 **wry and thoughtful:** Wendy Frith to author, July 2, 2012.
807 **being "looked over":** Rosanne Cerf to author, Feb. 18, 2004.
807 **wedding took place:** Rosanne Cerf to author; mentions of Rosanne in BAC diary, July 9 & 10, Oct. 2, 1969, Aug. 19 & 20, 1970. The wedding took place Sept. 1, 1970. Box 12, CP.
808 **Now it required agonized apologies:** CBC to author, Dec. 22, 2016.
808 **"too interesting by half":** MKF to author, May 31, 2012.
808 **set out to convince Bennett:** JFC to author, Oct. 8, 2014.
808 **giving off negative signals:** Helen Bernstein to author, Oct. 26, 2005; MKF to author, May 31, 2012.
808 **"darling":** BAC diary, July 5, 1971, Box 12, CP.
808 **Chris was crazy about:** Joan Ganz Cooney to author, Dec. 9, 2010.
808 **Whatever he did:** Christopher Cerf Oral History, Random House Oral History Project (hereafter CBC OH), 23.
808 **bought a townhouse:** BAC diary, July 28, 1968, Box 12, CP.
808 **"passions":** See, e.g., BAC diary, Mar. 16, 1969, Box 12, CP.
808 **"If you want laundry done":** Helen Bernstein quoting BAC to author, Oct. 26, 2005.
809 **"energy, creativity, and sweetness":** Joan Ganz Cooney to author, Dec. 9, 2010.
809 **"This is a good move":** DSK quoted by CBC in CBC OH, 8.
809 **there'd always be a place:** DSK quoted by CBC to author, Aug. 7, 2003.
809 **Jerry tried to turn back:** On the Weidman weekend, see BAC diary, July 18–19, 1971, Box 12, CP. On the encounter at the pool and BAC's reference to what happened to RLS, see Weidman, *Praying for Rain,* 355–63. Ample details are misremembered due to the passage of time and also, perhaps, Weidman's long history of writing fiction. His chapter makes for compelling reading, and there is a kind of truth in it. But RH had been sold five years, not two years, before the incident; the Sarnoff referred to is clearly the General, who was very much incapacitated by then; and JOH was dead. In a broader sense it seems unlikely that DSK, given all that had happened between them, harbored any hope of buying back RH with BAC.
810 **"Bill, I want to live":** BAC quoted by WS to author, Mar. 3, 2003.
810 **"Look after your mother":** BAC quoted by JFC to author, Mar. 4, 2003.
810 **Capote visited and felt odd:** TC to his biographer Gerald Clarke, undated interview notes, courtesy Clarke. TC's visit took place on Aug. 25, 1971.
811 **"The food is proving":** BAC to AAK and Helen Knopf, Aug. 26, 1971, AAKR.
811 **phone lines were down:** Leona Nevler, JHS's wife at the time, to author, Dec. 2, 2005.
811 **"You're not going to believe":** CBC to author, Mar. 4, 2003.
811 **Phyllis didn't want Chris to come:** Rosanne Cerf to author, Feb. 18, 2004.
812 **Rosanne and Jon had arrived:** Rosanne Cerf to author, Feb. 18, 2004.
812 **"I have to wash the sheets":** PC quoted by Rosanne Cerf to author, Feb. 18, 2004.
812 **"I know Bennett has left":** PC quoted by Rosanne Cerf to author, Feb. 18, 2004.

EPILOGUE: REVOLVING DOORS

813 **in shock:** Howard Goldstein to author, May 16, 2003.

813 **went together to lunch:** Susanna Styron to author, Nov. 18, 2003.

813 **looking out at ships:** Anthony M. Schulte to author, May 22, 2003.

813 **"I won't leave you":** Barber/Sinatra interaction per JFC to author, Mar. 11, 2003; Rosanne Cerf to author, Feb. 18, 2004.

813 **His sidekick Jilly Rizzo:** CBC to author, Dec. 18, 2002.

813 **terribly wan:** BK to author, Nov. 4, 2002.

813 **a lot richer than he actually was:** Per Sanford Kirschenbaum, BAC's last tax accountant, to author, Sept. 29, 2003. See also "Cerf Left Estate of Over 1 Million," *NYT,* Sept. 3, 1971.

813 **When it was probated:** Surrogate's Court, New York City, SCPA1406. PC's portion was almost $2.8 million, and each son received $746,000 in 1971 dollars, presumably after tax.

814 **Chris, bereft:** Helene Fagan Bidwell to author, May 25, 2005.

814 **come into his own:** FEP to author, Jan. 20, 2008.

814 **"trendiest couple":** Laura H. Stevenson, "Chris and Genevieve Cerf: She's Throwing Off Her Chains, but the Yoke Is on Him," *People,* Oct. 6, 1975.

815 **"said all the right things":** Pat Klopfer to PC, "Friday," Sept. 1971, Box 8, CP.

815 **she began lashing out:** Aileen Mehle (a.k.a. Suzy Knickerbocker) to author, July 6, 2003; CBC to author, Dec. 18, 2002; Rosanne Cerf to author, Feb. 18, 2004.

815 **On the boys' birthdays:** Sharon Lerner to author, Oct. 14, 2004.

815 **Sinatra, especially, helped:** CBC to author, Feb. 18, 2004.

815 **"That silly man":** FEP to author, Jan. 20, 2008. BAC being the only person who could keep PC in check per interviewee comment made to the author off the record.

815 **more than she cared to admit:** LH to author, Nov. 17, 2002. Abel Green, "Publisher, Author, Panelist, Punster, Partygoer, Bennett Cerf Dies at 73," *Variety,* Sept. 1, 1971; "Bennett Cerf Dies; Publisher, Panelist, and Lover of Puns," *LAT* (UPI), Aug. 29, 1971.

815 **Michener wanted to fund:** JFC to author, Jan. 28, 2010.

815 **It was Phyllis who persuaded:** On PC's role in Wells Rich Greene, the company Wells Lawrence founded, see Mary Wells Lawrence, *A Big Life in Advertising* (New York: Alfred A. Knopf, 2002), 139, 145, 146.

815 **"sparkle, smile, chill and sometimes freeze":** Enid Nemy, "Phyllis Wagner's New Job Is Hard, Which Suits Her Fine," *NYT,* July 21, 1978.

816 **Pressed by the company:** RLB to author, May 5, 2003, and June 13, 2012.

816 **a man without hobbies:** LKL to author, May 4, 2005.

817 **His letters are those of an older man:** For the DSK/MD letters, see MDP. DSK's last letter was Mar. 14, 1986, two months before he died.

817 **On one trip to Italy:** DSK and Pat's friend per Joyce Hartman to author, Sept. 12, 2004; LKL to author, Nov. 19, 2003.

817 **the marriage also survived a suicide attempt:** Found by her maid, she was rushed to the hospital. JE drove DSK to Tampa to catch the first flight back. JE to author, Dec. 9, 2003.

817 **quite solicitous:** Hartman to author, Sept. 12, 2004. Hartman said Pat told her that her heart was failing.

817 **A native New Yorker:** See Bart Barnes, "Poet, Democratic Official Katie Louchheim Dies," *The Washington Post,* Feb. 12, 1991; Glenn Fowler, "Katie Louchheim Is Dead at 87," *NYT,* Feb. 12, 1991.

818 **had briefly dated Bennett:** For correspondence between BAC and Louchheim, see Box 3, Katie Louchheim Papers, LoC.

818 **She moved to New York:** Pat inherited the Beekman apartment from her parents. LKL to author, May 4, 2005.

818 **Don had lost or grown bored with:** LKL to author, May 4, 2005.

818 **The marriage didn't work out:** LKL to author, May 4, 2005.

818 **graveside funeral:** LKL to author, May 4, 2005.

818 **Veterans who'd served:** LKL to author, Nov. 19, 2003.

818 **a later eulogy:** Aug. 25, 1986. The eulogy is in Box 65, REP.

818 **He never found:** LKL to author, Nov. 19, 2003.

818 **admitted that the men's relationship:** Pat Selwyn Klopfer to PC, "Monday" (Aug. 30, 1971), Box 9, CP.

818 **"My father felt closer":** LKL to PC, Aug. 29, 1971, Box 8, CP.

818 **"I've worked with wonderful":** DSK quoted in Herbert Mitgang, "Modern Library Giant, 80 Today, Still Active," *NYT,* Jan. 23, 1982.

818 **Although RCA had installed:** RLB to author, Apr. 1, 2003. RLB described Alexander "Sandy" MacGregor III as a "terrific" lieutenant.

819 **he reported only to God:** Interviewee to author. Interviewee wished to remain anonymous.

819 **fearing Federal Trade Commission scrutiny:** RH was among a group of publishers forced to sign a Department of Justice consent decree over school market price-fixing (see chapter 52). Oscar Dystel headed Bantam at the time. Dystel said RCA feared a new intervention from the FTC, and so sold the stake in Bantam's owner Grosset. He later cast doubt on that explanation, but gave no reason. See his Columbia OH, 164–65. RCA fears of FTC, FCC, SEC per Alexander MacGregor III to author, Oct. 29, 2003. RH's decision to sell had a domino effect: other publishers-owners also pulled out of Grosset. Dystel tried to buy it, but failed; it was bought by movie theater magnate National General.

819 **Ballantine Books, the brainchild:** RLB to author, May 5, 2003; Alexander MacGregor III to author, Oct. 29, 2003; "Ian and Betty Ballantine Off On Their Own," *PW,* Aug. 12, 1974; RLB with Merlino, *Speaking Freely,* 228–29. Ballantine was bought for $6.4 million. "Random House in Deal for Ballantine Books," *NYT,* Jan. 9, 1973. The president of Intext, Ballantine's owner, at the time was ex-RH executive Richard Kislik.

819 **largest corporate write-off:** Alexander MacGregor III to author, Oct. 29, 2003.

819 **the board rebelled:** RLB with Merlino, *Speaking Freely,* 166.

819 **his grandfather had helped:** RLB with Merlino, *Speaking Freely,* 6–7.

819 **he and two others went further:** RLB had considered trying to take a "sabbatical" from RH or to divide his time, either to work with the U.N. or the State Department or to become U.S. ambassador to Israel. Respectively on RLB choices, Herbert K. Schnall to author, Dec. 7, 2016; Martin P. Levin to author, Apr. 23, 2004; Howard Kaminsky to author, Sept. 29, 2003.

819 **RCA wanted to offload:** Herbert Mitgang, "Random House May Be Bought by the Times Mirror Company," *NYT,* Feb. 11, 1977. See also William D. Smith, "Random House Sale Talks Pushed; RCA Apt to Get Less Than It Paid," *WSJ,* Feb. 12, 1977.

819 **Times-Mirror Corporation again knocked:** RCA senior VP Rocco Laginestra made the approach to an Air Force buddy, Herbert K. Schnall, then-president of TM's NAL. Schnall to author, Dec. 7, 2016; see also "Times Mirror Co. May Purchase the Random House Unit of RCA," *LAT,* Feb. 10, 1977. Smith described TM and RH as "a perfect match." However, there were three impediments: RLB did not like his future reporting line should the deal go through; TM's reaction to RLB's desire to divide his time; TM deciding to decrease the price they would pay, claiming that RH overheads and advances were higher than originally estimated. *WSJ,* Feb. 12, 1977; Martin Levin to author, Aug. 11, 2010, Apr. 21, 2004; Schnall to author, Dec. 7, 2016. Levin headed TM's publishing division at the time and would have become RLB's boss. See also the comments on Levin in RLB with Merlino, *Speaking Freely,* 144–45, 168. On the other hand, DSK had supported TM's offer. DSK to Robert F. Erburu, TM CEO, Apr. 4, 1977, Box 1560, RHR.

819 **For a minute, Bernstein dreamed:** RLB said he did not or could not buy RH because Ballantine was "doing so badly." RLB to author, May 5, 2003.

820 **a half hour's notice:** RLB to author, May 5, 2003. The announcement was made on Sept. 6, 1979. See "RCA Says It Intends to Sell Random House," *PW,* Sept. 17, 1979, courtesy *PW* clipping files.

820 **Lazard Frères and Lehman Brothers:** Herbert Mitgang, "Whither Random House?" *NYT,* Oct. 15, 1979. Newhouse was mentioned as possible buyer. See "Page Six," *New York Post,* Sept. 19, 1979, courtesy *PW* clipping files. Press reports estimated RH 1978 sales of $150–170 million and earnings of $5–10 million, making $50–75 million realistic. See also "RCA Says It Intends to Sell Random House."

820 **No way would Advance:** Alexander MacGregor III to author, Oct. 29, 2003.

820 **private, family-owned New York company:** By the time Newhouse bought RH, about twenty family members were involved in the company, mainly on the newspaper side; at one time, sixty-four family members were involved. "Newhouse Discusses Parental Relationship to Random House," *PW,* Feb. 22, 1980, courtesy *PW* clipping files.

820 **made more than $100 million in profit:** The Newhouse family had owned TV stations and sold them to Times Mirror—indeed, TM had used funds earmarked for buying RH to buy those stations instead—so now Newhouse could tap into the TM money to buy RH. The $100 million was on sales of $1.2 billion. See N. R. Kleinfeld, "RCA Agrees to Sell Random House to Newhouse for $65–$70 Million," *NYT,* Feb. 7, 1980.

820 **memory of the $75 million:** The interest-free loan per Alexander MacGregor III to author, Oct. 29, 2003.

820 **the Newhouses were paying:** Kleinfeld, "RCA Agrees to Sell Random House to Newhouse for $65–$70 Million."

820 **Si wanted RH Inc. to grow:** Edwin McDowell, "The New Reach of Random House," *NYT,* May 5, 1985.

820 **Bernstein had clashed:** Howard Kaminsky to author, Oct. 10, 2003; RDL to author, Feb. 19, 2017, among others. Selma Shapiro was appointed RH publicity head after Jean Ennis's death. She and JHS became involved. At that time, JHS was married to Fawcett chief editor Leona Nevler; this was before Fawcett became part of RH. RLB thought Shapiro focused too much on JHS's books—some editors had complained. He fired Shapiro, who founded her own PR agency; JHS went to S&S, and they later married.

821 **Jason Epstein took over:** RLB with Merlino, *Speaking Freely,* 239; John Taylor, "The Book Makers," *Manhattan, Inc.,* Dec. 1984, 57, 58, courtesy AEP. In 1980, Marc Jaffe, the longtime president of Bantam, was recruited by RLB for a three-pronged position: to be editor-in-chief of Ballantine, to acquire books for the RH imprint, and to join Tony Schulte and Richard Krinsley, whom BAC had hired to run children's books and RLB later made head of Ballantine, to supervise the overall publishing program of the RH division. JE then reported to them. In 1983, Jaffe was moved from the RH imprint by RLB and taxed with establishing a fourth hardcover imprint, called Villard, focusing on highly commercial books. Howard Kaminsky was hired directly by his personal friend Si Newhouse in 1984 to run RH trade after Jaffe's move to Villard. On Jaffe and his role at RH, see Herbert Mitgang, "Jaffe Quits Bantam for Random House," *NYT,* May 1, 1980; "Jaffe Heads Villard Books, New RH Hardcover Imprint," *PW,* Feb. 18, 1983.

821 **With Bernstein often tied up:** On Newhouse's increasing role, see RLB with Merlino, *Speaking Freely,* 239–41; also Taylor, "Book Makers," 57, 58. RLB was aware of Kaminsky's ambition to succeed him, and didn't approve. When he forced the issue, Newhouse allowed him to fire Kaminsky in the fall of 1987. Kaminsky's replacement as head of the RH division was Joni Evans, who had run S&S trade (and had been married to S&S CEO Richard Snyder). See also Madalynne Reuter, "After the Un-Random Showdown," *PW,* Oct. 30, 1987; Alexander MacGregor III to author, Oct. 29, 2003; Kaminsky to author, Oct. 10, 2003. Kaminsky became president of Hearst. See Edwin McDowell, "Hearst Hires Fired Random House Exec," *NYT,* Dec. 25, 1987.

821 ***The Art of the Deal:*** RLB with Merlino, *Speaking Freely,* 239; Jane Mayer, "Donald Trump's Ghostwriter Tells All," *TNY,* July 25, 2016.

821 **"super-corporation":** DSK to Billy Collins, Nov. 27, 1961, Box 48, RHR.

821 **Si didn't have that:** Newhouse overpaid, and the London publishing houses he bought weren't properly integrated. Alexander MacGregor III to author, Oct. 29, 2003.

821 **Started as the Outlet Books:** Crown history and purchase per author's contemporaneous reporting for *PW.* See also John F. Baker and Calvin Reid, "Random House, in Surprise Move, Acquires Crown Publishing Group," *PW,* Aug. 26, 1988; Cynthia Crossen, "Random House Says It Will Buy Closely Held Crown Publishers," *WSJ,* Aug. 16, 1988; Edwin McDowell, "Nat Wartels, 88, the Chairman of the Crown Publishing Empire," *NYT,* Feb. 8, 1990; RLB with Merlino, *Speaking Freely,* 243–44; Alexander MacGregor III to author, Oct. 29, 2003.

821 **were losing a fortune:** Alexander MacGregor III to author, Oct. 29, 2003; also, Alberto Vitale to author, July 29, 2003. That Crown's mail-order operation had been peddling pornographic videos became common knowledge among senior RH staff after the fact. As a senior journalist at *PW,* the author was told about it repeatedly in the early 1990s.

821 **wasn't given to blaming himself:** N. R. Kleinfeld, "Heads Have a History of Rolling at Newhouse," *NYT,* Nov. 2, 1989.

822 **seems to happen every single time:** Betty Prashker (who witnessed RLB's ouster and the denouement) to author, Feb. 8, 2006.

822 **True, overheads were high, profits thin:** Alberto Vitale characterized it to me as having "very little profit" and confirmed "Crown was a substantial mess." He, too, had wanted to buy Crown—for BDD—but like RLB, he had no idea about the pornography. Alberto Vitale to author, July 29, 2003.

822 **Having executed that integration:** On the RLB ouster and Vitale's background, see Roger Cohen, "Changing Spirit at Random House," *NYT,* Mar. 19, 1990; Albert Scardino, "Bantam's 'General' Brings a Legacy of Discipline," *NYT,* Nov. 9, 1989. Meg Cox, "New Random Chief Knows

How to Handle the Books," Nov. 9, 1989, *WSJ,* all courtesy *PW* clipping files.

822 **"Look what I rescued":** Eleanor Carlucci, librarian and former secretary to AAK, to author, Sept. 11, 2003.

822 **big authors that would sell, sell, sell:** Betty Prashker to author, Feb. 8, 2006. During her long career in publishing, Prashker worked in executive positions at Doubleday and Crown.

823 **Bernstein had effectively exempted:** Pantheon's financial situation per Alexander MacGregor III to author, Oct. 29, 2003.

823 **"unfairly" asked to shoulder:** André Schiffrin to author, Dec. 1, 2005.

823 **The situation escalated:** Pantheon background and imbroglio per the author's own contemporaneous reporting at *PW.* Also André Schiffrin to author, Dec. 1, 2005; Alberto Vitale to author, July 29, 2003; Edwin McDowell, "Chief of Pantheon Is Said to Have Been Asked to Quit," *NYT,* Feb. 27, 1990; John F. Baker, "A Sad Day for André Schiffrin—and for Publishing," *PW,* Mar. 9, 1990; Doug Ireland, "The Fall of the House of Pantheon," *Village Voice,* Mar. 13, 1990; Madalynne Reuter, "Protests Mount over Events at Pantheon," *PW,* Mar. 16, 1990; Laura Shapiro, "Publisher at the Barricades," *Newsweek,* Mar. 19, 1990; "Newhoused," editorial, *The Nation,* Mar. 19, 1990; JAM, public letter released Mar. 19, 1990; "40 Random House Publishers and Editors Speak Out on Pantheon," *PW,* Mar. 23, 1990; Roger Donald, "Taking Issue with the Random 40," *PW,* Apr. 20, 1990; "Writers for Pantheon," advertisement, *PW,* May 8, 1990. All articles and JAM letter courtesy *PW* clipping files. See also David Streitfeld, "Life at Random," *New York Magazine,* Aug. 5, 1991; RLB with Merlino, *Speaking Freely,* 237.

823 **Appreciating the importance of history:** Harold Evans to author, Feb. 15, 2007.

823 **even talk of remaindering:** Alberto Vitale to author, July 29, 2003; Harold Evans to author, Feb. 15, 2007. Vitale considered transferring the ML to Everyman's Library at Knopf.

823 **As a graduate student:** Harold Evans to author, Feb. 15, 2007.

824 **"nudged" back to magazines:** Harold Evans's era and accomplishments per Alberto Vitale to author, July 29, 2003; Alexander MacGregor III to author, Oct. 29, 2003. See also Lorne Manly, "Can Mort Rescue the Amazing Harry?" *New York Observer,* Dec. 8, 1997, courtesy *PW* clipping files. Evans became editorial director of Mortimer Zuckerman's newspaper and magazine group for a time. He was replaced as publisher by Ann Godoff, who had been his chief editor; JE had ceded his position as "editorial director" several years earlier to "the brilliant" Godoff, as JE characterized her. See Jim Milliot, "Evans Leaving Random; Godoff Takes His Place," *PW,* Dec. 1, 1997.

824 **approached by Thomas Middelhoff:** Doreen Carvajal, "Book Deal: The Deal: German Media Giant Will Buy Random House for $1.4 Billion," *NYT,* Mar. 24, 1998.

824 **Quality spoke strongly to German pride:** Alberto Vitale to author, July 29, 2003.

824 **Newhouse wanted a week:** Sale to Bertelsmann per Alberto Vitale to author, July 29, 2003; Warren St. John, "So Why Did Newhouse Sell Random House to Bertelsmann?" *New York Observer,* Mar. 30, 1998; John F. Baker, "Bertelsmann's Buy of Random Completed," *PW,* July 6, 1998; Doreen Carvajal, "Newhouse's Legacy Lives in Publisher," *NYT,* Mar. 30, 1998.

824 **the acquisition was announced:** St. John, "So Why Did Newhouse Sell Random House to Bertelsmann?"

824 **The next year, New York became Bertelsmann's:** William Boston, "Bertelsmann Will Base Book Publishing in New York, Taps Olson to Head Unit," *WSJ,* Dec. 10, 1999.

824 **Newhouse, who now held the base lease:** Valerie Block, "Random Sites for Publisher," *Crain's New York Business,* Dec. 13, 1999, *PW* Records, Box 60, Columbia. See also Elizabeth Manus, "Random House Homeless! Office Space Vanishes!" *The New York Observer,* Nov. 8, 1999.

825 **A series of presidents, publishers, and chief editors:** Ann Godoff was ousted by Peter Olson in Jan. 2003, having paid one too many high advances and fallen short of profit targets for several years. She was almost immediately hired by Penguin and given her own imprint. Eschewing her name, she called it Penguin Press. The RH group was moved under the control of Gina Centrello, then the president of the Ballantine group, whose background in paperbacks had taught her to be very attentive to the balance sheet. Daniel Menaker, who had been fiction editor at *TNY,* was named chief editor. Four years later, he was gone. Centrello appointed Susan Kamil RH editor-in-chief and later publisher. Kamil died in 2019, and her chief editor, Andy Ward, moved up to become publisher.

825 **Bertelsmann plucked Markus Dohle:** Jim

Milliot, "Dohle Remodels Random House," *PW,* May 24, 2010.

825 **shocked the book world:** On the initial RH-Penguin merger, see Jim Milliot, "Dohle Remodels Random House," *PW,* May 24, 2010; Rachel Deahl, "The Building Blocks of Penguin Random House," *PW,* Jan. 21, 2013.

825 **No surprise that six months into her watch:** Gayle Feldman, "McIntosh Begins to Make Her Mark at PRH US," *The Bookseller,* Feb. 11, 2019.

827 **"a culture of talk":** Madeline McIntosh quoted in Feldman, "McIntosh Begins to Make Her Mark at PRH US."

828 **"At a meeting of the board of directors":** Box 64, CP.

828 **"If I'd been running":** DSK OH, 63, 70–71.

829 **every publisher tends to be:** The line is Erich Linder's. See Roberto Calasso, *The Art of the Publisher,* translated by Richard Dixon (New York: Farrar, Straus & Giroux, 2015), 94.

829 **Bennett Cerf, while not without his critics:** MacKinlay Kantor, who published eight books with RH and then left for other pastures, appended a three-page note in his papers at the LoC to tell future literary historians that although he found RKH and SC to be "heroic" and "very fine" human beings, BAC was "a pompous blow-hard and not to be trusted at all." One might ask why, then, both RKH and SC were so devoted to BAC? Folder 1, Box 51, MacKinlay Kantor Papers.

829 **"Who's Bennett?":** BK to author, Nov. 4, 2002.

829 **a period marked by the obliteration:** Calasso, *Art of the Publisher,* 126, 127.

829 **rendered increasingly faceless:** WS to author, Dec. 3, 2003.

830 **"style, splendor and swoosh":** Norman Cousins, "Bennett," *SRL,* Sept. 11, 1971.

830 **"the really noteworthy events":** BAC, obituary of Horace Liveright, *PW,* Oct. 7, 1933, reprinted in *AR,* 80–81.

Credits

Cover and Title page: Bennett Cerf in Vermont, 1938, Bennett Cerf Papers, Rare Book and Manuscript Library, Columbia University

p. 5: Fredericka Wise Cerf, Cerf Papers, RBML, Columbia

p. 8: Gustave Cerf, Cerf Papers, RBML, Columbia

p. 12: Fredericka and Bennett Cerf, Cerf Papers, RBML, Columbia

p. 14: Fredericka, Gustave, and Bennett Cerf, Cerf Papers, RBML, Columbia

p. 22: Bennett Cerf and Columbia classmates, courtesy Christopher and Jonathan Cerf

p. 25: Uncle Herbert Wise and Gustave Cerf, courtesy Christopher and Jonathan Cerf

p. 27: Donald S. Klopfer, courtesy Lois Klopfer Levy

p. 35: Bennett Cerf, Marian Ansbacher, and Donald S. Klopfer, courtesy Lois Klopfer Levy

p. 39: Boni & Liveright announcement card, 1923, courtesy Christopher and Jonathan Cerf

p. 48: Horace Liveright by Carl Klein, Cerf Papers, RBML, Columbia

p. 51: Boni & Liveright 1924 catalogue designed by Ralph Barton, Cerf Papers, RBML, Columbia

p. 56: Alfred A. Knopf, Cerf Papers, RBML, Columbia

p. 57: Blanche Wolf Knopf by Raphael, courtesy Alfred A. Knopf, Inc.

p. 60: Max Lincoln Schuster and Richard Leo Simon circa 1924, © Bettmann/Getty Images

p. 68: News! The Modern Library Has Changed Hands! Cerf Papers, RBML, Columbia. Used by permission courtesy *Publishers Weekly*. Copyright © PWxyz LLC. All rights reserved.

p. 69: Gustave Cerf, Bennett Cerf, and female staff at 71 West 45th Street office, courtesy Christopher and Jonathan Cerf

p. 76, top: Elmer Adler, Pynson Printers Collection, courtesy Princeton University Library, via Walter Weintz

p. 76, bottom: Lucian Bernhard's Modern Library colophon, Cerf Papers, RBML, Columbia

p. 77: Rockwell Kent's revised Modern Library colophon, Cerf Papers, RBML, Columbia. Used by permission courtesy *Publishers Weekly*. Copyright © PWxyz LLC. All rights reserved.

p. 79: Random House colophon, Cerf Papers, RBML, Columbia

p. 81: East 57th Street office reception room, courtesy Christopher and Jonathan Cerf

p. 83: *Candide,* Cerf Papers, RBML, Columbia

p. 88: Francis Meynell, reproduced by kind permission of the Syndics of Cambridge University Library

p. 93: "The Publishers' Weakly," courtesy Christopher and Jonathan Cerf

p. 94: "They Float!," courtesy General Research Division, New York Public Library. Used by permission courtesy *Publishers Weekly.* Copyright © PWxyz LLC. All rights reserved.

p. 99: Bennett, George Gershwin et al. in Cuba, Cerf Papers, RBML, Columbia

p. 107: Dr. Saxe Commins, Cerf Papers, RBML, Columbia

p. 110: Bennett and Eugene O'Neill by Fania Marinoff, Cerf Papers, RBML, Columbia

p. 111: Carl Van Vechten, *Portrait of Carlotta Monterey O'Neill,* 1933, Library of Congress, Prints & Photographs Division, Carl Van Vechten Collection, LC-DIG-ds-17335

p. 119: James Joyce by Ruth Asch, Viking Press, Cerf Papers, RBML, Columbia

p. 121: Sylvia Beach and James Joyce, Cerf Papers, RBML, Columbia

p. 137: Judge John Munro Woolsey, courtesy The Century Association Archives

p. 141: "How to Enjoy *Ulysses,*" Cerf Papers, RBML, Columbia

p. 147: Bennett and Harold Guinzburg in Egypt, Cerf Papers, RBML, Columbia

p. 152: Carl Van Vechten, *Portrait of Christopher Isherwood and W. H. Auden,* 1939, Library of Congress, Prints & Photographs Division, Carl Van Vechten Collection, LC-DIG-ds-17334

p. 153: William Saroyan, Cerf Papers, RBML, Columbia

p. 155: Bennett and Pauline Kreiswirth by Lisa Larsen, Cerf Papers, RBML, Columbia

p. 158: Carl Van Vechten, *Portrait of Gertrude Stein, with American flag as backdrop,* 1935, Library of Congress, Prints & Photographs Division, Carl Van Vechten Collection, LC-USZ62-103680. Scan from Cerf Papers, RBML, Columbia

p. 160: Carl Van Vechten, *Portrait of Bennett Cerf,* 1932, Cerf Papers, RBML, Columbia

p. 165: Glamour girls and Kathleen Winsor advertisements, Cerf papers, RBML, Columbia. Used by permission courtesy *Publishers Weekly.* Copyright © PWxyz LLC. All rights reserved.

p. 168: Sylvia Sidney, courtesy Academy of Motion Picture Arts and Sciences Margaret Herrick Library, Core Collection Biography Files

p. 176: Martha Dodd, The Hanna Holborn Gray Special Collections Research Center, University of Chicago Library

p. 179: Florence "Pat" Selwyn and her mother, Historic International Newsreel photo

p. 183: Robert K. Haas by Kaiden Kazanjian, Cerf Papers, RBML, Columbia

p. 193: Helen Thompson, Cerf Papers, RBML, Columbia

p. 202: Phyllis Fraser by Robert McAfee, Cerf Papers, RBML, Columbia

p. 205: Ginger Rogers, Phyllis Fraser, Lela Rogers, © Bettmann/CORBIS/Getty Images

p. 209: Bennett with Phyllis Fraser, Cerf Papers, RBML, Columbia

p. 213: William Faulkner by Phyllis Cerf, courtesy Christopher and Jonathan Cerf

p. 223: Anne Shirley and Leonora Schinasi (later Hornblow), Academy of Motion Picture Arts and Sciences Margaret Herrick Library, Arthur and Leonora Hornblow Papers

p. 225: 132 East 62nd Street, courtesy Christopher and Jonathan Cerf

p. 230: Budd Schulberg by Phyllis Cerf, courtesy Christopher and Jonathan Cerf

p. 234: Captain Donald S. Klopfer, courtesy Robert D. Loomis

p. 236: Trade Winds logo, Cerf Papers, RBML, Columbia

p. 241: Bennett in the studio for *Books Are Bullets* by Harold Stein, Cerf Papers, RBML, Columbia

p. 243: *Great Tales of Terror and the Supernatural,* book courtesy Christopher and Jonathan Cerf/ Gayle Feldman

p. 248: *The Pocket Book of War Humor,* book courtesy Christopher and Jonathan Cerf

p. 250: *Modern American Short Stories ASE,* book courtesy Christopher and Jonathan Cerf/Gayle Feldman

p. 281: North wing of the Villard Houses, 457 Madison Avenue, 1947, by Wayne Andrews. Geographic Images Collection, PR020, courtesy New-York Historical Society 101486d

p. 284: Robert Linscott, Harry Maule, Saxe Commins, and Bennett in Bennett's office in the Villard, by Lisa Larsen, Cerf Papers, RBML, Columbia

p. 289: Bennett, Phyllis, Christopher, Jonathan Cerf, Cerf Papers, RBML, Columbia

p. 290: Donald Klopfer, Bob Haas, Bennett in 57th Street office by Lisa Larsen, Cerf Papers, RBML, Columbia

p. 292: Truman Capote by Phyllis Cerf, courtesy Christopher and Jonathan Cerf

p. 303: John O'Hara by Phyllis Cerf, courtesy Christopher and Jonathan Cerf

p. 318: At La Quinta, photo by Gail B. Thompson, Gayle's Studio Archive, courtesy of the Palm Springs Historical Society

p. 334: Bennett Cerf by Gordon Parks, courtesy of and copyright The Gordon Parks Foundation

p. 349: James Michener, Billy Rose Theatre Division, The New York Public Library for the Performing Arts

p. 362: "Sioux City Welcomes Bennett Cerf," Cerf Papers, RBML, Columbia

p. 364: Leonora Hornblow by Phyllis Cerf, courtesy Christopher and Jonathan Cerf

p. 371: Landmark Books advertisement, Cerf Papers, RBML, Columbia

p. 379: William Faulkner by Phyllis Cerf, courtesy Christopher and Jonathan Cerf

p. 382: The Cerfboard, Cerf Papers, RBML, Columbia

p. 387: *What's My Line?* panel, courtesy Fremantle

p. 390: Arlene Francis, Bennett, and Bob Bach, courtesy Christopher and Jonathan Cerf

p. 401: "The Columns," courtesy Christopher and Jonathan Cerf

p. 407: Jonathan Cerf and Peter Gabel by Phyllis Cerf, courtesy Christopher and Jonathan Cerf

p. 412: "Success" greeting card by Whitney Darrow Jr., from Random House, Cerf Papers, RBML, Columbia

p. 417: Bennett, Phyllis, and Alicia Patterson Guggenheim, Cerf Papers, RBML, Columbia

p. 427: Ralph Ellison by Gordon Parks, courtesy of and copyright The Gordon Parks Foundation

p. 429: Bennett with Marilyn Monroe, studio publicity photograph from GENTLEMEN PREFER BLONDES © 1953 20th Century Studios, Inc. All rights reserved.

p. 437: Bennett with Quentin Reynolds by Lisa Larsen, courtesy Christopher and Jonathan Cerf

p. 439: "Fact Fiction" advertisement, Cerf Papers, RBML, Columbia

p. 442: Saxe Commins in the 1950s, courtesy Robert D. Loomis

p. 460: Store window filled with *An Encyclopedia of Modern American Humor,* Cerf Papers, RBML, Columbia

p. 463: Hiram Haydn, courtesy Robert D. Loomis

p. 475: Norman Mailer by Helen Marcus, courtesy Caleb Marcus

p. 480: Bennett and some of the books he authored, Cerf Papers, RBML, Columbia

p. 484: Bennett and Phyllis Cerf, courtesy Christopher and Jonathan Cerf

p. 490: The Cerf family visiting J. Edgar Hoover at FBI headquarters, Cerf Papers, RBML, Columbia

p. 495: Literary luncheon for William Styron by Barney Stein, Cerf Papers, RBML, Columbia. Permission, courtesy Bonnie Stein Crosby

p. 499: Ayn Rand by Phyllis Cerf, courtesy Christopher and Jonathan Cerf

p. 505: *Atlas Shrugged* jacket (design by George Salter), courtesy Christopher and Jonathan Cerf

p. 521: Bennett and Ted Geisel, Cerf Papers, RBML, Columbia

p. 531: Robert and Helen Bernstein by Dev O'Neill, House Creative Services, U.S. House of Representatives, courtesy Bernstein family

p. 536: Robert D. Loomis, courtesy Diana Loomis

p. 539: Jason Epstein and Nan Ahearn Talese by Hans W. Schoenlank, courtesy Talese family

p. 559: Random House, Inc., share prospectus, Cerf Papers, RBML, Columbia

p. 565: James A. Michener, Albert Erskine, Bert Krantz by Steven Baron, Cerf Papers, RBML, Columbia

p. 567: Kitty Carlisle Hart by Phyllis Cerf, courtesy Christopher and Jonathan Cerf

p. 569: Moss Hart by Phyllis Cerf, courtesy Christopher and Jonathan Cerf

p. 577: Alfred and Blanche Knopf and friends, courtesy Alfred A. Knopf, Inc.

p. 581: Alfred A. Knopf Jr., courtesy Alfred A. Knopf, Inc.

p. 593: Knopf, Random House in Publishing Merger, from *The New York Times*, April 17, 1960, © The New York Times. Knopf photo by Fabian Bachrach. Cerf photo by Phyllis Cerf

p. 600: Robert Penn Warren by Phyllis Cerf, courtesy Christopher and Jonathan Cerf

p. 606: Bennett reading the *Random House Dictionary,* Cerf Papers, RBML, Columbia

p. 625: Joseph M. Fox, courtesy Anne Isaak via Kay Eldredge

p. 633: At the NYSE. Used with permission of NYSE Group, Inc., © 2026 NYSE Group, Inc.

p. 638: Front jacket of William Faulkner's *The Town,* courtesy Christopher and Jonathan Cerf

p. 651: Cerf family on the *Queen Elizabeth,* Cerf Papers, RBML, Columbia

p. 664: James Silberman and Muhammad Ali, courtesy Selma Shapiro

p. 675: At the Haywards', Cerf Papers, RBML, Columbia

p. 688: Cormac McCarthy, Knoxville Journal Collection, McClung Historical Collection

p. 689: Toni Frissell, *Photo of Irwin Shaw,* 1959, Library of Congress, Prints & Photographs Division, Toni Frissell Photograph Collection, LC-DIG-tofr-16409

p. 700: Angelo Rizzuto, *Manhattan cityscape featuring the 30 Rockefeller Plaza skyscraper, formerly known as The RCA Building,* 1952, Library of Congress, Prints and Photographs Division, Anthony Angel Collection, LC-DIG-ppmsca-69571

p. 709: Radio Corporation of America (RCA)—David Sarnoff (President of RCA) dedicating building. New York World's Fair 1939–1940 records, Manuscripts and Archives Division, The New York Public Library, digital collection, 1681003

p. 719: Frank, Mia, Leonora, Phyllis, Cerf Papers, RBML, Columbia

p. 728: Truman Capote in bed by Phyllis Cerf, courtesy Christopher and Jonathan Cerf

p. 734: Truman Capote with book jacket by Phyllis Cerf, courtesy Christopher and Jonathan Cerf

p. 738: Invitation to a dance, Cerf Papers, RBML, Columbia

p. 749: Frank Sinatra by Phyllis Cerf, courtesy Christopher and Jonathan Cerf

p. 756: Toni Morrison by Helen Marcus, courtesy Caleb Marcus and The Century Association Archives

p. 767: Robert Gottlieb by Nina Bourne, courtesy Lizzie Gottlieb

p. 768: Nina Bourne by Dorothy S. Gelatt, permission courtesy Victoria Arthur and Gail Regina

p. 769: Anthony M. Schulte, courtesy Elizabeth Darhansoff Schulte

p. 774: William Styron by Dick Kallett, Cerf Papers, RBML, Columbia

p. 782: Philip Roth by Nancy Crampton

p. 785: letter to "Miss Snoony Lou Sherwood," Cerf Papers, RBML, Columbia

p. 791: Albert Erskine, John O'Hara, Bennett, Rolls Royce, Cerf Papers, RBML, Columbia

p. 794: Bennett being carried out, photograph by Christopher Cerf, Cerf Papers, RBML, Columbia

p. 798: Famous Writers School Advertisement, Cerf Papers, RBML, Columbia

p. 816: Donald S. Klopfer and Robert L. Bernstein, Jack Manning/The New York Times/Redux

p. 830: Bennett Cerf, Cerf Papers, RBML, Columbia

PHOTOGRAPH INSERT

p. 1: Inspirational Orgy for Rockwell Kent invitation, Cerf Papers, RBML, Columbia

p. 2, top: Ulysses by James Joyce, front cover designed by Ernst Reichl, Book Art Collection, RBML, Columbia

p. 2, bottom: Ulysses by James Joyce, opening spread designed by Ernst Reichl, Book Art Collection, RBML, Columbia

p. 3, top: Try and Stop Me by Bennett Cerf, cover, illustrations by Carl Rose, Cerf Papers, RBML, Columbia

p. 3, middle: Bennett's desk view of his office in the Villard, Cerf Papers, RBML, Columbia

p. 3, bottom: Invisible Man by Ralph Ellison, cover designed by E. McKnight Kauffer, Rare Book Collection, RBML, Columbia

p. 4, top: The Cat in the Hat by Dr. Seuss, cover designed by Theodor Seuss Geisel, Historic Children's Books Collection, RBML, Columbia

p. 4, bottom: Portnoy's Complaint by Philip Roth, cover designed by Paul Bacon, Rare Book Collection, RBML, Columbia

p. 5: Annual Report Random House 1960, Cerf Papers, RBML, Columbia

pp. 6–7: "The Structure of the American Literary Establishment," *Esquire Magazine,* July 1963, Esquire / Hearst Magazine Media, Inc. / Illustration by Rudolph de Harak, Cerf Papers, RBML, Columbia

p. 8, top: Bennett Cerf's The Sound of Laughter by Bennett Cerf, jacket photo and design by Alex Gotfryd, RBML, Columbia

p. 8, bottom: Declaration of Random House Directors, Cerf Papers, RBML, Columbia

Index

ABOUT THE AUTHOR

Gayle Feldman has written for *Publishers Weekly* for forty years, including as a senior staff editor. Since 1999, as U.S. correspondent for *The Bookseller,* she has analyzed the American book business for U.K. readers. She has also contributed features, reviews, and essays to *The New York Times,* the *Los Angeles Times, The Philadelphia Inquirer, The Times* of London, *The Nation, The Daily Beast,* and other publications. She is the author of the cancer memoir *You Don't Have to Be Your Mother,* first published by W. W. Norton, and was awarded a National Arts Journalism Program fellowship at Columbia University, through which she published *Best and Worst of Times: The Changing Business of Trade Books*. The National Endowment for the Humanities has supported her work on *Nothing Random* with a Public Scholar award. Feldman lives in New York City.